History of
PUBLIC WORKS
in the United States

1776
1976

Public works provide the physical base essential to the social and economic development of American civilization. Designed to protect and enhance the human environment, they represent investments in the future for the people who create them and for succeeding generations. The transportation networks; the facilities that control floods and provide drainage; the systems that supply water for domestic, agricultural, industrial, and power-generating needs; the public buildings required for health services, education, defense, housing, and recreation; the waste collection, treatment, and disposal systems as well as the facilities that harness the power of the atom and explore space have all contributed significantly to the growth of the nation.

Public works have made it possible for the people of the United States to achieve the highest standard of living in the world. Yet clean water at the turn of the tap; fresh vegetables year around; light and power at the touch of a switch; hard-surfaced roads that, during winter or summer, provide for the movement of people and goods; modern airports that make safe and convenient air travel possible; extensive educational facilities, hospitals, public libraries, theaters, stadiums, parks; and many other types of public works are often taken for granted by contemporary society. They did not, however, just appear when they were needed. They were created through the efforts of many people working together within the framework of the American system of government. Dedicated men and women dreamed, planned, and worked for a better life. And the nation's engineers, contractors, and public officials joined with them to make their dreams a reality.

This comprehensive publication about the development of public works systems in the United States is based on materials provided by federal, state, and local units of government. It was undertaken by the American Public Works Association to commemorate the 200th anniversary of the American Revolution. Responsibility for producing the publication was entrusted to the APWA Bicentennial Commission which undertook the task with the cooperation of a distinguished Advisory Board. It was prepared and edited by a team of professional historians under the leadership of a prominent public works engineer-administrator. Assistance was provided by an Editorial Board composed of persons with wide and diversified experience.

The American Public Works Association (APWA) is a nonprofit public service organization composed of more than 1,000 public agency members and a total of 16,800 public works executives, engineers, and administrators at the federal, state, and local levels of government. Many educators, consulting engineers, and contractors, as well as representatives of manufacturers and suppliers of public works products, are also members of the association. It was founded in 1894, maintains its headquarters on the campus of the University of Chicago at the 1313 Center for Public Administration, and has a Washington office at 1776 Massachusetts Avenue, N.W. Members of APWA are served through a network of sixty chapters located in the United States and Canada.

HISTORY OF PUBLIC WORKS IN THE UNITED STATES
1776 - 1976

By
American Public Works Association

EDITOR

Ellis L. Armstrong

ASSOCIATE EDITORS

Michael C. Robinson   Suellen M. Hoy

American Public Works Association
1313 East 60th Street
Chicago, Illinois 60637

TABLE OF CONTENTS

FOREWORD

The American Public Works Association (APWA) is dedicated to improving public works practices and enhancing public understanding and support for needed public facilities and services. From its origin in 1894 to the present, this 16,800 member organization has conducted activities to promote excellence in the mangement of public works and to inspire loyal, dedicated public service. At a special ceremonial meeting held at Congress Hall in Philadelphia in September 1971, the association adopted a resolution to undertake, as its official bicentennial project, the preparation and publication of the *History of Public Works in the United States, 1776-1976.* Public Law 92-564, enacted by the Congress and signed by the President of the United States, endorsed this important undertaking. The APWA resolution is as follows:

Whereas public works, constituting as they do the physical structures and facilities required to house all types of governmental functions and provide water, power, waste disposal and transportation service to the general public, have contributed significantly to the growth and development of the United States; and

there is a general tendency to take public works facilities and services for granted, not realizing how much people are actually dependent upon such systems, particularly in urban communities; and

members of the American Public Works Association are now assembling in the historic City of Philadelphia for the 1971 Public Works Congress and Equipment Show, while members of its Board of Directors, House of Delegates and Advisory Council, consisting of the Past Presidents of the Association, are now convened in joint session in Congress Hall where the founding fathers of this Nation took historic action of far-reaching significance to all mankind; and

President Richard M. Nixon has officially proclaimed the Bicentennial Era to extend from 1971 through 1976, and has requested that appropriate steps be taken to mark the observance of the 200th Anniversary of the United States of America; now, therefore, be it

Resolved that members of the constituent bodies of the American Public Works Association assembled here this eleventh day of September, nineteen hundred seventy one, do hereby adopt and authorize as the Association's official Bicentennial project, the preparation and publication of a history of public works in the United States from 1776 to 1976 so that future generations may benefit from a comprehensive review of public works in perspective; and

that the Executive Director be requested to seek the cooperation and endorsement of this project by the Senate and House Public Works Committees of the United States Congress and that he be charged with the responsibility of making appropriate arrangements for the successful completion of this project by early 1976 and empowered to enter into agreements and incur such expenditures as may be required subject to their approval by the Board of Directors.

This publication, designed to be of lasting value to this and future generations, is the result. It was produced by the APWA Bicentennial Commission with the counsel of a distinguished Advisory Board. It was prepared from numerous special reports and contributions from many sources by a team of professional historians under the leadership of a prominent public works engineer-administrator. Valuable assistance was also provided by an Editorial Board composed of persons with wide and diversified experience. The history is so written to be of interest not only to governmental officials, engineers, and administrators but to the citizenry as a whole, and especially to the youth of the nation.

The *History of Public Works in the United States, 1776-1976* describes this nation's efforts to protect and enhance the human environment. It also offers an historical analysis of some of the basic workings of self-government. This is especially important in 1976 as the United States struggles to determine the most rational way to use its resources and to provide essential services without jeopardizing the health, safety, and well being of its people. This history not only demonstrates the vitality of democracy, but it also rekindles confidence in the people of the United States—past and present—and their institutions.

Ray W. Burgess
President
American Public Works Association

AMERICAN PUBLIC WORKS ASSOCIATION
BICENTENNIAL COMMISSION

HONORARY CHAIRMEN

Hon. Jennings Randolph, Chairman
Committee on Public Works
U.S. Senate

Hon. John A. Blatnik, Former Chairman
Committee on Public Works
U.S. House of Representatives

CHAIRMAN

Ellis L. Armstrong
U.S. Commissioner of Public Roads (1958-61)
Commissioner of U.S. Bureau of Reclamation (1969-73)
Adjunct Professor, University of Utah

MEMBERS

Joseph F. Casazza
Commissioner of Public Works
Boston, Mass.

Keith P. Mazurek
President, Truck Division
International Harvester Co.

Victor W. Sauer
Public Works Director
Contra Costa County, Calif.

Louis R. Howson, Partner
Alvord, Burdick and Howson

E. J. Peltier, President
Sverdrup & Parcel and
Associates, Inc.

Joseph A. Seta, President
Joseph A. Seta, Inc.

John A. Logan, President
Rose-Hulman Institute
of Technology

J. Philip Richley
Former Director
Ohio Dept. of Transportation

Wilbur S. Smith
Wilbur Smith & Assoc.

A. R. Marschall
Rear Admiral, USN
Commander, Naval Facilities
Engineering Command

Carl D. Wills
Director of Public Works
High Point, N.C.

ADVISORY BOARD

Hon. James T. Lynn
Secretary (1973-75)
U.S. Dept. of Housing and
Urban Development

Hon. Rogers C. B. Morton
Secretary (1971-75)
U.S. Dept. of the Interior

Hon. William T. Coleman, Jr.
Secretary (1975-   )
U.S. Dept. of Transportation

Hon. Russell E. Train
Administrator (1973-   )
U.S. Environmental Protection Agency

Hon. Arthur F. Sampson
Administrator (1973-75)
U.S. General Services Administration

Henrik E. Stafseth, Executive Secretary
American Assn. of State Highway &
Transportation Officials

Elmer K. Timby
Vice President
American Consulting Engineers Council

Max O. Urbahn, FAIA
President (1972)
American Institute of Architects

PUBLIC WORKS HISTORICAL SOCIETY
PATRONS

The Public Works Historical Society was created in 1975 by the American Public Works Association. The society exists to foster historical research and publication in the field of public works and thereby promote understanding of the role of public works in the growth and development of civilization. The patrons listed below have graciously provided the society with the developmental support so necessary for any new institution.

ORGANIZATIONS

Cutler Repaving, Inc.
The Graham Foundation
Morrison-Kundsen Company, Inc.
Newark Brush Co.
Rockwell International

CONSULTANTS

Albert Switzer & Associates
Boyle Engineering Corp.
CH$_2$M-Hill
Harza Engineering Company
Keyes Associates
Murphy Engineering, Inc.
Wilbur S. Smith & Assoc.

INDIVIDUALS

George H. Andrews	Wesley E. Gilbertson
Ellis L. Armstrong	Herbert A. Goetsch
James E. Attebery	Jack M. Graham
Frank Bowerman	Erwin F. Hensch
Robert D. Bugher	Mark B. Owen
Ray W. Burgess	Lyall A. Pardee
David H. Burrows	Eugene J. Peltier
Myron D. Calkins	Michael R. Pender
David Caplan	Jennings Randolph
John T. Carroll	John J. Roark
Edward J. Cleary	Joseph A. Seta
Russell R. Doyle	W. Clement Stone
Donald S. Frady	Jimmie V. Thurmond

INTRODUCTION

The American Public Works Association (APWA) undertook the task of publishing a history of public works in the United States convinced that, with the perspective history offers, the public works profession will be better prepared to provide and maintain the facilities and services that comprise the foundation of America's civilization. If the men and women who serve the profession are acquainted with the advancements in their field, public works will be a more effective force in communities across the nation. A person who is proud of the accomplishments and contributions of those who have gone before will undertake his or her own work with new respect and renewed vigor. *The History of Public Works in the United States, 1776-1976* is, however, so written to be of interest not only to governmental officials, engineers, and administrators but to the citizenry as a whole and especially to the youth of the nation.

Since public works achievements have occurred with little fanfare, they are generally taken for granted. Clear, clean water at the turn of a tap; light and power at the touch of a switch; wastes disposed of with the turn of a handle—these and many other public works services are accepted as customary in our daily lives. Yet when they fail to function properly or to meet continually rising expectations, citizen disapproval is nearly unanimous. The public has infrequently recognized the accomplishments of the past.

Even before the United States won its independence 200 years ago, it was dependent on public works. The first American settlers recognized the need for facilities to help them survive and prosper in a hostile new world. The colonists needed harbors to maintain contact with families, friends, and business associates in the mother country; and as they began moving inland and expanding westward, they required overland transportation routes. Their challenge of occupying a vast and primitive land was certainly formidable, but it was completed in a relatively short period of time. However, it would not have been possible without concentrated public works programs of all kinds.

The United States is today a highly developed nation, but there is still a great need for public works programs. The country's present standard of living brings with it new requirements, new concerns, and new commitments. It is obvious that we cannot function with the same assumptions that guided our forefathers. We can, however, profit from their experiences as we strive to develop and manage both present and future public works systems. To do this, we need a record of past events.

Such a record can serve a very practical purpose. It not only illustrates the accomplishments of our ancestors, it documents their mistakes as well. By studying the actions of our predecessors, we can learn to emulate their achievements and perhaps avoid their mistakes. History demonstrates, for instance, that our forefathers were not as sensitive as we are today to environmental issues. They disposed of wastes by discharging them into the water and air; they sometimes built canals, dams, and highways without adequate concern for landscapes and communities; and they provided needed energy without always considering or minimizing the adverse effects of its production. But conditions have changed. Present generations can no longer afford to continue harmful practices. And we will not do so, if we are conscious of the past.

This nation's public works heritage has been neglected by most historians. It is the hope of APWA members that the *History of Public Works in the United States, 1776-1976* will be recognized as a beginning that will stimulate interest and additional research in a highly significant field. As a result of APWA's commitment to the collection, preservation, and dissemination of public works history, it has created the Public Works Historical Society to carry on the work begun by the APWA Bicentennial Commission. Assistance contributed by the society's patrons supported the production of this volume.

This publication is not an encyclopedia of public works history. Rather, it is a survey which traces the evolution of the most significant public works programs and facilities from the birth of the nation to its bicentennial. Various aspects of public works history are treated in different chapters. For instance, the constant political and legislative struggle to determine the areas of state and federal public works responsibility is treated in detail in Chapter 7, "Airways and Airports." Advancing technology's effect on design and construction methods is detailed in Chapter 9, "Flood Control and Drainage," and in Chapter 10, "Irrigation." Examples of specific projects are given, not on the basis of comparative importance, but to illustrate types of problems and accomplishments.

In preparing the history, assistance was received from numerous public agencies at all governmental levels as well as professional organizations and APWA Chapters located in the United States. Acquiring the data to prepare a 200-year survey of American public works presented immense problems. Very little historical investigation had been undertaken of most subjects, and draft chapters had to be written from original sources. In 1973 a tentative book outline was formulated and revised on the basis of discussions with the APWA Bicentennial Commission, Advisory Board, and Editorial Board. A questionnaire was sent to local, state, and federal agencies to identify and acquire relevant historical information. In addition, the APWA Chapters were requested to select and submit descriptions of landmark public works projects in their respective areas. The responses were enthusiastic; and from the results, specific requests for special reports and information were made to federal agencies and professional associations.

From the large amount of information that was collected, the editors prepared the *History of Public Works in the United States, 1776-1976*. The principal contributors are recognized in a footnote at the beginning of each chapter. Others are acknowledged in this introduction. Without the assistance of these individuals, it would have been impossible to produce this publication in the time allotted. It must also be stated that the contributions received from these individuals and the many public agencies contacted were not only carefully prepared but meaningful in content. Thus, any errors or imperfections remain the responsibility of the editors.

Many portions of the APWA bicentennial history are based on contributions from federal agencies. In accordance with Public Law 92-564, the public works oriented departments and independent agencies of the national government prepared special reports and submitted books, articles, photographs, and other historical data to the APWA Bicentennial Commission. Their efforts in the project's behalf raised understanding of the valuable perspective history gives to the formulation and implementation of public policy. Some agencies initiated or broadened historical programs as a result of participating in this project. Heads of federal departments and agencies served as members of the history's Advisory Board, and top-level administrative staff assisted the project by designating the following individuals to provide support.

The United States Department of Transportation was a major contributor to the history. John L.

McGruder and Walter F. Cronin led a task force of department personnel that included Nick Komons, Federal Aviation Administration; Joyce Ritter, Federal Highway Administration; and JoAnne Sloane, Federal Railway Administration. These individuals collected materials as well as prepared special reports that formed the basis of several chapters covering the development of American transportation. Special recognition is given to Frederich W. Cron of the department's Federal Highway Administration, who prepared extensive material on the history of highways. Furthermore, Truman Stubridge, United States Coast Guard, compiled a presentation that surveyed his agency's role in military public works. The APWA is also grateful to Diane Enos and Bob Abrams of the department's Urban Mass Transportation Administration, who extended courtesies and offered advice which strengthened the history's treatment of municipal mass transit.

All branches of the American military furnished materials that covered their respective roles in American public works history. Howard Stingle was retained by the Army Corps of Engineers to provide data on the corps' pivotal role in the evolution of military installations, navigation, and water resource development. His work was embellished by review and comments offered by Editorial Board member Lenore Fine, Albert Cowdry, and other members of the agency's Historical Division. Gratitude is also extended to Edward Greene, who coordinated the corps' assistance; and Roy Gordon and Doran A. Topoloski, who compiled an extensive collection of photographs. Colonel Charles Schilling, United States Military Academy, drafted a survey history of West Point's seminal role in the growth of the civil engineering profession. The APWA Bicentennial Commission member Rear Admiral A. R. Marschall, commander of the Naval Facilities Engineering Command, designated Judy Johnston to undertake a definitive survey of naval public works. Her lucid and illuminating manuscript was one of the finest contributions received by the project. A history of air installations, written by Major John McAndrews of the United States Air Force, was equally good.

Several agencies of the Department of Interior furnished material on their wide-ranging contributions to the development and preservation of natural resources. Jim Hart, Carlos Whiting, and K. K. Young assembled data that surveyed the Bureau of Reclamation's role in the development of irrigation, hydroelectric power, and domestic and industrial water supplies in the West. Dan Schausten and Vera Springer of the Bonneville Power Administration submitted an excellent historical survey of the effect of electric power transmission and generation on the growth of the northwestern United States. Douglas Baldwin, Bureau of Outdoor Recreation, provided a summary of the nation's parks and recreation programs.

The Department of Agriculture submitted documents and prepared special reports for several chapters. David Granahan and Wayne Rasmussen coordinated the agency's contribution and Glen Kovar, Forest Service; Louis L. Granados, Rural Electrification Administration; and Hubert Kelley and F. Glennon Lloyd, Soil Conservation Service provided specific assistance. The Department of Health, Education, and Welfare's Office of Education gave support to the Council of Educational Facilities Planners that enabled the latter to prepare a survey of educational facilities. Harold Arberg coordinated the agency's assistance and Dwayne Gardner, the council's executive director, directed his organization's efforts. The Economic Development Administration's contribution, which was submitted by Barbara A. Estabrook, consisted of case studies of significant public works projects. Special thanks are also due Leo Morris and E. J. Howenstine, Department of Housing and Urban Development, who provided documents and data.

The chapter on public buildings incorporates contributions from three independent federal agencies. T. L. Payton, Jr., Allan G. Kaupinen, Walter Roth, Peg Malloy, and Mickey Blackistone of the General Services Administration lent support. The agency retained eminent architectural historian Frederick A. Gutheim and his associate Antoinette Lee to survey the evolution of federal buildings and support facilities. The United States Postal Service's Rita L. Moroney and Linda Wilson prepared a treatment of their agency's growth that was used to write a history of postal buildings. John Garver and Larry Gorban of the Veterans Administration were enthusiastic and dedicated contributors to the history. They fashioned a thorough and informative treatment of the agency's hospitals and domiciliaries.

Since the responsibilities of the Environmental Protection Agency have a broad effect on the public works profession, it made important contributions to several chapters. William A. Schwartz and Gilbert M. Gigliotti, of the agency's National Environmental Research Center, compiled a large body of data on sewers, wastewater treatment, and air quality. Robert Griffin was designated to survey the evolution of solid waste collection and disposal practices, and the chapter on this topic was strengthened by Ralph Black's cogent advice and criticism. Richard Hewlett, Energy Research and Development Administration, offered data and guidance on atomic energy. The Federal Power Commission's submittal, written by Michael Walker, was a thorough analysis of hydroelectric power. Larry Calvert coordinated the Tennessee Valley Authority's contribution to several chapters on water resource and inland navigation development, and NASA's Frank Anderson, Jr., prepared an outstanding survey history of aeronautical research and space exploration.

The quality of the history was enhanced by the work of the six APWA Bicentennial History Fellows. In 1974 this group spent the summer in Washington, D.C., conducting research on selected topics in public works history. They subsequently submitted manuscripts which comprised the basis or formed integral parts of several chapters. Their respective names, universities, and topics follow: James Gardner, Vanderbilt University, Atomic Energy; Gordon Hendrickson, University of Wyoming, Water Quality; Richard Harland, George Washington University, Communications; Richard McEvoy, University of Maryland, Public Housing; Richard Nagle, Pennsylvania State University, Labor and Public Works; and Christine O'Conner, University of Arizona, Railroads. Furthermore, Frank N. Schubert and Jesse Smith, Jr., undertook supplemental research that improved several chapters.

In addition to the above contributions, many portions of the history were prepared from research conducted by the APWA Bicentennial Commission at institutions in the Washington, D.C. area. The project was expedited by special courtesies extended by the Library of Congress. Dudley Ball and John F. Brannigan, Stack and Reader Division, and Legare H. B. Obear, Loan Division, were gracious and helpful. James D. Walker and Albert U. Blair guided APWA researchers to relevant materials in the National Archives; and Robert Vogel and John H. White, Jr., offered advice, lent criticism, and located resources in the Smithsonian Institution.

In addition to supporting the project through membership on the Advisory Board, several professional organizations offered additional assistance. Through the efforts of George Symons, president (1973) of the American Water Works Association, and Eric Johnson, the association's executive director, the APWA Bicentennial Commission received a manuscript on community water supply development written by J. M. LaNier. Dwight F. Rettie, executive director of the National Recreation and Park Association, furnished a draft historical survey prepared by Peter S. Verhoven, Tempel R. Jarell, and Judith Goldstein that served as the basis for the chapter on parks and recreation.

Richard Fenton of the City of New York's Environmental Protection Agency and Rodney R. Fleming. American Public Works Association, presented incisive advice on the solid wastes chapter. John C. Duba, Air Transport Association of America, and Adele C. Schwartz, Airport Operators Council International, offered remarks and data that improved the discussion of airport development. Dorothy Gazzola, National Association of Housing and Redevelopment Officials, made insightful suggestions that strengthened the public housing chapter. A large measure of gratitude is tendered to Edward J. Cleary, University of Cincinnati, whose lifetime dedication to public works was reflected in his keen comments on several chapters. Finally, the following individuals assisted in formulating the structure and conceptual framework of the history's concluding chapter, "The Profession in Perspective:" Joseph P. Ashooh, Associated General Contractors; Robert D. Bugher, American Public Works Association; Donald A. Buzzell, American Consulting Engineers Council; Donald C. Stone, Carnegie-Mellon University; and Raymond H. Merritt, University of Wisconsin at Milwaukee.

Grateful appreciation is extended to the Editorial Board for reading the manuscript and making numerous thoughtful suggestions. Associate Editors Michael C. Robinson and Suellen M. Hoy's many contributions at every stage of the project deserve special acknowledgement. The enthusiastic drive, support, and review of Robert D. Bugher, APWA's executive director, made the undertaking possible. And special thanks are due Anne Spray, who typed and indexed the entire manuscript, and Paula Degen, who assisted in the final editing of the history. Many others also made contributions and their efforts are deeply appreciated. Special thanks are also due my wife, Florine, who has had a hectic two years, with many plans jettisoned, serving as supporter, reviewer, and critic.

Ellis L. Armstrong
Editor

CHAPTER 1

PUBLIC WORKS AND PRIVATE RIGHTS

Public works are developed by and for the benefit of people. Designed to protect and enhance the human environment, they represent investments in the future for the people who create them and for succeeding generations. "Public works" is a generic term broadly defined as: "The physical structures and facilities developed or acquired by public agencies to house governmental functions and provide water, waste disposal, power, transportation, and similar services to facilitate the achievement of common social and economic objectives." In the United States, questions such as when, where, and what kinds of public works should be constructed are largely determined by the actions of people exercising their private rights and responsibilities as individuals. These include but by no means are limited to, their right to vote.

Governmental institutions, land, capital, labor, and public support are prerequisites for the development of virtually all public works facilities. Since the nation was founded 200 years ago, states, cities, counties, townships, and special districts, as well as various agencies of the federal government, have contracted for the construction of thousands of

public works projects. In each instance, they were significantly influenced by the scope of power of the contracting authority and by the availability of land upon which the facilities were to be built. Because citizens have long considered their right to own land one of their most precious rights, a wide assortment of problems have arisen when privately owned land was needed for public improvements. Thus, any discussion of the development of public works systems must of necessity treat the relationship of land ownership and use to the construction of public improvements.

Capital is also essential in the creation of all public works facilities. Its availability is significantly affected by economic conditions throughout the nation. The federal government's fiscal and monetary policies have a direct bearing on both the public and private sectors and determine to a large extent the amount of tax revenues available to finance public works programs. Therefore, an awareness of this interrelationship is basic to an understanding of the problems associated with the development of public works systems.

Labor and public support are likewise important factors in the construction of public improvements. Although normally financed by various governmental units, public works are usually built by contractors who employ large numbers of individuals from the private sector. Yet many of the social gains of the

This chapter was prepared by Robert. D. Bugher, APWA Executive Director. Portions are based on a manuscript written by Richard Nagle, APWA Bicentennial History Fellow, and materials provided by the Economic Development Administration.

1

New York City-Newark, New Jersey metropolitan area. Public works facilities such as airports, ports, bridges, and highways foster commercial and industrial development.

country's work force have resulted from actions taken by the national government on federally funded projects. But, in the end, it is the people and their elected representatives who determine what projects are undertaken and how problems involving land, capital, and labor are resolved.

People are the basic source of societal power and customarily exercise it through a myriad of public and private institutions. Theoretically, the only authority that these institutions have is that which has been collectively relinquished to them by the people who created them. Private institutions, which are a vital part of the social and economic fabric of the nation, are generally organized and controlled by a limited number of persons who have special or personal interests to advance. But governments are formed as public institutions to serve the common interests of all people within the boundaries of their jurisdictions.

Different political philosophies describe the people's relation to their governments. Views vary from the belief that the most effective government controls virtually all aspects of the lives of its citizens to the conviction that

the best government is that which governs least. In *The Wealth of Nations*, published in 1776, Adam Smith stated that the functions of government should be limited to providing for external defense, affording legal protection, and undertaking indispensable public works. Government, he said, had "the duty of erecting and maintaining certain public works and public institutions, which it can never be for the interest of any individual, or small number of individuals, to erect and maintain, because the profit could never repay the expense to any individual, or small number of individuals, though it may frequently do much more than repay it to a great society." Although the multitude of functions performed by public institutions in the 1970s is far more extensive than those enumerated above, the planning, design, construction, operation, and maintenance of public works have always been regarded as appropriate responsibilities of government.

The United States has traditionally been called "the land of promises and opportunities." For over two centuries, the promise of self-fulfillment and the opportunity to be free and independent have attracted people from afar and motivated those who reside within the nation's boundaries. And the unalienable rights of "Life, Liberty and the pursuit of Happiness," proclaimed in the Declaration of Independence, have inspired the citizens of this country to develop one of the most creative, complex, and dynamic societies the world has ever known.

The Constitution, which is the fundamental "law of the land," provides for the separation of powers between the legislative, executive, and judicial branches of the federal government. Those not delegated to the federal government, nor prohibited by it, may be exercised by state and local governments. The basic authority and constraints of power regarding the building of public works are, therefore, found in the Constitution. Although state and local governments have been responsible for most public works projects, some of the largest undertakings have been constructed under the direction of federal agencies.

State and Local Units of Government

The states generally adopted forms of government patterned after the national system. They divided their power between legislative, executive, and judicial branches; and nearly all states created bicameral legislatures. Since the composition of these legislatures was determined by the number of people living in various districts, some state constitutions required that districts be reapportioned every ten years to insure more equal representation in state legislatures. Notwithstanding this requirement, elected officials often refused to vote for reapportionment because they feared that it would reduce their chances of being reelected. Thus, as population shifted from rural to urban areas, serious problems, adversely affecting public works programs and infringing on the individual's private rights, developed in many states.

By 1960, in every state, there was at least a two-to-one disparity in voter representation between the most and least heavily populated districts. In some cases, the disproportion was much greater. This imbalance tended to create financial problems for many large cities. For while they struggled to provide needed facilities and services for their growing populations, rural-dominated legislatures tended to remain unresponsive to their requests for additional revenue.

As late as 1946, the United States Supreme Court refused to consider reapportionment cases since they were considered "too political." But by the 1960s, more liberal-minded justices had been named to the court, and public sentiment favoring reapportionment had become more pronounced. Between 1962 and 1964, the Supreme Court assisted cities by rendering a series of landmark decisions. In each case, the court decided in favor of reapportionment, arguing that as nearly as practicable one person's vote is to be worth as much as another's. Within a five-year period, all but one state had carried out—or promised to carry out—some form of reapportionment. Only in a few instances in the history of the United States had the Supreme Court's rulings so directly affected local governments.

There were over 78,000 units of local government in the United States in 1972, including counties, townships, special and school districts, and municipalities (see Table 1-1). Virtually all of these units are responsible for the construction and maintenance of some kind of public works facility. Counties are formed by the sovereign power of the state without the consent or action of the people who inhabit them and exist in all states except Connecticut, Rhode Island, Louisiana, and Alaska. The principal political subdivision corresponding to the county is the parish in Louisiana and the borough in Alaska. The number of counties in each state varies from as few as 3 in Delaware to as many as 254 in Texas; most states, however, have from 60 to 100 counties. New York County is the smallest in area with only 21 square miles; San Bernardino County in California is the largest with 20,175 square miles. Each county usually comprises an area of about 400 to 500 square miles, even though their populations range from less than 100 to over 7 million persons.

The first county was established in Virginia over 200 years ago. This unit of government has always had important responsibilities in collecting taxes, in improving

TABLE 1-1
Total Number of Governmental Units in 1962, 1967, and 1972

Type of Government	1962	1967	1972
Total	91,237	81,299	78,269
U.S. Government	1	1	1
State governments	50	50	50
Local governments	91,186	81,248	78,218
Counties	3,043	3,049	3,044
Municipalities	18,000	18,048	18,517
Townships	17,142	17,105	16,991
School districts	34,678	21,782	15,781
Special districts	18,323	21,264	23,885

Bureau of the Census

roads, and in maintaining the rights of the individual by administering justice and conducting elections. In more recent years, the county has been assuming an increasingly significant role in providing public works facilities and services to those, particularly in rural areas, who cannot acquire them by other means. The inability of small towns and villages, located in metropolitan areas, to deal effectively with some of their public works

TABLE 1-2
Independent Special Districts within and outside Metropolitan Areas, Percent Distribution by Function: 1972

	Number of Districts	Percent of Districts Within SMSA's (1)	Percent of Districts Outside SMSA's (1)
Total all districts	23,885	32.8	67.2
Northeast	3,937	52.9	47.1
North Central	8,024	25.3	74.7
South	5,525	24.6	75.4
West	6,400	37.1	62.9
Single function districts	22,983	31.6	68.2
Cemeteries	1,496	10.5	89.5
School building	1,085	57.1	42.9
Fire protection	3,872	38.5	61.5
Highways	698	19.9	80.1
Health	257	39.3	60.7
Hospitals	655	22.9	77.1
Housing & urban renewal	2,270	30.4	69.6
Libraries	498	29.7	70.3
Natural resources, total	6,630	20.3	79.7
Drainage	2,192	19.9	80.1
Flood control	677	19.4	80.6
Irrigation, water conservation	966	28.1	72.0
Soil conservation	2,564	16.2	83.8
Other	231	39.8	60.2
Parks and recreation	749	50.3	49.7
Sewerage	1,406	58.5	41.5
Utilities, total	2,478	37.4	62.6
Water supply	2,323	37.8	62.2
Electric power	74	17.6	82.4
Gas supply	48	14.6	85.4
Transit	33	93.9	6.1
Other	889	37.0	63.0
Multiple function districts	903	60.2	39.8
Sewerage & water supply	629	60.3	39.7
Natural resource & water	67	65.7	34.3
Other	207	58.5	41.5

(1) Standard Metropolitan Statistical Areas (cities and adjacent areas with populations of at least 50,000)

Advisory Commission on Intergovernmental Relations

problems has led many counties to develop regional systems to serve such communities. In fact, many urban counties presently furnish the same kinds of facilities and services that at one time were found only in large American cities.

Townships, as subdivisions of counties, were established in the Middle Colonies during the seventeenth century. They were generally rural in nature and were responsible for performing limited public works and other governmental functions. Sixteen states still retain these subdivisions, and they remain a viable force. Various types of special districts were also established to provide essential public works facilities. As early as 1790, Philadelphia had organized a special district to administer prisons; and in the following years, districts were formed for many other purposes. The Port Authority of New York and New Jersey, created in 1921, is currently responsible for the management of three major airports as well as tunnels, bridges, port facilities, a rapid transit system, and an international trade center. Boston, Chicago, Seattle, and scores of other cities have established metropolitan sanitary districts for the treatment and disposal of wastewaters (see Table 1-2). Airport and transit authorities have likewise been organized to serve people living in large regional districts. But the most common of the many types that have been formed are the school districts. They were among the first to be created and have been largely responsible for the construction of the nation's schools.

New York City became the first chartered American municipality in 1652. However, the New England town, with its characteristic style of government, existed almost from the date of the earliest settlers' arrival in Massachusetts Bay. Jon C. Teaford, in *The Municipal Revolution in America,* traces the evolution of the city through colonial times and the early years of the nation's history. He explains that prior to the 1730s and 1740s, urban rule rested primarily with those concerned with the regulation and promotion of trade. An examination of ordinances enacted in Philadelphia from 1705 to 1724, for example, revealed that 53 percent of them dealt with trade and only 18 percent with public works. Whereas seventeenth- and early eighteenth-century municipalities regulated trade—often in favor of the well-to-do—because of the scarcity of goods and supplies, succeeding generations tended to regard such regulations as unnecessary and undesirable. By 1775 municipal barriers to growth, mobility, and enterprise gradually collapsed as people became more concerned with public health and safety, clean water, paved streets, and other public works.

The Revolution marked not only the beginning of a new nation but a broadening of opportunities to participate in the political life of the community. But, following the war, two conflicting views emerged which have influenced the scope and quality of public works programs for 200 years. There were those who stressed the need to give increased power and money to cities so they could, among other things, provide needed public works facilities. There were also those who were fearful that the entrustment of such power to government might pose a threat to both the political and private rights of the people. Ever since, the extent of support given public works programs has varied with the degree of confidence citizens have placed in their governments.

Although some states incorporated cities by special act, this practice often proved unsatisfactory. As a result, general laws for the incorporation of cities were usually enacted. Many municipalities still operate under charters adopted pursuant to these statutes, while others are governed by home rule charters. According to the United States Supreme Court, a home rule city "occupies a unique position. It does not, like most cities, derive its powers by grant from the legislature, but it frames its own charter under express authority from the people of the state, given in the constitution." The primary advantage of such charters is that they may be defended in the courts against conflicting statutes enacted by state legislatures. For it is only by constitutional amendment that a state may alter the power of self-government conferred upon cities by a state constitution.

City charters are similar to federal and

state constitutions in that they prescribe the legal framework within which public business is conducted and private rights are protected. The city council or commission serves as the municipality's legislative body and adopts plans, budgets, and ordinances and also often awards public works contracts. The council or commission is commonly composed of the people's elected representatives and thus functions as a policy-making body in a manner similar to Congress and the state legislatures. The public works issues on which legislative bodies must act are often clear cut. In such instances, laws can be tightly drafted and easily implemented. Where issues are complex, laws are frequently accompanied by administrative guidelines. These are intended to insure uniform interpretation and fair application of laws. Yet it is not uncommon for federal, state, and local courts to be called upon to resolve questions or rule on cases affecting public works programs and the private rights of individual citizens. Thus, virtually every level of government may, at one time or another, become involved with a public works project. Since people live within several governmental jurisdictions—one or more special districts, a city, county, state, and nation—it becomes important in the formulation and implementation of public works policies that their respective powers be carefully defined to minimize waste and conflict.

Responsibility for public works functions has shifted over the years. Activities that were once regarded as matters of strictly local interest are now issues of state and national concern. The increased mobility of Americans has made the environment and public facilities in one community more important to persons living in other parts of the country. Each year nearly one out of every three families pack up their belongings and move to another locality. A lack of adequate transportation and drainage systems in cities and towns situated in metropolitan areas can have an adverse effect on people living or working in neighboring jurisdictions who must pass through such communities. Since larger units of government are often in a better position to finance the many kinds of public works

facilities needed both within and beyond local boundaries, the states and the federal government have become increasingly involved in their development. Councils of governments, intergovernmental agreeements, and local governmental consolidations have all emerged to facilitate the delivery of such services.

Land Ownership, Use, and Development Patterns

The vast network of public works facilities which extends from coast to coast provides the life-support systems for the most productive nation in the world. Two-hundred years after its founding, the United States stands second to no other country in terms of wealth and power—characteristics which are both liked and disliked at home and abroad. Each, however, is generally considered essential for protecting the interests of Americans, increasing their standard of living, and assisting the people of other nations in obtaining a better way of life.

Natural resources, especially land, have been the primary source of wealth for large numbers of United States citizens. It was the quest for land that motivated thousands of Europeans to leave their native countries and establish colonies in North America. Even before the eastern coast was fully settled, many colonists moved westward to exploit the riches of their "new-found-land." Since they regarded America as the land of plenty, they used it—drew from it, built upon it—to make theirs and future generations prosperous. But to whom does the land belong?

There are presently some 2.3 billion acres of land in the United States. Approximately

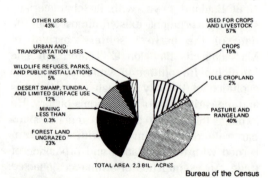

Figure 1-1.
Land Use in the 50 States 1969.

three fifths of this acreage is privately owned. Included in this amount are 99 percent of the nation's cropland, 61 percent of the grassland pasture, 56 percent of the forest land, 13 percent of the remaining land (mostly swamps, marshes, desert, and tundra), and about 40 million acres of urban land. Thus, a relatively large portion of the land, with all its favorable attributes, is in private hands.

Before the American Revolution, land was held primarily by the proprietors of the various colonies and their associates. After independence was won, those lands not already deeded to private landholders became a part of the public domain to be disposed of by the federal government and the states. But not until New York and Virginia had ceded their claims to land west of Pennsylvania and north of the Ohio River did the survey and disposal of public land become the concern of Congress. The initial arrangements for the disposition of the Old Northwest Territory were then set forth in the 1785 Land Ordinance, which provided for the rectangular survey and the establishment of the six-mile-square township as the basic land pattern.

These land townships served as convenient and easily identifiable local units of government. Many assumed responsibility for conducting elections, levying taxes, laying out roads, and building schools. The 1785 Land Ordinance specifically stipulated that a portion of the land be reserved for the benefit of common schools. Although land subsidies for public works facilities were not originally provided for, many land grants were made to subsidize road building, canal digging, river improvements, and, in later years, railroad construction.

The procedures for disposing of land in the public domain were also set forth in the 1785 Land Ordinance. Before the land was surveyed and offered for sale at auctions, all Indian titles were to be cleared; then, when the land was sold, a proper deed granting title in fee simple was issued by the federal government to the purchaser. The minimum amount of land that could be bought was initially 640 acres. This amount was, however, reduced several times until by 1834, forty acres became the minimum.

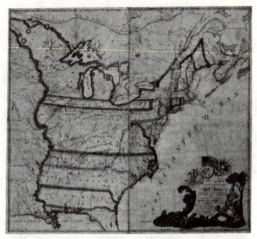

Abel Buell's 1783 map of the United States. The relinquishment of western land claims by the states enabled passage of the 1785 Land Ordinance.

The original legislation fixed the minimum price of public land at $1.00 per acre plus the surveying cost. In 1796 the price was increased to $2.00 per acre, and a year's time was allowed to complete payment. The law was changed in 1800 to give purchasers four years to pay for their land, but this credit feature was removed in 1820 when the minimum price was reduced to $1.25 per acre. The Graduation Act, adopted in 1854, authorized that land which had been on the market for a considerable period of time be sold below the $1.25 minimum price. Finally, in 1862 Congress passed the Homestead Act which provided that the federal government give title to 160 acres of land to heads of families who agreed to till the land for a minimum of five years. Although this measure helped to settle the West, most of the more productive land had already been claimed, including the sizeable areas added to the public domain during the intervening years.

In disposing of the public domain, over 380 land offices were established. However, the sale of these lands never provided a reliable source of revenue for the federal government. The Public Land Commission, created by Congress in 1880, reported that the public domain had cost the government over $322 million and that land sales had returned only $200 million to the Treasury. The primary objective of the federal government during this period was to place as much land and resources as possible in the hands of settlers and entrepreneurs. This course of action was not inconsistent with the "laissez-faire" policy espoused by Adam Smith and others who believed that "pluralistic decisions working their cumulative impact through the interplay of competition were far more efficient and more likely to achieve outcomes in the best interests of society than any heavyhanded attempt by government to direct the course of national development."

Much of the land disposed of by the federal government was placed under cultivation in the second half of the nineteenth century. The number of farms increased from 1.4 million in 1850 to 5.7 million in 1900. The value of farm property more than doubled during the following decade, and the average value of farmland rose from $13 per acre in 1900 to $32 in 1910. As in earlier years, land continued to be a speculative commodity; for once land became the property of private owners, it was the owners' right to do with it as they pleased. Since mineral rights were generally joined with surface rights when land was transferred from federal to state or private ownership, the speculative fever was especially high in those areas where rich mineral deposits had been discovered.

The rapid growth of the country was also accompanied by an increase in the use of natural resources, including mineral fuels and other materials. By 1972 the United States utilized 4.4 billion tons of new basic raw materials each year to sustain the nation's economy. The sizes of the rectangles in Figure 1-2 indicate the proportionate weight of each type of material required per capita. The mining, transportation, and processing of these huge quantities of materials obviously demanded large capital investments, provided employment for many segments of the populations, and had a significant impact upon the surrounding environment.

As land and natural resources were used more intensively, it became apparent that certain restrictions on the private rights of individuals were needed. The value of one piece of land, for example, depended to a

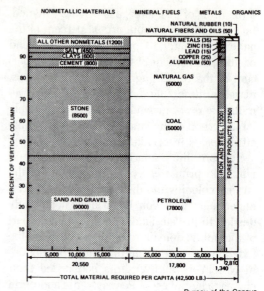

Bureau of the Census

Figure 1-2.
Weight of New Basic Raw Material Used Per Capita in the United States in 1972 (in Pounds).

large extent upon the availability of public works facilities and the uses to which the surrounding parcels were put. In the 1920s, local units of government began enacting zoning ordinances to regulate land use, particularly in urban areas. Zoning practices, however, have been severely criticized in recent years. Although they initially provided a reasonable degree of guidance to the developers of private property in urban areas, the limited jurisdictions of the many villages, towns, and cities adopting zoning regulations in metropolitan areas frequently resulted in a hodgepodge of land use patterns. These irregular patterns, in turn, created numerous problems, not the least of which was that of providing adequate public works facilities to the taxpayer at a reasonable cost.

During recent years, the public's attitude toward land and urban growth changed. Increased concern about the depletion of the nation's natural resources and the high cost of alleviating congestion and pollution prompted many persons to demand new policies to control all types of land development in both rural and urban areas. This altered attitude represented a significant departure from the modified laissez-faire traditions which governed private land developments during the last 150 years. Vermont, Maine, Florida, and North Carolina, spurred to action by the tide of public opinion, followed Hawaii's lead and enacted statewide land use control laws.

The resource demands that future urban growth may entail and the impact of public works on the shape and distribution of growth have promoted some—such as John A. Blatnik, former chairman of the House Public Works Committee—to call for the enactment of a National Public Works Investment policy. This would necessarily involve comprehensive regional planning and include an assessment of the collective impact of diverse public works projects on a given area and its capacity to assimilate the activities sustained by such projects. Federal funds for the construction of needed facilities would thereafter be allocated only for projects meeting pre-determined "carrying capacity" criteria. Greater consideration of the social and environmental stress that these projects may alleviate or induce would be taken into account along with economic impact and other factors that have guided public works investments in the past.

The idea that the population of an area will ultimately be limited by its resources, underscored in the nation's early history, has also received more attention in recent years. In a famous essay on population, Thomas Malthus noted in 1798 that while populations are capable of exponential growth the resources on which they depend only increase arithmetically. The demand for food can, therefore, be expected to exceed the available supply at some point in the future—even with the larger yields and the greater amounts of land placed under cultivation. The rapid growth of the world's population, which is expected to double from 4 to 8 billion in the next thirty-five years, has already placed a considerable strain on the economies of many nations. And although resources can be transferred from areas of abundance to areas of scarcity, this is both difficult and costly. Thus, problems continue to mount and become more acute as demands exceed supplies, whether it be wheat, oil, or any other essential resource. These conditions illustrate the importance of the current debate in international circles on population control and bring into sharp focus the interdependent nature of the world as it exists today.

The availability of adequate highways, water, power, and waste disposal systems may make a particular area attractive for development. However, history teaches that development actually occurs only when industries choose to locate in that area, individuals move there anticipating better employment opportunities, and developers build there. Thus, the timing, rate, and extent of growth is dependent not only on actions taken by governments but also on a myriad of decisions made by private institutions and individuals.

Some contend that the development of public works systems should be limited to accommodate the pre-determined carrying capacity of an area. Others point out, however, that to achieve the desired effect, it is also necessary to restrict the use of such systems to their design capacity. The problem, therefore, is basically one of regulating or restricting the use of available facilities. Limiting the number of private vehicles on existing streets to their design capacity, for example, obviously would alleviate air pollution and traffic congestion. However, proposals of this type have been strongly opposed in the past by those who objected to such restrictions and who preferred instead to put up with the prevailing levels of pollution and to use the streets at reduced rates of efficiency.

The fact that technological advances can often change alternatives and alleviate problems complicates matters still further. For instance, federally imposed air pollution standards have spurred the development of techniques which have significantly reduced pollutants in exhaust gases from automobiles. According to the United States Environmental Protection Agency, 1975 model cars showed a 90 percent reduction in hydrocarbons, 83 percent in carbon monoxide, and 48 percent in oxides of nitrogen over pre-1968 cars which had no pollution controls. Although further reductions are desirable—and anticipated, these figures serve to illustrate the dynamic nature of the scientific and regulatory processes as they interact in a pluralistic society.

Studies conducted in 1974 by the Academy for Contemporary Problems for the Public Works Committee of the House of

Representatives confirmed that natural resources served as the primary stimulant for national development in the United States during the eighteenth and nineteenth centuries. However, by the early twentieth century, the nation had become so influenced by laissez-faire doctrines that public actions were often taken only in response to the needs and problems arising from private decisions. Thus, government was expected to react to private initiatives rather than to lead—to provide the necessary public works systems in an effort to stimulate private investment. But in the 1930s, when employment became a serious problem, the federal government departed from its reactive policies and initiated thousands of public works projects as part of a comprehensive economic recovery program.

Labor, Prosperity, and Productivity
    The building, operation, and maintenance of public works have provided jobs, relieved unemployment during depressions, and helped establish fair wage rates and equal employment opportunities for millions of Americans. During the nineteenth century, large projects—such as those involving the construction of roads, canals, and railroads—employed thousands of workers, particularly new immigrants who obtained their first jobs on public works undertakings. As cities grew after the Civil War, workers found employment paving streets; building and maintaining sewer, water, and waste disposal systems; and erecting public buildings. Thus, in the past two centuries, public works have played an important role in the social and economic development of the nation.
    Funding public works to offset serious unemployment was advocated during the depressions of the 1850s and 1870s, but these proposals were not implemented. However, the Panic of 1893, which eventually threw 20 percent of the labor force out of work, prompted some cities to look to public works as a way to alleviate distress. In many instances, private groups such as churches and settlement houses worked with municipal governments to employ people. Projects included landscaping public parks, cleaning

refuse from alleys, and shoveling snow after storms. Municipal governments also attempted to accelerate their public programs. Rather than wait for summer, Holyoke, Massachusetts, employed 300 men to build sewers during winter months. In addition, Waterbury, Connecticut, inaugurated a winter street program to provide jobs. Although these efforts were spotty, they set important precedents for using public works to reduce unemployment. In the wake of the 1920-1921 depression, several plans were put forth by presidential commissions and congressmen to use public works to stabilize employment. Basically, the proposals advocated increasing expenditures for public works whenever private employment slacked off. However, public works were not used in an attempt to bolster an ailing economy until the Depression of the 1930s.
    The 1929 stock market crash touched off ten years of "hard times." Unemployment soared from 3 percent in 1929 to nearly 25 percent in 1933, creating widespread human suffering. Although public works programs are associated with the New Deal, President Herbert Hoover approved the 1932 Relief and Construction Act which made $300 million available for public construction loans. This law marked the beginning of direct federal efforts to alleviate unemployment through public works expenditures. During President Franklin D. Roosevelt's first two terms, a number of federal public works agencies were founded, including the Civilian Conservation Corps (CCC), Tennessee Valley Authority (TVA), Federal Emergency Relief Administration (FERA), and the Civil Works Administration (CWA). However, the Works Progress Administration (WPA) and the Public Works Administration (PWA) were responsible for executing the largest number of projects.
    The WPA was popularly regarded as a "make-work" agency, but actually over 75 percent of its funds went for construction. The WPA workers built or improved nearly 500,000 miles of roads, erected 78,000 bridges, and constructed thousands of schools, hospitals, courthouses, and sanitation facilities. About 8.5 million persons worked

U.S. Bureau of Reclamation

Hoover Dam construction, 1933. New Deal public works projects provided employment for millions of Americans.

for the agency in the 1930s. The PWA built federal facilities and made loans and grants to state and local public agencies for large, durable structures. Its projects literally changed the face of the country. The PWA's undertakings benefited 3,069 of the nation's 3,071 counties; and from 1933 to 1939, it accounted for 70 percent of school construction as well as 65 percent of the new courthouses and city halls. In addition, PWA and other public works programs indirectly stimulated employment through orders for construction materials. The New Deal public works programs did not completely revive the sluggish economy, but they cushioned the effects of the dislocation and relieved human suffering.

After World War II, the 1946 Employment Act announced a "continuing policy of the Federal Government" to insure that the economy "afforded useful employment oppor-

tunities . . . for those able, willing, and seeking to work . . . ." But no programs were established to meet this objective. The relatively prosperous 1950s and 1960s brought about a change in policy regarding public works and unemployment. Attention focused on distressed areas, pockets of unemployment that could be identified and countered selectively. In 1961 the Area Redevelopment Administration (ARA) was established in the Department of Commerce to provide technical assistance, loans, and grants to local governments for public projects—particularly those that would attract private businesses. The Appalachian Regional Development Act was adopted in 1965 in an effort to revitalize the sagging economies of West Virginia and parts of ten (later twelve) other states extending from New York to Alabama. Senator Jennings Randolph, chairman of the Senate Public Works Committee, was the author of this important legislation which resulted in the investment of over $3 billion in job-producing projects in these areas during the past ten years.

The 1965 Public Works and Economic Development Act replaced ARA with the Economic Development Administration (EDA) to continue federally assisted public works programs that relieve unemployment in depressed areas. It authorized the formation of additional multistate regions to stimulate economic activity in areas burdened with high unemployment and low family incomes. Multicounty cooperation was also encouraged under this legislation since funds were made available to counties that joined together to create economic development districts. More than 1,200 counties and scores of cities and towns are now working together, with the aid of grants and loans from the federal government, to spur economic development programs in these districts. An amendment to the act, passed in 1971, also authorized the initiation of additional federally funded public works projects to provide immediate construction jobs for persons in areas suffering from high rates of unemployment.

From 1965 to 1975, EDA channeled nearly $2 billion into public works projects in economically distressed areas. These outlays were augmented by nearly $500 million in planning, technical assistance, and business loans. Its programs are restricted to areas with low family incomes or unemployment rates significantly above the national average. The EDA funds act as a catalyst to local initiative and private enterprise and spur capital investment from the private sector by funding public works projects. The agency supports port development, vocational-technical schools, and recreational projects; but nearly two thirds of its public works grants have been related to industrial parks. During EDA's first eight years, approximately 600 industrial park projects were built for just under $1 billion. These undertakings involved site development and construction of related public works facilities such as water supply systems, sewer lines, and roads. Thus, EDA has assisted in rebuilding local economies that provide jobs to thousands of workers.

Since World War II, American society has been shaken by the civil rights movement. Blacks, women, and other minorities have pursued a campaign to better their social, economic, and political position. Frequently, the federal government's power and influence were arrayed on the side of equal opportunity, and public works policies have been used to further this objective. On June 25, 1941, Roosevelt issued an executive order which forbade discrimination of race, creed, color, or national origins in the employment of workers in government or defense industries. This proclamation marked the beginning of the federal government's effort to use its contracts to secure equality of opportunity. The Committee on Fair Employment Practice (FEPC) was founded to supervise compliance. The committee's efforts helped raise the percentage of Negroes in defense industry employment from 3 percent in 1942 to more than 8 percent in 1944.

The FEPC was terminated after World War II and was subsequently replaced by a Committee on Government Contract Compliance in 1951 and a Government Contract Committee in 1953. Although the precedent of using federal pressure for equal employment through contract provisions was kept alive, it was not used significantly until President John F. Kennedy founded a new Committee on Equal Employment Opportunity (EEOC) in 1961. The committee actively pursued discrimination complaints and achieved notable success. In 1963 the entire range of state and local projects that received federal grants or loans came under EEOC's scrutiny.

The 1964 Civil Rights Act dramatically expanded the federal commitment to equal opportunity. Its sections on voting rights and public accommodations were supplemented by others that affected public works. They outlawed discrimination on programs receiving federal assistance; and they forbade inequality in hiring, paying, promoting, or firing workers by employers, employment agencies, and trade unions. Subsequently, an Office of Federal Contract Compliance (OFCC) was founded in the Department of Labor to oversee and enforce equal opportunity on every contract in excess of $10,000 that involved federal funds. The 1972 Equal Employment Opportunity Act greatly strengthened the powers and expanded the jurisdiction of EEOC. For example, the act was broadened to encompass private employers, educational institutions, state and local governments, employment agencies, and labor unions. Under this legislation, EEOC was empowered to bring suits in federal courts to enforce the law.

Wage rates and working conditions on public works projects have also been affected by federal legislation. The 1931 Davis-Bacon Act has had a profound impact on those who build public works. It required that on all construction, alteration, or repair of public buildings or other public works done under federal contracts of more than $2,000 prevailing wages must be paid to workers. Prevailing wages were defined as those customarily paid for similar kinds of work in the public project's locality. The act remains in force and regulates wages on all projects financed wholly or in part by the federal government. More than thirty states have also passed similar legislation.

The Davis-Bacon Act has been attacked by some groups for many years. Critics contend that, while once needed to guarantee decent incomes, the law results in excessive expenditures because rates are usually based on wages paid to highly unionized workers. Thus, the act has increased the cost of public construction and fueled inflation. The 1936 Public Contracts (Walsh-Healy) Act set basic labor standards, including safety and health requirements, on federally funded projects exceeding $10,000. Model safety programs were established by the Bureau of Reclamation, the Army Corps of Engineers, and other construction agencies and incorporated in federal contracts. This law was the precursor of the 1970 Occupational and Health Act which extended protection to approximately 55 million private and public employees throughout the nation.

Attempts to mitigate unemployment, alleviate discrimination, and insure fair wages and safe working conditions have undoubtedly relieved human suffering and advanced the cause of individual rights. However, these positive measures have had some negative effects. Compliance with governmental regulations, for example, requires public works agencies to allocate money and staff time to undertake mountains of paperwork and monitor employment practices. Thus, guaranteeing individual rights frequently increases project costs, reduces productivity, and sometimes compromises the quality and scope of the services offered. These developments and the depressed economic conditions of the 1970s have caused many governmental agencies to expand the use of scientific management procedures to cut costs and increase employee productivity.

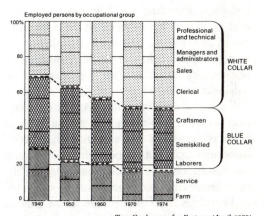

Tom Cardamone for *Fortune* (April 1975)

Figure 1-3.
Distribution of Employed Persons by Occupational Groups.

Labor-management disputes in the public sector have recently been underscored by work stoppages which have made citizens more aware of the essential tasks performed by public employees. Over 20 percent of the nation's labor force works for national, state, or local governments; and, in spite of a general leveling off of union membership in private industry, unions such as the American Federation of State, County, and Municipal Employees have been growing rapidly in recent years. The increased unionization of public employees and their demands for higher wages and fringe benefits, coupled with citizen campaigns calling for reduced taxes and increased productivity in government, illustrate the conflicting nature of some of the issues facing the American people at this time.

Capital for Public and Private Facilities

Money and credit have been prerequisites for the development of public works facilities since the first projects were constructed in colonial America. In the seventeenth and eighteenth centuries, precious metals served as money and were used for exchange. The value of gold, silver, and copper was established by weight and the price of each varied according to supply and demand. John Kenneth Galbraith has observed that, "discovery and conquest set in motion a vast flow of precious metal from America to Europe," which resulted in inflation. For "at work in a primitive but unmistakable fashion," according to Galbraith, "was the central proposition concerning the relation of money to prices—the quantity theory of money," which held that, "other things equal, prices vary directly with the quantity of money in circulation."

Since metallic circulation could not keep pace with the requirements of the economy, it became necessary to supplement it with fiduciary circulation. Credit permitted people and institutions to exchange monetary certificates representative of their wealth—property and earnings from rent, profits, or wages—to satisfy their wants and fulfill their dreams and aspirations. In 1767 James Steuart, in *Principles of Political Economy,* explained the difference between public and private credit. Acknowledging his preference for the term public "credit" over "debt," he stated that credit was an asset to the community, one of the tools of progress. For under a private debt contract, persons or institutions incurring debt became responsible to creditors for its payment; but those who contracted an obligation by borrowing money to construct a capital improvement in the name of the public were not themselves responsible for it. Thus, according to Steuart, public debts are essentially credits. Since they serve to increase directly and indirectly the productivity of people, public debts play a constructive role in the economy and create a new form of wealth—government bonds. Bonds, in turn, encourage thrift and savings by providing people with opportunities to make investments which are more readily accessible than land.

As people become owners of government securities (many of which are issued for public works), they also develop more interest in affairs of state. Alvin H. Hansen, former professor of economics at Harvard University, suggested that a widely distributed public debt is a sort of national insurance system: "we all get benefits more or less in proportion to our income in terms of the interest we receive on the bonds we hold; not exactly, but more or less as the bonds are in fact distributed. It is an insurance system to which we are all paying premiums more or less in proportion to our income status." It has also been noted that one who holds a government bond can sell it, borrow on it, and in case of distress have something that is of genuine value in terms of security—so long as the government has the confidence and support of its citizens.

There is a tenuous link between the financing of a public improvement and the establishment of the nation itself. George Washington, as a youthful surveyor, dreamed of a waterway linking the Potomac with the Ohio River. After the War for Independence, Washington became president of the Potomac Company, which was authorized to raise money to open the river to navigation at its highest point and also to construct a road to the Ohio. The states of Virginia and Maryland, eager to profit from tolls and land sales, provided funds for this venture as did many private citizens. Construction of the canal proved burdensome and toll revenues were never as great as expected; however, it did bring together two states in a common enterprise. Hoping to foster further cooperation, Washington called a conference at Mount Vernon in 1785 to discuss ways to improve navigation on the Potomac. This meeting led to subsequent meetings in Annapolis and in Philadelphia. At the convention in Philadelphia, a new Constitution was drafted under which Washington became the nation's first President.

The creation of private corporations to develop public improvements was more common in the eighteenth and early nineteenth centuries than it is today. However, the fact that physical structures and facilities which serve the public's needs have been developed by both public and private institutions demonstrates the flexibility of the American system of government. But because such systems or facilities usually have the characteristics of a monopoly, the ones that are privately owned frequently operate under local franchise agreements or are otherwise regulated by public agencies. The property as well as the income of these private corporations is also subject to taxation by one or more governmental jurisdictions.

Public works serve long-term needs. The Cabin John Aqueduct Bridge near Washington, D.C., has served the nation's capital for over a century.

Why, then, are there private institutions building and operating facilities similar to those developed by public works agencies? Simply stated, the real or perceived social and economic advantages are considered to be mutually beneficial to the people and their elected representatives and the private parties involved in the enterprise. Conversely, public works are conceived and developed because people, acting directly or indirectly through their elected representatives, determine that their collective interests are best served, if such facilities and services are provided by public rather than private institutions. The relative advantages of each method are influenced by a number of variables. For example, the scarcity or availability of money in the public and private sectors has been the decisive reason in some cases; while people's attitudes toward government and their views on what constitutes fair and equitable rates as well as excessive profits have been the determining factors in others.

The types of facilities that are built by either of these methods are usually designed to serve long-term needs and are generally amortized over extended periods of time. The rights of those who invest in private corporations that construct public facilities are protected by the Constitution which provides that private property may not be taken by the government without just compensation to the owner. The cost of operating these facilities, especially utility systems, can represent a sizeable portion of the total expense. Therefore, the comparative efficiency of public and private operations is a significant consideration. Equally important in the case of utilities are the amount of taxes that are paid, the competitiveness of utility rates, the extent to which utilities are regulated, the rates of return that private utilities pay their investors, and the ability of both public and private institutions to obtain the capital required for expansion and modernization.

Borrowing has always been a primary means of obtaining funds for projects requiring large capital investments. In January 1790, Secretary of the Treasury Alexander Hamilton, in a ''Report on Public Credit,'' placed the United States' total public debt outstanding at $77 million. The foreign debt amounted to $11.7 million; the domestic debt, $40.4 million; and state debts, $25 million. By 1976 the federal debt had climbed to over $500 billion; state and local governments had accumulated debts exceeding $200 billion (making the total public debt more than $700 billion); and private debts had topped the $2 trillion mark. Approximately 60 percent of the private debts were corporate, while the balance was incurred primarily by individuals with mortgages.

There has been a continued upward trend of government spending. Twenty years ago, as indicated in Figure 1-4, spending at all levels—federal, state, and local—represented approximately one fourth of the Gross National Product (GNP), that is, the total production of goods and services. Since that time, spending (including transfer payments) has nearly quadrupled and now accounts for one third of the GNP. While expenditures for defense, public works, and other direct operations of government have risen in dollar terms, they have been holding relatively steady as a percentage of the GNP. However, the so-called income transfer payments—represented in the form of government checks sent to individuals for social security, medicare, veterans benefits, welfare, unemployment compensation, and similar programs—have increased substantially during recent years. If these spending trends continue, government expenditures would account for more than half of the dollar value of all goods and services produced in the United States by the end of the twentieth century.

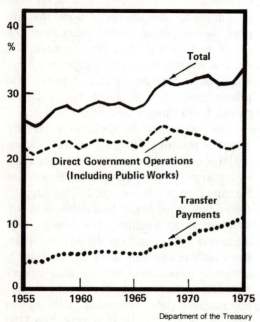

Department of the Treasury

Figure 1-4.
Total Government Spending as a Percentage of GNP.

States hold about one third of the total indebtedness of state and local governments, only about 5 percent of which is short term. Approximately 90 percent of the local debt outstanding is represented by long-term bonds. Over one half of the bonds issued by both jurisdictions are backed by the full faith and credit of state or local governments to minimize interest and carrying charges. Other bonds are simply secured by tolls, special assessments, or other income sources pledged by the state or local jurisdiction issuing the bonds. Most of these long-term bonds have been issued for some type of public works

project or capital improvement, while most of the federal debt has resulted from borrowing to finance wars in which the United States has been involved. Skyrocketing inflation and costly social programs have also added to the debt burden in recent years. Interest alone amounted to more than $30 billion in fiscal year 1975 and now represents one of the largest items in the federal budget, exceeded only by national defense outlays and income security payments.

Some contend that there is no reason for concern over the size of the national debt as long as the economy is growing and can bear the burden of taxes required to pay the interest and carrying charges. It is not size alone, they say, but size in relation to the national income that determines the relative burden of the debt. So long as national income rises at least proportionately to the cost of the interest and carrying charges, the burden on the taxpayer is not increased. Others, however, remain somewhat skeptical, noting that federal spending has grown during the past decade by 175 percent while the economy has increased by only 120 percent. Much of this imbalance, they note, has resulted from growing outlays for interest on the nation's debt and for unemployment benefits and other social welfare programs which do not increase the GNP as much as do direct expenditures for goods and services. Sharing the cost of facilities with future generations who will also use them can be understood and accepted; however, the idea of transferring social welfare costs from one generation to the next is a much more controversial issue. This does not mean that the problems giving rise to such social programs can be ignored. Yet, some approaches to their solution have a more drastic impact on the public and private sectors of the economy than others. The amount of funds available for public works facilities and for other important programs is significantly affected by the cost of the approach that is adopted.

The increase in the public and private debt during the past 200 years is matched and largely supported by the rapid growth of the American economy. By 1974 the GNP amounted to $1.4 trillion. Twenty-two percent of this total was attributable to expenditures (excluding transfer payments) by federal, state, and local governments; however, most of it resulted from spending by the private sector, thus generating tax revenues to finance government services and amortize a portion of its debts. Approximately 63 percent went for consumable goods and services, and 15 percent was invested in the replacement and expansion of productive facilities. Goods represented a little more than half of the value of total output, while the remainder was in the form of services.

Much of this growth took place during the last twenty-five years when the per capita GNP increased at the rate of approximately 3 percent per year. With 212 million persons, representing 6 percent of the world's population in 1974, the United States produced about one third of the world's output. There can be little doubt that the private enterprise system has served as the driving force of the nation's rapidly expanded economy. However, it should be noted that public policies have also been adopted to protect and assist private entrepreneurs since the start of the nation. Governments have not only provided essential public works facilities; but they have also furnished land at little or no cost, lent their credit, adopted laws to limit investors' risks, and protected them against unfair competition.

As communities grew and became more integrated into the market system, most segments of the economy prospered by providing added goods and services to the increasing population. But in some instances, unrestrained competition led to the domination of key industries by a handful of men who subverted the free enterprise system to reap unfair profits and gain great personal power. Their control over raw materials and markets was such that they adjusted both production and prices to changing conditions. As a result, large sectors of the economy were removed from the disciplines of the competitive marketplace, and the federal government was forced to intervene through various forms of regulation. Although local markets competed vigorously for consumer products, the basic industries sold large quantities of items such as steel and oil in national and international markets. Thus, different types of legislation were enacted to increase markets served by the free enterprise system on the one hand and to give the public needed protection against its abuses on the other.

Reliance on a pluralistic economy has helped make the American standard of living the envy of the world. Internal Revenue Service figures show that there are over 12 million separate businesses operating in the United States. Only 14 percent of these function as corporations; however, the non-financial ones accounted for 52 percent of the GNP in 1974. They also provided a sizeable amount of tax revenues to help finance needed public works facilities. Yet corporate profits in 1974, as a percentage share of the national income (after inventory adjustment), amounted to only 6.5 percent—less than half of what it was in 1950. Although profits declined, the amount of compensation paid to employees of such corporations increased considerably during the past twenty-five years.

Many persons, mindful of the exorbitant profits made by "robber barons" of yesteryear, feel that these developments are appropriate since they tend to equalize the nation's wealth. However, others emphasize that corporate profits help to finance public services and sustain the income-producing fabric of the nation itself. In 1974, for example, approximately 65 percent of such profits went to pay taxes; and a portion was paid to millions of stockholders in the form of dividends for the use of their money. But the largest percentage of corporate profits retained after taxes was plowed back into businesses to replace obsolete equipment, build up inventories, and modernize or expand productive facilities to provide additional goods, services, and jobs for a growing economy. The amount of funds needed to create a new job in private industry varies, but the average amount invested by the nation's largest industrial firms in 1974 was in excess of $41,000 for each new employee. Although somewhat higher than the cost of creating public service jobs, the fact remains that large amounts of capital are needed to provide additional jobs in both the public and private sectors.

The link between the nation's economic

policies and the job market has been recognized for many years. The 1946 Employment Act, for instance, specifically stated that federal economic policy should be designed to maintain full employment. Although this goal has not been realized, the act provides the basis for government action to combat unemployment. Since a large amount of the nation's productive capacity is used to supply goods and services to people in other parts of the world, the work of many Americans is dependent upon United States firms maintaining a competitive position in world markets. This can only be achieved if capital if available to both public and private institutions to enable them to make the necessary investments for the replacement and modernization of their facilities. From 1960 to 1973, business investments, as a percentage of the GNP and the growth rate of output per man hour, were lower in the United States than in several other industrialized countries. The reversal of this trend constitutes a major challenge to the nation during the last quarter of the twentieth century.

Large amounts of capital are also needed in the public sector for the replacement and modernization of highways, water and power systems, and other types of public works facilities which benefit commerce and industry as well as the general public. Failure to provide the necessary funds causes increased shortages, higher prices, deteriorated services, and greater unemployment. Private corporations use both internal and external sources for their capital requirements. Internally, money comes from retained profits and depreciation allowances; externally, it is obtained largely from borrowing or from the sale of stocks, representing equity in the corporation. During recent years, increasing amounts, exceeding half of the funds needed by private corporations, came from external sources. Since government also obtains capital for public works projects by issuing bonds, this places added pressure on the money market and tends to increase the cost of borrowing.

Throughout the nation's history, the development of public works facilities has been strongly influenced by the functioning of the private enterprise system. The availability of water, power, transportation, and waste disposal service has facilitated the growth of commerce and industry in every state of the Union. The service charges and tax revenues generated directly and indirectly by business firms and their employees have helped to finance such facilities. Thus, the ability of the private sector to operate successfully in the economic system that has evolved has a direct bearing upon the future funding of public works projects. For many of the same factors

U.S. Bureau of Reclamation

Expenditures for irrigation public works support agriculture and related industries.

that affect the financial affairs of private industry have an equally significant impact upon public works programs.

Inflation constitutes a sustained rise in the level of prices thus eroding the value of money. Theoretically, inflation is non-existent only when the rate of monetary expansion equals the rate of growth of real output of goods and services. This delicate balance cannot easily be maintained. Inflation results, in part, from the action of small firms and individuals but is especially influenced by the federal government, big business, and labor. The average annual rate of price rise during the past quarter century has ranged from roughly 2 to 10 percent (increasing at an average rate of 3.3 percent), reducing the purchasing value of the dollar by 41 percent during the past ten years alone. This obviously has had a significant impact upon the amount and cost of public works constructed during recent years. However, the nation has experienced periods of inflation in the past. In fact, during the American Revolution, the average rate of price rise per year was 26.7 percent; and during the War of 1812, World War I, and World War II, it averaged 18.8, 11.7, and 7.0 percent respectively.

Many factors—shortages of fuel and basic materials as well as crop failures, for examples—contribute to the rapid rise of prices in specific markets. However, the primary cause of inflation is generally attributed to the fact that aggregate expenditures increase faster than the flow of goods and services. In the private sector, higher prices are met by borrowing, by reducing the size of consumer money holdings relative to their incomes, or by granting higher wages which often raises prices still further. In the public sector, increased prices are met by borrowing, by increasing taxes, or, in the case of the federal government, by creating money. If this latter action is accomplished without a rise in prices, it is equivalent to the government borrowing funds at zero interest rate. But if prices rise, it has the same effect as if government taxed money balances to the extent of the rate of the price rise.

In the past 200 years, prices in the United States rose at an inflationary rate during about half of the period and were either stable or falling during the remainder of the time. Prior to World War II, rises in the level of prices were generally followed by a downward trend; however, since World War II, inflation has persisted and continues even today to erode the purchasing value of the dollar. Although some economists believe that inflation can be controlled by reducing the rate of monetary expansion to correspond to the rate of growth of real output, others contend that this will not assure full employment which is an equally important concern. Those holding the latter view argue that full employment, guaranteed by the pledge of government jobs if necessary, is a crucial element of an integrated plan for maintaining economic stability and for avoiding inflation as well as recession.

Taxes, paid by individual citizens and private corporations, provide the primary source of income for financing public works by federal, state, and local governments. The total tax burden in 1974 amounted to 32 percent of the GNP. During the same year, rent, interest, and corporate profits accounted for approximately 25 percent of the $1.1 trillion national income (GNP less capital investment allowances and indirect business taxes), while 75 percent went for wages, salaries, and other labor income. These statistics reflect the relative importance of the income tax structure, which is roughly proportional throughout the income range for 90 percent of all families and progressive for the top 10 percent. Personal taxes amounted to $171 billion in 1974.

Sales, excise, and personal income taxes were the primary sources of state taxes in 1974. They accounted for roughly 30, 20, and 23 percent respectively of all state tax revenues. The property tax, which generates about 83 percent of local tax receipts, represents the principal source of local tax revenues. Large variations exist in the relative roles of state and local government throughout the United States. In New York, for example, local governments account for 73 percent of all state and local expenditures, while in Hawaii they make up only 20 percent. Federal outlays to state and local governments for fiscal year 1975 amounted to over $52 billion. This represented about 23 percent of all state and local expenditures. A sizeable amount of these funds were invested in public works facilities. States are also providing increased financial assistance to local governments, much of which is used for the construction of elementary and secondary schools and related facilities.

One of the most important actions taken by the federal government in recent years was the enactment of the 1974 Congressional Budget and Impoundment Control Act. It provides for a systematic procedure by which Congress may consider the President's annual budget proposals as a whole and resolve conflicts among authorizations, appropriations, and tax measures; and it will undoubtedly have a far-reaching impact upon the funding of future public works programs. This act also permits planned expenditures for public works and other types of programs to be viewed in proper perspective. For example, in 1976 only about 25 percent of the federal budget is controllable in the sense that policy makers have an option to make adjustments in projected outlays. This new legislation requires the establishment of targets for a number of functional spending categories, total receipts, expenditures, and projected deficits. Moreover, it prescribes the process by which decisions are made, thus assuring that their impact on fiscal and monetary policies will be taken into account. Finally, the 1974 Congressional Budget and Impoundment Control Act enables Congress to consider, more effectively than in the past, the desirable long-term allocation of national resources between the public and private sectors of the economy.

Citizen Participation in Government

The extent to which people benefit from public works facilities and share in the cost of constructing and maintaining them is determined, in part, by their elected representatives. American citizens, exercising their right to vote, select individuals who best represent them and their views in the decision-making process. While it has been argued by some that the complexity of the issues often reduces the "average citizen" to a state of confusion and bewilderment, others

have reminded us of Winston Churchill's classic observation: "Democracy is the worst possible form of government, except for any other that has been tried." Viewed in this perspective, it behooves all who have the right to vote to do so, after becoming familiar with the candidates and informed on the issues.

The history of suffrage in the United States is, for the most part, a record of progressive extensions of the voting privilege to new groups of individuals. In the pre-Revolutionary era, the right to vote was restricted to those in the community who owned land, possessed vocational skills, or were born into prominent families. And municipal officials were usually appointed by colonial governors. However, closed municipal corporations virtually disappeared after the Revolution.

Under the federal system, each of the states became responsible for adopting its own suffrage regulations. But the Fifteenth, Nineteenth, and Twenty-sixth amendments— passed in 1870, 1920, and 1970 respectively— forbade a state (or the United States) to deny or abridge the right to vote to its citizens because of race or color, sex, or age (for persons eighteen years or older). Although voting was originally the exclusive privilege of white male property owners, property qualifications were largely abandoned by the middle of the nineteenth century. By the early twentieth century, some blacks and a substantial number of women had become part of the voting population.

The effects of increased enfranchisement of the nation's citizens are important. For it is the people's elected representatives who determine the scope and extent of public works policies and programs at the federal, state, and local levels of government. And even though many citizens frequently voice indifference when confronted with the issues, their deep-lying prejudices, fears, aspirations, and moral sentiments generally set limits to the area of choice in which decision makers function. Therefore, although the majority of the people rarely express themselves on specific issues, their elected representatives are usually aware of and sensitive to their opinions.

North Central Texas Council of Governments

Aerial view of Dallas, Texas. The complex public works systems that support American civilization require citizen participation in the decision-making process.

In the last presidential election (1972), approximately 145 million persons were eligible to vote. About 25 million of these individuals were newly enfranchised; some 11 million were eighteen to twenty years old. Over 60 percent of all eligible persons actually voted. For several reasons, the percentage of citizens exercising their right to vote increased in the last decade. Not only was the poll tax abolished, but the regulations governing absentee voting were relaxed as were state residence requirements. However, one of the reasons for the increased voter turnout was the concerted action taken by civil rights organizations to register blacks.

The efforts of these civil rights groups were supported by legislation, especially the 1965 Voting Rights Act, which provided for direct federal action to secure the registration of blacks. The impact of this law was most striking in Mississippi where only 6.7 percent of the blacks of voting age were registered in 1964. The percentage in 1968 rose to 59.4 percent. Equally significant was the fact that in 1960 the eleven states of the old Confederacy accounted for only 14.0 percent of the total national voter turnout; by 1968 the people in these eleven states accounted for 20.2 percent. The influence of these new voters on state and local public works programs and other important issues was, of course, much greater.

As the former Harvard University professor of government, V. O. Key, Jr., once remarked, "To speak with precision of public opinion is a task not unlike coming to grips with the Holy Ghost." Nevertheless, it is a

force that must be reckoned with. Over 1,000 books are published in the world each day. This fact plus the rapid growth of the nation's communications systems explains the problem of keeping abreast of current issues. To be well informed in the mid 1970s, one should presumably understand the United States' foreign policy alternatives and their consequences as they relate to the Middle East, China, and the Soviet Union; inflation and unemployment; and tax reform, to say nothing of energy conservation, air and water pollution, and transportation programs. Since it is impossible to be well versed on all these subjects, elected officials customarily listen to the conflicting opinions of different groups, often at public hearings, and then act in a manner which they perceive to be in the public interest.

Because public works programs must compete with many other programs, some leaders in this field use modern communications techniques to obtain public support for soundly conceived policies and projects. For the engineering of consent is the very essence of the democratic process—the freedom to persuade. It is based upon an understanding of those whom it attempts to win over and is designed to induce affirmative action through the favorable influence of public opinion. Public works administrators, however, are somewhat skeptical of public opinion polls. Although they are occasionally used, their value has long been questioned. In the December 1961 issue of *Harper's Magazine*, an article entitled "The Poll of 1774" reported that a survey was allegedly conducted by order of the First Continental Congress to determine if the people would take up arms to win independence from the British Crown. The article concluded: "When the entire survey is considered, the Interrogators are of the opinion that there doth not exist Public Support for the proposed War. Our people are ill-informed scantly concerned and sadly Muddy in their Thinking . . . . No cause can hope to succeed with so little backing." Although polls are not infallible, one thing is certain: "The people have the say so," as Carl Sandburg observed in his poem "The People, Yes."

Public support has always been and continues to be a prerequisite for the development of water, power, transportation, waste disposal, and other public works facilities in the United States. The difficult technical problems that were encountered were, however, overcome by the ingenuity and hard work of those who designed, constructed, and maintained these vital systems and services. Thus, the magnificent structures and facilities used by citizens everyday serve as an enduring tribute to the engineers and work forces who built them.

Yet, the greatest tribute belongs to the people themselves, especially to the voters and their elected representatives, who created and vested power and authority in the governmental institutions whose actions brought into being the public works facilities that serve the entire country. Continuing concern for protecting the private rights of individuals and groups of individuals, in the process of obtaining the necessary resources—land, capital, and labor—to build public works facilities, has tended to strengthen the fabric of the nation itself. For it has led to an increased understanding and appreciation of the complementary virtues of public and private enterprise as they function within the framework of the American system of government.

SUGGESTED READINGS

Advisory Commission on Intergovernmental Relations. *Regional Decision Making: New Strategies for Substate Districts, Substate Regionalism and the Federal System.* Washington, D.C., 1973.

Carstensen, Vernon. *The Public Lands: Studies in the History of the Public Domain.* 2d. ed. Madison, Wisconsin, 1968.

Christenson, Reo M., and McWilliams, Robert O., eds. *Voice of the People: Readings in Public Opinion and Propaganda.* 2d. ed. New York, 1967.

Galbraith, John Kenneth. *Money: Whence It Came, Where It Went.* Boston, 1975.

Hirsch, Werner Z., and Sonenblum, Sidney, eds. *Governing Urban America in the 1970s.* New York, 1973.

Karlen, Harvey M. *The Pattern of American Government.* Beverly Hills, California, 1968.

Moak, Lennox L. *Administration of Local Government Debt.* Prepared for Municipal Finance Officers Association. Chicago, 1975.

_____ , and Hillhouse, Albert M. *Concepts and Practices in Local Government Finance.* Prepared for Municipal Finance Officers Association. Chicago, 1975.

Ogg, Frederic A., and Ray, P. Orman. *Introduction to American Government.* New York, 1948.

Scott, Mel. *American City Planning.* Berkeley, California, 1971.

Snider, Clyde F., and Gove, Samuel K. *American State and Local Government.* 2d. ed. New York, 1965.

Teaford, Jon C. *The Muncipal Revolution in America: Origins of Modern Urban Government, 1650-1825.* Chicago, 1975.

U.S. Bureau of the Census. *Governmental Finances in 1973-74.* Series GF74-No. 5. Washington, D.C., 1975.

U.S. Department of Agriculture. *Major Uses of Land in the United States, Summary for 1969.* Agricultural Economic Report No. 247. Washington, D.C., 1973.

CHAPTER 2

WATERWAYS

Waterway development for navigation has been an integral part of America's founding and emergence as a great nation. From the colonial period to the present, harbors, lakes, and rivers have provided the United States with an extensive water transportation network. Natural streams and estuaries enabled the first access to the interior; and the history of these same waterways, improved, maintained, and linked together by canals, is a story of man working with nature to meet his transportation needs.

Origins of Waterway Improvements

To Old World settlers, the American continent offered among many other resources good natural waterways and safe harbors, which supported waterborne traffic and inland migration. The Atlantic Coast of North America was blessed with numerous large rivers—the St. Lawrence, Connecticut, Hudson, Delaware, James, and Savannah. New York, Baltimore, and other large cities emerged because of their fine harbors which could accommodate oceangoing vessels. These rivers and harbors served the colonists for nearly two centuries as nature provided them. The riparian dwellers felt little

Portions of this chapter are based on reports prepared by the Army Corps of Engineers and the Tennessee Valley Authority.

need to make more than the most elementary improvements. Nevertheless, the projects they undertook can be noted as the origins of American waterway development. These consisted of removing snags and other obstructions, extending private piers outward to navigable depths, and marking navigation channels.

The east coast rivers were navigable up to the fall line, the physiographic barrier at the foothills of the Appalachian Mountains which marked the initial limit of colonization. Between their upper reaches and the tidewater region, many of these streams were broken by rapids and waterfalls. Such obstructions required the portage of boats and cargoes. For many decades, settlers dreamed of building canals and locks to bypass these barriers, but the colonial era had nearly closed before the first artificial waterways were begun.

In 1750 Cadwallader Colden constructed a short canal in Orange County, New York, thought to be the first built within the territorial limits of the United States. George Washington was also a pioneer advocate of inland water transportation improvements. Prior to the Revolutionary War, he urged the Virginia House of Burgesses and the Maryland Assembly to make improvements on the Potomac River, but the plan was never adopted. Subsequently, Washington organized the Potomac Canal Company in 1784, which in 1802 completed a canal around the Great and Little Falls on the Potomac, and later built two other canals around the falls above and below Harpers Ferry, West Virginia. This work was a noteworthy engineering feat, but the cost was excessive, and the company went bankrupt in 1819.

Shortly after America achieved independence, other canal projects were undertaken. The most ambitious New England waterway improvement was construction of the Middlesex Canal in Massachusetts. Begun in 1789 and completed in 1804, the canal provided a 27-mile link between the Merrimack and Charles rivers, facilitating trade from New Hampshire to Boston. In the South, the Dismal Swamp Canal, one of the oldest in the United States, was completed in 1794 as a multipurpose undertaking to drain the swamp, make land available for cultivation, and provide a waterway. Running from Deep Creek, Virginia, to South Mills, North Carolina, the historic waterway is still in use as part of the Intracoastal Waterway.

The early attempts at artificial waterway construction were a reflection of the intense interest in transportation. The thirteen former colonies quarreled with one another over navigation rights on waterways they jointly bordered, and this was still an issue as the laws of the young nation developed. The Philadelphia Convention, which wrote the Constitution of the United States in 1787, actually grew out of a 1785 meeting at Mount Vernon, Virginia, where representatives from Maryland and Virginia met to resolve differences regarding navigation of the Potomac River. In the resulting "Mount Vernon Compact," they agreed to bilateral navigation of the Potomac and duty-free passage through the mouth of Chesapeake Bay. The next year the two states plus Delaware and Pennsylvania signed the Annapolis Convention which broadened the free commerce principle and recommended building a waterway between the Delaware and Susquehanna rivers. The participants issued a call for the Constitutional Convention, which wrote into the Constitution the "commerce clause." It remains as the basic authority for federal waterway improvements.

The new government immediately took

U.S. Department of Transportation

The original Cape Henry Lighthouse (foreground) was the first public works project undertaken by the federal government.

steps to upgrade navigation facilities. Realizing that coastal and foreign shipping was the lifeblood of the nation's economy, Congress passed a statute on August 7, 1789, authorizing construction of a lighthouse at Cape Henry, Virginia. It was the first public works project undertaken by the federal government. For years ships faced a hazardous journey through the mouth of Chesapeake Bay, and the light was needed to guide safe passage. Cost overruns and design changes delayed construction, but the beacon finally went into operation in October 1792. Though retired from service in 1881, the octagonal stone structure still stands near Virginia Beach, Virginia.

In 1790 Congress confirmed the right of states to enact statutes which imposed duties on cargoes as a means of providing for pier maintenance and construction. Congress later sanctioned a Georgia law for removing obstructions from the Savannah River and a Virginia statute for improving navigation on the James River. On April 6, 1802, an appropriation was made for the first federal funds for inland waterways. Congress granted $30,000 for repairing and erecting public piers on the Delaware River after the state ceded the property to the federal government.

So great was interest in internal improvements that in 1807 the Senate directed Secretary of the Treasury Albert Gallatin to make a thorough investigation of waterways, canals, and roads. Gallatin's 1808 report was an admirable summary of contemporary projects and a foresighted guide to future development. He outlined and advocated a comprehensive system of roads and inland water routes which would bind together the seaboard states and provide access to the interior.

Gallatin's ideas received enthusiastic support from some quarters, with their strongest advocacy coming from Henry Clay and John C. Calhoun. In 1817 they proposed a unified "American System" which was designed to foster economic self-sufficiency and to promote national unity. The proposal called for a protective tariff for manufacturers and a home market and better transportation for farmers. Calhoun believed these steps would "bind the republic together [and] . . . make the parts adhere more closely."

The plan received support from the pioneers who had rushed to settle the trans-Appalachian region. Between 1810 and 1820, the population of these areas doubled and four new states, Indiana (1816), Mississippi (1817), Illinois (1818), and Alabama (1819), were admitted to the Union. Owing to the difficulty of navigating the Mississippi and Ohio rivers, western supplies of manufactured goods came by wagon road from Atlantic seaports. The principal outlet for trans-Appalachian agricultural commodities was the Port of New Orleans via the Ohio and Mississippi river systems.

Consequently, Congress approved the so-called "Bonus Bill" in 1817, which would have created a permanent fund for internal improvements by setting aside the $1.5 million paid by the Second Bank of the United States for its charter privileges. President James Madison had earlier recommended a federally subsidized network of roads and canals, but he vetoed the bill on constitutional grounds, affirming that the commerce clause could not be stretched to cover internal improvements. He insisted that a constitutional amendment was necessary before such projects could be legally adopted by the federal government.

Seven years later, in the landmark case of *Gibbons* v. *Ogden*, Chief Justice John Marshall handed down the first decision which broadened congressional power under the commerce clause. The case involved a monopoly granted by the New York legislature for operating steamboats on the Hudson River. Marshall, in a complex and far-reaching decision, held that Congress was sovereign in all aspects of interstate commerce and could not be limited by state statutes. This "emancipation proclamation of American commerce" paved the way for federal improvement of rivers and harbors for navigation, and it firmly established the right of citizens to pass freely over the nation's navigable waterways.

Canal Era

When strict constitutional views and intersectional rivalries in Congress thwarted federal funding for internal improvements, the task of building waterways fell to the states. Canals became part of the American transportation pattern more slowly than needs might have dictated. By 1816 only about 100 miles of canals existed in the United States, but there were reasons why the boom in canal construction which swept Britain in the late eighteenth century had not reached America. Canals required far greater capital than could be raised easily in the United States, and in America canal engineering was in its infancy. In addition, the few miles of existing canals had proved so unsuccessful financially that it was almost impossible to find investors for new ventures.

The Erie Canal launched this country into its great canal age, which in turn helped bring about regional specialization and aided the growth of a national market economy. Its building required remarkable faith and dedication by New York leaders. The challenges seemed overwhelming: a 364-mile canal (by far the longest in the world) between Albany and Buffalo had to be built through largely unsettled wilderness;

Construction of the Erie Canal touched off a "canal craze" that swept the country.

engineering problems exceeding any previously solved in lock and aqueduct construction had to be surmounted; and the skepticism of critics who foresaw nothing but financial ruin and political corruption as the end product of the risky venture had to be overcome.

Governor DeWitt Clinton, more than anyone else, was responsible for this success story. The state legislature authorized the construction in April 1817, and work began the following July. The federal government denied any financial aid, so the state assumed responsibility for raising the necessary funds and directing the building. A lack of trained engineers forced the state to appoint a few experienced men who gave on-the-job training to aspiring engineers. These technological pioneers directed the work with an energetic resourcefulness and skill not uncommon in early America and acquired the skills which enabled them to later supervise other internal improvements. The ambitious undertaking,

along with a branch canal northward to Lake Champlain, was completed in 1825. Traffic was so heavy that nominal tolls enabled the state to recover the $8 million construction cost in just seven years. To provide for the ever increasing commerce, the state ordered enlargement of the entire canal in 1835. The width at the water surface was increased from 40 to 70 feet and the depth from 4 to 7 feet. Three later branches built southward from the Erie Canal did not succeed financially, but tonnage on the Erie system continued to grow until it peaked in 1880.

What was initially scorned as "Clinton's Big Ditch" cut freight charges between Buffalo and New York City from $100 to $10 a ton and reduced the hauling time from twenty-six to six days. Due in part to the large amount of canal trade, New York City grew rapidly in wealth and population, becoming the greatest port on the Atlantic seaboard.

The success of the Erie Canal provided the spark for a nationwide canal building boom. By 1840 various states had invested a total of $125 million in 3,200 miles of canals. A very common and important type of waterway constructed in the coastal regions during the boom era was the canal to tidewater, built to improve transportation between the upcountry and tidewater in states bordering the Atlantic. Three major ones were constructed in New England: the Cumberland and Oxford in Maine from Sebago Pond to tidewater near Portland; the Blackstone from Worcester, Massachusetts, to Narragansett Bay, Rhode Island; and the New Haven and Northampton from New Haven, Connecticut, to Northampton, Massachusetts. The most successful of the three was the Cumberland and Oxford Canal, which was chartered in 1820 and completed in 1827. It was only 20 miles long but was supplemented by lake and river systems which provided an important outlet for inland products.

In the middle Atlantic states, there was a demand for canals from points in eastern Pennsylvania to the Delaware River. The successful Erie Canal venture triggered the realization of this aim. Four such tidewater routes, all generally prosperous, were known as "the anthracite canals" because their principal business consisted of carrying coal to Philadelphia and New York markets. Of the four, only the Delaware and Hudson Canal was under state management. This particular waterway supplied coal to New York and New England cities. Completed in 1828, it had many prosperous years. A second notable water link south of the Delaware and Hudson Canal, was the Lehigh and Morris Canal system. It provided another major outlet for Pennsylvania anthracite. The Lehigh Canal ran from White Haven to Easton on the Delaware. From this point, boats could proceed by river to Philadelphia. The Morris Canal, which connected with the Lehigh at Easton, wound 102 miles through New Jersey to Newark. South of the Morris Canal in New Jersey and connecting Bordentown on the Delaware with tidewater at New Brunswick, the Delaware and Raritan Canal provided a large and well-constructed route from Philadelphia to New York. One of the most important transportation routes in the nation shortly before the Civil War, it actually carried greater tonnage than the Erie Canal for a few years. A fourth important canal network, the Susquehanna and Tidewater Canal and the Chesapeake and Delaware Canal, served both Baltimore and Philadelphia. Along with a less profitable canal, the Union, which connected Reading and Harrisburg, the Susquehanna and Tidewater Canal represented an important link in the Pennsylvania system of waterways.

Two major tidewater canals were built in the South after 1815, the James River and Kanawha and the Chesapeake and Ohio. The James River and Kanawha Canal was begun before 1800 and by 1840 was completed over the 146 miles between Richmond and Lynchburg, Virginia. The company which built the canal had intended to cross the Appalachian divide and connect with the Ohio River. This goal was never realized, but it did a substantial though not profitable business.

As mentioned, Washington founded a canal company which built canals around the rapids of the Potomac River north of what was to become the capital city bearing his name. He had wanted a canal to parallel the Potomac from Georgetown to Cumberland, Maryland,

and to extend from there to the Ohio River. Washington did not see his dream come to fruition, for it did not begin until the 1820s, when the Erie success story awakened greater interest. With a name reflecting optimism, the Chesapeake and Ohio Canal Company was formed to undertake the ambitious work. It was apparent that immediate extension to the Ohio River was financially impossible, so in 1828 work was begun on the 176-mile stretch from Georgetown to Cumberland. Despite generous stock subscriptions from Virginia, Maryland, and the federal government, the company was constantly short of funds. Futhermore, it faced competition from the Baltimore and Ohio Railroad, whose goal was also to reach Cumberland and then proceed to the Ohio Valley. The canal reached Harpers Ferry one year ahead of its rival, but it arrived at Cumberland eight years later than the railroad. Only the railroad pushed on to the Ohio Valley. The canal was expensive, exceeding the cost of the Erie. Built with generous dimensions (50 to 80 feet wide and 6 to 8 feet deep), the canal carried considerable coal from the Cumberland region and was used until the early twentieth century.

Fearful that the nearly completed Erie Canal would divert most of their trade with the West, Philadelphia merchants called for a Pennsylvania waterway that would extend from Philadelphia to Pittsburgh. Opposition came from those with vested interests in the turnpike system and from a few who foresaw railroads as the wave of the future. Nonetheless, the canal craze prevailed, and the ambitious scheme began to unfold in 1826.

Moving from east to west, the state built a railroad leg from Philadelphia to Columbia on the Susquehanna River. Westward, the canal followed the Susquehanna and Juniata rivers to the Allegheny Mountains near Hollidaysburg. At this point, the notable Portage Railroad carried canal boats over the mountains on specially designed cable cars. West of the Alleghenies, the canal followed the Conemaugh and Allegheny rivers to Pittsburgh. Opening in 1834, the so-called "Main Line" covered 395 miles and cost over $10 million to build. It was never a strong competitor to the Erie Canal, although it did substan-

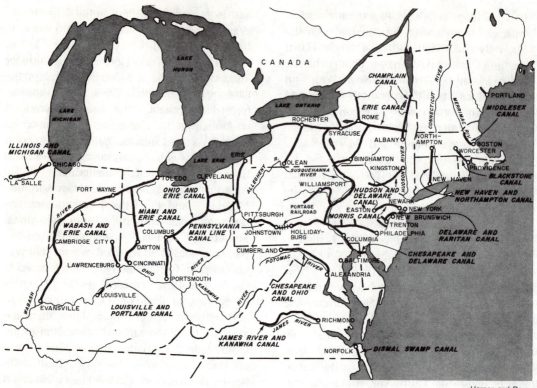

Harper and Row

Principal canals constructed by 1860.

tial business, even as the railroads boomed in the Civil War period.

In retrospect, the Pennsylvania system appears to be a shortsighted failure. It was built when construction costs were high and the railroad era was imminent. Topographically, the challenge was tremendous, as evidenced by the portage link, which added great cost and time to the passage. In its effort to meet the challenge of New York, Pennsylvania spent more on new canal construction than any other state. By 1860 the state's outlay for waterway public works totaled $65 million.

Eight months before the official opening of the Erie Canal, the Ohio legislature authorized the connecting of Lake Erie and the Ohio River by two major state-owned canals. Completed in 1833 at a cost of nearly $8 million, the 308-mile Ohio and Erie Canal joined Cleveland on Lake Erie and Portsmouth on the Ohio River. The Miami and Erie Canal was completed from Cincinnati to Dayton in 1832 and to Toledo on Lake Erie in

1845. Traffic peaked about 1851, and thereafter the Ohio waterways suffered an extraordinarily rapid decline from flood damage and railroad competition. In fact, railroad construction was so great in Ohio that by the mid 1850s the canals were obsolete. Nevertheless, during their two decades of service, Ohio's canals were a great boon to the state's growth.

Indiana's canal building experience was a woeful one. In 1827 the state received a federal land grant to aid in building a canal to connect the Ohio River with Lake Erie via the Wabash and Maumee rivers. This diagonal through the state would join a connecting link through a small portion of northwest Ohio to Lake Erie. When completed the canal stretched 450 miles, the longest in the nation. In addition to undertaking this big single canal project in 1836, the Indiana legislature passed a mammoth Internal Improvement Bill, which provided for an ambitious program of canal, turnpike, and railroad building. Incompetent work direction, political corruption, and depression took their toll.

By 1841 the state's debt exceeded $13 million, of which over $9 million was attributed to internal improvements. The Wabash and Erie Canal was completed in 1853, but flood damage and railroad competition gave it a short life. Operations ceased on the southern portion about 1860. This long canal helped open northern Indiana, but financially it was a disaster. Its cost exceeded $8 million; while during its operation, revenues totaled only $5 million, over half of which came from the sale of lands granted by the federal government.

The Illinois and Michigan Canal, connecting Lake Michigan at Chicago with the Illinois River and thereby with the Mississippi River, was begun in 1836 and completed in 1848. Barging revenues were insufficient to offset the huge debt incurred in building the project. This led, in part, to the ruin of the state bank in 1842 that seriously undermined the credit of the entire state. However, this canal contributed substantially to the phenomenal growth of Chicago. Traffic was heavy, almost from the date of opening. Enlarged and extended on several occasions, it is one of the few nineteenth-century canals to remain in service.

The total expenditure for public and private canal construction in the United States from 1815 to 1860 was about $195 million. Economic historian Carter Goodrich states that of this amount 62 percent was entirely public works, including the major programs of New York, Pennsylvania, and Ohio. Government participation in mixed enterprises such as the Chesapeake and Ohio Canal increased the public investment to about 70 percent of the total. The remaining 30 percent was privately financed.

It may seem strange that government aid for canal building was so extensive in nineteenth-century America, well known as an era of laissez-faire capitalism. In Great Britain most canals were built by unassisted private enterprise, but, unlike the young American nation, Britain had large amounts of available capital as well as experience in the formation and operation of private corporations. In America the large sums necessary for canal building were unavailable in the private sec-tor. Thus, canals were generally financed through public aid and usually owned and operated by state governments.

Government support for canal building was manifest in many different ways. Money might be spent directly on a public works project or aid might be granted to a corporation under various terms and conditions—stock subscriptions, loans, guarantees of company obligations, or simply outright subsidies. When all other means had failed, New York successfully raised large sums through the sale of state bonds. At first, the money came in small amounts and almost entirely from state citizens; but as the success of the canal became apparent, the securities were attractive to larger investors in New York City and London.

Although the federal government had refused to help New York in building the Erie, it later made some substantial contributions to canal building. By 1860 it had granted states approximately 4 million acres of public land for canal projects in Ohio, Michigan, Indiana, Illinois, and Wisconsin. In addition, it had subscribed over $3 million in canal company stock. Still, the states were the major financial contributors at the beginning of the canal era and for a time were generally blessed with little indebtedness and good reputations for meeting obligations. In the 1830s, state canal financing was facilitated by general prosperity and by an 1836 law which distributed federal surplus funds to the states. But by the early 1840s, a depression gripped the country and almost every state was in financial difficulty.

The Panic of 1837 contributed to the collapse of canal enthusiasm, but there were other factors which played a role. The ambitious enlargement programs undertaken on many canals were very expensive. For example, the Erie was enlarged at a cost of $44.5 million, almost six times the cost of the original project. In addition to the high cost of construction (the average for most canals was $20,000 to $30,000 per mile), maintenance and repair expenses were extremely high for most canals. Transit slowdowns caused by flooding, low-water levels, lock difficulties, and freezing meant loss of the revenue to pay off the huge indebtedness. Corruption and mismanagement were often factors in the financial pinch. All of this contributed to the passing of the canal age, which came about with the ascendancy of the versatile railroad as the major transportation facility of the nation.

On the average, rail freight rates were higher than those for water haulage; but when it came to dependable service, canals could not keep pace with the railroad. Bad weather was rarely an impediment to railroad travel. Railroads could build short lines and sidings right up to a shipper's loading dock, something seldom possible for the waterway. Unlike its competitor, the railroad could be taken through rough, hilly country and thereby tap remote markets. Finally, the rail lines could provide freight and passenger service that was significantly faster than water-borne carriers.

Those economically tied to the canal systems raised strong opposition to the railroad. Even the general taxpayer often opposed the railroad, fearing that his taxes would be increased if canal revenues were reduced. Consequently, for a short period a few states, including New York and Ohio, had laws requiring railroads to pay taxes to make up for reduced canal revenues. On the other hand, the federal government was well aware of the importance of railroad development. By 1857 federal grants of land for railroad expansion totaled 18 million acres. The advantages of the railroad were so great that even the strongest canals faced a losing battle, and by 1860 the railroad became the dominant factor in national transportation. By the end of the Civil War, most of the weaker canal systems had faded out of the transportation picture, while a few of the more notable operations continued for several years before they too declined.

Army Corps of Engineers

For the past century and a half, federal activity in the field of waterway improvement for navigation has been carried out primarily by the Army Corps of Engineers. The engineers first appeared in 1775 when the Continental Congress provided for one chief engineer and two assistants for the army. The corps was formally organized in 1779, but disbanded after the conclusion of peace in 1783. There were short-lived revivals in the 1790s when war again threatened, but the modern Corps of Engineers was created on March 16, 1802. President Thomas Jefferson was authorized by Congress to establish a corps of five officers and ten cadets, who "shall be stationed at West Point, in the State of New York, and shall constitute a Military Academy; and at all times to do duty in such places and on such service as the President of the United States shall direct." The Military Academy, deeply influenced by French professors and texts, formed the only school of engineers in the United States until the establishment of Rensselaer Polytechnic twenty-two years later.

Not until 1824 was Congress able to employ this engineering capability for waterway improvement. That year, the landmark *Gibbons v. Ogden* Case gave the national legislature power over "navigation within the limits of every state in the union." This decision permitted passage of two significant authorizations that laid the basis for federal navigation public works. The first asked the President "to cause the necessary surveys, plans, and estimates, to be made of the routes of such Roads and Canals as he may deem of national importance, in a commercial or military point of view, or necessary for the transportation of the public mail." The act also authorized employment of "two or more skillful civil engineers, and such officers of the Corps of Engineers" as the President "may think proper." The second authorization provided for improvement of navigation on the Ohio and Mississippi rivers, appropriated $75,000 for this work, and asked the President to employ "any of the engineers in the public service which he may deem proper." The act also authorized experimental work on two sandbars as well as the removal of snags and trees.

Such congressional authorizations for improvement of rivers and harbors for the benefit of navigation became known as a Rivers and Harbors Act. Since 1824 almost every Congress passed one or more of these acts to provide for maintenance and improvement on America's waterways. Each act contains two principal parts: a section authorizing and directing preliminary examinations and surveys at designated localities, and a section authorizing specific river and harbor works in accordance with reports previously submitted by the army's chief of engineers.

Before the Civil War, many worthwhile projects were undertaken to survey and improve the nation's rivers and harbors, but the work was often hampered by myopic politicians and strict constructionist Presidents. Because of the parochial interests of the legislators, Congress appropriated small amounts of money for primarily scattered projects of local or regional value. Support for internal improvements was only gained by adding improvements to districts of reluctant legislators. Sectional jealousies, constitutional questions, and conflicts between the legislative and executive branches further muddied the river-improvement waters, making comprehensive planning impossible.

States rights objections to river improvements were quieted after the Civil War and Republican administrations supported expenditures to facilitate commerce. By 1900 a com-

Army Corps of Engineers.
During the nineteenth century, government snagboats cleared dangerous obstructions from navigable rivers.

prehensive plan for developing the Mississippi River was in effect. In addition, the Army Corps of Engineers had divided the nation into five divisions each headed by a senior colonel to administer river and harbor projects.

By the beginning of the twentieth century, existing navigation river development plans were being challenged. People began to consider America's waterways as a multipurpose resource, to be developed not only for aiding navigation but for controlling floods, using stored water to irrigate crops, generating hydroelectric power, and providing water for municipal and industrial use. This emphasis on "beneficial use" and "multiple use" led to broader developmental plans for river basins. For example, in 1907 President Theodore Roosevelt announced formation of the Inland Waterways Commission. In so doing, he stated:

> Works designed to control our waterways have thus far usually been undertaken for a single purpose, such as the improvement of navigation, the development of power, the irrigation of arid lands, the protection of lowlands from floods, or to supply water for domestic and manufacturing purposes . . . . The time has come for merging local projects and uses of the inland waters in a comprehensive plan designed for the benefit of the entire country. Such a plan should consider and include all the uses to which streams may be put, and should bring together and coordinate the points of view of all users of water.

Congress authorized entry of the Army Corps of Engineers into the multiple-purpose, water resource planning field with its passage of a Rivers and Harbors Act in 1925. The act directed the secretary of war, in collaboration with the Federal Power Commission, to submit an estimate of the cost of making surveys of those navigable streams and tributaries throughout the nation where power development appeared feasible in combination with navigation, flood control, and irrigation development.

The 1927 Rivers and Harbors Act directed the secretary of war through the chief of engineers to prepare detailed comprehensive surveys and reports on the principal river systems of the United States. The ensuing studies became known as "308" reports and covered 191 rivers. They required a decade to complete and helped further establish the concept of multiple-purpose project planning. Thus, by 1930 the basis was laid for broadening and strengthening all water programs from the single-purpose, single-project approach to the planning, design, construction, operation, and maintenance of multiple-purpose, basin-wide projects which sought optimum use of river systems.

Since World War II, navigation improvements have been part of broader river basin development plans. In 1946 the Federal Inter - Agency River Basin Committee was established, mainly at the initiative of the agencies concerned with water resources, to discuss federal water resource plans. In January 1950, the President's Water Resources Policy Commission was appointed, and it formulated three volumes of reports and recommendations. That same year, President Harry S. Truman directed all federal agencies concerned with natural resources to become involved in water resource development and ordered that the states be allowed to participate. From this beginning came a great number of comprehensive river basin studies.

President Dwight D. Eisenhower approved an "Interagency Agreement on Coordination of Water and Related Land Resources Activities" in 1954 which led to replacement of the Federal Inter-Agency River Basin Committee by a similar Interagency Committee on Water Resources. This new committee was composed of the assistant secretaries of agriculture, army, commerce, interior, and labor plus the surgeon general of the Public Health Service and the chairman of the Federal Power Commission. Its responsibilities were to determine means to promote coordination of the water and related land resource activities of the agencies, to resolve interagency differences, and to suggest to the President changes in existing law.

In 1959 a Senate Select Committee on National Water Resources was formed to study the relation of water resource activities to the national interest and the extent such activities would be required to take care of water needs

for all purposes, now and in the future. This group, commonly known as the "Kerr Committee," held nationwide hearings from 1959 through 1961. They recommended that comprehensive water resource development plans be drawn up cooperatively by federal agencies, states, local governments, individuals, corporations, and others concerned.

Throughout the years of federal involvement, the Army Corps of Engineers has retained a pivotal role in water resource development, with prime responsibility for navigation and flood control. In addition to its complement of army engineer officers and 40,000 civilian employees, the corps works mainly through private contractors for construction, development, operation, and maintenance of improved rivers, canals, and harbors. The corps operates a fleet of 3,000 vessels consisting of dredges, barges, pontoons, and other floating equipment to support maintenance and operation work. The corps also cooperates with other federal agencies and the states in carrying out engineering feasibility studies and cost analyses and preparing reports which Congress uses to determine the nation's water resource programs.

During its century and a half of public works activity in the navigation area, the corps has undertaken work on coastal and inland harbors, rivers, and the Great Lakes. The following discussions of improvements on the Mississippi and Ohio rivers are representative of the navigation activities of the Army Corps of Engineers and other agencies.

Mississippi River

Before improvements were made, the Mississippi River joined the Gulf of Mexico by a series of passes and small mouths. In each of these outlets, the river lost velocity and dropped its burden of silt and bedload (heavy sand and sediment that is pushed along its bottom). These sediments piled up, forming bars which gradually blocked the passage of large oceangoing ships. Consequently, the Port of New Orleans became inaccessible for the most profitable forms of commerce.

Two schemes for deepening the mouth of the Mississippi River developed. The first was to dredge a channel through the sand bars. The other was to increase the velocity of the river by artificial extensions of its banks, known as jetties, and to let the river dig its own channels through the bars. Even before the Civil War, both methods were employed by various contractors and army engineers, but the results were unimpressive.

In 1873 the distinguished civilian engineer, James B. Eads, visited the mouths of the Mississippi River with a group of congressmen. He had won fame as the designer and builder of the iron-clad gunboats during the Civil War, as the manufacturer of a foolproof diving bell for recovering cargoes from sunken steamers, and as the engineer of the first steel bridge across the Mississippi River at St. Louis. Eads offered to open the mouth of the river and guarantee a 28-foot depth by building jetties in such a way as to utilize the river in scouring a channel.

After much debate and controversy, in 1875 Congress directed Eads to begin his work. He faced a difficult task, complicated by yellow fever and unfavorable financial arrangements. Eads staked his reputation and his personal fortune on the works he proposed; and on July 8, 1879, a 30-foot channel was officially declared to exist at the mouth of the Mississippi. Eads achieved the goal set by Congress, and large oceangoing ships were able to proceed upriver to dock at New Orleans.

Improvements were also badly needed on the river above New Orleans. Following the Civil War, the population of the lower Mississippi Valley was in a desperate situation. Not only had the area been ravaged by war, but it had never recovered from pre-war floods. Reconstructing the Mississippi basin meant two things: reopening the river channel to navigation and minimizing the effects of recurrent floods that devastated the land along its banks.

No snagging operations had been carried out since 1854. When operations resumed, the river was found to be a maze of wrecks, wartime casualties of the fighting that marked the passage of the Union and Confederate armies through the area. This wreckage added to the natural accumulation of obstructions, which

before the war annually caused snagboats to remove over 56,000 foreign objects from the river. By this time, the commerce clause of the Constitution had been interpreted to permit river improvements, but flood control was considered to be outside the legitimate concerns of the federal government. Federal statutes restricted levee construction and repair to work that was to aid navigation.

In 1874 Congress authorized surveys of river transportation routes to the seaboard, among which was reconnaissance of the Mississippi from Cairo, Illinois, to New Orleans. Five years later, a board of army engineer officers concluded that a complete levee system would aid commerce during periods of high water. Moreover, the board reported that if levees "were permanently established throughout the river, they would doubtless develop a large additional commerce and afford the kind of facilities for its transaction." The people of the valley were not impressed by legal technicalities. For them, prevention of recurrent floods demanded restoration of the levees, which had been built largely by local funding. They turned to the federal government for help. The Mississippi River Commission (MRC) was created in 1879, partly in response to the public demand for improving navigation and flood control on the Mississippi. As constituted, the commission consisted of seven presidential appointees, three from the Army Corps of Engineers.

The first problem MRC faced was bringing into focus its powers and responsibilities. The enabling legislation was vague, an omnibus bill which asked the commission to "deepen the channel and protect the banks of the Mississippi River," "prevent destructive floods," and "promote and facilitate commerce." But the limits of its authority were not carefully defined. The commission interpreted its authority liberally and in 1880 submitted its first report which called for construction of a complete system of levee and channel improvements.

In 1882 a decisive reorganization of the commission occurred. The river was divided into four districts, each under control of a corps officer. These men were to carry out the day-to-day executive work of MRC, interpreting its policies and recommending the appropriations it should request from Congress. In 1892 the chief of engineers was granted the power to veto, although he still could not initiate, the projects of the commission. The organization was fleshed out as the local districts hired bigger civilian staffs.

The MRC's primary tasks in the Mississippi Valley were to let contracts, inspect and maintain levees, and direct flood fights. After a flood in 1912, levee heights were raised 3 feet, but in 1927 an extremely severe flood proved that this was not enough. The subsequent 1928 Flood Control Act authorized the Mississippi River and Tributaries (MR&T) project and made MRC responsible for its construction. (See Chapter 9 for flood control features). In addition to flood control, this plan provided for improved navigation channels for river traffic between Cairo, Illinois, and New Orleans. Congress also authorized the establishment of a Waterways Experiment Station. Constructed at two locations, in Vicksburg and Clinton, Mississippi, the station developed a hydraulics laboratory which used small-scale models of the Mississippi and other river systems to study navigation, flood control, and related problems. It added a soil mechanics laboratory to analyze the characteristics of soils used in levees, dams, spillways, and canals. The Waterways Experiment Station has since become the outstanding installation of its kind in the world.

In 1928 the width of the Mississippi's navigational channel was increased to 300 feet, and in 1944 the authorized channel depth from Cairo to Baton Rouge was increased to 12 feet at low water. Since World War II, the 12-foot channel has been developed and maintained by a program of bank stabilization and dredging. Below Baton Rouge, the maintenance of sufficient navigation depth to the Gulf of Mexico is still a project of major importance. In the 1945 and 1962 Rivers and Harbors acts, several separate projects were combined to authorize development of a navigation channel for oceangoing traffic in the lower reaches of the river. The minimum allowable depths on various stretches of the channel were set between 30 and 40 feet. Perhaps the most significant aspect of this program was completion of the Mississippi River-Gulf Outlet in 1965. A dredged channel running southeast from New Orleans to the Gulf of Mexico, the 76-mile-long waterway is shorter and easier to navigate than the Mississippi River and is free of floating debris and dangerous currents.

The 200-mile reach of the Mississippi from the mouth of the Ohio to the mouth of the Missouri is called the middle Mississippi. This short section is the hub of a vast inland waterway system which totals 16,000 miles. In its original condition, the middle Mississippi channel was obstructed by numerous snags; the stream was divided at many places into separate channels or chutes; and sand bars sometimes reduced depths to less than 4 feet.

The rise of St. Louis, Missouri, as the major metropolis on this part of the river led to the first navigation improvements. As early as 1836, the federal government provided small amounts of money to improve the St. Louis harbor. With the rapid growth of river commerce, attempts were made to decrease navigation hazards by removing snags and wrecks from the channel. In 1872 a board of engineers presented a more comprehensive project for the middle Mississippi, including

Army Corps of Engineers

Models are used at the Waterways Experiment Station at Vicksburg, Mississippi, to determine the effects of proposed river improvements.

river development in the vicinity of St. Louis and a river survey to its confluence with the Ohio. The project called for improving the stream bed by means of bank revetments, reducing the channel width where excessive; and forcing low-water flow into the main channel by closing chutes and secondary channels. About $1.5 million was spent under the original project for the survey, dikes, retaining walls, and revetments. This project was interrupted in later years, but was restored by the 1910 Rivers and Harbors Act which also provided for channel maintenance by dredging. The revised project called for an 8-foot channel depth between St. Louis and the mouth of the Ohio River and a 6-foot depth between St. Louis and the mouth of the Missouri River.

The latest authorizations for navigation improvements on the middle Mississippi were contained in the 1927 and 1930 Rivers and Harbors acts. These provided for obtaining and maintaining a minimum channel depth of 9 feet and a minimum width at low water of 300 feet (with greater widths in the river bends). In contrast to the navigation pools of the upper Mississippi, the channel over most of the middle Mississippi is maintained by "open river" techniques involving the use of stone dikes, bank revetments, and dredging. These improvements have contributed to an increase in traffic on the middle Mississippi from 2.5 million tons in 1939 to 58.3 million tons in 1970.

In its natural state, the upper Mississippi was a series of deep pools separated by shoals and rapids. Its channel was obstructed by bars and snags, and during late summer and autumn little water ran in this reach of the river. In the nineteenth century, navigation on the Mississippi upstream from St. Anthony Falls (at present-day Minneapolis) was confined to floating or rafting logs, although small steamboats operated on some sections of this reach. Between 1875 and 1879, the federal government removed the worst obstructions between Minneapolis and St. Cloud, Minnesota, but this work ceased in 1879 because of lack of funds.

More important was the gradual development of canals on the river below St. Anthony

Falls to the mouth of the Missouri. Congress believed the river was important in developing this region and authorized expenditures for river improvements on troublesome reaches. Noteworthy was channel work carried out in 1837 at the Keokuk and Rock Island Rapids by Lieutenant Robert E. Lee of the Army Corps of Engineers. However, in the 1850s, railroad competition thwarted further efforts. Though more expensive, railroads operated on a year-round basis, often building tracks alongside the river. River communities and navigation interests sought ways to prevent the resulting loss of business and began to exert pressure on Congress to assist river navigation.

In 1868 the State of Minnesota was granted 200,000 acres of federal land to aid private interests in building a lock and dam on the Mississippi at Meekers Island, about 3 miles downstream from St. Anthony Falls. Excessive costs, however, prevented construction. Ten years later, Congress authorized a $4^{1}/_{2}$-foot channel on the Mississippi between St. Paul and the mouth of the Missouri River to be accomplished by erecting wing dams and closing chutes. The project's execution was slow and the results disappointing. Since transportation vessels were growing in size and carrying capacity, little interest could be generated for a channel only $4^{1}/_{2}$ feet deep. Nevertheless, in 1890 this depth was established from St. Paul to the Missouri.

Meanwhile, between 1884 and 1895, the Army Corps of Engineers built five reservoir dams at the headwaters of the Mississippi. Studies were also made on the feasibility of constructing reservoirs in the upper reaches of several tributaries—the St. Croix, the Chippewa, and the Wisconsin rivers—but these were judged impracticable. Reconstruction of the original five upstream dams and reservoirs became necessary between 1900 and 1911, and a sixth dam and reservoir, Gull, was placed in operation. Although these were great achievements, not everyone was pleased. According to a special board of army engineers, the reservoirs had not greatly improved the depth of the navigable channel below the dams; and the reservoir dams were vigorously opposed by property owners who

Army Corps of Engineers

Construction of dams and locks on the upper Mississippi has facilitated the flow of waterborne commerce.

wanted their inundated lands once again made usable for agriculture and manufacturing.

Following a careful study of proposed upper Mississippi improvements, in 1930 Congress approved construction of a 9-foot channel between Minneapolis and the mouth of the Illinois River. A system of twenty-eight locks and dams were subsequently built. These changed the upper Mississippi into a series of "steps," which river tows and other boats could climb or descend as they traveled the river. The lowermost dam, No. 26, is located at Alton, Illinois, 8 miles north of St. Louis. The uppermost at Minneapolis is located 660 miles above the Missouri River mouth. The dams are spaced at irregular intervals varying from 10 to 47 miles; the average pool length is 25 miles. At most of the sites a main lock 110 by 600 feet has been constructed as well as an upper gate bay of an auxiliary lock 110 by 360 feet to be completed when required by traffic. The entire authorized 9-foot navigation project, with the exception of the upper 4.6 miles, has been in operation since 1940. The latter was completed in 1963.

River traffic increased rapidly after completion of the project. Total commerce between Minneapolis and the mouth of the Missouri River rose from 2.4 million tons in 1939 to 54 million tons in 1970. The principal commodities that are transported include petroleum products, coal, and grain. Harbors, terminal facilities, and riverside industries have developed at many of the river cities and towns as a result of the improved navigation.

In recent years, a study has been underway to determine the advisability of providing a 12-foot navigation channel from Minneapolis to the mouth of the Ohio River. Such a change, of course, would affect the surface level of the waterway as well as pollution control and land drainage systems along its shores. Many communities and members of levee and drainage districts have thus voiced opposition to any plan that would involve raising present pool levels. Another proposal under consideration is the enlargement of present locking facilities. Tows are increasing in number and becoming longer; and breaking up the tows to get through the locks is a costly and time-consuming process. However, obtaining authorizations for such enlargements is difficult due to increasingly high costs and environmental concerns.

Year-round navigation on the upper Mississippi is projected for the future. Since World War II, all-season navigation has been maintained on the Mississippi as far north as the mouth of the Illinois River, but each year traffic has been stopped further north by ice conditions. Ice jams frequently develop early in the winter and block navigation pools. Ice sometimes clogs the river to depths of several feet and becomes a formidable barrier to river traffic. At present, reservoirs maintained by the Army Corps of Engineers are used to extend the navigation season by releasing water to break up ice blockages. Much more, however, needs to be done to insure year-round navigation on the upper reaches of the Mississippi.

Ohio River

The Ohio River Basin is a vast area of 204,000 square miles. It reaches northeast to Chautauqua Lake in northern New York, west to the flat land of Illinois, and south to the Tennessee River drainage which extends into Georgia, Alabama, and Mississippi. Over 20 million people live in an area that is expected to support 35 million by the year 2020. Through its heart, the Ohio River carries the largest volume of water of the six Mississippi tributaries. As the crow flies, it stretches 500 miles, but the winding river is nearly 1,000 miles in length.

Many kinds of floating craft were used to navigate the Ohio River of early days: canoes, rough timber rafts, keelboats, and steamboats. Following the Civil War, the use of barges pushed by towboats to move bulk materials proved to be a far more efficient system than the early packet boats. Unfortunately, the level of the river water was far from stable. After long dry periods of little or no rain, the Ohio would run so low that in many places a person could easily wade across. "A mile wide and a foot deep" was an early description of the river during summer. When the water receded to this stage, river traffic sat on its hulls in the mud and waited for higher water.

In 1866 a civil engineer, W. Milnor Roberts, was commissioned to study the Ohio and its problems. Until that time, improvements on the river consisted of open-channel work (clearing wrecks and snags, removing rocks, channel dredging, and building dikes and jetties) plus one canal bypassing the falls at Louisville. The shallow, meandering channels had been satisfactory for packet boats, but Roberts contended that tows of deep-draft barges required broad, relatively straight channels. He recommended transforming the Ohio by a system of locks and dams—called "canalization."

Roberts submitted his report in 1870 to a board headed by Major W. E. Merrill of the Army Corps of Engineers. In 1874 Merrill recommended construction of thirteen locks and movable dams between Pittsburgh, Pennsylvania, and Wheeling, West Virginia. The following year, Congress appropriated $100,000 to construct "a movable dam, or a dam with adjustable gates, for the purpose of testing substantially the best method of improving, permanently, the navigation of the Ohio River and its tributaries." As a result, the first dam and lock complex was built at Davis Island, 4 miles below Pittsburgh, and opened to traffic on October 7, 1885.

This movable dam was so successful that it became a prototype for further construction on the river. Most of the ensuing dams were of this "wicket" type, which had been in use for several years on the inland waterways of France and other European countries. The distinctive feature of the wicket dam was a navigable pass filled with a comparatively narrow line of shutters, or wickets, resting on a concrete foundation. By use of a "maneuver boat," these wickets could be raised or lowered. When the river rose and became navigable, the wickets were folded down flat against the foundation; and instead of using the locks, river traffic passed over the dam.

In 1910 Congress approved the complete canalization of the Ohio River; and by 1929 the system of forty-six locks and dams, which assured year-round navigation on the 981 miles between Pittsburgh and Cairo, Illinois, was completed. The system adequately handled the 20 to 30 million tons of freight that yearly moved on the river in the 1920s and 1930s, pushed mainly by steam-powered, stern-wheel towboats.

In addition, the Army Corps of Engineers built reservoirs inside the Ohio Basin for flood control and water storage. Among other purposes, these were used to augment stream flow during periods of low water. Since construction began, the low-flow record in the

Ohio River at Cincinnati occurred in 1963—about 4,000 cubic feet per second. Of this amount, 60 percent came from the reservoirs. Had all planned reservoirs been in operation, the flow could have been increased nearly three times.

Almost all the navigation planning was predicated on the continued supremacy of the steamboat in river transportation. After World War I, however, the more powerful diesel towboat appeared, and the new vessels found themselves inhibited by a navigation system designed for less powerful vessels. Diesels were capable of pushing loads twice as long as the old steamboats, which meant that some tows had to be divided in order to pass through the locks. Such double locking was costly and extremely slow, demanding up to an hour and a half at each lock. A tow passing all forty-six structures on the Ohio River could spend more than two days in locking alone.

Once again, a different kind of river improvement was needed. In 1955 a modernization program was begun which would replace the forty-six original dams with nineteen higher, gated dams, each with dual lock chambers and at least one 1,200-foot-long, 110-foot-wide lock. Making the dams higher provided longer distances and deeper water between lockages, thus reducing the number of dams and locking time. The estimated federal cost to complete the current modernization program is approximately $500 million. As of June 30,

1972, the number of dams was reduced from forty-six to twenty-six. Of these, seventeen were replacements begun under the 1955 modernization program.

These projects related primarily to navigation, but in 1955 the Senate Committee on Public Works adopted a resolution authorizing a survey of the Ohio River Basin to formulate a "framework plan of development which will serve as a broad guide to the best use, or combination of uses, of water and related land resources of the basin to meet short- and long-term needs." This study, exclusive of the Tennessee River Basin, has been completed. In general, it is an appraisal of existing development plans and projected requirements through year 2020. A study program is underway which investigates problem areas and recommends additions to the plan for economically feasible and environmentally acceptable projects.

An Ohio River Basin Commission was established in 1971 to coordinate the activities of federal, state, interstate, local, and nongovernmental agencies involved in planning and developing water and related land resources in the basin. Subsequently, a Water and Related Land Resource Development Program emerged to provide a framework for determining general approaches to mutual problems and to establish long-range objectives. For navigation, these include 2,187 channel miles of improvement to the existing system by 1980 and 527 miles of new waterways by 2020. In addition, there are specific goals for flood control, water supply storage, water quality control, hydroelectric power, recreation, irrigation, and drainage.

Though far from complete, these projects on the Ohio River have permitted an astonishing growth in waterborne traffic. The 22 million tons carried in 1929 increased to 136 million tons by 1974. During these forty-five years, the annual ton-mile figure grew twenty times to 31 billion in 1974. The program anticipates an increase to about 150 billion ton-miles by 2020.

Army Corps of Engineers

Long strings of barges can pass through modern locks on the Ohio River without being broken up.

Great Lakes and the St. Lawrence Seaway

The largest North American inland waterway system is the chain of five Great

Lakes and their long outlet, the St. Lawrence River. These bodies of water stretch for 2,340 miles from Duluth, Minnesota, on Lake Superior to the Atlantic Ocean. Throughout the system, the St. Lawrence Seaway permits seagoing ships to traverse the vast navigation network which is vital to Canadian and American commerce.

In discovering the Great Lakes, the French came by way of what the Indians called "the river without end," the St. Lawrence. The Indians had used this river as a highway for centuries before French explorer Jacques Cartier gave it its present name. The French, therefore, had a head start over other colonizing nations in penetrating the interior of North America. Nevertheless, their trading posts on the St. Lawrence grew slowly because their modes of transportation were canoes and bateaux, light craft they carried around the numerous rapids which dotted the river's course. These white waters were obstacles the French felt unable to remove. The only attempts made at improving the St. Lawrence were abortive efforts in 1689 and again in 1700 to build a canal around the Lachine Rapids near Montreal.

In 1779 the first successful canal construction on the St. Lawrence was carried out by the Northwest Fur Company, a British concern. It was a lock and canal around St. Mary's Falls, today's Sault Ste. Marie, to permit navigation between Lake Superior and the other Great Lakes. Shortly thereafter, the British also completed canals to pass the Cascades, Cedar, and Coteau rapids, up-river from Montreal.

The idea of creating an uninterrupted waterway navigable by seagoing ships is credited to the American statesman. Gouveneur Morris. Formerly an ambassador to France, Morris was elected to the Senate from New York and in 1800 made a visit to the St. Lawrence region. At one point, he speculated that "one-tenth of the expense borne by Britain in the last campaign would enable ships to sail from London through Hudson's River into Lake Erie." He helped promote the Erie Canal and advocated a comprehensive plan for canals along the St. Lawrence from the Great Lakes to the Atlantic.

A long history of political wrangling and other delays transpired before Morris' dream reached fulfillment. For a time, its future looked particularly grim. In the War of 1812, the Americans wrecked the British canal at Sault Ste. Marie; and when it was suggested that this waterway should be restored, Henry Clay insisted that the area served by the canal was beyond the pale of American settlement. However, in 1824 the Army Corps of Engineers undertook, as one of its first tasks, improvement work on Erie Harbor and Presque Isle in Lake Erie. The following year, Congress authorized the corps to study the harbors of Cleveland and Fairport, Ohio. Subsequent surveys were made at Buffalo and Ashtabula in 1826 and at Chicago in 1832.

On the Canadian side of the border, more positive steps were taken. In 1818 an astute businessman named William Hamilton Merritt petitioned the Upper Canada legislature for a canal survey around Niagara Falls. His plan was to build a diversion canal from the Welland River to Twelve Mile Creek where he owned a mill, thereby providing water power for his mill and a bypass for river boats around Niagara. Rebuffed, he borrowed private capital in 1823, obtained a charter, and began a job he thought could be finished in two years. In 1824 he began excavations. Merritt encountered many unanticipated difficulties, and his projected two years ran to five; but finally, on November 27, 1829, two ships, one American and one Canadian, were towed through the new Welland Canal. The venture was so successful that Merritt immediately organized a lobby for a full St. Lawrence Seaway.

An Upper Canadian Canal Commission was appointed, with Merritt as its chairman. Working with a similar commission from Lower Canada, they began constructing a canal around the Long Sault Rapids on the St. Lawrence in 1833. Since they projected all St. Lawrence canals to be 9 feet in depth, they also deepened the Welland Canal. By 1848 the Canadians had built a series of canals and fifty-three stone locks, bypassing Niagara Falls and all the St. Lawrence rapids; thereby creating a continuous water route from Lake

Erie to the Atlantic Ocean.

Americans suddenly discovered that improvement of a shared waterway was becoming a unilateral undertaking. What prompted this concern was the discovery of deposits of iron and copper ore on the shores of Lake Superior. As a result, Congress granted a right-of-way on the American side of the border at Sault Ste. Marie to an American company, and in 1855 a canal was built to replace the one that had been destroyed. The depth of this new canal, however, was increased from 9 to 11$^1/_2$ feet. This was the first canal built by Americans as part of the St. Lawrence system. The Canadians later countered by building a deeper canal on their side of Sault Ste. Marie.

In 1841 the United States Congress appropriated $15,000 to initiate a systematic survey of the entire Great Lakes. This study with additional funding continued from 1841 to 1882, when it was allowed to lapse for seven years. Then, in 1889 it was resumed as a data-gathering operation, which still continues to function. The purpose of the lake survey was dual in nature: to furnish charts to lake navigators and to determine improvements necessary to maintain lake commerce. These studies made systematic commercial use of the lakes feasible.

On March 2, 1895, Congress authorized the President to appoint a Deep Waterways Commission to report on the feasibility of building a deep-water channel from the Great Lakes to the Atlantic Ocean. The members of this commission met the following January with members of a similar Canadian commission and recommended examination and survey of the waterways between the Great Lakes and the Atlantic. This task was subsequently undertaken by the Army Corps of Engineers.

Beginning with President William H. Taft in 1909, a succession of American Presidents supported the St. Lawrence Seaway project, but all failed to convince a reluctant Congress, under pressure from railroads and east coast harbor interests, to fund the program. For example, in 1940 President Franklin D. Roosevelt allocated $1 million of special defense funds to the Army Corps of Engineers

and the Federal Power Commission to make engineering studies of the International Rapids section of the river. To Roosevelt, development of the St. Lawrence for deep-water navigation and the generation of power was vital to the security of the United States.

As governor of New York, Roosevelt had actively supported efforts to improve the International Rapids section for navigation and hydroelectric power. The state legislature created the Power Authority of the State of New York in 1931 to accomplish this task in cooperation with the Canadians. In spite of the fact that a special Army Corps of Engineers district office was set up at Massena, New York, and a report submitted in April 1943, work on the seaway was delayed by Congress. The Canadians were unhappy with American reluctance. In 1951 Canadian Prime Minister Lester Pearson stated: "The biggest and longest dragging of feet I have known in my entire career is that of the Americans on the St. Lawrence."

The key to the waterway's development was the dams and the reservoir area excavation required for hydroelectric power generation. The New York Power Authority obtained a license from the Federal Power Commission in July 1953 to construct, operate, and maintain the American portion of the power project. This cleared the way for the Canadians to build the seaway on the Canadian side and cooperate with the New York agency in the hydroelectric development. Congress then passed the Wiley-Dondero Act in May 1954 which established the St. Lawrence Seaway Development Corporation and authorized the creation of a 27-foot channel around the International Rapids on the American side of the river.

Agreements were then reached between the two countries to prevent costly duplication of navigation facilities. The Canadian canals and locks cost $330 million, mostly downstream from where the river served as the international boundary. The canals and locks on the American side cost $130 million. The design and supervision of construction in Canada was by the Canadian St. Lawrence Seaway Authority. The St. Lawrence Seaway Development Corporation utilized the Army

Corps of Engineers to design and supervise construction of the American navigation improvements. The $650 million cost for hydroelectric facilities was equally shared by the Hydroelectric Power Commission of Ontario and the Power Authority of the State of New York. (The power portion of the project is discussed in Chapter 11.)

In April 1959, the St. Lawrence Seaway was opened to deep-draft traffic. In June Queen Elizabeth and President Eisenhower formally dedicated the waterway, bringing to realization the dream of sailing oceangoing ships from the Atlantic Ocean to the heart of the American continent. Thus, for eight months of the year, vessels began to traverse the 1,000-mile-long reach up the Gulf of St. Lawrence and the St. Lawrence River to Montreal, ascending 20 feet in the process. At Montreal, they entered the first of seven new locks, five of which were in Canadian and two in American waters, raising the ships 226 feet in the 182 miles to Lake Ontario. After crossing Lake Ontario, the vessels bypassed Niagara Falls by the Welland Canal, equipped with eight locks to lift shipping 326 feet within 28 miles. The vessels moved from Lake Erie to Lake Huron through the connecting

link near Detroit, thence on to Lake Michigan or Lake Superior. In 1971 the Welland Canal carried 63 million cargo tons. The Sault Ste. Marie reported 91.5 million tons passing through the American locks and 1.5 million tons passing through the Canadian canal.

Not all problems have been solved. For example, at present the Great Lakes are experiencing a period of unusually high levels, which are causing damage to shore properties and difficulties in harbors and at terminals. Thus far this condition has not seriously affected navigation. A continuing problem, however, is disruption of navigation in the winter months. About 255 miles of the reach from Duluth (at the western end of Lake Superior) to Ogdensburg (on the St. Lawrence River) consists of connecting channels in which heavy ice forms each winter. Navigation on the Great Lakes and their connecting channels is suspended during the winter because of the effects of the ice from about mid December to early April. Commerce and industry served by navigation are forced to resort to expensive stockpiling to carry through the winter period or turn to more costly modes of transportation such as the railroads. Both "lakers" (giant, bargelike boats

Locks on the St. Lawrence Seaway, such as the Eisenhower Lock near Massena, New York, enable oceangoing vessels to enter the heart of the North American continent.

which carry mostly iron ore inside the Great Lakes system) and "salties" (oceangoing ships that carry cargoes between the Great Lakes and the world's market places) find themselves immobile for four months of the year.

Attempts have been made over the years to extend the shipping season. In 1965 Congress authorized the Army Corps of Engineers to take a limited look at the feasibility of extending the season. In the 1970 Rivers and Harbors Act, Congress authorized continuation of this study, and it voted a three-year, $6.5 million program to explore further its practicability.

Tennessee River

The 1933 Tennessee Valley Authority Act authorized, among other things, building a navigation channel adequate for 9-foot draft vessels on the Tennessee River from Knoxville, Tennessee, to Paducah, Kentucky, a distance of 650 miles. When the Tennessee Valley Authority (TVA) began constructing the waterway in the early 1930s, there were two dams with locks on the river: Wilson Dam near Florence, Alabama, which provided a 15-mile channel; and Hales Bar Dam near Chattanooga, Tennessee, which furnished a 6-foot depth for 33 miles. Under the TVA Act, seven more high dams with locks were built on the river. By 1944 the 9-foot channel was virtually completed. A larger main lock, 110 by 600 feet, was added at Wilson Dam in 1959; and in subsequent years, locks at other dams have been enlarged. A new dam and lock were completed in 1963 on the Clinch River, a tributary of the Tennessee, which increased the 9-foot channel on the waterway to 750 miles. Tellico Dam will add 33 miles of navigable stream when construction is completed in 1976.

The nine mainstream dams and locks raise vessels more than 600 feet, an average of nearly a foot per mile. The navigation channel is open year-round. The Army Corps of Engineers operates the locks and performs regular dredging, and the coast guard establishes and maintains the navigation aids as they do on other inland waterways. In addition to joining the Ohio River at Paducah, the Tennessee River is linked with the Cumber-

land by a canal in Kentucky Lake. The Tennessee-Tombigbee Waterway, which is being built, will tie the Tennessee to the Warrior River and provide access to the Port of Mobile, Alabama.

Oil companies were the first industry to recognize the utility and economy of the new waterway. They built terminals on the river in the 1940s and began sending cargoes from Houston and Port Arthur, Texas, up the Mississippi River to customers in the Tennessee Valley. Grain companies, recognizing the expanding livestock industry along the Tennessee system, built mills and shipped large quantities of corn, soybeans, alfalfa pellets, and other agricultural commodities. A brisk commerce in coal, forest products, chemicals, and steel has also developed. Industries were early attracted to the area because the multipurpose river development project provided low-cost hydroelectric power and abundant supplies of water. Moreover, TVA's resource development activities are "total" in concept and extend beyond the river. Its forestry activities provide an expanding source of raw materials for the paper, timber, housing, and furniture industries. Fertilizer production has made adjacent farmlands much more prosperous. The growth of industry and river commerce has been paralleled by the expansion of other forms of transportation. By fostering industrial growth, TVA's activities have led to the growth of an interdependent truck, rail, and barge transportation system in the region.

Since the 1930s, the partnership between TVA and the people has enhanced the quality of life in the Tennessee Valley. The navigable waterway is a tool for development, and TVA cooperates with state and local agencies and private organizations to promote orderly economic growth. Through their public and private organizations, the people stimulate investment in the valley's resources resulting in higher income levels and greater personal opportunities.

The TVA identifies land along the Tennessee River that has industrial potential. In some instances, waterfront land that is suitable for industry is also suitable for other public or private uses such as wildlife habitat

Tennessee Valley Authority

Tows pass through the lock at Wilson Dam, the oldest water control structure on the Tennessee River.

and recreational and residential development. The TVA cooperates with state and local planning agencies to determine jointly the future use of undeveloped waterfront property. The authority encourages communities on the waterway to reserve their waterfront for industries which require access to the barge channel or to the river for process water. It also assists in identifying lands as potential property for industries that do not require a waterfront location. Preliminary development plans for alternate potential industrial sites are prepared as joint efforts involving local leaders, economic development districts, state and regional industrial development agencies, and TVA. These preliminary plans help local leaders to evaluate development benefits and costs and to reach decisions that vitally affect the future of local and regional economies.

Shortly after its creation, TVA identified the need to build a system of public river terminals to increase use of the waterway and bring the advantages of water transportation to the region. Citizens of the valley, including representatives from the nine principal port cities on the Tennessee, formed the Tennessee Valley Waterways Conference whose

objectives were to secure optimum use of the waterway by developing adequate river terminals and water transportation services. The net, long-term result of these cooperative efforts is that public terminals are available along the entire waterway. In Mississippi, the Yellow Creek Port Authority and TVA are completing a joint project to create a transportation complex for trucks, barges, and railroads that will serve a 2,000-acre manufacturing area. The Yellow Creek Port project is located in northeast Mississippi at the juncture of the Tennessee River and the Tennessee-Tombigbee River waterway, which is under construction. The TVA assists state and local agencies by evaluating proposed terminal sites and by examining economic and engineering features of planned facilities. The federal agency also furnishes information on functions and operations of terminal facilities, identifies potential terminal users, and estimates shipping costs. In addition to its many other functions, TVA also participates in proceedings before the Interstate Commerce Commission in an effort to coordinate transportation rates and services between land and water carriers and to remove barriers to optimum use of the Tennessee River system.

More than fifty companies operate barges on the Tennessee River waterway. In 1973, 29 million tons of commercial freight moved on the river, setting a new tonnage record for the twelfth consecutive year. Along the shoreline, private industry announced in the same year investments of $329 million for new or expanded waterfront plants and terminals. The 41,000 workers employed by industries situated along the river are evidence of TVA's impact on the economy of the Tennessee River Valley.

The Panama Canal

The Panama Canal is a 51-mile-long, lock-assisted ship canal across the Isthmus of Panama that connects the Atlantic and Pacific oceans. The waterway was built and is operated by the United States under a treaty with the Republic of Panama, and it lies within the Canal Zone, a strip of land under American control that bisects the country. Control of the facility is exercised by the

Panama Canal Company, a self-sustaining government corporation that operates at no cost to the American taxpayer. The President of the United States has traditionally designated the secretary of the army to act on his behalf in Canal Zone and canal company matters. The Chief Executive also appoints a governor for the zone, who, after Senate confirmation, becomes president of the Panama Canal Company. The secretary of the army appoints the company's board of directors.

The French began the first attempt at building a water route across the isthmus in 1881, under the direction of Ferdinand Marie de Lesseps, the builder of the Suez Canal. After nearly two decades of frustration caused by engineering problems, tropical diseases, and labor shortages, the French company offered to sell their canal rights to the United States. In 1902 Congress approved the Spooner Act, which authorized the President to purchase the French property and canal rights for $40 million if Columbia ceded to the United States a 5-mile-wide strip of land across the isthmus. An agreement with Columbia was reached in 1903, but it was later rejected by the Columbian legislature. In November 1903, a revolt in Panama, encouraged by the United States, resulted in the creation of an independent Panamanian nation. Two weeks later, a treaty was signed with the new nation which enabled the United States to build the waterway. Under the agreement, America was given control over a zone extending 5 miles on either side of the canal. For surrendering its sovereignty over this territory, Panama received an initial sum of $10 million and annual payments of $250,000 which began in 1913. These annuities have since been increased to nearly $2 million.

The French rights and properties were officially transferred to the United States in May 1904, but work was delayed because of organizational problems. The first seven-member Isthmusian Canal Commission appointed John F. Wallace chief engineer, but bickering among commission members hindered his effectiveness. Wallace resigned soon after the creation of an executive committee, composed of the commission chairman, chief engineer, and governor of the canal zone. He was replaced by John Stevens, who was given complete charge of the project.

Stevens immediately recognized that the construction effort was hindered by poor organization and a lack of support facilities. Under his direction, the transisthmanian railroad was renovated, and construction camps were erected. Roads, docks, storehouses, water supply and sewage systems, and other public works were built. Stevens also recruited a skilled and unskilled labor force and arranged for an adequate food supply. Despite these efforts, Stevens received harsh criticism because comparatively little excavation was undertaken during the project's first two years. The controversy also raged over the canal's design. European consultants recommended a sea level canal, but Stevens and his team of engineers were convinced that a lock system was the best approach. Stevens returned to the United States to fight for his plan, and in June 1906 the Senate approved his design. Criticism of the project continued, however, and in 1907 Stevens resigned. President Theodore Roosevelt decided to fill the position with "someone who can't quit." He turned the project over to the Army Corps of Engineers and requested the canal commission to appoint Colonel George W. Goethals as chief engineer and commission chairman. Under the officer's direction, construction moved forward at a rapid pace.

The project's magnitude was without precedent. An earth dam was built on the Charges River to create a navigable lake. On the Atlantic side of the dam, a harbor was created and a channel dredged to the dam site. A set of 1,000-foot-long locks in the dam raised and lowered ships 85 feet to the level of the lake. At the other end of the lake, a cut 8 miles long was made through the mountains, where additional pairs of locks lowered ships to a channel on the Pacific side. The undertaking included building the largest earth dam and locks at that time in the world. It was also the largest excavation project in history.

The Americans benefited from the excavation done by the French which amounted to 78 million cubic yards, but only 40 percent

Nearly 14,000 oceangoing vessels use the Panama Canal annually.

of this cut could be used for the new canal. The task was further complicated by soft soil formations, particularly in the Culebra (later Gaillard) Cut area where serious landslides frequently slowed construction. Excavation on the canal exceeded 200 million cubic yards of earth and rock. The cost in human lives was an impressive testimonial to the perils of the project. During the ten-year construction period, more than 6,000 people lost their lives. The prevalence of disease, especially yellow fever and malaria, beleaguered the project during the first few years. However, the efforts of Chief Sanitary Officer Colonel William C. Gorgas against disease-carrying mosquitoes virtually eradicated yellow fever and significantly reduced the number of lives taken by malaria. Between 1906 and 1914, deaths from disease fell from 37 to 7 per thousand.

On August 15, 1914, the waterway opened and it subsequently altered world trade patterns. It reduced ocean voyages between the Atlantic and Pacific by 7,000 miles and saved shippers the several weeks sailing time required to round Cape Horn. Tolls based on net tons have not been raised since 1914. They average about $7,000 per oceangoing vessel and constitute one tenth of the cost of rounding South America. Since its opening, the canal has undergone many improvements. Dams have been built on feeder streams to control water levels; the Gaillard Cut has been widened; and the locks' efficiency has been increased. The Panama Canal is one of the most important waterways in the world. In fiscal year 1975, this public works facility was used by 13,779 oceangoing vessels.

Waterway Traffic

The Indian canoe was the first conveyance used on the North American rivers. Then came the flatboats and broadhorns, crudely box-like, flat-bottomed rafts that floated downstream to ports of call such as New Orleans. Often cheaply and poorly constructed of green timber, they were one-way craft, which were dismantled and sold for lumber after their cargoes were delivered. In his *Life on the Mississippi*, Mark Twain recalled these vessels: "I remember the annual processions of mighty rafts that used to glide by Hannibal . . . an acre or so of white, sweet-smelling boards in each raft, a crew of two dozen men or more, three or four wigwams scattered about the rafts, vast level space for storm-quarters."

The keelboat replaced the flatboat in the early nineteenth century. For two-way use, it was sturdily built with long, graceful lines and was constructed to survive many trips. It needed only skillful guidance for downstream hauls with as much as eighty tons of freight aboard. To "cordelle" it back upstream, a crew of hardy men walked the river bank tugging on ropes to pull it against the current. Sometimes they stood aboard and pushed it upstream by using iron-tipped poles that reached to the river bottom. One observer reported that 500 keelboats operated on the Ohio River in 1819. The number on the Mississippi was much greater.

The keelboat yielded to the wood-burning steamboat later in the century. The first American steamboat was launched in 1787 by James Rumsey of Maryland. It was propelled

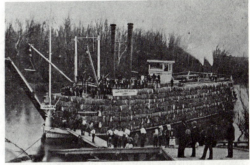

Packet boats carried freight and passengers on inland waterways during the nineteenth century.

by a stream of water forced out the stern by steam pressure and was able to attain a speed of about four miles per hour. Robert Fulton, who is often credited with being the inventor of the steamboat, was preceded by several others, including John Fitch, Samuel Morey, Nathan Read, and John Stevens in America, and by William Symington in Scotland. On the inland waterways, after the dramatic 1807 debut of Fulton's *Clermont* between New York and Albany, the most significant trip was that of another side-wheeler, the *New Orleans*. Owned by Nicholas Roosevelt, it opened service between Pittsburgh and New Orleans in 1811. In 1814 twenty-one steamboats arrived in New Orleans and by 1819 there were 191. By 1836 river steamboats were arriving at New Orleans at a rate of 1,000 per year. In 1852 the docks at Cincinnati reported 8,000 paddle-wheeler calls, about one every hour.

The steamboat first proved itself hauling freight upstream. Later it carried passengers in comfort and sometimes splendor. The stern-wheeled packet boat, so-called because it originally carried mail packets, began to travel regular routes, transporting passengers, freight, and mail. The packet boat increased river traffic greatly. In 1834 there were 230 packets; by 1849 there were about a thousand, with an aggregate cargo of about 250,000 tons. At the height of the packet boats just before the Civil War, the river fleet was reportedly carrying more tonnage than all the vessels of the British Empire.

The river fleet was devastated by the War between the States and only partially rebuilt after the end of hostilities because of railroad competition, which nearly finished river commerce by the end of the nineteenth century. Railroad companies expedited the demise of water transportation by buying up river and lake lines in order to destroy this competing industry. Vessels rotted at their moorings, and the docks and terminals rotted with them. These tactics were recognized in the 1912 Panama Canal Act which conferred upon the Interstate Commerce Commission power to divorce railroads from water carrier ownership. Railroads had so outstripped other forms of transportation in the late nineteenth century

that when the United States entered World War I, inland waterway traffic was comparatively minute.

Demands created by the war congested the railroads so alarmingly that Congress, on June 15, 1917, commissioned a study of the feasibility of utilizing the nation's navigable waterways to relieve the pressure. Pursuant to the report, the United States Shipping Board, upon the recommendation of the President, allotted $3.9 million from the funds of the Emergency Fleet Corporation for building barges and towboats to be used on the Mississippi River from St. Louis to St. Paul. By late 1917, some of the commissioned vessels were in use. This constituted the first direct government operation of water transportation facilities. Under the direction of the Railroad Administration, a wartime agency, the director general of this federal waterways venture commandeered all privately owned floating equipment on the New York State Barge Canal (formerly the Erie Canal) and the Mississippi and Warrior rivers; and it spent $12 million for more extensive operation on these three water routes. Losses of $1.3 million were suffered in the barge operations, however, the primary aim of the Railroad Administration was to help win the war rather than to have a profitable operation.

The 1920 Transportation Act reflected the prevailing sentiment that the experiment in waterway transportation should be continued by the federal government. Placed under the direction of the secretary of war, the barge service became known as the Inland and Coastwise Waterways Service. An unprecedented drop in the water level of the Mississippi River in 1922 brought staggering traffic dislocations. For the period of March 1920 to June 1924, losses soared to $8.3 million. The service depended upon yearly funding from Congress. The chief of the service argued that this year-to-year funding inhibited effective planning and improvement. He pointed out that a revolving fund, possible under corporate status, would encourage long-range planning and allow profits from plentiful years of operation to see the barge business through lean times.

The Congress was at first unwilling to

consider incorporation. By 1924, $175 million had been spent for improvements on the Mississippi River. Secretary of War Willard Weeks stated that those huge public expenditures could not be justified "unless we can use these waterways for transportation purposes." Proponents of incorporation insisted that it would free the service from its handicaps to the extent that it would show a profit and make itself desirable for purchase by private enterprise. Congress approved, and by an act of June 3, 1924, created the Inland Waterways Corporation (IWC) "for the purpose of carrying on the operations of the government-owned inland, canal, and coastwise waterways system to the point where the system can be transferred to private operation." The secretary of war was designated governor of the corporation and in 1939 this role was shifted to the secretary of commerce. He was empowered to appoint a six-member advisory board in place of the board of directors commonly found in a private corporation. The advisory board had little power; almost the entire responsibility for management was vested in a chairman-president.

The 1924 act further provided for a capital stock of $5 million which was subscribed by the United States. The corporation was prohibited from discontinuing operations on any existing routes, and new lines were to be opened only by authorization of Congress. From 1924 to 1938, IWC showed an overall profit of $3.3 million although a slight loss was registered for several of these years. The enabling act was amended in 1928 to permit extension of IWC operations to all improved tributaries of the Mississippi River. Barge traffic on the Illinois River was opened in 1931, and by June 1933 operations were extended to Chicago. The line supported the Army Corps of Engineers' plans for channelization projects on major rivers and with this improvement came a tremendous increase in private river transportation.

The 1940 Transportation Act provided for closer federal regulation of inland water transportation through the Interstate Commerce Commission. It required the commission to fix minimum rates of common and contract carrier water lines, to restrict operations to definite routes, and to otherwise exercise control through the issuance or withholding of permits. Advocates of inland water transportation saw this act as generally friendly. It indicated that this reawakened industry had matured, and it seemingly showed that Congress intended to continue the river improvement program.

The outbreak of war in Europe in 1939 disrupted export trade, particularly the shipment of grain from New Orleans. Corporation officials saw this as the beginning of steady financial losses which were incurred every year thereafter except for a slight profit in 1951. During World War II, IWC shipped huge amounts of freight. However, it was reimbursed only for direct expenses and at the war's end was left with obsolete equipment in poor condition. Reconversion woes were aggravated by shortages of materials and labor problems. While wage rates nearly doubled between 1938 and 1945, freight rates were not raised to compensate for the increased labor costs.

Until the post-World War II period, the principal opponent of the government-owned barge line was the railroads. Their spokesmen had earlier argued that when the World War I transportation crisis was over, it was no longer necessary for the government to be concerned with an auxiliary mode of transportation. In the 1930s, railroad proponents charged that the government was subsidizing water transportation in the Mississippi Valley as a competitive means of driving down railroad rates. In the post-World War II period, when IWC losses were heavy, private water transportation interests were numerous and vocal enough to add real force to railroad protests. Profitable operations by the corporation appeared hopeless under these conditions.

When the corporation was formed in 1924, Congress had expressed its intent that the government operation of the barge line continue until four main objectives were met. These were: (1) until navigable channels were completed in the rivers where IWC operated; (2) until adequate terminals were provided; (3) until joint rates with railroads were published, making joint rail-barge transportation generally available; and (4) until private capital engaged, or showed a willingness to engage, in common carrier service on the waterways. Secretary of Commerce Sinclair Weeks, son of the original governor of the corporation, expressed belief that these four goals had been met. Accordingly, on February 8, 1953, he invited purchasing bids for IWC. The corporation was subsequently sold to a private company for $9 million.

The IWC was a unique public works undertaking that contributed to the revitalization of a private transportation industry. By 1953 more than a dozen barge lines were operating on the rivers and canals of the Mississippi River system. In addition, a healthy commercial interchange had developed between the waterborne carriers and the railroads.

Today, the diesel-powered towboat has replaced the paddle-wheeled steamboat as the queen of river transportation. The name towboat is actually a misnomer because towboats usually push, not pull, their strings of barges. They have none of the grace or beauty of the stern-wheelers Mark Twain wrote about, but rather they have an austere appearance which harmonizes with the simple lines of their barges. Towboats are low in the water. At the bow are towing knees—pusher plates against which the barges are lashed. With the barges lashed together and fastened to the towing knees, the unit operates as a single vessel, often composed of forty barges extending more than 1,000 feet. Towboats ply the protected inland rivers and canals, but for open-water towing, such as along the coasts and in the Great Lakes, tugboats are employed.

Virtually any commodity can be shipped by water. The inland waterways industry has developed a variety of barge types and sizes for the efficient handling of various products. The most versatile, least costly, and most numerous is the hopper barge. It is basically a simple open-top box that carries coal and other heavy bulk commodities. The dry cargo barge is another common design. Equipped with watertight covers over the cargo hold, these carriers transport commodities such as grain, cement, iron and steel products, and packaged goods. For shipment of petroleum products and industrial chemicals, various types of tank barges are currently afloat which can accommodate pressurized liquids. Others haul cargoes which require extremely high or low temperature. Liquefied sulphur is moved at 280 degrees Fahrenheit, and barge-mounted tanks transport liquid hydrogen at minus 423 degrees Fahrenheit.

One of the most spectacular developments of recent years has been ocean barging, by which tows ranging up to 35,000 tons carry oil and dry bulk cargo along the Atlantic and Gulf coasts into the Caribbean and along the Pacific Coast to Alaska. Shipping interests have recently developed new types of vessels to speed international traffic by reducing or avoiding reloading at ocean terminals. They combine barges and oceangoing vessels into a new transportation system. Ships take aboard loaded river barges and transport them on the high seas. Vessels are also in use which carry truck vans and railway cars, thus providing waterborne linkage with other common carriers. The miniship, an oceangoing vessel with a draft of just 9 feet, is able to carry a thousand tons of general cargo. It can land foreign cargoes at inland ports, completely bypassing busy ocean terminals.

There has been a tremendous growth in waterborne shipping since World War II. In 1947 barges carried 262 million tons of cargo (exclusive of the Great Lakes); by 1973 the figure had climbed to almost 600 million tons. In 1975 about 2,000 companies were engaged in commercial inland shipping. They operated over 4,000 towboats and tugs which pulled and pushed a fleet of 21,000 barges with a total capacity of 27 million tons.

The growth and expansion of inland waterways transportation has resulted in the construction of modern terminals for handling barge freight and for exchange between water carriers and other transportation modes. The terminals represent substantial investments by private interests as well as public agencies especially created for this purpose. A great deal of waterfront land has been developed in these port cities, both for terminals and industrial production, thus increasing property values and creating new sources of municipal tax revenue. Waterway transportation re-

American Waterways Operators

Present waterways of the United States.

quires a variety of port services such as warehousing, boat supplies, dry dock and boat repairing, bunkering, marine insurance, banking, and harbor towing. All of these services add to the business development of the cities in which they are located.

The major portion of these facilities are privately owned, but the growth of barge transportation has also spurred interest in public terminals. States, counties, municipalities, and port districts are recognizing the economic benefits which result from publicly owned modern terminal facilities. Both private and public terminals generally provide docks, wharves, loading and unloading equipment, warehouses, tank farms, and open storage for the various commodities that move by barge. Along inland waterways, docks are built at proper elevations to insure that the rise and fall of the river will not affect operations. In some cases, privately operated terminals are designed and managed to meet the special needs of a single shipper or receiver. Modern terminals are highly mechanized installations which permit fast loading and delivery, eliminate unnecessary delays, and speed turnaround time. The variety of equipment available for handling barge cargoes is extensive. It includes various sizes of cranes, fork trucks, conveyors, pallets, power mules, and clam shells and hoppers for bulk commodities. Most ports along inland waterways also have railroad and highway connections which permit direct freight interchange between barges, trucks, and railcars.

Harbors and Ports

The excellent harbors and port facilities which exist at many American coastal cities have been developed because of the commitment of the private and public sectors to meet the requirements of expanding maritime commerce. In their natural state, there were few bays and tidal estuaries along the Atlantic,

Gulf, and Pacific coasts with depths of more than 20 feet. In some cases, harbor entrances were blocked by sand bars and shallow water. Some natural harbors were traversable by sailing vessels, but they have been improved in the past 150 years to meet the needs of larger sailing vessels and the greater drafts required by steam-powered ships.

While some early harbor improvements were undertaken by private initiative and local governments, because of the large costs and the engineering expertise such projects required, harbor development has largely been the responsibility of the Army Corps of Engineers. The first federally funded harbor improvements were carried out on the Great Lakes. In 1824 and 1825, the corps began work on Lake Erie at present-day Erie, Pennsylvania, and Cleveland and Fairport, Ohio. These projects included construction of breakwaters, jetties, piers, and the deepening of channels. In the following century and a half, nearly 300 harbors have been improved by the federal government. In addition to work at commercial ports, the program included development of fishing harbors and harbors of refuge for small commercial and recreational craft.

The following are but a few of the Army Corps of Engineers' achievements in port development. By 1852 the excellent natural harbor at New York City could no longer safely accommodate the large steamships that were being constructed. In that year, the corps executed the first improvement of the harbor by removing the rocks at Hell Gate in the East River. Since that time, the country's largest port has undergone subsequent improvement and enlargement, until today its 45-foot main channel depth provides one of the most modern harbors in the world. Army Corps of Engineers' improvements at the Port of San Francisco date back to the early 1850s. The natural harbor provided a broad and deep entrance, but it was hazardous because of submerged rocks. Blossom Rock, the most dangerous, sat in the main ship channel east of Alcatraz Island and was only 5 feet beneath the surface at low tide. It was dramatically removed in 1870 by one of the first efforts at submarine blasting. Today, the Port of San Francisco has the deepest improved harbor channel in the United States. The corps maintains a navigation channel 50 feet deep and 2,000 feet wide in the bay.

Twentieth-century changes in ocean transportation technology have had profound effects on American port development. Sailing vessels carried about 20 percent of the world's cargo in 1900, but by World War I most remaining sailing ships were replaced by coal-burning steamships. The latter, however, was gradually replaced by more efficient oil-burning ships. In 1914 oil-powered vessels carried only 3.4 percent of the world's merchant tonnage, but their share increased to 55 percent in 1939 and an overwhelming 96 percent by 1961. The change in power plants had broad implications for port development since most American ports did not have equally good access to coal and oil. For example, the Port of Los Angeles, which was handicapped for decades by a lack of coal, became a magnet for oil-burning vessels after the discovery of oil in California.

The increase in the sizes of oceangoing vessels has also wrought significant changes at American ports. For example, in 1939

American Association of Port Authorities

Modern facilities are provided at the Port of Los Angeles for containerized freight.

tankers had a capacity of 10,000 to 16,000 tons. By the 1970s, most tankers exceeded 60,000 tons, and a new generation of super-tankers, ranging between 150,000 and 300,000 tons, had been introduced to commercial shipping. Since relatively few deep natural harbors existed in the United States, the expanding size of cargo vessels required improvements in approach channels, docks, wharves, and terminal facilities. At the turn of the century, 30-foot-deep channels would accommodate virtually all ships. In subsequent decades, minimum harbor depths were increased to 35, 40, and 45 feet; and even the latter depth was inadequate for fully loaded supertankers. The cost of breakwaters, channel improvements, and related navigation features have usually been borne by the federal government under rivers and harbors legislation; but docks, wharves, and terminal facilities have been financed by individual ports. Investments in improvements to keep pace with the changing demand of shipping vary widely from port to port, but in general the federal government and state and local interests have been willing to spend large sums to improve harbors and dockside facilities. From 1966 to 1972, expenditures for improvements at American ports totaled $1 billion, and outlays of $1.4 billion have been projected for 1973-1977. The United States' 2,121 deep-draft port terminals handled 1.7 billion tons of cargo in 1974 which was valued at $38.5 billion.

The large expenditures have also occurred because of significant changes in the handling and carriage of cargoes. Multipurpose ships are being replaced by automated cargo vessels designed to carry a single commodity or narrow range of commodities in bulk. For example, specialized vessels have been designed to carry bananas, molasses, automobiles, liquefied natural gas, and even wine. In the 1960s, intercoastal traffic, which had been depressed by railroad competition, experienced a revival as a result of containerization. Containers are simply large steel cargo boxes which are designed to carry their contents from shipper to consignee. Standardized dimensions permit them to be loaded, stowed, unloaded, and easily transferred from one mode of transportation to another. The costs of building new container ships and specialized terminal facilities have been offset by reductions in cargo pilferage, reduced damage and handling costs, and lower unit costs resulting from larger ships, rapid turnaround time, and faster cruising speeds. By the early 1970s, virtually all American ports were handling containerized cargoes.

To manage this growing industry, a wide variety of port administrative arrangements have evolved in the United States. The public character of port functions was recognized before 1900; but except for the federal government's jurisdiction over navigable waters, the government's role was minimal at most ports until the twentieth century. Comprehensive public control over the Port of San Francisco was established by the State of California in 1863. However, in most coastal cities ownership of port facilities and effective control of operations remained in private hands, usually the railroads.

Railroad abuses of ports, particularly attempts to destroy intercoastal and coastwise traffic together with anti-corporate sentiment during the Progressive era, caused business, agricultural, and labor groups to demand that ports be placed under public control. Some groups sought merely to regulate port activities, leaving ownership and operation in the private domain. Other reformers argued that the public character of port facilities and the superior financial resources of government for future development made public ownership the appropriate solution.

Therefore, various administrative and ownership arrangements emerged during the first quarter of the twentieth century. Some port agencies were organized as a unit of municipal government; for example, the Board of Harbor Commissioners of Milwaukee and the Bureau of Port Operations in Philadelphia. Other agencies, such as the Port of Seattle and the Harris County-Houston Ship Channel Navigation District, were founded as public corporations with the authority to levy district-wide taxes. Many other port agencies were given substantial independence as a port authority or corporation but lacked the power to levy taxes. The latter version included units with bi-state jurisdictions, such as the Port Authority of New York and New Jersey; statewide jurisdictions, such as the Virginia State Ports Authority; and local agencies, such as the Board of Commissioners of the Port of New Orleans. Ports are, therefore, an integral part of the waterway system that facilitates commerce in the United States and with foreign countries. The interconnected network of improved rivers, canals, and shore facilities developed in the past two centuries comprises a significant aspect of America's public works.

SUGGESTED READINGS

American Association of Port Authorities. *Ports of the Americas: History and Development.* Washington, D.C., 1961.

American Waterways Operators. *Big Load Afloat.* Washington, D.C., 1965.

Barsness, Richard W. "Maritime Activity and Port Development in the United States Since 1900: A Survey." *Journal of Transport History,* 2 (February 1974), 167-184.

Chorpening, C. H. "Waterway Growth in the United States." American Society of Civil Engineers *Transactions,* CT (1953), 947-1041.

Clark, William H. *Railroads and Rivers: The Story of Inland Transportation.* Boston, 1939.

Corthell, E. L. *History of the Jetties.* New York, 1881.

Drago, Harry S. *Canal Days in America: The History and Romance of Old Towpaths and Waterways.* New York, 1972.

Goodrich, Carter, ed. *Canals and American Economic Development.* Port Washington, New York, 1960.

——————— . *Government Promotion of American Canals and Railroads, 1800-1890.* New York, 1960.

Hill, Forest G. *Roads, Rails and Waterways: The Army Engineers and Early Transportation.* Norman, Oklahoma, 1957.

Lippincott, Isaac. "A History of River Improvement." *Journal of Political Economy,* 22 (1914), 630-660.

Payne, Pierre. *The Canal Builders: The Story of Canal Engineers Through the Ages.* New York, 1972.

Poor, Henry V. *History of the Railroads and the Canals of the United States of America.* New York, 1970. Reprint of 1860 edition.

Quick, Herbert. *American Inland Waterways.* New York, 1909.

Rubin, Julius. *Canal or Railroad? Imitation and Innovation in the Response to the Erie Canal in Philadelphia, Baltimore, and Boston.* Philadelphia, 1961.

Sanderlin, Walter S. *The Great National Project: A History of the Chesapeake and Ohio Canal.* Baltimore, 1946.

Taylor, George Rogers. *The Transportation Revolution, 1815-1860.* The Economic History of the United States. Vol. 4. New York, 1951.

U. S. Panama Canal Company. *The Panama Canal, Fiftieth Anniversary: The Story of a Great Conquest.* Washington, D.C., 1964.

Waggoner, Madeline S. *The Long Haul West: The Great Canal Era, 1817-1850.* New York, 1958.

Wayman, Norbury L. *Life on the River.* New York, 1971.

CHAPTER 3

ROADS, STREETS, AND HIGHWAYS

A major factor in creating the good life of 1976 America has been the individual mobility made possible by motor vehicles operating on the 3.8 million miles of roads, streets, and highways that tie the nation together. In 1975, 135 million automobiles, trucks, and buses traveled about 1,310 billion vehicle miles, providing unprecedented freedom and convenience for the average American. The whole economy is directly dependent upon this mobility which makes the entire nation one gigantic assembly line for production and moving of goods to consumers and consumers to goods. Socially, it makes the country one big neighborhood.

In 1976 an average of 2.2 automobiles, trucks, and buses—public, commercial, and personal vehicles—meet the highway travel needs of each family. The vehicles travel an average of 10,000 miles each. They provide access to work, the grocery store, church, the doctor's office, school, and to recreational areas both near and far. This broadens each individual's opportunity for employment, widens his choice of residence, and expands his social horizons. The saying "If you've got it, a truck brought it" is actually true, as trucks handle virtually all products at various stages between raw materials, manufacturing,

and points of consumption.

When automobiles were first introduced in 1892, the nation essentially had an agricultural economy and was just beginning to become an industrial country. Distances were great, most cities were small, and the suburbs spread out. The character of 1976 America is largely the result of the automobile. Highway transportation provides one out of every six jobs in the nation and creates an industry—including manufacturing materials, building and maintaining vehicles, providing fuels, and constructing and maintaining the roads—of over $200 billion per year, 17 percent of the gross national product.

Until the twentieth century, travel for the average person was a luxury; now it is a necessity and a major part of life. This has created problems, but it has evolved from the freedom of choice that is basic to America. It has been made possible by the system of roads, streets, and highways, built by government public works organizations utilizing the nation's construction contractors and their workmen coupled with the automotive industry. The highway transportation dollar is divided into twelve cents for the roads and eighty-eight cents for the vehicle. In recent years, the construction and maintenance of roads has been financed primarily by highway user taxes on a pay-as-you-go basis.

The relationship of vehicles to population, since the beginning of the automobile age, is

This chapter was prepared mainly from reports and information from the United States Department of Transportation.

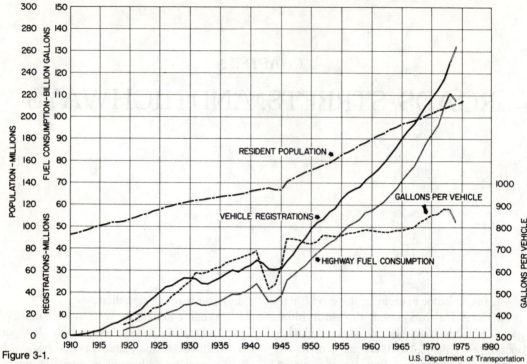

Figure 3-1.   U.S. Department of Transportation

Population, motor-vehicle registrations, and motor-fuel consumption in the United States.

shown in Figure 3-1. In 1968 there was a vehicle for every two persons; in 1976 the ratio is a vehicle for each 1.6 persons. The gross national product index is directly related to vehicle miles of travel. The figure also shows the increasing amount of gasoline consumed, which is one of the major problems of 1976.

At the birth of the nation, only a few hundred miles of relatively primitive roads provided a weak bond among colonies. As late as 1900, although there was a total of about 2.4 million miles of roads, only a few hundred miles had hard-surface paving, and most of those were within cities. In the bicentennial year, the nation has 1.8 million miles of bituminous and portland cement concrete surfaced roads, 1.3 million miles of gravel and stone surfaced roads, and about 900,000 miles of non-surfaced roads as shown in Figure 3-2.

Of the total, 630,000 miles of highways and streets in urban areas carried about 50 percent of the total traffic. The through routes were generally part of the state highway systems, administered by the states; but over 90 percent of the urban mileage was administered by local and municipal public works departments. State rural highway

systems totaled about 800,000 miles. Federal aid applied to 950,000 miles of road which carry about three fourths of all vehicle travel. The mileage under the various government administration jurisdictions are shown in Figure 3-3.

The disbursements for highways by the various governmental units are shown in Figure 3-4, the total of which has grown from about $1 billion in 1920 to $25.9 billion in 1973. Figure 3-5 illustrates the 1973 source and disbursements of the funds. Federal high-

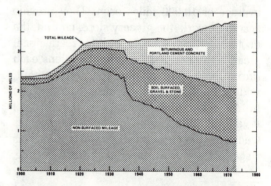

Figure 3-2.   U.S. Department of Transportation

Total road and street mileage in United States by surface types.

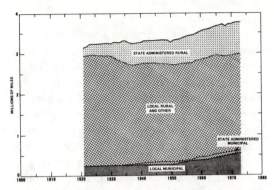

Figure 3-3.   U.S. Department of Transportation
Total road and street mileage in United States by administrative jurisdiction.

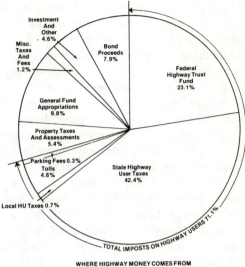

WHERE HIGHWAY MONEY COMES FROM

way trust funds are apportioned to the states as federal aid and are available only for construction. The amount of federal support has increased from 10 percent of the full program in 1956 to 23 percent in 1973. Over 50 percent of the expenditures by local municipal governments was for maintenance.

The growth of the road mileage, as it developed into street systems in the cities and as state and nationwide highway systems, underscores the country's political operations. It demonstrates the complex interplay of competing interests as well as dedicated, objective efforts to provide for the overall good at all levels—local, state, and national. It is an activity that, with the advent of the automobile in appreciable numbers, brought about revolutionary social and economic changes in little more than fifty years. And more changes are ahead as adjustments are made to enhance man's environment and as the problems of energy supply and utilization respond to changing attitudes, new sources, and advancing technology.

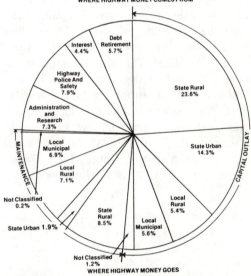

WHERE HIGHWAY MONEY GOES

Figure 3-5.   U.S. Department of Transportation
Highway funds — receipts and disbursements for 1973.

Early Development

The young nation that emerged from the War of Independence had a weak government and a primitive transportation system. The rivers and the sheltered coastal waters, such as Long Island and Albemarle sounds and Chesapeake Bay, provided the principal arteries for travel and commerce. Extending from these arteries were roads in various stages of development. A very few, near and within the largest cities, were "artificial roads," ditched and sometimes surfaced with gravel or with "pounded stones." The rest were improved only to the extent of having

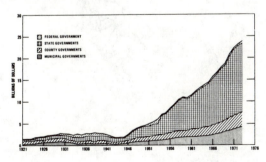

Figure 3-4.   U.S. Department of Transportation
Total disbursements for highways by governmental units.

stumps and boulders removed and the worst irregularities leveled. Many were impassable for wheeled vehicles in winter or during spring thaw. Travelers crossed small streams by fording and the large ones by ferrying. Bridges were few, small, and unreliable.

In the larger cities, the principal streets were graded and surfaced, generally with gravel but some with compacted broken stone. The remainder were primarily access ways with little improvement. On the fringes of settlement, however, the "roads" were really only horsepaths, unsuitable for wheeled vehicles. Although General Edward Braddock's 115-mile military road, constructed in 1755 from Fort Cumberland to the present location of Pittsburgh, was chopped out to a width of 12 feet—wide enough to pass his train of 150 Conestoga wagons in single file—within three years, it had reverted to merely a trace through the forest. The other principal transmountain road through Pennsylvania was widened in 1758, during the French and Indian War, to enable General John Forbes' wagon trains to pass but was otherwise unimproved. Even the Wilderness Road through Cumberland Gap, which Daniel Boone blazed in 1775, was nothing more than a pack trail.

Despite the primitive condition of the roads, colonial authorities established a land postal service between the principal cities of the eastern seaboard. For the most part, the mail was carried on foot or by post riders on horseback who averaged about four miles per hour, with no night travel. In 1729 a letter sent from Boston, Massachusetts, to Williamsburg, Virginia, required four weeks for delivery.

As early as 1750, a regular stage-wagon, a covered springless vehicle fitted with hard wooden passenger benches, provided service from Philadelphia to New York. Just before the Revolution, passengers could travel by stage from Philadelphia to the Paulus Hook (now Jersey City) ferry in two days in good weather, and public passenger stages were available for the journey from New York to Boston.

Under colonial laws, which were patterned after those of England, roadmaking and upkeep were responsibilities of the local governments—the towns in New England and the counties in other colonies. In New England, the elected town officers, among them a surveyor of highways, were charged with the upkeep of highways, private ways, causeys,

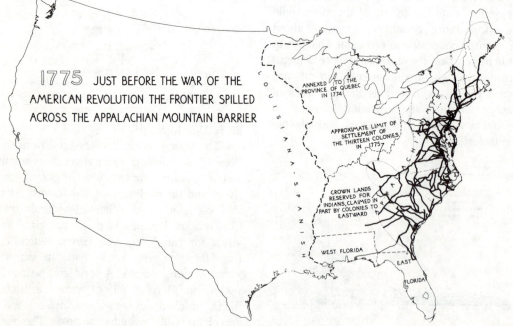

U.S. Department of Transportation

Roads in the United States at the beginning of the Revolution.

and bridges. They were authorized to remove obstructions from the highways; to dig for stone, gravel, clay, or marl in any land not planted or enclosed; and to command the labor, on appointed days after public notice, of all persons over sixteen years of age for work on the roads.

In Virginia, the county court, which was composed of eight or more "gentlemen" inhabitants elected by the freeholders and approved by the governor, was responsible for the condition of the roads and bridges. The court could contract for necessary road work or direct that it be performed gratis by the "tithable males" under the supervision of the precinct surveyor or foreman. Tithable males were local residents over sixteen years of age, whether free, slave, or indentured. Owners of two or more tithables could send them as substitutes in lieu of working in person.

The other colonies used similar procedures for repairing their roads. All of them authorized the local authorities to require compulsory road service or its equivalent in cash. For many years, this "statute labor" was the principal resource available to local governments for road work in the colonies and later in the states. But other resources, such as private subscriptions, donations by public spirited citizens, assessments on adjacent property, or the proceeds of public lotteries, were occasionally available.

By the close of the Revolutionary War and the birth of the new nation, road traffic had substantially increased, especially near the larger cities. The feeble efforts of the local authorities were ineffective in keeping the roads in repair, and there was widespread agitation for state assistance to help maintain the principal roads. The debt-burdened state governments met this challenge by chartering private turnpike companies, conferring on them authority to build roads and to charge user tolls. The first of these companies, chartered by Virginia in 1785, built a turnpike road from Alexandria, on the Potomac River, westward to the mountains near Berryville. However, the turnpike between Philadelphia and Lancaster, Pennsylvania, was the first to be completed for any considerable distance and one of the most financially successful.

Pennsylvania began what appears to be the nation's earliest statewide transportation plan. In February 1791, the Society for Promoting the Improvement of Roads and Inland Navigation submitted a plan to the Pennsylvania legislature. It proposed the appointment of a board of commissioners with power to decide the locations of the principal roads in the state and to determine which should be improved by turnpike companies and which ought to be built or repaired at public cost. The board would then have the authority to advertise and award contracts for building and operating the turnpikes and to employ persons to repair those roads deemed unsuitable for turnpikes.

In April 1791, the legislature appropriated 36,160 Pennsylvania pounds (equivalent to about $100,000) to be expended under the direction of the governor and council for sixty-eight road and navigation improvements in various areas of the state. A year later, legislative acts established the Philadelphia and Lancaster Turnpike Road Company. The Lancaster Pike that resulted became a prototype for the early turnpikes. Its charter required that it be laid out 50 feet wide between fences. At least 20 feet "shall be made an artificial road, which shall be bedded with wood, stone, gravel, or any other hard substance well compacted together, a sufficient depth to secure a solid foundation to the same; and the said road shall be faced with gravel, or stone pounded or other small hard substance, in such a manner as to secure a firm, and as near as the materials will admit, an even surface." The charter specifications limited the gradient to a maximum of 7 percent.

The turnpike company had no trouble selling its stock, and construction began in February 1793. In less than three years, the 62-mile road was completed—a remarkable engineering achievement for the period. Construction of the road cost $465,000 for an average of $7,500 per mile. This amount represented a great commitment of resources, for at that time the wage for farm and construction laborers was only sixty cents for a twelve-hour day.

The company collected tolls at thirteen points along the road. Rates varied from two and a half cents per vehicle-mile for stages and coaches drawn by two horses to five cents for four-horse freight wagons with 4-inch tires. Vehicles with wider tires could travel for lower rates, and a horse and rider could travel ten miles for six cents. During the first five years, the return on the invested capital was 2 percent or less; but as the western part of the state developed, the profits rose to as much as 15 percent in some years, the maximum permitted by the charter.

After 1800 most of the states adopted toll financing for main roads while retaining the old statute labor system for local improvements. By 1808 Connecticut had chartered fifty turnpike companies, which had completed 770 miles of roads. In New York, sixty-seven companies, capitalized at over $5 million, were chartered before 1807 to build 3,110 miles of turnpike roads costing $8 million.

At first the turnpike companies concentrated their efforts on the main roads between cities where traffic was heaviest. Since most of these cities were along the Atlantic Coast, the coastal highway (now U. S. Route 1) was the first to be improved over any considerable distance. By 1812 the entire distance of the New York-Philadelphia road was stone surfaced. This, and improvements to the coastal highway in other states, saved the country from a severe transportation crisis during the War of 1812 when the British blockaded coastal shipping.

The larger mid-Atlantic seaboard states had extensive areas of western lands which they were anxious to settle and develop. Also, the seaport cities were eager to trade beyond the Allegheny Mountain barrier. Four main transmountain roads were built to meet these needs: in Pennsylvania, the extension of the Lancaster Pike to Pittsburgh; in New York, a turnpike system from the Massachusetts boundary to Lake Erie; Maryland's turnpike connection with the Cumberland Road, which was then being built by the federal government with federal funds; and the Northwest Turnpike in Virginia, which was to extend from Winchester to "some point on the Ohio River to be situated by the principal engineer."

The Northwest Turnpike was a state-owned enterprise, with the governor as president of the board of directors. The principal engineer was Claudius Crozet, formerly professor of engineering at West Point and perhaps the ablest road engineer in America at that time. In 1838 this road was completed to Parkersburg on the Ohio River, a distance of nearly 250 miles, at a cost of $400,000.

The standards and costs of the many turnpikes varied widely. Some were graded and ditched but unsurfaced; most were surfaced with gravel or pounded stone. The latter was expensive because stone had to be quarried and broken by hand labor. Some roads after 1846 were surfaced with wooden planks laid on heavy sills. Average construction costs for turnpikes in this period ranged from $550 to as high as $14,000 per mile.

The turnpike movement eventually spread into all states, and by 1850 there were hundreds of companies operating thousands of miles of roads. They were basic to the nation's development, for along with the toll canals they opened new lands to settlement, reduced the cost of haulage from farms to markets, and stimulated the development of industries. Indeed, the construction of these privately financed public works was a major industry in the early 1800s.

Some states subsidized turnpike companies by giving tax exemptions and by purchasing shares in the ventures. With a few notable exceptions, the profits on toll road investments were modest at best. Most of the charters contained provisions for reducing tolls when profits reached a certain level, usually 12 to 15 percent per year. Generally, the toll roads and the toll canals served as complementary elements of an expanding transportation system.

The toll roads were built by contractors or by hired laborers supervised by trained road-builders. Usually the roads were well located and well built in order to meet the standards of their charters. Their construction was far better than that of the roads built by inefficient statute labor directed by amateur supervisors.

Paving of the early turnpikes conformed to the recommendations of J.P.M. Trésaguet, director general of France's roads from 1775 to 1785, with whose work many informed Americans, such as Benjamin Franklin, were well acquainted. Trésaguet's plans included adequate right-of-way and generous side ditches to carry away surface water which otherwise would saturate and soften the road. On a crowned and rolled subgrade, his road-builders placed a layer of heavy foundation stones, laid on edge, with the interstices packed solidly with smaller stones rammed into place by hammering. Above this course, they placed successive layers of broken stone, compacted and filled so that the stones interlocked with each other. The top 3 inches were of hard, specially selected stone, broken with hammers to walnut-size and placed on the road to form the surface course. The carriageways for these roads were 18 feet wide and about 10 inches thick. Most of the early American turnpikes were approximately this wide. Trésaguet's greatest contribution to highway administration was his insistence on prompt and incessant maintenance of the road by trained and adequately paid work-

men. His system of maintenance made France's roads the best in the world for two generations.

After about 1820, the ideas of the Scotsman, John L. McAdam, dominated American roadbuilding. McAdam, who was responsible for the good roads around Bristol, England, did not believe in massive foundation courses. He asserted that the native soil alone supported the road and the traffic; the road crust's only function was to protect the basement soil from wetting and abrasion. His macadam roads, named after him, were 6 to 10 inches thick and made of angular broken stones, all passing a 2-inch ring and packed by traffic until they interlocked into a dense mass. The first American road built according to McAdam's principals was the Boonsborough to Hagerstown Turnpike in Maryland, completed in 1822.

As might be expected, the administration of turnpikes varied widely from company to company, depending on the quality of the management, the amount of toll-paying traffic, and how well the roads were originally laid

The first American macadam road was the 10-mile turnpike between Hagerstown and Boonsborough, Maryland, built in 1823.

out and constructed. Many were underfinanced, and failures and reorganizations were frequent. Maintenance was often inadequate, especially for those roads which provided small returns to the investors. However, it was the arrival of rail transportation that dealt the death blow to the early turnpike era.

The advent of the steam engine and the full section steel rail encouraged the rapid extension of the railroads as discussed in Chapter 5. Their higher speeds, and their ability to haul large tonnages at low cost, gave them a tremendous competitive edge over both the turnpikes and the canals. For topographic reasons, railroad lines were located parallel or close to the previously established turnpikes. This direct competition was ruinous to the freight-wagon and stagecoach companies which eventually lost not only their passengers and freight but also their mail contracts to the railroads.

The National Pike, or Cumberland Road, entered upon an era of great prosperity when the Baltimore and Ohio Railroad reached Cumberland, Maryland, in 1842. Eleven years later, when the railroad reached the Ohio River at Wheeling, Virginia, the freight-wagon and stagecoach companies went into bankruptcy. Likewise, the great Pennsylvania wagon road to the west failed when the Pennsylvania Railroad was completed to Pittsburgh in 1854. Roadside businesses, such as inns and stables which depended on the road traffic, were forced to close. With no revenue coming in, the turnpike companies stopped maintenance, and the roads became so rough that travelers refused to pay tolls.

At the eastern end of the Pennsylvania Road, the Lancaster Turnpike, once the finest road in America, fell steadily into disrepair, as did hundreds of other turnpikes. Most of them eventually reverted to the local authorities for maintenance. The railroads became the backbone of the nation's transportation system. As the older and larger turnpikes collapsed, new charters were issued for relatively short feeder roads to the railroads. Many of these enjoyed a measure of prosperity and were passably maintained until condemned or bought out by the states or local governments in the early twentieth century.

Initial Federal Involvement

In 1796 Colonel Ebenezer Zane, the founder of Wheeling, Virginia (now West Virginia), received permission from Congress to build a post road overland through the territory northwest of the Ohio River to the important river port of Limestone, Kentucky (now Maysville). As his only compensation for building the road, Zane was allowed by act of Congress to locate three square miles of land, due him from his military bounty land warrants which he had received as a Revolutionary War veteran, where his road crossed the Muskingum, Hockhocking, and Scioto rivers. This was the first instance of a subsidy to local roads by the federal government and was a minor concession.

Zane's first road was only a pack trail, but it immediately became a mail route from Wheeling to Lexington, Kentucky, and eventually to Nashville, Tennessee. Zane's Trace, as it became known, played an important role in opening southeastern Ohio to settlement. It was also used by hundreds of flatboatmen returning on foot or horseback to Pittsburgh and to upriver towns from downriver ports as far away as New Orleans. They traveled first on the famous Natchez Trace, a pack trail hewed out as a military road from the lower Mississippi to Nashville, then connected with Zane's Trace northward. By 1803 Zane's road was chopped out wide enough for wagons to pass. The section between Wheeling and Zanesville, Ohio, became a part of the National Pike after 1825, and the remainder became an important turnpike in the 1830s.

The lack of roads and the resources to build them was a serious impediment to the development of the lands north and west of the Ohio River. The federal government owned practically all the undeveloped land, and sale of such land was its main source of revenue. To encourage expansion into the Northwest, the federal government agreed to provide a portion of the revenues from the sale of public lands for building roads and canals, thereby promoting not only the development of new territories but land sales as well.

Thus, Congress in 1803 established a "2 percent fund" derived from the sale of federal public lands to be used under the direction of

Congress for constructing roads "to and through" Ohio. Following the Ohio precedent, Louisiana, Indiana, Mississippi, Illinois, Alabama, and Missouri, on their admission to statehood, were given 3 percent grants for roads, canals, levees, river improvements, and schools. Congress later granted an additional 2 percent to these states, except Indiana and Illinois, which, with Ohio, had already received the equivalent in expenditures on the National Road. The remaining twenty-four states admitted to the Union between 1820 and 1910 received 5 percent grants, except Texas and West Virginia, which had no federal lands.

In March 1806, an act was passed by Congress directing the President, with the advice and consent of the Senate, to appoint three commissioners to lay out and build a road from the head of navigation on the Potomac River at Cumberland, Maryland, to a point on the Ohio River. The act set certain minimum standards for the proposed road and appropriated $30,000 from the proceeds of Ohio land sales to finance the location of the road and to start construction. Debates attending the passage of this act exposed bitter rivalries and jealousies between the eastern seaboard states over development of the lands beyond the Ohio River.

The seaport cities in particular feared the advantage that a federal government-built road might give in competition for the western trade. Strict constructionists of the Constitution denied that the federal government had the authority to build roads at all, except possibly in the territories. Proponents of federal roadbuilding, on the other hand, asserted that authority to build roads was implied under the "general welfare" clause of the Constitution. In the end, the issue was decided by those of both parties who felt strongly that the bonds between the East and the West should be strengthened in the interest of national unity.

It took four years to select the route and another eight years to push the construction through from Cumberland to Wheeling, the head of low-water navigation on the Ohio River. The road was 30 feet wide, with the central 20 feet paved by the Trésaguet method. The right-of-way was cleared 66 feet wide, ditched, and provided with drains and bridges. The cost of the Ohio section, paid out of Ohio's 2 percent land fund, was about $1.8 million, or an average of $14,000 per mile. The road was later extended westward toward Vandalia, Illinois, using macadam surfacing.

From the time the first section was opened in 1813, the Cumberland Road came under traffic so heavy that the stone surface was worn away almost as fast as it was built. The funds appropriated for maintenance were not sufficient to provide systematic and continual repair nor to protect the road from the depredations of travelers and local residents. Freighters ripped up shoulders of the road by descending the steep hills with locked wheels. Local inhabitants fenced parts of the right-of-way, dug into the banks, dragged logs over the road, and even stole broken stone from the road bed. Consequently, the condition of the road steadily deteriorated, despite efforts to repair the worst damage.

In order to provide a regular and dependable source of funds for maintenance, Congress passed an act in 1822 authorizing the collection of tolls from road users. President James Monroe vetoed this act as an unwarranted extension of the power vested in Congress to make appropriations "under which power, with the consent of the states through which the road passes, the work was originally commenced, and has so far been executed." Collection of tolls, the President said, implied a power of jurisdiction or sovereignty which was not granted to the federal government by the Constitution and could not be unilaterally conveyed to any state without a constitutional amendment. It was one thing to make appropriations for public improvements, but an entirely different matter to assume jurisdiction and sovereignty over the land whereon those improvements were made. Monroe's veto established the federal position on highway grants to the states which has since endured.

In the ten years that followed, Congress made occasional and minimal appropriations for maintaining the Cumberland Road, but they were inadequate to preserve it under ever-increasing traffic. Transferring respon-

The National Pike, or Cumberland Road, was the first important road built with federal funds. The first section was opened in 1813 and carried heavy traffic including the famous Conestoga freight wagons.

sibility for the road to the states for maintenance seemed to be the only solution to the dilemma. In 1835 the section of the road east of the Ohio River, after major repair and rebuilding work under direction of the Army Corps of Engineers, was placed under state control for operation as a toll road. Meanwhile the corps continued building the road on west; and by 1840 when funds ran out and Congress refused further appropriations, the partially finished road had reached Vandalia, Illinois. By 1856 all rights connected with the entire road had been ceded to the various states.

The first significant federal land grant for roads was made in February 1823 when Congress granted Ohio a 120-foot right-of-way for a public road from the lower rapids of the Miami of Lake Erie River east to the western boundary of the Western Reserve. In order to finance the road, Congress gave the state all the public lands for one mile on each side of the road, with the proviso that the land could not be sold for less than $1.25 per acre. In another land grant to Ohio, in 1827, Congress subsidized a toll turnpike from Columbus to Sandusky. Next, Indiana built the "Michigan Road" from Lake Michigan to Indianapolis and then southward to Madison, using funds from the sale of lands granted to them for that purpose by the federal government.

The course of highway policy in the United States was profoundly influenced by a second presidential veto. President Andrew Jackson's veto of a bill for funding the Maysville Turnpike in Kentucky in 1830 established national policy with respect to internal improvements of purely local character, which are not of national importance. Jackson was not personally hostile to internal improvements; in fact, in his first annual message to Congress he had recommended distributing the embarrassing yearly surplus of federal revenue among the states to be used by them

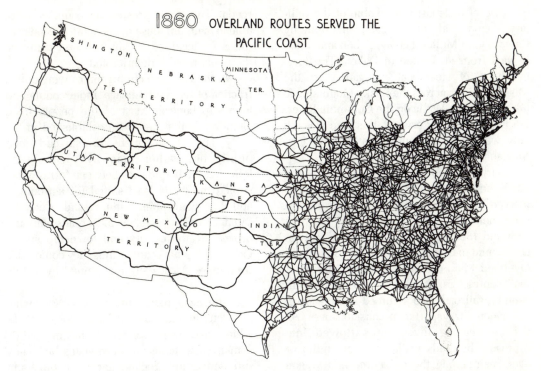

1860 OVERLAND ROUTES SERVED THE PACIFIC COAST

U.S. Department of Transportation

The road system in America in 1860 at the beginning of the railroad expansion era.

for internal improvements. However, the Maysville Turnpike veto put an end to national aid for local road improvements.

Except for military wagon roads, mostly in the territories, the Maysville Turnpike veto ended further wagon road subsidies, other than the National Road, until the Civil War. Between 1863 and 1869, Congress made ten separate grants of land to Michigan, Wisconsin, and Oregon for certain "military" wagon roads. These, with the previous grants to Indiana and Ohio, totaled about 5,500 square miles—an area somewhat larger than Connecticut.

Congress had authorized a more direct military road from Nashville to New Orleans, following the War of 1812, to shorten the distance between those cities by 220 miles. Utilizing army troops, construction on the 516-mile route began in June 1817 and the road was completed by May 1820. The work included a cleared 40-foot right-of-way through dense forests, a graded earth road 35 feet in width, over thirty-five bridges from 60 to 200 feet in length, and several miles of log corduroy causeways through swamps. However,

by 1824 most of the south half of the road was grown up with timber and abandoned.

The army built more than 100 other military wagon roads in the period from 1807 to 1880, most of them in the territories. Their total length was well over 21,000 miles, some built by troops and some by hired labor. They were crude—mere wagon tracks across the prairies or traces chopped through heavy timber—but in the early years of settlement, they were often the only roads.

Among them were the famous Santa Fe Trail from Kansas City, Kansas, to Santa Fe, New Mexico, marked by the army following a route originally beaten by traders and trappers; and Colonel Cooke's Road from Santa Fe to San Diego, pioneered by the army in 1846. The army reopened the 400-mile Old Spanish Trail from Pensacola to St. Augustine, Florida, between 1824 and 1830. Military roads radiated like the spokes of a wheel from strategic Detroit toward Chicago, Grand Rapids, Saginaw, and Cleveland; and in 1838 a 512-mile wagon road was made from Ft. Snelling in Minnesota Territory to Ft. Leavenworth in Kansas Territory.

One of the most remarkable of the military wagon roads was located and built by Captain John Mullen between 1858 and 1862. It went from Ft. Benton in Dakota Territory, the head of steamboat navigation on the Missouri River, across the Rocky Mountains to Old Fort Walla Walla on the Columbia River. For twenty years afterward, this road was the only way open to immigrants into western Montana and northern Idaho.

During the overland migrations of the 1850s and 1860s, the army improved and marked most of the pioneer wagon trails and used them to supply its garrisons. Between 1850 and 1869 some of these trails were transcontinental mail routes used by the Butterfield Overland Mail, the Pony Express, and other mail contractors. But by the mid-nineteenth century, railroads had assumed supremacy in the nation's transportation consciousness. As ever increasing investments flowed into railroads, the funds available for extending or even maintaining the old horse and wagon facilities steadily decreased and finally were discontinued altogether.

Rural Roads and City Streets

When railroad competition drove the long distance wagon freighter and stagecoach companies out of business in the 1850s and 1860s, many toll road facilities were taken over by local authorities and maintained as common roads. The more prosperous counties were able to maintain these roads in fairly good condition for local travel; but in poorer counties, the roads rapidly deteriorated.

In the East, the old turnpikes were only a fraction of the road mileage under county and township control. Most of the people lived along roads that had been established in the early days of settlement through continued public use rather than by plan. These followed the boundaries between farms or occupied the lands least suited for agriculture and thus were often winding and poorly located. Over the years, the local roads were improved by the county and township supervisors with what scanty funds they could raise from taxes. Most were maintained by statute labor.

The local road situation was somewhat different in the "public land states," those which had been formed from the public domain. The lands in these states had been subdivided into rectangular townships and sections according to an ordinance of the Continental Congress, May 29, 1785. These land lines became the boundaries between farms, and thus were the lines of least resistance for local roads. The customary rights-of-way for these roads was one chain wide (66 feet), and each property owner donated 33 feet on his side of the section line. As in the East, these roads were normally maintained by statute

U.S. Department of Transportation

During the last half of the nineteenth century, railroads took over long distance transportation and rural roads were neglected.

labor. In the Great Plains and the Far West, the tendency to fix the local roads on the section lines was strengthened by an act of July 26, 1866, in which Congress granted a free right-of-way for public roads over unreserved public lands.

The years between 1850 and 1900 have been called the "dark age of the rural road." Yet in this period, well over 1.5 million miles of rural road were built, primarily by counties. Most of them were unimproved, at best only ditched and graded; but in the aggregate they represented a great public works effort, particularly in the West where population was sparse and finances limited.

The first complete inventory of public road mileage made in the United States was compiled by the Office of Public Roads (OPR) in 1904. This inventory showed 2.2 million miles in existence at that time outside of incorporated cities, of which only 153,662 miles were improved with stone, gravel, sand-clay, or some kind of surfacing better than plain dirt. With a few exceptions, all of these roads were under county or township control. This mileage was distributed as shown in Table 3-1.

Until the early 1900s, the main sources of local road funds were taxes on property, poll taxes, and statute labor. In 1904 only twenty-five states had laws permitting counties, townships, or road districts to issue bonds for road improvement, and in these the privilege was used sparingly and usually only to fi-

nance a particularly expensive structure, such as a steel or concrete bridge.

Property taxes levied for road support varied widely from state to state and from county to county within the same state. As OPR observed in a 1904 report: "Unquestionably the bitterest controversies in counties and townships in connection with the subject of road improvement are over proposed increases in the rates of property taxation for road purposes. It is common in many parts of the United States for uninformed though honestly disposed citizens to make a determined opposition to a very moderate and perfectly reasonable increase in the tax rate." These taxes, together with poll taxes payable in cash, were by far the major sources of funds for building and maintaining the country roads, yielding about $54 million in 1904.

Even so, this large investment was spread so thinly that very few rural residents enjoyed adequate roads. In the northern states, earth roads were quagmires during the spring thaw and became distressingly soft during rains at any time of year. Deep sand was a problem in many parts of the South. The loads a farmer could haul with his teams were only a fraction of what they would have been on a reasonably good road. This difference was, in effect, a tax on everything the farmer bought or sold.

The high cost of transport from the farms was also a tax on the people of the cities who were forced to pay higher prices for locally grown food and farm products. In 1901, for

TABLE 3-1

Public Roads in the United States in 1904

Surfacing Type—Miles

Area	Earth	Gravel	Stone	Sand-Clay, Shells, etc.	Total
Eastern and Southeastern States	580,850	24,627	21,240	3,091	629,808
Texas	119,281	167	1,909	52	121,409
Public Land States	1,297,777	83,439	15,573	3,664	1,400,353
Total	1,997,908	108,233	38,622	6,807	2,151,570

There were also 1,101 miles of stone-surfaced toll roads in Pennsylvania and 497 miles of toll roads in Maryland.

example, fruit from California could be shipped to Raleigh, North Carolina, by rail for less than farmers living only 15 miles away could deliver their fruit to the Raleigh markets. One farmer wrote:

> You see by this that the railroads enable the fruitgrowers of California to compete with the fruitgrowers of our own county towns. The way to successfully compete with these people is to build good roads so as to enable us to get to market at any time and carry a full load, thereby reducing the cost of transportation. A bad road is a relentless tax assessor and a sure collector.

In American cities, street layouts during the colonial period were influenced by European practices. William Penn, who with Thomas Holme developed the original plan for the city of Philadelphia, was London bred and a frequent visitor to many of Europe's largest urban centers. Philadelphia's layout, as a result, was similar to those of many European cities. Its major features included a gridiron street pattern, uniform spacing and setbacks for buildings, and a series of open spaces. The network of streets consisted of nine parallel roadways, laid out between the Delaware and Schuylkill rivers, with twenty-one streets running perpendicular to them. All of the streets were 50 feet wide, except for the two streets intersecting at the center of the city which were 100 feet wide. A central square of 10 acres was located at the main intersection, and four additional 8-acre squares were placed in each quarter of Philadelphia for public use.

Although the gridiron street pattern was subsequently adopted by many American cities (Savannah, Pittsburgh, and Lexington, for example), other design concepts were introduced during the colonial period. Annapolis' plan featured a square and two large circles from which diagonal streets radiated. This innovative layout was developed in 1695 by Francis Nicholson, who designed Williamsburg's street system four years later. The primary elements in the Williamsburg plan were two intersecting roadways. One served as the major axis connecting the College of William and Mary with the capitol building; the other, located midway between these two points, was the perpendicular minor axis leading to the governor's palace. The city plan developed for Washington, D.C., by Pierre L'Enfant in 1791 combined diagonal and radial streets and superimposed them on the traditional gridiron.

As Americans moved westward during the first half of the nineteenth century, new urban design patterns emerged. But many of these plans, as well as those developed in the colonial and early national periods, were ignored or changed to permit more intensive land use. With the increasing value of land in urban areas, houses were built from lot line to lot line. And squares, once reserved for open spaces, were consumed in the process. These practices were reflected in the street plan adopted by New York City in 1811. It imposed a rigid gridiron—with few open spaces and little regard for topography—on all but the upper part of Manhattan Island.

In 1790 only 3 percent of the United States' total population lived in the fifteen cities of over 5,000 inhabitants. No city had a population of 40,000. By 1900 there were about 140 cities of more than 30,000 inhabitants. Of these, twenty three had populations between 100,000 and 250,000; nine had more than a quarter million people. The prosperity of these cities depended on their ability to move goods and people freely from place to place. Industry, powered by steam, used great quantities of coal which had to be hauled through streets from docks and railroad yards to factories and mills. The hauling of raw materials and finished goods to and from the factories, warehouses, docks, and railroads also generated a tremendous volume of wagon and dray traffic. Outside of the industrial areas, city dwellers depended on streets for access to their homes and for deliveries of coal, ice, and groceries.

The construction and maintenance of city streets for horse-drawn traffic presented problems far different from those associated with the building and upkeep of roadways for today's motor vehicles. Ezra C. Knowlton in *History of Highway Development in Utah* cites an 1892 report of the Salt Lake City engineer that illustrated the difficulties:

Many of our streets have an excellent natural foundation of clean gravel, the surface of which has, during the past forty years, been subjected to a process of grinding by the wheels of passing vehicles, and as a result we now have a covering of finely powdered stone several inches in thickness, which in summer is an unbearable dust, in winter an impassable mud, and in all seasons a detriment and disgrace to our city. No street cleaning having ever been done, this powdered surface has become foul with animal vegetable matter, and is no doubt pregnant with germs of fatal diseases. The continued inhalation of this polluted dust is a menace to the public health, and the concern of every thoughtful citizen.

Since streets were not only costly but vitally important to a city's future, it is surprising that prior to the automobile age they received so little attention. In 1904 John W. Alvord, supervisor of streets in Chicago, described many of the problems related to street paving. His statement was later summarized by Ira O. Baker of the University of Illinois in his book *Roads and Pavements:*

In no other branch of civil engineering is there expended so large an amount of money in so unsystematic a manner, and generally with such unsatisfactory results. Pavements are primarily designed to accommodate travel; but scarcely anyone in this country thinks of investigating the travel of a city systematically and thoroughly before proceeding to lay pavements . . . . Street pavements are by far the most expensive single improvement that the municipality undertakes; yet in hardly any of the cities of this country are there suitable laws, proper organization, or sufficient public spirit adequate to care for the investment after it is once made . . . .

These conditions, according to Alvord, were the result of numerous factors. Since American cities changed administrations every few years, the persons placed in charge had limited opportunity to acquire knowledge and experience in the design of pavements; taxpayers and their elected representatives, who were generally uninformed on road-building techniques, insisted on the right to determine the kinds of streets to be built; no one type of pavement satisfied the requirements of all the people; municipalities seldom called on specialists for advice on street pav-

ing; and cities customarily lacked adequate "general funds" for road maintenance and repair. Finally, concluded Alvord, "the street-paving problem is everywhere regarded as a local or neighborhood problem. The general public has not yet come to regard it as a national problem, or even entirely a municipal problem; and hence the lack of appreciation of the broader municipal requirements, and the insufficiency of the study of its fundamental principles."

During the colonial period and the Revolutionary era, efforts were made to get city people literally out of the mud by using cobblestone pavements, especially in localities where the material was readily available. Cobblestone proved durable. At the turn of the twentieth century, older cities still had many miles of this type of pavement. New York, for example, had 229 miles of cobblestone pavements in 1902, and Baltimore had 321 miles. Although 93 percent of Philadelphia's streets were paved in this manner in 1884, by 1904 the mileage had decreased to only 6 percent.

When the quarrying and shaping of stone became economical, stone blocks replaced cobbles. Blocks provided a smoother and more satisfactory pavement, and they were easier to clean and maintain. They were generally laid upon a 6-inch concrete base, with a 2-inch sand bed, and the joints were filled with either road pitch and pebbles or cement grout. Granite was commonly used for the stone blocks. Brick pavements also were widely employed. When burned hard enough and cooled properly, bricks made of shale and fire clay lasted nearly as long as granite and provided a smooth surface. Since block and brick pavements were noisy, cities began almost immediately to experiment with other materials to minimize citizen complaints.

Treated wood block paving, which had been used with some success in London and Paris, was introduced in the United States during the last half of the nineteenth century. It was first adopted in Boston and then in Galveston, Indianapolis, and other cities. Boston's specifications called for uniform blocks (4 inches wide, 4 inches deep, and 8 inches long) made of long-leaf Georgia yellow pine—no second growth timber was allowed. The blocks were placed in an airtight cylinder, where dry heat was used to expel the moisture, and patented wood preservative agents were applied by means of hydraulic pressure. The blocks were then laid, with the grain vertical, on a 6-inch concrete foundation with a 1-inch cushion of clean, screened sand; and they were driven tightly together at every sixth row. The joints were filled with dry, screened sand, and the pavement rolled with a five-ton steam roller until the blocks presented a firm, uniform surface. However, wooden surfaces, although less noisy than stone block pavements, were still not satisfactory. They were too slippery for horses, especially on inclined streets.

Asphalt paving, which had been used in Europe since 1849, was first tried in the United States in 1871. The previous year, E. J. De Smedt, a Belgian chemist working in the United States, received a patent for asphalt mastic pavement. It was made of asphalt from Trinidad, mixed with sand and limestone dust, and combined by fluxing with petroleum residuum. This material was first applied on an experimental basis in Newark, New Jersey, and then used on Pennsylvania Avenue in Washington, D. C., in 1872.

During the following decade, asphalt pavement was employed only sparingly, but it became increasingly popular in subsequent years. Omaha and Buffalo paved the streets of their cities with asphalt in 1882; and by 1900 there were 2,600 miles of asphalt in the

United States, representing an investment of $95 million. Most cities used Trinidad lake asphalt, but other types—Burmudez, Alcatraz, California, Utah, and Trinidad land asphalt—were also utilized. In an attempt to obtain reliable asphalt and workmanship from paving contractors, the majority of cities required maintenance guarantees.

In 1897 the American Society of Municipal Improvements (ASMI) conducted a survey of the types of pavement laid in United States cities. Of the 420 cities with populations of 10,000 and over contacted, 144 replied. Twenty-two cities indicated that none of their streets was paved. The remaining 122 cities reported the following miles of various kinds of pavement: asphalt 1,365; granite 1,151; wood 729; brick 705; and sandstone and trap rock 547. The average costs per square yard, according to the ASMI survey, were as follows: granite $2.26; asphalt $2.08; sandstone or trap rock $1.67; brick $1.56; and wood $1.18.

Although street pavements provided a smoother and more comfortable riding surface, they did not eliminate the dust and dirt tracked onto streets from adjoining property. Many miles of side streets were unpaved; therefore, streets were periodically sprinkled to minimize the dust problem. St. Louis voters, for example, adopted a charter amendment in 1888 authorizing "general street sprinkling" four times a day from March 15 through November 3 to keep their thoroughfares dust free.

The practice of tearing up pavements to install and repair gas, water, and sewer lines was particularly destructive to the life of street pavements. The magnitude of the problem was well illustrated in an 1896 report of the New York City Department of Public Works. It indicated that one in every four miles of paved streets was torn up for construction purposes during the year. The lack of care in refilling trenches and the carelessness in replacing pavements often presented serious problems for city officials. Different methods were suggested to cope with the situation. In 1899 an ASMI Committee on Street Paving recommended that "no excavations of any nature, except for emergency

U.S. Department of Transportation

A bicycle parade proceeds down Pennsylvania Avenue in Washington, D.C., in 1884 during the convention of the League of American Wheelmen.

repairs of existing pipes and fixtures, shall be permitted in any street except upon written application of the individual or corporation desiring to make said excavation, and the filing of a proper indemnity bond." Some engineers saw as the ideal solution, the construction of general conduits for service lines. The time is coming, they said, "when any city which can afford a brick, asphalt or modern wood-block pavement must afford to first place under it a conduit which will preserve it from premature disfigurement, deterioration and renewal."

Curbs, gutters, and sidewalks were constructed on the more heavily traveled streets of larger cities during the first half of the nineteenth century. The height of curbs was used as the basis for regulating the cross section of roadways and sidewalks and for fixing the elevations of buildings and houses. Granite curbs were common where such stone was available, but combined concrete curbs and gutters were also frequently constructed. Curbs and gutters improved the appearance of streets and were a source of great pride to property owners.

Under the impulse of new paving projects, cities sought in various ways to beautify their thoroughfares. In 1872, for example, a commission of public officials was appointed in Washington, D. C., to select, plant, and care for all trees along the city's streets; and, in the spring of 1873, municipal officials supervised the planting of more than 6,000 trees. Many of these were silver maples which the commission described as "perfect street trees"; they grew quickly, they were easily transplanted, and they had beautiful foliage.

At night, streets became hazardous, especially to pedestrians. Without proper street lighting, pedestrians were frequently the easy victims of reckless drivers or calculating thieves. Cities attempted from as early as the seventeenth century to illuminate their streets by the best and most economical methods available. By the end of the nineteenth century, electric arc lamps were becoming common for use in lighting streets. The growth of street lighting is discussed in Chapter 11.

In the 1890s, railroads and cities committed funds to abolishing railroad crossings that were considered either dangerous or annoying to local traffic. In 1895, by elevating the tracks, the Pennsylvania Railroad Company removed twenty grade crossings in Elizabeth, New Jersey. Because of the success of this undertaking, other railroads and cities followed suit. The City of Chicago achieved the most notable results. By 1901 it had abolished 389 grade crossings at a cost of over $17 million.

The impact of bicycle enthusiasts also was evident in cities at the turn of the century. Legislative action often was necessary before the bicycle was accorded the ordinary privileges of the road. Not until 1887 did the New York legislature give cyclists the right to pass through public thoroughfares. Yet one of the first bicycle paths constructed in the United States was built in 1895 by the Park Department of Brooklyn. The path, located in Prospect Park, was $1^1/_2$ miles long and constructed of broken limestone. It then was covered with a thin layer of small stone and cost $18,000. It was so popular that contemporary accounts reported 20,000 wheels passed over the path in a single day.

For the most part, even with the inadequacies of streets in many communities, city dwellers enjoyed reasonably good local transportation by the end of the nineteenth century. Even relatively small cities had horsecar lines, some of which persisted into the early 1900s. Small towns on the peripheries of the large cities were connected with the cities by steam railroads; and by the late 1890s, by electric, interurban railroads as well. Frequent services by these railroads made it convenient for thousands of the more prosperous city workers to live in the suburbs and commute to work.

Concentrated populations, trade, and industry built a solid base for property taxation in the cities. These taxes, supplemented by special assessments, provided the funds for thousands of miles of improved streets as well as sewers, water supplies, street lights, schools, parks, and other municipal services far beyond the reach of rural citizens. Most city street improvements were financed by bond issues, which were amortized out of general tax revenues, as the cities for the most part avoided "pay-as-you-go" financing. Construction was usually accomplished by public bidding and contract.

Practically all American cities enjoyed the right, conferred on them by state legislatures, to assess the cost of street improvements to the benefited property. This power, which greatly enlarged the financial resources available to cities for improvements, was uniquely American in origin. It was first used in New York City during the colonial era to finance streets and sewers. While city dwellers' taxes were greater, they were not obliged to perform statute labor to maintain their roads. Instead, cities accomplished street maintenance work with paid labor under the supervision of public works departments and knowledgeable road builders.

The great disparity between the cities and the rural areas in the quality of life was evident to everyone, but few city dwellers thought they had an obligation to do anything about it. They taxed themselves to build their roads and streets; the farmers should do likewise. Nevertheless, the impetus for road reform came from the cities, primarily from civic leaders who recognized the economic burdens to city dwellers and farmers alike caused by bad roads.

In an effort to bring about some improvement in the condition of rural roads, the first state road convention was held in Iowa City, Iowa, in 1883. The convention recommended the payment of road taxes in cash instead of labor, consolidation of road districts, letting road construction to responsible contractors and, most importantly, authorizing county boards to levy a property tax in order to create a road fund. These recommendations were adopted by the Iowa legislature in 1884, although the reforms were optional rather than mandatory for the counties.

While other states soon adopted similar "good road laws," the good roads movement did not get under way until 1890 when the organized bicyclists launched a national public relations campaign for more and better roadbuilding. Bicycles became practical for personal transportation after introduction of the "safety" design in 1884 and the pneumatic tire in 1888. Almost overnight, cycling became

a national craze. Wheelmen fanned out into the country in all directions, thereby having intimate contact with the deplorable country roads. Cyclists formed organizations that were vociferous advocates of road improvement.

A "Good Roads Association" was formed in Missouri in 1891, followed by similar organizations in other states. The first national conference, held in 1894, urged state legislatures to set up limited systems of state roads and to create temporary highway commissions to recommend suitable legislation for implementing good roads programs.

New Jersey was the first state to provide aid to counties for road support. Good road groups succeeded in getting a state aid bill passed in 1891, after pointing out that most of the travel was intercounty rather than local. The bill gave the initiation, planning, and supervision of state aided projects to county officials, while the state reserved the right to approve projects and to accept or reject contracts. The cost of improvement construction was to be split three ways: one tenth assessed to the holders of property along the road, one third to the state, and the remainder to the county.

The administration of the act was placed under a commissioner of public roads, appointed by the governor for a three-year term. The New Jersey state aid bill was a milestone in the history of highway administration in the United States. It established the principle that highway improvement for the general good was an obligation of the state and county as well as the people living along the highway.

U.S. Department of Transportation

New Jersey's first state aid road project under construction in 1892.

The act also imposed much needed reforms including the requirement that township committees adopt a systematic plan for improving the highways.

Massachusetts improved this approach by specifying a system of main highways connecting the municipalities of the commonwealth on which the state aid could be used and by maintaining control over standards for this system. The state aid principle spread slowly to other states. It took various forms, ranging from advice only, which might be accepted or rejected by local authorities, to a state highway commission which was given direct or indirect supervision over every public highway in the state. Four states gave minimal help by putting convicts from the state penitentiary to work on the roads; others authorized the employment of state and county convicts for road work and also gave cash grants. State aid did not extend to the cities since they generally were handling their street problems through the taxing authority available to them.

As the good roads movement gained momentum, there was pressure on Congress to provide federal assistance to highways. Articles promoting good roads appeared in influential newspapers, citing the contrast between poorly maintained American roads and those in Europe where well supervised road maintenance practices produced roads "far superior" to those in the United States. Many had reservations about how federal assistance might be accomplished and whether it was practical. A petition to establish a cabinet officer in Washington, D.C., evoked the following reaction in an editorial appearing in Salt Lake City's *Deseret News,* December 30, 1892:

Luckily we of the far West know something of a practical nature regarding the subject, and can make, repair, and maintain highways; but candor compels us to say that they are not all as good as they should be, and that there is a lack of system in either the construction or maintenance is painfully apparent. The thing to be done, therefore, is to expend less money in theorizing and circulating documents and more in work of a useful character. A bureau in every state and territory having this subject in hand and being charged with the full responsibility of it, would amount to very much more than an executive department at Washington whose occupants might or might not know something of the matter committed to them and who, under any circumstances, would run so largely to red tape and gold seals that little good would be accomplished.

Such concern was widespread and resulted in federal involvement taking a slow and cautious course.

The Chicago World's Fair, planned for 1893, prompted a Senate bill in July 1892 to create a National Highway Commission "for the purpose of general inquiry into the condition of highways in the United States and means for their improvement, and especially the best method of securing a proper exhibit [at the World's Fair] of approved appliances for road-making and of providing public instruction in the art . . . ." The Senate passed the bill, but it was not acted on by the House. However, in the next session, the Agriculture Appropriation Act provided $10,000 for the secretary of agriculture "to make inquiries in regard to the systems of road management throughout the United States, to make investigations in regard to the best methods of road-making, and to enable him to assist the agricultural colleges and experiment stations in disseminating information on this subject."

On October 3, 1893, the Office of Road Inquiry (ORI) was established within the Department of Agriculture and headed by Roy Stone, a prominent New York civil engineer and good roads booster. His authority was carefully limited, however, to developing and disseminating information. He was specifically forbidden to seek to influence or control road policy in states or counties.

Stone, with a staff of only himself and one clerk, sent letters of inquiry to the governors of the states and territories and their secretaries of state, members of Congress, state geologists, and railroad presidents. He solicited information on highway laws, the locations of materials suitable for roadbuilding, and rail rates for hauling such materials. By the end of June 1894, ORI had issued nine bulletins on these subjects, some of which were by then in their second printing. In the following year, ORI produced eight more bulletins, four of which reported the proceedings of national good roads conventions. Able and influential men were speakers at these programs and publication of their speeches at government expense was an easy and economical way to spread the gospel of good roads throughout the country.

Stone then proposed to build short "object lesson roads" near or on experimental farms in the various states, a system which Massachusetts had found effective in selling good roads. These would serve to instruct the road makers, to educate the visiting public, and to improve the economic conditions of the farms. The plan won approval, with the stipulation that ORI emphasize the practical side of roadbuilding. The total budget of ORI was still only $10,000, so Stone accomplished the first object lesson roads only by getting manufacturers to supply equipment and obtaining local support and funding for materials and construction. An ORI supervisor controlled the design, stake out, and construction "in order that the roads may be creditable to the government when done." The roads succeeded in being a forceful demonstration of the "seeing is believing" philosophy of selling good roads to the public.

Stone resigned in October 1899 to accept the presidency of the National League for Good Roads in New York, an organization he had helped establish. The name of the federal agency was changed to the Office of Public Road Inquiries (OPRI), and Martin Dodge, formerly president of the Ohio State Highway Commission, was appointed director.

The demonstration road program continued under the new director and was given a boost by the "Good Roads Trains" which were organized and provided by the National Good Roads Association in 1910. The trains carried information on road improvement throughout the country. Road machinery companies donated their latest models of equipment and trained operators to run them. Various railroads contributed the trains. The government provided a road expert to lecture on roads and to supervise demonstration of roadbuilding.

At this time, the railroads, secure in their position as the backbone of the American transportation system, were among the strongest supporters of good roads. They were anxious to extend their tributary traffic areas and also to overcome some of the widespread hostility engendered by their high-handed methods of dealing with the public. The association mounted a powerful publicity campaign to prepare the way for Good Roads Trains. Within three years, these trains demonstrated road construction practices in most of the large cities of the nation.

In welcoming the Southern Railway Good Roads Train to Lynchburg, United States Senator J. W. Daniel of Virginia said:

> An itinerant college on wheels has come among us. It brings its professors and its equipment with it. It is known as the "good roads train" of the Southern Railway system. This college does not teach out of books, nor solely by word of mouth. It teaches by the greater power of example. If you will watch its operation you will see a new good road grow over an old bad road at the magic touch of titanic machinery, and while an orator talks of road building, it will set his words to the music of practical accomplishment

Another change in the federal office occurred in 1906 when the Division of Tests of the Bureau of Chemistry merged with the Office of Public Road Inquiries to form the Office of Public Roads in the Department of Agriculture. The new agency had a statutory role and was to be headed by a director, "who shall be a scientist and have charge of all scientific and technical work," at a salary of $2,500 per year. The act also provided for a chief of records, an instrument maker, and six clerks. The total annual appropriation for the office's work increased to $50,000. Director Dodge was a lawyer and therefore could not qualify for the new post. Logan Waller Page, chief of the Division of Tests in the Bureau of Chemistry, was appointed to the position and held it until his death in 1918.

Arrival of the Automobile Age

The new federal office came into being at a momentous time in the history of land transportation. To Page's predecessors, good roads meant wagon roads, constructed according to the time-tested methods of Trésaguet, Telford, and McAdam and designed for

U.S. Department of Transportation

America's first gasoline engined automobile was tested on the streets of Springfield, Massachusetts, in 1893.

horse-drawn, steel-tired traffic traveling six to eight miles per hour. But in 1893, Frank Duryea tested the nation's first gasoline engined automobile on the streets of Springfield, Massachusetts, and changed the future. By 1905 the shape of things to come was dimly foreshadowed by 50,000 automobiles, primarily in the cities; by 1918 this number had increased to 6.2 million. The automobile age had arrived. With it would evolve new kinds of roads, streets, and highways designed specifically for motor vehicles to meet the needs of a different way of life.

Initially these early automobiles were simply "horseless carriages," but as they improved they became large, heavy, and clumsy. This was due, in part, to a lack of engineering knowledge and strong and light materials for their manufacture. About 1906 vanadium alloy steel and other alloys were developed which enabled Henry Ford of Detroit, Michigan, to redesign his big heavy touring car into a much lighter and smaller vehicle— the famous Model T. At the same time, he began to mass produce components for this one vehicle and designed a moving assembly line on which the cars were put together. Ford's contribution to industry was in organizing manufacturing into a smooth coordinated process, eliminating wasted time and effort, and applying technology to increase productivity.

By redesigning the vehicle and standardizing the production process, Ford was able to increase production from 1,500 units in 1905 to 14,877 units in 1907, while at the same time reducing prices. These lower prices, in turn,

opened the door to a mass market. As sales increased, Ford was able to realize economies of scale in manufacturing and further reductions in costs. By 1911 he was selling cars for less than $600 each, as compared to 1900 when prices ranged from $3,000 to $12,000.

As Ford's competitors adopted his methods in a rush to catch up with him, the automotive industry turned out more vehicles at lower prices. Annual production of American-made motor cars was 25,000 in 1905; 187,000 in 1910; and 969,930 in 1915. In that year, 2.5 million vehicles were registered in the United States, of which 158,506 were trucks. The average new motor vehicle price in the United States in 1916 was only about $600.

Increasingly, the owners of these automobiles began using them on country roads, raising clouds of dust, and creating a rural road crisis which began to be seriously felt about 1910. In the early 1900s, a motor trip for any considerable distance into the country was an uncertain undertaking. To run out of fuel was disastrous, mechanical service was practically unobtainable, and blowouts and tire punctures were frequent and not easy to repair. Dust was a major nuisance in dry weather. There were no comfort stations, and tourists were dependent on private kindness or the more secluded portions of the right-of-way for sanitary accommodations.

Furthermore, to the dismay of road officials, the automobile damaged macadam and gravel roads. Director Page of the Office of Public Roads (OPR) described the problem:

> The driving wheels of motor cars moving at high rates of speed exert a powerful tractive force on the road surface, which displaces the materials composing the surface. The result is that the finer particles and dust are thrown into the air to be carried off by cross currents of air. The rubber tire of the automobile does not wear any appreciable amount of dusk from the rock fragments, and consequently, the loss of rock dust is a permanent loss to the road. Under these conditions, the road soon ravels, making travel difficult, and allowing water to make its way to the earth subgrade or foundation.

The initial reaction to this destruction of rural roads was a clamor to bar automobiles from the highways or to limit severely their speed. But calmer counsels prevailed, and some observers, such as the editor of *American Highways* in 1904, even viewed dusting as a blessing in disguise:

> The motors are unquestionably here to stay and are going to play an important and very useful part in the lives of coming generations and instead of trying to bar them off the highways or misusing their owners, highway commissioners should attack the problems they present and should solve them as they have former problems. It is rather fortunate than otherwise that the motors have appeared upon the scene before road building in the better sense engaged public attention. Had their advent been postponed until the country had built up a complete system of roads, a tremendous expense would have been incurred for tearing up the old material and relaying it.

There were, as might be expected, conflicts between the early motorists and farmers. Most rural residents looked upon motorists as intruders. This feeling gradually changed as more farmers became motorists, and motoring ceased to be regarded as a rich man's plaything.

By 1905 only fourteen states had highway departments, and five of these were less than six months old. The mileage of roads under state control was small; and state expenditures, mostly in the form of aid to counties and townships, were only about 3 percent of total road outlays in the United States. It was evident that the main effort for improving rural roads would have to be directed toward counties and townships. Up to this time, OPR's most popular work with local governments had been the object lesson roads, and evidence of their effectiveness began to accumulate. The program was expanded, but its emphasis changed from macadam construction to a wider use of local materials, particularly earth, clay, and sands. Director Page wrote in 1909: "Experience has shown that our earth roads can, in general, be very much improved by proper construction and systematic maintenance at a cost well within the reach of almost any community. Furthermore, these improved earth roads serve as the best possible foundation for further improvements with a hard surface as the means

become available." This concept of stage construction became one of the guiding principles of federal road policy and was widely accepted by the states.

The object lesson roads were utilized to test various surfaces including brick, blast slag, and sand-clay mixtures. An important experiment in 1900 was the oil treatment of a 4,650-foot section of the Queens Chapel Road in the District of Columbia. At that time, road oiling was practically unknown outside of Los Angeles County, California. There, 6 miles of road were oiled in 1898 to lay the dust "which churned beneath the wheels of yearly increasing travel during the long dry season in that region, [and which] had become a most serious nuisance."

Hot-laid asphalt paving had been used on city streets in the United States since the 1870s, but it was considered far too expensive for country roads. Various experiments were tried, and by 1908 the tar and residual petroleum oil (asphalt) treatments were pronounced "on the whole very satisfactory." Field tests showed that both the penetration method and the mixing method of making bituminous macadam surfaces gave good results. By 1916 the dust abatement program included experiments on twenty-eight roads in eleven states and the District of Columbia, Gradually, the emphasis shifted from "dust prevention" to "road preservation" and provided for building up tar or asphalt wearing courses over macadam and slag or gravel bases. This led to the general adoption of bituminous surfaces wherever automobiles were an appreciable portion of the traffic.

At the same time, experiments were carried on to improve road maintenance. There were nationwide efforts to raise maintenance standards in the counties and to improve road management. The OPR, working with various local government road organizations, initiated training programs to try to meet the shortage of highway engineers. But an attempt to establish a national school for roadbuilding, patterned after France's successful system, failed to get adequate support.

The OPR, as the federal government's roadbuilding authority, began furnishing advice on forest roads to the United States Forest

Service in 1905 and to the National Park Service in 1910. This assignment grew rapidly, and by 1916 OPR was maintaining 160 miles of road, constructing another 170 miles, and making surveys and plans for another 477 miles—a program spread over federal lands in twelve states and Alaska. The 1916 Federal-Aid Road Act, which increased this far-flung program still further, made it a major activity.

By 1910 there were scores of organizations in the United States devoted to promoting good roads. A few of these were strong, effective, and national in scope. Among the most important were the American Automobile Association, founded by motorists in 1902, and the American Road Makers, established by state engineers, road contractors, and road machinery manufacturers. At Page's invitation, in 1910 the officials of some thirty state and interstate organizations, including highway departments, railroads, good roads associations, and others, met in Washington and formed the American Association for Highway Improvement. The association sponsored the first American Road Congress at Richmond, Virginia, in 1911. It passed strong resolutions which later became the basis for federal aid legislation.

A number of state highway commissioners and chief engineers assumed active roles in the American Association for Highway Improvement, but most of the state highway officials felt a need for an association more specifically tailored to their needs. Such an organization, with membership restricted to the chief officials of the state highway departments and their staffs, was organized in December 1914. At that time, only thirty-three states had highway departments. The organization was named the American Association of State Highway Officials (AASHO), and its declared purpose was for "providing mutual cooperation and assistance to the state highway departments and the several states and the federal government, as well as for the discussion of legislative, economic and technical subjects pertaining to the administration of such departments." One of the first acts of the executive committee was to prepare, for the consideration of Congress, a bill authorizing federal aid to highways.

Launching the Federal Aid Highway System

It is hard to comprehend the isolation in which most farmers lived in the nineteenth century. They had no rural mail delivery and no telephones. They also had to go to town, perhaps 4 or 5 miles away, to get mail or a newspaper. When the roads were bad, as they usually were in winter and spring, farmers had great difficulty in communicating with their neighbors. One of the strongest arguments of good roads advocates was that improved roads would reduce this isolation and would make it practical for the government to deliver mail to farms, as some European countries had been doing for decades. Furthermore, the establishment of "post roads" was the constitutional obligation of the federal government.

In 1893 Congress appropriated $10,000 for an experimental program of rural mail delivery. The first rural delivery routes to farms from Charlestown, Halltown, and Urvilla, West Virginia, were established in October 1896; and by July 1897, forty-four routes were in operation. Congress increased the appropriation to $50,000 in 1898, and thereafter the rural delivery system grew rapidly. By 1903 there were 8,600 carriers traveling 200,000 miles per day and reaching almost 5 million people.

The Post Office Department made a policy that rural delivery would be established only along reasonably good roads and that the carrier need not go out on his route unless the roads were in fit condition for travel. These requirements marshaled public opinion for better roads, and hundreds of counties undertook substantial road improvements in order to get rural mail delivery. In Texas, for example, 100 fords were replaced by bridges in 1901 and 1902.

Even so, these efforts did not meet the increasing demand for rural delivery service. Congress was generous with funds to operate and extend the free delivery system. It consistently appropriated more than the Post Office Department requested, but the problem was actually one of inadequate roads on which to carry the mails. For fourteen years, various bills were considered to provide funds for building post roads under provisions of Article 8, Section 1, of the Constitution, which states: "The Congress shall have the power to establish Post Offices and post roads . . . ."

U.S. Department of Transportation

The first federal Post Office Department funds to improve post roads was expended on this section of road in Alabama in 1913.

None was successful until 1912 when an experimental appropriation of $500,000 was added to the Post Office Department appropriation bill to provide one third of the cost of improving the condition of selected post roads. The act also instructed the secretary of agriculture, in cooperation with the postmaster general, to formulate a plan to provide national aid for postal roads, a large assignment which was to be done within the regular budgets of both departments.

In order to treat all states equally and to get information representative of all parts of the country, the two departments proposed to divide the appropriation among the states. They notified each governor of the apportionment and asked that he designate approximately 50 miles of road within his state on which rural mail delivery was or might be established as an experimental post road. Five governors did not even reply to this request; six refused to participate; and twenty-eight indicated that they were unable to comply for lack of legal power or because of conflicting state statutes. Only Alabama, Iowa, and Oregon agreed to designate post roads and accept the federal subsidy. This approach failed to get the program moving.

The federal officials then decided to work with the counties. They selected from two to eight locations representative of conditions in various sections of the country and concentrated the available funds on a few roads in these localities. Agreements were made for seventeen post road projects totaling 457 miles, located in thirteen states and twenty-eight counties. There were some practical and legal difficulties. For instance, one county in Virginia cancelled its agreement, having decided that it could build roads more economically by convict labor or by free labor working ten or eleven hours per day than by accepting the federal subsidy with its attendant "red tape."

The first post road to be completed, 14 miles of dirt road between Florence and Waterloo, Alabama, was opened to traffic in 1914. The program, after congressional extensions, dragged on for four more years. From the start, this program was burdensome, but it taught lessons about aid programs that proved valuable to the framers of the 1916 Federal-Aid Road Act. The most important of these recommendations was that federal aid should be dispensed only through the states, thereby avoiding the complexities of dealing with the nation's more than 3,000 counties.

The post road program of 1912 to 1918 was the first federal road policy which induced social change in the states by means of a public works program. Later legislation conditioned federal grants for roads upon compliance of the state with the maximum eight-hour per day law, the prohibition of convict labor, the use of hand labor methods, and numerous other requirements that were primarily social.

Early automobile trips across the continent inspired a growing interest in motorable long-distance roads. In 1912 Carl G. Fisher, builder of the Indianapolis Speedway, conceived the idea of building a "coast-to-coast rock highway" as a way to dramatize the need for interstate roads. The Lincoln Highway Association was formed to carry out the scheme and to collect public subscriptions to finance it. They selected the most direct route across the mid United States beginning at New York and proceeding by way of

Philadelphia, Chicago, Omaha, Cheyenne, and Salt Lake City to San Francisco, a total distance of about 3,150 miles. Funds were raised by donations to finance "seedling miles," short sections of a few miles improved with a good pavement, which were distributed throughout the length of the route as a means to educate the public regarding better roads.

The Lincoln Highway inspired arguments both for and against long-distance roads. The rural interests generally were against them, claiming that the nation would be drained of funds to build a few "peacock alleys" for the enjoyment of rich tourists. Urban spokesmen, however, argued that the country had been in bondage to the medieval English concept that roads were the responsibility of the smallest and weakest units of government, namely the road districts, townships, and counties. They also believed that the federal government should assume responsibility for "national routes."

The National Highways Association, a good roads promotion group, published a map showing a 50,000-mile system of national roads extending from coast to coast and from Canada to the Gulf, which it claimed should be the responsibility of the federal government to build and maintain. Such a system, its proponents stated, would not lay additional expense on the states and counties but, rather, would relieve them of the cost of maintaining their most heavily traveled roads, leaving more of the local funds to be spent on local roads.

These developments evolved into federal aid legislation for roads. The real questions before Congress were how much the aid should be and the form in which it should be granted. Extensive hearings were held and inquiries were sent to people throughout the country. Over 10,000 replies were received, 97 percent in favor of some form of federal aid. Various legislative proposals were considered, and finally, after being hammered out by the political process and establishing basic principles that have endured, the inevitable federal aid bill became law in July 1916.

As the nation adapted to the increasing numbers of automobiles on the roads, streets, and highways, problems changed; and the various entities of government became more involved in public works. While special interests were still important, their particular concerns increasingly became the interests of all. The evolution is exemplified in the federal aid highway program, in which the national concerns interacting with state and local interests, is well reflected by the development of the cooperative relationships.

It is not possible to cover all aspects of the highway program as they have evolved over the years. Only some of the most significant can be discussed here. The unique and highly successful federal-state relationship in the administration of the federal aid highway

U.S. Department of Transportation

A principal purpose of the 1916 Federal-Aid Road Act was to provide a national road system uninterrupted by state lines.

program and the well defined separate roles of the federal government and the states and their subdivisions are particularly important in the history of the nation's highways.

The 1916 Federal-Aid Road Act established the concept of a cooperative federal-state program and also prescribed the basic roles of each in administering the program. The federal government was to cooperate with the states and provide federal funding assistance through the respective state highway departments. On September 1, 1916, the secretary of agriculture issued "Rules and Regulations for Carrying Out the Federal-Aid Road Act." In them, he designated the Office of Public Roads and Rural Engineering, as it had then developed, as his representative in the administration of all sections of the act except Section 8, which applied to roads in national forests.

Before work could begin, however, many other problems had to be resolved in order to establish the new federal-state partnership. At that time, eleven states did not have highway departments that complied with the act, and the status of those in five others was doubtful. This meant that legislation creating acceptable highway departments was necessary in sixteen states, and some legislation was required in many others to fully meet the provisions of the law. Furthermore, all the states had to assent to the provisions of the act through their legislatures or temporarily through their governors. Fast action was taken, however, and by June 30, 1917, all states but one (Indiana was an exception until 1919) had highway departments that complied with the act and agreed to its requirements and terms.

The separate roles of the federal government and the states in carrying out the road programs were so clearly defined in the act that the basic principles were not only established but, with only minor refinements, have remained virtually intact. These basic principles were:

1. Participation of any state in the program was "permissive" not "mandatory."

2. If a state elected to participate, it must satisfy the requirements and comply with the provisions of the legislation and its implementing rules and regulations.

3. The authority and responsibility for initiation of proposed projects, their character, and method of construction were reserved to the states; federal fund participation was subject to compliance with the legislative rules and regulations.

4. The state highway department, or its equivalent, was required to represent the state in the administration of the program in cooperation with the federal government, as distinguished from the individual local governmental subdivisions.

5. The state highway department was responsible for the preparation of plans, specifications, and estimates (PS&E) with review and approval by the federal authority.

6. Upon approval of PS&E, the applicable federal funds were "obligated" and reserved for future payment to the state as progress payments for work completed.

7. The construction work in each state was to be done in accordance with its laws and under the direct supervision of the state highway department, subject to the inspection and approval of the federal authority.

8. Reimbursements to the states for the federal share of state construction progress payments could be made as work progressed, with full reimbursement upon federal approval of the completed project.

9. Proper maintenance of all roads constructed with participation of federal funds was the continuing responsibility of the states.

10. While not specifically stated in the 1916 legislation, it was clear that the states would retain full ownership of the roads constructed or improved with federal aid funds. The act did provide that they must remain free from tolls of all kinds.

Much had to be done at both the state and federal levels in order to implement the program. State legislation had to be enacted to satisfy administration, organization, maintenance, and federal aid matching requirements as well as to develop administrative and fiscal relationships with the states' local governmental subdivisions. At the federal level, the Office of Public Roads and Rural Engineering had to develop the implementing rules and regulations required by the act and formulate plans and organization for its role in administering the program, both in Washington, D.C., and at the field level in all the states.

Project costs eligible for federal participation were those directly involved in construction as defined in an agreement, and did not include design and specification, administrative, right-of-way, and related costs. The work had to be publicly advertised, and federal participation was limited to the costs established by the lowest bidder.

The first section of road completed under the 1916 act was a 2.6-mile project in Contra Costa County, California. The work consisted of grading the roadbed, installing culverts, laying a portland cement concrete base 20 feet wide and 5 inches thick, and surfacing it with a 1$^1/_2$-inch bituminous concrete pavement. The cost of construction was approximately $21,000 a mile.

Implementation of the 1916 act had just started when the United States entered World War I. The war curtailed road construction and limited it primarily to those roads needed for military purposes or war industry. The war effort put great demands on the country's railroad system. Serious railroad car shortages and congestion at freight depots developed. Despite the work of the specially created Railroad War Board, the freight problems increased to a point of creeping paralysis in railroad transportation by the fall of 1917. Coal shipments, normally carried by ships from Chesapeake Bay ports to New England, were shifted to rail, creating new burdens. Railroad beds deteriorated as maintenance workmen changed to war industries. Because of difficulties in getting long-haul freight into cities, railroads refused to accept short-haul shipments such as milk and farm produce. Out of these problems, the trucking industry was born.

In 1917 there were 391,000 motor trucks in the nation, most of them used in the cities for drayage and deliveries. A few trucks were on farms; and with the railroad problems, farmers began to drive them directly into the cities instead of only to railroad stations. Merchants in the cities began to send their trucks out into the country for loads of produce. Because of congestion at city railroad terminals, some consignees had their shipments taken to outlying towns and sent their trucks there to receive them, at the same time carrying outgoing shipments. Soon hundreds of trucks were being used and constantly increasing the radius of operation.

This added truck travel soon began to break up the roads. Although many of the roads were bituminous macadam, they generally were light, seldom more than 6 or 7 inches thick, and 14 to 17 feet wide. At that time, all trucks ran on solid rubber tires. There were no laws against overloading, and many were loaded to the full capacity of their engines.

Single, light trucks expanded into fleets with heavier units which, in turn, developed into long trains. Roads satisfactory for horse-drawn vehicle traffic with loads of three tons or less, traveling at four miles an hour, soon had to carry heavy motor trucks with loads of eight to twelve tons, thundering along at twenty miles an hour. This tremendous roadbed burden reached its peak during the spring thaw of 1918 and the results were critical. As an example, the passing of a single truck convoy reduced the Philadelphia Pike in Delaware from a good bituminous macadam road to a rutted quagmire. All across the country, supposedly high-quality roads of brick on concrete bases or bituminous concrete on macadam bases, warped and crumbled. A lack of railroad cars to haul repair gravel and paving materials intensified the problem. By the end of the war, thousands of miles of roads were barely passable.

There were 605,000 non-military trucks on the roads by the end of 1918. Even with fuel restrictions and the generally poor conditions of the roads, trucking for hire thrived, unencumbered by government regulation and charged by tough competition. The time saved in short hauls, door-to-door delivery, and reduced boxing and crating costs brought trucking more into favor. The result was a turning point in highway design to meet the need for heavier and more scientifically constructed pavements.

The wartime experience with truck damage to roads, resulted in development of sound policies for future improvements. Some wanted to ban heavy trucks from using the roads; others campaigned to have roads built heavy enough to carry the truck loads. Out of the discussions came cooperative efforts that have since continued. The roadbuilders and the truck manufacturers agreed on a truck capacity of 7¹/₂ tons for future production.

By 1917 a considerable number of the 43,565 rural mail routes were motorized. Some experimental routes were used to deliver farm products, such as fresh vegetables, by mail, and serious consideration was given to extending this service on a large scale. But when the war ended, the proposal failed to get necessary continuing support. Still, the problem of improving rural roads continued. The farmers were primarily concerned with getting out of the mud on the farm-to-market routes. Demands for connecting routes between towns, especially in the more populous East, conflicted with the farm-to-market concepts. The 1916 federal aid act failed to establish an accepted system of roads on which to apply federal funds. The question was whether to continue to expand the radius of the farm-to-market roads or to concentrate on the trunk through-roads.

The apportionment formula for determining the amount of federal funds to each state was based one third on miles of rural post roads, one third on population, and one third on area, each as related to the national total. However, the initial legislation did not require a designated state highway system. Recognizing the need for such a system, the secretary of agriculture required the states to submit proposed programs for the five years of the original authorizations and to file a "tentative" system in which improvements would be made. This gave additional impetus to sound highway system planning. The national need for a connected system of highways also was clear. Since such a system would accommodate most of the through traffic, the concept of the highway users paying for the improvements grew. Oregon in 1919 became the first state to enact a gasoline tax and provide income to be used for highway purposes. This practice quickly received widespread acceptance. Local roads serving primarily farms were considered the responsibility of the

Virginia Department of Highways

This principal rural road in northern Virginia in 1919 was similar to many at the close of World War I.

property owners and were financed largely from real estate taxes.

Congress accelerated the highway program at the end of the war, both because of the deteriorated condition of roads and concern over the unemployment that would result from demobilization of the armed forces and war industry. The 1920 Post Office Appropriation Act included $200 million for additional federal aid under the 1916 Federal-Aid Road Act. Further, it transferred most suitable surplus war materials and equipment to the secretary of agriculture to be distributed to the state highway departments for use on federal aid roads. The value of the surplus materials turned over to the states totaled $139 million when the distribution was essentially completed in July 1922. This transfer of surplus war equipment played a major role in postwar construction which began the national network of highways. Many states were able to continue construction and maintenance at that difficult time only because of this equipment.

The appropriations under the 1916 act, as amended, only extended through fiscal year 1921. Consequently, the Congress in 1921 had to decide whether to continue the program and, if so, in what manner. During the hearings on the proposed legislation, there was considerable debate as to whether the federal government should construct a system of national highways directly or continue with the federal-state cooperative plan.

There were also differences of opinion as to the classes of roads to be built with federal aid funds. One position was that federal funds should be used only for principal highways which would serve as main lines and which would connect with county and local roads. The other position was that the local roads, tying the farmer to his market, were the most important to the welfare of the country and that those should be built before the interstate roads, which would be used mostly by tourists.

Both issues were decided in the 1921 act. It reaffirmed the federal aid concept in a federal-state cooperative program. The "character of road" issue was resolved by a new requirement—that federal aid funds should be expended only upon a system of main connecting interstate (primary) and intercounty rural (secondary) roads, limited to 7 percent of a state's total road mileage, to be selected by the state. The 7 percent would limit the system to a mileage which could be constructed in a reasonable period of time and would provide a basic network. Not more than three sevenths of the designated mileage could be primary nor interstate in character. Thus, a balanced program was assured.

Another important provision of the act gave particular emphasis to the need for state highway departments to have adequate powers and be suitably equipped and organized for discharging their duties. The responsibility of the states for continuing adequate maintenance of roads constructed under the act was also strengthened. The secretary of agriculture was authorized to appropriately maintain any federal aid road if a state failed to do so, charging the costs of such work against the federal funds allotted to that state.

Two other fundamental provisions were included: (1) the requirement for state matching funds was liberalized by increasing the 50 percent federal share of project costs on a sliding scale in the states having large public land areas; and (2) a requirement was added that before any project could be approved, a state must make provisions for the state funds required each year by the act for construction and needed for maintenance of all federal aid highways within the state. Such funds were to be under the direct control of the state highway department.

In its entirety, the 1921 Federal Aid Act, while an amendment of the 1916 act, further formalized the basic principles, policies, procedures, and controls that would make possible the nation's successful highway program over the next several decades. Numerous legislative refinements have been made, yet the basic principles of the 1916 and the 1921 acts have remained essentially intact.

While Congress must be given credit for the federal aid highway programs, the state highway departments, highway industries, highway associations, and the Office of Public Roads also played important roles. Among all major federal assistance programs, the federal aid highway program has been most successful in its effectiveness, efficiency, and cooperative administration by the federal government and the states.

The initial work of Director Page, who died suddenly in December 1918, was strongly supported and advanced by his successor, Thomas H. MacDonald, who left the position of chief engineer of the Iowa State Highway Commission to accept the appointment as director in May 1919. In July the organization's name was changed to the Bureau of Public Roads. MacDonald provided strong leadership for the early development and continuing success of the cooperative federal-state relationship. He retained the position as head of the Bureau of Public Roads until his retirement in 1953 and deserves great credit for his contributions to America's highway system.

The framers of the 1916 and 1921 acts believed that the key to a successful federal-state relationship was interaction and cooperation of the federal government with the states founded on mutual respect. An appropriate vehicle for this was the American Association of State Highway Officials (AASHO) which, since its founding in 1914, had established itself as an effective organization for highway planning, design, construction, and administrative improvements.

The Bureau of Public Roads and its successor agency, the Federal Highway Administration, has been a "member department" of AASHO since 1919 and was a full member of the executive committee until

1953, when the revised AASHO constitution provided for the federal highway administrator to serve as an ex officio member of the committee. The principal interaction between AASHO and the bureau was in the areas of proposed legislation; interpretation of the effects of proposed or new legislation on the states; plans for implementation of legislation; necessary changes in policies, regulations, and procedures to meet new requirements; continual cooperative review and support of AASHO committees in resolving problems; the content and plans for the annual national and regional AASHO meetings; joint consideration of relationships with the many other national associations involved in the highway program; and other subjects of mutual interest that are not practical for direct handling with an individual state.

The separate roles of the states and the federal government in the project procedures established in 1916 and amended in 1921 set the basic pattern for the cooperative administration of the program. Some of the more important efforts and actions taken together included development of standard construction specifications and format; standards for uniform methods of sampling, testing, and reporting on road materials; minimum design standards for various classes of roads and structures; standard forms, such as bid forms including required general provisions, construction contract forms, performance and payment bonds, contractor qualification forms, and project agreement forms; and standards for highway numbering, signing, traffic controls, and highway markings.

The AASHO-bureau partnership has not always been "honey and roses." There were areas of disagreement as to what is necessary or desirable in complying with legislation, especially as new and complex provisions were passed. There problems were quite often the result of provisions in other legislation that interacted and sometimes infringed upon the highway program. In recent years, these problems have become more frequent and troublesome because of the increasing complexity of program impacts, the greater effectiveness of special interest groups, and the evolution of complex social values of public concern.

In order to carry out the broader requirements of the entire transportation program, AASHO officially changed its name to the American Association of State Highway and Transportation Officials (AASHTO) in November 1973. The association now represents all forms of transportation.

The Transition Years

With the assurance of a continuing federal aid program following the 1921 act, road improvements moved into high gear. State highway departments were developing more effective organizations and procedures as was the construction industry. During fiscal year 1922, 10,247 miles of road construction were completed at a cost of $190 million, three and a half times as much as had been completed since the beginning of the federal aid program. Commissioner MacDonald stated:

> But merely to say that this year has added 10,000 miles to the previously existing mileage conveys no adequate sense of the far-reaching effects of the work that is being done. The 10,000 miles completed represent something more than the equivalent of three transcontinental roads. They are not transcontinental roads. They are not even connected roads, though as the work continues they will be connected; but each separate project is to some community a new opportunity, a means of bettering in some respects, the economic and social status of the community, and together they form the new means of transportation, no less important to the country as a whole than that offered by the railroads.

About two thirds of the mileage was low type, such as graded earth, sand-clay, and gravel. This was in keeping with the stage construction policy which provided that roads first be pushed through and connections made; the refinements would come later as traffic increased. Most of the stage construction was in the sparsely settled South and West. The East concentrated on improving the roadbeds and pavements which had been severely damaged by wartime traffic.

By 1929 the states had improved about 80,000 miles on the federal aid system and an additional 57,000 miles on the state systems, financed wholly by state funds. During that period, motor vehicles had increased to nearly 27 million, two and a half times the number in 1921, and road user taxes had increased six times to over $763 million per year. The portion of the highway costs carried by road users had risen to 96 percent.

The number of horses and mules in the nation peaked at 26 million in 1918, and by 1929 the number was decreasing rapidly. Stage construction of roads was the best solution for the transition from horse-drawn to all motor vehicles, although few, if any, foresaw the great increase in motor traffic which actually did occur. In the years following, the nation's highway system, designed and built for horse-drawn vehicles with comparatively light loads, was transformed into the generally efficient, high-speed, automobile, truck, and bus highway system of 1976, carrying on the main routes as many as 225,000 vehicles per day. The transition has required strong public support along with the combined abilities of public works engineers and officials at all levels of government.

As road use increased, one of the big difficulties was to determine the number and kinds of traffic that should be provided for in the design of streets and highways and the overall highway and street system that should be developed. Good data on which to base these designs were generally not available, although some information had been assembled. For instance, Maryland made the first statewide traffic census in 1904. Illinois made one in 1906, and Massachusetts and New York in 1909. Census methods varied, and compared to today's sophisticated analysis, they were rather primitive. They included counting the number of vehicles, classifying them as to passenger cars or trucks of various sizes to aid in road design, and recording the state of registration to estimate lengths of trips and the proportion of interstate travel. The findings of these surveys and others similar in nature supported early economic studies and decisions leading to the development of the federal aid highway system.

The need for more accurate information resulted in the 1934 Federal Aid Highway Act providing for data collection in these terms: "With the approval of the secretary of agriculture, not to exceed 1½ per centum of the amount apportioned for any year to any state . . . may be used for surveys, plans, and engineering investigations of projects for future construction in such state, either on the federal-aid highway system and extensions thereof or on secondary or feeder roads." This is the basic and still controlling legislation that authorizes the ongoing highway planning process. The percentage figure has remained the same, but the "may" has changed to "shall," and the provision "with or without State matching," has been added. The funds have been used for the broad planning process so necessary for an effective program.

In 1934 and 1935, Herbert S. Fairbank, the Bureau of Public Roads' deputy commissioner for research, began "planning for planning." Fairbank was indeed the father of highway planning. He sketched out the data collection and analytical processes, and he wrote and spoke strongly on the necessity of planning and its use in policy, administrative, and engineering decisions. Early work undertaken for collection and analysis of data to be used in planning included highway surveys of three broad types—road inventory, traffic, and financial and road use.

The inventory phase involved driving over every mile of rural highway and recording its width, type, condition, and adjacent cultural features. The information was recorded on inch-to-the-mile county maps and the data tabulated in a variety of ways for analytical use. The traffic surveys counted and categorized traffic. The data was recorded on appropriate maps and tabulated for various uses. Coupled with the road inventory data, they showed the adequacy of existing roads to provide for the movement of traffic and to serve the needs of rural lands. Cost estimates of bringing road conditions up to a suitable standard could then be determined. The third general area involved the recording of expenditures and revenues for highways and all other purposes from all units of government, including special districts, to ascertain the degree to which user and other taxes were being applied to road purposes. In

1934 there was little information available upon which to estimate the propriety of highway financing. In addition, the financial survey consisted of studies which determined the use made of the roads in different systems. Also included in the financial surveys were road life studies, which permitted estimates of the physical life of roads making up the highway system.

The planning surveys required a great deal of manpower. In Ohio, for example, over 600 men were in the field within two months after the work got underway. Nationwide, at least 15,000 men, almost all from the relief rolls or the ranks of the unemployed, were given employment. Apart from the benefits of the planning surveys to highway administration, the work was a constructive expenditure of work relief funds during the Depression. In the years after 1934, the provision of federal aid funds for surveys, planning, and engineering investigations was broadened to include highway research, safety and other studies, and statewide highway planning surveys.

By using highway work, including highway planning, as one of the "make work" projects of the Depression years, the National Recovery Act brought employment opportunities close to the homes of the unemployed. Moreover, it was estimated that for every person directly employed on road work, there were at least two others working in the manufacture and transportation of road materials and equipment.

The requirements for state matching funds for the federal aid highway programs were temporarily lifted because of the Depression. This allowed roadbuilding to continue on a reduced scale, even with depleted state revenues. Also during the Depression, for the first time, federal aid funds were made available for extensions of the federal aid system into and through municipalities and for secondary feeder roads. Special funds were provided for the elimination of hazardous railroad grade crossings. In 1936 special "Works Program Highway" funds were made available as part of the Works Progress Administration program.

In July 1939 the Bureau of Public Roads was moved from the Department of Agriculture to the Federal Works Administration and renamed the Public Roads Administration. In 1949 it was transferred to the Department of Commerce and renamed the Bureau of Public Roads, where it remained until the Department of Transportation was established in 1966. It then became the Federal Highway Administration of that department.

The 1940 Federal Highway Act authorized the last apportionments for the regular federal aid highway program until the end of World War II. The next federal aid act was entitled the 1941 Defense Highway Act. It was approved on November 19, 1941, less than three weeks before Pearl Harbor, and it placed the road program on a war footing.

The effect of war on highway construction was felt in two principal ways: first, in revising the highway programs to concentrate on improvements important to the war effort; and second, to carry on the restructured program in the face of material shortages, loss of key personnel to military services and war industries, and reduced road user revenues. Congress authorized 75 percent, instead of the normal 50 percent, participation in projects on a designated strategic highway network and provided the full cost of access roads to military establishments and essential industrial plants. Close working relationships were maintained with agencies responsible for allocating critical materials in order to gain authorizations for supplies needed for the most essential projects.

An amendment to the Defense Highway Act, approved July 13, 1943, permitted the states to use any funds still remaining from the apportionment under the 1940 Federal Highway Act, not only for the "engineering and economic investigations" authorized in 1934 but also for the preparation of plans, specifications, and estimates. The purpose was to keep the collection of essential data going and to provide a reservoir of "plans on the shelf" to permit the immediate start of highway construction once the emergency ended.

All non-critical highway work was deferred during the war, and the use of critical materials was reduced to a minimum. New construction was mostly on access roads to military installations, defense plants, ports, and similar defense needs, thereby leaving many miles of highways, already worn and obsolete and scheduled for replacement, to carry the streams of war traffic. Routine surface maintenance, resurfacing, and resealing

Michigan State Highway Department

Traffic congestion in cities, such as this avenue in Detroit in 1940, resulted in a 1944 act allocating 25 percent of federal aid funds specifically for urban areas.

were intensified to protect the existing highways and keep them usable.

The 1944 Federal Aid Highway Act greatly expanded the highway program in several ways: (1) it authorized a $1.5 billion apportionment for a three-year period beginning at the termination of the war emergency; (2) it authorized funds specifically for the federal aid highway system in urban areas, which consisted of the connections into and through the urban areas on the existing federal aid systems; (3) it required the selection of a federal aid secondary system, to which secondary funds were limited; (4) it divided the funds as follows: 45 percent for the federal aid system (the primary system) to be expended on rural or urban portions at the state's election; 30 percent for the new secondary system; and 25 percent specifically for the routes in urban areas (this 45:30:25 ratio prevailed until 1973); (5) it authorized the designation of the National System of Inter-

state Highways "so located as to connect by routes, as direct as practicable, the principal metropolitan areas, cities, and industrial centers, to serve the national defense, and to connect at suitable border points with routes of continental importance in the Dominion of Canada and the Republic of Mexico . . ."; (6) it provided that on any highway or street thereafter constructed with federal aid "the location, form, and character of informational, regulatory, and warning signs, curb and pavement or other markings, and traffic signals installed or placed by any public authority or other agency, shall be subject to the approval of the state highway department with the concurrence of the public roads administration . . ."; and (7) it added to the authorization of the 1.5 percent highway planning funds the words "and for highway research necessary in connection therewith" to encourage specific research in the areas of economics and administration.

Postwar high prices and shortages of equipment and materials retarded construction progress throughout 1946. Considerable momentum was gained in 1947, and the volume of construction work on highways carried on in 1948 and 1949 taxed the facilities and resources of highway organizations. In 1950 legislation required that the states hold local public hearings with respect to any proposed project that would bypass any city or town.

Legislation enacted in 1954 permitted a major change in the basic federal-state roles through the initiation of "The Secondary Road Plan." Under the plan, any state could discharge most of its engineering and administrative review and approval responsibilities for secondary road system projects by making a "certification" that the projects had been designed and constructed in accordance with state standards and procedures which had been approved by the Bureau of Public Roads. Following World War II, there had been a concerted effort on the part of local agencies to improve local roads and streets, to which most states provided strong support. Engineering capabilities were strengthened through the activities of organizations such as the National Association of County Engineers and the

American Public Works Association. Designs and testing standards fitted to local roads and streets were established. Some states legislated a portion of the state gas tax directly to the counties and cities for use in local roadways. This made the federal "Secondary Road Plan" possible. It supported local road and street agencies, gave the states more independent responsibility, and permitted bureau staff to devote their principal efforts to the primary system.

Evolving Highway Standards

A great obstacle in adjusting the streets and highways to the automobile age was scarcity of basic information on how highways should be developed to meet economic and social needs and how they should be designed and constructed to withstand the increasing volume and weight of traffic. The initial efforts of the federal government were directed to providing information and demonstration of good practices. By 1912 a small nucleus of highway engineers, chemists, and research scientists was at work on experimental and demonstration roads in various parts of the country. Their main objective was to improve materials and methods of construction and the dissemination of information. In 1916 a survey showed that less than half of the states had adequate facilities for testing materials, and some had no facilities at all.

In 1917 a conference of the testing engineers and chemists from the highway departments was held to further cooperative efforts in meeting research needs and promoting the establishment of properly equipped highway laboratories in every state. Later that year, AASHO activated its committee on tests and investigations, with Thomas R. Agg, testing engineer of the Iowa State Highway Commission, as chairman.

A program was underway early in 1919 with the backing and support of the bureau and AASHO. The engineering division of the National Research Council began planning a national program of highway research and on October 31, 1919 created a Highway Research Committee "to coordinate and assist the highway research work now being conducted by the United States Bureau of Public Roads, by the state highway departments, by manufacturers, research departments and commercial laboratories." Dean Anson Marston, of the Iowa State College Division of Engineering, the chairman of the committee, wrote that: "The National Research Council merely fulfills the function for which it was organized by the United States Government, that of taking the initiative and of coordinating the work of all investigators, so that they will not cross each other's field, and so that the whole field will be covered adequately."

Over a year of deliberation and review followed. Public works officials, educators, and researchers had a vital stake and a common urgent interest in the total effort. Their work culminated in establishment of the Highway Research Board (initially called the National Advisory Board on Highway Research) in November 1920. The bureau took the lead by expanding its research activities and by cooperative research agreements with highway departments and universities.

Among the research programs instigated were the investigation and measurement of traffic, design of highway and street systems, driver behavior, properties of soil and pavement materials, geometric design, structural design of highways, maintenance and construction methods, highway finance, engineering economy, and comprehensive transportation economics. As rapidly as findings were made and verified, they were published in *Public Roads,* the research journal of the bureau, or in the proceedings of the Highway Research Board and the bulletins of a number of universities. These publications charted the course of the emerging discipline of highway engineering and then the full scope of transportation systems engineering.

The Highway Research Board (renamed the Transportation Research Board in 1974) included full representation of engineers, scientists, and researchers from all levels of government in the public works field, private organizations and industry, and educational institutions. The yearly conferences held in Washington, D.C., attract thousands of registrants. Since 1960 the board has administered a national research program supported by all the states. The projects and policies were determined by the states and the bureau and provided a yearly research program of several million dollars.

An area of vital concern, and a major factor in cost, is that of achieving the optimum pavement design to fit traffic conditions. Early in highway development, engineers recognized that the supporting ability required of a road pavement structure was determined principally by the axle loads of the vehicles it carried and their frequency of occurrence. More factual information on pavement and soil elements was necessary for determining just how good a road should be to service the traffic that uses it, and how best to meet the overall needs within the limitations of available funds. Between 1923 and 1930, several research projects, using specially constructed test tracks and roads, produced significant advances in the science of pavement design and construction. One such effort was the Bates Experimental Road, a test conducted by the Illinois Division of Highways in 1922 and 1923 near Springfield, Illinois. Trucks with solid rubber tires on which wheel loads were increased from 2,500 to 13,000 pounds were run on a 2.5-mile roadway divided into sixty-eight test sections of varied materials and design. The results clearly showed that the pavement structure should be designed in relation to the expected axle loads. Knowledge of this relation soon led to the adoption of laws regulating vehicle weights.

The need for large-scale highway research on controlled axle loadings became more apparent in the years following World War II. The National Governor's Conference in 1949 set up committees to address the need for uniformity among states in the motor vehicle and weight limitations. A rigid (portland cement concrete) pavement test road was established in Maryland, with participation by twelve state highway departments, the Bureau of Public Roads, auto manufacturers, and the petroleum industry. The purpose of the testing program was to determine the relative effects of various axle loads and configurations on distress of rigid pavement. The findings were utilized in future design and material developments. The Western Associa-

tion of State Highway Officials constructed a test road in Idaho in 1951 to determine load limits and to develop rational design methods for flexible (asphalt) pavements. A number of specially designed and constructed flexible pavements were carefully observed under the repeated application of selected heavy axle loads. The findings provided significant information on the materials and soil parameters for designing flexible pavements, especially in western states having conditions similar to those of the test road site.

In 1955 AASHO, with the support of the bureau, undertook a road test on a section of the Interstate Highway near Ottawa, Illinois. Various heavy truck loads were operated on specially constructed pavement sections of both rigid and flexible types. The Highway Research Board administered the project and a vast amount of data was collected and analyzed, providing engineering facts for highway design and construction nationwide. The test findings were aimed at determining maximum desirable weights of vehicles to be operated on federal aid highways, including the Interstate System. In addition, they helped determine an equitable distribution of the tax burden among various classes of vehicles using federal aid highways.

Other areas needing study and research were similarly investigated. The sophistication in traffic and transportation systems studies of the 1970s is a result of these programs. For instance, the Chicago Area Transportation Study was initiated in 1954, building upon an earlier Detroit study; and it became the first of the new generation of transportation planning procedures. Active work is going forward in the study of the complex problems associated with the task of providing optimum intermodal transportation in urban areas of the 1970s.

An area where research has been especially fruitful is that of the relationship of hydraulics to highway structures. While bridges and culverts have been used for centuries to cross streams and rivers, the advancement of design, materials, and methods of construction has been slow. Except for very large bridges over major rivers, little attention was given to the hydraulics of the designs, until the advent of the automobile and accelerated highway construction programs made drainage and water problems more critical. Washouts and flooded roadways were less tolerable, and paved surfaces required good drainage to prevent pavement failure.

For a long time, the designs were based on judgment without well-developed engineering technology. It was common to size drainage structures, including bridges, using a formula developed in the late nineteenth century by Arthur N. Talbot of the University of Illinois. The lack of flood runoff data and of information on highway structure hydraulics made development of design procedures difficult. Research on the hydraulics of highway structures and the collection of runoff data began during the 1920s. Culvert and bridge waterway hydraulics were initially investigated at the University of Iowa. In the 1940s, the Soil Conservation Service of the Department of Agriculture began establishing experimental watershed stations to study rainfall-runoff relationships.

The lack of stream flow data, especially on small watersheds and in urban areas, hampered the development of flood estimating procedures. Cooperative programs to collect flood data and prepare analyses were initiated by state highway departments, the Bureau of Public Roads, and the United States Geological Survey. During the two decades after World War II, this program accelerated and in the early 1970s reached an expenditure of about $1 million annually.

An extensive program of research on the hydraulics of culverts, bridges, and storm sewers was undertaken in the 1950s and 1960s, largely through the bureau's contracts with various universities and federal agencies, with some participation in funding by several state highway departments. A number of reports and design manuals were published recording the results of this research and providing practical methods for highway drainage design.

Good highway design results from anticipating the roadway requirements of motor vehicular traffic and satisfying these requirements in the construction plans. It involves the selection of dimensional values for geometric features such as widths, radii of curvature, rates of cross section slopes and longitudinal gradients; determination of requirements for the pavement and base course, roadway structure, and for bridges, drainage and other structures; preservation and restoration of ground cover plant growths; safety and efficiency of traffic operations, including all forms of traffic control devices; and melding of the highway's alignment and gradient with the landscape in a manner least disturbing to the natural environment. Engineering analyses must attain an acceptable balance between the broad controls of economic limitations, land use, and environmental and social considerations.

Early in this century, many of the newly organized state highway departments drew up their own versions of highway and street cross sections and other dimensional and structural controls. Broadly, these engineering and design features became known as "design standards," the expansion and refinement of which has continued into present practice.

Design standards generally provided norms from which engineering analyses could begin in developing details for specific highways. As highway design and operational experience progressed during recent decades, some individual items among these standards have become fixed (such as a 12-foot lane for main roads), but collectively they constitute basic guides rather than strict standards. In some cases, both "minimum" and "desirable" values were enumerated in the design standards to give broader guidance.

In 1937 the Bureau of Public Roads and the state highway departments established a small working committee to bring the available information on highway design up to date, to develop new data based on research and experience, and to present them in usable form. By 1944 the committee had developed individual design policy brochures on most basic highway design elements. In 1950 the brochures were reprinted in a single volume entitled *Policies on Geometric Highway Design*. A complete reworking into a single cohesive volume was issued in 1954 under the title *A Policy on Geometric Design of*

Rural Highways. This was commonly known as the "blue book" and received wide acceptance both in the United States and abroad. An updated version was prepared and printed in 1965. A similar "red book," entitled *A Policy on Arterial Highways in Urban Areas,* has become the accepted authority on urban design of highways financed with federal aid.

The committee developed other AASHO policies, reports, or guides which were separately published. By 1974 there were eighteen AASHO guide publications, each of which serves to provide needed national administrative design policy guidance. The subject areas include such elements as roadway lighting, bicycle routes, safety rest areas, accommodating utilities on highway rights-of-way, U-turn median openings, and private driveways to major highways. These elements are known as geometric design policy. All are based on research and experience data and significantly influence the design of modern highways.

The cloverleaf interchange structure permits free-flowing traffic between two major divided traffic-lane routes.

Special design standards were developed by AASHO and the bureau for the Interstate system and adopted in 1956. The major items included: control of access throughout the system; design adequacy for projected 1975 traffic; 12-foot travel lane width; 10-foot minimum shoulder width; elimination of railroad grade crossings; elimination of highway at-grade intersections; design speeds of fifty, sixty, and seventy miles per hour respectively for mountainous, rolling, or flat terrain conditions; curvatures and gradients consistent with design speeds; separated traffic lanes with variable median widths on a right-

of-way adequate in width to accommodate these standards; and minimum widths for highway bridges. All standards were formulated as minimum rather than fixed levels, with the expectation that minimum levels would be used only where higher ones would result in excessive cost.

The 1956 geometric standards were found to be inadequate to meet realistic needs for future traffic service. The statutory design year of 1975 was changed by Congress in the 1963 Highway Amendments Act to provide for traffic service adequate for a twenty-year period from the date of plan approval for the initial construction of the project. And a 1966 congressional amendment required "such standards shall in all cases provide for at least four lanes of traffic."

Reasonable uniformity prescribed through minimum standards was appropriate for geometric requirements of the Interstate as these features directly affect drivers and are the features they see. In contrast, characteristics which govern load carrying capacity and durability are hidden from the drivers' eyes. Moreover, structural design of a roadway is necessarily largely guided by localized physical conditions, availability of materials, and local experience and practice. Consequently, structural design standards provide only that the design be adequate to support anticipated traffic loads and be soundly determined.

Cities developed various standards to meet their specific needs, although not with the coordinated national attention that characterized the more rural-oriented federal aid program. The inclusion of the state primary and secondary routes through urban areas, as a result of the 1944 legislation, provided for more concerted attention on these routes and the adoption of standards that have been helpful, primarily in moving traffic.

Cities often have been forced to conform to street rights-of-way established long before the full impact of automobile usage was realized or even contemplated. This constraint, along with a strong desire for autonomous action by local authorities, limited funds and engineering personnel, and emphasis on short-range programs of city administrations had curtailed research into street design problems at the municipal level. Studies made in the 1950s by the Bureau of Public Roads on ways to increase capacity and safety of city streets resulted in the national Traffic Operations Program to Increase Capacity and Safety (TOPICS). This helped focus increased attention on the complex problems of streets in urban areas. It clearly revealed the diversity of public and private interests involved and affected by the design of streets to serve the people living and working in an urban environment.

Much has been and is being done to develop and improve standards for city streets. Systematic road life and performance studies have been underway in many cities for over thirty years, resulting in improved standards. In 1968 the American Public Works Association, through its Institute for Municipal Engineering, made a national survey and prepared recommendations on urban arterial street design standards. While the AASHO-developed standards have used urban studies and are valuable and satisfactory in many cases, municipal public works engineers feel that they must be modified and adapted to better fit the specific needs of urban situations.

The comprehensive transportation planning programs in urban areas, required by federal legislation since 1965, are bringing many specific problems into focus. Resolving these problems through further research, and effectively utilizing other modes of transportation in conjunction with present street systems, will help provide optimum mobility in urban communities.

Revival of Toll Roads

Heavy traffic demands coupled with inadequate highway funds led to a resurgence of construction of toll roads, or modern turnpikes, starting with the Pennsylvania Turnpike in the 1930s and reaching a peak in the late 1950s. These roads were high-standard, controlled access, high-speed highways. They were planned and built by special state authorities, utilizing private engineering firms for design and construction supervision, and financed from the sale of bonds to be amortized from the toll revenues. Such revenues are usually not available for general highway purposes, but they are pledged to the operating and capital costs of the specific road or bridge on which they are levied.

The Pennsylvania Turnpike, a 159-mile toll road between Harrisburg and Pittsburgh, constructed upon a partially built but abandoned railroad grade, opened just before World War II and proved to be a great boon to military convoy and general truck movement during the war period. The increase of traffic at the close of the war brought ample revenues, and this success gave widespread attention to toll roads in other states as a means of meeting traffic needs. When the New Jersey Turnpike opened its initial 120-mile length in 1952, it was immediately financially successful; and toll road construction quickly expanded to other states. Many of the toll roads, such as the New York Thruway and the Ohio Turnpike, were construction epics and demonstrated the effective capabilities of the private consulting engineering firms and the construction industry.

In the 1954 Federal Aid Highway Act, Congress authorized the secretary of commerce "to make . . . a study of the costs of completing the several systems of highways in the several states and of the progress and feasibility of toll roads with particular attention to the possible effects of such toll roads upon the federal aid highway programs . . . ." Data gathered during the ensuing study were analyzed to determine the characteristics of the traffic using the toll roads. Investigators analyzed the origins and destinations of trips, their purposes, the time and distances involved in the use of toll roads in comparison with alternate free routes, the tolls paid, and the proportions of travel on the existing roads that were diverted to the toll route. Information developed from these analyses was used in making toll road feasibility projections. All sections of the Interstate system and other routes believed to have toll potential were considered. Estimates were made of the probable use of toll roads and the revenue the traffic would produce as compared to the costs of maintaining, operating, and amortizing the investment in toll facilities.

It was concluded that it was economically feasible to finance the building of 6,700 miles of highway by the use of tolls. All but 200 miles were on the route of the 1944 established Interstate system. At the time of the study, 1,240 miles of toll road were open, 1,380 miles were under construction, 3,315 miles had been authorized for construction as toll facilities, and 2,250 proposed, exceeding somewhat the mileage estimated to be feasible by the study. A policy decision was made not to recommend any change in the 1921 federal aid requirement that "all highways constructed or reconstructed under the provisions of this act shall be free of tolls of all kinds." However, the study did recommend the inclusion of existing toll roads in the Interstate system, provided that adequate roads were available on another federal aid system which allowed for continuous travel without traversing the toll sections.

Most of the present turnpikes have been built as self-supporting facilities. That is, their cost has been met from the proceeds of bond issues to be amortized from toll revenues. In some cases, however, the states have pledged other revenues, such as road user taxes, to supplement tolls in order to assure solvency of the projects.

The toll road has proven popular in corridors of heavy travel because it provides a self-supporting highway facility relatively quickly, the costs are defrayed solely by those who use the facility, and it is financed outside of the state's usual highway budget without draining current highway revenues. The objection, of course, is the increased cost to the highway user. In 1973 there were about 4,100 miles of toll roads operating in twenty-three states. Another 1,400 miles were under active consideration as future toll roads.

The Interstate Highway System

The origin of the present Interstate Highway System was the report *Toll Roads and Free Roads* prepared by the Bureau of Public Roads in cooperation with the state highway departments and presented to Congress in 1939. Before then a few scattered parkways and urban arterials had demonstrated the virtues of controlled access highways with grade-separated interchanges. There had been some early visions of a transcontinental network of superhighways, usually bypassing all cities and serving only those that wanted to make long automobile trips. The Futurama exhibit at the New York World's Fair in 1939-1940, depicting controlled access highways, received wide public attention and increased support for a free-flowing superhighway system.

President Roosevelt appointed a National Interregional Highway Committee in 1941 to pursue the report's recommendation of a

Twenty-three hundred miles of toll roads, such as this section of the Massachusetts Turnpike completed in the 1950s, were made a part of the National System of Interstate Highways.

26,700-mile, non-toll, interregional network with the federal government sharing the construction cost at more than the traditional 50 percent federal aid rate. Commissioner MacDonald of the bureau was appointed chairman of the committee, and the resources and assistance of federal and state highway organizations were made available to it. Then in 1943, in the midst of World War II, Congress requested the Bureau of Public Roads to make a study of the need for a nationwide expressway system. The committee and the agency cooperated, with the help of state highway departments, and prepared a single report, *Interregional Highways,* which was presented to Congress in 1944.

This report considered systems of several sizes, testing each by a variety of criteria, and recommended as optimum a rural network of 33,900 miles, plus an additional 5,000 miles of auxiliary urban routes, bringing the total proposed system to about 39,000 miles. It suggested a postwar expenditure for construction of the system at $750 million a year, two thirds to be spent on the urban sections.

Congress utilized the 1939 and 1944 reports when it enacted the 1944 Federal Aid Highway Act, which directed the designation of a National System of Interstate Highways limited to 40,000 miles. Considerable study and discussion followed with important input from the United States Army. Selection of the general locations for the main routes of the Interstate system was announced on August 2, 1947. They totaled 37,700 miles, including 2,900 in urban areas. The remaining mileage within the 40,000-mile limit was reserved for auxiliary urban routes.

Congress had authorized a sizeable postwar federal aid highway program, but for the fiscal years from 1946 to 1953 no specific amounts were earmarked for the Interstate system. The 1952 Federal Aid Highway Act did authorize $25 million for the Interstate system for each of the fiscal years 1954 and 1955, to be matched on the traditional 50-50 federal-state cost sharing basis. And the 1954 Federal Aid Highway Act authorized $175 million for the Interstate system for each of the fiscal years 1956 and 1957, with the matching ratio changed to a 60 percent federal share.

During the first postwar decade, about 27 percent of the primary and 45 percent of the urban federal aid funds were used on the interstate system. However, this level of construction funding fell far short of advancing the system toward completion.

In a message sent to the National Governors' Conference on July 12, 1954, President Eisenhower called for a "grand plan for a properly articulated highway system." Later in 1954, a committee of the National Governors' Conference reported to the President its belief that the national government should assume primary responsibility, with state participation, for financing the interstate system. President Eisenhower appointed an Advisory Committee on a National Highway Program, with General Lucius D. Clay as its chairman. The committee's report, *A 10-Year National Highway Program,* was transmitted to the Congress in February 1955. Using estimates made jointly by the states and the Bureau of Public Roads of $23 billion and adding to it $4 billion for the urban auxiliary routes not included in that estimate, the committee arrived at an overall cost of $27 billion for completing the Interstate system in ten years. The federal share was estimated at $25 billion, or about 90 percent.

To finance the program, the committee proposed creation of a federal corporation which would issue $20 billion of long-term bonds to be repaid over the thirty-two-year period, 1956-1987, from the existing two cent federal motor fuel tax. While the proposal had attractive aspects, there were features that weighed heavily against it: (1) it placed a ceiling for thirty-two years on the regular federal aid program as a necessary part of the financing plan; (2) it would cost $12 billion in bond interest; and (3) it, in effect, removed fiscal control of the program from Congress.

Congress began to consider the highway problem early in 1955. While significant bills by Senator Albert Gore of Tennessee and Representative George Fallon of Maryland received long and serious consideration that year, no legislation resulted. The failure to enact legislation came as a shock to many. There had been almost universal testimony supporting an expanded highway program, but there were diverse proposals, each vigorously supported or opposed by various advocates. Among the issues to be resolved were the questions of toll financing and current revenue financing. Each highway beneficiary group expressed willingness to pay its fair share of the cost, but according to its own method of calculation.

When Congress returned to the problem early in 1956, user groups seemed more amenable to compromise, the public was better informed, and there was strong support for action. Earlier federal corporation and financing plans were abandoned, and the Administration endorsed the pay-as-you-go principle. The Senate-House conferees developed a compromise bill on June 25, and the next day both the Senate and the House approved it by overwhelming votes. On June 29, 1956, President Eisenhower signed the bill into law and launched the National System of Interstate and Defense Highways.

The act prescribed that standards for the interstate system be adopted by the secretary of commerce in cooperation with the state highway departments; that they should be adequate to accommodate the traffic forecast for 1975 (modified in later legislation); and that they be applied uniformly throughout the states. To preserve the operating efficiency and safety of this system, access points at interchanges on interstate highways were to be limited to those provided in the 1944 original project plans, except as approved by the secretary.

In authorizing interstate funds, the act significantly departed from the traditional biennial authorization pattern. For the first time, an accelerated program to complete a highway system was approved. The act authorized a total of $25 billion over the period 1957-1969 as the federal share of this construction program. It also established a new method for apportioning Interstate funds among the states, changing after the first three years from a formula based on mileage, area, and population to an apportionment factor for each state computed from the ratio of the cost of completing the system in each state to the total cost of completing the system in all states. The act further provided for a series of cost

estimates to establish these values on a current basis as construction of the system progressed. The federal share of Interstate project costs was set at 90 percent, except in states having large areas of federal public land. There the federal share increased proportionally up to a limit of 95 percent.

Service stations and other commercial establishments were barred from location on or access within the Interstate system right-of-way, on the grounds that highway users should not be subjected to monopoly and that highway-oriented business could compete freely. The act permitted use of space above or below interstate highways for parking purposes, a provision subsequently broadened to allow any public or private use that will not impair the highways.

The act required that Interstate highways have some protection against very heavy loads. The limits on vehicle weight and width were essentially those of the then current policy of AASHO, or alternatively, those legally permitted in a state on July 1, 1956, whichever was greater. The law provided that no federal aid apportionment would be made to any state that permitted vehicles on the Interstate system of a size or weight greater than these limits.

To some extent, Congress entered into problems of route location. The act proposed that "insofar as possible in consonance with this objective, prompt completion of the Interstate, existing highways located on an interstate route shall be used to the extent that such is practicable, suitable, and feasible, it being the intent that local needs, to the extent practicable, suitable, and feasible, shall be given equal consideration with the needs of interstate commerce." And while only 7 percent of the mileage was in urban areas, over half the total cost of the system was in the heavy volume urban sections of the highway.

Broadening a provision of the 1950 Federal Aid Highway Act, the 1956 act required that the state highway departments, in planning a federal aid project involving the bypassing or traversing of a city or town, must hold (or offer to hold) a public hearing and must consider the economic effects of such a location. This provision was subsequently expanded to cover rural interstate projects as well. Acquisition of right-of-way would be a large, costly, and complicated aspect of the Interstate system program. To ease the problem, the act authorized use of apportioned federal aid funds for advance acquisition of right-of-way, provided that actual construction followed within a specified period.

The act permitted toll roads, bridges, and tunnels to be included in the Interstate system if they met standards and if their inclusion promoted development of an integrated system. However, federal aid funds could not be used on toll roads, nor on toll bridges and tunnels, except under the special circumstances already covered by federal aid legislation. It did provide that federal aid Interstate funds could be used on an approach to a toll road incorporated in the system, if the toll road were to become free when the bonds were liquidated and if there were a reasonably satisfactory alternate free route available by which the toll section could be bypassed. As a result of these provisions, about 2,300 miles of toll facilities (roads, bridges, and tunnels) have since been incorporated into the Interstate system. Although there were proposals to reimburse the states for Interstate projects already built which had had less than 90 percent federal aid or none at all, they were not adopted by Congress.

The 1956 Highway Revenue Act (Title II) provided the funds for the authorizations, established the Highway Trust Fund, and

Modern highways provide pleasing landscapes as shown by this section of Interstate 91 in Vermont.

assigned specific motor-vehicle user taxes to the fund for the payment of highway construction costs. Thus, for the first time, federal excise taxes on highway users were designated for use as federal aid for highways. There were three major objectives: to provide financing for the long-range federal aid program, including the funds specifically authorized to complete the Interstate system, and the anticipated, but not legislated, escalating primary, secondary, and urban extension programs (often called the ABC programs); to provide revenue wholly from highway-user tax revenues; and to confine the program to a pay-as-you-go basis.

Thus, the overall legislation broke with tradition and established new principles. It authorized completion of an entire national highway network, the Interstate system, and provided for its financing on the basis of costs recognized at the time. It required the establishment of, and broadly defined, location and design criteria for the system. It departed from the 50-50 federal-state sharing of project costs and the fixed formula method of apportionment. It tied highway-user tax revenue to highway expenditure and established the Highway Trust Fund. The act began an accelerated highway improvement program which was to bring about a new era in highway transportation.

While the $27 billion cost estimated in the Clay committee report was used in the legislation, Congress recognized that requirements for the system would change following detailed studies and that there would need to be up-to-date periodic estimates of the cost of completing the system. The act provided for a series of such estimates beginning in 1958. The first of the series of periodic estimates was prepared by the individual states during calendar year 1957 and submitted to Congress in January 1958. At that time, the cost for completing the total system, expanded to 41,000 miles by subsequent action of Congress, was estimated to be $41 billion. This was the first detailed estimate encompassing the full system.

In 1958 the nation was in an economic recession. Accelerating the federal aid highway program was considered as a way to create jobs and bring about recovery. The 1958 Federal Aid Highway Act increased the annual Interstate authorizations in the 1956 act from $2.0 billion of $2.2 billion for fiscal year 1959, and from $2.2 billion to $2.5 billion for each of the fiscal years 1960 and 1961. More important, it set aside the pay-as-you-go provision of the 1956 act for two years and directed apportionment to the states of the full amounts authorized. This provision was not matched by a commensurate one for additional revenues. The net effect was to appreciably advance the time when the federal aid program annual expenditures would exceed trust fund revenues.

In an effort to correlate the level of anticipated trust fund revenues and expenditures, the Bureau of Public Roads in 1959 instituted a program of "reimbursement planning." Under this program, a limit was set quarterly on the rate at which each state could obligate funds to contracts. This was done to assure that federal payments of ultimate reimbursement to the states for work accomplished could be made within the available trust fund balance.

The highway cost allocation study, called for by the 1956 act, was reported to Congress in January 1961. It provided information on which Congress might make an equitable distribution of the federal tax burden for support of the program among the various users and beneficiaries of federal aid highways.

The need for additional revenue to meet the cost of the Interstate system program was evident from the 1958 and 1961 cost estimates. The 1961 act reaffirmed the Interstate program and increased the total authorized funds to $37 billion, the federal share of the cost. To provide the needed financing, the motor-fuel tax was continued at four cents per gallon, the tax per pound on highway vehicle tires was increased from eight to ten cents, on inner tubes from nine to ten cents, and on retread rubber from three to five cents. The use tax on heavy vehicles, those over 26,000 pounds gross weight, was increased from $1.50 to $3.00 per 1,000 pounds per year. All of the 10 percent tax on the manufacturer's sale price on new trucks, buses, and trailers was earmarked to the trust fund, instead of only half as provided by the 1956 act. By this action, both the necessary authorizations to complete the Interstate system and the required revenues were provided.

The provisions of the 1956 act and later legislation added to the complexity of the program and its administration. All contracts and subcontracts for interstate construction were made subject to the Davis-Bacon Act which required approval by the secretary of labor of prevailing wage rates to be determined for each project. The requirement for public hearings was broadened. The definition of construction costs was extended to include relocation of utility facilities. Authorization provided for and encouraged the advance acquisition of rights-of-way for federal aid projects to be built within five years, later changed to seven years, and then to ten years. Direct acquisition by the federal government of rights-of-way for interstate projects could be made where state laws did not provide the necessary control of access authority.

The 1962 legislation required state highway departments to furnish satisfactory assurance that relocation advisory assistance was available for families displaced by federal aid highway construction. It further provided for federal participation in the cost of relocating families and business concerns. This program, commonly called "relocation assistance," at first applicable only to highway programs, was broadened into the 1970 Uniform Relocation Assistance and Real Property Acquisition Policies Act, for application in all federal and federally assisted programs. A comprehensive study and report was subsequently required by Congress to determine what federal action could be taken to increase highway safety. This led to enactment of the 1966 Motor Vehicle Safety Act and further to the 1973 Highway Safety Act, which have concentrated additional attention on reducing accidents on the nation's highways.

A continuing flow of new legislation following the 1956 act brought refinements, additions, and controls into the highway program. In 1956 and 1957, a number of new features were added, and the primary, secondary, and urban extension system (ABC systems) were significantly expanded. In

1958 not only was the ABC program level supplemented but the normal 50 percent federal share was increased for one year to 66.7 percent as an anti-recession measure. The 1958 Federal Aid Highway Act also established the national policy of encouraging and assisting the states in controlling outdoor advertising on the Interstate system. The program became known as the "billboard control" program and has been strengthened in subsequent years.

The Interstate system is nearing completion in rural areas and in most urban areas. The benefits derived in freedom of movement and safety of travel have been enormous. The flow of people and goods on the system results in a user benefit of about $2.90 for every dollar invested in construction, estimated over the system's service life. The difference in operating safety of the Interstate over other highway systems saves an estimated 8,000 lives per year. The system contributes dramatically to the economic development of the areas it serves; and because of its advanced design features, it will continue to assist this development long after other highways would have become functionally obsolete.

Coordination of Highway and Urban Planning

As previously indicated, cities and towns initially took care of their own streets through various financial arrangements with local citizens. The state and federal levels of government were not generally concerned, as the population of the cities was dense enough to make relatively low per capita cost of streets possible. And most larger cities had substantial capabilities and experience to handle adequately their problems. However, the layout of streets tended to grow to meet changing needs of developers. Economic piecemeal approaches were often used rather than a well-designed, long-range plan. Too often, programs were not based on quantitative data and sound land use planning.

The 1944 legislation provided federal aid funds for urban extensions of the primary and secondary federal aid highway routes. The resulting origin and destination traffic studies and the land use and street network inventory data of the highway engineers gave a giant impetus to improved city planning based on factual information. The analysis of this great amount of data in a meaningful way was difficult until computers came into use. Since then, bringing an array of disciplines into the planning process has made possible a sophisticated approach that will have an impact for decades to come.

Cooperation with the housing industry also was important. The Federal Housing and Home Finance Agency "701" planning assistance funds became available as a result of 1954 legislation. The joining of the comprehensive land use and transportation planning processes was especially beneficial.

In 1954 a National Committee on Urban Transportation was created at the initiation of the Automotive Safety Foundation (now the Highway Users Federation for Safety and Mobility) and included nine other organizations concerned with transportation in the urban areas. The outcome was an unparalleled volunteer effort culminating in 1958 with the publication of *Better Transportation for Your City* and seventeen procedural manuals by the Public Administration Service. These procedures were successfully field tested as a demonstration in seven cities. This marked a significant gain in federal-state-local relationships in solving local transportation problems and resulted in many effective ongoing planning programs.

While the 1956 Federal Aid Highway Act placed major emphasis on completing the Interstate system, it did not neglect the transportation problems of urban areas. Many state highway departments were engaged in urban transportation studies in cooperation with the cities, but few states were actively working with the cities in solving urban transportation problems. States were more concerned with getting a highway through the city in an acceptable manner than in contributing to a solution of the city's internal transportation problems. But while the states were not prepared to work with the cities, the cities were generally no better prepared to cooperate with the states.

Early in 1957, the Automotive Safety Foundation, AASHO, the American Municipal Association (now the National

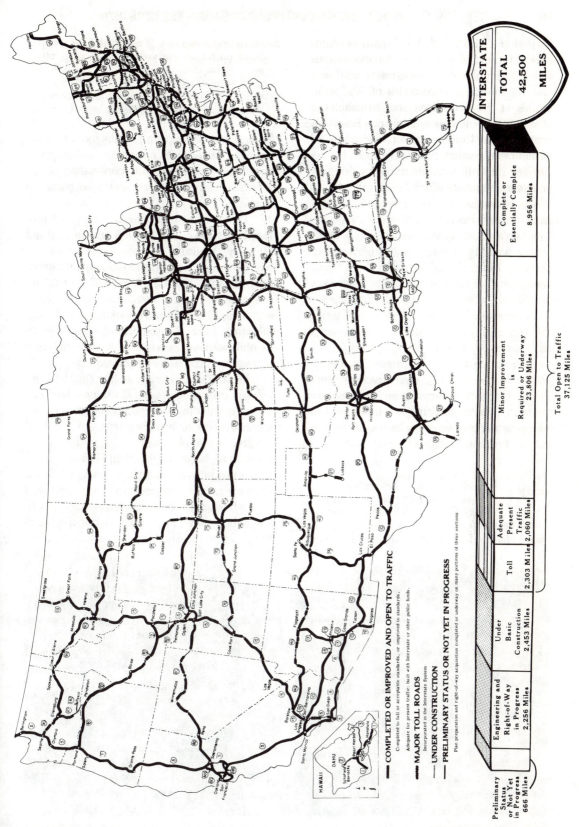

The National System of Interstate and Defense Highways — Status of improvements on September 30, 1975.

U.S. Department of Transportation

League of Cities), and the Bureau of Public Roads formed a committee to explore the state-city problems and to act as a catalyst in working toward solutions. One of the first activities of the committee was to cosponsor, along with the Highway Research Board, the first National Conference on Highways and Urban Development, held at Syracuse University in 1958. It was attended by highway engineers, transit officials, planners, and other professionals and interested leaders from the business and academic communities. The conference agreed that the final choice among possible alternatives in highway location and design should be guided by a "grand accounting" of costs and benefits. It also suggested that advantages and disadvantages of each alternative—to the highway user and to the community—be evaluated in relation to the total cost entailed.

The highway departments agreed to cooperate in developing a tentative program of urban highway improvement at least five years in advance to provide a basis for local planning and in developing tools to furthur the urban highway program. The conference noted that:

Urban planning can aid in determining the scale and character of the highway program by providing highway officials with estimates of urban growth and development likely to take place in a metropolitan area in the next two decades or more. If new highways are to accomplish their purpose and not become obsolete soon after completion, their planning must take into consideration the patterns of community growth, as well as the urbanizing influence of the highway itself.

Several similar meetings followed this conference, designed to encourage and improve effective cooperation and coordination of the efforts of city planners and transportation officials.

The 1962 Federal Aid Highway Act provided that after July 1, 1965 any federal aid highway programs in urban areas must be based on a "continuing comprehensive transportation planning process" carried on cooperatively by the states and the local communities. This forward-looking legislation, therefore, made it a requirement that governmental agencies in urbanized areas utilize a process that had already proved effective.

In principle the approach is simple. It involves developing several alternative land use plans, calculating the transportation requirements of each, determining from the people of the area which plan they prefer, and then proceeding with the development. The actual implementation is complex and difficult. However, as the process has improved through research and experience, the relationships between land use and transportation have evolved in such a manner that sophisti-

Virginia Department of Highways

Express bus lanes are provided on Shirley Highway in northern Virginia to provide fast commuter service.

cated models, with accompanying computer programs, have been created to quantify them. This has resulted in the development of an elaborate kit of planning tools and techniques and a highly skilled group of artisans to utilize them.

The key is land use planning that will meet the future objectives of the urban areas and the nation as a whole. This, of course, includes resource planning and the protection of the environment. The difficulty is in providing an organizational structure that is politically and technically able to do the job. Progress is being made, and the continuing comprehensive planning process required by the federal aid highway program was a step toward the development of sound transportation systems for urban communities of the future.

Public Works Historical Society

Horse-drawn scrapers and stone slips made up the excavation equipment on this road in Arizona in the 1890s.

Construction Methods and Equipment

Roadbuilding through the latter part of the nineteenth century was with hand labor, horse-drawn slip scrapers, and wagons. The steam shovel was utilized to a limited extent, and the steam roller was used in city pavement work. The first road grader, introduced in 1875, was a steel blade hung beneath a wooden wagon; but the steam tractor, with broad iron wheels, foreshadowed the retirement of the horse and wagon from the road construction scene by the 1930s.

Portland cement concrete was used in cities during the 1890s as a base for paving surfaces of brick, rock blocks, and asphalt, but it involved slow and costly hand work. The first rural section of concrete pavement was not constructed until 1909, when a one-mile section in Wayne County, Michigan, was built. Its use increased, however, as mixing and placing equipment improved and the pavement's durability was proven.

By 1907 a sheepsfoot roller was in use on embankment work in West Coast road construction. By 1910 steel forms were being produced for concrete work; and the gasoline engine had come to construction work as the power unit on hoisting and excavation equipment, marking the end of the cumbersome steam engine. The diesel engine was also being developed, and crawler tracks were being tried on tractors and cranes. A wooden-boomed excavator was first rigged with a drag bucket in 1903, making this the forerunner of the drag line. A rock crusher and elevator was mounted on a four-wheel truck in 1910 to become the first portable crushing and screening plant.

Equipment for highway construction underwent extensive changes as the national road program developed in the 1920s. The steam shovel had been replaced by gasoline engine-powered excavators. The lines of horse-drawn wagons disappeared as dump trucks took over their jobs. Crawler tractors pulling rotary scrapers replaced horse- or mule-drawn fresnos and drag scrapers. Shortly thereafter, large, early models of self-propelled scrapers were developed. A manually operated bulldozer blade was put on a crawler tractor in 1923, and by 1925 hydraulic controls operated the dozer blades. The self-propelled motor grader was introduced in the early 1920s. By 1922 R. G. Le Tourneau's all-welded, tractor-drawn scraper with a six-cubic-yard capacity was in use; and by 1924 electric hand saws were used in construction. During this period, the steam stone crushers were replaced by gasoline engine models with revolving screens and conveyor belts; in 1923 a complete portable stone crushing and screening plant was first marketed.

Probably the two most important advances in modernizing construction equipment during the next decade were: (1) the development of large pneumatic tires which were used on scrapers as early as 1932 and on dump trucks in 1934, making it easier for them to operate on soft ground; and (2) the introduction of the diesel engine on tractors and graders in 1931. The front apron was initially placed on scrapers in 1933, making a twelve-cubic-yard load a reality. Ballastable rollers were introduced in 1936 for compaction of earth. Hydraulic controls were placed on power shovels in 1937. Le Tourneau put his self-propelled scrapers on the market in 1938, which made it possible to move earth more economically and at a much faster pace. It changed the earth-moving industry.

Revolutionary developments were also occurring in paving equipment. The traveling paver was introduced in 1926; then, in 1932 the dual-drum traveling paver was put in use to increase production of concrete for pavements. Internal vibrators for portland cement concrete were patented in 1935, enabling better concrete consolidation. Bituminous paving equipment was also developed. The road mix machine was introduced in 1929, and the bituminous paver was placed on the market in 1932. This equipment provided more rapid construction of improved asphalt pavements at lower cost.

Unit prices of the various items needed for road construction were generally lower during the 1930s than in the 1920s because of equipment improvements. The progress in excavation equipment is especially noteworthy. Until the inflation effects since 1970, the unit cost of excavation had remained almost constant over forty years, while nearly all other items were quadrupling. For instance, with an excavation index of 100 in 1920, by 1960 the cost index would have been about 450 without improvements in methods and equipment, whereas the actual cost index was still about 100. This made larger excavations physically and economically possible; thus, the highway could be better adapted to the landscape.

The federal aid system of building roads was well established by 1926, and most projects were built in stage construction. That is, the roads were expected to be further im-

proved to higher standards as traffic volumes and the weight and speed of vehicles increased. This allowed more miles to be improved with the limited funds available. Stage construction also had other advantages. Projects could be let to contract for the grading work alone, or perhaps the drainage and grading work, leaving the surfacing work to be done at a later time, thereby taking advantage of contractors' specialties. This also permitted the embankments, built as part of the grading work, to settle before placing the surfacing material and better assured that back-slopes in excavation cuts were stable before the road was opened to traffic.

Although wartime highway construction activity was curtailed, the postwar period was one of greatly expanded activity as programs were developed to overcome wartime neglect of the highways and to catch up with expanding needs. The Bureau of Public Roads worked closely with AASHO, the Highway Research Board, and industry associations in coordinating construction and maintenance practices and in research and development of standard specifications. In 1948 AASHO published its *Policy on Maintenance of Roadway Surfaces* (revised in 1961). Then in 1949, AASHO published a *Manual of Highway Construction Practices and Methods*. These publications disseminated information to the states and their subdivisions so that they could benefit from the advancements made in construction and maintenance procedures. By 1951 about half of the state highway departments had adopted systematic procedures for determining the required roadway surface thickness for given conditions of load, traffic density, subgrade and conditions, climate, and related factors. This contrasted greatly with the situation a few years before when determination of the thickness of pavements was left to the judgment of the individual engineer.

Major advances in construction equipment have continued through recent decades. A significant improvement was the development of the self-powered, road-mix, earth-stabilizing machine in 1945, which greatly increased the productivity and control of stabilized bases and subbase courses. The rubber-tired bulldozer in 1947 and the vibrating roller in 1948 proved to be successful over the years. In rock excavation, the new carbide insert on rock bits lengthened their life and increased their effectiveness. In the development of construction equipment, the trend has been towards heavier and more powerful units to obtain more production at lower unit cost.

In paving equipment, significant advances were started in 1955 when electronic controls were put into use on concrete batch plants. The triple-drum concrete paver was introduced in 1959, producing 125 batches per hour compared to 87 batches for the dual-drum paver. Central-plant mixing with hauling by agitator trucks and transit mixers was also introduced. Slip form pavers became widely accepted for highway work. Spreading and finishing equipment for concrete pavement was also being improved. Some road contractors were able to pave more than a mile per working day of 9-inch thick, 24-foot wide portland cement concrete pavement with the modern equipment. In 1973 one contractor set a new record by placing 14,853 cubic yards of concrete in paving 4.7 miles of 8-inch-thick, 24-foot-wide pavement in a twenty-three-hour period.

Public Works Historical Society

Elevating excavators load 35-cubic-yard trucks in the 1960s.

By the 1960s, the Interstate program was in full swing. Excavation averaged 20 million cubic yards per working day during most of the years. Although production was still the main goal, there were other concerns as well—such as increased highway safety, highway beautification, and consideration of

wildlife, recreation areas, and historic sites. Construction procedures were implemented to reduce the erosion of soil during the construction process. Studies were undertaken to investigate ways to control noise and air pollution during construction. For instance, the dryer-drum process for hot mix asphalt plants and better mufflers for heavy equipment were developed to reduce adverse environmental effects.

New advances in tamping and vibrating rollers were helping to speed up compaction of embankments and base courses. Nuclear devices were used for testing compaction more quickly. New equipment was developed that provided more accurate information in subsurface investigations and resulted in more accurate bidding on excavation work. The laser beam became a useful tool in giving line and grade for various construction operations, such as drainage pipe laying, thus eliminating the need for offset lines and batter boards. New methods for handling concrete, such as concrete pumps, have made bridge work easier. Stay-in-place steel forms that act as part of the reinforcement for concrete bridge decks eliminated the need for the removal of the forms, a hazardous and difficult task.

Additives for concrete were developed and employed to control the set, giving better workability and producing more durable structures. The heavy use of salt as a deicing agent caused early deterioration of concrete bridge decks as the salt penetrated the concrete and the reinforcing steel. To counteract this condition, specialized construction methods for the protection of bridge decks, such as epoxy-coated or galvanized reinforcing steel and waterproof mastics or membranes, were developed.

Approximately one third of the total present-day construction costs of highways is attributable to each of the three major items of grading and drainage, pavement bases and surfaces, and structures. Wages for labor accounts for about 25 percent of the construction cost; material and supplies for about 40 percent; and 35 percent for equipment operation, including depreciation and repairs and overhead costs. This has changed from twenty-five years ago when a good rule-of-thumb was to estimate one third for each of these basic elements of cost.

Safety has become one of the most important aspects of highway building. Many kinds of new safety devices have been built into highways such as breakaway sign posts, safer guardrails, and several kinds of crash cushions. The development of occupational safety measures improved working conditions for the construction work force as well.

Other activities on construction projects have also changed over the years. For instance, construction contractors are sometimes required to furnish completely equipped material testing laboratories and to do their own surveying and layout staking, operations previously done by state highway departments. More states are also using aerial photography and new data processing procedures to speed up monthly progress estimates as well as for studies, designs, and specifications.

Maintenance

Adequate attention to maintenance has been difficult to achieve since roads were first built. It has evolved from a strictly local problem of adjacent landowners to a program of national concern that has resulted in a well-managed, generally effective and efficient program utilizing approximately one fourth the total expenditure on highways. This amounted to about $6 billion in 1975. Present-day motor vehicular traffic demands high standards of maintenance. In the horse and buggy days, maintenance usually failed to get adequate attention, except in the largest and best managed cities. As late as 1915, a convention of the American Society of Municipal Improvements concluded that "many cities spend large sums on roads and then do nothing to keep them in order, thereby losing outright a large part of their original investment." Discussions at the convention centered on the difficulty of obtaining understanding of and support for a maintenance budget.

The problems were greatest on county roads. Users of the road had to rely on maintenance by adjacent property owners working out their "road tax" by a few days labor each year, dragging the roads to smooth up the surface, and perhaps cleaning out drainage ditches. Until a good roadbed was constructed that would carry the loads, dragging of the roads was only a temporary expedient. The isolation of rural areas, except during dry weather, was an accepted fact of life well into the twentieth century.

In February 1796, Congress ordered a survey of roads to be made, financed by the federal government. The feeling was expressed that it was properly the business of the general government to provide roads, as the different states were incompetent to do so and their ideas in design clashed with each other. The construction of the National Pike was authorized as a federal activity in 1802, but funds were not provided for its construction until 1811. After construction, Congress was reluctant to furnish maintenance funds. It was not convinced that such funds were necessary, and the road rapidly deteriorated. When the pike was finally turned over to the states for local administration in 1835, the entire road including many of the bridges had to be rebuilt under the direction of the Army Corps of Engineers before the states would accept it.

The lack of skilled labor and supervision by local officials appointed almost entirely for political reasons did little for the roads. There was a general lack of knowledge of what ought to be done. In 1903 Ira O. Baker in the first edition of his *Roads and Pavements*

Virginia Department of Highways

Horse-drawn road drags provided the principal maintenance of rural roads in the early 1900s.

stated that "Although it is frequently claimed that the public would be benefited by placing the care of roads in the hands of engineers . . . there is no evidence that any considerable number of engineers comprehend either the principles of roadmaking necessary for the improvement and maintenance of our country roads or the economic limitations and political difficulties of the problem." Improvements awaited the pressures of automobile travel becoming the dominant problem, and then the gasoline tax provided an equitable and major source of funds. Maintenance in most states did not become a state function until well into the 1920s, when proper maintenance became a requirement for participation in federal aid for highways.

Maintenance of state highways was not generally considered to require special skills until about the middle of the twentieth century or, in some states, even later. In many states, the highway maintenance crews were replaced with a change in administration; qualifications were on the basis of political party affiliation. The high quality of maintenance required for high-speed, high-volume automotive travel by the 1960s made capability and experience increasingly important since proper maintenance of modern highways is an exacting operation, requiring the best of skills and supervision.

It was well into the last half of the nineteenth century before much paving of city streets was accomplished other than gravel surfacing and, in the larger cities, paving with cobblestones. Pavements were considered a luxury. The concept that the "cost of pavements not only comes high, *but like all luxuries,* need constant attention and outlay" (emphasis added) was not progressive. Charges for maintenance as well as construction were generally assessed to the property owners along the street, with the cost of the street intersections borne by the general fund. The efforts of the American Society of Municipal Improvements, in disseminating information at their annual conventions on methods of maintenance, did much to improve paving techniques. By 1900 there was general recognition that with the rapid growth of the cities, pavements were in the first rank of importance in municipal affairs and that maintenance must become a well-administered program. Then, as the number and speed of automobiles increased, new forms of road surface came into being that required new and more sophisticated maintenance. The broken stone pavements and surfacings, admirably adapted to horse-drawn vehicles, were rapidly destroyed by faster moving automobiles and trucks.

The early object lesson roads built by the federal government were used to demonstrate maintenance methods as well as construction operations. With the passage of the 1916 Federal-Aid Road Act, states were required to have an organization and program to perform maintenance. This began to be an increasingly important requirement during the big construction years of the 1920s. As more people obtained cars and traveled more miles, the proper maintenance of roads and streets became politically sensitive, resulting in gradual general improvements.

During World War II, as the roads were called upon to continue performance with a minimum of effort devoted to upkeep, better maintenance methods evolved. Cooperative efforts of federal, state, and local governments, along with industry, resulted in development of improved maintenance materials and methods. In 1948 the American Association of Highway Officials published the *Policy on Maintenance of Roadway Surfaces* that has been a valuable guide.

Intensive research on materials, methods, and management for maintenance have paralleled the increasing needs. For instance, beginning in 1939 a detailed study of all maintenance operations of the Iowa Highway Department was carried out and performance of equipment and men evaluated. Out of these and other studies, standards of performance, including materials, equipment, manpower, and management, have been established for different conditions. The information has been widely distributed and training programs have been and are being carried on extensively. More efficient operators are adapting to changing conditions as such studies and training continue.

For instance, the 1976 efficient street cleaning mechanized operations in cities have come a long way from the "White Wing" street sweepers of the 1890s. Snow removal has progressed to where winter travel is available to all with little inconvenience except during a heavy snowfall or blizzard. Until the 1920s, it was the usual practice to put an automobile in the garage elevated on blocks to relieve pressure in the tires until the spring thaw. Travel for any appreciable distances was limited to trains until the 1920s, when the main cross country highway routes began to be kept open during winter snow months.

Until the beginning of the twentieth century, city travel in the wintertime in the northern part of the United States was by horses and sleighs, and snow removal was limited.

Street cars had snow sweepers and plows to keep tracks clear, but most other streets relied only on horse-drawn traffic to open them up after a snowstorm. As motorized vehicles became more common, pressures increased to clear snow from at least the arterial streets. Heavy draft horses drawing four-wheeled road graders fitted with plow blades were initially used. Hand labor was extensively utilized to load wagons in the main downtown business areas.

By the 1920s, various kinds of snow plows attached to trucks and tractors came into use; and in the 1930s, single, horizontal curved blades mounted in front of trucks or tractors which pushed the snow to one side were in general use in cities and on rural roads and highways. Heavy snows required

Colorado Department of Transportation

Main traveled mountain routes are kept open during winter month with snow plows (left) and snow blowers (right).

V-shaped blades, similarly mounted. Efficiency dictated that equipment used for other purposes in non-winter seasons be converted to snow removal functions during the snow season. Rotary plows began to be developed for deep snows and drifts by 1920 and by the 1930s evolved into effective snow-moving machines. A common type was a horizontal, spiral rotor resembling an auger. The rotor broke up the snow and pushed it to the center of the plow where fans blew it out a spout. Heavy rotary snow plows are utilized on the Rocky Mountain and Sierra Nevada passes where snowfalls of over 30 inches are not unusual.

In the cities, snow loaded and hauled away was dumped on vacant land or bodies of water as near as possible to the loading points. By the 1960s, where hauling distances were great, both stationary and portable snow melters began to be used to cut hauling costs and reduce water pollution problems.

Snow fighting became a major activity of street and highway departments in the 1950s, as higher standards of street and highway snow and ice clearances were demanded by the public. Heavy snowstorms in the Northeast during the winter of 1960-1961 required especially large expenditures to clear city streets. New York City, for example, spent over $24 million on snow removal, and other cities had proportional expenditures. As a result, an annual Northeast Conference on Urban Snow Removal began in the spring of 1961; and by 1969, it had expanded to an annual North American Snow Conference, sponsored by the American Public Works Association. These conferences contributed greatly to improving the organization and management of men, materials, and equipment in snow removal and ice control programs. Effective parking restrictions during snow alerts have been planned, publicized, and supported by the public. The seasonal unpredictable nature of keeping streets and highways open during snowstorms has required the best in public service management and involves the cooperation of all city and highway forces and the public.

By 1976 snow removal and ice control programs were generally well-planned, organized, and effective operations providing dry, snow-free streets and highway surfaces most of the time. Snowstorm prediction methods had generally improved. While salt and grit applied to hasten snow and ice melting have created other problems, progress was made in improving effectiveness and in resolving adverse effects.

Various ways of performing general maintenance have been tried. In special cases, such as applying a seal coat to a pavement or a well-defined specific operation, a contract with private firms works well. However, for the regular maintenance program, the best practice generally is to have a maintenance supervisor with responsibility for a section of road and to provide him with the trained help he needs. This approach, plus sophisticated evaluation and control management, is producing good results.

Projecting ahead, it is expected that maintenance costs will increase, due to the higher costs of accomplishing work without appreciable interference with high volume traffic and as better service is required. As roadbeds and pavements wear out, maintenance costs rise. Skid-free pavement surfaces, such as diamond-cut grooves in portland cement concrete pavements and grit-embedded seal coats on bituminous concrete pavements, improve highway safety and service but cost more. Better and more effective signing; clear and well-maintained pavement lane markings; lighting of high-volume intersections and interchanges; improved landscaping and care; and rapid repair of defects contribute to better and more overall economical transportation but involve increased maintenance expenditures. However, these types of operations are sound expenditures from the standpoint of the cost of highway transportation, and they protect and extend the life of the initial investment. A continuing problem will be to provide sufficient funds to insure adequate and effective maintenance of America's roads, streets, and highways.

SUGGESTED READINGS

American Association of State Highway Officials. *The First Fifty Years: 1914-1964*. Washington, D.C., 1965.

American Public Works Association. *Snow Removal and Ice Control in Urban Areas*. 2 vols. Chicago, 1965.

——————— . Institute for Municipal Engineering. *A Survey of Urban Arterial Design Standards*. Chicago, 1969.

——————— . Research Foundation. *Street and Urban Road Maintenance*. Chicago, 1963.

Baker, Ira Osborn. *Roads and Pavements*. 3d. ed. New York, 1913.

Besson, Frank S. *City Pavements*. New York, 1923.

Borth, Christy. *Mankind on the Move*. Washington, D.C., 1969.

Coates, Albert W., Jr. *A Story of Roads in Virginia*. Richmond, Virginia, 1973.

Judson, William Pierson. *City Roads and Pavements*. New York, 1902.

Knowlton, Ezra C. *History of Highway Development in Utah*. Prepared for the Utah Department of Highways. Salt Lake City, Utah, 1964.

MacDonald, Thomas H. "The History and Development of Road Building in the United States." American Society of Civil Engineers *Transactions*, 92 (1928), 1181-1206.

National Academy of Sciences. Highway Research Board. *Ideas and Actions—A History of the Highway Research Board, 1920-1970*. Washington, D.C., 1971.

Owen, Wilfred. *The Metropolitan Transportation Problem*. Rev. ed. Washington, D.C., 1966.

Public Administration Service. National Committee on Urban Transportation. *Better Transportation for Your City*. Chicago, 1958.

Rose, Albert C. *Historic American Highways*. Washington, D.C., 1953.

Schlivek, Louis B. *Man in Metropolis*. New York, 1965.

U.S. Department of Transportation. *The 1972 National Highway Needs Report*. 2 parts. Washington, D.C., 1972.

Wixom, Charles W. *Pictorial History of Roadbuilding*. Prepared for the American Road Builders Association. Washington, D.C., 1975

CHAPTER 4

HIGHWAY STRUCTURES AND TRAFFIC CONTROLS

Structures and various types of traffic controls are an integral part of the nation's roads, streets, and highways. Their construction and maintenance involved about one third of the overall expenditures made for road systems during the past several decades. Some bridges rank among the most daring and spectacular public works achievements. Tunnels have presented great difficulties in construction. Structures to guide and control traffic and increase the safety of travel have involved ingenuity and imagination. In recent years, parking facilities have become increasingly important to the movement of street traffic in congested urban areas. All are required to expedite the flow of highway traffic in the cities and rural areas of America.

This chapter outlines the developments in highway structures and traffic controls that have occurred during the first 200 years of the nation. Only some of the unique and significant milestones can be mentioned here, but they demonstrate multiple effort, ingenuity, and accomplishment.

Early Bridges

A well-designed and functioning bridge evokes attention, admiration, and appreciation. Many lyrical writings have attested to the

majesty and beauty with which bridges perform their function. They are an essential part of a road and highway system. Some have called bridges an "index of civilization." They free man by overcoming obstacles to his mobility; they demonstrate man's inventiveness and achievement.

In 1776 there were few structures that could be classed as bridges. Natural waterways made up most of the transportation system. Boats, barges, and ferries of various kinds provided crossings for deeper streams, and those of shallow depth were crossed by fording. Bridges of a sort were first built by laying logs across streams, then by wooden beam type spans; but these were usually limited to 20 feet or less in length. On wider streams, some structures were constructed with bents, consisting of piles driven into the riverbed or of log or timber cribs filled with rock. These bents were placed on about 20-foot centers and provided support for the hewn timbers that served as girders. Light traverse beams were laid across the girders and a plank deck was nailed to these beams. Floating bridges, usually of large logs fastened together, were constructed at some crossings. Several pontoon floating bridges were used during the Revolutionary War.

There were some short stone arch bridges in the colonies north of Maryland. The first known stone arch to be built in this country was across Pennypack Creek in Philadelphia.

This chapter was prepared primarily from reports of the United States Department of Transportation and state highway departments.

Built in 1697, it was a three-span arch structure and is considered the country's oldest existing bridge.

It appears that the first highway bridge of importance was constructed across the York River at York, Maine, in 1761 by Samuel Sewall, the major American bridge builder of the eighteenth century. It was 270 feet long, 25 feet wide, and was supported by four pile bents spaced 19 feet apart. It is the initial bridge for which the builder's drawings survived, and some have suggested it was the initial American bridge built from plans prepared on the basis of a survey of the site. It remained in use, with repairs, for almost 175 years, and it provided a draw span which could be moved by manpower to allow the passage of sloops on the river.

Another bridge of special interest was across the Charles River, between Boston and then Charlestown, Massachusetts. It also was constructed by Sewall and was 1,503 feet long, with a 42-foot roadway and a 6-foot sidewalk. The pile bents were about 20 feet apart, and a draw span was provided for river traffic. Forty lamps were installed for night use. The bridge was built by private interests under a franchise that included toll charges. An interesting feature of the franchise was the requirement that the bridge owners pay $666.66 a year to a nearby ferry to compensate for "income loss for ferriage."

What is regarded as the first framed bridge structure was a 368-foot-long, two-span structure across the Connecticut River at Bellow Falls, Vermont. Built by Enoch Hale in 1785, the superstructure rested on abutment walls of rubble and a braced timber bent at the center. The deck planking and beams were carried on heavy braced timbers arranged in a trapezoidal archlike form, with four such arches set in parallel planes for each span. Records indicate the bridge was only in use about fifteen years.

Timber trussed arches were developed in the last decade of the eighteenth century to cross wide rivers where multiple spans of timber beams were impractical. The Essex-Merrimac Bridge near Newburyport, Massachusetts, was constructed in 1792 with two 160-foot arch spans. The Piscataqua River Bridge, built by Timothy Parker, about 7 miles above Portsmouth, New Hampshire, contained a wooden trussed arch span of 344 feet. The McCalls Ferry Bridge over the Susquehanna River at McCalls Ferry, Pennsylvania, built in 1814-1815 by Theodore Burr, contained a truss arch with a 367-foot span, said to be the longest ever built in America.

The first of many covered bridges in America was built in 1800 by Timothy Palmer at Middle Ferry, Philadelphia, Pennsylvania. The covering protected the bridge members from decay so that a properly maintained bridge would give many years of service. The Waterford Bridge over the Hudson River, about 10 miles upstream from Albany, New York—a covered wood truss bridge built by Theodore Burr in 1803-1804—had a service life of 105 years, until it was destroyed by fire in 1909. Most covered timber truss bridges did not endure so well; there were many failures due to lack of maintenance, fires, floods, and overloads.

U.S. Department of Transportation

The original wooden covered bridge at this site near West Cornwall, Connecticut, was constructed in 1837 and has since been restored and preserved.

Early bridge builders in America developed a timber construction craftsmanship that received worldwide recognition. Their work in the 1820s and 1830s led to the modern truss form of bridge. Initially, the design of the structures was based on trial and error coupled with an intuitive engineering judgment, but their increasing skill and the young nation's growing transportation demands accelerated the timber construction era.

The advent of the railroad, with heavier loads, longer crossings, and greater rigidity requirements, gave impetus to the development of various trusses named for their developers such as Howe, Pratt, Whipple, Fink, and others. Although the truss was a framing of relatively small members arranged and connected so that the assemblage had rigidity and behaved as a unit, any number of variations in the style of the truss was possible. The layout and relative position of the trusses and arches, the proportioning of the members, the method of supporting the floor system, and the type and magnitude of the connections were determined by the experience and judgment of the builder. While there is evidence that early developers used mathematical theory in determining the various styles, there was no published method of stress analysis available to the builders for proportioning members and connections until Squire Whipple's publication in 1847, *An Essay on Bridge Building*, and Herman Haupt's publication in 1851, *General Theory of Bridge Construction*.

The general use of timber trusses for highway bridges continued to the 1880s, even though cast iron, wrought iron, Bessemer steel, and basic open hearth steel bridge supporting members were developed and used during this period. After the 1880s, the construction of timber truss bridges gradually decreased, except in isolated areas where timber was readily available and used for scenic reasons. However, the use of timber-pile bent highway bridges did not materially diminish, especially after ways were found to prolong the life of timber in contact with earth and water. Early methods were tried with little success. However, the railroads continued searching for a satisfactory method for increasing the life of the ties and timber structures on their systems. In 1865 the first pressure creosote treating plant was constructed at Somerset, Massachusetts, primarily to treat timber railroad track ties. As the treatment plants emerged to supply the railroads, treated timber piles and lumber became available for use in highway bridge structures as well.

Cast iron, malleable iron, and wrought iron were introduced early in the construction

U.S. Department of Transportation

The nation's first iron bridge was completed in 1839 in Brownsville, Pennsylvania, as part of the National Pike.

of timber bridges for incidental parts. Use of iron facilitated construction, improved the rigidity of the structure, and reduced maintenance problems. Wrought-iron rods began to be employed for tension web members of trusses. The first cast iron arch bridge in the country was built by the Army Corps of Engineers over Dunlap Creek along the present main street of Brownsville, Pennsylvania. The span of the arch was 80 feet and the rise was 8 feet. The arch was composed of five similar ribs of nine equal length pieces. It was completed in 1838 and is still in use. This was one of several structures on the National Pike which required repair or reconstruction before the road was turned over to the states for operation.

Early highway truss bridges were also constructed of iron. The initial American use of iron truss superstructures was in 1840 for two highway bridges over the Erie Canal. The first to be completed was designed by Earl Trumbull at Frankfort, New York. It consisted of a truss, formed according to a combination truss and suspension principle, with an 80-foot span and a wooden floor system. The second bridge was a 70-foot span at Utica, New York, that was designed by Squire Whipple, the first example of his bow-string truss. The tension members were wrought iron and the compression members were cast iron. This bridge also had a wooden floor system.

Most other bridges built in the mid-nineteenth century following these first two iron bridges were railroad bridges. The increased use of wrought iron and cast iron for bridges, rails, and other related uses caused a boom in the iron industry as well as an increase in the size of plates and sections of wrought iron rolled. The use of steam power in production also increased the capacity of the industry and was an incentive to develop new processes for producing iron and steel. The Bessemer process for converting pig iron into steel began in 1860; the open-hearth steel making process followed in 1870.

The first all steel spans built in America were the five main span trusses of the Glasgow Bridge in 1878-1879, over the Missouri River at Glasgow, Missouri. Bessemer steel was used for the main spans of 315 feet. The remaining trusses and trestle work were made of wrought iron. Alloy steel had previously been used in the chords of the arch spans of the Eads Bridge over the Mississippi River at St. Louis, Missouri, completed in 1874. The longest span of this combination railroad-highway bridge was 520 feet.

The use of long-span, cantilever truss bridges in this country was initiated in 1876 when Charles S. Smith built a bridge with three 375-foot spans over the Kentucky River for the Cincinnati Southern Railway. Other long-span cantilever bridges included the crossing of the Monongahela River, built in 1904 at Pittsburgh, Pennsylvania, having a maximum span length of 812 feet, and the Queensborough Bridge, built in 1909 in New York City, with maximum span length of 1,182 feet.

Plate girders for short spans were used during the Civil War, primarily for railroad bridges. These spans were limited to moderate length by the size of the wrought-iron plates and shapes then being rolled. Early highway bridge construction of plate girders was generally limited to short spans because of the inconvenience and cost of transportation and erection, unless the bridge was located near railroad transportation. The first American plate girder arch bridge was the Washington Bridge over the Harlem River in New York City, built in 1886-1888. There were two 510-foot arch spans with plate girder ribs 13 feet deep. The flanges were 20 inches wide.

Beginning about 1850, companies were formed primarily for constructing truss bridges. Some companies were established by bridge patentees to build their type of structure, while others produced trusses for which they were patent licensees. These companies became well established since there were relatively few bridge engineers with a working knowledge of stress analysis and truss design in the early years of iron superstructure construction. For bridges with short- and medium-length truss spans, it became the practice to let bids permitting the bidder to furnish the superstructure according to his own plans. This was satisfactory when the contractor had a competent engineer or retained a knowledgeable consultant, but this was seldom the case. While many safe and satisfactory bridges were built by this procedure, there were also many unsatisfactory ones. During the third quarter of the nineteenth century, twenty-five or more bridge failures occurred each year. Attention, focused on the problem by such organizations as the American Society of Civil Engineers, resulted in improvements. By 1900 failures became rare.

In 1801 James Finley built the first highway suspension bridge in this country over Jacobs Creek near Greensburg, Pennsylvania. It had a span of 70 feet. The supporting members were wrought-iron chains made from 1-inch-square bars. The links were varying lengths, from 5 to 10 feet long, so that the horizontal component of each link was equal to the distance between floor beams. The hangers were connected to the chain with clamps at the intersections of the links and were stirrup-shaped at the lower end to support the floor beams. The timber floor system was made relatively stiff in order to distribute the floor live loads over several hangers and to resist deformation, undulations, and vibrations from the live and wind loads. Albert Gallatin's report of 1808 cited a similar bridge by Finley across the Potomac River near the site of the present Chain Bridge just upstream from the Georgetown area of Washington, D.C. He wrote that "the principle of this new plan, derived from the tenacity of iron, seems applicable to all rapid streams of moderate breadth."

Construction of the Finley type of chain suspension bridges was popular for awhile, and a number of single and multiple span bridges were built under the direction of Finley or his licensees. The maximum span lengths were about 150 feet. The cable supports were usually timber towers on stone masonry piers. The Finley type of suspension bridge at Lehigh Gap, Pennsylvania, apparently the last one in use, was replaced by a modern structure in 1933.

The first highway bridge in America with wire suspension cables was designed by Charles Ellet and was completed in 1842. It was built to replace Lewis Wernwag's famous "Colossus," the wooden 340-foot span trussed-arch covered structure, built in 1812 over the Schuylkill River at Philadelphia and destroyed by fire in 1835. Drawn wrought-iron wires were used for the cables, as was the case for all American suspension bridges built prior to the Brooklyn Bridge.

After 1840 several wrought-iron wire bridges were built in America under the direction of Ellet, John A. Roebling, Thomas M. Griffith, Edward W. Serrell, and others. These bridges were, in general, of the suspension system type developed and built under the supervision of Marc Seguin and his brothers in France. A suspension bridge from Wheeling, Virginia, to Zane's Island in the Ohio River was designed and constructed by Ellet from 1847 to 1849. The suspension span was 1,010 feet. There were ten large and two small cables. The large cables each contained 550 strands of No. 10 wrought iron and the small cables contained 140 strands. When completed this was the longest span suspension bridge in the world. It was badly damaged by high winds in 1854, apparently by aerodynamic forces not understood until nearly a century later.

John A. Roebling supervised the design and construction of nine suspension bridges during the period 1842 to 1855. One of these was the combination highway-railroad bridge with an 821-foot span over the Niagara Falls Rapids, completed in 1854. It had four suspension cables, each with 3,640 parallel wires. Roebling also designed and directed the building of the Cincinnati suspension highway bridge over the Ohio River. Built between 1856 and 1867, its construction was delayed by the Civil War. The main span, 1,057 feet long, was the longest in the world at the time of its completion.

The Brooklyn Bridge across the East River between Manhattan and Brooklyn frequently has been described during its ninety-three year history as "The Eighth Wonder of the World." Completed in 1883 at a cost of $15.5 million, it was 50 percent longer than any other span in the world and retained the title of the longest span for some twenty years. It was not materially exceeded in length for over forty years. The center span was 1,595 feet and the side spans were 933 feet each. Along with the Eads railroad bridge in St. Louis, Missouri, which was under construction at the same time, the Brooklyn Bridge was one of the first large bridges in which pneumatic caissons were used in building the foundations. One pier foundation extended 47 feet and the other 78 feet below water.

Like all public works undertakings of this magnitude, various plans for the bridge were discussed and promoted for many years before any definite action occurred. State legislative action in 1867 incorporated the New York Bridge Company to build and maintain the bridge. At first it was a corporation in which private investors and New York City and Brooklyn (then a separate city) bought stock, but in 1874 it was placed under complete control of the two cities. Roebling was retained as chief engineer. His skill with the suspension bridge had been established by his bridges across the Niagara gorge and the highway span over the Ohio River at Cincinnati. Although the Brooklyn Bridge was his conception, Roebling never saw it completed. He lost his life as work got underway in 1869. His foot was crushed by a ferry boat while he was standing on the edge of a dock, sighting across the river to line up the tower locations. Tetanus developed and two weeks later Roebling died.

His son, Washington A. Roebling, was only thirty-one years of age, but he had been associated with his father on several bridges.

The Brooklyn Bridge, completed in 1883, has been described as "The Eighth Wonder of the World."

He was appointed to his father's former position to complete the work. Within eighteen months, he too fell victim to the bridge. Young Roebling developed caissons disease—the bends—from extended activities in the pneumatic caissons and became permanently crippled. He finished the project confined to a wheelchair at home, where he watched the work through field glasses and directed the project with the capable assistance of his wife Emily.

Safety practices of the construction crews left much to be desired. Disregard of rules caused at least three deaths from the bends and injuries to over a hundred others. Line and derrick failures, loose boards, and falling objects accounted for many other injuries and over twenty deaths.

The case of the widow Delaney illustrates the lack of concern for workmen during this period. Mrs. Delaney's husband was killed when he fell from the bridge. The trustees paid the $51.12 funeral expense and donated a sum of $25 to the widow. However, she felt this was inadequate and threatened a lawsuit. After formal action by the trustees, "not as a legal obligation but as an act of charity," she was allowed a sum of $100 to be paid in installments. She seems to have fared better than most others who were widowed by the bridge. Workmen, incidentally, were paid $2.00 per eight-hour day for the most hazardous work, but this was increased to $2.75 for those who worked in the 87-foot-deep caisson.

The six-lane bridge, hung on four $15^3/_4$-inch diameter cables, had many innovations in its design and construction. It was the culmination of a series of outstanding accomplishments in suspension bridge building in the nineteenth century. Despite many problems during its thirteen-year construction, it set a pattern for future bridges. The formal opening of the bridge was a national event, attended by such dignitaries as President Chester A. Arthur and his cabinet; the governor of New York, Grover Cleveland (later President); several other governors; representatives from most of the states; and the mayors of nearly all cities in the vicinity. The Brooklyn Bridge had a major influence in consolidating and expanding the two cities into the major metropolis of America. The bridge was designated a historic site by the National Park Service of the Department of Interior in 1964 as a structure "possessing exceptional value in commemorating and illustrating the history of the United States."

The tolls established by the Board of Trustees for users of the Brooklyn Bridge were as follows:

Traffic	Cents Toll
Pedestrians	1
Railroad fare	5
One horse, or horse and man	5
One-horse vehicle	10
Two-horse vehicle	20
Additional horses, each	5
Sheep and hogs, each	2
Neat cattle, each	5

These were periodically adjusted and finally abolished in 1911.

Two other notable suspension bridges were built over the East River at New York City. The Williamsburg Bridge, erected in 1903, has a 1,600-foot main span with four cables, each containing 7,696 wires. The Manhattan Bridge, built in 1909, has a 1,470-foot main span with four cables, each containing 9,472 wires. The Point Bridge over the Monongahela River at Pittsburgh, Pennsylvania, built in 1875-1877, was a stiffened chain suspension span 800 feet long. The main span and backstay chains were of wrought-iron link bars 20½ feet long. Warren-type trusses supported the roadway floor and served as stiffening trusses.

The nineteenth century also saw changes in design of movable bridges. The early movable spans to accommodate river traffic in colonial times were light and relatively simple. They were opened and closed by manpower, since fast opening time was not necessary for slow-moving sailing ships. However, with the advent of railroads and steam-powered boats, the weight and maneuverability of the spans became more critical. Wrought iron and then steel came into use for the bridge members.

Although steam became the operating power for railroad and primary highway movable bridges as well as for those over frequently used waterways, manpower was still used for bridges over minor waterways and secondary highways and for action during power failure. There was a transition from steam power to electric power for movable bridges from about 1895 to 1910. As the larger rivers and tidal estuaries became more fre-

quently bridged and as rivercraft became wider and longer, broader channel openings were required, necessitating longer spans on more movable bridges.

Chicago has more movable bridges than any other area in the world. The city in 1975 operated fifty-five movable spans across the Chicago River and its tributaries. The development of these bridges enabled Chicago to fully utilize its strategic location astride the waterway connection between the Great Lakes and the Mississippi River Basin and as a railroad hub. The city's first movable bridge, a primitive castle drawbridge type, was constructed of wood across the Chicago River at Dearborn Street in 1834. Two movable sections were lifted by chains from a "gallows" type framework tower at the ends of two sections. The operation was unreliable and incurred such hostility from both land and water traffic that the axes of an irate group destroyed the bridge one night in July 1839.

The next crossing was a pontoon bridge at Clark Street constructed in 1840. It was a simple structure, anchored to each bank, which could be swung open for ships. Several similar bridges followed, but all were destroyed by the floods of early 1849. They were replaced by improved designs, based on trial and error. In 1854 a pivot or swing bridge was erected at Clark Street. This type was supported on a pier in the center of the stream. It rotated so that, when open, the span was parallel to the stream, providing a passageway on each side of the pier.

The first iron bridge west of the Alleghenies was of this pivot type, completed at Rush Street in 1859, at a cost of $50,000. The bridge met a disastrous end in 1863, as described in *Chicago Public Works: A History* (1973):

At about five o'clock in the afternoon, with a hundred head of cattle, a horse and buggy and a horse-drawn wagon at the bridge along with several people, a tugboat whistled about two blocks away . . . the cattle crowded to the south end of [the bridge] . . . the tender recklessly swung the bridge from the abutment. In an instant the north end of the bridge was twenty feet in the air, there was a snapping of iron, a creaking and crashing of timbers, a shriek of horror from the bystanders, and the bridge, breaking in two across the center pier, fell with all its burden of people, cattle, and vehicles splash into the river.

Most swing bridges were destroyed by the Chicago fire of 1871 but were soon replaced with larger and more substantial structures.

As ships became bigger and wider, the center pier was an obstruction. New types of bridges were developed. In the "jackknife" type, the action of each half of the bridge was similar to that of a loosely hinged jackknife. As it was raised to its vertical position, the hinged leaves pulled back against the supporting towers on each bank. Operation of this structure, however, proved unreliable and costly.

In 1894 the first modern vertical-lift movable bridge was built to replace a swing bridge at South Halsted Street. The structure operated as a giant elevator in which the center span of the bridge, a steel truss 130 feet long, 58 feet wide, and weighing 280 tons was raised 158 feet vertically between two steel towers. The lifting was done with wire cables passing over the large grooved wheels at the tower tops and down again to large cast iron counter weights operated by steam power. It was constructed at a cost of $243,000 and served traffic for forty years despite many operational problems.

The first rolling-lift bridge was built across the Chicago River at Van Buren Street in 1894. It consisted of two movable leaves

The 80-foot span Cassleman River Bridge near Grantsville, Maryland, was the largest single-span stone arch bridge in the United States when it was constructed in 1813. It has been rehabilitated and is still in use.

and was the forerunner of the modern trunion bascule bridge, universally known as the "Chicago" type. Each leaf had cogs on its runners matching cogged rails on its shore abutments, allowing it to roll up and down like a huge rocking chair.

An intensive international study of movable bridge types was carried out in 1899 by Chicago's Department of Public Works to determine the best design. It resulted in the development of the "bascule" bridge, a French term meaning teeter-totter. The principle was based on revolving counter-balanced leaves on fixed trunions or axles. The forty-eight movable bridges built in Chicago since 1903 have been modifications of this type.

Another bridge type in the nineteenth century was the stone arch. Stone arches have not been a major element in highway bridge construction in this country because of their high cost and the special craftsmanship they require. Nevertheless, numerous short-span stone arches have been built in areas where stone and skilled masons were readily available. Until early in the twentieth century, the world's largest stone arch was the Cabin John Bridge spanning the creek by the same name in Montgomery County, Maryland. Built in 1857-1864, under the direction of Captain Montgomery C. Meigs of the Army Corps of Engineers, it is a closed spandrel arch with a span of 220 feet and a rise of 57 feet. The spandrel fill under the roadway surface carries the aqueduct furnishing water to Washington, D.C.

Natural cement entered into bridge construction after it was first made in this country in 1818 by Canvass White from rock near Fayetteville, New York. It was used initially as mortar for stone masonry and, as early as 1849, for unreinforced concrete footings and substructures. David O. Saylor is generally credited with the first manufacture of portland cement in this country at Allentown, Pennsylvania, in 1871. The portland cement industry expanded rapidly as many users of natural cement switched to this more uniform and superior type. Even so, natural cement has continued to be used to some extent. Concrete was employed for a pedestrian underpass in Clefridge Park, Brooklyn, New York, in 1871. Its arch followed the design of stone arches and had a radius of 10 feet. This structure is considered the earliest concrete arch constructed in America.

The first reinforced concrete bridge in this country was the Golden Gate Park Bridge, San Francisco, California, in 1889. This 20-foot span bridge followed the design specifications of E. L. Ransome. Other early reinforced bridges included one in Rock Rapids, Iowa, with a 36-foot span, built in 1894; Eden Park Bridge, Cincinnati, Ohio, with a 70-foot clear span arch, 1894-1895; and a 100-foot bridge in Ice Glen at Stockbridge, Massachusetts, built about 1895. The first reinforced concrete bridge of considerable size, having one 125-foot, two 110-foot, and two 97-foot arch spans, was erected over the Kansas River at Topeka, Kansas, in 1896.

Twentieth-Century Bridges

Through the years leading to the automobile age, the methods, materials, and equipment for bridge construction improved steadily with experience. By the time the federal aid highway program got underway, steam-powered equipment supplanted men and horses for heavy lifting and excavation. Deep foundation excavations in open and cellular coffer-dams and in open and pneumatic caissons were developed and successfully used. Steam piston and pulsometer pumps replaced the chain and ship pumps of colonial days for unwatering foundation excavations. Improved timber sheet piling, such as the Wakefield type, and interlocking steel sheet piling were produced, resulting in relatively watertight cofferdams.

Many steel fabricating shops utilized power equipment for fabricating and handling steel bridge members. Power shears, punches, and drills were employed. Heavy hydraulic and pneumatic riveters for driving tight rivets were developed. Relatively efficient and structurally satisfactory standards for riveted connections, pin connectors, and other structural details were in use. Efficient and safer methods were established for erecting steel superstructures. Steam-powered cranes, derricks, and gin poles were available for lifting heavy members. Relatively light

pneumatic riveting guns were used for driving field rivets so that only small and minor structures had hand-riveted or bolted connections.

These construction improvements were documented in the literature; and engineers and technicians, who knew how to apply them, were available for bridge construction. In 1910 the federal Office of Public Roads established a Division of Highway Bridges and Culverts. Upon application from a state or local political authority, it sent a bridge engineer to assist with inspections, surveys, and estimates for proposed bridges and culverts. Assistance with design and construction was also provided. In addition, the office reviewed and advised on bridge plans and specifications prepared by states, local authorities, or bridge companies. These services were extensively used.

At the start of the federal aid road program in 1916, most states had essentially a system of country roads, located and designed for pre-automobile traffic. Many of the bridge standards being used were not adequate for the volume, weight, and speed of the growing automobile and truck traffic. An immediate task was to set standards for design and construction of bridges proposed under the federal aid act and to establish procedures for submission of data, plans, and reports, and for inspections. Circular No. 100, which had been issued by the Office of Public Roads in 1913, was initially used for design, review, and construction standards. Design stresses were based on a fifteen-ton road roller for live loading.

An American Association of State Highway Officials (AASHO) Bridge Committee, composed of the bridge engineer of each state and one from the federal Bureau of Public Roads (as the former Office of Public Roads had become) gradually developed bridge specifications. Important contributions came from other organizations such as the American Society of Civil Engineers, American Institute of Steel Construction, American Society of Testing and Materials, American Concrete Institute, Portland Cement Association, and others who were directly involved in various ways with bridges. Most of state, federal, and private bridge engineers had membership in one or more of these organizations.

As the several sections of the specifications were approved, they were made available to the state highway departments and other interested organizations. A complete specification, commonly called the Conference Committee Specification, was available in 1926. The first printed edition of the AASHO *Standard Specification for Highway Bridges* was issued in 1931 and revised editions have since been published regularly. These specifications have been, with a few exceptions, criteria for bridges on the federal aid highway system and have been used extensively as guides for bridges on other state, county, and municipal roadway systems.

Hennepin County Department of Public Works

The Franklin Avenue Bridge on County Road 5 across the Mississippi River in Minneapolis, Minnesota, was completed in 1923. The deck was recently widened to carry heavier traffic volumes.

The quality of bridges improved dramatically during the 1920s because of experience, improved criteria, specifications, and guides. While the federal aid system was only a small portion of the state highway systems, the example of the improved highways and bridges created a demand for similar improvements on other state and local highways. In general, bridges on the federal aid system were of the short- to medium-span type and built at moderate cost. Until the Interstate system was funded in 1956, high-cost bridges and tunnels were usually toll facilities, built by bridge and tunnel authorities or private interests. Studies, designs, and construction supervision were done by private engineering firms. Since 1929 the financing, construction, and management of toll facilities have been accomplished almost entirely with some type of state or local public authority or commission.

Federal law at first prohibited the use of federal aid funds in the building of access roads to toll facilities. In order to discourage their construction by private interests, Congress amended the law in 1927 to permit federal aid to be used for toll bridges built, owned, and operated by states, and for the construction of approaches to these bridges. This permitted the states to receive 50 percent of the facility cost in federal aid and to sell revenue bonds for the other 50 percent. The facilities were required to become free after the tolls had paid off the revenue bonds. However, the federal aid funds had to come out of the regular allocation to the state; and as a result, only six toll bridges have been funded with federal aid assistance.

A severe flood in November 1927 washed out many bridges on the Vermont and New Hampshire highway systems. Congress appropriated emergency relief funds to aid the states in the reconstruction of the flood-destroyed roads and bridges. Bureau of Public Roads engineers assisted the states in a survey of damages, and bridge engineers were assigned to aid the Vermont Highway Department in the design and construction of replacement bridges. Since that time, Congress has made regular provisions for federal funds to restore highway facilities on the federal aid system that are extensively damaged by natural disasters.

When the 1944 highway act authorized a Federal Aid Secondary Highway System for farm-to-market and feeder roads, minimum standards for roads and bridges on the system were established cooperatively by the Bureau of Public Roads, AASHO, and the National Association of County Engineers. Criteria for new bridges was based on traffic volume. Improvement required for existing bridges that were to remain in place was minimal. However, a safety provision was made that the roadway width of an existing bridge must be as wide or wider than the paved width of adjacent road improvements. Many bridges of the secondary system are still inadequate for the traffic they carry.

The construction of the Interstate system to meet current and future traffic needs required important changes in the character of highway bridges. Standards for traffic and load capacity, the various physical dimensions that affect safe movement of vehicles, and the appearance of structures were given careful study in order to provide for the safe and free movement of vehicles over bridges. Good architectural treatment of structures was encouraged, especially for improvements that could be made without substantial cost increases. Private engineering and architectural firms have designed most of the major bridges in urban areas and on the Interstate system.

Continuing study of bridge railings led to the use of wider curbs of adequate height and to streamlined railings of greater strength with wide, smooth-faced lower rails. Full width roadways, including the shoulders, were used for safety on bridges. Particular attention was given to horizontal clearance for vehicles at underpasses, and design policies were established for greater clearances to sidewalls and center piers than had been customary. Elimination of traffic hazards at the approaches to bridges and improvements in the arrangement of ends of curbs, walks, and railings were also encouraged.

The improved criteria also advocated continuous span construction. This type of construction, in which trusses, girders, or slabs are made continuous for two or more span lengths instead of using simple or separate spans between each pair of supports, usually saves material and is particularly advantageous in reducing the number of expansion joints which require maintenance and cause an uncomfortable riding surface for motorists. This type of structure has increased markedly in recent years.

The use of composite steel I-beam and concrete slab bridges increased rapidly after World War II. The critical item in this type of design was the shear connector between the steel beam or girder and the concrete slab. Extensive studies and research tests on the connectors and on full-sized composite beams developed sound requirements for composite

structures which were included in the AASHO bridge specifications. Another area of improvement was in welded steel structures. Failures in welding due to lack of toughness in steel were frequent until cooperative efforts by bridge engineers, the American Society for Testing and Materials, and steel producers created a satisfactory welding steel. The specifications were first published in 1954 and later revised in 1960. The availability of these steels rapidly expanded the scope and volume of welded structures, for they allowed more versatile and economical designs.

In the early 1950s, reports on European use of prestressed concrete bridges aroused the interest of engineers and cement producers in this country. The Bureau of Public Roads together with cement producers studied the theory, literature, and tests of prestressed concrete. In 1955 the bureau published a report, *Criteria for Prestressed Concrete Bridges,* the only such publication in the United States at the time. Guided by this pamphlet and standard plans prepared by the cement industry and the bureau, the use of prestressed concrete for bridges rapidly developed not only on the federal aid system but on all structures. Many of the overpasses are now being built with precast, prestressed concrete beams and girders. The first prestressed concrete girder was a 160-foot span in Philadelphia, built in 1949. The largest to date are the 269 post-tensioned girders, 196 feet long and weighing 240 tons each, placed in the South Channel Jamaica Bay-Cross Bay Parkway Bridge on Long Island, New York. This 3,100-foot, six-lane bridge was built by the Triborough Bridge and Tunnel Authority of New York City in 1970.

The improved techniques of bridge construction with precast, prestressed concrete members have had a great impact in recent years, especially in the construction of the Interstate system. A structure that dramatically demonstrates the potential of precast members is the 24-mile bridge across Lake Ponchartrain in Louisiana, completed in 1956. All the elements of this structure—the piles, pile-caps, girders, deck beams, and deck-slab units—were precast and prestressed on shore, floated to position on barges, and then put in place by pile drivers and cranes floating on barges.

Bridges of increasing size and span, during the first half of the twentieth century, have had a tremendous effect on American cities whose sites were limited by water barriers. The prolific building years of the 1930s produced many of the world's largest bridges and changed the character of cities such as San Francisco, New York, New Orleans, and Pittsburgh. The record-making Brooklyn and Williamsburg suspension bridges in New York City were surpassed by two bridges in the 1920s; first by the Philadelphia-Camden Bridge with a span exceeding that of the Brooklyn Bridge by 130 feet and with a deck 50 percent wider; and the Ambassador Bridge completed in 1929 at Detroit with its span of 1,850 feet, at that time the longest bridge span in the world.

In 1921 the states of New York and New Jersey established the Port Authority to finance, construct, and maintain various facilities in the New York City area. It demonstrated the success of financing large structures with revenue bonds to be repaid by tolls. The method has been widely followed elsewhere. The authority planned the George Washington Bridge from Fort Lee, New Jersey, to 179th Street in New York City, with a span of 3,500 feet, almost doubling that of the record bridge at Detroit.

The first stage of the bridge, one eight-lane deck (there were provisions for a lower deck to carry a four-track rapid transit line to be added later) was completed in 1931 at a cost of $75 million. The four 36-inch diameter cables contain 26,474 steel wires each, with a total length of wire of 107,000 miles. As the volume of traffic increased, plans were changed in order to make the lower deck a seven-lane vehicular facility. This was completed in 1962 and cost an additional $183 million. The steel space-frame towers are of unparalleled size and stand 635 feet above the top of the piers. Designed by the authority, with Othman H. Ammann as chief engineer, the bridge is still the world's greatest suspension bridge in total weight. The open caissons for the piers extended to 80 feet below water surface, a record at that time.

Another record bridge, also completed in 1931 by the authority, was the Bayonne Bridge across the Kill van Kull between Bayonne, New Jersey, and Staten Island, New York. It is a steel arch span of 1,652 feet, still the longest steel arch in the world, and it was the first to use carbon manganese steel. The Triborough Bridge, built by the Triborough Bridge and Tunnel Authority and connecting Manhattan, Bronx, and Queens, is a series of bridges and viaducts having a total length of 3½ miles. It opened to traffic in 1936.

Other important bridges followed. The 4,260-foot center-span suspension Verrazano-Narrows Bridge across the entrance to New York Harbor, between Brooklyn and Staten Island, opened for traffic on the upper six-lane deck in November 1964. Like the George Washington Bridge, provisions were made for adding a lower six-lane deck when traffic warranted, and this was completed and opened in June 1969. The bridge has the longest span in the world; its towers extend 693 feet above water, and the four 36-inch diameter cables contain 143,000 miles of

Triborough Bridge and Tunnel Authority

The four 36-inch diameter cables of the 4,260-foot center span of the Verrazano-Narrows Bridge, the world's longest, contains 143,000 miles of galvanized high strength steel wire. Extending across the mouth of New York harbor, it was opened for traffic in 1964.

galvanized high-strength steel wire. The special steel wire is four times as strong as ordinary structural steel. Wire of conventional steel suspended from tower to tower would not be strong enough to support its own weight. The construction cost of the bridge was $230 million; the total cost including land acquisition, financing, engineering, and administration was $320 million. By 1975 it was carrying over 40 million vehicles per year.

At the beginning of this century, San Francisco was a disintegrated community, somewhat isolated. Its narrow peninsula provided the only land access to the rest of the state. The changes in the social and economic pattern of the city have come about primarily as a result of the record bridges that now tie the communities around the bay together. The broad waterways of the bay, coupled with the history and future probability of earthquakes, presented great obstacles to bridge construction.

The rapid growth of automobile traffic in the early 1920s added to the need for bridges and offered a means of producing the necessary funds to finance construction costs, following the example of the authorities established in New York City. The use of revenue bonds amortized by tolls had proven to be an effective means of financing such facilities. The American Toll Bridge Company was formed in 1923 to finance and build the span at Carquinez Strait, the first of a great complex of bridges. This bridge joined the north and south halves of coastal California, cut off by Suisan and San Pablo bays. The truss bridge has two long spans of the cantilever-suspension type, the longest being 1,100 feet between bearings. The bridge was opened to traffic in 1927, and in 1958 a parallel structure of similar design was constructed as a part of the Interstate Highway System.

Crossings of the bay to San Francisco had been under study for years, and a series of proposals had been formulated as early as 1856. This resulted, in the 1930s, in two of the world's greatest bridges being under construction in the area at the same time: the 8$\frac{1}{2}$-mile-long San Francisco-Oakland Bay Bridge and the Golden Gate Bridge. The former is still the world's greatest overall bridge structure; and the Golden Gate Bridge, with its 4,200-foot center span, retained the title for the world's longest span for over thirty years. It was then exceeded by the Verrazano-Narrows Bridge in New York, which is 60 feet longer.

The Bay Bridge, started in 1933 and opened to traffic in 1936, is two different structures separated by Yerba Buena Island. The west portion is a double suspension bridge, and the east portion is a combination of through and deck trusses, with a cantilever channel span of 1,400 feet, a record in the country for over twenty years. It was designed and constructed for the California Toll Bridge Authority by the State Highway Department. The outstanding feature of the bridge is the center pier of two 2,310-foot suspension spans, which extends 220 feet below the water surface to bedrock, a record in depth and size of pier. A special caisson, consisting of fifty-five steel cylinders, 15 feet in diameter, sealed at the top with a removable cover, was devised for its construction. By an ingenious system of air ballasting of the capped steel cylinders to control alignment, the caisson was sunk through the bottom mud to bedrock.

The structure is double decked with six lanes on each deck and cost $76 million. Financial backing for the structure was difficult in the midst of the Depression years, until Congress approved a $73 million loan from the Federal Reconstruction Finance Corporation in June 1932. Construction began in July 1933 with fanfare; President Franklin D. Roosevelt touched off a blast by pressing a special key at the White House. Former President Herbert Hoover was the principal speaker at the site and stated that the structure, when completed, would be "the greatest bridge yet erected by the human race." The bridge was opened to traffic on November 12, 1936, as President Roosevelt pressed an electric button in Washington which flashed a green "Go" signal at the bridge.

The crossing of the one-mile waterway at Golden Gate presented unprecedented challenges from the standpoint of its span length and pier construction. The first specific

California Department of Transportation

The Golden Gate Bridge, across the entrance to San Francisco Harbor, is often acclaimed as the world's most beautiful bridge.

proposal for a crossing called for a combination suspension and cantilever bridge and was made in 1920 by Joseph B. Strauss, who eventually became chief engineer for the structure. In May 1923, a Golden Gate Bridge and Highway District was created by the state legislature to plan, finance, and construct the bridge. Doubts about its feasibility delayed getting the bond issue approved by the voters until November 1930.

Construction began in January 1933 and the $36 million bridge was opened to traffic in May 1937. The two towers are 746 feet above sea level and support the 36³/₈-inch diameter cables which extend across the 4,200-foot span. The south pier, extending 100 feet below water surface, presented problems due to the strong tidal currents. The pier location was finally enclosed within a concrete cofferdam, originally intended as a protective fender against the currents but then extended around the pier location to enclose it. The pier

was constructed in the dry. An item of special interest was the use of a safety net of manila rope, woven with a 6-inch mesh and extending under the entire structure and 10 feet out on each side. This net is credited with saving nineteen lives during construction. It has since been adopted as standard safety practice on bridge construction. The Golden Gate Bridge has been called "the world's most beautiful bridge" and deserves the title from its spectacular setting, its unity and simplicity of design, and its unique towers.

Like San Francisco, New Orleans is almost entirely surrounded by water. By the 1930s, studies had been made concerning ways to overcome the difficulties of a 3,000-foot-wide, 215-foot-deep river having a normal flow of about a million cubic feet per second. A minimum clearance of 135 feet was required for navigation, and the foundation was outwash from the Mississippi for a depth of over 4,000 feet to bedrock. However, borings indicated a compacted sand layer at the 180-foot depth that, with proper design, would support a bridge.

During the administration of Governor Huey P. Long, a Public Belt Railroad Commission was created, and revenue bonds were issued for financing a combination railroad and highway bridge. Construction began in 1933 on this 4¹/₃-mile continuous steel bridge. It is still the longest of its type in the world, although the cantilever channel span is a modest 790 feet in length. It was opened to traffic in 1935. Another crossing to New Orleans, a single deck highway cantilever bridge, was completed in 1958. The main span of 1,575 feet is the longest truss span in the United States.

Suspension bridges received a setback in 1940 when the Tacoma Narrows Bridge across Puget Sound collapsed. The main suspension span of 2,800 feet, the third longest in the world at the time of its construction, was designed with economy and beauty as foremost considerations. No special problems were encountered in construction and, in July 1940, it was opened to traffic. But, 130 days later, the Tacoma *News Tribune* printed one of its most astounding banner lines in large red letters: "NARROWS

BRIDGE COLLAPSES." For some time the structure had been undulating in the wind, so much that it had been nicknamed "Galloping Gertie." On the day of the collapse, the wind was blowing at forty miles per hour. Some had predicted that "Galloping Gertie" might twist herself into destruction, but the collapse was a shocking surprise to the ablest bridge engineers and to the public. Most startled of all was a Seattle insurance agent who had written some of the $5 million insurance on the bridge. Deciding it could not possibly fall, he had pocketed the premium. He was sent to the state penitentiary.

The bridge's failure resulted in extensive reevaluations of suspension bridge design theories and became a milestone in advancing the field. These intensive studies showed that the failure was caused by forces which had not, until then, been considered critical. It was demonstrated that the bridge created a turbulent flow of air around the structure causing whorls and vortices in the airstream. The small alternating forces synchronized and caused the structure to oscillate. Because of the adverse aerodynamic form of the 8-foot-deep girders and the lack of weight and stiffness, the bridge was not capable of nullifying the forces. Better understanding of the failure of the Wheeling Bridge in 1854 would have averted this disaster.

After being delayed by World War II, work on a new bridge began in April 1948. The second bridge—4,979 feet long and costing $16.5 million—was opened to traffic October 14, 1950, only a few days less than ten years after "Galloping Gertie" had collapsed. Today the graceful Narrows Bridge stands solid. It carries approximately 10 million vehicles a year between Tacoma and the territory to the west. The new bridge provides four lanes of traffic instead of two. Each driving lane is separated from the next by open steel gratings which not only serve as effective stabilizing agents, but as dividing strips to keep vehicles in their lanes. The sides or stiffening trusses of the new bridge are 33 feet deep.

These are examples of major bridges that have influenced the development of the nation. Others could be discussed, such as the

eight bridges across the Potomac River at Washington, D.C.; the Mackinac Straits Bridge in Michigan with its 3,800-foot main span and a total 8,614-foot suspension span, including anchor spans, completed in 1957; the several bridges across the Allegheny and Monongahela rivers tying the Golden Triangle of Pittsburgh to its surrounding area; the 1,271-foot steel arch bridge across the Colorado River canyon at Glen Canyon Dam in Arizona, 700 feet above the river; the two 1.3-mile concrete pontoon bridges across Lake Washington near Seattle; the 17.5-mile Chesapeake Bay Bridge-Tunnel and the two 7.7-mile Chesapeake Bay bridges in Maryland; the parallel and duplicate 2,150-foot-span Delaware Memorial bridges between Delaware and New Jersey; the 3-mile Pulaski Skyway between Newark and Jersey City, New Jersey; and still others that have been public works achievements of magnitude and have made great contributions to man's mobility. They demonstrate increasing understanding of natural forces and materials and the ability to apply this understanding to meet the needs of society. They also illustrate man's capacity to create, to achieve, and to resolve problems.

In 1975 there were about 567,000 bridge structures on the nation's highway system, of which 238,000 were on the federal aid system, and 329,000 were on the remaining state and local systems. Most of the major bridges are toll structures. There were 178 toll bridges in the United States in 1974; ninety-six were intrastate, fifty-eight were interstate, and twenty-four were international; with a total length of about 375 miles.

Tunnels

The first highway tunnel constructed in the United States was located in California. Built during the 1870s, the tunnel pierces a high rock cliff on the Pacific Ocean, about 6 miles south of San Francisco. The bore was constructed to provide the local ranchers with easy access to the city. The first tunnel of substantial length built to accommodate automobile traffic is also located in California. Completed in 1901, the Third Street Tunnel passes through Bunker Hill in the downtown

APWA New York-New Jersey Metropolitan Chapter

Mockups illustrate the Holland Tunnel under the Hudson River at New York City, with the proposed ventilating system, compared to the existing railroad tunnel. The vehicular tunnel was opened to traffic in 1927.

area of Los Angeles. Interestingly, the contractor made an unsuccessful attempt to use a tunnel boring machine on this project. Because his crude machine was able to travel only 80 feet, technical journals of the day held the idea up to ridicule.

Some of the most famous American highway tunnels were built in the 1920s. A comprehensive research program developed the fundamental data regarding vehicular tunnel ventilation early in the decade. The research was conducted for the design of the Holland Tunnel. Passing under the Hudson River between New Jersey and New York, it opened to traffic in 1927 as the nation's first major subaqueous vehicular tunnel. However, the drilling method had been pioneered in the Hudson railroad tunnel which was under construction for thirty-four years before its completion in 1908.

In 1924 the Liberty Twin tunnels were completed in Pittsburgh, Pennsylvania, and, at 5,800 feet, were the longest highway mountain tunnels in the country. At the same time, the Posey Tube under the estuary between Oakland and Alameda, California, was nearing completion. When opened to traffic in 1928, it became the first highway tunnel in the world to be built by the "trench method." An American innovation, this technique consists of sinking prefabricated tunnel sections into a prepared trench on the river bed. Thirteen highway tunnels have been built in the United States by the trench method, the latest being the Wallace Tunnel which opened to traffic in

1973 on Interstate Route 10 in Mobile, Alabama.

The majority of the tunnel construction in the 1930s was in the western states. Many of these tunnels were located on new access routes into national parks. Probably the most notable accomplishment during the 1930s was the Yerba Buena Island Tunnel connecting the San Francisco-Oakland Bay bridges in California. Completed in 1937, it remains the only double-deck highway tunnel in the country.

The first of the present three tubes comprising the 8,216-foot-long Lincoln Tunnel from New Jersey to Manhattan was completed in 1937; the other tubes followed in 1945 and 1957. Each has two lanes and directions are reversible as necessary to accommodate directional traffic peaks. Immediately following World War II, tunnel construction activity increased, and in 1950 another record was established. The 9,117-foot-long Brooklyn-Battery Tunnel under the East River in New York City had two parallel two-lane tunnels, 15 feet apart, and became the longest highway tunnel in the country.

Since the early 1960s, the bulk of highway tunnel construction has been on the Interstate Highway System. To date, fifteen major tunnels have been completed on the Interstate, four are under construction, and thirteen others are under design. These facilities are planned to handle safely high-speed, high-volume traffic.

One of the most famous of these is the

Colorado Department of Transportation

The Eisenhower Tunnel through the continental divide west of Denver, Colorado, was difficult to construct. It is one of 104 major vehicular tunnels in the United States.

Straight Creek, now designated the Eisenhower Tunnel, on Interstate Route 70 through the backbone of the Rocky Mountains west of Denver Colorado. This 1.7-mile tunnel was one of the most difficult to construct. Nearly 1,900 feet of bad ground required slow and costly drift excavations completely around the tunnel periphery. Concrete lining in some areas is as much as 10 feet thick. Upon completion of the tunnel in 1973, the contractors received the American Public Works Association's Contractor-of-the-Year award. Now that the $109 million tunnel is finished, there is no evidence of the construction problems; and travel through the tunnel is routine. The 19,000 vehicles that have driven through the mountain on a peak day have little feel for the drama of its construction. The two-lane bore will have a parallel tunnel as traffic volume increases.

In 1975 there were 104 major vehicular tunnels in the United States with a total length of about 90 miles. The highway lane miles of tunnels is 168 miles. Most of the tunnels are two lanes.

Signing and Traffic Controls

The first attempt to legislate road numbers and signs appears to be a 1704 Maryland statuate requiring that each road leading to a ferry, courthouse, or church be marked on both sides with two notches on each tree along the roadside. Those roads leading to a courthouse required an extra notch, higher up; to a ferry, another notch equal distance above the other two; and to a church, "a slipe cutt down the face of the tree near the ground."

Stone markers at 2-mile intervals were placed on sections of the principal road from New York to Philadelphia as early as 1743. The new nation's first turnpike, the Lancaster Road, was required by its charter to provide milestone and directional signs. Most companies that built turnpikes thereafter were obligated to furnish some type of direction signs and markers. As bicycling surged into popularity during the latter part of the nineteenth century, a flurry of improvements in signing took place, especially near the cities.

While traffic control signals and lights were used in London in the 1800s (the first traffic signal with colored lights was installed near the House of Parliament in 1868), they did not appear in the United States until well into the twentieth century. The Institute of Traffic Engineers report in their *Traffic Devices and Historical Aspects Thereof:* "when the twentieth century began, the only traffic signals in our own country were the ubiquitous red-globed kerosene lanterns hanging over holes or standing on obstructions."

Toledo, Ohio, in 1908 appears to be the first city to use manually operated semaphores; and then in 1913, one was installed in Detroit and another in Philadelphia. Flint, Michigan, provided a small booth to protect the operator from the elements at its semaphore erected in 1916. One of the first electric traffic lights was developed in 1912 in Salt Lake City, Utah, by Lester Wire, a detective on the city police force. It was described as a "wooden box with a slanted roof . . . . The lights were colored with red and green dye and shone through circular openings. The box was mounted on a pole and the wires were attached to the overhead trolley and light wires. It was operated by a policeman." In March 1917, Salt Lake City achieved another milestone. The world's first electrically interconnected signal system was developed by Charles Reading, an electrician who had worked with Wire on his signal. Six signals, three on Main Street and three on the adjacent State Street, were interconnected to provide uninterrupted traffic flow at twenty miles an hour. Although rather crudely built, they were effective.

Cleveland adopted an electric signal in 1914, reportedly patterned after one installed in St. Paul. Experiments in San Francisco in 1915 with signal lights and semaphores, bolstered by an automatic whistle, demonstrated ways to improve the systems. These were followed by traffic towers which began rising in all parts of the country about 1916 and started a "tower era" that extended into the late 1920s. As traffic congestion problems grew with increasing automobile travel, many other innovations were introduced to improve traffic flow. The "red, yellow, and green" traffic signal, as known today, is credited to William Potts of the Detroit police department and was installed in 1920 at the intersection of Woodward Avenue and Fort Street.

Effective road signing took a long time to evolve; for until a system of roads was developed, travel outside cities was limited. In Wisconsin in 1918 the state highway department began to erect official route signs as part of its regular maintenance functions, apparently the first such state effort. The AASHO at its annual meeting in Chicago in January 1923 adopted a signing and marking plan that became the basis for national standards to be agreed upon two years later. In April 1923, Minnesota published what is believed to be the first manual on markers and signs.

The growing congestion on streets in major cities increased accidents and adversely affected commerce. The expanding national concern for better methods and means to control traffic resulted in a National Conference on Street and Highway Safety being called in 1924 by Secretary of Commerce Herbert Hoover to consider the problem. The report of the conference stated that "Proper signs and signals are essential to the safe movement of traffic on any street or highway . . . . Signs should be uniform for a given purpose throughout the United States . . . . It can be assumed that the federal aid signs . . . will be uniform in every state, and will point the way for state and county highway authorities to follow the same standards . . . . All signs should be simple, with the least amount of wording necessary to make them readily understood, depending mainly on distinctive shapes, symbols, and colors."

The report further recommended familiar color indications (such as red for "stop," green for "proceed," and yellow for "caution") on control lights and at curves, and special cautionary indicators at crossroads. It also suggested that distance and direction signs be black and white; and railroad crossings remaining at grade be safeguarded in every reasonable way. Highway lane striping was prescribed, as were parking restrictions.

The secretary of agriculture appointed a Joint Board on Interstate Highways in March

U.S. Department of Transportation

Designation of a system of interstate roads and adoption of uniform indication signs was accomplished in 1925.

1925, including twenty-one members from state highway departments and three from the Bureau of Public Roads, to examine highway signing and route numbering. The board made recommendations for a proposed interstate route numbering system and a comprehensive set of designs. The system devised for numbering the interstate network of highways, now called the U. S. Route System, designated even numbers for east and west roads and odd numbers for north and south roads. Long-distance, cross-country routes, east and west, were given multiples of ten. The principal north and south routes were given ones and fives such as one, five, eleven, and fifteen. Other numbered routes could be used for shorter lines between main highways. The joint board sign standards followed closely the 1924 conference recommendations with the addition of the now familiar "U.S. Shield" marker for the new network. These were accepted by AASHO and subsequently adopted by letter ballot of the state highway departments.

In 1927 AASHO published its first *Manual and Specifications for the Manufacture, Display, and Erection of U. S. Standard Road Markers and Signs.* The manual set forth the design and use of each type of sign. It listed a series of working drawings of standard signs and alphabets, and it contained detailed specifications for materials and manufacture of various types of wood and metal signs. A second edition in 1929 authorized the use of a luminous element mounted below a standard sign or on a separate post. A 1931 revised edition added a number of new types, including another design for junction markers.

Two years after the publication of the 1927 AASHO manual, the National Conference on Street and Highway Safety, recognizing the need for greater uniformity in street traffic signs, signals, and markings, sponsored a national survey of existing urban sign conditions and prepared a recommended manual of practice. The resulting report accepted most of the AASHO sign manual standards for urban usage, but also included traffic signals, pavement markings, and safety zones. The recommendations included terms, systems, control types, colors, specifications, beacons, and "wigwag" and flashing light train signals. There were then two national manuals, one for rural use and the other for municipal use, with some significant differences between them. Representatives of the developers of the two manuals came together to form a Joint Committee on Uniform Traffic Control Devices. They prepared a combined manual which was subsequently approved as the standard code for application on federal aid highways. It appeared in printed form as the 1935 *Manual on Uniform Traffic Control Devices for Streets and Highways* (MUTCD). Several revisions and reworkings have periodically been issued.

In 1956 AASHO set up a committee to develop an Interstate system signing and marking manual, utilizing the best experience on rural and urban toll roads and freeways. After approval by the Bureau of Public Roads, it was adopted as standard for the Interstate system and was published in 1958 as the *Manual for Signing and Pavement Marking of the National System of Interstate and Defense Highways*. Some revisions have since been adopted.

The various standards, which generally reflect the best practices, have made traffic movement safer and more efficient on the existing streets and highways and have become of growing importance as interstate travel has increased. Some problems were encountered in getting nationwide standards accepted, but cooperative involvement in determining and adopting them has overcome differing local preferences. After approval by the federal government as standard for federal aid routes, adhering to the standards is mandatory in order for the states to receive federal aid funds.

The first interconnected stop and go signal in 1917 was refined over the next decade, and by 1929 the first traffic-actuated signal was installed in Chicago. Within a couple of years such signals were in use in over 150 cities. When a car approached an intersection, a pressure-sensitive device tripped the signal light cycle. Various types of detection devices were developed such as photoelectric cells. By 1933 Montreal, Canada, had a large-scale, traffic-actuated system covering fifty intersections. Many other cities followed suit. Washington, D.C., had a fifteen-intersection system in operation the following year.

Surveillance of traffic by television cameras at a central control point, where signals of various kinds could be controlled, was initiated in Detroit in the late 1950s. This has evolved into a variety of operating traffic control systems. In the 1950s, computers came into use in processing detector data to control signal light cycles in large areas to make them responsive to actual traffic movement. The first extensive system of this type was installed in Denver in 1952. Such installations have become increasingly sophisticated so that by the 1970s, data from detectors could be stored and processed in a variety of ways, making full use of analog and digital computers and centralized automatic controls. These improvements, along with standardized signs and markings, have assisted in making existing roadways more effective in moving traffic and safer for all concerned.

Parking

Off-street parking was provided for the farmer's horse and buggy, where the horses could rest and eat while farmers took care of their city shopping chores. These areas, often odorous from manure and feed refuse, attracted large swarms of flies. Curb parking was informal. As the cities grew in size, more attention was paid to sanitary conditions, but increasing congestion of horses, wagons, and buggies created insolvable problems. Abandoned vehicles on the streets of New York City, for instance, did not originate with automobiles, for abandoned wagons created big problems in the late 1800s.

The free use of the streets including parking was generally considered a right, but the growth of automobile travel into downtown areas created problems. In the early 1930s, the Hartford Municipal League reported that "Probably no problem is more continually annoying to both citizens and the city government than that of parking in the downtown area." While city ordinances early established street parking time limits, it was not until 1935 that the first parking meter was installed in Oklahoma City. The initial court decision establishing parking as a "privilege and not a right" was that of the Florida Supreme Court in 1936, concerning parking meters in Miami. They were strongly opposed by groups such as the American Automobile Association. Meters were regarded as an additional unwarranted tax on the overtaxed motorist, even though the initial charge, which continued for many years afterward, was only five cents per hour or longer.

By August 1936, eleven cities had installed parking meters, after passing appropriate city ordinances. Six years later, the number had grown to 320, and by 1949 the total was over 800. By 1953 parking meters were considered a mature American institution, for over 2,800 cities had more than a million meters, with an annual revenue of about $70 per meter.

Initially, private interests provided facilities for off-street parking. However, with increasing needs, private interests were unable to meet the demand because of financing problems or inability to acquire sites suitably located to fit the overall traffic needs. Thus, the municipalities became involved in providing parking space as a government function. In the latter part of the 1930s, municipalities began parking vehicles on vacant lots. A

survey in 1946 showed 344 cities were furnishing publicly owned off-street parking facilities, but only fifteen were charging for the privilege. The fee was usually ten cents a day; Miami, Florida, charged twenty-five cents. Four of the cities had metered lots. By then, five states had passed laws permitting the establishment of parking districts or authorities to finance and operate parking facilities.

The post-World War II years brought a crushing demand for parking space in commercial city center areas, not only in the large cities, but the smaller ones as well. These needs were met by public works facilities of various kinds to supplement those provided by private owners. In the 1960s, parking needs expanded to neighborhood shopping areas, sports stadiums, rapid transit connections, and—one of the biggest problems—airports. City ordinances were passed to cope with parking problems such as requiring off-street parking facilities to accompany new construction. Parking on alternate sides of the street every other day was necessary to facilitate street cleaning, and permits for all-night parking were required in some areas.

The needs in the central business districts have been met with multilevel parking structures. A survey made in 1972 by the National League of Cities showed that 6,464 cities (46 percent of the total) had municipally owned parking garages, carried on the books at $5 billion, with an annual revenue of over $250 million. The study further demonstrated that 8,246 cities had about 6.3 million parking spaces available; 67 percent of the total spaces were municipally owned; the remainder were provided by private interests. Several studies have indicated that at least $500 million a year will be expended in new parking facilities for the next ten to fifteen years.

Parking structures constructed in 1972 totaled 451; in 1973, 392 structures were completed; and in 1974 the number was 363, according to a report of the National Parking Association. The median size was approximately 500 spaces, ranging to a maximum of 5,000. About a fourth of the structures provided over 1,000 spaces. Approximately two thirds of the structures were in the city central

This Lakeland, Florida parking structure, completed in 1971, is representative of modern design.

business districts. The remaining were outside the central area in shopping centers and in outlying "park and ride" facilities at rapid transit stations.

An example of one of the better facilities that furnishes parking space as a key component of transport modal interchange is the Market Street East facility in Philadelphia. Under construction at a cost of $8.5 million, it will provide 850 parking spaces as a part of a commuter railroad, bus terminal, subway, and office and retail store complex. Other well-designed, similar installations have been built or are being planned across the nation. Another facility, with 750 parking spaces, which is well designed to fit its location architecturally and from the traffic standpoint, is the $1.4 million municipal parking structure built of cast-in-place concrete, completed in Lakeland, Florida, in 1971. Another example is a 350-space concrete municipal garage that was finished in Columbia, South Carolina, in 1966 at a cost of $652,000.

Structures and Highway Safety

Accidents in highway travel have long been a problem, and in the horse and buggy days, runaway teams often caused serious accidents and fatalities. Data is limited, but what is available indicates the accident rate per mile traveled may have been greater with horse and buggy travel than with automobiles. However, it was not until the increase in automotive travel in the 1920s that highway accident fatalities became a problem of national concern. By 1924 fatalities had reached almost 20,000 per year. This, along with problems of congestion on city streets, led to the National Conference on Street and Highway Safety in December 1924. The first of many similar conferences, it brought together representatives of state highway and motor vehicle commissions, police departments, insurance companies, railroads, safety councils, chambers of commerce, labor unions, women's clubs, automobile associations and manufacturers, and truck and bus operators. With this broad array of concerned and involved organizations working on the problem, much progress was made.

An index of articles on highway safety, prepared by the Bureau of Public Roads, listed over 2,400 articles published in American and European journals during the years 1923 to 1927, indicating an intense concern for the problem of highway safety. This work has since continued unabated, as accidents and death on the highways are still among the nation's greatest tragedies. Data on accidents has been collected, problem areas defined, and corrective measures formulated. Uniform traffic controls and signing, speed limits, improved safety features of vehicles and highway design, procedures for effective driver information and safety instruction, driving laws and enforcement, and many other items have been developed. The problems are complex and cut across many troublesome areas of today's society. For instance, statistics show that the use of alcohol is a contributing factor in about 50 percent of traffic accident fatalities.

One of the major safety issues in early automotive years was the railroad crossings on heavily traveled roads. As discussed in Chapter 3, cities and railroads cooperatively launched an extensive program to eliminate railroad crossings on streets in the 1890s. Elimination of rural road crossings, however, was slow in getting underway. Crossings were initially thought to be the responsibility of the railroad, but as automobile traffic grew, this idea gradually changed to place the main burden on highways. Starting in 1934, over $700 million from special emergency relief and other funds were made available during the Depression to correct railroad grade crossing hazards. In 1937 states eliminated over 1,300 railroad crossings, and by 1941 the majority of the most hazardous ones were removed or protected. However, many remained, and the program has since continued.

By 1975, 13,150 crossings had been eliminated or reconstructed, and activated lights and gates had been installed at 13,700 crossings at a cost of about $4 billion. A 1972 study by the Department of Transportation showed 223,000 locations where public roads cross railroads at grade, of which 48,500 have train-activated protective devices. The study recommended a program of protective devices for at least 3,000 crossings per year and the elimina-

tion of 200 crossings annually for the next ten years.

The accident rate per vehicle mile traveled is an index of progress made in highway safety. In 1920 it was 28.2 fatalities per 100 million miles traveled, eight times as high as the 1975 rate of 3.6. The decline has been generally steady as the result of safer highways and vehicles. The establishment of a 55-mile-per-hour speed limit in 1974, as a result of the energy crisis, decreased highway accidents at least 10 percent. The fatality rate in 1973 was 4.3. Controlled access highways with grade separations, the modern toll roads, and the Interstate system have had an accident rate half or less the overall average. In 1974 over 46,000 people were killed and 1.8 million suffered disabling injuries in 14.4 million highway accidents; property damage totaled over $10 billion.

The problem in providing the safety features in highways, so similar to most other public works undertakings, is that the needs keep far ahead of the funds allocated. It is probable that facilities will never catch up, thus judgment and careful management is a continual requirement in establishing priorities that will give the best returns among the many competing needs. The difficulties arise in determining where the most attention and funds should be directed.

The 1966 Motor Vehicle Safety Act focused on vehicle safety as well as providing for the establishment of standards to improve the safety aspects of highway design and construction. The act created an organization that evolved into the National Highway Traffic Safety Administration. Further concern of Congress, however, was that safety features were being added as incidental appurtenances to larger highway construction and reconstruction projects. This led to the 1973 Highway Safety Act, which authorized funds to concentrate on safety features of highways, as a gigantic demonstration project, and to test out new concepts and approaches. It initiated detailed evaluations to determine the most cost-beneficial way to reduce accidents and thus prevent injury and save lives. It was an attempt to temper "perfection" with common sense and know-how. Following the 1966 act,

The Asphalt Institute

Traffic lane markings, lighting, and signing on modern, well-located expressways, such as this Interstate belt route near the nation's capital, result in accident rates less than half the average.

much has been learned about crash energy control through development of various highway structures such as crash cushions, breakaway signs and luminair supports as well as improved guardrails, bridge railings, and median barriers. Cleaner and more gently contoured roadsides also have been provided. Studies have indicated these features alone reduced accidents about 25 percent. In 1974 the American Association of State Highway and Transportation Officials (formerly AASHO) issued its book *Highway Design and Operation Practices Related to Highway Safety.*

The problem of keeping abreast of the highway traffic needs, with increasing vehicles and travel, is a serious one, and a higher level of funding will be required. Ways to better manage traffic on existing facilities are being studied. Many roadbeds and pavements are wearing out and need reconstruction, and about 78,000 existing bridges are seriously inadequate for the traffic loads they carry. Realistic overall evaluation, including consideration of energy shortages, traffic congestion in cities, and accident problems, still projects a 1.5 to 2 million vehicles per year increase for the next fifteen years. The major operations will consist of reconstructing and modernizing highway structures and roadbeds already in place. There is a lack of public appreciation that structures and roads wear out and become inadequate for new demands. Many need to be rehabilitated, modernized, and rebuilt. During recession years, these highway improvements are great employment generators. Detailed studies of the Department of Transportation show a $1 billion expenditure on highways produces 26,000 on-site jobs, 28,700 off-site jobs, and 71,750 induced jobs for a total of 126,450 man-years of productive work.

Environmental Considerations

The stage construction concept for highways has been the policy from the beginning. The first effort was to get a roadway of sorts extended through the wilderness. It was then improved as traffic warranted. While aesthetic aspects were no doubt considered, they rarely affected design or construction plans; for the emphasis was to build as much road as possible with limited funds.

This was generally true until the recent three or four decades when the main-traveled routes have become hard surfaced. Traffic has increased, resulting in additional revenue for highways. With more people beginning to have marked adverse effects on the natural environment and with increasing general affluence, attention has extended to the environment and to ways in which it can be protected and improved. The parkways near New York City in the 1940s were some of the earliest large-scale efforts to make highways beautiful. Specially designed highways into national parks have also combined utility with beauty. Since then, steady improvement has made aesthetic considerations a part of highway design criteria.

Attention to the impact of the highway on the natural environment is increasing. In 1975 one dollar out of eight was being expended on adapting the highway to its setting. These expenditures included landscaping, designing

California Department of Public Works
Modern highways are fitted into the natural setting, as illustrated by this section of Interstate just south of San Francisco.

aesthetic bridges and other structures, rerouting to preserve and enhance streams, providing recreational amenities such as roadside rest areas and small lakes and parks, improving scenic views, and shaping excavations and embankments to make the highway more harmonious with their surroundings. It is a massive effort of architects, urban planners, sociologists, biologists, and other disciplines working with local communities and highway and street engineers and officials to optimize needed construction. Noise control by embankments, deflection fences, and foliage; elimination and screening of junkyards; and billboard removal and scenic easements are among the additions to highways of the 1970s which give promise for the future.

Air pollution from automobiles in congested city areas is one of the big problems being attacked from all sides. Ways to minimize downtown congestion by carpooling; more use of buses; rapid transit in major cities; various types of people movers such as moving sidewalks, bicycles, and electric minibuses; and many other approaches are being considered and put into effect. Improvement in combustion engines has the greatest promise, but it appears that several more years will be required to resolve this problem.

Sophisticated analysis to determine optimum pavement maintenance operations, periodic bridge inspections, detailed continuous traffic data, and identification of traffic bottlenecks are indicative of the progressive work being done. Providing balance in overall transportation by utilizing railroads, rapid transit, air travel, and highways will continue to challenge public works officials for decades to come. Most of the technical problems are resolved well ahead of appropriate application and available funding. The largest challenge will continue to be how to best meet the overall needs of people and still offer the widest possible freedom of choice.

SUGGESTED READINGS

American Association of State Highway Officials. *Manual and Specifications for the Manufacture, Display, and Erection of U.S. Standard Road Markers and Signs.* Washington, D.C., 1927.

American Society of Civil Engineers. "Verrazano-Narrows Bridge." *Journal of the Construction Division,* 92 (March 1966). 1-192

Billings, Henry. *Bridges.* Rev. ed. New York, 1967.

Chicago. Department of Public Works. *Chicago Public Works: A History.* Edited by Daphne Christensen. Chicago, 1973.

Condit, Carl W. *American Building Art: The Nineteenth Century.* New York, 1960.

Dooley, John H. "The Brooklyn Bridge After 90 Years of Service." *The Municipal Engineers Journal,* 59 (1973), 103-164.

Finch, James Kip. *The Story of Engineering.* Garden City, New York, 1960.

Gies, Joseph. *Bridges and Men.* Garden City, New York, 1963.

Jacobs, David, and Neville, Anthony E. *Bridges, Canals and Tunnels.* New York, 1968.

National Joint Committee on Uniform Traffic Control Devices. *Manual of Uniform Traffic Control Devices for Streets and Highways.* Washington, D.C., 1971.

Sandstrom, Gosta E. *Tunnels.* New York, 1963.

Sessions, Gordon M. *Traffic Devices: Historical Aspects Thereof.* Washington, D.C., 1971.

Silverberg, Robert. *Bridges.* Philadelphia, 1966.

Smith, Hubert S. *The World's Great Bridges.* New York, 1965.

Steinmen, David B., and Watson, Sara Ruth. *Bridges and Their Builders.* 2d. rev. ed. New York, 1957.

U.S. Department of Transportation. *The 1974 National Highway Needs Report.* Washington, D.C., 1975.

_____ . *Railroad-Highway Safety—A Report to Congress.* Washington, D.C., 1972.

_____ . Federal Highway Administration. *Highway Statistics.* Washington, D.C., 1944-1974.

CHAPTER 5

RAILROADS

Even though railroads are often thought to be in the private sector, their growth and development has been substantially assisted by public resources. In the early nineteenth century, public funds and land grants enabled the first lines to be built; some states directly undertook rail construction programs. Though virtually all railroads have since become privately owned, they have come under intensive governmental regulation to help insure they serve the public interest. They also have been taken over and operated by the government during national crises and shored up with public funds during economic downturns.

In recent years, some rail lines have been beset with bankruptcy and obsolete equipment. The federal government has responded with large outlays of emergency funds, but long-range planning, reorganizations, and consolidations are badly needed. Indications are that reorganization and revitalization may be achieved with direct public assistance and, perhaps, some type of public operation of some parts of this vital transportation system.

Early Years

The railroad originated in England, where foresighted inventors such as Richard

Trevithick, William Hedley, and George Stephenson developed the first primitive locomotives that made modern rail transportation possible. Their experiments during the first two decades of the nineteenth century culminated in the opening of a railway between Stockton and Darlington, England, in 1825. Promoted by Stephenson, it was the first railway to carry both freight and passengers, and it marked the birth of the railroad industry.

English railroad development was closely watched by American inventors and entrepreneurs. By 1818 Oliver Evans proposed a railway be constructed between New York and Philadelphia. Two years later, John Stevens received from the New Jersey legislature the first railroad charter granted in the United States. The proposed line between the Delaware and Raritan rivers was never constructed, but in 1825 he built the first American locomotive model and ran it on a half-mile circle of track at his home in Hoboken, New Jersey.

In February 1827, the first commercial American railroad, the Baltimore and Ohio Railroad Company (B & O), was chartered by the State of Maryland as a common carrier for freight and passengers. Its promoters envisioned it as a vital transportation link between the West and the eastern seaboard. The line was to run all the way to the Ohio River and channel the commerce of the growing trans-

This chapter is based on a manuscript prepared by Christine O'Conner, APWA Bicentennial History Fellow, and a special report provided by the United States Department of Transportation.

131

Appalachian region through the Port of Baltimore.

Railroads in America were initially considered a public facility similar to a turnpike or canal, an improved roadway to be used by and for the benefit of the public. The concept that the railroad was private property to be used exclusively by the owners, slowly developed as railroad locomotives and larger railroad cars became more costly and beyond the financial capability of individuals or single companies. For instance, the State of Pennsylvania built a railroad (timber rails with iron straps) from Philadelphia to Columbia and in 1829 licensed twenty different companies to run horse-drawn cars over it. In 1837 the chief engineer of the Madison and

Smithsonian Institution

Richard Trevithick's 1809 demonstration of an experimental railroad in England.

Indianapolis Railroad in Indiana recommended that the state furnish only the steam power for its railroads, "leaving the cars for the conveyance of freight and passengers to be furnished by individuals or companies, from whom the state will exact the proper toll for the use of the road and motive power."

Technological obstacles had to be overcome before railroads began hauling large quantities of goods and passengers. Companies found the British engines unsuited to America's rough terrain and began developing their own locomotives. The B & O commissioned Peter Cooper to construct the *Tom*

Thumb, a diminutive concoction of wheels, pulleys, and levers connected to an engine and boiler mounted on a flatcar. The little giant made its first run in the summer of 1830. The utility of this engine was limited and, except for a famous race with a horse and excursions for special guests, it remained idle. The B & O used horse-drawn cars until 1831 when the *York,* a practical and dependable steam locomotive, was placed into service.

With this auspicious beginning, other companies joined the race to find suitable engines. In the fall of 1830, *The Best Friend of Charleston* made its debut for the South Carolina Canal and Railroad Company. It reached a speed of thirty miles per hour without a load and twenty-one miles per hour when pulling cars containing forty to fifty passengers. This success was short lived, for its boiler exploded in the early summer of 1831. Undaunted, the company acquired the *West Point,* which had the unique safety feature of a "barrier car." The barrier car provided a virtual mountain of secured cotton bales to shield passengers from boiler explosions and was used until engines became more dependable. Meanwhile, in the North, the Mohawk and Hudson line running between Albany and Schenectady, New York, started laying track in the summer of 1830. A year later its engine, the *Dewitt Clinton,* made its first run.

Another northern company's work was

U.S. Department of Transportation

The *Tom Thumb* signalled America's new mechanical transportation era in running a 13-mile race with a horse-drawn railway car on August 28, 1830.

even more vital to the future of the railroad engine. In 1831 Matthias Baldwin built a small locomotive on a circular track inside the Peabody Museum in Philadelphia. His model so impressed the leadership of the Philadelphia, Germantown, and Norristown Rail Road Company that they contracted with Baldwin to build *Old Ironsides,* which in 1832 successfully ran at twenty-eight miles per hour. Baldwin invented a steam-tight metal joint that could contain 120 pounds of pressure without leakage. Well built and durable, Baldwin's engines formed an integral part of railroad history.

Still, the future of railroading appeared grim. A group of London scientists postulated that the top speed obtainable must not exceed thirty miles an hour, or "the passengers would suffocate." In Munich, Germany, a medical faculty admonished "that all railroad passengers were sure to contract a new type of mental illness termed delerium furiosum." Despite such dire predictions, early railroads eventually proved safe.

In New England, railways were introduced to counter the commercial success of the Port of New York which prospered from diverted trade from Boston after the construction of the Erie Canal in 1819. Boston merchants rejected the idea of constructing more canals because of their cost; but they were impressed by the success of the Granite Railway, a two-mile trainway built at Quincy, Massachusetts, in 1826 to transport granite for the Bunker Hill monument. Attempts to secure public funding failed, but three small private lines were built in 1830 and 1831 to form the matrix of the New England rail system. In 1835 the Western Railroad was chartered to link Worcester, Massachusetts, with Albany, New York, and thereby tap the rich Hudson Valley trade. The $2 million stock subscription was inadequate for the project, and the state purchased $1 million of the company's stock. Massachusetts subsequently loaned the line an additional $4 million before its completion in 1841.

Meanwhile, improvements continued to be developed for equipment on the various lines. One of the most significant improvements was made by John B. Lewis during his tenure as chief engineer on the Mohawk and Hudson. To overcome the problems caused by the rigid front axle and poor turning characteristics of English locomotives, Lewis designed the first swivel, or "bogie" wheels, which were mounted in a truck under the front of the locomotive. The *Experiment,* built by Lewis in 1832, easily negotiated curves and attained speeds of over fifty miles per hour. The equalizing beam, invented by Joseph Harrison, permitted equal pressure on each drive wheel on rough and uneven track. In 1836 Henry R. Campbell of Philadelphia designed an eight-wheeled engine (bogie plus four drive wheels) which dominated American locomotive types for a half century.

The cowcatcher prevented derailments caused by cows or other animals straying onto the track. It was invented by Isaac Dripps, the head mechanic of Robert Stevens' railroad. A slick track resulting from a grasshopper plague gave impetus to the apparently anonymous invention of the "sandbox," again demonstrating that "necessity was the mother of railroad invention."

Nearly all of the early railway tracks were built of long iron straps fastened to wooden rails, which in turn were secured to large stone blocks. However, this method was unsuccessful because the commonly used wooden rails with iron straps were incapable of supporting heavy engines. The use of heavier iron straps was also unsatisfactory because they loosened and curled up after prolonged wear making "snakeheads," which sometimes broke through the floor of a passing coach. In 1830 Robert Stevens, on his way to England to purchase strapiron rails, invented the "T" shaped iron rail which is still used. The "T" rails created from the prototype he whittled on a transatlantic voyage became standard equipment. The heavy granite blocks also were replaced because they were unresilient and hard on rolling stock. In the 1830s, rails were eventually attached to wooden ties buried in a gravel roadbed, a practice which has continued since.

Railroad expansion also required conquering geographical barriers. Construction of the Hoosac Tunnel is an example. The Hoosac Mountain in the Berkshires was a major im-

Smithsonian Institution

An 1842 drawing depicts early track laying with "T" rails and wooden ties.

pediment to trade between the Hudson River and Boston. A Boston-to-Albany railway was completed in 1842, but its exceptionally steep grades resulted in high shipping costs for New England merchants. In 1848 construction of a 4.8-mile tunnel through the tough granite mountain was proposed by the Troy and Greenfield Railroad. Work began in 1851. Constructing the tunnel by drilling and blasting with black powder was a slow process. In 1854 the State of Massachusetts loaned $2 million to keep the project alive, but by 1861 funds had run out and a year later the state foreclosed. A state commission subsequently undertook completion and hired Thomas Doane as chief engineer. Doane introduced nitroglycerin blasting and employed Charles Burleigh's compressed air powered drills, which bit into the rock at 300 blows per minute. Work progressed although the project was expensive. Originally estimated at $2 million, the tunnel eventually required $20 million and took the lives of 195 men. When opened to railroad traffic in 1875, the Hoosac Tunnel was the nation's longest tunnel and one of the engineering marvels of the nineteenth century.

From the earliest days of railroading, other designers labored on pieces of equipment that would add to passenger comfort. In 1829 in Boston's famous Faneuil Hall, R. F. Morgan unveiled the first design for a sleeping car. A double-decker, "Morgan's Rail Road Carriage" never received a patent and the car soon lost the public's attention. Yet the idea of a special car for sleeping continued to intrigue railroad managements. By 1838

several such cars operated on various lines. One of the earliest models contained three layers of bunks on each side, covered with thin straw mattresses.

At first, many railroads merely supplemented canals, but once the advantages of travel by rail were realized, track mileage increased dramatically. From 1830 to 1837, it rose from 23 to 1,497 miles and by 1840 to 2,818. The total length of canals was 3,200 miles in 1840 and increased only to 3,700 miles by 1860. At the opening of the Civil War, the United States had 30,600 miles of railway track, and it was evident that the railroads' battle with the canals as the main artery of travel had been won.

Expansion and Depression

The 1830s marked the beginning of a remarkable railroad expansion. By January 1837, over 200 railroad companies were in various stages of development. The need for capital to finance railroads caused lively debate. As the value of railroads become more apparent, the big question was how and where funds should be obtained, a debate which characterized most of pre-Civil War railroad history.

Part of the controversy concerned the role the federal government should play in financing internal improvements. Initially, Congress funded some internal improvements, but by the 1830s the states rights philosophy that such matters were the province of the states predominated. In 1828 a joint resolution of Congress made federal ownership of railroad or canal stock illegal. Even so, the federal government found other ways to encourage and support railroad development.

For a time, the government gave small but vital indirect support to the railroads. Under the 1824 General Survey Act (in effect until 1838), the Army Corps of Engineers completed sixty-one railway surveys at an estimated cost of $75,000. This was necessary since the army had the only pool of talent capable of planning and directing the surveys. Army engineers made the first federal railroad survey in 1826 for a line connecting the James, Kanowba, and Roanoke rivers. From the outset of construction, army engineers were also loaned to railway companies. The practice came under heavy criticism, but the government defended the policy on the grounds that this was the only way the work could be done and that it benefited the entire nation. The critics pointed out, however, that some engineer officers accepted payments from railroads and occupied company executive positions while holding positions in the military. Sectionalism also played a significant role in the outcries against the engineers. Stout opposition arose in the South because most railroads were constructed in middle and northern states. Furthermore, while some companies freely obtained technical aid from the federal government, others were required to pay for engineering assistance. By 1838, when the practice of loaning army engineer officers to railroads was finally prohibited, over sixty companies had utilized their services.

The federal government also aided railroads by remitting duties on imported iron. Because of their small capacities, United States iron factories could not meet the early railroad demands. Railroad promoters appealed to Congress for relief from an iron tariff which forced them to pay exhorbitant prices for foreign iron. An 1830 tariff revision provided a reduction of duties through a 25 percent refund on iron used for railroads. In July 1832, Congress passed an "act to release from duty iron prepared for and actually laid on railways or inclined planes." For the railroads, this meant a reduction of $15 to $20 per ton on the cost of rails. This act saved the companies approximately $6 million during the ten years it was in effect.

During the period before 1840, the federal government established precedents for land and right-of-way grants. The first land grant for railroad aid received congressional approval in March 1833. This statute allowed Illinois to use funds from public land sales for railroad construction. While the state never adopted this plan, an important precedent was established. In 1835 Florida and Alabama received the first right-of-way grants from the federal government. Four railroad companies in the two states received 60-foot rights-of-way, and one company received ten acres for

a terminal. Thus, the federal grant policy of the 1850s and 1860s did not suddenly appear. Rather it slowly emerged from tentative steps taken in recognition of public needs during the early days of railroad development.

Though the national government eventually took a larger role in railroad affairs, most public support came from the states. New York's success with the Erie Canal induced other states to fund internal improvements. The boom mood of the country made even wild schemes seem feasible. States wanted to enhance their economic position and chose railroads as the means for obtaining desired growth. In the period before the Panic of 1837, state investment steadily grew, and by 1838 state debts from railroad investment totaled nearly $43 million.

States became involved in railroads in a variety of ways. The federal government gave large land grants to the states. The states, in turn, freely gave these grants to corporations to build railroads. Though exceptionally large land grants did not occur until the 1850s, the initial grants fueled the building boom of the 1830s. Expansion also resulted from direct state building programs and subsidies. In 1828 Maryland pioneered state ownership with a $500,000 stock subscription in the Baltimore and Ohio Railroad Company. A Virginia law required state ownership of three fifths of the stock of any railroad within its borders. In 1834 Virginia acquired a controlling interest in the Richmond, Fredericksburg, and Potomac Railroad Company, and it continued to hold a portion of the company's stock until 1946.

From stock subscriptions, the states moved to actual construction programs. In 1828 the Pennsylvania legislature authorized state construction and operation of railroads. Though it stimulated trade, the resulting Philadelphia and Columbia Rail Road never showed a profit. Nevertheless, it merits distinction as the first railroad in the world undertaken by a government. Georgia also entered the railroad business by constructing the Western and Atlantic Railroad, another line that operated at a loss and subsequently passed into private hands in 1871. In the Midwest, Indiana also tried and failed to complete construction of a railroad, spending over $1.5 million on the ill-fated venture. The boldest scheme, however, was devised in Illinois. In 1837 the Illinois legislature committed the state to constructing more than 1,300 miles of railroad, but this ambitious project was stopped by the Panic of 1837.

Other states did not get so deeply involved as Illinois but did provide financial support. Loans were a popular form of subsidy, and states guaranteed railroad bonds. Favorable provisions were made in railroad charters. These charters contained special provisions that the companies used to attract investors. One of the most important provisions abolished the railroad's status as a public turnpike, thereby creating a monopoly. States also gave railroads immunity from taxation. In Ohio, for instance, the legislature did not tax the general property of railroads until 1852. The states also provided public lotteries as a means of raising needed capital to benefit the railroads.

While most special provisions evoked little criticism, some were contested. The states often found themselves caught in a dilemma. If they granted the promoters' demands for money, land, and freedom from state interference, their citizens grew restive. If, however, state laws were not attractive to investors, no railways would be built. Being practical, states usually acceded to the demands of investors because of the high value legislators placed on economic growth.

The states did, however, reserve some rights for themselves. They retained, for instance, the right to purchase the railroads in case of bankruptcy. State legislatures also freely gave local governments the privilege of granting subsidies to railroads. Local businessmen wanted railroads running through their counties, cities, and towns because transportation was vital to the growth of their area. If a town desired a railway, it was expected to pay liberally for it. Taxes for railroad subsidies or stock subscriptions were considered investments in the future. It is estimated that municipal and local contributions totaled one fifth of the costs of railroad construction undertaken by 1870.

Small private contributors offered another source of capital for railroads. Using pamphlets, newspapers, petitions, and committees, promoters scoured the countryside seeking money. Railroad agents held public meetings in towns located on proposed routes. These affairs served as social functions and were an effective device for obtaining stock subscriptions. Though most people expected to make a profit on their stock, many farmers and merchants bought stock primarily to obtain improved transportation. They received a severe blow with the Panic of 1837, however. This depression destroyed the expansionist enthusiasm of railroad construction. Private, local, and state subscribers suffered as their investments became worthless. In addition, fraud, deception, and corruption of the subsidy system were discovered and added to the general dissatisfaction with railroads. Railroad subsidies tended to attract financial adventurers who cared little for the public interest and who organized companies to obtain quick profits.

Such unethical behavior and poor planning put many states in financial trouble. Insolvent railroads forced the State of Michigan to take over lines and complete construction. In 1846 Michigan sold its railroad holdings, which had cost the state $3.5 million, for $1.8 million. Illinois also experienced financial difficulties. *Hunter's Merchant's Magazine* commented that of all the states, "none had more canvas spread, or so little ballast, as that gem of the West, Illinois." By 1841 the state's debt was $14 million and its treasury empty. Voters reacted to depression and disclosures of corruption by expressing opposition to public support for internal improvements. Beginning in the North, state legislatures enacted laws and amendments against state investments. These laws, which ranged from forbidding state loans or stock ownership to a ban on public investments for internal improvements, marked the end of direct state aid to railroads. By 1857 all of the states except Virginia and Georgia divested themselves of railroad holdings.

Westward Expansion

Aided by the telegraph and other innovations, railroads grew and changed in the 1840s and 1850s and played an important part in westward expansion. In spite of depression and corruption, by the Civil War, the United States had a fairly widespread rail system. By 1860 railroads had evolved from a group of unconnected lines to a 30,000-mile network.

The railroads had replaced canals as the chief means of transport by the end of the 1840s. The 1850s marked the continuing decline of canals as more railroad miles and cheaper rates cut into canal business. For instance, while shippers used the Ohio Canal to transport a million bushels of wheat to Cleveland in 1850, ten years later this figure dropped to barely 200,000. During the 1840s, the railroads constructed nearly 4,000 miles of track while only 400 miles of canals were built.

Smithsonian Institution

Boston & Philadelphia Railroad engine and shops in 1858. By the 1850s, railroads had replaced canals as the chief means of transportation.

Dreamers and promoters helped fuel the drive west. As early as 1819, Robert Mills, architect of both the Bunker Hill and Washington monuments, urged Congress to construct a railway from the Mississippi River to the Pacific Ocean. By the 1840s, the plan seemed more realistic and attracted strong advocates. Foremost was Asa Whitney, who for more than ten years promoted a Pacific railroad despite the apparent disinterest of Congress and the general public. His work sparked the first railroad convention, which met in 1849 to consider construction of a transcontinental road. This convention elected Stephen A. Douglas chairman and passed a resolution favoring a San Francisco-St. Louis route, with branches to Chicago and Memphis. Though success remained years away, such promotions excited the country about the potential of railroads.

Railroad transportation sparked the economy during this period and otherwise benefited the nation's growth. Most important was the railroads' role as a consumer. The railroads stimulated the iron industry by purchasing a great deal of the domestic iron output, and they exhibited the largest appetite for coal of any segment of the economy. Railroads also fostered urbanization. Chicago, for instance, grew because of its importance as a railroad junction. In 1860 eleven major railroads converged at Chicago, making it the greatest railroad center in the world. Its phenomenal growth was aided by the introduction of grain elevators which contributed to the city's value as a shipping center. Introduced in the 1840s, mechanical grain elevators enabled the rapid loading and unloading of railroad cars, canal boats, and lake vessels. Other cities experienced growth comparable to that of Chicago, thus helping to change the face of America.

Railroads became embroiled in sectional politics of the 1840s and 1850s. Disputes between northern and southern congressmen were a major barrier to construction of a transcontinental railroad. Each section vied for the privilege of building the line in its region and competed for control of western commerce. The majority of rail construction linked the West and Northeast, thereby diverting the flow of commodities from the Mississippi River and embittering southerners by the loss of economic status. Thus, the railroads helped forge close economic ties among the northern states, an important causal factor of the Civil War. Congressional action on railroad surveys reflected this conflict of sectional interests. In 1853, after much bickering, Senator William Gwin of California tacked an amendment onto an army appropriations bill to allocate $150,000 for surveys of railroad routes to the Pacific. The United States Corps of Topographical Engineers completed the surveys in December 1856, but Congress was unable to reach agreement on a route.

Railroads were an important factor in the

outcome of the Civil War as well. The North used railroad systems so effectively that one historian claimed they "did as much, certainly, as any one thing to settle the issue of the struggle." While this statement is perhaps exaggerated, the southern war effort was indeed enfeebled by the lack of an efficient transportation system.

Legislation was passed during the war for the construction of two northern transcontinental railroad routes. In 1862 Congress authorized the Union Pacific Railroad to lay track from the Missouri River to the Rocky Mountains, while the Central Pacific Railroad was chartered to build a road from Sacramento, California, to the connection with the Union Pacific. In 1864 Congress authorized construction of the Northern Pacific Railroad, which connected Duluth, Minnesota, with Puget Sound.

Land grants were made to railroads to encourage investments. Eventually, over 130 million acres were given to the companies, representing 9.5 percent of the land in the United States. The estimated value of these grants at the time they were made was between $1.7 and $2.5 billion. The Union Pacific and Central Pacific each obtained 200-foot rights-of-way and ten alternate sections of public land for each mile of track they laid. The secretary of the treasury was further authorized to sell large tracts of land and issue to the companies thirty-year United States bonds payable in treasury notes. These actions created tremendous incentives for investors. In addition, the railroad companies obtained loans from the states and towns along their lines.

With such lucrative returns to the investors, the railroad business boomed. In 1869 the Union Pacific and Central Pacific completed the nation's first transcontinental railroad with the "golden spike" ceremony at Promontory Point, Utah. The Northern Pacific Railroad took longer, but Henry Villard successfully directed its completion in 1883, the same year the "Sunset Route," running from New Orleans to San Francisco, was completed by the Southern Pacific Railroad Company. Cyrus K. Holliday's line, the famed Atchison, Topeka, and Santa Fe, reached Los

Angeles in 1887. James J. Hill's Great Northern Railroad, the last of the great transcontinental lines and the only one without public subsidy except for the right-of-way, opened its Pacific route in 1893.

The transcontinental rails opened land beyond the Mississippi to settlement. Railroad companies, anxious to see the land appreciate in value, promoted immigration and attracted a great many settlers to the West. Colorful

Smithsonian Institution

This poster announced the opening of the first transcontinental railroad.

posters, newspaper advertisements, and articles exhorted people to go west. Railroad agents held meetings to enlist pioneers for the frontier. Promoters exalted the promise of free land available under the Homestead Act and underplayed the hardships and sacrifices the plains demanded of settlers. In order to draw even larger numbers of people, railroad agents traveled throughout the European continent publicizing the supposed wonders of the new nation. Would-be pioneers received offers of free seed and other inducements, and most rail companies reduced rates or carried western immigrants and their baggage, freight, and livestock without charge.

The federal government supported western settlement, for the demand for land increased the value of public and private land and augmented the taxable wealth of the nation. The government also promoted railroads because they facilitated utilization of natural resources. For example, railroads running through such states as Kansas and Texas stimulated the growth of the cattle business. Many identify cattle drives with cowboys, dusty trails, and adventurers, forgetting that the railroad terminals in towns like Abilene, Kansas, made this colorful chapter in American history possible.

Leadership and Technical Progress

Although many of the railroad men were robber barons and corrupt opportunists, the period from 1865 to 1900 was marked by some outstanding industrial leaders. Foremost was James J. Hill, who molded the railroads of the Northwest into an efficient servant of the region's economic development. Building his road without land grants, Hill's efficiently managed Great Northern survived the 1893 depression that forced many other railroads into bankruptcy. John Edgar Thompson, president of the Pennsylvania Railroad, was another skilled railroad manager. Thompson routed his railroad's mainline and branch tracks with uncanny foresight and laid the foundation of an excellent system which never missed a dividend until 1946.

The conduct of the so-called "money men," however, cast a pall over the industry. Because of the large sums involved, oppor-

tunities for corruption were widespread. The Union Pacific Railroad was a classic example. Thomas Durant, one of the chief promoters and vice president and general manager of the company until 1869, organized the Union Pacific in 1863 as a moneymaking proposition. Helped by George Francis Train, Durant also founded an infamous construction company, the Credit Mobilier of America, which amassed huge profits through inflated contracts and shoddy workmanship. Congressmen became involved through the Ames brothers, Oakes and Oliver, wealthy Boston industrialists who invested in the Union Pacific. To influence congressional votes on railroad matters, Oakes Ames, himself a congressman, sold and gave other congressmen stock in both Union Pacific and Credit Mobilier. Schulyer Colfax, speaker of the house and vice president under Ulysses S. Grant, and future President James A. Garfield accepted shares. Even the government-appointed director of Union Pacific operations, Congressman James Brooks, owned 150 shares. In 1872 the activities of the two companies were exposed and the Credit Mobilier blew up into one of the major scandals in the history of the United States government. Congress eventually censured both Ames and Brooks for their activities, but that failed to check the disquieting conclusion that railroads were cheating the nation.

On the other side of the first transcontinental line, the Central Pacific leadership also contrived to fleece the government and public. One story about Collis Huntington, president of the Central Pacific, is particularly illustrative. He convinced a geologist to declare that the base of the Sierra Nevada Mountains extended 15 miles farther west than it really did and collected $48,000 per mile in government loans instead of the $16,000 paid for laying track on flat terrain. Other schemes to raid both public and private funds multiplied during these years. Some railroads withheld their land grants from sale to settlers in order to wait for a better price; others issued watered stock. Companies were also known to accept grants but never build the lines for which they had contracted. Railroads undervalued their assests for tax appraisals while overvaluing them for rate-making and stock-issuing purposes, other practices which angered taxpayers. In 1890 Kansas railroads were capitalized at $52,500 per mile and assessed for taxes at $6,500. To Kansas farmers and other citizens who paid heavy taxes to cover state and local railroad debts, these activities were reprehensible.

Despite the widespread corruption that existed in the railroad industry, advancements in technology during this period made rail transportation safer and more efficient. In 1868 Eli H. Janney invented the automatic coupler to replace the standard link and pin coupler which previously accounted for the majority of railroad worker accidents. George Westinghouse's invention also saved lives. In 1868, at the age of twenty-two, he patented the air brake, which eliminated another frequent cause of accidents. Manual braking, performed by workers twisting hand brakes atop moving cars, was extremely hazardous, especially during wet or snowy weather.

Smithsonian Institution

Until air brakes were adopted, railroad workers operated hand brakes from the top of freight cars.

Unfortunately, railroad companies often refused to use these safety features because of their added cost. Lorenzo S. Coffin, former Iowa farmer and school teacher, was the foremost leader in the battle for railroad safety. As railway commissioner of Iowa during the 1880s, he fought for and won legislation requiring all trains in the state to use automatic couplers and air brakes. Coffin was also instrumental in the passage of a national Railway Safety Appliance Act in 1893, which required all trains in interstate service to be equipped with the new coupling and brake systems. The effect of the statute was dramatic. Railroad worker accidents, which previously ran as high as 30,000 per year, were reduced by 60 percent.

Some of the most notable engineering progress was made in the field of bridge construction. Reliable wooden truss bridge structural designs had evolved by the 1830s, but by 1865 wooden structures were being rapidly replaced by iron bridges. The introduction of steel as a bridge material enabled engineers to span even greater distances. An important example of the early use of steel was the bridge built by James B. Eads across the Mississippi River at St. Louis. Though some iron was used in construction, it was the first major structure in the world to employ steel in its principal structural elements. The bridge was composed of three enormous piers set more than 500 feet apart. In constructing its piers, which reached 122 feet below water level to bedrock, Eads sunk pneumatic caissons that were the first built in America. The structure was double-decked, with trains running beneath an upper level that carried pedestrians, wagons, and carriages. On July 4, 1874, President Grant officially opened the bridge, an event which began an era of steel bridge construction.

Vast improvements were made in rails to enable railroads to move larger loads at greater speeds. The first steel rails were imported from England in 1862, and two years later the first domestic steel rails were produced in Chicago. By 1880 a fourth of the nation's rail mileage was steel, and by the turn of the century virtually all new track was made of this material. Rail transportation was also improved by nationwide adoption of the 4-foot 8½-inch "standard gauge." In 1861, 46 percent of America's track width was not based on this criteria, but the use of standard gauge

Public Works Historical Society

The bridge across the Mississippi River at St. Louis, completed in 1874, was the first major structure in the world to use steel as the principal structural element.

on the transcontinental lines led to wider adoption of this practice. By 1880 one fifth of the track mileage was of different gauges, most of it in the South where 5-foot gauge lines were built. Representatives of the southern lines met in February 1886 and agreed to change to the narrower gauge by the following June. Thus, southern railroads truly became part of the national rail network, easing the flow of goods and passengers to and from this section of the country.

As standardized gauge and safety equipment provided faster and more efficient rail service, improvements in train signaling and control were required. Ashbel Welch, vice president and chief engineer of the Camden and Amboy Railroad, developed the first manual block-signal system in 1865. Six years later, William Robinson devised a system for opening and closing signals electrically. During the 1870s, the fundamental principles of block signals and electrical track circuits were developed which by the 1920s evolved into automatic train control. This allowed one individual to manage switches, signals, and train movements over a wide area.

The longer and heavier trains introduced in the postbellum period also required major improvements in locomotive design. By 1865 steel wheels were in use, and experiments were being conducted with steel fireboxes and boilers which enabled engines to attain higher steam pressures and more power. During this period, railroads changed from wood- to coal-fired engines which further increased

locomotive efficiency. By 1890 ten-wheeled engines weighing as much as eighty tons were used to provide freight and passenger service throughout the country.

Freight equipment increased in capacity along with increases in motive power. Train loads grew from 200 to 2,000 tons between 1865 and 1900, and the average freight car capacity rose from 10 to 40 tons in the same period. A variety of special car designs were developed such as stock cars for western beef, refrigerated cars for meat and fresh produce, hopper cars for coal, and tank cars for oil. Passengers benefited as sleeping cars, dining cars, and steam heating were introduced to rail transportation. The remarkable increases in operational efficiency gave the railroads a virtual monopoly on domestic transportation. In the fifty years following the Civil War, track mileage expanded from 35,000 to 2.5 million miles.

Reform and Regulation

As the railroad industry expanded, the public began to demand more efficient service, fairer rates, and controls on illegal and unethical practices. As early as the 1860s and 1870s, the rate structure came under attack. In 1873 Ignatius Donnelly lamented that "it cost as much to ship wheat from Minneapolis to Milwaukee, as to ship the same wheat from Milwaukee to Liverpool." Companies used the "transit rate," which forced shippers to pay the full cost of shipping goods to eastern depots regardless of the consignment's destination. In addition, the roads negotiated agreements with grain elevator companies and commission agents to control both shipping and marketing rates at the farmer's expense. Initially, it was thought competition would keep rates down, but railroads consolidated or made rate-fixing agreements with each other.

Organized resistance to these practices developed. Hudson Kelley organized the Patrons of Husbandry, popularly known as the Grange, to improve the social and intellectual well being of the farmers. Established as a social organization, the Grange began the first full-scale assault on railroad privilege. State legislatures passed a series of so-called

"Granger laws" which established the principle of state regulation. For instance, an 1871 Illinois law authorized a rate advisory commission to fix and alter schedules of reasonable maximum rates. The board heard the cases of both the shipper and carrier and then determined a standard for tolls. If the railroads failed to comply, the commission could take them to court. In 1877 the United States Supreme Court upheld such laws, and the Grangers appeared victorious.

The statutes, however, never really solved the problems, and the very title, "Granger laws," is somewhat misleading. Many historians have asserted that the farmers did not represent the true strength of the railroads' opponents. The Granger movement was instead part of the reaction of the mercantile community to the rise of interstate railway systems. In most cases, initiative and leadership were provided by shippers and businessmen working through their boards of trade, mercantile associations, commercial conventions, and the regular machinery of the state. Farmers participated in anti-monopolistic conventions, but the leadership came from other professions.

However, the initial state successes in railroad regulation were set back in 1886 when the Supreme Court reversed its earlier position and in the landmark Wabash Case ruled that state commissions could not regulate interstate shipments. This decision contributed to the enactment by the federal government of the 1887 Interstate Commerce Act which created a five-member Interstate Commerce Commission (ICC) to regulate the nation's railway system. The law required that interstate freight rates be "reasonable and just" and prohibited railroad practices such as pools and rebates.

The new commission appeared to hold great promise, but by the twentieth century it had failed miserably. Under the law, the commission could not set rates, but only declare, after receiving a shipper's complaint, that rates were not just and reasonable. Overturning shipping costs required prolonged litigation. The average length of ICC cases was four years and in many cases even longer. Furthermore, the railroad companies usually won because of their highly paid corps of talented lawyers and judges who were unsympathetic to ICC objectives. Between 1887 and 1905, sixteen ICC cases reached the Supreme Court; fifteen were decided in favor of the railroads. Furthermore, the commission also had little power to control rebates and other illegal practices which remained commonplace throughout the industry.

In spite of their legal triumphs, the railroads' public image suffered. Because of discriminatory rates and the wheeling and dealing in railroad securities, the industry came under attack from reform groups. During the 1890s, the Populists promoted public ownership of railroads as one of their principal reforms and gained a wide following in the southern and plains states. Railroad companies retaliated by pouring money into the campaign chests of political candidates who would support their interests.

The reform fight was carried on by supporters of the Progressive movement, a broad-based early twentieth-century reform crusade which sought to end corporate and special interest domination of the American political and economic system. An outcome of this reform impulse was the 1903 Elkins Act which strengthened the prohibition of rebates. In 1901 President Theodore Roosevelt joined the battle by directing Attorney General Philander C. Knox to file suit under the 1890 Sherman Act against the Northern Securities Company, a giant railroad conglomerate organized by William Harriman and James J. Hill. The 1904 Supreme Court decision, ordering the company to be broken up, restored industry competition and was hailed as a significant reform victory.

Other legislation soon followed. The 1906 Hepburn Act increased the ICC from five to seven members and extended its authority to additional common carriers such as express and sleeping cars and pipeline companies. The act strengthened the prohibition against rebates and empowered the committee to set "just and reasonable" railroad rates on its own initiative. The new law, however, disappointed some reformers by still allowing railroads to use court action to delay or reverse implementation of commission orders. This practice was finally eliminated by the 1910 Mann-Elkins Act which allowed ICC rates to remain in effect during litigation. In addition, the burden of proof that proposed rates were reasonable was placed upon the railroads.

The 1913 Railroad Valuation Act was the culmination of over four decades of railroad reform. The statute required ICC to assess the value of all railway property. By doing so, the commission was able to base rates upon the real value of each company rather than upon their watered stock and inflated capitalization. In the same year, Congress passed the Panama Canal Act which made it illegal for railroads to control competing water carriers.

Thus, by the eve of World War I, the American railroads were regulated by a comprehensive system of government controls to insure that they operated in the public's interest. World War I created conditions which called for even greater government involvement. The demands of war required quick and efficient transfer of supplies and men, and the railroads tried to meet the challenge. On April 11, 1917, almost 700 railroad presidents met in Washington, D.C., and agreed to contribute to the war effort by running their lines as if they constituted a "continental railway system." A Railroad War Board was established to coordinate rail commerce. The board, however, was unable to meet the enormous demands, and the harsh winter of 1917-1918 cut into railroad efficiency. When the shortage of cars reached 158,000 in the fall of 1917, the federal government decided to step in. Enough cars existed to handle the nation's freight but there was no system to coordinate rail use. Lack of service in the face of dire emergency forced the government to consider nationalization. On December 26, 1917, Woodrow Wilson issued a presidential proclamation asking for nationalization, and Congress followed with the Federal Control Act which created the Railroad Administration. To the Congress, engrossed in a war effort, the matter was not a question of private versus public operation of the rail network. Unified operation had to be implemented quickly if the difficulties inherent in decentralized use of rail facilities were to be overcome.

President Wilson appointed William G. McAdoo to lead the new agency. McAdoo, a lawyer and Wilson's secretary of the treasury, spent part of his younger years working to complete railroad tunnels under New York's Hudson River. This venture was a financial and engineering success; and McAdoo had exhibited a particular flair for public relations, coining the phrase "The Public Be Pleased" for his company, the Hudson and Manhattan Railroad. McAdoo set up a central administrative system which welded the lines into a unified and responsive rail network. Many operational changes were made to augment coordination and efficiency. To discourage wasteful passenger traffic, duplicate service between cities was eliminated and sleeping car operations were curtailed. Stringent controls were also introduced for freight. Efficient management of routes and car allocation reduced the congestion on crowded lines and resulted in better utilization of track capacity. Efforts were made to coordinate shipments so they were promptly delivered. Government operation of the

Smithsonian Institution

A 1910 wooden cattle car. During World War I, the federal government assumed control of the railroads to resolve car shortage problems.

railroads meant a suspension of some state laws while others remained in force. Statutes relating to real estate taxes, Jim Crow laws, and other traditional taxing and police powers were enforced. Nationalization, however, shut the state out of matters such as rates, crew laws, and frequency and quality of service. By the spring of 1918, the car shortage crisis was over and the railroads were meeting the country's wartime transportation needs.

Prosperity Decade

When the war ended in 1918, the disposition of the railroads became a national issue. Some felt the war created an opportunity to make the federal takeover permanent. Glenn E. Plumb, lawyer for the four largest railroad unions, offered his "Plumb Plan." It proposed the government purchase the railroads which would be run by a fifteen-member board composed equally of labor, management, and government representatives. Railroad unions, the American Federation of Labor, and other labor groups endorsed this proposal. Retired Director McAdoo suggested five-year federal control. But the railroads fought any form of continued government operation and eventually won the struggle.

American railroads had been under federal control for over two years when, in compliance with the prevailing view that government should limit itself to regulating industry in peacetime, Congress passed legislation providing for the orderly termination of federal control of the railroads. The 1920 Transportation Act was signed by President Wilson on February 29, 1920. In addition to returning the railroads to private ownership, the act was designed to protect the public from unreasonable and discriminatory rates, to provide for an adequate transportation system, and to give railroads a fair return on their investments.

To protect the public from abuses that some railroads had perpetrated in the prewar era, ICC was given greater power. For instance, it gained increased authority to control rates. Prior to approval of rate changes, the commission determined fares or charges that would allow a "fair rate of return" on the total investment. A "fair rate of return" was determined to be equal to 5.5 percent of a railroad's investment and, further, the government acquired one half of all profits over 6 percent. The commission was also granted authority over mergers, new routes, abandonment of tracks, and railroad financing. To meet these increased responsibilities, the act expanded the number of commissioners from nine to eleven.

By creating a nine-member Railroad Labor Board, the transportation act also reflected concern for the welfare of workers. Of the nine members, three represented the railroads, three the railroad employees, and three the general public. This board was given jurisdiction over railroad labor disputes concerning grievances, rules, working conditions, and wages.

Intensive use of the railroads during World War I necessitated deferral of acquiring new or modernized equipment. Consequently, at the war's end, the railroads were under-maintained and under-equipped. In anticipation of the problems which this deficiency could cause, Congress devised a loan program to aid the railroads' recovery. This program, part of the 1920 Transportation Act, included a revolving fund of $300 million to make loans to seventy-seven railroad companies. From this fund, the government loaned a total of over $356 million at 6 percent interest. Although slightly more than $29 million of principal and interest was in default, by 1972 over $91 million in interest had been paid, and the United States Treasury had received more than $52 million in excess of what it had loaned.

Given the new regulatory and aid structure, the railroads were finally returned to their prewar owners on March 1, 1920, thus ending twenty-six months of government operation. With the exception of a switchmen's strike barely one month later, the railroads went about their business as the major mode of transportation for the nation. During the 1920s, railroads moved about 75 percent of the freight and over 25 percent of the passengers transported in the United States.

Returning the railroads to private control was a sound decision. Had the railroads remained in government control, the United

States Treasury would have foregone well over $270 million in taxes in 1920 alone. This figure rose each year, and in 1929 railroads were paying over $396 million in taxes. Nevertheless, government-railroad interaction did not end with the cessation of federal control. In an effort to avoid disruptions, which could be disastrous for the national transportation system, Congress passed the 1926 Railway Labor Act. This act provided a National Mediation Board with authority to reconcile disputing parties and created a National Railway Adjustment Board with management and union representatives to consider grievances, interpretations, and applications relating to complicated labor-management agreements. Congress also enacted the 1928 Dension Act which, although principally intended to aid inland waterways, a major competitor of the railroads, also allowed carriers to fix through routes and joint rates for rail and water transport.

Many changes and improvements were made relating to business management and planning during the 1920s. Two very important examples of organizational improvements were the creation of the Car Service Division and the development of various shipper's advisory boards. The Car Service Division was an industry organization created in 1920. The railroads gave this new body the power to marshal and allocate railroad cars in order to help avoid congestion or shortages both regionally and seasonally. Successful coordination among the railroads meant that when a freight car was needed in New England it was there rather than sitting idle in Texas. Such efficiency was crucial at harvest time and would become imperative during World War II.

In 1923 the Northwest Shippers' Advisory Board was organized in Minneapolis. This group of shippers and railroad customers sought to make rail transport more productive by anticipating needs for railroad cars and services. By estimating requirements in advance, it was possible to plan rail movement in order to minimize idle time for both cars and the commodities they carried. By 1926 fourteen regions had organized advisory boards that were effective in aiding railroads

to serve the nation. For example, in 1920 there was an average daily freight car shortage of 81,592 cars. Despite heavier traffic, the shortage fell to 47,882 cars in 1922, 29,216 in 1923, and 1,047 in 1924. The shortage was well below 100 cars per day by 1928. By maximum use of available freight cars, the American railroads were able to transport goods cheaper and faster.

Organization was not the only method by which railroads advanced the prosperity of this period. Major expenditures were made to modernize and rehabilitate existing equipment. In fact, from 1923 to 1930, over $6.7 billion was spent on capital improvements, and numerous innovations were developed to improve railroad performance. Among experiments in the early 1920s were containerization of freight, self-propelled passenger cars, and locomotives propelled by steam turbines or gasoline engines. Another major innovation was called Automatic Train Control. With this system, a train running through a stop signal or exceeding the speed limit could be stopped or slowed automatically, thus compensating for human error and increasing safety.

Completion of the federally owned Alaska Railroad was an outstanding public works milestone of the 1920s. After private efforts failed, the road was authorized by Congress in March 1914 and launched the federal government on an experiment in railroad ownership and operation that has successfully endured for half a century. Beginning in 1915, construction crews fought mountains, tundra, and brutal cold for eight years, until July 16, 1923, when President Warren G. Harding drove a golden spike at Nenana, Alaska, to mark completion of the 500-mile railroad. The Alaska Railroad was built from Seward and Whittier, on the south coast of the Kenia Peninsula, through Anchorage to Fairbanks, some 175 miles below the Artic Circle. By providing the mineral- and lumber-rich interior access to warm water ports, the railroad has been vital to Alaskan economic growth.

The Alaska Railroad has been an unusual public agency and represents a noteworthy departure from the view that government should confine itself to regulating transportation industries. From 1923 to 1966,

The Alaska Railroad is a federally owned transportation facility.

the railroad was operated by the Department of Interior. It was then transferred to the Federal Railroad Administration, an agency of the new Department of Transportation. Throughout its history the railroad has been managed in an enlightened and progressive manner. It has received no congressional appropriations to meet operating expenses since 1939 and, except for a reconstruction period after a 1964 earthquake, has received none for capital improvements since 1956. The railroad has proven to be an important economic asset.

Perhaps the most significant technological development during this decade was the perfection of a practical diesel locomotive. The first non-experimental diesel locomotive was used for switching operations by the Central Railroad of New Jersey in 1925. It weighed sixty tons and generated 300 horsepower and, because of its small size and low power, was used only for switching purposes. Later improvements, however, made diesel locomotion

The Central Railroad of New Jersey began operating the first diesel locomotive in 1925.

so superior to steam that by the late 1950s steam locomotives had virtually disappeared. The new locomotive required less maintenance, used fuel more efficiently, was quicker to start, and did not fill cities and stations with harmful smoke.

Other improvements were put into use throughout the industry. Telephones and teletypes were used to dispatch trains. Radio communication between locomotive and caboose was experimented with by various railroads and first adopted for permanent use by the Central Railroad of New Jersey in 1927. Experiments were performed in 1926 to test the "piggyback" concept of carrying trucks upon flat cars. Although this system used fuel more efficiently than highway transport and saved loading and unloading boxcars, it did not become widely accepted until the 1950s. Not all innovations were directed solely at improving freight service; railroads showed their concern for passenger comfort and convenience as well. By 1927, for example, the Pullman Company was experimenting with air-conditioned sleeping cars.

As the decade closed, the concept of centralized traffic control became a physical reality. Use of this system allowed one operator-dispatcher, sitting at a centralized control panel, to set switches and trackside signals for the movement of trains over distances ranging up to 400 miles. By having one man control several train movements, railroads could pass lower costs on to their customers as well as serve them more rapidly and reliably.

Such advances were augmented by outstanding engineering and construction efforts. For example, one of the decade's most noteworthy engineering feats was construction of the Cascade Tunnel in the state of Washington, still the longest railroad tunnel in North America. The possibility of such a tunnel had been part of the Great Northern Railroad's development plans since 1890. The original line was carried over the summit of the Cascades by a series of switchbacks which were often covered by snow slides in winter. A 2.7-mile tunnel was built in 1900, but the snowslide danger necessitated construction of costly snow sheds to protect tunnel entrances. In November 1925, the Great Northern approved plans for a 7.8-mile tunnel between Bern and Scenic, Washington. Work on the new Cascade Tunnel started in December 1925 and progressed around the clock, seven days a week. By driving a smaller, parallel working tunnel, the main bore was worked from as many as eleven places at once with total employment reaching 1,800 men. Dedication ceremonies on January 12, 1929 completed the $14 million project. President-elect Herbert Hoover hailed the accomplishment in a nationwide radio program which included a live broadcast aboard the first train through the tunnel.

Construction of this engineering benchmark enabled trains to avoid the snowslides, steep grades, and dangerous curves of the old route. The new tunnel also allowed ton-miles per train hour to increase from 11,520 to 70,000 on the Cascade section of the Great Northern route. Originally wired for electric locomotives, diesels were introduced through the tunnel in 1956 after construction of a highly sophisticated ventilation system to exhaust smoke and fumes.

Depression and Recovery

The prosperity of the 1920s ended with the stock market crash in the fall of 1929 and the Great Depression of the 1930s which lasted until World War II. Like the nation as a whole, American railroads fell upon hard times; but with some government assistance, they were able to recover and help the nation emerge from its deep Depression. Had the rail transportation system collapsed, the farms and industries could not have gotten their goods to market and consumers would have been cut off from essential supplies. The

railroads continued to function, however, and in so doing helped avoid an even more chaotic economic situation.

The federal government took an active part in aiding railroads during the Depression. The justification for some form of aid becomes apparent when the state of American railroads in 1930 is examined. First, they were faced with rising and generally unregulated competition from trucks, planes, and water transport. Second, though exacerbated by this increase in competition, rails were circumscribed by a regulatory structure designed to limit monopoly. Due to the reduced freight revenues created by the business depression and to high fixed costs, many railroads experienced financial difficulty.

The first federal response to railroad problems was made by ICC which authorized freight rate increases in October 1931. The proceeds from these increases were to be marshaled and distributed by the Railroad Credit Corporation (RCC). The corporation was empowered to make loans until May 31, 1933. However, inadequate proceeds as well as a banking crisis prevented RCC from accomplishing its goal. Thus, the corporation's importance began to decline when in February 1932 the Reconstruction Finance Corporation (RFC) was created. The RFC was empowered to make temporary loans to railroads with ICC approval. These loans were secured by adequate collateral and were made only if it was not possible to obtain the funds through private channels. A 1933 amendment to the act authorized loans to the trustees of railroads being reorganized under the Bankruptcy Act of the same year. In 1935 RFC was further authorized to cover railroad debts through the Public Works Administration (PWA). These loans enabled the railroads to continue construction and modernization resulting in money flowing through the economy and jobs for workers.

Another phase of government aid to railroads began in June 1933 with the passage of the National Industrial Recovery Act (NIRA). This legislation authorized the President to aid in the financing of railroad maintenance and equipment upon approval by ICC. As a result, about $200 million was loaned by PWA to thirty-two railroad companies. As with loans under the 1920 Transportation Act, the government made a profit while at the same time aiding the economy. Approximately 95 percent of the principal of the loans made to railroads under NIRA was repaid, and interest and other benefits received by the government amounted to $4.7 million more than the defaulted interest.

In addition to lending money, the federal government also promoted a more efficient transportation system. Upon the recommendation of ICC, the Emergency Railroad Transportation Act was passed by Congress in 1933. It established the position of federal coordinator of transportation whose duties included coordinating the work of various modes of transportation as well as improving the efficiency of individual modes.

The federal government also tried to cope with the difficulties experienced by railway employees during the Depression. One example was the "Dill-Crosser Act," or the 1934 Railway Labor Act. This act amended the 1926 Railway Labor Act by abolishing the Board of Mediation and substituting a national board composed of three members appointed by the President. This board was created "to provide for the prompt disposition of disputes between carriers and employees." The act also created the National Railroad Adjustment Board. This body, composed of eighteen management and eighteen labor representatives, was divided into four sections (corresponding to employee classifications) and held hearings to interpret agreements and hand down other quasi-judicial decisions. One week after passing the Dill-Crosser Act, Congress approved the 1934 Railroad Retirement Act. This legislation provided a retirement and unemployment relief system for railroad employees.

Although the government contributed significantly to the railroads' success in weathering the Depression, the roads themselves took initiative in providing many improvements. A variety of innovations and engineering accomplishments were achieved during the 1930s. Many of these occurred for public comfort even though railroads lost money on passenger transport in every year of the decade.

One of the first improvements for passenger comfort was the introduction of air-conditioned coaches on scheduled trains by B & O in 1930. The B & O continued to pioneer in this field when, at a cost of about $5,000 per car, it introduced the first all air-conditioned train the next year. The Illinois Central followed suit and soon other railroads added this comfort system to their trains. Another technical advance was the use of welded rails. Avoiding independent rail sections virtually eliminated the possibility of two connecting rails being misaligned. This, plus various signalling and other safety innovations, enabled railroads to reduce by one half the likelihood of accident.

Perhaps the greatest progress in rail transportation during this period was the introduction of lightweight diesel-powered locomotives for passenger service. Although still limited in their capacity to haul heavy loads, diesel locomotives were capable of attaining high speeds. This ability coupled with the new streamlined design enabled railroads to provide rapid and practically smokeless intercity passenger transportation with excellent operating efficiency. The enthusiasm that railroads and the public had for this new concept is exemplified by the popularity of the Burlington Zephyr and other streamliners. The diesel revolution also stimulated vast improvements in freight services during the 1930s. For example, the average locomotive had 10 percent more tractive power in 1939 than in 1930. Freight capacity and train speed

Library of Congress

In the 1930s, rail passenger service was improved by diesel-powered streamliners.

increased which improved efficiency and lowered freight rates.

Government support of railroads was a major force in the process of recovery during the 1930s. Without the increasingly efficient and inexpensive carriage of goods, the American economy could never have recovered so completely and rapidly. Without the railroad investment and government loans, unemployment and industrial failure would have exceeded their high levels. Railroads were the backbone of the nation during the Depression, and when World War II broke out the country had a high-capacity, high-performance rail system ready to respond.

War Years

Before the United States entered World War II, Congress passed legislation based upon an evaluation of changes in transportation over the past two decades. By 1940 rail transport, though still the dominant mode of freight carriage, was far from the near monopoly it was in 1920. In passenger movement, railways dropped from a position of dominance to the point where they carried only a small fraction of the passengers transported by buses and private automobiles. Furthermore, partly because they were much more strictly regulated than their growing competition, many railroads were in severe financial straits. To deal with these developments, Congress passed the 1940 Transportation Act which empowered ICC to set rates for all interstate common carriers to insure competition.

The act released land grant railroads from their obligation to carry government property and mail at reduced rates. The immediate effects of this provision were minimal because most of the government rail traffic was military until 1945, when the railroads' obligation to military traffic was also released. In return for the release, the railroads surrendered to the government the unused and unsold portions of their land grants.

Even before Pearl Harbor, the war in Europe had a profound effect on rail transportation. After serving the relatively meager need for freight transportation during the Depression, the railroads were confronted with the growing demand to carry freight to eastern ports for use in Europe. The United States was supplying vast quantities of goods to the allied combatants, and the requirements of the Lend-Lease program generated extensive business for the railroads. Ton-mile requirements jumped approximately 60 percent between 1938 and 1941. Railroads consequently emerged from the Depression to show a positive net income in 1939 which more than doubled in each of the next two years. However, with this prosperity came disputes as to whether labor elements were receiving their fair share. When labor troubles arose in 1941, an emergency mediation board was convened to avoid a disruption of transportation. The board's recommendations were unsatisfactory to the workers and a strike was called for Sunday, December 7, 1941. Fortunately, President Franklin D. Roosevelt intervened and the strike was cancelled on December 2.

Gearing up for the tremendous demands placed upon railroad facilities and maintaining the levels reached were not simple tasks. The most serious obstacle was the sheer volume of demand. The number of ton-miles carried by railroads during each of the war years was more than twice the amount handled in 1938. Number of passenger miles in 1942 was more than twice as great as 1938 and over four times as great during each of the following three years. Between Pearl Harbor and V-J Day, American railroads provided 97 percent of all domestic troop movements and about 90 percent of all domestic movements of army and navy equipment and supplies. In the less than four years of war, troop trains transported an average of nearly a million servicemen per month.

Not only was the volume of goods greater, but the variety of types of materials changed with the war. Special loading techniques were necessary to handle various types of explosives. Handling large pieces of equipment, such as tanks, boats, artillery, and aircraft parts, caused great difficulties. These bulky items created clearance problems and required special routings. An unusually large proportion of military shipments required open-top cars which were scarce at the beginning of the war.

Many other products were transferred by rail instead of by sea. For example, prior to the war, New England got 70 percent of its coal by ship; by 1943, 50 percent of this traffic was handled by rail. Lumber from the Pacific Northwest which had previously come via the Panama Canal was transported by rail during the war. Sugar and other commodities from South America were unloaded at gulf ports and carried by train to East Coast destinations instead of traveling by ship directly to Atlantic ports. The wartime limitations on gasoline and rubber for commercial use meant that railroads were substituted for highway transportation. Railroads were expected to adjust quickly to new destinations. Instead of carrying commodities to industrial or population centers, many trains were routed for army bases or naval facilities. Hastily made military plans were frequently changed, with corresponding changes in transportation arrangements sometimes affecting troops and supplies already en route.

Railroads carried large quantities of military equipment during World War II.

The railroads were aided in their attempts at coordination by the Office of Defense Transportation. Directed by Joseph B. Eastman, former ICC commissioner and former federal coordinator of transportation, the federal office was to see that the various transportation modes operated at maximum efficiency. Railroad companies cooperated to avoid any necessity for government control. By running faster and longer trains (now possible with improved locomotives), the enormous quantities of war materials were moved by fewer engines. The use of Centralized Traffic Control expanded greatly during the war, resulting in time and manpower savings.

American railroads were expected to accomplish all of this despite a severe manpower shortage. About 300,000 prewar railroad workers were in the armed services. Labor disputes arose during the period. In late December 1943, the government took over the railroads to avoid a strike called for December 30. Under federal control, which lasted less than a month, management and operation were handled by railroad personnel without any significant deterioration of service. Despite all the problems facing them during the war, railroads logged more passenger and freight miles than ever before. All this was done without restricting the use of common carrier service to the public. Not until 1945 was it necessary to limit civilian travel in any way.

As the war wound down, many railroads began to concentrate on improving public passenger travel. One innovation popularized by the Burlington Railroad was the dome car. First used between Chicago and Minneapolis in July 1945, the glass dome on top of the car allowed passengers to have a better view of the scenery and was such a success that forty more were immediately ordered by the Burlington. Many other railroads introduced similar dome cars. Passenger pleasure was further improved the following year when the first through sleeping car service between the Atlantic and Pacific coasts was inaugurated.

Improved service was also a result of better communications. Beginning in 1945, the Federal Communications Commission (FCC) began issuing radio licenses to railroad companies. Radio then allowed intertrain contact and improved train-to-station communications. By the end of the decade, 190 railroad and terminal companies had FCC licenses.

The prototype diesels of the late 1930s were mass-produced and came into common use for hauling freight during the 1940s. At about the same time that the Santa Fe Railroad was putting diesels into regular service, the Union Pacific was giving steam's last gasp. In

1941 and 1942, this railway unveiled its "Big Boy" locomotives, weighing 534 tons each with a tractive force of 135,000 pounds and generating 7,000 horsepower. Nevertheless, during the decade, the more efficient diesels began to replace the steam engine as the principal source of railroad locomotion.

Diesel Era

The 1950s was a period of unparalleled advances in technology. Partly as a result of the wartime demand for new and better weapons, and the Cold War competition between East and West, the demand for innovative science increased rapidly. As the nuclear age began, the need for engineers, physicists, and other scientists accelerated. In response, educational institutions, encouraged by the government, expanded their science departments. American railroads reflected and participated in this era of technological progress.

In the Korean conflict as in other wars, rail transportation played a key role in supplying troops and moving equipment. The Defense Transport Administration was established to aid in coordinating rail movements during the emergency. This agency was similar to the World War II Office of Defense Transportation but somewhat more restricted. Its primary functions were to determine transportation priorities, encourage development and use of new techniques to transport material, stimulate efficient use of facilities, and maintain the expeditious movement of

traffic. To insure uninterrupted rail service, the railroads were placed under federal control from August 25, 1950 to May 23, 1952. However, as in World War II, day-to-day operations were performed by the existing management and labor.

Perhaps the greatest advance in railroad operation during the 1950s was the virtually complete replacement of steam power by diesel. New engineering improvements continued to increase diesel locomotion's superiority over steam. Freight hauled by steam engines declined from 54 percent in 1950 to less than 1 percent in 1959. Diesels increased their share of rail passenger service from 57 percent in 1950 to over 94 percent in 1959. Although simpler maintenance, greater range, quicker start-ups, and better fuel efficiency were among the reasons for changing to diesel power, the fuel economy of diesel rail locomotion was its best selling point.

Although the concept had originated years earlier, the 1950s saw the piggyback system, or TOFC (Trailer on Flat Car), become widely accepted. This system combined the flexibility of trucks for door-to-door service with rail economy. Some railroads used existing flat cars and others designed special new TOFC cars, and the system expanded rapidly, increasing more than threefold between 1955 and 1959.

Improved rolling stock contributed significantly to better rail service. Insulated boxcars with underframe heaters were used to

Southern Railroad Company

In the 1950s, piggybacking became a widespread transportation practice.

keep perishables from freezing. Built-in compartments in boxcars to prevent shifting helped prevent damage to goods. Installation of cushioned underframes to reduce shocks further protected rail freight. Smoother rides also resulted from increasing the amount of welded rail which eliminated vibrations at rail junctions.

Passengers as well as freight became more comfortable during the 1950s. "Slumbercoaches" were introduced to rail travelers by the Burlington Railroad on its Denver Zephyr in October 1956. These new cars offered the coach passenger a private roomette with a bed for the night, a private toilet, and baggage facilities. Slumbercoaches proved so enjoyable that by the early 1960s they were filled to 83 percent of capacity on the Chicago-to-Denver run. By 1960 several other railroads included similar economy sleeping cars in their passenger trains.

Many other innovations were on the drawing boards, encouraged by an optimistic view of the railroads' future. This hopeful outlook was at least partially attributable to provisions of the 1958 Transportation Act which appeared to relieve some of the burdens upon rail transportation. The act's history began in 1958 when the Senate Committee on Interstate and Foreign Commerce created a subcommittee on surface transportation. After several months of hearings on all aspects of transportation, the subcommittee recommended a bill which was passed by Congress with unusual speed. This legislation gave direction in three major areas. One provision authorized ICC to guarantee up to $500 million in emergency loans under somewhat restrictive conditions. Another portion of the new law gave ICC increased authority regarding modifications or discontinuances of service for trains operating at least partially in interstate service. This jurisdiction replaced, to some extent, the power of states to require the continuance of unprofitable lines. Perhaps the most important and most controversial aspect of the act, however, directed the commission to allow competitive rates where reasonable, without regard to protecting certain carriers. The railroads saw this as a chance to recapture some of the traffic they had lost to less

strictly controlled modes of transportation.

Decade of Advancing Technology

The 1960s exhibited a general expansion of research and development for further improvements. Containerization or COFC (Container on Flat Car) began to be widely used. This system, a modification of the piggyback concept, used a standard-sized container (height and width remained constant, and only length varied), which was carried on a flat car and could be fitted with wheel apparatus to become a trailer. Like piggyback trailers, these containers were sealed to prevent pilferage and reduce loading and unloading costs. The COFC avoided hauling the weight of axles, wheels, and other trailer apparatus. Containers were also more flexible in that they could easily be carried by ship or air freight as well. This improvement also eliminated air turbulence between the flat car and piggyback van, thereby decreasing drag and increasing fuel efficiency.

By 1959 only about 10 percent of the new automobiles produced each year were shipped by rail. This fact was attributable to the shipping method—stuffing three of four autos into a boxcar, while highway rack trucks could carry six cars. Railroads began operating tri-level rack cars capable of transporting twelve to fifteen automobiles. This saved car buyers $25 to $60 per car in freight costs. By 1966 about one half of the annual production of automobiles traveled on railcars. Rack cars were also built to accommodate farm machinery, small trucks, and boats.

Additional rail car improvements resulted from the research of the previous decade. In the mid 1950s, officers of the Southern Railroad had become aware of large quantities of grain being hauled into the southeast by unregulated "gypsy" truckers. The Southern decided to build 500 enormous hopper cars (named Big John cars) at a cost of $13 million. Each of these covered hopper cars had a capacity for over 100 tons of grain and enabled a possible 60 percent decrease in shipping costs. A legal furor arose when Southern published a new rate schedule with charges reduced by 60 percent. A variety of government organizations at all levels, trade associations, corporations, businessmen, unions, consumers, and others became involved in the long dispute. After ICC reversed itself twice and several judicial appeals were heard, the new rates were finally allowed. As a result, the Southern Railroad's grain traffic ballooned from 700,000 tons per year to over 2 million.

Southern Railroad Company

Employment of 100-ton Big John hopper cars enabled railroads to cut shipping costs for grain and other bulk commodities.

A new system of train organization called a unit train was also devised during this period. Perhaps the most important stimulus to the development of the unit train was the use of coal slurry. Under existing methods, pipeline transportation of slurry was less expensive than rail transportation of solid coal. Since the utility companies using coal were among the biggest railroad customers, the planning and construction of pipelines and facilities for using slurry aroused the concern of railroad officials. In order to compete with the pipelines, B & O experimented with huge, permanently coupled hopper cars which went to the same destination. This concept was soon adopted by other railroads, and service was so improved that some pipelines were shut down and plans for new pipelines were abandoned.

Unit trains were also utilized for a variety of bulk goods which could be regularly scheduled. For example, the Santa Fe Railroad shuttled 100-ton gondola cars loaded with ore between New Mexico and California. Other railroads began transporting grain, steel, lumber, and other bulk items via unit trains. Such trains, pulled by new diesels, were hauling record loads of freight. The "rent-a-train" practice evolved from the unit concept. Using the rent-a-train system, a large shipper, such as a grain exporter, would organize a train of its cars for which the railroad company would provide locomotion.

A major catalyst to continued technological research was the 1965 High Speed Ground Transportation Act, which authorized $90 million for research, experimentation, and demonstration projects over a three-year period. A supplemental appropriation of $18 million was approved in 1966. The results and importance of such research were recognized by Congress when, in 1968, it extended this project for two more years and added $50 million to its funding. Later amendments in 1970 and 1972 extended High Speed Ground Transportation research through 1975 and appropriated nearly $400 million in additional funds.

The federal government began to consider transportation as an entity rather than an aspect of other functions, and on October 15, 1966, Congress passed the Department of Transportation Act. The department thereby created was officially activated April 1, 1967. It was authorized to coordinate and administer federal transportation programs, encourage cooperation between private industry and various levels of government, stimulate technological improvements, and recommend policies, all toward the goal of assuring fast, safe, efficient, and convenient transportation at low cost. Included in the department was the new Federal Railroad Administration (FRA), which absorbed functions formerly belonging to ICC and the Department of Commerce. Under this reorganization, a variety of research and experimental projects were undertaken in cooperation with the railroad industry to improve the operation of rail transport.

Metroliners provide high-speed passenger service between Washington, D.C., and New York City.

One government-sponsored program, the Northeast Corridor Project, was created to provide passenger service between Boston, New York City, and Washington, D.C., at high speeds (sometimes exceeding 100 miles per hour.) For its part, the Pennsylvania Railroad, which later became the Penn Central, installed continuous welded rail along most of the 227 miles from New York to Washington. The railroad also purchased fifty new self-propelled cars capable of high speeds. The trains, called Metroliners, travel at speeds limited only by safety considerations. By connecting the centers of these major cities, this train was able to compete with air travel which required time-consuming circling of airports and slow rides through traffic from airports to downtown destinations. As rail travel came closer to air transportation in the time required for shorter trips, other conveniences such as lower fares, comfort, and telephones (in Metroliner cars) began to convince travelers once again of the value of railroads for passenger service. This project was so successful in attracting passengers that by 1972 twice as many round trips were run as had been scheduled initially, and Metroliner service was showing a profit.

A related project originally cosponsored by the Department of Transportation and the Penn Central Railroad was the Turbo-Train connecting Boston and New York. First run in April 1969—just three months after Metroliner service was inaugurated—the Turbo-Train had a potential speed in excess of 150 miles per hour. Since its propulsion system did not require electrified tracks, it offered a less expensive alternative to the Metroliner system. These trains included many innovations adapted from aircraft engineering such as a rounded shape similar to that of an airplane fuselage; flush doors and windows also similar to an airplane; meals served at the passengers' seats by hostesses; and music via personal headphones. The Turbo-Train also featured domed observation cars to allow a panoramic view of the New England countryside.

One major engineering advance in the Turbo-Train was its pendulous banking suspension system. Because each car of the train was suspended on an A-frame system, centrifugal force allowed the cars to remain steady while the train banked around curves. This offered a potential 40 percent increase in safe speed. Within two years, the Turbo-Train's New York terminal was switched from Grand Central to Pennsylvania Terminal to connect with the Metroliner. These two demonstration trains signalled a resurgence in rail passenger travel made possible by space-age technology and the realization by the federal government of the potential of rail transportation.

In the latter 1960s, American railroads were active in adapting computers and other technological systems to improving rail service. One such innovation is known as Automatic Car Identification (ACI). In the ACI system, all locomotives and cars are identified with plastic labels on their sides. The label consists of thirteen strips of colored plastic which identify the car by color combinations. Trackside scanners located at strategic points read these labels in any weather and at train speeds of up to eighty miles per hour. The information gathered is then relayed to a computer which records the location of all cars. The computer records are pooled by the Telerail Automated Information Network (TRAIN). The TRAIN system links forty-four data terminals to a central computer at the headquarters of the Association of American Railroads. Made operational in 1969 and 1970, TRAIN maintains records on 98 percent of the freight car interchanges between railroads. With these records, it is easier to plan car distribution to avoid shortages.

Government Involvement

By the end of the 1960s, a few of the railroads in the United States were prosperous and progressive; others were in bankruptcy or in severe financial difficulty. Most railroads were surviving but were often more nearly bankrupt than prosperous. The difficulties were attributed to a variety of causes—over-regulation, inability of railroads to control their own rate-making, the burden of unprofitable passenger service, excess facilities, and inept management. The deteriorating situation, especially in the northeastern states, and the vital role the railroads must play in a viable national transportation system led to government involvement to assure continued availability of railroad service.

Despite the technical advances of earlier decades, great difficulties remained. Among the most pressing were safety problems related to equipment and cargoes. In 1972, for example, more than 7,500 railroad accidents occurred, killing 1,945 persons and injuring almost 17,900. In addition to direct damage caused by collisions and derailments, further harm resulted from leakage from railroad cars of hazardous substances shipped by the Department of Defense and gases of various types shipped both by the Department of Defense and commercial companies. Commodities such as propane, liquid natural gas, and agricultural chemicals exploded or burned following railroad accidents.

While much of the damage resulted from factors not subject to the railroads' control, an increasing number of derailments and other accidents were attributed to the inability of the railroads to maintain their rolling stock and rights-of-way in top condition. As the financial state of railroads deteriorated, they were forced to cut corners by reducing the level of maintenance of roadbeds and equipment.

Prior to 1970, there were no government regulations for conditions of railroad track or cars. In the 1970 Railroad Safety Act, this area became the concern of the Department of Transportation. This first specific railroad safety legislation was designed to promote safe railroad operation and reduce railroad-related accidents, deaths, and injuries. The act authorized the secretary of transportation to prescribe regulations for railroad safety to supplement existing rail safety statutes and regulations; to conduct research, testing, and hearings on the subject of rail safety; to study and report on eliminating problems concerning grade crossings and transporting hazardous materials; and to prohibit the use of any facility or equipment found to be unsafe.

The act also allowed states to adopt and enforce laws and standards relating to railroad safety. A state law more stringent than the federal would be acceptable unless the statute was an oppressive burden on interstate commerce. State cooperation in inspection and enforcement was provided by granting the Department of Transportation the power to subsidize 50 percent of the state's cost in carrying out these functions. The penalty set for violations of safety requirements was a fine of up to $2,500 per day per violation.

The law was used to require safe railroading practices. For example, in August 1974 FRA ordered the Penn Central to terminate all service over sixty-seven miles of track between Chicago and Louisville because the track failed to meet minimum standards as tested by the FRA Track Geometry car. Later that month, another section of this statute was the basis for requiring protective head shields on certain tank cars.

The FRA's Office of Safety is also concerned with prevention of grade crossing accidents, inspection of railroad rolling stock, and investigation of complaints about safety and signalling equipment. The office has helped develop track safety standards, health standards for railroad personnel, a reporting system for personal injury accidents, and numerous regulations concerning safe carriage of hazardous materials.

Undoubtedly, the most significant event in rail passenger history since World War II was the formation of the National Railroad Passenger Corporation. Created by the 1970 Rail Passenger Service Act, the corporation (originally referred to as "Railpax" but soon known as "AMTRAK") was authorized to manage the operation of intercity passenger trains. The purpose of creating AMTRAK was to revitalize ailing passenger service as well as to relieve railroad companies of a service which had become financially burdensome. Specifically, AMTRAK was incorporated by Congress to provide modern, efficient intercity rail passenger service by employing innovative operating and marketing techniques. AMTRAK's board of trustees was composed of nine presidential appointees, three railroad executives, and the secretary of transportation. Although not a public agency, the corporation was to receive federal funds to offset deficits.

AMTRAK began with considerable handicaps. Rail passenger travel was declining so rapidly that, excluding commuter runs, the number of passenger miles on trains in 1970 was one half that logged in 1966, and the latter figure was one half of the 1951 total. The 40 billion passenger miles logged in 1947 fell

to just over 6 billion in 1970. There were about 25 percent as many rail passenger cars in operation in 1970 as there were in the late 1940s. Since competition from other modes had drastically reduced the demand for railroad passenger service, there was little incentive for the railroads to spend money on modernization and promotion.

Before AMTRAK could begin operation, the 1970 act required the secretary of transportation to designate a basic system of intercity routes for AMTRAK. On January 28, 1971, the secretary issued a final report describing essential service which would be provided and additional optional routes. The routes in the secretary's report were analyzed individually in relation to the entire system. Route selections were announced after such factors as market size, physical characteristics of the route and track, current demand, operating costs, and relationship of the line to other routes and modes had been considered. On May 1, 1971, AMTRAK assumed responsibility for most of the intercity rail passenger transportation in the United States. Under the law, AMTRAK acquired the rail passenger service components of railroad companies in exchange for stock of the Rail Passenger Service Corporation. There were some additional conditions. For example, a railroad divesting itself of its passenger service was required to make provision for the protection of workers who would be displaced when AMTRAK took over its passenger operations. Only a few of the railroads declined the opportunity to turn over their services to AMTRAK.

In its effort to solve the problems it had inherited, AMTRAK experimented with potential route changes, a limited amount of improved new equipment, and some expanded services. In its first year of operation, provisional service was inaugurated on five new routes. The following year experimental routes were extended across the Canadian border from Seattle to Vancouver and between Washington, D.C., and Montreal. By the winter of 1972, AMTRAK had scheduled trains to Mexico. The number of trains on some routes was increased to meet growing demand, but some experiments were unsuccessful and trains were discontinued.

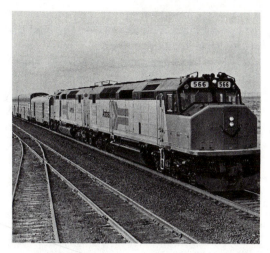

AMTRAK

AMTRAK was created in 1971 to revitalize rail passenger service in the United States.

AMTRAK made a notable effort to obtain new and to modernize old equipment. The improvements and expansion of Metroliner and Turbo-Train demonstration projects were partially attributable to AMTRAK after May 1971. Over $28 million worth of new locomotives were ordered during the first two years of operation. In addition to initial refurbishing of existing rolling stock, AMTRAK ordered $63 million worth of new equipment in October 1973. Turbine-powered trains were soon operated on Midwest runs, and by 1974 seven new Turbo-Trains costing $30 million were ordered to supplement the existing ones as well as conventional trains on the Boston-New York route. Other new equipment was also provided. For example, a national computerized reservation system allowed passengers to purchase tickets quickly by telephone. Refurbishing of equipment to encourage increased patronage included new paint, carpeting, and upholstery. Movies were made available and a piano player was added for entertainment on weekend runs of the Washington, D.C., to Montreal train. Credit card payment for tickets was initiated in 1972. Tours of Disney World and ski excursions in Vermont were just two of many travel package plans which AMTRAK arranged.

Perhaps most important from the passengers' point of view, there were fare reductions on many runs. For calendar year 1973, AMTRAK experienced a 24 percent rise in revenue over that of the previous year, indicating an heightened level of acceptance by the public. But persuading people to change travel habits is a slow process, so that even with the increased revenues, AMTRAK operations showed a deficit that year of $158.6 million.

Several factors affected the industry's solvency. For instance, there was a surplus of railroad capacity in certain areas—especially in the Northeast—where two or more rail lines were built to compete for freight and passenger shipments. One railroad spokesman characterized this as "redundant, obsolete, duplicative, parallel facilities." The existence of competing means of transportation for both passengers and freight was another factor. The airlines and truck carriers both received indirect aid from the federal government, in that air facilities, highways, and waterways were subsidized by public funds. These problems existed most acutely in New England and the Midwest areas served by the Penn Central Railroad and certain of its competitors, five of which were in bankruptcy proceedings by 1973.

Some of the blame for the industry's shaky financial condition is attributable to out-dated government regulatory policies. Railroads no longer monopolize freight and passenger traffic as they did sixty years ago. Conditions in American transportation have changed drastically since World War I. Rigid regulation is no longer required and often retards the industry's ability to respond quickly to changes in the marketplace. A railroad cannot cut off a train, close a station, or change freight rates without obtaining ICC approval. The ICC hearings and decisions on rate changes are often slow and have been characterized as "a carnival of oratory." The commission has been reluctant to allow railroads to merge or reduce rates, and it often required the companies to keep their rates high to assure trucks and barges a large share of the total commercial traffic. In a sense, ICC has moved from protecting the public against abuses to sheltering other transportation forms from railroad competition. The result has been high shipping costs.

To help meet the problem of railroad solvency, Congress enacted the 1973 Regional Rail Reorganization Act. This statute provided for the establishment of a new nonprofit corporation called the United States Railway Association (USRA) to prepare and implement a plan for systematic rail service in the Northeast and Midwest. Once it had determined the routes to be included in the system, USRA was charged with the task of planning, organizing, and financing the acquisition and improvement of the rail properties to be operated by the Consolidated Rail Corporation (CRC), also created by this law. The corporation was designed to be profit-making and was to be responsible for the operation, rehabilitation, improvement, and modernization of rail properties in order to maintain adequate and efficient rail services. The act was intended to provide for a new rail system for the Northeast which would not displace profitable operating railroads but would assure that rail transport would be available wherever in the Northeast it is the proper and most cost-effective mode of transportation.

The Regional Rail Reorganization Act was challenged as unconstitutional by major creditors and the Penn Central Company. For they argued, that if Penn Central entered the Consolidated Rail Corporation by transferring its assets to that corporation, the assets would erode during the process and the stockholders would suffer loss of property without proper compensation. However, the act was declared constitutional by the Supreme Court on December 16, 1974. The court rejected the allegations of the plaintiffs, ruling that if the stockholders do suffer losses they may sue the government in the Court of Claims to regain the assets lost in the transfer.

On February 26, 1975, USRA unveiled its plan for rail reorganization in the Northeast which called for the most massive corporate reorganization in American history. It supported combining the Penn Central and five other lines to form the CRC or ConRail. By eliminating 6,200 miles of branch lines, the new system would create a unified 15,000-mile system that would be modernized through massive transfusions of federal money. The proposal called for $9.3 billion to rehabilitate rails and equipment and to buy freight cars and locomotives over the next fifteen years. To reduce ConRail's initial debt, the plan also suggested government ownership of tracks, yards, and rights-of-way with the company paying an annual fee for their use. A coeval event reaffirmed the magnitude of the northeastern railroad crisis. The day the USRA report was issued, the Senate approved $347 million in emergency aid to keep the Penn Central limping along.

The USRA submitted a Final System Plan to Congress on July 26, 1975 which was approved the following November. This action set the stage for the Railroad Revitalization and Regulatory Reform Act which President Gerald R. Ford signed February 5, 1976. The law's principal provision authorized ConRail, a new government-assisted private corporation, to be formed by consolidating the Penn Central and six other bankrupt northeastern railroads. The government authorized $2.1 billion in loans over the next five years for modernizing and rehabilitating plants, acquiring equipment, refinancing indebtedness, and providing working capital. ConRail was due to begin operations April 1, 1976.

The act also changed federal regulatory practices. Railroads were given more freedom to change their rates, and ICC was required to implement decisions on rates and mergers more rapidly. In addition, loans were made available for financially unstable railroads throughout the country.

The Outlook

The future of rail passenger service and of rail freight transportation in the United States will depend on many factors. It can be expected that long-distance rail passenger travel will continue to lose ground to air transportation. However, the passenger service provided between cities up to 300 to 400 miles apart will become more attractive with the speed and facility improvements being made by AMTRAK. The existing railroad facilities and rights-of-way into downtown areas offer great potential for increased passenger service. Many railroad terminals, designed for a different age and different conditions, will be renovated and remodeled to fit new and increasing needs. As for freight, it has long been obvious that no other reasonable available transportation mode could replace railroads for the long distance, overland hauling of such heavy and bulky commodities as coal, iron ore, steel, or other products that are basic to the health and growth of the national economy.

However, as essential as rail transportation is, railroad companies have not been financially stable, and in the Northeast and Midwest at least six major railroads have filed for bankruptcy. Both government and private specialists have given time and effort to making the railroads in these areas viable again.

The industry will continue to be affected by the pressing energy shortage of the 1970s. Yet, in a fuel-short situation, railroad transportation offers great advantages both in economy and convenience. First, the railroads are already built, so they are available without overwhelming costs for land acquisition and roadbed construction; second, for long hauls, rail transportation is efficient and relatively inexpensive; third, when operating long trains, railroads produce significantly less air pollution than any other mode carrying the same material.

Even though advantages will accrue from greater utilization of railroads in the future, problems will arise from subjecting them to more intensive use. The most serious problem is the maintenance backlog that will require many years and billions of dollars to remedy. Another problem which will shortly become acute is a shortage of rail cars, particularly boxcars and gondola cars for hauling freight, and modern passenger cars. The anticipated great increase in the hauling of coal in the next few decades to meet the nation's energy needs will place additional demands on the railroads.

In recent years, the federal government has taken an active role to help insure the nation will have a reliable freight and passenger rail network. This commitment is consistent with a long tradition of public regulation, financial support, and operation of railroads. The railroads have been and will continue to be vital to America's commerce and productivity. Nevertheless, large segments of this industry are beset with bad roadbed, obsolete equipment, and operating deficits. These are portents that modernization and efficiency can only be achieved through expanded public expenditures and perhaps some type of direct involvement of government in some features of the railroad system.

SUGGESTED READINGS

American Society of Civil Engineers. *The Eight-Mile Cascade Tunnel, Great Northern Railway—A Symposium.* New York, 1931.

Association of American Railroads. *American Railroads and the War.* Washington, D.C., 1943.

Beebe, Lucius M. *Trains in Transition.* New York, 1941.

Bruce, Alfred. *The Steam Locomotive in America.* New York, 1952.

Carper, Robert S. *Focus: The Railroad in Transition.* Cranbury, New Jersey, 1968.

Condit, Carl. *American Building.* Chicago, 1968.

Dick, Everett. *The Sod-House Frontier, 1854-1890: A Social History of the Northern Plains from the Creation of Kansas and Nebraska to Admission of the Dakotas.* New York, 1937.

Dorin, Patrick. *The Domeliners.* Seattle, 1973.

Dubin, Arthur. *Classic Trains.* 2 vols. Milwaukee, 1964.

Fishlow, Albert. *Railroads and the Transformation of the Antebellum Economy.* Cambridge, Massachusetts, 1965.

Holbrook, Stewart H. *The Story of American Railroads.* New York, 1947.

Johnson, Emory R. *The Railroads and the Public Welfare.* New York, 1944.

Lyon, Peter. *To Hell in a Day Coach: An Exasperated Look at American Railroads.* Philadelphia, 1968.

Martin, Albro. *Enterprise Denied: Origins of the Decline of American Railroads, 1897-1917.* New York, 1971.

McCague, James. *Moguls and Iron Men: The Story of the First Transcontinental Railroad.* New York, 1964.

Miller, George H. *The Railroads and the Granger Laws.* Madison, Wisconsin, 1971.

Norton, Hugh S. *Modern Transportation Economics.* Columbus, Ohio, 1963.

Nye, Russell B. *Midwestern Progressive Politics: A Historical Study of its Origins and Development, 1870-1920.* East Lansing, Michigan, 1951.

Stover, John F. *American Railroads.* Chicago, 1961.

Southerland, Thomas C., Jr., and McCleery, William. *The Way to Go: The Coming Revival of U.S. Rail Passenger Service.* New York, 1973.

United States Railway Association. *Preliminary System Plan for Restructuring Railroads in the Northeast and Midwest Region Pursuant to the Regional Rail Reorganization Act of 1973.* 2 vols. Washington, D.C., 1975.

U.S. Department of Transportation. *A Statement of National Transportation Policy.* Washington, D.C., 1975.

White, John H., Jr. *The American Locomotive, 1830-1880.* Baltimore, 1968.

CHAPTER 6

URBAN MASS TRANSPORTATION

The availability of local mass transportation has been a determining factor in shaping the pattern of large American cities. Twentieth-century urban centers are characterized by a sharp distinction between residential, commercial, and industrial land use; but during the early years of the republic, the metropolitan landscape was decidedly mixed. Rather than a central business district ringed by industrial and residential areas, large communities were an unorganized hodgepodge of private dwellings, factories, warehouses, and stores. The transformation of the urban environment from this unintegrated condition into highly segregated working, shopping, and living areas largely resulted from the development of mass transit systems. For without effective intraurban transportation, it is difficult to see how the great cities which emerged during the nineteenth century could have developed as they did.

Until the onset of industrialization in the early decades of the nineteenth century, the principal American cities flourished mainly because of foreign and domestic commerce. They served as exchange points for raw and finished goods, and along their fine harbors emerged the first American metropolises. Near the waterfronts, in close proximity to one

another, sprang up public buildings, churches, warehouses, shops, and the homes of wealthy businessmen and skilled and unskilled workers. This tendency for economic activity to focus near the docks accelerated as foreign trade broadened and industrialization was introduced. As the pace of the economy quickened, the cities grew at an astonishing rate. In 1790 only five cities had a population in excess of 8,000. But by 1840, forty-four were in this category.

This influx of people produced overcrowding because city dimensions were constrained by the distances most residents could walk to work. A few members of the upper classes owned private carriages or hired hackneys, the small public coaches of the period, but these modes of travel were beyond the means of most wage earners. Therefore, as the city's population grew, so did its density, and the urban environment became more crowded and less comfortable for all classes of citizenry.

Workers pressed into the residential areas nearest the center of commercial or industrial activity. The more affluent then sought relief from the filth, stench, noise, and confusion endangered by human compaction. By the third decade of the nineteenth century, a latent demand existed for a means of public conveyance that would allow residents to live greater distances from their work.

This chapter was prepared by Michael C. Robinson, Associate Editor.

The Omnibus

The omnibus was the first innovation in local transportation to significantly alter the living and working habits of some urban dwellers. First appearing in Paris, France, this common carrier was introduced into the United States in the 1830s and dominated mass transit until the 1860s. John Stephenson, a New York City coach builder, constructed the first American omnibus. His gaily decorated *Sociable* began operating on New York streets in 1831 and was so popular that it was followed by a fleet of similar vehicles. The long coaches, pulled by two-horse teams, seated about twelve passengers, and unlike hackneys, passed along specific routes. Fares ranged between twelve and thirty-five cents and seldom varied with the distance traveled. By 1855, 583 omnibuses were operating along twenty-seven routes to New York. The enterprise proved so profitable that omnibuses spread to other large American cities such as Boston, Philadelphia, Baltimore, and Pittsburgh.

Despite heavy public patronage, the omnibus was far from an ideal transit mode. Passengers rode in cramped and stuffy coaches, sat on hard wooden benches, and endured clatter and bone-jarring bumps as the iron-rimmed wheels jostled the omnibus along the cobblestone or deeply rutted dirt streets of the era. Patrons had to guard against pickpockets and short-changing drivers, and they traveled in constant fear of runaway horses and collisions with other vehicles. The danger to riders was compounded by the reckless, competitive drivers who raced and jockeyed along the streets in search of customers while shouting oaths at one another. As street traffic increased, accidents became commonplace, and omnibuses posed an evergrowing threat to pedestrains crossing busy thoroughfares. After viewing a typical 1850 street scene, a vexed New Yorker aptly characterized this pioneer transit system as "a perfect bedlam on wheels."

In response to public outcry, municipal governments passed regulatory ordinances to reduce danger and bring order to the streets. In most cities where omnibuses operated, drivers and conductors were licensed, and companies were given designated routes. In addition, vehicle capacity was limited, and speed and other driving regulations were imposed. These laws, which established the principle of common carrier regulation, were the forerunners of ordinances which govern city traffic today.

Public patronage of the omnibus began to alter significantly the urban landscape. These early transit lines laid the foundation of a new community structure, characterized by a vibrant central business district encircled by residential areas. By expanding the effective commuting radius of the city, the omnibus allowed some urbanites to flee the congested inner city for more salubrious and less hectic outlying residential areas. Unfortunately, the introduction of mass transit did little to ease the plight of the poorer classes. Prevailing transit fares were beyond the means of a vast majority of the laboring population. As the more prosperous elements of society moved to the city's perimeter, those who still walked to work huddled ever closer together in deteriorating housing adjacent to commercial and manufacturing centers.

Horsecar Period

Although the omnibus led the way in providing public conveyances, it became apparent that another system was needed to meet increasing user demand. The introduction of the horsecar brought about the first transit system that was relatively safe and comfortable. Horsecars originated as a result of public antipathy to the operation of noisy, smoke- and cinder-belching steam railroads in congested urban areas. To transport passengers into cities, some railroads built tracks down streets and hitched horses to their passenger cars. Before long this innovation was applied to intraurban transit needs. In 1832 John Mason, president of the New York and Harlem Railroad Company, commissioned Stephenson, builder of the first American omnibus, to design and construct a railcar for use on New York City streets. The first horsecar, named the *John Mason*, went into operation in New York City on November 14, 1832.

The new transit system was an improve-

The first street railway began operating in New York City in 1832.

ment over the omnibus. By placing the public vehicle on rails, friction was reduced and horse power was more efficiently utilized. Horsecars provided a comparatively smooth, bump-free ride. They held two or three times more passengers than the omnibus, thereby reducing traffic congestion and eliminating the hurly-burly of omnibus competition. They traveled about seven miles per hour and increased the half-hour commuting distance for city workers from 2 to 3 miles. It is no wonder that promoters hailed the horsecar as "the improvement of the age" and claimed it was a panacea for public transportation needs.

In spite of its attributes, horsecar development was delayed by opposition from the public and from omnibus companies. Some citizens objected to laying track down city streets because carriage and wagon traffic would be disrupted. Other cities suggested that vehicles moving at the unheard of speed of seven miles per hour would cause horses to bolt and threaten pedestrians crossing busy streets. The business community was especially hard to convince that track construction would not reduce adjacent property values. Omnibus companies fought the in-

troduction of horsecars tooth and nail and stirred up public opposition. Even amateur sociologists chimed in, insisting that the glamorous new vehicles would undermine American democratic values because horsecar passengers would become snobbish and would view with disdain lowly pedestrians and omnibus patrons.

Horsecar development was further hindered by pre-Civil War economic conditions. A considerable capital outlay was required to put a system into operation, and investors hesitated to gamble on the unproven and unpopular enterprise. The depression of the late 1830s and early 1840s dried up possible funding sources. More delays occurred as mass transit became a factor in the political arena. Because streets are in the public domain, construction of city rail systems required approval of local governments through the granting of franchises. In seeking these privileges, prospective transit builders were often hindered by partisan bickering or by venal politicians who demanded bribes in exchange for right-of-way approval. It was not uncommon for early street railway investors to regard outlays to mayors, common councils, and aldermen as part of construction costs.

New York's pioneer horsecar line was a success, but there was no significant expansion of the industry until the 1850s. In 1856 a highly publicized horsecar system was constructed in Boston, and other cities began to follow suit. Horsecars were introduced into Philadelphia in 1858, and a year later Baltimore, Cincinnati, and Pittsburgh joined the ranks of street railway cities.

Although opponents sought injunctions to stop construction and insisted the new transit mode was a public nuisance, opposition gradually eroded as the new systems proved the criticisms unsound. A significant factor in moving construction forward was the conversion of the business community. Capitalists began to realize that street railways were a profitable investment and a boon to retail businesses and real estate values. As systems expanded and usage increased, stores bordering horsecar lines experienced accelerated sales, and builders discovered that homes on or near rights-of-way sold at a premium. With fares pouring into company coffers, street railway operators had little trouble attracting investment capital.

Street railway expansion was retarded by the Civil War as resources were diverted for this epic conflict. But from 1865 to 1890, the horsecar reigned supreme as the principal urban common carrier. Cities large and small adopted the vehicles, and by the mid 1880s over 100,000 horses and mules were pulling 18,000 horsecars on 3,500 miles of track throughout the country. This growth permitted cities to enlarge and encouraged suburban development.

Although horsecars provided the first efficient means of local transit, inventors and entrepreneurs sought a wholly mechanical means of conveyance. The principal shortcoming of this mode was the horse itself. Each animal could work only four hours a day, requiring frequent team changes. Companies maintained large and expensive stables which demanded substantial outlays for feed and caretaking personnel. A good horse cost over a hundred dollars, required forty to sixty cents a day to feed, and was replaced after three to four years of grueling labor on

city streets. In addition, street railway companies came under fire from groups who asserted it was cruel and exploitive to have horses pull the heavily laden cars.

Horses were prone to frequent injury and disease. The roughly paved streets cracked hoofs, induced lameness, and fostered other disabilities. The dank and fetid stables, where the animals spent most of their day, were breeding places for communicable diseases. In 1872, when the horse population of the United States was ravaged by a plague of equine influenza known as the Great Epizootic, horsecar companies were especially hard hit. Some firms suspended operations, while others hitched up oxen or ordered their idled drivers and conductors to pull the cars themselves.

Perhaps the most vexing problem was disposing of the animals' waste. Each horse daily discharged gallons of urine and nearly twenty pounds of fecal matter onto the streets, which deteriorated the rails and posed a serious public health hazard. Furthermore, horsecar firms habitually maintained a manure pit to supplement their income. Though these stable gleanings were sold as fertilizer, storing the offensive resource did not endear the companies to local residents. As people grew increasingly public health conscious, it became apparent that a substitute for the horse was necessary.

Horsecars had additional drawbacks. In the winter, snow removal from the tracks was

Smithsonian Institution

Boston horsecar in 1870. Horsecars provided the principal means of urban mass transportation until the 1890s.

laborious and expensive, and it raised public ire because it disrupted sleighing, a popular recreational activity. External heat created other problems. In the summer, horses fatigued rapidly and required more frequent team changes. Because of their limited pulling power, horses had difficulty in negotiating steep grades. Relay teams had to be stationed at the bottom of hills, and in some instances passengers were requested to disembark and walk up. Thus, street railway expansion was limited to relatively flat terrain. To these inconveniences were added traffic safety risks. Some horses were temperamentally unpredictable and tended to disobey driver commands. Injuries to patrons often occurred when a fidgety nag lurched forward while the car was taking on or letting off passengers.

In the quest for a wholly mechanical form of traction, mid nineteenth-century technology offered the steam engine as the most likely candidate, but public opposition to using locomotives on city streets remained firm. Although citizens gradually became inured to having tracks traverse major streets, they rightly believed that the noise, smoke, ash, and steam of steam engines would foul the urban environment and damage property values along streets where it operated. Proponents of "dummies," as the small transit engines were called, praised the system's attributes. They argued that because of more reliable control, the locomotives afforded greater safety than the horse and could transport more passengers; but their use in urban areas remained severely circumscribed.

Engineers, mechanics, and inventors sought to overcome this antipathy by reducing emissions and noise, but their combined efforts achieved little success. Others tried alternative power sources. Between 1865 and 1900, the United States issued patents for vehicles propelled by compressed air, ammonia, caustic soda, and natural gas. However, none of these exotic inventions proved to be applicable to the country's transit needs.

Another approach to overcoming the objections of property owners to steam engines were schemes for elevating railroads above the street surface. The major selling point was that separating mass transportation from pedestrians and other traffic would permit higher speeds, reduce congestion, and promote safety. In especially crowded urban centers, the el was viewed as the central component of an integrated transit system which would carry passengers to the suburbs while being served by a feeder system of horse railways.

The four elevated lines which began serving New York City in 1879 were immensely profitable. Patronage increased from 60 million the first year of operation to nearly 190 million a decade later. Although the el succeeded in New York, other cities resisted it until the 1890s. Several factors caused the delay. Financial wheeler-dealers such as Cyrus Field and Jay Gould controlled the transit corporations and operated them in an unethical fashion which gave els an unsavory image of stock watering and manipulation. Complaints about accidents and pollution were aired, and noted medical authorities alleged the noise and vibration from the els retarded child development and caused nervous disorders, paralysis, deafness, and even death. When property owners along streets where els operated sued the transit companies for structural damage to their buildings, civic leaders in other cities took heed and blocked el construction.

Cable Cars

The cable car was the first replacement for the horsecar to gain widespread acceptance. In 1869 Andrew S. Hallidie, a San Francisco wire rope manufacturer, began working on a means of conveying transit cars by cable. The technology had been available for several decades, and Hallidie was convinced a cable system could be devised for street railroads.

Hallidie's invention basically consisted of an endless cable, which stationary steam engines propelled through a conduit under the surface of the street. Beneath each railcar extended the grip, a clamping device that would engage the fast moving cable and move the car along the rails. To pick up or discharge passengers the operator, or "gripman," released the device and applied a brake.

In many respects, the opening of the first cable railway in San Francisco on August 1, 1873 was a triumph of engineering over geography. The city's hilly terrain was not conducive to widespread employment of horsecars; the grades of many streets were so steep that horses pulling streetcars could not ascend them, restricting population mobility within the city.

The cable offered numerous advantages over the horse. Hills could be surmounted at no reduction in speed, and inclement weather offered few impediments to effective operation. The cable car could run twelve miles per hour as opposed to seven for the horsecar, thereby nearly doubling commuting distances. Moreover, since one gripcar could pull several large passenger cars, street congestion was reduced in dense traffic areas. By 1881, 12 miles of cable railway were operating in San Francisco with 3 more under construction.

In spite of the apparent advantages of Hallidie's invention, no other American city adopted cable railways during the 1870s. The paramount factor inhibiting expansion was the cost of putting a line into operation. Building the power stations and the elaborate underground network of pulleys, cable, and conduits cost at least $100,000 per mile, five times more than a horse railway. Most street railway owners and operators thought the expense too great and chose to retain their old equipment.

Efforts to introduce this new technological breakthrough encountered opposition from familiar sources. Owners of homes and businesses along rights-of-way were outraged by the temporary disruption of water, gas, and sewage services that constructing underground conduits entailed. Tearing up city thoroughfares temporarily disrupted traffic flow and raised the hackles of businessmen who complained of reduced commercial activity. The increased speed of the new vehicles also gave rise to shrill protests regarding the safety of riders and other street users.

City governments and potential investors were especially wary of cable cars because the system encountered many operating defi-

Smithsonian Institution

Baltimore, Maryland cable railway system. Cable railways required large expenditures for a power plant, cars, and equipment.

ciencies and was prone to breakdown. The cable followed a very circuitous and tortuous route over sheaves, through pullies, around corners, and through the power mechanism. The bending and twisting, as well as wear from the grips and the strain of pulling heavily laden cars, damaged and even broke the cable. When breaks occurred, the entire railway had to be shut down until repairs were made.

After San Francisco, Chicago was the next city to operate a cable railway, which opened in March 1881. Chicago's cable railway system was acknowledged as one of the technological wonders of the 1880s and 1890s. Horsecar operators came in droves to the windy city to inspect the new system and ponder its applicability to their respective communities. Philadelphia organized a cable railway in 1883 and was followed by New York, St. Louis, Oakland, Denver, Washington, Cincinnati, and a number of other large American cities. By 1890, 223 miles of cable railways operated in the United States. However, the cable railway never replaced the horsecar. In 1890, 4,061 miles of horse railway were in use, a total nearly twenty times greater than the cable. Despite the advantages of the cable, economics continued to thwart widespread substitution. By 1890 the cost of building a cable line had risen to well over $150,000 per mile as compared to $34,000 per mile for a horse railway. Operating expenses for the new system were less than half of the old, but these savings only offset the high initial investment where patronage was especially heavy. Therefore, cable cars primarily operated in established business districts where they carried nearly 20 percent of the nation's passengers in spite of accounting for only 5 percent of the trackage. By the end of the nineteenth century, it was apparent that the cable railway would remain confined to the high-density area of the inner city and contribute little toward urban expansion.

Trolley Era

The search for a safer, more efficient, and less costly means of motive power for urban transit engaged numerous inventors who sought to harness electrical energy. In 1834

Thomas Davenport, a Vermont blacksmith, built a miniature electric railcar operated by a battery. He was followed thirteen years later by Moses G. Farmer who operated small battery-powered electric cars at Dover, New Hampshire. The most noteworthy of these early experiments in electric traction was conducted by Charles G. Page. In 1851 he ran a small car from Washington, D.C., to the nearby suburb of Bladensburg, Maryland, over the tracks of the Baltimore and Ohio Railroad. Before his batteries failed, Page achieved a speed of nineteen miles per hour, thus demonstrating the potential electricity held for mass transit.

These pioneer attempts produced no immediate, practical results because of their dependence on storage batteries. It was not until the development of the electrical generator, or dynamo, in the 1870s that a practical power source became available for the development of electric street railways. The German inventor, Werner Siemens, designed the first successful electric locomotive to receive its power from a stationary generator. In 1879 he introduced his invention at the Berlin Industrial Exposition and thereafter constructed electric railways throughout Europe.

Meanwhile, during the 1880s, several Americans wrestled with the technological challenges that had to be met before widespread electric traction became a reality. By this time, efficient generators and motors were available, but other problems remained. The first was to decide whether the current should be transmitted to the cars via the rails, overhead wires, or a transmission line running through conduits under the streets. Inventors were also faced with developing a reliable power return system, producing efficient brakes and devices to control motor speed, and solving the riddles of complex linkages between the motor and the car's axle.

The earliest experiments in the United States on dynamo-powered electric railways were conducted in 1880 and 1881 by Thomas Edison. As builder of the first municipal lighting plants, he viewed electric railways as a means of keeping his generators operating during daylight hours when they were normally shut down due to low demand. In 1881

Smithsonian Institution

Thomas Edison developed this experimental electric locomotive in the early 1880s.

at his Menlo Park, New Jersey laboratory, Edison designed and built an electric locomotive which attained a top speed of forty miles per hour. The dynamo and motor performed efficiently, but there were other shortcomings. The current was carried by one rail and returned by the other to complete the circuit, and it was apparent to observers that transmitting electrical current at ground level would pose too great a danger on crowded city streets. Furthermore, the vehicle's speed was hard to control, and it could be stopped only by breaking the circuit and applying hand-operated wooden brakes against the wheels.

Edison temporarily lost interest in electric traction, but others continued to push back the technological frontiers. The first attempt to electrify a municipal railway was undertaken by Edward Bentley and Walter H. Knight. They opened an electrified section of the East Cleveland Railway in 1884, using a charged rail in an underground conduit to transmit the current to the cars. This new line attracted a large ridership and intensive publicity, but it was abandoned after two years of operation. The owners discovered the conduits were prohibitively expensive to construct. Furthermore, the motors frequently malfunctioned and were difficult to control because of inefficient gearing and braking devices. Short circuits, induced by water, mud, or pieces of metal grounding the wire in the conduit, also plagued the line.

John C. Henry, a former Kansas farmer and telegraph operator, is generally credited with overcoming the dangers, cost, and inconvenience of conduit or electrified rail transmission. An ambitious amateur mechanic, Henry purchased a dynamo, borrowed a used horsecar, salvaged a steam engine from a wheat threshing machine, and began tinkering in a shed near his home in Kansas City. What he came up with set the pattern for future street railway development in the United States. He solved the transmission problem by attaching the electrified lines on tall poles next to the track and connecting them to the car by means of a wire and a wheeled carriage running along atop the wires. The innovation was called a "troller"; hence, the term "trolley car" became part of our national vocabulary. Henry operated his experimental system in Kansas City from 1885 to 1887 but was beset with many of the same problems which confounded his peers. Without effective gearing and a means of regulating current flow to the motor, the car was hard to control and unsafe for use on street railways.

Another electric railway pioneer, Charles J. Van Depoele, built the first citywide trolley system in America. It was installed in Montgomery, Alabama, in 1886. Van Depoele had earlier introduced experimental lines in Detroit, Toronto, South Bend, and Minneapolis, but the southern city was the first to adopt exclusively electric railways for its transit needs. Van Depoele's major contribution to streetcar technology was attaching the trolley mechanism to the end of a rigid pole extending from the car's roof and holding it to the underside of the transmission wires by a strong spring. This innovation reduced stoppages caused by overrunning carriages which tended to disengage from the wires.

The most ambitious and successful of the early electrified systems was Frank Sprague's Richmond, Virginia line which opened in 1888. Sprague, a former navy officer, electrical engineer, and erstwhile employee of Thomas Edison, contracted to build a forty-car electric line for Maurice B. Flynn, a New York financier and politician. Flynn had obtained a franchise for a route which was too hilly for horsecars, so he sought out Sprague who had been experimenting with electric traction on New York's elevated railroads. In building the Union Passenger Railway in Richmond, Sprague developed many new and ingenious techniques which became standard in all electric railways. Among these were spark arrestors, a more efficient underrunning trolley, better gearing, and stronger suspension. He was the first to mount electric motors directly onto each axle, thereby eliminating complicated motor-axle transmission linkages, the universal bane of early streetcars. During the following two decades, deployment of electric railways in virtually every sizeable community in the country, earned for Sprague rightful enshrinement as the father of the trolley industry.

This early period of electric railways was marked by intensive competition and then consolidation of manufacturing companies. In the late 1880s and early 1890s, several firms actively competed for street railway business. Trade journals ran full-page advertisements extolling the low cost and remarkable efficiency of the Sprague, Bentley-Knight, and other electric railway systems. Within a few years, however, consolidations reduced the field to two. In 1890 the Edison General Electric Company merged with the Sprague Electric Railway and Motor Company. Concurrently, the Thompson-Houston Company of Boston acquired patents held by Van Depoele and Bentley and Knight and became a major force in street railway construction. These two large corporations were joined in the same year by a third with the entrance of the Westinghouse Company into the traction field.

In 1892 Edison General Electric and Thompson-Houston consolidated, establishing the General Electrical Company. Thus, General Electric and Westinghouse became the principal competitors in the traction field; and with their respective financial resources and intensive research programs, they steadily advanced electric railway construction and technology. By 1895 the industry developed safety devices for the electric cars. These included power brakes, headlights, fenders, and enclosed vestibules to protect motormen from the elements. Cars became larger and quieter, and manufacturers gave increasing attention to rider comfort by introducing efficient heating devices and upholstery.

An important technological breakthrough in 1894 was the development of long-range transmission of alternating electrical current. Until then, electric railways were limited to comparatively short lines because of the transmission limitations of 500 volt direct current generators. The possibility of sending great quantities of electric power over long distances broadened the potential field of trolley expansion and ushered in an enormous increase in urban electric railway construction. A census of street railways in 1902 revealed that 22,000 miles of trolley tracks had been built and only 250 miles of horse railway were still in operation. By this time, cable cars were still running in only a few cities.

Much like earlier transportation entrepreneurs, the trolley promoters had to fend off critics before electric railways could be built. The major impediment was the public's fear of electricity. To many, this unseen, magical power source was a sinister intrusion into community life, if not the devil's work, at least the invention of lesser demons. Unfortunately these misgivings were nurtured during the early years of electrification by fatal accidents caused by faulty equipment. "Man roasted by electricity" was a common headline in newspapers because wires frequently tore from their moorings in strong winds or fell on unsuspecting citizens during blizzards and ice storms.

The trolley wires had other unseemly and hazardous characteristics. The wires and poles cluttered the landscape and interfered with the operations of the fire department. Occasionally telephone and streetcar wires came into contact, causing spectacular short circuits, disruption of service, and fires at telephone exchanges. Furthermore, the early direct current systems posed a danger to other public utilities. Leakage of current interrupted gas and water service when the process of electrolysis ate away the pipes. Thus, there were still problems to be worked out in developing a satisfactory urban transportation mode.

Street Railways and City Development

Prior to the automobile age, the electric streetcar proved to be the most potent force in determining the shape, quality, and direction of American city growth. American social and economic conditions were propitious for the development of the trolley industry. Older cities were literally bursting at their seams, and newer communities were expanding at a rapid rate. In the closing three decades of the nineteenth century, the country doubled in population. By 1900 the national population growth rate steadily advanced with nearly 1.5 million new citizens being added each year. It was an area of unparalleled urban expansion, and the electric streetcar became an important symbol of municipal vitality and pride.

The electric streetcar offered many advantages over previous public transportation modes. It was able to achieve more than twice the old horsecar speeds; and in contrast to the cable, electric railways were mechanically simple and easy to put into operation. Moreover, operating expenses were not significantly different from cable systems, and the initial investment was even lower than for horsecars. In sum, it was regarded as a panacea, an engineering marvel that promised the creation of cities free from overcrowding. The "lightning cars" also intoxicated investors with prospects of windfall real estate profits and visions of residential areas springing up within commuting distance of the central business destrict. If no body of water or other topograhical feature interfered, electric cars increased the half-hour commuting distance from 3 miles to 6 and the potential urban area from 28 to 113 square miles.

A major contribution of the elctric streetcar was to accelerate the tendency for the downtown or central business district to serve as a nodal point. The developing street railway network radiated out from the core making it the easiest single place in the city to reach. Customers and workers from throughout the urban area could gather together in a relatively short time at in-creasingly lower cost. As a result, stores and specialized services which could lead only the most precarious existence in thinly populated outlying neighborhoods could thrive on high-customer volume in the central business district.

Not only was the downtown a market for goods, it was also a market for jobs. The ease of reaching the central point made it possible to recruit a work force from all of the city and thereby to concentrate a variety of skills in one place at low cost to worker and employer. Whether his operations depended upon highly paid professionals or sweated labor, the employer with a downtown location could look to the whole urban area as a source for prospective employees.

Smithsonian Institution

Denver, Colorado's 1885 street railways encouraged economic activity to focus in the central business district.

On the other hand, the centralization of jobs was also a boon to workers, since it offered a wide range of opportunities. Furthermore, the mobility afforded by the streetcar also meant that larger numbers of workers were not forced to reside within walking distance of their jobs. This mobility was a product not only of the availability of transportation but also of the almost universal nickel fare levied for any journey, regardless of its length. Middle-class employees followed the rich to the city perimeter where they could live in more pleasant, salubrious suburban surroundings free from the congestion of the downtown area.

In the horsecar era of transportation growth, the street railway operators were conservative and followed the outward thrust of population. However, with the rush of rural and foreign-born peoples to cities in the 1880s and 1890s, the streetcar companies often led the way in the development of new residential areas. Developmental activities by street railway companies capitalized on demands by immigrants for living space near the core, and the desire by an increasingly large part of the middle-class population for more spacious living. This movement reached its zenith during the heyday of the electric car in the 1890s and the first two decades of the twentieth century.

As might be expected, a symbiotic relationship between real estate developers and street railway companies occurred. Indeed, many trolley firms went into the real estate business, profiting from the sale of land and houses while building new markets and new revenues for their transit operations. When a streetcar line pushed out into undeveloped areas, housing typically sprang up two to four blocks on either side of the route. The form of the neighborhood depended upon the persons who planned the development and the features other than transport availability that added or detracted from the potential quality of the neighborhood. Once an area was opened up to home building by street railways, the other utilities such as gas, sewer, water, and refuse collection were provided to meet potential needs.

Residential development of an area began along the streets served by the streetcars. During the expansion of horescar lines, these streets were initially the most attractive residential locations because of transportation convenience. But when the trolley was substituted for the horse, this ceased to be true. Poles and wires, the universal adjunct of the electric car, ignited spontaneous outrage from proud homeowners who bemoaned the spoiling of their front-yard view. The cars were noisy, particularly in the early days of electrification. They moved along the right-of-way with an accompaniment of gear-grinding and motor whine, and the heavier cars also produced loud thumps when passing over bad rail joints or poor trackage. As a result, property immediately along the streetcar route became less desirable for residential purposes by those who could afford a choice in the matter.

Although the clank and grind of the electric cars drove householders away, the access afforded by the street railway made the "trolley street" appealing to commercial development. Often the property could be purchased for a reasonable price and the houses cheaply converted into stores and shops. As a result, the trolley streets became long, strung-out shopping areas, dubbed disdainfully by urban planners of today as the "strip shopping streets." The market area tapped by these establishments extended along the streetcar line for some distance and included the three- or four-block residential area on either side of the transport route. In general, shops on such streets supplied necessities; the purchase of more expensive goods or shopping in connection with costly purchase required a ride downtown.

Expanding streetcar service eventually developed some commercial competition for the core area. The junction points of major car lines outside of downtown became the site of shopping centers of considerable size. Service by several car lines meant that an even larger market area was accessible to a given location. What happened, in effect, was that two strip shopping streets merged to produce a miniature downtown. Such areas offered excellent business opportunities because riders often took a few minutes to shop before transferring to another line and continuing their journey.

At the close of the nineteenth century, factory districts grew up in certain parts of urban areas. These districts encouraged development of small public streetcar lines within the overall transit system for the entire city in order to meet the needs of the blue-collar workers. But these lines were generally not too well integrated into the rest of the public transport system. Thus, certain parts of town became dominated by people working in factories close to their homes. Choice of dwelling place was limited by accessibility of the factory area to the rest of the city. As factories came to be located farther and farther from the downtown, workers became, in large part, captives of their occupation and segregated from the city activity as a whole. White-collar workers, who held jobs downtown, chose dwellings near main streetcar lines providing maximum mobility. Downtown occupations became increasingly white collar.

The construction of crosstown lines, beginning in the 1890s in larger cities, was a by-product of consolidating streetcar companies. It gave added flexibility to the street railway system as a whole, and it also proved to be a boon to day laborers, whose work location varied considerably throughout the course of a week or month. These unskilled, low-income, often immigrant workers usually lived near to downtown in order to walk to a job site or have the greatest choice of streetcar service available to them.

The crosstown lines and transfer privilege permitted the day workers a greater choice of dwelling place. Conversion of older, less attractive housing, in what were once relatively high-class residential districts, resulted in overcrowding and a general lowering of neighborhood tone. In more modest residential areas, the pattern was similar. Rising incomes of the early inhabitants, coupled with the availability of property farther from the core that better fitted their aspirations, led to their movement out of the original middle-class neighborhoods. High-density housing replaced single-family dwellings as the housing demand of low-income groups became more acute. Squalor and slums were often the products of transport-related living and working patterns.

Suburbs provided temporary relief from the vexations of crowded urban living even for those who could not afford to live there. As cities and towns began to grow to more substantial sizes, cemeteries were located away from the downtown area in places that offered abundant land at reasonable cost. Since most antebellum United States cities were bereft of parks and recreational areas, cemeteries were popular visiting places on Sundays and holidays. Besides paying respect to the dead, residents of crowded or unpleasant cities were able to enjoy fresh air, greenery, and sunshine by excursions to the cemetery. The development of northern industrial cities led to establishment of outlying public beaches, parks, and picnic groves for recreational purposes. Streetcar service was provided, which gave companies a means of balancing traffic and revenues throughout the week.

Another source of recreation for urban residents soon developed, for electricity not only provided power for streetcars but also for a public attraction that bloomed in the 1890s—the amusement park. Usually, the pleasure-dromes were owned by streetcar companies to augment income and generate weekend passenger traffic. Roller-coasters, merry-go-rounds, toboggan-slides, swings, zoos, and band concerts were among the attractions trolley riders enjoyed. Thus, by the turn of the century, traction trade journals were carrying advertisements for public amusements alongside those for standard streetcar hardware.

A definite general pattern for urban development was thus observable by World War I. As the lines of transport radiated from the downtown area, an urban configuration emerged resembling the outlines of a starfish. Between the starfish arms, the majority of the landscape remained rural in character. Indeed, in some midwestern cities, it was possible to find land still used for farming relatively close to the core and between the developed arms of the city. Along the commuter railroads, the technology and economics of the steam locomotive made it impractical to space stops closer than two or three miles apart. Towns developed around small villages having railway stations, but because the technical and economic capabilities of the electric car permitted rapid acceleration at modest cost, the electric interurban railways were able to space their stops more closely together. Nearly 16,000 miles of electric interurban railways were built in the United States, but they were largely abandoned during the 1930s Depression. In either case, satellite communities grew along the lines of public transport like so many beads on a string, augmenting the starfish pattern.

Bus Ascendancy

The statistical record bears testimony that from 1890 to 1917 the trolley companies enjoyed uninterrupted growth and financial success. Ridership on street railways jumped from 2 billion in 1890 to more than 5 billion in 1902. By 1917 it had expanded to 11 billion. Per capita patronage of street railways increased faster than did urban population until the end of World War I; hence, investment in urban mass transportation was extremely attractive so long as operating costs remained stable. In the peak year of 1917, the United States' trolley industry had 80,000 passenger cars operating on 45,000 miles of track.

In the midst of this heady prosperity, the trolley operators suddenly faced a threat that touched off a revolution in urban transportation. By 1915 the development of cheap automobiles had made some impact on mass transportation, but it was not until the outbreak of the jitney craze that the trolley industry realized that motor vehicles were a serious competitive threat. Between 1914 and 1920, jitneys, secondhand automobiles operating along trolley routes for a five-cent fare, swept the country like a fire storm, skimming off the cream of the trolley ridership. In virtually every large city, swarms of flivvers jockeyed in and out of traffic reaping a rich harvest of fares and leaving many trolley companies financially crippled.

The response of the transit operators was to drive out these upstart competitors by asking city governments to "regulate" the jitneys out of existence. The companies argued that the jitneys were a traffic nuisance and constituted a direct violation of their franchise agreements. Therefore, in city after city, burdensome license fees, liability insurance requirements, and route restrictions were imposed on the wildcat drivers. By 1920 most were forced out of business.

The jitneys were not the first common carrier motor vehicles in America, but they accelerated development of a transportation mode which today dominates the industry—the motor bus. Credit for introducing the motor bus as an intracity passenger vehicle belongs to New York's Fifth Avenue Coach Company which put a single twenty-four passenger bus into operation in 1905. Few other firms followed suit until the jitney phenomenon made it apparent to transit operators that the public was fond of riding in motor vehicles. After driving its competitors

from the marketplace, the streetcar firms adopted the idea and began supplementing their trolley lines with buses.

By World War I, the automobile was giving way to larger passenger vehicles. The first makeshift attempt was to place a boxlike body on a truck chassis. This provided increased carrying capacity; however, usually the vehicle's power plant was inadequate for large passenger loads, and the riding conditions were extremely poor. It was not until buses were designed from the ground up that they became a real success. The first major step in this direction was the introduction of the Fageol Twin Coach in 1927. It had a powerful engine and was built low to the ground which provided a low-entrance step for passengers. The bus' springs and interior fittings set new standards in riding comfort and design aesthetics.

At first, buses were primarily employed by street railway companies as feeders for their trolley lines. They could efficiently operate in areas of low-population density and were free to maneuver unconstrained by a fixed right-of-way. In the early 1920s, street railway companies all over the country began buying buses. At the end of 1922, fifty transit firms were operating 400 buses; eight years later the respective totals had climbed to 390 and 13,000. Companies discovered during this time that if a lightly traveled streetcar line required track replacement, the costs were sufficiently high to warrant the substitution of buses.

Changes in the street environment also

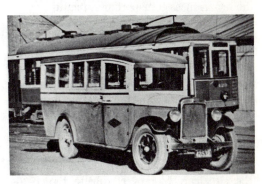

By the early 1920s, a Dallas, Texas transit firm was using small feeder buses to supplement trolley service.

made buses an attractive investment. When street railways were first constructed, many firms simply laid ties and track on the ground or on cobblestone streets, at a relatively low cost. By 1930, however, most trolley streets were paved for automobiles, and the cost of laying and maintaining track had increased greatly. Thus, although buses were at first more expensive to operate, there were strong fixed investment incentives to adopt the new system.

The introduction of a hybird vehicle—the trolley bus—presented a compromise between the motor bus and streetcar. Trackless trolleys, essentially rubber-tired streetcars, made their first appearance in 1900 and in 1910 were commercially introduced in Laurel Canyon near Los Angeles, California. At first, the system was not popular, but by the mid 1920s some street railway owners viewed trolley buses as a means of avoiding burdensome track maintenance and paving costs. Trolley buses were also attractive to trolley firms because, unlike streetcars, they could swing over to the curb to pick up passengers and travel at higher speeds in the center lane. More significantly, they offered an opportunity to continue electric operations. Although writing off track meant heavy capital losses, companies could continue to use their investment in overhead trolley wires and electrical distribution systems. After Salt Lake City, Utah, established a trolley bus system in 1928, other companies converted to the new equipment. They operated in a large number of American cities until the early 1950s, when they began to rapidly fade from the urban mass transportation picture.

Although the trolley bus forestalled conversion to internal combustion power, the motor bus eventually swept electric transit vehicles from the streets. One factor which brought about this change was the continued development of bus technology. In 1930 buses were about 30 feet long and carried forty seated passengers. By 1939 they were 35 feet long and carried forty-five passengers. This brought the bus capacity up to 75 percent of the streetcar. Moreover, during the 1930s, reliable automatic transmissions and diesel engines were introduced, a combination that

upgraded passenger comfort and lowered operating costs.

A few trolley operators tried to limit bus encroachment by improving street railway technology. In 1929 a group of transit owners formed the Electric Railway President's Conference Committee which resolved to design an efficient and comfortable streetcar that would recapture public favor. Under the committee's sponsorship, a team of researchers developed the PCC Car (named after the committee) which was introduced in 1936. The new vehicle was faster, braked better, was less noisy, and offered patrons new standards of interior lighting and seating comfort. It was 50 feet long, seated about fifty-five passengers, and weighed less than earlier vehicles.

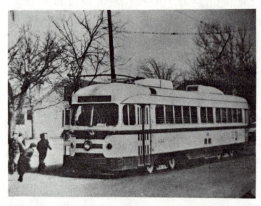

Dallas Transit System

PCC Cars upgraded trolley comfort and service, but they could not compete economically with buses and automobiles.

PCC Cars were bought by public transportation firms throughout the United States, but the changing character of urban travel continued to make streetcar operation financially uncertain. When the automobile began to replace public transit for recreational travel, off-peak revenue declined. Nevertheless, the companies had to maintain the capital investment necessary for rush hour service. In addition, during the Depression, the work week was reduced in many cities from six to five days, which cut ridership further. Both bus and street railway operations were affected by these factors; however, the trolley companies lost more heavily because their fixed costs were higher. By the end of World War II, the operating cost of diesel buses became less per seat than for streetcars. The trolley's doom was sealed. No new streetcars were purchased or manufactured in the United State from 1952 to 1974.

In recent decades, there have been several important developments in bus transportation. Bus design has not fundamentally changed, but in general buses have become larger, more powerful, more attractive, and more comfortable to ride in. They are a highly flexible transit mode that is better suited than the streetcar to the more diffuse and changing passenger demands of the modern metropolis. By the 1970s, the bus was the king of intracity public transportation. Of the 946 transit systems in the United States in 1974, 930 were all-bus operations.

Impact of the Automobile

The decisive role of public transportation in shaping American cities was ended by the automobile shortly after World War I. In 1926 transit ridership peaked at 17 billion passengers and entered a steady decline which has continued virtually unabated for fifty years. Automobile ownership leaped from 9.2 million in 1929 to 105 million in 1970 and authored dramatic changes in the size and composition of large cities.

Although first regarded as a recreational vehicle, the automobile proved to be a highly flexible transportation mode that could serve areas where population density was too low to warrant investment for public transportation equipment. In providing this service, the automobile's dramatic expansion was indirectly subsidized by substantial public outlays for road and highway improvements. Pressure for improved roads was initiated by bicycle enthusiasts in the 1880s and augmented by farmers and early automobile owners after the turn of the century. The greatest success of highway support began in 1916 with federal participation in highway expansion. All levels of government have since been engaged in developing and improving highways, and highway lobbies have fought for and won huge public outlays for road improvements.

In urban regions, the areas between the radial arms of settlement not served by public transportation were soon crisscrossed with new roads; and new housing developments sprang up as this territory became readily accessible to the automobile. The most spectacular consequence of the motor car was this astonishing expansion of suburbia. The suburban movement began with street railways, picked up speed in the 1920s, and exploded after World War II. Between 1920 and 1940, almost every city of 25,000 or more lost population to the suburbs. By 1950 a fourth of the population of the United States lived in suburbs; by 1975 it had risen to half. The automobile provided a means of low-cost, multidirectional travel that made suburban development independent of public transportation. According to the Bureau of the Census, there were 50 million commuters in the United States in 1963; 82 percent—41 million—commuted by automobile, and 40 percent—20 million—had no available public transit.

The automobile has had a positive impact on the American way of life. Distribution methods have been revolutionized, market areas have widened, population and industry have become decentralized, better schools and medical care for rural areas have been brought within reach, and new forms of recreation have developed. Road construction, the oil and gas industry, hotels, and the tourist trade, as well as hundreds of support industries such as glass, rubber, nickel, and plastics have boomed because of the motor car revolution. The process has also enabled people who would otherwise be jammed into city apartments and tenements to live more comfortably in less crowded suburban homes.

On the other hand, the exodus from the central city has had its deleterious effects. Much of the suburban development has spread out at random over the countryside, reproducing the clutter and congestion of the city in a slightly different form. In many instances, inadequate planning and ineffective zoning have produced unsightly suburban sprawl that provides sparse access to recreational facilities and other amenities. The automobile has also depleted the nation's energy reserves, fouled the air with pollution, and caused traffic congestion.

At the time the motor vehicle was gaining prominence, the pattern of urban transportation was designed to serve the central city, and the car was initially regarded as a more convenient way to get from the outskirts to the downtown area for business, shopping, or entertainment. The inevitable result of this swelling torrent of traffic was congestion, engendered by introducing a new form of transportation into an old form of urban organization. There was considerable dispersal of businesses and industry to suburban locations, but the fact remained that the volume of traffic converging on central business districts kept getting heavier. The accepted nostrum to cure this problem was to reshape the urban habitat to fit the new technology. Streets were widened, traffic control devices implemented, lines painted, parking restricted, and limited access highways plowed through residential neighborhoods and commercial districts. In short, Americans tried to adapt a road and street system designed for horse-drawn traffic to the requirements of the automobile.

The introduction of the automobile dealt a telling blow to mass transit. However, the industry and local government bore their share of responsibility for its inability to keep pace. At the very time the motor car became popular, the public transportation companies were weakened by unethical financing, myopic and incompetent management, and poor government regulatory and taxing policies.

By World War I, the trolley companies were burdened by over-capitalization. The face value of company shares were far in excess of assets, and thus of the earning power of the company. Even worse, a substantial part of the transit firms' capital was in the form of bonded debt, which meant that interest charges had to be met annually, regardless of revenues. Moreover, in return for franchises to lay track on public streets, the street railway companies assumed certain obligations. These included limiting fares to five cents, giving free rides to city employees, and sweeping, plowing, and repairing city thoroughfares. When profits ran high, transit operators became overly confident and offered only minimal comfort and convenience to their patrons. The industry became neglectful of public relations, conservative toward new operating practices, and insensitive to consumer complaints.

Such negligence and shady business practices were possible during the boom period from 1890 to 1910, but by World War I, rising costs for manpower, equipment, and supplies began to spell trouble for the poorly run firms. Spiraling inflation and the jitney threat increased operating costs and cut patronage. Furthermore, per capita ridership began to fall; and since companies used their depreciation reserves to defray bonded indebtedness, equipment fell into disrepair and the quality of service declined. By the end of World War I, one third of the transit companies were bankrupt. So serious was the plight of urban railway transportation that in 1919 President Woodrow Wilson appointed a Federal Electric Railway Commission to investigate the industry's afflictions. Findings confirmed that street railways were overly capitalized, poorly managed, and alienating riders because of poor service. Thus, at the very time when the automobile was beginning to capture public interest, the crippled mass transportation companies were unable to offer either an attractive transit alternative or fight the burgeoning power of the highway interests.

During the 1920s, motor car ownership tripled, but transit firms, after hitting a peak of 17 billion riders in 1926, began to lose patrons to their rival. The affluence of the decade created a continued rise in workers' relative wages, making automobile ownership possible for the common man. This change in lifestyle and mobility created changes in land use patterns and attitudes toward public transportation. The car became an attractive status symbol, and public transportation became increasingly less appealing.

In spite of the conversion from streetcars to buses and trolley coaches in the 1920s and 1930s, the transit companies continued to lose riders and revenue. Funds were needed for new capital expenditures and operating expenses; but as the Depression set in during the

1930s, many firms went bankrupt or were forced to cut services.

In addition to the hard times, the 1935 Public Utility Holding Company Act had a devastating effect for the transit industry. By this time, about 80 percent of the public transportation passengers rode bus and streetcar lines owned by public utility holding companies. In many cases, the lines incurred operating deficits, but the companies continued to operate them for fear that divestment or dissolution would invite public wrath with respect to more profitable franchises. The 1935 act gave the companies a convenient escape. Its key provision ordered them to "limit operations . . . to a single integrated public utility system." The Security and Exchange Commission could modify this provision, but in most cases the holding companies were glad to rid themselves of transit operations. Thus, in a period when capital sources were contracting, the industry's last internal support was removed.

A sharp upturn in patronage occurred during World War II. The imposition of gas and tire rationing and a halt in car production turned people once again to public transportation. Ridership climbed from 13 billion in 1941 to 23 billion in 1945, but this sudden influx of passengers did little more than tax equipment beyond operational limits. Shortly after the war, some firms were able to make capital investments for new buses, but after 1947 patronage steadily declined. By 1960 it had fallen to 9.5 billion and in 1973 bottomed out at 6.6 billion.

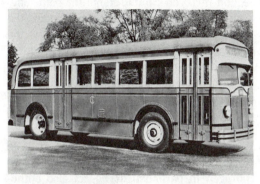

A 1934 Chicago motor bus. The shift from trolleys to buses provided a more flexible transit system, but ridership declined due to automobile competition.

This loss of business to the automobile forced a gradual shift from private to public ownership of citywide transit systems. As a public utility, transit companies were best operated as regulated monopolies. The alternative operation of several competitive firms, each with a huge investment in equipment, resulted in high consumer costs and sometimes redundant service. Originally transit operations fit logically into the regulated utility concept, but as the ratio of people to motor cars moved downward from eleven in 1920 to two in 1970, investor-owned transit systems could no longer meet expenses. This set of circumstances led to city ownership of transit systems.

In 1912 San Francisco was the first city to enter the electric street railway field. In 1919 Seattle took over a bankrupt system, followed by Detroit in 1922, New York in 1932, Cleveland in 1942, and Boston and Chicago in 1947. Until 1956 public ownership had come in only those seven cities; but since then there has been a virtual parade of changeovers from investor to public ownership, among them Los Angeles in 1958, Miami in 1962, Kansas City in 1969, Washington, D.C. in 1973, and Milwaukee in 1975. By the latter year, publicly owned companies carried over 91 percent of the United States' total transit riders.

The switch to community operation did not generally make transit systems more efficient or profitable. As a whole, the industry suffered operating deficits every year between 1963 and 1974. To offset these losses, fares were raised during the same period by an average of 60 percent, but rising labor and equipment costs outran revenues. The simple fact remained that the use of automobiles, encouraged and fostered at all levels of government, had taken such a huge portion of intracity travel that there were too few passengers left to share the rising costs of operating the nation's transit systems.

Since "let's get the farmer out of the mud" became a call for road improvement, highway building programs have made allies of auto clubs, petroleum refineries, cement producers, contractors, and government officials. These powerful lobbying interests have pushed for ever-larger highway expenditures.

Through their efforts, America has developed an excellent road system. But overreliance on the automobile all but destroyed public transportation and produced an imbalance in intraurban travel in many cities. Therefore, many people became convinced that government should broaden its transportation program to include expenditures for urban mass transportation.

The Federal Role

As traffic congestion grew worse and public transit declined, it became painfully obvious that there was no governmental authority at the local level that could effectively deal with metropolitan transportation problems. As suburban development increased, the tendency was for each community to maintain its political and fiscal individuality and shun comprehensive urban transportation planning. Many residents who had fled to the suburbs to escape the central city's problems resisted overtures for political union. Consequently, when a problem such as transportation arose, which affects an entire metropolitan community, it was difficult to marshal broad support for its solution. The unwillingness or inability of most state and local governments to take effective action eventually made the search for solutions the responsibility of the federal government.

The 1961 Housing Act was the first modest effort at federal assistance for mass transit. Backed by President John F. Kennedy and a coalition of central city and transportation pressure groups, the act opened the way for more ambitious programs that would follow. Though buried in this omnibus housing bill, it had three provisions concerning urban mass transportation. First, $25 million was authorized for transit demonstration projects. Second, the act specified that transportation planning should be included as an integral part of comprehensive federally financed urban planning programs. Finally, $50 million in loans for mass transport undertakings was authorized to be administered by the Home Finance Agency. Despite its limited funding, the program had seminal value. The novel demonstration projects would generate public interest and help prod the federal government to commit greater resources to America's public transportation needs.

A follow-up measure was needed to complement the foregoing legislation. Specifically, capital funds were required to provide necessary operating equipment, but such legislation was blocked in the House of Representatives by a strong coalition of rural and conservative members. A 1962 Urban Mass Transportation bill died in the House Rules Committee. However, by 1964 prospects looked brighter. A pressure group was formed to push for more federal aid. As the Urban Passenger Transportation Association (UPTA), it represented the central city interests, organized labor, the transit industry, and railroads. Their efforts and the backing of President Lyndon B. Johnson turned the tide, and in June the 1964 Urban Mass Transportation Act narrowly passed in both houses of Congress.

The aim of the legislation, which became the cornerstone of the federal transit program, was not only to provide aid for the improvement and development of mass transportation systems, but to encourage the planning and establishment of areawide coordinated transport. In conjunction with the planning provisions of the 1962 Highway Act, incentive was given to develop integrated transport systems combining both the private automobile and mass transportation.

The first two of the law's three main provisions basically expanded the loan and demonstration project provisions of the 1961 Housing Act. The third and most important section involved capital grants for both long-term and short-term programs. Under the former program, a city had to satisfy the government that "the facilities and equipment for which the assistance is sought are needed for carrying out a program . . . for a unified or officially coordinated urban transportation system as a part of a comprehensive and continuing program of planned development." While all grants or loans were to be made to public agencies, private enterprise was encouraged to participate. The act also authorized $75 million for 1965 and $150 million each year for 1966 and 1967.

As with many embryonic federal public

works programs, the 1964 act was a positive step, but it soon exhibited several deficiencies. Its most conspicuous shortcoming was parsimonious funding in comparison with other federal transportation expenditures. Between 1961 and 1966, approximately $375 million in federal funds was spent for mass transportation. During the same period, about $24 billion was appropriated for highways, airways, and waterways.

In many cities, capital expenditures were not enough to cure transit ills. Operating deficits plagued municipalities which were often unable to match funds for federal grants. Another problem that grew out of the 1964 act was providing the plans and cost estimates to qualify for capital grants. For large-scale projects, thousands of dollars were needed to undertake engineering and planning studies. No federal aid was available for such purposes. Futhermore, more research money was needed. Although the demonstration program had provided a valuable tool for increasing knowledge about mass transit, the program was uncoordinated and unsystematically administered.

In 1966 amendments to the 1964 act put the federal program on a somewhat sounder footing. One-hundred-fifty million dollars was made available for each of the fiscal years from 1967 to 1969, and the scope of activities was substantially broadened. Aid was provided for planning, engineering, and designing mass transport systems, for training programs to upgrade transit management, and for colleges and other nonprofit institutions to conduct research in this field. In addition, a New Systems program was inaugurated which involved developing future-oriented research projects to meet America's transportation needs. The research focused on three periods: the immediate future (up to three years), fifteen to twenty years ahead, and, finally, up to the turn of the century.

Until 1968 the federal mass transportation responsibilities were administered by the Department of Housing and Urban Development (HUD). However, the agency's handling of the program drew criticism. Progress was slow, not only in carrying out transit improvements, but in working efficiently and

diplomatically with Congress to secure more funding. The great difficulty with HUD was that the mass transit program was buried within the departmental structure, and administrators often gave relatively short shrift to transit programs. Consequently, when the Department of Transportation (DOT) was organized in 1967, Congress ordered the secretaries of DOT and HUD to submit recommendations as to whether the program should be moved to the new agency. In 1968 the President and Congress concurred that the change should be implemented, and subsequently the Urban Mass Transit Administration (UMTA) became a full-fledged DOT agency. In the meantime, the mass transportation program bogged down because of the changeover. New administrators were reluctant to make important decisions in an election year. Furthermore, the election of Richard Nixon made lame ducks of Johnson-appointed officials and exacerbated the slowdown.

By 1969 the mass transit industry was in a steep decline. The burgeoning inflation of the late 1960s was a severe blow to this labor- and capital-intensive industry. Labor costs rose sharply as new union contracts were made, and outlays for equipment and sup-

Bay Area Rapid Transit District

Approximately 15 percent of the funds for San Francisco's BART rapid rail system came from the federal government.

plies spiraled upward. Marginal private operators all over the country began to fail, forcing more cities to take over transit systems in order to continue service. As a result, pressure mounted on Congress and the President to augment the federal commitment to mass transportation.

The most serious problem, as far as cities were concerned, was that future funding of public transportations were not conducive to planning long-range construction programs. To remedy this situation, bills were introduced calling for trust fund financing that would guarantee sustained support. President Nixon's advisors, however, were opposed to any new trust funds since they limited the President's authority to manage the economy. The President urged Congress to adopt a twelve-year, $10 billion program, with funds being obligated no more than one year in advance. Congress countered with a compromise plan which the Administration accepted. The 1970 Urban Mass Transportation Assistance Act authorized $3.1 billion to finance UMTA projects over a five-year perod and adopted the general outline of Nixon's twelve-year plan. After almost ten years, the mass transportation program was finally beginning to receive substantial support.

With this victory achieved, transit proponents sought to attain two new goals: (1) obtaining operating subsidies for public transportation, and (2) diverting some of the Highway Trust Fund money to mass transit. The former was strongly opposed by Administration officials, but the latter received support on Capitol Hill and at the White House. Consequently, the 1973 Highway Act marked a decisive shift away from the highway orientation of federal transportation programs.

The act gave cities and states much more latitude in determining the type of transportation system they wished to have. Beginning in 1974, cities could use their share of the Highway Trust Fund's $800 million Urban Systems road apportionment for mass transportation. Cities, working together with their state governments, were also allowed to trade trust fund money earmarked for the Interstate Highway System for an equal amount

from the general fund for mass transit. The law also provided $3 billion in contract authority to UMTA for 1974-1976 and increased the federal portion of capital grants projects from two thirds to 80 percent. It was difficult to predict how the 1973 Highway Act would affect the fortunes of mass transportation. But one thing was certain, the Highway Trust Fund was no longer a sacred cow, and communities were free to choose the best solution to their transportation needs.

The next stumbling block to crumble was opposition to funds for operating subsidies. During the energy shortage of the 1973-1974 winter, the Nixon Administration reevaluated its position and pushed for a revenue sharing program that would give cities an option on spending block grants of federal money for either capital investments or operating expenses. This approach was upheld by Congress and President Gerald R. Ford. In November 1974, the Urban Mass Transportation Act was signed and provided $11.8 billion over a six-year period. Of that total, $7.8 billion would go to extend existing capital investment programs. But the remaining $3.9 billion could be used at local option either for operating subsidies (up to 50 percent of total operating costs) or for capital outlay. This was a landmark event, which dramatically increased federal support of the sagging mass transportation industry and suggested that the nation was on the brink of major transit activity.

Modern Transit

The most spectacular urban mass transportation development in recent years has been the planning and construction of "heavy rail" rapid transit systems in several American cities. In the past, heavy rail transit (intraurban rail vehicles operating on exclusive rights-of-way) has been limited to large metropolitan areas with high-population densities. During the late nineteenth and early twentieth centuries, downtown traffic congestion forced city planners in cities such as New York, Boston, Chicago, and Philadelphia to place commuter railways either underground or on stilts above the streets. Chicago's elevated Loop—from which downtown Chicago got its name—is America's most famous elevated railway and has served the windy city since 1897. The alternative construction of subways was extremely expensive. They were undertaken on a massive scale only in New York City, which built 150 miles of subway during the twentieth-century's first four decades.

Progress in rapid transit remained at a virtual standstill until the San Francisco Bay Area, where the cable car was born, once again brought forth a landmark public transportation system. The Bay Area Rapid Transit System (BART) had a tremendous impact on the revitalization of rapid transit in the United States. Its design, planning, and construction have brought about the development of new and unique transit equipment and management ideas that will serve as models for cities seeking to find solutions for their mass transportation needs.

As the first all new regional rail transit system built in the United States in over sixty years, BART was the product of farsighted thinking nearly a quarter century ago. Following the post-World War II bay area building boom, there was local concern that the metropolis might be badly disrupted if it became entirely dependent upon the automobile. In 1951 a regional transit commission was established to study transit problems; and as a result of its recommendations, the state legislature created a five-county BART District in 1957 to implement the construction of an areawide rapid transit system. Two counties eventually withdrew, but in 1962 residents of the remaining three approved the $792 million BART bond issue; the largest fiscal referendum ever passed in the United States. Action was delayed because of a suit questioning the legality of the bond issue; but in June 1964, President Johnson touched off an inaugural dynamite charge and construction began.

Like many public works undertakings, BART was beset with financial ills as inflation added to development costs. By 1966 cost overruns totaled $164 million; and at one point in 1968, the original bond proceeds were so low that it appeared system cutbacks would be made. Pressure mounted to reduce trackage from 75 to 57 miles, but BART supporters stood their ground. Finally, after much debate, in 1968 the state legislature authorized BART to levy a half-cent sales tax in its three counties to cover deficits. Federal capital grants also bailed out the troubled transit system. Of BART's total $1.4 billion cost, $207 million, or about 15 percent, came from federal funding.

The BART was dedicated on October 11, 1972. In his remarks on that occasion, Secretary of Transportation John A. Volpe captured the new system's significance: "It marks a turning point, a Renaissance in the redevelopment and re-construction of the cities of America."

The BART provided an opportunity for engineers to develop a totally new rapid transit system incorporating the exciting technological spinoffs from the aircraft, aerospace, and electronics industries. After more than fifty years of technological stagnation in the transit field, available cars, controls, and operating procedures were far below BART aspirations. In 1963, after an exhaustive investigation of monorail and other alternatives, a dual-track system was adopted. The passenger cars are powered by a third rail which carries 1,000 volts of electrical current. The 5½-foot track gauge is nearly a foot wider than standard railroad track and provides great stability at high speeds in the bay area's strong crosswinds. In addition, a new generation of automated and computerized equipment was developed for controlling cars and collecting fares.

The BART cars transport seventy-two passengers in great comfort. They are decorated with wall-to-wall carpeting, wide foam padded seats, and large tinted windows. There are no overhead straps or luggage racks, and advertising posters are limited. The ride is smooth, relatively quiet, and fast. Top speed is 80 miles per hour; and since the rails are welded together, there is none of the clickety-clacking, swaying, and jiggling experienced on passenger trains.

Through mutual cooperation between the California Department of Transportation and the Bay Area Rapid Transit District, an 11-mile-long rail and highway multimodal

Bay Area Rapid Transit District

A passenger station and parking facilities were built within the Route 24 multimodal transportation corridor in Contra Costa County, California.

transportation corridor has been built along Route 24 in Alameda and Contra Costa counties. The joint project has saved millions of dollars in shared construction costs and land use. Unified planning, design, financing, and construction reduced community disruption and the amount of land removed from the tax rolls in areas served by the combined facilities. Under the agreement, the transportation department purchased the right-of-way, designed the roadbed, and supervised construction. The cost of frontage roads and freeway fencing and landscaping was shared equally by the two agencies. They also made joint expenditures for building retaining walls, overpasses, and drainage structures. The eight-lane improved highway facility through the dual-modal corridor was opened in the summer of 1970. The BART began rail operation on the medial strip in May 1973.

Rapid transit development is also underway in Atlanta, Georgia, and in Washington, D.C. In January 1966, the Metropolitan Atlanta Rapid Transit Authority (MARTA) was established to build and operate a coordinated bus and rail system. After voter approval was given in 1971, MARTA began designing a 50-mile rapid rail and 14-mile rapid busway

system which is scheduled to begin operation in 1979. Construction of the regional transportation network is being funded by UMTA grants and through a 1 percent sales tax levied by the two participating counties. The system also includes provisions for expanding into adjacent counties at a later date. The MARTA is by far the largest public works project in Georgia history; and despite economic troubles, it continues to adhere to its production schedules.

In early 1976, the first 4.6 miles of Washington, D.C.'s 98-mile Metro system was scheduled to go into operation. The modern rapid rail facility is the product of nearly two decades of congressional and citizen efforts to relieve oppressive traffic congestion and improve the physical character of the Capital region. The project is administered by the Washington Metropolitan Area Transit Authority, an interstate agency composed of representatives from the District of Columbia and the three Maryland and five Virginia counties Metro is scheduled to service by 1980. Since its ground-breaking in December 1964, the transit authority has gained valuable experience in construction and construction management which it has shared with other transit systems in planning or early construction stages. The majority of the system is subway, which has made the cost very high. Originally set at $3 billion in 1970, projected costs soared to over $4.5 billion by 1975.

The search for answers to America's public transportation problems has also involved development of relatively low-cost solutions. In recent years, reexaminations of transportation planning and urban objectives have raised serious questions about capital intensive responses to public transportation requirements. The costs of rapid transit systems have accelerated significantly to the point where development costs would exceed benefits. Furthermore, the resulting environmental and neighborhood disruption has generated substantial public concern and, occasionally, active resistance.

The high cost of rapid rail systems has convinced some communities to examine the feasibility of returning trolleys to city streets.

"Light rail transit," as it is now styled, may bring about the rebirth of the street railways that shaped urban development patterns in the late nineteenth and early twentieth centuries. In 1975 Boston and San Francisco ordered 275 trolley cars, the first to be built in the United States since 1952. The same year, Dayton, Ohio, developed a comprehensive light rail system plan, and Rochester and Buffalo, New York, and several other cities began to consider using the system to meet transit requirements.

Among the most promising public transportation innovations are "demand-responsive" systems which provide personalized home-to-destination service in response to travel requests. Typically, there are no set routes and schedules. Instead, a dispatching center receives customer requests and assigns a bus to pick up the caller. The object is to group passengers with similar destinations on the same buses. In this way,

U.S. Department of Transportation

Modern light rail transit vehicles may bring about a new trolley era.

vehicles operate only when they are needed, and the passengers avoid the disagreeable aspects of traditional bus service such as long walks to stops and outdoor waits during inclement weather.

Demand-responsive transit can either supplement or replace fixed route systems. In low- and medium-density suburban areas, they provide a total transportation service where bus lines are not economically feasible. In high-density areas, they provide feeder service to rail and bus lines, filling the void between conventional transit and taxi service.

This service is generally referred to as dial-a-bus or dial-a-ride and has been implemented since 1964 in more than eighty municipalities in North America and Europe. The largest demand-responsive system began operating on November 24, 1974 in Santa Clara County, California. Called Arterial/Personalized Transit (APT), the bus service combines the convenience and flexibility of dial-a-ride transit with the traditional fixed route busing. For service, customers call a reservation number and a transit controller feeds the caller's origin, destination, name, and phone number into a computer terminal. The computer selects the nearest available bus, calculates the pickup time, and flashes the information to the controller, who relays the data to the caller. If the passenger's destination is within a specified service area (roughly ten square miles), he is directly delivered. If, however, the person is going outside of the APT area, the bus will take him to the most convenient fixed bus route.

The APT also offers special services. Customers may subscribe for daily pickup, and commuters who work in the same place may form a buspool, which provides convenient nonstop service from their neighborhood to work. In March 1975, the Santa Clara County Transit District deployed four specially equipped buses which accommodate wheelchairs; thus, providing mobility for handicapped people in a way never before possible.

The comfortable APT buses are air-conditioned and carpeted, and they feature panoramic tinted glass windows and padded seats. They also have clean-burning propane engines which give off neither the roar nor foul-smelling fumes of diesel buses. It is believed that with this modern equipment, APT will reduce pollution and traffic congestion in Santa Clara County and demonstrate that automobile trips can be cut by substituting comfortable and efficient transit service.

The search for low-cost transportation alternatives has also involved developing ways to utilize more effectively existing facilities. One of the most promising has been reserving one freeway or street lane for bus traffic, thereby augmenting public transit flow during rush hour periods. Some traffic planners suggest that rather than widening highways or building expensive rapid transit networks, urban traffic congestion can be relieved by convincing commuters to ride buses. For the typical rush hour, private automobiles occupying one lane of freeway carry about 2,600 commuters per hour, but theoretically the same road space could transport over 50,000 persons per hour if buses were substituted. Costs vary for the creation of busways. In some cases, new lines of pavement are constructed either parallel to existing traffic arteries or along abandoned railway rights-of-way. However, because costs for new busways are high and a lengthy period of construction is required, some metropolitan areas have converted existing streets and limited access highways to busways.

Bus lanes can be operated either with or against the normal traffic flow. The most successful plan has been adoption of the "contraflow" method. The success of a contraflow lane is largely due to its intrinsic self-enforcing nature which keeps the lane free from private automobile encroachment. Motorists are reluctant to drive in lanes which normally carry opposite directional traffic and are further intimidated by the bus' size and weight. Several cities have incorporated contraflow busways into their transportation planning. For example, in May 1971 the Massachusetts Department of Public Works instituted an 8.4-mile exclusive bus lane on Boston's Southeast Expressway. The lane normally used by outbound motorists was reversed for bus use during the morning rush hour. While automobiles pile up waiting to use exit ramps, the buses are able to circumvent the queues, thus avoiding delays. Travel time for bus passengers on this section of the expressway has been reduced from twenty-four to ten minutes.

Demand-responsive transit service and contraflow bus lanes are but two of the innovative transportation ideas which have proliferated in recent years. Several of the other more noteworthy plans follow: (1) staggering working hours and reducing the work week to four days in order to cut extreme peaking of traffic demand which now occurs during a few hours each day; (2) providing free or heavily subsidized service to convince commuters to abandon private automobiles; (3) collecting commuters into mandatory carpools and buspools; and (4) developing dualmode vehicles that can travel on either roads or under-utilized rail rights-of-way.

None of the aforementioned systems will usher in a public transportation millennium, but there are signs that America's over-reliance on the automobile is beginning to diminish. In 1974 urban mass transportation usage rose 342 million over the previous year, the first significant increase since World War II. The rising concern for more efficient utilization of fossil fuels and the commitment of the federal government to foster public transit suggest that the corner has been turned. The heyday of the private automobile is far from over, but the desirability of improving mass transportation is now firmly entrenched in the United States. The problems remain pandemic. However, progress will be made if all levels of government resolve to once again make mass transportation an efficient servant of the community.

SUGGESTED READINGS

American Public Transit Association. *Transit Fact Book*. Washington, D.C., 1930-1974.

Barger, Harold. *The Transportation Industries, 1889-1946: A Study of Output, Employment, and Productivity*. New York, 1951.

Burby, John. *The Great American Motion Sickness*. Boston, 1971.

Dewees, Donald N. "The Decline of the American Street Railways." *Traffic Quarterly*, 24 (October 1970), 563-581.

Gilmore, Harlan W. *Transportation and Growth of Cities*. New York, 1953.

Hilton, George W. *The Cable Car in America: A Treatise Upon Cable or Rope Traction As Applied to the Working of Street and Other Railways*. Berkeley, California, 1971.

Jones, John P. "Development and History of Mass Transportation." *Proceedings of the Lecture Series on Urban Transportation*. Edited by Kumares C. Sinha. Milwaukee, Wisconsin, 1973.

McShane, Clay. *Technology and Reform: Street Railways and the Growth of Milwaukee, 1887-1900*. Madison, Wisconsin, 1974.

Meyer, John R.; Kain, John F.; and Wold, Martin. *The Urban Transportation Problem*. Cambridge, Massachusetts, 1965.

Miller, John A. *Fares Please!: A Popular History of Trolleys, Horse-Cars, Street-Cars, Buses, Elevateds, and Subways*. 2d. ed. New York, 1960.

Mossman, Frank H., ed. *Principles of Urban Transportation*. Cleveland, Ohio. 1951.

Owen, Wilfred. *The Accessible City*. Washington, D.C., 1972.

Rae, John B. "The Evolution of the Motor Bus as a Transport Mode." *High Speed Ground Transportation*, 5 (Summer 1971), 211-225.

——————— . "Transportation Technology and the Problem of the City." *Traffic Quarterly*, 22 (July 1968), 229-314.

R. H. Pratt Associates. *Low Cost Urban Transportation Alternatives: A Study of Ways to In-*

crease the Effectiveness of Existing Transportation Facilities. Prepared for the U.S. Department of Transportation. Washington, D.C., 1973.

Rowsome, Frank. Trolley Car Treasury: A Century of American Streetcars, Horsecars, Cable Cars, Interurbans, and Trolleys. New York, 1956.

Saltzman, Arthur. "Para-Transit: Taking the Mass Out of Mass Transit." Technology Review, 75 (July-August 1973), 46-53.

Smerk, George M. "The Streetcar: Shaper of American Cities." Traffic Quarterly, 21 (October 1967), 569-584.

——————— . Urban Mass Transportation: A Dozen Years of Federal Policy. Bloomington, Indiana, 1974.

Solomon, Richard J., and Saltzman, Arthur. History of Transit and Innovative Systems. Cambridge, Massachusetts, 1971.

Taylor, George R. "The Beginnings of Mass Transportation in Urban America, Part I." Smithsonian Journal of History, I (No. 2, 1966), 35-50.

——————— . "The Beginnings of Mass Transportation in Urban America, Part II." Smithsonian Journal of History, I (No. 3, 1966), 31-54.

Walker, James B. Fifty Years of Rapid Transit. New York, 1918.

Warner, Sam Bass. Streetcar Suburbs: The Process of Growth in Boston, 1870-1900. Cambridge, Massachusetts, 1962.

Weber, Robert D. "Rationalizers and Reformers: Chicago Local Transportation in the Nineteenth Century." Unpublished doctoral dissertation, University of Wisconsin, 1971.

CHAPTER 7

AIRWAYS AND AIRPORTS

Air carriers were used to fly mail for the first time in the United States on May 15, 1918, when United States Army pilots using army equipment carried letters from New York City to Washington, D.C. By August 1918, the Post Office Department had assumed the army's mail carrying duties, and by 1920 it operated an airmail service from coast to coast. However, in 1925 the Air Mail Act authorized the postmaster general to award contracts to private carriers, and these contracts marked the beginning of organized air transportation in the United States.

During the years that have followed, Americans have become more and more dependent on air transportation. Even though it is only fifty years old, it has superseded every other means of transportation in terms of passenger miles traveled except the private automobile. Not only is air transportation the fastest and one of the most comfortable ways to travel over long distances, it is frequently the most economical. And in some instances, it is the only way to travel, since there is no longer rail passenger service to many places, and bus accommodations are often inadequate.

During 1974 commercial airliners recorded 207 million domestic passenger trips as Americans traveled by air for personal and business reasons. During the last two decades, American business, governmental, scientific, technological, and educational institutions have come to rely heavily on rapid travel, face-to-face meetings, and direct supervision in the execution of their responsibilities. But not only people travel by air. Goods of all kinds—mail, bank checks, video tapes, medical supplies, farm produce, machine parts, and countless other items—are also transported by air.

Airports and related aviation activities play a vital role in the nation's economy. Besides aiding air travelers, airports provide jobs. More than one-half million people are employed in the country's 500 airports served by scheduled air carriers. The annual salaries of these employees totaled more than $6 billion in 1974. In addition to the economic activity generated by the regular expenditures of resident aviation employees, airports also stimulate the economy through the use of local services for air cargo, aircraft maintenance, food catering to the airlines, and ground transportation in and around the airports. Regular purchases of fuel, supplies, and equipment from local distributors inject further income into local communities; while airport retail shops, hotels, and restaurants "re-cycle" money among community members. This multiplier effect operates in all cities as aviation dollars are channeled throughout the community.

This chapter is based primarily upon materials provided by the United States Department of Transportation.

Land located near airports usually increases in value as the local economy begins to benefit from the presence of an airport. Land in proximity to Chicago's O'Hare International Airport, for example, which sold for no more than $800 an acre in the 1950s, had a 1975 market value of $100,000 an acre. Near Phoenix's Sky Harbor Airport, commercial land value has risen from $26,000 per acre in 1961 to a record high of $130,000 per acre in 1974. Property near the Louisville Airport, which sold for $4,000 per acre in 1959, sold for $18,000 per acre fifteen years later. Similar property value increases have been experienced near small, medium, and large airports across the country.

Good airports are an attraction to business firms requiring air cargo and passenger service. Statistics indicate that companies seeking to relocate or to open branch offices consider airport accessibility in the area a prime requisite in site selection. Thus, cities with superior air transportation facilities continue to grow and enjoy the economic benefits brought to the community by new and expanding businesses.

The Nation's Early Airports

Airports of the early twentieth century were very different from those of 1976. From the time of the Wright brothers' flight until after World War I, any level field or pasture was looked upon as a potential landing strip. It was generally believed that merely installing a gas pump made such an "airport" ready

Federal Aviation Administration

The Douglas M-4 was used to carry mail in the 1920s and 1930s. Landing fields were similar to the one shown.

for operation. More elaborate airports of the period had wooden loading ramps and cleared runways for aircraft takeoffs and landings. Although the physical facilities of airports have changed considerably during the past fifty years, their basic function remains the same—to furnish aircraft with an adequate surface for takeoff and landing.

The first aircraft were light and needed only short runs to reach a speed sufficient to support flight. However, as aircraft became heavier in relation to their wing area and power, longer distances and harder surfaces became essential for takeoffs. Airplanes attain their required speed more easily when headed into the wind rather than when headed crosswind or downwind. Therefore, as airplanes were flown more regularly and in varying wind conditions, they needed more than a single runway. These requirements led to the conversion of grass pastures into airfields.

Support for the improvement of airfields was not won easily. Although the Post Office Department began awarding mail contracts to private airlines in 1925, aviators were not taken seriously by most government officials, military officers, or businessmen until much later. Early airline companies received no federal appropriations and few private donations and thus were forced to operate on a shoestring. They flew planes purchased from army salvage and rebuilt in company shops. Paid only for the mail they carried, they continually complained that the mail sacks weighed more than the letters inside. Before his spectacular flight in 1927, Charles Lindbergh observed that Americans thought of aviation only in terms of barnstorming and flying circuses. He vowed, therefore, to demonstrate the airplane's range, speed, and overall efficiency.

Lindbergh's flight from New York to Paris, the most dramatic illustration of the airplane's transportation potential, served to stimulate interest in aviation. It failed, however, to arouse the same kind of enthusiasm for airports. The 1926 Air Commerce Act had authorized the secretary of commerce to establish, operate, and maintain civil airways, but left the airports to be provided for on a local basis. Not until 1938, with the passage of the Civil Aeronautics Act, did this change. Yet even then, primary consideration in airport development was reserved for national defense. While it is true that federal funds were made available to airports in the early 1930s, these funds were appropriated for work relief in general—not for airport work per se. Until the mid 1930s, airport development remained, for the most part, the responsibility of private investors and local governmental units.

City officials and airport owners across the nation were unable to meet the needs with their limited resources. Whenever possible, they constructed new airports or expanded old ones in an attempt to keep pace with the

United Airlines

Chicago's Midway Airport in 1953. This was the nation's busiest airport during the 1950s and early 1960s.

rapidly developing aircraft technology. In 1927 Chicago built an airport in the corner of an open area one mile square near the intersection of Cicero Avenue and Sixty-third Street. Two years later, when passenger flights were introduced, the city expanded its airport. Then, in 1937, Chicago extended the airport's runway space the entire south half of the square mile and constructed a larger terminal building along Cicero Avenue. Although air traffic continued to increase during World War II, northward expansion of the field was blocked by the tracks of the Belt Railway. In 1940 these tracks were relocated; and in the following year, the entire 620 acres were opened up to hangars, runways, and other airport facilities. During the days of the

propeller-driven planes, Midway Airport served Chicago well. It became the world's busiest airport in the 1950s. With the appearance of jet-propelled planes, however, the city once again had to build a larger airport.

In the late 1920s, there were about 1,000 airports in the United States. By 1975 there were nearly 13,000. Many of these airports began as small, low-activity fields and gradually expanded to their current sizes and capacities. For example, Newark Airport in Newark, New Jersey, has developed in its present location over a long period of time. But in other instances, where runway lengths could not accommodate jet aircraft, early airports were closed and new ones opened to replace them. In the 1930s, Washington, D.C., provided airline service through its Washington-Hoover Airport. When it became apparent that this field could not handle the increased air activity, Washington National Airport was constructed on the Potomac River. When this airport proved inadequate, Dulles Airport was built in nearby Virginia.

Newer, faster, and heavier air transports were introduced during the 1930s. The first modern airliner, the Boeing 247, began regular flights in March 1933; it was soon outclassed by the Douglas DC-2, which began scheduled service in May 1934. Two years later, in June 1936, one of the most famous airplanes—the Douglas DC-3—began operations. Larger and faster than the DC-2, the DC-3 quickly became standard equipment on major trunk airlines.

The DC-3s demanded takeoff and landing strips that were long and hard. A smooth 100-acre field or a 1,500-foot stretch of cinders or gravel was unacceptable. By 1938 the majority of the nation's airports still had takeoff and landing strips that were too short and lacked adequate support strength. Local airport and government officials, especially in small- and medium-sized cities, insisted that they could not make the necessary adjustments. They argued that the costs had become too great, and they demanded more federal assistance. It became evident that localities needed aid to meet the needs of the nation.

State support for airport programs was minimal. Connecticut enacted a state aeronautical law in 1911, and in 1921 Oregon was the first state to establish a state aviation agency. By the early 1940s, twenty states had followed suit. Although their activities varied widely, they were primarily involved with coordinating airport programs within the state for intrastate aviation.

Federal Civil Aviation Agencies

Federally sponsored public works programs designed to foster and regulate civil aviation development fall into two distinct, but related, categories: the establishment of civil airways equipped with air navigation aids and the promotion of civil airports through grants-in-aid to local sponsors. In the history of federally sponsored public works, these activities are relatively new. They date back to 1919, when the United States Air Mail Service designated the first segment of the old transcontinental airway. However, since moving the mail by air was never regarded as a permanent federal function, the commencement of the federal government's involvement in aviation-related public works is better dated May 20, 1926—the day on which President Calvin Coolidge signed the Air Commerce Act into law.

Prior to the Air Commerce Act, commercial air transportation—except for the New York to San Francisco airmail route—did not exist. This was true primarily because the federal government did not perform certain functions that were critical to aviation's development. Ground-based air navigation aids, for instance, were unknown. Pilots were not licensed. Aircraft were not certified for air worthiness. Safety rules and air traffic regulations were non-existent.

In the absence of these kinds of guides and directives, the airplane's use was limited. Before 1926 many people looked upon the airplane as little more than a curiosity, a kind of hayfield sport. This view was changed, however, with the passage of the Air Commerce Act.

The Air Commerce Act instructed the secretary of commerce to designate and establish civil airways; to operate and maintain air navigation aids; to improve such aids through on-going research programs; to license pilots; to issue air worthiness certificates for aircraft; and to investigate accidents. To insure that these duties were carried out, the secretary was given the authority to create an Aeronautics Branch in the Department of Commerce. In 1934 this branch was redesignated the Bureau of Air Commerce and placed under a director of air commerce. This arrangement lasted until 1938 when the Civil Aeronautics Act went into effect.

The Civil Aeronautics Act, which initiated a new phase of government intervention in civil aviation, did not entirely repeal the earlier law. A number of Air Commerce Act provisions (notably those authorizing the secretary of war to designate military airways and the President to make airspace reservations) were left untouched. However, those provisions fostering and regulating civil aviation were superseded by the new law. Under the Civil Aeronautics Act, not only the functions formerly assigned the secretary of commerce by the 1926 act but also those relating to the economic regulation of civil aviation were to be performed by a new independent agency, the Civil Aeronautics Authority (CAA).

Until 1938 economic regulation was carried out under a series of airmail acts and consisted of awarding airmail contracts to individual carriers and adjusting rates under those contracts. The Post Office Department performed both functions until 1934, when the Interstate Commerce Commission began handling airmail contracts. But with the passage of the Civil Aeronautics Act, the airmail-contract system was changed. Like the railroads, the airlines were to carry mail in accordance with regular schedules rather than individual contracts. Since airmail rates still had to be determined, the airlines became subject to the economic regulations of CAA.

The CAA was composed of nine officials (an administrator, an authority of five members, and a three-member Air Safety Board) appointed by the President and subject to confirmation by the Senate. The administrator was authorized to establish civil airways, provide technical improvements for air navigation facilities, and regulate air traffic along the airways; the authority was responsible for all safety and economic regulations; and the safety board was to investigate accidents and make recommendations for accident prevention. To coordinate these functions, the authority created the office of supervisor of the Bureau of Safety Regulations and assigned the duties of that office to the administrator. Thus, the administrator directed, on behalf of the authority, the latter's safety inspection and certifying activities. The authority, however, reserved the power to suspend or revoke certificates after a hearing.

Another period of government intervention in civil aviation was inaugurated by President Franklin D. Roosevelt's Reorganization Plans III and IV, which took effect in June 1940. The purpose of these plans was "to clarify the relations of the Administrator of the Civil Aeronautics Authority." The five-member authority was transferred to the Department of Commerce and renamed the Civil Aeronautics Board (CAB). The Air Safety Board was abolished and its accident investigating responsibilities were transferred to the new CAB. The administrator was also assigned to the Department of Commerce and placed under the supervision of its secretary.

As head of the new Civil Aeronautics Administration, the administrator's duties included the ones assigned to him by the Civil Aeronautics Act—fostering air commerce, establishing and equipping civil airways, improving air navigation facilities, and regulating air traffic—plus those he had performed on behalf of the Civil Aeronautics Authority as supervisor of the Bureau of Safety Regulations. Then, in 1950, President Harry S. Truman's Reorganization Plan V transferred all functions of agencies or persons within the Department of Commerce (except those of CAB and certain similar agencies with rulemaking and adjudicatory powers) to the secretary.

By 1950 the federal government and the aviation community had begun to turn attention to other aviation problems. Following World War II, it became increasingly clear that a single national air navigation and traffic control system was needed to serve the increased demands of both civil and military aviation. With aircraft constantly expanding in number and in speed, a modernized common system was imperative for the safe and efficient use of the nation's airspace.

The principal interagency body established to implement a central control system was the Air Coordinating Committee (ACC). It was created in March 1945 and made responsible primarily for international aviation matters. It was also charged with developing integrated policies for all agencies in the aviation field. In the mid 1950s, ACC came under the review of Edward P. Curtis, special assistant to the President for aviation facilities planning. Following his recommendations (submitted in a report on May 10, 1957), two pieces of legislation were passed which significantly affected governmental aviation organization. The first, approved in August 1957, created the temporary Airways Modernization Board (AMB). This agency was to develop, test, and select procedures and facilities "to meet the needs for safe and efficient navigation and traffic control of all civil and military aviation except for those needs of military agencies which are peculiar to air warfare and primarily of military concern." In addition, AMB was to determine the systems, procedures, and devices that would best coordinate air traffic control and air defense systems.

The second piece of legislation passed on the heels of the Curtis recommendations was the 1958 Federal Aviation Act. It repealed the 1926 Air Commerce Act, the 1938 Civil Aeronautics Act, the various presidential reorganization plans, and the 1957 Airways Modernization Act. The tasks formerly distributed among CAB, CAA, and AMB were now divided between two independent agencies: CAB, which continued with the same composition but was freed of its administrative ties with the Department of Commerce; and the Federal Aviation Agency (FAA), which was created by the 1958 act.

Although CAB retained responsibility for the economic regulation of air carriers and for accident investigation, it lost most of its former authority in safety regulation and enforcement to FAA. Under the law creating it, FAA was to make and enforce all safety rules. However, any FAA order involving suspension or revocation of a certificate could be appealed to

CAB for a hearing, after which CAB could affirm, amend, modify, or reverse the FAA order. The Federal Aviation Act also provided for FAA participation in accident investigation, although the determination of probable cause was a function of CAB alone.

In addition to the authority acquired at the expense of CAB and from the superseded or absorbed agencies, FAA was assigned sole responsibility for managing the nation's airspace. The FAA administrator was obligated to give "full consideration to the requirements of national defense, and of commercial and general aviation, and to the public right of freedom of transit through the navigable airspace." Provision was also made for accommodating the rule-making authority of the administrator to meet military needs in emergencies. When an appropriate military authority determined that an emergency existed, aircraft of the United States' national defense forces were permitted to deviate from the air traffic rules established by the administrator.

In 1967, with the creation of the Department of Transportation (DOT), the Federal Aviation Agency became the Federal Aviation Administration—a major component of the new department. The CAB's functions of determining the cause of civil aviation accidents and exercising appellate jurisdiction over safety-rule enforcement were assigned to the National Transportation Safety Board, a departmental component authorized to act independently of the secretary in these matters. The creation of DOT reflected a growing awareness by the public, the government, and the transportation industry that an integrated and balanced transportation system under the control of a single agency was essential if the nation's transportation needs were to be met.

Federal Support, 1926-1945

Federal sponsorship of airport development through grants-in-aid is one of the largest federal aviation programs in existence today. But fifty years ago, when the federal government first became involved in civil aviation, the prevailing opinion about federal aid to airports was quite different. Indeed, the 1926 Air Commerce Act specifically pro-

hibited the secretary of commerce from establishing, operating, or maintaining airports. This prohibition remained law for twelve years.

In drafting the Air Commerce Act, Congress drew heavily on precedents in maritime law and on the testimony of Secretary of Commerce Herbert Hoover. In 1925 Hoover testified before a board established to study aviation needs that he saw a complete analogy between air and water commerce. The needs of air navigation, he maintained, paralleled those of water navigation for the kinds of services the latter had been receiving from the federal government. A special committee of the National Advisory Committee on Aeronautics (NACA) came to the same conclusion:

> Federal policy toward airports should be analogous to its policy regarding seaports and the encouragement of water navigation. In the latter field the Government makes charts, establishes and maintains lighthouses, dredges channels, furnishes weather forecasts and storm warnings, and provides for inspection and licensing, but leaves to municipal authorities the control of port facilities. In aid of air navigation the Federal Government should chart airways, establish and maintain emergency landing fields, furnish weather-report service, and provide for inspection and licensing, but leave to municipal authorities the control of airports.

In other words, the airports of air commerce were like the docks of waterborne commerce; and docks, under traditional policy, were provided by private enterprise or municipalities.

The NACA subcommittee did not rest its case with one analogy. It argued further that, if the federal government were to assume control of airports, the initiative of municipalities would be destroyed and strong pressures would continually be applied on Congress to make large appropriations for airport land acquisitions. "The financial burden on the Federal Treasury would be so tremendous," the subcommittee said, "that it would take a great many years to carry the policy into effect, if, indeed, the responsibility thus assumed would ever be discharged." According to the subcommittee's predictions, airports would not be established in the numbers needed, and "the primary object of the bill—the encouragement of commercial aviation—would be defeated." Thus, when Congress wrote the 1926 Air Commerce Act, it prohibited federal involvement in airport development.

The absence of federal funding did not completely deter airport development in the 1920s. Spurred on by the speculative fever of the decade as well as by the Air Mail Act, the Air Commerce Act, and the Lindbergh flight, municipalities and private investors did build airports. Between 1925 and 1928, the number of airports increased by 30 percent. But when the stock market crashed in 1929, airport development immediately declined. In 1930 private investors and muncipalities spent $35 million on airports; in 1931, $20 million; in 1932, $5 million; in 1933, a mere $1 million. By the time Roosevelt became President, airport development was at a standstill.

The Port Authority of New York and New Jersey

In 1932 the Old North Beach Airport, on the site of what became LaGuardia Airport, served New York City and the surrounding area.

The federal relief and recovery programs inaugurated during the Great Depression worked to change the "dock" concept of the airport. In providing construction projects to combat the economic emergency, Congress took two basic approaches, both of which affected airport development. On the one hand, Congress demanded prompt and continued relief through work for the jobless; on the other, it urged well-planned projects to rehabilitate the country's disorganized industry and trade and to conserve its natural resources. Therefore, in 1933 Congress created the Federal Emergency Relief Administration (FERA) to accomplish the first

objective and the Public Works Administration (PWA) to achieve the second.

The first work-relief projects on airports, however, were administered by a temporary third organization—the Civil Works Administration (CWA). Roosevelt saw the need for CWA as the winter of 1933-1934 neared. Although more than $3 billion had been appropriated under the National Industrial Recovery Act for a national program of public works to be administered by PWA, these projects were still in the planning stage in the fall of 1933 and would not have any substantial impact before the spring of 1934. The FERA alone, the President feared, would not be able to cope with the impending winter-aggravated crisis; for it had a comparatively modest fiscal-year appropriation and was limited to the employment of persons on relief rolls. On November 9, 1933, Roosevelt created CWA to step into the breach with allocations from both FERA and PWA. By the end of the following March, CWA had provided work relief for more than 4 million persons and had spent nearly $1 billion. Of this sum, about $11.5 million had gone to airports.

In the spring of 1934, airport projects in progress under CWA were transferred to FERA and continued through annual appropriations acts. One of these, the 1935 Emergency Relief Appropriation Act, authorized the President to create the Works Progress Administration (WPA), which supervised all airport projects from 1935 to 1939. Then, in 1939, the President's Reorganization Plan I established the Federal Works Agency (FWA) to consolidate some of the agencies that had burgeoned during the previous six years. The WPA and PWA were included among its components.

In the years between the creation of CWA and the passage of the 1938 Civil Aeronautics Act, an important change occurred in the sources of funds directed to civil airport development. From about 1911 through 1932, the municipalities and the owners of private airports had shared almost equally all but a tiny portion of the total cost: the muncipalities' share had been 47.6 percent; the private-airport owners' share, 49.7 percent. Before 1933 the federal government had provided only 0.7

percent—primarily through the Post Office Department's Air Mail Service in the early 1920s—and the states had contributed the remaining 2 percent. From 1933 to 1938, all of these shares except that of the states changed drastically. The federal share rose to 76.7 percent while that of the municipalities dropped to 17.7 percent and that of the private sector to 3.6 percent.

Although federal expenditures for airport construction between 1933 and 1945 were extensive (see Table 7-1), many of these funds were ill spent. Shovel labor was not only frequently inefficient, but often it built airports for communities that did not need them and could not support them. Nevertheless, it must be remembered that when these programs were initiated, the overriding consideration was unemployment relief, not airport development. This fact alone explains why CWA projects included the construction of 566 new airports; funds were given where men were out of work. Most of these "New Deal" airports were minimal facilities, and about 60 percent of them subsequently reverted to grass. By contrast, practically all of the airports built under later programs (the Development of Landing Areas for National Defense Program, for instance) were still in existence long after World War II.

TABLE 7-1

Federal Expenditures for Airport Construction, 1933-1945

Agency	Airports New	Im- proved	Total	Expenditures
Civil Works Administration	566	386	952	$ 15,222,000
Federal Emergency Relief Administration	55	888	943	17,650,000
Public Works Administration		35	35	28,850,000
Works Progress Administration & Work Projects Administration	197	367	564*	331,585,000
Civil Aeronautics Administration	248	287	535	383,032,000
CAA, DCLA** Program			29	9,514,000

*Number of locations to June 30, 1940.
**Development of Civil Landing Areas, begun September 1944.

A comparison of the funds allocated for airport construction and improvement in the periods before and after 1931 show a highly significant shift. Before 1931 land and buildings received the lion's share of the total funds expended—more than three fifths between them. Land was by far the single largest item, accounting for 43.4 percent of all expenditures. Hangars accounted for 19.0 percent; other buildings, 8.3 percent; and seed, fences, and miscellaneous, 5.4 percent. All together, these items amounted to 76.1 percent of the total expenditure. The other 23.9 percent was devoted directly to runway construction or maintenance: clearing and grading, 13.1 percent; lighting, 4.0 percent; drainage, 3.8 percent; and paving, 3.0 percent.

After 1931 about three fifths of the total expenditure was spent on items in the runway category. Clearing and grading received 30.0 percent; paving, 21.5 percent; drainage, 6.3 percent; and lighting, 2.0 percent—these items totaled 59.8 percent. The other category, which had received more than three fourths of all funds in the period before 1931, received only 40.2 percent—less than was spent in the earlier period for land alone. The expenditure for land was 12.9 percent; hangars, 11.4 percent; other buildings, 12.2 percent; and seed, fences, and miscellaneous, 3.7 percent.

During the mid 1930s, most large municipalities had managed to prepare their airports for the twenty-one passenger, twin-engined DC-3s. By 1938, however, they were being urged to make further improvements to receive the forthcoming forty-passenger, four-engined airliners. There were only five airports in the United States—Cleveland, Oakland, New Orleans, Memphis, and Wichita—that could accommodate these forty-passenger planes. Some of the nation's largest and busiest airports—Kansas City, Newark, Detroit, Chicago, and Washington—were not ready for the newest aircraft. Needless to say, city fathers were not enchanted with the prospects of financing the necessary improvements. They knew all too well that following the forty-passenger airplanes would come even larger passenger carriers. If the New Deal relief and recovery programs had undermined the "dock" concept, these financial prospects demolished it.

In December 1937, the Bureau of Air Commerce held a National Airport Conference in Washington, D.C., in which the states actively participated. Its purpose was to deal with an acute problem—the gap between airport resources and air commerce needs. The conference resolved that there should be a "national system of public airports" and that responsibility for the system should be shared by federal, state, and local government. It also resolved that the phrase "except airports" be deleted from that part of the 1926 Air Commerce Act which authorized the secretary of commerce to provide and maintain air navigation facilities along designated airways.

Before the conference adjourned, it established a permanent Airport Advisory Committee to give the Department of Commerce a standing source of expert opinion on airport matters. The membership of the committee was made up of representatives from fourteen national associations. Three months later, this committee met in Washington and adopted a resolution stating that it was the proper interest and responsibility of the federal government to participate in the cost of establishing, constructing, developing, improving, and maintaining publicly owned airports. It appointed several of its own members to present the committee's views to the White House, the Bureau of the Budget, and Congress.

Although the Bureau of the Budget reluctantly approved the "national system of public airports" recommendation, it took a firm position against deletion of the phrase "except airports." To delete this phrase, the bureau argued, would be to commit the government to expenses for which there were no limits. Meanwhile, Congress was considering legislation that would revamp the entire civil aviation structure in the federal government—legislation that would eventually result in the 1938 Civil Aeronautics Act. Consequently, neither the House nor the Senate was prepared, at that time, to go beyond the position of the Bureau of the Budget.

The Senate hearings, conducted by the Committee on Interstate Commerce, took place on April 6 and 7, 1938. The views of the Airport Advisory Committee were best expressed by its chairman, Floyd E. Evans, who argued that the 1925-1926 concept of the airport was no longer valid and that the new law should reflect a revised concept in keeping with the 1938 realities. "We believe," Evans told the Senate hearings, "an airport is very similar in its Federal-local characteristics to our channels, harbors, and docks." He than stated the familiar federal-local division of responsibility: "The Federal Government makes the waterways safe for the operation of commerce; the local government or private interest build the docks used for the actual loading and unloading of cargo." An airport was in part like a waterway, he explained, "in that the actual landing area constitutes part of an airway and is surely interstate in character"; similarly, "the field lighting equipment, radio facilities, and traffic control facilities are of urgent necessity for the safe operation of air commerce into and out of the airport." Therefore, the landing area and its associated air navigation and traffic control equipment come within the federal sphere of responsibility.

Such was not the case, however, with "the area outside the actual landing area, comprising the hangars, airport offices, depots, repair facilities, and so forth." In a word, they were the "dock." Hence, they "should be furnished and maintained by the local community or private interests."

Evans further observed that thus far the federal government had participated in the construction or improvement of airports only in economic emergencies. This, he contended, was not enough. For mounting airport requirements—longer and wider hard-surfaced runways, more complete drainage systems, better field lighting equipment, radio facilities for instrument landings, and traffic control equipment—were "far more" than could be met by relief agencies. Evans cited an example from his own state of Michigan to illustrate the problems faced by airports: after investing over $35.2 million in its airport, Detroit found that the newer, larger planes had nearly rendered it obsolete. Newark, Kansas City, and Chicago, he argued, were in similar positions.

Congress agreed with Evans. The phrase

"except airports" was omitted from that part of the 1938 Civil Aeronautics Act covering federal provision and maintenance of air navigation facilities. The CAA was directed to make a survey of the existing airport system and to present to Congress, not later than February 1, 1939, definite recommendations on "whether the Federal Government should participate in the construction, improvement, development, operation, or maintenance of a national system of airports," and, if so, "the extent to which, and the manner in which, the Federal Government shall so participate."

In taking this action, Congress was governed by one basic consideration, the growth of aviation since 1926. It was apparent that 1938 aircraft could not be served adequately by 1926 airports. Hoover's comparison of airports with waterway docks was made when airports were simple, but by 1934 municipalities were arguing that the airport was a harbor, not a dock. And by 1938 a clear distinction could be made between the "harbor" (the runway and its associated air navigation and air traffic control facilities) and the "dock" (the terminal buildings, hangars, and other service structures).

Since Congress did not consider the Civil Aeronautics Act a policy statement, it was not accompanied by an appropriation. But the deletion of the phrase "except airports" at least suggested what Congress thought the policy should be. In March 1939, CAA recommended that airports be considered a "proper object of Federal expenditure" in normal times as well as when emergency public works programs were in progress. It also suggested that preference be given to airports "important to the maintenance of safe and efficient operation of air transportation along the major trade routes of the Nation" and to those "rendering special service to the national defense." Because of World War II, the authority's recommendations were not implemented. But they did pave the way for the 1946 Federal Airport Act.

Developments under the 1946 Federal Airport Act

President Truman signed the Federal Airport Act into law on May 13, 1946, one week before the twentieth anniversary of the Air Commerce Act. This provided a major responsibility to the federal government for developing the nation's airport system. Even so, at times the federal government acted reluctantly, unevenly, and ineffectively. Although Congress appropriated some $1.2 billion for airport development over the twenty-five-year life of the Federal Airport Act, it was not enough to meet the growing needs of a rapidly expanding industry. But the Federal Airport Act was better than no act. Indeed, what progress was made in developing and modernizing the nation's airport system in the twenty-five years following World War II was due largely to this legislation.

The Federal Airport Act contained two key provisions. The first required the formulation of a National Airport Plan (NAP) in which the CAA administrator specified the projects considered necessary to provide a public airport system adequate to meet and anticipate the needs of civil aviation. In accordance with NAP, the act then appropriated $500 million for the continental United States and $20 million for Alaska, Hawaii, and Puerto Rico over a seven-year period beginning on July 1, 1946. Appropriations for any one fiscal year were not to exceed $100 million; but if these appropriations were not spent, they remained available until the end of the seven-year period (June 30, 1953). All federal allotments to airport sponsors were, however, to be matched by local funds.

States increased their activity in aviation following World War II and the passage of the 1946 Federal Airport Act. By 1950 all except two states had established state aviation agencies, but their activities remained limited. Coordination efforts were made with federal activities, and some developments of small, low-volume, general aviation airports were undertaken.

From the beginning, Congress established a pattern that it would follow throughout the program's existence. It appropriated less—sometimes substantially less—than the level of funding authorized. If the program had proceeded at the required level, Congress would have appropriated funds at an average annual rate of $74.3 million. Instead, it appropriated

$42.8 million for fiscal year 1946 and $30.5 million for fiscal year 1947. In fact, the first appropriation proved to be the largest during the entire seven years. Thus, even though Congress extended the program another five years, by June 1953 it had appropriated only $194 million, an amount far short of the authorized $520 million.

Congress justified its failure to live up to the commitments of the Federal Airport Act by pointing to CAA. Each year, CAA found itself with large carry-over funds. By the end of fiscal year 1953, for example, CAA had spent only $168 million, some $26 million less than was appropriated. This can be explained by a number of factors. Aviation did not grow as rapidly during the late 1940s as had been anticipated, thus carry-overs quickly accumulated. Then, during the early 1950s when the need for funds increased, the demand was never as great as the actual need. Many local officials believed that federal administrative requirements were too complex, and airport sponsors complained that they could not rely on the availability of federal funds. Because of the time required to raise local funds, sponsors drew up airport development plans two to three years in advance of federal funding. But often they found that two or three years later, federal funds simply did not exist.

By 1953, when Dwight D. Eisenhower took office, the federal aid airport program had come to a halt. One government official remarked that the amount of federal funds going to states about equaled "the sum one large city might have to spend for the removal of an unexpected April snow." Despite this fact, the Eisenhower Administration decided that it would not ask for a federal-aid-to-airport appropriation for fiscal year 1954. Instead, it instructed the Department of Commerce to appoint a committee composed of federal, state, municipal, and aviation industry representatives to determine whether or not there was a definite need to continue federal assistance to airport development.

In the fall of 1953, the committee submitted its report to the secretary of commerce. It concluded beyond a doubt that civil airport facilities were incapable of meeting the needs of civil aviation either for the present or the future, that the investment required to provide the nation with an adequate system could not be borne by cities and states alone, and that the federal government must provide financial assistance to local sponsors to the extent that their airports serve the national interest.

The Eisenhower Administration accepted the committee's findings and requested $20.8 million for fiscal year 1955. In the following year, the Administration asked for only $11 million. Once again, faced with further delays in accomplishing badly needed airport repairs and with the prospect of suffering financial losses from wasted planning, public airport officials converged on Congress. As a result, Congress amended the Federal Airport Act and appropriated twice the amount requested by the Administration.

The nation's airport program finally received the funding stability it had lacked in the past. The amended Federal Airport Act established a new four-year program, running through June 30, 1959, with contract authorizations amounting to $63 million per year for each of the three fiscal years between 1957 and 1959. For fiscal year 1956, it authorized $42.5 million which, when combined with an earlier appropriation of $20 million, brought the fiscal year 1956 total to $62.5 million. This time Congress was as good as its word. It appropriated funds at the authorized level for the entire length of the program.

In 1959 the Eisenhower Administration submitted a bill to Congress proposing another but "final" four-year program. It was to be funded at a lower level ($200 million on the aggregate or $50 million a year) and would constitute a period of "orderly withdrawal" from the air program. Seeing that the recent appearance of jet transports would impose new pressures on the nation's airport system, Congress disagreed. The Senate approved a four-year program with a $465 million authorization; the House, with a $297 million authorization. In the end, a makeshift compromise was struck: a two-year program at the old $63 million level per year.

The Kennedy Administration was more receptive to a strong airport program. In September 1961, it increased the yearly level of authorizations to $75 million and maintained it, by periodic amendments, throughout the life of the act. But for a variety of reasons even $75 million was not enough.

Crisis at the Hubs

Civil air traffic grew at a very rapid rate during the 1960s (see Table 7-2). Between 1963 and 1967, the number of aircraft using the airways increased from 87,267 to 116,794 (34 percent). The number of people passing in and out of terminals also rose. In 1967, 126.4 million passengers were enplaned—almost double the number enplaned in 1963. This surge in air traffic outstripped the growth in airport capacity and resulted in unprecedented congestion which by 1975 was alleviated somewhat as indicated in the table.

Congestion was most severe at the great commercial, industrial, and population centers of the United States—New York, Chicago, Atlanta, Los Angeles, and Washington, D.C. While air carrier operations in the United States rose 16 percent between December 1963 and June 1967, operation at the ten largest hubs rose 29 percent. Moreover, these ten hubs received 31 percent of all air carrier traffic, and they originated nearly half of all air carrier passengers.

The expansion of air carrier operations was only a part of the overall aviation problem. For every air carrier aircraft flying, there were forty-five general aviation aircraft; and for every air carrier pilot, there were nearly ten private pilots. While air carrier growth had been rapid, general aviation

growth had been phenomenal. Between 1963 and 1967, the number of general aviation aircraft rose 34 percent; the number of private pilots increased 66 percent; and the number of itinerant general aviation operations recorded by air traffic control towers rose 64 percent.

These aircraft contributed substantially to the congestion at the hubs, for, in keeping with the principle of freedom of the skies, they had nearly unrestricted use of the airspace around the hubs. They also enjoyed use of the major airports. Hence, they not only occupied airspace around the airports; they also occupied the runways and taxiways. According to Port Authority of New York and New Jersey figures, 51 percent of the traffic at La Guardia Airport and 52 percent at Newark Airport during the busiest hours of 1967 consisted of general aviation movements.

Conditions such as these prevailed for many reasons. There was, first of all, a lack of general aviation "reliever" airports in the large metropolitan areas. Secondly, there was the problem of planning. Although FAA issued an annual National Airport Plan, it simply identified airport needs—it did not plan for them. No one, then, assumed the responsibility for airport planning, unless it was the local airport official who, understandably, could rarely see beyond the needs of his own operation. Thirdly, the $75 million authorized by Congress was insufficient to meet the demands of aviation's accelerated growth. In fiscal year 1968, for example, FAA obligated $70.2 million but had requests for

TABLE 7-2
Airport Landings and Takeoffs, 1950-1975
(Ranked in order of most landings and takeoffs in 1975)

Airport	1950	1960	1969	1975
Chicago, Illinois—O'Hare International	94,855	244,479	676,473	685,255
Long Beach, California—Long Beach	193,065	271,818	550,867	537,531
Los Angeles, California—International	172,411	289,026	613,938	458,514
Phoenix, Arizona—Sky Harbor Municipal	161,943	294,044	347,867	423,112
Denver, Colorado—Stapleton	139,650	308,194	365,135	395,464
New York City, New York— John F. Kennedy International	29,642	274,634	436,298	340,714
New York City, New York—La Guardia	176,689	242,843	335,848	330,547
San Francisco, California—International	121,038	235,944	391,334	325,944
St. Louis, Missouri—Municipal	199,955	235,041	342,258	315,464
Miami, Florida—International	210,181	321,017	407,277	314,429
Washington, D.C.—National	156,420	316,597	337,084	309,178
Honolulu, Hawaii—International	174,943	253,742	339,645	263,287
Chicago, Illinois—Midway	233,995	376,030	194,343	168,414

$339.3 million. Furthermore, with the United States' increasing involvement in Vietnam, Congress found it easier to cut back airport appropriations. Beginning with fiscal year 1967, Congress, for the first time since fiscal year 1955, appropriated less than the amount authorized by the Federal Airport Act. It continued to do so through the end of the decade.

States increased their activities during the late 1950s and the 1960s and became more involved in coordinating the various aviation programs within their jurisdictions, providing support for the establishment of small airports, and developing statewide airport plans. The objective was to cooperate fully with federal agencies in matters of mutual concern and to provide needed facilities and services not furnished by the federal government. About one fourth of the states passed legislation to channel federal funds to local airports through the state agency. All airports in Alaska, Hawaii, and Rhode Island are owned by the state.

Airways Modernization, 1961-1970

Although a significant program to modernize the nation's airways was initiated with the creation of FAA in 1958, it had barely begun when President John F. Kennedy took office. The change of political parties in the White House produced a major reexamination of the federal government's role in fostering and regulating civil aeronautics and air commerce. The new Administration, having promised decisive action in those areas affected by the rapid transformation of American society, felt that it had been given a mandate to carry out such a program. In early 1961, Kennedy requested the FAA administrator to "conduct a scientific, engineering review of our aviation facilities and . . . prepare a practicable long-range plan to ensure efficient and safe control of all air traffic within the United States." In addition, he was asked to investigate the development of military, commercial, and general aviation during the 1960s and recommend national aviation goals for the 1970s.

"Project Horizon," released on September 10, 1961, laid out the basic policies for the federal government's role in aviation under the Kennedy Administration. Generally, the report advised coordination of the nation's aviation program with an overall transportation system. Specifically, it recommended changes in the CAB regulation of route allocation and pricing to allow American air carriers to compete effectively with foreign carriers; support for research and development into future civilian aircraft to compensate for the slowdown of military research in those areas; study in federal aviation agencies on the needs of the general aviation community; and creation of a commission to study amendments to the Railway Labor Act that would include airlines and would eliminate the threat of strikes in the nation's airline industry.

On the following day, the "Project Beacon" task force for air traffic control delivered its report to the FAA administrator. It recommended the employment of radar as the primary means of traffic control; extension of positive control to all aircraft flying above 14,500 feet and to all aircraft above 8,000 feet on high density airways; segregation of controlled and uncontrolled aircraft on high density airways and congested terminal areas; and increased use of general purpose computers to process flight plans, issue routine clearances, make conflict probes, and generate display information. The "Horizon" and "Beacon" policy studies were completed in a relatively short time, but their implementation took much longer. Nevertheless, throughout the early 1960s, FAA made a concerted effort to upgrade its operational air traffic control system through the acquisition of new radar and communications equipment.

The original plan envisioned by the "Beacon" task force concentrated on aircraft control along the nation's airways. But it became increasingly clear to planners at FAA that an even more immediate problem in air safety was developing in the airspace surrounding the nation's airports. The 1960s proved to be a decade of tremendous growth in aviation, so much so that it began to overwhelm the ability of the airport system to handle it. The crowded skies of terminal areas posed real threats to aviation safety. The very nature of terminal airspace made traffic more difficult to handle there than between terminal points. In a terminal area both high- and low-performance aircraft were forced to mix because of takeoffs and landings; and with the rapid transition of the airlines to jet aircraft, even for short haul service to smaller airports, the air traffic control system faced a problem of crisis proportions.

The FAA launched an experimental program in area positive control at Atlanta's airport in 1964. Although it produced some delays and irritation to those persons landing and taking off, the automated radar terminal system (ARTS) provided an invaluable source of information to FAA for developing plans for a semi-automated traffic control system for airports. The ARTS displayed the information supplied by the beacon transponders in airborne aircraft on the ground controller's radarscope. Each radar blip showed aircraft identification, altitude, and ground speed for a particular aircraft. The ARTS was implemented on a modular and evolutionary basis to permit the addition of improvements as they became technically possible.

The explosive growth of aviation in the 1960s made it extremely difficult for FAA to keep pace in its modernization efforts. Furthermore, FAA's problems were compounded by the public's increasing concern over noise and pollution—the by-products of aviation development. Public concern for protecting the environment blocked the building of new airports, delayed the expansion of existing ones, and put even more pressure on the already congested airspace. By the late 1960s, before a semi-automated air traffic control system was fully operational, the airways and airport system appeared to be reaching the point of saturation. Responding to this threat, FAA limited the flow of traffic into the most congested areas in an effort to maintain an acceptable level of safety. These measures, however, resulted in frustrating delays for passengers and pilots alike.

A landmark in the struggle to keep ahead of aviation growth was reached in May 1970, when the Airport and Airway Development Act and the Airport and Airway Revenue Act became law. These measures committed the federal government to the modernization of airways through revenues generated from user taxes and held in a special trust fund for that purpose alone. By the middle of 1974, the results of FAA's efforts were beginning to bear fruit, as the National Airspace System (NAS), a semi-automated air traffic control system, was completed and installed in the major air traffic control centers and terminal areas across the country.

1970 Airport Legislation

In August 1967, the Senate Aviation Subcommittee held hearings on the growing air crisis. Among those invited to appear before the subcommittee were Secretary of Transportation Alan Boyd, FAA Administrator General William F. McKee, and Civil Aeronautics Board Chairman Charles S. Murphy. Boyd, who spoke for the Administration, readily admitted the inadequacy of the Federal Airport Act but said that an expanded airport program was not realistic. "Airport development," he insisted, "is only one of many pressing national problems which require expenditure of large amounts of money. Important as it is, however, it is simply not the top priority program at either the Federal, State, or local level." Boyd's solution was for the users—passengers, shippers, and aircraft operators—to begin assuming "a much greater share" of airport costs.

Federal Aviation Administration

The small feeder airport at Medford, New Jersey, is typical of the construction in the 1960s.

Murphy disagreed. He declared that airport inadequacy was already constraining air transport growth in some cities and that unless something were done immediately, airports would become even more unsatisfactory. More important, he contended that no solution would be found until the federal government accepted "the primary responsibility for getting the job done." Airports, he argued, were more than a series of local problems; they were an integral part of a nation's entire air transport system and had to be developed according to a comprehensive plan. Murphy concluded his remarks by insisting that only the federal government was in a position to formulate and implement such a plan.

As a result of these hearings, President Lyndon B. Johnson wrote Boyd in September 1967 that he was aware that the rapid growth of commercial and private flying was creating "demands for substantial expansion and improvement in the Nation's air traffic control system." But he also said that the people who would benefit most from these improvements were the users—the aviation industry and the flying public. He suggested that these people "should pay their fair share of the costs of the system . . . ." Johnson then asked Boyd for two items: a long-range plan setting forth the facilities, equipment, and personnel required to meet aviation's present and future needs and a detailed proposal for financing these improvements through a system of user charges.

An FAA task force, headed by Associate Administrator Oscar Bakke, was assigned to draw up a plan. In a lengthy and detailed blueprint, known as the Bakke plan, the task force contended that airports were "the greatest limitation upon the capacity of the air traffic system . . . ." They were inadequate in number, deficient in design, and lacking in proper location. Concentrating on four major areas—facilities and equipment, airports, research and development, and financing— the task force predicted that over the next decade the nation would require $7 billion in federal, state, and local funds for airport construction and improvement. Since current FAA funds were meeting only 20 percent of the demand, the Bakke plan proposed that federal funds be raised from their annual level of $75 million to $200 million.

From where was the money to come? Approximately $1.1 billion would be paid by the Defense Department for its share of the common civil-military system. The remaining costs could not come entirely from user charges nor from appropriations. Therefore, the task force suggested: (1) increasing the current 5 percent tax on air passenger tickets to 8 percent, (2) imposing a new tax of 8 percent on air freight waybills, (3) raising the existing tax on general aviation gasoline from four to seven cents per gallon, (4) placing a new tax of seven cents per gallon on jet fuel used in general aviation. Passenger head taxes, aircraft registration fees, and landing and parking fees were purposely avoided. The task force wanted to leave some forms of taxation exclusively to the state and local governments to be used in financing their part of airport development. However, the Bakke plan did propose that the federal government be given the power to regulate local assessments and operating restrictions to insure reasonable uniformity throughout the national airport system.

Finally, the task force recommended establishing an aviation trust fund, modeled after the highway trust fund. All revenues generated by the proposed user taxes and all FAA appropriations would be deposited in the fund. Similarly, all federal costs for running, maintaining, and improving the national airport and airway systems would be handled through the fund. The objective was to "make the trust fund the sole source of money for the Federal airport and airway programs."

The task force was convinced of the overall merit of the trust fund. Not only had it worked well for the Federal Highway Administration, but it would provide a predictable and increasing source of funds, a systematic way for determining whether or not airport and airway programs were operating on a break-even basis, and the flexibility to meet unforeseen requirements promptly. In addition, the task force believed that a trust fund would help win acceptance of the proposed tax program; it would assure the civil aviation community that revenues generated by taxes would be used solely for airport facilities and services.

Boyd and M. Cecil Mackey, assistant secretary for policy development in FAA, disapproved of the trust fund concept. They argued that since the fund would require appropriations to be fed into it, what the Bakke plan proposed was a trust fund in name only. They pointed out the risk that Congress might take the position that FAA should make do with the user-tax revenues. Finally, Boyd insisted that "when you set up a trust fund for airports, for highways, for water resources or whatever, you are saying that no matter what happens to the Federal Government, no matter what happens to the budget, these funds mean that this has a higher priority than the national defense or anything else."

What Boyd and Mackey had in mind was not to reform the federal-aid-to-airport program but to abandon it. In place of the FAA's proposed five-year, billion-dollar grant program, they proposed a $10 million-a-year grant program for local service air carrier airports. They also recommended a billion-dollar federal loan/loan guarantee program for air carrier airports that might have difficulty borrowing money at reasonable rates for capital expenditures.

Under their plan, general aviation airports would get nothing—no grants, no loans. "I know," Mackey declared, "of no overriding interest which warrants Federal participation . . . in airport development costs for general aviation." It is "a useful but generally expensive form of private transportation which has reached a stage of maturity where it should be able to pay its own way . . . and its growth should be governed by this ability." Mackey further reasoned that the major airports had enough traffic to generate sufficient revenues for their own improvement programs. Thus, Mackey asked, "if money could be generated at the local level, why should the federal government raise and distribute airport development funds?" Why should the federal government function as a broker?

This was an important question. Where did federal responsibility for civil aviation begin and where did state and local responsibility end? Mackey's position was reminiscent of the philosophy underlying the 1926 Air Commerce Act which had specifically excluded airports from federal responsibility. Far more important, however, was the FAA

contention that runways and their associated navigational aids were indispensable to safe flight and, therefore, within federal responsibility.

Having cleared the Department of Transportation's airport and user-charge programs with the White House, Boyd sent them to Congress in late May 1968. Congress reacted unenthusiastically. Senator Mike Monroney, chairman of the Senate Aviation Subcommittee, felt strongly that a trust fund should be established. Mackey was apprehensive, and he urged Boyd to meet with Monroney and find an appropriate forum for the Administration to state its case. The Senate Aviation Subcommittee ultimately provided the forum. Testifying before the subcommittee on June 18, 1968, Boyd made his case for the Department of Transportation's airport and user-charge proposals and outlined the Administration's airways program. While no serious resistance to the airways program materialized, the airport and user-charge proposals were another matter. Joseph B. Hartranft, Jr., president of the Aircraft Owners and Pilots Associations, recommended that FAA be reestablished as an independent agency. Before long it became clear that the Johnson Administration's program stood no chance of clearing the subcommittee.

On July 1, the Senate Aviation Subcommittee issued its report. As expected, the Administration's proposals did not fare well; neither, for that matter, did those of the various aviation groups. If any group fared well, it was FAA. The subcommittee's recommended user taxes were the same as those proposed in the Bakke plan, with the exception of the cargo tax which was reduced to 5 percent. Estimating that the tax program would bring in revenues of $2.9 billion over the next five years, the subcommittee recommended the creation of a trust fund and earmarked the revenues in the following manner: $250 million annually for facilities and equipment and $150 million annually for airport construction. The FAA's airport program was to be extended another five years and to function as before, except that it would receive twice as much money. The subcommittee also suggested a billion-dollar federal loan program for terminal area development at publicly owned airports.

The Senate Commerce Committee reported out a bill based on these recommendations, but a stalemate ensued. The Ninetieth Congress failed to act on the measure. Nevertheless this bill, along with the Bakke plan, served as a blueprint for the Ninety-first Congress when it undertook consideration of a new airport-airway proposal submitted by the Nixon Administration in June 1967. With minor differences, the Nixon program was essentially the program supported by FAA during the Johnson Administration and approved by the Senate Commerce Committee during the previous Congress. One difference was the Nixon Administration's preference for a designated account rather than a trust fund.

In May 1970, Congress passed the Airport and Airway Development Act (Title I of Public Law 91-258) and the Airport and Airway Revenue Act (Title II). Title I increased the total annual authorization to $280 million (by nearly four times for each of the next five fiscal years) and provided a wider distribution formula. Title II established a trust fund modeled after the highway trust fund. Thus, it was no longer necessary for airport and airway development to compete for money in the general treasury—the basic reason for the financial uncertainties of the past.

The new legislation also provided for planning grants—again marking a significant difference between it and the old legislation. The secretary could make grants to private agencies for airport system planning and to public agencies for airport master planning. Although a total of $75 million was reserved for such grants, planning grants could not exceed $15 million in any one fiscal year; nor could any such grant exceed two thirds of an airport project's cost.

During the first year of operation, the Department of Transportation submitted a budget request to Congress that proposed to obligate less than the minimum annual levels specified in the legislation for airport-airway development. The department planned to use the difference between the revenues generated by user taxes and the amounts requested for airport-airway development to help meet the operational needs of air navigation and traffic control. Although the department believed that it was acting in accordance with the 1970 act, Congress disagreed. It maintained that the minimum levels for airport-airway development specified in the act should be met first before any revenues generated by user taxes could be applied for operational purposes.

In November 1971, the act was amended accordingly. It specified that no trust fund money could be appropriated to carry out any program or activity other than "acquiring, establishing, and improving air navigation facilities"; that any excess of trust fund receipts over airport-airway capital investments could be applied toward the cost of administering the airport and airway development programs; and that funds equal to the minimum authorized for each fiscal year for airport ($280 million) and airway ($250 million) development must remain available in the trust fund until appropriated for that purpose. As a result of the specifications, surpluses began to accumulate in the trust fund, and Congress was forced to amend the act again in June 1973. The annual authorization for airport development grants was raised from $280 to $310 million.

Although surpluses continued to mount, there was little question that the Airport-Airway Act was more effective than its predecessors. Commitments were made under the Airport Development Aid Program (ADAP) at a rate five to six times greater than under the FAA's airport program. During ADAP's first four years of operation, the funds allocated to airport sponsors for development projects surpassed the $1.2 billion mark—the level attained by the FAA program during its quarter century of existence. And though the pressures of inflation inevitably affected ADAP, the future of the nation's airports was decidedly brighter in the 1970s than at any time since the federal government assumed a role in airport development.

Various studies were undertaken in the early 1970s to determine the proper role of state governments in the aviation program. Some studies indicated that the states could oversee the airport development aid program and most of the general aviation functions. By 1976 several plans for increasing state participation were still being considered by Congress, but all states had statewide airports plans under active study and were working closely with federal agencies to prevent duplication of efforts and insure full coverage and wide opportunities even for small communities. Each state also worked closely with the airline companies to provide needed services into all parts of the state.

State funds for local airport development were increased during the 1970s. For instance, in fiscal year 1972, $220 million of state funds were made available. This included $2 million for navigation aides and $3 million for aviation safety and educational programs. All but five states provided funds. In fiscal year 1973, allotments were approximately the same. However, only about 55 percent of the construction funds were expended because of the difficulties encountered by local agencies in providing matching funds.

Airports of the Seventies

Passenger convenience, airline efficiency, economy in construction, and operational safety are the keystones of airport design in the 1970s. Every major new airport in the United States has been planned around these goals. Since passenger convenience means simplicity, speed, and limited walking, airports of the seventies employ vehicular systems to move passengers between arrival points and boarding gates. These systems range in sophistication from an ordinary shuttle bus in Kansas City to a fixed guideway of concrete in Dallas/Fort Worth.

The Dallas/Fort Worth Regional Airport, a portion of which opened in the fall of 1973, occupies a plot of ground nearly as large as Manhattan Island. Stretching across the North Texas plains midway between Dallas and Fort Worth, this $700 million airport covers 17,500 acres. Its area—almost 10 miles from north to south and 8 miles at its widest point—is big enough to contain Chicago's O'Hare International, New York's John F. Kennedy International, and Los Angeles' International airports combined. Designed to meet aviation needs into the twenty-first century, the entire Dallas/Fort Worth airport will be completed by the year 2000 at a projected cost of $1 billion.

The Dallas/Fort Worth Regional Airport has a long history. The first discussions regarding its creation were initiated in 1927, as Fort Worth began constructing Meacham Field on the city's north side. Because officials

Dallas/Fort Worth Regional Airport

The Dallas/Fort Worth Regional Airport covers 17,500 acres. It is nearly 10 miles from north to south and 8 miles at its widest point.

in Fort Worth and Dallas could not agree on the location of the regional airport, Fort Worth completed Meacham Field and in 1928 Dallas purchased an airport (Love Field) of its own. Throughout the 1930s, each city improved and expanded its airport. But as larger aircraft were introduced and airport costs increased, the question of a regional airport was raised again in 1940 when both cities turned to the federal government for assistance.

In 1941 the army asked CAA to help it select an airfield for training between Dallas and Fort Worth. The CAA recommended Arlington, a city of 4,000 people, which was ideally located between the two large cities. Dallas and Fort Worth were also asked to participate in the project. Plans were then formulated for Midway Airport, a 1,000-acre facility to be governed by a seven-member board drawn from all three cities. Once again difficulties arose between Dallas and Fort Worth; this time the dispute concerned the location of the terminal buildings. So, in 1943, at the request of Secretary of Commerce Jesse Jones, Arlington agreed to operate the airport without the help of either Dallas or Fort Worth.

In 1947 Fort Worth bought Midway Airport from Arlington and enlarged it into what was the Greater Southwest International Airport. Dallas, for its part, expanded Love Field and made it a major aviation center. But the federal government continued to press for a single regional facility. Finally, in 1968, following years of negotiations, hearings, amendments to the state constitution, and voter referendums, the Dallas/Fort Worth Regional Airport Board was formed. A consulting firm was engaged to prepare a site selection report, an airport master plan, and a highway development program. All of these tasks were completed by 1969.

When the Dallas/Fort Worth airport was designed, its planners rejected the traditional concept of working from the ground up. They decided, instead, to plan from the "air down." They also chose to design for "tomorrow," arguing repeatedly that "you can't design for today's airport problems and today's aircraft." Working from the "air down" and for "tomorrow" meant that the airport's planners had to

analyze trends in aircraft technology and to determine through simulation programs the maximum number of aircraft their airspace could accommodate in the 1980-2000 period. Once these studies were completed, they planned ground facilities to handle this number—300 visual flight rule operations an hour—in the most efficient manner. When the Dallas/Fort Worth airport opened, there were four half-loop terminal superstructures, with a total of sixty-six passenger gates (by 2001 there will be thirteen half loops and 260 passenger gates); a series of modular "miniterminals" within each terminal loop, enabling passengers to park directly opposite their boarding gates; and an automated AIRTRANS mover system that transports people and baggage (as well as refuse, supplies, and mail) through each half loop and throughout the airport.

Dallas/Fort Worth Regional Airport
AIRTRANS transports both people and goods throughout the Dallas/Forth Worth Regional Airport.

Environmental considerations—particularly noise levels—also played an important part in the design of the Dallas/Fort Worth airport. Noise levels, in fact, were prime factors in determining the airport's size. Computers were used to simulate the noisiest airplane in existence, operating on a hot day at full capacity. Once agreement was reached on an acceptable noise level, the airport's boundaries were established. As a result, even when fully developed, the airport's northern and southern boundaries will be more than

3 miles from the ends of the primary runways, and the crosswind runways will end 2 miles from the airport's limits. Neighboring municipalities have agreed to rezone land adjacent to the airport to discourage the construction of residences, schools, or hospitals.

The Dallas/Fort Worth airport opened with three runways. There are two north-south runways 11,400 feet long and one crosswind runway 9,000 feet long, all of which can be expanded in the future. Ultimately, a total of nine runways is planned: two north-south parallels expandable to 20,000 feet; two 13,400-foot north-south parallels; two 11,000-foot southeast-northwest parallels; one 5,000-foot executive runway; and two 2,000-foot short takeoff and landing (STOL) strips. The original taxiway design was changed when computer simulation studies showed that some of the pavement could be eliminated without significant aircraft delays. During peak hours, Dallas/Fort Worth taxi layout accounts for an average delay of 1.24 minutes—four times less than most airports.

The regional airport is a self-supporting facility. Land costs of $62 million were paid by the two cities. The construction, however, was financed through the sale of revenue bonds made possible by airport use agreements signed by the airlines. The airlines agreed to pay a level of fees sufficient to cover all costs of maintenance and operation plus debt service after applying concession income against costs. The debt service on the bonds as well as the operating costs will, therefore, be liquidated with revenues acquired principally through landing fees, concession fees, and rentals. State and federal funding, together with participation by the cities of Dallas and Fort Worth and the airlines, approximates $800 million.

The Dallas/Fort Worth Regional Airport is the United States' first "jumbo jetport." By 1985 daily population figures (including employees, passengers, and visitors) are estimated to reach 220,000. During the period from January 13 to September 30, 1974, enplanements totaled 5.1 million and some 52,500 tons of air cargo were processed through the airport. Projections indicate that air cargo traffic will total 160,000 tons in 1980 and will rise to 410,000 in 1985. The airport's planners expect that Dallas/Fort Worth will

Kansas City International Airport

The Kansas City International Airport completed in 1973. The drainage lake in the background retains runoff from the site including the runways and taxiways.

remain the world's most sophisticated airport, known especially for its passenger comfort and its operating efficiency.

The Kansas City International Airport, like that of Dallas/Fort Worth, was planned to accommodate the supersonic transport, jumbo, and wide-body jets. One of the nation's largest airports, Kansas City International covers more than 5,000 acres. It is located in the rolling terrain adjacent to the Missouri River flood plain, 15 miles north of the central business district in Platte County. Todd Creek, a tributary of the Little Platte River, lies between the primary runways, and its grade variations range in depth from a few feet to 60 feet in some places. Since aircraft pavements (designed for 350,000 pounds dual tandem wheel loading) and linear terminals were eventually to be placed on these extreme variations of fill depth, the site preparation, excavation, and embankment required careful analysis, design, and construction control.

Extensive mucking operations were necessary in the area of deep fills, primarily in the head of the Todd Creek channel. Materials of insufficient strength to support massive fills were removed. The problem of controlling the fills to achieve minimum subsidence was compounded by the 200 different soil classifications used in the fills. A complete soils laboratory was established on the site; a rigorous testing program was carried out to insure compliance with the limits specified; and settlement gauges were installed to maintain a continuous field check on the rates of subsidence.

Kansas City International's terminal facility can serve up to 6 million enplaning passengers annually. When the airport began commercial operations in the fall of 1972, it had two main runways: an east-west runway 9,500 feet long and a north-south one 10,800 feet long. Eventually there will be six main runways—some capable of expansion to 13,500 feet. Kansas City International has more than 12 miles of vehicular roadways, enough electric power for a city of 20,000 people, storm drains totalling 26 miles in length, 8 miles of water lines, 6 miles of gas lines, and nearly 5 miles of ordinary sewer lines.

But the key to Kansas City International is not its size. It is its layout. The passenger terminal consists of three large doughnut-shaped buildings arranged in a partial circle around a central administrative complex which contains the air traffic control tower, central utilities building for heating and cooling equipment, airfield lighting control, and management and maintenance facilities. Each circular structure is 2 stories high, 65 feet wide, and 2,300 feet long. As many as 900 cars can be parked in the depressed, well-landscaped "hole" of each "doughnut," while the airplanes load and unload around fifteen gate positions along the outside perimeter of the building. Additional parking for automobiles is provided nearby.

Although each building has 2,300 feet of concourse, end to end, its 65-foot width puts most parked automobiles within 300 feet of the nearest airplane. About one fifth of each "doughnut" is cut away to permit vehicles to drive around the inner roadway and park. Airport planners call this the "gate arrival" concept. It stands in marked contrast to conventional airports where tickets are processed and baggage checked in a central terminal building, and passengers then walk as far as a half mile to their boarding gates. In the Kansas City airport, the functional elements have been decentralized. Carried to the extreme, each aircraft loading position could conceivably—although not practically—become a total terminal facility, insofar as passenger services are concerned.

The Newark International Airport has a history dating from 1928, but it cannot be overlooked as an airport of the seventies. The increased air traffic of the late fifties and sixties made it clear to the commissioners and planners at the Port Authority of New York and New Jersey that expansion was no longer sufficient. They believed that if Newark's airport were to meet the air needs of the future, it would have to be redeveloped completely. In September 1963, the Newark Redevelopment Program commenced with the construction of a huge drainage ditch extending 4 miles around the airport perimeter to direct storm water from the airport and adjoining communities into Elizabeth Channel.

The original Newark Airport of 1928 was billed as the "Airport of the Future."

Ten years later, in September 1973, the Newark International Airport—like the Dallas/Fort Worth Regional and the Kansas City International—opened its gates to scores of new passengers and wide-body jets. Three massive multilevel terminals, each branching to three circular satellite structures, provide eighty-three gates for the loading and unloading of the largest aircraft. There are 4,000 feet of terminal building curb frontage, about 3 miles of airside apron, and 15,000 public automobile parking places. There is also an aviation fuel storage farm, with a capacity of 9.6 million gallons.

In redeveloping the airport, there was special care taken that passengers would not be overpowered by its gigantic size nor lose orientation as they moved through the various stages of departure or arrival. Similar consideration was given to the planning of the new network of access and departure roads which take drivers to arrival, departure, or garage levels of the desired terminal buildings, to parking lots, or to operations facilities. Pedestrians are not required to cross any vehicular road. It is remarkable that the complete transformation of the Newark International Airport took place during the lifetime of many of the pioneer aviators who flew their simple aircraft in and out of Newark in the 1920s and 1930s.

Lighting the Airways

One of the most important elements in the expanding aviation business was the lighting of airways. The basic ideas for aerial lighting developed from marine lighting. However, since the navigational problems confronted by oceangoing craft were not precisely analogous to those confronted by aircraft, modifications had to be made.

In the United States, where the differ-

The redeveloped Newark Airport, with three multilevel terminals each extending to three circular satellite structures, opened its gates in 1973.

ences between marine and aerial lighting were quickly recognized, the two systems developed differently. Other countries used virtually the same principles in aerial lighting as they did in marine lighting. Widely spaced lighthouses, having either shielded lights throwing a beam in an approximately vertical line or simple high-powered lights radiating in all directions, were common. Intermediate or emergency landing fields were not provided. The American method of lighting, on the other hand, involved the use of two types of lights—rotating beacons and course lights—as well as intermediate landing fields located at strategic points along the routes.

The earliest standard airway beacon consisted of a single 110-volt, 1,000-watt Mazda lamp set in a 24-inch parabolic reflector. It was numbered and installed at the top of a 51-foot steel tower. The tower was mounted in the center of a concrete slab, approximately 70 feet long and arrow shaped. The arrow, black on the edges and yellow in the center, pointed to the next higher numbered beacon. Each facility produced a beam of 1 million candlepower, which was directed at a point of 1.5 degrees above the horizon and rotated so that it was visible to the pilot at 10-second intervals from a distance of 40 miles.

Two course lights were mounted on the platform of the beacon's tower, pointing forward and backward along the airway in the same direction as the airbeacon's ground arrow. These were 500-watt searchlights that projected a beam of 100,000 candlepower when fitted with either red or green lenses. Every third beacon had green course lights, indicating it was an intermediate landing field. All others had only red. As the beacon mechanism revolved and the clear flash of the beacon passed beyond the pilot's vision, the red or green flash of the course lights came into view. It was the timed regularity of these flashing lights and the distinctiveness and brilliance of the beam that enabled pilots to distinguish them from other competing and stray lights and even pick them out from varied clusters of lights in and around large metropolitan areas.

In 1931 the Aeronautics Branch of the Department of Commerce dispensed with the two course lights and adopted a new standard beacon. It featured a single 1,000-watt incandescent lamp and a double lens system at each end of a 36-inch drum, thus projecting two beams, 180 degrees apart. Each optical system consisted of an inner and outer prismatic lens. The outer lens and one inner lens were clear; the other inner lens was either red or green, depending on the beacon's location on the airway. The beacon, making six revolutions per minute, flashed alternately white and colored every five seconds. The clear lens projected a beam of approximately 1.6 million candlepower, the colored one about 400,000 candlepower. Since these beacons were more powerful than the earlier ones, they were placed 15 rather than 10 miles apart. This system, originally designed for use in the Southwest where commercial current was scarce, eventually became standard for all airways.

An intermediate landing field was a rectangular or triangular space that covered at least fifty acres. At altitudes of less than 4,000 feet, each field had two landing strips between 2,600 and 3,000 feet long and 400 to 600 feet wide. (Above 4,000 feet, runway length could be 3,500 feet.) The two strips formed either an "L" or a "T" or a cross, with the inner angles rounded off to provide additional landing space in the event of strong winds. For easy identification from the air, landing fields were marked at the intersection of the runway centerlines by circles measuring 50 feet in diameter. A central disk 12 feet in diameter was placed inside the circle. From the circle's outer border 40-foot panels ran along the runway centerline to indicate landing directions. The circle, disk, and panels were made of crushed stone, flattened to the field's surface, and painted yellow.

A variety of lights, including the airway beacon, lighted the field and marked its borders. These lights were made of waterproof prismatic globes and fittings, mounted on iron standards that stood 30 inches above the ground, and spaced at 300-foot intervals around the perimeter of the field. Approach lights, installed within the boundary lights at each end of the runway, had a slightly higher wattage and were green rather than clear. All obstructions were lighted by red lights. These landing fields were not owned by the federal government; they were leased from either private owners or municipalities for $400 to $500 a year, because the actual cost of establishing such a field—including surveying, site selection, grading, and lighting—was over $5,000.

The Airways Division installed its first airway light beacon on December 7, 1926, near Moline, Illinois. Six months later, there were 4,000 miles of lighted airways. The records for fiscal year 1929 report 263 intermediate landing fields, 881 revolving light beacons, and 10,000 miles of lighted airways. By 1933 there were 272 intermediate fields, 1,550 beacons, and over 18,000 miles of lighted airways.

During this time, the need to carry mail was the governing factor in determining airway lighting. From 1926 to 1933, the Department of Commerce lighted either airways that had daytime mail flights or those for which the Post Office Department had let a mail contract. Thus, the only lighted routes were airmail routes. In rare instances an airmail contractor might light a route, such as the one from Phoenix to Los Angeles that was lighted by American Airlines. Usually, however, the airlines operated only where the Post Office Department wanted them, since routes were profitable only if the airlines carried mail along them.

Because the United States has such a varied terrain, the problems of building and lighting airways were gigantic. High mountain ranges, low swamplands, dense forests, and rolling prairies often presented extreme difficulties to the airway engineer. Pack mules were used to carry beacons to the top of Sexton Mountain in Oregon; newly constructed cable cars moved equipment up Desert Peak in Arizona; and foundations for beacons were built on piles driven deep through mud and swamp land for the New Orleans-Atlanta airway. Mindful of such instances, the chairman of the aviation law committee of the American Bar Association, once said: "I want the record to show that the airway superintendents who went up there and the construction crews and gangs who went along with them to erect the beacons were the real American heroes."

Emergence of Radio Aids

Lighting the major airways was a great stimulus to the growth of aviation, but it was insufficient to insure and encourage the development of a reliable transport system. In the final analysis, flying a lighted course was a fair-weather activity. If air transport companies were to compete with the established carriers—railroads, steamships, and buses—they had to offer at least the same comfort, regular service, and safety. This they could not do if their services were subject to the vagaries of the weather. Scheduled flying required a two-way communications system as well as a reliable and safe navigation system. To provide such a system, the engineers turned to radio.

In 1927 the Aeronautics Branch assumed control of the transcontinental airway and seventeen radio stations. The stations were equipped with outdated arc transmitters and were capable of only point to point communication. The Aeronautics Branch immediately began replacing these transmitters with radio communication stations capable of ground-to-air communication. By 1930 twenty new standard radio stations were installed along the airways. Each of these stations maintained a 2-kilowatt transmitter for radio-telephone-and-telegraph work as well as two receivers and a 400-watt, crystal-controlled radio telegraph transmitter for point-to-point communication.

During this same period, the Bureau of Standards was developing an airborne receiver. It was to be light in weight, compact in size, easily installed, capable of receiving both radio beacon signals and voice communication, adequately shielded from engine ignition system interference, ruggedly constructed to cope with vibration during flight, and highly sensitive. A set possessing these characteristics was produced in 1928.

The Federal Radio Commission then cleared the way for air transport companies to develop a communications network which supplemented other facilities. By the close of 1929, a number of airlines were maintaining two-way voice communications between planes in flight and their own ground stations. However, it was the four-course radio range, which provided a basic all weather navigation system, that was responsible in large measure for making American air transport second to none. Developed also in the late 1920s, it remained the standard civil air navigation aid on United States airways until after World War II.

A typical four-course range was composed of two ground-based loop antennas set at right angles to each other and a signal-switching arrangement that caused the signals from the two antennas to merge into a steady dash at the zone of equal intensity. A single vertically placed loop radiated energy in a figure-eight pattern; two such loops placed at right angles to each other produced a pair of overlapping figure-eight patterns. One of these figure-eights was keyed to the Morse character "A" (dot-dash), the other to the character "N" (dash-dot). At the four intersections of the two figure-eight patterns, the "A" and "N" signals were of equal length, forming four zones of equal intensity. When the transmission of the "A" and "N" signals was properly timed and had the same tone, they interlocked at the zone of equal intensity. Thus, within that zone, neither letter could be distinguished from the other and all that could be heard was a monotone signal or continuous dash. This was the on-course signal.

A pilot flying the range in an aircraft equipped with a simple receiver and a non-directional antenna could follow the on-course signal by listening for the steady hum. If he drifted to one side or the other, the "A" or "N" signal would become audible, warning him to correct his course. Beacons with a range of 100 miles were spaced 200 miles apart so that when a pilot reached the limit of one, he turned his receiver to the next station 100 miles ahead on his course. Unitl the late 1930s, the on-course signal was interrupted every twenty-four minutes for station identification and every fifteen minutes for regular weather reports. With this radio beacon, aircraft could navigate in nearly all weather and without visual contact with the ground.

Airport Pavements

The past fifty years of air transport development are best reflected in the changes in airport landing strips. As aircraft became larger and faster, landing strips of necessity became heavier and longer. By the early 1930s, a freshly mowed swath in an alfalfa field or a 1,500-foot stretch of compacted cinders or gravel was already inadequate. Thus, when the first portland cement concrete pavement was completed in 1928 at the Ford Airport in Dearborn, Michigan, it was considered a turning point in airport construction and improvement.

Dearborn airport officials wanted a smooth uniform surface for their heavier planes. They complained that, although the airfield was well-drained and covered with good-quality turf, during the winter months the turf was either frozen or soggy. The first portland cement concrete pavement, which was 2,653 feet long and 7 inches thick with steel wire mesh reinforcement, provided a suitable surface for Ford planes weighing 10,000 pounds. Airport officials reported that with this pavement "the expense of keeping the surface of the field smooth" was lessened and that takeoffs on "the smooth uniform surface" were "always positive."

During the following year, many other airport runways were paved with concrete. Among them were those at the Grand Central Airport in Glendale, California; at Lunken Field in Cincinnati, Ohio; and at Bowman Field in Louisville, Kentucky. Runway pavement thicknesses were usually between 6 and 8 inches with various types of subgrades. In each instance, design followed established highway practices for both bituminous and portland cement concrete pavement. These design programs proved satisfactory until the 140,000-pound B-29 superfortress was developed during World War II.

The air force was then faced with the formidable task of rebuilding almost all existing airport runways in order to meet load requirements that were without precedent. The need for this was vividly illustrated when the first newly assembled long-range bomber, the XB-19, broke through the apron at Clover Field in Santa Monica, California. Takeoff was delayed for two months while a 9-inch portland cement concrete pavement was hastily constructed. Even though the plane was lightly loaded, the weather dry, and the groundwater low, when the plane finally flew from the runway, stress was still evident in the pavement and aprons. This event triggered an extensive search by the Army Corps of Engineers for a method of designing and constructing runways for these high loads.

Many pavement theories and formulas were available, but there were no easy solutions. Since no two airports were exactly alike, numerous factors had to be taken into consideration: size and distribution of the load; thickness of the pavement, base, and subbase; climatic conditions; basic soil characteristics; drainage; position of the water table; and so on. Finally the Corps of Engineers adopted the California Bearing Ratio (CBR) method of design for airport runway construction and improvement. While this method was based on empirical relationships, it proved generally practical for the rush program.

However, public works engineers continued to be challenged by the advent of larger aircraft. In the 1950s and 1960s, with the production of the B-36 long-range bombers, the B-707s, and the DC-8s—each weighing over 300,000 pounds—airport designers were forced to direct their attention once again to landing strips. To insure smoothness and durability, strips had to be redesigned and constructed for heavier loads. With the introduction of the 700,000-pound B-747s in the 1970s, some of the most recent airport pavements have been redesigned to accommodate ultimate loads of 2 million pounds.

Many airport officials used overlays to strengthen airport runways. Although it was difficult to evaluate existing pavement capabilities, a combination of elastic theory, load deflection measurements, and sound engineering judgment generally produced good results. At Salt Lake City, for instance, a 6-inch overlay of asphaltic concrete was laid in order to handle B-727 planes. In Palmdale, California, between 7 and 16 inches of reinforced concrete overlaying an existing 12-inch concrete pavement was used to provide for planes weighing a million pounds.

Throughout the 1960s and early 1970s, numerous innovations were made in pavement design and construction methods. In Newark, for example, the marsh land upon which the city's airport is located was loaded with 20 feet of sand for over two years to squeeze out the water and consolidate the muck. The sand was then mixed with fly ash, lime, and portland cement; compacted into a 30-inch maximum thickness pavement in 8-inch layers; and topped with a 4-inch asphalt concrete surfacing. This resulted in pavement that cost about half that of most other pavements and that could support a 700,000-pound plane. At the Dallas/Fort Worth Regional Airport, the pavement is composed of 18 inches of well-compacted, lime-stabilized clay and is covered with an asphalt emulsion seal, 9 inches of soil-cement compacted subbase, and 16 to 21 inches of portland cement concrete. Stronger, smoother, and more economical pavements are now being made through the use of slip-form paving with very low slump concrete.

Air Traffic Control

Shortly after World War I, when the federal government put its surplus military aircraft on the market at bargain prices, the chances of air collisions increased dramatically. The United States and other industrial countries expressed concern and, in 1919, created the International Commission for Air Navigation to develop general rules for air traffic. Among the regulations agreed upon were these elementary rules: "Every aircraft in a cloud, fog, mist or other condition of bad visibility shall proceed with caution, having given careful regard to the existing circumstances." The "risk of collision," the commission counseled, is determined by "carefully watching the compass bearing and angle of elevation of an approaching craft"; if neither changes "such risk shall be deemed to exist."

These rules were appropriate for the days of the uncrowded sky, but they were inadequate for the jet age. Their purpose, however, was similar to today's complex and sophisticated air traffic control system. In general they sought to prevent aircraft collisions, either with other aircraft or with ground objects; to provide for a fast, safe, and orderly flow of air traffic; and to make available advice and information useful in the planning and execu-

Federal Aviation Administration

The nation's first control tower to be equipped with ground-to-air radio transmitters and receivers was at Cleveland, Ohio, in 1930.

tion of flights.

Traffic rules for civil aircraft did not exist in the United States until the establishment of the Aeronautics Branch. The 1926 Air Commerce Act required the secretary of commerce to "establish air traffic rules for navigation, protection and identification of aircraft, including rules as to safe altitudes of flight and rules for the prevention of collisions." Once completed, these traffic rules were a distinct improvement over the rudimentary rules of the International Commission for Air Regulation. Yet, even though the federal government laid down air traffic rules, it by no means controlled traffic. What control did exist took the form of directing airplane traffic on the ground and was exercised either by state or local governments, airport operators, or in rare cases by airline operators. No one assumed control over en route traffic.

During the 1920s, terminal traffic control consisted of flagmen, stationed on the ground, who supervised aircraft takeoffs and landings. These flagmen were gradually moved into towers that overlooked the landing field. Then, in 1930, the City of Cleveland took a major step forward by equipping its control tower with ground-to-air radio transmitters and receivers. Within five years, twenty major United States cities had followed Cleveland's lead. The first air traffic control facilities at terminal areas were financed and operated by local or private capital.

En route air traffic control facilities were also begun by local or private initiative. By 1935 en route traffic conditions had become particularly hazardous near busy terminal areas when aircraft on the same or converging airways were navigating in the clouds by radio. A test pilot for a major airline described the situation at Chicago and Newark: "We have planes coming in . . . from different directions at about the same time. They are coming in on the radio beams with no visibility, so that it is of great importance that each of those airplanes know where the other man is and know exactly where he is going to stay and know the order in which they would come in and land." Yet no one was responsible for separating these aircraft either horizontally or vertically; no one saw to it that aircraft proceeded in an orderly sequence on arrival at an airport.

Airline operators and Bureau of Air Commerce officials discussed these conditions during a three-day conference in Washington, D.C., in November 1935. The operators asked the bureau to assume responsibility for controlling en route traffic. Federal officials said they recognized the seriousness of the situation but argued that they had neither the people nor the money to assume control.

The bureau proposed that the airlines establish and operate air route traffic control stations until such time as the bureau could secure the funds necessary to assume the responsibility. Beginning in December 1924, a consortium of airline operators established three airway traffic control stations (later called air route traffic control centers) in Newark, Chicago, and Cleveland. Then, in July 1936, the Bureau of Air Commerce took these centers into the federal airways system. By the end of the year, the bureau had established two more centers in Detroit and Pittsburgh; and by the end of the decade, another six had been commissioned in Los Angeles, Washington, Oakland, Fort Worth, Salt Lake City, St. Louis, and Atlanta.

Compared to standards of the 1970s, the en route air traffic control procedures of the 1930s were crude. Unlike today, controllers did not communicate directly with pilots. Instead, they received reports from airline dispatchers, airport officials in control towers,

The traffic control room at Newark Airport in the 1930s.

and Bureau of Air Commerce radio station operators, who had voice contact with the pilots. The controller would coordinate the information received from all sources and issue any instructions necessary to bring about a smooth flow of traffic. Again, the controller's instructions would be relayed to the pilot via airline radio stations, government stations, or airport control towers.

The jurisdiction of airport control towers varied. There were no set boundaries in which a tower's authority was always exercised. Rather, as conditions of visibility decreased or ceilings lowered, the radius of a tower's control was reduced and the authority of an air route center was expanded. Under minimum visibility conditions, a center might control a flight until the aircraft broke from underneath the overcast or until it reached the airport boundary in a landing attitude. In short, a tower controlled an aircraft only as far as the tower operator could see it or as far as the pilot could see the airport. The remainder of the flight was under control of the air route center.

At first, air traffic control centers were served only by telephone circuits. As traffic mounted, a communications system that could handle more messages became necessary. The one teletype network that existed (known as the "black" or meteorological net) was overburdened. There were periods as long as three hours when this network transmitted only weather information. Thus, beginning in 1937, a "white" net was established for the

exclusive use of air traffic control. This was later supplemented by leased interphone circuits connecting centers with remote locations. By 1944 there were 40,000 miles of interphone circuits and nearly 25,000 miles of teletype circuits used for air traffic control.

It was not until the eve of the United States' entry into World War II that the Department of Commerce took control of terminal air traffic. The unevenness of control tower performance from city to city was a subject of considerable concern. Some cities certificated controller personnel, others did not. Some required high standards, others had virtually none. This situation, plus the need for close interlock between en route and terminal control, prompted municipalities, airlines, and some federal agencies to urge the Department of Commerce to supervise tower control. Nevertheless, when the federal takeover did come, it came not as a way to improve the flow of commercial traffic but as a wartime measure.

Dissatisfied with the lack of uniform service provided by the various municipalities and disturbed by what this might mean in an emergency, the military services insisted that the federal government become involved in terminal control. Persuaded of the necessity, Congress provided in the Supplemental National Defense Appropriation Act of August 25, 1941, that either the secretary of war or the secretary of the navy could certify airports as essential to national defense, whereupon CAA would operate the towers at these airports. One million dollars was appropriated for this purpose. Accordingly, on October 17, 1941, the secretary of war certificated a list of airports as essential to national defense. By the middle of the following month, eight airport control towers were under CAA's supervision. At the height of the war, CAA operated 104 towers.

A small number of these towers were returned to their original operators both during and after the war. The majority, however, remained permanently under federal control. By the end of the first peacetime year, CAA operated 115 airport traffic control towers and 29 air route traffic control centers. The towers counted about 12 million aircraft operations, while the centers handled 8.8 million aircraft flying under instrument flight rules. By 1945 air traffic control had become the agency's largest single program.

Introduction of Radar

Radar (an acronym for radio detection and ranging) was patented in 1904 by a German engineer, who was looking for a way to detect radio waves from ships. It was later offered to the German navy but refused since it had a range of only 1 mile. No one took the invention seriously until 1922 when the United States Naval Research Laboratory set up a detection experiment using a five-meter, continuous-wave radar with a separate receiver and transmitter. During the testing, navy scientists detected a wooden ship passing between the receiver and transmitter.

Federal Aviation Administration

The Instrument Flight Rules Room at Washington, D.C.'s National Airport illustrates the complexity of traffic control procedures of the 1970s.

Eight years later, a researcher working on direction-finding equipment noticed that the received signal changed whenever an airplane passed between the receiver and the transmitter. The Naval Research Laboratory pursued this lead, and by 1932 it could detect aircraft as far away as 50 miles. Although the continuous-wave radar could discover a plane or target, it could not determine its location or distance from either the receiver or the transmitter. By changing to a non-continuous or pulsed system, a more workable radar was produced. In 1936 a detection ranging apparatus was created; and by 1938 the first anti-aircraft, fire-control radar was placed in operation.

One of the major factors contributing to the success of the Allied Powers in World War II was their superior radar systems. With the development of the magnetron (capable of producing 20,000 watts of power) in England in 1939, the Allies could pinpoint an object with a radar beam. Modern radar was, in fact, born with this invention.

At the end of the war, scientists began looking for ways to adapt radar to civil aviation. Development work commenced in 1945 at CAA's Indianapolis Experimental Station with equipment supplied by the armed forces. One year later, in May 1946, the first radar-equipped control tower for civilian aircraft was unveiled at the Indianapolis airport. By modifying the basic devices developed for the armed services, CAA and aviation industry engineers improved the equipment to include such items as moving target indication and more sensitive search antenna.

Two types of radar facilities were installed in terminal areas from the very first—airport surveillance radar (ASR) and precision approach radar (PAR). The PAR provided one more method, along with the widely used instrument landing system (ILS) and the standard instrument approach, for directing landings during low ceiling and poor visibility conditions. As an aircraft approached a runway, PAR monitored its progress and relayed its range, azimuth, and elevation to the controller. Using this information, the controller would "talk" the pilot down to a landing.

Whereas PAR scanned only the approach area leading to an instrument runway, ASR scanned an entire terminal area. When a radar pulse struck an aircraft, it was reflected back to a receiver and appeared as a pip of light on a radar scope. With each sweep of the rotating antenna, a new picture appeared on the scope's face. Thus, air traffic controllers observing the scope had a continuous picture of all aircraft traffic within their control area.

Progress in equipping the airways with radar facilities was painfully slow. Wartime radar, which was not altogether suited for civil uses, had to be perfected before CAA could confidently order it in large quantity. And funds were not readily available. By

1950 only three ASRs and three PARs were in use in the entire airways system. In 1952 there were only ten ASRs. But beginning in 1953. ASR installation began to accelerate; and by the end of 1960, more than fifty terminal areas were equipped with this facility.

Every society has modes of transportation upon which it depends. During the past fifty years, air transportation has assumed such a position in American society. Americans have become as dependent on airplanes as they have on automobiles, telephones, and televisions, for to a greater or lesser degree, all of these inventions make possible the rapid exchange of information, goods, and services. Wedded to the concepts of fast communication, easy access, and widespread distribution, the United States has become a nation of airplanes and airports. Without them, American society could hardly exist as it does.

SUGGESTED READINGS

Briddon, Arnold E.; Champie, Ellmore A.; and Marraine, Peter A. *FAA Historical Fact Book: A Chronology, 1926-1971*. Washington, D.C., 1974.

Champie, Ellmore A. *The Federal Turnaround on Aid to Airports, 1926-1938*. Washington, D.C., 1973.

Cohen, Stanley. "Dallas/Fort Worth to Open World's Largest Airport This Month." *Consulting Engineer*, 41 (September 1973), 72-81.

Condit, Carl W. *Chicago, 1930-1970: Building, Planning, and Urban Technology*. Chicago, 1974.

Dellinger, J. H., and Pratt, Haraden. "Development of Radio Aids to Air Navigation." *Proceedings of the Institute of Radio Engineers*, 16 (July 1928), 890-920.

Gilbert, Glen A. *Air Traffic Control*. New York, 1945.

Jackson, William E., ed. *The Federal Airways System*. Washington, 1970.

Kelly, Charles J. *The Sky's the Limit: The History of the Airlines*. New York, 1963.

Komons, Nick A. *The Cutting Air Crash: A Case Study in Early Federal Aviation Policy*. Washington, D.C., 1973.

Paradis, Adrian A. *Two Hundred Million Miles a Day*. Philadelphia, 1969.

Pratt, Haraden, and Diamond, Harry. "Receiving Sets for Aircraft Beacon and Telephony." *Bureau of Standards Journal of Research*, 1 (October 1928), 543-563.

Radio Technical Commission for Aeronautics. *The Air Traffic Story*. Washington, D.C., 1952.

Redford, Emmette S. *Congress Passes the Federal Aviation Act of 1958*. No. 62 of Inter-University Cases in Public Administration and Policy Formulation. University, Alabama, 1961.

Roberts, Henry W. "Radio Developments of the Bureau of Air Commerce." *Aero Digest*, 31 (December 1937), 34-37, 94.

Roose, R. S. "Airway Traffic Control." *Journal of Air Law*, 9 (April 1938), 271-274.

Schwartz, Adele C. "Airports—Patterns of Progress: Dallas/Ft. Worth." *Airline Management* (April 1971), 30-31.

Smith, Henry Ladd. *Airways: The History of Commercial Aviation in the United States*. New York, 1942.

Ward, Earl F. "Airway Traffic Control." *Air Commerce Bulletin*, 9 (October 15, 1937), 73-77.

Whitnah, Donald R. *Safer Skyways: Federal Control of Aviation, 1926-1966*. Ames, Iowa, 1966.

CHAPTER 8

COMMUNITY WATER SUPPLY

The development of clean, palatable community water supplies was vital to the growth of American civilization. In the past two centuries, cities and towns have built facilities that provide potable and wholesome water to about 80 percent of the United States' population. Thus, the public wells of the colonial era have evolved into sophisticated public works systems comprising collection works that tap surface water and ground-water supplies, plants that treat and purify raw water, transmission conduits that convey it to cities, and networks of distribution mains that transmit this precious resource to domestic and industrial consumers.

Early Water Supply

Before the American Revolution, colonial cities obtained water from nearby streams, wells, and springs. However, these sources became overtaxed and contaminated as urban populations grew. Concern for public health and ever-present fire dangers prompted city officials to look beyond local sources for water supply. Water was sought from outlying rivers and lakes, impounded in reservoirs, and distributed through citywide pipe networks. These first attempts were beset with technical problems, financial difficulties, and

political bickering. Nevertheless, by the 1840s, the development of publicly owned water systems was firmly established in the United States.

The first American municipal water works was built in 1754 by Hans Christopher Christiansen for the Moravian settlement of Bethlehem, Pennsylvania. Spring water was forced by a pump through bored hemlock logs into a wooden reservoir that provided the town with a plentiful water supply. Philadelphia, however, was the first large city to complete a water works and municipal distribution system. The city was endowed with one of the most wholesome and abundant water supplies in the American colonies. The first two wells were sunk before 1682; and by the early eighteenth century, the town was dotted with wells and pumps located on private properties or in the streets. Persons who built wells charged for their use and leased the site from the city for twenty-one years for a twenty-one shilling annual fee. In 1744 a visitor to Philadelphia reported there was "plenty of excellent water in this city, there being a pump at almost every fifty paces" in the streets. Good drinking water was also obtained from the adjacent Delaware River. In the mid 1750s, the city began purchasing private pumps and assessing fixed charges to residents who drew water from the city wells. By 1771 Philadelphia had 498 pumps, 120 of which were publicly owned.

Portions of this chapter are based on a manuscript prepared by the American Water Works Association.

A series of yellow fever epidemics in the 1790s prompted city officials to consider developing an outside water supply to end reliance on contaminated public wells. In 1798, during the midst of a devastating outbreak of the disease (which they erroneously believed to be waterborne), the common council retained Benjamin Latrobe to conduct a survey and prepare recommendations for a city water system. The engineer proposed installing two huge steam engines to pump water from the Schuylkill River to a reservoir on the site of Philadelphia's present City Hall. The water would be conveyed to consumers by 4½-inch inside diameter log water mains. The plan was accepted and work commenced on the two pumping stations and the pipe grid in March 1799. The system was dedicated in January 1801 and marked the first use of large steam engines for municipal water conveyance.

APWA Delaware Valley Chapter

Philadelphia's Centre Square Engine House marked the first use of large steam engines for water conveyance.

The Lower Engine House drew water from the river and pumped it over a half mile through a 6-foot diameter brick tunnel to the Centre Square Engine House. At this point, the water was lifted to two wooden tanks with a total capacity of 20,000 gallons. The Centre Square water works was a beautiful classical revival building that housed the company offices, steam engine, pump, and reservoir tanks. The grounds were attractively laid out and adorned with a fountain.

Unfortunately, this pioneer public works enterprise was a dismal failure. The enterprise operated at a loss, and the equipment could not keep pace with Philadelphia's growing population. Laying the wooden conduits was expensive, and the bored logs constantly sprung leaks that taxed available supplies. The steam engines were primitive. They frequently broke down and consumed huge quantities of coal. Furthermore, the city was unable to develop an efficient system for collecting water fees. In 1815 a new pumping engine and two reservoirs were built on the Schuylkill at Fairmount Hill north of the city. Despite its greater capacity, the new steam engine blew up twice—in 1818 and 1821—and as its predecessors burned coal voraciously.

In 1818 the city authorized $70,000 for 2 miles of 20- and 22-inch iron pipe to replace unreliable wooden mains. This installation marked the first extensive municipal utilization of cast iron pipe in the United States. By 1820 Philadelphia was disillusioned with steam engines and investigated alternative power sources. A dam was eventually built across the Schuylkill at Fairmount that supplied water to a mill race and water wheels that pumped water to the distribution reservoirs. The new system began operations in July 1822; and the following October, the troublesome steam engines were shut down. The total cost of the improvements was $426,000. For the first time, Philadelphia possessed a reliable system that met immediate needs and offered a comfortable margin for expansion. When the three waterwheels began operating, the Fairmount Water Works served 4,800 customers who daily consumed 1.6 million gallons. Fifteen years later, six wheels and pumps supplied 3.1 million gallons per day to 19,600 users. By 1840 Philadelphia had the best water system in the nation, and a water official justifiably claimed that the city was "not excelled by any in the world in the cheap and abundant supply of pure and wholesome water we now enjoy."

The townsite for Boston was primarily chosen because of available spring water. These natural supplies initially met most of the settlers needs, but by 1640 private wells were sunk after permission was obtained from the town's selectmen. A private Water-Works Company was chartered by the Massachusetts General Court in 1652. The proprietors built a 12-foot-square reservoir filled with spring water by log pipes. The project was abandoned after a few years of operation. By the eighteenth century, the town was abundantly supplied with water and residents reimbursed well owners for their use and maintenance. A few publicly financed wells were dug to supply the poor and provide for fire protection.

In June 1795, a group of investors obtained a charter from the Massachusetts legislature to found a water company. The Aqueduct Corporation was authorized to pipe water 4 miles from Jamaica Pond in Roxbury to Boston. The company was required to repair streets torn up during main construction and to provide free water to Boston and Roxbury for fire protection. The project got underway in November 1795 and began supplying customers in 1798. A bored-log aqueduct conveyed the water to a distributing reservoir in Boston. By 1817, 40 miles of pine water mains served about 800 families that paid a $10 annual utility fee. The city's principal source of water, however, continued to be 2,800 wells that had been dug in the city.

Boston began seriously considering the development of additional supplies after an 1825 fire destroyed over fifty houses and stores. Several good sources were near the city at Spot Pond, Long Pond, and the Charles River. However, over twenty years of clamourous debate occurred before a new supply was obtained. Proponents of the publicly owned Long Pond plan were opposed in the city council by a Spot Pond faction that supported private ownership. The tide of opinion turned in favor of the public plan when a report commissioned by the city and prepared by John B. Jervis, chief engineer on New York City's Croton project, revealed that Spot Pond was inadequate to meet municipal needs. After a state charter was granted, voters approved the Long Pond project by an overwhelming majority in April 1846.

The Cochituate Aqueduct was a notable antebellum engineering achievement. It extended 14 miles from Lake Cochituate to a

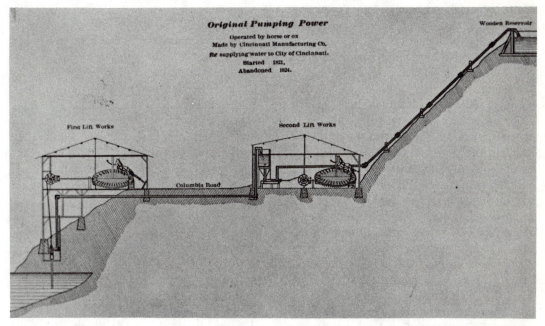

Original Pumping Power
Operated by horse or ox
Made by Cincinnati Manufacturing Co.
for supplying water to City of Cincinnati.
Started 1821.
Abandoned 1824.

Wooden Reservoir

First Lift Works

Second Lift Works

Columbia Road

Public Works Historical Society

Horse-driven pumps drew water from the Ohio River for Cincinnati's first water supply system.

receiving reservoir at Brookline. The eliptical conduit was constructed of masonry and was 6 feet high. Cut-and-cover construction was used along most of its course, however, iron pipes conveyed water over an arched bridge at the Charles River crossing. The masonry reservoir at Brookline held 100 million gallons and served two distributing reservoirs; one on Beacon Hill the other on Telegraph Hill in South Boston. Sixty miles of iron water mains were laid in the city to distribute the new and abundant water supply. The public works project cost about $4 million. On October 25, 1848, the citizens of Boston celebrated the project's completion with a water festival.

Cincinnati was the first western city to install a citywide water system. In 1817 the city council granted the Cincinnati Manufacturing Company a ninety-nine year monopoly for the exclusive right to construct a water works and lay mains within the city. The firm paid a $100 annual fee for its privileges and promised to complete the job in two years. The deadline was later extended and construction commenced in 1819. Water was initially drawn from the river by horse-driven pumps; but by the mid 1820s, a forty horsepower steam engine was lifting water 150 feet to a 200,000-gallon wooden reservoir that served 254 commercial and home users. Water was distributed through 5 miles of oak pipes connected with iron joints.

The company was a successful commercial enterprise. It showed profits of $1,600 in 1824 and two years later netted $2,900. However, after it was later sold to the private Cincinnati Water Company it encountered financial reversals. The system was costly to maintain; the log pipes leaked excessively and created "great sinkholes in the streets." System losses resulted in an incredible daily use of 360 gallons per family. As service declined, the water system became the center of a debate over private versus public ownership. A government committee, after assessing the problem, maintained that the water works "should be directed more to the public interest than to individual emolument." Defenders of private ownership were equally outspoken. The editor of a local newspaper warned that "public ownership would be a sink of corruption" because the "patronage of the council would be so much augmented that it would lead to endless contests and appointments." Proponents of private ownership prevailed until the city purchased the water company for $30,000 in 1839. Cincinnati later replaced most of the oak pipes with cast iron mains that provided exemplary service.

Wells were first sunk on Manhattan Island in the 1660s, and by 1696 sixteen wells had been built with public and private funds. These public supplies were supervised and maintained by a member of each ward who was compensated by the city. By the 1720s, the city abandoned its policy of well construction and allowed residents in each neighborhood to dig wells in public streets with the approval of the mayor and aldermen. Water was drawn from these first New York wells with either ropes and buckets or balance poles, but in 1741 a law was passed that required aldermen to install pumps at the expense of users. The water drawn from the wells was so brackish and foul tasting that drinking water was acquired by "tea-water men" at outlying springs and sold to residents. In 1753 the city began repairing and maintaining its water supply by an annual tax on residents and subsequently sank several new wells at public expense.

In 1774 Christopher Colles, an English engineer, convinced officials to build a public water works and citywide distribution system. Colles constructed a 20,000-gallon covered wooden reservoir fed by a steam engine that pumped well water. The water was to be distributed through a 13-mile grid of pine log pipes jointed with iron fittings. The undertaking cost the city 3,600 pounds and was complete except for the pipe system when it was abandoned at the outbreak of the American Revolution.

After the Revolution, many plans were submitted to the common council by private individuals who wished to supply the city with water. In 1799 the privately owned Manhattan Company obtained a state charter to provide water to the city, but its principal accomplishment was one large well 25 feet in diameter that fed a small distribution tank. Following the failure of the Manhattan Company, several proposals were offered for bringing the water of the Bronx River and other rivers into the city, but legal and political complications prevented easy solutions. Public ownership drew opposition, and various plans became embroiled in partisan politics. In the meantime, the city's water problems became acute. A cholera epidemic that claimed 3,500 lives in 1832 was largely attributed to polluted city wells. In 1835 a ruinous fire swept through the business district because there was not ample water to extinguish the blaze.

DeWitt Clinton presented a report in 1832 which led to the construction of the historic Croton Aqueduct. He advocated obtaining water from the Croton River in the highlands 30 miles north of the city. The enabling legislation for the publicly financed project was passed by the state legislature in May 1834, and a year later the electorate approved the bond issue by a three to one margin. Work began in 1837, and commissioners in charge of the project encountered the same problems occasionally experienced on modern public works undertakings. Additional funding had to be periodically sought, property owners refused to sell their land along the route, the courts acted slow in condemnation cases, and friction developed between the commissioners, designer, and chief engineer. David B. Douglass, a former army engineer, initially supervised the project, but he was replaced by John B. Jervis who completed the undertaking.

Croton Dam, a masonry structure 270 feet long and 50 feet high, was built 6 miles above the confluence of the Croton and Hudson rivers, forming the 5-mile-long Fountain Reservoir. In January 1841, the dam was overtopped as a result of an unusually heavy rainfall, and the earthen abutments washed out. It was reconstructed with triple the original spillway capacity. From the dam, the aqueduct paralleled the Croton River to the east bank of the Hudson River which it followed south to Yonkers, 33 miles from the dam. The aqueduct then followed a valley for 7 miles, crossed the Harlem River, and terminated at the 35-acre Central Park Reservoir that held 180 million gallons. This impound-

ment facility fed a 20-million-gallon distributing reservoir at Murray Hill, the present location of the New York Public Library. The masonry reservoir was built almost entirely above ground, and a staircase leading to the top provided New Yorkers a view of the aqueduct and a panorama of the city.

APWA New York-New Jersey Metropolitan Chapter

A high-arch bridge carried New York's Croton Aqueduct across the Harlem River to the Central Park Reservoir.

Constructing the aqueduct was a difficult feat. The terrain was characterized by ridges and deep ravines that necessitated excavation and tunnelling to maintain a uniform grade. Sixteen tunnels of varying lengths lined the aqueduct's course. Aqueduct bridges were built over streams, roads, and deep ravines. The eliptical conduit was constructed of dressed stone, brick, and cement, and its inside dimensions were $8^1/_2$ by $7^1/_2$ feet. An underground network of cast iron pipes branched out from the distributing reservoir, conveying water throughout the city.

Crossing the Harlem River was a complex engineering problem. The first design called for taking the water pipe across the river by cast iron pipe laid on a masonry bridge 50 feet above the river. But the state legislature decreed that either a submarine tunnel or a high-arch bridge should be built for the aqueduct. The city chose the latter alternative, and the masonry bridge consisted of fifteen arches that crowned 100 feet above the river's surface. The original estimate for the Croton system was $5 million, but the final cost was $13 million. Funding was extremely difficult because the aqueduct was built during the depression following the Panic of 1837.

New Yorkers celebrated the opening of the Croton Aqueduct in 1842. Brief ceremonies were held in June and July, but October 14 was set aside for a special festival. The day opened with cannon and church bell salutes. Spectators later lined streets, windows, and balconies to view a parade of brightly costumed military companies, fire brigades, temperance societies, and other organizations. In the evening, the festivities continued at public gardens, theaters, and fountains.

Water for Urban America

The public works engineers and city officials who supervised construction of the first municipal water systems believed their cities had ample supplies to last for decades. However, they could not foresee the burgeoning growth of America's cities that took place after the Civil War. To keep pace with increasing demands, cities made large expenditures for monumental public water systems. The quest for new supplies required creation of new governmental agencies, a rapid expansion of water technology, and cooperative efforts by cities, states, and the federal government.

The builders of the Croton Aqueduct assumed it would meet New York's water requirements for at least thirty years, but by the Civil War modifications were required. The masonry aqueduct had a potential daily capacity of 90 million gallons, but its effective capacity was only 42 million gallons because of the small diameter of the iron pipes that conveyed the water across the Harlem River. To remedy this shortcoming, the original 36-inch pipes were replaced by 90-inch conduits 'hat increased daily capacity to 72 million

gallons. In 1862 a billion gallon reservoir was completed in Central Park to receive and impound the greater volume.

By the early 1880s, the city was in the midst of a water crisis caused by increased population, leaks in the distribution system, and a rise in per capita withdrawals. The capacity of the Croton Aqueduct was exceeded, but reserve supplies existed in the Croton Watershed. After state legislative authorization was granted in 1883, construction commenced on the New Croton Aqueduct in 1885. The conduit increased daily capacity to 300,000 gallons and was completed in 1893. The Croton system was enlarged further by building several storage reservoirs in the watershed and constructing New Croton Dam 3 miles below the old one. The 1,600-foot-long, 235-foot-high structure was the highest masonry dam in the world at its completion in 1906. Unlike the original aqueduct, the new line was laid for most if its 33-mile length through a brick-lined tunnel. The 12-foot conduit fed several 48-inch iron mains that filled the Central Park Reservoir and a new reservoir at Jerome Park that was put into service in 1906.

Despite the new capacity, the race between supply and consumption continued. In 1898 the five boroughs of the Bronx, New York, Brooklyn, Queens, and Richmond were consolidated. The reorganization immediately confronted city authorities with supplying water to almost 3.5 million people who used nearly 370 million gallons per day. The Croton system, the sole source for Manhattan and a portion of the Bronx, had reached the limit of practical development. A much smaller water system, that obtained supplies from wells and Long Island streams, was inadequate in quantity and polluted .by the area's growing population and commercial development.

In 1899 a private company sought an exclusive forty-year contract to supply New York with 200 million gallons per day from the Ramapo River and the Catskill Mountains. The dubious features of this proposal were revealed in a city-sponsored study by John R. Freeman, an outstanding consulting engineer. His report revealed that 500 million gallons per day were needed and recommended that the city immediately develop its own supply. New York's Merchants Association, after studying the engineering, legal, and financial aspects of the problem, also condemned the private company's proposal. After several years of legal and political wrangling, the state constitution was amended to place capital expenditures for water supply outside the municipal debt limit. A 1905 law created the New York Board of Water Supply to oversee the city's water development. Simultaneously, the legislature founded the State Water Supply Commission that was given jurisdiction over the allocation of water supply resources in the state.

With the institutional entities in place, New York was ready to reach out for a new source of water. After reviewing findings of a special engineering study, the water board decided to tap the Catskill Watershed 100 miles to the north. The first stage of construction commenced in 1907 and was completed ten years later. Its principal features included building Ashokan Reservoir to store the water of Esopus Creek, that drained the southern slope of the Catskill Mountains. Water was conveyed to the city by the 92-mile-long Catskill Aqueduct, consisting of cut-and-cover conduits, steel-pipe inverted siphons, and pressure tunnels. After passing through a deep rock tunnel 1,000 feet beneath the Hudson River, the aqueduct fed the Kensico and Hill View storage reservoirs north of the city. Water entered New York through the City Tunnel No. 1 and large branch lines that served each of the five boroughs and the Silver Lake Terminal Reservoir in Richmond. This stage was finished in 1917, just in time to avert a serious water shortage.

The second stage expanded the system northward to the waters of Schoharie Creek. There, Gilboa Dam was built to create Schoharie Reservoir. The reservoir was joined to the Ashokan Reservoir by the 18-mile-long Shandaken Tunnel. This project, that was begun in 1917 and finished in 1927, raised New York's daily water supply to 525 million gallons. The Catskill water supply system was an outstanding engineering achievement that established modern water supply development and distribution practices. Because of its

landmark significance, descriptions of some of its principal features follow.

The 130-billion-gallon Ashokan Reservoir is 12 miles long and has an average depth of 50 feet. During construction the bottom and slopes of the basin were cleared of trees, brush, and debris. To control adjacent sources of pollution, the city acquired a wide strip of land around the shoreline. The reservoir was divided into two basins to provide greater operating flexibility. Since water quality seasonally varies, gate houses can divert water to the aqueduct from different reservoir depths. Leaving the reservoir, the water is screened, chlorinated, and aerated. The 1,600 nozzles in the aerator basin neutralize organic contaminants and improve water taste.

The aerator basin below Ashokan Reservoir restores depleted oxygen to New York's water supply which neutralizes organic contaminants.

Unlike Schoharie Reservoir, which was formed by a single dam across a deep, narrow valley, Ashokan was created by the Olive Bridge Dam and a series of earthen dikes that closed gaps in adjacent hills. The 4,650-foot-long dam consists of a 1,000-foot masonry portion flanked at both ends by earth embankments or dikes with concrete core walls.

The rugged and diversified topography traversed by the Catskill Aqueduct required several types of construction, including cut-and-cover, gravity and pressure tunnels, and steel-pipe siphons. When topography permitted, the less expensive, cut-and-cover method was used. This process consisted of excavating a trench or building an embankment to maintain grade. A concrete floor was laid, and concrete was placed between steel forms to create the side walls and arch of the horseshoe-shaped conduits. Where hills and mountains were encountered, tunnels were driven through the rock and lined with concrete. In these tunnels, the water flowed by gravity, but wide valleys presented special engineering problems. Since aqueduct bridges were prohibitively expensive, inverted siphons of steel pipe and pressure tunnels were built.

The Kensico Reservoir in Westchester County, New York, 30 miles north of Manhattan, was designed to provide the city a two-month reserve water supply. It has a 350-billion-gallon capacity and is formed by a dam across the Bronx River. The Kensico Dam is built of cyclopean masonry, and it is faced with concrete blocks on its upstream side and granite masonry on its downstream side. The great size of this dam and its location near a large population center prompted builders to make it architecturally attractive.

Water is conveyed through the City Tunnels No. 1 and 2, 40 miles of deep rock tunnels 200 to 780 feet beneath the Bronx, Manhattan, Queens, and Brooklyn, that feed large cast iron transmission lines. The former was put into service in January 1917, the latter was completed in 1936. Both tunnels are lined with concrete and are similar in design to pressure tunnels of the Catskill Aqueduct. Water is raised to the street mains by risers, smaller cement-lined steel pipes that extend vertically through thirty-seven shafts sunk throughout the city. Each tunnel is divided by section valves, and drainage shafts and pumping equipment were installed so that tunnel sections can be isolated for inspection and repairs.

New York recently began building a third city tunnel that will be completed in four suc-cessive stages. The first stage is under construction and consists of 13.7 miles of 20- to 24-foot diameter deep rock tunnels. Three major construction shafts and fifteen supply shafts were sunk along the route. The new tunnel will provide additional delivery capacity and augment existing feeders that are aging, overburdened, and experiencing pressure inadequacies.

Following the introduction of the first Catskill water in 1917, New York's average daily rate of consumption increased an unprecedented 30 million gallons per year. An investigation of new sources by the water supply board led to selection of Rondout Creek, a tributary of the Hudson River, and certain tributaries of the Delaware River that drained the western and southern slopes of the Catskill Mountains. Since the Delaware River was an interstate waterway, consent of New Jersey and Pennsylvania was required to divert the water for New York City's use. After long negotiations and subsequent litigation, in May 1931 the United States Supreme Court ruled that New York could obtain 440 million gallons per day from the Delaware Watershed subject to various safeguards. The decree secured for New York the right to develop the Neversink and East Branch rivers. The Rondout Creek project was not affected by this litigation. The entire plan consisted of building three interconnected impounding reservoirs on the three respective streams and the 85-mile Delaware Aqueduct to carry the supply from Rondout Reservoir to the city.

Despite the legal victory, the Depression slowed the new system's development. The sum of $49 million authorized in 1931 was withdrawn and additional funding was not obtained until 1936. Construction on the Rondout Reservoir began in 1937, and in 1941 Neversink Reservoir got underway. Work in the Pepacton Reservoir on the East Branch River began after World War II. The city began receiving water from the Delaware Aqueduct in 1944; by the mid 1950s, the three reservoirs and the tunnels linking them were completed. Earthfill construction techniques were used for the dams. In 1954 the city received from the Supreme Court an amendment to the 1931 decree that enabled it to de-

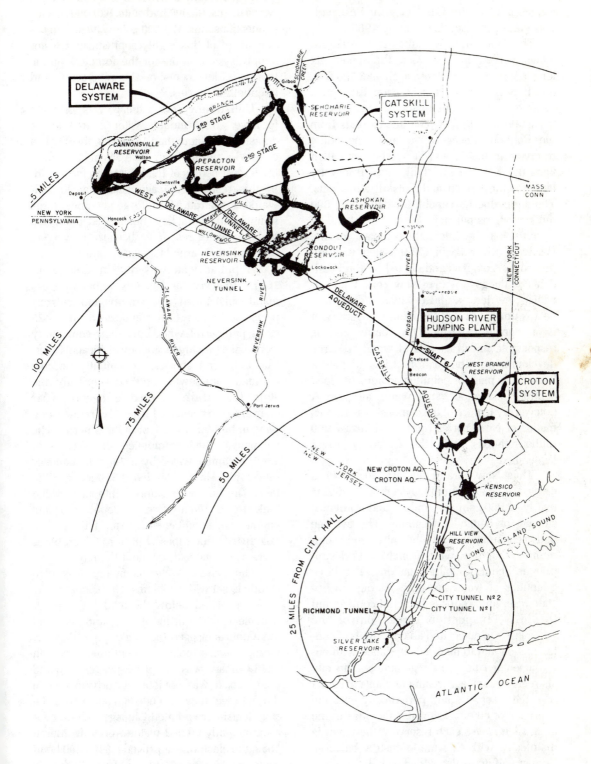

The water supply systems of New York City.

velop the West Branch of the Delaware River. Subsequently, the Cannonsville Reservoir was placed into service in early 1965.

The Delaware Aqueduct is a pressure tunnel drilled in bed rock throughout its length. Its maximum depth is about 2,500 feet, and it passes under the Hudson River at a depth of 600 feet. The inside diameter varies from 13$^1/_2$ to 19$^1/_2$ feet. The line extends from the Rondout Reservoir to an impounding reservoir in the Croton Watershed and then joins the Kensico and Hill View reservoirs built for the Croton and Catskill aqueducts. The adqueduct is capable of delivering 890 million gallons per day.

In 1963 the interstate compact for the Delaware River Basin Commission was approved by Congress and signed by the President and the governors of New York, Pennsylvania, New Jersey, and Delaware. This compact is unique in that the federal government is a signatory party. The commission is responsible for all aspects of water resource development in the basin and has adopted a basin-wide plan for pollution abatement, flood control, recreation, and water supply. A noteworthy feature of the compact was reaffirmation of New York's right to withdraw 800 million gallons from the Delaware River Watershed.

Thus, New York in the past 140 years has created a water supply system that drains nearly 2,000 square miles and provides storage for 548 billion gallons. The average daily consumption in the city and communities that draw water from New York supplies is about 1.5 billion gallons. The large quantities of water are pure. Storage in upstate reservoirs reduces bacterial content and turbidity. Inspection forces patrol the watersheds to detect and abate sources of contamination and to insure compliance with environmental rules and regulations. The city also operates sewage treatment plants in towns near the reservoirs and periodically tests the operation of other wastewater facilities in the area. As it leaves each reservoir, the water is disinfected with chlorine to destroy bacteria. Copper sulfate is also added to kill algae and coagulants are applied to promote clarification. The distribution system which delivers

water to consumers consists of 6,000 miles of water mains, 95,000 hydrants, 820,000 service connections, and 170,000 gate valves. The development of this highly sophisticated water supply system is one of the foremost public works achievements of the nineteenth and twentieth centuries.

Unlike New York, Chicago was fortunate to have an abundant water source at its doorstep. For more than 140 years, the city has drawn its supply from Lake Michigan, one of the largest bodies of fresh water in the world. In this respect, Chicago is similar to Milwaukee, Detroit, Buffalo, and other large municipalities that have not needed to develop outlying water resources because they were founded near large lakes or streams.

A public well was dug in Chicago in 1834. However, as the city expanded, demand outstripped this supply and citizens purchased water from vendors for 10 to 25 cents per barrel who drew their commodity from Lake Michigan and the Chicago River. The river and shoreline eventually became polluted with sewage and, consequently, the state legislature granted a seventy-year charter to the private Chicago Hydraulic Company to build a water works for Chicago. The company, which completed the system in 1842, obtained water by a 14-inch diameter intake pipe that extended 150 feet into the lake. The flow was pumped into an elevated tank by a twenty-five horsepower steam engine that simultaneously ran a flour mill. Log distribution pipes with 3- to 5-inch bores carried the water throughout the city.

The private water company was constantly beset with problems. Occasionally, the lake's level fell below the intake, the water became turbid during storms, and fish and large debris clogged the intake pipe. Furthermore, sewage pollution continued, and in 1848 Chicago was swept by a severe typhoid epidemic. It was obvious the private system did not meet the city's needs, and in 1851 the state legislature granted Chicago a charter for a municipally owned water works. In March 1852, the electorate approved a $400,000 bond issue for the new Chicago City Hydraulic Company. Construction commenced the following summer, and the project was completed in 1854. A pumping engine with a capacity of 8 million gallons per day drew water through a 3- by 4-foot timber intake pipe that reached 600 feet out into the lake to a brick suction well. Three elevated distribution reservoirs were constructed that supplied a water main grid consisting of about 9 miles of cast iron pipe. A second pumping station was installed in 1857.

By the early 1860s, the intake point in the lake was seriously polluted by sewage from the Chicago River. Furthermore, the supply capacity of the existing water works was exceeded. The next improvement in Chicago's water supply was one of the foremost public works projects of the nineteenth century. The responsibility for designing the system was given to Ellis S. Chesbrough, one of the era's leading civil engineers. Chesbrough proposed building a timber intake crib 2 miles from the shore and conveying lake water to the city via a 5-foot diameter masonry tunnel 60 feet beneath the lake's bottom. The project cost $465,000 and got underway in March 1864. Work continued in spite of the resources of money and men demanded by the Civil War. The project was dedicated on March 25, 1865, and the tunnel became the prototype for many

Chicago's famous water tower and pumping station were completed in 1869.

others built throughout the world.

The original pumping station was replaced in 1869. Large steam engines were installed, and an ornate water tower was constructed that is still a Chicago architectural landmark. These structures survived the 1871 Chicago Fire, but the pumping machinery was damaged and service was interrupted for eight days.

City engineers continued to be faced with meeting the demands of Chicago's growing population. At first, additional engines were installed to draw more water from the crib. The demand, however, soon exceeded the capacity of the plant. A second tunnel 7 feet in diameter was completed in 1874 that connected a new pumping station on the city's West Side to the intake crib. Because of problems of interference with the deep foundations and substructures of multistory buildings, the masonry tunnel was replaced by a deeper concrete tunnel in 1909. Another water system, finished in 1890, included two new pumping facilities connected by transmission tunnels to a new crib placed 4 miles from the shoreline. The intake facility designed by Chesbrough was replaced by the Carter Harrison Crib in 1897, and in 1927 the William F. Dever Crib was built next to it. A larger tunnel parallel to the original line was extended to the city's distribution system. Chicago's South Side receives water from two adjacent cribs located 3 miles from shore. The 68th Street Crib was built to provide water for the 1893 Columbian Exposition and was supplemented by the Edward F. Dunne Crib in 1911. The conduit from these facilities was the first lake tunnel constructed through rock instead of the lake's clay bed.

In spite of locating intake works well out into the lake, Chicago had to undertake the largest earth-moving project in the history of municipal public works to preserve the quality of its water supply. In 1892 the city began constructing the 28-mile-long Sanitary and Ship Canal to reverse the flow of the polluted Chicago River and divert industrial and sanitary wastes from Lake Michigan to the Mississippi River via the Des Plaines and Illinois rivers. Over 30 million cubic yards of earth were excavated and 12.2 million cubic yards of rock were blasted and hauled away before the canal was opened in 1900.

In spite of the protection afforded by the canal, the lake continued to be contaminated by lake traffic and cities north of Chicago and on the Indiana shore. Chlorine was added at the pumping stations by 1916 to disinfect the city supply, but the water was often excessively turbid because of lake wind and wave action. To remedy this problem, city engineers created an experimental filtration plant in 1928 and, based on their findings, prepared plans for a major installation on the South Side. In 1930 the city voted to build the plant, but the onset of the Depression delayed construction until Chicago received a $5.5 million grant from the Public Works Administration (PWA) in 1938. World War II slowed completion until the 320-million-gallon facility was put into full operation in 1947. A major plant expansion in the 1960s increased its processing capacity by 50 percent. Chicago's South Water Filtration Plant was the largest water processing facility in the world until the city's Central Filtration Plant was completed in 1964. The operation of the latter facility is discussed later in this chapter.

The development of Chicago's vast water supply system was a remarkable public works achievement. It is operated by the Chicago Department of Water and Sewers and in 1971 provided a daily per capita use of 255 gallons. In addition to 72.6 miles of water supply transmission lines under the lake and city, the agency maintains 4,100 miles of water mains, 46,000 fire hydrants, and 164,000 water meters.

Seattle's first water system consisted of a small wooden tank and an elevated open V-shaped trough which conveyed water from a hillside spring to the shores of Elliott Bay. Henry L. Yesler built this system in 1854 to supply his lumber mill. By the 1870s, the open trough was replaced with small fir log pipes with 2-inch bores. In 1881 the Spring Hill Water Company was organized to provide the first integrated water system for Seattle. It augmented its supply source of hillside springs with a pipeline from Lake Washington where a steam-powered pump was installed in 1886.

The Seattle Fire of June 6, 1889 prompted Seattle citizens one month later to approve development of a municipal gravity-fed water system. The city took over the Spring Hill water system and, based on the findings of Benezette Williams, a nationally known hydraulic engineer from Chicago, decided to draw its supply from the Cedar River 25 miles southeast of the city. A diversion facility was built on the river at Landsburg in 1901. A 42-inch woodstave pipe delivered the first Cedar River water to the city. At this time, steps were also taken to acquire the heavily timbered watershed in the Cascade Mountains above the diversion point. In order to provide storage upstream from the intake, a crib dam was constructed in 1905 at the outlet of Cedar Lake. In 1915 a masonry dam was completed 2 miles below the crib dam that raised Cedar Lake by 25 feet.

The Klondike gold rush and the rapid settlement of the Northwest caused Seattle's population to expand nearly fivefold from about 60,000 in 1895 to 311,000 in 1923. In 1908 a second woodstave aqueduct was constructed parallel to the first Cedar River pipeline. The two conduits provided the city a supply of 67 million gallons per day. In subsequent years, the original transmission lines from the Cedar River were replaced by larger 78-inch aqueducts (one steel and one woodstave) that raised supply capacity to 225 million gallons per day by 1960. Portions of the 78-inch woodstave pipeline are still in service.

The City of Seattle's system was developed to serve not only the city itself but the entire population of the Seattle metropolitan area. It became apparent that a second supply source was necessary to supplement the Cedar River supply. In 1958 development commenced on the Tolt River, about 30 miles east of Seattle; and by 1964, the Tolt Dam and a 60-inch aqueduct were completed. Combined management of the Cedar and Tolt River supply system together with distribution system storage can meet peaking rates of 400 million gallons per day. The peak day rate for the system, which serves nearly a million people or about 25 percent of the state of Washington, has been 348 million gallons.

As a result of the program initiated at the turn of the century to acquire the Cedar River Watershed, which was formerly owned by the Forest Service, Seattle has obtained ownership of nearly 80 percent of this 90,000-acre watershed. The city restricts public access and controls logging operations in the area to prevent pollution. The quality of the water diverted further downstream was maintained at such a high level over the years that only chlorination is required to insure suitable drinking water quality. Thus, the city has been able to avoid constructing expensive treatment plants. This closely regulated watershed along with a similarly controlled watershed on the Tolt River makes Seattle's water supply sources one of the most unique in the nation.

The use of water from federal reservoirs for municipal consumption is a relatively recent practice. During the early twentieth century, advocates of multiple-purpose water resource development proposed that comprehensive plans be developed and implemented for flood control, waterway improvement, irrigation, and hydroelectric generation. Except in western states, municipal water supply was rarely regarded as an important factor in river basin planning. However, as populations grew in areas without abundant supplies, federal assistance was provided.

The withdrawal of water for municipal consumption from the Army Corps of Engineers' reservoirs did not begin until the mid 1940s. Nevertheless, in the early nineteenth century, the corps was the leading engineering organization in the country, and former officers played important roles in the construction of municipal water works. Washington, D.C., however, used the corps to build its first water supply system. In the 1850s, Congress was concerned by the fires that frequently broke out in the capital city and appointed Lieutenant Montgomery C. Meigs to investigate sources of water supply. Meigs recommended building a 12-mile-long aqueduct from above the Great Falls of the Potomac River to a series of pumping stations and reservoirs near or within the city. Congress approved the plan in March 1853, and construction commenced the following November. The aqueduct required ten years to complete. The most impressive feature of the system was the 200-foot-long Cabin John Bridge, a combination water supply and roadway structure, that was the longest masonry arch in the world for over fifty years.

The corps' involvement in providing municipal water was first authorized in the 1944 Flood Control Act that included a provision for using federal multiple-purpose reservoirs to supplement domestic and industrial water supplies. The act authorized the secretary of the army to contract with cities, states, and private companies for sale of surplus water from corps public works projects. In the 1958 Water Supply Act, Congress made water storage available to cities and industries in federal multiple-purpose reservoirs. Local interests were required to reimburse the federal government for their share of construction costs over a period of fifty years beginning with the first withdrawals of the stored water. The act was subsequently amended in 1961.

Since passage of the 1958 law, large cities, small towns, water districts, and private companies have availed themselves of water impounded in corps reservoirs. As new dams and reservoirs were built, the corps sometimes emplaced outlet pipes in the event municipalities required future water supplies. Oklahoma City, Oklahoma, makes annual payments of $148,500 for rental of 90,000 acre-feet of storage space in Canton Lake on the North Canadian River. The City of Waco, Texas, relinquished to the federal government control of Lake Waco in exchange for equivalent storage in a new lake impounded by Waco Dam, a flood control and water conservation project.

Water storage capacity frequently results from state initiative. Kansas, upon recommendation of the Kansas Water Resources Board, requested that plans for Milford Reservoir on the Republican River be modified to include 300,000 acre-feet of storage for anticipated municipal and industrial water needs. The project's design was subsequently changed to meet this request. Private firms, including power utilities and oil companies, also purchase storage space for industrial purposes in federal reservoirs.

Water consumption by domestic and industrial users from Bureau of Reclamation projects predates the Army Corps of Engineers' involvement in this field. Early reclamation legislation was specifically designed to promote irrigation in the western United States and contained no provisions relating to municipal and industrial water supplies. However, the economic growth and development stimulated by the 1902 Reclamation Act resulted in the establishment of townsites in arid areas. Accordingly, the 1906 Reclamation Act authorized the secretary of interior to contract with communities to furnish them with water under comparable terms established for agricultural consumers. This practice was expanded by the 1939 Reclamation Project Act which recognized domestic water supplies as a major factor in planning and constructing multiple-purpose projects. The provisions of the aforementioned 1958 Water Supply Act supplemented the general provisions of reclamation laws.

The reclamation program is a unique public works undertaking in that most of the funds appropriated by Congress for project construction are returned to the federal government over a period of years. Municipal and industrial water contractors are required to reimburse the Department of the Treasury with interest for construction costs as well as annual operating and maintenance expenditures. The secretary of interior is authorized to enter into water supply contracts with municipal and industrial entities only if this use will not compromise the project's irrigation commitments. However, in recent project authorizations, where municipal and industrial water supply is a predominant purpose, Congress has specified that the above provision does not apply. These exceptions reflect the growing demand for water in the West to meet steadily increasing municipal and industrial needs. The following projects illustrate the bureau's expanding role in developing and furnishing water to small municipalities. Its involvement in the development of the Salt Lake and California aqueducts is discussed in Chapter 10.

In 1938 the W. C. Austin project began in Oklahoma. A combination of private irrigators and city and state officials petitioned the Bureau of Reclamation to construct a project which would provide water for irrigation and the city of Altus. The project was authorized in 1938 and work started in 1941 on the storage reservoir. Construction was delayed by World War II; but work was resumed in 1944, and the first water deliveries were made in 1946. The 110-foot-high storage dam is a concrete structure faced with quarry stone. The distribution system includes 52 miles of canals and 218 miles of laterals that serve 489 farms. The City of Altus built a pumping plant and 3.2 miles of pipe from the canal to the city to serve 18,000 people and nearby Altus Air Force Base.

In 1948 the bureau began the Cachuma project near Santa Barbara, California. By 1900 some irrigation had begun in the area by diverting water from nearby streams. The local county irrigation district constructed a storage reservoir and transmission tunnel several miles long. In addition, local residents pumped water from the ground, which so lowered the groundwater levels that by 1941 the Santa Barbara County Board of Supervisors requested a study be made to help solve local water problems.

In 1945 the Santa Barbara County Water Agency was formed and contracted with the Bureau of Reclamation to repay the cost for storage facilities and related water carriage works built by the federal agency. The local agency consisted of the City of Santa Barbara and four local water districts that had previously constructed some storage facilities. In 1948 work began on Cachuma Dam, a 3,350-foot-long earthfill structure 271 feet high. To convey water from Cachuma Dam to the area, Tecolote Tunnel was built. It was 6.4 miles long and 7 feet in diameter. In addition, four equalizing storage reservoirs and 25 miles of pipeline, ranging from 27 to 48 inches in diameter were constructed. This system also required the installation of five small pumping plants that provided both municipal and irrigation water.

The first project that was built by the Bureau of Reclamation exclusively for municipal and industrial water supply was the Canadian River Project in the panhandle

U.S. Bureau of Reclamation

The Bureau of Reclamation's Canadian River project included construction of a main aqueduct to convey water for domestic and industrial use.

of Texas. Eleven cities, including Amarillo, needed additional domestic and industrial water supplies, and they believed that the Canadian River would provide sufficient quantity and quality to serve their needs. The area was settled after 1876 by ranchers. As the number of settlers rose, there was more production of forage and other crops irrigated by well water. The drought of the 1930s increased consumption of groundwater, and studies were made of utilizing the Canadian River to supplement and conserve local supplies. The Canadian River Water Authority, consisting of the twelve cities, was founded and agreed to pay the cost of needed facilities. The federal agency made its final report in 1960 that recommended building public works that would assure a water supply for over 375,000 people and industry in the area.

Construction was started in 1962 on Sanford Dam and Reservoir. A five-unit pumping plant at the reservoir site was built to lift 183 cubic feet per second of water 296 feet into the distribution lines which extended 322

miles. This system consisted of underground concrete pipe, ranging in size from 15 to 96 inches; temporary storage-regulating reservoirs; and eleven smaller pumping plants. The operation of the plants and control of the system are automated and remotely controlled. The Canadian River Municipal Water Authority member cities constructed facilities to treat the water for domestic use. The project plan was based upon the cities continuing to rely in part on water from wells.

During the Depression, small and large municipalities were able to build or upgrade water supply systems with the assistance of PWA and federal work relief agencies. From 1919 to 1929, municipalities annually spent an average of $119 million for water works construction. However, by 1933 new construction fell to $47 million because of the onset of hard times. Much of the slack was taken up by PWA financing. The agency made allotments for 2,419 projects, costing $312 million from 1933 to 1939, that accounted for 50 percent of the total water works expenditures by all levels of government. During the same period, approximately $112 million was spent by the Civil Works Administration, Federal Emergency Relief Administration, and Works Progress Administration for work relief municipal water projects.

An outstanding feature of New Deal public works programs was that they enabled many small communities to install wholesome public water systems. Hundreds of communities which had been unable to afford treatment plants and pipe grids formed water districts in order to obtain PWA support. Approximately 75 percent of the projects funded by the agency were built by communities with populations of less than 1,000. In towns such as Goose Creek, Texas; Tyronza, Arkansas; and Cunningham, Kansas, community life was transformed by federally supported projects. Householders that formerly relied on private wells and public pumps were provided with pure water at the turn of a tap. The Department of Housing and Urban Development has continued the federal commitment to assist with water projects in cities and towns on a much smaller scale. Between 1966 and 1972, the federal agency spent nearly $1 billion on water supply projects that included pumping stations, treatment and storage facilities, and desalting plants.

Since the 1930s, the Department of Agriculture's Soil Conservation Service has assisted communities through its small watershed program (discussed in Chapter 9). In addition, the department's Farmers Home Administration (FmHA) administers a program through its 1,750 county offices that is upgrading water supply in rural and outlying suburban areas. Thousands of small water systems have been built to replace wells, springs, cisterns, and other private supplies that frequently become depleted and polluted. Some of the new systems receive their water from central wells drilled deep enough to obtain an adequate supply of pure water. In other instances, small dams are built to create lakes, or water is drawn from a nearby city reservoir and piped to farm homes.

The program was established in the late 1930s. However, all but a few hundred of the 7,000 water systems built with FmHA support were constructed after 1965 when the program was vastly liberalized to include grants as well as loans. By 1975, $1.9 billion in loans and $258 million in grants were made by the agency. Some officials believe that within a few decades all but the most isolated rural residents will be served by community water systems as they are now by rural electric cooperatives.

Land prices have increased in areas served by the systems, and in some instances introducing reliable water supplies to open areas has produced urban sprawl. Real estate speculators have discovered that a dependable water system is a sure-fire way of promoting housing developments. In addition, land conversion in rural areas is seldom controlled by planning and zoning. Despite these problems, the program has improved the quality of farm life and revitalized rural areas. Farmsteads that had been vacant for years have been bought by new farmers and put back into production.

Water Distribution

Municipal water distribution systems consist of networks of pipes and appurtenances extending from pumping stations, wells, and treatment plants. Lateral lines connect fire hydrants to water mains laid out along street patterns, and shutoff valves are located at strategic points to close down pipe sections for maintenance and repair. Water enters homes through service lines that tap street mains. The development of pipe grids that deliver water to residential, commercial, and industrial consumers was made possible by the creation of strong, corrosion-resistant pipe material.

In the seventeenth, eighteenth, and nineteenth centuries, wooden mains, consisting of bored and charred logs, were used to convey water within American cities. These early pipes were usually made of cedar, oak, or pine, and an iron ring was shrunk on the end of each section to prevent splitting. The first wood conduits were laid at Boston in 1652; and Winston-Salem, North Carolina, built the first citywide domestic water system with log pipes in 1776. Bored wood pipe was used well into the nineteenth century. The use of wood for water conveyance was improved with the development about 1850 of mains constructed of wooden staves bound with iron bands. Water utilities installed banded-stave mains until the 1930s, and this type of pipe was widely employed in the West for large aqueducts for city water supplies, irrigation, hydroelectric plants, and hydraulic mining. This type of pipe was best suited for low-pressure gravity systems. The introduction of high-pressure pumping engines spelled the end of wood as a major pipe material due to leakage caused by higher pressures and greater flow volumes.

Cast iron pipe was introduced to the United States from England shortly after 1800 and was first employed for city water distribution by Philadelphia. The city began laying iron pipes in 1819 to replace leaky wood conduits and increase water main life. By 1850 iron pipe was the preferred material for water mains, and it is still the major pipe material. Municipalities, however, discovered that the interior walls of cast iron pipe became tuberculated (the formation of encrustations of iron oxide) which deteriorated the conduits, reduced carrying capacity, and imparted a foul taste and red coloring to domestic water supplies. In the late 1840s, a process was developed that abated tuberculation by lining pipes with a tarlike substance. Thereafter, cast iron mains were the foremost means of conveying city water, except in areas where transportation charges for the heavy pipes made the utilization of wood preferable. For over a hundred years, cast iron pipe was pit cast; but in the early 1920s, centrifugally cast pipe was introduced and, because of its strength and durability, became the most common type used for water conveyance.

In the late 1800s, many miles of so-called cement pipe were put into service by American cities which consisted of a central core of thin sheet-iron surrounded inside and out by cement mortar. The pipes were less costly to make and lay than iron mains; but as pumping pressures increased, they were prone to leakage and breakage and were often replaced. Cement mortar, however, was eventually used as an interior coating for iron pipe, and a process for cement-lining water mains in place was introduced in 1939 at Charleston,

Seattle Water Department

In the early 1960s, Seattle, Washington, replaced banded-stave aqueduct conduits with steel pipe.

South Carolina, and Falmouth, Massachusetts.

By the 1970s, a broad spectrum of pipe materials was developed. The types of pipe presently used to distribute community water supplies include cast and ductile iron, asbestos cement, concrete, steel, and plastic. Whatever type a water utility opts for, efficient pipe systems exhibit the following characteristics: the ability to resist external pressure from trench backfill and earth movement caused by freezing, thawing, or unstable soil conditions; high bursting strength to withstand internal water pressures; the capacity to endure shocks and impacts encountered in transportation, handling, and installation; smooth, non-corrosive interior surfaces for minimum resistance to water flow; and an exterior unaffected by corrosive soils and groundwater.

Both ductile and cast iron are popular pipe materials because of their long life, toughness, ease of tapping, and ability to stand up to heavy internal and external loads. The production of ductile iron involves introducing magnesium into molten iron to create pipe that is stronger, less corrosive, and more elastic than cast iron. To inhibit exterior corrosion, a coating of bitumastic tar is applied to the surface. Iron pipe is usually lined with a thin coating of cement mortar that protects against tuberculation. The lining is applied while the pipe is rotated at a high speed so that it closely adheres to the surface and will not separate during maintenance operations. Asbestos-cement mains are made from a mixture of asbestos fiber, portland cement, and silica sand. A slurry of the ingredients is prepared, placed in molds, and heat dried. Although weaker than cast iron pipe, it is immune to electrolysis, resistant to corrosive soil and water, and smooth; thus, providing minimum resistance to hydraulic flow.

Several types of reinforced concrete pipes are employed in modern water distribution systems. Concrete pipe is durable, easy to maintain, and saves transportation costs because it can be manufactured at or near construction sites. Non-prestressed, steel-cylinder pipe is produced by surrounding a welded steel pipe with concrete. For high pressure, the pipe is prestressed by winding wire around the steel core before the concrete is applied. The concrete protects the steel from corrosion, provides a smooth interior surface, and enables the pipe to resist stresses from external loading. Although not as popular as cast iron, asbestos-cement, or concrete pipe, some steel pipe is used in water transmission lines.

Plastic pipe was first used for household service lines and plumbing fixtures in the late 1940s. However, more recently it has been employed for water distribution mains and large inplant piping systems. Of the various plastic materials developed for water conveyance, polyvinyl chloride and polyethylene are the most widely used. Pipes made of these substances are strong, extremely smooth, and—because they are chemically inert—corrosion resistant.

Pipe sections are fitted together by several joint types. The bell and spigot connection was first used for connecting wood pipes. This process initially involved inserting the plain end of one pipe into the flared end of another and sealing the joint with lead or some other caulking material. This principle is carried on by the compression joint, some-

times called a slip or push joint, which is the most popular type used in water distribution. The beveled spigot end is inserted into a bell that contains a rubber ring gasket that produces a tight seal when compressed. Flanged joints are made by threading pipe ends and screwing on flanges that enable pipe sections to be bolted together. This type is commonly used for interior piping in water plants. Joint types have also been developed for special distribution systems. Underwater lines, for example, require very flexible connections and use ball-and-socket jointing methods.

To check waste and develop equitable fee schedules, the water works industry developed metering devices that measured the amount of water customers drew from the mains. The cost of installing meters and the continuing expense of reading and repairing the devices were substantial; but they encouraged thrift, reduced expenditures for new processing plants, and delayed development of new sources of water supply. The first United States water meter patent was issued in 1850, and by the mid 1870s meters had been developed with legible dials that facilitated meter reading. Several common types of meters have been introduced in the past century. The *displacement* or *disk* meter is commonly used for small customers such as private homes and apartments. Its central component is a measuring chamber containing a rotating disk linked to a recording mechanism. As the chamber fills and empties, the quantity of water passing through is registered. *Velocity* or *current* meters contain a bladed wheel that rotates at a speed in proportion to the water flow rate. The turbine wheel is connected to a recorder by a series of gears. A *compound* meter incorporates features of the aforementioned types. Low flow is measured by a rotating disk; but after the water velocity reaches a predetermined rate, measurement is shifted to a turbine. Compound meters accurately measure water consumption during peak and low-use periods. They monitor water use of customers with varying flow rates such as motels, office buildings, factories, and other commercial properties.

Venturi meters are used to measure flows

in large pipes such as outlets from reservoirs and pumping stations. The device was invented in 1887 by Clemens Herschel, a noted hydraulic engineer, and is based on the hydraulic principle that when the velocity of water flow increases, there is a corresponding reduction in pressure. The apparatus consists of a short section of pipe called a reducer inserted in a water main to restrict the pipe's size, usually by about 75 percent. Downstream from the reducer, a connecting tapered piece of pipe gradually increases the conduit's size to the original pipe diameter. By simultaneously measuring the water pressure in the reducer and the main, it is possible to compute the velocity of the water and determine the amount flowing through the pipe.

Water metering was vigorously fought when it was introduced in the late nineteenth century. Prior to that time, customers paid a set fee regardless of the quantity of water they used. For example, in 1815 a Boston water company supplied 1,000 families through log pipes for an annual charge of $10. In planning the Croton water supply of New York City, officials estimated that the charge for each householder would be $8 per year. The flat rate persisted well into the twentieth century; and by the late 1930s, many cities charged domestic users according to the number of faucets and only metered large consumers. Many large cities, such as New York, continue to meter only industries, commercial establishments, and large apartment houses. However, in spite of the cost of meter installation, repair, and reading, most communities use metering to promote efficient water consumption and establish equitable water rates.

In recent years, some metropolitan areas have developed water rate schedules that recover the costs of serving different classes of customers while maintaining reasonable equity. Factors considered in determining rates include the cost of supplying the amount of water consumed, rate of use, and expense of maintaining the service. Simply put, charges are commensurate with the service rendered. For example, a customer with a high peak rate of use would require the municipality to build and maintain larger capacity pumps, pipes, and other facilities

than a user with a comparable total consumption that uses water at a constant rate. Some water utilities encourage off-peak hour consumption by lowering rates for large customers during periods of low flow. The purpose is to offset peaking and thereby reduce capacity requirements of system components.

Water Processing

Nearly all community water supplies are processed to render them fit for human consumption and industrial use. Water for domestic supplies must be chemically and bacteriologically safe and free from turbidity, color, odor, and bad taste. Before water reaches a treatment plant, it often collects debris and a broad spectrum of soluble organic and inorganic substances. The net effect is to add varying concentrations of algae, minerals, bacteria, toxic chemicals, and other pollutants that must be removed or neutralized. The development of water treatment systems was vital to the growth of large metropolitan areas.

The first means of water purification was filtration through a bed of sand and gravel to remove suspended matter. This process was initially undertaken to improve clarity, odor, and color; but as understanding grew of the bacterial origin of disease, it became fundamental to the preservation of public health in American cities. The origins of water filtration can be traced to ninth-century Venice, Italy, where water from city cisterns was filtered through sand. The first public water supply filtering system is generally believed to have been established at Paisley, Scotland, in 1804. A textiles factory owner constructed the filter to provide clear water for his plant and sold the remaining supply to the townspeople. Glasgow, Scotland, installed sand beds in 1807 and became the first city to pipe filtered water to customers. Despite these early efforts, filtration processes were primitive until James Simpson and Robert Thom designed the first efficient sand filters. Simpson, an English engineer, was commissioned in 1827 to design and build a filtration system for the Chelsea Water Works in London, England. This plant was the prototype for *slow sand* filters that were subsequently established in England and the United States. Thom, a Scottish engineer, designed and constructed a filter for Greenock, Scotland, in 1827 and improved and expanded the pioneer works at Paisley in 1838. His filters featured reverse-flow washing, a practice still used in modern plants to clean water filters.

The slow sand filters that were built in the United States were based on Simpson's design. They consisted of large masonry beds, filled to a depth of about 5 feet with sand and gravel, graded from top to bottom from fine to pea-sized rocks. The water was applied to the surface of the sand bed, flowed through the filter media, collected in drains, and carried to a reservoir or directly into the distribution system. As the water passed through the filter, insert solids and organic and bacterial matter adhered to the sand particles in the upper layers. When accumulations of material blocked the water flow, the clogged sand was removed from the surface and washed.

In 1832 the first attempt to filter a public water supply in the United States was made at Richmond, Virginia, by Albert Stein, designer of the city's water works. Water was pumped from the James River to a 194- by 104-foot reservoir that contained a sand filter in its bottom. This system and a second built the following year failed to operate effectively. During the next four decades, several cities including Boston, Cincinnati, and Philadelphia considered installing sand filters but demurred because of the high cost of installation and operation.

The next landmark in the development of water filtration was James P. Kirkwood's 1869 *Report on the Filtration of River Waters.* In 1865 Kirkwood was commissioned by the City of St. Louis, Missouri, "to proceed at once to Europe, and there inform himself in regard to the best process in use for clarifying river waters used for the supply of cities." The engineer was to prepare specifications based on his findings for a plant to filter the turbid Mississippi River water used by the city. Although St. Louis rejected his recommenda-

Public Works Historical Society.

Top layers of slow sand filters had to be periodically removed and cleaned.

tions because of high costs, Kirkwood's plans were implemented by other communities. Slow sand plants, based on Kirkwood's designs, were built at Poughkeepsie, New York, in 1872 and at Hudson, New York, in 1874.

The reluctance of United States water utilities to install filters was based in part on a poor understanding of disease transmission. The germ theory of disease, which was first announced by Louis Pasteur in 1857 and more firmly established by Robert Koch in the mid 1870s, gave considerable impetus to the study of water filtration. Once it was established that impure water was often the cause of cholera and typhoid epidemics, scientists and engineers investigated the effectiveness of using sand filters to screen out microorganisms and organic matter.

Research on filtration was carried out in several American cities in the 1880s, but the work of the Lawrence (Massachusetts) Experiment Station placed water filtration on a sound scientific footing. The facility, which was founded by the Massachusetts Board of Health in 1887, pioneered the inter-disciplinary approach to solving public health problems. A brilliant staff of young engineers, chemists, and biologists investigated water purification and sewage treatment techniques. One of the station's important findings was confirming the ability of slow sand filters to remove typhoid germs in river water supplies. When the city of Lawrence, Massachusetts, was threatened by a typhoid epidemic in 1892, the city council authorized Hiram F. Mills, director of the experiment station, to build a filtration plant for the city. The facility was dramatically successful in reducing the incidence of disease and prompted other communities to construct slow sand filtration plants. About twenty American water utilities constructed filters in the 1890s. A large facility built at Albany, New York, in 1899 served as a model for slow sand filtration systems later constructed at Washington, D.C., Philadelphia, and many other large cities. The Albany filter, which was designed by Allen Hazen, was covered to prevent disruption of service during freezing weather.

In America slow sand filters were eventually superseded by *rapid sand* or *mechanical* filters. Slow sand filters were effective for purifying water drawn from relatively clear streams, but some suspended particles of dirt and clay in highly turbid midwestern rivers did not adhere to sand and passed through the media carrying infectious bacteria. In addition, slow sand filters became frequently clogged by solids, and the sand had to be washed too often to make the process efficient for municipal use.

Mechanical filters were first adopted by paper making and other industrial plants which required clear, colorless water for production processes. The devices could be operated at a high-flow rate and were cleaned by reverse flow, thus eliminating labor costs for sand scraping and washing. The mechanical filters could clarify very turbid waters without presedimentation. Iron sulfate, alum, or other coagulants were added to the water so that suspended matter would bunch together and be trapped in the upper layers of the filter media. When the bed became clogged, the water flow was reversed and the waste material carried off. Most rapid sand filters were similar in general appearance to slow sand filters, but they were smaller in size and about 8 or 9 feet deep.

The most notable tests on mechanical

PITTSBURGH GRAVITY FILTER
WITH MECHANICAL AGITATION

The introduction of mechanical filters in the late 1800s increased water processing efficiency.

filters were conducted from 1895 to 1897 by George W. Fuller and a team of engineers at Louisville, Kentucky. These investigations of clay-bearing Ohio River water established the feasibility of using mechanical filters to purify municipal water supplies. The first large municipal rapid sand plant was installed at Little Falls, New Jersey, in 1902 to treat water drawn from the Passaic River. This structure was built of reinforced concrete and employed pretreatment coagulation and sedimentation to clarify the water before filtration. The plant is still in operation.

In the twentieth century, filtration systems have become larger and more efficient and complex, but their basic operating principles remain unchanged. The principal improvements have been the refinement of filtration materials and backwashing processes. One of the earliest modifications was to increase the size of sand particles used in the filter's upper layers. This augmented penetration of filtered wastes into the bed and decreased the frequency of filter cleansings. Early rapid sand filters were prone to form mud balls or other heavy impurities that dropped down to the course underlayers when the bed was backwashed. Higher pressures for backwashing were employed to solve the problem, but this often resulted in sand being carried off by the wash water. Several devices have been developed that increase scrubbing action during backwashing by spraying water onto the top surface of sand.

Some modern plants employ mixed media filter beds composed of coal, sand, and garnet. After backwashing, the media stratifies with the larger, lighter coal particles settling at the top and the heavier but smaller sand and garnet at the bottom. When the filter is operated, larger particles are trapped in the surface coal layer, while finer material is captured in the lower levels. Thus, the bed filters water to a great depth, and premature surface blockage is prevented.

Most modern water works pretreat raw water by sedimentation and coagulation before the flow is filtered. These processes remove most of the suspended matter and increase filter efficiency. Storing muddy water

to promote clarification was first practiced in ancient Rome. Many American cities built reservoirs in the eighteenth and nineteenth centuries to improve water quality as well as provide storage. By the twentieth century, coagulation was employed in conjunction with sedimentation to clarify water. Alum was first used as a coagulant for municipal water treatment at Kansas City, Missouri, in 1887. Settling basins in modern water processing plants remove solid matter from raw water after coagulants have been applied to promote flocculation. Water entering the basin is forced to the bottom behind a baffle wall and rises vertically to a discharge channel at the tank's surface. The bunched particles settle out and are removed by a mechanical scraping device.

To supplement sedimentation and filtration, most city water utilities disinfect their supplies with chlorine. Chlorine destroys disease-causing microorganisms, improves taste and odor, and helps remove iron manganese. Chlorine compounds were used as early as the 1830s to combat foul smells emanating from water supplies. Until the germ theory of disease transmission was established in the 1880s, it was commonly believed that odor control would limit the spread of typhoid and cholera. In the late 1890s, chlorine was found to be effective against pathogenic organisms. Experiments on chlorine disenfection were undertaken in conjunction with filtration studies at Louisville, Kentucky, in 1896. In this case and most other early experiments, chlorine gas was produced by electrolysis of salt water. In the late 1890s, bleaching powder was employed in England and Europe to sterilize water mains after typhoid epidemics; and the world's first permanent chlorination facility was founded at Middelkerke, Belgium, in 1902.

The first continuous application of chlorine to municipal water began in the United States in 1908 at Boonton Reservoir which supplied water to Jersey City, New Jersey. Construction of the chlorination facility resulted from a claim by the city that the private Jersey City Water Company had violated its contract by failing to provide a supply of "pure and wholesome water." To combat sewage pollution of the reservoir, the city demanded that the company build an intercepting sewer and a treatment plant. The company refused and conducted experiments with chlorine gas and bleaching powder. After subsequent litigation, the court held that chlorine was an effective disinfectant and the company installed a plant to add bleaching powder to Jersey City's water supply. This landmark case paved the way for the rapid expansion of chlorine treatment for municipal water supplies.

In 1909 liquid chlorine (compressed chlorine gas) became commercially available and in the following year was experimentally employed by the army to treat the water supply of Fort Myer, Virginia. Two years later, the water works at Baltimore, Maryland, and Niagara Falls, New York, began regularly applying liquid chlorine to their flows. Liquid chlorine was adopted by most water utilities because early chlorine compounds were chemically unstable and contained varying chlorine concentrations. However, in 1928 high-test calcium hypochlorite was developed. This material was more stable and active than the various bleaching powders and solutions previously available. Most modern plants employ liquid chlorine treatment, but calcium hypochlorite and some other chlorine compounds are used by small treatment facilities.

Improvements in chlorine analysis and disinfection techniques contributed to the widespread adoption of water chlorination. Disinfection dosages were originally based on the application of fixed amounts of chlorine. However, since raw water quality often varies from day to day, different amounts of chlorine are needed to neutralize pollutants. Gradually, the concept of varying chlorine applications on the basis of residual chlorine levels was adopted, and testing procedures were developed by the 1920s that enabled cities to regulate chlorine applications.

Several other processes have been developed to disinfect water, but only ozonization seems to have potential for widespread use. Ozone is a faintly blue gas that readily breaks down and becomes a powerful oxidizing agent. Ozone was employed for water treat-

ment in Europe before 1900 and is still widely used in France. A few plants were established in the United States before 1940, but most were abandoned because operating costs were higher than with chlorine. However, recent rises in chlorine prices, improvements in ozone production, and the efficacy of ozone as a viricide, have caused some cities to reconsider ozone disinfection of their water supplies.

One of the most troublesome aspects of water treatment has been making water palatable and aesthetically pleasing. The presence of objectionable tastes, odors, and coloration lowers public confidence in water supplies. Flavor can be affected by inorganic salts and metal ions, natural organic compounds, or industrial wastes. Algae, however, has been the most frequent cause of taste and odor problems in surface water supplies. Their metabolic activities impart compounds that produce fishy, musty, and other foul smells and tastes. A century ago, water utilities were powerless to combat these problems. During the 1880s and 1890s, George C. Whipple conducted research on factors relating to taste and odor in the surface supplies of Boston and New York and established algae growths as a major cause of water quality retardation. In 1904 copper sulfate was discovered to be an effective algicide, and cities throughout the country began using the substance to control algae growth in reservoirs.

The expansion of chemical industries after World War I added to the problem of taste and odor control by introducing into water supplies substances that are difficult to process. Oxidants such as chlorine, potassium permanganate, and ozone are effective for both odor control and disinfection. However, when chlorine is combined with waters carrying some types of industrial wastes, complex compounds are produced that are difficult to remove. Activated carbon has been used to improve taste and odor since the late 1920s. The carbon particles, which absorb odorous substances, are introduced to the flow during filtration. Since carbon absorbs chlorine, the two chemcials must be added at different points in the water treatment process. The removal of dissolved salts from water by distillation, electrodialysis, ion exchange, and reverse osmosis is discussed in Chapter 12.

Aeration also improves water taste and odor. Exposing water to the atmosphere was first employed by cities to restore dissolved oxygen depleted by water impoundment and to remove odors caused by decomposing organic matter and microorganisms. In the early twentieth century, aerator basins were built below reservoirs to combat the effects of water stagnation. Aeration is also used in modern systems to remove hydrogen sulphide and odors and tastes produced by the addition of chlorine to public water supplies.

Hardness in water results from dissolved minerals such as calcium and magnesium. These substances are a nuisance to consumers. They cause excessive soap consumption in laundering and produce scale in pipes, hot water heaters, and boilers of large industrial concerns. The ability of lime and soda ash to soften water by chemical precipitation was discovered in the 1840s. The first municipal water softening plant in the United States was opened at Oberlin, Ohio, in 1905. Subsequently, the zeolite or cation exchange method was developed which is the most common water softening process used for cities, industries, and homes. In this process, magnesium and calcium ions are displaced by sodium compounds. This treatment method was initially practiced on a municipal water supply at Wyoming, Pennsylvania, in 1923.

Since 1945 many communities have added fluoride compounds to their water supplies to reduce tooth decay. The practice has often engendered strong resistance from opponents who argue that fluoride treatment is detrimental to health and a violation of civil liberties. Proponents maintain that fluoridation will reduce dental cavities by 60 percent, and the practice has been endorsed by many national scientific and public health organizations. Approximately 50 percent of the United States population consumes water containing near optimum fluoride levels (one part per million). In most instances, the substance is added to supplies, but some water sources contain natural fluoride concentrations.

Chicago's Central Water Filtration Plant (1964) is the largest water processing facility in the world and incorporates advanced treatment and filtration techniques. Constructed by the city's Department of Public Works and operated by the Department of Water and Sewers, the plant daily processes an average of 960 million gallons and is capable of delivering 1.7 billion gallons. The plant serves a population of 2.7 million and, together with Chicago's smaller South Water Filtration Plant, supplies water to the entire city and sixty-six suburban communities.

Chicago draws its water from two intake cribs located in Lake Michigan 2½ miles offshore. Before entering the plant, the water passes through eight screens which remove fish and large debris. The half-inch mesh strainers are regularly cleaned by high-pressure water jets. Next the flow is raised 21 feet above lake level by eight pumps that have a combined capacity of 1.9 billion gallons per day. Once the water is elevated, it flows by gravity through the plant and is not pumped again until it reaches outlying booster stations. It takes approximately eight hours for raw water to pass through the various treatment processes that render it fit for human consumption.

A variety of chemicals are added to the water as it enters the plant. Alum produces floc, a gelatinous substance which enmeshes silt and other impurities making their removal easier. Chlorine is added to the influent to destroy bacteria, and water leaving the facility receives additional chlorine if needed. Activated carbon combats unpleasant tastes and odors and anhydrous ammonia neutralizes the taste of chlorine. Hydrated lime augments coagulation by adding weight to the floc and, by increasing the water's alkalinity, it inhibits corrosion in the distribution system. When constructed, the chemical feeding systems were considered the most advanced installed in a water treatment plant. The amount of chemicals is regulated by water flow through the facility so that applications are made according to the amount of water being treated. An average of over sixty-five tons of chemicals are added to the city's water supply each day.

After the admixture of chemicals, the water passes through a series of mixing

APWA Chicago Metropolitan Chapter

Chicago's Central Water Filtration Plant is the largest water processing facility in the world.

basins. The rate of flow and the motion of rotating paddles produce a helical flow pattern that thoroughly mixes the chemicals. The chemicals begin to process the water as it flows into settling basins where from 85 to 90 percent of the impurities are removed by sedimentation. To aid the process, the velocity of the water is sharply reduced. The flow is first passed through the basin's upper level where most of the floc produced by the alum settles out. The remainder is collected in the lower level. To remove the sediment without interrupting the process, continuous chain-type scrapers and sediment trenches were placed in the bottom of the basin. The collected waste material flows by gravity or is pumped through a discharge conduit to a point in the lake a mile off shore. Periodically, each settling basin is taken out of service and drained, and the sediment that has accumulated in the lower level is flushed away.

After most of the foreign matter is removed by the settling basin, the water is polished by filtration. The filters are located in two ten-acre filter buildings. They consist of ninety-six concrete boxes, each containing two filter sections. The 192 filters are 71 feet long, 25 feet wide, and 13 feet deep. The water flows down through beds of sand and gravel into underdrains. The filters are cleaned by backwashing. The wash water flows upward at a velocity eight times the normal rate, carrying away the waste but leaving the sand and gravel intact. Simultaneously, wash water is sprayed over the top of the filter to loosen and carry away encrusted matter from the sand particles. Approximately 2 percent of the plant's volume of filtered water is used to clean filters.

After passing through the filters, the water flows into clearwells located beneath the plant. From the clearwells, the water is conveyed to an outlet control structure, which contains a complex system for regulating filtered water flow to an impoundment reservoir and to two 16-foot diameter tunnel outlets. The plant has eight clearwells, each with a capacity of about 5 million gallons. When added to the 68-million-gallon capacity of the filtered water reservoir, the total plant storage capacity is about 111 million gallons. This large capacity is necessary to help balance supply and demand and is available for use in case of an emergency plant shutdown.

All phases of plant operation are controlled by a complex array of special instruments that measure water flow, regulate the application of chemicals, and check water quality at the plant's outlet. In addition to many monitoring and control stations located throughout the facility, a central control panel with a 60-foot-long instrument panel supervises all phases of the operation. A computer collects readings from over 300 instruments at regular intervals, computes the results, and prepares them for analysis. The information is primarily used to increase the plant's efficiency. A savings of 5 percent in the amount of chemicals used each year, for example, would amount to more than $100,000. A closed-circuit television system makes visual checks of key points in the facility, and a communications system controls processes in all parts of the plant.

The facility is located on a man-made, one-acre peninsula that extends from Chicago's shoreline into Lake Michigan. A 6,500-foot cofferdam was built to enclose the site and enormous quantities of construction materials and supplies were used to complete the facility. Over a million cubic yards of sand fill, for example, were required to raise the lake bed to the bottom of the present substructure. More than 120,000 wood pilings were implanted to support the structure, and 88 million pounds of steel and 570,000 cubic yards of concrete were used during construction.

The plant's structures are sited both above and below ground level and are arranged in quadrants, each capable of functioning independently. The substructures include the filtered water reservoir, clearwells, and mixing and settling basins. The headhouse is located above ground and includes the pumping, chemical, administration, and filter buildings.

Careful planning make this public works facility an adornment to Chicago's lakefront. The buildings are of an attractive, functional design, and the grounds are landscaped with thousands of bushes, plants, and trees. The ten acres of land that cover the filtered water reservoir is a public park featuring five large circular fountains representing the Great Lakes. At night colored lights are shown on the 105-foot-high water jets. During the winter, steam is used in place of water. The park also has walks, benches, and an observation platform for viewing the city's skyline. The entire cost of constructing and operating the filtration plant is paid for by revenue from the sale of water to area consumers. Chicago's water system is a self-supporting utility, and no tax revenues are used for system improvements.

Water System Management

The design and construction of community water systems involves the collective efforts of water works professionals and consulting engineers. Plans and specifications for publicly owned water systems are usually prepared by engineers employed by cities, towns, or large metropolitan water districts that serve several communities. Since 70 percent of the United States water systems are public works, municipal and metropolitan governmental agencies are responsible for constructing and maintaining most domestic water works. Engineers employed by manufacturers of pipe and water works equipment also play an important part by improving water system technology.

The huge volumes of water supplied by the water utility industry require large expenditures for facilities and manpower. The quantity of water needed by municipalities varies widely and depends upon local industrial demands, climate, and economic conditions. In 1970 the quantity of water withdrawn for public supplies was estimated by the United States Geological Survey at about 27 billion gallons per day, an average of 166 gallons per person served. The same year public systems supplied water to nearly 165 million people, about 80 percent of the total population. One third of public supplies is withdrawn by industrial and commercial establishments, and an additional third is lost through leaks in distribution systems or is used for carrying out public services such as fire fighting and street cleaning. The remaining third is supplied to residences. The average home uses water in the following manner: 41 percent for toilet flushing; 37 percent for bathing; 6 percent for kitchen use; 5 percent for drinking water; 4 percent for washing clothes; 3 percent for general household cleaning; 3 percent for lawn and garden watering; and 1 percent for car washing. These relative figures vary regionally and from season to season. For example, in arid western states as much as 60 percent of residential consumption results from summer lawn watering.

In 1974 water utilities employed approximately 115,000 people and spent $1.9 billion for construction of distribution networks, treatment plants, and processing equipment. Over 20,000 treatment plants are operating in the United States, and 12 million miles of transmission and distribution lines are currently in use by water supply systems. Systematic inspection and maintenance is essential to the efficient operation of water systems. Valves and water hydrants are usually operated at least two or three times annually to detect defects. Large mains are periodically flushed to carry away deposits and are inspected for corrosion. Dead-end lines need particular attention because sluggish water flows can compromise water quality. To control water losses, leak detection crews constantly monitor pipe conditions and conduct pressure tests during periods of maximum consumption to locate hydraulic deficiencies in distribution systems.

Records management is essential to efficient maintenance and operation. Public water utilities maintain maps and card files that provide the exact location of mains, valves, manholes, hydrants, and other water system appurtenances. This information is particularly valuable when large main breaks occur and the flow must be shut off before repairs can be undertaken. Most communities have emergency crews constantly on duty or on call who are dispatched to meet emergencies. To carry out repairs, municipalities maintain inventories of pipe, excavating machines, pumps, and electrical generating and welding equipment.

The major problem of some water utilities is deterioration of unlined cast iron pipes. These conduits often become encrusted by iron oxide that reduces pipe capacity and gives a red coloring to water. To remove encrustations, maintenance personnel use hydraulic pressure in conjunction with a pipe scraping tool generally called a pig. This device consists of a series of flexible steel blades mounted on a rod. First, several feet are removed from the pipe that is to be cleaned and the pig is inserted. The cutting device is propelled through the main by water pressure. At the discharge point, the pipe is cut and a snorkel pipe is installed that carries the wash water and scrapings out into the street and allows the cleaning tool to be removed.

Cleaning provides only a temporary solution to pipe corrosion unless some type of protective coating is applied to the walls of the mains. Several processes have been developed to line conduits with cement or bituminous substances without unearthing them. For example, lining machines are used to centrifugally apply cement mortar to the pipe wall that are followed by rotating steel trowels that smooth the surface. This and similar processes extend the life of old mains and reduce the need for costly and time-consuming pipe replacements which disrupt service.

Small water distribution systems are generally managed from a central treatment plant that processes water and controls flow volumes and line pressures. Large cities have built sophisticated control centers to gather water system data that enables operators to simultaneously regulate the production rates of several treatment plants, booster stations, and reservoirs. Flows and line pressures throughout the region are telemetered to the station and hourly printouts are made to warn controllers of low-pressure conditions, depleted water storage, and equipment malfunctions. Service can then be equalized by increasing pumping speeds, stepping up reservoir outflows, and adjusting valves that regulate flow rates in water mains. Thus, central control stations enable public works professionals to make and implement rapidly sound operational decisions.

The concern for safe, palatable water supplies and advancements in testing techniques led to the establishment of drinking water standards. The first set of standards was formulated by the Public Health Service in 1914 to protect the health of the traveling public and to assist in the enforcement of interstate quarantine regulations. The standards, which were changed and updated in 1925, 1942, 1946, and 1962, set limits on the amounts of substances such as toxic chemicals, bacteria, and soluble minerals that are contained in drinking water. In addition to protecting public health, the standards required water supplies to be colorless, odorless, and pleasant to the taste. These federal standards were later supplemented by the World Health Organization's International Standards for Drinking Water (1963) and the American Water Works Association's (AWWA) Quality Goals for Potable Water (1968). The AWWA's report deferred to the Public Health Service standards for criteria concerning health, but it focused attention on aesthetic and other water characteristics that concern consumers. These criteria included clarity, taste, odor, hardness, color, temperature as well as staining and corrosive properties.

By 1970 the Public Health Service drinking water standards were only applicable to the approximately 800 municipal water supplies subject to federal interstate quarantine regulations. However, the endorsement of the standards by AWWA and their partial or complete adoption by most state health departments resulted in their general application to public water supplies throughout the United States. Most large water utilities developed their own laboratories or had access to a state, county, or federal facility. In large systems, reservoirs and other impoundment facilities were frequently tested to insure a high level of water quality. Until recently, water research and testing was the responsibility of water utilities with some state support. However, as understanding of water quality increased, materials such as trace mineral elements, asbestos, chlorinated organics, and carcinogenic substances were discovered to effect public health. The costs of financing and equipping modern laboratories, capable of identifying concentrations of these substances, exceeded the resources of many water utilities.

The heightened concern for the environment in the 1960s focused national attention on the quality of public water supplies. In 1970 the Environmental Protection Agency (EPA) conducted a survey of drinking water systems in several states which revealed that half of the systems did not meet optimum bacterial standards. An additional quarter of them failed to meet bacterial standards for at least one month during a year testing period.

The 1974 Safe Drinking Water Act (SDWA) was passed to establish national drinking water standards. Under this law, EPA was given authority to establish national drinking water criteria. The states were required to enforce the standards and supervise public water supply systems and sources of drinking water. The law is applicable to systems with at least fifteen service connections or that regularly serve at least twenty-five customers.

The SDWA empowered EPA to set standards for maximum limits on levels of contaminants permitted in drinking water. They operate on two levels: primary standards to "reasonably protect human health" and secondary standards to govern aesthetic qualities including taste, odor, and appearance. The primary standards will ultimately be expanded to include treatment techniques and general criteria for operation, maintenance, and intake water quality. The states can continue to enforce their own laws and regulations governing drinking water supplies until EPA's national interim primary regulations go

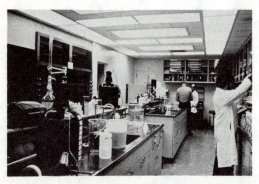

Public Works Historical Society

Public works agencies maintain water laboratories that constantly monitor the quality of public supplies.

into effect in December 1976. These primary regulations will later be revised based on findings of a two-year contaminant health effects study by the National Academy of Sciences. Standards relating to taste, odor, and appearance will be enforced at the states' discretion. A state will continue to implement drinking water standards if it adopts regulations that meet or exceed federal regulations; initiates proper surveillance and enforcement procedures; provides variances and exemptions that meet federal requirements; prepares plans for maintaining safe drinking water under emergency conditions; and keeps records and prepares reports that inform EPA of its activities. In the event of noncompliance, EPA may offer technical assistance, assume enforcement powers, and impose fines.

In addition, SDWA requires EPA to support research on the health, economic, and technological problems of drinking water supplies. Specifically required are studies of viruses in drinking water and contamination by cancer-causing chemicals. A survey of the quality and availability of rural water supplies was authorized as well as development of measures to protect underground drinking water sources. The act also included aid to states to improve drinking water programs through technical assistance, training programs, and grant support. Loan guarantees were provided to assist small water systems to meet regulations if other means of financing are unavailable. A National Drinking Water Advisory Council was founded to advise the EPA administrator on matters relating to SDWA, and $156 million was authorized for the 1975, 1976, and 1977 fiscal years to implement the act's provisions.

The SDWA has placed a heavy burden upon the water utilities industry. In the future, all communities will be required to monitor, evaluate, and in some cases take steps to upgrade the quality of their drinking water supplies. The SDWA has confronted public works officials with unprecedented technical, fiscal, and administrative problems. However, in the past two centuries, the water works profession has met the challenge of providing growing city populations with palatable and safe water supplies. Through public support, research, and hard work, America's civilization will continue to be preserved and enriched by the complex systems that supply and process this precious resource.

SUGGESTED READINGS

Ackerman, Edward A. *Technology in American Water Development*. Baltimore, 1959.

American Water Works Association. *Water Chlorination Principles and Practices*. New York, 1973.

—————— . *Water Quality and Treatment: A Handbook of Public Water Supplies*. New York, 1971.

Baker, Moses N. "Sketch of the History of Water Treatment." *Journal of the American Water Works Association*, 26 (July 1934), 902-938.

—————— . *The Quest for Pure Water: The History of Water Purification From the Earliest Records to the Twentieth Century*. New York, 1948.

Blake, Nelson M. *Water for the Cities: A History of the Urban Water Supply Problem in the United States*. Syracuse, New York, 1956.

Bridenbaugh, Carl. *Cities in Revolt: Urban Life in America, 1743-1776*. New York, 1955.

—————— . *Cities in the Wilderness: Urban Life in America, 1625-1742*. New York, 1938.

Chicago. Department of Public Works. *Chicago Public Works: A History*. Edited by Daphne Christensen. Chicago, 1973.

Clark, John W.; Viessman, Warren; and Hammer, Mark J. *Water Supply and Pollution Control*. 2d. ed. Scranton, Pennsylvania, 1971.

Davies, Delwyn G. *Fresh Water: The Precious Resource*. Garden City, New York, 1969.

246 HISTORY OF PUBLIC WORKS IN THE UNITED STATES 1776-1976

Draffin, Jasper B. *The Story of Man's Quest for Water.* Champaign, Illinois, 1939.

Durfor, Charles N., and Becker, Edith. *Public Water Supplies of the 100 Largest Cities in the United States, 1962.* Washington, D.C., 1964.

Hammer, Mark J. *Water and Waste-Water Technology.* New York, 1975.

Hirshleifer, Jack; Dehaven, James C.; and Milliman, Jerome W. *Water Supply: Economics, Technology, and Policy.* Chicago, 1960.

McWilliams, Mary, and Morse, Roy W. *Seattle Water Department History, 1854-1954.* Seattle, 1955.

U.S. Geological Survey. *Estimated Use of Water in the United States in 1970.* Washingotn, D.C. 1972.

U.S. Water Resources Council. *The Nation's Water Resources: The First National Assessment.* Washington, D.C., 1968.

Wade, Richard C. *The Urban Frontier: Pioneer Life in Early Pittsburgh, Cincinnati, Lexington, Louisville, and St. Louis.* Chicago, 1965.

Weidner, Charles H. *Water for a City.* New York, 1974.

Wolman, Abel. "75 Years of Improvement in Water Supply Quality." *Journal of the American Water Works Association,* 48 (August 1956), 905-914.

——————— . *Water, Health, and Society: Selected Papers.* Edited by Gilbert F. White. Bloomington, Indiana, 1969.

CHAPTER 9

FLOOD CONTROL AND DRAINAGE

The protection of life, land, and property from damage by excess water, whether in motion or standing, is the purpose of various flood control and drainage measures. Flooding occurs from storms that produce runoff exceeding the capacity of the normal stream channels. Long, heavy, widespread storms, or rapid melting of snow from a large area, cause floods on main stem rivers. Concentrated, local, high-intensity storms damage and flood headwater areas. Effective flood control requires both large control facilities on main stem rivers and upstream local watershed protection, including erosion protection and the drainage of excess waters. Waters from upstream, which may be confined in pipes or channels to prevent local damage, may still present major flood control problems further downstream.

Responsibility and Benefits

Responsibility for flood control and drainage depends on the magnitude of the problem. As the population grows, the overall concern for flood control becomes greater; and the benefits become more widespread. Present programs demonstrate how the need for public works increases as population den-

sities become greater. Pressures have mounted for utilizing land and water resources more fully and for minimizing damages from the vagaries of nature. These programs also show the difficulties of determining and following the best route between freedom of the individual to use his land as he considers in his best interest and the need for imposed controls for the overall benefit of communities and the country. These determinations can be made more rationally and effectively with a better understanding of weather, storms, and runoff.

Early settlements developed along the waterways of the nation because these were the early transportation arteries. Sometimes the danger of damage from river floods could be avoided by building on high ground, but often the risk was accepted. The problem of determining responsibility for recovery after a flood and for providing protection from future damage is illustrated by the poem of Douglas Malloch on "Uncle Sam's River" written about the beginning of the twentieth century:

The river belongs to the Nation,
The levee, they say, to the State;
The Government runs navigation,
The Commonwealth, though, pays
  the freight.
Now, here is the problem that's heavy—
Please, which is the right or the wrong—
When the water runs over the levee,
To whom does the river belong?

For the reason implied, the history of

This chapter was prepared mainly from reports of the Army Corps of Engineers, the Soil Conservation Service, the Tennessee Valley Authority, the Bureau of Reclamation, and the City of Chicago.

river flood control programs in the United States is relatively short. Many persons want to live or work near a river, it seems, but "when the water runs over the levee," no one wants responsibility. Though some national leaders very early alluded to the need for flood control on the country's rivers, most considered it a local problem; and the federal government for many years refused on constitutional grounds to become involved.

Throughout the nation's history, serious flooding on America's inland waterways demonstrated the need for means to control high waters. In 1692 a flood occurred on the Delaware River at Trenton, New Jersey, which, if repeated today, would be disastrous. In 1763 the "Point" at Pittsburgh, Pennsylvania, was submerged by a flood. The Los Angeles River flooded in 1770, and in 1771 the rivers in Virginia east of the Allegheny Mountains went on a rampage described as "probably the most devastating act of God experienced in Virginia in its history." In 1785 the Connecticut River in Massachusetts and the Androscoggin and Kennebec rivers in Maine spilled destructive waters into their regions. In 1861, 700 people died in a deluge on the Sacramento River in California. In 1889 at Johnstown, Pennsylvania, uncontrolled

waters killed 2,209 persons and destroyed over $10 million in property. In 1894 the Columbia River leaped its banks with a flow of 1.2 million cubic feet per second. Floods on the unruly Colorado in 1905 broke into the Imperial Valley in California, and for over a year, the uncontrolled flow into the valley created the Salton Sea. In 1913 the Great Miami River caused widespread destruction in Ohio. The nation's most devastating flood occurred on the Mississippi in 1927; and in 1937 the Ohio River Valley suffered its worst flood in history.

Great progress has been made, especially during the last three decades, in providing public works flood control facilities on most drainage areas to reduce the threat of destructive, uncontrolled flood waters. Unlike the past, storm runoff in urban areas rarely causes problems; and flood protection and drainage measures have made agricultural production possible and have increased yields on millions of acres of rich farmlands previously underutilized.

While there are varying opinions on how to measure the benefits of water control and especially flood control projects, accomplishments have been impressive in recent years. Values change with economic conditions and

Los Angeles County Flood Control District

Flood damages have occurred throughout the nation's history.

population pressures; and perspectives from the fairly comfortable, affluent America of the 1970s are quite different from those of earlier days. Many value judgments have been made and seem to have worked well, even with the difficulties of providing public works through America's complex political process and in its democratic, multi-institutional society.

One measure of the value of flood control facilities is an evaluation of the damage that would have occurred had control works not been provided. Sophisticated methods have been developed to measure such benefits as well as to better understand and predict storm and flood behavior. For instance, the approximately $8 billion that the Army Corps of Engineers has expended on completed flood control measures up to 1976 has prevented about $40 billion of flood damages. The Department of Interior's Bureau of Reclamation costs allocated to the flood control features of its projects in the West totaled $600 million by 1975. Since records began to be kept in 1950, these efforts have saved $1.2 billion in damages. In 1974 alone, the saving in damages was $176 million. Other programs are equally impressive.

Additional benefits accrue from the control facilities. The sixty hydroelectric power installations of the Army Corps of Engineers' flood control projects, for example, now total over 14 million kilowatts; and in 1974 produced 77 billion kilowatt hours of electric energy. The artificial lakes created by the Corps of Engineers' flood control dams have become popular recreational areas. These provided 400 million visitor-days in 1975, almost twice as many as were offered by the country's national parks. These outdoor, water-based recreational opportunities are available to many who otherwise would not be able to afford more expensive or less accessible experiences. Furthermore, flood control has improved the navigation waterways developed and maintained by the Corps of Engineers, which by 1975 were carrying 1.6 billion tons of cargo per year. Still another, and perhaps the most important benefit of flood control programs, is making agricultural land, and other land needed for urban and industrial space, available for man's productive use and enjoyment.

The task of providing full flood control may never be finished. However, a reasonable program is underway and is resulting in a better understanding of the vagaries of nature, in more effective use of flood plain areas, and in programs to minimize or eliminate flood risk. A comparison of today's water control programs with that of only a few decades ago clearly demonstrates accomplishments. Progress is and has been made toward the objective of a reasonable, balanced program of flood control and flood plain management.

National Flood Control Policy

The flood control problems of the Mississippi River were the first to receive national concern and continued in the forefront of slowly developing flood control programs. The Mississippi River Commission, created by Congress in 1879, gradually put the federal government into flood control work; and the federal legislation establishing the California Debris Commission in 1893 further recognized the nation's concern and responsibility. The conservation movement led by President Theodore Roosevelt, Gifford Pinchot, and others at the beginning of the twentieth century and the passage of the 1902 Reclamation Act (discussed in Chapter 10) still further involved the federal government in land and water resource development and management. The appointment of the Inland Waterways Commission in 1907 (discussed in Chapter 2) emphasized the national concern for multipurpose water control and use. While the capabilities of a local organization to handle its flood control problems were demonstrated in the early 1920s by the Miami Conservancy District in Ohio, this was a unique situation since it was geographically confined to only one state. The basin topographically lent itself to a well planned and effective flood control system; and it was a relatively rich area able to finance the needed works.

The 1920 Federal Water Power Act, creating the Federal Power Commission (FPC) and establishing procedures to help provide for the orderly development of the na-

Army Corps of Engineers

Providing flood control measures, such as this levee, became national policy with passage of the 1936 Flood Control Act.

tion's waterways, reiterated widespread concern for all aspects of water resource development. This was further emphasized by 1923 legislation directing the Army Corps of Engineers and FPC to submit an estimate of the cost of preparing studies of all the nation's rivers, except the Colorado which was being studied by the Bureau of Reclamation, where power development appeared feasible. The object of the studies was to formulate plans to improve navigation in combination with the development of water power, flood control, and irrigation. The report was submitted in April 1926 as House Document No. 308. The studies were authorized the following January and resulted in the important and extensive "308" river basin reports by the Army Corps of Engineers. These formed the basis for much of the project legislation adopted since.

The 1928 Boulder Canyon Act authorized the first large multipurpose water resource project to include vast flood control benefits. This was followed by the various programs of the Reconstruction Finance Corporation (RFC), Works Progress Administration

(WPA), and Public Works Administration (PWA) for river basin projects of the 1930s. The 1933 Tennessee Valley Authority Act established a regional resource development program to prevent floods and fully utilize water resources of the Tennessee River.

Proponents of federal responsibility for flood control argued that as rivers were under the jurisdiction of the United States there was an obligation to prevent damage from floods. Furthermore, the interstate character of rivers and the effects elsewhere of any local actions taken required federal responsibility for coordination. Levees and other water control works were being built by several agencies of the federal government as well as states, levee boards, cities, counties, districts, railroads, and various other groups and individuals; thus, making a consistent public works policy almost impossible to formulate without federal action. Added to this problem were considerations of interstate commerce, postal service, public health and safety, national defense, and the general welfare, As early as 1879, James A. Garfield, two years before he became President, stated in the House of Representatives that the problem was "too vast for any state to handle; too much for any authority other than that of the nation itself to manage."

To many, the government had as much right to make lands suitable for habitation and use by protecting them from flooding as it had to give the public domain to settlers. Furthermore, Congress had recognized and acted upon the need to provide flood relief to minimize human suffering and hardship. As the nation's population increased, arguments that flood control was unconstitutional were overcome. It became generally accepted that the widespread benefits of flood control extended to all. The rise of public concern for the general welfare finally resulted in passage of the 1936 Flood Control Act. This established flood control, including channel and major drainage improvements, for navigable waters or their tributaries as a proper activity of the federal government. Provisions were made for local participation in providing right-of-way and for protecting the United States against damages from construction of the works.

The act gave the secretary of war, acting through the Army Corps of Engineers, responsibility for supervising the federal river flood control functions. And the secretary of agriculture was made responsible for waterflow retardation and soil erosion prevention in the small watersheds. The act stipulated that this authority was not to interfere with river improvements in progress nor to be undertaken in connection with reclamation projects of the Bureau of Reclamation, pursuant to any general or specific authorization of law.

Through the 1936 act and subsequent project authorizations, including various modifications and refinements of the act, the Army Corps of Engineers has completed about 3,400 projects and project modifications that have some flood control benefits, as their part of the overall federal program. This includes over 400 dams and reservoirs located in forty-two states. Generally, the projects are planned and designed by corps personnel assisted by private consulting engineering firms. Construction is usually under contracts

awarded as a result of public bidding. Some of these programs are described in the following sections.

The other major federal water-related construction agencies, the Bureau of Reclamation and the Soil Conservation Service, have also planned and built hundreds of water control projects having flood control benefits. Various agencies of state governments have built projects for which they have received federal funds to compensate for the flood control costs of the projects. Operation of the flood control aspects of these projects is generally controlled by criteria developed and monitored by the Army Corps of Engineers.

By the 1960s, increasing attention and importance were being given to comprehensive flood plain mangement to minimize flood damage exposure. This involved, in addition to the flood control structures, restricting new construction and flood-proofing existing structures in flood-prone areas. This was not a new concept as it had been considered to some degree from the beginning of the flood control programs. Even so, flood damage is still high, averaging nationwide about $1.3 billion a year. It is not possible to provide control of all severe storm and flood hazards, but much can be done to minimize the impact of such disasters.

Until recent years, there was little unified effort to zone and control building on flood plains. However, programs, such as that of the Tennessee Valley Authority begun in 1953, have demonstrated what can be accomplished. The report of the federal flood control policy task force, presented to Congress in 1966, resulted in 1968 legislation establishing the National Flood Insurance Program in the Department of Housing and Urban Development. Further broadened in 1969 and 1973, the program is a comprehensive approach to flood damage protection. It enables property owners in areas subject to frequent flooding to obtain flood insurance at affordable rates, as the overall insurance is subsidized by the federal government. In turn, communities with designated flood areas are required to develop flood plain management measures to minimize future flood devastation. Such a plan must be adopted, or measures underway to establish the plan by 1976 or the area will be ineligible for federal assistance.

The flood-prone areas are those that would be flooded by a 100-year frequency flood; that is, one that has a 1 percent chance of happening in any one year. The Federal Insurance Administration (FIA) has notified over 15,000 communities that they are flood prone and has supplied them with maps tentatively identifying these areas. By the end of 1975, the majority of these communities had applied for the program. Detailed surveys and flood data follow their applications in order to develop adequate measures to minimize damage on the flood plains. The FIA calls upon other federal agencies, such as the Army Corps of Engineers and the Geological Survey, for basic data or utilizes private consulting engineers. The mandatory provisions of the act should help develop more balanced flood plain management programs.

The 1960 Flood Control Act authorized the Army Corps of Engineers to prepare flood hazard information on specific areas at the request of states or communities. This includes not only identifying areas subject to inundation by floods of various magnitudes and frequencies but also encouraging optimum use of flood-prone lands. Considerable work is being done; in 1974 over 12,000 requests were handled. The 1974 Water Resources Development Act provides for consideration of the full range of structural and non-structural approaches in all water resource planning where federal interests are involved, a concept that has been generally followed for several years.

The evolving flood control and drainage policies are demonstrated by the projects discussed in the following sections. The programs described are representative of the numerous problems encountered and illustrate public works that are in operation as well as the multipurpose nature of most flood control undertakings.

The Mississippi River and Its Tributaries

For floods, the Mississippi River is in a class by itself, draining with its 250 tributaries 1.3 million square miles, 41 percent of the contiguous forty-eight states. The yearly average flow into the Gulf of Mexico is about 610,000 cubic feet per second, and peak flood flows just below the entrance of the Arkansas River into the main stream have reached almost 3 million cubic feet per second. It was by flooding that the river built its long alluvial valley carrying silt to form new delta upon new delta as it worked its way from southern Illinois to southern Louisiana. The Mississippi received the first national attention for flood control. The river and its major tributaries, the Missouri, the Ohio, and the Tennessee, contain some of the major flood control facilities in the nation.

The Mississippi River: The written history of the Mississippi began with a flood. In 1543 Garcilliaso de la Vega, in his annals of the expedition led by Hernando de Soto, described the first recorded flood of the Mississippi as being severe and of prolonged duration. It began about March 10 and crested forty days later. By the end of May, the river returned to its banks, having been in flood for eighty days. French documents indicate that a Mississippi flood in 1735 was marked not only by high stages but by a duration of six months and destruction of most of the levees erected by the New Orleans colony along the river's edge. Other records indicate occurences of several more great floods in the latter part of the eighteenth century and of thirteen during the nineteenth century. In the twentieth century, eleven major floods had taken place by 1975.

The public works concept for control of floodwaters developed largely on the Mississippi, beginning in 1712 at New Orleans, six years before it became a permanent settlement. A young engineer, Blond de la Tour, was given the task of planning a levee system so that a town site could be developed. By 1727 the French had built a levee over 1 mile long and 3 to 4 feet high, along with a system of drainage ditches. Since that time, in attempts to confine flood flows within the river channel, the levees have been greatly increased in height and extent.

The French required owners of land abutting the streams to build and keep levees in repair. Many plantation owners constructed sections to protect their rich bottomlands against too frequent flooding. These were piecemeal local approaches which were not very effective. When the Mississippi Valley passed into the hands of the United States in 1803, crude levees extended about 100 miles upriver from New Orleans, but there were no other attempts to control the river. Congressional concern was expressed about the problem of flooding, but flood control was regarded as beyond the scope of federal responsibility and beyond the authority granted in the commerce clause or elsewhere in the Constitution. Though provisions of the Constitution were interpreted in 1824 to permit improvements for navigation; for many years, no constitutional way was seen to permit the government to assist afflicted localities and states to reduce flood damage. A majority of early congressmen concluded that although improvements to navigation fostered and encouraged the commerce of the whole nation, flood control on the same rivers amounted to "reclamation of overflow lands for the benefit of private owners." This was regarded as advancement of personal and local interests and not of national responsibility.

In 1835 Henry Clay proposed a measure that seemed to place some obligation for flood prevention on the federal government. He introduced a resolution in Congress directing the secretary of the treasury to have an estimate made "of the probable expense of constructing a levee on the public land on the western bank of the Mississippi, and the southern bank of the Red River." The study was made, but no further action was taken. Ten years later, John C. Calhoun suggested assigning certain public lands to the riparian states in the Mississippi Basin, proceeds from which would be used for flood protection works. The avowed purpose was to reclaim "millions of acres of public domain on the Mississippi River and its tributaries, now worthless." His proposal languished for four years, as Congress was reluctant to vote any kind of support for flood control. More such legislation died in committees or in floor votes, the ascribed reason being that such assistance amounted to "unwarranted appropriations for the illegitimate purpose of protecting the private property of citizens living adjacent to the Mississippi River." This manner of thinking continued the French policy that only those who lived alongside the river should provide flood protection works. As a result, not only was flood protection inadequate, but riparian farmlands often were so heavily taxed that many owners were unable to pay and lost their lands.

The State of Mississippi passed the first legislation in 1819 authorizing construction of levees and providing for collection of levee taxes from riparian owners. Then in 1846, the state began to tax backlands to help the land-

Army Corps of Engineers

Early levee construction on the Mississippi River was performed with wheelbarrows, often using convict labor.

owners on the river. In 1856 Louisiana developed a complex system aimed at the same end, whereby levee districts of parish size or larger were empowered to tax everyone in the district for flood control support.

After devastating floods in 1849 and 1850, the federal government enacted the Swampland Acts that were precedent-setting legislation. They were the outcome of twenty years of discussion in Congress concerning ways to make the wetlands of the public domain productive. The acts granted, among other provisions, about 28 million acres of periodically flooded lands lying within their borders to the riparian states of the lower Mississippi Valley. Other states were granted 36 million acres. The states were to drain the lands and then sell them to secure funds for further flood control. The plan was not successful in producing sufficient funds for accomplishing drainage and flood control, but it did form the basis for projects developed later. It accomplished the vast transfer of lands from the federal government to the states and soon thereafter from the states to counties and levee boards and later to private ownership.

Even if the acts had succeeded in providing funds for flood control, such efforts in the Mississippi Valley would have ended with the Civil War. When peace returned, residents along the Mississippi had become so impoverished that they could do little to restore levees or remove hazards to navigation. In the Mississippi Valley, reconstruction meant two things: reopening the navigation channel and rebuilding the protective works, mainly levees, against devastation of recurring floods.

In some ways, these two problems were intimately related. In 1866 the Senate directed the army's chief of engineers to investigate the repairs necessary to prevent extensive damage to agriculture along the river. The resulting report suggested a need for federal aid in flood damage reduction. The committee that considered the matter in Congress reported favorably on the expenditure of federal funds for rebuilding flood protection works. In 1867 the Senate Finance Committee stated that it was satisfied with the "constitutional power and the expediency and good policy" of granting federal aid for this purpose.

Still the bill did not pass, and responsibility for rebuilding protective works remained in the hands of those who lived beside the big river. Pressure from powerful northern business interests then began to arise, as they invaded the South in the wake of the Union armies. Buying into commercial real estate and the rich agricultural lands, eastern capital acquired a practical interest in flood control, an interest that became even greater as railroads built lines across the flood plains of the Mississippi.

In 1874 Congress created a joint commission of three army engineers and two civilian engineers to investigate "the best system for the permanent reclamation and redemption" of the alluvial basin of the Mississippi River which was subject to inundation. This led to further surveys to determine the optimum locations for preventive works. A recommendation was made that a general levee system be built, extending from the head of the alluvial region to the Gulf of Mexico, including the valleys of tributary streams. The commission determined that a system of double embankments should be adopted, with small front levees following the bends of the river and main levees set farther back and high enough to prevent inundations by the biggest known flood. The existing levees would become the front line, and new back levees would be the shoreline of the waterway in a major flood. The commission also found the existing system of local levee boards inadequate and stated:

> The experience of over 150 years has utterly failed to create the judicious laws of effective organization in the several states themselves, and no systematic organization has ever been attempted between them. . . . It is a common and apt figure of speech to personify the Mississippi and to speak of the conflict waged to protect the country against the inroads of a terrible enemy, and yet the army of defense has always been content to remain a simple aggregation of independent companies, with here and there a battalion under the command of a board of officers. That victory has not more frequently perched upon their banners is surely not surprising.

These problems were made the responsibility of the seven-member Mississippi River Commission (MRC) when it was created by Congress in 1879. Among its other duties, was the charge to "prevent destructive floods." In its sphere of responsibility, focusing primarily on navigation, MRC proposed to start building levees. The constitutional interpretation compelled MRC to show that levees were essential to navigation rather than for flood control.

Before construction got underway, a giant flood in 1882 wrecked the partially restored levee line along the Mississippi and almost destroyed the remaining financial credit of the impoverished levee districts. In the Rivers and Harbors Act of that year, Congress placed direct responsibility for construction in the hands of the Army Corps of Engineers but also authorized MRC to "build and repair levees if in their judgement it should be done as a part of their plan to afford ease and safety to the navigation and commerce of the river and to deepen the channel."

The commission furnished approximately one third of the funds for subsequent levee building, while the levee districts supplied the rest. The MRC's investment allowed it to introduce advanced techniques and organization into levee building. Proper selection of levee sites, often considerably back from the river to the dismay of riparian landowners; complete clearance of the topsoil under levees and removal of stumps; construction to specified heights and cross sections; prohibition of cuts and drains through the levees; and outlawing use of them as roadways were requirements of the construction "standards."

Another flood in 1890 brought renewed appeals from local groups for help in completing their levees. The "navigation plea" was often omitted as local officials claimed their burdens of debt were too great to finance needed levee construction or upgrading. The 1890 Rivers and Harbors Act, therefore, omitted the proviso against building levees for flood control only. This cleared the way for flood control to be recognized in its own right. As work progressed, the Mississippi came to be "walled in" by a patchwork of levees— some federal, some private, most built by levee districts with or without federal aid. In 1899 MRC was able to report: "For the first time in the history of the river, a great flood passed between banks from the Red River to the Gulf. The whole sugar country, where inundation means destruction, was saved from overflow."

The first Flood Control Act, approved March 1, 1917, extended the jurisdiction of MRC to "all water courses connected with the main river to such extent as might be necessary to exclude flood waters from the upper limits of any delta basin." Though this law did not represent the actual entry of the federal government into flood control, it was important for two reasons: (1) it swept away the pretense that levee building was intended only to benefit navigation and proclaimed openly that flood control was a proper activity of the federal government; and (2) it established standards for federal-state cooperation, providing that one third of the cost of flood control works should be paid by the national government and two thirds by local interests. The law continued the prevailing piecemeal control works, however, by requiring heavy participation by the local interests.

Eight years later, the 1925 Rivers and Harbors Act established another precedent by providing for comprehensive waterway planning. It declared that flood control, navigation, power production, and irrigation were interdependent aspects of such development and must be considered together in planning for the use of the country's inland waterways. The bankruptcy of halfway measures was demonstrated in 1927, when the most disastrous flood in American history struck. A month-by-month story of that tragedy was related by Albert E. Cowdrey in The Delta Engineers:

By 1926 the Commission felt that the flood problem had been nearly solved by the levees, and that maintenance and bank protection would be the concerns of the future. Yet in the autumn of that year certain signs began to appear that the levees were about to be subjected to another test.

In October, Major John C. H. Lee, the newly appointed District Engineer at Vicksburg, noted that the river had risen to 40 feet on the Vicksburg gage. He . . . found that it had reached 30 feet or more in October only six times in 54 years, and each time the spring following had brought extremely high water. . .

The new year opened ominously, with a minor flood in January, and a somewhat higher one in February. In early March, the waters fell somewhat, but toward the end of the month the seasonal rises of the Ohio, Missouri, and Tennessee showed not only a magnitude but also a degree of synchronization that plainly warned of a major flood on the way. . . .

The worst sign of all was the weather. . . . The spring rains, especially in the middle valley, were exceptionally heavy and on the night of April 15 New Orleans had a deluge of almost Biblical dimensions—14.01 inches. On April 18 the river stood at 56.2 feet at Cairo, and the lowlands were flooding rapidly; there were 25,000 homeless, and at least 12 dead. The worst sufferers so far were Missouri, Arkansas, and Mississippi, with lesser areas inundated in Illinois, Kentucky, Tennessee, and Louisiana.

Cloudbursts fell in southern Kansas, raising the Arkansas, which broke through the levees in Pulaski County and flooded 15,000 acres of Arkansas' richest land. . . .

Following the cloudburst of the 15th, New Orleans enjoyed several days of sunshine. . . . But the river was rising at every gage from New Orleans to St. Paul, and every major tributary except the Cumberland and the Tennessee was also rising. On 20 April the gage at New Orleans stood at 20.0, up 0.1 foot from the day before. The reports from upriver were an excruciating mixture of good and bad news. Whenever the Mississippi broke its levees the danger to New Orleans from the gigantic flood crest moving downriver was lessened to some degree. And as the crisis of 21-30 April began, there was little to be heard but this sort of tragic blessing. The levees upstream were being overwhelmed.

On the 20th the river reached 44.7 feet at Memphis and the levee broke at Clarendon, Arkansas. . . .

The mainline levee broke the next day above Greenville, Mississippi, flooding an area 50 miles wide and 75 miles long. Recalling the night of 20-21 April, Major Lee wrote, "No steamer was able to stem the current. . . . So we rushed in sacks (for sand bags) by airplane and by small boats braving the swirling current of the Arkansas South of Pine Bluff. Labor consisted of white volunteers, of drafted Negroes, of National Guardsmen, and of convicts from the state

A refugee camp was established along a levee near Arkansas City, Arkansas, during the Mississippi River flood of 1927.

farm. All worked side by side just as they would fight in a trench. They held this levee ten days and nights through wretched weather, cold and wet, until another attack developed just below and the forces had to be divided. It was then that the crisis came and South Bend went out. . . ."

The refugee camps were flooding, and epidemics of mumps, measles, and whooping cough were reported among the survivors. The Corps of Engineers reported to President Coolidge that the flood would be the worst in a generation. . . .

Meanwhile the federal government mobilized its resources, not to prevent ruin—it was too late for that—but to minimize the human suffering along the river. Major Gen. Edgar Jadwin, the Army Chief of Engineers, went to Memphis to take personal charge; a presidential commission under Herbert Hoover, the secretary of commerce, was set up to deal with the disaster; the President appealed for $5 million needed by the Red Cross; the activities of seven agencies of the government were integrated in a massive effort at relief. But the greatest question of the flood remained unanswered: what would happen to New Orleans when the crest reached it?

On 26 April, late in the evening, Governor Oramel H. Simpson ordered the levee to be cut at Poydras Plantation, below the city. One hundred thousand acres were expected to be flooded, the water eventually to find an outlet through natural drains into Lake Borgne and the Gulf of Mexico.

The finale went with a bang—and a fizzle. Trappers and farmers from the area to be flooded were reported guarding the levee. . . . Riotous public meetings were held, and state authorities made cheap and abundant promises of compensation, few of which were to be honored. Meantime, in New Orleans 500 "pump guns" were issued to patrol squads to guard against possible reprisals. An embargo was placed on dynamite sales, and 400 National Guardsmen were encamped above the city.

On 29 April six successive charges of dynamite breached the Poydras levee. Though 1500 pounds had been exploded, a reporter wrote angrily that "awe-inspiring spectacle that had been promised was lacking. There was no gigantic torrent. . . . Hours passed before the crevasse slowly grew to the needed dimensions. . . .

Coming at the end of that terrible April, when the levee system had been overwhelmed, 200 people killed, and 700,000 driven from their homes, the valley devastated, and $200 million in property losses recorded, the uninspiring blast at Poydras might have been taken as a far more significant sound. A policy had been breached, and the pouring waters were sweeping an era away.

As a consequence of the disastrous flood, President Calvin Coolidge directed the Army Corps of Engineers to prepare a comprehensive plan for a federal flood control program on the Mississippi River. The program was prepared and submitted in 1928. This so-called "Jadwin Plan" was adopted as the 1928 Flood Control Act, sometimes called the

"Flood Emancipation Act." The legislation authorized MRC and the corps to use federal moneys to develop a unified flood control system in the entire alluvial valley. The resulting project, still under construction nearly fifty years later, became known as the "Mississippi River and Tributaries Project" (MR&T). Its objective was to shackle the mighty Mississippi.

According to General Edgar Jadwin: "The plan set forth in the adopted project is to protect the alluvial valley of the Mississippi from the maximum flood predicted as possible." He and the designers of MR&T believed that flooding even greater than that of 1927 could occur. So they conceived a hypothetical deluge, a forerunner of similar approaches used for flood control designs on other rivers, which resulted by combining the most severe storms of record and placing them in a pattern to produce the worst possible runoff conditions. This flood proved to be 11 percent greater than the flood of 1927 at the Arkansas River. Below Natchez, Mississippi, it would be 29 percent greater.

The MR&T project was designed to control this flood. It comprised four major elements: (1) levees to contain flood flows; (2) floodways to detour excess flows past critical areas; (3) channel stabilization and improve-

The Mississippi River and Tributary Project, of which this levee in New Orleans, Louisiana, is a part, provides protection against floods on the Mississippi River.

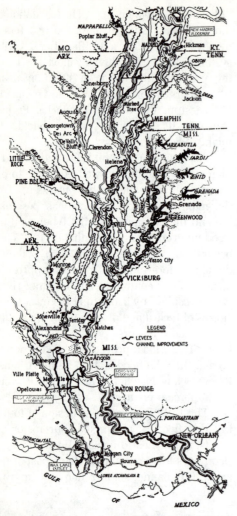

Flood control measures on the Mississippi River and tributaries downstream from Cairo, Illinois.

ment, to keep the river where it was, increase its flood-carrying capacity, protect the levee system, and provide a better navigation channel; and (4) tributary basin improvements, including dams and reservoirs. To protect against the flood, the planners of MR&T found that levees would have to average about 25 feet in height, with some as high as 40 feet.

Four floodways on the main stem have evolved from the planning, one in Missouri and three in Louisiana. The one in Missouri, the New Madrid Floodway, was designed to protect the city of Cairo, Illinois, as well as to reduce the amount of water that might combine with the Ohio River. A spillway, the Bonnet Carre, was built to carry off floodwaters from above New Orleans into Lake Pontchartrain. A third set of structures, at Old River, would help to divert waters from the flooding Mississippi into the basin of its sister distributary stream, the Atchafalaya River. This was also the purpose of the fourth, Morganza, located in the same vicinity.

Stabilization of the river channel and protection of the banks were included to protect flood control features and to insure the desired alignment of the river's navigation channel. This phase of the MR&T project later included a program of channel cutoffs, which in the flood of 1941, lowered river stages over 12 feet at Arkansas City and 11 feet at Vicksburg.

The fourth element of MR&T was tributary basin improvements. In this category, however, the 1928 Flood Control Act made provision only "for flood-control work on the tributaries and outlets in so far as they are affected by backwater from the Mississippi." It failed to recognize that these tributary streams themselves cause frequent damage which could not be prevented by mainstream control works, and that unbridled tributary waters make up much of the mainstream's flooding. After 1936 new flood control acts included protection of the major tributary lands by levees, dams, and reservoirs.

The Mississippi drainage area upstream of the Missouri River is considered the upper basin. The Mississippi rises in tiny Lake Itasca in Minnesota and descends through a region sometimes called the "breadbasket of America." It touches the five states of Minnesota, Wisconsin, Iowa, Illinois, and Missouri. The drainage area, approximately 189,000 square miles, also includes parts of Indiana and South Dakota. The topography of the basin varies from flat prairie lands in Iowa and Illinois to gentle rolling hills in Minnesota, Wisconsin, and Missouri. Storms precipitate an average of thirty-two inches of water over the basin during the year.

The region is susceptible to flooding each year in early spring, especially after heavy snowfalls during the preceding winter. Floods in 1881, 1952, and 1965 occurred after persistent below-freezing temperatures in the month of March, followed by sudden increases in temperature triggering snow melts and rapid runoff. Below Minneapolis, the upper Mississippi has been canalized by a system of twenty-eight dams and locks built primarily for navigation. While flood control measures are not so far advanced as on the middle and lower reaches of the river, there are local, state, and federal projects. These ranged from reservoirs to control floods in major tributary basins to levees and floodwalls for the protection of individual cities and some agricultural areas. The area still suffers annual flood damages estimated at about $30 million. In 1965 a destructive flood involved nearly every tributary to the Mississippi in the central and southern portions of the upper basin and resulted in nearly $50 million in flood damages.

In 1973 another devastating flood inundated most of the area. River locks began to be covered with water, forcing removal of electric motors and consequent closing of the river to traffic. The current crumbled private levees and flooded many business districts. In Hannibal, Missouri, for example, the Mark Twain Hotel had 5 feet of water in its lobby.

Flood control is included as part of the Upper Mississippi River Comprehensive Basin Study, now being implemented. In 1962 Congress assigned sponsorship of this cooperative investigation to the Corps of Engineers, with the understanding that the Departments of Agriculture; Commerce; Interior; Health, Education, and Welfare; and the Federal Power Commission would be full-study partners, along with representatives of the seven riparian states. The study was completed in 1972 and, in addition to flood control, included navigation, hydroelectric power generation, water supply, and other purposes coordinated with related land resources.

Controlling floods on this reach of the Mississippi is largely accomplished by regulating the waters of the tributaries. For instance, Central City Lake, on the Wapsipinicon River in Iowa, has been authorized as part of the comprehensive plan. On the Cedar River, a similar project, Rochester Lake, helps hold back floods. On the Iowa River upstream from Iowa City is a completed flood control project, Coraville Lake, con-

structed under the 1938 Flood Control Act. On the Des Moines River, the Red Rock Dam and Lake Red Rock were also authorized by this act. Farther up the river, near the city of Des Moines, the Saylorville Lake was authorized by Congress in 1958 to supplement the flood control capacity of the Red Rock projects. Mercer Lake was authorized by the 1965 Flood Control Act as a unit in the flood control and water resource development plan for the Grand River Basin. The Clarence Cannon Reservoir, on the Salt River was authorized by the 1962 Flood Control Act. This is a multiple-purpose reservoir with a total storage capacity of 1.4 million acre-feet, of which 884,000 are for flood control, in a 2,920 square-mile area in northeastern Missouri. Completion is scheduled for 1976.

Typical Flood Control Measures: The best flood control system for a river basin will depend upon many variables including topography; storm and runoff patterns; size and shape of watershed and of the flood plain; slope of the streambed; silt, bedload, and debris carried by the stream; extent and intensity of development; and many other factors. The following descriptions of the flood control measures undertaken by MRC illustrate the various methods that are used.

Although MRC at first accepted the building of levees as the only protective works that could be supported by federal action, several others were considered. The MR&T Flood Control Plan used most of these methods in various combinations to give the best results. The methods include (1) levees; (2) floodways, diversion channels, and other outlets; (3) dams and reservoirs; (4) bank and channel stabilization; (5) cutoffs; and (6) contour plowing and reforestation.

Levees. The name "levee" came to the United States with the French. Since these earth ramparts were elevated sections of the riverbank, they were called "elevees" by the early French settlers. The first levees built by the French at New Orleans, while extremely small, were adequate for the unconfined Mississippi of that day. Later, the inadequate levees built by riparian residents were substandard, primarily because of the financial inability of private landowners to provide the larger embankments required by a more confined channel.

The levees that protected the land against ordinary high water continually raised the crests of great floods by cutting off the river's natural overflow areas. As industry and agriculture prospered behind the earthen walls, potential losses from floods increased as well. The dimensions of levees on controlled rivers had to grow with the degree of confinement.

When the 1717 New Orleans levee was first constructed, the high-water mark was about 3 feet above the river banks. The levee, therefore, could be built to a height of only 4 feet, with side slopes of one vertical on two horizontal. This levee, with a crown width of 18 feet, was designed to be a flood embankment, a public landing, and a walk. By 1858 the Mississippi was more or less confined within 2,000 miles of embankments, with an average height of more than 8 feet. In many places, however, levees were only 4 to 5 feet high. Such levees were designed to provide a foot or two of freeboard above the highwater mark of the 1851 flood, the greatest known to that time. The disastrous flood of 1858 swept away miles of such levees.

When it considered the levees in 1879, MRC had a complicated problem, for it had to build onto the existing systems. Over a period of years, the commission adopted a "provisional grade" of 3 feet above the 1912 high water and a standard cross section to establish what became known as the "commission grade and section," the accepted mark of a "completed levee." These standards, however, again proved inadequate in the flood of 1927, and a new levee standard was adopted in 1928. It was based on a determined amount of freeboard above the maximum probable flood rather than any actual flood history. The following table illustrates the evolution of the standard levee section from 1882 to the present:

Year	Height (feet)	Base Width (feet)
1882	9.0	53.0
1896	15.5	120.5
1914	24.0	200.0
1928	27.0	260.0
Present	30.5	315.0

The width of the crown of most levees was increased to provide access roadways. During periods of high water, levees are routinely patrolled to detect and promptly correct weakness that might develop. In most instances, such corrections require hauling in construction material; thus, a roadway on the levees is essential. The 10-foot crown width of the initial standard levee section was increased for roadway needs, sometimes as much as 15 feet.

Size, grade, section, and slope, however, were still not the only factors which affected the strength of the levees. Until the twentieth century, little was known about soil properties, especially the permeability, shrinkage, and compactability of different kinds of earth from which levees are made. Knowledge was borrowed from the construction of earth dams. A new science called "soil mechanics" showed the advantage of giving greater attention to materials and their compactability. It became possible to construct levees having lower permeability, fewer and smaller voids, and lower shrinkage factors. As a result, few levees have failed in recent years because of inadequate compaction or improper materials.

These demands called for a corresponding improvement in building methods. Because the first levees were rarely more than a few feet in dimension, they were derisively called "potato ridges." They were often built by hand with shovels and wheelbarrows. The large "borrow pits," from which material for present levees is taken, are the descendants of smaller "barrow pits" of an earlier day. As larger levees became necessary, mules with drag scrapers, then wheel scrapers, then dump wagons were employed, until the construction needs of the extended levee systems passed the capacity of wagons and mules. Not only had the cost per cubic yard mounted, but there were not enough mules, wagons, and laborers to do the work. Draglines with large buckets and long booms were put into use.

The next step was the adapting of a commercial cableway to levee building. This involved two movable towers, running on steel tracks, one tower placed back of the levee, and the smaller tower at a distance of 500 to 1,000 feet from the levee on the riverside. A taut cableway was stretched between two towers. The bucket, supported from a trolley, was lowered for digging and elevated for traveling. This cableway functioned well and placed dirt more cheaply than the wagon; but by the early 1920s, it was superseded by the slack cableway tower machine with its greater capacity averaging 300 cubic yards an hour.

Since the 1940s, the tower machine, or cableway, has gradually faded out of the picture because the conditions that originally made it useful have disappeared. Levees on the Mississippi, at least, were completed to grade and section under the MR&T project. During this period, hauling units with capacities of 13 to 40 cubic yards replaced earlier 6 to 10 cubic yard units; and rubber tires replaced the caterpillar crawlers formerly used. Also, self-loading scrapers with capacities of 18 to 20 cubic yards were employed, and dump trucks began to be loaded by small draglines.

Some leveee construction is still performed by large draglines, generally possessing 150- to 180-foot booms with 5- to 8-cubic yard buckets. On new work, it is not unusual to see large draglines operating in tandem. For this, one machine casts material from the back to near the front of a borrow pit; and the second machine moves the material into the levee section.

Floodways. The purpose of "walling in" the Mississippi River was to "protect the Mississippi Valley from inundation, reclaim 15 or 20 million acres of overflow lands, and perfect approximately 20,000 miles of precarious navigation." There was, however, a price to be paid for these intended benefits. The overflow lands constituted the normal flood plain of the river. Before levees were built, in times of high water, the river rose to overtop the banks of the main channel and flowed into the vast adjacent low grounds, which served as temporary sumps for the storage of the flood waters. When levees were constructed, they closed the normal exits by which river water could reach the flood plains; and little by little those plains were utilized by homes and industry. With the extension of the levee system, waters in-

creasingly were confined within the narrow river channels, unable to escape laterally. Under these conditions, the waters rose between the levees, forcing the construction of higher and stronger embankments. Use of the flood plains for agriculture also contributed to increased stages, since removal of natural ground cover accelerated drainage of surface runoff into tributaries and the mainstream.

As early as 1851, Charles S. Ellet, Jr., a noted civil engineer making studies for the Army Corps of Engineers, realized that levees alone would not shackle the mighty Mississippi. He reported that "the most that can be expected from these embankments is to preserve the country against the effects of moderate floods, which do not reach their summit." He, therefore, recommended that other measures be used to supplement the levees. One of his suggestions was the use of artificial outlets to draw off surplus water from the river and discharge it through new channels into the Gulf of Mexico. In his report of 1852, he proposed an outlet from the Mississippi into Lake Borgne, about 11 miles below New Orleans, to form a "vent that would reduce the surface of the Mississippi at high water as nearly as possible to the level of the Gulf." An investigating commission disagreed; it concluded that such "artificial outlets, although correct in theory, had no useful application to the Mississippi."

In 1879 another civil engineer, John Cowden, proposed a series of outlets as the best method of relieving the alluvial region of the Mississippi basin of excess water. The MRC did not accept the proposal because of local opposition. In 1922 a crevasse occurred in a levee at Poydras, Louisiana, a few miles below New Orleans. When immediately thereafter high waters began to recede, New Orleans became convinced that a controlled outlet similar to the Poydras breach could carry off the crest of any flood when it reached a moderately high stage. The following year, MRC agreed that New Orleans should have a floodway, but that it should be located above the city.

In 1928 the "Jadwin Plan" incorporated the idea of floodways into the MR&T project. Jadwin proposed to restore to the river by ar-

The Bonnet Carre spillway, just upstream from New Orleans, released floodwaters into the floodway leading to Lake Pontchartrain to control the flood of April 1975.

tificial means what the levee system had taken away. That is, a system of floodways and spillways would restore the effects of the flood plain natural reservoirs while levees continued to protect the rest of the flood plains from inundation. The controlled entry of water into floodways would be by "fuse plug" levees. These were low embankments designed to hold out ordinary stages of the river but to crevasse in great floods. Once inside the floodways, the overflow water would be guided by a system of lateral levees.

In the dozen or so years that usually elapsed between great floods, land within the floodways would be made available for a variety of uses, including cattle raising and many types of farming. In Jadwin's view, residents of these unfavored areas would have no valid reason for complaint, since the proposed floodways were all overflow areas that would go under water anyway during great floods.

Dams and Reservoirs. Ellet's report also recommended creating flood control reservoirs by constructing dams in the upland areas of tributary streams of the Mississippi. Like floodways, these artificial lakes would help compensate for the loss of flood plain sumps, access to which had been cut off by the levees. He recommended that the federal government construct the reservoirs and pointed out they would also aid navigation by storing floodwaters for release when the natural flow was low, thus insuring sufficient depth for a navigable channel.

However, Congress saw this approach as primarily flood control, and it was seventy-five years before this responsibility was accepted. In the interim, a number of studies were made concerning the effects of reservoirs. Then the 1928 Flood Control Act provided that projects for control of all flood-prone tributary streams of the Mississippi River system should be studied. A report was prepared to show the effect that might be attained by establishing a reservoir system. This led to construction of five storage reservoirs in the MR&T project. Four of these are in the basin of the Yazoo River (Sardis, Arkabutla, Enid, and Grenada), and one is in the basin of the St. Francis River (Wappapello). None is on the main stem of the Mississippi.

Over 200 major reservoirs containing flood control features are now completed in the Mississippi River drainage area. Except the original five, all are outside the lower alluvial valley. Notable are the Tennessee Valley Authority structures on the Tennessee River; those of the Corps of Engineers in the basins of the Ohio, Missouri, Arkansas, and other tributaries; and those of the Bureau of Reclamation on the Missouri and its tributaries. In the Far West, dams and reservoirs provide the fundamental portion of the flood control development of the Columbia and the Colorado river basins as well as the control of water for irrigation, power, municipal, and related uses.

Channel Stabilization. High flood waters erode river banks, widen riverbeds, and sometimes cut new channels. On major rivers, widening of the riverbed can destroy forests, farms, buildings, roads, and railroads. In cutting new channels, the river may abandon bridges, towns, industries, and flood control improvements. Then in low-season flow, the wider riverbed may become too shallow for navigation. Bars may form to harass river transportation. Single channels may divide into two or more, each too narrow for barge tows. The purpose of bank and channel stabilization is to prevent such occurrences—to guide the river into the best alignment and hold it there. This means that the channel must be capable of safely carrying flood flows.

On the Mississippi River, since levees were completed to MR&T standards, probably the most important phase of improvement has been the stabilization program. It has two essential objectives: (1) to protect the banks from caving, thus preventing meandering and changes of course; and (2) to insure stability of the main channel for navigation. The 1928 Flood Control Act provided that this should be accomplished by means of revetments, contraction works, and improvement dredging. These three are the most commonly employed methods in stabilization programs on other rivers as well.

A revetment is a protective covering placed on riverbanks in locations most susceptible to erosion—the outer banks of river bends. Down through the years, those who have tried to prevent the river from caving its banks have tested all kinds of protection. In 1878 willow type revetments were first used in the harbor of New Orleans. These were basically willow trees wired together to form a mattress and weighted by stone to keep them submerged. Another form of revetment was the abatis, a barricade of felled trees and bushes with branches facing the river. Then there were permeable cribs or retards, spur dikes, and sunken groins. At one time, some experimented with hot asphalt dumped directly on the river banks.

The most economical and effective means of protecting the banks of the Mississippi is the articulated concrete mattress. This is made of twenty concrete blocks or slabs, each 4 feet long, 14 inches wide, and 3 inches thick. They are cast into unit squares 4 feet wide and 25 feet long, using corrosion-resistant reinforcing fabric. The blocks are manufactured at special casting yards on the banks of the river. The revetment-building season begins when the river is low and the rate of flow is slow enough to permit laying of the mattress. The rough bank to be revetted is first graded to the proper slope and then covered with gravel.

The unit squares are then loaded onto a mat barge and towed to the site of revetment construction. There, on the launching ways of a specially designed "sinking barge," they are assembled and fastened together with twist wires and cable clips to form a mattress 140 feet wide along the riverbank. The first section of the mattress is attached to a "mat-puller," which pulls it up the bank above the waterline where it is fastened to anchor cables and held securely in place. The other end is then lowered by moving the sinking barge out into the river.

Additional sections are assembled on deck and connected to the first section. As the singking barge is backed still farther out into the stream, the assembled mattress is laid onto the riverbank below the water surface. This

Army Corps of Engineers

An articulated concrete mattress revetment is being placed to protect the banks of the Mississippi River against erosion.

continues until the mattress is laid to the deepest part of the channel, sometimes as far as 600 to 700 feet out into the river. When all sections of the underwater mat are in place, the upper bank is covered with stone riprap to protect it during higher river stages. This method is repeated, with each succeeding mattress overlapping the previous one like shingles on a roof. Normally, the entire bend is revetted from the upstream point of river-current attack to the point where the channel begins to cross to the opposite bank. After the revetment stops the caving, the energy of the river, once destructively uncontrolled, deepens the main channel.

Between the bends of the river, there is a straight reach where the channel crosses from one side of the stream to the other. Here the flow spreads out over a larger area, and depths are shallower. Contraction works are used in these reaches to train the current in the desired direction and to contract the width, thereby deepening and stabilizing the low-water navigation channel. These works consist mainly of dikes, placed more or less perpendicular to the current and far enough out in the channel to develop the desired contraction.

Dikes are usually made of timber piling, stone, or a combination of the two, depending upon the degree of permeability required to arrest traveling sediment and cause it to build up as accretion. The dikes are built to relatively low elevations so that they are effective during low water but do not obstruct the flow during high water. By concentrating the flow of the river, dikes use the hydraulic force of the stream to deepen the navigation channel. Another purpose of dikes is to close secondary channels and undesirable chutes. Where there is an island or sandbar in the middle of the river, minor channels sometimes form on both sides. To stabilize the river, the less desirable channel is closed by dikes, directing all flow to the development of one main channel.

The third method of stabilization, improvement dredging, is used primarily to expedite the work of the dike system in realigning and developing the channel. After the dikes begin to do their work and revetments

keep banks from caving, the amount of dredging can be reduced greatly, since the river then scours its own channel.

Between 1896 and 1928, dredging was the principal means of maintaining navigation channels. After the 1928 act provided for river regulation on the Mississippi by systematic construction of contraction works, the amount of dredging was reduced. When a program of shortening the river by cutoffs was instituted, dredging was used for excavating the cutoffs.

For the rough work of channel stabilization, cutterhead dredges make cuts that lead the channel into the desired alignment. Once the channel is established, it is maintained by use of dustpan dredges, which move up the channel like giant vacuum cleaners, loosening the material on the bed of the river so that it can be sucked up and pumped away through large pipes.

Cutoffs. Rivers that flow through soft alluvial lands tend to meander, forming great loops that sometimes double back on themselves to the point of nearly touching. When high waters occur on such streams, the land inside an overdeveloped bend is often completely inundated. Later, as the floods recede, the river sometimes takes a shortcut as it returns to its banks, scouring across the narrow neck of land and forming a natural cutoff.

Pilots and barge companies usually favor cutoffs because they shorten the length of the river. Those living along the water's edge, however, often fear them, as homes and industry can be left abandoned by the change in the river's course. Historically, those concerned with flood control have had mixed attitudes. Some claimed that the cutoffs were useful in relieving floods; for in the area above a cutoff, it serves somewhat like an outlet or floodway, permitting stage reductions as the waters flow rapidly to areas farther down the stream.

Man-made cutoffs were considered early. In 1831 Henry Shreve cut off one of the many loops of the Mississippi to shorten navigation and thereby created Old River in Louisiana. Another cutoff was made in 1848 at Raccouri Bend by the State of Louisiana. As early as 1850, proposals were made for the federal government to construct artificial cutoffs on the Mississippi. They were not acted upon, however, and in 1885 MRC took a stand against cutoffs, both natural and artificial. It employed special measures, such as construction of dikes and revetments, to forestall impending natural cutoffs whenever they occurred.

This attitude still prevailed in 1928 when the MR&T project was adopted. During the following year, however, "Mother Nature" provided a demonstration that changed this thinking pattern. At Yucatan Bend, about forty miles south of Vicksburg, the Mississippi River took a short cut as it entered the low-water season, creating the first cutoff since 1884. Within two years, the shortcut had become a wide and nearly straight channel with ample depth for navigation. By April 1932, it was carrying 60 percent of the river's flow. The old looping channel deteriorated until November 1933, when the entire main stem flow passed through the cutoff. The Yucatan incident demonstrated that a cutoff was not necessarily detrimental to the river's regimen.

Meanwhile, General Harley B. Ferguson, who was soon to become president of MRC, was studying the subject of possible cutoffs for the lower Mississippi. When he took office in June 1932, he launched the commission for the first time on a cutoff program. His purpose was to lower flood stages, utilizing, as far as possible, the energy of the river itself to excavate new channels and fill those to be abandoned.

The program was pursued vigorously. By 1939 eleven cutoffs had been opened between the mouth of the Arkansas River and Baton Rouge, Louisiana. These, together with the natural cutoff at Yucatan and another at Leland, Mississippi, shortened the river a total of 116 miles. In 1941 and 1942, three additional cutoffs were made between the mouth of the Arkansas River and Memphis, Tennessee. These sixteen cutoffs, shortened this section of the former low-water river length about 25 percent or 170 miles. During the period these cutoffs were being developed, however, current velocities increased the water's erosion on banks, and the river began to regain some of its former length, a natural phenomenon of

rivers. As a result, since 1931 the shortening has been reduced from the original 170 to 114 miles.

The cutoff program has been suspended for the past thirty years, although many new projects have been proposed. The most promising of these is for construction of a cut across Slough Landing Neck of the meander loop at Bessie Landing, Tennessee. This cutoff site, in the vicinity of New Madrid, Missouri, straddles the land of three states and would require over 10 million cubic yards of excavation for the new channel. The last time the Bessie cutoff was considered, however, the commission recomended that the proposed construction not be undertaken.

Contour Plowing and Reforestation. After the turn of the century, advocates of multiple-purpose, beneficial-use projects set forth recommendations for improving flood control measures. One idea was to use contour plowing and deep plowing to retain "the greater part of the precipitation on or in the lands on which it fell." Demonstration farms were established to teach farmers these new methods and to encourage their practice.

In 1914 the Board of Officers on River Floods made an investigation of these demonstration farms and of the proposed new methods of flood control. They reported that the methods had merit if they could be practiced. However, there was no way to compel owners of the lands involved to practice them. Furthermore, many lands were not susceptible to treatment of this kind. It was concluded that "it can be part of the program but by itself is not the solution." Later studies have shown this approach may be effective for smaller storms, but that the soil does not have holding capacity for intense, large storms. These principles of upstream control of runoff have been incorporated into the soil conservation, small watershed program to be discussed later.

Another proposal for flood control was the planting of forests to retain moisture that might otherwise run off as floods. The Board of Officers on River Floods saw the merits of this proposal but questioned its feasibility. "It would be impossible," the board asserted, "to expect that any large amount of cultivated land can be returned to the state of forests, or even that further clearing of tracts suitable for cultivation can be prevented." However, the reforestation of public lands is a part of many programs and is an element of sound management and utilization of basic resources. The effect on runoff from severe and intense storms is probably small.

Missouri River Basin: The Missouri River, nearly 2,500 miles in length, has a ten-state drainage area of 530,000 square miles, one sixth of the contiguous United States. It is an area of contrasts. The river flows from the Continental Divide with 10,000- to 12,000-foot mountain peaks in southwestern Montana, through mountain valleys, the plateau regions of the semi-arid western plains, the semi-humid plains of the Dakotas, Nebraska, and Kansas, and on to the Mississippi River at St. Louis through the humid areas of Iowa and Missouri. The river system is thus complex, and the problems are immense.

Major difficulties have revolved around water, either too much or too little, as the

Soil Conservation Service

The Missouri River area has suffered from periodic floods, such as this one in 1952 which inundated the village of Percival near Council Bluffs, Iowa.

basin has suffered severely from periodic floods or drought. It early earned the title "The Big Muddy." Its average natural flow of about 65,000 cubic feet per second, varying from a maximum of 900,000 to a minimum of 4,200, transported an average of 250 million tons of silt each year from eroding highlands and deposited it in the lower reaches of the Mississippi Valley or carried it out to sea.

The drainage area was of little concern to Americans until after the Louisiana Purchase, and little was known of it until Meriwether Lewis and William Clark reported on their explorations of 1804-1806. The lower reaches were used for navigation during the early western movements, and the first steamboat ventured up the river in 1819. During the next forty years, some effort was made to remove snags in the navigation channel, but the boats were usually on their own. The hazards were great. More than 300 steamboats were destroyed by accidents on the river during this period. Some small piecemeal flood control levees were built, but they were local and generally ineffective.

Under the impetus of various land settlement legislation (discussed in Chapter 10), irrigation projects were begun in the more arid regions in the latter part of the nineteenth century. These were accelerated with the initiation of the reclamation program in 1902. By 1940 thirteen projects involving twenty-one reservoirs with a storage capacity of 3.6 million acre-feet had been completed to provide irrigation water to 877,000 acres of farmland. While these developments were of the single-purpose type, to store and control water for irrigation, most also provided flood control benefits.

The Army Corps of Engineers' "308" reports and the studies by the Bureau of Reclamation during the 1920s and 1930s began to define the overall problems. During the 1930s, construction was initiated on Fort Peck Dam on the mainstream in Montana, designed primarily to provide water for navigation in the lower reaches during dry seasons. Several reservoirs, primarily for irrigation, were built in the upper reaches of the Platte River tributary.

During the extended drought of the 1930s, when over 750,000 people left the area, PWA programs and the 1936 Flood Control Act combined to intensify studies for the overall basin development. The Army Corps of Engineers prepared a plan for the region emphasizing flood control and navigation, designated the "Pick" plan after Division Engineer Colonel Lewis A. Pick. The Bureau of Reclamation's plan for development of the

U.S. Water Resources Council

The Missouri River Basin system of mainstream and major tributary reservoirs.

basin stressed irrigation and hydroelectric power and was designated the "Sloan" plan after William G. Sloan who headed the study. These two proposals were reconciled with relatively minor adjustments, and the development of the Missouri River Basin by the "Pick-Sloan" plan was authorized by the 1944 Flood Control Act. It provided a comprehensive program for the conservation, control, and use of the water resources of the entire river basin. A major purpose of the plan was flood control, and this portion of the program has been actively supported with funding.

Five dams were authorized and completed on the Missouri River downstream from Fort Peck Dam, which was completed in 1940. These are Garrison Dam, 175 miles northwest of Bismarck, North Dakota; Oahe Dam near Pierre, South Dakota; Fort Randall Dam, near Lake Andes, South Dakota; Gavins Point Dam, on the Nebraska-South Dakota border near Yorkton; and Big Bend Dam, upstream from Chamberlain, South Dakota, built primarily for power production and

regulation of flows from Oahe Dam.

The combined capacity of these reservoirs, including the one behind Fort Peck Dam, is over 75 million acre-feet. They form the backbone of the flood control and navigation storage system. Releases from these reser-

Army Corps of Engineers

Fort Peck Dam on the Missouri River in Montana, completed in 1940, contains 126 million cubic yards of earth and rock.

voirs also produce hydroelectric power. The dams are all earthfill, faced with rock for wave protection, and have a total volume of over 350 million cubic yards of compacted earth and rock. The cost of these five dams, including all facilities, was about $1.2 billion, of which $840 million is being repaid with interest to the United States Treasury from power revenues.

In addition to the main stem dams, 103 dams and reservoirs that will provide an additional 110 million acre-feet of storage were authorized on the headwaters and various tributaries. All the projects are multipurpose. The Army Corps of Engineers is responsible for the main stem dams and those with flood control and navigation as the primary functions. The Bureau of Reclamation is responsible for upstream reservoirs whose primary functions are irrigation and hydroelectric power generation, and for the irrigation control and distribution works, the electric power transmission systems, and municipal water supplies. By 1976 eighty-one of the tributary reservoirs were completed or under construction.

In addition to the work of the two principal agencies described above, the Soil Conservation Service was given the responsibility for a program of flood runoff control on small watersheds, including soil and water conservation practices on individual farms. The initial program, termed the Missouri Basin Agricultural Plan, which was presented to Congress in 1949, proposed structures costing about $1 billion. While this program as such was not authorized, work has gone forward under the various soil and water conservation programs.

By 1972 land conservation measures were installed on 146 million acres, including about $60 million expended on land improvements, such as contour farming and contour dikes. Approximately 314,000 small farm ponds had been constructed, and 123 small watershed projects, with a cost of about $122 million, were partially finished. Work completed on these latter projects included 1,270 small reservoirs, 550 miles of channel improvements, and about 2,000 erosion control grade stabilization structures.

These programs also involve fish and wildlife considerations, Forest Service and Bureau of Land Management land and water conservation and development programs on public lands, Bureau of Indian Affairs programs on Indian lands, and activities of the National Park Service. In addition, state programs have developed 700,000 acre-feet of storage, primarily for irrigation, but including flood control and other benefits. The State of Montana has most of these, thirty-four projects totaling 400,000 acre-feet of storage. Development of local, district, and municipal programs were early, low-cost projects, although a few have been accomplished since the initiation of the Pick-Sloan program. Strictly private developments have been small and few in number.

The size of the overall program and the number of governmental entites involved made the problem of coordination and cooperation one of sobering complexity. Initially, a four-agency committee composed of the chief of engineers, the commissioner of reclamation, the land use coordinator of the Department of Agriculture, and the chairman of the Federal Power Commission worked to coordinate studies and proposals. After the 1944 authorization act was passed, the Missouri Basin Inter-Agency Committee (MBIAC) was formed. It included representatives of seven federal agencies and the states. The function of the committee was to provide a way for field representatives of the various participants to exchange information and coordinate activities. The Interior Department, with its Bureau of Reclamation, Fish and Wildlife Service, National Park Service, Bureau of Indian Affairs, Bureau of Mines, and Bureau of Land Management, formed an Interior Field Committee to coordinate the department's activities. These committees were effective during the years program details were being formulated.

The consistent and timely development of the program was prevented by higher priorities during wartime. Thereafter, competition with other programs for limited funds and the changing emphasis on objectives delayed work. However, the flood of 1947, which caused over $200 million in damages, gave impetus to the flood control portions of the program, which then received concentrated attention. Later, the growing demands for electric power encouraged hydroelectric development, and about 90 percent of the feasible hydropower has been developed. Irrigation lagged, as priority rating was affected by surplus farm production, but by 1975 it was getting additional support. The political process has acted to emphasize the immediate problems; even though it often failed to provide adequate support for objectives requiring long lead times.

The overall coordinating functions were taken over in June 1972 by the Missouri River Basin Commission when it was organized under provisions of the 1965 Water Resources Planning Act. The membership includes representatives of the governors of each state and of the ten federal departments involved with the basin programs. The commission has the responsibility for preparing and keeping current a comprehensive, joint plan for resource development and recommending long-range schedules of priorities for data collection and investigation, planning, and construction of projects. As a new regional institution for water and related resource planning, the commission has established a partnership in which state and federal representatives, with the assistance of an independent staff and a presidentially appointed chairman, work together as equals in carrying out their coordination and planning responsibilities. By 1975 it had demonstrated its ability to coordinate a complex and extensive program.

The major portion of the flood control works had been completed by 1975, including nearly all of the primarily flood control projects. In addition to the projects built as part of the Pick-Sloan plan, the Army Corps of Engineers' program, providing flood protection to localized areas has been impressive. Generally, these projects are in the $50,000 to $1 million range and may consist of a few miles of levee building and strengthening; channel improvements by clearing, snagging, dredging, or stabilizing with earth or concrete floodwalls; and floodways. Since 1944 about eighty projects of this type, costing over $150 million, have been finished.

The completed and partially operative portions of the overall program for the basin have prevented flood damages of well over $2.6 billion through June 1973, according to records of the Army Corps of Engineers. This is about equal to the total funds expended for all the developments since 1944 when the Pick-Sloan program was initiated.

The Ohio River: The 982-mile-long valley of the Ohio River is prone to flooding. Its watershed is frequently subjected to excessive rainfall during the months of January through May because of its position in the path of winter and spring storms moving from west to east across North America. During this period, the soil usually approaches saturation; the relationship between rainfall and runoff is high; and the occurrence of floods is frequent.

Later in the year, the eastern portion of the Ohio basin is vulnerable to storms spawned by hurricanes on the eastern seaboard. The average annual flow of the Ohio River ranges from 32,700 cubic feet per second at its head to 258,500 where it joins the Mississippi. Maximum discharges of record at the same localities are 574,000 and 1.9 million cubic feet per second. Under calculations for the maximum predictable flood, it is estimated that the Ohio could discharge 2.3 million cubic feet per second into the Mississippi.

In the historic flood of 1937, over 500,000 people were driven from their homes, and 65 lost their lives. Along the river and its tributaries, virtually all telegraph, telephone, electricity, highway, and rail facilities were interdicted. The economy of the valley was paralyzed. Flood damage was estimated at $400 million. As a result, the 1938 Flood Control Act initiated a basin-wide flood control program by authorizing a system of reservoirs and local protection projects. Then the 1954 Watershed Protection and Flood Prevention Act was passed to fill the gap in resource development between larger flood control projects and individual on-farm conservation measures.

The flood control plan was included in a comprehensive basin study for the Ohio River Basin. It included seventy-nine reservoirs and 235 local-protection projects. Subsequent legislation authorized additional projects, modified several, and deauthorized others. By 1965 the program included seventy-five major reservoirs, eighty-six large local-protection projects, and fifty-six small flood control projects. The reservoirs are located on tributaries and designed to contain about 17 million acre-feet of storage space for flood control. The other projects comprise 372 miles of levees and floodwalls and 207 miles of improved stream channels.

In Indiana seven reservoirs were completed or under construction by 1975. In Kentucky seven reservoirs were completed. In Tennessee the Center Hill, Dale Hollow, and J. Percy Priest reservoirs were in operation in addition to the series of reservoirs on the Tennessee River constructed by TVA. West Virginia had the Tygart, Sutton, Bluestone, and Summerville reservoirs. Virginia had obtained the John W. Flannagan Reservoir as part of the Ohio system. In Pennsylvania the Tionesta, Crooked Creek, Mahoning Creek, Conemaugh, Shenango River, and Allegheny River reservoirs were completed. By far the largest number of Ohio River system reservoirs are in the state of Ohio. On the Muskingum River alone, there are fourteen flood control reservoirs. In addition, Ohio has reservoirs at Mosquito Creek, Berlin, Pleasant Hill, North Branch of the Kokosing, Dillon, Burr Oak, Delaware, and West Fork of Mills Creek.

Flood-forecasting services for the Ohio River and its major tributaries are credited with the potential of reducing flood damage in this basin by another 5 to 10 percent as the services are expanded. It is estimated that the flood control projects in the Ohio basin in 1975 had already returned two dollars in prevented flood losses for every dollar spent.

An Ohio River Basin Commission was established in 1971 to coordinate activities of federal, state, interstate, local, and non-governmental agencies involved in planning and development of water and related land resources of the Ohio River basin. The commission estimates that when the plans for development of water and land resources of the commission are all put into effect, about 75 percent of potential future flood damages in the river basin will be prevented.

The Tennessee River: The Tennessee River Basin, because of its location with respect to the line of travel of storms of intense rainfall and the characteristics of its drainage area and river system, has historically experienced extreme floods and devastation. The drainage basin encompasses an area of nearly 41,000 square miles in portions of seven states—Virginia, North Carolina, Georgia, Tennessee, Alabama, Mississippi, and Kentucky. It is a watershed of contrasts. Rugged mountains and green forests dominate the eastern portion of the valley; rolling hills, open fields, and woodlands lie to the west.

The Tennessee River system has its headwaters in the mountains of southwestern Virginia and western North Carolina, eastern Tennessee, and northern Georgia. Two rivers, the Holston and French Broad, join at Knoxville, Tennessee, to form the Tennessee River—a 650-mile stream. Below this point, the river flows southwest through the state of Tennessee, gaining water from three other principal tributaries, the Clinch, the Little Tennessee, and the Hiwassee rivers.

The Tennessee continues flowing southwest into Alabama as far south as Guntersville and then westward, picking up water from another large tributary, the Elk River, in its course through the Muscle Shoals area of northern Alabama. The river turns north at the northeast corner of Mississippi, recrosses the state of Tennessee, and continues to Paducah, Kentucky, where it enters the Ohio River. During the river's second passage through Tennessee, it is joined by another large tributary, the Duck River. Water from tributaries in the northeast corner of the valley flows more than 900 winding miles to the mouth of the river at Paducah.

The watershed drains one of the wettest regions of the United States. For the valley as a whole, rainfall averages about fifty-two inches a year, and in some of the eastern mountains the average exceeds eighty inches. The Gulf of Mexico and the Caribbean Sea provide major sources of moisture. Prevailing winds from the south and west bring it across the watershed, and the area is also within range of hurricane storms that move across the southern coastline. Just as rainfall is not evenly divided among different areas of the watershed, it is not equally distributed throughout the year. Almost half of the annual total is received in winter and early spring, from December to mid April. March is generally the wettest month, although at some locations in the eastern sections of the valley, midsummer brings the most intense rainfall.

Tennessee Valley Authority

Completed storage reservoirs and channel improvements in 1967 protected Chattanooga, Tennessee (bottom) from floods such as the one in 1867 (top) which inundated most of the city.

While floods in past years have ravaged the whole basin, Chattanooga, Tennessee, with its population of 120,000, has suffered most. The city is highly vulnerable to flood damage because of its location on a low-lying flood plain at the entrance to the narrow gorge where the river twists its way through the southernmost arm of the Cumberland Plateau. Between 1874 and 1937, fifty-four floods ex-

ceeded peak floodstage discharges of 200,000 cubic feet per second at Chattanooga, which gives a depth of 30 feet. Twenty-eight of these exceeded a stage of 35 feet, eleven exceeded 40 feet, and seven exceeded 42 feet. The most serious flood occurred in March 1867, when the river reached a stage of 57.9 feet and the discharge peaked at about 459,000 cubic feet per second. It is said that a steamboat pushed down the main business street during the crest of this flood.

As the largest tributary of the Ohio River, the Tennessee system is one of the most important factors in Mississippi River floods. In the great Mississippi River flood of January 1913, the Tennessee River contributed over 240,000 cubic feet per second at the time of the Mississippi River crest, or 18 percent of the peak flow of the Mississippi just below the mouth of the Ohio. In the flood peak the following April, the Tennessee reached a flow of 275,000 cubic feet per second. The Tennessee Valley's flood problem was further compounded, prior to the founding of TVA, because conservation farming was virtually unknown and the heavy rainfall took a great yearly toll from the eroding soil. Forests had been cut and burned over, baring the mountainsides and speeding storm runoff.

The passage of the 1933 TVA Act was the culmination of decades of public interest and engineering investigations concerned with the conservation and best use of the natural resources of this area. Most of the early engineering studies were conducted by the Army Corps of Engineers and published as one of the "308" reports. The mandate from Congress was to develop the full resources of the river, regulating and conserving its floodwaters and using them for navigation and electric power generation. In 1933 the existing navigation improvements on the 650-mile-long main stem of the river consisted of only four isolated, widely separated, lateral canals with locks; one navigation dam; one federally owned power-navigation dam; one privately owned power-navigation dam; and numerous lateral dikes and dredged cuts. From the mouth of the river to Florence, Alabama, the controlling depth was only 4 feet and to Knoxville, Tennessee, only 18 inches.

By the terms of the TVA Act, Congress directed that the dams constructed on the mainstream produce the maximum benefit for navigation and hydroelectric generation and at the same time contribute to the control of destructive floodwaters in the Tennessee and Mississippi River basins. Detailed studies of costs and benefits for several low- and high-dam plans revealed that a system of high, multipurpose projects on the main stem offered the optimum solution. This type of development, summarized in the authority's 1936 report to Congress, made possible a fully effective system for flood control, hydroelectric power generation, and navigation, including reduction of flood stages on the lower Ohio and Mississippi rivers.

By 1975 thirty-three major dams regulated the Tennessee River and its tributaries. The TVA had built twenty-three of these and acquired four others. Three other units were under construction—Tellico Dam on the Little Tennessee River and Normandy and Columbia dams on the Duck River. Nine dams on the main river provide a continuous chain of pools which afford a minimum navigable depth of 9 feet from Kentucky Dam to Knoxville and, in addition, allow space for regulation of flood peaks. Kentucky Reservoir near the mouth of the river, had a flood detention capacity of 4 million acre-feet during the winter and early spring, and the other main river reservoirs upstream have an additional 2 million acre-feet. The tributary dams provide 7.5 million acre-feet of storage.

The annual cyclical pattern of runoff in the valley governs the operation of the reservoir system. Operating guides, derived from many years of runoff records, show the water levels in each of the reservoirs needed to meet the varying conditions during the seasons of the year. Using these guides with a complete storm, stream flow, and reservoir capacity data-gathering system, computers quickly analyze the data and provide operating directions. These enable the system of dams and reservoirs to respond in an optimum way to potential flood situations. Flood control needs have priority over power generation. The system of operation is sophisticated and effective.

The TVA flood control operations began with the closure of Norris Dam in 1936, and its operation that year cut more than 4 feet from a Chattanooga flood and saved $2 million in flood damages. As other dams were added to the system, flood control benefits were provided along major tributaries, and still further down on the lower Ohio and Mississippi rivers. By 1973 the system flood control benefits had accumulated to over $1.2 billion, more than five times the investment in flood control facilities.

Many communities with varying degrees of flood problems lie outside the influence of the TVA reservoir system. The TVA engineers had identified over 150 communities within the valley upstream from the dams or on small streams that suffered significant damage from floods. It was impractical to construct flood control facilities for more than a few of these areas. One solution was to keep structures away from flood plains by proper land use controls.

The agency was in a unique position to test this concept. By 1953 TVA had twenty years of experience in flood control operations. A vast amount of hydrologic data was available, as were experienced engineers capable of developing workable flood plain management programs. Of greatest importance, a working relationship with people of the valley and their state and local institutions had been carefully nurtured over the years.

The TVA initiated its flood plain management assistance program in 1953 with a fairly fixed formula. It visualized that flood damages could be substantially reduced by using the police power of local government to control land use by including flood plain provisions in zoning ordinances, subdivision regulations, and building codes. This approach required close cooperation between federal, state, and local institutions. The program depended upon factual flood information, which TVA would supply; planning assistance, which the states would furnish; and administration, which local governments would provide. As a first step in planning the program, TVA and the state agencies agreed on an order of priority for initiating the studies and preparing reports for communities with known flood problems. The program was vigorously pushed by both state and TVA personnel through contacts and the news media.

The finished report of a community was presented at a meeting of the local agency, usually the planning commission requesting the study. The report gave the history of past floods and described potential future floods that might reasonably be expected. Maps were provided showing areas inundated, and data was included concerning depth and duration of flooding, floodflow velocities, and rates of rise. The community was encouraged to initiate a flood damage prevention planning study as a second step, using the same local-state-federal cooperative approach.

These early planning studies evaluated flood control works and flood plain regulations and usually concluded that large engineering works could not be justified. In such cases, the study recommended adoption of flood plain regulations as the solution. Maps provided limits of the floodways. Specific provisions for inclusion of regulations in local zoning ordinances and subdivision regulations were in the proper format and complied with other plans for community development. Public hearings were held in accordance with state law before such regulations were adopted. In 1959 TVA utilized its experience in these cooperative efforts to prepare and submit to Congress a report entitled "A Program for Reducing the National Flood Damage Potential." A part of TVA's recommendations were put into effect a year later when Congress authorized the Army Corps of Engineers to provide information and technical assistance for such a program to local communities throughout the United States.

A broadening of the program occurred in 1960. More attention was given to flood proofing, urban renewal, and open spaces as parts of the program. The twin cities of Bristol, Tennessee-Virginia, provided the catalyst. Teams of planners worked out the optimum program, which called for two small flood detention reservoirs, channel improvements, flood proofing, and urban redevelopment, in addition to flood plain regulations. The program was endorsed by the cities and the states, and the responsibilities of the parties were out-

lined in a contractual agreement. The major elements of the program were in effect by 1975. By then, ten communities had joined with TVA in similar local flood protection projects. TVA had supplied flood reports for about 140 communities by 1975 in response to requests, and others were in preparation. Using TVA technical reports and assistance, ninety communities adopted zoning ordinances and subdivision regulations. Others were making studies in preparation for adopting regulations.

Tennessee Valley Authority

Flood damage is reduced in upstream drainage areas of the Tennessee Valley by a cooperative program of flood plain controls, flood-proofing existing facilities, channel improvements, and small retention dams.

In August 1966, President Lyndon B. Johnson transmitted to Congress "A Unified National Program for Managing Flood Losses" which was printed as House Document No. 465. The report was prepared by a task force on federal flood control policy that included the chief of TVA's local flood regulations staff. It reflected many of the ideas and concepts developed in the TVA program and stressed actions that could be undertaken to manage the nation's flood plains.

As an example, several months prior to the March 1973 flood, a businessman requested TVA's advice with regard to a proposed motel at South Pittsburg, Tennessee. The flood dangers at the site were evaluated and the floor level of the proposed structure was raised several feet. The businessman wrote TVA a thoughtful letter following the March flood. "Had we not listened," he said, "there is no telling what our loss would have been."

Regional Rivers and Tributaries

Flood problems on rivers other than the Mississippi also influenced the broadening of responsibility for flood control. Problems on the Sacramento River in California, for instance, received early federal attention as well as local and state involvement. As populations increased in all areas of the nation, flood control and drainage became more important. Problems and solutions are different in each drainage basin. The following five sections describe flood control programs in representative regions of the nation.

Sacramento River: The Sacramento River begins at the northern end of California's great Central Valley, where Mt. Shasta towers over 14,000 feet. Yearly precipitation at the higher elevations averages about 70 inches, most of it in snow. From Mt. Shasta, the river flows in a southerly direction between the Sierra Nevada and the Coastal Range to Surisun Bay, a distance of 375 miles. It drains 27,100 square miles and has flood discharges of up to 600,000 cubic feet per second.

The Sacramento Valley has always been subject to floods, the natural river channels having sufficient capacity for only a small part of the maximum flow. As a result, when a flood comes down the river, it gradually pours over the banks in thin sheets. In the course of succeeding floods, the land immediately adjacent to the river builds up with sediment, which the floodwater carries in suspension as long as it stays in the river channel, but drops as soon as it spreads out over the land where current slackens. Over its history, this process has caused a general sloping away from the river and has formed low basins, paralleling the course of the Sacramento River. These basins have become natural floodwater storage reservoirs which hold excess winter floodwater until it can drain off during the spring and early summer.

As the Sacramento Valley became populated, inhabitants settled along the higher ground next to the river channels and built levees to protect their farms from floodwaters.

The first levees were constructed by individual farmers, for each thought that just a little levee along the riverbank would keep the water from his farm, as it had never flowed deep over the land. Unfortunately, as fast as these levees were raised, the flood heights also went up, for the river flood plain became more confined. Farmers of the same vicinity organized themselves into a district to fight flooding more effectively; and in this way, reclamation districts sprang up all along the Sacramento. But plans were piecemeal, and when floods came, the districts with the lowest levees went under.

U.S. Bureau of Reclamation

Floodwaters of the Sacramento River are now being retained in reservoirs for later use during low-flow seasons.

In addition to these problems, gold was discovered on the Sacramento in 1849, and in 1852 hydraulic miners in the mountains began to unload their debris into the channels of the river and its tributaries. This became a major problem when the floods of 1861 and 1862 washed large quantities of the placer mining and other debris into the lower levels of the basin, filling old channels, and causing major flooding.

By 1870 hydraulic giants were developed for sluicing. Old gold-bearing channels, higher than the existing channels, were opened up; and it was a simple matter to sluice large masses of gravel from them into the present channels. By that time, nearly all of a million acres granted to California by the 1850 Swamp Act (much of it in the Sacramento Valley), was in private ownership; thus, problems multiplied, and court fights developed between miners and farmers. Congress in 1873 authorized an irrigation study in the valley; and the Army Corps of Engineers, in the next year, presented a plan for controlling and using the waters. In 1877 the state passed legislation creating the office of state engineer, and various plans were studied by the state as well.

The court fights continued between valley residents and the miners, and in the historic Bloomfield Case, hydraulic mining was virtually halted. Both sides appealed to the federal government for help; and in the 1893 "Caminetti" Act, Congress created the California Debris Commission to regulate hydraulic mining in the state and permit its resumption if it could be done without injury to navigation or to adjacent lands. The commission was also instructed to study and report on control plans for the rivers, including protection against floods. The state provided a debris commissioner and appropriated $25,000 for joint construction of debris barriers.

Renewed demands for flood control followed disastrous floods of 1904, 1907, and 1909. Part of the 1910 Sacramento River Flood Control Plan was adopted by Congress in the Rivers and Harbors Act of that year, provided California matched the $500,000 appropriated. During the next seven years, over 25 million cubic yards were dredged from the river.

The debris commission's flood control plan for the Sacramento River was adopted by Congress in 1917 in its first Flood Control Act, along with the provisions regarding the Mississippi. The plan had three parts: (1) to confine as much water as possible by straightening the river channel and building levees; (2) to bypass excess water over weirs and conduct it through the low basins paralleling the general direction of the river; and (3) to increase the capacity of the lower 15 miles of the river to carry the total runoff by widening, deepening, and straightening. The federal government was assigned responsibility for certain items of work, including construction of weirs and cutoffs in the river. State and local interests were required to do the remainder and to maintain the work after completion.

The state, working with federal agencies, was developing its own plan for control and use of the water in the valley. In 1933 the plan was approved by the voters and a bond issue authorized. However, due to economic conditions, the bonds could not be sold; and the state sought help from the federal government. In 1935, under the Emergency Relief Appropriations Act, President Franklin D. Roosevelt authorized the construction of Shasta Dam by the Bureau of Reclamation, as the first unit of the multipurpose Central Valley Project. It became a federal reclamation project after confirmation by Congress. Construction of the dam was completed in 1944.

The main purpose of the Central Valley Project is to store the surplus floodwater of the Sacramento River and provide for its use in the San Joaquin to the south. Shasta, the key structure of the project, is a 602-foot-high gravity concrete dam, 3,460 feet long, which creates a reservoir of 4.5 million acre-feet. It affords flood protection and river regulation to repel salt water encroachment in the delta area; and it furnishes water for irrigation in the Sacramento Valley and for export to the San Joaquin Valley. Its 154,000-kilowatt power plant produces about 1.5 billion kilowatt hours of electric energy per year. In 1974 the reservoir demonstrated its flood control value by containing a flood with an inflow of 215,000 cubic feet per second. Savings in downstream damages were calculated at $58 million.

Since Shasta, about twenty additional multipurpose dams have been constructed on the Sacramento River and its tributaries by the Bureau of Reclamation, the Army Corps of Engineers, the State of California, and utility districts. The operations of the reservoirs are synchronized by the flood control office of the corps to maximize flood benefits consistent with the other purposes of the reservoirs.

Great Miami River in Ohio: The most notable and successful flood control program carried out by a local district on a relatively small drainage basin is that of the Great Miami River Basin in southwest Ohio. The river has a drainage area of 5,433 square miles and enters the Ohio River just west of Cincinnati at approximately the Ohio-Indiana state line. The main urban centers are Dayton and Hamilton, with 1975 populations of 242,000 and 67,000 respectively. The valley has a population of over a million.

The river valley of rich, level land was the site of important Indian villages before the advent of white men. Dayton was laid out in 1795, the year a treaty was signed with the Indians. By 1810 the population was 383, and contact with the rest of the world was by navigation on the river. Conflicts occurred between fishermen, with their brush dams and fish baskets, and river boatmen, until a navigation canal from Dayton to Cincinnati was completed in 1829. It was extended north to Lake Erie in 1845. For twenty-five years, these canals contributed greatly to the development of the valley, following which the railroads supplemented the canals. The valley became an important part of a major industrial area.

The first flooding of Dayton occurred in 1805 when water was 8 feet deep on the main street. Protective levees were built that washed out and overflowed every few years throughout the remainder of the nineteenth century. Damages sometimes ran as high as $1 million.

During the last of March 1913, a disastrous flood occurred after four days of heavy rainfall of up to five inches per day. The peak discharge was over 250,000 cubic feet per second. When the flood receded, over 360 people had been drowned; and property damage was well over $100 million, not including extensive damage to the valley farms. Rescue work was followed by relief activities which continued into the following winter.

Various local committees were formed to consider flood control improvements. On May 25, cooperative action by the nine affected counties began with the formation of the Miami Valley Flood Control Association. Funds of over $2 million were raised for engineering and legal studies and for real estate appraisals. As Ohio had no provisions to enable formation of such a cooperative enterprise, legislation was prepared; and the Conservancy Act of Ohio became law on February 17, 1914. It provided for the establishment of a district by a court consisting of representatives of the common pleas court in each county of the proposed district. This Conservancy Court would appoint the board of directors, consisting of three landowners of the district, to supervise an appointed general manager and staff. Petitions were then filed for formation of the Miami Conservancy District.

Arthur E. Morgan served as consultant in formulating plans for the program and was later appointed chief engineer for the district. He assembled an outstanding engineering organization which applied many sound approaches and innovations in developing the plans for the project. Morgan later became the first chairman of TVA, where he utilized technologies and ideas developed at the Miami district. Other members of the early organization also influenced flood control plans elsewhere.

Even though the public was kept informed of progress and was able to review and discuss proposed plans, violent opposition developed, mainly in towns upstream from Dayton and downstream from the proposed reservoirs. It finally required a decision of the State Supreme Court in June 1915 to sustain the Conservancy Act.

In the meantime, a plan was adopted which provided for five large retarding reservoirs, with a combined storage capacity of 841,000 acre-feet and with channel improvements including about 60 miles of dikes and levees, balanced to obtain protection at minimum costs. The official plan was filed in May 1916, and information concerning it was widely distributed. Public hearings lasted seven weeks. A former chief of the Army Corps of Engineers testified that the plan had been worked out with more care and thoroughness than any engineering project of his knowledge; and technical papers published since, as well as the actual operations of the project, have confirmed the soundness of the program.

The plan was approved in November 1916, and appraisals of benefits and damages got underway. Over 60,000 pieces of property of 40,000 owners were evaluated. The tax role value of the property benefited was $1.2

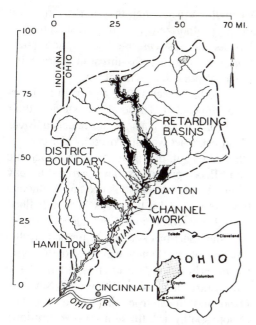

American Society of Civil Engineers

The features of the flood control district of the Miami River Basin in southwestern Ohio.

billion. The appraised benefits of the plan totaled $77 million; and as the estimated cost was $27.8 million, each property was assessed 36 percent of its appraised benefit. Thirty-year bonds bearing 5½ percent interest secured by the assets of the district were issued, and construction commenced in 1918. Because of war conditions, the district was unable to obtain satisfactory bids for the work. It, therefore, formed a construction organization of its own and completed the work in about three years at a construction cost of $30.8 million.

Floods in April 1922 tested the project, and all parts worked according to plan. Other notable floods have since occurred in twelve different years. The severest test was in 1959 when the rainfall was almost as great as that causing the disastrous flood of 1913. The controlled stage at Dayton was 16 feet, compared to a danger stage of 18 feet, and the 1913 stage of over 30 feet.

The bonds were paid off on schedule, and delinquencies in payment from the various properties were less than 0.4 percent. This project has been cited as the outstanding flood control project carried out by local initiative, planning, and financing; and it demonstrates

the results of careful planning and full participation by those immediately affected. It is in an area of high property values, one of the reasons it has been so successful. The American Society of Civil Engineers recognized the project in 1972 as a National Historic Civil Engineering Landmark.

The original purpose of the district was to combat floods. By 1975, however, it was best described as a water management organization. It had limited governmental power to implement water management programs and to levy assessments and user charges to finance them. It is a good example of a single-purpose water program, in this case flood control, evolving into multipurpose, comprehensive water management programs.

In 1967 the district was charged by the state with responsibility for planning, developing, and guiding an effective program for improving water quality in its watershed. This work is being funded by the beneficiaries—the six countries directly involved, and fifty industries and municipalities holding Ohio permits to discharge wastes into the Great Miami River and its major tributaries. Some grants to assist with the program have been received from the federal government.

The district is also participating in plans to make maximum use of the river corridor in the Dayton area that relate to flood control responsibilities. These projects include acquisition of 2,800 acres of flood plain lands, two low dams in the Miami River in downtown Dayton, a levee-top walkway, eight miles of bikeways, and a riverfront plaza. The plans provide for recreational areas and for beautification and improvement of the environment.

New England Rivers: The problem of flooding in New England has a long history involving all rivers that are affected each spring by a combination of rainfall and snowmelt and that are often wracked in the summer and fall by hurricanes. The federal government became involved in an effort to control three major rivers after heavy flooding in 1936. The Flood Control Act of that year initiated a comprehensive study of high waters on the Connecticut, Merrimack, and Winooski rivers.

The Connecticut River Basin extends

from northwestern New Hampshire and the Canadian province of Quebec to Long Island Sound below Hartford, Connecticut, a total length of about 392 miles. The watershed is bounded on the east by the White Mountains and on the west by the Green Mountains in Vermont and the Berkshire Hills in Massachusetts. Its greatest width is about 62 miles, and the basin covers an area of 11,260 square miles. Its principal tributaries are the Chicopee and White rivers. Feeder streams to the north and west drain precipitous rocky country and cause flash floods that quickly reach high peak discharges. On the eastern side, tributaries have flatter slopes, with basins containing many lakes and swampy areas that do not produce the high flood discharges of the western streams. Because of the numerous tributaries of the Connecticut River and because of its long, narrow watershed, floods on the lower main river do not attain high-peak discharges. Floodwaters from the downstream tributaries, in general, flow into the main stem before the arrival of floodwaters from the upper valley. Thus, floods on the main river are of relatively short duration.

The three largest recorded floods on the Connecticut occurred in November 1927, March 1936, and September 1938, the largest being that of 1936. Previously, a Army Corps of Engineers' "308" report had been prepared for the river, proposing a scheme of combined flood control and power reservoirs and suggesting an initial plan of ten such lakes. The study authorized by the 1936 act made a more exhaustive investigation, having flood control as its primary interest. As a result, a comprehensive development plan was submitted in which it was proposed that twenty reservoirs be built for the general protection of the valley—supplemented by levees, walls, and other protective works for the seven most populous communities of the basin.

The 1975 plan for flood protection in the Connecticut River Basin consists of twenty-eight reservoirs and twenty local protection works. Of these, seventeen reservoirs had been completed and put into operation and fifteen local protection works had become operational. The grades of levees and floodwalls along the main river are designed for a flood somewhat greater than that of 1936, reduced by the authorized system of reservoirs. As long as the upstream reservoir system is incomplete, however, the threat of overtopping the local protection will remain.

The basin states have agreed in an interstate compact to cooperate in solving their flood control problems. The Connecticut River Flood Compact was approved by Congress in 1953. Under it, downstream states benefiting from flood protection have agreed to pay equitable portions of the tax and economic losses suffered by the areas in which flood control reservoirs have been placed.

The Merrimack River is formed by the junction of the Pemigewasset and the Winnipesaukee rivers at Franklin, New Hampshire. It is located in central New England and flows from the White Mountain region southward through New Hampshire into the northeastern corner of Massachusetts. Its basin has a total length of about 134 miles and a width of 68 miles. Its drainage area is approximately 5,015 square miles.

The upper portion of the Merrimack basin above the Contoocook River is fan-shaped, and its tributaries are characterized by steep gradations and rapid runoff. This sector has serious local flood problems and contributes to floods in the lower valley. The southern part of the basin contains more sluggish tributaries, along which flood flows are generally absorbed by channel storage. The 1936 Flood Control Act authorized construction of a system of reservoirs in the New Hampshire part of the Merrimack Basin: at Franklin Falls, Hopkinton-Everett, West Petersboro, and Mountain Brook. Local protection was built at Fitchburg, Haverhill, Lowell, and Leominster, Massachusetts; and at Lincoln and Nashua, New Hampshire.

The Winooski River and its tributaries lie inside the state of Vermont. It rises in Washington County and flows westward to Lake Champlain, a distance of 90 miles. The Army Corps of Engineers did their first flood control work in New England on the Winooski—three earth-filled dams located at East Barre, South Barre, and Wrightsville, together with the channel clearing and enlargement of a 15-mile section of the

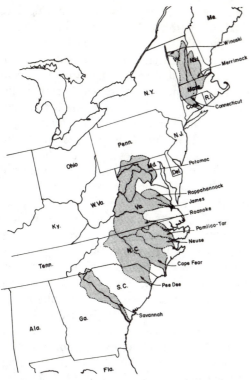

Public Works Historical Society

Drainage areas of the New England and South Atlantic rivers discussed in text.

Winooski between Montpelier and Middlesex.

South Atlantic Rivers: In the southern part of the eastern seaboard, many rivers cross the coastal plain after rising in the Appalachian highlands and flowing to the Atlantic or its estuaries. Those of major length often follow a broad diagonal course, usually southeastward. Of these, the Potomac, Rappahannock, James, Roanoke, Pamlico-Tar, Neuse, Cape Fear, Pee Dee, and Savannah rivers have basins that have required flood control attention. A brief description of some of the programs follows.

The basin of the Potomac River has a drainage area of 14,670 square miles in the District of Columbia and the states of Virginia, Maryland, West Virginia, and Pennsylvania. The river originates in the Allegheny Mountains and flows eastward to empty into Chesapeake Bay. It is tidal from Washington, D.C., to its mouth. Floods in the Potomac River Basin can happen in all seasons of the year. Most of the major high-water periods

have occurred between February and April, when heavy rains accompany snowmelt; or in the summer and fall, as a result of hurricanes or tropical storms. Major floods inundated various portions of the basin seven times between 1924 and 1972. The most damaging was in 1936 when a flow at Washington, D.C., of 484,000 cubic feet per second was recorded.

In the Maryland portion of the basin, three local flood protection projects have been completed. Two are on the Potomac, at Kitzmiller and Cumberland-Ridgeley, and one on the Anacostia River, a tributary in Washington, D.C., and Maryland. The Cumberland-Ridgeley project, located on the North Branch Potomac River near Cumberland, Maryland, provides 17,000 feet of channel improvements on the North Branch and Wills Creek; it is supplemented by 13,000 feet of earthen levees and 1,600 feet of concrete floodwalls, plus three pumping stations. The Kitzmiller project in western Maryland provides 4,700 feet of channel improvement, 5,800 feet of levees, and a drainage structure. The Anacostia River project consists of 14,400 feet of improved channels, 28,000 feet of earthen levees, four pumping stations, and interior drainage facilities.

In the Virginia portion of the Potomac basin, local protection is being provided for Bridgewater and Fourmile Run. At Bridgewater the plan consists of an earth levee 4,610 feet long to cut off overland flow through the town from a point at the con-

Army Corps of Engineers

Floodwalls are constructed to protect built-up urban areas.

fluence of the North and Dry rivers. At Four-mile Run, a levee and floodwall in the cities of Alexandria and Arlington were approved under the 1965 and 1970 Flood Control acts. Neither project is yet completed.

There exists an important need on the river for storage for municipal water supply of the nation's capital. Several comprehensive plans of development have been proposed and studied over the past twenty years but have failed to get approval. In the meantime, the water needs have grown and now exceed the recorded low flow of the river. Thus, the area can experience a water shortage at any time.

On the Rappahannock River, which drains 2,848 square miles of northeast Virginia, a dam facility was proposed at Salem Church. It will consist of a concrete spillway with crest gates, concrete non-overflow sections on both sides of the spillway, and earthen wing dikes on both abutments. This dam will create a lake with storage capacity for water supply, and flood, water quality, and salinity control.

The James River Basin is the largest watershed inside Virginia, covering one fourth of the state's total area. The river, formed by the union of the Cowpasture and Jackson rivers, drains approximately 10,102 square miles. One multipurpose control project, Gathright Lake, which was authorized by the 1946 Flood Control Act to provide flood control, low-water augmentation, and recreation, is now under construction. The Gathright Dam site is located about 4.3 miles above the mouth of the Jackson River.

The Roanoke River, located in southern Virginia and northern North Carolina, has a drainage area of 9,580 square miles. It flows in a southeasterly direction to empty into Albemarle Sound. The plan for development of the Roanoke River Basin includes two multipurpose projects: The John H. Kerr Dam and Reservoir and the Philpott Lake. The Kerr project provides a storage capacity of about 1.5 million acre-feet, primarily for the control of floods and the generation of electricity. The Philpott Lake project furnishes flood protection and hydroelectric power to cities and towns in the Smith River Valley. The two projects prevented an esti-mated $9.6 million in damages during the floods of the tropical storm Agnes in 1972.

The Pee Dee River Basin extends southeastward from western North Carolina and a portion of Virginia to the Atlantic Ocean at Georgetown, South Carolina. The upper or western part of this river is known as the Yadkin, which unites with the Uwharrie to form Pee Dee. The Yadkin is 103 miles and the Pee Dee is 253 miles in length. These two reaches drain a basin 16,340 square miles in area. The major improvement of the basin is the W. Kerr Scott Reservoir, with a total capacity of 153,000 acre-feet, of which 112,000 are for flood control. This is equivalent to the runoff from the flood of 1940, the greatest of record in the basin. In a 1970 flood, the W. Kerr Scott facility pre-vented damages in excess of $4 million.

The Santee River Basin extends diagonally southeastward from the western part of North Carolina, through South Carolina, to the Atlantic Ocean, draining 15,700 square miles. The Santee is formed by the confluence of the Congaree and Wateree rivers. The only project within this basin is at Sugar and Briar Creeks—3.2 miles of channel excavation on Little Sugar Creek and 4.4 miles of channel excavation on Briar Creek.

The Savannah River is formed by the junction of the Tugaloo and Seneca Rivers, and flows along the South Carolina-Georgia border to enter Tybee Sound, an arm of the Atlantic Ocean. A plan was approved for eleven dams to develop the Savannah basin. and by 1976 two, Clark Hill and Hartwell, had been completed. The Clark Hill project, situated on the Savannah River 22 miles above Augusta, Georgia, provides for flood control, navigation, and the generation of hy-droelectric power. It was one of the first large multipurpose water control projects built by the Army Corps of Engineers in the eastern part of the nation. The 200-foot-high concrete gravity dam contains 4.6 million cubic yards of concrete. The powerhouse has a generating capacity of 280,000 kilowatts. Completed in 1954 at a cost of about $80 million, the 2.6 million acre-foot reservoir forms one of the largest inland bodies of water in the southeastern part of the United States.

The Hartwell project, located on the Savannah River 67 miles above the Clark Hill Dam, is also multipurpose in nature. A concrete gravity dam, with a height above foundation of 240 feet, it contains 5 million cubic yards of concrete and has a 264,000-kilowatt powerhouse. It was completed in 1964 at a cost of $88 million. The two reservoirs are outstanding recreational attractions of the southeast; in 1975 they recorded about 13 million visitor days. The hydroelectric power is marketed by the Department of the Interior.

Rio Grande: The Rio Grande begins in the 12,000- to 14,000-foot high peaks of the San Juan Mountains of southern Colorado and flows for about 180 miles through Colorado and then 470 miles through New Mexico to El Paso, Texas. There it becomes the international boundary between Mexico and the United States and extends 1,240 miles to the Gulf of Mexico near Brownsville, Texas. The principal United States tributary is the Pecos River, originating in eastern New Mexico and entering the Rio Grande about 30 miles upstream from Del Rio, Texas. The drainage area of 182,215 square miles (93,247 in the United States and 88,968 in Mexico) varies from high mountains with heavy snowfall to some of the continent's most arid lands. Of the total watershed, approximately 39,000 square miles are in New Mexico and Colorado upstream from El Paso. Control works in the river are the concern of the three states and various local entities above the international boundary, involving an interstate compact and state laws. The 1,240-mile international boundary section is under the jurisdiction of the International Boundary and Water Commission of the United States and Mexico. It is administered in accordance with several treaty arrangements.

The mild climate, rich soil, and easily accessible irrigation water have attracted human habitation for several hundred years. When the Spanish explorers arrived in the first half of the sixteenth century they found Pueblo Indians irrigating crops and using primitive methods which persisted until the early part of the twentieth century. American settlers began to arrive about 1840 in the middle Rio Grande Valley, the portion primarily in New

Mexico; and irrigation increased following the end of the Mexican War in 1847. Simple temporary diversion structures and irrigation canals were soon supplying water to 125,000 acres of previously dry land in the 150-mile reach of the river downstream from Santa Fe, New Mexico.

The extensive water diversions in Colorado and New Mexico caused the river to periodically dry up at El Paso. In 1888 a drought caused great hardships downstream and evoked protests from Mexico. The International Boundary Commission (later changed to the International Boundary and Water Commission by the 1944 Water Treaty) created by the treaty of March 1, 1889, placed an embargo on further water development in Colorado and New Mexico until facilities could be built to control floodwaters for use in the summer drought periods. Following the passage of the 1902 Reclamation Act, the Rio Grande Valley was one of the first areas examined. A feasibility study in 1904 concluded that a reservoir meeting the needs could be created by building a dam at Elephant Butte, New Mexico. The structure was authorized in 1905 as the major structure of the Rio Grande project.

An international treaty was negotiated in 1906 which guaranteed Mexico an annual delivery of 60,000 acre-feet of water at El Paso in perpetuity. Construction of the Rio Grande project then got underway, first with perma-

Elephant Butte Dam, completed in 1916, was the first major project constructed to control Rio Grande floodwaters.

nent structures to replace the makeshift works destroyed by floods almost every year. The project was to store floodwaters to insure meeting the commitment to Mexico. It also provided irrigation water through a permanent diversion and delivery system to 178,000 acres of land with full supply and an additional 18,300 acres with a supplemental supply. Besides the Elephant Butte Dam, it involved five diversion dams, 140 miles of main canals, 460 miles of laterals, and 460 miles of drains.

After a delay caused by reservoir right-of-way problems, the construction of Elephant Butte, a 300-foot-high concrete gravity dam, began in 1912 and was completed in 1916. Flood problems downstream in both the United States and Mexico resulted in the development of a Rio Grande Rectification project by the International Boundary Commission. In 1933 PWA allotted the State Department $1 million for Caballo Dam, an earthfill structure 20 miles downstream from Elephant Butte, as a unit of that project. Further studies resulted in increasing the reservoir size to provide additional flood control benefits and to furnish a control reservoir for power generation at Elephant Butte. Subsequently, the 96-foot-high dam was constructed in 1936-1938 and a 24,300-kilowatt powerhouse was added at Elephant Butte in 1940, along with 490 miles of power transmission lines.

After years of effort, an interstate compact dividing the Rio Grande waters between Colorado, New Mexico, and Texas was negotiated and approved by Congress in 1939. One of the complex problems, still not fully resolved, was the relationship of underground water to surface runoff, and the way state laws treat the problem. A detailed study of the full development of the river above El Paso was begun in 1942 as a cooperative undertaking of federal and state agencies; and a comprehensive development plan was formulated, encompassing flood control, sediment retention, drainage, and irrigation. Under the plan, the Bureau of Reclamation rehabilitated the project built by the Middle Rio Grande Conservancy District prior to 1935 and channelized the river for 130 miles to reduce loss of water. The channelization

had become necessary because of aggradation in the stream channel and transpiration losses from heavy growths of salt cedar.

The Army Corps of Engineers' work, primarily for flood control but also for multiple benefits, consists of four earthfill dams and many miles of levees and flood channelization. The Jemez Canyon Dam, about seventeen miles north of Albuquerque, is located on the Jemez River just above its confluence with the Rio Grande. This 136-foot-high dam was completed in 1953, the first of the program. Its 112,000 acre-foot reservoir is primarily for flood control and sediment retention.

The 325-foot-high Abiquiu Dam, creating a reservoir of 1.4 million acre-feet, contains 13 million cubic yards of earth and rock and was completed in 1962 at a cost of $21.2 million. It provides needed storage for runoff from the Rio Chama tributary, provides flood control and sediment retention benefits, and has become an important recreational attraction. The 158-foot-high Galisteo Dam, authorized solely for flood control and sediment retention, was completed in 1970. Located just south of Santa Fe, it controls the arid Galisteo Creek which has a long history of violent flash floods that have carried hundreds of tons of sediment, rock, and other debris into the Rio Grande.

The $91 million Cochiti Dam is located on the main stem of the Rio Grande, 50 miles upstream from Albuquerque, and is scheduled for completion in 1976. The 251-foot-high dam contains 60 million cubic yards of earth and rock, making it one of the largest in the nation. Its main purpose is for flood control and sediment retention, but it also provides municipal water storage and recreational benefits. It will furnish storage space for part of the million acre-feet of water imported over a ten-year period from the Colorado River tributaries in Colorado by the San Juan-Chama diversion project, twenty-six miles of tunnels piercing the continental divide. Nearing completion by the Bureau of Reclamation, this project will provide irrigation and municipal water for central New Mexico.

Local flood protection for the urban areas of Albuquerque and El Paso encompasses diversion channels, levees, and debris reten-

Falcon Dam on the Rio Grande, 75 miles downstream from Laredo, Texas, was completed in 1953 as a joint flood control undertaking of Mexico and the United States.

tion dams. This has involved close cooperative planning and construction with municipalities, various water districts, and the state highway departments.

The Pecos River has four reclamation projects which have flood control benefits, and seven flood control projects of the Corps of Engineers have been authorized and are partially completed. Two dams were built by the International Boundary and Water Commission on the international section of the river: Falcon Dam, located 75 miles downstream from Laredo, Texas, was finished in 1953; and Amistad Dam, located 12 miles upstream from Del Rio, Texas, was completed in 1969. The costs of these two structures were shared between the United States and Mexico. The year after its completion, the $32 million Falcon Reservoir completely controlled the greatest flood of record on the Rio Grande and prevented damages of over $50 million. Other flood control projects that have been jointly planned and carried out by the two governments include 165 miles of river levees and 215 miles of flood waterways.

Small Watershed Program

A small watershed public works project is a means of developing, improving, and managing land and water resources through joint planning and execution by local, state, and federal government agencies with the full support of a large majority of the private landowners and operators in the watershed. The objective is to increase economic return, minimize flood damage and other related problems, and improve the environment and public enjoyment of the area. A watershed project meets such needs as flood prevention and control, drainage, land stabilization, soil improvement, irrigation, municipal and industrial water supply, pollution abatement, fish and wildlife improvement, and recreation opportunities. Such projects are significant to both agriculture and non-agriculture areas of the country. What is done or not done on farms, ranches, forests, and wildland is critically important to alleviation of floods in thousands of small communities.

Early day considerations of the flood problem were generally limited to disastrous floods on main stem rivers. The solutions considered were primarily channel improvements and levee construction to carry the flood peaks within the channel; large flood control reservoirs that would confine them to existing channel capacities; or a combination of these two types. In relatively recent years, it has become apparent that a large part of the nation's flood damages occur in the small watersheds above the main stem rivers. Estimates of the amount of such damage have varied; the first national assessment by the Water Resources Council in 1968 estimated that about 60 percent of the nation's flood damages occur in upstream areas. These upstream flood control problems require a different approach than those of main river floods.

Much of the main stem river flood damage affects urban areas. Therefore, a high degree of protection is needed, usually against severe floods likely to occur only once in 100 years. In contrast, most upstream damages are to agriculture, and the degree of protection desired is usually for flood frequencies of fewer than ten years.

On the rural upstream watersheds, the most efficient type of control is usually a combination of watershed land treatment and comparatively small detention structures. The land treatment measures are most effective in reducing runoff from the more frequent rainstorms; generally they become progressively less effective as the storms grow larger. As the watersheds become saturated they cannot retain additional rainfall, and most of it runs off. This combination of control by watershed land treatment measures and small detention structures in the upstream watershed requires the full cooperation of the landowners on whose property the works must be installed and maintained.

Congress took action toward protecting watersheds in 1891, when it authorized setting aside the first forest reserves from the national domain. In 1897 it passed the Organic Administration Act for National Forests and established the "securing of favorable conditions of waterflows" as a principal purpose of such forests. Consequently, the 1911 Weeks Act and the 1924 Clarke-McNary Act authorized purchase and protection of forest land in the interest of floodwater and sediment control.

As this legislation reveals, until the mid 1930s, public action in watershed land treatment was confined almost entirely to public land and directed primarily toward preserving and improving forest cover. But the unfavorable effects of farmland erosion on agriculture production had been recognized since colonial days. Many early agricultural leaders, including George Washington and Thomas Jefferson, not only wrote about soil erosion but also carried out effective soil conservation measures on their plantations. However, public action before 1933 was confined to sporadic investigations, conferences to deplore the ravages of erosion, and erosion research begun by state experiment stations in 1917 and the federal government in 1929.

Growing problems and concern, coupled with the severe Depression of the 1930s, changed public opinion about the role of the federal government in carrying out public works, including the conservation of soil, water, timber, grass, and mineral resources on privately owned land. The commerce and general welfare clauses of the Constitution were interpreted during these years to permit action of a kind and scope not previously conceived. The groundwork was laid by conservationists like Gifford Pinchot, Hugh Hammond Bennett, and President Roosevelt. The usefulness of massive public works projects in providing jobs for the unemployed combined to produce a national conservation effort which, with all its growing pains, has never lost its momentum.

One of the fruits of the 1933-1936 programs to restore the national economy was the creation by executive action in June 1933 of a Soil Erosion Service in the Department of the Interior. Bennett was appointed to head this new agency and $5 million of public works funds were allocated to it. As in other public works areas, the initial program of the federal government was to carry out demonstration projects. These small watershed projects were to focus technical skills in fields such as soils, agronomy, forestry, engineering, and biology on planning the use of every acre of privately owned farmland. The application of vegetative and structural treatments to protect each acre from erosion was also included. The program, carried out as a public works undertaking, required the landowner to sign an agreement and provide some labor and materials. The Soil Erosion Service did the technical planning and supervision, furnished materials, and provided large amounts of WPA and CCC labor for the construction. The projects were intended to demonstrate not only the increased economic returns resulting from erosion control, but also the decreased flooding and sedimentation downstream.

New developments came rapidly following the dramatic dust storms of 1934 and 1935. They blew great clouds of dust from Great Plains fields over Washington to settle on the decks of ships far out in the Atlantic. In the month following the 1935 dust storm, Congress established, by unanimous vote, a permanent Soil Conservation Service in the Department of Agriculture to take over the activities of the Soil Erosion Service.

By the end of fiscal year 1936, the Soil Conservation Service was operating 147 demonstration projects averaging 25,000 to 30,000 acres each, 48 soil conservation nurseries, 23 research stations, and 454 CCC camps. About 50,000 farmers in the demonstration areas had applied for programs for soil and water conservation on 5 million acres. Thousands more were asking for an opportunity to participate in the program.

A report sent to Congress by President Roosevelt on January 30, 1936 resulted in more legislation. The report, "Little Waters: A Study of Headwater Streams and Other Little Waters: Their Use and Relation to the Land," was prepared under the direction of R. G. Tugwell, Bennett, and Morris L. Cooke, heads of Department of Agriculture agencies; and the chairman of the National Resources Committee, Secretary of the Interior Harold L. Ickes.

In his message of transmittal, the President pointed out that, while the nation had grown accustomed to dealing with great rivers and their problems, the little rivers and streams had been neglected. His message emphasized the need to control water from its ultimate source and to develop an effective national policy on flood control and proper land and water use. He stated:

Our disastrous floods, our sometimes equally disastrous periods of low water, and our major problems of erosion . . . do not come full grown into being. They originate in a small way in a multitude of farms, ranches, and pastures. It is not suggested that we neglect our main streams and give our whole attention to these little waters but we must have, literally, a plan which will envision the problem as it is presented in every farm, every pasture, every woodlot, every acre of the public domain.

Five months later, Congress passed the 1936 Flood Control Act, which authorized the secretary of agriculture to make preliminary examinations and surveys to determine measures needed for erosion and flood control on the watersheds upstream from the flood control programs under the jurisdiction of the Army Corps of Engineers. Under this act, the Department of Agriculture surveyed and reported on more than 200 watersheds; but, partly because of World War II, it had sent Congress only twenty-six reports, including the Missouri Basin Agricultural Plan, by 1954.

Shortly after the 1936 Flood Control Act was passed, President Roosevelt suggested to governors that state legislation be passed authorizing farmers, ranchers, and other landowners and managers to organize districts specifically to conserve soil and water. Legislatures of twenty-two states enacted laws that year providing for districts, and the rest followed suit. Districts, legal subdivisions of a state, are managed by supervisors elected by the landowners and operators of the districts. It is significant that the nation's first soil conservation district was a watershed, Brown Creek in Anson County, North Carolina. These soil and water conservation districts, which now serve almost every community in the country and 95 percent of agricultural land, are the principal sponsors of today's watershed projects. Thus, between 1933 and 1937, federal and state legislation established a far-reaching program to protect and manage watersheds consisting mainly of privately owned land, even though no improvement works were authorized at that time. It took almost twenty years before the small watershed program began to have a widespread impact.

The 1944 Flood Control Act included land treatment but only on eleven watersheds, involving about 30 million acres. The House Agriculture and Public Works committees

Soil Conservation Service.

The Willow Creek Watershed Project in Minnesota includes contoured fields, stripcropping, and terracing. The small flood retention dam holds back floodwaters for release at a safe rate into the streambed below.

could not agree on the authorization process, so the number was kept low and structures on the projects were not authorized. The responsibility of the Agriculture Department for flood control was divided between the Soil Conservation Service and the Forest Service.

When work started on the initial eleven basins, it became apparent, as many people had long maintained, that the land treatment measures authorized by the survey reports would provide only limited flood protection. Demand grew for better flood protection in the small tributaries. The 1951 Department of Agriculture Appropriation Act contained language that permitted the eleven watershed projects to include upstream floodwater detention reservoirs, channel improvements, and other structures. In 1953 Congress appropriated $5 million for sixty-two pilot watershed protection projects under the broad provisions of the 1935 Soil Conservation Act.

Starting in 1950, a number of studies were made, extensive hearings held, and various legislation considered, which in August 1954 resulted in passage of Public Law 83-566. Known as the Watershed Protection and Flood Prevention Act, it was amended by subsequent actions, and it is still the authority for small watershed projects. The new act repealed the authority of the secretary of agriculture to make surveys and investigations under the 1936 Flood Control Act,

but it permitted the eleven authorized river basin projects and the pilot watershed projects to continue. Section 6 of the act authorized the secretary of agriculture to cooperate with other federal, state, and local agencies in investigating and surveying watersheds of rivers and other waterways as a basis for developing coordinated programs.

For watersheds no larger than 250,000 acres, the law authorized the secretary of agriculture to help local organizations plan and carry out works of improvement for flood prevention and the agricultural aspects of water conservation, development, use, and disposal. This assistance included conducting investigations and surveys, determining the engineering and economic feasibility of plans, and furnishing financial and other support. The law was thus designed to fill the gap between water-related practices on individual farms and the large downstream river basin projects.

A project plan could provide for no single structure with more than 5,000 acre-feet of total storage capacity. In the original law, local organizations were to pay an equitable share of construction costs for flood prevention, as determined by the secretary of agriculture. Federal construction funds were to be used only for flood prevention. Although the original act provided planning assistance for such agricultural water management purposes as irrigation and drainage, in practice the financial limitations of local organizations restricted the program almost wholly to flood prevention.

The scope of the small watershed program has since been greatly enlarged by a series of congressional amendments. The 1954 act was first amended in 1956 in response to complaints that it gave its local clientele less financial assistance than the programs of the Army Corps of Engineers and the Bureau of Reclamation and that local interests that wished to participate were unable to meet the costs.

These key 1956 amendments provided that the federal government would pay all construction and engineering costs for flood prevention and share in construction costs for agricultural water management. The secretary of agriculture determined the equitable share for local organizations in consideration of national needs and assistance authorized for similar purposes under other federal programs. All other costs were to be borne by local sponsoring organizations. The amendments provided for loans up to $5 million, at low interest, to local organizations to finance their share. Currently, the federal share is limited to a maximum of 50 percent of engineering and construction costs for agricultural water management, which includes both drainage and irrigation, with the continuing stipulation that cost sharing be consistent with other similar government programs.

The 1956 act also authorized works for municipal and industrial water supply, but these were to be paid for by local interests. In addition, the limit on total storage capacity of individual structures was increased from 5,000 to 25,000 acre-feet, but no more than 5,000 acre-feet could be for flood protection. It also simplified the time-consuming and involved procedures for authorization. The smaller projects, under the amendment, required neither authorization by Congress nor review by other construction agencies. Such projects may not require federal funding of more than $250,000 for construction costs, nor may they contain a structure larger than 2,500 acre-feet in total storage capacity.

Larger projects require review by the Army Corps of Engineers. If they include irrigation works or affect public land or wildlife, they must also be reviewed by the Interior Department. Each of these larger projects must be authorized by resolution of the appropriate committees of Congress. If a plan does not include the construction of a single structure larger than 4,000 acre-feet in total storage capacity, the plan requires approval by the Agriculture committees of the two houses of Congress. If a structure exceeds 4,000 acre-feet, the plan must be approved by the two Public Works committees.

A 1958 amendment added fish and wildlife development as a project measure under the same federal cost-sharing measures applied to agricultural water management at that time. The 1962 Food and Agriculture Act added recreation as a purpose eligible for cost sharing in watershed projects; authorized the Department of Agriculture to advance funds to preserve sites; and permitted projects to include capacity for future industrial and municipal water storage with repayment and interest charges deferred up to ten years. In 1963 the limit for water storage capacity was increased from 5,000 to 12,500 acre-feet, and in 1970 the Soil Conservation Service was authorized to do construction contracting if requested.

The 1972 Rural Development Act further broadened the Watershed Protection and Flood Prevention Act by including conservation and proper utilization of land in watershed planning. Groundwater recharge and water quality management were also added as project purposes. Further amendments added authority for long-term contracting up to ten years, cost sharing for water storage capacity to meet present needs, and use of federal funds appropriated for other programs to help pay the sponsors' share of the project. The 1974 Water Resources Development Act supplemented Public Law 83-566, by directing federal water resource planning agencies to consider non-structural measures for flood prevention in planning water resource projects.

Most of the states have enacted legislation to meet the requirement of the Watershed Protection and Flood Prevention Act that local organizations have the authority under state law to carry out, maintain, and operate the projects when completed. They include legal authority for local organizations to furnish land, easements, and rights-of-way; arrange for cost sharing; install, maintain, and operate works of improvement; acquire needed water rights; obtain loans and advances from the federal government; levy taxes or assessments; exercise the power of eminent domain; and obtain agreements from landowners for recommended land treatment. Public Law 83-566 projects have received widespread attention and support. By July 1974, 2,902 applications covering 226 million acres had been approved by designated state agencies and transmitted to the Department of Agriculture. Approved plans have authorized 1,096 projects for construction covering about 69 million acres.

The activity under this program indicates that it meets the long-felt need for public works to fill a gap in national resource conservation and development. Earlier legislation had provided for programs of public land conservation and for technical, education, cost-sharing and credit assistance to individual private landowners and operators. Large programs authorized under the reclamation, flood control, TVA, and other acts provided for federal development of downstream river resources, including large irrigation, hydropower, flood control, and navigation undertakings as well as projects or project features for fish and wildlife development, recreation, or municipal and industrial water supply. The void left by these programs in the smaller, upstream watersheds, which have the same basic needs for land and water management as the large rivers, is being filled by the small watershed program. Its fundamental principles are (1) local initiative and responsibility, (2) federal technical and financial assistance, and (3) state review and approval of local proposals with an open opportunity for state financial and other assistance.

One of the most rewarding features of the small watershed program has been its favorable effect on the economy of areas in which projects have been developed. They have helped stem low income, underemployment, rural poverty, and declining small-town population. For example, in Culpeper, Virginia, the adequate water supply and protection from floods brought about through the Mountain Run Watershed Project have attracted four new industries, employing more than 500 local people. One of the new industries is a $2 million flour mill that produces more than a million pounds of flour and animal feed a day. A community hospital, previously delayed because of a lack of enough municipal water, has also been completed. Without the watershed project, many local people would have been forced to migrate to the larger metropolitan areas in search of employment. In addition to a growing economy, the entire area now enjoys three new reservoirs with flood storage capacity of 2,860 acre-feet. A 4-acre picnic area is being developed at one of the reservoirs. It brings fishing and boating facilities to the town's back door. The completed work has been so successful, the sponsors are now revising the original plan to add two structures that will prevent flooding of urban property, furnish 1,000 acre-feet of additional municipal water storage, and provide public recreation.

A reliable municipal water supply is also a rewarding feature of other watershed projects. For example, twenty years ago people of Pittsfield, Illinois, were stymied by having too much water at certain times of the year and not enough at others. The area had a long history of severe spring floods and summer water shortages. The city's primary water source, a small reservoir built in 1924, had lost nearly half its capacity from silt washed down from surrounding corn fields. Even after two deep wells were drilled to supplement the reservoir, the supply failed to keep pace with the city's increasing water consumption. During the long, dry summers of 1953 and 1954, water was hauled from the Mississippi River, resulting in common monthly water bills of over $30 a family. This problem brought farm and city people together to find a solution. They began the Big Blue Creek Watershed Project, sponsored jointly by the city and the Pike County Soil Conservation District.

The project provided conservation measures on farmland to conserve water and reduce runoff and two floodwater retarding dams to catch and temporarily store the excess water that poured off 10,000 acres of surrounding farmland during heavy rains. One dam, enlarged at local expense, now backs up a 240-acre lake holding more than a billion gallons of water for municipal and industrial use. The adequate water supply has attracted a new $500,000 nursing home to Pittsfield and permitted the town to build a sewage oxidation basin costing $200,000. Several new housing developments have also been completed. This area is reaping other benefits as well. For instance, new public recreation facilities provided by the project include picnic and camping areas, fishing, and boating. The floodwater retarding structures proved their effectiveness in October 1969 when 9 inches of rain fell on the watershed in one weekend. Although other creeks in the area flooded and caused considerable damage, Blue Creek was contained within its banks.

Most projects are built primarily for flood prevention, since floods are the principal spoilers of natural resources as well as the major cause of property damages. Although upstream floods are usually not sensational in a national sense, they occur more often and as a result do more total damage than the bigger, less frequent, and more publicized floods downstream.

Until the small watershed program was enacted, there was little rural and small urban areas could do to lessen the threat of damaging floods. In some areas, annual floods were an accepted occurrence. Lampasas and Brunet counties in Texas experienced catastrophic damages when Sulphur Creek flooded in 1957. Total direct damages were estimated at $5.5 million with indirect damages an additional $800,000. Before the debris was cleared from the streets, the farmers and townspeople got together to start action. The next year, construction of floodwater-retarding structures under Public Law 83-566 was started. The nine works, now completed, successfully held a major 1965 flood within the streambanks through the city of Lampasas. The local people were reassured that the project would

perform as promised, and the town of Lampasas has grown steadily. The town's largest industrial plant, which burned down in 1968, was rebuilt and expanded in part because the owners felt they could rely on the flood protection. A house trailer construction firm and a garment factory are among the new industries attracted to town by the security from floods. Sediment deposits in the city water supply have been reduced, as has silt in fish-spawning areas. More fishing and recreation are available due to the project.

Utah's American Fork-Dry Creek Watershed, once flood-plagued and approaching economic stalemate, won the National Watershed Congress watershed-of-the-year award in 1966 after the Public Law 83-566 project had transformed the area. From the time this area was settled until the project was completed, the people of this 118,000-acre watershed had been troubled by periodic flooding. Water from sudden downpours in the mountains, and sometimes from rapid snowmelt, plunged down the stream courses, bearing thousands of tons of sediment.

The watershed project was designed to reduce floodwater and sediment damages and improve the efficiency of water use in the valley. The plan called for four debris basins strategically located to hold storm water temporarily and permit it to drop its sediment load. The project also included an irrigation reservoir paid for by local users of irrigation water. Recreation benefits were provided. Reseeding and special flood retarding trenches on large areas that previously had little vegetation have benefited wildlife. The area's more dependable agriculture has given the economy a healthy boost. The conservation work has meant improvement of water control and of the native grass resources. The livestock industry is growing. New schools, homes, and community centers and increased land values also attest to the benefits.

Another benefit, water-based recreation, is rapidly becoming one of the most popular purposes in watershed project development. Since 1962 over 200 recreation developments centered on retained floodwaters have been approved for construction. Many of the watershed recreational areas help the local economy by enhancing tourist industries. For example, thousands of people are taking advantage of the recreation development in the Mud River Watershed Project in Kentucky. There, one of twenty-five detention reservoirs was enlarged to include an 800-acre lake. The Kentucky Department of Fish and Wildlife Resources, one of the project sponsors, helped finance the recreation development and is managing it. A 300-acre park has been developed along part of the lake's shoreline. More than 200 privately owned cottages, valued at over $2 million, have been built along the lake. Other development, both public and private, around the lake includes 50 miles of new and improved roads, a bridge, a sportsman's lodge, and 20 miles of hiking trails.

Soil Conservation Service

The Mud River Watershed project in Kentucky provides a wide array of benefits.

A major aim in the Flat Creek Watershed in Lawrence County, Arkansas, was helping people enjoy a variety of outdoor fun in an attractive setting. The efforts of state and federal agencies and the town of Walnut Ridge were profitable. Before 650-acre Lake Charles was built, economists figured it would someday return $277,000 a year in community benefits. In 1970 recreation activities at Lake Charles pumped approximately $642,000 into the local economy—more than double the original estimates. Benefits to the region were nearly $1.5 million, almost as much as the cost of building the lake and park. The winding, all-weather trails in the park allow intense use of wooded

areas without destroying vegetation or causing soil erosion. People are using boat ramps, picnic tables and grills, playground equipment, and campsites. Besides boating, fishing, and swimming— and its primary role of keeping floodwaters off farmland and out of Walnut Ridge—Lake Charles performs another valuable job. It stores water for flooding several hundred acres on the Rainey Brake wildlife refuge every fall, giving migratory waterfowl a place to rest on their way south. It also supplements water supplies for the public hunting and fishing area in Rainey Brake during dry periods.

These are examples of the small watershed projects. What had started out as a hopeful experiment has rapidly become a strong public works program of resource development carried out by local people. Water, a common denominator that brought rural and urban interests together around local conference tables, catalyzed the solution of many other problems as well. The groups have found that problems such as faltering rural economics, the need for outdoor recreation, and vanishing fish and wildlife habitat, often can be solved at the same time as flood protection and water supply.

Drainage of Rural Areas

Flood control and drainage are closely interrelated. From the early days of settlement, various public works programs to drain flood waters from land have been undertaken. One of the first large efforts of this kind was by the Dismal Swamp Canal Company, chartered by Virginia and North Carolina, to drain the Dismal Swamp area for land reclamation and inland water transportation. The dual-purpose canal was opened in 1794 and is still in operation.

Originally about 275 million acres across the nation, one acre in seven, were poorly drained. Nearly a fourth of the nation's potential agricultural land, approximately 216 million acres, was too wet for farming. Most of these problem areas were in the South Atlantic Gulf Coast, the Mississippi Delta, and included much of the presently productive agricultural land in Ohio, Illinois, Wisconsin, Iowa, and Minnesota. Drainage work was carried out under state laws that provided for establishment of drainage districts or for the counties to plan, finance, and construct drains utilizing authority to levy special taxes or assessments on the lands benefited. Among the earliest laws were those of Maryland in 1790 and Delaware in 1816.

The first drainage work consisted mainly of small open ditches to drain low spots and of cleaning out small natural streambeds. Modern tile drainage began in 1835 when John Johnson of Seneca County, New York, brought patterns from Scotland from which clay tile was molded by hand. By 1880 over 1,140 factories were providing clay drain tile, mainly in Illinois, Indiana, and Ohio. Over 30,000 miles of tile were laid in Indiana in 1882. By 1884 Ohio had 20,000 miles of public works drainage ditches, benefiting 11 million acres of land and removing a major threat to settlers' health. By 1975 about 30 million acres had been added to the tillable area of the North Central states, and production was increased on 37 million more.

The first extensive census of drainage of rural lands was made in 1920 and showed approximately 66 million acres were benefited and assessed in public districts. Over 157,000 miles of open ditches and tile drains had been provided on these lands. It was estimated an additional 55 million acres of wetlands, not included in public drainage districts, had been improved by farm drainage. By 1970 there were about 2,500 public drainage districts, of which a little over 300 were counties. Acreage included within the districts totaled 137 million acres, greater than the combined area of the four states of Illinois, Ohio, Indiana, and Iowa. About half the districts' acreage was directly drained by tiles or ditches.

The 1920 census figures show the cost of the public drainage enterprises was $183,000 prior to 1860; $10 million by 1880; $61 million by 1900; and $435 million by 1920. The total cost of all drainage, including that of the drainage work done by the individual farmers was difficult to estimate, but fragmentary data indicated that by 1920 it was between $1.2 and $1.5 billion. Today the rural land drainage facilities include about a million miles of subsurface tile drains; 25,000 miles of

farm drainage ditches; 500,000 miles of main and lateral drainage ditches; 17,000 miles of large open collector drainage channels; 13,000 miles of dikes and levees (for farm or small group of farms); and 126,000 pumping plants. The total replacement cost is about $7 billion.

There has been a surge of drainage activity during times of food need such as war periods. With worldwide food shortage problems, it can be expected additional drainage work will be undertaken in the years ahead, especially in improving drainage of lands now under cultivation. Careful environmental evaluations will be required elsewhere as plans are considered to expand cropped acreages through drainage.

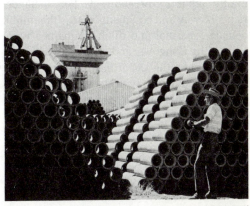

U.S. Bureau of Reclamation

About a million miles of subsurface pipe drains have been placed for rural land drainage.

Most of the drainage works have been planned and financed locally. Too often they have reduced local damage but have increased drainage and flood problems lower in the drainage area. Many have been inadequately planned and built and have failed. The increasing need to correlate all plans over a major watershed and to fully consider all consequences of actions taken has brought state and federal activities directly into the drainage program.

The financing of the drainage systems by the drainage districts was generally by bonds issued by the districts or counties and paid off by taxes or assessments on the lands benefited. The federal government had done little in direct land drainage until the

U.S. Department of Agriculture

Over one hundred million acres of the nation's productive farmland have been made available for agriculture by drainage works.

emergency public works programs of the 1930s. Prior to then, its function had been mostly advisory or indirect. For instance, rights-of-way and easements across the public domain for canal and ditch companies were granted by Congress, and research work was carried out by the Department of Agriculture.

In recent years, with the expansion of activities by the water resource construction agencies and with the organization of various federal financing agencies, federal functions have expanded considerably. Flood control works by the Army Corps of Engineers have helped with large drainage channels; the Bureau of Reclamation provides drainage systems as part of its irrigation projects; and the Soil Conservation Service has been active, especially with the individual farmer and with small watersheds.

These public works drainage activities have accomplished much. First, by draining swamps and stagnant water areas the health of the communities and rural areas where they have been constructed has improved; second, over 100 million acres of the best lands in the nation have been made available for agriculture that otherwise would have been of little value except for wildlife; third, yields of farm lands have been improved and losses from flooding have been reduced; and fourth, excess water has been removed which has benefited the construction of highways and railroads.

Urban Runoff and Flood Control

As urban density increases, so do the problems of flooding from storm water runoff. There is no sharp distinction between storm runoff, drainage, or flood control problems, except possibly in degree in a specific area. Land drainage of flood waters was one of the first public works services and has been increasingly vital to the health, welfare, and safety of all citizens, especially in today's urbanized society.

In 1776 urban drainage works existed only as natural ditches and perhaps some type of grading for swales or ditches to drain low spots and carry the storm runoff to the nearest stream channel or lake. It was possible, generally, to locate buildings and farms where danger of damages from runoff flooding was small. Drains were built by individuals or a small group for a specific local drainage problem. By 1790, at the time of the first national census, there were only four cities in the nation with more than 10,000 population: New York City had 33,131; Philadelphia, 28,522; Boston, 18,320; and Baltimore, 13,305. The rest of the nation was rural or semi-rural. Boston appears to have been the first city to become involved in community-wide drainage needs, and in 1823 it took over the maintenance of existing drains within the city.

As urbanization expanded, increased population, commercialization, and industrial development imposed demands upon citizens, especially property owners, to develop ways to safeguard their health and property. As communities grew, it became necessary to protect transportation arteries and divert water away from unsurfaced roadways, or they became quagmires. Stagnant pools were offensive because of their appearance and odor. Effective drainage became the goal of progressive communities. The storm drainage systems developed from the primitive hand-ditch and paved gutter for a small local area to the present day generally underground storm sewer systems. They include inlets, manholes, and catch basins integrated into a network of laterals, mains trunks, and outfall sewers.

Many early drains were apparently built without technical direction, and there were problems in getting them to function properly. It appears that engineering skills were not generally applied to designs until after 1850. The first community-wide sewerage system for drainage appears to be that designed by Julius W. Adams for Brooklyn, New York, in 1857, followed by a comprehensive plan for Chicago developed by Ellis S. Chesbrough in 1858. As the water-carrier system of waste disposal came into use, there was marked prejudice against the discharge of excretal matter into the drains, as their poor design and construction usually resulted in offensive odors considered detrimental to health. In fact, in Baltimore, Maryland, the direct discharge of such matter into drainage sewers was prohibited by law until 1911, when a new and comprehensive system of domestic sewers and a sewage treatment plant, the country's largest separate system, was put into operation.

Severe epidemics of yellow fever in the late 1870s resulted in the nation's first separate storm discharge and domestic sewage system, begun in 1880 in Memphis, Tennessee. That same year a separate system was undertaken in Pullman, Illinois. While the trend has since been away from a combined storm water and domestic waste sewer system, and new systems built today are generally separate, it will be many years before all existing ones will be converted to separate systems. Other solutions, such as the present Chicago plan discussed later in this chapter, may prove to be more effective.

A survey of expenditures for capital improvements in storm drainage systems in 1965 was made by the American Public Works Association Research Foundation. It estimated a yearly expenditure of $1,740 million. The breakdown is as follows:

Expenditures by	1965 Yearly Amount
Private Developers	$720 million
Local Governments	$360 million
Streets and Highways—Urban	$240 million
Streets and Highways—Rural	$420 million
Total	$1,740 million

With higher construction costs and projected volume increases, the estimated expenditure during 1976 may reach $4 billion.

Private land developers usually provide the storm runoff facilities for their development, the cost of which is included in the cost of the lots. Ownership then is generally turned over to the local municipal governmental authority for maintenance by the public works department. Local public agencies are usually responsible for construction of main and trunk sewers and drainage canals, although federal and state flood control programs are helpful in some areas. The expenditures for storm runoff drainage for streets and highways are made from highway funds, which include local, state, and federal sources. Maintenance is the responsibility of the appropriate local or state highway organization.

Public Works Historical Society

Providing drainage for urban areas includes placing large pipes to carry away the storm waters.

In recent years, the need for carefully coordinated and integrated drainage systems, flood control programs, and flood plain management has become increasingly apparent. Also, water quality is becoming a more important factor because of the pollutants from street, highway, and urban runoff. Sewers, levees, ditches, impounding basins, and corrective works must be designed with full consideration of zoning, flood plain regulations, subdivision controls, and land use plans. Many innovative ways to retain storm runoff to improve the environment and reduce lower basin flooding problems are being utilized.

For instance, in San Clemente, California, a flood channel and retention basin doubles as a golf course. In Bloomington, Illinois, a system of detention reservoirs utilizing the stream flood plain saved nearly one half of the cost of traditional underground drainage piping, reduced downstream problems, and improved aesthetic and recreational values of the development. In Montgomery County, Maryland, the flood plains of streams are retained by the county as wooded open spaces, with hiking and riding trails and parks.

The following three examples—New Orleans, Los Angeles, and Chicago—illustrate the range of problems in protecting large urban areas from flooding and standing water, and the innovative methods developed to meet the special difficulties. They demonstrate effective planning and action by public works officials.

New Orleans Drainage System: Not only did New Orleans pioneer in flood control work to protect urban sites from river floods with its initial levees, but the measures to provide drainage of storm runoff within the city were among the earliest in the nation. The location of New Orleans at the mouth of the Mississippi had many natural resource, commercial, and strategic advantages, but it presented a major storm water and surface drainage problem. The city's flat swampy saucer-like terrain, coupled with a yearly rainfall of 55 inches earned it titles such as "the pest-hole of the world" and "the city of the wet grave."

After the Louisiana Purchase in 1803, which lifted trade restrictions, and the introduction of the paddle-wheeled steamboat in 1812, which solved the problem of upstream navigation, New Orleans prospered. By 1840, with trade reaching $200 million per year, New Orleans rivaled New York in European commerce. However, the growth of the city was limited by lack of drainage.

In 1835 the New Orleans Drainage Company received a charter to drain the city by excavating open canals and erecting drainage "machines" along a natural bayou that discharged into Lake Pontchartrain, the northern boundary of the city. The machines were large, ranging in diameter from 28 to 34 feet, and raised 240 to 480 cubic feet per second of water from the bayou several feet into the lake. They could handle a rainfall of 0.12 inches in one hour. However, this rate was in-

adequate, for the city frequently received rains up to 2 inches per hour. The result was epidemic diseases, such as the yellow fever outbreak of 1878 that brought death to nearly 5 percent of the population.

It became obvious by 1893 that adequate drainage must be provided if the city were to expand. The first topographical survey of the city was made and a master drainage plan was formulated to drain the city by an extensive system of canals and pumping stations, discharging into Lake Pontchartrain. In 1896 the Louisiana legislature established the Drainage Commission of New Orleans to finance and construct the drainage public works. In 1899 the legislature created the Sewerage and Water Board primarily to establish an underground sewer system separate and distinct from the storm drainage system. Four years later, the commission and the board were merged and the modern Sewerage and Water Board, responsible for the city's water, drainage, and sewerage system, came into being.

The difficult problems of providing the large pumping capacity required were overcome in 1913 by A. Baldwin Wood, the superintendent of the Sewerage and Water Board. Wood invented a low-head, high-volume screw pump. Four of his 12-foot diameter pumps, each discharging 550 cubic feet per second, were installed in 1915. Wood improved the pumps a few years later by a 14-foot diameter pump which almost doubled the capacity of the 12-foot ones. When installed, the Wood screw pumps were the biggest and most powerful in the world, and by far the most efficient. They made New Orleans the mecca for the world's urban drainage public works officials and engineers. The designs are still being used throughout the world. In 1975 these pumps were designated as an American Society of Mechanical Engineers National Historic Mechanical Engineering Landmark.

The city's primary drainage system presently includes 170 miles of open and covered canals and 45 miles of large diameter pipelines with fifteen pumping stations housing pumps having a total capacity of over 29,000 cubic feet per second. Wood's original pumps are still in operation. The system is considered one of the largest and most efficient urban storm runoff drainage systems.

Los Angeles County Flood Control and Drainage Program: The Los Angeles basin illustrates the flooding problems and solutions of many of the nation's arid and semi-arid urban areas. It is unique, however, because the attractions of the mild climate have resulted in the explosive growth of urbanization in the basin within the past several decades. The population of the Los Angeles County Basin, enclosed within the boundaries of the 2,700-square-mile flood control district, has increased in the past sixty years from 700,000 to over 7 million. The assessed valuation has grown from $800 million to about $20 billion.

The San Gabriel and Santa Monica mountains to the north dominate the basin. The area is subjected to heavy winter rainstorms which move in from the Pacific Ocean, and the intensity of rainfall is increased by the orographic effect of the mountains. From the 11,000-foot peaks, the mountain canyons discharge into the detrital cones that have been built over the past ages by deposits from debris-laden flood waters. During recurring storms, rock slides, uprooted trees, brush, and other debris have been swept downstream to the mouth of the canyons. There it has been deposited, has filled the channels on the cones, and has caused the flood waters to turn and traverse the cones in an unpredictable and continually changing manner. The depositing of silt and debris in the Los Angeles and San Gabriel river channels and their tributaries has changed their courses over the centuries back and forth across the 25-mile-wide coastal plain.

As major floods have occurred at the rate of six or eight every fifty to sixty years, and not at regular intervals, periods of ten years or more pass without demonstrations of the potential damage of building within the stream channel areas. A flood in 1814, for example, cut a channel across what became the downtown district of Los Angeles. After the river changed again to its present channel, the city expanded into the old 1815 channel. A large part of the low-lying land of the basin was utilized for buildings, even though much of it was natural overflow areas. Small communities were built on the debris cones along the base of the mountains.

Although there were six major floods in the fifty years prior to 1914, it was not until the severe flooding in February of that year, causing over $10 million in structure damage and isolating the basin from the outside world for several days, that action was taken. Bridges, roads, railroads, buildings, telephone and telegraph lines, and utilities were destroyed; and the Los Angeles and Long Beach harbors were nearly blocked through siltation of the channels. A three-member Board of Engineers was appointed by the county to recommend remedial measures. They had difficulties reaching agreement on the relative emphasis and reliance to be placed on upstream measures (reforestation, check dams, and impounding dams) as compared to extensive downstream works (levee construction and channel bank revetments). However, a report was finally submitted July 27, 1915.

In the meantime the Los Angeles County Flood Control District (LACFCD) was created by state legislative action on June 12, 1915. The legislation defined the boundaries of the district and established the administrative procedures to carry out the objectives of control and conservation of flood and waste waters of the district. A limited *ad valorem* tax was authorized, then 0.1 percent but later increased to 0.15 percent, to support the activities and retire the bonds issued to finance the programs. Building upon the Board of Engineers' report, a bond issue of $4.5 million was passed by a narrow margin in 1917. He enabled the district to cooperate with the federal government in construction to remove the threat of silting the harbor, and to provide the most urgently needed levees, channels, and check and debris dams. The harbor work, directed by the Army Corps of Engineers, was federally financed except for lands required for right-of-way. The initial program, delayed by World War I, was completed in 1921.

The district's chief engineer, James W. Reagan, was supported in his enthusiasm for combining flood control and water conservation through construction of impounding dams and reservoirs. In 1924 a $3.3 million bond issue was passed by a large majority. The plan provided for several dams, including a large concrete gravity dam in San Gabriel Canyon intended to impound 240,000 acre-feet of water. Construction of the dam was started in 1925, but excavation revealed unsatisfactory foundation conditions. A site several miles downstream was selected for a rockfill dam, but material problems resulted in further delays and design changes. This 377-foot-high earth and rock dam, containing nearly 12 million cubic yards of material, was not completed until 1938, just a few days in advance of the great flood of March 1938. Containing this one flood prevented damages greatly in excess of the cost of the project.

These first two bond issues were for the most urgent work, and a long-range plan covering all major flood channels was not completed until 1931. This plan became a basis, with additions and modifications, for future work. In the meantime, a bond issue for $27 million in 1926 was defeated, at least partly because no major flood had occurred since 1916. A damaging localized flood upstream from Glendale on January 1, 1934 caught people unaware. Forty-one lives were lost, and damage was in excess of $6 million. The flood demonstrated the precarious position of the suburban developments in the foothill region, the destructive power of debris-laden water, and the enormous amount of material that could be carried by a single flood confined to a small area. The inclusion of debris basins then became a major part of the overall flood control plan.

Another bond issue of about $27 million failed to pass in 1934, probably because of economic conditions. The district then submitted a comprehensive plan as support for federal unemployment relief (WPA) funds in 1935, which was approved. From August 1935 to August 1936, approximately $20 million of WPA funds were expended on the flood control features. Seventeen thousand men were put to work, 95 percent from unemployment relief rolls.

The 1936 Flood Control Act put the federal government in the flood control business. The largest project included in the act was the "Los Angeles and San Gabriel Rivers,

California." The $70 million construction costs were to be from federal funds, and the $5 million for lands, right-of-way easements, and reconstruction of bridges were to be supplied by the district. Subsequent congressional actions changed the project title to "Los Angeles County Drainage Area" (LACDA) and expanded the program to include the main features of the district's comprehensive plan. It included building a series of basins at the canyon mouth of the tributary streams to collect mud-and-rock-flow debris, constructing flood control basins in the upper reaches of the main drainage systems to contain peak discharges and regulate downstream flow, and rectifying and stabilizing the channels throughout the coastal plain for rapid drainage.

This portion of the overall project was completed by the Army Corps of Engineers at a cost of $355 million in federal funds and $37 million in district funds for land and right-of-way. Included were five major dams, 205 miles of concrete channels, 99 miles of levees, and twenty-two debris basins. The total non-federal expenditure of the district for the entire flood control system, exclusive of the underground storm drains, was approximately $772 million.

In 1941 the district joined with the Department of Agriculture's Forest Service and Soil Conservation Service in a program to diminish the soil erosion problems in the mountain watersheds aggravated by several forest and brush fires. A large number of debris control and streambed stabilization structures, small debris basins, and check dams were constructed in a continuing program that involved expenditures of $26 million by 1975.

Provisions were made in the various projects to conserve water as well as to control floods. A substantial portion of the area is formed from huge gravel deposits, outwash from the canyons, which readily absorb water. This provides an ideal way to replenish the groundwater for recovery through wells further downstream. The flood channels themselves were built with porous bottom paving of large boulders and with ponding in the channel. Provisions were also made for

Santa Fe Dam and flood control basin is located at the mouth of San Gabriel Canyon in Los Angeles County. Percolation ponding areas are at middle left.

diversions to outside ponding areas for percolation of the groundwater. Reservoirs retained late spring runoff when flood storage capacity was not needed, and then released it for summer spreading. Over 300,000 acre-feet per year are now percolated into the groundwater reservoir in this manner.

By 1950 enough progress had been made to demonstrate the effectiveness of the plan in the most vulnerable areas. But problems were still occurring from accumulation of flood waters in streets and homes in low-lying areas due to lack of storm drains. An overall storm drainage plan was worked out and has been periodically financed and developed since 1952. By 1975 approximately $1 billion had been expended by the district on this under-

ground storm drain program.

The system was fully tested with the floods of 1969 when one of the largest storms of record occurred during the nine-day period between January 18 and 26. Over 45 inches of rainfall struck in the San Gabriel mountains. Thirteen inches fell in downtown Los Angeles, a storm considered to have a frequency of once in a hundred years. The system performed well and prevented over $1 billion in damages that otherwise would have occurred. Approximately 25 million cubic yards of outwash debris, mud, and rock were retained in the debris basins and in the reservoirs.

Recreational features are also a part of the overall program. For instance, the flood reten-

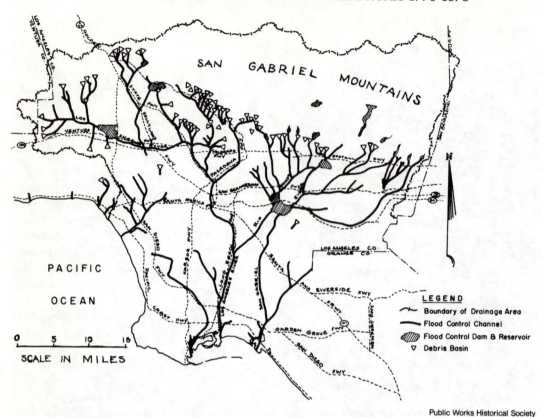

Flood control features of the Los Angeles County Flood Control District in California.

tion area in the reservoirs, that is under water only for a short period at the time of a flood, is utilized for golf courses, parks, playgrounds, and hiking and riding trails. Maximum public use is made of all the land in the rights-of-way for facilities such as utility corridors. Project areas are landscaped to enhance the environment.

By 1975 the district was operating and maintaining 20 major dams and reservoirs, including 5 maintained by the Army Corps of Engineers; 106 debris dams; 80 miles of leveed flood control channels and 344 miles of concrete-lined channels; 1,665 miles of underground storm drains; 29 spreading grounds covering 2,235 acres for percolation into the underground reservoir; and 15 miles of a fresh-water, injection-well barrier to protect against sub-surface intrusion of salt water into the basin from the ocean. In addition, 215 bridges across the various channels were constructed as part of the project and are maintained by various highway departments.

The Los Angeles program has received national and international recognition as an effective solution to a most difficult flood and debris control area. Extensive research has been carried out by the district in cooperation with other agencies involved in land use, flood warning systems, hydraulics of debris-laden high velocity flood flows, groundwater recharging, drainage, soil stabilization, and related problems. It is an example of coordinated, cooperative efforts of a local public works organization and state and federal agencies working together to resolve problems.

Chicago Drainage System: The 1½-mile marshland separating Lake Michigan and its tributary, the Chicago River, from other rivers that were headwaters of the vast Mississippi, was an ideal location for Chicago as a water transportation hub. But in its natural condition, the area was essentially hostile to human habitation. Problems of properly draining the flat swampland and of handling floods and storm runoff plagued the city. A series of innovative and extensive public works programs were necessary to enable Chicago to become the dynamic metropolis that it is today.

By 1854 Chicago had some drainage channels and 4 miles of crude triangular-shaped oak drainage structures below the principal streets, but there was not enough fall for them to drain properly. That year a typhoid and cholera epidemic resulted in the death of 5.5 percent of the area's population. A search for an experienced engineer resulted in the appointment of Ellis S. Chesbrough, famed for his drainage and sewer system work in Boston, as chief engineer for the city. Chicago became the first major city in the nation to formulate a comprehensive drainage plan. Over a series of years, the streets were raised approximately 11 feet, along with the adjacent buildings, to conform to the higher street grades. The latter operation, instigated by George M. Pullman, later to become famous for the Pullman railroad cars, was hailed as one of the nation's engineering wonders.

The drainage sewers initially emptied into the Chicago River. The Illinois and Michigan Canal, which had been opened in 1848 for navigation between the lake and the Mississippi, was deepened by 1871 to carry some of the drainage away from the lake and south into the rivers where dilution helped reduce pollution dangers. However, a "cloudbuster" of over 6 inches in August 1885 flooded the city and washed the polluted debris from the streets, sewers, and drains into the lake. After the storm, for miles offshore and out beyond the city's water supply intake, the lake was afloat with "an immense foul mass of wastes teeming with virulent bacteria." The resulting epidemic of waterborne diseases such as cholera, typhoid, and dysentery caused the death of about 90,000 people, 12 percent of the population.

Action was immediately taken to prevent a recurrence. By July 1889, a plan was developed to reverse the flows of the Chicago and Calumet rivers and to intercept all storm and sewer discharges into the lake and direct them into the rivers to be diluted by flow from the lake. The Metropolitan Sanitary District was formed by legislative action to carry out the plan. By 1892 the largest single earth and rock moving project in the history of municipal public works got underway. The Sanitary and Ship Canal was dug to reverse the flow of the Chicago River so that water flowed from the lake by gravity south to the Des Plaines River, a tributary of the Mississippi. By 1900 over 42 million cubic yards of earth and rock had been excavated for the canals; and by 1907 all interceptor sewers, 6 to 27 feet in diameter, were completed to prevent further drainage discharge into the lake.

Because of the growing population, downstream areas soon began complaining of the pollution of their river by Chicago wastes. This problem became worse with a 1930 court decision that limited the quantity of water that could be drawn from the lake. Treatment plants were constructed to reduce pollution of the canal waters, and by 1940 they were removing up to 90 percent of the pollutants. By 1970 Chicago had the largest treatment facilities in the world, processing 1.3 billion gallons of sewage wastes daily. Improvements underway as a result of continuing research and more sophisticated methods are expected to discharge effluents into the waterways that are over 99 percent pure by 1977. In 1975 these plants were handling the storm and wastewater flow from 860 square miles, including Chicago and 116 surrounding communities, with a population of 5.5 million and an industrial wastewater flow equivalent of another 5.5 million.

In 1975 the biggest problem facing the district was overflow of the combined sewers from storm water. As in other urban areas, more buildings, rooftops, and paving results in faster runoff and greater peak flows from storms. The excess of mixed storm water and sewage overflows sixty to seventy times per year and carries polluted water into the surface waterway system. Heavy storms have at times resulted in polluted water flowing into Lake Michigan. Many studies have been made of the 5,000 miles of sewers and their 640 overflow points to find ways to correct this problem, including the separation of the storm and sanitary sewer systems. Such a solution would not meet all requirements, for storm runoff, especially the initial flow, from streets and drains is generally heavily polluted.

U.S. Bureau of Reclamation

Modern tunnel boring machines make possible extensive underground drainage projects such as the Chicago Tunnel and Reservoir Plan.

A Tunnel and Reservoir Plan was adopted in October 1972 and work is underway. It will include about 120 miles of 10- to 35-foot diameter tunnels, drilled mostly in watertight dolomite rock 250 to 300 feet below the city streets. The excess flow of the existing sewers will be intercepted by 240 vertical drop shafts leading to the tunnels before it reaches the overflow points that now line the metropolitan river-canal complex. These tunnels will lead to existing rock quarries, 300 to 350 feet deep, which will serve as reservoirs to contain the storm water runoff. The reservoir capacity, with water 200 feet deep, will be 82,000 acre-feet and will contain the heaviest rainfalls in Chicago's history. After the storm, the polluted water will be pumped back through the treatment plants for

purification before discharge into the canals. To prevent odor, aerating pumps will continually agitate the wastewater prior to its being rationed out to the treatment plants. This will allow full utilization of the treatment plants, which have a capacity to handle 1.5 times the normal dry weather flow. Thus, all wastewater will be treated. Pollution of groundwater will be prevented as the tunnels will generally be in impervious rock. They will be grouted and lined where necessary and under hydrostatic pressure, which will prevent outflow. Flooding of streets, homes, underpasses, and other urban areas will be prevented. Greater flows will be provided for the navigation canals, which yearly have up to fifty delays of a few hours to a day or more. Treatment will allow for clean water standards to be met. The downtown section of the city, as well as the suburbs, should be revitalized due to the removal of flood threats.

Development in underground excavation methods and equipment makes projects such as this feasible. It is planned that the tunnels will be driven by mechanical moles. The 1975 cost of the project is estimated at $1.53 billion, about a third of the cost of providing completely separate sanitary sewer and storm water systems. Financing will be by local, state, and federal funds, and the work will proceed as fast as funds can be made available. At the beginning of 1976, 13 miles of tributary tunnels had been drilled, and contracts were being awarded for another 17 miles. Chicago expects to complete the project in the 1980s.

The Chicago drainage system, as with the others discussed, demonstrates an innovative and carefully designed solution to difficult problems. Such systems are made possible by greater knowledge of natural occurrences, by better methods of controlling undesirable effects, and by constantly improving design and construction technology. Public works of this kind can be accomplished when supported by the general public. The Chicago system also illustrates the contributions well-designed and constructed public works make in improving the environment in which people live and in protecting them from the vagaries of nature.

SUGGESTED READINGS

American Public Works Association. *Practices in Detention of Urban Stormwater Runoff.* Chicago. 1974.

_____ . *Urban Drainage—Practices, Procedures and Needs.* Chicago, 1966.

Arthur D. Little, Inc. *A River Basin Management Post-Audit and Analysis.* Prepared for the U.S. Department of Interior. Washington, D.C., 1973.

Ayres, Q. C. *Drainage and Flood Control Engineering.* New York, 1928.

Clapp, Gordon R. *The TVA: An Approach to the Development of a Region.* Chattanooga, Tennessee, 1955.

Cobb, W. C. "The Passes of the Mississippi River." *American Society of Civil Engineers Transactions,* CT (1953), 1147-1163.

Cowdrey, Albert E. *The Delta Engineers.* New Orleans, 1971.

Etcheverry, Bernard A. *Land Drainage and Flood Protection.* New York, 1931.

Feringa, P. A., and Schweizer, Charles W. "One Hundred Years of Improvements on Lower Mississippi River." American Society of Civil Engineers *Transactions,* CT (1953), 1100-1125.

Humphreys, Andrew A., and Abbott, Henry L. *The Delta Survey.* Washington, D.C., 1861.

League of Women Voters. *The Big Water Fight.* Brattleboro, Vermont, 1966.

Maass, Arthur A. *Muddy Waters: The Army Engineers and the Nation's Rivers.* Cambridge, Massachusetts, 1951.

Missouri Basin Interagency Committee. *The Missouri.* Washington, D.C., 1958.

Missouri Basin Survey Commission. *Missouri: Land and Water.* Washington, D.C., 1953.

Moore, Norman R. *Improvement of the Lower Mississippi River and Its Tributaries, 1931-1972.* Vicksburg, Mississippi, 1972.

Moreel, Ben. *Our Nation's Water Resources: Policies and Politics.* Chicago, 1956.

President's Water Resource Policy Commission. *A Water Policy for the American People.* Washington, D.C., 1950.

_____ . *Ten Rivers in America's Future.* Washington, D.C., 1950

_____ . *Water Resources Law.* Washington, D.C., 1950.

Schneider, George R. "History and Future of Flood Control." American Society of Civil Engineers *Transactions*, CT (1953), 1043-1099.

U.S. Army Corps of Engineers. *Water Resource Development in* . . . . (each of the states). Washington, D.C., published biennially.

───────────── . *History of the* . . . *District*. (Histories are available for each of the Army Corps of Engineers' districts). Washington, D.C.

U.S. Department of Agriculture. *Land: 1958 USDA Yearbook*. Washington, D.C., 1958.

U.S. Department of Housing and Urban Development. *National Flood Insurance Program*. Washington, D.C., 1974.

CHAPTER 10

IRRIGATION

In many ways, irrigation played the major role in the growth and development of the western half of the United States. It furnished the means for making areas of the West suitable for settlement and created a frontier where people could find opportunity for economic betterment. Vital centers of the West owe their very existence primarily to irrigation and, in a large measure, to those irrigation public works provided with federal government assistance. Included among these centers are the Salt Lake City area of Utah; the Rio Grande Valley of Colorado, New Mexico, and Texas; the Phoenix area of Arizona; the Central Valley of California; the Boise Valley of Idaho; the Yuma, Imperial, and Coachella Valleys of Arizona and California; the Yakima Valley and the Columbia River Basin in Washington; and the North Platte River Valley of Wyoming and Nebraska. Without irrigation, little would have happened in these areas, and public works have been the key to stable irrigation development.

Irrigation is the artificial application of water to plants to produce growth and, of most importance to man, to crops for food and fiber. Generally, crops cannot be produced without irrigation in areas having less than ten inches of annual precipitation. Some crops, such as

wheat, can be grown in areas with ten to fifteen inches of precipitation, depending upon distribution during the year, but yields are usually low. Yearly fluctuations in amounts and timing of rainfall and the grouping of a series of dry years, where moisture may be only 50 percent or less of normal, make crop production uncertain.

One third of the land area of the world is arid, where otherwise potentially productive regions require irrigation for crop production. About the same percentage exists in the continental United States. In recent years, irrigation has increased in the humid areas of the nation to assist intensified farming and to provide insurance against weeks without rain. In 1975 an estimated 45 million acres of croplands in the United States were irrigated. Of the 3 billion acres under cultivation worldwide, between 550 and 600 million were irrigated.

Irrigation has been practiced for thousands of years, but it is only since the late nineteenth century that man has applied scientific knowledge to watering dry places to make them productive. Civilizations of the past have disappeared from lack of understanding of the relation of water, land, and crops and from inadequate, improperly operated and maintained water control public works. One of the first areas of activity of the agricultural experiment stations, established by the land-grant colleges in the western half

This chapter was prepared primarily from various reports of the United States Bureau of Reclamation.

of the United States, was investigation of water, plants, and soil relationships. The permanence of irrigated agriculture depends upon the application of knowledge based upon scientific understanding of these relationships. Intelligent water management and effective irrigation practices are a necessity for maintenance of irrigated lands.

Providing water control works, including storage, for large irrigation projects involves the pooling of cooperative efforts by large groups. Some authorities suggest that civilization began because cooperative efforts were required to divert waters for the irrigation of crops on the flood plains of river basins. It is now the usual practice worldwide for irrigation projects to be built, operated, and water supplied to farmers by public organizations, sometimes with the entire cost borne by the government. In the United States, federal involvement was a natural result of the national interest in settling the West, in bringing vast areas of the public domain into production, and in providing capital and institutions to accomplish river basin developments extending into several states.

While the federal involvement in irrigation has been a program confined to states west of the hundredth meridian, it has proved a sound national investment. For example, an economic study in 1972 showed that a national investment of $6 billion in reclamation public works, made by the Bureau of Reclamation during the seventy years through 1971, produced an annual economic activity in 1971 of about $4.3 billion. This, according to the study, was over and above that which would have occurred without the projects. The projects that year paid taxes of $800 million to the federal government as well as over $300 million to state and local governments. In addition, in accordance with reclamation laws, the costs of the projects were being repaid into the United States Treasury on schedule; the costs of the irrigation features were repaid without interest. In many of the areas, without federal investment, nothing would have happened. Besides the 10 million acres of farmland receiving full or supplemental irrigation from the federal reclamation investments in 1971, 168 communities (over 14 million people) obtained municipal water; 54 million visitor-days of recreation were provided; and about 47 billion kilowatt hours of hydroelectric power were marketed. Many other benefits such as flood control, fish and wildlife enhancement, and water quality improvement also resulted.

The types of irrigation organizations within the United States and the irrigation water supplied in 1969, according to the Bureau of the Census, are shown in Table 10-1.

U.S. Bureau of Reclamation

Irrigation converted deserts into productive farmlands in the Coachella Valley in California.

TABLE 10-1
Irrigation Organizations in the United States

Type of Organization	Percentage of Total Irrigation Water Supplied
Bureau of Reclamation (Federal) Constructed and Operated Projects	38.5
Districts (Irrigation and other)	24.7
Incorporated Mutual Companies	21.8
Unincorporated Mutual Companies	6.9
Commercial Companies	4.0
Bureau of Indian Affairs (Federal) Projects	2.7
State and Local Governments	1.4
Total	100.0

Irrigation is the nation's major consumptive user of water. The irrigation projects include many of the most spectacular public works structures. Such projects demonstrate the responsive role of public works undertakings to provide basic resource facilities to meet growing needs. They also reflect the rapid advance of technology that has enabled large construction programs to adapt the environment to meet people's needs. These accomplishments embody the resolution of many conflicts that arise in managing water resources, the problems of environmental effects, and the gradual evolution from a single-purpose localized development to the river basin, regionwide, multiple-purpose water programs of 1976.

This chapter outlines the history of development that has been motivated primarily by irrigation needs and is concerned mainly with the western half of the nation, where natural rainfall is generally not sufficient to insure crops. The flows of most western rivers vary widely from flood stage, during the melting of snows in the spring or following torrential rainfall, to little or no flow during the dry summer and fall months. The public works programs have been designed to control the floods, level out the wide fluctuations, and provide water when and where it is needed. The cooperative efforts of farmers with water resource engineers, agriculturists, and various governmental entities have advanced the science of irrigation.

Early History of Irrigation

Earth's first civilizations developed in mild, dry climates along the flood plains in the delta areas of great rivers. The seasonal flooding of the Nile, Euphrates, Indus, and Hwang rivers made it possible for the people of these areas to grow abundant crops in areas of low rainfall. With stores of food beyond their immediate needs, the inhabitants of these fertile lands found time and energy for endeavors other than survival agriculture. These included city building, writing, literature, religion, and law making. The earliest written records refer to irrigation and even water law. Hammurabi, King of Babylon circa 1700 B.C., in his famous "code" established regulations to govern water use and reduce waste on his kingdom's complex irrigation systems.

The flooding of the rivers was a kind of natural irrigation, which permitted the growing populations to convey and spread life-giving river waters to additional lands through construction of dikes, check dams, and canals. While irrigation became more sophisticated and increasingly important in these early civilizations, water lifts to bring water to higher lands depended upon the muscles of slaves and animals. At first, these lifts were one-man, counter-weighted scoops; then animal-powered wheels and screw lifts were constructed, followed by water-powered lifts.

It appears none of the very early irrigators built storage reservoirs as safeguards against periods of drought and seasonal low river flow. Probably there was no great need, as cyclical flooding and the availability of sufficient lands for irrigation by simple diversion may have met the needs of the limited population. However, the early Egyptians may have conceived stream-valley dams and storage reservoirs, for they had a natural reservoir as an example. Lake Moeris, in the Fayoum of Upper Egypt, filled each year through a 12-mile channel when the Nile was at flood; irrigators then drew upon this water supply to mature their crops. There is evidence that an irrigation storage dam was built about 1700 B.C.

The first known water storage systems were developed on the Indian subcontinent and in Ceylon. Several hundred years before Christ, the Aryans and Dravidians of this vast area demonstrated remarkable engineering skills in the construction of cities, sewers, canals, and "tanks." These tanks or storage reservoirs fed a complex and extensive irrigation system. One of the largest reservoirs was the Kalabala Tank, formed by an earthen dam 79 feet high and about 4 miles long. The artificial lake thus created had a circumference of nearly 40 miles.

Not only the Egyptians and East Indians, but also the Chinese, Assyrians, Babylonians, Arabs, and Persians built water control structures and dams. In both North and South America, the early Indian civilizations were based in large part on irrigated agriculture. Their works included terracing, cisterns, water diversion structures, and irrigation

Salt River Project

From 700 to 1400 A.D., the Hohokam Indians built over 150 miles of canals to irrigate the desert in the vicinity of Phoenix, Arizona.

canals and laterals. There were extensive irrigation works in the Pisco Valley of Peru before the birth of Christ, and the pre-Mexican civilizations were based in part on irrigation. The Hohokam Indians of the Salt River Valley in Arizona dug hundreds of miles of canals about the first century but lacked storage facilities. They disappeared about 1400 A.D., apparently as a result of a prolonged drought, but some of their canals still exist.

Modern dam building found its genesis in pre-Roman Spain. By the time the Romans arrived with Scipio in 208 B.C., the Spaniards were constructing small earthen and masonry dams for irrigation storage. The Romans extended existing irrigation in Spain to increase production of wheat and olive oil, Spain's major exports to Rome. In the process, Roman engineers absorbed knowledge of irrigation works and added dams and other features of their own design. The Romans also learned from the Tripolitanians of northwestern Libya, who from antiquity had had experience with irrigation in the Near East.

The Muslims, invading Spain from Africa in the sixth century A.D., brought many refinements to the practice of irrigation, both in engineering and the evolution of water codes. Peoples from Syria, Egypt, Persia, and Iraq added their centuries-old skills and practices in water use and management. Nearly every river in Spain was eventually dammed for irrigation and mechanical power.

The Spanish influence in irrigation engineering and water law was brought to Mexico and to what is now the American Southwest by laboring monks, settlers, army engineers, and retired civil servants. The wealthy Mexican Don Juan de Õnate established a colony on the west bank of the Rio Grande (New Mexico) in 1598 and dug five Spanish irrigation ditches in what is now the United States.

The Spanish Catholic missionaries also led their Indian converts in the partial rehabilitation of long-abandoned Indian irrigation systems. The several Spanish missions in the American Southwest were largely supported by irrigated agriculture. The mission at San Diego established in 1769 included an irrigation system. About 1776 the Spanish government built an irrigation community near the present site of Santa Cruz, California. Irrigation techniques first came to the attention of American travelers and settlers in California, Arizona, and New Mexico in the gardens and fields of these early Spanish missions.

American irrigation began on a modern scale with the Mormon pioneers in the valley of the Great Salt Lake. On the day of arrival, July 24, 1847, Brigham Young set his followers to work diverting small streams to low-lying adjacent land. This softened it for plowing and then provided water to the hastily planted crop of wheat and potatoes assuring harvest. The next spring 5,000 acres were placed under irrigation; by 1850 this was increased to 16,000 acres. Fifteen years later, 1,000 miles of canals had been dug in the west, 150,000 acres were under irrigation, and 65,000 people were living in comfort on the reclaimed land.

The early Mormon irrigation farmers worked their relatively small farms intensively and derived a remarkable amount of production from them. Their small diversion structures and generally short canals, rarely over 3 miles long, were usually cooperative projects of neighborhood families. They established organizations that made it possible to build communities that were comparable to those in humid regions from which they had come.

Various Mormon practices in the appropriation of water—the idea of prior use and attaching water rights to the land—and organization of mutual companies to build and manage irrigation works, became important concepts of irrigation in the West. A Mormon farmer could apply for and develop water sufficient to the needs of his family-size farm. In cooperation with other farmers, he contributed a proportionate amount of work and capital to develop water diversions and canals and in turn received proportionate shares in the water. For instance, a farmer who helped develop water for twenty acres had to contribute twice as much as the farmer who joined the cooperative undertaking to obtain water for ten acres.

The first Mormon water master to manage a cooperative water district was appointed on August 22, 1847. In 1850 the Mormon "state" of Deseret established its own office of superintendent of public works. Local communities could then obtain planning, managing, and technical and financial assistance in the construction and operation of irrigation works. This was important as irrigation was a new experience to the pioneers with eastern United States and Anglo-Saxon backgrounds.

The practice of the Mormon Church "calling" industrious and relatively prosperous farmers to resettle in new communities—not only to establish the physical boundaries of the "state" of Deseret, but also to open new communities to settlement for the continuing inflow of converts from overseas—widened and extended irrigation techniques and efficiencies. Mormon colonies ultimately extended from Mexico into Canada, bringing the practice of irrigation, with the necessary cooperative institutions to support it, to much of the West.

The California Gold Rush of 1849 gave an unexpected impetus to irrigation. The growing numbers of miners and other settlers, with their ready cash, put economic pressure on food suppliers to step up agricultural production. Also, the engineering ingenuity which the miners had shown in sluicing for gold was put to good use by farmers. Not only the skills but sometimes the actual water works of the miners—including both open and closed flumes gradually descending the face of

mountains, frequently abandoned as the gold ran out—were subsequently repaired and turned to irrigation by homesteaders.

Another important irrigation development was undertaken in 1857 in southern California southeast of Los Angeles. A group of German farmers and tradesmen who had migrated to San Francisco formed a cooperative group to establish a colony on the Santa Ana River. This Anaheim Colony developed several thousand acres, and it was successful in large part because of careful advance planning and because its supporters in San Francisco remained at their trades to earn money to sustain their brethren on the project until it could be well established.

The Greeley Colony, in northeastern Colorado, was initiated in 1870 by Nathan Meeker, agricultural editor of the *New York Tribune,* who the editor, Horace Greeley, had sent to Utah to study the irrigation practices of the Mormon pioneers. He convinced Greeley of the possibilities of development and settlement in the area of what is now Greeley, Colorado; and the "Union Colony of Colorado" was established by prospective settlers solicited in New York. Supporting the development financially and through newspaper promotion, Greeley contributed substantially to this major non-Mormon cooperative irrigation project. Although four ditches to irrigate 120,000 acres were planned, there were difficulties with construction, and only one ditch serving 32,000 acres was completed.

Although other similar cooperative settlements were undertaken in the West by various groups, the next step in irrigation development was the speculative, for-profit ventures of water companies. The cooperative colonies, founded upon irrigation, were usually successful in their limited areas but often were not strong enough to compete with and survive the great speculative boom in irrigation. Between 1880 and 1900, however, the stock companies were marked more often by failures and foreclosures than by successes.

While private irrigation development played an important role in early settlement of the West, it also produced many failures. After unpredictable droughts followed by the

Panic of 1893, it became apparent to many that major participation by the federal government would be necessary to develop the vast public lands of the West and enable the arid and semi-arid states to grow and contribute to the welfare of the nation.

A major proponent of federal assistance for western irrigation was Major John Wesley Powell. He was a natural scientist and a man of energy and action. Wishing to push the frontiers of science as well as civilization in the West, he secured federal backing for two expeditions along the Colorado River in 1867 and 1868. Then in 1869 he boated down the turbulent Colorado and became a national figure.

Powell's popularity helped gain support for his conclusions that settlement of the West would be difficult and probably impossible without large-scale development of water resources. His 1878 *Report on the Land of the Arid Region of the United States* had a sober but initially unheeded warning that western drylands could not be left to "development" by land, cattle, mining, and timber interests. He advocated more study of the West and stressed the importance of carefully developed plans for water control. He felt that large-scale federal programs would be required for lasting results, rather than solely private short-range development of water and land resources. In 1881 Powell became the director of the United States Geological Survey (the agency he helped create), and for many years he was the principal advocate of a federal irrigation agency.

American Water Law and Western Settlement

Panning and sluicing for gold had other direct influences besides providing a market for farm products—most noticeably in the evolution of American water law and irrigation practice. The gold miners took and used available water as needed. The rights thereto were defended by every means available including force. Whether by coincidence or otherwise, the California Forty-Niners followed customs characteristic of the Old World. The Germanic miners of the Middle Ages had declared the principle of "mining

freedom" in their use of water.

In contrast, other concepts of water rights in the West grew out of common law, which is the origin of the riparian doctrine. This held generally that, apart from modest water needs of those living along the streams, water could not be taken from a stream unless it could be returned undiminished in quantity or quality. Thus, stream flow was protected for powering grist and saw mills and to assure continuing water transportation and operation of locks. This doctrine was the basis of water law in the East.

In the arid West, settlement and use of land depended on the full use of the available water. Since old riparian concepts could not hold, modification was inevitable. This was seen in the Mormon settlements, which ini-

U.S. Bureau of Reclamation

In the arid West, rights to use water for irrigation are established by prior appropriation for beneficial use.

tially were not part of the United States but belonged to Mexico. These early Mormons, much like the California miners, were a law unto themselves. They refined the doctrine of prior appropriation of water. Those who first made beneficial use of water had a preference in its continued use. In turn, water rights became tied to the land where the water was applied. Moreover, the Mormons also recognized community responsibility in the use of water. From almost the beginning, water development was not an individual or profit-making effort; it was a cooperative undertaking. From these community efforts grew the idea of developing and managing water through the legal instrument of a water district, where the total need of the community was recognized. The first irrigation district legislation in the United States was enacted in the Territory of Utah in 1865.

The modification of old rules and creation of new water law was also to be seen in rights to underground water. In England and early America, underground water was associated with the soil and the right to the land. Water which percolated under the land could be exploited without limitation. Gradually, as it became recognized that underground water was limited in supply and was affected by an overdraft anywhere, the doctrine of reasonable use and correlative rights evolved. This, to an increasing extent, recognized the joint rights of all water users.

With the coming of territorial and state governments, local practice became codified into law with varying degrees of recognition of the public interest. In 1866 Congress first confirmed the water rights of vested individuals on the public domain under local customs, laws, and court decisions. Thus, state laws became the basis for water rights in the West. The 1877 Desert Land Act, intended to promote settlement in the West, declared that the right to use water depended upon prior appropriation. In this way, "free development" of waters on public land became national policy.

Territorial and state laws reflected the continuing conflict between riparian and appropriation adherents, but generally the more arid the land, the stronger were laws that recognized prior beneficial use. In the period between 1882 and 1921, the eight generally arid states in the West strengthened their laws reflecting prior appropriation and beneficial use. The riparian doctrine was recognized in greater or lesser degree in the nine less arid western states, but eventually the appropriation doctrine took precedence. Nevertheless, throughout the West, in law and in the courts' interpretation, there has been little tolerance for the waste of water.

The ownership and distribution of water is the single greatest problem in western agriculture. The division of water supplies determines the pattern of settlement and the degree of success in farming. A need for con-

struction of large-scale public works in the community interest was demonstrated early. As population increased and the readily available water supplies were tapped and distributed according to new laws and regulations, the natural flow of the streams during the growing season put a ceiling on development; and it became apparent that large storage reservoirs would be required. Ample land was available, the limiting factor was water.

The vast area beyond the Mississippi River had beckoned settlers from the beginning of the nation, even though some considered it the "Great American Desert." But even while the lands were Mexican, French, or British, American explorers and settlers had moved West. As the United States took title to the area, it looked to the sale of the lands and resources as a means of providing public coffers with much-needed funds. However, by 1841, with the Pre-emption Act, the sale of 160 acres for $1.25 an acre was no longer deemed so much a revenue-producing device as a means of occupying and developing the West. It became national policy, in the interest of strengthening the nation, to encourage western migration.

The 1862 Homestead Act designed more specifically for the sub-humid plains states, provided additional encouragement to western migration. The law enabled settlers to acquire 160 acres by filing on a tract, living on it, and developing it. For the more arid lands, without an adequate water supply, 160 acres proved insufficient to support a family, and subsequently the law was modified so that a settler could acquire 320 acres. This limit was again increased to 640 acres in an effort to provide an economic unit. The 1873 Timber Culture Act, requiring the planting and cultivation of at least 40 acres of trees out of 160, was tried as an experiment but proved generally unsatisfactory in stimulating settlement.

The 1877 Desert Land Act provided that 640 acres could be acquired for $1.25 an acre in payment plus satisfactory irrigation of the land within three years. As with previous experiments in settlement, this act looked to private efforts to populate the West; but under

Horse and ox teams were used to construct irrigation canals at the beginning of the twentieth century.

the act, it was possible to acquire more land than could be successfully farmed with available water. The energy and capital invested in homesites were frequently forfeited in periods of drought.

The attempts of innovative farmers to build ditches to irrigate their land were often nullified by the laws and regulations intended to encourage them. Speculators would move into a likely area where ditch enterprises were contemplated and lay claim to land before bona fide prospective settlers could acquire tracts. Since they were required to buy the land from speculators and in addition pay their share of the cost of the ditch, the capital burden was frequently too great and the entire project would fold.

During this period, Congress reviewed the problems of settlement in the West and the laws which were intended to stimulate a general western movement. Major Powell's idea that the federal government would need to play a direct role in developing water resources to provide for successful settlement began to take shape. The act of October 2, 1888 reserved from public settlement "all the lands which may hereinafter be designated or selected by such United States surveys for sites for reservoirs, ditches, or canals for irrigation purposes." It directed the Bureau of Geological Survey to undertake this study and

the selection of potential irrigation project lands. In 1890 Congress published the report of the Select Committee on Irrigation and Reclamation of Public Lands and began consideration of various bills that would provide for an irrigation service.

Congress passed the 1894 Carey Act, hoping to overcome the difficulties that were slowing irrigation progress. This act permitted land grants to each western state, up to a million acres, on condition that the state would provide for irrigation of the land. However, this was not generally successful because of financing difficulties, failure to tie the land to the water, and water supply problems. In twenty years, only about 750,000 acres had been patented to the states, and most of the projects, except for the Twin Falls Project in Idaho, were in trouble. Neither the Carey nor the Desert Land acts solved the basic problem of constructing bigger and more extensive works to supply water to lands distant from the streams and to provide necessary storage of early season flood waters to eliminate late season water shortages.

About 7.5 million acres were irrigated by the end of the nineteenth century, but they were restricted to areas with easy diversions, short canals, and limited storage. The need for more widespread and successful settlement of the West became so apparent, particularly as it related to development of water resources, that both major political parties supported federal financial and technical assistance in development of western lands. The goals were the dispersal and growth of the American population, economic development of the West and its resources, and integration of the regional economies of the nation.

Federal Involvement in Irrigation

In 1901 President Theodore Roosevelt precipitated action by his first message to Congress, in which he allied his Administration with proposals for federally constructed engineering works for water storage. He stated: "It is as right for the National Government to make the streams and rivers of the arid region useful by engineering works for water storage as to make useful the rivers and harbors of the humid regions by engineering works of another kind. Our purpose as a whole will profit, for successful homemaking is but another name for upbuilding the nation." He endorsed the major principles of a bill introduced by Congressman Francis G. Newlands of Nevada. In due course, this bill passed and became the 1902 Reclamation Act.

The act provided for federal planning, construction, and development of irrigation works as a public works program, under the direction of the secretary of interior, to reclaim public lands. It established a revolving reclamation fund from the sale of public lands to finance the program. Irrigable lands were then to be disposed of under provisions of the Homestead Act, with the additional provision that the settlers would contract, either individually or through water users associations, to repay to the federal government the costs of constructing the works that would deliver an assured supply of irrigation water.

The Reclamation Act established a program for the purpose of developing water supplies for irrigation in the arid and semi-arid areas of sixteen western states and territories. Texas was included later. In 1902 there were 353.5 million acres of public land still held by the federal government and subject to entry in the sixteen states and territories, and it was estimated at the time that 35 million acres could profitably be reclaimed by the construction of irrigation works. Since its enactment, the Reclamation Act has served as the foundation for federal water resource development in the seventeen western states and has been assisted by various flood control and navigation legislation. The United States Supreme Court has sustained the act a number of times, as in the 1963 *Arizona v. California* Case which ruled that "the Congress may promote the general welfare through large scale projects for reclamation, irrigation, or other internal improvements." Amendments enacted in subsequent years expanded the water development authority to full multipurpose status.

The Reclamation Service was established in 1902 within the Geological Survey of the Department of Interior to carry out the program. It was given bureau status in 1907, and in 1923 its name was changed to the Bureau of Reclamation, headed by a commissioner of Reclamation to be appointed by the President.

Almost at the outset of the program, it was recognized that single-purpose irrigation development was far too limited to develop fully the potentials of the West's water resources. Thus, in 1906 the Reclamation Act was broadened to permit the secretary of interior to allow the sale of municipal water supplies and hydroelectric power from reclamation projects.

The initial requirements were for the project costs to be repaid in ten years, which proved entirely unrealistic. In 1914 the repayment period was extended to twenty years. Problems encountered with inexperienced settlers, low-quality lands included in some of the projects, and the low prices of farm products following World War I resulted in the secretary of interior appointing a special commission to examine the program in detail. Subsequently, the 1924 "Fact Finders Act" provided for a detailed classification of project lands; repayment based on a percentage of farm returns rather than an average cost per acre; rigorous standards regarding physical and economic factors to be applied to new projects; and more detailed requirements of settlers regarding essential experience, capabilities, and capital necessary to make the project a success.

While several other acts between 1907 and 1927 led to the expansion of the program, 1928 marked a milestone in reclamation law with legislation for multipurpose project development. The Boulder Canyon Project Act, which among other provisions authorized construction of Hoover Dam, included such functions as power generation, flood control, municipal and industrial water supply, and other beneficial uses as well as irrigation. It also provided for appropriation from the general fund, in addition to the monies available in the reclamation fund, to finance the work. This practice has since continued.

The 1939 Reclamation Project Act was significant in that it established procedures to control authorizations for projects and for repayment of costs to the United States Treasury. A forty-year repayment period was provided, following a farm development period which could be as much as ten years. The non-reimbursable functions under the 1939 act, however, were limited to those costs for assistance to flood control and navigation. The 1944 Flood Control Act, authorizing the construction of the Pick-Sloan Missouri River Basin Project by the Army Corps of Engineers and the Bureau of Reclamation, further established full river basin development as a federal activity. In the Missouri basin, the Army Corps of Engineers was given responsibility for the mainstream dams and for flood control and navigation, while the Bureau of Reclamation had responsibility for the structures in the tributaries where irrigation and municipal and industrial water supply were the primary purposes.

The 1956 Small Reclamation Projects Act was enacted to provide loans and grants to state and local organizations for planning and developing water resources. This legislation extended the scope into the federally assisted projects' area. In 1966 the act was amended to offer grants for the development of recreation and fish and wildlife enhancement facilities.

In 1958 two pieces of legislation were passed that furthered the outdoor recreational objectives of the reclamation program. They were the Water Supply Act and the Fish and Wildlife Coordination Act. The latter placed the expenditure of federal funds for purposes of wildlife conservation on equal terms with other functions of water resource development programs.

In 1965 the Federal Water Project Recreation Act was passed which called for full consideration of recreation and fish and wildlife enhancement in the planning of all future water resource projects. Authority under the act limited the allocation of costs to recreation and fish and wildlife to 50 percent of total project costs. It also provided for similar developments on existing projects and established the cost-sharing concept under which costs would be shared with non-federal entities. More recent legislation has dealt with the formulation of evaluation policies and procedures for the inclusion of environmental considerations in project planning and management on the basis of national rather than only local benefits. These acts are the 1965 Water Resources Planning Act, the 1968 National Water Commission Act, and the 1969 National Environmental Policy Act.

Twenty years after the first irrigation at City Creek in Salt Lake City, the irrigated land in the West had only grown to about 155,000 acres, mostly in the areas of Mormon settlement. By 1880 there were about a million acres under irrigation, but during the next ten years the speculative boom development increased the irrigated acreage threefold. Some of the projects had sound merit; and after the elimination of the excessive speculation profit through mortgage foreclosures and new financing, they became successful.

The problem of irrigation on Indian reservation lands received early attention by the federal government in its capacity as guardian of the Indians. The first federal government venture in direct construction of irrigation works occurred in 1867 when appropriations were made for construction of a canal for irrigating lands on the Colorado River Reservation in Arizona. Other authorizations followed on an individual project basis.

Legislation by states during the last decade of the nineteenth century encouraged irrigation development. Also, existing projects were extended and improved, and some new diversions and canal systems were constructed. The 1910 census listed 14 million acres under irrigation of which 395,000 were federal reclamation projects just coming into production, 172,000 were Indian Service projects, and 288,000 were Carey Act projects. By 1940 one fifth of the 20 million plus acres under irrigation were on federal projects. During World War II, extensive irrigation was developed from groundwater, primarily by private capital.

The 1970 census indicated that approximately 40 million acres were under irrigation nationwide, 35 million of which were in the seventeen western states and about 5 million in the eastern humid states. Most of the irrigation in the East is on an individual farm basis, water being obtained from wells or adjacent streams or ponds by pumping. Mobile pumps and lightweight pipe is resulting in the rapid growth of irrigation in the East to insure against droughts reducing production and to maximize returns from intensive farming. Of the 35 million acres in the West, approximately 10 million receive water from federal projects. Various estimates indicate that irrigated acreage in 1975 was at least 10 percent higher than in 1970, and some suggest it had increased as much as 20 percent because of increasing use of deep wells and sprinkler systems.

The Unique Decade of the 1930s

Progress was made by 1930 in furthering the development of the West through federal irrigation public works. Forty projects had been or were being completed and water had been made available to irrigate 3.6 million acres, which in 1930 produced crops valued at $120 million. However, a number of factors during the 1930s had great impact on future programs involving water resources. Technology was well advanced and tested, as demonstrated by the large dams and conveyance structures that had been completed and were in operation. Basic information was available, and becoming more detailed, concerning precipitation, runoff, physical and geological characteristics of river basins, and potential projects for multipurpose utilization and control of rivers. The comprehensive "308"

reports of the Army Corps of Engineers (discussed in Chapter 9) were completed during the decade; the Geological Survey of the Department of Interior had compiled stream runoff records and completed topographic and geological mapping of major areas of the public domain. Reconnaissance studies of potential irrigation and hydroelectric projects in the West had been made by the Bureau of Reclamation and some of the states.

The decade of the 1930s was one of abnormal climatic and hydrologic conditions. It produced widespread drought conditions during more than half of the period and a series of devastating floods in all areas of the nation. Following the great Mississippi River flood in 1927, events brought into sharp focus the need for national programs to control and conserve soil and water resources. The 1927 flood and the widespread drought of 1930 did much to establish land and water planning as an important federal function. The recurring droughts throughout the decade enlarged the federal reclamation program. It expanded from large developments on arid lands to an all-inclusive use of water for irrigation in large and small areas as a means to provide stability on marginal lands and to open new opportunities for population shifts and resettlements. The widespread disastrous floods established federal flood control on all streams as a general welfare function of the federal government and extended activities to small upstream watershed areas as an integral part of water and soil conservation programs.

The national economic crisis of the Depression years and the change in political leadership accelerated the need for assisting various segments of the society to cope with conditions over which they had no control. A major concern was to make new opportunities available to people, since the great western frontier was gone, and to stabilize economic boom and bust cycles. Thus, public works programs, and especially those involving basic land and water, provided means to accomplish both economic and social goals.

Interagency coordination came into being from a number of actions. Some were aimed primarily at establishing priorities for public works projects as work-producing programs to help alleviate unemployment. This need culminated in the establishment of the National Resources Planning Board and similar groups that followed it. Their activities laid the groundwork for further comprehensive, multipurpose planning for water resource development.

Factors such as available technology, recognition of the need for land and water control and conservation programs, the demand for work-producing projects that would contribute to the economic base of the nation, the growing importance of electric power and the public-private controversy over the best way to produce it, governmental institutions capable of planning and carrying out large programs came together during the decade to formulate public works programs. And the effort to build national morale had its effect. The quotation "Make no little plans. They have no magic to stir men's souls" was often used to describe programs of the 1930s.

Far-reaching legislation included the founding of the Tennessee Valley Authority; the 1936 Flood Control Act specifically establishing federal responsibility for flood control; initiation of the comprehensive

U.S. Bureau of Reclamation

This 1000-cubic-feet per second canal is a part of the Central Valley Project in California initiated during the 1930s.

programs of water resource development in the Columbia River, the Central Valley in California, and the Missouri River Basin; creation of the Soil Conservation Service, the Farm Security Administration, and the Rural

Electrification Administration in the Department of Agriculture; the Case-Wheeler Act which coordinated the efforts of the departments of agriculture and interior to construct water conservation and utilization projects for relocating people from poverty areas; and programs that accelerated hydrologic fact-finding and research. These actions established the direction of future water resource programs.

Changes did not come easily. The literature of the period abounds with discussions and warnings of the "white elephants" being created such as Grand Coulee and Fort Peck dams. It was a period of shifting emphasis and new approaches to secure opportunity and stability for America. By 1940 federal expenditures for activities designed to control, conserve, regulate, and use water resources were about $600 million per year, a tenfold increase from 1930.

In view of the national emergency created by World War II, the country was fortunate that the programs of the 1930s were undertaken. The electric power generated from the Columbia, Colorado, and Tennessee rivers became the basis for much of the industrial war effort in the West and South. The agricultural production capacity built into irrigation projects and protected by flood control projects supplied food to the United States and war-ravaged areas all over the world. The organizational, engineering, and construction institutions and capabilities developed in the large water resource projects made important contributions to the great construction programs at home and abroad required by the war effort.

Early Reclamation Technology and Construction

When the West was thought of as the Great American Desert, its lands had not been extensively surveyed. While there was some basic geologic information, distances were often roughly measured by the number of revolutions of a wagon wheel or more accurately by the use of a Gunter chain of 66 feet. Land boundaries in many areas were set forth in metes and bounds. Land markers were frequently only easily moved boulders or charcoaled stakes, and elevations were often estimated solely with a barometer. Streamflow data was either non-existent or only short term. Size of flood flows and frequencies were estimated by probing the memories of old timers, by examining newspaper accounts where available, and by observing the location of flotsam along the banks.

To acquire the hydrologic and geologic data necessary to evaluate a proposed water resource project, early survey teams gathered up equipment and supplies of salted meat, coffee, lard, flour, and dried fruit and "headed for the hills" by pack train. Some of the "hills" were forested, with verdant valleys between; others in the Southwest were barren, inhospitable jumbles of hot rocks and sand with scant ground cover; and some lands were western grass-covered plains. Except for the chief of a survey party and his transitman, the other helpers—chainmen, axmen, teamsters, and cook—were local laborers and sometimes Indians. These conditions were common when private companies and individuals drew up their plans for diversion structures, for ditching the land, and subsequently for building of irrigation works. Most of these early irrigation developments did not include the essential storage facilities.

These physical conditions and state of technology existed when the Reclamation Service was established, but the need for storage facilities was well recognized. Its engineers had to survey the drainage basins, locate the lands, and classify the types of soils that were suitable for farming under irrigation practices. They had to determine the long-time quantity of water available from a stream and the size of dams and storage reservoirs needed to supply the potential farms with the water required. Also needed was an estimate of the size and frequency of floods that would have to be handled by the dam's spillways. The locations of the canals, tunnels, bridges, and other structures had to be determined and geologic studies of project sites made.

Not all projects planned and undertaken under the reclamation program were so successful nor so bountiful as envisioned. Some of this was due to the lack of knowledge in the classification of lands suitable for irrigation and failure to confine projects to the productive lands. Some of the early project plans were based upon insufficient stream-flow records, which resulted in planning less water storage than needed. Public pressure to develop a project quickly often did not permit sufficient detailed investigations and adequate economic studies to determine project feasibility. Sometimes the pressures forced commencement of a project of only marginal quality.

Many of the early privately developed irrigation projects ran into difficulty because control works were of a temporary nature; they were not well constructed; and they lacked storage reservoirs. They were dependent upon diverting a quantity of water from a flowing stream by means of a brush dam, a log and rock crib structure, or a rock dike. These temporary structures were often destroyed by flash floods from summer rainstorms. Some systems were extensions of old placer mining canals and flumes; and during the hot summer, they could dry up when the farmer's crops needed the moisture most.

As diversions increased in number and available free-flowing water decreased, needs for storage became more acute. The necessity for storage reservoirs had long been recognized as the key to additional settlement of the arid West, but storage was costly and involved complex technology. In the semi-arid areas, many homesteaders could not exist with "dry farming" and the one crop harvested every three to five years. Also many of the early farmers and settlers realized that their simple irrigation systems were temporary and undependable for assured operation. For many years, there had been studies and discussions of the needed assistance and support of the federal government in developing the West through irrigation. Thus, the general sentiment was favorable when the Reclamation Act became law in 1902.

Because of its origin, history, and achievements, the federal government's Bureau of Reclamation has been the dominant agency in arid land irrigation in the United States and has worldwide recognition as the leading institution in irrigation engineering. The bureau

U.S. Bureau of Reclamation

A woman survey crew on the Minidoka Project in Idaho in 1918 gathered data for reclaiming the desert.

has researched and pioneered in all phases of water control works such as dams, hydroelectric power plants, water conveyance structures, tunnels, and related structures. Six successive bureau dams were each in turn the highest in the world, and reclamation projects included the world's largest pumping plants and canals. Training in irrigation technology has been provided in the United States and other countries.

Within the first five years following passage of the Reclamation Act, twenty-five projects were examined by a top-level federal commission and authorized for construction by the secretary of interior. Of these, fifteen were started by private companies or a group of cooperating farmers, but who, because of various financial and technical difficulties, sought the help of the Reclamation Service in building storage and control facilities. Three of the newly authorized projects immediately introduced international problems with respect to water rights in the rivers. One project was in Montana, involving the Milk River which flows through Canada. There were two in the South, one on the Rio Grande and one on the Colorado River, both of which involved Mexico.

The undertaking authorized by the Reclamation Act was to expand irrigation farming by construction of large-scale irrigation works. Building large water control facilities was dependent upon the machinery, materials, and transportation available in the sparsely settled West at the beginning of this century. Railroad transportation, which had been in operation only about thirty years, was usually remote from proposed project areas and dam sites.

People and supplies were ordinarily moved by horse-drawn stages or wagon trains. When available, the needed cement, timber, and miscellaneous manufactured items were hauled by wagons from a railroad siding or station. In many of the early projects, machinery and steam engines for power were laboriously hauled in and sawmills and cement plants constructed to produce needed materials. Camps—sometimes tent cities— had to be built to house the engineering and construction workers, and stables were needed for their stock.

Building irrigation and water storage works consisted primarily of moving and placing earth and rock and mixing and placing concrete. Steam shovels were in use for digging the Panama Canal in the early 1900s; but because of their huge size, they were not readily adapted to the type and smaller scale construction required in building most early irrigation works. They could be used where large volumes of earth and rock were to be moved, provided a railroad spur was built to move them to the site. Electric power was new, limited, and used principally for lighting. Thus, most of the digging, transporting, and placing of earth and rock on early irrigation projects made little use of motorized machinery; these tasks were accomplished mainly by horses.

Horse-drawn slips or scoops that bit into the earth were then dragged along the ground to the point of unloading. These had handle bars, like a wheelbarrow, that the teamster used to load and up-end the device. New improvements on this operation consisted of a cylinder with one side cut away which was drawn along on the ground so that the cut-away section scooped up the earth. This famous "Fresno Scraper" had a long handle that controlled the digging and emptying, and it became the principal excavation tool on the early irrigation projects. Later, wheels were added to these pieces of equipment. They were used to dig many miles of canals and pile up thousands of cubic yards of earth for dams and waterway embankments.

Teams, wagons, and slips dug out and transported sand and broken rock or gravel to a concrete mixing plant. Steam engines usually ran the rotary mixers. Laborers with shovels and wheel barrows loaded the mixers, hauled the wet concrete to a structure site, and loaded it into the forms.

The early day construction of tunnels was even less mechanized. The operation was largely a pick and shovel affair. Holes into the rock face were drilled by a two-man crew, one to hold and turn a steel bit while the other drove it into the rock with a sledge hammer. After these holes were packed and the explosives detonated, the blasted rock was loaded by hand into small horse-drawn cars on rails and hauled outside for dumping. On the return trip, timbers were usually brought in to form supports to hold the roof and sides of the tunnel in place. On the 6-mile-long Gunnison Tunnel, one of the earliest tunnels undertaken in Colorado, every foot of advance made in digging the 11-foot-wide by 12-foot-high arched roof opening required about five cubic yards of rock to be hauled out as far as 3 miles.

U.S. Bureau of Reclamation

Workmen drilled blasting holes for the 6-mile-long Gunnison Tunnel in Colorado, under construction in 1904.

A progressive step in early operations was the construction of a steam-driven generating plant in 1905 used in building the Roosevelt Dam. It furnished electric power for operating a cement mill, for hoisting operations at the quarry, and for the overhead cableways employed in placing the rubble masonry in the dam. These types of innova-

tions to advance construction were made possible by the rapidly developing machinery industry in the first years after passage of the Reclamation Act.

Earth Dams: Early Reclamation Service earth dams were usually less than 100 feet high. The Minidoka Dam on the Snake River in Idaho is a significant structure in reclamation's early history. Work on construction of the 86-foot-high dam, with a crest length of 4,475 feet and a volume of 250,000 cubic yards, was undertaken in 1906 to provide storage for a project that had been established using only stream diversions. The Idaho state engineer in 1902 requested the assistance of the Reclamation Service in developing water storage to more fully develop the farming potential of the Snake River Valley.

Such early dams were constructed with several combinations of equipment. Steam shovels were used for excavating and for loading small railroad cars carrying one to three cubic yards of earth. Steam-powered "dinkey" engines hauled the cars to the embankment where they were dumped. In other cases, teams and scrapers accomplished this excavation and transportation of earth. If the operation were big enough and involved a long haul, sixteen-horse scrapers were used to dig, elevate the material, and discharge it into bottom-dump wagons which then hauled it to the embankment.

U.S. Bureau of Reclamation

Earthfill being placed for the Strawberry Dam in Utah in 1912. When completed in 1913, the 72-foot-high dam contained 118,000 cubic yards of earth and rock.

The dumped material was then spread in layers by scrapers, leveled out with drags or road graders, sprinkled with water from tanks pulled by horses, and usually compacted by the trampling of the horses. In a few instances, steam-powered rollers were used. Heavy rocks for facing the dams were placed by hauling them to the proper position by teams pulling stone boats. The rocks were then tipped into position. The voids between the larger rocks were filled with smaller, hand-placed stones. In some few instances, steam-powered cableways were used to pick up the large stones and transport them to their approximate positions. Meanwhile, concrete work was also going on to build the spillways, designed to pass floods downstream when the reservoir was full, and the outlet works to control water discharge into the river below the dam or into the irrigation canals.

The early earth dams were built by government forces. Simple contracts were made with the teamsters for their work and the services of their horses. The heavy equipment, such as steam shovels and locomotives, were owned by the government. Their operators were on the federal payroll. During one year of canal construction work in Idaho, some 500 teamsters with teams of horses were used.

The first earth dam built by the Reclamation Service to exceed 100 feet in height was Lahontan Dam on the Carson River in Nevada. This 114-feet-high structure was completed in 1915. Between then and 1938, when construction of the Green Mountain Dam in Colorado began, many advancements were made in construction equipment and methods as well as in design of such structures. The science of soil mechanics had advanced to where the Green Mountain Dam could be designed and built to a height of 309 feet and a volume of 4.4 million cubic yards with full confidence.

When internal combustion engines, and especially diesel engines, became practical, and the wheeled earth moving equipment had advanced through the slower caterpillar treads to the faster, large rubber-tired vehicles, earth dam construction methods changed so that larger dams could be built economically. While other unit prices steadily increased with the cost indices, earth moving unit prices decreased and then remained stationary over forty years because of the dramatic improvement in equipment. Progress in design analysis and construction methods made possible the building of the 456-foot-high Anderson Ranch Dam on the Boise River in Idaho, for more than twelve years the highest earth dam in the world. It was started in 1943 and, after interruption by World War II when a part of the dam was used to provide early storage as a war-food measure, was completed in 1950.

One of the unusual construction operations at Anderson Ranch Dam was the belt conveyor system used to transport the earth from the borrow area to the dam embankment. The borrow area was 1,200 feet above the dam area and over 2.5 miles distant. The 2-mile-long system consisted of six flights of 36-inch-wide endless belts that moved 1,000 cubic yards per hour. At the loading end, two 5-cubic-yard electric shovels loaded a large pendulum hopper that regulated the flow of material onto the belt. At the damsite, the belt discharged onto a stockpile adjacent to the embankment, from which 20-cubic-yard scrapers transported the material and spread it on the embankment for compacting with 20-ton sheepsfoot rollers. The belt was activated by 150-horsepower motor-generators which, after getting the belt underway, acted as generators returning power to the line that operated electric shovels. These generators also acted as brakes to provide speed control to the lines. By way of comparison, in 1906 the teamster and his equipment could dig and place on the embankment about 35 cubic yards of material in a day; while at Anderson Ranch Dam, over 20,000 cubic yards were excavated daily, moved over 2 miles, and placed in the embankment.

The highest dam in the nation is the 770-foot-high Oroville Dam, completed by the California Department of Water Resources in 1968 as a part of the California State Water Plan. It contains 80 million cubic yards of compacted earth and rock and creates a reservoir of 3.5 million acre-feet. Since 1902 the Bureau of Reclamation has built 300 dams to create storage reservoirs for the conservation and utilization of the West's water resources. Most of the dams have been constructed of earth materials.

Masonry and Concrete Dams: Some of the reclamation dams are made of concrete and a few are rock masonry. Roosevelt Dam in Arizona, started in 1905 and completed in 1911, is a masonry structure, and it is the key feature of the successful Salt River Project in central Arizona. Its location was in a remote area, 35 miles from the nearest railroad and difficult to reach by road. However, since it was in an area of hard, durable rock, the decision was made to build a rock masonry dam. Rock masons were imported from Italy to provide needed skills, and a quarry was opened nearby.

Electric power both to handle the rock in the quarry and to place the shaped rock in the dam was needed, and it was decided to utilize the difference in the elevation of the river 20 miles upstream from the damsite to generate the electricity. A small diversion dam was built with a 20-mile-long canal to carry 225 cubic feet of water per second to a forebay 220 feet above the plant site. Steel penstocks carried the water to a water wheel located in a cave. A belt-driven electric generator provided 950 kilowatts. The electrical energy

U.S. Bureau of Reclamation

The 280-foot-high, rock-masonry Theodore Roosevelt Dam was constructed between 1903 and 1911 and provides 1.4 million acre-feet of storage for the Salt River Project in Arizona.

from this plant was used to operate the lifting device at the quarry and the overhead cableways that brought the hand-quarried blocks into position on the dam for the laborers to place and grout.

Cement was needed to hold the blocks in place and make the dam watertight. However, this presented a problem, for cement manufacturing plants were distant and transportation costs prohibitive. Since good components for the manufacture of cement were nearby, a cement mill was built near the damsite; and during the period of project construction, the mill produced over 338,000 barrels of cement. Much lumber was also needed for construction. Sources of commercially produced lumber were far from the damsite, so this problem was also solved by establishing a local source of supply. A logging operation was activated in the upstream forested area by the operation of a portable sawmill which produced about 3 million board feet of timber for the dam's construction.

This 280-foot-high structure retains the record as the highest rock masonry dam in the world. The 356,000-cubic-yard rock structure has two features unusual for the time of its construction. A hydroelectric generating plant, containing three turbines with 1,080-kilowatt generating machines to operate at 25 cycles of alternating current (in 1976, 60 cycles is universal), was built at the foot of the dam in the deep canyon. This power plant became the first on reclamation projects to produce power for commercial use. The other noteworthy feature is the design of its spillways, the dam's safety valves used to pass flood flows harmlessly to the river below the dam. At Roosevelt, two spillways at its ends utilized the natural hard rock for their floors rather than the usual concrete-lined chute. The flow, as well as the upper level of the reservoir, is controlled by nineteen radial gates, each 20 feet by 15 feet 9 inches in size.

During the same early period, two vastly different dams were being constructed in Wyoming. One was a high masonry storage dam, Pathfinder, located in an almost ideal damsite on the headwaters of the Platte River to assist irrigation in Nebraska; and the other, Shoshone, a high concrete dam to provide for irrigation storage in northern Wyoming. Irrigation along the Platte River was practiced by the early settlers in the late 1800s with systems built by private firms. As elsewhere in the West, it soon became obvious that because of the erratic streamflows, storage reservoirs were required. The local irrigation district sought the assistance of the Reclamation Service immediately after the Reclamation Act was passed, and the project was authorized for construction in 1903.

Pathfinder Dam, a masonry structure like Roosevelt Dam in Arizona, is 214 feet high, has a crest length of 432 feet, and contains a volume of 65,700 cubic yards of granite rock. A rock quarry was established nearby to provide the masonry blocks, and a cableway was built to place them on the dam. Coal-fired steam engines were used for operating the hoisting and cableway equipment. All other materials, equipment, and supplies were hauled by teams and wagons up the Platte River from the railroad at Casper.

While this storage dam was being built piece by piece, other works necessary to bring stored water to the land were under construction. Some 175 miles downstream in Nebraska, the 35-foot-high and 2,360-foot-long concrete Whalen Diversion Dam was built; and the 2,200-cubic-foot per second, 95-mile-long Interstate Canal was dug. These features were constructed largely by horse-drawn equipment and manual labor.

To the north, Shoshone Dam (since renamed Buffalo Bill Dam), the Reclamation Service's first concrete gravity-type dam, was being constructed. This irrigation project had been conceived and started by Buffalo Bill Cody and his associates, but it was unsuccessful because no storage had been provided for summer irrigation when stream flow was low. In 1903 officials of the State of Wyoming requested help from the federal government to complete the project. The dam is 325 feet high, with a crest length of only 200 feet and a volume of 82,900 cubic yards of concrete. Cement and other materials and equipment to build it were brought in by wagon trains over 50 miles from the railroad at Powell, the last 10 miles of which were roads hewn out of the canyon walls. There were two and a half

years of preparatory work before a construction contract was awarded for the dam. While the dam is arched upstream, it is considered a gravity-type structure; that is, the weight of the dam is designed to resist the force of the water on the upstream face. However, the abutments were lodged into the sidewalls of the canyon for greater stability. In addition to storage of irrigation water, pipes placed through the dam supply municipal water to Cody, Wyoming.

Another early landmark structure was the Arrowrock Dam on the Boise River in Idaho. The Boise River Project was approved in 1905 for assistance under the Reclamation Act. This project had been under development by private companies following receipt of permission to divert water in 1864. By 1900 about 148,000 acres of land were under irrigation. When the Reclamation Act was passed, the landowners organized and petitioned assistance from the federal government in building storage reservoirs. The first to be undertaken was Arrowrock Dam, some 22 miles up the Boise River from the city of Boise. This all-concrete dam was the first of the curved gravity type.

The damsite was a fairly narrow canyon with high, steep, granite sidewalls. At the time of completion, its 350-foot height made it the highest dam in the world. It has a crest length of 1,150 feet and a volume of 636,000 cubic yards of concrete. While Arrowrock Dam is arched, the state of dam engineering had not progressed to the point of considering the value of the stresses developed by the arch action and resistance of the canyon sidewalls as abutments. It was designed as a gravity structure to resist sliding and overturning from the force of the water behind it; but no allowance was made for the possibility of uplift, a floating effect, from the pressure of the water seeping under its base.

Considerable preparation was required prior to starting work on the dam. This included the construction of 17 miles of standard gauge railroad into the site, facilities to house and care for 900 workmen, a sawmill, wagon roads, 54 miles of telephone lines, several miles of electric transmission lines, and excavation for diversion of the river. At another location, about 14 miles below the damsite, the Boise Diversion Dam was constructed, a concrete and masonry-type structure 39 feet high and 500 feet long, with a 216-foot overflow section on which the water level was controlled by planks between piers. The purpose was to divert part of the river flow into a powerhouse to operate three turbines with 500-kilowatt generators to furnish the electric power for construction at Arrowrock Dam.

After preparatory work, placing concrete in the dam began in November 1912, and it was finished three years later. The cement was brought in by railroad to a mixing plant, where two overhead 1,500-foot cableways transported the sand and other ingredients, and after mixing, it carried the concrete to the forms for placing. The mixing plant, the rock crushing and screening operations, and the cableways were electrically operated. While Pathfinder and Shoshone dams in Wyoming were being built largely by contractors, the whole operation in connection with the construction of Arrowrock Dam was by engineers, laborers, mechanics, teamsters, and others who were government employees.

Between 1902 and World War I, the bureau constructed twenty-six storage dams: seventeen earth, seven concrete, and two masonry. No significant work was undertaken during the war. From 1921 to 1928, six more earth dams and three small concrete dams were built. Great advancements in engineering technology occurred during this time, including understanding of the properties of concrete, of the stresses induced in arch-type structures from the water pressure and from the expansion and contraction of the concrete, and of earthquake stresses.

The 417-foot-high, 538,000-cubic-yard concrete gravity Owyhee Dam in eastern Oregon became the next step in technology; and when completed in 1932, it replaced Arrowrock as the world's highest. Several irrigation districts had been operating for many years by pumping from the Owyhee River. They petitioned for help in providing storage and enlarging the project. Studies were undertaken by the Reclamation Service in 1903, and the plan for constructing a storage dam

and other irrigation facilities—which would expand the project from 32,500 to 119,000 acres—was approved for construction late in 1926. Immediately thereafter a great deal of preparatory work was started, leading to the construction of Owyhee Dam. This dam was located in a narrow rocky canyon, 25 miles west of the nearest railroad. The railroad was extended to the site to transport the construction equipment and the cement, sand, aggregate, gates, valves, and other required materials. Telephone and power transmission lines and a camp to house the workers also had to be built.

A unique feature of the dam is a "glory hole" spillway chosen after extensive hydraulic model tests were made of various plans. It consists of a 22½ foot diameter vertical shaft, about 300 feet in length, which surfaces in the reservoir and connects with a diversion tunnel. The diameter at the top of the shaft is 52 feet 4 inches, and discharges are controlled by a circular steel gate 12 feet high. It is designed to handle a flood flow of 31,000 cubic feet per second.

When the contract was awarded for construction of this dam in 1928, construction equipment and methods had progressed to the point where horses were seldom used. Standard railroad equipment, power shovels, huge mixing plants for concrete, and a remote controlled cableway with a movable tower were used. Concrete mixing plants had grown to 4-cubic-yard capacity, two of which were required for Owyhee. The mixed concrete was moved to the cableway in 4-cubic-yard steel cars powered by a large gasoline locomotive. Except for encountering a narrow fault zone, which was cleaned out to a depth of 120 to 150 feet below the normal foundation, no unusual difficulties were encountered.

Experiments were made to develop methods for removing excess heat of cement hydration from mass concrete to bring the dam to a stable temperature. A 28-foot-square section extending up through the dam was cooled artificially by circulating river water through 1-inch pipes spaced at 4-foot intervals. The results of these tests formed the basis for the decision to use such a system at Hoover Dam, soon to be undertaken. As

Hoover was a project characterized by many innovations and by unprecedented magnitudes of size and technical problems, a separate section of this chapter describes its construction.

Other representative pioneering milestones in dam construction included Grand Coulee Dam, the largest concrete structure in the world; Morrow Point Dam, which is a thin, double-curved arch; and Pueblo Dam, a buttressed structure with a flip-type spillway. Each of these, as with others in the program, resulted from numerous studies of economics and structural suitability and were selected as being optimum for the specific site. Advances in methods of stress analysis in large dams, analysis of earthquake effects, strengths and durability of various materials, hydraulic design for controlling water flow and discharges and energy dissipation, all resulted in continuing improvements.

At Grand Coulee Dam, the volume of 10.6 million cubic yards of concrete required special measures to insure that the dam acted as an integral structure. Although it now appears to be a solid mass of concrete, it was built as a group of interlocking columns, varying in size from 50 feet square to 25 by 44 feet. These columns were built up, 5 feet at a time, with seventy-two-hour intervals between concrete placements. Because concrete shrinks as it cools, the columns were cooled to a stable

U.S. Bureau of Reclamation

Morrow Point Dam on the Gunnison River in Colorado was completed in 1968.

temperature before the joints between the columns were grouted solid. Since several hundred years would be needed to cool the concrete at the normal rate, pipes were embedded in the concrete as it was placed, and river water was pumped through them to cool the structure. It cooled in a matter of months, and the joints and pipes were then filled with grout. A total of 1,700 miles of this pipe were buried in the dam for the cooling and grouting process.

Morrow Point Dam is a 468-foot-high double curvature thin arch concrete dam in a deep narrow canyon of the Gunnison River in western Colorado, a part of the Upper Colorado River storage project. It is only 12 feet thick at the crest, 52 feet thick at the base, has a crest length of 720 feet, and contains only 380,000 cubic yards of concrete. It had substantial savings in concrete volume and costs over other types. The highest of several of this type, it is curved in both a horizontal and a vertical direction, utilizing arch action both ways for strength. The spillway is an overflow type, over which water plunges nearly 400 feet into a large stilling basin at the base of the dam. The 122,000-kilowatt powerhouse was built within the canyon wall.

The dam construction got underway in 1965 and was completed in 1968. Due to increasingly modern technology, such a complex structure could be built with assurance. Engineers and geologists carried out extensive investigations to determine characteristics of the canyon walls and the foundation. Over 100 diamond-core drill holes were drilled and observed with a television camera lowered into the 3-inch holes. Exploratory tunnels were driven into the abutments and the powerhouse location, where tests were made of the rock in place to supplement the testing of the cores. Geophysicists carried out seismic investigations to further evaluate the foundation rock reaction under stress. Using modern computers, complex studies were made to assure structural competency, economy, and safety. A plaster structure model was made, and deflections measured under various loadings. The dam is heavily instrumented to provide data concerning its behavior under project operation.

The roof-arch and the sidewall of the underground powerhouse were supported with over 50,000 feet of rock bolts, and the walls above the generator floor remained as exposed. Wire mesh was pinned to the arch to prevent small rock spalls from falling, and a light metal ceiling was installed the length of the chamber. The power generated is transmitted through underground high-voltage cables out of the canyon to a switchyard on its rim. The underground powerhouse eliminated dangers from falling rocks or slides in the steep canyon; expedited construction, as work could be carried on during winter months; and prevented scarring of the canyon walls. These innovations illustrated that advanced technology can result in cost savings and can adapt a structure to fit its environmental setting.

Hoover Dam

Hoover Dam on the Colorado River is perhaps the outstanding "glamor" public works project of the first half of the twentieth century, not only because of its economic worth and stimulus to the Southwest, but also because it was the first large multipurpose water resource project of modern scale. The unprecedented 726-foot-high structure, the highest dam in the world by about 300 feet at the time of its construction, captured the imagination of the nation as a demonstration of man's technological ability to control rampaging rivers so that water, otherwise destructive and wasted, could better meet the needs of people. Built during the years of the Great Depression, it also served as a positive focus for the attention of a troubled people, and thus it has been considered the best known of America's public works efforts. Other projects that followed such as the Grand Coulee and Bonneville dams on the Columbia River, Fort Peck on the Missouri River, and Shasta in California also received national attention; but Hoover has remained foremost because of its timing and challenge.

The Colorado River, originating in the Rocky Mountains of Wyoming and Colorado, drains 250,000 square miles of the arid Southwest, including areas in seven states. It was an unruly river, varying from rampaging,

destroying floods—heavy with silt and debris in the spring or following cloudburst storms—to low flow in the hot, dry summer months when water was needed. Irrigation had just started in Imperial Valley in California when the river, in the spring floods of 1905, smashed out of its banks and destroyed highways, farms, and lands as it ran uncontrolled into Imperial Valley, creating the 300-square-mile Salton Sea. It took two years of effort and over $3 million to get the river back into its channel and headed again for the Gulf of California.

While several projects had been formulated to utilize waters from the river, the wasted floodwaters needed to be controlled and put to use. The rapid increase in population in Southern California focused attention on the Colorado River as a possible source of water and of electric power generation. As water was the factor limiting growth in the Southwest, the other basin states were concerned that their rights to the waters of the Colorado be protected. Years of study and effort were involved in determining how to share the waters among the states. In 1922 an interstate compact dividing it between the upper and lower basin states was signed by a commission of state representatives chaired by Herbert Hoover, who was then secretary of commerce, representing the federal government.

The years of study also resulted in a report to Congress that formed the basis for the Boulder Canyon Project Act which became law in late 1928. After ratification of the Colorado River Compact in June 1929 by six of the seven states (Arizona withheld approval until 1944), the project got underway. A dam and power plant in Black Canyon, 25 miles southeast of Las Vegas, Nevada, was authorized along with the All American Canal into Imperial Valley.

A condition necessary to construction of the dam was that the secretary of interior should provide for revenues adequate to insure operation, maintenance, and amortization of costs. These revenues were to repay within fifty years all advances for construction of the Hoover Dam and power plant with interest, except for $25 million allocated to flood control. Repayment of the latter, without interest, could be deferred until after the interest-bearing portion of the debt was paid. Revenues were to come mainly from the sale of electrical energy generated at the dam. Contracts to cover the sale of electricity were speedily negotiated.

While intensive investigation of the damsites had been made in preliminary studies, much work had to be done before construction got underway. The damsite was in a desolate region where there were no living quarters for the workers; therefore, essentials for living and working in the forbidding desert had to be planned and constructed. Facilities were needed for transporting material and equipment over miles of burning sand and onto the construction site, 800 feet below the rim of the canyon.

Transportation facilities were provided first. The Union Pacific Railroad constructed a 23-mile branch line from Las Vegas to the site of the construction camp. From that point, the Bureau of Reclamation built its own 7-mile railroad to the damsite. Highways were required. Machine shops, air-compressor plants, garages, and warehouses had to be erected. The canyon had to be spanned, first by foot bridges and later by aerial cableways. A great gravel-screening plant and two huge concrete-mixing plants had to be designed and constructed; and power draglines and shovels, trucks, cars, derricks, and cranes had to be acquired in great numbers. Electric power for construction was obtained by building a powerline 220 miles across the desert from San Bernardino, California.

Living quarters for project workers were a special problem. There was no "labor pool" in the area, and construction workers were recruited from all parts of the nation. Homes had to be provided. The workers could not be expected to live in the immediate vicinity of the damsite where temperatures in summer often reached 110 degrees, with heat waves rising from the canyon as from a blast furnace. After studying climatic and soil conditions in the area, bureau engineers selected a high plateau location, 7 miles southwest of the damsite; and a complete town was constructed as Boulder City, Nevada. Modern

homes were built; lawns and parks were planted; streets were laid out and paved; and schools, churches, and stores were erected. A sewer system was installed, and Colorado River water was piped into the town. A modern desert oasis was brought into being.

The design of the dam, directed by John L. Savage, chief designing engineer of the Bureau of Reclamation, who had worldwide recognition for his work, was completed after years of study. Specifications were then rushed to completion, and the project was advertised for bids. The bids were then opened by Walker R. Young, the bureau's construction engineer for the project, who had directed the investigations. On March 11, 1931, the secretary of interior awarded a contract for the construction to the Six Companies, Inc., of San Francisco, a joint venture of several of the largest construction companies in the nation. Frank Crowe, veteran dam builder of the Bureau of Reclamation, was selected construction superintendent by the constructors.

The amassing of specialized machinery in quantities greater than ever before assembled demanded meticulous attention. Huge trucks were procured to haul men, materials, and equipment. Some trucks were of 16-cubic-yard capacity, others for operation as 100- and 150-man transports. Air compressor plants of 14,500-cubic-feet per minute capacity were built near the damsite. The sand-and-gravel-screening and washing plant that produced the aggregate was the largest of its type. It could screen, wash, and place aggregate in readiness for mixing with cement and water at the rate of seventeen tons per minute.

Recruiting over 5,000 qualified workmen for the job presented special problems, despite the fact that the Depression had resulted in large numbers of unemployed workers. Many of them came to the area in broken down cars, and some walked. Some were undernourished and had difficulty adjusting to the heat of the desert. Sixteen workmen died of sunstroke in the first year. Methods were devised to select men with the proper qualifications and physical capabilities for the work at hand. During the construction period, over 20,000 men passed the examinations by government physicians and were ac-

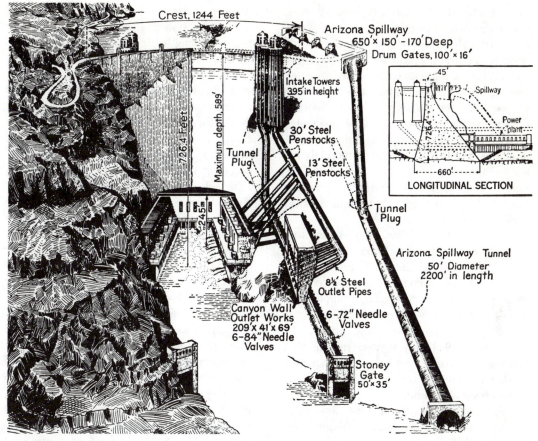

An artist's sketch showing how Hoover Dam operates. The reservoir, Lake Mead, provides 32 million acre-feet of storage.

cepted for employment by the contractors. Many worked long enough to get a "grub stake" and then moved on, but in general the turnover rate was low. The dispatch with which the job was accomplished bears lasting testimony to efficient planning and effective execution.

The general plan of attack in building Hoover Dam was to drive tunnels through the canyon walls around the site, divert the Colorado River through the tunnels, build coffer-dams to block off the river from the damsite, excavate the site, and build the dam and power plant. The narrowness of the canyon, the intensive activity up and down the river, and the possible large fluctuation of the river's flow made diverting the Colorado a major challenge.

Four 56-foot diameter tunnels, two on each side of the river, were built around the

damsite through the solid rock of the canyon walls and lined with concrete. The tunnel headings were attacked first by batteries of compressed-air drills. When the drills had bitten 10 to 20 feet into solid rock, a ton of dynamite was loaded into the holes. The electrically fired blast shook the walls of the canyon and the resulting loose rock and debris was loaded into trucks which roared away to dump their loads in side canyons.

With the completion of the two tunnels on the Arizona side of the river in November 1932, steps were taken to begin actual diversion of the river's flow. A temporary dam of earth and rock was thrown across the river just below the inlets of the two tunnels. Within twenty-four hours after starting this work, a dam of sufficient height to block the channel and force the water through the tunnels had been formed. Meanwhile, downstream from the damsite, another cofferdam was pushed across the river's channel just above the tunnel outlets. This prevented the river from backing into the construction area. With the cofferdams in place and the water diverted around the construction site, the dam area was pumped dry and excavation for the foundation of the dam and power plant proceeded swiftly. Manning huge power shovels, draglines, and other equipment, men labored around the clock digging down through the mud and slit of the channel before reaching solid rock. More than half a million cubic yards of muck were removed.

By April 1933, the Nevada diversion tunnels were completed in time to share in handling the spring runoff. On June 6, 1933, the first bucket of concrete was placed. Six months later, a million yards of concrete were in place. Another million were placed in the following half year; the third million by December 6, 1934, only eighteen months after starting placement; and all of the concrete work was finished by May 1935, over two years ahead of schedule.

As soon as construction of the dam, intake towers, and outlet works were sufficiently advanced and the upstream portions of the two inner diversion tunnels were plugged with concrete, a steel bulkhead gate was lowered at the inlet of the outer diversion tunnel on the Arizona side of the river. This was in February 1935. Back of the unfinished dam, water started to rise. By mid summer, the new reservoir held more than 3 million acre-feet of water, having a maximum depth of over 270 feet. The Nevada diversion tunnels were used to release water downstream until the reservoir reached a depth of about 280 feet when the water could flow through the intake tower gates.

The power plant at Hoover Dam is located at its base and is U-shaped. In the Nevada wing, there are eight huge units; seven are 82,000 kilowatts each and one is a 95,000 kilowatt unit. In the Arizona wing, there are nine primary units; seven generating 82,000 kilowatts each, one 50,000 kilowatts, and one 40,000 kilowatts. Two small units (one in each wing) are used in the operation of the facilities. The several generators were installed over a twenty-five-year period to match the power needs. The first power began flowing in 1936, and installation of the final unit was completed in 1961.

All principal generating units are operated under a contract with the City of Los Angeles Department of Water and Power and the Southern California Edison Company. The energy is sold to eight entities, consisting of two states, four municipalities, one water district, and one private utility company. Fourteen high-voltage transmission lines, built by the purchasers of power, connect the Hoover plant energy to market areas. Revenue from the sale of electric energy is repaying the cost of the construction of the dam and power plant, with interest, in accordance with contract provisions. The electrical facilities at Hoover involved design, construction, and operation of equipment of greater capacity and higher voltages than previously existed. Thus, the Hoover power development played an important part in advancing technology of the electric power industry.

The dam and power plant structure, which contains nearly 4.5 million cubic yards of concrete and 44,000 tons of steel, was completed in May 1935, just four years after start of construction at the site. Finishing other items, such as various metalwork and cleanup, required another nine months. The dam still holds the distinction of being the western hemisphere's highest concrete dam. It's reservoir, Lake Mead, backing up 115 miles behind the dam and providing storage space for 32 million acre-feet of water, is the nation's largest man-made lake.

Water Conveyance Systems

The rather short, small ditches and canals built during the early irrigation days of the nineteenth century, when design was often by cut and try and construction control was from sighting across a pan of water, are a far cry from today's conveyance systems that move millions of acre-feet of water hundreds of miles, with centralized automatic computer control of flows and discharges. But the application of developing scientific knowledge to move water from where it is to where it is needed for man's use has transformed millions of acres of once barren wastelands and desert into productive farms supporting and providing favorable environmental settings for prosperous communities. The basic technology was similar to works that transmitted water to cities for municipal and industrial use, but generally larger and more specialized structures were required.

The conveyance system to bring water to the land usually starts at the headworks, a diversion structure or a storage dam in the hills which regulates the flow of water into the main canal or pipe system that brings it into the irrigable area. From this main artery, smaller canals or laterals are built along the higher elevations, with turnouts or gates, through which the farmer's quota of water is released into his ditches or pipe systems. These systems almost always involve excavation of earth and rock. They usually require such structures as checks to control the velocity of flow and elevation of the water in the canal, pipes or concrete pressure conduits to carry it under streams or across valleys, and tunnels, flumes, and bridges. Unusual structures are frequently required to transfer the water from a higher to a lower elevation and to dissipate the energy without damage.

Changes in the types of materials used (wood, concrete, and steel) and in the shapes of canal cross sections and control structures evolved as the technology advanced through discovering and understanding hydraulic flow and energy control phenomena. While much of the increased knowledge came from development of theories and confirmation by laboratory tests, application of them improved as structures were built and their operations carefully observed and measured. Both theories and structures were modified when operating performances were different from those envisioned from model studies.

Changes in the method of excavating the canals and laterals kept pace with the evolution of construction equipment and machinery. Horse-drawn plows and scoops dug and shaped many miles of early day canals and laterals. The size of the canal in cross section usually dictated whether two-, four-, or six-horse teams were required. Later horse-drawn roadgraders helped smooth the base

and side slopes and spread the excavated earth on the canal banks. The adoption of the internal combustion engine as motive power replaced the huge steam shovels and the awkward steam-operated dragline excavators. As the mobility of such machines increased, they replaced horses.

Perhaps equally dramatic was the introduction of tracklaying or caterpillar treads on excavators, adapted from World War I tanks. On other operations, the gasoline- or diesel-powered engines, when mounted on caterpillar treads and fitted with a steel blade, the bulldozer, dug the earth as well as spread the dumped material. Then came the self-loading scoops or carry-all scrapers, usually tractor-drawn, which both dug and then carried the material away. Further improvements resulted with the replacement of the caterpillar tread with huge rubber tires. Also, the horsepower of engines was increasing rapidly. Such changes in types and capacity of earthmovers decreased the unit cost of earthwork and made larger canal projects progressively more feasible.

Specially designed pieces of equipment are noteworthy. The "walking" dragline excavator used on the All American Canal is an example. This 15,155-cubic-feet per second canal was dug through 80 miles of desert sand in southeastern California and was over 250 feet in width at the top. The work required long booms on the draglines and heavy and powerful motors. To support this equipment on the sand, the excavator was mounted on large pontoon type treads. The machine was capable of lifting these treads and moving them forward independently, thus shifting itself forward onto the pontoons for further digging. Another development was the ripper, a tractor-drawn heavy hook which when drawn through broken rock or shale fragmented the material and thus minimized blasting. A more recent development is the front-end loader, which scoops the earth, raises it vertically, transports it, and unloads it into trucks or onto a stockpile.

Where construction of small canals and laterals was extensive, contractors devised and used a wheel-type excavator which dug the canal's trapezoidal section in one pass

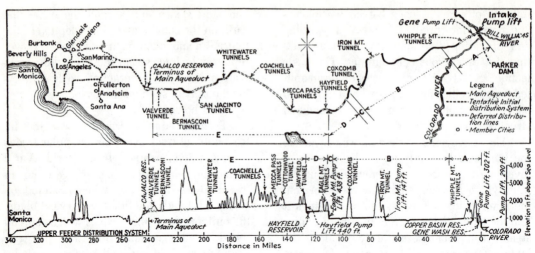

Engineering News-Record

The Colorado River Aqueduct crosses 242 miles of desert and mountains from the Colorado River to the coast cities and rises to 2,600 feet above sea level.

with a modified broad-based plow, the trailing edges of which carried the excavated material into banks on each side. Canals are often lined with concrete to prevent the loss of water from seepage. Early practice was to place the mixed concrete in timber forms in alternate panels on the banks. When the first concrete panels were firm, the rest of them and the bottom would be placed. This method was time consuming and costly.

However, over a period of years a more efficient method developed. Machinery passed along the dug canal, trimmed the bottom and sides to proper dimensions, and disposed of the excess material on the banks. This machine was then closely followed by one similar in shape (trapezoidal) that distributed the mixed concrete evenly on the sides and bottom, compacted it with vibrators, and troweled the surface to a smooth finish, all in one pass. Such machines usually ride on steel rails placed on each canal bank; frequently they are self-propelled. The evolution of such types of construction machinery has made it possible to economically build thousands of miles of water transport systems to bring water needed for irrigation and domestic purposes to the growing population of the arid West.

Some of the early tunnels built on Bureau of Reclamation projects were constructed by essentially the same methods as those used many years earlier. They were built by workmen using picks and shovels and hand-held, sledgehammer-driven rock drills. The rock was shattered by explosives and transported to the outside by men or horse-drawn carts. Many such tunnels were just large enough in diameter to accommodate the height of workmen and to be internally supported by heavy timbers. As the size of the projects and the amount of water to be transported became greater, the tunnels were increased in diameter, but the methods used for construction were slow to change. One of the first advancements was the use of compressors driven by steam engines that provided compressed air to drive the drills for blasting-powder holes. Tunnels were usually far removed from sources of electricity; but some builders provided it from on-site, coal-fired steam plants or by developing nearby hydroelectric plants to provide lighting, run the compressors, or power the engine for the muck cars.

The advent of gasoline and diesel engines did little to assist operations inside a tunnel because of harmful exhaust fumes. The internal supporting systems improved with the use of steel beams bent to the shape of the tunnel and around which were inserted heavy planks next to the rock. The use of electric power gradually improved to better light the working areas, operate the ventilation system, transport the tunnel muck, and run machines to pick up and load the broken rock or muck into rail cars. One of the longest tunnels built under Bureau of Reclamation direction was the concrete-lined, 9.8-foot inside diameter Alva B. Adams Tunnel drilled through the Continental Divide in Colorado from 1940 to 1946. Conventional drill and blast methods were used for the 13.2-mile-long tunnel.

With the exception of the use of long anchor bolts to bind the layers or rock together as a part of the tunnel support systems, tunneling methods changed little until the introduction of the electric-powered tunneling

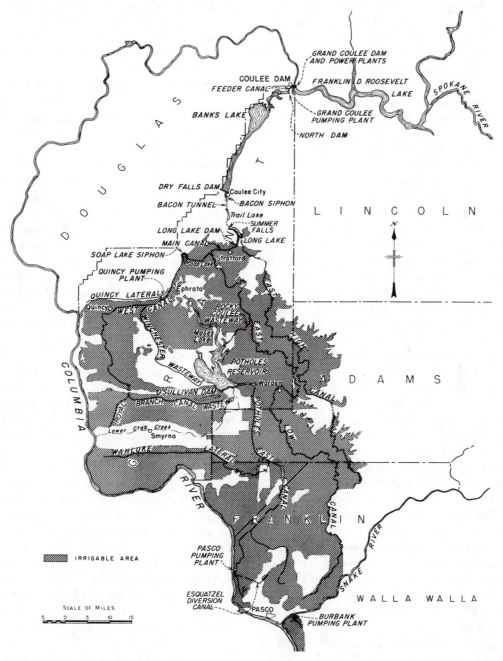

U.S. Bureau of Reclamation

The Columbia Basin Project in the State of Washington includes a million acres of irrigated land, of which 525,000 acres were well established farms by 1975.

machine or mole. It was first introduced in the diversion tunnel at the Army Corps of Engineers' Oahe Dam on the Missouri River, a 26-foot diameter tunnel through shale. In 1964 an electric-powered mole, guided by a laser beam, was used to chew its way mechanically for 13 miles to form a 13.3-foot diameter tunnel through a mountain on the San Juan-Chama Project in New Mexico. The rock was hard sandstone and shale, and the advance averaged 55 feet per day.

A contract was let in early 1975 for the 7-mile Buckskin Mountain Tunnel on the Central Arizona Project. The 20-foot diameter tunnel through hard sandstone will be machine-bored and lined with precast concrete segments, a decided cost saving over previous methods.

A large number of notable water conveyance systems have been constructed as part of the irrigation and related projects of the West. One of the largest, most diversified, and most difficult water conveyance systems in history, and an outstanding milestone of public works technology, is the Colorado River Aqueduct. It delivers Colorado River water made available by Hoover Dam storage to the Los Angeles area. One billion gallons of water a day are lifted 1,600 feet from the reservoir behind Parker Dam, crosses mountain ranges, and flows 242 miles to a reservoir near Los Angeles. Additional distribution aqueducts extend the total length to over 400 miles. The main aqueduct involved 92 miles of 16-foot diameter concrete-lined tunnels, thirty-one in number ranging from a few hundred feet to 18.3 miles in length; 30 miles of pressure inverted syphon structures with 16-foot diameter single barrel or 12-foot diameter twin barrel structures; 55 miles of 16-foot diameter horseshoe-shaped, cut-and-cover structures; and 65 miles of canals. Built across some of the most forbidding desert topography in the nation, the $200 million plus project was constructed between 1932 and 1939 and furnished jobs to over 45,000 workmen.

Extensive design studies were made to provide the most economical combination of structures. This classic in aqueduct design provided an important prototype for many projects that followed. It was constructed by the Metropolitan Water District of Southern California, formed under state laws to build and operate the project. The organization formed to design and build the project was headed by F. E. Weymouth, a former chief engineer of the Bureau of Reclamation; and many of his staff had years of experience with the bureau. On this project, as with many of the early large water control projects of the nation, key personnel were often alumni of the bureau.

Another milestone was the Salt Lake Aqueduct on the Provo River Project in Utah. This 42-mile aqueduct, including 3.5 miles of tunnel, was started in 1939; and after several years delay caused by World War II, it was completed in 1951. The 150-cubic-foot per second aqueduct was constructed primarily with 25-ton, 20-foot length sections of 69-inch diameter precast concrete pipe. The pipe was reinforced and used for hydraulic heads of up to 150 feet. A specially designed joint with a rubber gasket in slot indentations was an innovation that has been used extensively ever since. About 4 miles of the line, where heads ranged from 150 to 325 feet, utilized $1/2$-inch steel pipe, fabricated in 30-foot sections and coated with coal tar enamel on the inside and with gunite on the outside. All of the aqueduct is underground with a minimum cover of 3 feet. The water is delivered to the Salt Lake City system at a 40-million-gallon terminal reservoir, and it is used for municipal and irrigation purposes in the Salt Lake Valley.

The Columbia Basin Project includes one of the nation's largest water conveyance systems and irrigates a million acres of former desert. The history of the overall project, the Grand Coulee Dam, and the power features of the project are discussed in Chapter 11. The construction of the project was started in 1934; the pumping plant to lift water 310 feet into the 1.2 million acre-foot irrigation storage reservoir (the Grand Coulee) got underway in 1946 along with the primary irrigation conveyance system. By 1952 the first irrigation water was delivered to an initial area of 66,000 acres, and the work has since gone forward on a regular schedule. In 1974, 525,000 acres were well-established farmlands and produced crops with a gross value of $265 million. Towns and agricultural industries have been created to support this production. The map shows the 90-mile-long, 60-mile-wide irrigation area and the major features of the project.

By 1976 the major part of the main distribution system, consisting of 317 miles of canals, 12 miles of pipelines, and 4 miles of tunnels—with capacities from 3,900- to 16,000-cubic-feet per second—was completed. Four earth fill dams that create three regulating reservoirs are part of the system. Lateral canals to deliver water to the farms total 1,960 miles with capacities up to 2,000-cubic-feet per second; and 2,600 miles of drainage pipelines and waterways had been constructed. Completion of the distribution system to the remaining project lands had been delayed by funding problems. In 1975 about $1 billion of work remained to be completed on the $2.1 billion project including the power facilities.

The redistribution of excess water from northern California to water-short Southern California has resulted in the construction of the most extensive water conveyance system in history. Plans for the utilization of the water resources of the state have been underway since the beginning of the twentieth century, and intensive studies by the state resulted in formulating the first basic comprehensive plan for the state in 1921. It has since been periodically updated. Attempts by the state to finance the starting of the projects failed, and federal assistance was requested. Funds were made available during the Depression; and the Central Valley Project, a part of the overall statewide plan—primarily to control flood flows, provide storage, and transport water for distribution within the Central Valley itself—was undertaken by the federal government as a Bureau of Reclamation project. (See discussion of Sacramento River in Chapter 9.) When completed this project will provide irrigation water to almost 3 million acres of land and about a million acre-feet per year will be supplied for municipal and industrial use. Conveyance structures to transport water south include 623 miles of canals with capacities up

to 13,100-cubic-feet per second. Thousands of miles of drains have been constructed; and on the west side of the valley, 1,200 miles of underground concrete pipelines up to 96-inch diameter provide the distribution system to serve 575,000 acres of irrigated land. By 1975 over $1.5 billion had been invested in the project, most of which is being repaid under provisions of the reclamation law. Approximately $1 billion of work remains to be completed.

The initial phase of a state water plan, developed to correct the water imbalance statewide (much as the Central Valley Project had done within the valley), was adopted by California in 1959 and got underway the following year, financed primarily by state general obligation bonds. In developing the plan, cooperation with the federal agencies, primarily the Bureau of Reclamation and the Army Corps of Engineers, resulted in an overall coordinated plan and operation. Some of the features were joint undertakings with the Bureau of Reclamation's Central Valley Project. Basically, the first phase of the state water plan, constructed by the California Department of Water Resources, is to

Public Works Historical Society

Twenty-foot diameter prestressed concrete pipe is utilized for distribution of water from the California State Water Project. Each 20-foot section weighs 150 tons.

transport 4.2 million acre-feet of water annually to thirty-one public agencies in Southern California who repay costs allotted to water supply. The estimated cost at the time of authorization for this project was $2.3 billion; but by 1975, escalation and some added features increased this amount to $3.9 billion. The distribution systems required to convey water from the project aqueducts to users, financed and constructed by the entities contracting for water, were estimated in 1975 to cost $3.9 billion. By January 1975, the state had expended $2.2 billion on its project, and the distribution entities had expended a similar amount.

This storage and conveyance system is the largest public works program undertaken by a state in the history of the nation. Moving the water nearly 700 miles south involves 475 miles of canals with capacities up to 21,000-cubic-feet per second; 175 miles of pipelines and 20 miles of tunnels up to 30 feet in diameter; twenty-two pumping plants including the world's largest, the A. D. Edmonston plant, which lifts 4,095 cubic feet per second of water, 1,926 feet over the Tehachapi Mountains; twenty-five earthfill dams involving 271 million cubic yards of compacted earth and rock embankments; and seven power plants with an installed capacity of 1.3 million kilowatts and a pumped storage facility that when completed about 1978 will have a capacity in the pump-turbines of about 1.2 million kilowatts.

The initial features of the California State Water Project were essentially complete in 1975, although controversy had delayed the 43-mile, 21,800-cubic-foot per second Peripheral Canal across the Sacramento Delta waterway area. It has the primary purpose of improving the water quality for the project and in the various estuaries of the Delta. As with most large public works, the issues are complex and involve value judgments. The state has developed a sophisticated computer-controlled, semi-automatic system for centralized operation of the project.

These examples, while of the largest projects, are illustrative of the public works irrigation and municipal water conveyance systems throughout the West. Extensive research and development programs to improve materials, structure, and operation methods have been carried out by both state and federal agencies. The Denver, Colorado engineering laboratories of the Bureau of Reclamation are recognized as among the world's best. The pioneering work in improving portland cement, concrete, structure analysis, soil mechanics, hydraulic design, and related problems has had worldwide impact.

Studies have been made by various public and private entities of long-distance water transport that dwarfs even the California state water plan. For example, a number of different ways to import water from the water surplus rivers in Alaska and northern Canada over 1,500 miles to the southwest United States as well as into the Great Lakes system have been suggested. One privately financed study involved a yearly diversion of 78 million acre-feet of water to the United States' Southwest, 25 million acre-feet into Mexico, 22 million acre-feet into the Great Lakes, and 40 million acre-feet for use in Canada. A detailed study was recently completed of transporting about 6 million acre-feet of water per year from the lower Mississippi River over 700 miles to Texas and eastern New Mexico. The initial capacity of the canal would be about 40,000 cubic feet per second.

Technology and construction capability exist to accomplish such projects. However, many environmental, economic, and social problems are yet to be clearly defined and solutions formulated before such projects are built. Furthermore, there are many opportunities for greater returns from better management and more efficient and effective use of present facilities and supplies before proceeding with these more costly projects. The overall environmental effects will require careful and extensive studies to formulate the optimum long-range plan and to determine if the projects should be attempted at all. However, they do indicate some of the possibilities of what can be done to make the world more productive.

Irrigation Public Works Accomplishments

While the Bureau of Reclamation has

been the primary agency providing public works for irrigation development, other programs are also important. The Bureau of Indian Affairs supplies 900,000 acres with water under its irrigation program. The Small Watershed Program of the Department of Agriculture (described in Chapter 9) presently provides irrigation water to a million acres. Most of the western states have state programs, usually limited to relatively small projects generally involved with improving operations of existing systems by rehabilitation, canal lining programs, and similar work. California is an exception with its massive California Water Plan development. Most of the western states have now prepared, or have in preparation, a statewide plan for utilizing their water resources. These are cooperative undertakings with the various federal agencies involved to encompass the overall program.

Some of the bureau's projects have already been described. The following outline notes several additional projects, representative of the 165 projects in the total federal reclamation program.

By 1974 the Bureau of Reclamation program included 165 operating projects which delivered 30 million acre-feet of water, mainly for irrigation. Water was available to about 11 million acres of croplands on 145,000 irrigated farms. The gross value of the crops produced in 1974 was $4.7 billion. In addition, 52 billion kilowatt-hours of hydroelectric power were marketed; municipal and industrial water was supplied to approximately 16 million people; the recreational use of the project's 256 recreation areas totaled 64 million visitor-days; and flood damages of $176 million were prevented.

A total of $5.9 billion had been invested by June 30, 1974 in completed project facilities since the establishment of the program by the 1902 Reclamation Act. This included $1.2 billion in specific irrigation facilities, $1.4 billion in electric power facilities, and $3.3 billion in multipurpose and other facilities. About 84 percent of the total investment is reimbursable to the United States Treasury and $1.4 billion had been repaid. Another $1.4 billion had been ex-

pended on projects still under construction.

The physical works constructed include 300 dams creating 230 reservoirs with a storage capacity of 135 million acre-feet. A total of 140 diversion dams were completed to divert water from rivers into conveyance facilities that include 7,000 miles of canals, 890 miles of pipelines, and 220 miles of tunnels. Pumping plants of over 1,000 horsepower capacity totaled 130. Project lands were provided with 34,000 miles of laterals and 15,000 miles of drains, of which about three fourths were constructed by the bureau. The fifty completed power plants had an installed capacity of 7.8 million kilowatts, and plants with a capacity of 4.5 million kilowatts were under construction. The Bureau-constructed powerlines totaled 16,200 circuit miles with 295 substations.

The 335,000-acre North Platte project extends for 110 miles along the North Platte River from Guernsey, Wyoming, to 15 miles beyond Bridgeport, Nebraska. Settlement of the valley began in Nebraska in the 1880s with small diversions into the river bottom lands. Some of the early projects failed because of lack of storage reservoirs. Authorized as a reclamation project on March 14, 1903, it was one of the first three projects that came under the Reclamation Act. Construction commenced on the Pathfinder Dam, described earlier, and the 95-mile main canal in 1905. All of the canals were constructed by 1925 and the Guernsey Dam was completed in 1927. The project includes five storage dams providing reservoir capacity of 1.2 million acre-feet, four diversion dams, 337 miles of main canals and 1,260 miles of laterals, 370 miles of drains, and two power plants.

The North Platte Valley's sagebrush and rangeland was transformed into stable productive farmland by the $37 million spent for construction. A full supply of water is now provided to 335,000 acres. In 1974 these lands produced crops valued at $131 million. From 25 to 30 million kilowatts of electricity are generated each year, and flood control benefits are provided along with fish and wildlife and recreation opportunities.

The 390,000-acre Boise Project is located

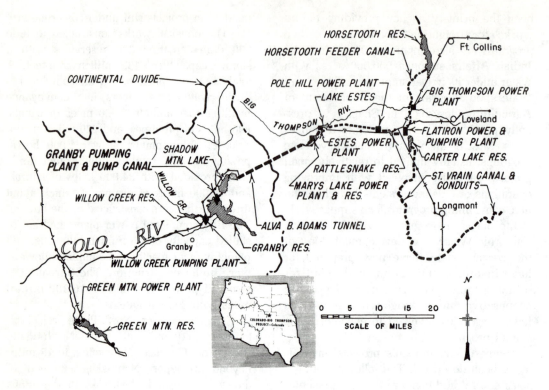

U.S. Bureau of Reclamation

The Colorado-Big Thompson Project in northeastern Colorado diverts water through the continental divide and includes over 100 major engineering features.

in southwestern Idaho along the Boise and Payette rivers. Water was first diverted for the townsite of Boise in 1864, and agricultural activity in the valley got underway in the 1880s as settlers began filing on the desert lands under small-scale private irrigation diversions. By 1900 about 148,000 acres were being irrigated. Planning for storage works and project expansion began with the passage of the 1902 Reclamation Act, and the first stage of the project was authorized in 1905. An orderly program of development has been carried on since with the key Arrowrock Dam, previously discussed, constructed during the period from 1911 to 1915. The project now includes five storage reservoirs including Anderson Ranch Dam, two diversion dams, 560 miles of main canals, 1,200 miles of laterals, seven pumping plants, and 400 miles of drains. Three power plants have a combined capacity of 36,500 kilowatts.

The project area was once entirely desert wasteland, except for small sections of river bottom. Water has transformed it into one of the nation's most stable productive areas, producing diversified crops of all types. The 340,000 acres irrigated in 1974 produced crops valued at $120 million. The project also provides flood control, water quality, fish and wildlife and recreation benefits, and usually it generates over 250 million kilowatt-hours of electricity per year. The $69 million project is being repaid on schedule.

The Colorado-Big Thompson Project in northeastern Colorado is a complex multipurpose project, including over 100 major engineering features. It diverts about 260,000 acre-feet of Colorado River water each year through the Continental Divide which provides supplemental irrigation for 720,000 acres of fertile land in the South Platte River Basin. The project area includes Horace Greeley's Union Colony which began irrigation about 1870. With the success of the early projects, irrigation rapidly expanded; and by 1900 the natural flow of the streams was overappropriated and attention was given to the development of reservoirs to store the high spring flows. By 1910 the reservoir sites in the plains area were utilized and attention focused on the costly tapping of the Colorado River by piercing the Continental Divide.

A preliminary survey by local interests was begun in 1933 and the resulting 1934 report indicated the project was feasible. A $150,000 Public Works Administration grant was made to the Bureau of Reclamation in 1935 for engineering studies that led to the project's authorization and the beginning of construction of the Green Mountain Dam in 1938. Work was curtailed during World War II, but water was delivered through the 13.1-mile Adams Tunnel in 1947. All features of the project were completed by 1959.

In addition to the Adams Tunnel, the project features, scattered over an area of 150 miles east-west and 65 miles north-south, include twenty-seven dams and dikes, over 130 miles of canals, twenty short tunnels, fifteen pumping plants, five power plants, and nearly 700 miles of electric transmission lines including thirty-seven substations. The 2,800-foot drop down the eastern slope of the Rocky Mountains is utilized in the 184,000-kilowatt capacity of the power plants, including a 8,500 kilowatt pumped-storage facility, one of the first in the nation. About 760 million kilowatt-hours of electricity are generated each year, of which 70 million are used for project pumping. Water is delivered to the existing 120 canals and sixty small reservoirs serving the project lands. In addition, about 45,000 acre-feet per year of municipal water is furnished to eleven communities. The proj-

ect also provides flood control, fish and wildlife enhancement, and recreational features which yearly result in 2 million visitor-days of water-oriented recreation.

In 1974 the project lands produced $269 million worth of crops. In drought years, 50 percent or more of the value of crops is attributed to the project water. Studies indicate that in normal years, about one fourth of the crop value can be credited to the project. The $162 million federal investment is being repaid on schedule.

The Frenchman-Cambridge Division of the Missouri Basin Project is located in the southwest corner of Nebraska and extends 70 miles along the Republican River and about 10 miles along Frenchman Creek, a tributary. The project provides irrigation water to 66,100 acres of farmland. It includes four storage dams, three constructed by the Bureau of Reclamation and one by the Army Corps of Engineers; four diversion dams; 110 miles of canals; 66 miles of laterals; and 20 miles of drainage channels.

According to anthropologists, the area was first inhabited in the fifteenth century by agriculturally minded Indians who subsisted for a time on corn and fish until driven from their homes by large floods, followed by several years of drought. A similar fate awaited early settlers in the late nineteenth century; but dry-farmed wheat areas on the highlands, along with some irrigation in the river bottomlands and buffalo grass rangeland, provided an agriculture base. However, a combination of extreme drought years and a

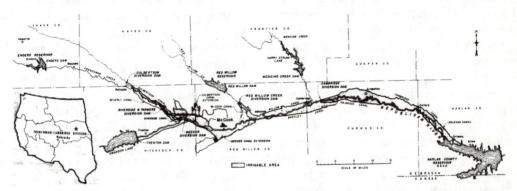

U.S. Bureau of Reclamation

The Frenchman-Cambridge Division of the Missouri Basin Project in southwestern Nebraska supplies irrigation water to 66,100 acres.

disastrous flood in 1935, when 135 people were drowned, gave emphasis to the need to provide a more stable economic base.

Following intensive investigations, the project was formulated in 1940 and was authorized as part of the Missouri Basin Project in 1944. Construction commenced in 1946, and the last feature, the Red Willow Dam which was primarily a flood control structure, was completed in 1962. The project was the testing ground for multiagency coordination of the Missouri Basin Project, with eight or more federal and state agencies actively involved in the development. Approximately $60 million of the $82 million project is being repaid to the federal treasury, $10 million by the irrigators and $50 million from the Missouri River Basin power revenues. The remaining $22 million is charged to the flood control features of the project, which are non-reimbursable.

As with other similar projects in the Missouri River Basin and elsewhere in the West, the value of the project comes from the widespread benefits of a stable agricultural base for the area. This enables full use of adjacent range lands by providing winter feed for livestock. It also supports a large enough assured production to prevent bankruptcy of the area during drought years, as has happened in the past. In 1974 the 43,850 irrigated acres produced crops valued at $17 million.

The Garrison Diversion unit is the largest irrigation feature of the Missouri Basin Project. The initial phase, which was 22 percent completed by the end of 1975, will provide irrigation water to 250,000 acres extending over 200 miles down the central part of North Dakota. It will also furnish water to fourteen towns and cities and four industrial areas, enhance fish and wildlife at thirty-six major areas and numerous smaller ones, and develop recreational opportunities at eight major water impoundments. Designed to bring a stabilized and diversified agriculture to North Dakota, the $250 million initial stage is expected to assure an increase in farm income of $34 million and an agricultural benefit of $88 million per year (all 1968 prices). New opportunities will be created that will serve to decrease emigration from the state and revive the small towns of the area. The facilities include a pumping plant near the Army Corps of Engineers' Garrison Dam on the Missouri River, 1,865 miles of canals and laterals, four regulating reservoirs, 141 pumping plants, and 2,800 miles of drains. The cost of the project, except for the 14 percent assigned to flood control benefits, will be repaid by the water users and from Missouri River Basin power revenues.

Plans for the ultimate development involve irrigating over a million acres and providing water to forty communities for municipal and industrial uses. The project has been under consideration for more than eighty years, with early investigation financed by the state. It is now supported by the Garrison Diversion Conservancy District, which includes 45 percent of the state's area, 60 percent of its population, and 60 percent of its valuation. The district has the power to tax to support its activities and contractual obligations. It has contracted with the federal government for the supply works of the project and will in turn contact with individual irrigation districts, municipalities, and other entities included in the overall development.

The project has been involved in controversy since its early days. It is located in a semi-arid area, where wheat is produced in some of the years. However, the area has steadily lost population since the 1930s, and diversification and stability is needed to utilize better the resources available and create opportunities for economic improvement.

Problems and Future Programs

America of 1976 faces many problems, changing concepts, and competing needs for the nation's water supplies. The available quantity of water is ample to meet foreseeable requirements; but problems arise from the geographic and time distribution of both water quantity and quality. This is especially true in the western arid states, where available water supply is generally the determining factor in agricultural production and development of many energy resources as well as in meeting urban needs and environmental considerations.

In the river basins of the Southwest, such as the Rio Grande and the Gila River, water is already completely consumed. And in basins such as the Colorado River, water will be entirely utilized by projects that are under construction or being planned for the immediate future. Competing requirements for the limited water supply are growing and reflect changing and differing local and national priorities. Institutional controls, such as water laws established to meet conditions at the beginning of the twentieth century, can become serious obstacles to the best use of water to meet future needs. For instance, in settling the West, irrigation water was essential in many areas to establish and grow. Now that most of the West is populated—and with the development of modern transportation facilities providing flexibility to obtain food and other basic needs from anywhere in the nation—water for irrigation is no longer necessarily the principal use. The problem of the future is to determine the optimum use of water to meet regional and national needs. Difficult economic and value judgments are required. The planning process is made especially complex by the long lead times

generally necessary to provide water supply and control systems and by the difficulty of adjusting institutional constraints to change.

One of the nation's most critical problems of 1976 is that of energy, as discussed in Chapter 11. Most undeveloped energy resources in the United States are in the eleven western states. Over 70 percent of the nation's strippable coal resources are in the West; and virtually all of the nation's oil shale deposits are in Colorado, Utah, and Wyoming and contain over 600 billion barrels of extractable oil. The major uranium resources are in the Rocky Mountain states, and most of the geothermal resources are in the West. The development of these resources to meet the nation's energy needs will have great impact on the water supplies of the region and their use for irrigation. The energy problems will have other effects. Studies have shown that irrigated agriculture requires less energy for crop production than production on non-irrigated land. For instance, studies in Nebraska have demonstrated the production of a bushel of corn on irrigated land needs only 60 to 80

Irrigation assures dependable food production.

percent of the energy required to produce a bushel on non-irrigated land. Also the production of food near areas of consumption requires less energy for transportation; thus, the growth rate of the West, estimated to be over twice that of the rest of the nation for the next twenty-five years, will dictate more irrigation for agricultural production.

As stream flows decrease from irrigation use, water quality becomes of greater concern. Return flows from irrigation add nutrients from fertilizers and dissolved salts to the streams. The consumption of water for irrigation decreases the amount available to dilute salts from natural sources and pollution from urban and industrial areas.

The concern for outdoor recreation opportunities, especially related to "wild" rivers and related fish and wildlife needs, have an impact on the development of water resources in arid areas. Determining the proper balance between utilitarian, aesthetic, and fish and wildlife considerations involves value judgments which are variable and complex. There are no easy solutions; choices must be made after careful, objective analysis of all alternatives.

The worldwide food crisis of the 1970s emphasizes the productivity and dependability of irrigated argiculture. From a 1976 perspective, it appears food demands will be difficult to meet. Maximum food production is important to help fulfill world nutritional needs. In view of the large imports of petroleum products to satisfy United States energy requirements for the next several decades, food exports are also essential to maintain a proper balance of payments.

The future of irrigation in the West, and also in the humid areas of the East, requires objective analysis. Full cooperation between all government entities and the private sector will be required. The objective must be to control and manage the available water supply to best meet the nation's needs. This will require greater treatment and recycling of wastewater, control of floodwaters, development of water storage and transport facilities, and careful consideration of environmental problems.

Areas that show promise include more efficient use of water: increasing the water supply in arid areas by cloud seeding; treatment and recycling wastewaters; control of natural and man-caused salt input to streams; desalting plants where appropriate, especially where waste heat from geothermal energy or from nuclear energy plants can be utilized; and effective overall management. Water conveyance losses can be reduced, and greater efficiency in the use of water by plants can be obtained. For instance, drip irrigation where a small outlet provides water directly to the individual plant, such as in an orchard, can result in water savings of 50 percent or more. An extensive and intensive program of salts control on the Colorado River is getting underway, including control of discharges from natural and man-made salt sources and construction of a $100 million desalting plant.

Weather modification by cloud seeding has a promising potential for increasing precipitation in selected areas. Intensive research studies by the Bureau of Reclamation over a fourteen-year period have established that carefully designed cloud seeding operations can increase runoff in water-short areas, such as in the upper Colorado River drainage by 6 to 9 percent, and in the upper Rio Grande from 8 to 11 percent. The costs of the additional water are estimated at $2.50 per acre-foot ($1.50 for seeding operations and $1.00 for environmental protection and contingencies). Studies and intensive observations have shown the environmental effects of this program would be miniscule. Generally, the program would be managed to reduce the amount of shortages during low-flow years. The technology is reasonably developed, and the research program is continuing. Many social, legal, and environmental problems remain to be fully resolved. However, experience to date indicates an effective educational program coupled with involving local people in the planning process can solve most of the sociological problems.

It is expected that irrigation developments will continue, although not at the same rate as in the past. Emphasis will be on better management and more effective utilization of existing facilities and more sophisticated controls and management techniques. Government assistance will continue to be required in building up sparsely settled areas, which offer opportunities to disperse population and revitalize declining rural areas.

Many improvements will occur if stable demand and higher prices provide farmers with capital and incentives to make improvements. Large-scale development of federal irrigation projects can be expected if food shortages persist and other lower-cost, short-term measures are unable to meet demands. The intensive, multidiscipline, multiagency planning that was demonstrated by the work on the Western U. S. Water Plan, directed by the Bureau of Reclamation, shows great promise. Irrigation public works demonstrate the flexibility and adaptability of America's pluralistic society in responding to the people's needs.

SUGGESTED READINGS

Bickert, Browne, Coddington, & Associates, Inc. *The Federal Reclamation Program: Its Impacts, Issues, and Future Considerations.* Denver, 1972.

Brough, Charles H. *Irrigation in Utah.* Baltimore, 1898.

Clyde, George D. "Irrigation in the United States." American Society of Civil Engineers *Transactions,* CT (1953), 311-341.

Dickerman, Alan R.; Radosevich, George E.; and Nobe, Kenneth C. *Foundations of Federal Reclamation Policies: An Historical Review of Changing Goals and Objectives.* Fort Collins, Colorado, 1970.

Eckstein, Otto. *Water Resource Development.* Cambridge, Massachusetts, 1958.

Golze, Alfred Rudolph. *Reclamation in the United States.* 2d. ed. Caldwell, Idaho, 1961.

Harding, S.T. *Water Rights for Irrigation.* Stanford, California, 1936.

Henny, D.C. "Some Phases of Irrigation Finance." American Society of Civil Engineers *Transactions,* 92 (1928), 541-581.

Huffman, Roy E. *Irrigation Development and Public Water Policy.* New York, 1953.

Hutchins, Wells A. *Irrigation Districts, Their Organization, Operation and Financing.* U.S. Department of Agriculture Technical Bulletin 254. Washington, D.C., June 1931.

Israelsen, Orson W., and Hansen, Vaughn E. *Irrigation Principles and Practices.* 3d. ed. Logan, Utah, 1962.

Moss, Frank E. *The Water Crisis.* Washington, D.C., 1967.

Pelz, Richard K. *Federal Reclamation and Related Laws Annotated.* 3 vols. Washington, D.C., 1972.

Powell, John Wesley, *The Explorations of the Colorado River and Its Canyons.* New York, 1961. Reprint of *Canyons of the Colorado.* New York, 1895.

Select Committee on National Water Resources. *Future Needs for Reclamation in the United States.* Washington, D.C., 1960.

Smythe, William E. *The Conquest of Arid America.* New York, 1911.

Thomas, George. *Early Irrigation in the Western States.* Salt Lake City, Utah, 1948.

U.S. Congress, Senate. *National Irrigation Policy: Its Development and Significance.* 76th Cong., 1st Sess., Washington, D.C., 1939.

U.S. Department of Interior. Bureau of Reclamation. *Dams and Control Works.* 3d. ed. Washington, D.C., 1954.

——————. *Federal Reclamation Projects: Water and Land Resource Accomplishments.* Washington, D.C., annually since 1902.

——————. *Western U.S. Water Plan: 1971 Progress Report.* Washington, D.C., 1971.

_____ . *Critical Water Problems Facing the Eleven Western States*. Washington, D.C., 1975.

_____ . *Reclamation Project Data*. Washington, D.C., 1961. Supplement, 1966.

U.S. Library of Congress. Legislative Reference Service. *Reclamation: Accomplishments and Contributions*. Washington, D.C., 1959.

University of Nebraska. Bureau of Business Research. *The Economic Impact of Irrigated Agriculture on the Economy of Nebraska*. Lincoln, Nebraska, 1968.

Warne, William E. *The Bureau of Reclamation*. New York, 1972.

Washington State University. Agriculture Experiment Station. *The Economic Significance of the Columbia Basin Development*. Pullman, Washington, 1966.

CHAPTER 11

LIGHT AND POWER

Modern America depends upon low-cost energy being widely and easily available as light and power, generally in the form of electricity. Yet, the large-scale conversion of energy into light and power for man's use is a comparatively recent development, nearly all occurring since the birth of the nation. In 1900 the estimated energy utilization in the nation in all operations including electricity was about two manpower per capita; by 1976 it was over 100 manpower per capita. The increasing use of energy in providing a higher standard of living has highlighted the fact that there is a limited quantity of energy resources as well as dangers to the natural environment in using these resources. More public involvement can be expected in planning, regulation, and control, and to an increasing extent in construction and operation in order to solve the difficult and complex problems of energy consumption. Providing an optimum balance between meeting energy needs and maintaining a healthy and attractive natural environment will require understanding.

The ways that power public works have evolved are described in the following sec-

tions. The earliest energy public works were for street lighting: from candlepower, to gas, to electric-arc lights, and then to improvements leading to the sophisticated city lighting systems of 1976. The first power for work came from mechanical hookups to waterwheels, followed by the development of steam engines. The generation of electricity from falling water and steam started a revolution that is still underway. Heat for steam to turn turbines came first from wood and coal, then oil and gas; and by 1976, heat from nuclear fission was beginning to have an impact. Even greater changes are ahead as research and development continue in the areas of nuclear fusion, solar, geothermal, and other energy sources.

Although public involvement has varied widely, the common objective of furnishing the nation's people with the benefits of energy has remained constant. Since the supplying of electricity is a monopolistic type of utility because of the fixed distribution systems, there have been differences of opinion from the beginning concerning public versus private ownership of electric power facilities. A pluralistic industry has evolved and provides a competitive stimulus to make electricity available to all segments of society. Table 11-1 shows the various types of publicly and privately owned utilities involved in the generation and marketing of electricity. In one sense, with the control exercised by federal, state,

This chapter is based upon special reports prepared by the Tennessee Valley Authority, Bonneville Power Administration, Rural Electrification Administration, Federal Power Commission, and a manuscript on nuclear power prepared by James B. Gardner, APWA Bicentennial History Fellow.

TABLE 11-1
Electric Utility Statistics — 1972

Type of Utility	No. of Systems	No. of Customers (Thousands)	Kwh Generation in (Billions Kwh)	Kwh States to Ultimate Customers (Billions Kwh)	Electric Operating Revenues (Million $$)	Net Electric Plant Investment (Million $$)	Installed Capacity (Million Kw)
Systems	2,251	10,405	156.9	207.6	3,564	13,205	39.5
Investor-owned Power Companies	284	59,325	1,356.9	1,244.4	25,355	92,780	312.1
REA Systems	915	7,076	32.3	84.6	2,025	6,014	7.0
Federal Agencies	10[1]	9[2]	206.7	62.0[2]	1,072	10,119	37.3
Total	3,460	76,815	1,752.8	1,598.6	32,016	122,118	395.9

1. Five major marketing agencies.   2. Power is primarily sold wholesale.

and local government agencies on the investor-owned power systems, they are all public works.

Street Lighting

In 1776 lack of artificial light was one of the greatest handicaps to towns and cities. The main source of lighting was still the candle, which was not only expensive but inefficient. Oil burning lamps using animal or vegetable oils were in use, and some streets were poorly lit by candle lanterns. As late as 1890, an article in the Literary Digest stressed that dark city streets were associated with crime, ignorance, and sloth in city administration and pointed out that "moonlight is far too uncertain a quantity to be reckoned with in so vital a thing as street lighting. A city should be kept lighted up during the entire part of the twenty-four hours when sunlight is not available."

At the birth of the nation, over 90 percent of Americans lived and worked on farms and daylight was sufficient for their activities. They went to bed early, not only because of exhaustion from the day's hard labor, but also because artificial light was primitive and expensive, illiteracy was general, and books were few. The hours of labor might be extended with light from burning pine knots or from tallow dip.

It appears the earliest community effort to light streets was in Rome about 200 A.D., when lamps were hung from each door. By 1630 Paris had only three fixed lanterns,

although portable ones were placed on streets during periods of unrest. In 1684 London streets were lit up during fall and winter, but only on moonless nights by lighting a candle in a lantern at every tenth house. But in 1736, 15,000 oil lamps were set up throughout the city and kept burning from sunset to sunrise. By 1776 improvements were being made in types of flames from oil such as the Aagand lamp in 1783, by better wicks and enclosed oil containers, and by polished reflectors which directed light rays for more effect.

Illuminating gas was developed in the late eighteenth century by heating coal and drawing off volatile compounds. The first gas light in America was in Newport, Rhode Island, in 1812. The first American city to have a gas lighting system, and the third in the world, was Baltimore, Maryland, in 1817. This came about because of the imagination and promotional talents of Rembrandt Peale, a gifted portrait painter and amateur scientist.

Peale built a museum, and being constantly alert for new attractions, purchased and installed a "gas making machine." With effective publicity, he launched gas illumination at his museum on June 13, 1816. He quickly followed up the enthusiastic reception by organizing the Gas Light Company of Baltimore, which was chartered by the city council four days later to lay gas pipes in the city streets. A gas plant was then erected, and the first lamp was lighted at Market and Lemon streets on February 7, 1817. The present Baltimore Gas and Electric

Company is a descendant of the founding group and operates under the original franchise and charter, as amended and extended for 160 years. The company still provides street light energy and maintenance under contract to the city.

Following the success in Baltimore, gas lighting spread to other American cities—New York in 1823, Boston in 1828, New Orleans and Louisville in 1832, Philadelphia in 1836, and Washington, D.C., in 1847. Gas lights spurred competition among oil lamp businesses which greatly improved the quality and candlepower of their product. The use of whale oil as a lighting fuel increased, and whaling boomed between 1830 and 1860. New Bedford, Massachusetts, for instance, had a whaling fleet of over 300 vessels. After 1859 coal oil or kerosine from petroleum became the chief lighting fuels and remained so in rural areas until nearly the middle of the twentieth century. Even so, by 1850 there were over 300 gas light companies, with a capitalization of $50 million, providing manufactured gas to more than 5 million people.

Natural gas was first used in Fredonia, New York, in 1821, when a 1½-inch pipe driven into a gas spring provided fuel for thirty street lights for many years. However, it was not until 1858 that the first company to engage in the natural gas business was formed. In 1883 pioneer legislation placing

Peoples Gas Light and Coke Co.

A street in Chicago in 1850 when "gas lights seemed to turn night into day."

gas companies under state supervision was passed by Massachusetts. Various arrangements were made by municipal public works departments for handling street lighting by gas, ranging from public ownership of all facilities to service contracts with regulated utilities.

Use of gas for cooking did not get underway until electricity began replacing gas for lighting at the beginning of the twentieth century. By this time, the gas industry was well established. Its pipelines were already in place and connected to millions of homes and industries to provide lighting; so its conversion to a cooking and hot water heating utility, and then a space heating and energy source for industry, was able to proceed at a rapid rate. With long-distance pipeline transmission of natural gas from fields to centers of need, uses increased. The first long-distance transmission line, 126 miles, was built by the Lone Star Gas Company in 1910. In the 1940s, the "Big Inch" pipelines were constructed from the Texas gas fields to the New York area. In 1975 260,000 miles of large diameter pipelines carried natural gas to most of the nation, supplying about one third of the total energy needs. Natural gas companies were well-established public service utilities, regulated and controlled by local, state, and federal government agencies. By 1975 there were 950 municipal and other local publicly owned gas systems serving 10 million people in communities throughout the nation and providing about 5 percent of the nation's total use. The remainder was furnished by investor-owned utilities with over 1.5 million stockholders.

Benjamin Franklin's kite experiment demonstrated the identity of electricity and lightning in 1752. It was followed by many important developments leading to the use of electricity by Davy's arc lamp in 1812; the first crude incandescent lamps about 1845; and Thomas A. Edison's development of the first practical incandescent electric lamps in 1878. The main initial use of electricity was for municipal street lighting. As the use of electricity grew, so did public utilities.

America's first electric street lights appear to have been twelve carbon arc lights

Con Edison Co. of New York

The dynamo room of the nation's first central electricity generating station at Pearl Street in New York City. Operations began in 1882.

erected in 1877 by Charles F. Bush around a public square in Cleveland; although Moses G. Farmer had exhibited three huge glaring arc lights at the Philadelphia Exposition in 1876. San Francisco adopted the new technology for city public illumination in 1880, using Bush company equipment. New York erected arc lights on Broadway in 1880, and the first electric arc street lights were installed in Philadelphia in 1881. When New York's first central generating system was placed in service at the Pearl Street station in late 1882—having a steam-powered generator serving 5,500 lamps—a new era in street lighting was begun.

In 1882 there were four municipally owned electric systems in operation to provide electricity for street lighting. Ten years later, the number had increased to 235, and electricity was beginning to be extended for residential use in cities as well as for street lighting. In 1887 the Common Council of the City of Detroit was considering whether to own and operate an electric arc lighting system, to rent a system, or to contract for lights. It appointed a special committee to report on the problem, and its secretary, Fred H. Whipple, made a national survey and report of the street lighting practices of the day. His study was so well received that he

published the information in a book in 1888. He surveyed 147 cities that used the contract or rental systems and found a wide variance of costs and extent of service. Typical examples follow:

Washington, D.C. 87 public lamps—burn all night every night—cost 65 cents per night each. Lamp on poles, wires underground—yearly contract.

Wichita, Kansas. 75 lights—located at street intersections—burn until midnight—costs $100 per year each. Also use 120 gas lamps and 300 gasoline lamps.

Chattanooga, Tennessee. 30 lights burning all night—cost 33 cents per night—2-year contract.

Ogden, Utah. 18 lights at street intersections, 673 feet apart in the business section—cost $133 per year each.

Sacramento, California. 36 intersection lights, burn all night except on moonlight nights—cost $252 per light per year—2-year contract—overhead wires—city also has 193 gas lights.

Whipple then surveyed the cities with municipally owned systems and reported strong support for this approach. Most cities claimed that large savings, as much as 50 percent, resulted from municipal ownership. He reported that the cities considered lights as a monopoly-type utility in the same category as water, and that one was "as much a government question as the other." He concluded that the problem of public versus private ownership "will undoubtedly soon become, if not already, a leading topic in municipal ethics." The dynamo and light systems of the twenty leading manufacturers were described in his book and presented a bewildering array of equipment. He warned the common council, however, that "it may be considered as practically certain that whatever be the system put in, patent litigation will be likely to follow." It took many years for patent rights on the various systems to be clearly established.

Public power originally meant city power. In 1902 there were 851 municipally owned electric systems in the United States, mostly small, isolated hydroelectric or steam plants. By 1924 the number reached 3,047. Thereafter, the number declined somewhat as investor-owned utilities constructed larger generating units and, with interconnected transmission, were able to provide low-cost energy from larger, more efficient systems. It is also probable that the financial and political influence of the private owner companies was an important factor in the decline in the numbers of municipal systems in the 1920s. As shown in Table 11-1, in 1972 the number of locally owned systems was 2,251.

The development of street lighting in Chicago was similar to that in many other cities, although Chicago had more lights than most. Its electric street lighting began in 1887 when lights were placed on the Chicago River bridges. Power was supplied by city-owned steam electric generating stations. Then Chicago's World Columbian Exposition of 1893, with its "Great White Way," stimulated electric street lighting throughout the country. In 1907 more economical electricity became available from the city's water-driven generators at Lockport, Illinois; and the following year, 8,200 arc lamps replaced one half of the city's 50,000 gasoline and oil lamps. Metallized carbon and long-burning flame arc lamps were introduced in 1912, with tungsten incandescent lamps following in 1914. During subsequent years, a series of bond issues were approved for new and improved lighting. In 1932 Chicago had 93,374 electric street

lights, the largest municipal system in the world. From 1947 to 1965, a $130 million alley lighting program was completed; and during one six-month period, 45,000 lights were installed.

Over the years, additional improvements in street lighting facilities have been made, with mercury vapor lamps and then high

U.S. Bureau of Reclamation

Modern street lighting is illustrated by this night view in Billings, Montana.

pressure sodium lamps. These two types by 1975 were generally standard. Street lighting is usually managed by the traffic divisions of municipal public works departments, since it is related closely to traffic control and the movement and safety of vehicles.

Water Power

Flowing water to turn wheels was utilized by the earliest settlements as a source of power. These early water power projects were mostly in New England, along the streams where the power was used directly at the site, for grist and saw mills. Towns such as Lowell and Lawrence, Massachusetts, and Manchester, New Hampshire, grew up around such mill sites.

About 1850 turbines, such as the one developed by James B. Francis, began to replace the old overshot and breastwater wheels; and water was brought by canals to the point where power was to be used. The developing factory system required greater amounts of power resulting in still larger developments, built mainly on a cooperative basis. However, water power lagged after 1860, for suitable sites within the limitations of mechanical power transmission were scarce. Furthermore, the more flexible steam engines were being improved in both dependability and economy.

Rensselaer Polytechnic Institute

The 20-foot-wide, 60-foot-diameter overshot water wheel, built in, 1853 to operate Troy (New York) Iron Works, was in service until 1898.

With the advent of electricity in the 1880s and the alternating current transmission of it developed by George Westinghouse, the flexibility and adaptability of electric power became apparent. The nation's first hydroelectric plant was built at Appleton, Wisconsin, in 1882 and produced 12.5 kilowatts from a direct current generator driven by a small vertical turbine. A major technological achievement occurred on June 3, 1889, when the Willamette Falls Electric Company transmitted electricity by direct current from the falls at Oregon City to Portland, Oregon, 14 miles away, to power a street lighting circuit.

Developments followed rapidly. In 1891 the Montana Power Company plant at Great Falls on the Missouri River went on the line. In 1892 electricity at 10,000 volts was transmitted 14 miles to Pomona, California. In 1895 the Folsom Water Power Company in California supplied Sacramento with power over a 22-mile, 11,000-volt line. Most of the early hydro plants were small and served a very limited locality.

The first large hydroelectric installation in the United States started operation at Niagara Falls in 1895, when three 3,728-kilowatt generators began producing electric current at 2,200 volts. The development was the beginning of a private versus public power fight which remained a political issue in New York for over half a century. Ultimately, in 1963 Niagara hydropower was fully developed, consistent with the preservation of the scenic value of the falls, by the Power Authority of the State of New York.

In October 1904, the City of Seattle put its two city-owned, 1,200-kilowatt generators on the line. Discussions were beginning concerning hydropower at Muscle Shoals, a 37-mile rapidly falling stretch of the Tennessee River in Alabama. This too became a battleground of public versus private power and later became the nucleus of the Tennessee Valley Authority.

The public versus private power development controversy has been long and bitter, but in recent years, it has become rather generally accepted that each has its place and that the full resources of both are needed to meet power needs. For example, the cooperative programs developed in the Northwest and in the Missouri River Basin demonstrate the successful workings of America's pluralistic system. The combination of private and public enterprise that has produced the supply of low-cost electric power across the country represents the best of the nation's technological workings.

The generation of electricity from falling water is unlike the production of power from coal or other fuels. It is clean and non-polluting. Water is a renewable natural resource—inexhaustible in nature in its continuous solar energy cycle from the sea, to the air, to the ground, and back again to the sea. Water out of control is destructive; most of the natural catastrophe damage comes from flood waters. Controlled, it becomes a servant of man.

Most modern water resource projects involve more than one state and require local, state, and federal agreement for development. Water power in all its aspects is not limited to the site of generation but extends to the area where the water begins its flow to the sea. Upstream water storage, both natural and manmade, is directly related to the supply of power to be spun from downstream turbines and generators. For example, a lake in one state and reservoir in another may be the water source for hydropower developed in still another state; and the electric current may be distributed over several states through interconnecting transmission systems. Thus, federal involvement comes naturally.

From the founding of the republic, it was generally considered that the Constitution gave the federal government jurisdiction over the navigable waters of the United States. There existed some doubt as to the extent of this jurisdiction, even though the Supreme Court's *Gibbons v. Ogden* decision in 1824 established the power of Congress to regulate interstate commerce on navigable streams. Provisions in the 1889 Rivers and Harbors Act established federal government control of structures on navigable waters by requiring review of plans, by the secretary of the army through the Corps of Engineers, of any dam, bridge, or similar facility in navigable waters to assure against unreasonable obstructions to navigation. In 1901 Congress passed a bill giving the secretary of interior the power to grant rights-of-way over public lands for water power plants, dams, reservoirs, and transmission lines. These actions were of a regulatory nature.

By the 1902 Reclamation Act, the federal government became directly involved in the production of hydroelectric energy through its commitment to irrigation in the arid West. The stored waters behind western dams, which were the storage and control facilities for irrigation and flood control, needed only the ingenuity of the engineer and the approval of the public to make them significant producers of electricity. Hydroelectric power from an irrigation project storage reservoir was planned in 1903. By the 1906 Town Sites and Power Development Act, Congress stipulated that, whenever a power development was necessary for the irrigation of lands under a reclamation project or an opportunity was afforded for a power development under a project, any surplus power or power privilege could be leased for a period of not more than ten years, giving preference to municipal purposes, provided that the lease would not impair the efficiency of the irrigation project.

A regulatory milestone was passed in 1905 when the Forest Service was transferred to the Department of Agriculture, and the secretary of that department began issuing permits up to fifty-year periods for rights-of-way in national forests for the generation and transmission of electricity from falling water. The fee system established for developers was nominal, and right-of-way permits were granted as a matter of course. Power sites were routinely awarded by Congress to private power interests. Efforts made to coordinate the many different uses of public lands and waters to accomplish comprehensive development in the overall public interest had little success.

A step toward correcting this situation was taken in 1906 with the passage of the General Dam Act. It stated that, when federal permission was granted to construct a dam for water power or any other purpose on any navigable waterway, the plans and specifications for the dam and all accessory works had to be submitted to the secretary of war for approval. The secretary could require conditions to protect navigation for the present and future interests of the nation. A 1910 amendment to this legislation required that in acting on the plans submitted, the secretary "shall consider the bearing of said structure upon a comprehensive plan for the improvement of the waterway over which it is to be constructed with a view to the promotion of water power."

President Theodore Roosevelt in his message to Congress in 1908 had called attention to the importance of the nation's water power and urged Congress to provide for its regulation in the public interest. In his speech, he said:

We are now at the beginning of a great development in water power. Its use through electric transmission is entering more and more largely into every element of the daily life of the people. The present policy pursued in making these grants is unwise in giving away the property of the people in the flowing waters to individuals or organizations practically unknown, and granting in perpetuity these valuable privileges in advance of the formulation of definite plans for their use.

The 1909 Rivers and Harbors Act directed the

Army Corps of Engineers to plan hydropower and other multipurpose features into waterway improvement projects.

By 1912 a major congressional battle was taking place between legislators representing private power interests and conservationists favoring public ownership. It was touched off by an omnibus water bill that would have authorized the construction of seventeen major dam projects with no provision for regulation by the federal government. President William Taft, however, vetoed the bill.

The special problems of the arid West, whose needs for water were unlike those in the East, resulted in different concepts concerning the use of water as discussed in Chapter 10. A conference of nine western governors in 1914 focused attention on each state's claim to all water within its boundary. Several bills were introduced in Congress over the next few years by contending interests, but none was able to pass both houses. For it was a period of searching to determine the appropriate way for government to facilitate and control the development of water power resources, consistent with overall water use needs.

In 1920 a Wilson Administration bill was introduced calling for federal regulation of the construction of water power projects on navigable waters, public lands, forest reserves, and government dams. There was by then a growing awareness that the nation's development of its resources was inadequate for a growing population and economy. Coupled with this was the strong desire for effective water power regulation so the full public interest would be protected. After compromises, a bill was passed by both houses and signed by President Woodrow Wilson on June 11, 1920. This was the Federal Water Power Act (now Part I of the Federal Power Act), which among other things created the Federal Power Commission and established as national policy the principle of federal regulation of non-federal water power projects to assist with the orderly development of the nation's water resources.

When Congress authorized the Army Corps of Engineers' entry into the field of flood control in 1917, it required hydroelectric power potential to be considered along with flood control. In the corps' "308" river basin reports in the late 1920s and early 1930s (discussed in Chapter 9) the hydroelectric potential was an important part of the studies.

In the meantime, several hydropower developments were made in connection with federal irrigation projects. The 1909 Rivers and Harbors Act also authorized the acquisition of an existing water power plant on the St. Mary's River in Michigan. This was done to provide water flow control for navigation between Lake Superior and Lake Huron. The four 450-kilowatt generators were utilized only when such use did not interfere with the navigation requirements. The construction of Wilson Dam, begun in 1918 by the Army Corps of Engineers to harness Muscle Shoals on the Tennessee River in order to produce power for the manufacture of munitions, brought the federal government still further into hydroelectric power operations.

U.S. Bureau of Reclamation

Hoover Dam on the Colorado River, completed in 1935, was the first large federal multipurpose water resource project.

Federal government entry into hydroelectric development accelerated with the 1928 Boulder Canyon Project Act, which authorized construction of the unprecedented multipurpose Hoover Dam on the Colorado River. This was followed by the large multipurpose river developments, with major electric power installations initiated by various federal laws during the Depression. These included such projects as Grand Coulee and Bonneville dams on the Columbia, Shasta Dam in California, Fort Peck Dam on the Missouri, and the Tennessee Valley Authority developments.

Franklin D. Roosevelt, delivering a campaign speech in the Northwest on September 12, 1932, focused national attention on federal development of hydroelectric power, touched on the controversies, and heralded developments to come. In the speech, the future President declared:

> The next great hydroelectric development to be undertaken by the federal government must be that on the Columbia River. This vast water power means cheap manufacturing production, economy and comfort on the farm and in the household. Your problem with regard to this great power is similar to our problem in the state of New York with regard to the power development of the St. Lawrence River. Here you have the clear picture of four great government power developments in the United States—the St. Lawrence River in the Northeast, Muscle Shoals in the Southeast, the Boulder [Hoover] Dam project in the Southwest, and the Columbia River in the Northwest. And from there, my friends, in each of the four quarters of the United States, there will exist forever a national yardstick to prevent extortion against the public and to encourage the wider uses of that servant of the American people—electric power . . .

These projects are generally considered the most spectacular public works of the nation's history.

The following discussions of selected river basin programs show the development of hydroelectric power, its relation to fossil fuel steam power, and the transition into nuclear power developments. They demonstrate that public works programs do adapt to meet the needs of a growing population with an improving standard of living. They also illustrate the value of full multipurpose utilization of the nation's water resources. The process has involved a continuing interplay of a wide array of economic, social, and multi-institutional forces.

Tennessee River Basin

Years of controversy over the hydroelectric development of Muscle Shoals focused national attention on the Tennessee River. Several attempts to obtain licenses for private development either failed to get through Congress or met presidential veto. The beginning of World War I precipitated action when Congress in 1916 authorized the

Tennessee Valley Authority

Wilson Dam and powerhouse was completed in 1925 to harness the power of Muscle Shoals on the Tennessee River. The navigation lock is at upper left.

project for the dual purpose of improving navigation and providing electricity for production of nitrates for munitions. Construction of the Wilson Dam, power plant, and locks was begun in 1918 by the Army Corps of Engineers; and the first eight generating units, with a total capacity of 184,000 kilowatts, began operation in 1925.

After the war, there was a continuing debate regarding disposal of the government nitrate plants and Wilson Dam and powerhouse. As the plants were designed to produce fertilizer in peacetime, the various proposals were acted upon by the Senate Committee on Agriculture and Forestry, chaired by Senator George W. Norris of Nebraska. A stern advocate of conservation and public power, Norris opposed various attempts by private interests to obtain public property at little cost. His bill to provide for public operation of the Muscle Shoals development was vetoed by President Calvin Coolidge in 1928. A similar bill was passed by Congress in 1930 but was vetoed by President Herbert Hoover. With the full backing and support of President Roosevelt, the act creating the Tennessee Valley Authority (TVA) was passed and signed into law in May 1933. The characteristics of the river basin and the flood control features of this region-wide, multipurpose project are described in Chapter 9 and the navigation features in Chapter 2.

The objective of the TVA Act was to provide for the economic and social development of the region through the coordinated use of basic resources. Low-cost power was considered to be one of the best instruments to achieve the program's goals. It had been stated of the Tennessee Valley that all it needed was "energy and the intelligence to use it wisely." Energy wisely used, similar to other needs assisted by public works, contributes substantially to creating and sustaining a strong economic and physical base on which the conservation of human resources is founded. In 1933 in the Tennessee Valley region, electricity was scarce, expensive, and little used. After the resource development programs of TVA got underway, however, electricity became abundant, less costly, and a widely used tool for improvement. How this

change came about is a demonstration of unified resource development by public works through successful cooperation between people and their various agencies of government.

A valuable opportunity in developing the Tennessee River was the large amount of waterpower that could be harnessed by the same dams that provided flood control and navigation benefits. Congress had obtained the "308" Army Corps of Engineers' studies showing this potential before it passed the law creating TVA. The studies estimated that 3 million kilowatts of electricity could be supplied from a system of dams on the Tennessee and its tributaries. This amount was several times greater than the available power supply in the Tennessee Valley at that time. Thus, there was an opportunity to bring low-cost electricity to millions of people in several states, including rural families who still used oil lamps.

While dams were being built, TVA's power program was begun. It started with the 189,000 kilowatts of generating capacity provided by Wilson Dam, which was made a part of the TVA system under the initiating legislation. But the program faced tremendous opposition. Announcement of TVA's electric rate schedules in 1933 met with predictions that they were too low to succeed. There was not a market for TVA power, the critics said, because the region was already amply supplied.

City after city voted to buy and distribute TVA power. Only a few were able to participate, however, for most were unable to purchase the existing privately owned distribution systems. Tupelo, Mississippi, with a publicly owned system, became TVA's first customer early in 1934. The same year, in Alcorn County, Mississippi, the first rural electric cooperative began functioning; and Tupelo distributed TVA power to 1,335 customers. The first TVA annual report said: "The new rates placed in effect under the contract resulted in savings of approximately 55 percent to residential customers, 58 percent to commercial customers, and 48 percent to industrial customers. The rate reductions stimulated a marked and almost instantaneous increase in the demand for electricity and for electrical appliances." Electricity consumption rose rapidly, and it was soon demonstrated that a locally owned system could distribute TVA power at low rates and still keep out of the red.

Tupelo became a proving ground. With the coming of abundant, low-cost electricity, the drudgery of home life could be relieved. After the first full year of TVA power, the number of residential customers had increased 30 percent; and the average saving per kilowatt-hour was about four and a half cents, from a cost of a little over seven cents to about two and a half cents. It was a good beginning and a demonstration to the entire country that electricity could become a useful human and economic development tool if it could be made widely available at a reasonable cost. In most of the region, however, lawsuits and injunctions by power companies and their supporters impeded the wide use of TVA power. The Ashwander Case, which reached the United States Supreme Court in early 1936, upheld the constitutionality of public power sales from Wilson Dam.

While TVA and the valley awaited that decision, other events were occurring. Private power companies adopted an "objective rate plan," with the result that rates went down and electricity consumption and the profits of the private electric utilities went up. The TVA helped rural and farm people organize cooperatives, which signaled a new contest. In a final court action of the eighteen companies' challenge of the TVA Act, the constitutionality of the act was upheld. This decision and the report of a specially appointed Joint Investigating Committee of Congress early in 1939 opened the way for the TVA power program. In August of the same year, negotiations were concluded for purchase of the electric properties of the Tennessee Electric Power Company. The purchasers were TVA, twenty-two municipalities, and eleven rural cooperatives. With this purchase, TVA became the supplier of power for an integrated service area in which it could develop and carry out the congressional objectives of widespread use of electricity at low rates.

However, a new challenge arose almost at once, as World War II took over the shaping of TVA and its role. Two weeks after the Tennessee Electric Power Company purchase, Hitler marched into Poland. President Roosevelt set the highly improbable goal, later to be greatly exceeded, of building 50,000 airplanes a year. Electric power was crucial. The aluminum plants in the valley were kept

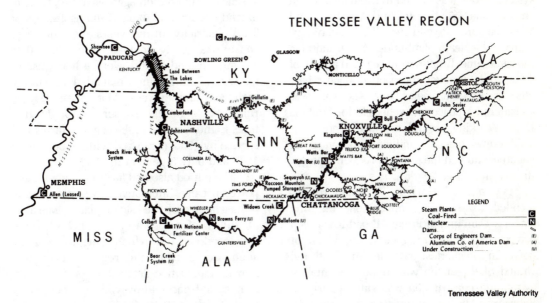

Tennessee Valley region in 1975 showing the multipurpose dams and reservoirs and the steam power plants, both coal-fired and nuclear.

running at capacity. But war production demanded more power, and TVA planned and organized to provide it. Its groundwork, both in resource development and in organization, enabled it to shift smoothly and quickly to support the nation's defense. With seven years' experience, TVA's engineering and construction organization was ready for the task. Under TVA operations, construction was carried out by forces directly on the agency's payrolls. This organization thus was able to program a series of construction projects with minimum time and effort and with well-trained crews.

In 1940 four new dams were in operation on the mainstream, and three more were under construction. Two tributary storage dams were completed, increasing power output at all the downstream dams. Cherokee Dam on the Holston River and Watts Bar Steam Plant were undertaken on emergency schedules. Cherokee Dam was built in less than sixteen months. (Norris Dam, the first construction project, had taken three and a half years.) On December 5, 1941, Cherokee Reservoir began to fill.

Two days later, the Japanese bombed Pearl Harbor and the United States was at war. By then TVA had four additional dams under construction on the Hiwassee River system. Work was started in rapid succession on Fontana, South Holston, Douglas, and Watauga dams. By mid 1942, TVA had twelve dams and a steam plant under construction at the same time. Employment reached a peak of 42,000, a total never approached since. Many other records were set. Five or six years was considered a peacetime schedule for Fontana Dam. Working around the clock, however, TVA crews placed 3 million cubic yards of concrete and had the project producing power in less than three years.

Before Pearl Harbor, TVA had recommended, over strong opposition, building Douglas Dam on the French Broad River as a project that could produce a big block of power in the shortest possible time. With the United States in the war, opposition melted away; and construction was started early in February 1942. Twelve months and seventeen days later, the gates dropped into place and

water storage began; a month later the dam was producing power. In 1939 the TVA system had produced less than 2 billion kilowatt-hours of electric power; in 1945 it generated nearly 12 billion.

In 1942 the huge, mysterious Manhattan project got underway in the hills of eastern Tennessee, with the new city of Oak Ridge being built around it. Then, on August 6, 1945, the first atomic bomb was dropped on Hiroshima signalling the end of World War II. Shortly thereafter, when the mystery of Oak Ridge was made public, it was revealed that one of the major reasons for locating the atomic plant in the Tennessee Valley was the availability of dependable electric power.

Wartime restrictions on manpower and materials were lifted. Rapid construction had expanded the power resources and brought the navigation and flood control features of the basic multipurpose reservoir system to near completion. For a brief period, TVA critics, noting that 75 percent of TVA power had been devoted to war efforts, raised the old battle cry of 1933. They claimed to again see a valley region vastly oversupplied with power. But this was short-lived as the peacetime use of electricity soon surpassed wartime demands.

Local municipal and cooperative electric systems embarked on aggressive programs to extend service and expand the usefulness of TVA electricity. In five years, the number of consumers nearly doubled, from 600,000 to 1.1 million, and so did average home use of electricity. Rural lines extended down the highways and byways. More than 311,000 rural people got electric service for the first time. Eighty percent of the region's farms had service by 1950, compared with 28 percent in 1945 and only 3 percent in 1933.

The period also had its crisis. When more power became imperative, TVA proposed to build a large coal-fired steam plant, since most of the region's waterpower had been developed and that which remained was not adequate to meet the region's economic growth. Opposition delayed action for a time. Congress finally approved the necessary funds, and in 1949 TVA commenced construction of the Johnsonville Steam Plant.

The need for electric power for defense dominated the period after 1950. The Atomic Energy Commission asked TVA and a group of private power companies which formed Electric Energy, Inc., to build new steam plants and jointly supply a new atomic plant at Paducah, Kentucky. The TVA continued to serve the Oak Ridge complex. Between 1950 and 1957, the atomic plants and other federal installations multiplied their use of TVA power over fifteenfold, from less than 2 billion kilowatt-hours per year to about 32 billion—almost double the electric energy used in New York City and well over half of TVA's entire output.

The potential for further hydroelectric projects in the valley was small compared to the rapid growth of these and other power demands. How to supply this need for power became an urgent problem. When Congress failed to provide appropriations for a new TVA steam plant, an amendment to permit the agency to issue electric power bonds was proposed. However, it was sidetracked by other proposals coming from outside TVA.

By 1954 TVA's generating capacity had increased to 6 million kilowatts. For the first year, generation of electricity by TVA coal-fired steam plants exceeded hydro generation. With the region's power requirements continuing to grow, TVA stepped up the building of coal-fired plants to meet additional power needs. Coal was the logical fuel for steam-electric generation, since it was an abundant resource in and near the region. That year was noteworthy for other reasons—TVA entered into an agreement with the Atomic Energy Commission providing for a study by TVA of the methods, feasibility, and economics of producing electricity from atomic energy. The annual report for 1954 stated that the results of the study "encourage the hope that nuclear power plants may in the not-too-distant future provide power competitively with coal-burning plants."

Congress in 1959 passed an amendment to the TVA Act authorizing the sale of electric power bonds to the public. No longer dependent on appropriations from Congress for the necessary funds, the TVA power system was free to orderly plan and build adequate power facilities on a dependable schedule to keep pace with the growing use of electricity. The amendment also included new requirements for payments to the United States Treasury, to continue repaying the previous appropriation investments in the power system and to provide an established return or dividend on that investment. It also placed a limit on the area to be served by the TVA power system, which had not changed substantially since the mid 1940s.

As the 1950s ended, TVA was generating nearly 60 billion kilowatt-hours annually—four times as much as when the decade began. The average residential use of TVA electricity had tripled, from 3,000 to nearly 9,000 kilowatt-hours per home, more than twice the national average. As use grew, the average residential rate dropped to about one cent a kilowatt-hour, less than half the national average.

Tennessee Valley Authority

TVA's Browns Ferry Nuclear Powerplant, constructed from 1967 to 1975, has three 1.15-million-kilowatt units.

The use of electricity continued to grow at a rapid pace during the 1960s. The number of electric customers in the region passed the 2 million mark. Well over a half-million homes were heated electrically, about 30 percent of all homes in the region. Average residential use reached 14,000 kilowatt-hours a year, still double the national average. The homes and farms of the region in 1970 used nearly 200 times as much electricity as they had in 1933 when TVA operations began. Continuing growth in the region's consumption of electricity required increases in the generating capacity of about a million kilowatts a year. In 1967 TVA started construction of the world's largest thermal power plant—Browns Ferry Nuclear Plant in north Alabama, with a capacity of nearly 3.5 million kilowatts in three units.

The growing size of power facilities required more vigorous efforts to deal with the environmental effects of operations. Increasing demands for coal and the development of giant earth-moving machinery resulted in expanded strip mining nationally. The TVA established demonstrations of strip-mine reclamation methods, and it urged passage of effective state reclamation laws. In 1965 it began including a requirement in its contracts that mine operations supplying strip-mined coal for TVA minimize the initial undesirable effects of this activity and reclaim and revegetate the stripped areas—even though in states where TVA bought fuel, about four fifths of the strip-mined coal was going to other purchasers. By 1970 all of these states had some type of strip-mining regulation laws.

To maintain air quality around its coal-burning plants, TVA designed generating units built in the 1960s to include electrostatic fly ash collectors. It also began adding them to earlier plants that had less efficient mechanical collectors. New plants were equipped with stacks up to 1,000 feet tall to avoid potentially harmful concentrations of furnace emissions at ground level. In cooperation with the national air pollution control programs, TVA began installing experimental equipment at two plants to test processes for removing sulfur dioxide from furnace gases.

In 1967 the long-time downward trend in the region's average residential electric rate turned upward. Rapidly rising costs for fuel, interest, labor, and materials forced TVA and the local power distributors to begin increasing their rates. In 1973 TVA power sales totaled over 100 billion kilowatt-hours for the first time—about 50 percent more than in 1963 and four times as much as in 1953. The added use of electricity had made possible more efficient service at lower cost per kilowatt-hour. But the large demand for electricity also produced new problems in maintaining a reliable power supply, at a cost

the consumer could afford, while meeting the stringent environmental protection standards established for the 1970s. To meet the growing demand, TVA, like other electric power utilities, plans generating plants eight to ten years ahead of the time they will be needed.

While there are still reserves of coal, oil, and gas in the earth, they are being used at a rate that makes it essential to develop new sources of energy. Nuclear power will be an important source for the future; but uranium reserves will be depleted in a matter of decades without a more efficient way of using them. A new kind of nuclear fission reactor, the fast breeder, offers the hope of extending the uranium supply for centuries. By 1974 development of the breeder reactor in the United States had reached the point where the next step was to build a full-scale prototype power plant. The first such plant in this country will be built on the TVA system at a site near Oak Ridge. It will be a demonstration project sponsored by the Energy Research and Development Administration and the electric power industry. The TVA and the investor-owned Commonwealth Edison Company have jointly established an organization to build and operate the plant. The project is expected to begin producing electricity in 1982.

Beyond the fast breeder is the prospect of generating electricity through thermonuclear fusion. Other possibilities for future energy supply lie in the synthetic production of crude oil and gas from coal, and solar energy. The TVA is supporting research in nearly all energy fields, both on its own and through its membership in the national Electric Power Research Institute.

A race has begun nationally between power demand and power supply, and no region is immune from the probability of serious power shortage problems. One approach in meeting the growth in power demands is to curb the growth itself. There are ways to save on power consumption, and TVA and local power systems in the valley are conducting campaigns to encourage more efficient use of electricity. Voluntary power conservation can provide only part of the answer to power supply problems, since there is a limit to the reductions in use that can be

TABLE 11-2
TVA Power System—Generating Capacity

Type of Capacity	March 31, 1974		Planned 1984	
	Capacity in Megawatts	% of Capacity	Capacity in Megawatts	% of Capacity
Hydroelectric	4,469	19	5,999	13
Coal-fired	17,750	76	17,750	38
Combustion turbines	1,097	5	1,097	2
Nuclear	—	—	21,501	47
Total	23,316	100	46,347	100

readily made. In the Tennessee Valley region, power demands continue to grow despite more efficient use and strong incentives for conservation resulting from highly publicized electric rate increases. The 1974 and planned 1985 TVA power system capacity is shown in Table 11-2.

By 1975 TVA power revenues approached $1 billion per year. The funds were used to repay federal government power costs with interest, to make payments in lieu of taxes to local entities of government, to pay interest on retirement of TVA bonds, and to provide for further development of the power system. Power generated in 1975 was about 110 billion kilowatt-hours.

The TVA Act provided for the production of fertilizer from the plants at Muscle Shoals and established the National Fertilizer Center. It not only has produced fertilizer for the valley, but it has taken the lead in research and development of fertilizers nationwide. The increased agricultural production from the use of these fertilizers in the Tennessee Valley attracted world attention. Plants licensed to use TVA-developed processes are located throughout the country and in many other nations. Cooperative farm and industry demonstrations are also a part of the program.

The recreation areas around the lakes created by the TVA dams have been showcases of the nation. In 1974, for example, over 61 million recreation visits were recorded at TVA lakes. Fish and wildlife facilities tied to a sound land use program are highlights of the

success story as are the forestry management activities.

New challenges steadily unfold to dictate the role of TVA in a changing society. The emphasis and methods in its public works resource development program have met new challenges far more complex than the urgent and obvious needs of the 1930s. But the planned, unified approach to resource development and use, with flexibility to adjust to changing conditions, is still the key to the TVA program. It demonstrates the positive results that accrue from competent, dedicated effort in providing for the needs of people— the basic purpose of public works.

Columbia River Basin

From the beginning of settlement, the Columbia River has been considered a challenging water power, irrigation water, and navigation resource. It also was a flood threat. The Columbia drains 259,000 square miles of territory—220,000 in the northwestern section of the United States and 39,000 in Canada. Its average yearly flow of 195,000 cubic feet per second makes it one of the world's largest rivers. And its hydroelectric potential of about 50 million kilowatts, half of which was developed by 1975, makes it North America's largest hydroelectric power resource.

The new United States Reclamation Service first investigated the possibility of irrigating areas along the Columbia in 1904, utilizing power developed by the river to pump water out of the canyon onto the highlands. Local leaders began promoting an irrigation and power project which, with the strong support of the Washington State's Columbia Basin Survey Commission over thirty years later, resulted in Grand Coulee Dam and the related Columbian Basin Irrigation Project. The Army Corps of Engineers' "308" report of 1931 recommended a ten-dam comprehensive plan including irrigation, flood control, power, and navigation with Grand Coulee Dam as the uppermost in the chain and Bonneville Dam as the key downstream project. The Bureau of Reclamation's detailed review of this report resulted in National Industrial Recovery Act funds being provided for Grand Coulee Dam by President Roosevelt in 1933.

The history of the promotion of this project is an interesting one. Spearheaded by Rufus Wood, publisher of the Wenatchee *Daily World,* and the Columbia River Development League, the publicity for the project evoked the full gamut of public reaction. An eastern congressman declared: "Grand Coulee is a vast area of gloomy tablelands interspersed with deep gullies . . . there is no one in the region to sell power to except rattlesnakes, coyotes, and rabbits." This viewpoint prevailed and was widely accepted until the power from Grand Coulee Dam became the cornerstone of the World War II effort in the Northwest.

The Depression and the need for jobs by the unemployed; Roosevelt's interest in public power as a "yardstick"; Washington's Senator Clarence C. Dill's personal promotional efforts with the President; and the desire to arouse the nation with imaginative challenging public works combined to get the development of the Columbia underway. The initial program was only for the Grand Coulee Dam; the irrigation features were to come later. The studies provided for a dam on the river that would generate power for the pumping of the irrigation water into the Grand Coulee, some 310 feet above the dam, and from there distribute it to project lands extending 130 miles to the south. It was started as a staged project, initially to be a low dam with power generation only; with provisions to later raise the dam, provide pumps and facilities for water storage in the Grand Coulee, and build

hundreds of miles of canals to irrigate about a million acres of desert lands. After construction of the dam had begun in August 1934, the plans were changed to complete the dam and powerhouse in one stage, with the irrigation features to follow repayment contract negotiations with the irrigators.

The 530-foot-high dam—4,173 feet long, containing over 10.5 million cubic yards of concrete—is still the world's largest concrete structure. It is a gravity dam, depending upon the weight of the concrete for stability. A spillway, 1,650 feet long, is designed to pass a million cubic feet of water per second over the center portion of the dam. The two powerhouses, one on each side of the canyon, contain eighteen 108,500-kilowatt generators. Part of the power generated is used to pump the irrigation water into the storage reservoir, and the remainder is sold to repay project costs. At the time of completion, the generating units were the world's largest, as was the power plant with a capacity of almost 12 million kilowatts. Before the plant was finished, the need for power in the Northwest resulted in the temporary diversion of two 75,000-kilowatt units, manufactured for Shasta Dam in California, to the project for operation while the Grand Coulee permanent units were still being manufactured.

The construction of Grand Coulee Dam gave a tremendous boost to the region's economy. Men who needed jobs found them at the dam site, and almost every building trade was represented among the more than 7,000 workers. From the beginning of construction in 1933 through the end of the decade, not only the Pacific Northwest but nearly every section of the country benefited from the massive public works program involved in the building of the giant Columbia River dams and the network of high voltage transmission lines and substations required to transmit their power.

Since the installation of the last of the initial power units in 1951, the characteristics of the widely fluctuating river flow have changed with controlled flow provided by dams in the upper reaches of the river in the United States and in Canada. Also the power demands have increased to where steam

Grand Coulee Dam on the Columbia River. The third powerhouse with 3.9 million kilowatt capacity, at left center, began producing power in 1975.

plants will soon be furnishing the baseload for the region, so hydropower can best be used for peak loads.

Construction of a third power plant got underway at Grand Coulee in 1968 by excavating the cliff at the right end of the main dam and extending the dam to an L shape. The first stage, including three 600,000-kilowatt units and three 700,000-kilowatt units, will be completed in 1978; and construction for six more 700,000-kilowatt units is planned to begin soon thereafter. The power plant, with the irrigation pumps converted to pump-generator units, will then total about 10 million kilowatts, which will again make Grand Coulee the world's largest hydropower plant. However, plans are already in preparation for larger installations on rivers in South America and Russia.

Oregonians had been urging the construction of Bonneville Dam at the upstream tidal influence on the Columbia for navigation and flood control as well as for power generation. It was also authorized as a Public Works Administration project soon after Grand Coulee, and the Army Corps of Engineers was designated as the government agency to construct and operate the project. It includes a 70-foot-high dam and spillway, a powerhouse with ten main units which have a total capacity of 518,000 kilowatts, a navigation lock, fish-passage facilities, and various public use developments. A second powerhouse is planned which will add another 335,000 kilowatts.

An average of 3,000 workers was employed during the construction of Bonneville Dam. Another 4,000 or more were employed in providing portland cement, steel, lumber, generators, and other materials for the dam. The economic impact on the area was impressive; the cost of over $83 million placed new money into the economy. The first generator began commercial power production on July 9, 1938, when the nearby city of Cascade Locks was supplied with electricity.

The Columbia River provides spawning grounds for large runs of salmon, steelhead trout, and other migratory fish. The salmon is an anadromous fish; at certain seasons, it returns from the Pacific Ocean to its native river to spawn. Obviously, the construction of huge concrete barriers at two sites on the Columbia would prevent the fish from returning. However, measures were taken to meet this problem in recognition of the legitimate concerns of fishermen, conservationists, and Indian tribes.

At Bonneville Dam, three fish-ladders

Bonneville Power Administration

The fish ladders at Bonneville Dam have more visitors than any other place in Oregon.

were built, consisting of long stairways with wide pools. Each was about a foot higher than the last. By passing up these ladders, the fish are able to reach the 70-foot-deep pool behind the dam and to the spawning grounds beyond. Baby salmon, known as fingerlings, are helped downstream by means of five bypass channels. Approximately a million fish pass up the ladders each year. The fish ladders at Bonneville, in a beautiful parklike setting, attract more visitors than any other spot in Oregon.

Grand Coulee, which is three times higher than Bonneville Dam, would forever block the upstream salmon migration. As a part of the fisheries' mitigation measures, hatcheries were built to handle the returning spawners; the eggs were incubated under ideal conditions; the young were raised in an optimum environment; and the fingerlings were released with the hope that they would return as adults to spawn. Anthony Netboy, in his book *Salmon of the Pacific Northwest,* com-

ments on the experiment: "Despite severe problems, the relocation of the Upper Columbia salmon and steelhead trout runs to areas below the Grand Coulee Dam was successful to a degree exceeding expectations." Later projects have built upon this experience and have improved fish mitigation measures. The facilities provided at Dworshak Dam, for example, have received special commendation.

Most of the early opposition to the Columbia River projects ceased after construction started. There were, however, still some critics who called the giant dams "White Elephants in the Wilderness." As Bonneville Dam neared completion, conflicts arose as to how the power should be distributed. Proposals included a Columbia Valley Authority, patterned after TVA; distribution by the construction agencies; and the creation of a new independent commission, endowed with corporate powers, as the marketing agency.

The Bonneville Project Act, after a number of studies and compromises, was passed in August 1937. It created a new bureau within the Department of Interior, which was formally named the Bonneville Power Administration (BPA) in 1940. The construction agencies operate the power plants with the new bureau building transmission facilities and marketing the power. The act directed BPA "to encourage the widest possible use of all electric energy . . . and to prevent monopolization thereof . . . to insure that the facilities for the generation of electric energy shall be operated for the benefit of the general public, and particularly of domestic and rural consumers . . . and to give preference and priority in the use of electric energy to public bodies and cooperatives." On September 28, 1937, as President Roosevelt dedicated Bonneville Dam, he stated: "The more we study the water resources of the Nation, the more we accept the fact that their use is a matter of National concern."

In November 1937, J. D. Ross was appointed the first BPA administrator, and the first Bonneville Advisory Board was established. On it were representatives of the Interior Department, the War Department, the Agriculture Department, and the Federal Power Commission. Its role was confined to discussions of major problems, primarily costs, rate schedules, additional generators, and transmission system funding. The energy and interest of the early Bonneville bureau was directed toward establishing the market for power and building the transmission system. Portland, Oregon, was designated as the headquarters of BPA, and a nucleus of able professionals was organized. The first challenge was development of the transmission system. Its construction involved the basic steps of surveying territory, acquiring rights-of-way, system designing, setting standards of equipment, letting bids, and the actual building of the power lines.

Before power came on line from Bonneville Dam, rates had to be established. The act provided that the rates may be uniform throughout the area to extend the benefits of an integrated transmission system and to encourage the equitable distribution of electric energy. The act further stated that the rate schedules were to recover the costs of producing and transmitting electric energy, including the interest and amortization of the capital investment—the cost of dams and a transmission network—over a reasonable period of years. As a matter of national power policy, it was considered necessary to establish a yardstick rate that could be applied to other federal hydroelectric projects and a goal to be met by private power utilities.

Hearings held in communities throughout Oregon, Washington, and Idaho provided an opportunity to explain Bonneville policy and procedures and for local residents to state their views. Special questionnaires were distributed to individuals and organizations throughout the Northwest. The response was excellent: 30,000 questionnaires were returned. A direct result of the hearings was the acceptance throughout the region of uniform rates for public power. The power purchased 200 or 300 miles from Bonneville Dam was priced the same as that sold to a customer 15 miles from the generator; within 15 miles a special rate applied. The clause in the Bonneville Project Act giving "preference and priority in the use of electric energy to public bodies and cooperatives" encouraged the formation of public utility districts and in-

creased the demand for low-cost public power, a demand that had grown rapidly during the Depression.

Public power had been an issue in Washington since the beginning of the century. The state constitution permitted a municipality to raise revenues to provide its residents with water, sewer, and electric power services. Under this authority, Seattle and Tacoma pioneered in establishing municipal electric systems; and within a few years, their successful operations set a yardstick that private companies had to meet.

Oregon's public power laws are markedly different from those of Washington, since they do not specifically authorize issuance of revenue bonds for financing the acquisition and extension of power systems. They do not make provision for financing distribution systems directly out of earnings, nor do they provide for the formation of districts with boundaries coextensive with county lines. The difference in the two state statutes is reflected in the number of public utility districts in each state. By the winter of 1938, twenty-five Washington public utility districts, the Seattle and Tacoma public systems, and a number of smaller municipalities were eligible to receive Bonneville power under the preference clause. Only two power districts and six municipalities in Oregon had requested service from BPA. The controversy over the merits of public versus private power continued in the Northwest until the defense effort drew all factions together in a common cause.

The BPA began transmitting energy over its own facilities, a 230,000-volt line from the Bonneville powerhouse to Portland, on December 1, 1939, when 26,000 kilowatts were delivered to the Portland General Electric Company's lines. The marketing of Columbia River power proceeded at a rapid rate. Because of the increasing demand for power, the Army Corps of Engineers advanced the completion date for the second two generator units at Bonneville Dam. These units and the two generators already on line gave a capacity of 194,400 kilowatts by 1941.

Construction began in 1939 on the 230,000-volt line, extending 234 miles from the powerhouse at Grand Coulee Dam to the substation at North Bonneville, Washington. Its completion in July 1940 brought the major population centers on the Columbia River within immediate reach of two of the greatest hydropower projects in the country (a combined capacity of nearly 2.5 million kilowatts). The coordination of power from both dams created the world's largest single source of electricity at that time.

The war clouds in Europe resulted in the establishment of the National Defense Power Committee in September 1938. A major consideration was the possibility of linking the nation's power resources together to meet not only peacetime needs but also national emergency demands for large blocks of power. As the nation's largest hydroelectric potential, the Columbia River received intensive study. This gave additional emphasis to the BPA transmission network to transport power from the federal dams to market and to tie together all the power generating capabilities of the region. The available electric power became the important factor in establishing defense production in the Northwest.

President Roosevelt declared in 1941 that "Airplanes are the key to victory." Prior to the President's call for greatly expanded aircraft production, the Aluminum Company of America had begun operation in September 1940 at its Vancouver, Washington plant. Additional aluminum production sites at Spokane, Longview, and Tacoma, Washington, and at Troutdale, Oregon, were developed. At the peak of their operation, these five plants utilized nearly 500,000 kilowatts of electrical energy. Of the major wartime industrial expansions in the region, aluminum was one of the most important as a power consumer, as a major contributor to the war effort and as a potential peacetime industry. During the war years, BPA developed a power transmission system that sold and delivered more electricity for war purposes—26 billion kilowatt-hours—than all of the other power systems in the region had developed and marketed up to that time. Its high-voltage, high-capacity transmission system grew from 37 miles of lines in 1939 to 2,720 miles in

1945, with an investment of about $75 million—at that time, the second largest power system in the nation.

In March 1943, the War Production Board directed BPA to provide power for a "mystery load," estimated to require from 75,000 to 150,000 kilowatts, through its substation at Midway. This order resulted when scientists and engineers from the Manhattan Project, searching for an isolated area with vast quantities of electricity and cooling water, found "an almost perfect site" on a remote, gray expanse of undulating tableland. It contained 630 square miles on the Columbia River near Hanford, Washington. At that site was built the Hanford Engineer Works, which produced the plutonium for the atomic bomb. From a small community of about 200 persons on the bend of the river, the region expanded to house a wartime construction force of 45,000. The Tri-City area—Richland, Pasco, and Kennewick—has since continued in its role as a major nuclear research center and as the site of the Northwest's first nuclear-fueled thermal generation plant.

In addition to war loads served directly by BPA, the early construction of the high-voltage grid also served as a "lifesaver" to all utilities in the Pacific Northwest. None of them was in a position to serve the large power load additions resulting from ship, aircraft, and munition production and the establishment and expansion of navy yards and military installations. Through the Northwest power pool, by which the eleven major power systems in the region were interconnected, over a billion kilowatt-hours of electric power from Grand Coulee and Bonneville dams were supplied to war industries and establishments located on the lines of other utilities.

Cessation of hostilities in August 1945 brought large cutbacks in the use of electric power as the wartime industrial machine converted to civilian production. But the lightmetals field replaced the wartime power load far sooner than expected, due in part to policies that encouraged new entrants into the aluminum field by making wartime plants and low-cost power available. This, coupled with an unprecedented increase in consumer demand for electric energy, partly due to the large number of defense workers who remained in the Northwest after the war, created added power demands and reduced reserves to a minimum. It resulted in an urgent need for continuing development of the hydroelectric potential of the basin.

The next project was the 564-foot-high Hungry Horse Dam on the South Fork of the Flathead River. It was authorized in 1944 as a Bureau of Reclamation project, with the power from the 300,000-kilowatt powerhouse to be marketed by BPA. Along with power at the dam, the storage provided by the reservoir enabled additional generation downstream at Grand Coulee and Bonneville. The next year, passage of the 1945 Rivers and Harbors Act authorized the Army Corps of Engineers to construct McNary Dam on the Columbia, 150 miles upstream from Bonneville; and four dams on the lower stretch of the Snake, a major tributary of the Columbia. In 1946 Chief Joseph Dam on the Columbia, 50 miles downstream from Grand Coulee, was approved. The authorization of these dams strengthened the concept of multiple-purpose development; since the projects provided for irrigation, flood control, and navigation as well as hydroelectric power.

Army Corps of Engineers

Columbia River Basin showing the major hydroelectric projects.

A major development in 1947 was BPA and the British Columbia Electric Company completing construction of a 230,000-volt line, linking the two power systems at Blaine, Washington. This was one more step in the evolution of the system to increase benefits through power exchanges. It was also a forerunner of the giant intertie that twenty-five years later would connect the West Coast from Canada to Mexico.

The demand for full development of the Columbia River reached a crescendo following the tragic flood of June 1948. The twenty-day flood was the greatest single disaster in the history of the Columbia River Basin. Thirty-eight persons lost their lives in the Portland area, when the raging Columbia broke through the dike surrounding Vanport and totally destroyed the community of 18,000 people. Nearly 5,000 other homes were devastated; 50,000 people were forced to leave their residences; and the measurable loss to the region exceeded $100 million.

While the Columbia was still at high flood stage, President Harry S. Truman inspected the inundated area and, upon his return to Washington, D.C., ordered that the plans of all federal agencies for development of the river be coordinated and expedited. The resulting complex eight-volume interdepartmental report, which had an important impact on all postwar river development work, was completed in early 1950. The 1950 Rivers and Harbors and Flood Control Act authorized construction of The Dalles and John Day dams on the main stem of the Columbia; and two upstream storage projects, Albeni Falls on the Pend Oreille River and Libby on the Kootenai River, both tributaries of the upper Columbia. Five additional dams, making a total of seven, were also authorized on the Willamette River and its tributaries, which added another 440,000 kilowatts of hydropower to the Bonneville system.

While the Army Corps of Engineers was getting these projects underway, the area experienced a critical power shortage. Since 1940 the region had had an increase in population of 44 percent, as compared to a 13 percent increase in the country as a whole. Net immigration exceeded a million between

1940 and 1949. Oregon led all states in growth with an increase of 59 percent; Washington, 48 percent; and Idaho, 13 percent. In addition, farms and businesses were rapidly finding new uses for power; and electric consumption in the home increased as new labor-saving devices were added and better lighting introduced.

In 1951 two policies, tax incentives to encourage private utility construction of hydroelectric plants and "no new Federal starts," resulted in greater private utility construction as well as that by public utility districts of the State of Washington. Controversy raged for several years over the proposed federal high dam at the Hells Canyon site on the Snake River. But it ended in July 1955 when the Federal Power Commission granted the Idaho Power Company a fifty-year license to build three low dams on the Middle Snake. The three public utility districts in eastern Washington, encouraged by the federal policy that welcomed local hydroelectric development, built four great power dams on the middle Columbia; Priest Rapids, Wanapum, Wells, and Rocky Reach. They added substantially to the Northwest power supply.

To facilitate the coordination of power utilization from non-federal projects, the proposal was advanced to make the federal transmission grid available for wheeling non-federal generation to load centers, whenever it was feasible to do so. Legislation to accomplish this was passed in August 1957. It was a significant milestone in achieving coordinated and efficient service to Pacific Northwest power customers. It virtually eliminated duplications of lines and assured maximum use of the transmission grid serving federal dams. An outstanding technological addition to the network was the completion of a 345,000-volt line from McNary Dam to Portland and Vancouver, the first extra-high voltage transmission west of the Rockies.

Over a span of twenty years (1937-1957), the wholesale power rates charged by BPA had not changed. In this period, BPA sold 247 billion kilowatt-hours of electric energy at an average rate of 2.36 mills per kilowatt-hour. The sales to publicly owned utilities accounted for 59 billion; to privately owned utilities, 56 billion; and to industry, 132 billion. On June 30, 1957, BPA had repaid $512 million on schedule to the United States Treasury.

The Columbia River flows across the boundary between the United States and Canada. In anticipation of problems that might arise over joint use of this great resource and other international rivers, the governments of Canada and the United States ratified the 1909 Boundary Waters Treaty which provided machinery to settle questions concerning these waters. The treaty established fundamental principles for the regulation of international waters and created the International Joint Commission (IJC). The first step was taken toward cooperative development of the Upper Columbia River when IJC was asked by the two governments in March 1944 to determine how greater use could be made of the Columbia River system in the public interest of both countries. The IJC established the International Columbia River Engineering Board to undertake the investigation.

Two decades later, on September 16, 1964, the President of the United States, the Prime Minister of Canada, and British Columbia's Premier met to acknowledge full ratification of the Columbia Treaty. The intervening twenty years had been filled with studies, hearings, and negotiations carried on by representatives at every level of government of the two countries in reaching a settlement mutually advantageous to both nations. The objective was the full multipurpose utilization of the river.

Under the treaty, Canada was to construct three great storage projects on its side of the border. The United States was permitted to build Libby Dam which backs water into Canada. Two of the Canadian storage dams, Mica and Keemleyside, are on the main stem of the Columbia. The third dam, Duncan, is on a tributary. In addition to providing storage, Mica, one of the world's largest earthfill dams, will have its own generating plant of 2 million-kilowatt capacity. Treaty dams are to supply 15.5 million acre-feet of storage usable for the production of power downstream in the United States. Libby Dam provides 5 million acre-feet of usable storage as well as power at the site. Together, these dams furnish more than double the amount of previously available storage. Added to storage in other United States projects—existing, authorized, and under construction—there is a total of 41 million acre-feet in the Columbia River Basin. The United States agreed to pay Canada $64.4 million for flood control benefits in the United States derived from Canadian projects.

Libby Dam is on the Kootenai River, a tributary of the Columbia, in northwestern Montana.

An account of record flood years on the Columbia and its tributaries illustrates the benefits gained by the United States from this use of upstream storage. The greatest floods on the Columbia since man began to record its flows occurred in 1894 and 1948. These floods reached a maximum river level of 35.5 feet at Portland, Oregon, and Vancouver, Washington. If a flood of this size were to hit again, storage built in the United States before the treaty dams would have held the level of the river 31.7 feet—only 3.8 feet less. But the three Canadian storage dams and Libby and Dworshak dams in the United States would reduce the flood level to a 26.1-foot level. Thus, thousands of valuable acres of land and homes along the lower Columbia have been made safe from flooding.

The three Canadian storage dams enable downstream facilities in the United States to produce 2.8 million kilowatts of additional firm power (available full time). Libby Dam will add 750,000 kilowatts of firm power in the United States. Under the treaty, half of the additional power generated downstream in the United States as a result of the floodwater storage in the Canadian dams belongs to Canada.

When arrangements between the two countries got underway to implement the terms of the treaty, a basic problem was the inability of British Columbia to raise the capital to proceed with construction of the treaty projects. To provide an acceptable method of financing, BPA, as the principal agency of the United States government involved in the power sale transactions, acted as a catalyst in forming a nonprofit corporation, known as the Columbia Storage Power Exchange (CSPE). It issued bonds to finance prepayment to Canada to purchase its share of the treaty power. The Canadian treaty entitlement power was sold to CSPE for thirty years at an agreed price of $254.4 million. Forty-one Northwest utilities participated in the bond issue. In return, BPA guaranteed specific amounts of capacity and energy to each of the forty-one utilities in direct proportion to its participation in the financing.

Concurrent with the Columbia River Treaty, a thirty-nine-year coordination agreement was executed in the United States by BPA, the Army Corps of Engineers, and fourteen non-federal generating utilities in the Pacific Northwest. It insures that all of the major hydroelectric projects in the region, including Canadian storage, will operate as though there were but one owner. With all of the region's hydro projects operating in concert, maximum power, consistent with flood control requirements, will be generated to best meet the load demands.

The additional storage made more power generation possible at Grand Coulee. The bill authorizing the third powerhouse, already described, was signed into law on June 14, 1966. This legislation contained other important provisions, one of which established a "Basin Account" for the Pacific Northwest. It provided for use of power revenues to repay irrigation costs for reclamation projects, thereafter authorized within the Pacific Northwest, that were beyond the ability of the farmers to repay within the prescribed period and that could not be repaid from other sources. A new repayment schedule, which gave explicit congressional authority covering the payout program for the Columbia River system, was also contained in the measure. This new payout method, which met the federal requirement of repaying each project within fifty years, had a broad impact on the financial structure of all government hydroelectric power operations.

The nation's first plutonium production reactors at Hanford, built to produce weapons, offered a potential for power production. In September 1962, Congress authorized the Atomic Energy Commission (AEC) and BPA to enter into the necessary contracts for non-federal financing, construction, and operation of steam-generating facilities at the Hanford works. Under this authorization, AEC contracted with Washington Public Power Supply System (WPPSS), a group of sixteen Washington State public utility districts, for the sale of by-product steam from the Hanford New Production Reactor. It also contracted for the subsequent lease of the reactor to WPPSS to produce steam for power whenever it was not being used for the production of plutonium.

The Hanford atomic steam plant began delivering power to the Bonneville grid in April 1966. When the generating facility went on line, it was the world's largest nuclear power plant; and its rated output of 865,000 kilowatts was almost equal to all the nuclear plants then in operation in the United States. It opened a new era of industrial growth in the region and marked the start of the transition of the Pacific Northwest from an all hydro power supply to a combination of hydro and thermal power.

Pacific Northwest - Pacific Southwest Power Intertie: The Pacific Northwest - Pacific Southwest Intertie became a reality in the 1960s through a culmination of three crucial forces—technological, political, and economic. Its history, from conception to completion, covered over half a century. Integration of electrical power systems was an idea suggested as early as the 1920s. The concept

arose because of the double diversity of loads and resources of the two regions. The Southwest has summer peaks due to irrigation pumping and air conditioning. The Northwest has winter peaks due to electric heating. In terms of resources, the Northwest rivers predominantly run off as the snow melts during the late spring and summer months, whereas the Pacific Southwest rivers peak in the fall and winter. Thus, the two regions had strong economic incentives for interconnecting.

Bonneville Power Administration

The world's longest 800,000-volt, direct current line extends 846 miles to provide an intertie between the Pacific Northwest and the Pacific Southwest power transmission systems.

Detailed investigations of a possible intertie between the Bonneville system and the Central Valley Project of California were made by the Bureau of Reclamation in 1949. This study proved the feasibility of a 230,000-volt interconnection between the two regions. In 1953 a Federal Power Commission study reaffirmed the economic advantages of a strong intertie between the Pacific Northwest and Pacific Southwest. However, studies and negotiations were carried on for over ten years before Congress, in August 1964, put its stamp of approval on legislation to appropriate $42 million to initiate construction of three transmission lines between the federal Columbia River Power System and the Pacific Southwest. The biggest single electrical transmission program undertaken in this country was underway.

The uniqueness of the Pacific Northwest - Pacific Southwest Intertie lies in its scale. This huge transmission project, with an investment of about $700 million, was built by two agencies of the Department of Interior, four private utilities, and the City of Los Angeles. One leg, the first and longest ultra-high-voltage, direct current transmission line constructed to date, 800,000 volts, stretches 846 miles from the Celilo converter terminal near The Dalles, Oregon, through central Oregon and Nevada to the Sylmar converter terminal near Los Angeles. This direct current line can carry 1.4 million kilowatts of power. It was first energized in May 1970. Two 500,000-volt alternating current legs of the Intertie, each with a capacity of a million kilowatts, extend from the John Day Dam on the Columbia River through the Central Valley of California to a substation near Los Angeles.

The successful operation of the Intertie has strengthened and stabilized the power systems of both regions. It holds great promise for the future through its proof of shared economies and reliabilities and its advancement of technology. It foreshadows a broad schedule of plans to build high-capacity electrical interconnections between neighboring major power systems throughout the continent. New and perhaps even bigger interties will come to diminish the chance of electrical brownouts and blackouts and to make the most effective use of North America's energy resources.

The Northwest Hydro-Thermal Power Program: For thirty years, the Pacific Northwest enjoyed the economic advantage of the lowest-cost electricity in the nation due to the hydropower generated at the great dams on the Columbia River. Dam construction reached a new high during 1966 and 1967. By then twenty-two federal dams were delivering over 6 million kilowatts into BPA's high-voltage lines, and eight projects under construction would add another 8.5 million kilowatts. Paradoxically, just at that period

when generation and transmission construction peaked, it became apparent that power needs would require new energy sources to augment the hydro potential of the Columbia River that would be developed by the mid 1970s. It was a problem involving regional, multi-institutional responsibilities.

The BPA joined with the utilities of the region in forming a joint power planning council. After two years of intensive study and negotiations, an agreement was reached on a Hydro-Thermal Power Program. This cooperative plan called for a $15 billion construction effort over the next twenty years of new thermal, hydro, and transmission facilities. The agreement derived from the basic understanding that the federal government would continue to construct the high-voltage transmission system and additional hydro capacity; public and private utilities would build and operate thermal plants—sized, located, and scheduled to meet regional loads; and BPA would acquire or exchange power from the utilities' plants using the high-voltage transmission system.

The need for joint action by all of the utilities in the region was based on these facts:

1. The most economical size thermal plants are large units, those of a million kilowatts and larger.
2. No single utility or small group of utilities could absorb a plant of such size in its normal load growth pattern.
3. The existence of an extensive hydroelectric power system in the region allows the addition of low-cost peaking capacity at existing and proposed hydro sites.
4. The use of the low-cost hydro peaking will allow the operation of the large thermal plants in the most economical manner as "baseload" plants, that is, operating at full capacity.
5. The BPA transmission grid will permit the output of these large thermal plants to be wheeled to utility loads throughout the region and will deliver peaking capacity from hydro plants at the time of regional peak loads.
6. The federal hydro system and BPA's sale of interruptible power to industry provide a portion of the "forced outage" reserves

for the integrated hydro-thermal system, without which additional generation would have to be built.

7. When water conditions are favorable in the region, low-cost surplus hydro energy can displace thermal energy with savings in fuel costs.

The first plant completed under the program was the coal-fired facility near Centralia, Washington, built by the Pacific Power and Light Company, Washington Water Power Company, and several other utilities. The steam plant consists of two 700,000-kilowatt generators, which began producing power in August 1972. Located near Rainier, Oregon, the Trojan Nuclear Power Plant, with a generating capacity of a million kilowatts, was the second facility to get underway and was constructed by the Portland General Electric Company with the City of Eugene as one-third owner. This project, the first nuclear plant built under the program, was completed by the beginning of 1976.

By 1976 five other thermal plants were in various stages of planning and construction. Throughout its history, BPA had focused its concern on forecasting power requirements, planning programs to meet those requirements, and implementing the programs. Thus, a key element in the Hydro-Thermal Power Program was BPA's ability to continue long-range, areawide planning and to enter further into long-term commitments. It was imperative that customers know with certainty the role the federal system would continue to play in the region so they could proceed with plans for development. While congressional approval of the program helped assure them of continuity in the region's power supply, successful implementation of the program depended upon the federal Columbia River power system and the non-federal utilities meeting their construction schedules.

Studies were made and varied legislation was considered that would insure that federal funds would be available to meet the scheduled needs for the transmission system. Finally, President Gerald R. Ford signed the landmark Columbia Transmission System legislation on October 18, 1974. It permits BPA to use its revenues from electric power sales, any appropriations from Congress, receipts from sales of bonds, and other BPA receipts without necessitating further appropriations but subject to the presentation of an annual budget to Congress. It also authorizes BPA to issue bonds and sell them to the secretary of the treasury to assist in financing the construction, acquisition, and replacement of transmission system facilities. This permits sound, long-range planning with assured continuity.

By 1976 the United States' part of the Columbia basin had thirty-one federal multipurpose dams with powerhouses, having a capacity of over 18 million kilowatts. The BPA high-voltage transmission grid for marketing the power extends over 12,000 circuit miles, serving a land area of 300,000 square miles and a population of 6.6 million. The federal investment in the multipurpose projects and the transmission system in the Columbia River Basin, by the end of 1975, was $6 billion. Revenues from federal power for 1975 totaled about $170 million; the wheeling of non-federal power over the government transmission system produced $17 million. Repayments to the United States Treasury from power revenues totaled approximately $790 million at the end of 1975. The power revenues will pay 81 percent of the total federal investment including interest. The remainder includes irrigation costs, which will be repaid, and flood control, navigation, and fish and wildlife features which are non-reimbursable.

In a historical sense, electricity is still a relatively new province of technology. The BPA over the last thirty years has pioneered in the development of high-voltage transmission of electrical power. In the 1940s, BPA made successful use of large auto-transformers and series capacitors in high-voltage transmission networks. Milestones for the 1950s included the development of an advanced design for a 230,000-volt, alternating current submarine transmission cable and the country's first microwave system for communicating signals to the relays that trigger equipment protection devices. In the 1960s, BPA built the world's longest 800,000-volt, direct current transmission line as part of the Pacific Northwest - Pacific Southwest Intertie. It began building the first 500,000-volt, alternating current transmission lines in the West. The early 1970s marked the beginning of the construction of what will be the world's first operational compressed gas insulated transmission system near Ellensburg, Washington.

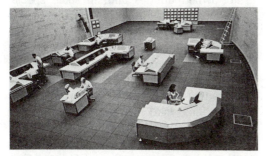

Bonneville Power Administration

Dittmer Control Center provides for centralized control of the electric power network of the Northwest.

The inauguration of operation of the fully computerized Dittmer System Control Center at Vancouver, Washington, in 1975 marked the fruition of two decades of pioneering digital computer application. At the center, which is the hub of digital and analog communications systems that extend over the entire Pacific Northwest, the dispatcher has at his fingertips complete immediate information about the full system performance. Centralized remote switching gives him the capability of making operational changes in the entire system simply by pushing buttons.

The power generation and transmission system in the Columbia River Basin has demonstrated the dynamic effect of a multi-institutional approach in providing services. It also shows the adaptability of the free enterprise system. The Pacific Northwest has become almost 100 percent electrified, with the families in the area enjoying one of the highest electrical standards of living in the world.

Missouri River Basin

Power production developed slowly in the Missouri River Basin to meet localized needs, and even by 1940 about 90 percent of the farms were still without central station service. Urban and industrial loads were generally small, of low load-factor (ratio of the average load to the maximum load), widely scattered, remote from water power sites, and not interconnected by transmission systems. Many small thermal and hydro plants had been built, some investor-owned and some publicly owned, each taking care of its peak demand and standby needs. It was only in the late 1930s that the utilities and the Rural Electrification Administration (REA) cooperatives began to distribute electricity to rural areas. But by 1940, many of the old plants approached obsolescence.

Army Corps of Engineers

Three 35,000-kilowatt generators in the powerhouse at Fort Peck Dam.

The first federal power plant in the Missouri River Basin was a 600-kilowatt hydroplant on the Bureau of Reclamation's North Platte Project in southeastern Wyoming. It began operation in 1919. It was located along the Fort Laramie Canal, a 1,500-cubic-feet per second capacity irrigation water conveyance facility, having a drop of about 100 feet at the power site. Initially, two 300-kilowatt units were installed, and in 1927 two 400-kilowatt units were added. Power was used in the immediate project area until the operation of the plant was discontinued in 1956 because of high costs of operation.

In 1924 the Shoshone power plant, located at the base of the Bureau of Reclamation's Buffalo Bill Dam, went on the line with two 800-kilowatt units. Another unit of 4,000-kilowatts capacity was added in 1931. In 1925 the Pilot Butte power plant on the Riverton project in central Wyoming began production of electricity from one 800-kilowatt unit, and another unit of the same size was added a couple of years later. The power plant at Guernsey Dam on the North Platte River in southeastern Wyoming was next in 1928, when its two 2,400-kilowatt units began producing power.

Only one other federal power plant was completed before the passage of the 1944 act establishing the Pick-Sloan Missouri River Basin program, the 32,400-kilowatt plant with three equal size units at the base of the Seminoe Dam. The first 35,000-kilowatt units of the Fort Peck project came on line in 1944. Thus, with the beginning of the accelerated program of water and related resources development, besides Fort Peck, there were only five federal hydropower installations having a combined capacity of 45,800 kilowatts, about three fourths of which was in a plant only four years old. Transmission was limited to 800 circuit miles, mostly at 34,500 volts; and the power was used primarily in the reclamation project areas for domestic use and pumping for irrigation.

The overall Pick-Sloan Missouri River Basin project is described in Chapter 9. By 1970, twenty-seven years after the beginning of the Pick-Sloan plan construction, the installed electrical generating capacity in the full Missouri River Basin had increased over six times to about 15 million kilowatts, of which 50 percent was that of investor-owned utilities, 32 percent was that of non-federal publicly owned and cooperative utilities, and 18 percent was that of federal hydroelectric plants. Of the total, about 25 percent was hydroelectric power and the remainder mostly thermal power.

Nearly all of the federal public power was marketed to the consumer through local public power utilities. Unlike TVA, which has the responsibility of providing for the growing energy needs of its market area, the power generated at the federal hydroelectric plants is available for sale to others having responsibilities for their own market areas. Preference is given to publicly owned utilities. Initially, power in excess of the needs of preference customers was sold to investor-owned utilities and, in some special cases, to private industry; but there were provisions to withdraw the commitment, as necessary, to meet the later needs of the preference customers. Now that all the federal power is committed, the local public systems and cooperatives are responsible for meeting their market areas, growing power needs from other sources.

This is being done by organizations such as the Basin Electric Power Cooperative, through which 118 rural electric cooperatives began to combine in 1961 to plan and then build the Leland Olds station on the Missouri River at Stanton, North Dakota. The first unit of 216,000 kilowatts went on the line in 1966, and the second unit of 460,000 kilowatts began operation in late 1975. Another large coal-fired plant to meet 1980 loads is under study, and it probably will be located in Wyoming. This plant will be a three-unit, 1.5 million-kilowatt station, and it will involve five other cooperatives and public agencies in addition to Basin Electric.

Public power entities in Nebraska have been active in developing their own power sources on a large scale since construction of the Platte River hydroelectric developments during the 1930s, which were financed partly with PWA loans. The Central Nebraska Public Power and Irrigation District built Kingsley Dam, a 170-foot-high earthfill structure, located on the North Platte River in western Nebraska. Construction was started in the 1930s; and when completed in 1942, its 32 million cubic yards of earth and rock made it one of the largest dams of its type in the world. The dam diverted water into a high-line canal that had three powerhouses with a total generating capacity of 54,000 kilowatts. The Loup Public Power and Irrigation District developed 48,150 kilowatts of hydro capacity on the Loup River. Other developments followed. The Nebraska Public Power District built the Cooper nuclear station, having an 800,000-kilowatt boiling water nuclear reactor facility, at Brownville. Nebraska. It went into operation in July 1974. The Omaha Public Power District's 500,000-kilowatt Fort Calhoun nuclear power station also went on the line during 1974. Other thermal plants, both nuclear and coal-fired, are being considered to meet the growing needs.

The large federal hydroelectric installations have been important in launching the use of electric power throughout the region. Along with the REA consumer distribution systems, they were responsible for providing electricity to practically all the farms in the basin. However, the future needs will be met with large coal-fired and nuclear plants, utilizing hydropower as much as possible to meet peak loads, where its flexibility and fast and efficient starting and stopping characteristics make it especially valuable. In 1975 the Army Corps of Engineers conducted a study of increasing the generating capacity at the six mainstream dams to meet short-time peak loads. The Nebraska public utilities were considering an all underground pumped storage facility to meet peak loads. Other such possibilities have been identified which could provide over 25 million kilowatts of peaking capacity, utilizing fifteen or twenty different locations.

The transmission system extends throughout the basin and has connections with the Colorado River system of the Bureau of Reclamation and with other systems to the east and south. It includes major plant interties, transmission to load centers with appropriate substations, and a system-wide dispatching and operations center. The twenty-three federal power plants have a total installed generating capacity of 2.7 million kilowatts, of which 2 million are in the six mainstream dams of the Army Corps of Engineers. All the federal power is marketed by the Bureau of Reclamation through its transmission system, which had 10,600 circuit miles of line and 174 substations by 1975. The power was delivered to 348 municipalities, cooperatives, irrigation districts, state and federal agencies, and a few investor-owned utilities. By the 1970s, the yearly federal power marketed was about 13 billion kilowatt-hours. The investment in these facilities was approximately $1 billion and was being fully repaid with interest to the United States Treasury. The wholesale rate for the federal hydroelectric power in the eastern division in 1974 was 4.83 mills per kilowatt-hour; and in the western division, where plants are small and far apart, the rate was 6.40 mills per kilowatt-hour. Substantial increases in rates were under review in 1975.

The planning to meet growing power needs, plus the various environmental problems encountered, has resulted in increasing cooperation among various public and private entities. In 1970 the North Central Power Study was jointly launched to identify the region's needs and ways to meet them. The cooperatives, utility districts, municipalities, and investor-owned utilities cooperated with the federal government in developing the basic program. The study identified forty-two strip-mine coal sites, providing coal for at least thirty-five years for fueling generating stations with capacities upward from a million kilowatts each. The study indicated that sufficient water was available in the basin for cooling thermal plants of more than 70 million-kilowatts capacity, and it then could still serve as industrial water for various coal-processing plants such as gasification or liquefaction. However, long and costly aqueducts would be needed, and each proposed plant would require extensive detailed study.

While the cooperative and coordinated efforts to meet the demands of the area have been slow in developing, they have grown stronger. The involvement of the federal government has had an important influence in bringing them into focus, and the Missouri River Basin Commission is increasing their overall effectiveness. However, the cooperatives working in close association by 1975 were playing a key role.

The Colorado River Basin

Events leading to the construction of Hoover Dam to control the waters of the Colorado River and to generate hydroelectric power are discussed in Chapter 10. Contracts for sale of the power delivered at the damsite were negotiated with nine entities, and 92 percent went to the publicly owned power groups. Southern California contracted for about 65 percent, including 35 percent for the Metropolitan Water District to be used for pumping Colorado River water through the

Colorado Aqueduct. The contracting entities built and operate the transmission lines to the dam. The powerhouse is operated by the Los Angeles Water and Power Board and the Southern California Edison Company, (each with one side of the plant) under contract with the federal government.

The power plant is located at the toe of

National Academy of Science

The Colorado River Basin showing the major water control reservoirs.

the dam, and it extends 650 feet along each canyon wall. Fourteen 82,500-kilowatt units and five smaller units provide a total capacity of 1.3 million kilowatts. The first unit went on the line in 1936 and the last one in 1952, the units being added as the power load increased.

Parker Dam, located 155 miles downstream from Hoover, was constructed in the mid 1930s. It provides a 648,000 acre-foot forebay and desilting basin, from which the Metropolitan Water District pumps water into its Colorado Aqueduct. A powerhouse, consisting of four 30,000-kilowatt generators, was added from 1939 to 1942. The dam is a 320-foot-high concrete arch structure, of which 235 feet is below streambed.

The construction of Davis Dam, a 200-foot-high, 3.3-million-cubic-yard earthfill dam, located 67 miles downstream from Hoover, started in 1942, was interrupted by World War II and completed in 1953. The powerhouse includes five 45,000-kilowatt generators, all of which were producing power in 1951. The Bureau of Reclamation built a 1,600-mile, high-voltage transmission system, including thirty-six substations, to connect Davis with Parker and Hoover powerhouses and deliver power to the public power entities in Arizona, California, and Nevada.

The use of the Colorado River above Hoover Dam began on a small scale with the early settlements in the last half of the nineteenth century. Studies for additional developments were initiated soon after the 1902 Reclamation Act. The flow of the Colorado is extremely erratic, varying between 4 and 22 million acre-feet annually at Lee Ferry, near the northern border of Arizona. It is considered the dividing point between the upper and lower basins of the Colorado. The 1922 Colorado River Compact divided the flow between the two basins and provided 7.5 million acre-feet for yearly consumption in the upper basin. However, this allocation was contingent upon delivery to the lower basin of 75 million acre-feet in any ten consecutive years and delivery of additional water for use in Mexico under certain circumstances. Agreement on division of the upper basin

waters among the five states of Wyoming, Colorado, Utah, New Mexico, and Arizona was established by the Upper Colorado River Basin Compact in 1948.

As the low-flow years and the high-flow years tend to be grouped, the problems of river regulation and use were accentuated. In prolonged dry periods, there was not enough water to allow the use in the upper basin and at the same time meet requirements downstream. In wet years, the flows were more than sufficient for these purposes. Thus, large reservoirs were required that could be filled when flows were high and have carryover storage to insure meeting downstream requirements through the low-flow years.

A plan to provide the required storage, about 27 million acre-feet, was cooperatively formulated and presented to Congress in 1950. It included a series of dams to supply the storage capacity to meet compact requirements, along with power development, and to provide storage and control for other uses including irrigation, municipal and industrial use, and wildlife and recreation. After years of debate and refinement, the project was authorized by the 1956 Colorado River Storage Act. Provisions included a power-generating capacity of approximately 1.3 million kilowatts, which is completed except for 50,000 kilowatts that will be built by 1978.

The largest structure in the upper basin of the Colorado is the 710-foot-high Glen Canyon Dam with a 950,000-kilowatt power plant

U.S. Bureau of Reclamation

Glen Canyon Dam on the Colorado River has a 950,-000-kilowatt power plant.

built on the Colorado River just south of the Utah-Arizona state line. Completed in 1964 at a cost of $245 million, it generated 4.6 billion kilowatt-hours in 1973. The reservoir has a capacity of 27 million acre-feet. It received the American Society of Civil Engineers' Outstanding Civil Engineering Achievement Award for 1964.

The 502-foot-high concrete gravity Flaming Gorge Dam is located in northeastern Utah on the Green River tributary of the Colorado, and the 3.8 million acre-foot reservoir extends into Wyoming. The power plant at the base of the dam has three 36,000-kilowatt units. The three hydroelectric plants on the Gunnison River tributary in Colorado have a combined capacity of 208,000 kilowatts. The 408-foot-high, 26-million-cubic-yard earthfill Navajo Dam in the San Juan River tributary in New Mexico has a storage capacity of 1.7 million acre-feet, and two 11,500-kilowatt generators are scheduled to produce power in 1978.

The 10 billion kilowatt-hours of electricity produced in the upper Colorado River power plants in 1974 were distributed to seventy-eight public power entities through the project's 1,860 circuit miles of high-voltage transmission lines, including fifteen substations. These connect the power plants in the upper Colorado River Basin and tie to the adjacent power transmission grids, both publicly and privately owned, and to other power plants to the southwest and in the states east of the Rocky Mountains. A remote control center, located in southwestern Colorado, coordinates the operation of the power plants for water releases as required and for load demands on the power system. It is a cooperative effort of the federal government, local utilities, and investor-owned power systems.

The Colorado River projects were designed and constructed by the Bureau of Reclamation with construction through competitive bidding by private contractors. The design and various specialized laboratory testing work was done at the bureau's engineering center in Denver, Colorado.

Water from the Colorado River projects is being and will be used in developing electrical energy from the vast coal and oil shale deposits in the upper river basin. The amount of water available will limit the development, although a reasonable, well-managed program can be accomplished. Studies are being made to find ways the existing reservoirs can be better utilized for supplying peaking power.

The Federal Power Commission

Controversy over development of hydroelectric power finally resulted in the 1920 Federal Water Power Act, which established the Federal Power Commission (FPC) specifically to control and license non-federal development of hydroelectric power. The commission originally consisted of the secretaries of interior, agriculture, and war. Ten years later, it was made into an independent agency having five full-time commissioners appointed by the President with the advice and consent of the Senate. Subsequently, in 1935 its regulatory powers were broadened to include licensing of investor-owned electric utilities engaged in interstate commerce. In 1938 the Natural Gas Act gave FPC jurisdiction over sales of natural gas in interstate commerce, and this too became an important part of the commission's work. In addition to the hydro licensing requirements, the commission is empowered and directed to promote the adequacy and reliability of the nation's electric power supply; establish fair wholesale rates for electricity in interstate commerce; and continually evaluate the hydroelectric power resources of the fifty states. This includes encouraging voluntary cooperation in interconnecting and coordinating facilities to provide the best possible efficiency.

Ten regional reliability councils have been formed, which have among their members representatives of the utilities within each region. These councils, covering all the continental states, have received strong encouragement and support from FPC. They have made positive contributions in coordinating the electric industry's regional and inter-regional planning, and they carry out continuing analyses of electric power fuel use and fuel substitution potentials.

In addition to other functions, FPC carries on a continuing national power survey to

TABLE 11-3
Hydroelectric Installations and Class of Ownership

Class of Ownership	Installed Hydroelectric Capacity in millions of Kilowatts			
	1920	1940	1960	1970
Investor-owned utilities	3.5	8.5	13.4	16.6
Non-federal publicly owned utilities	0.2	1.1	4.4	12.1
Federal	*0.0	1.7	14.6	22.9
Industrial	1.1	1.1	0.7	0.7
Total, all plants	4.8	12.4	33.1	52.3

*Less than 50,000 kilowatts

analyze issues and alternatives relating to the nation's future electric power supply. Also, emergency plans and procedures of power suppliers are under continual review. Each licensed hydroelectric project must be adapted to its particular site and to a comprehensive plan for its river basin. In addition to structural integrity and public safety requirements, licenses may contain special provisions relating to water supply for domestic and industrial use, flood control, navigation, water quality, public health, recreation, scenic preservation, and fish and wildlife. Since 1970 environmental impact statements are required before licenses are granted.

Table 11-3 shows the conventional hydroelectric capacity by class of ownership in the forty-eight contiguous states from 1920 to 1970. The data is drawn from the FPC 1970 national power survey.

The licensed hydroelectric projects are expected to serve almost indefinitely because, like their federal counterparts, they have distinct advantages over thermal generating plants. They are non-polluting, operating and maintenance costs are low, and there is no fuel cost except for energy at pumped storage plants. Hydroelectric installations have long life and low rates of depreciation. Unscheduled outages are less frequent and downtime for overhaul is of short duration, for generating units operate at relatively low speeds and temperatures and are less subject to damage. A hydroelectric unit is normally out of service about two days per year due to

forced outages and about one to two weeks for scheduled maintenance. The average outage rates of modern steam-electric units are several times greater. The ability to start quickly and make rapid changes in power output make hydroelectric plants particularly well adapted for serving peak loads, for frequency control of electric current, and for spinning reserve capacity to meet quickly unexpected power loads. They have great value as a source of starting power to steam plants following a major power failure.

Some of the public hydroelectric projects licensed by FPC in New York State and in the Columbia River Basin are described elsewhere in this chapter. An example of other public power projects licensed by FPC is the Toledo Bend Project on the Sabine River, where it forms the boundary between Texas and Louisiana. The two-state development is a cooperative project built and operated by public authorities of the two states. The 8 million-cubic-yard earth dam provides a 4.5 million acre-foot, multipurpose reservoir; and the powerhouse has a generating capacity of 115,500 kilowatts. Besides the power, flood control, water quality, and conservation benefits, it has become an outstanding recreational area with facilities available for all types of activities.

The City of Seattle, Washington, operates several projects dating back to the first two 1,200-kilowatt generators which went into production in 1904. Later developments have required FPC licenses. These include the

Seattle City Light

Seattle's 450-foot-high Ross Dam provides a maximum capacity at the downstream powerhouse of 450,000 kilowatts.

three dams on the Skagit River: 390-foot-high Diable Dam completed in 1933; 540-foot-high Ross Dam completed in 1949; and 300-foot-high Gorge Dam redeveloped in 1960. These dams provide an overall normal rated capacity of 623,000 kilowatts in the three power-houses. Peak capacity at full reservoir is considerably higher. Another Seattle project is the 360-foot-high Boundary Dam, located on the Pend Oreille River, which has a power-house with a capacity of 700,000 kilowatts at full reservoir. All four dams are concrete, are located in spectacular scenery areas, and provide extensive recreational attractions.

The 480-foot-high rockfill Exchequer Dam, with its 87,000-kilowatt power plant operated on the Merced River in California by the Merced Irrigation District, is an example of the special type funding secured by some public FPC-licensed projects. The licensee financed the project through a contribution from the federal government for providing flood control benefits and through the sale of revenue bonds. The bonds were secured by a long-term power sales contract with a large investor-owned utility. Besides offering flood control and power, the project furnishes irrigation from its large reservoir as well as a variety of outdoor recreational activities.

There are many other projects equally impressive.

Power Authority of the State of New York

The hydroelectric power potential of the St. Lawrence River was recognized early in this century. With a drainage area of 300,000 square miles in the United States and Canada and with the 100,000 square miles of equalizing reservoir surface in the five Great Lakes, it has the most uniform flow of the world's great rivers. The maximum discharge is only twice the minimum flow of record, and the average flow since 1860 is about 250,000 cubic feet per second. Below the outlet of Lake Ontario, where the river originates, it drops 92 feet in less than 50 miles through the International Rapids along the United States-Canadian border. It then continues another 580 miles, all in Canada, to the Gulf of St. Lawrence dropping another 154 feet.

An Army Corps of Engineers' report in 1911 stated that the river from Ogdensburg, New York, to Montreal could develop 4 to 5 million horsepower of electrical energy. In 1913 the Hydro-Electric Power Commission of Ontario (Ontario Hydro) began detailed studies of the power possibilities of the St. Lawrence; and eight years later, it presented the results to the International Joint Commission(IJC), established under the 1909 Boundary Waters Treaty between Britain and the United States. This commission recommended that a joint board of engineers be appointed to determine the best method of harnessing the International Rapids section. In 1924 three members were named by Canada and three by the United States to form the board. Two years later, the board presented its findings that the seaway and power projects in the International Rapids section were feasible. On the basis of this report, the 1932 St. Lawrence Deep Waterway Treaty was signed, but it failed to receive ratification by the United States Senate.

Again in 1941, an agreement was signed by the representatives of the two nations providing for development of the International Rapids section. Like the earlier treaty, this one also was not ratified by the Senate, although Congress held intermittent hearings on the proposal for the next ten years. Also in 1941, the Army Corps of Engineers, with FPC, completed a detailed engineering study of projects in the International Rapids section of the river.

In June 1952, the governments of Canada and the United States filed application with IJC for permission to develop the power potential of the International Rapids section. The Canadian application included a proposal to provide all-Canadian, deep-craft navigation between Montreal Harbor and Lake Erie. The commission issued an order of approval for the power works in October 1952.

The Power Authority of the State of New York (PASNY) was established by the state legislature in 1931, primarily to cooperate with the United States and Canadian authorities in developing the hydroelectric power resources of the International Rapids section of the St. Lawrence River. The Power Authority Act has been periodically amended to fit changing needs. Initially, the concept was that the authority would operate the power facilities after construction by the federal government, so that it would be in a position to market the power and then take over the project when the costs were repaid. Legislation considered in Congress during the 1940s included such provisions.

In 1951 the dominion government of Canada and the province of Ontario signed an agreement providing for the latter to construct and operate the power facilities in the International Rapids section. The province named Ontario Hydro as the Canadian entity. With Congress refusing to act, PASNY prepared an application to FPC for a license to develop the power, which it presented on July 16, 1948, along with supporting applications to IJC. Following several years of considerations, submittals, and court actions, FPC issued a fifty-year license to PASNY on July 15, 1953. Then on November 4, 1953, President Eisenhower named PASNY as the designee of the United States for construction of the power works. Governor Thomas Dewey appointed Robert Moses as chairman of PASNY in early 1954, and he aggresively supported the project. However, further legal actions delayed start of construction until Supreme Court action on June 7, 1954 cleared the way

for the project. Construction was begun in August 1954, and the first power went out over the lines less than four years later. Private consulting engineering firms were utilized for the planning, design, and construction management; and the construction was contracted after public competitive bidding.

In the meantime, the Wiley-Dondero Act was passed in May 1954, creating the St. Lawrence Seaway Development Corporation to construct the part of the seaway in the United States and to cooperate with the Canadian entities in the construction and operation of the seaway. Thus, the seaway portion of the project also became an international undertaking.

The PASNY portion of the project was financed by the sale of thirty-year revenue bonds to private investors without governmental credit or tax support. Revenue from the sale of power would pay interest on the PASNY bonds, retire them according to schedule, and cover the cost of operation and maintenance. Under the terms of the license granted by FPC, and within the framework of the New York law establishing the authority, the power was marketed by contract with existing private utility companies, industries, municipalities, and rural electric cooperatives. The contracts with the utilities required them to pass savings on to their customers. Virtually all the St. Lawrence power was contracted before any generation equipment had been installed.

The major features of the project include the Robert Moses-Robert H. Saunders Power Dam, a 167-foot-high concrete dam and powerhouse structure, 3,300 feet long, which is bisected by the international boundary. With its 57,000-kilowatt capacity generators, sixteen on each side of the boundary, the power plant has a rated capacity of 1.8 million kilowatts, one of the world's largest at the time of its construction. Its total cost was approximately $170 million. The Long Sault Dam, located on the channel south of Barnhart Island, is a curved concrete gravity structure, 132 feet in maximum height and an overall length of about 3,000 feet. It is all within the United States and provides the spillway for discharges from the reservoir, other than through

Aerial view of St. Lawrence Power and Seaway Project looking upstream.

the hydraulic turbines in the powerhouse. Its cost was $41 million.

Iroquois Dam, located near the upper end of the reservoir, provides control of Lake Ontario levels, replacing the natural control of a rock ledge upstream from the dam that was removed to provide depth for the navigation channel. It is a gated concrete gravity structure, having a maximum height of 74 feet and an overall length of about 2,000 feet. Its construction cost was $23 million. Massena Intake is a concrete gravity structure, 710 feet in length with a maximum height of 118 feet. It controls flow into the Alcoa power canal during construction of the project and provides the intake for the Massena area water supply. The construction cost $12 million.

Channel enlargements, involving over 63 million cubic yards of excavation, extend up the reservoir area. These excavations were to meet criteria: (1) for navigation of a velocity not exceeding 4 feet per second during the most critical flow conditions; (2) to produce a velocity not exceeding 2.25 feet per second during the ice forming period to insure a solid ice cover on the reservoir and prevent formation of ice flakes that would build up flow bar-

riers under the downstream ice cover; (3) to reduce head loss as economically justified for the conservation of power; and (4) to provide a minimum depth of 27 feet for the navigation waterway.

Sixteen miles of compacted earth embankments were built, which, with the power and spillway structures, confine the power pool (Lake St. Lawrence), having a capacity of 760,000 acre-feet and covering an area of 27,500 acres. The embankments have a maximum height of 85 feet and contain 17.5 million cubic yards of compacted earth and rock. Relocations involved railroads, highways, utilities, and related features as well as the moving and rehabilitation of seven towns with a total population of 6,700 on the Canadian side of the power pool. The total cost of the project in the International Rapids section was about $650 million; the cost to the United States for two locks and the 10-mile navigation canal was $130 million; and the cost of the Canadian locks at Iroquois and the canals and locks in the all-Canadian reach of the river was $340 million.

While the power project is separate from the seaway navigation project, the joint use of the river and the reservoir for power and navigation required the two projects to be completely coordinated in planning, construction, and operation. Thus, the entire operation had to be carefully managed as one program.

There were a number of features of the St. Lawrence Project that were unique to a public works program. The project was an international undertaking involving the United States and Canada, with the international boundary approximately bisecting the overall project. The IJC and the Joint Board of Engineers had responsibility for seeing that the provisions of international agreements were met.

The project had to be constructed without interfering with navigation in the existing Canadian 14-foot draft canals, including twelve locks that extended around the rapids in the 50-mile reach of the project. Furthermore, there could be no interference with the natural level of Lake Ontario or of the river levels downstream from the project. As one

operation would lower the river level in a reach of the river, another compensating operation had to be made to maintain the river level. This was carefully monitored by the International Board of Control to insure compliance. In addition, the Canadian Department of Transport and the Army Corps of Engineers had regulatory responsibilities in all operations affecting navigation. A large number of local governmental entities were involved on both sides of the river, including state and province highway departments, county and township public works organizations, municipalities, and utilities of all kinds. Both Canadian and American railroad organizations with respective regulatory bodies participated in relocations.

The construction schedule was tight. As there was a pressing need for power, the most expeditious, economically sound building program was developed; and the first power was on the line less than four years after the start of construction. The major item of con-

Power Authority of the State of New York

Niagara Power Project with powerhouse in the foreground and the Lewiston pumped-storage reservoir in the background. The outlet from the river above Niagara Falls is at the right of the Lewiston pump-generating plant in center.

struction involved in the International Rapids section, including the seaway portion, shows the magnitude of the project: 150 million cubic yards of earth and rock excavation, of which 42 million was the seaway portion of the project; 5 million cubic yards of concrete, of which 1 million was in the seaway portion of the project; and 180 thousand tons of steel. At the peak of construction, there were approximately 17,000 workmen on the project; about 60 prime contractors and 100 subcontractors were engaged in various phases of the work. The value of the construction equipment on the project during the peak period was about $90 million. The major items included: 140 shovels and draglines up to 15-cubic-yard capacity, 400 large tractors, 735 trucks, 85 scrapers, 9 dipper dredges, 250 railroad cars, 9 large concrete plants, and 6 large aggregate crusher plants. Difficult problems were encountered with excavation. Most of the material was glacial till which had been overlain during the ice age with 5,000 to 6,000 feet of ice and thus was as heavy and dense as concrete. Large deposits of marine clays became almost a liquid when disturbed.

In addition to the positive returns from the 13 billion kilowatt-hours of electric power utilized in the United States and Canada each year and the passing of 7,000 or more oceangoing vessels with over 50 million tons of cargo through the locks, the project is an environmental showcase on both sides of the river. Broad environmental considerations were an integral part of the design and construction of the project, including protecting and restoring scenic areas; providing parks, camping grounds, beaches, and playgrounds; and furnishing attractive access to the project facilities. The project features themselves were designed and built for aesthetic purposes, are carefully maintained in their natural landscaped settings, and offer informative and illustrative visitor centers. For instance, on the American side of the river, over 2,500 acres are included in five parks, five marinas, and five beaches. A 3,000-acre waterfowl management area, including 1,900 acres of water, with a constant water level controlled by a specially constructed control dam, was provided and has become a major

nesting area for flocks of wild Canadian geese and other waterfowl. In addition, 2,700 acres of islands in the reservoir have been preserved in their natural condition for wildlife and conservation. The facilities are equaled on the Canadian side.

Near the completion of the St. Lawrence Power and Seaway Project, years of negotiations, private versus public power disputes, and various legal problems were resolved so that the Niagara Falls power project could be undertaken by PASNY. Action became necessary when a rock slide in 1956 destroyed two thirds of the existing 365,000-kilowatt Schoellkopf plant of the Niagara Mohawk Power Company. Construction of the 2.19-million-kilowatt plants—including the main powerhouse of thirteen 150,000-kilowatt generators with a 313-foot head and the twelve 20,000-kilowatt pump-turbines in the pump storage portion of the project—got underway that same year. The first power was generated a little over three years later.

To preserve the scenic value of Niagara Falls, the flow over it is maintained in daytime and evening hours. The water diverted through the powerhouses during the nighttime is shared by the United States and Canada. The power facilities in Canada were built during the 1950s and are similar to those of PASNY. The power on the United States side that is not needed to meet power loads is used to pump the water into the Lewiston reservoir, an energy storage facility. It is then released during the daytime peak load hours, generating power by reversing the pump turbines into generators as well as through the 317-foot head powerhouse.

The project was financed by $737 million in revenue bonds sold to private investors, the same as for the St. Lawrence power project. The plant had the nation's greatest capacity at the time of completion, replacing Grand Coulee Dam as the largest. It ranks as one of the nation's largest public works construction projects. Besides the development of power, the project greatly improved the environment around the American side of the Niagara Falls area and financed remedial measures for the falls themselves. The FPC license provided that PASNY could expend up to $15 million for a scenic drive and park near the falls, with the cost to be considered part of the project investment. Since completion of the Niagara project, PASNY has been directed by state legislation to construct three additional power plants to assist in meeting the requirements of New York State. Under May 1972 legislation, the state is making studies of ways to provide base-load power to the Metropolitan Transportation Authority which operates the subway and commuter railways in New York City and nearby counties as well as bridges, tunnels, and other facilities.

The FitzPatrick Nuclear Plant is located on Lake Ontario, half way between the St. Lawrence and Niagara power projects. It has a capacity of 821,000 kilowatts. Construction started in May 1970, and the project was completed in about three years at a cost of $320 million.

The Blenheim-Gilboa Project is a four-unit, 1 million-kilowatt pumped-storage project located in the Schoharie County towns of Blenheim and Gilboa, about 35 miles southwest of Albany. It consists of a lower and an upper reservoir, with a head differential of 1,000 feet, connected by a 28-foot diameter tunnel through the powerhouse. Such installations are an integral part of an electric power system that contains large fossil-fuel or nuclear-powered steam turbines. The economy of these big thermal units comes from continuous operation. Thus, when the electricity load is down during nighttime, the excess capacity can be used to pump water into the upper reservoir, which becomes in effect a large energy storage battery. When the peak power demands occur during the day, the water flow can be reversed through the pump-turbines to generate electricity. While about one third of the energy is lost in the process, the power is available when and as needed to meet the peak loads. The excess base load, the lowest-cost power, is used provide the storage. Construction of this project began in July 1963 and was completed four years later. The cost, including all related environmental benefits, was about $163 million.

The Breakabeen Pumped Storage Project, located about 5 miles north of the Blenheim-Gilboa, has a planned generating capacity of a million kilowatts, and it will be similar to the latter plant. Final environmental and design studies were completed and the application for construction was submitted to FPC in 1975.

The first transmission line constructed by the authority was 70 miles of a 230,000-volt line from the St. Lawrence project to Plattsburgh, New York. Ties are made into the Ontario Hydro grid system in Canada at both St. Lawrence and Niagara. High-voltage lines connect the projects to enable flexibility for maximum use of the two projects. Two 345,000-volt circuits, the first of such voltage to be placed in service in New York State, extend eastward from Niagara Falls to Utica where ties are made to other power grids. Authority transmission lines total about 820 circuit miles and tie into existing lines of other utilities. Power is delivered to the various customers through cooperative wheeling arrangements.

An environmental problem of the 1970s is the large transmission lines needed to transport electric energy. The work of PASNY is illustrative of how this problem is being met, both by public- and investor-owned utilities. The PASNY policy has been, wherever possible, to provide for the multiple-use of land along the power line right-of-way. Generally, permanent easements are acquired, by which the right to set up and maintain the lines is obtained. They allow the owner to use the land on the right-of-way for any purpose that does not interfere with operation of the line. The uses to which land has been put include farming, recreation, wildlife management, and even Christmas tree farming. Cooperative efforts on outdoor recreation and wildlife conservation are carried out with state and federal agencies.

The lines are designed to transmit electricity reliably and economically under conditions which will preserve and enhance environmental values. Scenic, historic, and populated areas are avoided whenever possible. Besides multiple-use of the right-of-way land, features of the program include selective clearing and screen planting to preserve the aesthetics of rights-of-way in the project areas, especially at major highway and stream crossings and in certain naturally scenic areas. The goal is to minimize or eliminate an adverse impact on the environment and to give careful consideration to physiographic, socio-economic, and other features of the surrounding areas. Selective clearing maximizes the use of existing vegetation, and screen planting is undertaken where appropriate.

The public works power program of the State of New York demonstrates how natural resources can be used to provide wide benefits to the public. It also illustrates the benefits of cooperating with existing investor-owned utilities in meeting demands for electric power. The PASNY generates about one fourth of the electrical power used in New York State. The PASNY total in 1974 was over 25 billion kilowatt-hours, the largest of any non-federal public power agency.

Rural Electrification Administration

Although electricity had come into widespread commercial use in the United States by 1900—there was about 5 million-kilowatt capacity with 10 billion kilowatt-hour production in the United States in 1909—by 1935 millions of Americans were still without the benefits of electric power. Only about 10 percent of the farms had central station electric service. A few farmers generated their own current, despite its high cost. The rest of American agriculture was burdened by inconvenience, drudgery, and spirit-numbing labor which often began an hour before dawn and ended well after dark. Heavy work was done by steam engines, horses, and human muscle. Some farmers had telephones and battery-powered radios; many had cars; but electric wires did not reach out to them.

America lagged behind other nations in rural electrification. Most European countries, for example, had a much higher proportion of electric service for rural populations. This was partly because European farmers usually lived in villages, going out to work on farms and returning home at night. Also, their farms were small, and the villages were close together. Government interest also counted heavily. For instance, by 1934 there were 5,000 cooperative societies in Germany serving rural areas. Over half of Germany's

electricity, 53 percent, came from publicly owned plants. By 1935 Holland served 100 percent of its farms with electricity, and 93 percent of French rural communities had electric service. By 1930 American cities had become a vast network of wires with everything from elevators to hospitals depending on them, but 90 percent of the rural areas remained without electricity.

As early as 1900, John Martin, a founder of the Pacific Gas and Electric Company (PG&E), had introduced an electric irrigation pump on a Yuba County, California farm to promote rural use of electricity. The PG&E overcame farmer skepticism by paying all costs and guaranteeing satisfaction. The pump was successful and helped sell rural electrification in the state. By 1923 there were 32,064 electrified farms in California and 81,100 by 1935, when 54 percent of the state's farms were served with highline power.

In 1912 the Middle West Utilities System formulated a rural policy which recognized that service could be profitably extended only to "compact groups of small towns." This position was generally in line with that of the industry as a whole. Of necessity, power companies had to provide a return on investments, and usually this was considered to require a minimum of thirty-two customers per mile of transmission line. Early in 1923, the Committee on the Relation of Electricity to Agriculture (CREA) was formed by the Department of Agriculture, partly in response to agitation for rural electrification in Pennsylvania. The CREA surveys showed that at the end of 1923 electricity was available on 177,560 farms, only 2.8 percent of the total number in the country.

Agriculture in 1925 used about 47 million horsepower in addition to human labor. This was twice as much power as was used in all other manufacturing, and it was exceeded only by that utilized in transportation. Electricity accounted for only 4 percent. The yearly cost of this farm power, derived from animals, gas and oil engines, wind, water, and electricity, was about $3 billion. There was a huge potential market for anyone who could show farmers a savings in cost. Utility experts estimated, however, that farm work was so heavy that electric power could not be used without a capital outlay that the farmer could not afford.

During the quarter century preceding creation of the Rural Electrification Administration (REA), a movement developed concerned with electrification as a public interest beyond mere regulation of commercial electric corporations. Great men—such as Gifford Pinchot, George W. Norris, Franklin D. Roosevelt, Morris Llewellyn Cooke, and others—were involved in persistent educational programs concerned with conditions of adequacy and cost of electric service. Not until the 1936 Rural Electrification Act established REA was there an agency whose primary purpose was development of rural electrification. But for the men who helped establish the agency, its realization capped years of devotion at times in the face of apparently insuperable difficulties.

Outstanding among these men was Senator George W. Norris of Nebraska. Throughout the 1920s, Norris fought to keep the great power site of Muscle Shoals on the Tennessee River from being transferred to private ownership and paved the way for TVA. The support of Norris and others for public power was one of the forces that helped to make rural electrification possible.

Morris Llewellyn Cooke studied the cost of power distribution for many years and held important positions with public works in Pennsylvania. For example, he served as director of public works in Philadelphia from 1912 to 1916. While working as director of Pennsylvania's power survey in 1925, Cooke wrote: "From the power field perhaps more than from any other quarter we can expect in the near future the most substantial aid in raising the standards of living, in eliminating the physical drudgery of life, and in winning the age-old struggle against poverty . . . . Our first concern must be with the small user, particularly the farmer . . . ." He served as the out-of-state member of PASNY from 1932 to 1934. He was also chairman of the Mississippi Valley Committee in 1933-1934 that defined the need for a rural electrification program. Cooke was also one of a group close to President Roosevelt and

Senator Norris who perceived in the 1935 Emergency Relief Act appropriation an opportunity for the beginning of a program of rural electrification under federal auspices. It was in the logic of events that he should be appointed the first administrator of REA.

The fledgling federal public works program to provide electric power to rural areas received neither a warm reception nor a hopeful appraisal from the industry. A special committee of utility executives convened at the suggestion of Cooke to "survey the approximate extent to which development of rural electrification may be effected promptly in cooperation with the Rural Electrification Administration." Their report of July 24, 1935 expressed the judgment that, in light of earlier extensive research, "there are very few farms requiring electricity for major farm operations that are not now served." And, the report continued, "Additional rural consumers must largely be those who use electricity for household purposes . . . the problem is a social one rather than an economic problem; not one of rates, but of financing the wiring and purchase of appliances."

Shortly after establishing REA, President Roosevelt issued regulations that set down uniform conditions for applying relief funds. Some of these presented problems to REA: at least 25 percent of the funds were required to be spent directly for labor; and 90 percent of the labor had to be procured from relief rolls with certification by the United States Employment Service. The REA staff found itself unable to employ grants or grants-in-aid on REA projects under these conditions. Construction of electric lines called for skilled labor not often found on relief rolls in areas where projects were planned.

In August 1935, the President issued the regulation that established the agency as a rural electrification banker and set the permanent pattern—REA became a lending agency, freed from the unworkable requirements in the earlier regulations. It established rural electrification as an orderly government lending program on an interest-bearing, self-liquidating basis. The REA program thus became a national business investment with low interest rates and a long loan retirement period.

During the next forty years, over a thousand borrowers, independent business cooperative enterprises, directly and indirectly increased the number of farms electrified from about 10 percent to over 98 percent.

After a slow start of the REA program, private companies abandoned the position that neither they nor the farmers could afford to bring power to the farm. During 1935 the number of farms newly electrified by private companies increased by 175 percent. However, the private company rural lines extended only to selected areas, and they were unable to provide full area coverage.

These and other problems led to the 1936 Rural Electrification Act, which provided for several types of loans. Those under Section 4 were to be used to build electric power lines and for generating and transmitting electricity. Preference was given to borrowers other than private companies; loans were self-liquidating within twenty-five years; and the borrower was to pay the same rate of interest that the government paid on its long-term obligations. Section 5 loans enabled the farmer to buy electrical equipment. Thus, REA as it operates today came into being. The cooperative was to do the job that private industry had been unable to do.

It was necessary for REA to devise legal, economic, and engineering analyses to appraise the ability of a proposed cooperative to become a financially sound business. Legal codes, varying from state to state, determined the form the co-op could take. The REA drafted a model state law for rural electric co-ops to help insure sound organizational structure and urged its passage where needed. Engineers had to design lines that were less costly, yet durable. Negotiations had to be carried on to obtain wholesale power. Each cooperative needed a capable manager who would be both engineer and administrator.

The purpose of the program, to help people cooperatively meet their needs, was sound. The many problems were gradually overcome and the program was launched. "Electricity at reasonable rates," stated the Arkansas Extension Service's 1935-1936 annual report, "represents one of the greatest needs of a large percentage of Arkansas farms. Its effect on home life, community development and agriculture efficiency is of real value, economically and socially, to the area served." Hard work, dedication, and determination began to show results and; as the lights came on down the country road, rural America was changed.

Bonneville Power Administration

A group of electric cooperative members in Washington State review their plans for 1940 with the co-op manager (extreme right).

Cooperatives, owned by the people they serve, are controlled through a system of one member, one vote. Members have a vital interest, not only in their dollar investment, but also in the type, adequacy, and cost of service they receive. Cooperative boards of directors are elected by the membership on the basis of their knowledge of, and interest in, the organization. Generally, they serve without pay or for nominal fees to cover expenses. The board hires a manager to take charge of operating the public works business for the benefit of the member-consumer-owners.

Since the earliest days of rural electrification, there have been charges that cooperatives do not pay their fair share of taxes that other businesses are forced to pay. Rural electric cooperatives paid $83 million in taxes in 1973, mostly state and local taxes. In some areas, the rural electric cooperative is the largest taxpayer. Tax situations vary, of course, from one locality to another. A few states enacted special tax rulings for certain types of businesses to enable them to serve thinly populated areas or otherwise provide needed services. In certain instances, rural electric co-ops, qualified for this type of help, thus making it possible to serve sparsely settled territory.

Before REA, the cost of building rural power lines was between $1,500 and $2,000 per mile. The REA engineers concentrated on finding new and cheaper ways that would be both simple and sturdy; and by the end of 1936, REA announced nine projects completed in as many states at an average cost of $941 per mile of line. By 1939 REA systems were building lines for an average of less than $825 per mile including overhead. A combination of several innovations reduced the cost of rural construction. High-strength conductors, which came on the market about the time REA began, were a major development. Longer spans could be used, dropping the number of poles needed per mile from about thirty to eighteen. Another cost-saver was the adoption of so-called vertical space line construction rather than the familiar cross-arm.

Large-scale bidding and construction were made possible by standardization of poles, pole-top hardware, transformers, and conductors. Simplified construction procedures with specialized crews were developed. Strong motivation played an important part in the program. Crews sensed they were part of an important adventure, one of filling a human need.

Other cost-reducing programs included a "group wiring plan" which cut wiring costs for farm homes from $70 to around $55. Manufacturers, in cooperation with REA, offered "lighting packages" containing fixtures for a six-room house—nine modern fixtures sold for around $18, about half the cost of comparable fixtures bought separately. Group plans were developed for installation of plumbing—an electric water-pressure system with kitchen sink, water and drainage pipes; and a disposal system with seepage drains. The down payment was $24; monthly installments were $1.90 each. These various plans helped farmers, aided the struggling co-ops, and by opening up tremendous new markets for electrical equipment spurred an ailing economy.

In 1939 REA was placed under the aegis of the Department of Agriculture. By then more than 30 percent of American farms were receiving central station electric service, three times the number at the start of the program. On September 12, 1940, the loan was approved to serve the millionth consumer on REA lines. There were 732 REA systems by 1941, and the program assisted in supplying electric power to new military installations. The same year, REA headquarters offices were moved to St. Louis, Missouri, to free Washington office space for war agencies.

Shortages caused by the war effort adversely affected the rural electrification program. Authorization of the War Production Board (WPB) was required before REA borrowers could purchase construction materials. The WPB permitted completion of thirty-four projects already underway. Because the war effort increased badly needed farm production, in 1943 WPB eased restrictions to permit REA borrowers to build short extensions to farmers.

In order to encourage rural electric cooperatives to serve areas in which returns would be even smaller than the average to 1944, Representative Stephen Pace drafted a bill designed to ease the financial burden and difficulties of reaching and serving isolated farm sections. In September 1944, the Pace Act set a uniform interest rate of 2 percent on REA loans and gave the co-ops a longer time, thirty-five years, in which to repay the principal. The act extended the life of the agency indefinitely.

When World War II ended in 1945, REA headquarters returned to Washington, D.C., and an REA loan provided for service to the 2 millionth consumer. "Area coverage" was reemphasized. The first loans were approved to serve areas in the Great Plains and in the West. By 1946 materials for construction began to be available to private contractors. On November 10, 1948, a loan was approved that provided electric power to the 3 millionth consumer, and during 1949 REA loans passed the $1 billion mark.

On October 28, 1949, President Truman signed H.R. 2960 amending the Rural Electrification Act to provide for a rural telephone loan program to be administered by REA. It authorized self-liquidating loans at an interest rate of 2 percent for a period up to thirty-five years for the extension and improvement of telephone service. The reason was clear. By 1940 there were fewer farms with telephones than in 1920. Most small communities had some service, but neglect and lack of capital caused many lines to deteriorate into disrepair or total disuse.

The REA helped farmer mutuals merge into new cooperative or commercial systems. Although cost of rural telephone construction in thinly settled areas was high, REA borrowers achieved satisfactory operating margins by combining the rural areas with an associated town and community center. Telephone systems were designed to serve "communities of interest." Also, cost-saving improvements were made in technology to provide the service to remote areas.

By 1975 REA had advanced a total of $2 billion to 656 commercial telephone companies and 242 cooperatives to finance rural telephone facilities in forty-six states. Over 700,000 miles of telephone lines were in operation. More than 6 million rural families, businesses, and establishments received service. In fiscal year 1974, REA loan funds to rural telephone systems totaled $303 million, a record high. Of this amount, REA loaned $140 million and the Rural Telephone Bank (RTB) approved loans of $163 million. Part of this money provided for new services for 145,000 telephone subscribers. The total loan commitment for 1975 was over $400 million.

The RTB was established in 1971 by amendment to the Rural Electrification Act to provide a supplemental source of financing for rural telephone systems. An agency of the United States, the bank is managed by a governor and a board of directors. It utilizes the staff and facilities of REA and other Department of Agriculture agencies to administer its program. Bank ownership, shared by the federal government and the bank's borrowers, ultimately will become completely borrower-owned and controlled. Originally, the interest rate established for bank loans ranged from 4 to 8 percent and was based on the borrower's ability to pay. Later, this was changed to the bank's cost of money.

Two policies especially have been reaffirmed and adhered to by REA administrators over the years—"area coverage" and "progressively diminishing agency assistance for its borrowers." The implementation of the latter is demonstrated by 1,300 REA employees in 1950 being reduced to 754 in 1974, handling more borrowers, more money, and different kinds of loan procedures. In June 1953, the census reported less than 10 percent of farms without central station electric service. The net worth of REA electric borrowers passed the $200 million mark. The Inter-Industry Farm Electric Utilization Council (later called the Farm Electrification Council) was organized in 1954 to draw all segments of the electric industry into an organization where "cooperation" was possible, encouraged, and realized in promoting wider and better use of electricity on the farms. That year, REA officials and co-op leaders made their first explorations into the possibilities of atomic energy. In 1956 REA approved its first loan for conventional components of a nuclear power plant to the Rural Cooperative Power Association, Elk River, Minnesota.

By April 1958, REA had approved a loan to provide service for the 5 millionth rural consumer, and total electric repayments to the government passed the $1 billion mark. By 1976 over $13.5 billion had been loaned by REA to rural electric systems. Of this amount, less than $45,000 had been lost through foreclosure.

The largest single generating unit financed by REA, a 100,000-kilowatt steam plant, went into operation May 31, 1958 near Lexington, Nebraska. The REA also funded the first 230,000-volt transmission line in that state. The REA and its borrowers were moving into the big time in power supply and transmission. On February 6, 1974, Administrator David Hamil signed loans that would be part of a package involving $537 million for the Cooperative Power Association, Minneapolis, and the United Power Association, Elk River, Minnesota, to finance a 900,000-kilowatt, coal-fired complex near Underwood, North Dakota.

The rural cooperatives have slowly earned acceptance as partners in the electric utility industry. For instance, REA groups are

Rural Electrification Administration

The REA program includes 1.8 million miles of power transmission lines, 50 percent of the nation's total mileage. By 1975 over 98 percent of the farms of America had central station power.

members of the Mid-Continent Area Power Pool, and they have power supply arrangements with the Otter Tail Power Company, Minnesota Power and Light Company, Interstate Power Company as well as with the United States Bureau of Reclamation. While REA-financed systems generate approximately 2 percent of the nation's total power and serve about 10 percent of the country's consumers, they have built and are operating over 1.8 million miles of transmission lines, about 50 percent of the nation's total.

Pooling arrangements and interconnections are becoming more commonplace among REA power suppliers and neighboring investor-owned utilities. For instance, Central Iowa Power Cooperative (CIPCO) of Marion, Iowa, has been operating under coordinating arrangements with the Iowa Electric Light and Power Company for almost thirty years. The CIPCO and Corn Belt Power Cooperative, at Humboldt, Iowa, with REA financing, all share ownership in the Iowa Electric Light and Power's nuclear generating facility, the Duane Arnold Energy Center near Cedar Rapids. In Missouri, the Associated Electric Cooperative, working with forty distribution co-ops, commercial power companies, and private credit sources, is constructing a 600,000-kilowatt generating unit and related transmission facilities at New Madrid, Missouri. Intra-industry cooperation is im-

proving in all the states.

Financing capital and interest rates came under severe scrutiny in 1972. However, after a year of hard-questioning and review, Public Law 93-32 was signed in May 1973, providing guaranteed loan which expanded resources for financing capital needs. Borrowers still had the protection of the historic 2 percent interest rate under certain special conditions, but the bulk of REA financing would be at 5 percent.

Rural non-farm use of electricity is increasing. Commercial and industrial loads are being added to lines of REA-financed systems at a rate of more than 21,000 a year. These users double their power consumption every five years, compared with seven years for residential users. The REA-financed systems account for 5.4 percent of all electric energy sold to ultimate consumers—including farm and non-farm.

The REA systems are active in fuel conservation and energy research and development, and they participate in the Electric Power Research Institute. The REA conducts annual rural community development surveys. From 1961, when the agency began the surveys of their borrower local area development programs, to 1975, more than 467,000 new jobs have been created in rural areas through the 7,336 local projects these borrowers helped establish. The REA power supply borrower needs are expected to be at least $1.6 billion each year over the next five or six years. As REA systems improve their capabilities for dealing with the private money market, sources of capital are expected to expand. This is in keeping with the act that directs that "rural electric and telephone systems should be encouraged and assisted to develop their resources and ability to achieve the financial . . . organizations and other sources at reasonable rates and terms consistent with the loan applicant's ability to pay, and achievement of the Act's objectives."

The progress of REA has been beneficial to the entire nation; it helps make agriculture more productive, improves rural living, creates a large rural market for goods and services, and stimulates the rural growth that helps alleviate urban congestion. There was evidence in 1975 that the population flow from rural to urban areas was being reversed, and this will be of increasing importance to REA activities in the years ahead. Thus, the rural electrification accomplishment is another example of the flexibility of the American system in developing a public works program to meet the needs of people. It demonstrates again that government and industry, even with the conflicts that arise, can cooperate and work together to provide a dynamic, vital program to make life better for all.

Municipal Public Power

The earliest public works providing central station electric service were municipal electric street lighting systems beginning in 1882, the first year of central electric service. The lighting systems grew rapidly, and it soon became evident that these new, flameless lights could be adapted to homes, businesses, and industry. Lines were strung from street lighting circuits to nearby homes and other buildings and the electric service for lighting expanded. With the availability of electricity came the development of electric motors to perform an ever-increasing variety of tasks. A new energy era had begun.

Typically, the first municipal systems used steam engines to generate electricity with direct current dynamos, although some communities were able to utilize primitive hydroelectric installations at local streams. The coal-fired steam engine continued to be the principal prime mover in municipal electric plants for nearly three decades. But about 1910 the diesel engine and related internal combustion engines were introduced and within a few years became dominant in municipal electric plants. The quick success of the internal combusion units was explained in part by the fact that the steam engine plants required fifteen to twenty pounds of coal to generate a single kilowatt-hour of electricity.

The earliest electric generating stations, whether publicly or privately owned, provided direct current from small, isolated plants. During these early years, it was not so much a question of quality of service as of providing any service at all. The development of alternating current technology made possible long distance transmission of electricity, and the introduction of the steam turbine marked the beginnings of modern thermal generation around the turn of the century.

The numbers of both privately and publicly owned electric systems grew rapidly from a handful in 1882 and reached a peak after World War I. Through a continuing trend of mergers and consolidations, the numbers of private power companies declined from more than 4,000 around 1920 to fewer than 300 in 1975. Municipally owned utilities numbered 3,047 in 1924 and declined to fewer than 2,000 in 1930. A 1975 listing shows about 2,100 municipal electric utilities, slightly more than the 2,020 reported in 1929. These municipal systems vary in size from those serving only a few customers to the Los Angeles Department of Water and Power which serves over 1.1 million. Although there continues to be public versus private power disputes in various communities from time to time, the number of municipal electric systems has remained stable for a period of more than forty-five years.

The following are examples of municipalities that operate some of the oldest hydroelectric projects in the country. The Marquette Department of Light and Power in Michigan, for example, owns a hydroelectric project (3,700 kilowatt) dating back to the previous century. The first facility was built in 1890 to provide for street lighting. Others were added in 1900, 1918, and 1924.Today, the project functions as a peaking plant serving community power needs. The town went into the power business because no private enterprise was available to furnish the service in the upper peninsula. The town of Marshall, Michigan, became involved in the electric business in 1892, when it purchased a 319-kilowatt hydro project from a private owner. The town's City Water and Electric Works has since operated the project. Its original purpose was to serve as the source of power for street lighting; but the purpose has evolved to providing peaking power for general community use.

In Alaska, Petersburg Municipal Light and Power Agency's hydroelectric project dates back to 1916. Capacity of the project has increased to 1,600 kilowatts, and the output serves as the base load for the entire community. The original project provided power for street lighting and for canning fish at a local cannery. Lack of private enterprise to do the job led the municipality to act on its own.

The Kaukauna Electrical and Water Department in Wisconsin in 1974 purchased hydroelectric facilities that date back to 1907. The plant was built by the Green Bay and Mississippi Canal Company, which began in 1866. In 1872 the company's canal operation was taken over by the Army Corps of Engineers. Originally, the company used falling water to generate mechanical power for grinding, but then it established hydroelectric generating facilities for street lighting. The plant operates as base-load, run-of-the-river plant, serving the entire community of Kaukauna.

Salt River Project

Theodore Roosevelt Dam and powerhouse produced the first electricity for the Salt River Project in 1911.

In addition to the more than 2,000 municipal electric utilities serving individual communities in forty-eight of the fifty states (only Montana and Hawaii do not have municipal electric systems), there are other types of local, non-federal, publicly owned electric systems. In the West, a number of irrigation districts entered the electric power business by developing hydroelectric potential along with water storage for agricultural use. The Salt River Project, the first multipurpose project authorized under the 1902 Federal Reclamation Act, now serves more

than 240,000 electric consumers in the fast-growing Phoenix area. In Washington State, an agrarian movement in the 1920s led to the creation of county public utility districts; and twenty-two such districts now furnish electric service to nearly 400,000 consumers in that state. Four public utility districts serve counties in Oregon.

Development of water power resources has spurred the expansion of local public power in several states. A water project program in Nebraska led to the acquisition of private power company properties and the creation of the nation's first all-public power state. Thus, all electric service is consumer-owned, either by public agencies or cooperative systems.

The PASNY, which constructed the St. Lawrence and Niagara projects, is now moving into nuclear and pumped-storage projects, as has been discussed. Other major state power projects include the South Carolina Public Service Authority (Santee-Cooper) and the Grand River Dam Authority in Oklahoma. Offshore public power agencies include the Puerto Rico Water Resources, the Virgin Islands Water and Power Authority, Guam Power Authority, the Electrical Division of the publicly owned Panama Canal Company, and the Electric Utility Division of the government of American Samoa.

Municipal electric systems and other local publicly owned electric utilities remain a vital segment of the pluralistic electric utility industry after more than nine decades of central station service. They serve more than 10 million customers, about 13.5 percent of the total, providing a competitive stimulus in an essential but otherwise monopolistic industry.

To meet the challenge of growing loads in an era of large-scale electric generating units, the generally small local public power systems are banding together in joint action projects to furnish the economies of scale to numbers of independent electric systems. These projects, sometimes including rural electric systems, encompass construction of large new generating stations and the purchase of shares in large plants being built by private power companies. An example of the cooperative programs being developed is the 2.3 million-kilowatt, coal-fired steam plant in Page, Arizona. Municipal and other local public power entities, along with the federal government and investor-owned electric utilities, joined together to build and operate the plant under mutually beneficial arrangements. The local public power systems will continue to be a significant segment of the electric utility industry.

Nuclear Power

The American public became aware of the nation's commitment to atomic energy development in August 1945, when the first atomic bombs were dropped on Hiroshima and Nagasaki, Japan, in the last days of World War II. The initial discussions of atomic energy naturally concerned the dreadful responsibilities and consequences this new weapon brought to the United States and the world. The destructive potential of the atom seemed a threat to life itself. At present, with even more advanced weaponry, this is still a basic concern.

While the atomic bomb was the initial result of "history's largest crash construction program," a $2 billion industrial and supporting works project was accomplished in a little over two years and created a new source of energy for man's constructive use. In the earliest days of research, scientists were aware of the potential of peaceful application of the energy from the atom being used for generation of electric power. In over three decades of research and development, the United States has pursued this goal of atomic power; and by the beginning of 1976, about 42 million kilowatts of electricity were being generated by nuclear power stations. The amount is expected to triple by 1985. Accomplishments have been accompanied by many difficulties of both technology and policy.

In the project that produced the facilities for controlled nuclear power, the United States was working under a sword of Damocles. In 1938 German scientists discovered that it was possible to split the uranium atom. The following year, several of America's new refugee scientists—Albert Einstein, Leo Szilard, and others—warned President Roosevelt that Hitler might be able to build on this knowledge of uranium fission and develop a terrible superweapon. Consequently, in the fall of 1939, the President established a government-backed program of nuclear energy research for the United States.

A little over three years later, December 2, 1942, a telephone message was flashed from Chicago: "The Italian navigator has landed. The natives are friendly." To those who knew the code words, the message meant that Enrico Fermi, a refugee scientist from Italy and a team of other scientists, had unleashed and controlled the energy of the atom by accomplishing the world's first controlled nuclear chain reaction. Their work took place in a crowded room underneath the stands at the University of Chicago football stadium.

However, before this experiment succeeded and while much research still remained to be done, the decision had been made to create the huge industrial plants required to produce an atomic bomb. Utilizing the Army Corps of Engineers, an organization was established that became known as the Manhattan Engineer District. And the "Manhattan Project" was placed under the command of Brigadier General Leslie R. Groves, deputy chief of construction of the Office of the Chief of Engineers. The facilities necessary to unleash and control the power of the atom were constructed in deepest secrecy in several locations across the country and involved about 100,000 workmen at the construction sites and an equally impressive number producing construction materials and plant equipment.

The principal facilities required to effect atomic fission and produce the bomb were located at three sites: the Clinton Engineer Works near Knoxville, Tennessee; the Hanford Engineer Works in Washington State; and research and bomb-assembly facilities at Los Alamos, New Mexico. The most extensive of the resulting industrial plants was the Clinton Engineer Works situated in the foothills of the Cumberland Mountain Range in the isolated Clinch River Valley of Tennessee. Three methods of separating uranium isotopes were carried on at Clinton—electromagnetic, gaseous diffusion, and thermal diffusion. In addition, there was a pilot plant for plutonium production. Together with the full-fledged city of Oak Ridge, built for its construction and operating personnel, the Clinton facilities cost $1 billion. At the peak of construction, 47,000 workmen were on the site. Clinton's residential complex, Oak Ridge, grew into the fifth largest city in Tennessee. The new community included nearly 10,000 family dwelling units, 13,000 dormitory spaces, 5,000 trailers, and more than 16,000 hutment and barrack accommodations, complete with public works support facilities.

Bonneville Power Administration

Atomic works under construction in 1945 at Hanford, Washington.

In Washington State, the Hanford Engineer Works, a plutonium production plant, was built on a 630-square mile site near a big bend of the Columbia River. It included three huge reactors spaced miles apart on the right banks of the river; two chemical separation areas some distance to the south; a plant for making uranium slugs and testing pile materials; a large construction camp at Hanford; and a town for operating personnel at Richland. Construction forces reached a peak of 45,000. The Hanford reactors were large-scale versions of the small, crude "pile," or reactor, developed by Fermi in Chicago. For nuclear weapons, these reactors produced plutonium, a radioactive metallic element that exists in nature in such minute quantities that it can be detected only with great difficulty

and not in sufficient quantities to be processed. The reactors produced plutonium artifically by a process known as transmutation—the conversion of one element to another. Inside the reactors, transmutation took place when the internal structure of uranium atoms was violently rearranged.

The most secret and sensitive of the Manhattan projects, the Los Alamos research and bomb-assembly laboratory, was located at a 54,000-acre, isolated site in New Mexico. Conceived initially as a physical laboratory with a staff of 150 scientists and technicians, it became a quasi-military compound jammed with 7,000 people whose purposes involved ordnance, metallurgy, and engineering as well as physics. By 1975 Los Alamos had grown to a city of 17,000. In addition to housing and support facilities, the project included an extensive air-conditioned and dustproof chemical-metallurgical laboratory, a proving ground, enlarged water and power supplies, and various other public works support facilities such as schools and municipal buildings. The University of California operated the new laboratory under contract with the Manhattan District.

The wife of one of the first scientists at the project wrote: "I felt akin to the pioneer women accompanying their husbands across uncharted plains westward, alert to dangers, resigned to the fact that they journeyed, for weal or woe, into the 'Unknown'." It was indeed a journey into the "Unknown," for the world's first man-made atomic explosion took place only twenty-eight months after the arrival of the first scientific contingent at the project.

Three weeks later, on August 6, 1945, the B-29 *Enola Gay* flew 31,600 feet above Hiroshima, the second most important military center in Japan. At 9:15 a.m., the atomic bomb was dropped on the target below; and a few seconds later, some four square miles of the city lay completely razed. On August 9, a second bomb was dropped over Nagasaki. On August 14, Emperor Hirohito sued for peace, and World War II was over. The basic knowledge had been developed, and the initial facilities were in place from which to build a nuclear power program.

To produce electricity with atomic energy, a nuclear reactor is needed. The reactor starts and controls the self-sustaining chain reaction necessary to generate heat for production of electric power. The reactor merely replaces the boiler in a conventional steam power plant. Instead of coal, oil, or gas producing heat and steam to operate a turbine generator, atomic fuel is used in a reactor to perform essentially the same function. The differences in types of reactors are in the ways the nuclear reaction is controlled and the heat utilized to produce steam.

During the war years, scientists had resolved most of the basic problems such as the maintenance of the chain reaction, the effects of fission upon the reactor itself, control of the reactor while in operation, fuel processing, and heat utilization. By the end of the war, the basic technology necessary for a reactor program had been developed. However, the first reactors did not reach a high enough temperature to produce the high-grade steam necessary for power production. Although as early as 1944 designs were being considered for a power plant, the general conclusion was that the technology was not yet sufficiently developed to deal with the problems of a high-temperature reactor.

After considerable debate in Congress and elsewhere concerning the way to manage the future of atomic energy and the relative roles civilian and military control would play, the Atomic Energy Act was signed into law by President Truman on August 1, 1946. The act provided for a five-member civilian Atomic Energy Commission (AEC) with full management and advisory support, including a Military Liaison Committee, to insure absolute government monopoly and control over atomic energy development. At that time, atomic energy was still basically a weapons technology. Therefore, control and administration were approached cautiously to insure full, rational development of this new technology without jeopardizing the United States' monopoly and security. The AEC was given extensive power over the development and use of fissionable materials, which were to remain government property. An unprecedented security and information control system was established. Congress also founded a Joint Committee on Atomic Energy to maintain a measure of legislative control.

Following the end of the war, the Manhattan District concentrated on producing fissionable materials and began the first United States atomic power program. When AEC, with Chairman David E. Lilienthal, former chairman of TVA, took over the program on January 1, 1946, it continued the high priority of fissionable material production, but it made a careful two-year review of the entire reactor program. By late 1948, a program was formulated, directed primarily at development of a naval propulsion reactor, central-station electric power reactors, and basic technology.

The prototype submarine *Nautilus* was constructed and brought to full power by 1953 and launched in 1954 with its reactor propulsion system. An experimental breeder reactor was built at the 400,000-acre National Reactor Testing Station near Idaho Falls, Idaho. In 1953 it demonstrated for the first time that breeding (that is, producing more fissionable material than is consumed while producing power) was possible. New discoveries of high grade ore in the continental United States established a firm base for a civilian power industry as well as for defense requirements. By 1950 industry had a growing interest in development of nuclear power by private enterprise. As the problems and issues clarified, AEC issued a policy statement in 1953 that power development as a "national objective" and that a part of the policy was to promote and encourage free competition and private investment in the development work while at the same time accepting "certain responsibilities for furthering technical progress . . . to provide a necessary basis for such development." However, AEC and others recognized many problems remained before economically competitive nuclear power could be a reality.

On December 7, 1953, AEC asked for bids from industry to engage in a cooperative arrangement for the construction and operation of a nuclear power plant "to determine the practicability of nuclear power for civilian purposes." From this proposal came the Pressurized Water Reactor Shippingport Atomic Power Station in Pennsylvania, which, with its 90,000-kilowatt station going into production in 1957, became the first full-scale civilian nuclear power project. The agreement provided for AEC's ownership of the reactor and company ownership of the generating facilities.

Westinghouse Atomic Power Division

The world's first nuclear power station to generate commercial electrical power was this 90,000-kilowatt plant at Shippingport, Pennsylvania, which began operation in 1957.

A significant development was President Eisenhower's "Atoms for Peace" speech delivered to the General Assembly of the United Nations on December 8, 1953. In it he outlined a plan for international cooperation in developing the peaceful uses of atomic energy under an International Atomic Energy Agency and pledged full United States support. This gave added incentive to an accelerated nuclear power program by attaching national prestige and foreign policy to domestic power goals.

Debates during the first half of 1954 primarily centered on how best to encourage nuclear power development as well as on public versus private development issues. The taxpayers' investment in overall atomic energy expansion by that time was about $12 billion, and public advocates wanted assurance that the distribution of future benefits of atomic energy would be fair and equitable. Furthermore, there was a concern that private development was not yet economically feasible since turning the program over to private industry would mean unpredictable delays. The private enterprise advocates felt that government military priorities had held power development in check and that only they could offer the rivalry and incentive that would accelerate the program.

The 1954 Atomic Energy Act became law on August 30. It permitted AEC to license private industry to possess and use, but not own, special nuclear materials and to own reactors to build and utilize the materials. The AEC would continue to regulate development against "special interests" and to protect public health and safety. A clause gave public utilities preference in the disposal of by-product energy from government reactors. Tight security measures were provided so that a would-be developer was subject to a long list of restrictive rules and regulations.

To stimulate private development, in January 1955 AEC invited industry to submit proposals for building power demonstration reactors. Four proposals, using all but one of AEC's five basic designs, were accepted and subsequently completed. One of these was a public power station in Nebraska. That fall, invitations for units smaller that 40,000 kilowatts resulted in four small generating plants, two of which were consumer-owned, one municipal, and one rural electric cooperative. Two large utility companies also elected to build central-station nuclear plants without government support.

Seven experimental power reactors were in operation in 1957, and nine other projects were under construction. In June 1960, the 200,000-kilowatt Dresden Nuclear Power Station, 50 miles southwest of Chicago, started operation. This was followed by the 175,000-kilowatt Yankee Nuclear Power Station at Rowe, Massachusetts, which began commercial power production in 1961. Although it appeared that economical nuclear power was imminent, recurring technical difficulties in some of the prototype and demonstration plants continued to frustrate hopes for an early new power source. However, problems were slowly overcome and confidence gradually built up in the prospects for economical power. By 1962 the government had expended $1.3 billion on the civilian reactor program; and industry, $500 million. By 1963 the reactor technology was proven so that true commercial development could begin.

In 1964 the Jersey Central Power and Light Company announced a contract for a 515,000-kilowatt nuclear reactor at Oyster Creek near Toms River, New Jersey. This was the first nuclear plant selected on purely economic grounds, in direct competition with a fossil-fuel plant, and without government assistance. In the next few years, more than half of the new electric generating plants announced in the United States were nuclear powered.

With the increasing interest within the private sector, there was concern regarding government monopoly of fissionable materials as a limitation on economic nuclear power growth. In August 1964, a law was passed that provided a transition period for a changeover from government ownership to private ownnership. Power reactor fuels were to be in private ownership by June 30, 1973. The act further authorized AEC to offer uranium enriching services to both domestic and foreign customers under long-term contracts. Tight security control and accountability of the fission material was maintained.

During 1965 momentum began to build for private construction of nuclear reactors. Technology focused on light water reactors that fit United States fuel availability and development progress, although gas-cooled reactors continued to be developed. It was becoming apparent that problems of fossil fuels lie ahead: the possible decrease in United States' production of petroleum and the environmental concerns about the sulphur and nitrogen

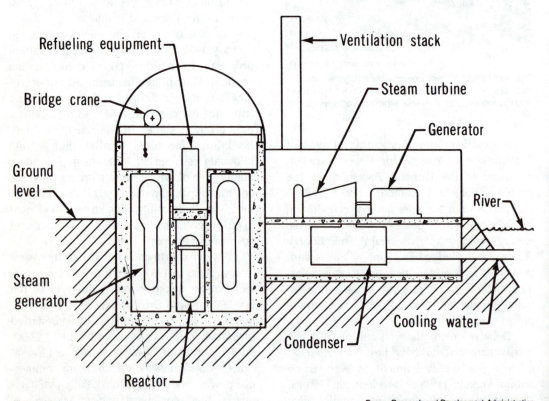

Figure 11-1.
Principal components of a pressurized-water nuclear power plant.

Energy Research and Development Administration

oxides produced from the burning of fossil fuels. Also a factor was the marketing drive of the reactor and generator manufacturers as their productive capacities increased. The goal of economically competitive nuclear power was in sight, and government participation in the facilities, except for fuel enrichment, ceased. Furthermore, the economies of size were also being demonstrated.

Environmental concerns were a problem, and the Calvert Cliffs court decision in July 1971 ruled that all nuclear plants licensed after January 1, 1970 would require an environmental impact statement in accordance with the National Environmental Policy Act. This created a hiatus that stopped further licensing for almost a year, but since that time the licensing has continued at a steady rate. By the end of 1970, there were 108 nuclear central-station generating units in operation, under construction or on order in the United States, with a total electrical capacity of over 86 million kilowatts. By March 31, 1975, the total had increased to 213 central-station, generating units with a total capacity of 218 million kilowatts. Fifty-five were licensed for commercial operation and were producing 36.7 million kilowatts. Of the plants in operation by the beginning of 1976, about 17 percent of the capacity was from publicly owned utilities, the remainder were investor-owned utilities. Of those under construction or with nuclear reactors ordered, about 15 percent were publicly owned utilities. Units as large as 1.3 million kilowatts were being ordered. As the various construction and operation problems were solved, dependability equaled or exceeded that of large fossil-fuel units.

With the growing operation of nuclear power generation, there are still major misgivings among some groups over safety. Concerns involve the handling and transporting of the enriched fuels, the reactor operations, and the handling and disposal of radioactive wastes. The dual role of AEC as both promoter and regulator of nuclear energy was attacked, even though the two functions were handled by separate divisions. There also were problems in delineating state responsibilities for regulation in relation to federal control.

While problems still remained, it appeared by 1975 that most were yielding to additional research, experience, and perseverance. Attempts were being made to reduce the ten-year period required from decision to go-ahead with a project to power production, by streamlining some of the licensing requirements. With additional experience and information, this appears possible. However, the delaying actions of several groups showed that greater efforts had to be made to demonstrate the safety of nuclear power to the general public.

A three-year study had been undertaken to evaluate risks to the public from the operation of large commercial nuclear power plants of the type in use. The results were published in August 1974. The study was headed by Norman C. Rasmussen of the Massachusetts Institute of Technology, assisted by a technical staff of about sixty scientists and engineers plus specialized consultants. The report's basic conclusion was that the risks were "very small." The designs of nuclear reactors, based on a in-depth concept that includes a series of "fail-safe" systems of protection, made the possibility of adverse health accidents remote. The study examined the various paths leading to a core melt accident to determine the probability of occurrence. With 100 reactors operating, as is anticipated for the United States by 1980, the study found that one such accident would occur about once every one and three-quarter centuries. However, only one in ten potential core melt accidents, occurring once in seventeen centuries, might produce measurable health effects.

As nuclear technology has advanced, it has done so with a close step-by-step assessment of its safety and reliability. With the establishment of a broadly based nuclear industry, a separation of the development and regulatory functions was accomplished after much debate by legislation signed October 11, 1974. This law dissolved AEC, effective early in 1975, and created the Energy Research and Development Administration (ERDA) and the Nuclear Regulatory Commission (NCR). The ERDA absorbed the research and development functions of AEC plus some of the energy research development activities of other agencies. The NCR, as an independent agency, extended progress already made in the complex area of nuclear regulation.

To support the programs of these two new agencies, by 1975 AEC had built up a research, development, and testing plant with a capital investment of about $9 billion, in addition to the wartime facilities in fifteen major installations across the nation. The experienced manpower developed in those installations and in associated industries, along with the physical plant, is a great national asset. Over thirty years of constantly improving technology in manufacturing, transporting, and protecting nuclear materials had been accomplished. By 1976 the 2,000 reactor years' experience of nuclear power plant operation, without a single accident that injured a member of the general public, demonstrated that progress was being made.

Power in the Future

During the 1960s, electricity use increased at a rate of 7.2 percent per year, compared to the overall energy use increase of 4 percent. By 1975 approximately a fourth of America's energy was going into the generation of electricity. By the end of the century, most studies estimate that this will grow to 50 or 60 percent. Electricity has become the very lifeblood of modern life and will continue to be so in the future.

There are many reasons why this is true. An important one is the shift of the basic energy resources. At the birth of the nation, wood supplied nearly all the energy needs; by the end of the Civil War, wood was still supplying 80 percent of the energy used. However, coal was coming into use and by 1910 supplied 79 percent of the energy; wood furnished only about 10 percent; and petroleum and natural gas accounted for another 10 percent. By 1972 petroleum and

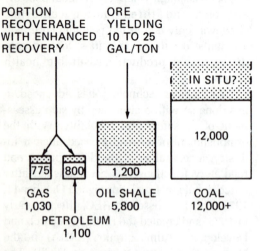

AVAILABLE ENERGY IN QUADS (10^{15} BTU) SHOWN GRAPHICALLY BY AREA.

TOTAL U.S. ENERGY CONSUMPTION IN 1974 WAS 73 QUADS

(One million barrels of oil per day for a year is equal to approximately 2 quads)

PORTION RECOVERABLE WITH ENHANCED RECOVERY

ORE YIELDING 10 TO 25 GAL/TON

IN SITU?

12,000

775 800 1,200

GAS 1,030

OIL SHALE 5,800

COAL 12,000+

PETROLEUM 1,100

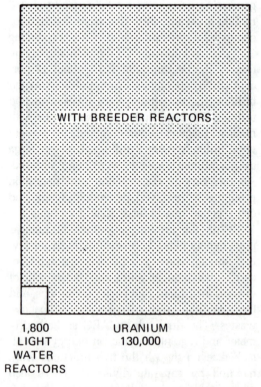

WITH BREEDER REACTORS

1,800 LIGHT WATER REACTORS

URANIUM 130,000

Figure 11-2.
Energy available from recoverable domestic energy resources.

Energy Research and Development Administration

Artist's rendering of the nation's first large-scale Liquid Metal Fast Breeder Reactor demonstration plant. Construction is scheduled to begin in 1976.

natural gas provided 78 percent of the nation's energy, but then they began to decline because of domestic production decreases. Coal production again increased, and nuclear energy began to be used. The problems of shifting the energy base were highlighted by the Arab countries' oil embargo in 1972, followed by the cartel of the Organization of Petroleum Exporting Countries (OPEC). It increased the price of petroleum from about $2 per barrel to about $11 per barrel within only a few months. This disrupted the existing worldwide economic balance. The basic problem remained in 1975 that, with the projected use of oil and gas estimated, worldwide reserves would be exhausted in fifty years or less. The OPEC actions brought the world's dependence on the limited oil and gas resources into sharp focus.

The production of oil and gas in the United States decreased from 1972 to 1976 at a rate of about 6 percent per year. While oil from the North Slope of Alaska will be available in 1978, it is not expected to compensate for the decreasing production in the rest of the nation. Thus, in its bicentennial year, the United States faces hard decisions that must be made regarding energy and the nation's future.

Figure 11-2 illustrates energy available from recoverable domestic energy resources. It shows, for instance, that domestic petroleum alone would be able to supply the nation's anticipated energy needs for not much more than ten years. The same is true of natural gas. Oil shale has a greater potential— in fact the oil shale energy potential may be as great as the Middle East petroleum reserves— but mining and processing the shale will require a large capital outlay, will need a long lead time, and will present many environmental problems. For instance, a plant that would produce 100,000 barrels of oil per day had an estimated cost (1975 prices) of about $1 billion and would require at least seven or eight years for development from the point of decision to the production of oil.

Coal is a great energy resource, but it also involves many problems. The adverse environmental impact of mining and air pollution from burning coal creates issues that by 1976 are not yet satisfactorily resolved. Despite progress, long lead times and large capital requirements persist.

The uranium supply for light water reactors of the type in use in the United States would be ample to provide all energy needed by the country for fifteen to twenty years. Problems again are large capital requirements and ten years or so lead time from decision to production. However, the breeder reactor has promise of furnishing adequate energy for nearly a century. Construction of the first liquid-metal, fast breeder reactor was underway as a commercial demonstration in Oak Ridge, Tennessee, by the beginning of 1976. This 380,000-kilowatt plant is estimated to cost about $1.7 billion, and it is scheduled to be in production by 1982. From this demonstration plant to large commercial production, however, is at least fifteen to twenty years away.

The commercial development of controlled fusion will provide an unlimited energy source for the future. However, the general consensus is that it will be well into the twenty-first century before fusion power can be demonstrated on a commercial scale. Using coal and uranium for energy is best done by generating electricity, thus creating the big increases that are projected for electricity growth. No doubt liquefaction and gasification of coal will begin to have a sizeable commercial impact by 1990. Other sources, such as solar and geothermal energy, have potential; but technology must be developed and demonstrated before they have any appreciable impact on the overall energy needs. Hydroelectric generation of electricity, while it has been the prime catalyst in the development of electricity use, provided only about 4 percent of the total energy needs in 1975. Most of the good hydroelectric power sites have been developed. However, it is expected that additional development will occur, especially in providing for peaking power by pumped storage installations. But the growth at best is expected to keep pace only with the growth of energy needs. The percentage of energy from hydroelectric power will probably decrease.

The energy problems facing the United States in 1975 were serious. However, they were becoming well-recognized, and many programs were beginning to show results. The research, development, and demonstration plan was beginning to come into focus, with the government funding about $2 billion per year and an equal or greater amount coming from industry. Means of cooperative assistance by government for industry to provide insurance and capital support were being developed. One proposal under consideration was formation of a government corporation, capitalized at $100 billion, to give support for energy installations. Many ramifications of such proposals were being examined.

The dilemmas are well illustrated in the oil shale area. Four government-owned tracts in Colorado and Utah have been leased to energy companies for development. An investment of over $1 billion (1975 prices) will be required for one 100,000-barrel-a-day plant. This would produce oil costing about $11 per barrel. But uncertainties exist: the changing environmental requirements that could increase the cost; the escalating costs of plant and construction; the possibility of the OPEC countries reducing the price of foreign oil if the oil shale potential appears threatening to their objectives; and the large financial commitments required for a long period of time before any returns are evident. Adverse actions in these areas could be catastrophic for the industry. The magnitude of the problems are far beyond past risks and, in the opinion of many, require support that can only be provided by the federal government.

The conclusion of numerous studies was summarized by the ERDA report of June 1975. It states that:

> National security, the nation's economy, and the ability to determine life style are all in peril today. Substantial assistance from new technology is critically needed, but significant results are not expected before 1985. Major efforts must be pursued now on all national energy technology goals because of the time required to research, develop, and implement new energy technologies . . . . The nation's energy plan must provide multiple options which, taken all together, could exceed perceived needs . . . . The task of creating choices for the future must be urgently addressed now and with full public participation.

There will be a marked increase in the

use of coal and nuclear fuels in the immediate future to make up for the decreasing petroleum production. It is quite likely that the breeder reactor will follow by the end of the century, supplemented by solar and geothermal sources. These should provide energy until the fusion of nuclear material becomes feasible, which will provide energy indefinitely. This will involve more electricity as the energy transport means. Another energy transport is hydrogen gas, obtained by the hydrolysis of water. This has the potential of utilizing the natural gas pipeline networks. Direct generation of hydrogen from water, either from nuclear fission or fusion, is potentially attractive. Thus, research and development programs must pursue all the energy possibilities so that sound choices can be made for the future.

The nation, in its bicentennial year, faces a challenge without precedent. From a technological standpoint, it appears that conservation and production solutions to the energy problem can be obtained. The challenge is to obtain public understanding and support for the institutional arrangements that will enable the problems to be resolved. They are complex, far-reaching, and of great magnitude. However, the adaptability demonstrated in the history of public works during the first 200 years of the nation and the dynamic record of accomplishment offer great promise for the future.

SUGGESTED READINGS

American Public Power Association. "Public Power Directory." *Public Power,* 33 (January-February 1975), 28-76.

Childs, Marquis. *The Farmer Takes a Hand.* New York, 1952.

Dill, Clarence C. *Where Water Falls.* Spokane, Washington, 1970.

Groves, Leslie R. *Now It Can Be Told: The Story of the Manhattan Project.* New York, 1961.

Gunby, F. M. "Supply of Water Power in the United States." American Society of Civil Engineers *Transactions,* CT (1953), 461-475.

Hammond, Allen L.; Metz, William D.; and Maugh, Thomas H. *Energy and the Future.* Washington, D. C., 1973.

King, Judson. *The Conservation Fight from Theodore Roosevelt to the Tennessee Valley.* Washington, D. C., 1970.

Larned, A. T., and Salzman, M. S. "Evolution of the Modern Hydroelectric Power Plant." American Society of Civil Engineers *Transactions,* CT (1953), 536-555.

Lyerly, Ray L., and Mitchell, Walter. *Nuclear Power Plants.* Understanding the Atom Series. U. S. Atomic Energy Commission. Rev. ed. Washington, D.C., 1973.

Netboy, Anthony. *Salmon of the Pacific Northwest: Fish vs Dams.* Portland, Oregon, 1958.

Power Authority of the State of New York. *1973 Annual Report.* New York, 1974.

Rocks, Lawrence, and Runyon, Richard P. *The Energy Crisis.* New York, 1972.

Seaborg, Glenn T., and Corliss, William R. *Man and Atom: Shaping a New World through Nuclear Technology.* New York, 1971.

Twentieth Century Fund. *Electric Power and Government Policy.* New York, 1948.

Uhl, W. F. "Water Power over a Century." American Society of Civil Engineers *Transactions,* CT (1953), 451-460.

U. S. Atomic Energy Commission. *The Nation's Energy Future.* Washington, D. C., 1973.

—————————— . *Annual Report to Congress, 1974.* Washington, D. C., 1975.

U. S. Congress. Joint Committee on Atomic Energy. *Understanding the "National Energy Dilemma."* 93rd Cong., 2nd. Sess., 1973.

—————————— . Senate Select Committee on National Water Resources. *Electric Power in Relation to the Nation's Water Resources.* 87th Cong., 1st Sess., 1961.

U. S. Department of Agriculture. *Water: 1955 Yearbook.* Washington, D. C., 1955.

U. S. Department of Interior. *The Colorado River.* Washington, D. C., 1946.

————————— . Bonneville Power Administration. *Annual Reports.* Washington, D. C., 1937-1974.

U. S. Federal Power Commission. *Annual Report.* Washington, D. C., 1972.

————————— . *The 1970 National Power Survey.* Washington, D. C., 1971.

U. S. Rural Electrification Administration. *Rural Lines: U.S.A.* Washington, D.C., 1960.

U. S. Tennessee Valley Authority. *Annual Reports.* Knoxville, Tennessee, 1934-1974.

Whipple, Fred H. *Street Lighting.* Detroit, Michigan, 1888.

CHAPTER 12

SEWERS AND WASTEWATER TREATMENT

The development of America's urban civilization required the construction of public works systems that control and treat wastewater. During the last two decades, the problem of maintaining a clean environment has become increasingly difficult as industrialization and urbanization intensified. In spite of past efforts, the discharge of partially or untreated wastes continued to pollute rivers and lakes. The ever-increasing amount of such contaminants and the growing understanding of the complexity of their composition raised public concern for the safety and usefulness of the nation's water resources. Therefore, federal, state, and local governments have jointly launched a massive cleanup of wastewater flows. The United States celebrates its two-hundredth birthday in the midst of an intensive nationwide effort to improve water quality.

Concern for water pollution, however, began long before the ecological thrust of the 1960s and 1970s. The so-called environmental movement is an intensification of efforts to control and neutralize wastes that reach back to the beginning of the eighteenth century. Since the colonial era, American cities have built sewers to control and dispose of urban wastewater. After the discovery of the bacterial origin of disease in the nineteenth century, pioneer environmental engineers and scientists developed wastewater treatment systems which municipalities adopted for processing sewage flows. By 1975, 76 percent of the American population was served by wastewater treatment facilities. The current surge of attention to pollution control and the increased expenditures for sewage system construction are rooted in past efforts to protect public health by controlling and treating wastewater.

Sewer Systems

The first sewers were built during the colonial era to collect wastewater in the commercial centers of the largest cities. At the beginning of the eighteenth century, Boston, Philadelphia, New York, and several other communities began paving their thoroughfares with gravel and stone blocks. Surface and subsurface drainage was provided to keep the streets dry.

In Boston most newly paved thoroughfares were built with a crown in the center and gutters along side, although in some cases the gutters were placed in the center. Subsurface drainage was also developed in Boston. During the seventeenth century, some urban dwellers employed wooden drains to rid their cellars of wastewater. By the early 1700s, these lines were being connected to common

Portions of this chapter are based on manuscripts prepared by Gordon Hendrickson, APWA Bicentennial History Fellow, and Morris Cohn, Consulting Engineer.

sewers which ran beneath the streets. Most of the early sewers were built with private capital. In 1704 Bostonian Francis Thrasher was given permission by the city government to construct a sewer which was "not only a Generall good and Benefit by freeing the Street from the Usual annoyance with Water and mire by the Often Stoppage and breaking of Small wooden Truncks or drains . . . but a more perticular benefit to ye Neighbourhood as a Common Shore [sewer] for draining of their Cellars and conveying away their waste water." In view of the need for this undertaking, the city's selectmen ordered all residents who connected their drains with this sewer to help pay for the project.

This underground sewer in Boston was so popular that others were built. Users were required by law to assume part of the construction and maintenance cost. From 1708 to 1736, Boston authorities issued 654 sewer construction permits, with the attached requirement that street pavements be carefully replaced when projects were completed. By the mid eighteenth century, few cities of the world were as well drained as Boston. A 1740 observer wrote: "the streets are well paved, and lying upon a descent, the Town is, for the generality, as dry and clean as any I remember to have seen."

Other towns were less progressive in providing urban drainage. In Pennsylvania a law for "Regulating of Streets and Water Courses in Cities and Towns" was passed by the Provincial Council in 1700 which required that all subsurface sewers be built of brick or stone. Six prominent Philadelphians were appointed by the governor to assure that drains in the city were maintained in good condition. By the 1750s, masonry culverts and underground sewers had been constructed in some parts of the city. New York was even farther behind in sewer construction. In 1696 the town's council agreed to build a "Common Sewer in the Broad Street," but during the next six decades little subsurface drainage was undertaken. Surface water drained in open channels or "kennels," which ran down the middle of streets and emptied into the Broad Street Sewer. In 1769, however, city authorities began building trunk sewage lines in several wards.

The early sewers were constructed piecemeal without a sound technical basis of design. They were usually built of stone, brick, or wood and came in varying shapes and sizes. In many cases, their slopes were inadequate and sometimes were actually pitched the wrong way.

Throughout the colonial era, and until the mid nineteenth century, city governments made a sharp distinction between disposal of general wastewater and human wastes. The common sewers carried storm runoff water, overflow from public and private pumps, and household wastewater, but citizens were prohibited from discharging fecal matter into common drains. This distinction between drainage and waste disposal was due to mistaken concepts of disease transmission.

Until the microbiological source of disease was discovered, the "miasma theory" was accepted by medical and scientific authorities. This theory held that exudations from swamps and other low-lying damp areas where organic matter decayed gave off vapors detrimental to public health. Therefore, it was deemed appropriate to keep the poorly constructed public drains as free as possible from contamination that would produce dangerous fumes. To curb improper use of sewers, local governments prohibited the discharge of fecal matter and other home wastes into public sewers and imposed fines on violators. These bans were in effect in Boston until 1833, in Philadelphia until 1850; and in some cities, they were not lifted until the twentieth century.

Removal and disposition of sanitary waste was regarded as a private responsibility. Homes and buildings had privy vaults, backhouses, and in some cases cesspools to collect waste. Garbage was thrown into gutters to be consumed by roving herds of pigs. Private contractors cleaned cesspools and privies and dumped the foul contents in convenient places—usually the nearest body of water. In most large cities, health officers were appointed to respond to citizen nuisance complaints of overflowing cesspools and backhouses. In crowded slum areas, conditions were intolerable. A New York City inspector

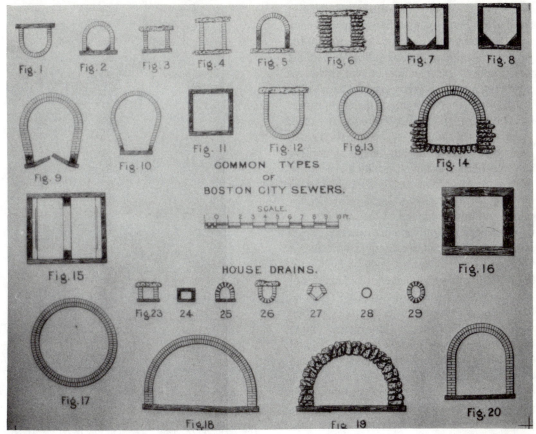

Sewers of various designs and dimensions were built in Boston, Massachusetts, during the eighteenth and nineteenth centuries.

reported families "living in basements with privy vaults located at higher levels than the apartments and oozing their contents into them, amidst offensive odors." Another New York officer described the "insalubrity of privies in which masses of human excrement were found on the seats and floors."

The most tragic consequence of these waste disposal practices was the spread of disease. Public wells and cesspools existed in close proximity, and as disease organisms leached into the ground they contaminated public water supplies. Outbreaks of cholera and other epidemics scourged American cities during the nineteenth century. Six serious cholera epidemics swept the nation between 1832 and 1873, and cholera and typhoid killed more soldiers in the Civil War than did hostile action.

The rapid growth of urban centers in the

pre-Civil War era rendered existing drainage systems obsolete. As cities expanded, greater land masses became covered with streets, sidewalks, and buildings, and the increased volume of runoff water exceeded the capacities of sewers and drains. To provide coordinated drainage systems, cities took over the maintenance of sewers and incurred public indebtedness to fund new construction. Boston, for example, assumed public control of its scattered private sewer lines in 1823. The increased volume of water runoff resulted in a need for comprehensive sewerage systems with more liberal flow capacities. This job required the talents of trained civil engineers.

The first extensive sewer systems were some of the largest public works undertakings of the mid nineteenth century. American engineers borrowed heavily from European designers. In 1843 Hamburg, Germany, became the first city to build a comprehensive sewerage system. It served as a model for American builders such as Julius W. Adams who prepared the specifications for Brooklyn, New York's drainage system in 1857 and Ellis S. Chesbrough who completed his report on the sewerage of Chicago, Illinois, in 1858. These pioneer undertakings established basic principles of sewer design that were applied and improved upon in other cities.

Although human and household wastes were originally excluded from storm drains, public pressure mounted to use them to dispose of these and other urban wastes. Cesspools and privies were fouling the urban environment, and industries such as slaughterhouses and tanneries created huge volumes of liquid by-products. In his 1857 report, Philadelphia's chief sewage engineer recommended that "there should be a culvert on every street and every house should be obliged to deliver into it, by underground channels, all ordure or refuse that is susceptible to being diluted." The introduction of public water supply systems added to city wastewater problems. With more abundant water supplies came the development of indoor plumbing and bathtubs. Increased volume of wastewater prompted Boston to pass an ordinance in 1844 prohibiting the taking of baths without a doctor's order. The first flush toilet, invented in 1809 but only minimally used until the 1880s, further increased wastewater volume; and its discharges and other effluents were eventually diverted into street drain conduits in most cities. Objections to using storm sewers were eventually overcome by building separate systems to handle sanitary flows. The first separate sewer systems were concurrently designed in 1880 by George E. Waring, Jr., at Memphis, Tennessee, and Benezette Williams at Pullman, Illinois.

The fundamentals of sewer system design and construction were well established in the early twentieth century. Improvements have been made, however, in sewer pipe and pumping machinery. Construction methods dramatically changed with the replacement of hand labor by heavy machinery. Public workmen have also been aided by the accumula-

Library of Congress

The adoption of water closets in the 1880s increased wastewater loads on municipal sewers.

tion of accurate data on rainfall and runoff, permitting more accurate design of both combined systems and storm water drains.

The system of conduits that transports wastewater in most communities generally consists of the following. Laterals collect the discharges of homes and other buildings and feed them into collectors or sub-mains. The sub-mains carry wastewater to large mains or trunk sewers which are connected to treatment plants by interceptors. After the wastewater is treated, the outfall usually carries the water to a stream or other body of water.

Early builders of sewer and drainage facilities relied on available materials such as natural clays and brick and mortar. The first planned citywide systems constructed in the mid nineteenth century were generally built of vitrified clay or cement mortar conduits for small lines and brick or wood staves for the large sections. In 1885 concrete sewer mains were introduced in Washington, D.C. Since then a wide range of sewer construction materials have been developed. Contemporary sewer pipe is made of clay, asbestos-cement, cast iron, steel, or plastic and can be lined with protective coatings to reduce deterioration. These advances resulted in materials which are stronger, weigh less, and are easier to install and maintain. Jointing methods have been developed which provide watertight bonding and flexibility between line sections. Excavations for early sewers were by hand, but the development of steam shovels and trenching machines made sewer construction less labor intensive.

The first sewers and drains received little maintenance except when stoppages occurred. With the organization of municipal sewer departments, however, regular maintenance programs were generally implemented to supplement emergency service. In progressive municipalities, the maintenance program includes periodic cleaning of all sewers and preparing specialized operation and maintenance manuals. Accurate records are kept of trouble spots, the cleaning of lines,

Maintenance crews use cutting tools to clear sewer blockages caused by tree roots.

and line maintenance. Sophisticated television and photographic systems enable sewer departments to inspect new construction to determine the quality of workmanship and location of possible sources of infiltration. The techniques are also used to inspect and forecast maintenance needs of older sewers, an important factor in preparing public works departmental budgets and work schedules.

Public works agencies fight a day-to-day battle against sewer line blockages. The most common obstructions are roots and accumulations of grease, grit, and miscellaneous debris. There are several effective methods of removing stoppages and cleaning sewers. Power rodding with roots saws and auger tools are the most common methods for emergency service. Stoppages caused by accumulations of grease, sludge, and sand are scoured from pipes by high-pressure hydraulic cleaning devices. After the material is flushed downstream, it is removed by vacuum units or other eduction equipment to prevent further disruptions of service.

Public education and strict enforcement of sewer regulations can minimize system abuse. Root growth problems can be reduced by discouraging the planting of certain tree varieties such as elm, poplar, willow, sycamore, and soft maple near sewer lines. Grease clogging is also preventable. Since wastes from restaurants, service stations, meat packing plants, and grease and soap from cleaning establishments can cause severe clogging; grease traps and screens are often required by law to remove these substances from wastewater before they pass into the sewer system.

In the 1960s, public works agencies became increasingly conscious of the problems of infiltration and inflow. Infiltration is the groundwater which enters sewer systems through broken pipes, defective pipe joints, and manhole walls. Inflow is wastewater collected from such sources as manhole covers, yard and cellar drains, catch basins, surface runoff, and cross connections between storm and sanitary sewers. These extraneous waters sometimes exceed the capacities of sanitary sewer systems, resulting in flooding and serious public health hazards.

They may also exceed the capacities of sewage treatment plants so that wastewater is bypassed into receiving streams with a full load of pollutants. Recent environmental legislation, which requires treatment of all discharges, has caused public works agencies to step up their infiltration-inflow (I/I) abatement programs. All applicants for federal grants to construct treatment plants must demonstrate that their sewers are not excessively subject to these twin problems. After a careful analysis of the overall system, new treatment facilities are designed to handle the normal sanitary flows plus the I/I load that cannot be practically eliminated.

Cities are meeting the problems of infiltration and inflow with a dual strategy of prevention and cure. The use of improved types of sewer pipe and modern jointing practices in new construction makes sewer systems virtually watertight. Better methods of trench preparation and pipe laying provide proper alignments and full soil support. In addition, new methods of testing for sewer leaks insure compliance with infiltration standards. Since extraneous sewer flows result from hundreds of sources, I/I correction initially involves a system-wide analysis of general sewage flow conditions and the location of serious I/I sources. This data enables officials to develop cost estimates and comprehensive repair and replacement plans. I/I abatement and other sewer rehabilitation measures are great environmental challenges of the 1970s. A 1974 survey by the United States Environmental Protection Agency (EPA) concluded it would require $61 billion to upgrade America's sewer lines to acceptable performance levels.

America's sewage systems have been rightly proclaimed "conduits of civilization." By 1975, 590,000 miles of sewer lines were in service in the United States. Virtually every municipality is served by some type of sewer system. In spite of a rise in environmental expectations which have focused attention on sewer system shortcomings, the public works profession can take pride in its accomplishments in this field. Seventy-six percent of the American population is served by sewers which free man from contact with his wastes.

What began as piecemeal storm drains in colonial cities has evolved into intelligently administered public utility systems.

Growth of Wastewater Treatment

By the last quarter of the nineteenth century, the wastewater of many urban centers was being disposed of in watercourses, but pollution remained a detriment to public health. Cities initially sought to disperse wastewater more efficiently or irrigate farmland with their effluents, but by the late 1880s treatment methods were being developed which removed many organic pollutants before the wastewater was discharged into receiving waters. The creation of these basic primary and secondary sewage treatment processes inaugurated pollution control practices that are still being used.

Massachusetts was the cradle of American sanitary engineering. Because of its early industrial development, this state began the first systematic studies of water quality. In 1850 Lemuel Shattuck, the only active member of a special state sanitary survey commission, issued his *Report of a General Plan for the Promotion of Public and Personal Health*. This report on the effects of water pollution went virtually unnoticed, but in 1869 the state created the Massachusetts State Board of Health (MSBH), the first state agency to seriously investigate water pollution and waste treatment methods. Its first chairman, Henry I. Bowditch, made a study of sewage disposal practices in England and guided the agency's investigations in its formative years. The second annual report of MSBH in 1871 explored the causes of typhoid fever and observed the causal relationship between pollution and disease. The report also urged removal "even of the present small nuisance, because the very filth, which tends to contaminate, might be saved and used for beneficial purposes, whereas it is now lost and at the cost, perhaps, of human health and life." The agency's 1873 report concluded that water supplies were threatened by stream contamination. The study recommended that sewage be applied to land areas to abate water pollution. These initial studies were followed by investigations of stream self-purification and wastewater treatment processes.

The agency's most important sanitary engineering experiments were conducted at the Lawrence Experiment Station which was founded in 1887. This group of scientists and engineers, initially headed by Hiram Mills, represented the first American effort to investigate scientifically waste disposal practices. Its 1890 report, which documented the facility's engineering research, established a technical basis for the purification of water and the treatment of sanitary sewage and industrial wastes. Perhaps the most lasting contribution of the station was bringing together a brilliant group of young chemists, engineers, and biologists. Men such as Allen Hazen, George W. Fuller, and William T. Sedgwick acquired their early training at the station and became leaders in the water pollution control field. In 1889 the Massachusetts Institute of Technology established the first American sanitary engineering curriculum, and the school subsequently founded its own pollution research laboratory in 1903. In the late nineteenth century, Massachusetts was clearly the center of water pollution research, and many of the following treatment methods were initially practiced in the state.

The first common sewers discharged their wastes into the nearest stream or other body of water. The practice of disposing of wastewater by dilution was justified on the basis that water had the capacity for self-purification. The outfalls of the earliest sewers were generally located near the shoreline; but as cities grew and waste loads increased, the receiving waters often became grossly polluted. To rid themselves of nuisances such as sludge banks and scum, cities relocated discharge points by constructing interceptor sewers, extending outfalls into deeper water, and dispersing sewage through multiple outlets. These attempts to increase sewage dispersion were paralleled by efforts to evaluate scientifically the nature and dangers of water pollution and set standards for dilution disposal.

In 1876 James P. Kirkwood delivered a report to MSBH on stream pollution which offered evidence that streams had the capacity to cleanse themselves. Rudolph Hering's 1888

Public Works Historical Society

This apparatus was used in 1913 to collect river water samples for biochemical oxygen demand (BOD) tests.

recommendations on disposal of Chicago's sewage by dilution led to the construction of the Chicago Drainage Canal, which diverted that city's wastewater from Lake Michigan to the Illinois River. Subsequent studies by the United States Public Health Service and several state and municipal public agencies resulted in procedures to evaluate accurately the effects of sewage effluents on receiving waters. Shortly before World War I, "biochemical oxygen demand" (BOD) was developed as the basic measure of water quality. This procedure established pollution levels by determining the amount of dissolved oxygen required by aerobic bacteria to break down organic matter present in water. Until recently, this has been the principal means of judging water quality. However, in the last two decades, more sophisticated analytical methods and monitoring devices have been developed to evaluate pollutants. New industrial wastes, interactions among pollutants, and higher water quality standards have broadened the spectrum of water contaminants which must be identified and treated.

The advent of sewage pumps in the 1880s led to the development of cage screens, grit chambers, and bar racks to remove insoluble matter from wastewater flows. To protect the pumps and other mechanical equipment from clogging and injury, preliminary treatment devices were used to remove trash, grit, and large suspended organic substances. The first cage screens in the United States were constructed for the Boston Main Drainage Pumping Station in 1884. Grit chambers for removal of mineral solids were introduced at Worcester, Massachusetts, in 1904.

The advent of sewage treatment plants required more advanced preliminary treatment. The use of finer screens and other straining equipment produced clogging. To remove these substances, sewage workers initially used hand-operated brushes and scrapers. The first mechanical screen cleaning device was installed at Sacramento, California, in 1915. As the use of screening became widespread, however, trash disposal became a serious problem. Municipalities usually returned the screenings to the land or burned them in incinerators. To avoid separating and disposing of these substances, municipalities began using comminution equipment to grind suspended garbage. The first comminutor was installed in Durham, North Carolina, in 1933 to reduce large volumes of melon rinds during summer months.

Wastewater pretreatment has also involved the removal of grease and floating oils from sewage. Before the employment of secondary treatment plants, "sleek" was removed by skimming these substances from the surface. Washington, D.C., pioneered this technique in 1908. Grease removal continued as an adjunct to more advanced treatment processes. It is usually affected by vacuum flotation, aeration flotation, and the use of chlorine and chemical coagulants to agglomerate suspended oils.

Sewage treatment was undertaken before the basic principles of disease transmission were understood. *Broad irrigation* or sewage farming was initially practiced in sixteenth-century Germany and subsequently in France and England during the eighteenth century. Sewage was applied to relatively level land areas where it could be absorbed and purified by soil. Large areas of easily drained soil were required. Due to flies and odors, the tracts were usually well isolated from population centers. Because of the fertilizer value of the sewage, crops were grown on the irrigated fields.

The first sewage farm in the United States was created at the State Insane Asylum near Augusta, Maine, in 1872. Lenox, Massachusetts, opened a municipal broad irrigation facility in 1876. Due to the large tracts of land required and the insect and odor problems, sewage irrigation was not widely adopted in the East; however, in the arid West, sewage farming gained greater acceptance. The first sewage irrigation system in the western states was at Cheyenne, Wyoming, in 1883. Land application is still widely practiced in Texas, California, New Mexico, and Arizona. Texas has been particularly progressive in adopting this system. By 1970, 30 percent of Texas' wastewater treatment plants used some form of land irrigation. This waste treatment process became popular with small communities and industrial plants in the 1950s and 1960s. Unlike nineteenth-century practices, however, contemporary irrigation wastewater is usually pretreated to some degree, depending on the type of land and crops irrigated, the method and rates of application, and other considerations.

As a result of experiments in England and at the Lawrence Experiment Station, a modified form of broad irrigation known as *intermittent filtration* was developed in the late nineteenth century. Raw sewage was applied evenly to the surface of beds of sand or other fine material, underdrained by open-jointed tile conduits. During its passage through this crude filter, the wastewater was purified by aerobic bacteria nurtured by the atmospheric oxygen present in the sand. The process derived its name from the need to apply the sewage intermittently so that air could periodically enter the voids in the sand. In New England, where soil conditions were especially favorable, this method was promptly adopted by many towns because it required far less treatment area than did broad irrigation. Although this treatment approach was superseded by more sophisticated processes, it established the practice of treating sewage biologically.

The large land areas required and the necessity of specific soil composition for broad irrigation and intermittent filtration remained a problem for some regions, and the search for new methods continued. *Contact beds* were developed in England in the 1890s, and they were subsequently introduced to America in 1899. The first was installed at a golf club near Chicago, Illinois. Contact beds essentially consisted of tanks filled with broken stones, slate, or other coarse, inert substances, which provided a relatively large surface area for the growth of microorganisms. The device was operated on a fill-and-draw basis, and the organic matter in the sewage was decomposed by the bacteria on the filter bed. When the filter was empty, bacteria growth would be stimulated by the flow of air through the voids between the filter material. Contact filter installations were relatively small and cumbersome to operate. The filter materials often clogged with sludge and the system's treatment capacity was limited.

Trickling filters were also developed in England before they were introduced to the United States. The process fundamentally involved sprinkling untreated effluent over a bed of coarse rocks covered with biological growths. Wastewater was intermittently applied to the surface of the filters by rotating spray nozzles or other mechanical devices. As the sewage was sprayed into the air and passed through the layers of stone, atmospheric oxygen was absorbed to increase the biological oxidation and mineralization of organic matter. The first municipal trickling filter was placed into service at Reading, Pennsylvania, in 1908. The principal advantage of the trickling filter was its ability to treat high volumes of wastewater. Since the 1920s, major advancements in this treatment process have been improvements in sewage application devices, the use of plastic for filter

beds, and the treatment of plant outflows with chlorine prior to discharge into receiving streams.

Chemical precipitation was another early sewage treatment method. This process involved adding lime, iron sulfate, and other coagulants to wastewater. The chemicals stimulated reactions in sewage causing organic and inorganic solids to settle out. The procedure was initially used at Coney Island, New York, in 1887 and at East Orange, New Jersey, a year later; but chemical treatment was largely abandoned by 1900 because of high costs, excessive sludge production, and competition from simpler, more efficient biological treatment processes. Interest in chemical treatment was revived in the 1930s because of improved sludge collection and disposal techniques and the production of cheaper ferric coagulants and other chemicals. Even so, widespread use of chemicals did not occur until the 1960s. This revival was caused by higher water quality treatment standards and the inability of biological methods to neutralize toxic industrial wastes such as heavy metals.

One of the earliest primary treatment methods reduced the organic content of wastewater by retaining the flow in tanks and allowing solid matter to settle out. The process removed a substantial portion of the suspended material, but disposing of the foul-smelling sludge was a costly and difficult problem. This was partially solved by the adoption of septic tanks in which sewage solids were digested by an anaerobic bacteria. It was originally believed that this process would liquefy almost all solids, but the results were often unsatisfactory. The tanks were extremely odoriferous and covered with scum. In order to avoid these objectionable features, tanks were developed which separated the sedimentation and sludge digestion processes.

In the first decade of the twentieth century, several two-chambered tanks were introduced to the United States from Germany and England, but only the tank designed by Karl Imhoff was widely adopted. In the Imhoff tank, solids dropped through slots in the bottom of the sedimentation chamber into a sludge compartment. The sludge was allowed

Chicago began operating the first municipal sludge incinerator in 1932.

to digest until most of the organic matter was gasified or liquefied. After it was stabilized, the remaining material was dried and subsequently dumped or used for fertilizer. The first tanks of this type were built at Madison-Chatham, New Jersey, in 1911 and at Atlanta, Georgia, in 1912. By the end of the 1930s, Imhoff tanks accounted for nearly half of the treatment works in America. Although they have since been superseded by other processes, they are still used by smaller communities for wastewater treatment.

Activated sludge was the next process to be widely employed in the United States. The method basically involved combining raw sewage with heavy concentrations of aerobic microorganisms. Air was pumped into the mixture by mechanical aerators to stimulate bacterial reduction of organic pollutants. After this process was completed, the activated sludge and residue was allowed to settle out and was subsequently retrieved to work on new wastewater. This process was the prod-

uct of a series of experiments on sewage aeration conducted in the United States and England shortly before World War I. Notable American experiments were carried out by the Lawrence Experiment Station in 1912 and the Chicago Drainage District in 1914. In 1914 Milwaukee, Wisconsin, initiated large-scale investigations of this process leading to completion of what was the world's largest sewage treatment plant in 1925. The first activated sludge facility, however, was installed in 1916 at San Marcos, Texas. Because activated sludge plants require a smaller land area than trickling filter systems, they have been widely adopted by large municipalities. The introduction of pure oxygen aeration in the past decade has made this process even more efficient.

The accumulated solid materials, known as sludge, which result from wastewater treatment processes in the United States annually amount to approximately seventy pounds per person. Sludge easily becomes putrid and can become a major pollutant if it is not biologically stabilized and disposed of in a suitable manner. Only two sludge handling methods were available in 1900. Smaller plants drained and air-dried sludge by spreading it over sand beds. At larger chemical precipitation works, the sludge was partially dewatered by cumbersome plate presses and used for landfill, given to farmers for fertilizer, or placed on barges and dumped in the ocean.

The advent of activated sludge processes caused new disposal problems because the diluted sludge produced by this method was difficult to dry on sand beds. Various solutions were investigated. In 1917 the Stockyards Testing Stations of the Sanitary District of Chicago initiated chemical conditioning experiments. Vacuum filters were introduced at Milwaukee in 1921, and the first large-scale sludge incineration facility began operating at Chicago's West Side Sewage Treatment Plant in 1932. The most common present-day activated sludge systems involve digesting the sludge in heated tanks, dewatering it with vacuum filters or centrifuging it, and then incinerating or disposing it at a sanitary landfill. At many plants, the methane gas produced by anaerobic digestion is recovered and used to heat the tanks, thereby increasing the efficiency of the process.

Although first promoted in the 1920s, *oxidation ponds* or *stabilization lagoons* did not receive wide acceptance until after World War II. A lagoon is a large shallow pond in which sunlight, algae, and oxygen interact to restore water to a quality that is often equal to or better than effluent from secondary treatment plants. Ponds can provide primary and secondary treatment or they can supplement other processes. In some cases, the wastewater is artificially aerated while microorganisms feed on the raw sewage. Suspended solids settle to the bottom and bacterial actions reduce the organic pollutants to relatively harmless matter. After sufficient retention in the pond, the effluent is chlorinated and delivered to the receiving stream.

Although oxidation ponds are relatively inexpensive to build and operate, they require spacious land areas. As a result, they are not

Public Works Historical Society

Some communities use wastewater lagoons for recreational activities.

applicable for treating wastes in large urban areas. Many smaller communities, however, have turned to stabilization lagoons to upgrade their treatment capacities. Between 1962 and 1967, oxidation ponds accounted for almost 36 percent of the new waste treatment plants constructed in the United States. Because lagoons can handle fluctuating flows more easily than can mechanical treatment works, they are often used to treat organic industrial effluents and are particularly effective for handling agricultural wastes.

The foregoing treatment methods which were developed in the late nineteenth and early twentieth centuries remain the standard means for processing wastewater. There have been many improvements and modifications of these processes, but until recently sewage treatment basically consisted of separating solids, digesting and disposing of sludge, and neutralizing suspended organic matter. The concern for water quality during the 1960s, however, touched off development of waste treatment systems that provide a much higher degree of purification.

Advanced Treatment

Industrial development and the rise in standards of living in the twentieth century produced new challenges to engineers. Prosperity and economic expansion increased the volume and added to the complexity of wastewater flows. New home plumbing devices—showers, dishwashers, automatic clotheswashers—vastly increased per capita water consumption. In addition, food waste disposal units changed wastewater composition. Shredded household food wastes have become an integral part of sanitary sewage flows, adding enormously to the amount of organic matter treated by sewage plants.

Furthermore, controlling water pollution has become increasingly complex because many municipal sewer systems accept industrial wastewater. In addition to the normal load of organic matter, modern treatment plants must remove various toxic substances including trace metals, complex organic compounds, and other substances which may produce carcinogenic reactions in humans.

Industrial wastes are difficult to process. The industrial capacity of the United States has grown enormously in the last two centuries. Early factories were often located on streams to allow nature to carry away and dispose of wastes. Few people were concerned about water pollution; in fact, many community leaders regarded belching smokestacks and multicolored liquid wastes as signs of economic progress. States and cities in the nineteenth century sought to attract industries and seldom imposed stringent wastewater regulations. In 1900 the pollution load on American rivers was 40 percent industrial in origin; by 1968 this figure had risen to 80 percent.

Prior to 1940, most industrial effluents responded to conventional treatment, but subsequent advances in chemical production and other types of manufacturing created new waste products that existing plants could not process. In addition to organic wastes, industrial by-products include toxic chemicals, oil and grease, radioactive materials, and heat. The technology exists for removal of nearly all industrial wastes, but the methods are usually costly and often require large capital investments for treatment facilities.

In response to environmental challenges in recent years, industries have reduced pollution loads in their wastewater to avoid outlays for new treatment plants. Some companies, for example, changed raw materials to lessen the impact of by-products on water quality. Perhaps the classic example of employing production changes to overcome pollution is the synthetic detergent industry. When critics pointed out that its product was not biodegradable, the industry developed a substitute manufacturing process. By changing from alkyl benzene sulfonate to linear alkyl sulfonate as a basic ingredient in detergent manufacturing, the industry eliminated its product's ability to survive conventional waste treatment processes. In addition to altering raw material, industries can change production techniques to reduce pollution loads. For example, by substituting sulfuric acid for hydrochloric acid in steel production, acid waste is reduced from about thirteen pounds per ton to less than one fourth of a pound per ton.

Many companies have found that careful waste handling can lead to considerable savings. By recovering materials from waste products, some industries are able to retrieve raw materials and recycle them into the production process. A steel mill in East Chicago, Indiana, for example, noted a savings of $1,925 per day by recovering mill scale. Similarly, materials retrieved from wastes can often be transformed into salable commodities. Whey, a by-product of cheese production, can be turned into protein supplements. Monosodium glutamate and potash are valuable resources recovered from sugar beet processing.

While production changes can remove significant amounts of water pollutants, industrial waste control remains a major concern of public works professionals. Fifty percent of the waste loads currently treated in municipal plants originate with industry. Recent federal environmental legislation, which seeks zero discharge goals, requires that industries using public sewage works bear their fair share of plant construction, operation, and maintenance. The difficult process of working out cooperative agreements between the public and private sectors involves establishing equitable user fees and setting criteria for assessing waste loads.

In the past hundred years, sanitary engineers have developed complex systems to treat industrial and sanitary wastewater. But the recent focus of state and federal water pollution control authorities on "non-point" pollution sources has broadened the scope of municipal treatment responsibilities. Non-point pollutants include soil erosion, pesticides, herbicides, fertilizers, feedlot runoff, and salt used on roads for ice and snow abatement. These substances enter sewage processing plants through area-wide drainage systems, creating additional treatment problems for public works agencies.

Non-point pollution is part of a larger concern for contaminants carried by storm runoff water. In the past, wastewater treatment focused on processing the substances in sanitary flows. Runoff water was a major problem only during storms when wastewater from combined sewers exceeded treatment plant capacities. The accepted solution was to separate sanitary wastewater from storm runoff flows and to discharge the latter directly into receiving waters. However, investigations in the 1960s revealed that storm drainage systems also carried a heavy load of pollutants. Rainfall scours the urban environment and transports pollutants such as street litter, salt, animal droppings, petroleum products, industrial wastes, and fertilizers. A 1967 study by the American Public Works Association (APWA) for the Federal Water Pollution Control Administration revealed that street litter alone accumulated at a rate of between 0.4 and 5.2 pounds per day for every 100 feet of curb. Some of this residue can be collected through efficient street cleaning practices, but the zero discharge goals contained in new federal legislation suggest that treatment of urban stormwater runoff will be needed. In January 1974, an amendment to the 1972 Water Pollution Control Act required each state to develop estimated costs for treating storm runoff water. The projected costs are astronomical. After surveying state reports, EPA estimated in 1974 that it would require $235 billion in capital expenditures for stormwater runoff control and treatment facilities to meet zero discharge goals by 1983.

Technological progress in the field of wastewater treatment and disposal has required increased training for management, operation, and maintenance personnel. Treatment plants may embody the most skillful application of research and experience in their design, but if operation is careless and haphazard, performance will be unsatisfactory. Fortunately, municipal, state, and regional pollution control organizations have established short- and long-term operator training

Public works personnel receive specialized training in order to operate modern wastewater treatment plants.

schools. Many states require registration and certification of operating personnel and set standards of staff competence for different types of treatment facilities. Public works personnel enhance their understanding of water pollution control processes through memberships in professional organizations and attendance at meetings, workshops, and exhibits featuring new equipment and treatment methods. The professional staffs at modern treatment plants differ greatly in background and experience from the political appointees who often operated early sewage works. In the larger cities, top management and technical staffs are usually selected by civil service.

Water pollution control is also fostered by professional societies. Perhaps foremost among these groups is the Water Pollution Control Federation (WPCF) founded in 1928 as the Federation of Sewage Works Associations. The WPCF was formed out of individual state organizations, the oldest of which was established in New Jersey in 1915. The American Society of Civil Engineers founded a Sanitary Engineering (now Environmental Engineering) Division in 1922. The journals of these and other societies, such as APWA and the American Public Health Association, serve as valuable exchange media for information on operations and research.

Administration of wastewater control and treatment systems varies widely throughout the country. The first public sewer works were usually built and maintained by commissions established by state or local governments. During the late nineteenth century, professional engineers were placed on city payrolls to head up sewage departments. In today's large municipalities, the sewage unit is usually part of a broad public works agency that coordinates the planning, operation, and maintenance of public services. Some communities administratively divide sanitary sewer and storm runoff management functions. The Department of Sanitary Sewers in Tampa, Florida, for example, operates independently from the Public Works Department's storm sewer unit. Because of the ecology thrust of the 1960s, metropolitan areas have incorporated wastewater management

into public agencies having broad environmental responsibilities. The recent trend toward water reuse has caused many municipalities to combine their water supply and wastewater handling agencies into one organization. This concept is exemplified by Philadelphia's Water Department which has total responsibility for water supply as well as sewage collection and disposal.

Closer relationships between sewer and water departments have also been established through the imposition of sewer service fees. This financing method helps solve the frequently troublesome problem of securing adequate operation and maintenance funding for wastewater systems. In the past, once a bond issue was floated and new facilities constructed, municipal governments often failed to appropriate adequate operating funds. Today, however, regular sewer service charges are invoked to support operation and maintenance activities as well as to liquidate capital costs. Since sewage flows are not normally metered, various means have been established to determine reasonable service charges. The most common is to base sewer fees for households and businesses on a percentage of their water billing. The imposition of service charges was given great impetus by the 1972 Water Pollution Control Act which requires all applicants for EPA wastewater project grants to establish self-sustaining sewer utilities through equitable service charge formulas.

The most significant organizational change in recent years has been the expanding geographical scope of sewage system management agencies. Cooperative wastewater collection and treatment networks have been established to serve multicommunity areas. Under these arrangements, local municipalities maintain control of their collector lines, but a broad-based governmental entity controls the interceptor sewers and wastewater processing works. The constituent communities, in such cases, are billed for this service either on the basis of flow readings taken at metering stations or by other equitable fiscal procedures. In Minnesota, for example, the Metropolitan Wastes Control Commission serves over 100 communities in the Minneapolis-St. Paul area.

The problems of industrial and non-point pollution have placed heavy burdens upon existing wastewater treatment systems. In the future, these problems will be met through more complete methods of removing pollutants. However, the immediate answer to these problems is wider application of existing waste treatment methods. Some cities have only primary treatment facilities, and many other communities need to enlarge or modernize primary and secondary treatment plants. But this is only a partial solution. Conventional treatment processes are already losing the battle against tougher wastes. Advanced waste treatment techniques which range from extensions of biological treatment capable of removing nitrogen and phosphorous nutrients to physical-chemical separation techniques are now under investigation. These new processes can achieve a high degree of pollution control so that discharges from treatment plants can be reused for agriculture, industry, recreation, and public drinking water supplies. These third generation processes, collectively known as advanced treatment, offer the promise of virtually complete pollution control and more efficient utilization of water resources.

Coagulation-sedimentation is a process being used to increase the removal of solids from effluent after primary and secondary treatment. Besides essentially removing all settleable solids, this method is capable of reducing phosphate levels by over 95 percent. To achieve these results, alum, lime, or iron salts are added to water as it leaves the secondary treatment facility. The flow passes through tanks where the chemicals cause smaller particles to floc (bunch) together into large masses. These lumps of particles then settle out in a sedimentation tank. In many cases, this process is employed as a pretreatment step for some of the other advanced treatment methods.

Processes have also been developed to remove refractory organic materials which resist normal biological treatment. *Adsorption* consists of passing wastewater through a bed of activated carbon granules which can remove more than 98 percent of the organics.

To reduce the cost of the procedure, the carbon granules can be cleaned by heat and reused. Another carbon system is also under study in which, instead of passing the effluent through a bed of granules, powdered carbon is put directly into wastewater flows. The organics attach themselves to the carbon, and the carbon is subsequently removed from the effluent by chemical coagulants.

The separation of salts from sewage has been a vexing problem for environmental engineers. Salts, in this sense, encompass many minerals dissolved by water as it passes through the air as rainfall, trickles through the soil and over rocks, and is used in homes and factories. *Electrodialysis* is a rather complicated process by which electricity and membranes are used to remove salts from wastewater. A membrane is usually made of chemically treated plastic. The salts are forced out of the water through the membrane by an electric field. As an example, the two elements of common table salt are sodium and chlorine. When salt is dissolved in water the sodium and chlorine particles separate to form ions. When the effluent passes through an electrodialysis cell, the positive sodium ions are attracted through the membrane by a negatively charged electrode. The negative chlorine ions are separated from the water by an electrode with a positive charge. With the salts removed, the water can be reused or discharged into a river or lake.

Water can also be purified by *distillation*. Distillation or evaporation basically consists of heating effluent to the boiling point. The steam is piped to another chamber where it is cooled and returned to liquid form. Most of the unwanted impurities remain in the original chamber. However, some volatile substances may distill along with the water and carry materials that contribute objectionable taste. To most people, distilled water has a flat, disagreeable taste caused by the absence of minerals and air. But by blending this pure water with the standard water supply, a better tasting drinking water results. Distillation remains an important adjunctive process to other treatment methods, but it is costly and energy intensive.

Reverse osmosis is another treatment process now under investigation. When liquids with different concentrations of mineral salts are separated by a membrane, molecules of pure water tend to pass by osmosis from the more concentrated side to the purer side until both liquids have the same mineral content. Scientists are exploring ways to reverse the action of this natural phenomenon to cleanse wastewater. When pressure is exerted on the side with the most minerals, the natural force reverses itself, causing molecules of pure water to escape the compartment containing a high salt concentration. Rather than taking pollutants out of water in the traditional way, this process draws water away from the pollutants. Tests have shown that the process results in clean drinking water.

Discharges from conventional secondary treatment plants often contain many organic materials. Oxidants such as ozone and chlorine have been used for many years to improve the taste and odor qualities and to disinfect municipal drinking water. However, the concentration of organics in waste-bearing water is much higher than in municipal water supplies. Until recently, cost of the oxidants prevented their widespread use in waste treatment. Improvements in the production and application of ozone and pure oxygen have reduced costs sufficiently to make their use practicable. When employed in conjunction with other processes, oxidation effectively eliminates wastes resistant to other processes.

During the past twenty years, the chemical industry has been working on synthetic organic chemicals, known as polymers, to improve waste separation. Polymers were initially used to augment sludge dewatering. By introducing polymers into the sludge, the physical and chemical bonds between the solids are tightened. When this occurs, the water can be separated more rapidly from the sludge. By putting the compounds directly into streams, it may be possible to capture silt at specific locations so that it can be removed in quantity. If polymers are put into raw sewage, waste treatment plants are able to combine a chemical process with the standard primary and secondary stages. This solids removal method can immediately upgrade

Public Works Historical Society

Advanced wastewater treatment technology and legislation are cleaning up polluted streams such as this.

plant efficiency without costly investments for new facilities.

Within the past two decades, the public works profession has responded to challenges arising from the increased public concern for water quality. The combined effects of a better understanding of wastewater composition and federal environmental legislation have spawned innovative waste treatment technologies, increased capital expenditures for wastewater systems, and stimulated the creation of public agencies with broad environmental responsibilities. Wastewater control, once confined to the field of sanitary engineering, has evolved into a multifaceted discipline which plans, administers, and maintains complex environmental systems.

Water Pollution Control Legislation

While there has been a flurry of federal water quality legislation in recent years, significant attempts to identify and develop effective means of water pollution abatement actually have been underway for more than a century. Early steps to preserve the quality of streams and lakes originated with state and local governments. Only in the last quarter century has the federal government developed an extensive program to control water pollution.

The first measure to control water pollution was adopted in colonial Massachusetts. In 1647 the provincial government passed an act making it "unlawful for any person to cast any dung, draught, dirt or anything to fill up the Cove, or to annoy the Neighbors, upon penalty of forty shillings." Nearly eighty years later, South Carolina's provincial assembly authorized the assessment of fines for actions which reduced the economic value of rivers. To protect the navigability of rivers, the legislature prohibited inhabitants from leaving felled trees in waterways for more than a specified time. A second section decreed that "in case any white persons by any means shall poison any creek in this Province; he or they upon proof made thereof before any of his Majesty's justices of the peace in this Province, shall forfeit the sum of ten pounds." The latter measure was not, however, a general ban on water contamination. It was designed to protect an important food source by prohibiting fish poisoning.

Extensive legislative action to curb pollution in the interest of public health did not emerge until governments became aware of the relationship between contaminated water and disease. The first efforts to control water pollution were undertaken at the local governmental level. Municipalities, counties, and townships imposed sanitary regulations; and water supply and waste disposal were regarded as local problems. Buttressing this parochial viewpoint were state constitutional provisions which limited state indebtedness in such a way as to force most public works expenditures down to the local level of government. Thus, water supply and sewage disposal systems were financed by municipal bonds payable out of local taxes or sewage service charges. By American custom, the unit of government which financed and administered projects also was responsible for regulation.

During the nineteenth century, a great deal of state legislation was passed to enable local jurisdictions to meet water pollution hazards. Administrative agencies were created to deal with the problems of waste disposal, water pollution control, and water purification. Institutional arrangements varied widely from state to state, but basically water quality control was sought by three means: delegation of power to local governments to prevent or abate pollution nuisances; legislative mandates enforced by local officials with set fines and sentences; and authorization of civil suits for damages by aggrieved individuals.

These local agencies, usually boards of health, were the first public pollution fighters. Their duties included inspecting public wells, outhouses, and cesspools; answering citizen nuisance complaints; and preparing reports on their cities' public works needs. They also made surveys of births and deaths, administered medical programs for the poor, and coordinated responses to epidemics. These efforts were partially successful in coping with local problems; but in some instances, success was purchased at the expense of other cities. Sometimes local governments cleaned up their own water supply, but they flushed their wastes downstream to foul the supplies of their neighbors.

The only other line of defense against pollution was for aggrieved individuals to initiate civil suits for damages caused by pollution. Under common law, water pollution constituted a violation of riparian rights, and property owners could obtain relief by suing for damages or seeking injunctions. The basic doctrine found in many nineteenth-century judicial decisions was that individuals could not abuse water to the detriment of downstream users. However, such cases were extremely difficult to win because of the difficulties in obtaining proof. Most streams were polluted by the cumulative effects of discharges from several sources; and until the end of the nineteenth century, there was no sound scientific understanding of water pollution effects. Furthermore, the judicial process was costly, time consuming, and offered remedies only after the damage was done. A North Carolina politician once offered a laconic observation of water quality litigation: "The longest way to controlling pollution is through the courthouse door!"

At the end of the nineteenth century, state governments began to tackle water pollution on a broader scale. State health departments were created, which became responsible for protecting public water supplies from sewage contamination. At about the same time, parallel responsibilities were given to fish and game departments to enforce waste discharges harmful to wildlife. By the early twentieth century, most states had developed comprehensive water pollution control programs.

Under the state programs, laws were passed to forbid specific substances from streams and lakes. Most states, for example, enacted statutes that prohibited dumping dead animals into municipal or other domestic water supplies. State laws also banned sawdust, slaughterhouse waste, oil and tars, and other products harmful to fish and aquatic life. Violations of these environmental laws were misdemeanors; and violators were subject to fines, injunctions, or administrative orders to terminate pollution. However, enforcement was lax.

Since the Korean War, there has been a movement away from reliance on public health agencies and a movement toward the creation of either autonomous water quality control agencies or comprehensive environmental protection units. In addition to enforcing pollution control statutes, these agencies supervise federal sewage treatment grants and plan general water resource programs. In the same period, the scope of water pollution control laws has broadened. Some state statutes protect the recreational uses of waters so that wastes will not render streams and lakes unfit for swimming and boating. In most states, laws have been expanded to cover disposal of industrial by-products and to regulate the quality of groundwater as well as surface water. These changes have expanded government's regulatory role from prohibiting sewage pollution to protecting water from contamination.

Two avenues have been followed by states to resolve interstate water disputes: court action and interstate compacts. Shortly after the turn of the century, a series of celebrated cases were fought in the United States Supreme Court. From 1900 to 1906, Chicago was the object of legal action arising out of its famous drainage canal. St. Louis, Missouri's officials held that diverting Chicago's sewage from Lake Michigan into the Mississippi River via the Illinois River posed a hazard to St. Louis' water supply. The Supreme Court decided in Chicago's favor, ruling that since the Illinois River was less contaminated than

the Mississippi at their confluence, no hazard had been demonstrated. In 1908 New York sued New Jersey for polluting its harbor; but in 1921, the court ruled in New Jersey's favor, once again claiming a lack of proof of damage.

Interstate compacts have offered a more effective means of promoting regional water pollution control. These agreements require the sanction of participating state legislatures and the approval of Congress. The Ohio River Valley Water Sanitation Commission (ORSANCO) and the Delaware River Basin Commission (DRBC) are the most significant interstate agencies that have been created. The ORSANCO began operating in 1948 and consists of three representatives from the federal government and three members from each of the eight member states—Ohio, West Virginia, Virginia, Illinois, Indiana, Kentucky, New York, and Pennsylvania. The commission has authority to issue enforcement orders and bring polluters to court, but it has relied primarily on promoting voluntary compliance by municipalities. The DRBC was formed in 1961 under an agreement by the federal government, New York, New Jersey, Pennsylvania, and Delaware and provided the first pollution abatement compact within the context of a basin-wide water resource development and control program. The agreement instituted an organizational innovation: it allowed the commission's decisions to be determined by majority vote, foregoing the veto power given to each participating state in other interstate water quality agencies.

The national government did not adopt pollution control legislation until comparatively recently. Only in the last quarter century has the federal government taken a direct role in water pollution control.

In the early nineteenth century, Congress promoted the economic growth of the country by aiding the development of transportation systems. In 1824 the Army Corps of Engineers was first given responsibility for developing and maintaining navigable rivers; and during the rest of the century, projects were funded to expedite the flow of commerce on rivers and lakes. The concept of pollution was limited to objects or substances that impeded waterborne traffic. Section 13 of the 1899 Rivers and Harbors Bill, for example, prohibited the discharge of "any refuse matter of any kind or description whatever other than the flowing from streets and sewers and passing therefrom in a liquid state" into any navigable waterway without obtaining a permit from the army. Although recent environmentalists rediscovered this act and dubbed it the 1899 Refuse Act, it was designed to keep rivers open, not to control water pollution.

The first federal water pollution control efforts involved indirect aid to state health agencies. The Marine Hospital Service and the Public Health and Marine Hospital Service, forerunners of the United States Public Health Service, studied the relationships between polluted water and certain diseases and shared their knowledge with state agencies. After the turn of the century, however, federal officials cooperated in water quality studies. In 1908, for example, the Public Health and Marine Hospital Service joined the states surrounding Lake Michigan to form the Lake Michigan Water Commission. The commission studied pollutants discharged into the lake, evaluated lake conditions, and assessed future problems. While the agency lacked congressional authority to investigate pollution in specific bodies of water, studies relating to public health were undertaken. In 1910 Allan J. McLaughlin directed the first health service investigation of stream pollution to determine the "extent of pollution of water supplies [of Great Lake cities], and its relation to the prevalence of typhoid fever and other water-borne diseases." This investigation was the beginning of many federal inquiries; but like the earlier study of Lake Michigan, it was conducted in cooperation with state boards of health.

Recognizing the need for greater knowledge of pollutants and their effects prompted Congress in 1912 to change the name of the Public Health and Marine Hospital Service to the Public Health Service. It authorized the new agency to study "the pollution either directly or indirectly of the navigable streams and lakes of the United States." Quickly rising to the challenge, the Public Health Service initiated a detailed

study of water quality problems on the Ohio River. Officials selected the Ohio for investigation because it was a large, major river, and its problems seemed representative. The Public Health Service hoped the questions asked and the solutions found with regard to Ohio River pollution would be of assistance on many other rivers. Investigators of the Ohio sought to define the character of wastes discharged into the river, the effect of the pollutants on the stream, and the relationship of pollutants to public health in the adjacent communities. Similar investigations of other streams commenced prior to American entry into World War I. The agency also established a research center in Cincinnati, Ohio, which studied water pollution and wastewater treatment processes.

Although World War I reduced the agency's work force, results of studies continued to be published aiding local and state governments in maintaining high-quality water. Following the war, the Public Health Service resumed its stream and pollution studies with new vigor. Some investigators examined streams to determine their water quality. Others experimented with different sewage treatment and water purification methods. Still other scientists investigated natural stream purification and laboratory controlled sewage treatment methods to determine the best way to secure high-quality water. During the interwar years, studies of streams and stream pollution continued to develop important information. Public awareness of the danger of water pollution, particularly its relation to public health problems, stimulated the construction of numerous waste treatment facilities in the 1920s.

The advent of the Depression, however, brought about a sharp decline in the number of treatment plants constructed with state and local financing. As the Depression affected state and local governments, progress slowed in the field of water pollution control. To revitalize the economy and provide jobs to the unemployed, the federal government established agencies such as the Civil Works Administration (CWA), the Public Works Administration (PWA), and the Works Progress Administration (WPA). These organizations

During the Depression, a submarine interceptor sewer was built to Coney Island, New York, as part of a PWA-funded project.

spurred the construction of public works, including improvements in sewer systems and waste treatment facilities. The CWA, although designed simply to carry the unemployed through the winter of 1933-1934, assisted in the construction of sewage treatment plants and laid or repaired more than 2,300 miles of sewer lines. In addition, 8,000 communities built or repaired their water and sewer systems with WPA assistance by 1936. The PWA also funded sewage projects. After 1933 PWA spent nearly $1.2 billion for the construction of over 500 waste disposal plants.

The only attempt to establish federal water pollution regulations prior to the Depression had accomplished little. Congress designed the 1924 Oil Pollution Control Act to reduce the amount of oil polluting the nation's coastal waters. The secretary of the army was authorized to establish rules and regulations governing the discharge of oil from ships for the purpose of protecting public health, navigation, and persons and property engaged in commerce on the coastal waters. While the act granted sufficient power to regulate effectively oil discharges, it was difficult to enforce.

In the 1930s, several water pollution control measures failed in Congress. The most significant was a bill Senator Alben Barkley of Kentucky introduced in 1936 that provided the basis for later pollution control legislation.

Barkley's proposal included federal investigation of pollution and a capital grants program to states, to be administered by the Public Health Service. After incorporating some changes suggested by the Conference of State and Territorial Health Officers, Congress passed a revised version of the bill, but it was defeated by a last minute call for reconsideration. Nevertheless, the water pollution control bills drafted by Barkley and others before World War II heralded the 1948 Water Pollution Control Act.

Congress resumed consideration of water pollution control following the war. Early in the Eightieth Congress, Representatives Brent Spence and Charles Elston introduced identical pollution control bills to the House of Representatives; and Senators Robert Taft and Barkley cosponsored a companion bill in the Senate. The Taft-Barkley bill, including the same basic provisions as the previous Barkley bill, received congressional approval. President Harry S. Truman signed it on June 30, 1948, and the Water Pollution Control Act became the basic federal water quality law. It provided for comprehensive planning, technical services, research, interstate cooperation, financial assistance, and enforcement. It authorized $2.3 million in annual low-interest loans for constructing sewage abatement facilities from 1949 to 1953. An additional $800,000 a year was authorized to develop plant designs. Congress extended the act in 1952, and in 1956 placed the Water Pollution Control Act on the books as permanent legislation. Larger pollution control expenditures were also authorized. The law granted $3 million a year to state agencies and $500 million a year for local sewage treatment construction from 1957 to 1966.

Public concern for conservation and protection of natural resources eased adoption of the 1965 amendments to the Water Pollution Control Act. The 1965 legislation stated that one purpose of the act was "to enhance the quality and value of our water resources and to establish a national policy for the prevention, control, and abatement of water pollution." Previous legislation provided financial and technical assistance for sewage treatment plant construction but contained no measures to establish uniform water quality standards. The 1965 Water Quality Act, as the amendments to the basic 1948 law were titled, required all state and territorial governments to establish minimum water quality standards. The federal government would review these standards to assure their compliance with acceptable minimum levels. Thus, a truly national water quality policy could be developed. A system of standards, roughly uniform in scope, was established throughout the United States as a result of the 1965 legislation.

In 1966 additional amendments to the Water Pollution Control Act further expanded the role of the federal government in the water pollution control area. The new amendments provided for greater federal research, demonstration, and construction grants. In addition, the federal government agreed to assist state governments in developing comprehensive plans for cleaning interstate rivers and lakes. The 1966 act also extended the jurisdiction of the 1924 Oil Pollution Control Act from coastal waters to all navigable waters.

The 1965 and 1966 amendments to the act brought a changed emphasis in pollution controls. Public health concerns remained important catalysts, but more recognition was given to the value of preserving the environment for aesthetic purposes. In accordance with changing attitudes, President Lyndon B. Johnson transferred control of water pollution programs from the Department of Health, Education, and Welfare (HEW), where it had resided since 1961, to the Department of Interior.

Even though important changes in the administration and regulation of water pollution controls occurred in the late 1960s, many problems remained for the following decade. In order to resolve some of these issues, Congress adopted the 1969 National Environmental Policy Act, which established EPA and assigned to it water pollution control responsibilities. The most important provisions of this act required all federal agencies to include "in every recommendation or report on proposals for legislation and other major federal actions significantly affecting the quality of the human environment" a detailed

statement on the possible and expected environmental impact of the proposed action, plus a list of alternatives to that action. While environmental impact statements were not always as effective as some desired, they required agencies to consider the environment when developing new projects. Continuing the environmental thrust of the decade, President Richard M. Nixon issued executive orders in February and March 1970 requiring governmental projects to conform with water quality standards and calling on government agencies to guard against pollution when issuing "loans, grants, contracts, and licenses."

Throughout 1968 and 1969, Congress could not reach agreement on the principles of further water pollution legislation. Heavy public pressure following oil spills along the California, Louisiana, and Florida coasts, however, stimulated Congress to strengthen regulations against oil pollution. To correct some inadequacies of previous legislation, Congress adopted the 1970 Water Quality Improvement Act. This new law required owners or operators of ships or offshore oil facilities to pay for cleaning up oil spills. In addition, the 1970 legislation authorized demonstration projects for controlling acid mine drainage, ordered the development of criteria to cover pollution effects of pesticides, prohibited dumping of raw sewage from boats, and placed stronger restrictions on thermal pollution discharges from electric generation plants.

The entire spectrum of pollution control philosophy was revised in 1972. With the funding programs of the Water Pollution Control Act due to expire in mid 1972, public pressures mounted for new environmental legislation. The Senate prepared a bill seeking elimination of all water pollution by 1985. To secure this goal, it established a five-year, $20 billion matching fund program. Industries and municipalities were required in stages to employ progressively better treatment techniques that would eliminate all pollutant discharges by 1985. The Administration, displeased with the high price tag and stringent time schedule of the Senate bill, sought adjustments in the House of Representatives. The House approved regulations more closely aligned with Administration's desires, but differences in the two pieces of legislation were resolved.

A conference committee developed an acceptable bill which authorized expenditure of $24.6 billion for research and construction grants from 1972 to 1975. In addition, new requirements based on the Senate bill were adopted for industrial and municipal treatment. All industrial and agricultural polluters were to use the "best practicable control technology currently available" by July 1, 1977. Municipalities were to employ secondary treatment facilities by the same date. By July 1983, industries were required to use the "best available technology economically achievable." The 1972 Water Pollution Control Act established, as a national goal, elimination of pollutant discharges into American waters by 1985 and, as an interim goal, achievement of water quality safe for fish, shellfish, wildlife, and recreation by July 1, 1983.

Waste discharge permits were retained under the 1972 Water Pollution Control Act, but the procedures for granting permits and the governing authority were changed. The 1899 Refuse Act was superseded by a new permit system administered through EPA. Industries, when applying for permits, had to meet EPA discharge requirements and could not pollute the waters of a downstream state. The EPA could reject a permit application if it did not meet established discharge guidelines, or if governors of downstream states could prove that discharges polluted the waters of their states. Viewing the bill as expensive and impractical, President Nixon vetoed the legislation, only to be overriden with but thirty-five votes in support of the veto in the House and Senate combined.

The final adoption of the 1972 Water Pollution Control Act did not, however, terminate the legislative-executive confrontation over water pollution problems. In November 1972, President Nixon ordered EPA's administrator to withhold $3 billion of the $5 billion for expenditure in fiscal year 1973 and half of the 1974 authorization of $6 billion. Nixon thus exercised a "second veto" of the 1972 Water Pollution Control Act. However, in 1974 the courts ruled that the full funding be made available as authorized by Congress.

Wastewater Treatment Landmarks

Water quality control is a broad and complex field encompassing a wide variety of problems which can be met by different technological solutions. Each community selects its treatment system after evaluating factors such as cost, annual rainfall, population size and density, topography, sludge disposal alternatives, and the volume and content of wastewater flows. The following sketches of innovative sewage treatment systems are a few examples of imaginative and ambitious attempts by American communities to protect water resources.

Milwaukee, Wisconsin's Jones Island West Plant was one of the first major treatment facilities to use the activated sludge process. This historic public work which began operation in 1925 was the product of nearly two decades of sewage treatment research conducted by the City of Milwaukee. In 1909 the Milwaukee Common Council authorized the appointment of a commission of three engineers to make a comprehensive study of sewage disposal for the city. Among their recommendations was one calling for the construction of sedimentation tanks and facilities to clarify and disinfect sewage. After considering this engineering report, the Common Council recommended that the state legislature permit the city to establish a sewerage commission. The legislation was adopted in 1913, and five citizens were made responsible for planning and constructing a sewage system for the collection, transmission, and disposal of Milwaukee's wastewater. The commission's first action was to establish a sewage disposal testing station where the most recent methods of sewage treatment could be applied to local wastewater. During 1914 and 1915, the commission experimented with coarse and fine screening, grit chambers, Imhoff tanks, intermittent filters, trickling filters, chemical precipitation, and chlorination. They also investigated the activated sludge process developed in England by Gilbert J. Fowler. The studies showed this process to be superior to the others, and a

Public Works Historical Society

Milwaukee, Wisconsin, began operating the world's first large activated sludge treatment plant in 1925.

2 million gallon per day (mgd) pilot plant was built. Further experiments were conducted, and in 1919 construction began on an 85 mgd plant, which was placed into operation at the Jones Island site in 1925. Subsequent expansion has increased the plant's daily treatment capacity to 200 million gallons.

The Jones Island plant pioneered the production of commercial fertilizer from sludge. Since the 1920s, the city has sold Milorganite (Milwaukee Organic Nitrogen), a product that is an excellent nutrient for lawns and gardens. This recycling of wastes is made possible by Milwaukee's unique industrial sewage from breweries, tanneries, and meat packers which gives Milorganite its high-nitrogen content. Approximately 80,000 tons of the fertilizer are produced annually by the Jones Island plant.

In accordance with the federal program to encourage development of new and practical methods of pollution abatement, in 1966 the City of Milwaukee submitted a project proposal for a detention tank to collect combined sewage overflows for later return to intercepting sanitary sewers and eventual full treatment. In times of heavy rainfall, untreated sewage overflowed directly into the Milwaukee River an average of fifty-six times a

year. With the detention tank in operation, the annual number of overflows was reduced to approximately sixteen, and the sewage received partial treatment. These overflows may still occur during periods of extremely high rainfalls and when maintenance or repairs are required on the detention tank or intercepting sewer. However, all overflows in excess of tank capacity are chlorinated to provide an effluent compatible with Milwaukee River water.

The detention tank has a capacity of 3.9 million gallons, was constructed at a cost of $1.2 million, and was placed into operation on October 11, 1971. It is located on the north bank of the Milwaukee River and serves an area of 570 acres. An additional $281,000 was spent to build and equip eleven monitoring stations to obtain data relating to the quantity and quality of flow in combined sewers, intercepting sanitary sewers, and the Milwaukee River. The detention tank is not designed as a primary treatment plant. Instead, coarse screens collect all large debris at the inlet to the tank. A chlorine solution is injected into the overflow at this point. The remaining combined sewage, liquid and solid, is retained in the detention tank until it is feasible to return it to the intercepting sanitary sewer. Mixer agitation equipment is employed to resuspend solids before repumping the mixture into the sewer. During the first year of operation, the detention tank prevented approximately 120 million gallons of combined sewage containing 225,000 pounds of suspended solids from being discharged into the Milwaukee River.

The restoration of the bodies of water surrounding Seattle, Washington, is one of the great public works success stories of the 1960s. Greater Seattle is 80 percent surrounded by water; and by the mid 1950s, the area was seriously polluted. Crowded between salty Puget Sound and the fresh waters of Lake Washington, the region included more than thirty uncoordinated sewerage agencies and was particularly vulnerable to water pollution. In Lake Washington, the discharge of effluent rich in nitrogen and phosphorous from sewage treatment plants caused severe eutrophication. More than 20 million gallons of phosphorous-rich treated wastewater were being dumped into the lake each day. The water was turbid, emitted unpleasant odors, and was a hazard to swimmers. In Puget Sound, the discharges of raw sewage through shallow outfalls made the beaches unsafe for swimming and further contributed to the decline of water quality.

Because of citizen concern for degrading water quality, the Municipality of Metropolitan Seattle (Metro) was founded in 1958. Its formation was a community achievement and resulted from a successful educational campaign to persuade voters to approve the largest and most costly sewage construction program of any metropolitan area of comparable size. Metro is a federation of local governments and special governments whose elected representatives sit on a thirty-six-member Metropolitan Council. This corporation is empowered to prepare comprehensive plans; acquire, construct, and operate metropolitan sewage facilities; fix rates for use of the facilities; and approve plans and establish minimum standards for construction of local sewer facilities. The Metro system was built and is maintained through the sale of sewer revenue bonds, federal and state grants, and local user charges. Metro does not operate local sewage systems; instead, it connects to them, transports and treats their sewage, and discharges it into receiving waters.

To clean up the waters, Metro adopted and implemented a comprehensive plan that involved building a collection system to transport sewage to modern treatment plants. Twenty-eight small plants were replaced by five larger, more efficient ones. The plan also included constructing interceptor sewers along the shore of Lake Washington and Lake Sammamish to divert all sewage from the lakes; treating all effluent entering salt water and discharging plant outflows into deep water through special diffusers; and constructing interceptors along the banks of the Duwamish River to free the river from sewage contamination.

The first stage of the program was completed in October 1970 at a cost of $120 million—only 1.5 percent over original estimates. This ambitious public works project succeeded in halting the eutrophication along the 22 miles of Lake Washington and eliminated raw sewage contamination along the beaches of Elliott Bay, a Puget Sound inlet and the site of Seattle's harbor. The second phase of the comprehensive plan is being implemented and is scheduled for completion in 1985. It will cost in excess of $186 million and will provide sewage treatment and collection services to additional outlying communities.

The impact on the area's quality of life has been profound. The community takes pride that much of the cleanup of Lake Washington was a local effort and occurred before a great deal of federal aid was available to combat pollution. The water quality of Lake Washington has been improved so that it is once again a year-round center of recreation. The beaches of Elliott Bay are safe and the Seattle harbor is one of the cleanest in the world.

Metro's West Point Treatment Plant is the keystone of the system. Completed in 1966, this plant is located only 4 miles from downtown Seattle and sits on a small point of land which juts into Puget Sound. Since Seattle has combined sewers, the facility was designed to respond to the area's frequent rainstorms as

APWA Washington Chapter

The West Point Treatment Plant was completed in 1966 as part of Metropolitan Seattle, Washington's efforts to control water pollution.

well as sewage from domestic and industrial sources. The plant has an average dry-weather flow capacity of 125 mgd and a daily peak capacity of 325 mgd. With two sources of water to process—sewage and storm runoff—the West Point plant has adopted an innovative Computer Augmented Treatment and Disposal (CATAD) system to abate plant overflows. The principle behind CATAD is simple. A central computer monitors the flows within the system's interceptor and trunk lines. During rainfalls the computer determines if too much water is filling these conduits. When an overflow threat occurs, the computer activates gates in the pipes to block water and store it in different parts of the system until the plant can handle the flow.

The West Point Treatment Plant is also participating in a unique method of sludge disposal. Prior to January 1973, sludge was disposed of through the plant's outfall which reaches three quarters of a mile into Puget Sound. But federal and state requirements halted this practice. The possible value of dewatered sludge to improve the productive capacity of low-quality forest soils is being studied by the University of Washington at

the Pack Demonstration Forest west of Mount Rainier. Tests are being conducted to determine the ability of sludge to promote seedling growth on cutover forest land and to enhance the growth of various tree varieties.

At the West Point plant, sludge is treated by anaerobic digestion and dewatering. The process creates methane gas which is used to power seven huge sewage pumps and to heat the plant and digesters. Most of the solid material is removed through sedimentation and skimming, and the effluent is disinfected by chlorination before being discharged.

The sewage treatment facility at Santee, California, stands as another model of progressive water treatment systems. When faced with difficult waste disposal problems in 1959, the San Diego Metropolitan System proposed an ocean dumping system to the communities in the vicinity of the Pacific port. Basically the San Diego plan called for treating all sewage and disposing of the effluent in the Pacific Ocean. Such a plan would be costly for participating communities and provided no adequate safeguards against ocean pollution in the area designated for the dumping zone. Santee decided not to participate in the system. The community developed an alternative which involved extensive treatment of sewage wastes and reuse of the wastewater for recreational purposes.

Since the town already had a new secondary treatment plant, the proposal simply required the addition of a final cleaning stage. Several means could have been used to achieve the goal, but a natural system seemed to be the best available and the least expensive alternative. When the San Diego Board of Health rejected a proposal that would have utilized a series of three oxidation ponds providing progressively cleaner effluent prior to releasing the water for public and recreational use, officials of the city looked elsewhere for a solution to their problem.

Sycamore Canyon on the western edge of the community, which carried the effluent from the existing treatment plant, was well suited for use as a sand filtration system. The geological formation of the canyon, an impervious clay layer beneath a layer of sand and gravel, provided a natural sewage filter. A sand and gravel excavating firm was working its way up the canyon, leaving abandoned gravel pits behind; and the city decided to seek the firm's cooperation in developing the recreational potential of the canyon. The pits with clay bases were ideal for artificial lakes. Sanitation officials at Santee decided to supplement the existing secondary plant, which used activated sludge as the basic treatment technique, by constructing an oxidation pond in one of the abandoned gravel pits. After a thirty-day holding period in the pond, where natural biological processes further purified the secondary effluent, the wastewater was pumped up the canyon and spread over a series of sand beds. Gradually, the effluent seeped through sand and gravel, working its way downhill to be recaptured, chlorinated against undesirable bacterial growths, and released into a series of recreational lakes constructed in other abandoned gravel pits.

Since not all of the effluent could be used in the recreational area, about two thirds of the effluent from the oxidation pond was released directly into Sycamore Creek and used downstream for irrigation. Essentially, the process gave all sewage from the community tertiary treatment through use of the oxidation pond. The filtration system in the canyon removed additional organic matter and protected it against viruses and bacterial growths. Scientific investigation of the system proved the efficiency of sand filtration. Approximately 99 percent of the biochemical oxygen demand (BOD) and about 95 percent of the viruses, bacteria, and organic nitrogen were removed after 200 feet of filtration in the canyon. When measured after 1,500 feet of filtration, other pollutants such as alkyl benzene sulfonate were almost completely removed from the recaptured wastewater.

The collected effluent in the recreational lakes has been tested and approved. The San Diego Board of Health approved public use of the lakes in 1961, shortly after the treatment began. Gradually, over the next four years, more uses of the lakes were approved and in 1965 a new swimming pool, filled with reclaimed water from the city's sewage treatment plant, was opened. Picnicking, boating, and fishing had been a part of the project since 1961, and with the addition of swimming a complete recreational facility was in use.

The facilities in Sycamore Canyon have been expanded to meet the demands of Santee's growing population. The secondary treatment plant's capacity was met in the latter part of 1967, and the canyon's filtration capacities were exceeded in 1970. As a result, Santee officials began developing processes which would purify wastes sufficiently, without filtrating lake water in the canyon. In January 1968, a new secondary treatment plant opened. It continued the high level of BOD removal obtained in the canyon while working to remove phosphorus and nitrogen dangerous to the life of the lakes. Effluent from the new plant continues to be used for recreational purposes in addition to fulfilling existing irrigation needs.

Muskegon County, Michigan, has developed an innovative and efficient tertiary treatment system. Muskegon, a growing metropolitan area on the eastern shore of Lake Michigan, had been indirectly discharging its treated wastes into the lake. Recognizing the need for pollution control in the late 1960s, community leaders sought ways to alleviate the problem. A plan was devised whereby sewage from all communities in the county would be treated in stabilization lagoons and the effluent applied to unproductive land. The naturally low fertility of the sandy soil in the area prevented extensive agricultural development. The economy of Muskegon County relied mainly on heavy industry, especially primary and fabricated metals, non-electrical machinery, and transportation equipment. With 80 percent of the population living on 33 percent of the country's land, and only 10 percent of the land area under cultivation, a sizable portion of Muskegon County was unproductive. By spreading treated sewage effluent on the idle land, the soil would act as a "living filter," trapping organic materials and excess nutrients from the sewage and purifying the wastewater. At the same time, the nutrients would increase the productivity of the land, providing an additional boost to the economy of the county.

A system was developed whereby all wastes in the county would be collected and pumped inland to aerated lagoons which would provide the equivalent of secondary treatment. The treated effluent would then be held in storage lagoons prior to being spread on the selected acreage through a sprinkler irrigation system. Since Muskegon is in a cold northern climate, the system would not be operable during the winter months. As a result, the storage lagoons were designed to be large enough to retain effluent for the months when the soil was frozen. The original design called for treating only domestic sewage, leaving industries to purify their own wastes; but the plan, as implemented in May 1973, provides treatment for all municipal and industrial wastes in the county. In addition, storm-water runoff is sent through the system making it one of the first to provide total tertiary treatment for an entire county. The Muskegon County irrigation system differs from others in the country mainly in its size. Whereas most land application plants dispose of wastewater on no more than a few hundred acres, the Muskegon system irrigates 6,000 acres of unproductive scrubland in the northeastern part of the county. Upon reaching full capacity, the system will process 43 million gallons of sewage per day and irrigate 10,000 acres of land.

In recent years, many smaller communities have renovated and expanded their sewage facilities to provide more efficient wastewater treatment. The Wastewater Treatment Plant at Marinette, Wisconsin, is a well-designed public works facility that utilizes modern waste treatment techniques. The plant was originally constructed in 1938 and subsequently expanded in 1954, 1956, and 1972. The 1972 renovation and expansion program which cost $2 million provided facilities to handle the wastewater generated by a projected 1990 population of 17,000. The plant can process a daily flow of 4.3 million gallons and an average daily organic loading of 3,000 pounds. All sewage undergoes primary and secondary treatment, disinfection, and phosphorus removal at the site.

The initial treatment phase involves the removal of settleable solid materials present in the raw wastewater. Wastewater collected in Marinette's sewer system enters the plant through a 30-inch sewer. Upon entering the Main Service Building, the wastewater passes through a grit chamber where heavy inert materials are allowed to settle for later disposal. The wastewater then flows to the comminutor which shreds the coarse organic solids into particles of a smaller, more uniform size. From the comminutor, the wastewater is pumped by three sewage pumps to the settling tanks. At this point, chemicals are added to promote settling in the primary clarifier. Additional suspended solids are removed in settling tanks that detain the wastewater for a period of time and allow the solids to settle to the bottom, thus forming the primary sludge. This primary sludge is mechanically thickened by a screw conveyor in the bottom of the clarifier. Grease and floatable solids that rise to the surface are removed by a mechanical skimmer. The scum and primary sludge are gathered in the Primary Sludge Pump Building and pumped to the sludge storage tank in the Solids Handling Building for further processing.

The secondary phase of treatment involves the removal of dissolved pollutional

Marinette, Wisconsin's Wastewater Treatment Plant is a modern, efficient public works facility.

matter. A large portion of the dissolved solids in wastewater are organic and cause oxygen depletion in receiving water if not properly treated. These dissolved solids are removed through a combination of biological and physical treatment processes. The plant utilizes the activated sludge process to remove dissolved organic solids. From the primary settling tanks, the wastewater enters the aeration tank in which the microorganism growth takes place. Air is pumped through the liquid in the tank to promote microorganism growth. The aeration tank is divided into three bays through which the wastewater flows. Operation of the activated sludge process and the amount of air pumped to the tanks is automatically controlled by electrical components in the Main Service Building. The wastewater flows from the aeration tank to the two secondary tanks. Here the sludge mass

produced in the aeration tank, settles from the wastewater and is removed by mechanical scrapers. A portion of the sludge is pumped back to the aeration tanks to assure a steady supply of fresh microorganisms.

The remaining matter, or waste activated sludge, is pumped to a flotation thickener unit located in the Solids Handling Building. As the sludge enters this unit, tiny air bubbles attach to the sludge solids, causing them to rise to the surface. The accumulated solids are then skimmed off by mechanical scrapers into a hopper. The process of air flotation reduces the amount of water present in the sludge, making additional dewatering more efficient. This sludge is then transferred to a storage tank and mixed with the primary sludge prior to ultimate disposal.

Disinfection destroys any disease causing microorganisms which are present in the effluent wastewater. It consists of a two-step operation involving chlorine application and wastewater detention. All flow through the plant enters the chlorine application manhole where a chlorine solution is added. Sufficient detention time for disinfection to occur is achieved in a chlorine contact chamber, a circular tank in which the effluent is held for a period of time. After passing through the tank, the treated wastewater is discharged to the Menominee River.

Because phosphorus causes accelerated growth of algae and weeds in lakes and rivers, this potential source of pollution is eliminated by the addition of ferric chloride to the wastewater at a manhole upstream from the plant. The chemically treated wastewater is held briefly in flocculation chambers located in the center of the primary settling tanks. The chemically bound phosphorus compounds settle out with the sludge.

The conditioning and disposal of sludge constitutes the final step in the wastewater treatment process. Due to the high moisture content of sludge, a vacuum filter unit is used to dewater the material. This device consists of a revolving drum to which the sludge is drawn by vacuum. The surface of the drum is covered by a fine filter which allows the passage of water while withholding the solids. The water is returned to the plant for treatment while the dewatered sludge is conveyed to the incinerator. The solids from the incinerator are disposed of in a landfill, and the exhaust gases from the incinerator are purified by an intense water spray before release to the atmosphere.

New York City's response to the demand for wastewater treatment is dramatically illustrated by the North River Water Pollution Control Project, currently under construction. This 220 mgd facility, scheduled for completion in 1982, will serve an area of more than 6,000 acres with a population of approximately 1 million persons. This project, including the plant and 11 miles of interceptor tunnels, represents the largest non-military, competitively bid project in the nation's history. It will cost $700 million to complete. The plant is being constructed in two phases. Phase I, which is scheduled for completion in

1976, involves construction of a thirty-acre concrete platform extending almost 750 feet into the Hudson River. This substructure, the largest marine platform in history, will be supported by 2,300 concrete-filled steel caissons socketed into rock as much as 250 feet below the river's surface. The treatment plant, with walls 55 to 69 feet high, will be constructed on this base. It will be fed by an 11-mile-long interceptor sewer system which has been completed along Manhattan's west side. The North River project will meet or exceed all existing state and federal sewage treatment requirements.

When the project was proposed in the early 1960s, it encountered stout opposition. The site borders West Harlem, a community largely black in racial composition. The inflammatory charge was raised of bringing the white man's waste to the black man's doorstep, and the aesthetic impact of a thirty-acre plant on the waterfront was assailed. After four years of interaction between the community, state, and city, an acceptable solution was found. The city was allowed to build the plant, and the state agreed to create a thirty-acre park on the plant's roof. The recreational amenities of the park, the sixth largest in New York City, will include football and baseball fields, handball and tennis courts, community buildings, and a restaurant and cafe. The park will also give the community direct access to the waterfront.

The Metropolitan Sanitary District of Greater Chicago (MSD) recently embarked on a unique sludge disposal project, using its "liquid fertilizer" for reclamation of several thousand acres of strip-mined land in Fulton County, Illinois. The district's sewage treatment system is the largest in the world, serving an area covering 860 square miles; it involves water use by 5.5 million people and an industrial use equivalent of another 5.5 million. On an average day, 1.3 billion gallons of wastewater are processed, resulting in an accumulation of 900 dry tons of disposable solids.

In the mid 1960s, MSD recognized the need for a better sludge disposal method. At that time, about half of the area's sludge was heat dried and sold. The rest was digested and

Sludge from Chicago's West-Southwest Wastewater Treatment Plant, the world's largest treatment facility, is used to reclaim strip-mined land.

stored in eleven sludge lagoons. The sludge drying process created air pollution, consumed large quantities of natural gas, and was costly. Space for new lagooning was running out, and existing lagoons occupied large tracts of valuable urban land.

The MSD "Prairie Plan," begun in 1972, expands the concept of utilizing sludge as a fertilizer. It is designed to revitalize an entire region through multiple-use land development. The agency believes that using digested sludge to reclaim strip-mined areas offers several advantages over its utilization as a fertilizer on normal agricultural land. Strip-mined land is deficient in organic matter and has a great assimilative capacity for plant nutrients and other wastes, thus reducing the risk of soil and water contamination. Land that has been surface-mined for coal generally offers large, contiguous acreages

which simplifies sludge transportation and distribution. Furthermore, sludge is an excellent soil builder. Digested sludge contains respective percentages of 5, 3, and 0.5 for nitrogen, phosphorus, and potassium. Because the waste product is a natural organic material, it also provides increased humus content, greater soil fertility, improved soil structure, and more water holding capacity.

To implement the Prairie Plan, MSD purchased over 10,000 acres in Fulton County, about 200 miles southwest of Chicago. To reach the project's goals, MSD will eventually require 30,000 usable acres. Sludge leaves digesters at a Chicago treatment plant and is piped to storage tanks at a nearby loading dock. There, it is pumped aboard barges which travel down the Illinois River to a depot at Liverpool, Illinois. The sludge is then piped to holding basins 11 miles away where it is retained until it is ready for land application. The sludge is applied only eight months a year because distribution lines freeze in winter. This detention allows the sludge more time to age, thereby guarding against objectionable odors. The distribution system consists of pipes, an above-ground header system, and a "big-gun" spray vehicle that travels across the fields applying a 300-foot-wide spray. In 1975 about 9,000 wet tons were being disposed of per day, about 50 percent of the sludge produced daily by the communities MSD serves.

Experiments are taking place in several areas on a promising new development, a swirl concentrator device, for regulating and concentrating combined sewer overflows. During wet weather, a regulator is used to prevent overloading a treatment plant. Usually, the combined sewage that cannot be accommodated is bypassed by the regulator directly into the receiving waters, resulting in heavy pollution loads. In the late 1960s, experiments were launched on the swirl concentrator device which uses circular flow patterns to regulate flow and remove solids, thus providing a dual function at low cost. This principle was first demonstrated at Bristol, England, and became the subject of full-scale investigations in the United States by APWA and several private firms under an EPA contract. This simple, practical structure offers the advantages of low capital cost and short detention time. The absence of moving parts reduces maintenance problems. The device is also self-cleaning by virtue of its low-flow patterns; the various traps and outlets are easily cleaned during low-flow periods. The first full-scale unit was built in Onondaga County, New York, in 1973 and was followed by a 300,000-gallon per day unit in Toronto, Canada, in 1974.

The swirl concentrator differs from a sedimentation tank in that it utilizes the differences in inertia between particles and liquid as well as gravitational forces to effect separation of solids and liquids. Sewage is introduced close to the bottom of a circular chamber and guided by a vertical deflector that makes the flow take the "long path" around the chamber. This is called the primary current. A secondary current is introduced to make the surface portion of the liquid flow outward from the center and the bottom portion flow toward the center of the chamber. This secondary current forces solids to the center, just as a river deposits sediments on its inner bank. Thus, most of the settleable solids and grit become concentrated and are swept to an outlet and exit to the treatment plant. The larger volume of liquid, which is relatively free of solids, is relieved of floatable matter by a trap and discharged into receiving waters. The swirl concentrator is the first regulating device to offer the advantages of simultaneously controlling the quantity and quality of combined sewer overflows. Unlike many advanced treatment methods under investigation, it is a simple, practical device that can effectively reduce the quantities of grit, settleable solids, and floatables over a wide range of overflow rates.

The foregoing case studies illustrate the ability of the public works profession to respond to new challenges. The first treatment systems were developed near the turn of the twentieth century to protect urban inhabitants from their own wastes. The recent demand for tertiary treatment has led to new systems to supplement or replace traditional primary and secondary practices. America's endeavor to strive for zero pollution discharge has produced the dawning of a new wastewater treatment era. The costs are enormous, and the engineering, legal, and administrative challenges are far-reaching; but the technology is being developed that will enable communities to effectively process their wastewater flows.

SUGGESTED READINGS

American Public Health Association. *A Half Century of Public Health*. New York, 1921.

American Public Works Association. *Prevention and Correction of Excessive Infiltration and Inflow into Sewer Systems*. Prepared for the Environmental Protection Agency, Water Quality Office, and Thirty-Nine Local Governmental Jurisdictions. Washington, D.C., 1971.

————— . *Water Pollution Aspects of Urban Runoff*. Prepared for the Federal Water Pollution Control Administration. Washington, D.C., 1969.

Besselieore, Edmund B. *The Treatment of Industrial Wastes*. New York, 1969.

Blake, John B. *Public Health in the Town of Boston, 1630-1822*. Cambridge, Massachusetts, 1959.

Bridenbaugh, Carl. *Cities in Revolt: Urban Life in America, 1743-1776*. New York, 1955.

————— . *Cities in the Wilderness: Urban Life in America, 1625-1742*. New York, 1938.

Cleary, Edward J. *The ORSANCO Story: Water Quality Management in the Ohio Valley Under an Interstate Compact*. Baltimore, 1967.

Cohn, Morris M. *Sewers for Growing America*. Amber, Pennsylvania, 1966.

Davies, J. Clarence III, and Davies, Barbara S. *The Politics of Pollution*. 2d. rev. ed. Indianapolis, 1975.

Duffy, John. *A History of Public Health in New York City, 1625-1866*. New York, 1968.

Heath, Milton S. *A Comparative Study of State Water Pollution Control Laws and Programs*. Raleigh, North Carolina, 1972.

Hyde, Charles Gilman. "Review of Progress in Sewage Treatment During the Past Fifty Years in the United Sates." In *Modern Sewage Disposal*, edited by Langdon Pearse. New York, 1938.

Metcalf, Leonard, and Eddy, Harrison P. *American Sewerage Practice*. 3d. rev. ed. 3 vols. New York, 1935.

Moss, Frank E. *The Water Crisis*. New York, 1967.

Murphy, Earl F. *Man and His Environment: Law*. New York, 1971.

————— . *Water Purity: A Study in Legal Control of National Resources*. Madison, Wisconsin, 1961.

Research and Education Association. *Pollution Control Technology*. New York, 1973.

U.S. Environmental Protection Agency. *A Primer on Waste Water Treatment*. Washington, D.C., 1971.

————— . *Costs of Construction of Publicly-Owned Waste Water Treatment Works, 1973 "Needs" Survey*. Washington, D.C., 1973.

CHAPTER 13

SOLID WASTES

Most solid wastes in the United States originate from agricultural or mining activities. Solid wastes include large amounts of animal, crop, and mineral wastes as well as those materials discarded by a highly urbanized and industrialized society. Although increasing attention is being directed to problems associated with wastes produced in the agricultural and mining sectors of the economy, refuse collection and disposal systems have been designed primarily for handling wastes generated in urban communities.

Solid wastes from urban and industrial sources in the United States totaled more than 360 million tons in 1975. This included 250 million tons of residential, commercial, and institutional wastes and 110 million tons of industrial wastes. As the handling of solid wastes is estimated to cost over $5 billion per year, it is not only one of the most perplexing of public works services but also one of the most costly. In the last half century, the amount and type of wastes have changed radically. In 1920 Americans individually produced an average of 2.8 pounds of solid wastes daily; in 1975 they produced about 6 pounds, and some estimates indicate that the amount will reach 8 pounds by 1980. With the

increased emphasis on packaging in the post-World War II era, the ratio of paper in municipal solid wastes has risen almost 50 percent.

Of the more than 230 million tons of residential, commercial, and institutional solid wastes discarded by Americans in 1971, approximately 190 million tons were collected by public agencies or private refuse firms. These collected wastes included 30 million tons of paper and paper products; 4 million tons of plastics; 100 million tires; 30 billion bottles; 60 billion cans; millions of tons of demolition debris, grass, and tree trimmings; food wastes; and millions of discarded major appliances.

Not all solid wastes are collected and disposed of by public or private collectors. Some wastes are abandoned, dumped, or disposed of at the point of origin; others are hauled away by the producer to dumps, landfills, or incinerators. More industries are finding ways to reprocess materials they formerly discarded. Paper is often salvaged without ever entering the wastes stream. The amount of paper saved depends upon the price paid in the market, although the paper recycling rate has declined from 35 percent in 1944 to about half that amount in 1973.

The term "solid wastes" refers to the useless, unwanted, or discarded materials resulting from society's normal activities. Wastes may be solids, liquids, or gases. Solid wastes

This chapter is based primarily on materials provided by the Office of Solid Waste Management, United States Environmental Protection Agency

TABLE 13-1

Classification of Refuse Materials

Garbage	Wastes from the preparation, cooking and serving of food Market refuse, waste from the handling, storage, and sale of produce and meats		
Rubbish	Combustible (primarily organic)	Paper, cardboard, cartons Wood, boxes, excelsior Plastics Rags, cloth, bedding Leather, rubber Grass, leaves, yard trimmings	From: households, institutions, and commercial concerns such as: hotels, stores, restaurants, markets, etc.
	Noncombustible (primarily inorganic)	Metals, tin cans, metal foils Dirt Stones, bricks, ceramics crockery Glass, bottles Other mineral refuse	
Ashes	Residue from fires used for cooking and for heating buildings, cinders		
Bulky Wastes	Large auto parts, tires Stoves, refrigerators, other large appliances Furniture, large crates Trees, branches, palm fronds, stumps, flotage		
Street refuse	Street sweepings, dirt Leaves Catch basin dirt Contents of litter receptacles		From: streets, sidewalks, alleys, vacant lots, etc.
Dead animals	Small animals: cats, dogs, poultry, etc. Large animals: horses, cows, etc.		
Abandoned vehicles	Automobiles, trucks		
Construction & Demolition wastes	Lumber, roofing, and sheathing scraps Rubble, broken concrete, plaster, etc. Conduit, pipe, wire, insulation, etc.		
Industrial refuse	Solid wastes resulting from industrial processes and manufacturing operations, such as: food-processing wastes, boiler house cinders, wood, plastic, and metal scraps and shavings, etc.		From: factories, power plants, etc.
Special wastes	Hazardous wastes: pathological wastes, explosives, radioactive materials Security wastes: confidential documents, negotiable papers, etc.		Households, hospitals, institutions, stores, industry, etc.
Animal and Agricultural wastes	Manures, crop residues		Farms, feed lots
Sewage treatment residues	Coarse screenings, grit, septic tank sludge, dewatered sludge		Sewage treatment plants, septic tanks

are classed as refuse. Liquid wastes are mainly sewage and industrial wastewaters, including both dissolved and suspended matter. Atmospheric wastes consist of particulate matter such as dust, smoke, fumes, and gases. The physical state of wastes may change in conveyance or treatment. Dewatered sludge from wastewater treatment plants becomes a form of solid wastes; garbage may be ground and discharged into sewers, becoming waterborne wastes; and fly ash may be removed from stack discharges and disposed of as solid or as waterborne wastes (see Table 13-1).

Early Solid Wastes Practices

Visits to historic sites of colonial America leave modern day tourists with various impressions. Independence Hall, the birthplace of the Declaration of Independence and the Constitution, often evokes a sense of patriotism and drama; while the architecture and formal gardens of Mt. Vernon and Colonial Williamsburg inspire a certain admiration for the style and gentility of southern life. But if today's tourists were actually carried back in time to the colonial era, their first impressions might be mild shock or perhaps disgust. Heaps of garbage lying about the streets and odors of decaying refuse close to even the most elegant homes were not uncommon. Nor were the dozens of pigs squealing through unpaved streets in competition with dogs, rats, and vermin—all busily rooting through the wastes for a meal.

For all the creativity shown by eighteenth-century Americans in political philosophy and the practical art of governing, very little imagination was applied to supplying such civic amenities as solid wastes collection and disposal. In most cities, no collection was provided. The streets were considered perfectly legitimate receptacles for household refuse. In unusual instances, wastes were carried to vacant lots or dumped at the edge of town. Scavenging animals were welcomed for their role in reducing the volume of wastes from the streets. And since most wastes were edible or organic, the combination of animal scavengers and the natural process of decay did, in fact, serve to keep the level of wastes accumulation within bounds.

Thomas Jefferson's home, located on a mountaintop outside Charlottesville, Virginia, offered an architectural exception to this general lack of concern for the disposal of household wastes. Monticello, designed and built by Jefferson between 1770 and 1809, featured an elaborate system of underground tunnels through which garbage, ashes, and human wastes were conveyed in buckets by means of ropes and pulleys. Slaves then emptied the buckets and disposed of their contents some distance from the house.

Benjamin Franklin is credited with an even more significant contribution to solid wastes management in the United States. In 1792, according to a plan devised by Franklin, servants were engaged to collect and carry the solid wastes of Philadelphia (then boasting a population of 60,000) to the Delaware River where they were dumped. These practices constituted the first systematic garbage collection and disposal service for Philadelphia and perhaps the first for any city in the United States. Franklin's very real contribution to city sanitation was, however, marred by his choice of disposal method. But many years passed before Americans began to understand the serious environmental consequences of continued use of the nation's waterways as convenient vehicles for waste disposal.

One of the first known city ordinances pertaining to solid wastes was passed in 1795 by the Corporation of Georgetown (now a part of Washington, D.C.). The ordinance prohibited the storage of refuse for extended periods of time on private property and outlawed dumping in the streets. But, since no provision was made for collection by the city, each citizen was left to haul his own refuse or to hire the services of a "carter." John Adams, the first President to reside in the new capital city of Washington, D.C., was also first (in 1800) to hire a private carter to carry refuse away from the White House. Private haulers have ever since provided this service to the first family.

Solid wastes were initially hauled only from the White House to a distant point for dumping. Refuse from other buildings, including those occupied by federal employees, was burned each day on the premises of several buildings located throughout the city. But one hot summer afternoon as President Jefferson was riding in his carriage, he reportedly became sickened by the odor of burning garbage. Returning to the White House, he instructed his secretary to discuss with the presidential hauler a plan for collecting the refuse from all government buildings and removing it to a dump outside the city. Thus, Jefferson initiated the first contract for the collection of wastes from federal buildings.

Although Washington's streets were cleaned periodically by private contractors since about 1800, it was not until 1844 that these contracts were extended to include the collection of wastes from households. And it was not until 1856 that residential wastes were removed at public expense. Even then, combustible wastes and ashes were left for disposal by the individual citizen.

Despite occasional efforts to organize regular solid wastes collection services for cities, the practice of dumping in the streets persisted in most communities with little change until the latter part of the nineteenth century. After a visit to New York City in 1842, British novelist Charles Dickens reported that pigs roamed all of the major streets, including Broadway, feeding on garbage. So important were scavenging animals for reducing waste volumes that cities sometimes protected certain of them by law, including carrion-eating vultures.

Considering these appalling sanitary conditions, it is not surprising that during the nineteenth century epidemics of yellow fever, cholera, small pox, typhoid, and typhus fever were frequent throughout the United States. In 1849 Lemuel Shattuck, a Boston bookseller, was appointed by the governor of Massachusetts to head a three-member commission charged with preparing "a plan for a Sanitary Survey of the State, embracing a statement of such facts and suggestions . . . to illustrate the subject." Shattuck submitted a "Report of a General Plan for the Promotion of Public and Personal Health" the following year. The commission stressed the need to improve city sanitation and recommended establishing an office within the state government to administer a public health program. The commission's recommendation went unheeded until 1869 when the Massachusetts State Board of Health was organized as the first state public health agency.

Shattuck apparently recognized the cause-and-effect relationship between poor sanitary conditions and the incidence of disease. Twenty years passed after Shattuck's report was submitted before the pioneering work of Louis Pasteur and Robert Koch in bacteriology revealed that microorganisms cause disease. It was not until the 1890s that the role of animal and insect vectors in disease transmission was discovered.

The "Rise of the City" and Wastes

The modern American city emerged between 1860 and 1910. During these fifty years in which the total population increased from 31 million to 91 million, the number of people living in municipalities of 2,500 or more increased from 6 million to 44 million. In 1910, 46 percent of the United States' total population lived in cities of over 2,500; only 20 percent had done so in 1860. The trend was unmistakable — the United States was becoming a nation of cities.

With the emergence of cities, especially large and congested ones, residents could no longer ignore the mounds of wastes at their doorsteps. The horse, which was the prime source of motive power for transportation well into the twentieth century, contributed generously to the accumulating refuse in every city. Each horse daily discharged gallons of urine and pounds of fecal matter onto the streets. Municipal engineer George A. Soper estimated in *Modern Methods of Street Cleaning* (1907) that 1,000 horses deposited about 500 gallons of urine and 10 tons of dung on city pavements during an eight-hour working day. As late as 1914, it was reported that the 82,000 horses, cows, and mules maintained in the city of Chicago produced annually 600,000 tons of manure.

Although the early public health movement generated discussion about the need for better sanitation, refuse collection and disposal practices improved very slowly in most urban areas. Wastes from such large cities as Chicago, St. Louis, Boston, and Baltimore

Horse-drawn wagon in Philadelphia, 1900. In most large cities, wastes were carried in horse-drawn carts to open dumps or to the sea.

were simply carted to open dumps. Until the turn of the twentieth century, Cleveland had no public provisions for collecting household refuse; while New York and many other coastal cities customarily dumped substantial percentages of their wastes into the sea.

Newfound knowledge concerning the origins and spread of disease inspired some cities to apply chemical disinfectants to their solid wastes. Many others, however, began to burn their refuse, using combustion as a method of disinfecting wastes as well as a way of reducing volume. The first municipal incinerator was built in 1885 in Allegheny, Pennsylvania, but before long many other cities constructed "crematories" for their wastes. During the 1890s, the incinerator serving the District of Columbia was operated only in winter months. In summer, wastes were shipped by barge down the Potomac River to a dump site in the river south of Alexandria, Virginia. On one occasion, the citizens of Alexandria became so offended by the passage of garbage-laden barges that they took the matter into their own hands and sank several of the barges.

Widespread interest in municipal incinerators resulted in a number of technological innovations, some of which were accompanied by strong rivalries between their inventors. During the 1890s, two distinct types of incinerators were in common use in Chicago: the stationary furnace and the portable burner. A. M. Brainard, designer of the stationary furnace, threatened to throw the

portable burner invented by George S. Wells into a stationary furnace. Wells, for his part, offered a $1,000 wager (which was not accepted) that he could reduce all of the city's wastes to ashes within days. Harper's Weekly applauded the bravado of both men, for "out of this picturesque rivalry grew a startlingly clean condition of alleys in the city."

Colonel George E. Waring, Jr., was probably the most outstanding administrative figure in the municipal sanitation field during the late nineteenth century and certainly one of the most interesting. He was trained in scientific agriculture, but he chose to devote his energies to municipal engineering and sanitation. During the 1880s, Waring developed a sewer system for the City of Memphis, Tennessee; in January 1895, he became commissioner of street cleaning for New York City. His administration as commissioner was marked by innovation and reform because he believed he was responsible not only for making New York clean and disease free but for improving the total quality of urban life. Although Waring was not the first to advocate making refuse collection and disposal a wholly municipal function, he was one of the first to implement the idea. Because of his endeavors, New York City became a model for other cities throughout the nation.

Colonel Waring, whose military title was earned during the Civil War as a volunteer in the Missouri Cavalry, imposed a quasi-military discipline and organization on the Department of Street Cleaning. At first his actions drew ridicule from the press, but later he received praise from the same sources. As a result of the efforts of Waring and his department, New Yorkers could drive through streets and walk down sidewalks that were cleared of garbage and manure. To facilitate street cleaning operations, Waring immediately removed some 60,000 unharnassed trucks and wagons that had been abandoned on public thoroughfares. He then directed his attention to enhancing the image of his department and to improving its morale. Drawing on his military experience, he outfitted sweepers and drivers in smart looking white uniforms, which gave them a sense of pride and instilled in them a feeling of solidarity. No longer were

Because of the efforts of Colonel George E. Waring, Jr., and his "White Wings," New Yorkers could walk down sidewalks and drive through streets cleared of garbage and manure.

New York's street cleaners looked upon as the dregs of society—Waring's "White Wings" were respected by the community.

Much of Waring's success resulted from freeing his department of political influence. He had accepted his appointment as street cleaning commissioner on the condition that he would have "his own way." Thus, he was able to fill department vacancies with men of his choosing. Waring usually hired young men with technical training or military experience, and he boasted that his policy in hiring for menial jobs, such as hand sweeping, was to place "a man instead of a voter" at the end of the broom.

Waring improved the working conditions of his employees and in novel ways encouraged public support for keeping the city clean. During his administration, collectors were paid generously ($2 per day); and committees, established to hear grievances and receive suggestions, met regularly. Waring also created a Juvenile Street Cleaning League. Its membership initially consisted of

500 young people—the majority of whom lived in New York's Lower East Side—who were instructed in good sanitation practices. The league quickly increased its membership by recruiting students from the city's entire school system. Waring hoped that by discussion and example, league members would influence the behavior patterns of their parents.

As commissioner, Waring was as innovative in the technical aspects of city sanitation as he was in the areas of personnel administration and public relations. In 1896 he initiated a system of primary separation which required householders to store organic wastes, rubbish, and ashes in separate containers for collection. He then persuaded Mayor William L. Strong to assign a contingent of forty policemen to the Department of Street Cleaning to explain the new primary separation requirements to citizens and to insure compliance.

Waring intended that New York City benefit from the separation process by selling the materials recovered from the wastes. For many years, he had watched private scavengers collect resalable waste materials from individual homes and scow-trimmers work through refuse-laden garbage scows, picking out items of probable value such as old shoes, carpets, paper, and rugs. Waring was well aware of the money that could be made in scavenging and trimming. He, therefore, recommended that the city perform these services and reap the profits.

Many other cities subsequently adopted the practice of on-site separation for a variety of reasons. It became popular where household and commercial garbage was fed to hogs. But the practice continued to survive even after the original reasons for it had disappeared. In 1974, for example, when the price of salvage paper soared, more than 100 municipalities in the United States either required or requested householders to separate newsprint for recovery.

Despite New York City's early success in reusing and recycling wastes, a substantial residuum continued to be disposed of at sea. Waring recognized the hazards and shortcomings of this process, including the resultant fouling of beaches and harbor waters, but he was not opposed to sea disposal. He believed primary separation would alleviate many of the problems. Thus, at various times, he attempted to improve New York's sea operations. He strongly urged use of the Delehanty Dumping Scow, a self-emptying catamaran-type vessel, as a replacement for the Barney Self-Dumping Scow which was less sanitary.

The results of Waring's administration were apparent in the community's aesthetics, and they were no less evident in New York's public health statistics. According to the board of health, both the death rate and sick rate for New Yorkers declined. From 1882 to 1894, the average annual death rate in the city was 26.8 per 1,000; during the first half of 1895, the rate fell to 19.6 per 1,000. Diarrheal diseases also decreased significantly. Although these reductions were due in part to an improved water supply, protection of produce in markets, and better sanitary standards in public eating places, Waring and the health board attributed much of this to improved solid wastes collection and cleaner streets. Yet

these functions were accomplished with such efficiency that the daily cost per mile to clean streets dropped to half that of 1895.

Waring probably contributed more to the reform of refuse collection and disposal and to street cleaning than any other individual in his era. Besides organizing a disciplined and efficient administrative system, he introduced the concepts of refuse classification and primary separation. He also demonstrated the potential value of wastes. By reducing garbage, he salvaged important by-products such as ammonia, grease, glue, and dry residuum for fertilizer which, when sold, substantially increased the city's revenue. And finally, Waring brought a new and deserved respectability to his occupation.

In his quest for a cleaner city, Waring inspired a reform spirit among professional scientists and engineers. They urged a "scientific" response to municipal wastes, contending that wastes problems in the United States could best be solved through engineering knowledge and skill. By systematically applying developments in the biological sciences to engineering, a distinct branch of engineering emerged in the first half of the twentieth century—sanitary engineering. (In the 1960s, as the field became more inclusive, it began to be referred to as environmental engineering.) The first sanitary engineers were primarily concerned with problems of water supply and sewage or wastewater disposal; but by the 1920s, many of these same practitioners had begun to turn their attention to solid wastes management.

Women also became interested in refuse reform. In large cities across the country, women played prominent roles in local public health movements and in efforts to promote civic improvements. In Chicago, a women's club secured better solid wastes services by demanding "scientific" garbage collection. In Philadelphia, in 1916, Edith W. Pierce became the first female city inspector of street cleaning in the United States. Following Waring's example, she formed a Junior Sanitation League and vigorously supported many programs to help solve Philadelphia's wastes problems. In smaller communities, the reform impulse often took the form of cleanup or

Horse-drawn wagons, pulling rotary sweeping brushes, were replaced by mechanical sweepers after 1914.

beautification campaigns. In 1912 a women's league in Kirksville, Missouri, promoted a cleanup drive that led to permanent improvements in solid wastes collection and disposal; and in Sherman, Texas, a women's civic league sponsored a campaign that resulted in the enactment of an ordinance establishing four annual cleanup periods and regulations to ensure proper solid wastes services.

The effects of many civic improvement projects were short-lived. Even the more substantial reforms instituted by Waring were temporarily undone by the Tammany administration immediately after the colonel left office in December 1897. They were, however, largely reinstated and improved upon by the energetic John McGaw Woodbury, who was appointed street cleaning commissioner in 1903. But the work of professional engineers and activists in the public health movement, supported in no small measure by citizen-sponsored community improvement campaigns, had enduring value. And while the development of solid wastes

services was frequently slow, inadequacies of an earlier era were no longer considered acceptable.

Street Cleaning Trends and Developments

Street cleaning continued to pose difficult problems to public officials in the early twentieth century, particularly because of the wastes discharged by horses. Although some administrators believed hand sweeping was the most inexpensive and thorough street cleaning method, others were convinced that machines would replace "the man behind the broom" and began experimenting with new street cleaning equipment. As early as 1882 in New York City, horse-drawn wagons were pulling rotary sweeping brushes, but the most popular device by far was the mechanical sweeper.

The first practical and commercially successful self-propelled mechanical sweeper was used in 1914 in Boise, Idaho. Three years earlier, a self-powered mechanical street sweeper had been introduced but was not widely accepted because it lacked maneuverability, a hopper for the sweepings, and sufficient power. Its two-cylinder engine was unable to supply power to the sweeping apparatus and provide mobility for the unit as well. Thus, the pick-up sweepers which were adopted in many cities after 1914 not only furnished adequate power, but they usually provided a sprinkler attachment that wet the streets immediately ahead of the sweeper and loosened street grime. Sprinklers were later adapted for settling dust on unimproved streets, and flushers were frequently added for cleaning streets that were hard surfaced.

A number of cities began using squeegees to scrape pavement surfaces clean and to force excess water into the gutters. A squeegee consisted of rubber blades or fins attached to a central core that formed a cylindrical brush. The brush, which was mounted diagonally on the chassis, revolved mechanically. When the rubber blades came in firm contact with the street surface as they turned, they wiped the dirt and water from the surface and pushed it toward the curb. Parked wagons and then automobiles interfered with the squeegee process. Thus, as more and more city residents acquired automobiles, the squeegee system became less and less popular.

A vacuum device adopted by many cities in the 1920s and 1930s was employed principally, although not exclusively, to remove dust from pavement surfaces after the heavier particles had been swept away. Since water was not required, its chief value was that it could be used in freezing weather. But it was noisy and unreliable. Unlike the squeegee, however, the vacuum device was never completely abandoned. In the early 1970s, the vacuum or airsweep system was reintroduced by several manufacturers of street cleaning equipment, since vacuum sweepers reportedly picked up a much greater portion of the particulate matter than did mechanical sweepers that relied entirely on the flicking action of brush fibers. Research studies by the Environmental Protection Agency (EPA), the American Public Works Association (APWA), and others indicate that if particulate matter is not picked up it is washed into sewers and streams where it contributes to pollution.

The advent of the automobile affected street cleaning practices. Before widespread use of the motor car, horse manure was a major source, if not the prime source, of street debris. Not only did the automobile help to reduce the manure problem, but the vehicle's rubber tires did less damage to streets than did horseshoes and iron wagon wheels. With the automobile came demands for smoother streets made of concrete and asphalt, and pavements made of blocks and bricks which collected dirt became obsolete.

As the horse was gradually replaced by the automobile and the truck, one source of street pollution disappeared. But a demand for frequent street cleaning arose as more motorized vehicles, traveling at increased speeds, appeared on the streets and their tires picked up quiescent dust and litter. During the 1920s and 1930s, municipalities of all sizes purchased mechanical sweepers to satisfy this demand. They began using them to clean the business districts several times each week, but many swept residential areas only sporadically or not at all.

Sweeper technology improved slowly during this period. Gutter brooms were added and engines became more powerful, but payloads remained rather low. A vacuum sweeper was introduced in the 1920s to pick up the dust missed by mechanical sweepers, but few cities adopted it. World War II brought sweeper production to a standstill. Not until the 1950s did the production backlog disappear entirely. As municipalities increased in size, residents wanted cleaner streets; since more sweepers were needed, new companies entered the field.

Mechanical sweepers increased in capacity and power during the 1950s. Long lasting man-made fibers were used for the main broom. Although they cost more than brass, palmyra, and other natural fibers which were good for only a few hundred sweeping miles, they lasted several times as long. The replaceable hopper was also introduced in the 1950s. No longer was it necessary to dump the contents of a hopper on the street for subsequent cleanup or to drive to a designated dumping area. When a hopper

American Public Works Association

Sweepers of the 1970s have hopper capacities that often exceed 4 cubic yards as well as twin gutter brooms which clean areas adjacent to curbs.

was full, the operator set it aside and picked up an empty one. A special tractor then collected the full hopper, dumped it, and returned it for future use. During the 1960s, manufacturers developed sweepers that fit on truck chassis as well as self-unloading sweepers that hoisted their hoppers and dumped directly into trucks.

Both the equipment and methods used in the 1970s are much different from those of even a few decades ago. Today's sweepers are much bigger. Hopper capacities commonly exceed 4 cubic yards. Twin gutter brooms are mounted on some sweepers to clean areas adjacent to both curbs on one-way streets. Many are self-dumping units, while others are mounted on truck chassis for sweeping expressways at higher speeds. Improved vacuum machines are appearing on municipal streets as officials become aware of their unique ability to pick up the particulate matter that is otherwise flushed through sewers into lakes and streams where it contributes to pollution. These improvements in equipment help keep streets clean. Some developments, however, have the opposite effect.

A 1973 survey by APWA's Institute for Solid Wastes reflected a trend away from backyard refuse collection which was quite common prior to the 1950s. The survey found that 68 percent of 637 municipalities collected from the curb line in some or all of their resi-

dential neighborhoods. Thus, when accidental spills occurred or collectors were careless, refuse littered the street. If the spills took place at the back door, most householders removed them; but, at the curb, many persons simply ignored them and waited for the city's street cleaning crews to take care of them. Since there is a high paper content in today's solid wastes, even a light breeze distributes spilled paper over a wide area. To alleviate these effects, many municipalities design their sweeping routes to follow solid waste collection routes.

The effectiveness of street cleaning programs depends to a great extent on the cooperation of those served. Detailed regulations and new equipment in and of themselves do not insure effective and economical operations. Public officials must secure the assistance of the citizens in their communities. This cooperation is best acquired through public education. For more than two decades, Keep America Beautiful (KAB), a national nonprofit public service organization, has sponsored programs to instill in Americans an awareness of their environment and a concern for its appearance.

On the national level, KAB has used methods similar to those employed by Waring in teaching good sanitation practices to New York youngsters. KAB's litterbug, although unappealing to many adolescents and adults, was successful in making children conscious of the litter problem. Acknowledging that "there is more to litter than meets the eye," KAB dropped "litterbug" from its vocabulary in the mid 1970s and limited the poster contests and cleanups that once constituted its "litter prevention programs" to the elementary schools. In place of the litterbug, KAB adopted a more comprehensive, systematic program to achieve a litter-free environment.

The primary thrust of KAB's current program is a behaviorally based systems approach to the problem of littering. It is an outgrowth of a project, Action Research Model (ARM), initiated by KAB in the early 1970s and tested by broad-based Clean City committees in Charlotte, North Carolina; Macon, Georgia; and Tampa, Florida. It is a community change process designed to educate

Charlotte Clean City Committee

Action Research Model demonstration site in Charlotte, North Carolina. Two receptacles were placed at each of the three department store entrances. ARM reduced litter accumulations by at least 60 percent at most sites.

citizens as to the source of litter (pedestrians and motorists are presently responsible for approximately 20 percent of the litter in most communities; 80 percent comes from poorly containerized household and commercial refuse, loading docks, construction and demolition sites, and uncovered trucks) and to involve them in reducing the amount of litter by supporting the use of updated ordinances, technology (including modern equipment and an adequate number of properly located litter receptacles), education, and enforcement. Research shows that people are more likely to litter where they see that trash has already accumulated, where they feel no sense of property ownership, and where they are not responsible for the cleanliness of the area. Programs to change these practices must, therefore, be community-owned and community-implemented.

Under a KAB grant, APWA developed a method for measuring litter accumulation. The method is widely applicable, relatively simple, generally inexpensive, and sufficiently accurate to document the results of litter-reduction programs. It requires the cooperation of public officials and the assistance of an engineer or statistician only at the outset. After the initial phase, volunteers can utilize this litter-measuring technique. The beginning phase consists of identifying and photographing random samples of streets and alleys. With the aid of grid overlays, they are then rated for the level of litter accumulation; sources are subsequently identified and strategies developed to control them.

An important part of KAB's program is education. Although updated ordinances which bring together all regulations affecting community cleanliness and vigorous enforcement with citations, reasonable fines, and work penalties (rather than arrests) are recommended; residents' motivation to obtain clean streets and discourage littering is the vital facet of KAB's program. Since good public communication is required to insure the necessary behavioral changes, community involvement is pursued through workshops, club and school presentations, and the media.

Refuse Collection Practices

During the nineteenth and early twentieth centuries, refuse collection practices were largely limited to periodic removals of accumulated wastes by horse-drawn wagons. The wastes generated in business districts of cities as well as refuse produced in industrial plants were normally collected and disposed of by private haulers. Municipal operations were primarily confined to residential areas; however, city crews collected wastes from commercial establishments in some cases. In the 1920s and 1930s, many municipalities began to use open trucks instead of horse-drawn wagons for garbage, rubbish, and ash collection; and by the beginning of World War II, the motorized truck had replaced the horse and cart as the primary refuse collection vehicle in American cities.

Although the hourly costs for loading a truck were initially greater than those for a horse-drawn wagon, the costs of transporting wastes by truck were less. Many cities overcame the high-loading costs by using trucks for transfer or by the so-called tractor-trailer system. In 1922 Chicago introduced this system in six of its fifty wards. Four wards were selected because their ash and refuse teams were able to collect only one load a day since the disposal dumps were 8 to 9 miles away. The cost of collection was almost prohibitive. The two remaining wards were chosen for experimental purposes. They were "short hauls"; the distances to their respective dumps were 3 and 5 miles.

Tractor-trailer trains made from five to six trips daily on the 3-mile haul, four on the 5-mile haul, and three on the 8- or 9-mile haul. The motor tractors were operated by a chauffeur and a conductor; the trailers were horse drawn and manned by a driver and a helper. Once the refuse and ashes were collected by the trailers, the tractors picked up the trailers from a central point and hauled them to the dump site. At the end of 1922, Chicago's Bureau of Streets recommended that the tractor-trailer system be introduced into all fifty wards. According to its estimates, the city could save at least $717,500 annually for the collection and hauling of refuse and ashes. By 1928 eighty-two cities reported that they were using the system on a regular basis.

Alley collection in residential areas was the norm in many municipalities. However, collection from the rear of the house was also widely used. Only a few cities required residents to place their containers at the curb. Collection from alleys or curbs seldom required a crew of more than two or three persons. But several cities employed special set-out crews, which began work about an hour before the collection point. In some cases, two set-back employees followed the collection crew and returned the cans. When collection was made from the rear of the house, two to four "tote men" often emptied the contents of the containers from several houses into burlap bags or folded squares of canvas. When they had collected thirty to sixty pounds of waste, they walked to the alley or street and dumped it into the wagon.

Collection frequency for garbage was commonly two or three times a week. Many of the cities that picked up three times a week during warm weather reduced the number of collections to twice a week when the weather turned cold. Even though there was less garbage during winter months, the total manpower requirements remained steady due to the need for ash collection.

Snow removal operations developed in many cities during the 1920s. As the number of automobiles and trucks increased and as emergency, waste removal, and commercial delivery services became motorized, provisions were made to insure that vehicles could function and that services could continue throughout the entire year regardless of the amount of snow that fell or ice that formed. Thus, most cities located in the snow belt learned quickly to adapt their regular street cleaning and refuse collection equipment and practices to snow removal, as discussed in Chapter 3.

During the period from 1930 to 1940, more trucks supplanted horses and wagons; more cities added ashes and trash collections; and more emphasis was placed on sanitation. In 1937 Samuel A. Greeley, chairman of the Committee on Refuse Collection and Disposal for the newly formed APWA, observed that "one of the most encouraging aspects is the general acceptance on the part of public officials and citizens of the real connection between public health and the handling and disposal of refuse." He noted that evidence during 1936 showed that the public and its officials recognized that the health and well-being of their communities depended "to a considerable extent on the promptness and effectiveness with which refuse is collected and disposed of."

Although no significant developments took place in collection methods during the Depression and World War II years, manufacturers made some progress in the design of collection equipment. The "dustless" collection vehicle first appeared on the market in the 1930s. These covered trucks were designed to permit easy loading of refuse without spilling. As a result, they helped to minimize the amount of dust from ashes, newspapers from rubbish, and drippings from garbage on streets. Compaction vehicles, however, were practically unknown.

During the 1930s and early 1940s, many cities hesitated to enforce ordinances which required residents to furnish sturdy receptacles for solid wastes. Many householders, as a result, used cardboard boxes and similar unsatisfactory units. Because of an increased awareness of sanitation, however, a few cities such as Lansing, Michigan, furnished cans to its citizens, picked up both can and contents, dumped the refuse at a transfer station, cleaned the cans, and returned them to the householders.

The problems related to the handling of solid wastes changed profoundly after World War II. While better packaging and marketing practices enabled more high-quality food to reach the consumer, the rise of the packaging industry and the wide acceptance of packaged and canned foods caused a substantial increase in the per capita generation of wastes. The present average of six pounds per capita per day is more than double that of fifty years ago. During the 1950s, packaging companies, which specialized in making "disposables," doubled and tripled their sales as they satisfied America's demands for convenience. Products from these companies—"trays that can be cooked, bags that can be boiled, bowls and other eating utensils that can be discarded to eliminate dishwashing"—and an economy that frequently made it cheaper to replace worn items than to repair them were large contributors to the nation's high per capita wastes production.

But besides increasing the volume of wastes, these technological changes and new marketing techniques affected the character of refuse and, in some cases, the points at which it was generated. For example, the trend toward the consumption of processed foods (canned and frozen) was largely responsible for the relatively low percentage of putrescibles and the high percentage of paper, plastics, and metals in the wastes stream following World War II. Fruit and vegetable trimmings, which presently accumulate in enormous quantities at canneries and food processing plants, were formerly found in the kitchens of individual dwellings.

Hundreds of chemical substances and solid industrial wastes that are now discarded were unknown only a few years ago, and many are explosive or highly toxic. Some are proven carcinogens, while others are thought to be cancer-producing agents. These materials present special challenges to public works officials who are responsible for solid wastes disposal. If particular care is not exercised, the wastes may migrate from disposal sites to contaminate ground and surface waters; if they are burned in the open air, or

even if they are burned in incinerators without adequate emission control equipment, they may cause air pollution of an especially hazardous nature.

Although there is some geographical variation in the characteristics of municipal solid wastes, social and economic factors cause the major variations in their physical and chemical composition. However, with standardized data and reporting methods, it was possible to determine the materials in the nation's solid wastes stream in 1975. In gross terms, the physical composition of municipal solid wastes by weight was 50 percent paper, 10 percent glass, 10 percent metal, 20 percent food wastes, 3 percent yard wastes (grass clippings and tree trimmings), 1 percent wood, 1 percent plastic, 1 percent cloth and rubber, and 4 percent inert material.

Refuse collection includes those practices involved in the handling of solid wastes at their source and conveying them to a final disposal site, to a transfer station, or to a processing plant where materials having value may be recovered. The rise in wastes volume and the changed character of refuse in the immediate postwar years placed new burdens on municipal collection systems. And in recent years, with air pollution regulations that prohibit leaf burning and the use of apartment and household incinerators, these demands have increased once again.

Several devices have been made to facilitate the handling and temporary storage of wastes prior to collection. Probably the most important of these is the kitchen sink garbage grinder or disposal unit. After grinding, food scraps or organic wastes are discharged immediately to the sewer, thereby reducing the volume of wastes that must be collected. In the past, a few cities prohibited the installation of grinders because of the added load ground garbage placed on their wastewater treatment plants. Many cities, however, required their installation to minimize the problem of storing putrescibles, thus permitting less frequent collections. Although the widespread use of grinders has reduced the nation's volume of collected wastes by less than 10 percent, this amount represents that portion of refuse most troublesome to store and most attractive to rodents and insects.

Over the last decade, trash compactors for home use have been marketed widely as convenience items. These devices compress household wastes to 10 or 20 percent of their original volume and neatly package them in throw-away plastic or paper bags. Large stationary compactors that can handle commercial, institutional, or industrial wastes have also gained wide acceptance since they reduce wastes to about one fourth of the original volume. The containers of these large compactors are emptied by dumping the contents into a collection truck, by replacing a full container with an empty one, or by removing the compressed contents in a plastic-lined bag.

American Public Works Association

During the 1960s, many homeowners adopted large plastic bags for waste storage and collection in place of the 30-gallon garbage can.

Householders have traditionally used grocery bags to hold wastes during storage in the ubiquitous 30-gallon metal or plastic garbage can. But during the 1960s, more homeowners adopted single-use containers—large plastic or paper bags designed for waste storage and collection. As a result, many municipalities have begun to require the use of such disposable containers and have established citywide bag collection systems. There are numerous advantages to this system. For example, it is less noisy than those involving the use of metal containers, and it eliminates the need for collectors to handle heavy receptacles. But most of all, it saves the time required to return reusable containers to the point of storage. One study indicated that through the use of bags each refuse collector lifted two and one-

half tons less refuse each day and that the incidence of sprains and other injuries to sanitation workers was reduced considerably. Since single-use containers were sealed more tightly than regular garbage cans, bags were generally a better deterrent to rats and to spillage by stray animals.

Three basic types of waste collection vehicles have been in common use since the late 1940s: the open-body truck, the closed-body truck, and the compaction vehicle. A national survey published in 1968 reported that out of some 272,000 collection trucks in use, one third of them were compactors. But the trend toward compaction trucks is strong, for over one half of the collection vehicles now in service are compactors. Their increasing use is partly because disposal sites are presently located at greater distances from collection points.

The typical open truck has a capacity of between 10 and 20 cubic yards and a mechanism to tilt the bed for unloading. Although many open trucks are being replaced by the more sanitary and efficient compaction vehicles, especially in larger cities, open trucks nevertheless have some advantages that assure their continued use. They are less expensive than other equipment; their open tops permit them to accommodate awkward or oversized items that could not be compacted or loaded through a truck door; and, as a less specialized vehicle, they can perform a variety of public works functions such as snow removal. Many cities, such as New York and Milwaukee, mount plows on compactors to remove snow. The disadvantages of the open truck are its relatively small capacity, its generally high and inconvenient loading height, and its open top which allows odors from collected refuse to escape into the air. Closed non-compaction trucks are similar to open trucks except that since the tops of the trucks are closed they have doors on the side or rear for loading. Although a certain degree of compaction can be obtained by closing the doors and tilting the truck bed, closed trucks have far less capacity than compactors of similar dimensions.

Compaction vehicles are more costly to purchase and to operate than open or closed

American Public Works Association

Typical refuse compactor. Many cities increased their use of compactors during the early 1970s because disposal sites were located at greater distances from collection points.

trucks, but their expense is justified by the large loads they carry to disposal sites. Some models compact wastes by means of sliding partitions that compress the refuse; other models grind the refuse as it is loaded to achieve even greater volume reduction. Where there are substantial volumes of wastes, portable containers are frequently used; and where disposal sites are long distances away, many cities have established transfer stations.

There are three basic types of loading systems that handle portable containers. These systems (front, rear, and side) are commonly used in industrial, commercial, multiple-dwelling, and rural areas. Containers with as much as 10-cubic-yard capacities are placed at convenient locations. Wastes are deposited in these units which are then collected by special hoisting trucks on a regular basis. Containers with capacities not exceeding 6 cubic yards can be emptied into regular hatch-loading collection trucks. In rural areas, the front-loading containerized system is the most popular because it requires a minimum crew size and has the fastest servicing time.

Where huge amounts of solid wastes are generated, roll-off containers are often utilized. Empty units are delivered to the point of collection to replace loaded containers which are transported to the disposal site. Where lengthy hauling distances are involved, portable containers are sometimes used in conjunction with transfer trucks or trailers. These permit the dumping of their entire contents at one time, and the trailers are usually large enough to service from ten to twenty portable containers.

Transfer stations provide points at which the contents of collection trucks are unloaded into a larger vehicle or temporary storage bin. The accumulated wastes from many individual collection trucks are then transported in large volume—and far more economically—to the disposal area. In some cases, refuse is moved by barges over long distances. A study by APWA in conjunction with twenty-two municipalities, EPA, and the Penn Central Railroad indicated that rail haul is also feasible for long-distance transport.

The City of San Francisco operates one of the world's largest transfer stations. It can accommodate 5,000 tons of refuse which is considerably more than the city's present daily average of 1,800 tons. Built on a 12-acre tract at a cost of $2.5 million, the enclosed main building is capable of handling 200 collection trucks per hour on a twenty-four-hour basis. As the trucks enter the building, a computerized device weighs their contents and records the name of the collection firm or agency for billing purposes. The trucks then drive further into the building where they dump their loads into receiving pits. Bulldozers in the pits push the refuse into chutes through which it falls to larger tractor-trailer vans parked on a lower level. The vans haul their loads to a sanitary landfill 32 miles away.

Transfer stations increased tenfold during the 1960s when the location of disposal sites became an acute problem in the largest urban areas as well as in some intermediate- and smaller-sized cities. A 1974 APWA survey indicated that seventy municipalities operated one or more transfer stations and that almost half of the communities of more than 500,000 population had such facilities. Smaller cities, as would be expected, reported less of a need for these stations; but by and large, municipalities found that by using transfer stations they were able to reduce the high cost of equipment and labor normally required for hauling wastes long distances to disposal sites.

A few cities still use the patronage system to fill some jobs in solid wastes agencies. However, many cities have adopted civil service or merit systems to obtain qualified employees. According to two APWA surveys, the percentage of municipalities that place refuse collection personnel under civil service has nearly doubled in the last decade. A 1964 survey showed only 24 percent coverage; the 1973 survey indicated 46 percent coverage. In general, more large cities have civil service systems that do small ones. Public agencies with formal merit systems customarily have position classification and compensation plans. These systems, for the most part, protect municipal administrators and departments from political patronage and rapid turnover of personnel.

The unionization of both public and private refuse collection forces has also increased substantially during the past ten years. In 1964 about 30 percent of the collection employees in both the public and private sectors were members of unions. In 1973 employees of 59 percent of the municipal collection agencies belonged to unions, and 45 percent of the cities using the contract method reported that their contractors' employees were unionized. Although strikes against solid wastes collection agencies by union members create health hazards and cause substantial inconvenience to the public, they often result in higher pay and greater fringe benefits for refuse collection employees. These developments in this high labor-intensive field of activity will undoubtedly have far-reaching implications for other segments of society.

Municipal, Contract, and Private Collection

The goal of solid wastes collection is a clean and sanitary city. Municipalities employ various methods of collection depending upon specific local situations. Some collect all wastes with municipal forces; others contract with private firms to perform the task; and still others rely on private contractors to deal directly with the customers they serve. But regardless of the method used, most municipalities have ordinances that require wastes to be collected and stored in a sanitary manner. Still the question is asked again and again: should a community's solid wastes be collected by municipal forces, firms under contract with a public agency, or private haulers?

Collection by municipal forces have certain inherent advantages over services provided by private firms such as exemption from taxes and freedom from the need to earn a profit. These two factors give the public agency a significant economic head start over contract or private franchise operations. There are, however, negative aspects to municipal solid wastes operations such as possible political interference, outdated-equipment policies, or resistance to change. A few cities such as Akron, Ohio, and Kansas City, Missouri, have begun to do both—to operate their own municipal collection systems and to contract for collection with private firms. This dual arrangement provides an element of competition that assists public works officials in evaluating both types of services.

During the 1960s, a business phenomenon occurred which had far-reaching effects on solid wastes collection systems. A few large hauling firms began buying up smaller companies in a number of cities across the country. These large firms or agglomerates soon acquired both industrial and residential customers. With the economies of scale, sophisticated management techniques, and efficient collection practices, agglomerates expanded rapidly. By 1974 they collectively held contracts to provide solid wastes services to over 300 municipalities.

Since some of these agglomerates furnished total services, including collection and disposal, many cities found it convenient to contract with such firms. This seemed especially important at a time when federal, state, and local regulations were requiring strict adherence to environmental controls. Equally significant were financing and labor-management considerations. The opportunity to shift responsibility for financing from the public to the private sector was particularly appealing to elected officials who were being pressured by union representatives to provide higher salaries and more fringe benefits for city and county employees. Strikes by government

TABLE 13-2
Type of Residential Solid Waste Collection in 661 North American Cities in 1973

| Method | Population in Thousands | | | | | | | Total | Per-cent |
	5-10	10-25	25-50	50-100	100-500	Over 500	Not Stated		
Municipal	11	51	73	64	43	14	1	257	39
Contract	11	19	41	22	9	1	3	106	16
Private	2	12	34	25	5	2	3	83	12
Municipal and Private	2	14	30	23	32	3		104	16
Municipal and Contract	1	4	7	14	7	5		38	6
Municipal, Contract, and Private	1	3	5	9	4	6		28	4
Contract and Private	1	8	14	9	7	4	2	45	7
Total	29	111	204	166	107	35	9	661	100

TABLE 13-3
Type of Collection Agency Used in 995 North American Cities in 1964

| Method | Population in Thousands | | | | | | | Total | Per-cent |
	5-10	10-25	25-50	50-100	100-1000	Over 1000	Not Stated		
Municipal	116	172	92	34	29		3	446	45
Contract	54	70	30	13	7		1	175	18
Private	49	43	20	12	3		3	130	13
Municipal and Private	15	46	27	22	34	4	3	151	15
Municipal and Contract	1	10	12	8	1		1	33	3
Municipal, Contract, and Private	3	4	6	1	1	1		16	2
Contract and Private	8	14	12	7	3			44	4
Total	246	359	199	97	78	5	11	995	100

APWA, *Solid Waste Collection Practice*

workers often persuaded legislative bodies to accept union demands so that the elected officials' constituents would not retaliate for the inconvenience they experienced by voting against them in the next election. The much larger waste volume handled by private companies was particularly advantageous in developing solid wastes recycling systems. Thus, by early 1974, these firms operated at least sixty processing and recovery centers.

Table 13-2 indicates that 39 percent of the 661 North American cities surveyed in 1973 had municipal collection exclusively. This was more than twice the number with contract collection (16 percent) and more than three times the number with private collection (12 percent). Adding the percentages for all combinations of municipal collections shows that 65 percent of these municipalities operated their own collection systems. The 1964 survey (see Table 13-3) produced the same total of 65 percent, although the distributions were somewhat different.

A comparison of the two tables demonstrates that the proportion of cities with exclusively municipal collection declined from 45 to 39 percent during the nine years between surveys. However, the total percentage of cities with municipal collection remained stable at 65 percent. The increases appeared in combined methods. Municipal and private collections increased from 15 to 16 percent; municipal and contract doubled from 3 to 6 percent; and municipal, contract, and private also doubled from 2 to 4 percent.

Conventional Refuse Disposal Methods

In the late 1800s, American cities disposed of their refuse in a variety of ways. According to a survey conducted by the Massachusetts Institute of Technology at the turn of the twentieth century, forty-five cities deposited refuse on land; nine burned it in dumps; eighteen plowed it into the ground; fourteen dumped it in water; forty-one fed it to stock; twenty-seven incinerated it; nineteen

View of feeder pigs just out of quarantine. Between 1953 and 1955, hog feeding fell into disfavor when the spread of vesicular exanthema necessitated the slaughter of more than 400,000 swine.

employed reduction processes; and eleven used "irregular" methods. Twenty years later, when the American Society of Municipal Improvements (ASMI) collected information on "the present status of refuse collection and disposal methods" in some 200 cities, ASMI found that few changes had occurred.

The practice of feeding garbage to hogs was extensive in the early decades of the twentieth century and remained in relatively common use until the mid 1950s. In 1941 the Bureau of Agricultural Economics of the Department of Agriculture questioned authorities in 412 cities with populations of 25,000 and over as to their garbage disposal methods. Returns from 247 of these cities indicated that approximately 27 percent of their garbage was fed to swine. And from an estimated 8 million tons of garbage produced by 412 cities, it was calculated that approximately 2.2 million tons were fed to hogs.

Flint, Michigan, operated a 260-acre hog farm for over twenty-five years. Feeder pigs weighing about 125 pounds were purchased at regular intervals from markets in Detroit and St. Paul. Once transported to the farm in Flint, the hogs were vaccinated for cholera. During a three-week quarantine period, they were fed no garbage. Thereafter, they were gradually given more garbage until they fed on nothing else. When the hogs reached the desired weight of 200 to 250 pounds, they

were sold. During the fiscal year ending June 30, 1943, Flint's total income from the sale of hogs and farm produce amounted to approximately $152,000. Hogs sold, numbering 3,840, accounted for more than $67,000 in income. Operating expenses—including operation of the farm, maintenance of the grounds, taxes, and overhead—amounted to only $23,000. The profit was credited to the city's revenue and used to reduce the overall waste collection expenses.

Although the practice of feeding raw garbage to swine put organic wastes to beneficial use and increased the income of many municipalities, this method of disposal contributed to the spread of trichinae infection in humans. During the 1940s, an average of 400 cases of trichinosis was reported yearly to the United States Public Health Service at a time when one third of the states did not report incidents of this disease. Between 1953 and 1955, when the rapid spread of vesicular exanthema necessitated the slaughter of more than 400,000 swine as a livestock-disease control measure, hog feeding fell into disfavor. Most states passed laws requiring that wastes be thoroughly cooked before being fed to hogs. In the early 1970s, only about 4 percent of food wastes collected in the United States were consumed by swine.

Since hog feeding was but one way of disposing of garbage, the advantages and disadvantages of other disposal methods—most notable, reduction and incineration—were debated regularly by public works officials. Most of these discussions took place at conferences and meetings sponsored by professional societies concerned with the management of municipal affairs. Representatives from large cities frequently spoke in favor of the reduction process. They argued that, whereas incineration almost completely destroyed garbage, reduction produced salable materials, namely grease and tankage.

But public administrators, especially from small cities and towns, contended that the reduction process was too costly. It was a viable method, they insisted, only in big cities where large amounts of garbage were collected or in wealthy areas where residents were extravagant in their use of meat, butter, and lard. Officials also noted that the first cost of a reduction plant was comparatively high since expensive equipment was always required. Even large cities could afford only one plant. Administrators warned, therefore, that entire solid wastes systems could be seriously crippled if the operations of a reduction plant were halted by fire or strike. Since offensive odors and nuisances resulted from the reduction process, it was observed that citizen complaints were common unless plants were located far away from the city which, in the end, increased the total refuse collection and transportation costs.

During the first half of the twentieth century, most small municipalities and many large ones disposed of refuse by dumping it on land, feeding it to hogs, or incinerating it. Incineration—a controlled process by which combustible wastes are burned to produce gases and a residue containing little or no combustible material—had many advantages. No other method surpassed it from the standpoint of volume reduction and sanitation; the process destroyed most organic matter and germ life and was considered thoroughly sanitary according to the standards of the times. Research conducted in later years, however, revealed that stack emissions contributed significantly to air pollution. Since incinerators were neither so costly nor so malodorous as reduction plants, municipalities often owned

several incinerators and located them in interior sections of the city near the largest refuse producing centers. Transportation costs were automatically reduced, and some cities even collected revenue from incinerator residue and steam.

In 1924, for example, the City of Atlanta and the Atlanta Gas Light Company signed a contract permitting the gas company to use surplus steam from the incinerator for a fee. The contract required a minimum of 260,000 pounds of steam every twenty-four hours at sixteen cents per thousand up to 70 million pounds and twenty cents per thousand pounds above that figure. During 1925 a total of 79 million pounds of steam was generated from 126 million pounds of refuse. Of this amount, 63.5 million pounds were sold, and 15.5 million pounds were used by plant auxiliaries.

Atlanta built a second incinerator adjacent to the first in 1927. At the end of the following year, with the new unit in operation, the steam supply was much greater than the demand at the gas works. To prevent waste, a steam line was constructed from the second incinerator to the steam-heat mains of the Georgia Power Company, furnishing an outlet for all steam produced at the incinerator. Figures for the period from 1925 to 1935 showed a gain in refuse of 30 percent; in steam generated, 124 percent; in steam sold, 103 percent; and a money gain of 138 percent.

Oversized or bulky burnable wastes such as logs, tree stumps, mattresses, large furniture, tires, and demolition lumber were not usually processed in municipal incinerators. These objects were either too large to charge, burned too slowly, or contained steel frames of such size and shape that they could foul grate operations or residue removal systems. Ashes, which were a major constituent of refuse before World War II when coal was the common fuel for heating, were, of course, never incinerated. They were either dumped on land outside the city limits or used for filling purposes.

During the late 1930s, the number of incinerators in the United States declined substantially. Shortly thereafter, with pressures to reduce municipal costs and with improvements in sanitary landfilling techniques, public works officials introduced the landfill method of disposal as an economical alternative to incineration. Sanitary fills had their origins in Great Britain in the 1920s, where they were called "controlled tippings." They were first used in the United States in the mid 1930s by New York City and Fresno, California. But it was not until after World War II, during which time the United States Army experimented with landfills, that many other American cities began employing this disposal method.

The sanitary landfill not only proved to be the most economical of the acceptable disposal methods but could receive almost all kinds of refuse, including bottles, cans, and lawn trimmings. The objectionable features—unsightliness, disagreeable odor, rat and vermin nuisance, and smoke from fire—which ordinarily characterized the open dump were not present. Thus, well-planned and well-integrated landfill operations turned land that formerly had little or no value into parks, playgrounds, golf courses, botanical gardens, or parking lots.

Three general methods of landfilling gradually evolved: the area method, the trench method, and the ramp method. In an *area* sanitary landfill, solid wastes were placed on the land; a bulldozer spread and compacted them; the wastes were then covered with a layer of earth obtained from adjacent areas; and finally the earth cover was compacted. This method was best suited for flat areas or gently sloping land; it was also used satisfactorily in quarries, ravines, valleys, or where other land depressions existed. In a *trench* sanitary landfill, a trench was cut in the ground and solid wastes were placed in it. The wastes were then spread in thin layers, compacted, and covered with earth excavated from the trench. This method was used where the land was flat and the water table was not near the ground surface. In a *ramp* sanitary landfill, solid wastes were dumped on the side of an existing slope. After spreading the refuse in thin layers, bulldozing equipment compacted it. The cover material, usually obtained just ahead of the working face, was spread on the ramp and compacted. Unlike the trench

method of landfilling, only one piece of equipment was needed to perform all ramp operations.

During the 1960s, several innovative landfill projects were undertaken in various parts of the country. In 1967 the City of Madison, Wisconsin, in conjunction with EPA, the University of Wisconsin, and the Heil Company tested the potential for milling refuse prior to landfill. After the refuse was pulverized in a mill and the ferrous metals were magnetically separated, the milled material was spread uniformly over a landfill site. Even without daily cover, the project participants found the method satisfactory. Rats rarely survived on the refuse; fly populations did not increase; the higher density reduced the danger of fire; and the lifetime of the landfill's available area was extended.

Experiments were also conducted in St. Paul, Minnesota, and San Diego, California, with another landfill variant—the balefill. In both instances, baling stations were built for compacting the wastes. Collectors dumped refuse at the station, where it was processed and then shipped in trailers to balefill sites. One of the stations was a completely automated plant with a hydraulically controlled three-stroke compressor unit. It molded 2,800 pounds of refuse into 3- by 4- by 4$\frac{1}{2}$-foot bales. Lift trucks loaded the bales onto a flatbed truck for the trip to the disposal site where they were piled in tiers. Since the bales had about the same density as the soil, they could support the heavy trucks. Few problems were encountered with insects, rodents, fires, or blowing trash.

Farmers and gardeners have been composting wastes for their own use for centuries. But beginning in the 1920s, a number of attempts were made to apply engineering methods to make compost on a large scale from municipal wastes. Compost is produced by reducing organic refuse to an inert, humus-like material through biological decomposition under controlled conditions of aeration, temperature, and moisture. Compost is useful as a soil conditioner, but contains only small amounts of nitrogen, phosphate, and potassium. It can, however, be enriched with sewage sludge or chemicals to make it more

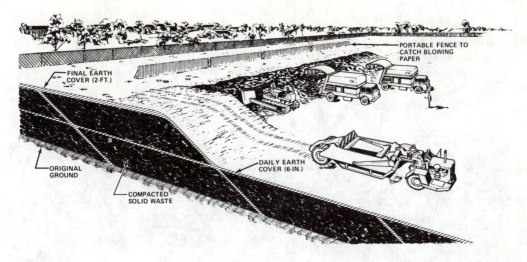

AREA METHOD.

TRENCH METHOD.

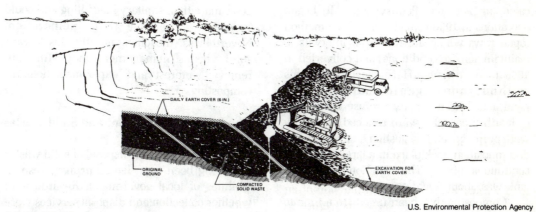

U.S. Environmental Protection Agency

RAMP METHOD.

Figure 13-1.
Three General Methods of Landfilling.

This standard bulkhead flatcar, loaded with fifty-six bales weighing a total of seventy-seven tons, was used in St. Paul, Minnesota, to transport compacted wastes to the disposal site.

desirable for agricultural purposes.

Although a significant proportion of organic wastes are composted in a few foreign countries, notably India and the Netherlands, only a negligible fraction of municipal solid wastes is composted in the United States. One of the few successful composting plants is located in Altoona, Pennsylvania. It began operations in 1950 using the windrow method (open rows which are turned at intervals to maintain aerobic conditions) and converted in 1963 to the Farfield-Hardy method. In this method, non-organic material was handpicked from the city's refuse for salvage or landfill; particles were reduced in size by wet pulping; and digestion, or biological decomposition, took place in a large tank with continuous mixing. The retention time in the tank was about five days.

Composting has been urged from time to time as a disposal method. However, the cost of processing and distributing compost produced from municipal refuse has been too high for it to be competitive with commercial fertilizers and soil additives. Thus, most of the composting plants that have been built in the United States have been forced to close. An EPA report entitled "Composting of Municipal Solid Wastes in the United States" concluded that, while composting of wastes on a municipal scale is technically possible, it costs more than sanitary landfilling and could be more expensive than incineration. Nevertheless, the changing attitudes toward solid wastes management may stimulate renewed interest and experimentations in composting.

The Federal Government and Solid Wastes Management

The handling and disposal of solid wastes have long been regarded as primary responsibilities of local government. Regardless of whether collection and disposal services were provided by public employees or private contractors, city, township, and county ordinances have traditionally specified how wastes are to be handled and disposed of.

Since the states have given responsibility in this area to local governments, states have not been directly involved with the management of solid wastes collection and disposal systems.

Until the 1960s, the federal government displayed little interest in solid wastes management. The only exceptions were the military, whose interest was limited to handling wastes in encampments and on reservations, and the United States Public Health Service, which conducted a modest research program under its general authority in matters of public health and sanitation. But by the early 1960s, accumulated changes in the volume and nature of solid wastes had created problems of growing concern to local officials. In 1963 a National Conference on Solid Waste Research was held in Chicago under the auspices of APWA. Messages from Richard J. Daley, mayor of Chicago; Paul R. Screvane, president of the New York City Council; and others urged the federal government to take prompt and direct action since the problems were of such magnitude as to warrant its special attention.

Two years later, Congress passed the Solid Waste Disposal Act which laid the groundwork for a greatly expanded federal role in the solid wastes field. The legislation provided for a national research and development program to foster new and improved methods for all aspects of solid wastes management. No regulatory authority was included. The act was to be administered jointly by the Department of Interior, which had responsibility for wastes arising from mining and minerals extraction processes; and by the Department of Health, Education, and Welfare (HEW), which was made responsible for wastes from all other sources, including residences, commercial establishments, industry, and agriculture.

The role of the federal government in solid wastes management was reaffirmed in 1970 with passage of the Resource Recovery Act. This legislation basically continued the earlier programs authorized by the Solid Waste Disposal Act. But with the creation of EPA in December 1970, the responsibilities of HEW in the solid wastes field were transferred to EPA. The legislation directed EPA to carry out a number of special study and demonstration projects. Among these were studies of methods to recover materials and energy from solid wastes, of ways to reduce the generation of solid wastes through changes in product characteristics and packaging practices, and of incentives and disincentives to recycling and reuse of wastes.

Grants were given to state, interstate, municipal, and intermunicipal agencies for solid wastes planning. Federally assisted programs included surveys of disposal practices and problems as well as plans for regional or local recycling systems and for the removal or processing of abandoned automobiles. Public agencies received grants for resource recovery systems and for new or improved disposal facilities, and funds were made available to train instructors and supervisory personnel working in the solid wastes field.

The EPA was directed to publish guidelines on the collection, separation, recovery, and disposal of solid wastes consistent with public health and protection of the environment. These guidelines were not binding except as they applied to waste handling practices of other federal agencies or to anyone receiving a permit to dispose of solid wastes on federal land. However, EPA was authorized to recommend model codes, statutes, and ordinances in order that states and municipalities could implement its guidelines. The agency was also called upon to issue technical and cost information on various processes and methods of dealing with solid wastes.

A particularly important feature of the Resource Recovery Act was the stipulation that EPA prepare plans for a national system for the storage and disposal of hazardous wastes. All materials—including radioactive, toxic chemical, and biological wastes—were to be identified; methods of disposal were to be catalogued; and recommendations were to be made concerning the reduction, neutralization, recovery, or disposal of such wastes. In addition, an inventory of possible disposal sites for hazardous wastes was to be presented.

The Solid Waste Disposal Act (as amended by the Resource Recovery Act) was due to expire on June 30, 1973. The legislation was, however, extended by Congress to June 30, 1975 to provide time for a reevaluation of the federal government's role in the solid wastes field. The EPA proposed a drastic cutback in the federal program. It encouraged elimination of planning grants and the demonstration grant program and decreases in technical assistance. Agency representatives argued that all feasible approaches to recycling technology had been demonstrated, that most state plans had been completed, and that the private sector could best provide technical assistance services. Thus, in place of its earlier, more comprehensive role, EPA recommended that federal activities be limited to the regulation of hazardous wastes.

Opposition to EPA's proposal was immediate. Resistance came from Congress; from groups such as the Council of State Governments, the National Association of Counties, the National League of Cities, and the United States Conference of Mayors; and from many professional, environmental, and citizen organizations. They disputed EPA's contentions and attributed the cutback to an overall economy move to reduce mounting deficit spending by the federal government. The EPA later amended its position, indicating an interest in continuing efforts to improve methods for disposing of hazardous wastes and to further develop and promote resource recovery technology.

Resource Recovery

Americans use more materials, produce more finished goods, and generate more wastes than any other people in history. These materials are generally taken from the earth, processed into consumer goods, used for a time, and then significant amounts are either incinerated or dumped into landfills. Items that are discarded are lost as commodities of economic value and often create health hazards and environmental problems. The reuse of discarded materials—salvaging them for a useful purpose—is called resource recovery. Until the late 1960s and early 1970s, resource recovery seemed to offer little poten-

tial for the future. Given the volatility of the secondary materials market, public agencies and private companies were reluctant to invest heavily in the sophisticated industrial technology required for resource recovery. Only with the federal government's assistance has resource recovery become a viable alternative to waste disposal.

The 1970s' "energy crisis," which caused fuel shortages and higher costs, stimulated renewed interest in the possibility of recovering energy from wastes. As a result, cities such as Chicago, Illinois; Harrisburg, Pennsylvania; and Braintree, Massachusetts have begun experimenting with waterwall incinerators. Incinerators of this kind are not built simply to contain burning wastes but also to convert the heat of combustion into steam. In the waterwall incinerator, refractory brick is used only near the base; and the walls are lined with closely spaced metal tubes in which water is converted to steam. The steam can be used for heating, industrial processes, or—when converted via a steam turbine—electricity. Chicago's incinerator can handle 20 percent of the city's total refuse output. The incinerator consists of four furnaces, each capable of generating 110,000 pounds of steam per hour. About half of this steam is used to provide power to inplant equipment; the remainder is sold.

Several techniques are also being developed to prepare solid wastes for use as fuel. They all require that combustibles be separated from non-combustibles and that burnable wastes be reduced to a uniform size. In some instances, the wastes are pelletized or compressed into a briquette-like form; in others, the wastes are wet pulped to form a slurry from which ferrous metals are removed magnetically and non-burnables are taken out by screening and centrifuge. The remaining burnable material (organics, plastics, and others) is then dewatered and pressed into cakes suited for use as boiler fuel.

The means for recovering energy from solid wastes are not, however, limited to the heat of combustion. By employing a process known as "pyrolysis," it is possible to convert organic wastes into gaseous and liquid substitute fuels. Pyrolysis consists of heating

Chicago's Northwest Incinerator, which can handle 20 percent of the city's total refuse output, produces steam to power inplant equipment and for sale.

substances in an oxygen-free or low-oxygen atmosphere; for without an adequate supply of oxygen, combustion cannot be sustained but chemical decomposition does occur. Depending upon the particular process used, pyrolysis of wastes may yield a relatively low Btu gas, a heavy oil-like liquid similar to No. 6 fuel oil, or a solid char with a heating value comparable to coal. Since these fuels can be transported easily and stored until needed, pyrolysis has distinct advantages over the heat of combustion.

The Monsanto Landgard system, which has been installed in the city of Baltimore, utilizes pyrolysis to produce a low Btu gas. The gas is burned on site to provide steam sold to the Baltimore Gas and Electric Company. The Landgard system is designed to handle unseparated municipal refuse, which passes through a kiln where it is subjected to a heat of 1,800 degrees Fahrenheit. Besides producing gas, the system also forms a residue with an iron and glass aggregate. Ferrous metals, recovered from the residue, are also sold.

The County of San Diego, California, has recently contracted with a private research and development corporation to construct a pyrolysis plant that will make a synthetic fuel oil. It is reported that for a ton of input refuse the plant can produce more than a barrel of oil with a heating value of 10,500 Btu per pound. Unlike the Landgard system, which accepts whole refuse after shredding, the process to be used in San Diego requires the separation of combustibles prior to charging refuse to the pyrolysis reactor.

Although these are only two of the most promising of the new technological approaches to recovering energy from solid wastes, there are other techniques and processes under investigation. One technique, for example, would use anaerobic-digested refuse to produce pipeline-quality methane gas. Another would employ hydrogenated waste paper, plastics, and sewage sludge to produce liquid fuels. Because of the soaring costs of fossil fuels and the increasing environmental constraints being placed on other disposal alternatives, it is expected that these and other experiments in energy recovery will continue into the 1980s.

SUGGESTED READINGS

American Public Works Association. *Public Works Engineers' Yearbook*. Chicago, 1936-1944.

_____ . Street Sanitation Committee. *Street Cleaning Practice*. Chicago, 1938. 2d. ed. 1959.

_____ . Committee on Refuse Collection. *Refuse Collection Practice*. Chicago, 1941. 2d. ed. 1958.

_____ . Institute for Solid Wastes. *Municipal Refuse Disposal*. Chicago, 1970.

_____ . *Solid Waste Collection Practice*. Chicago, 1975.

American Society of Municipal Improvements. *Proceedings*. Chicago, 1894-1930.

Branch, Joseph. *Heating and Light From Municipal and Other Waste*. St. Louis, Missouri, 1906.

Corey, Richard C., ed. *Principles and Practice of Incineration*. New York, 1969.

Hering, Rudolph, and Greeley, Samuel A. *Collection and Disposal of Municipal Refuse*. New York, 1921.

Melosi, Martin V. "'Out of Sight, Out of Mind': The Environment and Disposal of Municipal Refuse, 1860-1920." *Historian,* 35 (August 1973), 621-640.

National Academy of Sciences—National Research Council Committee on Pollution. *Waste Management and Control*. Washington, D.C., 1966.

National Center for Resource Recovery, Inc. *Municipal Solid Waste Collection: A State-of-the-Art Study*. Lexington, Massachusetts, 1973.

National Commission on Materials Policy. *Material Needs and the Environment Today and Tomorrow*. Washington, D.C., 1973.

Parsons, H. de B. *The Disposal of Municipal Refuse*. New York, 1921.

Soper, George A. *Modern Methods of Street Cleaning*. New York, 1907.

Sorg, T. L., and Hickman, H. L., Jr. *Sanitary Landfill Facts*. Washington, D.C., 1970.

U.S. Environmental Protection Agency. *Decision-Makers Guide in Solid Waste Management*. Washington, D.C., 1974.

Venable, William M. *Garbage Crematories in America*. New York, 1906.

CHAPTER 14

PUBLIC BUILDINGS

Throughout American history, public buildings have served as symbolic expressions of the institutions, culture, and ideals of the nation. The structures which house government offices, offer cultural inspiration, and provide entertainment and other public services account for nearly half of the non-residential building construction in the United States. Many public buildings such as capitols, courthouses, and city halls are sources of community identity—physical manifestations of the dignity and power of America's system of government. Because of their monumentality and symbolic importance, aesthetic considerations have always been a paramount concern of public building architects. In the past, their designs were inspired by classical ideals, and derivations of Greek and Roman architectural precepts were reflected in American public buildings. In the twentieth century, more functional styles have emerged. The stress on utilitarianism has been accompanied by technological and engineering advancements that have made buildings self-contained environmental systems. As a result, the services of highly trained building managers, engineers, and

The first section of this chapter, covering the evolution of federal buildings, is based on materials prepared by the General Services Administration. The discussions of postal buildings and veterans medical facilities incorporate reports contributed by the United States Postal Service and the Veterans Administration.

custodial personnel are required to maintain these complex public works.

FEDERAL BUILDINGS

The settlers in the New World emerged from a tradition of government housed in structures that bespoke grandeur, power, and aristocracy. The democratic ideals of America, however, called for a new relationship between government and citizens. Over the past two centuries, concepts of how the federal government ought to house itself have produced various styles ranging from those reminiscent of the opulent grandeur of the Old World to those characterized by simple frugality and functionalism. Such questions as whether government architecture should adapt itself to the prevalent styles of its time and locality or whether aesthetic concerns should be secondary to the values of economy, flexibility, and simplicity have influenced federal design since the founding of the nation in 1776.

Likewise, various responses to the question of who should provide the designs for the structures—government or private architects—have evolved through the years. Until the mid nineteenth century, architects were hired to design buildings in Washington, D.C., while federal buildings elsewhere in the country were under the jurisdiction of local commissioners who hired their own architects under the general supervision of the secretary of the treasury. The increasing number of federal buildings required throughout the country prompted the secretary of the treasury to wrest control of the design and construction of the buildings from the treasury-appointed local commissioners and consolidate their tasks into an office of construction. This consolidation led to nearly four decades of fairly uncontested reign by the office of the supervising architect. This office provided all designs for federal buildings throughout the country; but by the 1890s, the workload of the supervising architect had expanded, and new measures were created to give private architects the opportunity to aid the overworked supervising architect's office by offering designs and consultations to the government. This arrangement of both the federal government and private architect supplying designs has continued in the twentieth century. Since the creation of the General Services Administration in 1949, private architects have dominated federal building design.

From the time of the occupation of a permanent seat of government in 1800, there have always been more federal employees outside Washington, D.C., than in the city. Many governmental service buildings, post offices, and customhouses were built throughout the nation as it expanded westward. However, since the buildings housing these functions were dispersed over a wide area, Washington became the center stage for observing public building construction and design. Few large cities possessed federal buildings of sufficient mass or of such great numbers to rival the attention focused on structures in Washington.

The New Nation's Capital City

After the seven years of war that affirmed America's independence from the ties and influences of the Old World, the housing of the government under the Articles of Confederation was makeshift and unstable. The new government moved between such diverse capital seats as Philadelphia, Trenton, Princeton, and New York, often occupying buildings that were constructed for the colonial capitols.

By the end of the confederation period, the government's structures consisted of merely a few arsenals, military posts, and seventy-five post offices.

The Constitution specifically provided for a Congress, President, and both a Supreme Court and lower courts, implying the need to house these functions in appropriate buildings. Congress was empowered to pass legislation to create a capital city. It could also "exercise authority . . . for the erection of Forts, Magazines, Arsenals, Dock-Yards, and other needful Buildings." Furthermore, the powers of the United States as enumerated in the Constitution also included the right to lay and collect taxes, duties, imports, and excises (customhouses); to coin money (mints); and to establish post offices, implying that all of these functions would be housed at key locations throughout the country.

A statute, generally called the Residence Act, was passed in 1790 to carry out the dictates of the Constitution regarding the designation of the federal city. Although the Constitution did not specify that it be a new city, Congress believed that the nation's fresh start called for a new location. The Residence Act provided that the city be located on the Potomac. Three commissioners were to be appointed by the President to "provide suitable buildings for the accommodation of Congress, and of the President, and for the public offices of the government of the United States."

After Congress first met in New York in 1789, Philadelphia served as the capital city for ten years (1790-1800) while Washington, D. C., was being developed. During the government's residence there, Congress met in the English-styled brick State House, and the Supreme Court sat in an adjacent county court house. A three-story, red-brick mint building was completed in 1792. By 1800 the government had increased its stock of buildings to fifteen lighthouses, several military installations, and the New York Customhouse at Fort George. None of the federal buildings, in either Philadelphia or the rest of the nation, was specifically designed to serve as a symbol of the new government. Rather, these aspirations were part of the plans for the new federal city rising on the Potomac.

Three individuals played important roles in shaping the capital city: George Washington, Thomas Jefferson, and Pierre C. L'Enfant. Washington induced landowners to cede their property for the new city, selected the three commissioners who took charge of the city's development, and appointed L'Enfant to create "drawings of the particular grounds most likely to be approved for the site of the federal town and buildings." Although these appointments constituted Washington's primary contributions to the physical form of the city, he also had definite ideas about the location of the President's House (in its present location), and he recommended founding a national university.

Jefferson's interest in the capital city was more aesthetically oriented and encompassed both the city plan and public architecture. His advice was frequently sought because of his reputation as an authority on architecture. While in Europe, between 1784 and 1789, Jefferson collected and studied city plans of many European municipalities which he made available to L'Enfant. Jefferson suggested that the new federal city have a Capitol, a President's House and gardens, townhouses, a market house, public walks, and a hospital. He sketched a plan for the new federal city, consisting of a street grid with the President's House and Capitol located where they are now, connected by a public walk. The physical separation between the two buildings reflected Jefferson's convictions that a "strong nationally elected executive should balance the congress of locally elected legislators."

The first public buildings in Washington, D.C., the President's House and the Capitol, were largely inspired by Jefferson's views of classical architecture, which he considered to be ideal for expressing the majesty of the new republican state. To Jefferson, the Roman-temple style was especially suited to public architecture. He had earlier designed the Virginia state capitol building (1785) as the full embodiment of this new republican style. As the first American classical revival building, it was the prototype for the structures that dominated the nation's architecture until after the Civil War.

L'Enfant, drawing on the advice of both Washington and Jefferson, designed the city as a radial plan superimposed on a grid. He was acutely aware of problems in draining the adjacent flood plain of the Potomac, an expanse of marshes and lagoons; and he proposed a network of canals to drain the lowlands and subsequently aid the city's commercial development. Cascades, pools, and fountains were also planned. The avenue connecting the Capitol with the White House (Pennsylvania Avenue) was envisioned by L'Enfant to be "magnificent, with the water of the cascade [falling] to the canal which will extend to the Potomac." Major public buildings were to adorn the avenue: "the Judiciary Courts, the National Bank, the grand Church, the plan house, markets and exchange, offering a variety of situations unparalleled for

Library of Congress

One of the first designs for the White House envisioned it flanked by large executive office buildings.

beauty, suitable for every purpose, and in every point convenient." The sites for the major public buildings were tied by public walks, and major settlements were to develop around fifteen public squares. The execution of the plan prompted L'Enfant to demolish new private buildings which blocked his intended radiating avenues. The resulting controversies led to his dismissal in February 1793.

By 1800 many of the characteristics of public buildings in the city had already taken root. Jefferson's classical revival style dominated both the city's and the nation's public building facades for decades to come, and L'Enfant's city plan gave Washington, D.C., its basic structure.

Federal public buildings during the first half of the nineteenth century were designed by a series of multitalented men adept at all types of design and construction. Benjamin Henry Latrobe was the first of these designers to have a lasting impact on the architecture of the federal city. Latrobe had acquired national fame by designing the Bank of Pennsylvania (1800) in Philadelphia, one of the first Greek revival structures built in America. Thus, President Jefferson invited him to design public buildings for the new federal city. Latrobe's work in Washington, D.C., included the Washington Canal, which he viewed as crucial to the city's development as a commercial center. The simple Greek revival style and masonry vaulting which Latrobe first practiced so successfully in Philadelphia were applied to Washington's public buildings. His major buildings included parts of the Capitol, both before the War of 1812 and after it was burned by the British; the Navy Yard in the northeast section of the city; and a fireproof annex to the Treasury Building. When he departed Washington in 1817, Latrobe left a legacy of the simple Greek revival public building which endured for the next four decades. Latrobe also trained many architects and engineers, including Robert Mills who carried on the Greek revival tradition in the captial city.

Mills, a native of Charleston, South Carolina, was Latrobe's close associate on projects in Washington and other cities. In 1808 he left Latrobe's employ and moved to Philadelphia where he designed bridges, churches, and private residences. He later worked in Richmond and Baltimore, and in 1820 returned to South Carolina to serve the next ten years as state engineer and architect. In 1830 President Andrew Jackson invited Mills to Washington, D.C., where he took on various public building projects, including a design for a Potomac River bridge. Six years later, Jackson appointed him the first architect of public building. In this capacity, Mills designed public buildings both for the federal city and the rest of the nation, making his position the precursor to what in the early 1850s became the position of supervising architect in the Treasury Department's office of construction.

As architect of public buildings for the next fifteen years, Mills exerted enormous influence on the government's physical presence in many cities and towns as well as in the nation's capital city. Mills developed theories about public buildings—what they should look like, how their design and construction process could be economized, and how they should function—and the results were early examples of standardized design in public building. Of all Mill's work, his three public buildings in Washington—D.C.—the Treasury Building, the Patent Office, and the Post Office—were his masterpieces in size, design, and continuous use by the government.

Expansion of Federal Building

During Mills' tenure as supervising architect, serious problems arose in the construction of public buildings outside Washington, D.C. Although the treasury secretary was responsible for federal construction, local commissioners selected architects, administered the funds, and supervised construction. Quarrels between architects, commissioners, and the Treasury Department often resulted in costly delays and design changes. The series of quarrels that characterized local public building projects multiplied as the government's responsibilities for providing customhouses, courthouses, and post offices increased.

By 1853 the Treasury Department owned

and maintained twenty-three customhouses and eighteen marine hospitals, with fifteen additional customhouses underway. In that year, Secretary of the Treasury James B. Guthrie turned to the War Department for aid and appointed Captain Alexander J. Bowman as engineer in charge of the Treasury Department's office of construction. The duties of the engineer in charge included "the selection and purchase of the sites for all buildings" and the "making of plans and estimates for custom houses, mints, and marine hospitals."

The power of the engineer in charge over the designs eliminated bitter situations in which a series of architects were retained and then dismissed by local commissioners. However, other problems remained at the local level. Construction was supervised by local superintendents who were responsible for contracting materials, for the payroll, and for all other duties connected with the construction process. Because the supervising engineer (later the supervising architect) was unable to make frequent trips to local building sites, the process of construction was less controlled than were the location and design of the public buildings. The government was authorized to take over the work if superintendents and contractors for materials failed to fulfill their obligations. Blatantly inferior work could be referred to special boards to deter-

mine whether poor workmanship should be condemned and taken down. However, uncertainties in all three phases—site selection, design, and construction—were exacerbated by the need to make annual requests to Congress to appropriate sufficient funds for carrying on the work in succeeding years.

Bowman's annual reports to the secretary of the treasury revealed the perils of the building process. Congressional control over site selection and funding prompted Bowman to complain that some other system be adopted "by which a more equal distribution may be made among the several states, and a just discrimination between the cities and towns of each state, based upon the actual need of such buildings." He was chagrined to report, for example, that an appropriation was made for a courthouse at Memphis, Tennessee, although no courts were in session in that city.

Bowman's assistant, Supervising Architect Ammi B. Young, represented the last gasp of the Greek revival in public building design. During Young's tenure (1853-1862), he designed about seventy buildings. He was the first supervising architect to vary the style of building facades, perhaps an attempt to adapt the design to the community in which the federal building was to be located. For example, in New England cities, he often designed small classical-styled build-

Antebellum Greek revival design precepts were reflected in the Boston Customhouse (1849).

ings, continuing the Mills tradition of simplicity and economy. Young moved from the standardized building plans developed by Mills to a collection of standardized building types in the belief that the varieties of communities necessitated flexibility in the size, scale, and appearance of federal buildings.

A. B. Mullet became supervising architect in 1865 and continued Young's regionalism in his building designs. Mullett hoped to avoid the repetition of style and design that he found so prevalent in the Greek revival public buildings. He recommended that designs be adapted to the local material, the peculiarities of soil and climate, and the "necessities of various localities."

Until his resignation in 1874, Mullett presented an annual tabulated statement of buildings, both owned and under construction by the federal government, and recommended decentralization of his office. He suggested appointing resident government architects for various sections of the country to relieve the Washington office of its increasing work load and to "enable the department to avail itself of their knowledge of local peculiarities and prices." Mullett also sought to improve management. He developed a system of checks on errant superintendent architects, instituted a uniform system of measurement, completed an inventory of furniture, and issued monthly reports. One result of these improvements was that construction costs were less than those for buildings constructed by his predecessors. Mullett objected to Congress retaining control of site selection. Unnecessary public building construction prompted him to remark that in many cases the motive for site selection was a "desire to expend money in the locality in which the buildings were located."

The location and appearance of public buildings within even insignificant cities and towns were given a grander vision by Mullett. As part of a fire preventive measure, Mullett suggested that federal buildings be located where the adjoining land was unencumbered in order to assure good natural light and to provide sufficient isolation to minimize fire danger. "Fire proofing," said Mullett, "means more than just materials . . . it means having

wide streets and open spaces." Thus, Mullett recommended surrounding public buildings with landscaped grounds providing both an appropriate setting for the building and an urban amenity to the residents of the community.

A "superior building" in Mullett's view was exemplified by the French renaissance style. Buildings constructed in the ten years of Mullett's tenure often replaced Greek revival public buildings designed by Mills and Young only a decade or so earlier. They were monumental in scale. Greater floor-to-ceiling heights were made possible by iron frames, and the visual effect was further enhanced by Mullett's mansard roofs crowned by cast iron crestings and sculptures.

The succession of James G. Hill to the post of supervising architect in 1876 marked the first abandonment of classical forms in federal architecture. During Hill's nine years of government service, his designs for public buildings were a sharp break with those produced by Mullett. While Mullett thought classical forms were as "adaptable to a larger building as a small one," Hill established in federal public buildings a decorated red brick rectangular style, known as the "romantic style," which was already widespread in religious, commercial, and residential architecture as well as in other public buildings. Whereas Mullett achieved an impressive governmental presence in communities with his large-scale buildings topped by enormous mansard roofs, Hill inspired a similar awe with lofty clock towers similar to London's "Big Ben." At a time when few buildings rose more than ten stories, an observer could pick out from a distance the government building as easily as he could church spires. The old Bureau of Printing and Engraving in Washington, D.C. (1879) portrays Hill's concept of a functional brick building with open courts, dramatized on the exterior by arched windows and the pointed tower. The impact of Hill's standard exterior design on federal architecture for the next twenty years was enormous—few of his successors strayed from the basic elements of this form.

After Hill's departure in 1883, most succeeding supervising architects recommended open competition among private architects for public buildings designs. The work load had become more difficult to handle. Between 1880 and 1895, the federal inventory of public buildings increased from 163 to 382. Furthermore, the newer structures were becoming larger and more complex. The introduction of iron and steel for building frames dramatically increased their size. Sophisticated lighting, plumbing, and temperature control systems became part of the design process. As a result, the supervising architect was daily faced with complex engineering and architectural problems which often exceeded his experience.

The cry for reform was taken up by the American Institute of Architects (AIA) which pressed Congress to permit design competitions. In 1891 AIA formed a committee to draw up model legislation which was later presented to the House of Representatives by Missouri Congressman John C. Tarnsey. The Tarnsey Bill became law in 1893 and gave the treasury secretary the authority to designate which public buildings would be open to design competition and which would be designed by the supervising architect. Still, even with the new law, few private architects were employed on federal public building projects until James Knox Taylor became supervising architect in 1898. During Taylor's fourteen-year term (1898-1912), the dramatic increase in the number of public buildings made the use of private architects a necessity. His office's inventory rose from 399 in 1899 to 1,126 in 1912. Taylor awarded the first private contract in 1899 for a new customhouse and post office at Norfolk, Virginia. In succeeding years, private architects designed and superintended construction of public buildings throughout the country. The government, however, provided a superintendent of construction at each building site to guard the public's interest.

The necessity of paying both a government resident architect and the private architect's fee raised the cost of designing and supervising some public buildings above the cost of projects wholly undertaken by the supervising architect's office. Taylor found "private architects [to be] failing in matters of administration," and he suggested that the Tarnsey Act be modified to limit private architects to supplying designs and specifications, leaving all supervising work to the federal government.

In 1913 the experiment in privately designed public buildings ended with the repeal of the Tarnsey Act. Distrust between private and government architects and the added costs of employing private architectural firms made the practice unsatisfactory. The repeal of the act did not spell an end to private architects' participation in the growing demand for public buildings. The secretary of the treasury and the supervising architect were no longer empowered to retain private architects, but Congress was. Congress could employ private architects where "the prospective building [was] . . . monumental in character, or when it forms part of a city plan grouping in a community or involves the expenditure of a larger sum of money." This nebulous line between expensive, monumental public buildings and all others was never clarified, and until the creation of the General Services Administration (GSA) in 1949 all classifications of public buildings were designed by both architectural sectors.

The repeal of the Tarnsey Act was only one symptom of what Attorney General J. C. McReynolds termed "conditions in the supervising architect's office [which] appear unfortunate and . . . demand radical treatment." The 1913 Public Buildings Act appropriated nearly $100 million for new public buildings and created a Public Buildings Commission (PBC) to recommend new public building policy. The act instructed PBC— composed of the secretary of the treasury, the postmaster general, congressional members of the Public Buildings committees, and the supervising architect—to frame cost and design standards for all federal public buildings. The PBC report followed a year later. It recommended the adoption of utilitarian and efficient building design, the creation of a permanent bureau of public buildings to relieve the supervising architect of administrative responsibilities, and a zone system of public buildings management across the country. With the exception of the second recommendation, the

1914 report laid the groundwork for federal public building policies until the 1950s. Reviewing what the commission saw as "indulgence" in ornamented public buildings, it suggested a "durable, simple, and architecturally desirable construction," permitting economical operation and maintenance.

Meeting New Emergencies

The outbreak of World War I brought about a sudden demand for office space to accommodate the large number of federal office workers employed in the support of the overseas forces. Several temporary buildings containing a total of more than a million square feet of floor space were rapidly constructed in Washington, D.C. Within a matter of months, temporary three-storied buildings rose on the Mall. These uninviting "tempos" were subsequently removed when the war ended.

The nation began the post-World War I era with the realization that the federal government was the "biggest business in the world." The larger government establishment required erecting large public buildings in Washington and throughout the country. Providing space for the expanded federal work force also involved recognition that the nature of government work was changing. From the traditional activities found in courthouses, marine hospitals, customhouses, and mints grew the large service bureaucracies which engaged in research, prepared statistical reports and surveys, and administered federal assistance programs. In these latter categories, it was increasingly difficult to distinguish federal activities from the work of insurance companies, industrial management, or publishing. As in the world of private business, the federal government establishment became increasingly characterized by purely administrative tasks.

Until the mid 1920s, few new federal buildings were constructed despite the fact that after World War I, federal departments endured extremely cramped conditions. By 1926, however, support had grown in Congress and PBC for constructing a complex of public buildings in the "Triangle"—the area between the Capitol and White House bounded by Constitution and Pennsylvania

avenues. In that year, Congress appropriated $50 million to construct public buildings to house governmental functions in the District of Columbia. The PBC was designated as the supervising agency, with planning assistance to come from the supervising architect's office.

In PBC's subsequent reports, the configurations of the Triangle's form emerged. Each of the twelve buildings would "enjoy separate architectural treatments," but they were to be developed in a unified architectural plan so that there would be no chance of further additions of "incongruous new buildings." "Uniformity without monotony" was the key phrase. The grouping would fulfill the "need for a great single architectural composition, unique in America and surpassing in scale and extent anything heretofore attempted for similar purposes abroad." Rather than attempting to copy similar groupings of buildings in Europe, the Triangle was intended to be a product of the modern age: "An architectural composite that will be a distinctive product of the early twentieth century, depicting the revival of classic architecture for the use of modern business demands."

This impressive grouping of buildings on seventy acres of land had a great emotional impact. Government functions, once relegated to a few monumental buildings or hidden in numerous vernacular structures, came together in one place to proclaim their power and dignity. President Calvin Coolidge wished for such a vivid architectural statement when he signed the 1926 bill. He had previously admonished planners and architects that the federal city should be "symmetrically laid out and adorned with the best that there is in architecture, which would arouse his [an American's] imagination and stir his patriotic pride."

In addition to the aesthetic aspects of the Triangle project, the economic justifications were also stressed. The prior dispersal of government agencies in privately owned buildings scattered throughout the city fostered the ominous "million-dollar rent bill." Coordinating activities within a department was inefficient both to employees and to Washington visitors who came to transact business with the department. Many of these private buildings were old and originally built for commercial purposes. The increasing number of government workers in them were depicted as "suffering from unbearable heat in summer, drafts, and poor ventilation and from lack of natural light as well as from congestion and other insanitary conditions." In such situations, many working hours were lost to illnesses and early closing days in the summer. Building new public edifices in one large grouping cut down the government's rent bill, improved intradepartmental communication, upgraded heating and ventilating standards, and provided predictable working conditions.

Construction of the Triangle project began in the affluent years of the 1920s and continued into the 1930s. As the full human effects of the Great Depression became apparent, PBC altered its dual emphasis on inspirational design and economics and stressed strict utilitarianism. In 1932 PBC justified the project, which eventually cost $190 million, on the premise that it "was not primarily concerned with beautification, but rather with the utilitarian problem of adequately housing the federal activities in such a way as to provide for most efficiently carrying on the public business in the most economical manner." One of the last Triangle buildings, the Federal Trade Commission, reflected this changed emphasis. Its simple facade contrasted sharply with the adjacent, ornate National Archives Building.

A sudden surge of construction occurred during the Depression years, both as a response to the need for buildings and to provide employment to architects, engineers, construction specialists, artists, and laborers. The extraordinary economic conditions called for new administrative mechanisms to deal with the crisis. In 1933 an executive order reorganized the Treasury Department. A procurement division was established to determine "policies and methods pertaining to property, facilities, and structures exercised by any Federal agency, with the exception of work performed by the Corps of Engineers." The activities of building commissions, architectural boards, and private architects

under contract were administered by one office. Paralleling the new division were other relief agencies such as the Public Works Administration (PWA), created specifically to provide employment, stimulate private industry, and give many communities a building through which federal services could be more effectively extended.

By 1939 much of the construction work of the Treasury Department and other agencies such as the Works Progress Administration (WPA) and PWA was nearing completion. An era of administrative reform succeeded the New Deal. In 1939 the building programs were more strongly unified. The Public Buildings Administration (PBA) was created in order to bring about closer cooperation between engineers and architects. The building process was thus removed from the Treasury Department and, in 1940 PBA became one branch of the Federal Works Agency (FWA), sharing equal and often overlapping roles with the Public Roads Administration, PWA, United States Housing Authority, and WPA.

Both functionalist and traditionalist architectural styles were reflected in the design of federal buildings in the 1930s. These treatments seemed to struggle for dominance—the functionalist being more apparent in public buildings outside of Washington, while the traditionalist, being aided by the extant classical environment, predominated in the federal city. As large public buildings rose across the country, they were no longer devoted to a handful of services—a post office, courthouse, or customhouse. The Depression created new demands on the federal government for social services, relief coordination, and the administration on the local level of federally funded jobs. The public buildings constructed to house these services were called variously "Post Office and Court House," "Post Office and Federal Building," or simply "Federal Building."

The Pittsburgh Post Office and Federal Building (1934) was one of the largest public building projects of the decade. The postal functions were relegated to the three basement levels and the first three floors above ground. The six courtrooms and various federal offices occupied the fourth to the tenth

National Archives and Records Service

The Pittsburgh Post Office and Federal Building was one of the largest federal buildings constructed during the Depression.

floors. Like other federal buildings constructed in the 1930s, transportation connections were critical, and it was located adjacent to the Pennsylvania Railroad Station.

During the Depression, artists were employed by federal agencies to enhance the interiors of public buildings. In 1933 the Public Works of Art Project hired nearly 4,000 unemployed artists who completed more than 15,500 works of art. The Treasury Department organized a section of painting and sculpture to "secure suitable paintings and sculpture for public buildings," including the new buildings rising in Washington, D.C., and the post offices and federal buildings across the country. The agency also employed artists through the Treasury Relief Art Project and commissioned thousands of paintings which adorned public buildings. The WPA also employed artists, including many who became nationally and internationally famous in the 1950s and 1960s. When WPA became absorbed into FWA, the arts projects were incorporated and continued to function until 1943.

During World War II, as in the previous war, buildings were rapidly constructed to provide space for the increase in federal office workers. Public office buildings often housed the activities of several agencies, and new designs stressed the flexibility of office space. Public buildings were anonymously designated Federal Building No. 1, No. 2, et cetera.

Building planners became increasingly concerned with efficient utilization of floor space and office accommodations, often at the expense of the symbolic qualities of the exterior facade.

When the war ended, the government began to evaluate its past fifteen years of frantic building activity. The Hoover Commission was created in 1947 to improve federal purchasing and management procedures. Its foremost problem was to determine how the government should administer the programs created during the Depression and World War II. In 1949 the commission made 273 recommendations, mostly of a housekeeping and management nature. In the area of public buildings, the commission noted the need for the impending GSA to "set standards of efficiency in building management, to supervise space allotments, and to keep adequate records of all buildings owned or leased by the government." It made no concrete recommendations as to the supervision of the public building design and construction.

In 1949 FWA was absorbed into the new GSA. The PBA, as part of FWA, was brought into GSA along with the Bureau of Federal Supply, the War Assets Administration, and the National Archives. Re-created as the Public Buildings Service (PBS), its functions at the time were regarded as "just another over-the-counter purchasing job." In the late 1940s and early 1950s, federal building activity was at a low ebb, and PBS had little noticeable effect on the design and construction of public buildings. However, in the mid 1950s, building activity increased.

The Cold War created a new concern about federal building design, especially those intended for defense and other highly sensitive purposes. The theory prevailed that government operations ought to disperse into the Washington suburbs and to regional centers in cities across the country. Buildings constructed for the military in the postwar era incorporated such bomb-resistant features as massive underground quarters, windowless exteriors, thick reinforced concrete walls, and special blast doors.

By 1954 newly dispersed public services across the country were crammed into extant public buildings and had flooded over into rented private buildings. Although there was a need for new public buildings, GSA administrators were unwilling to follow the tortuous route of annual congressional appropriations. In 1954 a new system of financing was devised—"lease-purchase." By this method, public buildings were financed by private investors. Once the building was completed, the government agreed to purchase it by paying the investors back with interest over an agreed number of years. The advantages of this financing method to the government were several: rent paid for private office space, often considered to be higher than comparable government-built space, was reduced; the actual construction of the buildings could be more predictably financed; and, during the period of payment, the property remained on local tax rolls. In adopting lease-purchase, GSA did not abandon the traditional methods of renting and capital appropriations, but it added this alternative for greater financing flexibility. In addition, Congress did not loosen its influence over public building projects, for its approval was necessary before PBS could invite bids for financing and construction.

In announcing this new funding method, GSA outlined for the first time the values sought in new public architecture. Economics, simplicity, and comfort headed the list of priorities. Economy was achieved by reducing the square feet per employee from 125 to 75. Standardization of mechanical equipment, paint, ceiling heights, and window sizes resulted in additional savings.

The lease-purchase arrangement did not garner all the advantages of speed and economy in public building construction, and in 1958 Congress altered the program. In discarding the lease-purchase arrangement, Congress codified and remodeled federal building legislation and simplified procedures and controls. The outcome was the 1959 Public Buildings Act in which seventy-five projects were authorized. Once the building projects reached this authorization stage, the Public Works committees of both houses of Congress worked over the appropriations for the buildings. The 1959 law included controls to prevent any free-and-easy authorizing or appropriating for new government buildings. In 1960 Congress authorized sixty-four new federal buildings and set the stage for a decade of significant public building activity. By this date, GSA had built ten regional offices and had spent several years searching for appropriate values to be reflected in public buildings. However, a renewed aesthetic concern did not lead PBS back to the classical genre. The sleek glass curtain-walled skyscraper towers of private corporations presented a powerful symbol of prestige and efficiency in office building design, and this form was incorporated into public buildings. Office tower public buildings rose across the country in the late 1950s and early 1960s, with little obvious distinction made in their facade from those of private corporate towers.

In 1961 President John F. Kennedy reviewed the scattered collection of new public buildings, both completed and under construction, and assessed their aesthetic qualities as "dismal." In that year, he convened the Ad Hoc Committee on Federal Office Space to make recommendations as to how public architecture might be improved. One year later, the committee issued the 1962 *Guiding Principles for Federal Architecture.* In this treatise, the committee made three major recommendations: (1) public architecture should reflect "the dignity, enterprise, vigor, and stability of the American National Government," incorporating regional traditions and the fine arts; (2) the development of an official style must be avoided; design must flow from the architectural profession to the government, and not vice versa; and (3) the selection of the site, complete with streets, public places, and landscapes should be the first consideration in the design process.

The celebrated Chicago Federal Center reflected this new concern for design. Three structures covering several city blocks were erected and linked by a granite paved plaza. Completed in 1964, the thirty-story United States Court House and Federal Office Building is a beautiful blend of glass, steel, and aluminum sheathing. The floor space and mechanical equipment were based on a 5-foot-square module, allowing for flexibility of

The nineteenth-century flavor of Lafayette Square was preserved by retaining old residences as a foreground for new federal buildings.

space. Fifteen courtrooms occupy the building, and the skyscraper provides a marked contrast to older courthouses. The forty-four-story tower, completed in 1974 and devoted solely to offices, was constructed at a ninety-degree angle to the courthouse and differed little in appearance from a private corporate skyscraper; its location and associations define it as a public building. Adjoining the office tower, a single-story post office was built in 1973.

The 1960s marked a return to the aesthetic and inspirational concerns in the design of public buildings of the 1920s and 1930s and recognition of artworks as an integral part of the architectural environment. A renewed interest in art and the unity of art and architecture was reflected in a GSA policy that permitted one half of 0.5 percent of the total estimated construction costs to be devoted to the procurement of artworks.

The concept of good public building was broadened beyond new architecture to the preservation of historically significant old public buildings. The most impressive example of this change in attitude is the area encompassing Lafayette Square across from the White House. Throughout most of the 1950s, plans for the area included the demolition of the Old Court of Claims building (formerly the original Corcoran Museum and now the Smithsonian's Renwick Gallery) and many of the nineteenth-century residential buildings that lined the square. Historians, architects, and planners were outraged by the radical changes intended for the area surrounding this historic American park. Much national attention was focused on the square, and its destiny spelled similar fates for historical buildings nationwide. In 1962 plans for modernizing the square were reviewed and rejected. A new design was developed which provided the government increased office space in the form of two high-rise structures which were placed behind a row of restored and redesigned nineteenth-century residences facing the square. By blending the new office towers with the residences in the foreground, the character of the square was preserved. The large Court of Claims building was retained and restored as an outstanding example of the government's commitment to the preservation of historic landmarks. Following the success of Lafayette Square, GSA took steps in other communities to save, restore, and use public buildings. The first, in 1965, was the Galveston, Texas customhouse, post office, and courthouse.

The Lafayette Square project added to the search for excellence in public architecture, and it became part of a unified concern for excellence in all aspects of design. These values were carried over into subsequent administrations and broadened into an interest in

America's man-made and natural beauty. In 1965 the White House Conference on Natural Beauty examined townscape, roads, utilities—all elements that made up the environment. During the proceedings, buildings were regarded as a praiseworthy national objective. In 1968 the President's Council on Recreation and Natural Beauty further underscored the importance of public buildings in the following analysis: "A large measure of the symbolic appeal and significance of downtown often derives from its function as the seat of government . . . that gives recognition to art, decoration, and sculpture otherwise absent in the community." Following in this vein, in 1972 President Richard M. Nixon requested that the National Endowment for the Arts review and expand the 1962 guidelines and coordinate efforts of the federal agencies to improve design in architecture, graphics, and publications. A few months later, the Civil Service Commission and the endowment were requested to form a task force to review personnel recruitment policies so that the country's best designers would be attracted to government employment. The task force's 1973 report, *Excellence Attracts Excellence,* recognized the enormous influence of public buildings upon the government's reputation in the design field and thus its attractiveness as an employer to designers: "Federal buildings make impressions . . . . Government architecture provides an image of Government, an idea of its accessibility and, by extension, an impression of our national life."

Recently, the federal government has overcome the problem of annual congressional appropriations as the primary source of funding. Beginning on July 1, 1974 the "Federal Buildings Fund" went into operation. Modeled after the Highway Trust Fund, individual government agencies are required to pay for the office space they use through a user charge equivalent to commercial rent. These monies come to GSA to be set aside in a revolving fund for its building financing and management needs. The predictability and availability of funds, unobtainable under the former system of congressional appropriations or lease-purchase, has been secured.

The advances made in public building

planning, design, and construction since the early 1960s have freed public buildings from the burden of traditional concepts of an official style and a monumental setting, and simplistic concepts like functionalism and economy have given way to a complex of values reflecting human and aesthetic needs.

Support Services and Management in Federal Buildings

Public buildings have steadily evolved over the past 200 years from the few functional and monumental buildings of the early republic to the highly integrated and specialized office buildings, warehouses, laboratories, and institutional structures of today. An important part of this story has been the advance of the mechanical equipment and building support services and the growing army of increasingly skilled personnel responsible for their maintenance and management. Today more than 10,000 buildings stand throughout the nation to shelter and support the activities of the federal government.

Before the mid nineteenth century, public building was a spasmodic activity. Outside of the capital city, federal buildings were provided whenever the limited resources of the federal government allowed and the need for them was demonstrated. This meant that the individual buildings were authorized, architects were chosen to design them, and local commissioners were appointed to superintend their construction. At the conclusion of such an effort, the building was managed by whatever agency occupied it. Because of its far-flung system of customhouses, the Treasury Department administered the nation's public building programs until almost the end of the nineteenth century.

A long series of engineering developments during the nineteenth century caused radical changes in the construction of buildings and in their heating, lighting, and ventilation. This progress required highly trained building managers and maintenance personnel who contributed not only to more efficient mechanized buildings management but who also influenced the design of new buildings.

The mechanization of public buildings, which began in the late nineteenth century, has progressed through the years to the point that today new federal buildings often differ only in exterior architectural design. The working heart of each building—the lighting, heating, ventilating, air conditioning—are all part of a kit of identical, interdependent parts that can be erected on different sites regardless of climate. The technical capability to build from the inside, ignoring the amount of natural daylight, the extremes of heat and cold, and the effects of high humidity, is the result of a century and a half of inventions which collectively have made the building environment self-contained and more comfortable.

Typical of the pre-technological government buildings was the original red brick Treasury Building constructed in 1800 beside the White House. This structure was similar to many eighteenth-century Georgian buildings, with each room organized around a window for light and an individual fireplace for

Library of Congress

Lighting in the Treasury Building was originally provided by ornate gas light fixtures.

heat. There is evidence that both wood and coal were burned, and some of these fireplaces may have been fitted with a form of the Franklin stove. Since government office hours before the Civil War were from 9 a.m. until 3 p.m., relatively little work was done at night, and candles and lamps were used only to supplement natural light on dark winter days. The later four-story Treasury Building designed by Robert Mills and completed in 1842 introduced a new lighting medium to federal buildings—gas light. The open-flame lamps improved illumination but gave off carbon monoxide which caused office workers to suffer from headaches, drowsiness, and dizziness. In addition, windows were often kept shut to guard against drafts. Consequently, the working environment was often hot, humid, and befouled with tobacco smoke and body odor.

Montgomery C. Meigs, an army engineer, pioneered solutions to the problems of lighting, heating, and ventilation in public buildings. In 1850 Congress voted $100,000 for the construction of two new wings to the Capitol for the House and Senate. The marvel of gas lighting had just been introduced in the Capitol Building, but heating and ventilating systems were non-existent. Meigs designed a novel environmental system by drilling a million holes in the floor through which air was forced by powerful fans driven by a steam engine. His originality was further demonstrated in designing the conference, committee, and office rooms without windows to end drafts and outside distractions.

The luminous cove ceiling presently lighting the House and Senate chambers was originally designed as a skylight—the first in a public building in Washington, D.C.. Nineteenth-century interior lighting standards were far lower than today because it was generally thought that an excess of daylight was unhealthy. The unevenness of daylight coming through the glass roof apparently prompted Meigs to place movable metallic plates under the skylight to regulate illumination. Glass architecture, so typical of contemporary office buildings, was costly and used sparingly in early nineteenth-century buildings; but by mid century, large plate glass could be economically manufactured and its use became popular. The essential difference between nineteenth-century and modern glass architecture was that the former was for the most part invisible from the street. Following Meig's example in the Capitol wings, there was widespread use of glass skylights and broad areas of glass in the interior walls of public buildings.

Near the end of his career, Meigs became the architect of another building that reflected his concern for lighting, heating, cooling, and ventilation. Environmental considerations were the primary rationale behind the design of the Pension Building which was built between 1882 and 1887. When Meigs submitted his plans to the secretary of war, Robert Todd Lincoln, he gave his reasons for adding a unique clerestory to augment the building's gas lighting system: "It will have no dark corridors, passages, or corners. Every foot of its floors will be well lighted and fit for the site of desks at which to examine and prepare papers." Over a hundred windows installed in the clerestory were hinged at the center and opened by a chain-operated mechanism. Meigs introduced the thermal pane—two panes of glass with an intermediate air space—for the same reasons it is popular today: to avoid excessive summer heat from entering and to prevent winter heat from escaping. Meig's ventilation plans thirty years earlier in the legislative chambers of the Capitol met with great resistance from congressmen who disliked having air continually blown at them from underneath. The million holes in the floor gradually were covered with carpets, and Meigs did not repeat the system in the Pension Building. He returned to the use of windows for light and ventilation. In his report to Robert Todd Lincoln, he stated: "every room having windows on two sides, one opening to outer air, the other to the central court covered from the weather by a non-conducting fire-proof roof."

The growth of large multistoried government buildings before the invention of fluorescent lighting necessitated interior light courts. By 1888 it was federal building practice to construct large glass ceilings in the central part of the building on the second floor to light the working area below. Above this glass ceiling, a well extended to the top of the building which was covered with a glazed

roof to light the interior and the colonnade at each floor. Throughout the country, large post offices of the 1880s and 1890s used this new glass architecture; interior light courts could be surrounded by any desired architectural treatment.

Typical of the way architects adopted new technology to improve the working environment of public buildings was the lighting in the State, War, and Navy Building (currently the Executive Office Building). "Old State" was completed in 1888 when gas light was still the sole illuminant, but the building became a pioneer in technological improvements. In the absence of a citywide electrical system, an electric generator was connected to the building's boiler system, giving it a few electric lights. Reflecting the ambivalence of the day in the contest between gas and electricity, combination gas and electric fixtures were installed in the building about the turn of the century.

General Services Administration

Built in 1917 to house the Interior Department, this structure was the first of the "wing buildings."

Whereas the Pension Building was an experiment in combining exterior light with gas light, the 1917 Interior Building (presently the General Services Administration Building) increased lighting by using incandescence and sunlight as the new architectural design determinant. It was the first of Washington's "wing buildings," a design that ended dependence on interior light courts and skylights for supplementary illumination. Lighting was the primary consideration in the building's general plan which took the form of the letter *E*, having three arms extending south from the spine. The rooms were lit with electric lights and designed to permit the maximum entry of sunlight. In order to avoid shadows and poor lighting, a shallow 20-foot room depth was adopted and large windows ranging from $7^1/_2$ to 10 feet high lined the face and interior courts of the building.

Through the difficult Depression years, the federal government engaged in a massive building program, and the environmental ingenuity of the National Archives Building affected the mechanical core of the buildings constructed in its wake. The Archives was essentially a building within a building. The outer structure, with its imposing Corinthian columns and porticoes, formed a monumental enclosure around an inner core which was equipped with the latest environmental controls of the mid 1930s. The windowless inner building protected documents and papers from sunlight. The humidity and temperature of the air was regulated for additional security and employee comfort.

Once the ability to control humidity and regulate air temperature was demonstrated, a move began to introduce air conditioning in all monumental buildings. Until the 1930s, ventilation demanded open windows. Dust and dirt from the streets flew in the open windows, accompanied by the noise of the surrounding urban activity and the fumes from the growing number of automobiles. Fans had been in general use since the first decade of the twentieth century, but they achieved little improvement in comfort, while drafty working conditions and the blowing of papers were a marked nuisance.

Improvements in lighting and air conditioning accelerated environmental services and made possible a new building type—the block building—first illustrated in the General Accounting Office (GAO) completed in 1951. The invention of the fluorescent lamp in the late 1930s revolutionized public building architecture. Until then the need for good natural lighting was the principal determinant in the design of all major buildings. This was true whether the solution was skylights, light courts, or wing buildings.

The GAO was conceived at the very end of the 1930s. The seven-story building, with a basement and sub-basement, covers an entire city block and has no wings or courts to provide light to the interior rooms. Since the agency is the "watchdog of the Treasury," its office workers are daily involved in reading columns of figures and small print. Therefore, a higher level of illumination was needed, and the white, glareless fluorescent light promised to be the answer. New standards for office lighting, not only for government offices, were established in GAO. The outstanding characteristic of this general office lighting was the quality of the illumination. It was comfortable to the eye; and when office layouts conformed to the fixture lines, it was free from shadows and direct or reflected glare. The uniform intensity throughout all work areas created an unusually good visual environment.

In 1951 the government felt it had mastered the luminous environment, and without this mastery all the subsequent technological accomplishments would have been unlikely. With new standards in the quality and quantity of lighting, new developments in air conditioning were made. However, government work was especially elusive, and it was difficult to determine if significant gains in efficiency would result from air conditioning and hence justify the considerable expenditures it would require. Experiments of employee behavior in large industrial plants showed that any change in working conditions, whether for better or for worse, led to at least a temporary increase in production. A further complicating factor was that in many of the situations in which increased productivity had apparently resulted from installation of air conditioning, other changes such as painting and better lighting had also affected productivity. To determine more precisely what benefits would result from air conditioning public buildings, a significant experiment was conducted in 1958 by the research division of the Office of Buildings Management.

The experiment was conducted in a wing-type federal office building. One wing was air conditioned for the test, while another was used as a control. Similar work was done in both areas, and it was possible to maintain records of errors in filing and other comparable work. Both the test area and the control area were first painted and illuminated to provide identical working conditions, and the work force in both areas was structured to offer further comparability (especially as to the proportion of men and women and the experience of the workers). The result of the experiment showed an overall average increase in productivity of more than 9 percent in the test area. Since it had been established that an increase of only 1.5 percent in productivity would justify the cost of air conditioning the building, this was a compelling finding. Of further significance was the reduction by 2.5 percent of absenteeism in the air-conditioned area and an increase in accuracy of nearly 1 percent. Further changes noted in the survey were higher employee morale, less soiling of clothing, and a lower consumption of iced drinking water. The study also noted that many of the environmental improvements and changes in building design, if reflected in the design of a new building, would result in further economies.

National Archives and Records Service

In 1946 public offices were lighted by incandescent fixtures and cooled by pedestal fans.

The efficiency of a building is closely related to its function. Over its lifetime, a building's operating characteristics will be of greater economic importance than savings from design and construction. Modern office buildings provide better working conditions which lead to greater productivity and a closer suitability of the building to the working tasks performed in it. Of greater significance,

however, is the capability of a building to accommodate more people and thus "do more work." This is directly translated into value for money; a cheaper building that is well designed will do the same job that would otherwise require a larger and more costly building.

While concern for the functional efficiency of office buildings is contemporary, architectural design has always had this capability. In functional buildings, like factories, mills, housing, or prisons, the concept of efficiency has been fully articulated. The environmental aspects of design have become increasingly recognized; and a great change affecting the building's use has come about with the introduction of mechanical equipment. The result of better heating, ventilating, air conditioning, illumination, and other environmental support services is that the space per person in new buildings has been steadily reduced.

In 1912, 1,800 cubic feet of space per person was the standard; today this has been cut in half. Ceiling heights have been lowered, floor space per worker has been reduced, dark spaces in working areas have been eliminated, and space utilization enhanced. Modern office layout and improved design of furniture have led to a more efficient use of space. Acoustical controls have reduced noise levels and removed the need for greater space to provide relative quiet and to avoid distraction and interferences. One architectural expression of these changes has been the provision of larger and unobstructed working areas. Not only structural limitations but social and psychological factors are recognized as primary considerations in architectural design and space control.

Whereas older buildings were cut up into small offices by partitioning to secure privacy, quiet, and temperature control, modern buildings are laid out in work areas of as much as 10,000 square feet. In such areas, the emphasis is upon working groups rather than individuals. The size of the groups and the working conditions they require periodically change, and the space (both building space and furnishings) is flexible to permit adjustments. The new science of ergonomics (human factors engineering) was borrowed from experience in designing submarines and space vehicles in which crews remained confined for months. Improved office lighting derived from the shadow-free conditions that safety engineering had developed in industry. The creation of central air conditioning in office buildings emerged from more than a quarter century of experiences in printing plants, cigarette factories, textile mills, and theaters. Environmental experience was gained by the management of post office work rooms and other specific situations in which measurable criteria of light, ventilation, temperature, and other work conditions had been identified and compared.

In the past, office layout mirrored the institutional hierarchy. Executives as a matter of rank got the best space, the light, the view, the privacy, whether or not the nature of their work required it. Stenographic and clerical workers were given inside office positions, often in the main traffic arteries, when they were not marshaled in "typing pools" under close supervision. Emancipation from these

conditions was a further factor in the popularity of office landscaping. The reorganization of interior working spaces has produced profound changes in office routines and offers the creative evolution of new work patterns.

Throughout this period of growing sophistication in support services and office organization, there has been a comparable increase in the professionalism of those who manage and maintain federal buildings. In the early 1800s, when the first monumental buildings in the new federal city were occupied, the need arose for building managers. For most of the nineteenth century, the manager of each building was employed by the occupying agency and, in the smaller buildings, his duties included repair work and custodial chores. The records of public architecture which give information on numbers of government clerks and administrative personnel are available, but the records are scant for the workers who carried the wood and coal, stoked the fires, cleaned the flues, trimmed the candles, filled the oil lamps,

When completed in 1883, the State, War, and Navy Building (presently the Executive Office Building) was the largest public building in the nation.

repaired the furniture, and washed the floors and windows. Prior to the advent of the civil service in the 1880s, many of the lower echelon jobs in building management were filled by patronage. Although skilled labor was in short supply in Washington, D.C., there was an unskilled labor pool to draw upon and apparently little difficulty in obtaining people to do the simple, repetitive tasks.

The greatest number of people involved in the daily operations and maintenance have been and are the custodial force. The first chronicle of maintenance operations appeared in the records of the State, War, and Navy Building. When this massive, elaborately appointed building opened in 1883, it was the country's largest public building, greater in size than the Capitol. To supervise this vast structure, Congress created a federal agency solely for the purpose of managing its daily operations. For many years, the President appointed a superintendent from either the army or navy. The original work force consisted of 152 employees, over half of whom were charwomen.

The architect of the building, A. B. Mullett, had a great interest in mechanical devices and incorporated into the structure several new ideas and inventions. Although not the first public building to have central heating, it was the first to have central hot water heating and the first designed with steam elevators. Engineers, firemen, and plumbers were needed to run the boiler equipment which, in addition to supplying heat and propelling the hydraulic elevators, pumped the water into the attic tanks which was then distributed to the washrooms and bathrooms throughout the buildings. Engineers were also hired to operate and maintain 6,000 gas jets, most of them ornately custom-designed for the building.

In spite of the increasing number of technical people needed to run the building, the largest numbers of employees were hired to clean it. In an era of labor-saving inventions—the typewriter was rapidly coming into use for office workers—it was natural for the building superintendent to look for ways to mechanize his greatest number of employees, the charwomen. Their primary task was cleaning eight acres of offices and two and a half acres of black and white marble corridors each evening. In 1899 Superintendent George W. Baird bought a mechanical scrubber resembling a bicycle with two large rotary brushes. Two women pedaling the machine around the corridors could do the work of eight to ten women mopping by hand. To Baird, as to many of his successors, mechanical equipment permitted him to raise the level of cleaning the building. But the charwomen organized a strike, the first by civil service federal employees against the United States government. It was effective, and the initial attempt to mechanize custodial workers failed.

A new electrical era arrived in the 1920s and dramatically affected the work of custodians. Following the development of electrical refrigerators and stoves, more powerful motors led to the invention of a vast number of labor-saving devices such as central vacuuming systems. New buildings were equipped with hundreds of outlets that could be reached by a 50-foot length of cleaning hose. Although a hose was an efficient way to clean a corridor, it was unwieldy in offices. Furthermore, they tended to wear out quickly, and in the 1950s construction of buildings with central vacuuming was discontinued.

After steam elevators proved successful, elevators were incorporated in new public buildings and installed in older ones. As elevators were introduced, the operators were drawn from the custodial force, and they participated in the government's earliest training programs for operation of new machinery. Such training programs are now a common practice. When automatic elevators were first installed in public buildings after World War II, there was strong resistance from office workers who felt insecure inside a moving elevator with no person in command. By the time the General Accounting Office was completed in 1951, however, the safety of automatic elevators was fully established, and it became the first public building with completely automatic elevators. They paid for themselves in five to six years by eliminating the expense of manual operators.

The amount of office space operated by the federal government substantially increased following World War II, and building managers realized the need to develop work standards for the various maintenance jobs. Time studies were conducted on every aspect of a cleaning job; an examination was made of the efficiency of equipment; and a review was conducted of cleaning standards in private institutions. These studies resulted in regulations for all phases of the cleaning program: room cleaning, floor maintenance, toilet cleaning, stair cleaning, cleaning of public spaces, high cleaning, venetian blind cleaning, window washing, outside maintenance, and insect and rodent control. As a result of the extensive research program, the federal government now requires a work standard of 19,000 square feet per employee per night, compared with 8,000 square feet expected in the late 1930s.

Library of Congress

Government charwomen cleaned federal buildings by hand until the introduction of labor-saving machines.

In 1974 there were 160 million square feet of federally owned space and 60 million square feet of leased space to be cleaned nightly. In spite of new machines and more efficient methods of cleaning, the greatest number of people involved in building management today, as always, are the custodial force. Forty-two percent of all GSA employees are cleaners, the remainder are craftsmen, guards, elevator operators, and central and regional office staff. The skills of operating engineers, general mechanics, elevator mechanics, painters, electricians, carpenters, plumbers, and miscellaneous tradesmen are all needed to make the complex heating, ventilating, plumbing, and air-conditioning systems in today's public buildings function smoothly.

The trend toward professionalism in buildings management is further demonstrated by the evolution of building guards into the present Federal Protective Service. In the 1960s, anti-war and civil rights demonstrations made existing security measures obsolete. Most dissident groups did not intend to destroy federal buildings, but some chose to illustrate their grievances by physically occupying an agency or generally disrupting the normal operations of government. The surrounding of a building by guards holding hands was no longer an adequate solution to the problem. In 1970 the Federal Protective Service was created; and by the end of 1972, it included 5,264 uniformed personnel.

Under normal daily conditions, all federal buildings are offered round-the-clock protection services. Whereas formerly protection entailed guards assigned to fixed posts, today, with the use of modern communications equipment, federal buildings are protected under the mobile patrol concept. Walkie-talkies, electrical or mechanical devices and sensors, and closed circuit television connect to a central control center which transmits messages to nearby federal protection officers. This flow of communication through a control center allows more protection to encompass larger areas on a continuous basis.

Technology had long been used in fire alarm systems. In the 1970s, similar technology, particularly new communications systems, was introduced to aid in protecting people, safeguarding property, and preventing disruptions of normal government operations. The men and women of the Federal Protective Service are trained in bomb search and reconnaissance and emergency medical assistance to handle bomb threats. The government has recruited college graduates with training in criminal psychology and law to lead this program and to conduct intensive training for all guards in the history of law enforcement, criminal justice, and the nature and control of civil disorders in a democracy.

In addition to the professionalization of the custodial force, building engineers, and the protective services, there has been an extensive upgrading of the people who manage federal buildings. Formerly, most building managers rose from the ranks of mechanical or electrical engineers in the manner of noncommissioned officers entering the officer corps of the military. By 1975, however, 90 percent of the top management positions were filled by college graduates with relevant training.

Current Federal Building Policies

The progress of public building has been accomplished with scarcely a thought of the increasing amounts of energy required to maintain the new working conditions. Yet the air conditioning, higher levels of lighting, and other services were all accompanied by increases in electricity, fuel, and other energy demands. The new architectural aesthetic of glass facades was a further factor in increasing energy consumption. In the whole march of architectural progress, almost the only energy gain was in the increased use of thermal insulation.

The assumptions of architectural design were abruptly challenged by the environmental awareness that arose toward the end of the 1960s and became dramatically expressed in the power shortages, brownouts, and finally in the energy crisis of the winter of 1973-1974 when fuel oil, electricity, and gasoline shortages became acute. The GSA's leadership in energy conservation was evident to every occupant or user of federal buildings as a variety of conservation measures were put into effect. But of greater significance in the long run was the new attitude toward energy conservation that was reflected in the design of new buildings and in building maintenance. Energy conservation became a permanent factor in the public buildings program.

An environmental demonstration project was undertaken in the design of the new Federal Office Building in Saginaw, Michigan, in 1972. It contains many elements of energy conservation which will influence the design of all future federal buildings. In Manchester, New Hampshire, another federal office building has been designated by GSA as a still more specialized demonstration of energy efficiency. These buildings have become research laboratories in which a new technology for office buildings is being formulated and tested.

The most dramatic design feature of the Saginaw building is the solar energy collector. All of the hot water and approximately 60 percent of the heating will come from this pollution-free device. The large, flat solar collector rises above the surrounding peninsular landscape, but most of the building itself is underground to reduce heat loss. This low single-story structure will require no elevators. Its low-wattage lighting systems are a sharp departure from past office building lighting standards.

Improved fire prevention measures are another vital concern in federal building programs. Fear of fire pervaded all colonial and nineteenth-century building. The first District of Columbia commissioners specified in the building code that the new city on the Potomac be built of brick for just this reason; but these regulations proved inhibiting to the growth of the city, and before the capital was moved, they were rescinded. Before the days of a paid fire department in Washington, D.C., even the most prominent statesmen and leading citizens were seen in volunteer bucket brigades. The first Treasury Building fire, which occurred when the city was only a few months old, reportedly enlisted the aid of President John Adams; the scene was repeated by his son John Quincy Adams passing the bucket in the Treasury fire of 1833. After the first fire, Secretary of the Treasury Oliver Wolcott was accused of burning down the Treasury to conceal a corrupt administration. The charge was never proven, but throughout the century arson was not uncommon in public buildings.

The first public building specifically designed to be fireproof was an archival depository for official records, designed by

Benjamin Latrobe as an annex to the Treasury. One of its outstanding features was the omission of fireplaces. It proved its worth by surviving two Treasury fires and was only torn down to make way for the greatly expanded—and fireproof—new Treasury Building in 1836.

Nineteenth-century architects experimented with new materials in their continuing search for fireproofing. Iron became the most favored construction material. Even if the building were not constructed of iron, it was freely used in fire escape stairs. In the 1880s and 1890s, fire fighting equipment and techniques rapidly improved. After the turn of the century, sprinklers and sensors were introduced to identify and fight building fires. The development of alloys, combined with other techniques, created structures in which steel was encased in concrete for fire security.

The growth of high-rise buildings has added a new dimension to the problem of fire prevention. Any building over eight stories high can create a "stack" effect. The structure becomes a chimney for fire and smoke, and evacuation is difficult, if not impossible. Most buildings are filled with combustibles such as wood, cloth, plastics, and paper. Stairways, elevators, air-conditioning ducts, and corridors become highways for smoke. Heat-sensitive call buttons for some types of automatic elevators can send people to the floor of the fire and fling open the doors. Even if the elevator is somehow prevented from going to the floor of the fire, its shaft can become a conduit for smoke.

There have been many fires in public buildings over the years, but the potential for a high-rise holocaust especially concerned GSA after major fires in New York in 1970 and New Orleans in 1972. To offset this threat, the prototype of a truly firesafe building has been developed in GSA's Seattle Federal Building. It gathers and concentrates in a single system proven fire prevention meaures as well as many innovations to provide a new concept in fire safety. Basic to the plan for this thirty-eight story building is tight control of its fuel supply, heat-activated sprinklers, and non-combustible walls and

General Services Administration

GSA's Seattle Federal Building pioneered fire prevention features that will be incorporated in future high-rise public buildings.

ceilings. "Security islands," zones sealed from smoke and fire and equipped with self-supporting communications systems, are a unique feature of the building. Rather than attempting to evacuate it, people either assemble in safe areas to wait out the fire or they are guided to elevator shafts that open only on the ground floor. An elaborate fire control center, tied with the environmental and security services in the total building system design, acts as a security monitoring system.

Over a fifty-year period, building experts estimate that 100 fires of some kind will occur in each high-rise, but the new system demonstrated by the Seattle Federal Building suggests that fires can be controlled by new design approaches. The knowledge gained from this building has caused GSA to reassess fire safety in its old buildings. The importance of this program was underlined in July 1973 when the six-story GSA building in suburban St. Louis, occupied by the Military Personnel

Records Center, was burned with the irreparable loss of vital records. For three days, the fire burned out of control despite fire department efforts to extinguish the blaze. The lack of a complete sprinkler system was a factor in the extent of the damage. Installation of such automatic systems is probably the largest single item in the $40 million fire control system that GSA has programmed for its older buildings.

Also reflected in current federal building programs is the structure's contribution to its urban environment. Large public buildings have a tremendous impact on urban areas. They provide a major source of employment to their localities, require construction of transportation facilities, and influence development of surrounding residential and commercial areas. In recent years, attempts have been made to locate new public buildings where they will provide major benefits to urban areas.

In February 1970, President Nixon issued Executive Order 11512 outlining new concerns in the planning of federal buildings. The GSA was asked to "coordinate proposed programs and plans for buildings and space in a manner designed to exert a positive economic and social influence on the development or redevelopment of the areas in which such facilities will be located." In order to be compatible with local policies, "proposed developments shall be, to the greatest extent practicable, consistent with state, regional, and local plans and programs."

Two public buildings illustrate the incorporation of these factors. The Internal Revenue Service Building in Fresno, California, was located in a low-income residential area in order to provide employment opportunities where few had existed in the area before. Accommodating the visual effect of the building to the area, the completed building covered nearly thirteen acres in a single-story configuration. Whereas the Fresno building revitalized a residential area, the Social Security Administration Center in Birmingham, Alabama, displayed a commitment to rejuvenate the inner city. Located in the city's newly designated Civic Center area, the building took its place within a cluster of museums, gardens, state and municipal buildings, and hotels. Looking upon these examples of structures built according to Executive Order 11512, in 1974 GSA viewed itself as being in a "leadership position in the urban development process."

TYPES OF BUILDINGS

The development of federal buildings is illustrative of most public buildings, especially in regard to support facilities such as heating, lighting, ventilating, and the custodial and management services. All buildings benefited from the interchange of technology and its application. Various public buildings which serve specific needs are described in the following sections. All levels of government are often involved in community public buildings such as courthouses, jails, and medical facilities. Private donation funds contribute heavily to some community buildings such as libraries, museums, and theaters. The operation and maintenance of buildings are accomplished in many ways. While the federal buildings are managed by GSA, state and local government buildings may be managed by a public works department or by the specific agency which the building serves.

Capitols

Capitol buildings are the legislative headquarters of American state and national governments. In the state capitols, a single building initially housed the chambers, committee rooms, offices, libraries, and lounges of the legislature; the offices of the executive branch; and the chambers and offices of the state supreme court. As government functions and services increased, states constructed additional buildings or groups of buildings to house their rapidly growing executive departments.

In addition to being the center for the affairs of government, a capitol, better than any other building, transmits a sense of a state's heritage. In approaching a capitol's entrance or passing through its main hallways, one's awareness of the state's past and present is enhanced by paintings, sculpture, displays, and design features. A glance at the 32-foot bronze figure of the Sower atop Nebraska's State Capitol, for example, dramatizes one of that state's sources of wealth. The statue of William Jennings Bryan just outside the building represents the Great Commoner's influence on the nation's history.

The physical bearing of America's state capitol buildings is consistent with the dignity of their role. Some capitol buildings are located on elevations to enhance their prominence. Though their architectural styles vary, all exhibit a strength and beauty in keeping with their functions. Bicameralism in every state legislature except Nebraska (which was bicameral when its capitol was designed) has influenced the winged symmetry common in American capitol buildings.

Before the twentieth century, America's capitols were patterned after the great architectural achievements of the past. The United States Capitol and the state capitols of California, Connecticut, and Maryland respectively drew from Classical, Roman, Gothic, and Georgian architectural traditions. Typical of the features found in many capitols are the dome, rotunda, pediment (the decorative triangular piece atop a front entrance), Greek columns, and a monumental flight of steps. In the first half of the twentieth century,

The Nebraska State Capitol marked a distinct break with classical architectural styles.

however, a controversy developed between advocates of traditional architectural styles and those favoring contemporary forms. Modern architectural expressions became generally accepted; and when the Nebraska State Capitol was completed in 1932, it represented a distinct break with former architectural patterns. Lacking a dome or pediment, the Nebraska Capitol is notable for its majestic tower which soars 400 feet into the air. That same year, Louisiana opened a similarly styled "skyscraper" capitol. North Dakota completed a nineteen-floor capitol building in 1934 which resembled the best commercial buildings of the era.

In recent years, states have built annexes to provide office space for the expanding functions of governments. Many of the older capitols have been completely renovated to accommodate growing work loads. Support services such as printing and restaurant and parking facilities are being incorporated into the design of modern capitols. In 1976 costly replacement or expansion programs are underway in several states. The new $8.5 million Memorial Plaza, largest office building in Tennessee, is designed to serve the needs of the state legislature for many years to come. Florida is building a $42 million "skyscraper" capitol, and a new multimillion-dollar capitol complex is also nearing completion in New York. Maryland is constructing a Legislative Services Building in the same modified Georgian style of its Old State House—the nation's oldest capitol building (1772).

The United States Capitol, which houses the legislative chambers of Congress, symbolizes the United States of America more fully than any other single building. Finished in resplendent white marble, this majestic structure's hilltop site was selected by Pierre L'Enfant, who had observed "a pedestal waiting for a monument."

President Washington laid the cornerstone of the Capitol in September 1793. Despite difficulties in obtaining finances, supplies, and workmen for construction, the original section was completed in 1800 and accommodated the House, Senate, Supreme Court, and Library of Congress for the next seven years. In 1803 Benjamin Latrobe was appointed superintendent of construction and in 1807 completed the separate south wing of the building. Following the burning of the Capitol by the British in 1814, it was Latrobe's task to direct the reconstruction of what he called "a most magnificent ruin." In 1827 under Charles Bulfinch, Latrobe's successor, the central link between the two wings was completed. The building was given a plain dome, and the 155-acre grounds were terraced and landscaped. Under succeeding superintendents, major wing extensions were pursued. The House extension was completed in 1857, and two years later the Senate wing was finished. The present dome was completed during the Civil War. In spite of wartime demands for federal resources, President Abraham Lincoln pushed forward the construction because he believed that "if people see the Capitol going on . . . it is a sign we intend the Union shall go on."

By 1965, $50.5 million had been spent on the Capitol, not including additional millions for furnishings and the inspiring works of art throughout the building. Statuary Hall houses bronze and marble monuments to some of America's great leaders. Eight historic paintings located in the rotunda portray important events in the nation's history such as the landing of Columbus and the embarkation of the Pilgrims. Although the art treasures of the Capitol are numerous, the artistry of Constantino Brumidi is especially noteworthy. Brumidi was employed in 1855 to paint murals in the Capitol; and his works such as the spectacular fresco, "The Apotheosis of Washington," on the ceiling of the dome, enhance the magnificence of this impressive building.

City Halls

City halls are the headquarters of municipal government. They have traditionally housed a meeting room for the city council, offices for the mayor, courtrooms, and space for public ceremonies and receptions. In large cities, the offices of the executive departments have traditionally occupied most of the city hall. In contrast, the legislative meeting rooms and ceremonial areas dominate the buildings in small communities. In towns and villages, a large number of the citizens regularly attend council meetings and participate in decisions involving zoning, public health, fire and police protection, and public works. Small city halls consist of a few offices grouped around a large meeting room. In the large cities, the city council chamber provides seating for the public to carry on the tradition that legislative meetings should be open to the citizens. Many of the largest cities have built separate municipal office buildings to house executive departments and utilize the city hall to legislative and ceremonial uses.

Builders of early American city halls sought to convey through architecture the spiritual and emotional values of their city. In the early 1800s, New York built a city hall that was one of the most beautiful buildings in the United States. The cornerstone was laid in May 1803, but construction was slowed by lack of funds and the building committee's whimsical design changes. The city wanted a costly marble structure but eventually compromised and faced the front and two sides of the building with marble and the rear with brownstone. Completed in 1812, the city hall won lasting recognition as a beautiful combination of French renaissance and American colonial architectural influences.

In 1858 fireworks celebrating completion of the Atlantic Cable started a fire that destroyed the cupola, dome, and much of the second floor. In 1917, during repairs to the roof, sparks from a charcoal burner again set fire to the cupola and required another restoration. By the 1940s, the deterioration of the exterior stonework had reached the point that weak and damaged overhanging masonry posed a threat to pedestrians. To save this civic landmark, New York appropriated $2 million in 1954 for the building's restoration.

To restore its exterior, the old veneer was replaced with stone work similar in appearance but more durable than the original. To secure the new surface, the 15,000 new stones were attached to the old inner wall with bronze anchors. Steel supports replaced deteriorating wooden lintels over the tops of the basement-level windows. The cupola was repaired and given three coats of paint. While the paint was still tacky, the surface was sprayed with pulverized limestone to match the stonework as closely as possible. By restoring its city hall, New York retained a historic landmark that continues to serve as the focal point of the Manhattan Civic Center.

In 1847 Jackson, Mississippi, constructed a city hall in the Greek revival style that was popular in the antebellum South. The building survived a fire that almost destroyed the city during its capture in the Civil War. In 1963 the city began a restoration project that preserved the building's classic beauty while adding 10,000 square feet of floor space on a new fifth story. This was done by lowering the old-fashioned high ceilings and adding steel support beams. A new lighting system, central air conditioning, and new floors were installed; and deteriorating masonry was replaced. The renovation cost $450,000, and Jackson officials believed that preservation of the historic landmark fully justified the commitment of public funds.

Twentieth-century city growth and expansion of municipal services have forced cities to erect larger city halls. For example, in 1871 when Phoenix, Arizona, was a small village of adobe huts, the local government met in a butcher shop; and four years later it moved to a larger adobe building. Phoenix completed its first city hall in 1888, which also housed the territorial government. In 1929 the city erected a City-County Building that presently houses the Phoenix police department and the Maricopa County offices. In the early 1960s, as its population passed a half million, Phoenix built a modern ten-story municipal

City of Philadelphia

Philadelphia's City Hall was the largest public building in the United States after its completion in 1901 and is still the tallest structure in the city.

building that features precast concrete walls and small deep-set window openings reminiscent of early buildings in the Southwest. The Council Chamber occupies a separate one-story round concrete building with rose quartz facing that seats 200 persons. A colorful mural depicting ancient and modern Phoenix decorates the entrance vestibule. In the functional municipal building, the windows for tax and municipal service payments, and the zoning, building inspection, and licenses offices are located on lower floors that are accessible by escalator. Offices that have less frequent contact with the public, such as the water and sewer, engineering, and transportation departments, are located on the upper floors.

To accommodate its rapidly increasing city service requirements, Las Vegas, Nevada, built a complex of buildings devoted to municipal government. This civic center consists of a ten-story tower for the executive and administrative offices with lower structures grouped around it that house the courts, the police department, and the city council chamber. They are connected to the central tower by passageways and corridors. The entire city hall complex contains 341,640 square feet of floor space and cost $9 million to build. Construction began in May 1971, and the building was occupied in June 1973.

Thus, many municipal governments have outgrown their city halls and have created new complexes to provide space for expanding city services. Whether the functions of city governments are housed in modern civic centers or stately city halls, these structures are a source of civic pride and community identity.

Courthouses

There are approximately 25,000 public buildings which house the activities of federal, state, and municipal courts in the United States. While other public functions are often carried out within these structures, their character and form have been predominately influenced by the judicial process. Courthouses are usually monumental buildings which visually convey the majesty of America's common law tradition.

Courthouses of the colonial era differed little in appearance from residences of the period. These structures were usually simple wooden buildings, and the offices for judges and clerks were provided nearby. But during the nineteenth century, many distinctive courthouses were constructed in county seats throughout the nation, and no other building type had such a widespread impact on local history. The site and monumentality of county courthouses have made them symbols of the physical and social organization of countless American communities. The county courthouse which housed the judicial and administrative offices for the county was often located on the highest hill or on the town's central square. In their pomp and style, they represented a visual locus surrounded by the region's chief commercial buildings. Because of generations of deferred maintenance, some of these stately structures have been torn down and replaced. Many counties, however, have restored and modernized their historic courthouses because of the identity and cohesion these structures give to their respective communities.

Courthouses built in the early and mid nineteenth century usually reflected the adoption of classical design ideals such as a porticoed front. They usually contained a single courtroom with adjacent rooms for the judge's offices and the jury. In many instances, these structures were two-storied and provided offices for county or municipal officials. Larger courthouses became more common after the Civil War because of the growth of population and the expansion of county and municipal services. These buildings were usually stately and ornate, exhibiting the era's fondness for Renaissance and Romanesque architectural styles. Courthouses constructed after 1900 and for the next forty years returned to a more restrained neoclassic image. The exteriors were usually of smooth stone, and columns were placed along the front.

The United States Supreme Court Building (1935) near the Capitol in Washington, D.C., epitomizes the classic influence on American courthouse architecture. The extraordinary building embodies classic Corinthian design precepts and is finished in white marble from Italy and Spain. Interior features, such as the spiral staircase and the magnificent chamber room, give the building its beauty and solemnity.

By World War I, courts in major cities required larger and more sophisticated buildings to house their functions. Because of the increase in the size and complexity of them, serious problems developed regarding the movement of people within the buildings. In the early courthouses, the courtroom was the building's central feature and little concern was given to auxiliary functions. Gradually, during the 1920s and 1930s, there was a tendency to give the court staff and public officials their own restricted areas, including separate corridors, stairs, and elevators. The movement of prisoners within court buildings was also improved in order to avoid their contact with the public. Whereas in older buildings the different parties involved in trials used common corridors, stairs, and elevators, the new trend was to provide several access routes to the courtrooms to avoid confrontations that might be detrimental to the administration of justice.

Court buildings constructed after World War II have assumed more modern forms and are often indistinguishable from office buildings, schools, and other institutional structures. This trend toward functional anonymity is also characteristic in the interior. Improvements in environmental design and circulation patterns have been accompanied by a corresponding decline in the spatial and visual importance of the courtroom. There tend to be more courtrooms in each courthouse and they are usually smaller. Except for some ceremonial and high courts, they have much lower ceilings than most courtrooms of the past. Furthermore, modern courtrooms are better lighted and better ventilated than in the past, and they tend to be less dramatic in appearance. Most modern courthouses also provide an efficient separation of staff, public, and prisoner traffic by a system of corridors, stairs, elevators, and entrance doors.

The Sedgwick County Courthouse, completed in Wichita, Kansas, in 1958, is a prime example of modern courthouse design. The ten-story structure provides an environment for the operation of police, judicial, and other

Sedgwick County Commissioners' Office

The Sedgwick County Courthouse in Wichita, Kansas, provides a functional environment for various public services.

public functions. The first two floors are set aside for offices frequently used by the public—county clerk, tax offices, and the sheriff's department. The county jail extends from the third through the eighth floors on the west side of the building and assumes about a quarter of the building's total volume. The remaining space on the third floor is set aside for commissioners' offices and meeting rooms, but there are two or three courtrooms on the other floors. Thus, on five of the six floors, the jail is adjacent to the courtrooms. The building, therefore, has three zones—public, staff, and prisoners—each with its own clearly delineated traffic system.

In recent decades, America's overburdened courtroom dockets have dictated pronounced changes in the design of the nation's courthouses. The former emphasis on monumentality and architectural prominence has shifted to functional design. Nonetheless, many of these new structures continue to express the dignity and stateliness that have always been reflected in the public buildings which house the administration of justice.

Postal Buildings

In 1639 the Massachusetts General Court designated Richard Fairbanks' tavern in Boston as the colony's repository for incoming and outgoing overseas mail, thereby establishing the first post office in the colonies. Other colonies located their post offices at taverns, inns, or coffeehouses because they were the centers of colonial community life. Postal service developed slowly, and Benjamin Franklin's work as postmaster general in the mid eighteenth century provided faster and more efficient service and extended postal service from Maine to Florida.

On July 26, 1775, the Second Continental Congress established the post office to provide communication among the colonies during the Revolution. The post office was the only agency to remain intact after the Articles of Confederation was replaced by the Constitution. In 1785 the post office made the first of many contributions to improve national transportation when it began using stagecoaches on heavily used postal routes. The newly established federal government viewed the post office as its means of conveying knowledge of its laws and proceedings to all parts of the country and devoted postal revenues to expanding services to scattered settlements on the frontier.

Between 1789 and 1849, the number of post offices expanded from seventy-five to 16,749. Postal mail contracts contributed to the development of steamboats, and in 1835 the post office signed the first railroad mail contracts. Public demands for fast, continuous postal service caused the railroads to begin running trains at night which aided the growth of passenger service.

In 1847 the post office began a period of innovation in mail handling with the introduction of postage stamps. In the 1850s, it added registered mail and street letter boxes to its services and began requiring prepayment of postage. The growth of the United States after the Civil War stimulated more postal improvements including free urban delivery, uniform rates for domestic letters, and postal money orders. The urban delivery service fostered the use of mail boxes or door slots in city homes, the building of sidewalks, and the installation of cross walks, street lights, and signs.

In 1896 rural areas began receiving free mail deliveries. Rural free delivery created a demand for better transportation, and local governments began increasing outlays for road improvements. In 1912 the parcel post system was established and brought rural residents into the mainstream of American economic and intellectual life with deliveries of newspapers, magazines, catalogs, and merchandise. In 1911 the post office began experimenting with airmail service, which subsequently aided the development of a new form of transportation. Postal requirements and subsidies stimulated airport construction and installation of safety devices in aircraft and at airfields.

To provide postal services for the expanding population, the post office built structures for receiving, processing, and distributing mail. For the smallest communities, a special counter in the general store served as the post office. In larger villages and towns, a separate postal building was constructed with a public service counter, workroom for mail processing, and loading dock. Urban post offices handling volumes of mail required large buildings with extensive workrooms, offices, employee facilities, loading platforms, and windows or counters to serve the public. Urban post offices often shared space in large federal buildings with courts and the branch offices of federal agencies.

City post offices were usually located adjacent to the railroad tracks. More recently, truck loading areas covered by a marquee to protect the mail from inclement weather have been constructed. In the early twentieth century, most post offices had service windows that separated the public area from the workroom. Recently, more open counters have been installed that have separate areas for stamp sales, parcel post, and money orders.

The annual per capita mail volume increased from 211 pieces in 1940 to 429 pieces in 1974. Particularly heavy increases occurred in periodicals, advertising, and business letters; while personal correspondence, including postal cards, declined to 14 percent of total mail volume. In spite of these developments, Congress failed to provide adequate funding for capital improvements. By 1970, 95 percent of the large urban post offices that handled most of the mail had been built before 1940. Postal efficiency was compromised by inadequate dock space, poor layout, crowded and noisy work areas, and poor lighting, heating, and cooling. By 1970, 11,000 of more than 32,000 post offices were badly deteriorated and 90 percent of the mail was still sorted by hand.

Inadequate facilities were only part of a growing problem of postal inefficiency resulting from political control of the postal operations. In response to demands for reform, on August 12, 1970, Congress enacted the Postal Reorganization Act. This law created the United States Postal Service as an independent agency within the executive branch, but under the direction of a bipartisan Board of Governors. It also changed the traditional postal policy of deficit spending to a policy of self-sufficiency in which all categories of mail paid the costs directly traceable to their handling. The law also authorized the Postal Service to borrow up to $10 billion from the general public to finance postal building and mechanization.

In the four years after reorganization, the Postal Service allocated over $2 billion for construction and modernization that added 16 million square feet of space to its facilities. By 1975 half of the mail was processed in post offices with facilities for machine sorting. Advancements in mail processing technology include conveyor belt systems that move mail through mechanized operations. Incoming mail is dumped into conveyors that funnel it into an edger/feeder that sorts mail by envelope size. The mail is then fed into a facer/canceller that stacks letters face up, cancels the stamps, and postmarks the envelopes. Next a letter sorting machine, capable of processing 30,000 letters an hour, channels the mail into over 200 destination bins.

On October 20, 1960, the first post office specially built to house new processing machines opened in Providence, Rhode Island. The Providence center revealed that to be cost effective these mechanized centers must handle a large mail volume. Consequently, automated post offices were designed to serve several communities. A typical example was the postal center opened in 1970 at Riverdale, Maryland, to process mail for post offices in the Washington, D.C. suburbs.

U.S. Postal Service

Sorting machines enable the Postal Service to efficiently handle growing mail volumes.

These new sectional centers have been built outside of congested downtown areas where transportation of mail to and from the older post offices had often been difficult. The Postal Service is building twelve bulk facilities and twenty-one auxiliary facilities to handle mechanically newspapers and magazines, advertising, and packages. Five of these automated plants were in operation by 1974, and the rest were expected to be in place by 1976. The Postal Service plans to spend $5 billion in the last half of the 1970s for construction and modernization.

In the past 200 years, the United States mail system has grown from a handful of small post offices into one of the world's biggest businesses. The Postal Service handled 90 billion pieces of mail in 1974, which was almost half of the world's mail and included 1.2 pieces of mail each day for every person in the nation. It employs 750,000 people with an annual payroll of $8.1 billion. The service operates a fleet of 227,600 vehicles, and it annually spends $770 million for air, rail, and highway transportation. Almost 90 percent of the 32,000 buildings maintained by the Postal Service are leased. As a result of reorganization, the Postal Service is upgrading its ability to provide the nation with an efficient, dependable mail service.

Medical Facilities

Veterans hospitals represent the earliest participation of the federal government in providing medical facilities. The tradition of public responsibility for the care of disabled servicemen dates from America's colonial era. The first veterans program was enacted in 1636 by Plymouth Colony during a conflict with the Pequot Indians. The law provided that "if any man shalbee sent forth as a souldier and shall return maimed hee shalbee maintained competently by the Collonil during his life." During the seventeenth and eighteenth centuries, other colonies adopted similar programs; and by the outbreak of the American Revolution, the concept of veterans benefits was firmly established. The Second Continental Congress passed a pension law for disabled veterans in August 1776. In September 1789, the first pension bill approved under the Constitution was signed into law. Since that time, the veterans program has broadened to include facilities which offer medical care and hospitalization for men and women who served in the armed forces.

Medical care for veterans was inaugurated by a 1798 law which provided relief for sick and disabled seamen. In 1801 a temporary marine hospital was opened in a converted building at Norfolk, Virginia. Three years later, a new hospital was completed at Charlestown, Massachusetts, which later became the Boston Marine Hospital. Construction of marine hospitals continued during the nineteenth century, and these facilities offered care to all sailors, including merchant seamen. In 1826 the navy purchased a tract of land near Philadelphia to build a naval asylum. This handsome gray stone classical structure opened in 1833.

Bills were introduced in Congress in 1828 and 1841 to found an army asylum but they were unsuccessful. Interest in veterans hospitals subsequently lapsed until after the close of the Mexican War. Then, in March 1851, an act was passed to establish a "Military Asylum for former soldiers of the Army." It was financed by $100,000 in surplus military funds offered by General Winfield Scott and $500,000 appropriated in 1847 to aid returning Mexican War veterans. In addition to a main Washington, D.C. facility (the present Soldiers and Airmen's Home), three temporary branches opened at New Orleans, Louisiana; East Pascagoula, Mississippi; and Harrodsburg, Kentucky.

The tragic human consequences of the Civil War accelerated the construction of facilities for disabled veterans. The findings of the United States Sanitary Commission, established in 1861 to study the medical needs of the Union Army, aroused concern over the need for veterans care. In 1865 Congress authorized a veterans hospital construction program called the National Home for Disabled Volunteer Soldiers (NHDVS). In October 1866, the first patient was admitted to the Eastern Branch (NHDVS homes were referred to as branches), a former hotel purchased by the government at Togas Springs, Maine. A year later the Central Branch opened near Dayton, Ohio, where the patients were temporarily housed in a farmhouse, barn, and log cabins, while permanent brick and stone buildings were being erected. Homes were also opened near Milwaukee, Wisconsin; Hampton, Virginia; Leavenworth, Kansas; Los Angeles, California; Marion, Indiana; and Danville, Illinois.

The NHDVS board of managers established a policy of locating homes in suburban settings. Each facility was a complete community where veterans were cared for amidst landscaped grounds and attractive, comfortable buildings. At Milwaukee the patients could enjoy the home's bowling alley, billiard room, and 2,000-book library. The inmates also periodically gave public concerts and dramatic performances and spent their leisure hours playing croquet, chess, and backgammon.

At least twenty-eight state homes for Union soldiers were built before 1900, some of which provided care for veterans' widows and orphans. In the South, fourteen state homes were established for Confederate veterans. During the Spanish-American War and the Philippine Insurrection, disabled veterans were treated in army and navy hospitals. Those who required prolonged hospitalization were transferred to state veterans' facilities or were cared for at army expense in civilian hospitals near their homes. In January 1901, all disabled veterans of the Spanish-American War and former conflicts became eligible for NHVDS facilities. The only federal construction for veterans from 1898 to 1914 were two NHVDS branches at Mountain Home, Tennessee, and Hot Springs, South Dakota, to meet the needs of aging Civil War veterans.

Obtaining care for the majority of World War I disabled veterans was initially the responsibility of the Bureau of War Risk Insurance (BWRI). Founded in 1914 to provide war risk insurance for neutral American merchant ships, the agency later became responsible for administering a broad range of services including payment of allowances to families of servicemen and providing medical and surgical treatment for veterans with service-connected disabilities. In 1921 Congress founded the Veterans Bureau to consolidate the activities of BWRI and other federal agencies providing care. The agency contracted with private and public hospitals, leased and operated former military facilities, and in some cases converted vacant public buildings to medical use. During the 1920s, the Veterans Bureau opened twenty-five new hospitals and acquired fifty-seven veterans' hospitals that had been opened during World War I by the Public Health Service.

In July 1930, President Herbert Hoover formed the Veterans Administration (VA) by consolidating the functions of the Veterans Bureau, Pension Bureau, and the NHVDS. From 1930 to 1941, VA opened thirty-four new hospitals and combined hospital-domiciliary facilities. There were also temporary openings and closings and replacement construction at existing sites. Until after World War II, the VA's general medical and surgical hospitals were located near large population centers, although rural locations were preferred for centers offering neuro-psychiatric and tuberculosis care. By December 1941, VA was administering ninety-one hospitals and combined hospital-domiciliary facilities.

The VA's planning and construction was drastically curtailed during World War II because of other priorities for personnel and materials. From 1945 to 1948, part of the demand for veterans care facilities was met by transferring armed service hospitals to VA. In addition, a modest new construction program was undertaken. These efforts added 11,000 new beds, yet VA facilities were taxed beyond their limits. To meet this need, Congress approved construction programs in 1947 and 1948 to add 152,000 new hospital beds (a 16,000 bed cut was later made). Although the VA design staff was substantially expanded,

Veterans Administration

The local Spanish Pueblo architectural style was adopted for the main building of the Veterans Administration Hospital in Albuquerque, New Mexico.

the Army Corps of Engineers undertook the major portion of this building program, including the supervision of design and construction. Eighty-four new facilities were built at a cost of $832 million. Twenty-four hospitals built between 1951 and 1974 have added 16,000 beds to the VA's inventory. In addition to these major construction programs, VA has renovated older facilities in order to modernize and improve the quality of medical care.

Advances in medical research and treatment have required new construction standards. Intensive care units give concentrated attention to patients following major surgery or injury, to critically ill medical patients, and to patients who have suffered acute heart attacks. The three basic principles involved in these units are concentration of personnel, continuous visual observation from a strategically located Life Surveillance Center, and monitoring major physiological functions at the bedside and life center. Provisions are also made for prevention of bacterial cross-contamination of patients. Resuscitation and inhalation therapy equipment is available if a life-threatening emergency arises.

Spinal Cord Injury Centers provide specialized training, treatment, and rehabilitation for paraplegic and quadriplegic veterans. The facilities are designed to offer wheelchair mobility and specialized training facilities for bowel and bladder rehabilitation and care. Equipment such as swivel bars, loop lifts, and special beds are necessary assists.

The VA has eliminated many psychiatric hospitals in favor of more general hospitals with facilities for treating psychiatric patients. These hospitals are located in urban and suburban sites, close to medical and educational centers. This conversion began with the inclusion of such facilities in most larger post-World War II general medical and surgical hospitals. Dramatic successes in treating mental patients with drugs has reduced the need for exclusive psychiatric hospitals. Since 1945 seven formerly exclusively psychiatric hospitals have been converted to general hospitals. Facilities which care for long-term patients provide bowling alleys and swimming pools for recreational therapy.

Chemotherapy treatment (which VA research helped develop) for patients with tuberculosis has made it possible to eliminate the twenty-one tuberculosis hospitals the agency once operated. Thirteen were converted to general hospitals and eight were closed and their patients moved to modern, better located general hospitals.

Research and innovation are an integral part of the VA construction program. Over the years, improvements have occurred in the design of nursing units and hospitals to achieve optimum efficiency within the limits of space, available funds, and the type of facilities required. During the 1960s and into the 1970s, rapid advances in medical research and treatment methods required hospitals that were more complex and intricate to construct. This made some relatively new hospitals obsolete and presented unusual problems for hospital designers. The demand grew for facilities that could be altered to meet changing requirements for medical research and treatment.

Through its VA Hospital Building System (VAHBS) research program, the agency has achieved better cost control and has reduced the time required for hospital design and construction. New and renovated VA facilities are easier and more economical to operate and maintain and can be remodeled to meet changing medical requirements. One new feature employed to achieve adaptability is the use of "interstitial space" between functional hospital floors to house utilities, service lines, and equipment. As a result, all utilities are readily accessible for maintenance and modification. The VAHBS has also developed modular designs with common characteristics which permit their incorporation in hospitals of widely different size, medical program, and appearance. The VA's architects and engineers developed for medical researchers a plan to provide changeable room configurations and functions at a reasonable cost. Basic 10- by 20-foot modules can be divided or expanded into larger areas to meet different laboratory requirements. Laboratory technicians are able to completely disassemble and rebuild partitions and change the locations of shelves, cabinets, benches, and sinks.

In addition to their many other contributions to medical research and human care, VA facilities have a beneficial impact on surrounding communities where they are located. In recent years, VA has encouraged employees to cooperate with medical programs of federal, state, and local governments in their respective communities. Even before the recent sharing of medical and educational facilities, most VA units have trained doctors, nurses, medical, paramedical, and other hospital service personnel. In addition to offering a complete range of medical care and related services, VA hospitals provide emergency medical care in case of accident or community disaster. Many veterans' hospitals offer an open space and attractively landscaped area within an urban environment. In addition, a number have space for community activities including recreational and playing fields as well as meeting rooms for approved community projects.

Federal and other public funds have also helped provide medical care for general patients. The general hospital is the most common type of hospital and offers basic services in medicine, surgery, and obstetrics. There are also many hospitals which offer specialized care such as pediatrics, obstetrics and gynecology, orthopedic surgery, cancer, venereal disease, and mental disorders. Hospitals are owned by corporations, churches, nonprofit organizations, and are also financed and operated by federal, state, and local governmental agencies.

Early hospitals were generally established to care for the indigent and protect the community from communicable disease by isolating the afflicted. Because of primitive medical knowledge and the lack of sterile surgical techniques, mortality rates were so high that hospitals were generally regarded as way stations to the grave. Churches had a particularly large role in early hospitals which functioned primarily to make patients comfortable and minister to their souls while they awaited the inevitable. In early hospitals, the ill were isolated from the outside public but were not segregated from one another by the nature of their ailments. It was not until the development of bacteriology and efficient life saving aseptic surgery in the nineteenth century that hospitals became important institutions.

The first successful American effort to establish a general hospital occurred in 1751 with the opening of the Pennsylvania Hospital in Philadelphia. The country's second oldest hospital—the New York Hospital—opened in 1791. Nevertheless, American hospital development was slow. By 1825 New York had obtained two additional ones, and general hospitals had also been established in Boston, Baltimore, Cincinnati, and Savannah. During the nineteenth century, medical care facilities expanded rapidly as the country became more urbanized.

The hospitals established in the eighteenth and nineteenth centuries were constructed and run by proprietary groups and church and other nonprofit organizations. This form of ownership remains the predominant characteristic of United States medical facilities. However, of the 8,297 United States hospitals functioning in 1974, 3,180 were owned by federal, state, and local governmental agencies.

Hospitals of the late nineteenth century were ornately designed and reflected the more elegant tastes of the Victorian era. Pillars, pediments, domes, and turrets were common features of such hospitals as the old Garfield Memorial Hospital, which operated in Washington, D.C., until 1958 and Baltimore's Johns Hopkins Hospital. In recent decades, however, hospital design has become more simple and functional. Rapidly rising costs in medical care have been a major factor in seeking savings through simplicity of design and construction. Technological progress and hospital experience have brought vast improvements in safety features and floor plan design. The modern hospital has sound-proofing features and environmental controls. Modern fireproof construction and protection against smoke have removed objections to multistory hospitals. In modern facilities, floors of operating rooms are grounded to prevent dangerous discharges of electricity where flammable anesthetics are used. These safety features have led to construction of the large, single-building hospitals rather than the older, multiunit facilities.

Interior design is especially important for

the smooth, safe functioning of a hospital. To minimize patient travel, related services are usually located in close proximity. For example, hospitals often have admissions, emergency room, and x-ray facilities on the ground level, surgical suites and rooms for surgery patients on one floor, and delivery rooms and other maternity services on another. Yet in spite of careful planning, rapid advances in medical technology and patient care tend to make many hospitals outdated within a relatively few years. The trend toward private and semi-private facilities has made many old public hospital wards undesirable by comparison. Recent developments in the field of radiology, such as for cancer treatment, have limited the offerings of hospitals which lack underground, lead-shielded radiation rooms. Modern hospital floor plans offer obstetrical areas designed so that fathers have access to labor and recovery rooms without passing the sterile delivery areas and risking contamination. Surgical suites are designed to keep the sterile areas away from entrance doors, to channel the direction of air flow within the suite from the cleaner to less clean areas, and to allow for the safe removal of contaminated materials.

The federal government has played a major role in the post-World War II improvement of hospital and health care facilities. The 1946 Hill-Burton Act authorized the federal government to aid localities by providing a federal share of up to two thirds of hospital construction costs. The purpose of the act was to stimulate projects where financial help was required. The percentage of federal funding was based on the degree of need for the project. With the help of these funds, the United States has experienced a spiraling growth of hospital facilities since World War II. In 1945, $122 million was spent nationwide for public and private medical care construction. By 1974 the yearly total had climbed to $4.5 billion, about one fourth of which was public funds. Health is the third largest industry in the United States, ranking only behind agriculture and construction. In 1974, 4.5 million people worked in America's health facilities.

Because of the modernization and expansion of hospital facilities in recent years, the cost of care has risen greatly. From 1950 to 1975, the cost per patient day in non-federal, short-term general hospitals rose from $15 to $65. Whereas many industries have been able to lower per unit operating costs through technological advances and increased output, hospital costs have continued to soar. The high quality medical care made possible by the diagnostic and treatment facilities means added costs not only for these facilities but also for the increased per patient hospital staffing required to offer these modern services. The average number of employees per hospital patient has increased from 1.8 in 1950 to 3.1 in 1972. Thus, as a general rule, the larger the hospital, the more expensive the facilities.

Community hospitals are expensive to build and to operate. To help cope with high hospital costs, administrators have coordinated the planning of services that each hospital will offer. In one large city, for example, there were seventeen open heart surgery units. Expert observers concluded that for quality care and economy of operation, four units would be sufficient. While the tremendous rate of progress in medical treatment makes effective hospital planning difficult, nonetheless, spiraling cost increases in medical care facilities have caused hospitals to coordinate the joint planning of medical services wherever possible.

Libraries

During the colonial era, American libraries consisted of small private collections or the books owned by Harvard and other early colleges. Attempts to establish public libraries at Boston, Massachusetts (1656), and New Haven, Connecticut (1659), from the bequests of prominent citizens were short-lived failures. The former was destroyed by fire, and the latter aroused so little interest that it was sold to a minister in 1689. After 1700 some churches provided small collections of religious works for public use, but few Americans had access to books.

In the eighteenth century, establishment of subscription libraries was the most successful attempt to make books available to a general reading public. Benjamin Franklin founded the first such library at Philadelphia in 1731. Following a pattern already popular in England, Franklin and a small group of friends formed the Philadelphia Library Company. About fifty members paid two pounds each to join and ten shillings in annual dues. Franklin played a major role in selecting and obtaining the books from England. They at first were kept in a member's home, but in 1740 they were moved to the Pennsylvania State House which later became Independence Hall. The success of this first colonial subscription library prompted the formation of others. During the Revolution and Constitutional Convention, the Philadelphia Library Company made its books available to the founding fathers. Thus, the collection briefly served as the national library of the infant nation.

From the time of the Revolution to about 1850, many readers were served by the social library, which adopted the general form of the subscription library. The social library often catered to individuals with very specialized rather than general reading tastes. After 1800 it spread from eastern cities to smaller towns, the West, and, to a lesser degree, into the South. The collections were housed in a member's home or office, in a public building, or, in the case of larger collections, in a separate building. Other notable library services were provided by businesses for the improvement of their employees and by organizations such as temperance societies which stressed the moral uplifting of the populace.

The Peterborough (New Hampshire) Public Library is usually regarded as the pioneer in public library service. In 1832 the town decided to use a part of the State Literary Fund, usually applied to the support of schools, for the purchase of books for a free public library. Other donations increased the book collection, which was maintained in a store that housed the post office. By 1837 the collection contained 465 volumes on religion, history, and biography.

The public library movement took hold at mid century when several New England states (beginning with New Hampshire in 1849) passed laws authorizing towns to appropriate money for the establishment and maintenance of public libraries. The first

large one was opened in Boston in 1854. By 1877 it contained nearly 30,000 volumes and was circulating over a million volumes per year. In 1866 Samuel Tilden left the bulk of his estate, including his personal library of about 20,000 volumes, to enable New York City to build a free public library. The initial lack of a library structure was remedied in 1901 when Andrew Carnegie donated $5 million for the erection of sixty-five branch libraries. In 1911 the famous central library building known as the New York Public Library was opened. This reference library is recognized as one of the world's finest research institutions.

The greatest expansion in American public libraries resulted from the generous aid of Carnegie, who by 1920 provided financial aid for 2,500 library buildings in the United States, Canada, and Great Britain. Regionally, the West and particularly the South lagged behind the East in establishing public library services. The development of public libraries in the South came largely after 1900, and many offered services only to white readers. As late as 1947, only 188 of 597 southern public libraries were open to Negroes. This unfortunate situation changed rapidly with the civil rights movement of the 1950s and 1960s.

Public libraries suffered major difficulties during the Depression years. Budgets and services were reduced and some branches were closed. The federal government came to their aid after 1933 through the WPA which made funds available for both staffing and new construction. Through WPA efforts, public library facilities were extended to areas where none had previously existed. By 1939, 3 million additional Americans obtained library service because of these efforts.

Since World War II, there has been special emphasis on expanding library services to rural areas. The 1956 Library Service Act provided federal aid for library extension in rural areas and in towns of less than 10,000 population. This act was amended in 1964 to include matching grants for library construction. From 1965 to 1973, $167 million in federal money was expended for library buildings. This program has since been terminated, although some libraries continue to receive indirect federal support through block grant and revenue sharing programs. Local government bears the greatest share of library construction costs. Of the $82.8 million spent nationwide for public libraries in 1974, $67.4 million represented outlays by county and municipal governments.

Unlike the ornate Greek-temple styling of earlier library buildings, those built in recent years tend to be more rectangular and resemble modern office buildings. Inside, the newer buildings are characterized by bright colored furnishings, open stacks, and audio-visual services which supplement the traditional book collections.

Most states maintain one or more libraries designed to serve governmental agencies and the public. Owing to the large amount of legal materials maintained by these libraries, many states have established separate law libraries. In some of the larger states, state agencies have developed special libraries of their own. Likewise, more than 2,700 libraries serve the executive departments, independent agencies, and the legislative and judicial branches of the federal government. Congress has appropriated funds to acquire the papers of the United States Presidents, which are deposited in the Library of Congress. In addition, Congress has established separate presidential libraries for materials of Herbert Hoover and the presidents who followed him. The federal government has also established three national libraries. The National Library of Medicine, in Bethesda, Maryland, is the world's largest research library in a single scientific and professional field. The National Agricultural Library in Beltsville, Maryland, serves the Department of Agriculture, colleges and universities, and research institutions. The best known of the three is undoubtedly the Library of Congress.

The Library of Congress began in 1800, when Congress appropriated funds for the purchase of books. The library was initially housed in the Capitol but was destroyed in the burning of the Capitol in 1814. The Library of Congress was reconstituted when Congress purchased Thomas Jefferson's private collection of 6,700 volumes, providing a library

Library of Congress

The Main Reading Room of the Library of Congress accommodates 202 researchers.

superior to the one that had burned. It continued to grow through regular congressional appropriations and acquisitions until another fire in 1851 destroyed more than half of the volumes. These losses were quickly replaced, and in ensuing years many valuable collections were added to the library. A major source of books commenced in 1870, when the registration of copyright was placed under the librarian of congress, and two copies of each work printed in the United States came into the library's possession.

The present main building of the Library of Congress was completed in 1897 equipped with the latest facilities then available—well-lighted rooms, steel stacks, and book conveyors. To meet the increasing classification demand, a new system adapted to the needs of the Library of Congress was developed; and, under the "LC system," the entire library was reclassified and cataloged. The Library of Congress card distribution program is one of its most valued services. Any library in the world can order these standardized book listings and incorporate them into their card catalogs. The Library of Congress is the premier public library in the world. In 1975 its collections included 16.7 million books, 31 million manuscripts, 8.5 million photographs, 202,000 motion pictures and slides, 3.5 million maps, 3.4 million music scores, and 609,000 reels of microfilm.

Museums

Throughout the seventeenth and eighteenth centuries, the collection of scientific specimens and works of art became popular in Europe. Frequently, these collections were begun by learned men who were anxious to preserve objects associated with their fields of knowledge. The first public museum was founded in England, when in 1683 the Ashmolean Museum, part of Oxford University's School of Natural History, was opened to the public. During the eighteenth century, many large private collections were transformed into public museums. The world famous British Museum (1759) was established after the government purchased Sir Hans Sloane's extensive holdings, which, under the terms of his will, were to serve for the "benefit of mankind." During the French Revolution, the republican government declared the king's art collection at the Louvre in Paris to be a public museum.

The first American public museum was founded in 1773 in Charleston, South Carolina, where it still exists as the Charleston Museum. At its opening, the public was invited "to procure . . . the natural productions of the country, either animal, vegetable, or mineral . . . together with explanations of the use of the articles in agriculture, commerce or medicine." Before the end of the century, museums were also established in Philadelphia, New York, and Salem, Massachusetts. The first federal museum was founded by Congress in 1790. Named the National Cabinet of Curiosities, this collection was maintained by the Patent Office and included patent models as well as "specimens of compositions . . . fabrics and other manufactures and works of art."

Financial problems beset many of the early museums during the nineteenth century and caused their closure. In their efforts to survive, some institutions turned to various devices to attract greater audiences. For exam-

ple, in 1842 the Philadelphia Museum turned to the showmanship of P. T. Barnum who included performances by trained dogs and ventriloquists as part of the museum's attractions. The same period, however, witnessed the origins of the Smithsonian Institution, which would become the largest museum complex in the United States. The institution was based on the collections of English chemist James Smithson, who in 1829 bequeathed his property to the young republic for the "increase and diffusion of knowledge among men." In 1846 Congress founded the Smithsonian Institution which became the governing body in charge of federally owned museum collections.

In the twentieth century, museum facilities have expanded greatly. Over 70 percent of the 4,800 American museums operating in 1975 were built after 1930. Attendance at the nation's museums is estimated by the American Association of Museums at well over 700 million visits a year. A significant twentieth-century trend has been the tendency to replace the multiple-interest museum with more specialized structures, each having a particular focus such as natural science, science, history, archeology, ethnology, or art. Nevertheless, all modern museums have the same basic functions—collecting, presenting, and preserving noteworthy objects. Modern museums generally allocate about 40 percent of their floor space to public exhibit areas, 40 percent to storage, and 20 percent to office and work space. The latter category includes administrative offices; laboratories; classrooms; reference libraries; and studios for photographers, artisans, restorers, and preparators. These structures have flexible lighting systems, extensive safeguards against fire and theft, and temperature and humidity controls that help preserve the institutions' collections.

The museum's principal contribution to the general public is educational—offering exhibits that reinforce classroom teaching for children and provide new knowledge and insights for adults. In response to shortened work weeks and the availability of more leisure time, many museums have extended their hours and offer classes, lectures, concerts, and films. Checkrooms, lounges, snack bars, and sales desks are usually provided for the comfort and convenience of the visitor.

Until well into the twentieth century, museum design reflected the architectural elegance of the past with styles reminiscent of Greek temples, Gothic churches, and Italian renaissance palaces. Since the 1930s, however, museum architects have stressed functional aspects in museum design. For example, the New York Museum of Modern Art (1939) has a beautiful sleek exterior, but its flexible, partitioned interior enables officials to vary the size of exhibits. In the past decade, traditional American styles have begun to reemerge. History museums, for example, are often located in buildings that reflect or preserve architectural patterns of the past. Many communities are incorporating museums into old buildings to save these historic structures from destruction. For instance, small collections may be housed in former railroad stations, private homes, factories, and municipal buildings. Some older museum buildings are as distinctive as the collections they house. The original Smithsonian Institution building in Washington, D.C., the famous "red castle on the Mall," is one of the most spectacular Gothic revival buildings in America. Built in 1849 of local sandstone, it originally included a museum, lecture hall, art gallery, laboratories, offices, and living quarters for officials. Today, it is the Smithsonian's administrative center.

Private, nonprofit organizations own 57

American Association of Museums

The Los Angeles County Museum of Art is a beautifully designed contemporary structure.

percent of the museums in the United States. Local governments own 19 percent; state governments, 12 percent; the federal government, 7 percent; and proprietary organizations, 5 percent. Since World War II, slightly less than half of the nation's total museum construction has been publicly funded. In spite of increased public expenditures, museums have been hard hit by inflation in recent years. The operational costs of museums is extremely high. Several major art museums, for example, pay over $1 million each year for maintenance and guards. Endowment income has not kept pace with rising costs, large donors are becoming scarce, and museums have been forced to charge admission fees.

Still, it is important to maintain these institutions despite their rising costs. The collections in America's museums illustrate the beauty and variety of nature and preserve creations of man in history, art, and science. These institutions reflect changes in mankind's view of himself and the universe, and they bear witness to the diverse interests, achievements, and attitudes of the world's civilizations.

Theaters

Since ancient times, the evolution of drama has been reflected in changing forms of theater buildings. Recently, these changes have occurred more frequently than in the past, and theater buildings now outlast styles of play production. Therefore, theaters must be able to accommodate several dramatic formats. Modern architectural forms and building engineering have made such flexible theaters possible.

During most of the colonial period, America had no permanent theaters, and dramatic productions took place outdoors or in borrowed or converted buildings. The Southwark Theater, built in Philadelphia in 1766, was the first permanent American theater. Philadelphia's Chestnut Street Theater (1793) is the earliest one of which interior views have survived. The architects copied English theaters and constructed an apron stage 71 feet wide that extended into the auditorium and placed the actors in the midst of the audience. The horseshoe-shaped auditorium seated 2,000 patrons on backless benches.

By the 1820s, every major city in the United States had a theater, and the new theaters accommodated increasingly larger audiences. In 1854 the New York Academy of Music opened with a seating capacity of 4,600. It offered patrons the luxury of upholstered chairs and gas lighting which enhanced the stage production by providing uniform illumination. During the nineteenth century, the romantic attitude in drama demanded elaborate scenery and special effects that stimulated innovations in stage design and equipment. Stage braces were installed that allowed flats to be mounted at any angle, and theaters were built with large lofts above the stage so that entire sets would be rapidly raised and lowered.

Most nineteenth-century theaters were built with a proscenium arch that framed the stage and created a greater distance between the performers and the audience. The proscenium style of theater architecture was suited to plays in which illusion and setting were important to dramatic impact. Proscenium theater usually had an auditorium depth of only 65 feet and seats at wide angles from the center of the stage that offered poor sight lines. High urban land prices limited both the backstage area and the seating arrangements. Patrons sat in steeply raked cantilevered balconies.

In the 1920s and 1930s, German and Russian dramatists experimented with new forms of production that used arena staging and actors planted in the audience to break down barriers between performers and spectators. After World War II, these experiments began to influence theater in the United States. The open or thrust stage represented a return to the stage apron of the Chestnut Street Theater, and it provided a setting in which the actor was a free standing element against a scenic backdrop. With the audience on three sides of the stage, it gave a three-dimensional quality to dramatic productions and increased the number of entrances and exits. Arena stages provided seating on all four sides of the stage and required actors to increase movement to convey the drama to the entire audience. They

APWA Ohio Chapter

The University of Akron's Edwin J. Thomas Performing Arts Hall (1973) features flexible staging, lighting, and acoustical arrangements.

also demanded even greater simplification of scenery than thrust stages, because large flats interfered with sight lines. These developments made scenery more abstract and often limited it to elements of pure design instead of the elaborately detailed realism of romantic sets. Set changes took place in view of the audience and were often integrated into the performance. These new techniques were influenced by revivals of Shakespeare and other dramatists who wrote before the introduction of the proscenium stages and from intimate modern dramas that focused on interpersonal relationships.

In the 1950s and 1960s, resident theater companies developed in many American communities, and large cities built performing arts complexes. In 1959 American colleges presented 4,000 full-length play productions, and 1,500 civic and community theater groups were active in the United States. All of these theaters required facilities that they could adapt to various styles of dramatic production. New mechanical and electrical equipment made it possible to change the configuration of stages. The same auditorium could be used for both popular plays for large audiences and experimental plays that required more intimate settings. Proscenium theaters added forestages or built mechanized orchestra pits that could be raised to form a thrust stage. Most modern theaters feature open stages, flexible seating arrangements, and a total absence of physical barriers within the theater.

Whatever the style of production, theaters have common requirements. They are usually ventilated with special duct linings, noise traps, and resilient mountings to silence the noise from air-conditioning machinery. The scene shop is insulated from the rest of the theater, so that the noise of set building does not interfere with rehearsals. In the backstage area, theaters have space for costume storage, dressing, and makeup. Theaters also need adequate electrical capacity; lights are suspended above the stage and spotlights are located at several places in the ceiling and walls of the auditorium.

The Vivian Beaumont Repertory Theater at New York's Lincoln Center, which opened in 1965, can be adapted to several production styles. It can house both thrust and proscenium productions in its main auditorium, and a smaller auditorium was designed for intimate arena productions. The thrust stage extends 28 feet into the audience and can be removed and replaced by rows of seats for proscenium productions. When the thrust stage is used, the actors can enter or exit through tunnels that open in front of the stage. The mechanical and electrical equipment is carefully concealed to keep the audience's attention focused on the stage.

The Kennedy Center for the Performing Arts in Washington, D.C., is a focal point for America's cultural activity. Completed in 1971, the $70 million structure features a 2,800-seat concert hall, a 2,200-seat opera house, a 1,100-seat main theater, and a 500-seat film theater. These are supported by automobile self-parking underground plazas, great halls including a six-story high grand foyer, restaurants, and galleries. Financed by donations as well as government funds, it is a fitting cultural public works structure for the nation's capital.

Trade and Convention Centers

Several cities have built trade centers which provide a central location for activities relating to international trade. Until the building of the World Trade Center, the international trade community had been scattered throughout the New York City area. Believing a central location for exporters, importers, American and overseas manufacturers, international banks, and transportation lines was needed, in 1962 the states of New York and New Jersey agreed on a sixteen-acre site along the Hudson River in lower Manhattan.

The project consisted of two 110-story towers, the highest in the city, and four low-rise plaza buildings grouped around a five-acre landscaped plaza with a pool and fountain in the center to "become the working symbol of America's leadership in international economic progress for trade." The two towers and two of the plaza buildings were essentially completed by 1973. The United States Bureau of Customs is located in one of the plaza buildings to provide a modern and specially designed customhouse at the center of the complex. The last unit, a hotel for international businessmen and visitors, is scheduled for completion in late 1976. When the $600 million plus complex is finished, 50,000 people will work at the center and 80,000 people are expected to visit it each day. For the tenants of the 9 million square feet of office space, the center provides a 35,000 square-foot shopping mall containing 100 shops, restaurants, and service establishments. Subways and the terminal of the Port Authority of New York's Trans-Hudson rail system are accessible from the mall.

Construction began in 1966, and in December 1970, the North Tower was ready for its first tenants. The South Tower was occupied in 1972. Both rise 1,350 feet above the plaza and provide 40,000 square feet of space on each of 110 floors. The exterior walls of the towers carry the vertical loads and provide column-free interiors except within the elevator service core. This eliminates columns from the office space and provides the tenants with maximum flexibility in office layout. Each tower is divided into three elevator zones. The forty-fourth and seventy-seventh floors serve as skylobbies where passengers transfer from the fifty-five express elevators to local elevators serving particular zones. Elevator shaft requirements are reduced by limiting local runs to one third of the building with three local elevators operating at different levels within a single shaft.

The twin towers of the World Trade Center are the tallest structures in New York City.

American cities have built public auditoriums and meeting facilities to provide for national business and professional meetings, trade fairs, and exhibitions. Since World War II, cities have competed with each other to build larger and more elaborate facilities. A convention center usually consists of large exhibit areas, smaller meeting rooms, restaurants, and other facilities for the use of conventioneers or visitors. Cities often combined the convention center with a performing arts complex or a sports stadium. Frequently, a convention center was a major component of a downtown urban renewal program. New York's Coliseum, Detroit's Cobo Hall, and Phoenix's Convention Center were all partly built to revitalize decaying central city areas. Many cities used modern design techniques and construction methods to create buildings that serve a variety of convention, artistic, and athletic purposes. Modern exhibition facilities are located in cities such as Los Angeles, Las Vegas, Miami Beach, Dallas, Denver, Atlanta, and Milwaukee.

Chicago's McCormick Place is an outstanding modern convention center. The present McCormick Place is a replacement for a building that was largely destroyed by a fire in January 1967. Work began on the new building in May 1968, and it was completed in late 1970 at a cost of $83 million. Architects incorporated remnants of the original structure into the new building. They placed a platform on the same level as the main exhibition floor of the original structure and restored the lower levels that had escaped destruction. On the platform, two new buildings with 50-foot-high glass walls were built. One contains the 302,000 square-foot main exhibition area. The other houses a 4,450-seat theater with full stage and orchestra facilities. Restaurants and meeting rooms flank the theater.

The exhibition building and the theater share a common twenty-acre roof. The roof covers the mall between the two buildings and overhangs them for 75 feet on all four sides to protect both visitors and the loading docks from inclement weather. The level directly below the platform contains a 60,000 square-foot registration lobby, the main entrance for the theater, a 291,000 square-foot secondary exhibition area with its own loading dock facilities, and a vehicular tunnel as well as restaurants and meeting rooms. The lowest level houses the cafeteria and snack bar, the offices and building service facilities, and a tunnel that connects the center with the Soldier Field parking lot. McCormick Place provides a gross floor area of 1.8 million square feet on a 30-acre site. It contains 600,000 square feet of exhibition space, 100,000 square feet of meeting rooms, and 42,000 square feet of restaurants and cafeterias. This functional and elegant structure reflects the commitment of large cities to provide facilities that will attract the trade and convention business that strengthens local economies.

Jails and Prisons

The origins of the county or city jail can be traced to tenth century England, where local jails were established to hold arrested felons until they could be tried. The early English jail was rarely a distinct structure. It was often contained in a castle, tower, or public building. Although the jail keeper was unpaid, the crown-appointed position was highly prized and notably profitable. By selling goods to the inmates, the jailer made a living from the prisoners entrusted to his care.

As in England, early American jails were used to detain individuals awaiting trial. In colonial America, punishment for crimes rarely involved long-term imprisonment. Instead, convicted offenders were sentenced to death, mutilation, whippings, and branding as payment for their debt to society. Near many jails, stocks and pillories were erected where offenders were publicly humiliated by taunts and barraged with stones, rotten vegetables, and fecal matter. In 1642 the Virginia General Assembly authorized the first jail system in America. The act required that persons awaiting trial be retained in jails in their home county. Most of the earliest county jails were simply built structures which resembled dwelling houses. Since taverns were frequently used as courtrooms, the prisoners often awaited trial in a back room. By the late eighteenth and early nineteenth centuries, most states had adopted the county jail system.

The first reform efforts were undertaken by Pennsylvania Quakers. In 1682 that state's jails were replaced by workhouses or houses of detention where imprisonment was substituted for corporal punishment. In 1725 the state adopted a county jail system and vested control of the facilities in a sheriff who often exacted exorbitant fees from his charges. While wealthy inmates lived well, it was not uncommon for poor inmates to die of starvation.

Throughout most of the eighteenth century, American jails provided no differentiation in treatment nor segregation in confinement regardless of the prisoner's age, sex, previous record, or mental condition. The problems of the American jail system mounted considerably as the United States became a populous urban nation. The condition of over-crowded jails in urban areas and nearly empty rural jails became common throughout the country.

Since the majority of the states lacked standards for the physical well-being of jails or their inmates, the conditions in many jails became a national disgrace. In 1930 the Bureau of Prisons was authorized to inspect jails to ascertain if they were suitable for holding persons charged with federal offenses. Less than a third of the three thousand jails inspected were placed on the acceptable list. Pressure mounted to improve facilities and to staff them with competent individuals. In the past four decades, there has been some improvement in inmate care and professional training for jail personnel. There has also been increased emphasis on jail security and inmate well being through limiting the number of prisoners assigned to each cellblock and through separating juveniles from adults. America's recently built jail facilities range in size from structures for as few as two men to institutions designed to house over 3,000, though the average capacity is fifty-six inmates. Costs of new jails vary greatly depending on size, location, and custody requirements. In 1966 per bed construction costs ranged from $888 for a 250-man addition to the county jail in Oklahoma City to $17,000 for a 38-man jail in Manitowoc County, Wisconsin. The need for new jail construction is great. A comprehensive 1970 study revealed that approximately half of the jails in the United States are over fifty years old. At this time, the Federal Jail Inspection Service estimated that one third of America's jails still failed to meet minimum standards for housing federal prisoners.

Whereas jails exist for pretrial confinement or for the containment of minor offenders serving short sentences, prisons generally house felons committed for long-term sentences. Historically, early European prisons were commonly used to coerce payment of debts. These places of confinement were often cages within a fortress or castle or subterranean, dungeon-like enclosures. As early as 500 A.D., persons found guilty of serious offenses were often held in prisons lacking either a door or window, the only entrance being through a vaulted ceiling. The renaissance spirit of the sixteenth century brought some reforms, such as the workhouse, which stressed the rehabilitative value of regular work and the formation of industrious habits.

The studies and writings of John Howard played a leading role in a major reform movement that began in England in the 1780s and spread to America. Howard recorded the wretched conditions he observed—crowded, unsanitary living quarters; poor, inadequate food; general lack of supervision and control over prisoners; shakedowns and assaults as common practice; and corruption of the younger, more naive inmates by ruthless and experienced felons. Until Howard's study was published in 1777, prisons were notably lacking in functional architectural characteristics. Thereafter, distinct styles emerged in response to prevailing penal philosophy and technological progress.

The decreasing cost of iron made its extensive use for bars and doors feasible, thus facilitating the segregation and surveillance of prisoners. These objectives also contributed to a radial design for prisons. By building them in the form of the spokes of a wheel, it became much easier to segregate prisoners and to watch them from a centrally located guard station. Constructed in 1829 on this architectural plan, Philadelphia's Cherry Hill Prison

became the first large prison in the United States. Each cell contained hot water heating, a water tap, and toilet. First floor cells had individual exercise yards. Prisoners remained in their cells during their entire sentence except for serious illness. The architecture and solitary confinement practices of Cherry Hill served as a model for many European and American prisons built during the nineteenth century.

In the second half of the nineteenth century, the characteristic layout for American prisons consisted of a central building containing offices, mess hall, and chapel, usually joined on each side by a multitiered cellblock. The Cherry Hill system of solitary confinement was gradually replaced by penal practices pioneered at the Auburn (New York) Prison—congregate work for prisoners in daytime and solitary confinement in sleeping cells at night. By 1910 nearly all states had built maximum security prisons and very little prison construction occurred during the next two decades.

American prisons constructed during the past forty years have often adopted the telephone pole design. These structures are characterized by a series of cellblocks, service facilities, and shops joined by a long central corridor. Application of the telephone pole

U.S. Bureau of Prisons

The United States Penitentiary at Altanta, Georgia, includes old and modern prison buildings.

plan is exemplified in the state prisons of Minnesota, New Mexico, Ohio, Oregon, Texas, Massachusetts, Connecticut, Oklahoma, and the federal penitentiary at Lewisburg, Pennsylvania.

The modern trend toward limiting the harshness of prison life and the adoption of therapeutic techniques to treat criminal behavior have spawned a wide variety of prison structures. Prisons are classified by three general levels of security: minimum, medium, and maximum. Minimum custody institutions, such as forestry camps, farm camps, and some youth facilities, usually have no fences, walls, or towers. These institutions tend to be small, housing 60 to 300 inmates in dormitories or individual rooms rather than in cells. Medium custody institutions usually have a capacity of 300 to 800. They provide a variety of housing facilities, particularly dormitories and one- or two-man cells. They are surrounded by fences and have guard towers placed at strategic points. Maximum custody institutions are double-fenced or walled facilities with guard towers that furnish very tight security. The cells are of varying sizes. These institutions are usually large (capacities ranging from 500 to 3,000) and are designed for long-term, serious offenders.

In spite of progress which has been made in penal architecture, many prison facilities are overcrowded and provide substandard living conditions. Much work remains to be done if the jail and prison systems are to rehabilitate criminal offenders so that they can become productive members of society.

Stadiums

No permanent stadium facilities existed in the United States prior to 1900. The wooden stands built in the late nineteenth century for professional baseball teams were precarious structures; and in 1902 a stand collapsed in Philadelphia, killing two persons and injuring more than a hundred. The first permanent stadiums were built by the owners of baseball clubs. In 1909 Forbes Field was opened as the home of the Pittsburgh Pirates and during the ensuing two decades ball parks were erected for all the major league teams. These facilities included Ebbets Field (1913), home of the

Brooklyn Dodgers; Wrigley Field (1916), the Chicago Cubs' ball park; and massive Yankee Stadium (1923), probably the most architecturally impressive of the early privately financed stadiums.

While the major league ball parks were erected by baseball club owners, universities and municipalities built giant football stadiums. In 1912 the U-shaped Harvard Stadium was built; two years later, the 70,000 seat Yale Bowl was completed. The Los Angeles Memorial Coliseum was finished in 1923 and later enlarged to accommodate 105,000 spectators for the 1932 Olympics. Philadelphia's Municipal Stadium (now John F. Kennedy Stadium), which seats 102,000, was built in 1926; and Chicago's Soldier Field went up the same year. Many of these mammoth college and municipal stadiums were constructed in the relatively inexpensive single-tiered, bowl shape. For example, the Los Angeles Memorial Coliseum was built for $800,000. Excavation costs were reduced by selecting an abandoned gravel pit as the location for the structure.

During the 1930s and 1940s, there was a lull in stadium construction, but by the late 1950s a need was felt nationwide for updating or replacing old sports facilities. Many of the old baseball parks could not accommodate the growing numbers of fans who attended professional football games. Baseball fans and officials complained about the wide variance in field conditions and dimensions that existed at ball parks. Furthermore, by the late 1950s many older facilities were located in declining neighborhoods and lacked parking spaces for suburban fans. Spectators also objected to the narrow wooden seats, girder posts that obstructed vision, and sloppy field conditions after rainstorms. These factors forced some ball club owners to obtain new facilities or face dwindling attendance and possibly the transfer of their franchise to another city.

Pittsburgh's Three Rivers Stadium and other municipally owned modern stadiums built in the 1960s and 1970s have solved these shortcomings. Three Rivers, for example, is a multitiered circular structure that will accommodate over 50,000 spectators. It is designed to provide good viewing for both football and baseball. The seats are padded and wider than those of older stadiums, and its cantilever design eliminates the need for supporting girders that block the spectator's view of action on the field.

The new generation of stadiums also includes spacious parking facilities and giant scoreboards which instantly project electronic messages and animated images. In the mid 1960s, artificial turf was developed for use in the Astrodome in Houston, Texas. Since then, many stadiums have installed Astroturf or the more recent Tartan Turf to provide excellent playing conditions in spite of inclement weather. The famed Astrodome began a new era in stadium construction when it opened in 1965. This air-conditioned, domed structure

Louisiana Superdome Board of Commissioners

New Orleans' $164 million Superdome is the largest enclosed stadium in the United States.

allows fans to watch the Houston Astros in comfort, free from the city's summer heat and humidity. In 1975 New Orleans completed its enclosed stadium—the $164 million Superdome—and Atlanta had already invested $400,000 for air-conditioning ducts in its new stadium. The great height of modern stadiums (many are as tall as a twelve-story building) allows the lighting system to be installed along the roof contour. The newest lamps, such as those installed at Philadelphia's new Veterans' Stadium, provide 3.5 times more illumination than lighting used in the 1950s.

Due to their great cost, almost all modern stadiums have been publicly financed.

Because these newer facilities are multipurpose and can accommodate several sports, public support has been easily obtained. Nevertheless, some controversy has arisen. Stadium construction costs have climbed rapidly—more than 50 percent between 1960 and 1971. The original cost estimate for Three Rivers Stadium was $28 million, but the structure required $36 million to complete. The 1958 cost estimate for Washington, D.C.'s Robert F. Kennedy Stadium was $8.6 million. In 1960, a month before the construction contract was awarded, the estimate had jumped to $16.6 million, and the project eventually required $19.8 million to finish. In addition, the federal government contributed 160 acres of land and Congress appropriated $2.7 million to provide parking areas, roadways, and landscaping.

Only four of the early twentieth-century ball parks remain standing: Boston's Fenway Park, Chicago's Wrigley Field and White Sox Park, and Detroit's Tiger Stadium. These stately structures and the modern multipurpose stadiums provide citizens with an opportunity to enjoy the spectator sports that have become favorite American pastimes. They instill a sense of community pride and identification and stand as architectural monuments to the American public's sports enthusiasm.

Fire Houses

Until the mid 1800s, fire fighting equipment consisted of water tanks and hand operated pumps mounted on wheels and pulled by volunteer manpower and of equipment for bucket brigades. Gradually, steam-operated pumps, drawn by horses and mounted by career firemen, replaced the volunteers in the cities. The first self-propelled, steam-powered fire engine was used in Cincinnati, Ohio, in 1852. By 1900 steam fire engines were in use in thousands of cities. With the advent of the automobile, fire fighting equipment on trucks evolved to the modern and efficient equipment and facilities of the 1970s.

Traditionally, fire houses have been utilitarian structures that house and service fire fighting equipment and provide living quarters for firemen. In the mid twentieth century and later, the fire houses have been designed that are more symbolic of their protective service to the community and blend well with the architecture of their neighborhoods. The apparatus room forms the main section of the ground floor of every fire house. Modern fire departments include one pumper or engine company and ladder, rescue, or other specialized units. Each company must have reserve apparatus to use in emergencies or when its first line is under repair. Most fire houses contain at least two major fire fighting vehicles. Within the apparatus room, each pumper truck requires a 16- by 32-foot area, and each aerial truck requires a 75-foot-long parking area. The apron or ramp in front of the station is large enough to permit the washing of fire fighting equipment and the maneuvering of vehicles safely into traffic.

Nineteenth-century fire houses had watch towers which were used to locate municipal fires. Modern fire houses have watchrooms containing alarm and communications facilities from which the watchman can alert and dispatch the fire crews. The watchroom is located adjacent to the apparatus room but insulated from outside noise, drafts, and apparatus movement. A glass window provides a view of the apparatus floor and the street in front of the fire house.

To provide lodging for the firemen on duty, the fire houses contain a dormitory, kitchen, and recreation room. Older fire houses had drying towers to dry hoses, but electrical drying equipment has saved fire departments thousands of dollars in construction and maintenance costs in recent years. Fire houses also provide space for classroom instruction and a library. In order to keep apparatus repaired, fire houses have a maintenance shop with facilities for wood and metal working, lifts and hoists, and a paint shop.

Large cities, such as Houston and New York, have built special training centers for their firemen. These centers include both classrooms and practical training areas. The facilities feature an apparatus room where trainees can be shown how to operate various types of fire equipment and areas where fire fighting problems can be simulated. New York's training center includes replicas of loft

buildings, tenement houses, and frame dwellings.

In the past twenty years, several innovations have been made in design and construction. In 1955 Wichita, Kansas, built a one-story fire station with overhead doors at both ends of the apparatus room to speed operations and avoid backing-in the fire equipment. All other rooms were located along either side of the apparatus room making it immediately accessible from every other room in the fire house. The one-story brick structure blended well into its residential surroundings.

In 1960 New Haven, Connecticut, built a new central fire station to house three fire fighting companies and the fire department headquarters. City officials wanted the station to be an attractive gateway to the Wooster Square Neighborhood, one of the city's major redevelopment areas and a symbol of its entire urban renewal effort. Therefore, they built a structure that related well with the new and old buildings surrounding it. The apparatus room occupied the ground level with living quarters on the second level and the department's central offices on the third. A 60-foot hose drying tower added a strong vertical element to the building's design. The structure was built of reinforced concrete which gives it a rugged and forceful character that symbolizes the nature of fire fighting. In southwestern states, fire houses are frequently built with glass-walled apparatus rooms to display the fire engines for the community. In such fire houses, the living quarters and offices were enclosed in brick and placed to the rear of the apparatus room to provide both privacy and shade from intense sunlight. Thus, in addition to housing a vital public service, modern fire houses architecturally enhance their communities.

Municipal Service Centers

Since World War II, many cities have replaced their scattered system of offices, garages, and unsightly barns and tool houses with a single complex of administrative, maintenance, repair, and storage buildings. These new centers coordinate the day-to-day water, sewer, street maintenance, and refuse functions of municipal public works departments.

The results have been impressive. Cities that have adopted this approach have experienced improved materials handling, quicker and easier vehicle servicing, and a general upgrading of community services.

The center of activity in most service complexes is a shop for the repair and maintenance of municipal vehicles and heavy equipment. The spacious, high-ceiling structures have several large doors to facilitate the rapid entrance and exit of trucks and other vehicles that come in for lubrication, tune-up, and major repairs. In some instances, the building is divided into two service areas: one for light vehicles, the other for heavy equipment. Layout and equipment vary from facility to facility, but most have hydraulic lifts, a wheel alignment pit, work benches, and overhead cranes and hoists. The repair shop at Sheboygan, Wisconsin, for example, contains a ten-ton traveling crane that can span the length and width of the shop. Thus, heavy components and even complete vehicles can be easily hoisted and moved to any part of the building.

The wide range of municipal public works activities require separate rooms or work areas for "speciality shops." An important adjunct to the main vehicle maintenance activities are designated rooms for welding, steam cleaning, body and tire repair, carpentry, and painting. Shops are also outfitted for the repair and maintenance of electrical equipment, signs, and parking meters. Adjacent to the shops are the general administrative offices which include the superintendent's office, first aid room, records vault, and conference or class rooms. Although the buildings are functional in design, they also meet the personal needs of all employees. A spacious parking lot is provided, and workers have access to locker rooms and wash and shower areas. Most service centers also have a large, attractive lunchroom which doubles as an assembly room for group meetings. These facilities boost employee morale and increase productivity.

Storage facilities for equipment and materials are another important part of these service centers. Building space is usually set aside for snow plows, spreader bodies, and

Covina Public Works Department

The Covina, California City Yard is walled and landscaped to insure that maintenance work will not disturb nearby residents.

other seasonal equipment that would deteriorate if left outdoors. Outside storage is provided for pipe, electric light poles, wire, transformers, and other items that do not require building protection. Separate bins are sometimes erected to store rock, sand, bituminous mix, and similar road building materials. In northern states, public works departments maintain large inventories of chemicals for ice and snow abatement. For example, the Canton, Ohio service center has two 480-ton-capacity silos which contain salt and calcium chloride. When a winter storm occurs, trucks can be filled at five-minute intervals and dispatched to meet the emergency.

The telecommunications center is vital to the efficient operation of each maintenance center. The complex is covered by a paging system, and speakers are placed in every building. Telephones are also conveniently located to provide prompt communication between shop workers and administrative personnel. A dispatcher coordinates the movements of the radio-equipped public works vehicles. This command post is usually manned twenty-four hours a day and insures rapid responses to emergencies such as disruptions of sewage service and breaks in water, gas, and electrical lines.

In spite of the stress placed on the functional aspects of service center design, the complexes are usually architecturally attractive and compatible with their surroundings. Since new centers are often built near residential neighborhoods, steps are taken to minimize noise and unsightliness. Covina, California's city yard is enclosed by a high decorative wall and bordered by trees and shrubs. These features enable most maintenance work to be undertaken out of sight and earshot of nearby homes.

Construction of service centers has resulted in savings to taxpayers. Because of its rapid growth and diffused urban pattern, Phoenix, Arizona, built four satellite service centers to augment its central garage facility. This measure reduced non-productive travel time to and from jobs. Employees now report to centers located within a defined work district. By placing workers and vehicles nearer the jobs, worker productivity rose and vehicle

expenses fell. Canton, Ohio's new service center, which opened in 1968, increased the productivity of motor vehicle repairmen by 30 to 50 percent. In reflecting on these statistics, Wilbert H. Schultz, Canton's motor vehicle superintendent, offered an observation that is applicable to all the nation's municipal service centers: "We have always felt . . . that if a man is comfortable, works under safe conditions, and has the proper tools and equipment, he will produce a far better day's work."

Thus, even the most utilitarian public structures reflect a dual concern for aesthetics and functions. In the past two centuries, public buildings have become sophisticated public works systems that require the expertise of skilled management and maintenance personnel. Whether their purpose is to house administrative functions, provide vital public services, or offer culture and entertainment, public buildings are structural embodiments of community pride and identity. Federal, state, and local governments strive to create functional buildings that architecturally enhance their surroundings as well as efficiently meet public needs.

SUGGESTED READINGS

American Public Works Association. *Centralized Maintenance of Public Buildings: A Report on the Importance of Adopting Centralized Building Maintenance Programs.* Chicago, 1964.

Banham, Reyner. *The Architecture of the Well-Tempered Environment.* London, 1969.

Burchard, John E. *The Architecture of America: A Social and Cultural History.* Boston, 1961.

Burns, Henry. *Origin and Development of Jails in America.* Carbondale, Illinois, 1971.

Christofano, S. M. "How to Design a Municipal Maintenance Facility." *American City,* 83 (September 1973), 80-85.

Daniel, Hawthorne. *Public Libraries for Everyone: The Growth and Development of Library Services in the United States.* Garden City, New York, 1961.

Fitch, James M. *American Building: The Environmental Forces that Shape It.* 2 vols. Boston, 1972.

Fuller, Wayne E. *The American Mail: Enlarger of the Common Life.* Chicago, 1972.

Gutheim, Frederik A. *One Hundred Years of Architecture in America, 1857-1957.* New York, 1957.

Hamlin, Talbot F. *Benjamin Henry Latrobe.* New York, 1955.

Johnston, Norman B. *The Human Cage: A Brief History of Prison Architecture.* New York, 1973.

Luciano, Michael J. "A Study of the Origin and Development of the General Services Administration as Related to Its Present Operational Role, Direction and Influence." Unpublished doctoral dissertation. New York University, 1968.

Mandell, Muriel. *The 51 Capitols of the USA.* New York, 1965.

Michigan University. Law School. *The American Courthouse: A Planning and Design Guide for Its Future Development.* Ann Arbor, Michigan, 1971.

Mumford, Lewis. *Sticks and Stones: A Study of American Architecture and Civilization.* New York, 1955.

Risley, Mary. *House of Healing: The Story of the Hospital.* Garden City, New York, 1961.

Schwartz, Alvin. *Museums: The Story of America's Treasure Houses.* New York, 1967.

Sexton, Randolph W. *American Public Buildings of Today.* New York, 1931.

Smith, Darrell H. *The Office of the Supervising Architect of the Treasury: Its History, Activities and Organization.* Baltimore, 1923.

Tidworth, Simon. *Theatres: An Architectural and Cultural History.* New York, 1973.

U.S. Public Works Administration. *Public Buildings: A Survey of Architecture of Projects Constructed by Federal and Other Government Bodies Between 1933 and 1939 with the Assistance of the PWA.* Washington, D.C., 1939.

Weber, Gustavus A., and Schmeckebier, Lawrence F. *The Veterans Administration: Its History, Activities and Organization.* Washington, D.C., 1934.

Williams, Ralph C. *The U.S. Public Health Service, 1798-1950.* Washington, D.C., 1951.

CHAPTER 15

EDUCATIONAL FACILITIES

In the past 200 years, educational facilities have evolved from crude, one-room, wooden schoolhouses to multipurpose brick and steel campuses that provide comfortable learning environments. Public investments for educational facilities have paralleled the growth of the United States from an agriculturally based group of colonies to the foremost industrial nation on earth. Once an individual's responsibility, education has become a basic right. Virtually every American has access to twelve years of publicly financed schooling and the opportunity to attend college. Public education is the touchstone of American democracy and enables citizens to acquire skills that are essential to personal as well as national development.

Educational facilities are a basic part of every community and require extensive public works efforts in addition to the public buildings and equipment. Streets, water supply, sewers, drains, and waste disposal activities are all involved. Many university campuses are virtually self-contained communities with public services provided by the institutions.

Origins of Public Education

In the colonial era, education was con-

This chapter is based on a special report prepared by the Council of Educational Facility Planners, International and data provided by the Department of Health, Education, and Welfare's Office of Education.

sidered to be a private responsibility. Since few parents had the means to educate their children, only the wealthy received schooling. In the North, students were taught in tuition-supported private and religious schools; while in the South, children were either educated by private tutors or were sent to Europe for schooling. Education for the poor was also privately financed. Some "pauper schools" were established by philanthropic and religious groups, but they inhibited the growth of public education because free schools and pauperism became synonymous.

The Massachusetts Bay Colony established antecedents for publicly financed education. The 1642 Massachusetts Bay Law and the 1647 "Old Deluder Satan Law" required localities to provide reading and writing instruction for all children. Although these laws were not always adhered to, they were a first step to establishing education as a public responsibility. Townships of over fifty households were required to appoint "one in their towne" to teach all children to read and write. Townships of more than 100 households were required to "set up a grammar school, the master thereof being able to instruct youth so far as they may be fitted for the university." Education in colonial Massachusetts was religiously based and prepared students for divinity school.

As families began to move away from the town centers, the single school concept began to change, and district schools were founded.

Each section or district of a township was responsible for maintaining its own school, and township tax revenues were divided equally among the districts. "Moving schools" also developed which involved a single school master moving from district to district to teach students. Under this system, the school session often lasted only two months. Thus, New England colonies established precedents for a tax-supported public school system.

The founding fathers did not directly address education in the Constitution because it was assumed that education was a state responsibility. Some states included provisions for education in their constitutions. Pennsylvania's 1790 constitution supported public education but limited it to schools where "the poor may be taught gratis." The Massachusetts constitution encouraged "spreading the opportunities and advantages of education in the various parts of the country, and among the different orders of the people," and asked "legislatures and magistrates in all future periods of the Commonwealth, to cherish the interests of literature and the sciences, and all the seminaries of them." The western states that were founded in the early 1800s all made provisions for public schooling. The most ambitious plan was adopted in Indiana, which required town school and university education to be "free and open to all."

Nevertheless, education was not universally considered as an individual right nor a governmental responsibility. Opponents argued that it was unfair to take one individual's assets to educate someone else's children. Many property owners having this viewpoint were adamantly opposed to free schools. There was also opposition in rural areas, where residents saw little practical value in public education.

In spite of such opposition, government support for schools developed. Shortly after independence was won, the Continental Congress passed two laws, the 1785 Land Ordinance and the 1787 Northwest Ordinance, that included provisions for education. The 1785 ordinance, which governed the sale of public lands in the Northwest, required that the lands be divided into townships comprising thirty-six sections of 640 acres each. The revenue from one section of every township was used to maintain public schools. The 1787 ordinance reaffirmed government support for education and stated: "Religion, morality, and knowledge being necessary to good government and the happiness of mankind, schools and the means of education shall forever be encouraged."

Although no states produced so dramatic a piece of legislation, a few backed public schooling. By 1784 New York was appropriating money for elementary schools. An 1809 Pennsylvania law provided education for poor children, and in 1811 South Carolina passed a law giving $300 to each state school district. In 1825 Ohio passed a law requiring establishment of school districts and county school taxes.

HEW Office of Education

During the early 1800s, pupils attended school in crude one-room schoolhouses.

Before 1830 few local governments supported education. Most states passed legislation that enabled them to levy taxes for schools, but most communities did not take advantage of the opportunity. Since public support was insufficient to provide a free educational system, the parents of students were required to pay for their children's schooling. In some states, this was accomplished through a rate bill, which taxed families on the number of children enrolled in public schools and the number of days of at-

William and Mary College in Williamsburg, Virginia, the second oldest college in the United States, was founded in 1693 and supported by a special tobacco tax.

tendance. Almost all public education funds were spent at either the elementary or college level; secondary education was almost totally private.

Colleges received some aid from public funding. When Harvard was founded in 1636, the General Court of the Massachusetts Bay Colony appropriated 400 pounds for its construction and operations and continued to aid the school financially. William and Mary, which was established in 1693, was supported by a special tobacco tax adopted by the Virginia legislature. Most private colleges founded in the early 1800s received some public funding. In addition to direct aid, states granted colleges land and allowed them to hold lotteries to raise funds. Some state governments also established public institutions. In 1785 Georgia became the first to charter a public college. In 1809 Ohio University and Miami University of Ohio became the prototypes for state universities assisted by the sale of public lands. Thus, the tradition of public support for colleges extends back to the beginnings of the nation.

The school facilities of the pre- and post-Revolutionary War period were usually austere. Children attending a New England "Dame" school usually met in the kitchen of a private home. A fireplace, some stools, and perhaps a table comprised the only furnishings. Sometimes the meeting house, designed essentially as a place of worship, was used as a schoolhouse. Eventually the one-room schoolhouse dominated public education architecture. Constructed of boards or logs, the small, crowded building was poorly lit and lacked proper heat and ventilation. The schools were constructed on the least valuable land available, usually along a road or on the fence line of a field. In the South, school was held in log shacks erected in rocky or abandoned fields. These were known as "old-field" schools and were usually tended by a minister.

The interior of the early schoolhouse was spartan and simple. The teacher taught from a platform at the front of the room, and the students sat in rows on crude benches or desks. Classroom equipment consisted of basic primers, slates, and goose quill pens. The teacher, armed with a pointer (also used as a switch), moved about the room listening to recitation. In winter, heat was supplied by a fireplace or a stove which was usually inadequate for the room. Walls and floors were seldom weatherproof; the roof often leaked; and the building depended upon natural light,

Westmoreland, New Hampshire school interior circa 1820. Early school furnishings included blackboards, the teacher's rostrum, and hard wooden benches.

which was limited by window space and location. Restroom facilities consisted of outhouses at the rear of the building.

An educational movement developed in England by a Quaker schoolmaster, Joseph Lancaster, spread in urban areas in the 1800s. Though a simple system, it allowed a single teacher to work with large numbers of students. The teacher would train older students in the lesson for the day. Each student (monitor) would instruct ten younger students; and each group would then present itself for recitation before the teacher. The Lancasterian method was popular because it provided an inexpensive and apparently functional method of training. The facilities consisted of a single large room with rows of benches facing the teacher's platform. A few such rooms could accommodate as many as 350 students in a single structure. Small siderooms were provided for small group preparation. The system depended upon a high degree of discipline to control the students and keep the groups progressing in an

orderly manner. Lancaster's approach was abandoned as more liberal attitudes toward learning developed.

Private academies provided the major portion of secondary schooling. The regimen at these institutions was strict. Besides teaching arts and sciences, the academies sought to instill in the minds of pupils "moral and Christian principles and form in them habits of virtue and the love of piety." The campus atmosphere that characterizes modern secondary schools was non-existent in this period. The academy was generally a single building, much like Deerfield Academy in Massachusetts which opened in 1799. Deerfield had 269 pupils the first year, who attended school in a two-story brick structure surmounted by a cupola. Ten years later, a third story and a wing were added to the original structure which allowed twelve rooms to be fitted for boarding students at a weekly cost of $1.50. Most students roomed at home or in local residences. The building consisted of austerely furnished lecture and recitation rooms and a meeting room or chapel.

Like the academies, colleges generally consisted of a single hall or in some instances a small complex of buildings. Sometimes the halls provided living quarters for students on upper floors and lecture rooms and meeting rooms on lower levels. Because colleges were highly respected and well supported, these buildings were often architecturally impressive. Such famous inidividuals as Christopher Wren (William and Mary) and Thomas Jefferson (University of Virginia) designed structures for the nation's early colleges. Many colleges and universities have managed through renovation and reconstruction to maintain their original buildings.

Education for an Industrial Society

The period from 1830 to 1860 was the "Age of the Common School." Although secondary and higher education also expanded, elementary education became an integral part of the American way of life. While the basis for publicly financed education was laid in the colonial era, only New England was committed to public education by 1830. The middle and southern states had almost no publicly financed educational system. Three major obstacles inhibited the development of free schooling: the granting of public monies to private schools; sectarian religious jealousies; and the equating of public education with pauperism.

During the Jacksonian period of the 1830s, the country was swept by democratic fervor. State and national leaders believed it was essential for the nation to have an educated electorate. States began to fund schools more generously, and in 1837 the federal government dispersed $28 million in surplus revenues to the states for education. Thaddeus Stevens, a supporter of free schools in Pennsylvania, implored the legislature to establish a state system of free schools. He argued it was essential for governments to provide education because "free schools plant the seeds in the desire of knowledge in every mind." In 1834 Pennsylvania passed "An Act to Establish a General System of Education by Common Schools." In 1849 the legislature made local financing of education mandatory rather than discretionary.

To establish control of its education system, Massachusetts established a State Board of Education in 1837 and appointed Horace Mann as its secretary. Although the board had no direct control over schools, it developed an awareness of education in all its aspects—teaching, facilities, and finances. Mann, a tireless worker, is considered the father of the common school. In his eleven years as secretary, he traveled the state, the country, and the world observing educational practices, compiling statistics, and arguing for reform of teaching practices and training. Mann instituted programs for teachers, wrote annual reports on the state of education, and edited the *Common School Journal* a leading educational magazine. Mann's support for common schools was grounded in his belief that: "If one class possesses all the wealth and education, while the residue of society is ignorant and poor, it matters not by what name the relation between them may be called: the latter, in fact and truth, will be servile dependents and subjects of the former."

Other states also established agencies to promote public schooling. Pioneer educator Henry Barnard headed Connecticut's education office. Barnard, like Mann, was deeply interested in the development of education throughout the nation. In 1855 he began publishing the *American Journal of Education*. Barnard wrote the magazine almost

Kalamazoo, Michigan's high school was a typical "stacked building" of the last half of the nineteenth century.

single-handedly and covered virtually every subject relating to education. In the *School Architecture,* Barnard compiled information that became the "bible" for school building construction and established the relationship between architecture and pedagogy. Barnard, an architect by profession, drew up detailed plans for school buildings and recommended proper furnishings, lighting, and ventilation. The relation of learning to environment, a theme which dominates present architectural design, was first recognized by Barnard.

As populations increased and public schools became widespread, buildings were constructed on a larger scale. The graded elementary school and the high school required multiple classrooms, office space, and large meeting rooms. The form which these buildings took was the "stacked building," in effect one-room schools piled atop one another. Unfortunately, this design dominated school building construction for the next century. Even so, these structures were improvements over those of earlier schools. Wood structures gave way to brick and stone, and wooden benches were replaced by desks that accommodated different sizes of pupils. Fire places and pot-bellied stoves were replaced by centralized furnaces that provided even temperatures throughout the buildings. And recreational space became an important consideration in site selection.

Changes in facilities were the result of a transformation in educational philosophy. The educational system which was dominated by religion and strict discipline gave way to a new philosophy that embodied the thinking of Johann Heinrich Pestalozzi. He sought to establish order and social harmony through education and eschewed punishment and intimidation in favor of cooperation between teacher and student. He limited traditional booklearning and drill and stressed equipment and space that would challenge the senses. Thus, children were no longer looked upon as insufferable creatures in need of discipline and training, but they became regarded as developing persons in need of experience and assistance.

As a system of free elementary schools gained strength, reformers turned their atten-

tion to secondary schools. Private academies dominated secondary education by the mid nineteenth century. In 1855, 6,185 academies existed in the United States with an enrollment of 263,000 students. Facilities at academies were little different than those of the public elementary schools. Generally, students lived in private homes, but occasionally academies provided dormitory space. Ironically, they lost prominence because their success spurred the growth of public secondary schools. By 1860 public high schools existed in most of the New England and Middle Atlantic states and were growing rapidly in the West. Cleveland and Columbus, Ohio, for examples, established public high schools in 1846; and by 1853 public schools had totally replaced academies in New York City. The situation in the South was different. There remained a great deal of opposition to free schools, especially in rural areas. Only North Carolina had state-supported secondary schools before the Civil War.

During the antebellum period, financial aid to higher education was dramatically reduced. Georgia, for example, stopped supporting its state university. However, some states created state-financed higher education. Michigan founded the University of Michigan in 1841. In spite of the decline in public support, private colleges grew rapidly. The

HEW Office of Education

One-room elementary schools characterized American rural education well into the twentieth century.

Utah State University in Logan, Utah, is a representative institution founded as a result of the Morrill Act. Established in 1888, it now includes seventy-two buildings on campus and another sixty-six on experimental farms and research facilities in locations throughout the state.

western United States experienced the founding of eleven colleges in Kentucky before 1865, twenty-one in Illinois before 1868, and thirteen in Iowa before 1869. College buildings in the first half of the nineteenth century were usually rectangular, brick structures four or five stories high with one or two square projecting bays or towers containing stairways.

The six decades between the Civil War and World War I were a period of consolidation and expansion in public education. The public high school that was emerging by 1860 became a viable institution by 1917. The kindergarten, which first appeared in 1855, was accepted as part of most school systems. Higher education evolved from small liberal arts colleges to great universities offering training in a large number of fields. Education was improved by the establishment of state departments of education, national study committees, and compulsory attendance laws. Expen-

ditures for elementary and secondary education grew from $69 million in 1870 to $215 million in 1900. This growth was augmented by the 1874 Kalamazoo Case, which established the constitutionality of publicly financed secondary education.

Perhaps the most significant change during this period was the expansion of curriculum. Early schools placed heavy emphasis upon religious instruction and the classical languages. Curricula were gradually expanded to include geography and some arithmetic. In the 1860s, private academies added courses such as modern language, natural science, English literature and composition, and bookkeeping.

Changes in educational philosophy and the needs of a growing nation led to expansion of the secondary school curricula in two other major areas: vocational training and science. The first demonstration of manual training in the United States took place at the 1876 Centennial Exposition in Philadelphia. The concept of technical education was adopted in the American high schools. The first manual arts school was established in St. Louis in 1880; and within the next ten years, schools in major cities were providing classes in woodworking, pattern making, forging, and machine work. Courses in sewing, cooking, and dressmaking were introduced, and by 1900 fourteen cities provided manual training in high schools and elementary schools. A national educational program in agriculture, manual arts, and home economics was firmly founded by 1920. Science made significant progress as a curricular offering in the public schools. The science that was taught in the elementary and secondary schools was "book science." About 1875 the first laboratories appeared in the public schools, and the study of science advanced rapidly in the later decades of the nineteenth century.

Despite advances in elementary and secondary education, the greatest progress was made in higher education. The period from 1860 to 1917 was an era of unprecedented growth for public universities. College education had been essentially private, church-related, and classical in its curriculum. The private university continued to flourish, but the major growth occurred in the development of the public university, open to all graduates of

public secondary schools. The state college movement presented the opportunity for public education from kindergarten through college. The college in this period evolved from purely liberal arts training to developing practical skills. Emphasis was placed upon training in agriculture and engineering to aid states in their economic development.

The 1862 Morrill Act provided the financial impetus for establishing public institutions of higher learning. It authorized the donation of lands to the states and territories for the establishment of colleges that would give instruction in agricultural and technical education. Experimental research stations were developed at the land-grant colleges by the 1887 Hatch Act, and the second Morrill Act passed in 1890 provided annual federal funds for each land-grant institution. The impact of these acts has been tremendous. Sixty-nine colleges created by it still exist; and although this figure represents only 4 percent of the colleges in the United States, land-grant schools account for 20 percent of all college students in the country.

The design of facilities for schools underwent changes in this period. As the population of towns and cities increased, the one-room schoolhouse, with its emphasis upon a single instructor teaching several grades, became outmoded and gave way to the graded

HEW Office of Education

West Denver High School is a typical urban high school of the 1930s.

elementary school. This concept consolidated the activities of one-room schoolhouses into a single building. Instead of having many grade levels in one room with a single teacher, each grade level was assigned a separate room and instructor. Specialization, economy, and ease of operation were the principal arguments advanced for the grade school. Rooms were furnished with desks, slate boards, and other equipment designed for appropriate age levels, and special rooms were built to meet the needs of the expanding curriculum. Even the smallest graded schools usually contained an auditorium or large meeting room and administrative offices. As the movement for science and the manual arts took effect, rooms were provided for technical training and science laboratories. School buildings were also improved by centralized heating, plumbing, and artificial lighting which made the school environment more conducive to learning.

During this period, normal schools were established to give college training to teachers. To oversee the quality of secondary education, accrediting agencies were formed, and state education departments were founded to supervise educational institutions. In short, the educational establishment evolved from a haphazard collection of district and private schools to publicly supported and supervised educational systems.

Development of Universal Education

The twentieth century has been a period of expanding enrollment in the public schools, particularly the secondary schools where enrollment rose from 2.5 million students in 1918 to 14.4 million in 1975. To some degree, this increase is attributed to population growth, but a much more significant reason is the need for a highly educated citizenry. Child labor laws coupled with compulsory attendance effectively decreased the number of school-age children in the labor market and increased enrollment in public schools.

The shift from a predominantly rural to an urban population expanded the schools' role. In pre-industrial, rural America, the school provided literacy and some degree of moral training. In the industrial, urban

HEW Office of Education

The Gordon C. Swift Junior High School of Watertown, Connecticut, is representative of educational facilities built during the 1950s.

culture, the school was asked to foster socialization and to develop technical as well as agricultural skills that would prepare students for the changed society. Therefore, the 1914 Smith-Lever Act authorized federal funds to promote the study of agriculture, and the 1917 Smith-Hughes Act provided for vocational education.

By the 1930s, many existing facilities were inadequate because of age or design. In 1932 there were 245,940 school buildings in the United States. However, 58 percent of those structures were one-room schoolhouses. In addition to the demand for more classrooms, space was needed to improve and expand curriculum. Unfortunately, the demand for facilities occurred in the midst of the Depression, which virtually halted school construction. A 1935 National Education Association study revealed that only 5 percent of the nation's schools had been constructed since 1930, and 40 percent were more than forty years old.

Since the efforts of local and state governments to alleviate the problem of inadequate facilities were often insufficient, the federal government became directly involved in aiding education. The agency that had the greatest effect on education was the Public Works Administration (PWA). Between 1933 and 1937, PWA helped to finance 70 percent of the school construction in the United States. Loans and grants of $300 million were made for education. More than 6,300 building projects created 33,718 additional classrooms with seats for 1.4 million pupils. The agency also funded construction of 2,165 auditoriums,

HEW Office of Education

Modern public schools offer spacious, well-lighted learning environments.

1,720 gymnasiums, 884 libraries, 676 shops, 443 cafeterias, and approximately 6,000 other units including laboratories and study halls.

The following PWA projects are illustrative of the agency's nationwide improvement of school systems. In Lyme, Connecticut, a central public school was constructed to replace five one-room schools which "erected from 92 to 150 years ago, had no sanitary appointments, inadequate lighting and ventilation, no janitor service and were heated by stoves." The new facility was a one-story, four-classroom elementary school building with an auditorium and manual training facilities. In Henderson County, Kentucky, a modern, two-story brick facility replaced ten one-room school houses, only one of which had sanitation facilities. In Carthage, Illinois, a two-story addition to the high school was constructed with a combination gymnasium and auditorium.

The federal government continued to take an active role in primary and secondary as well as higher education. The 1941 Lanham Act provided assistance to schools in communities affected by the federal government's activities and was extended in 1950 to include funds for school construction. The 1945 National School Lunch Act gave school districts surplus agricultural products, and the 1946 George-Barden Act increased aid for vocational education. But the 1944 GI Bill was perhaps the most significant piece of federal legislation for support of higher education. It gave World War II veterans an opportunity to receive a college education by providing funds for tuition and books and living allowances.

In the first half of the twentieth century, the secondary school assumed an expanded role in American education. Traditionally, the basic purpose of the secondary school was to prepare students for college. As compulsory attendance and manual training were introduced, most high school graduates moved directly into the labor market. As a result, vocational education was expanded beyond manual arts training. Courses in woodworking, metalworking, agriculture, and home arts were joined by training in mechanics, business machines, cosmetology, and the graphic arts. By the 1950s, most high schools had fully integrated their vocational and college preparatory curricula.

Expanded enrollments were accompanied by improved educational facilities. In many states, building standards for schools were established. In 1921 a National Council on Schoolhouse Construction was founded to deal with problems of school plant planning and construction. The primary purpose of this professional group was "to promote the establishment of reasonable standards for school buildings and equipment with due regard for economy of expenditure, dignity of design, utility of space, healthful conditions and safety of human life." In 1930 the council published a *Guide for Planning School Plants* which established minimum standards for school buildings. In the 1940s, building standards became a governmental responsibility, and states began maintaining divisions to oversee school construction and maintenance.

School construction reflected changing attitudes toward education. For a century, school buildings had been multistory, box-like structures. In the 1950s, the relationship between students and the environment in which they worked was a major theme in the design of facilities. Consequently, buildings became more attractive and comfortable, and rigid institutional architecture was replaced by campus planning. Schools became single-story clusters of buildings spread out across sites with adequate recreational and athletic facilities. Movable furniture and flexible classroom sizes allowed for the adoption of new programs and the introduction of creative teaching methods. Modern construction techniques enhanced the new educational environments. Steel, brick, and glass were used to create functional buildings pleasing to the eye. Lights were replaced by flourescent lamps with rheostats to regulate lighting conditions. Classroom comfort was improved by ventilation systems that circulated warm or cold air throughout the building. Sanitation facilities were also improved.

Public schools have been supported primarily by local tax revenues, most of which are derived from local property taxes. When this system was devised in the mid nineteenth century, most areas had approximately equal tax bases, but this has changed greatly over the years. Some areas are able to raise much more revenue per levied mill than others, and some school districts must spend more money per pupil due to the specific needs of the students they educate. This has been a continuing problem, and by 1975 twelve states had made provisions to equalize per pupil expenditures.

Inequities in school funds have come under legal scrutiny. In at least nine states, courts have ruled that educational financing systems resulting in large discrepancies in expenditures per pupil violate the equal protection clauses of state constitutions. The first such ruling was the 1971 California decision, *Serrano* v. *Priest*. In the only case to reach the United States Supreme Court, *Rodriguez* v. *San Antonio Independent School District,* the court ruled that education did not represent a "fundamental interest" under the Constitution, but allowed state constitutions and statutes to declare disparities in educational financing unconstitutional. These legal pressures have stimulated an increasing role for state governments in financing local education expenditures through state aid programs based on equalizing formulas.

Because local governments and states could not or did not provide sufficient funds for education, the federal government became a source of financial support. The 1958 National Defense Education Act was a reaction to Russian advances in technology. Federal aid was given to support science, mathematics, foreign language, counseling and guidance, and educational technology. This assistance took the form of grants for school equipment and teacher training. The act was extended in 1964 to include English, history, reading, and geography. The most far-reaching piece of federal legislation was the 1966 Elementary and Secondary Education Act, which attempted to equalize educational opportunities for all students. The act issued grants to states for allocation to school districts with low-income families to upgrade the education of poor students by providing remedial reading, additional counseling, and teacher retraining. Other federal legislation included Head Start, which attempted to support compensatory education for pre-school children; the 1963 Vocational Education Act which financed the construction of vocational schools; and the 1964 Higher Education Facilities Act which gave federal grants to public and private colleges for facility improvements.

Closely aligned with federal assistance to

HEW Office of Education

Clemson University's attractive new library in Clemson, South Carolina, is beautifully landscaped.

public education was the attempt to end discrimination in public school systems. Despite the growth of universal public education, some school systems failed to provide equal educational opportunities. Since the 1954 *Brown* v. *Topeka* decision, the federal government has sought to remove injustices against blacks and other minorities by integrating schools and meeting special educational needs.

As the schools and universities have expanded their curricula and services, special types of facilities have been added to the basic classroom. The library has undergone significant changes in appearance and function. The traditional arrangement of card catalogues, book stacks, and quiet study areas has evolved into a research and media center providing television, microfilm, and audio tapes in addition to books and magazines. The library has become a center where students can seek information in a comfortable, well-furnished environment. In addition, the development of computer services has increased the capacity for data storage and retrieval.

School auditoriums have been transformed at the university level into convocation centers with seating capacities of up to 20,000. At the high school level, the auditorium which generally shared space

with the gymnasium has taken on new dimensions. It serves as a school-wide meeting area; and because of innovative design, it can be divided to provide large or small group instruction areas. The gymnasium, which became part of the educational system because of the influence of European immigrants in the 1800s, has become a separate facility from the auditorium, for their functions are recognized as being unique and distinct. Traditionally, the gymnasium was a basketball court occasionally used for physical education. In recent years, however, interest in athletics and recreation has expanded the gymnasium's uses. The growth of intramural programs and federal attempts to provide equal opportunities for women in physical education have led to athletic facilities that can accommodate a wide range of activities.

In recent years, school systems have stressed total community involvement in education. Schools have expanded community recreation and adult education programs. Community colleges, which are experiencing tremendous growth, enable citizens to acquire two additional years of education at a minimal cost and provide vocational training that is unavailable elsewhere. A new educational concept is just beginning to gain widespread acceptance—community education. Its basic premise is that combining educational and other community services enhances education and saves tax dollars. Some educators believe students have been receiving their education in a vacuum, cut off from the rest of society. The American Association of School Administrators' book, *New Forms for Community Education,* points out that "reconceiving education on an interagency, community-wide basis makes a lot of sense economically in terms of both capital and operational budgeting." The movement is beginning to take hold. Atlanta, Georgia, and Pontiac, Michigan, for examples, have established centers which house schools, several public agencies, and community college programs. The Thomas Jefferson Community Junior High School in Arlington, Virginia, has become a prototype for community planned and developed multiagency facilities. Colleges are training educators to meet this new need.

The availability of universal education has become a fundamental part of the American way of life. The commitment of national resources to education has been enormous. In 1972 there were 1.9 million public elementary and secondary classrooms in the United States having a replacement value of over $150 billion. In that year, 60 million students were enrolled in America's schools, of which 50.8 million were in primary and secondary schools and 9.2 million were in the 3,000 colleges and junior colleges. Eighty-eight percent attended public schools and the

remainder private schools, although nearly all obtained some public assistance. During the next decade, primary and secondary school enrollments are expected to decline about 1.2 percent per year, and college enrollment to increase about 1.3 percent per year.

According to the National Center for Education Statistics, of the total estimated expenditure of $107.5 billion for education in the school year 1974-1975, local government funds supplied 30.3 percent; state funds, 33.4 percent; federal funds, 10.7 percent; and 25.6 percent was provided by tuitions and private funds. Even with the growth of federal aid, most of the money is still supplied by local and state taxes. Of the $87.5 billion expended for public institutions, federal funds accounted for 10.5 percent. Of the $20 billion expended for private institutions, federal funds provided 11.5 percent; state funds, 1.5 percent; and local funds 0.5 percent. Public capital outlays for construction of educational facilities, including rehabilitation and equipment, has averaged about $5 billion per year during the 1970s for primary and secondary schools and about $3.5 billion for institutions of higher learning. This rate is expected to continue.

The United States' public education system, though recently beset with rising costs and some decline in enrollments, strives to provide equal educational opportunities to all citizens. The development of facilities responsive to the educational needs of the public will continue to play an important part in the development of American public works.

HEW Office of Education

This suburban Chicago high school illustrates school architecture of the 1970s.

SUGGESTED READINGS

American Association of School Administrators. *New Forms for Community Education.* New York, 1974.

Binder, Frederick M. *The Age of the Common School, 1830-1865.* New York, 1974.

Cohen, Sheldon S. *A History of Colonial Education, 1607-1776.* New York, 1974.

Educational Facilities Laboratories. *Bricks and Mortarboards.* New York, 1966.

———————— . *The Greening of the High School.* New York, 1973.

Furnas, J. C. *The Americans: A Social History of the United States, 1587-1914.* New York, 1969.

Good, H. G. *A History of American Education.* New York, 1956.

Graham, Patricia Albjerg. *Community and Class in American Education, 1865-1918.* New York, 1974.

Gumbert, Edgar B., and Spring, Joel H. *The Superschool and the Superstate: American Education in the Twentieth Century, 1918-1970.* New York, 1974.

Johnson, Clifton. *Old-Time Schools and School-Books.* New York, 1965.

Klauder, Charles Z., and Wise, Herbert C. *College Architecture in America and Its Part in the Development of the Campus.* New York, 1929.

Rudolph, Frederick. *The American College and University.* New York, 1962.

Sloane, Eric. *The Little Red Schoolhouse.* Garden City, New York, 1972.

U.S. Department of Health, Education, and Welfare. Office of Education. *Projections of Educational Statistics to 1982-83.* Washington, D.C., 1973.

CHAPTER 16

PUBLIC HOUSING

Adequate shelter is one of the basic necessities of life. Yet many persons do not have the means to acquire it. The desire to possess land and own one's home predates the nation itself. And housing statistics, compiled by the federal government since 1890, show that progress has been made toward satisfying the aspirations of those who seek this goal. In 1890, for example, 48 percent of the 12.7 million housing units in the United States were owner-occupied, while 52 percent were renter-occupied. By 1970 the percentages of owner- and renter-occupied units had changed to 63 and 37 respectively, and the total number of occupied units had risen to 63.5 million. Of this total, plus over 4 million units that were unoccupied, 47 million were one-unit dwellings, 19 million were structures with two or more units, and about 2 million were mobile homes or trailers. Publicly constructed housing units constituted approximately 3 percent of the total.

The construction of housing is only one of the many ways that the federal government has assisted its citizens in obtaining adequate living quarters. In fact, the meaning of the term "public housing" has shifted over the years. In the mid 1930s, it meant publically financed, low-cost housing for persons with low incomes. Since that time, a wide variety of programs have been adopted to assist those with low and moderate incomes finance the cost of their housing. In 1970 the federal government provided assistance by guaranteed loans, secondary financing, and direct financing to 431,000 units, 29 percent of the 1.5 million conventionally constructed home starts of that year. A significant number of these units were for moderate, rather than low-income households. The favorable federal tax treatment of home purchasers has been a substantial incentive; and interests costs and local and state taxes on purchased homes have reduced the homeowners' income on which federal income taxes are based.

Estimates from Department of Labor statistics indicate that in 1972 the average annual cost of housing for a four-person urban family was $2,387 for homeowners and $1,566 for renters. These figures represented about 20 percent and 13 percent respectively of the homeowners' and renters' total budget. Comparable figures in 1972 for retired couples, sixty-five years and older, were $1,128 and $1,226 or 22 and 24 percent respectively of the homeowners' and renters' entire budget.

Although income levels vary, in 1972 a family of four with earnings ranging from $4,000 to $8,000 per year was considered a moderate-income household. An annual income of $4,000 or less qualified a four-person

Large portions of this chapter were prepared by Richard McEvoy, APWA Bicentennial History Fellow.

household for low-income housing. According to figures from the Department of Commerce, over 5 million families were below the low-income level in 1972. Included in this number were 2 million families with female heads of households.

While it is generally considered that no one should pay more than 25 percent of his or her income in rent, at least 6 million renter households actually paid more than this amount in 1972. In addition to excessive payments, other housing deficiencies persisted. It was estimated in 1973 that there were over 3 million households that still lacked plumbing facilities and some 4 million households that were living in overcrowded quarters (more than one person per room). Many housing units were also located in undesirable environments. Thus, in 1973 at least 13 million households were "housing-poor" since they were living in dwellings they could not afford, in overcrowded conditions, in unsatisfactory locations, or in units without adequate plumbing.

Although various federal programs have been introduced in recent years to help moderate-income groups obtain better quality housing, the construction of public housing was designed primarily to assist low-income families. Many Americans have not welcomed traditional public housing. They have regarded it as a costly benefit to those who have not been as diligent or thrifty as themselves and as a competitor of private enterprise. During its existence, the federal government's housing program has failed to obtain continuous financial support and to win widespread acceptance by local government officials who often find public housing a liability rather than an asset to their communities. It has alienated both vocal representatives of the poor and spokesmen for the physical and social betterment of urban areas. Yet, despite these negative aspects, public housing is almost the only new housing that has been constructed for those who cannot afford standard housing, especially racial minorities and the elderly.

Housing, whether it be public or private, normally requires substantial financial outlays by governmental agencies. For without adequate public facilities and services, no housing is decent. In 1934 Catherine Bauer, one of the early advocates of public housing wrote:

> Perhaps there was a time when the individual dwelling, in a strictly physical sense, was more or less self contained, when a man was quite free to consider a house his castle, and, if he had a mind to, build a moat around it. Curiously, however, this ideal never made any sort of general headway until after the technical developments of the nineteenth century had rendered it thoroughly impracticable. Today, physically speaking again, a dwelling is little more than a ganglion on a network of interlacing wires and pipes, pavements, school districts, fire districts, shopping districts, transportation lines, and mail delivery lines. If a man were to put a moat around his house today, he would find himself cut off from every comfort and convenience and economy that the past hundred years has produced.

Although contemporary standards for public facilities and services vary widely, public or community overhead for items such as streets and alleys, water supply, sewers and treatment plants, and parks and playgrounds costs thousands of dollars per family housed. Similarly, operating expenses for these facilities and services are large and growing. However, even with these costs, the United States has a good record in building housing for its middle and affluent classes. The efforts of private enterprise account for most of the construction, but government policy has provided assistance and incentives through mortgage guarantees, secondary credit facilities, and favorable tax treatment.

In contrast, the United States' housing record for low-income groups has been less than satisfactory. This is due largely to differing viewpoints on the kind of assistance that should be provided. Some persons insist that public housing is merely an interim program; they argue that once the income level of the poor is raised, whether through employment or a guaranteed annual income, the need for such a program will be removed. Others contend more realistically that, while increased incomes would reduce the need for public housing, there will always be individuals who lack earning capacities and who need aid in obtaining decent housing. Therefore, in the years to come, the question will center on the manner in which public housing assistance is offered to those who need it. Will it be given mainly through the construction of housing by public agencies or through subsidies by which low-income families may rent or buy private housing?

FIGURE 16-1
DECLARATIONS OF HOUSING AND COMMUNITY DEVELOPMENT POLICY IN NATIONAL HOUSING LEGISLATION
Excerpts from major national housing acts, 1937-1974

Declaration of Policy in the United States Housing Act of 1937
It is "The policy of the United States to promote the general welfare of the Nation by employing its funds and credit . . . to assist the several states and their political subdivisions . . . to remedy the nonsafe and unsanitary housing conditions and the acute shortage of decent, safe, and sanitary dwellings for families of low-income. . . ."

Declaration of Policy of the Housing Act of 1949
"The general welfare and security of the Nation and the health and living standards of its people require housing production and related community development sufficient to remedy the serious housing shortage, the elimination of substandard and other inadequate housing through the clearance of slums and blighted areas, and the realization as soon as feasible of the goals of a decent home and suitable living environment, for every American family, thus contributing to the development and redevelopment of communities and to the advancement of the growth, wealth and security of the Nation."

Amendments to the Housing Act of 1954
These amendments broadened the slum clearance and urban renewal programs authorized by the 1949 housing act by providing federal assistance in "preventing the spread of slums and urban blight through the rehabilitation and conservation of blighted and deteriorating areas."

Title I of the Demonstration Cities and Metropolitan Development Act of 1966
This title, which established the model cities program, stated that "improving the quality of urban life is the most critical problem facing the United States" and that in connection with physical renewal programs, it is essential to "provide educational and social services vital to health and welfare."

The Housing and Urban Development Act of 1968
This act established national housing goals by stating that the 1949 goal of "a decent home in a suitable living environment for every American family" can be "substantially achieved within the next decade by the construction or rehabilitation of twenty-six million housing units, six million of these for low- and moderate-income families."

The "Urban Growth and New Community" Title of the Housing and Urban Development Act of 1970
This act established a new "urban growth and new communities" policy by stating that the "rapid growth of urban population and uneven expansion of urban development, together with a decline in farm population, slower growth in urban areas and migration to the cities, has created an unbalance between the Nation's needs and resources . . ." requiring the "Federal Government, consistent with the responsibilities of state and local government and the private sector, to assume responsibility for the development of a national urban growth policy which shall incorporate social, economic and other appropriate factors."

Section 8 of Chapter II of the Housing and Community Development Act of 1974
This act established a new era in public housing by stating "for the purpose of providing a form of low-income housing which will aid in assuring a decent place to live for every citizen, which will take full advantage of vacancies in the private housing market and which will provide economically mixed housing" public housing agencies may house low-income families in private accommodations in accordance with the provisions of this section.

Nineteenth-Century Tenement Housing

During the early national period, most families in the United States provided for their own housing in addition to many of their other needs. But during the nineteenth century, a massive housing problem evolved as urban populations increased from 3 percent of the national population in 1790 to 25 percent in 1870. Early in the century, New York City began housing its large immigrant population in one-family dwellings that had been partitioned into apartments for several families

Congested Hester Street in New York City in 1900. Most of the city's large immigrant population was housed in one-family dwellings divided into apartments for several families.

and in new houses built on every available piece of yard or garden space. When land in a given neighborhood was developed to capacity, overcrowding occurred; whole families sometimes lived out their lives in a single room. In 1834 a New York City building inspector lamented that "we have serious cause to regret that there are in our city so many mercenary landlords who only contrive in what manner they can to stow the greatest number of human beings in the smallest space."

Serious cholera epidemics in New York City during the 1830s and 1840s together with frequent cases of typhoid and other contagious diseases revealed some of the dangers that bad housing posed for city populations. Many tenement residents shared their neighborhoods with slaughterhouses and distilleries which were not required to operate safe and hygenic plants. The lack of adequate water supplies prevented private cleanliness. And city officials often failed to provide proper refuse collection and disposal services; to repair buildings in danger of collapse; or to

establish sanitary standards for privies, cesspools, and sewers.

The New York Association for Improving the Condition of the Poor organized the Workmen's Home Association in the mid 1850s to design and construct a model tenement. It built the "Workmen's Home," a substantial brick structure containing eighty-seven apartments on Mott and Elizabeth streets. But the Workmen's Home Association perpetuated one of the worst evils in New York tenements when it made three of the four rooms in most apartments totally inaccessible to outside light or ventilation. Thus, rather than becoming an example of better housing, it became one of the city's most notorious slum dwellings.

Chicago builders constructed the first "balloon-frame" structure in 1833. Until then, Americans had erected wooden houses as Englishmen had for centuries. They built their homes on a sturdy frame of timbers held together by one beam shaped to fit into the hole of an adjoining beam. Where there was a pull on the joint, the pieces were fastened by a wooden peg. The balloon-frame merely substituted a light frame of two-by-fours nailed together for the heavy frame of timbers joined by pegs. While the term balloon-frame expressed the traditional builders' disdain for the "flimsiness" of such structures, balloon-frame houses actually proved as substantial as older houses in which moisture tended to accumulate in the joints and rot the timbers. But even more important, especially in areas where there was a scarcity of labor, balloon-frame houses could be built quickly by persons with minimum carpentry skills and a few common tools. "To erect a balloon-building," noted writer Solon Robinson, "requires about as much mechanical skill as it does to build a board fence."

Wooden structures were, however, fire hazards. In 1867, 1879, and 1884, New York City enacted laws requiring fire escapes for tenement buildings, light and ventilation in interior rooms, and one water closet for every twenty inhabitants. These laws, which were not always effective, gave the New York City Board of Health too much authority in determining what specific facilities met minimum standards. The laws permitted the board of

National Archives and Records Service

Dumbbell airshaft in a New York City tenement. These airshafts provided little ventilation and light; instead they were often used as receptacles for garbage.

health, for instance, to certify that "dumbbell" tenements provided adequate light and ventilation. Yet a dumbbell tenement (the structure acquired its name from the indentation at its middle) usually stood five or six stories high with fourteen rooms on each floor. Ten of the fourteen rooms opened on an air shaft about 28 inches wide and indented into the side walls of the buildings. These shafts actually provided little light or ventilation. Instead they served as ducts that allowed fire to spread rapidly from one floor to another and as receptacles for garbage and filth. Public halls and stairs were often so dark and narrow that two persons could not easily pass each other.

In the 1880s, Jacob Riis, a Danish immigrant and newspaper reporter, wrote dramatic articles describing the feelings of tenement dwellers toward their surroundings. In 1890 Riis' *How the Other Half Lives,* a vivid account of the degradation of life in the East Side wards of Manhattan, awakened the consciences of middle- and upper-class Americans. As they discovered slums in their own localities as bad as those portrayed by Riis, they demanded the construction of model tenements and stricter enforcement of housing regulations.

Alfred T. White became the most significant builder of model tenements in New York.

In May 1890, he opened the Riverside tenement in Brooklyn with six-story buildings forming three sides of a quadrilateral. The Riverside covered only 50 percent of the lot, leaving the remainder for grass plots with gravel walks and a playground. White built completely fireproof brick buildings with a window in every room. He also furnished each apartment with a private water closet, sink, and washtub. But these model tenements provided better housing for only a small number of New York's tenement dwellers. Most investors with enough capital to construct model dwellings found more profitable ventures; and since the majority of landlords had only enough money to build and operate a few dumbbells, they were unwilling to sacrifice their earnings for the good of the community. A breakthrough finally came in 1901 when New York State enacted a Tenement House Law which prohibited future construction of dumbbell tenements; it required a separate bathroom in each family unit; and it provided more stringent fire protection measures.

Boston, Cincinnati, and Hartford had tenement-house problems similar to those of New York. Boston's tenements were, however, less offensive than New York's because they were lower in height, covered less of the lot, and housed fewer people. The majority of Cincinnati's working people lived in large brick tenements. They resembled New York's tenements except that those in Cincinnati had fewer floors. Hartford copied New York's dumbbells and added them to an assortment of dilapidated wooden and brick houses and converted private dwellings.

Tenements posed serious problems for many nineteenth-century cities; yet cities without tenements had housing problems as well. Chicago contained many overcrowded and dilapidated one- and two-story wooden structures. Frequently, three of these houses occupied a single 25- by 100-foot lot with a three-story house in front and two two-story houses in the rear. While Pittsburgh had a few large wooden tenements, its greater supply of inferior housing included overcrowded one- and two-story houses, cellar dwellings, and wooden shanties on the city's outskirts.

Homestead, a Pittsburgh industrial suburb, erected houses on its alleys as well as on its main streets. In 1907 most Homestead houses had no running water nor inside private toilets. Still, many Homestead families took in lodgers, and sometimes as many as four or five people shared one room. Alley dwellings in Baltimore and Washington, D.C., like those in Pittsburgh, lacked proper water supply and sewer connections. None of these cities had laws regulating occupancy, ventilation, or sanitation.

Low-Cost Housing Experiments

The demand for public housing in the United States began in the early twentieth century when social reformers discovered that building code enforcement did little to improve the housing needs of low-income groups. It merely raised the price of standard housing beyond their ability to pay. Massachusetts was the first state to undertake constructive housing reform. In 1911 the legislature created the Massachusetts Homestead Commission to plan and build low-cost housing developments in rural or suburban surroundings. The legislators believed that by removing working-class families from the cities and providing them with better homes in healthier environments they would be cured of their social ills.

Massachusetts' experimental housing program encountered many difficulties and delays. In early 1917, when the commission requested $100,000 to erect fifty houses costing $2,000 each, the legislature granted it only $50,000. Once construction began in October 1917, the project was crippled almost immediately by rising costs and labor shortages caused by World War I. With only twelve houses completed in Lowell, Massachusetts, the commission discontinued the housing experiment; and the Massachusetts legislature chose not to revive it when the nation returned to peacetime conditions.

Although World War I stifled homebuilding in Massachusetts, the war forced the federal government to experiment with low-cost housing. There was a real shortage of dwellings at reasonable rents for workers in shipyards and munitions plants. The Emergency Fleet Corporation was created to provide housing near shipyards, and the United States Housing Corporation was established to construct homes at other defense installations. Both agencies employed leading architects and planners who were committed to the garden city ideal of British wartime housing programs. They also maintained standards for safe and sanitary housing that exceeded those usually followed by commercial builders. These two wartime agencies completed 15,183 family dwellings and 14,745 accommodations for single persons.

However, these high standards of construction and community planning were not well received by an economy-minded postwar Congress. On July 30, 1919, the House Committee on Public Buildings and Grounds reported favorably on a bill to repeal the wartime housing provisions; it argued that Congress intended them to exist only during the war emergency. In the committee's opinion, "College professors and alleged experts in various lines were called in and placed on the payroll at large salaries and designated as 'town planners,' 'town managers,' etc., ad nauseam and ad absurdam." To insure that the government spent no more of the taxpayers' money for housing or community planning, the committee called for the immediate termination of the war housing program.

Edith Elmer Wood, a leading advocate of government homebuilding for low-income families, saw special interests at work. She observed that "speculative builders and tenement house owners," who saw their investment threatened should workingmen become accustomed to living in a better type of house, were "raising the cry of extravagance and trying to get Congress to call a halt on all unfinished housing projects." Representative George Holden Tinkham of Massachusetts wanted to use war housing programs as models for civilian low-cost housing projects. He, therefore, introduced a bill to create a bureau of housing and living conditions in the Department of Labor. Tinkham envisioned the bureau functioning as both a research agency to study housing conditions and an educational agency to instruct builders in design, construction, town planning, property management, and financing. The House Committee on Public Buildings and Grounds took no action on Tinkham's bill.

During the 1920s, speculative builders constructed nothing in the way of housing for low-income families. A few states experimented with various plans to aid the home-building industry, but only New York State registered any significant accomplishments. In 1926 New York enacted a law providing state aid to private limited-dividend housing corporations to ease the scarcity of low-rent housing, particularly in New York City. Under this program, limited-dividend corporations completed nine projects for 1,700 families. The Amalgamated Clothing Workers of America constructed one of these projects on New York's Lower East Side. The project's buildings were made of light brick and were six stories high. Since they covered only 60 percent of the building site, the tenants were able to enjoy an interior court containing plants, flowers, and fountains. In 1930 the project won a medal from the American Institute of Architects for its simple but dignified architectural style. It was described as one of the best apartment houses in New York.

Homebuilding was one of the industries that declined significantly before the 1929 stock market crash. The industry reached its nadir in 1933 when builders completed only 93,000 housing units. During these years, construction workers accounted for one third of the total number of unemployed workers. Thus, the Depression added the immediate need of finding work for unemployed building tradesmen and laborers to the long-standing need of providing safe and sanitary dwellings for people with low incomes. The two problems stimulated the first political pressure for public housing. New York's Senator Robert F. Wagner led the movement in Congress. In 1931 the National Public Housing Conference was founded to generate popular support and act as a legislative lobby for public housing. President Herbert Hoover's 1931 Conference on Home Building and Home Ownership further dramatized the national complexion of the issue and challenged private enterprise either to provide decent low-income housing or to accept federal intervention in this area.

Beginning of Public Housing

The national housing program for economic recovery began with attempts to expand New York's projects and provide federal loans to limited-dividend housing corporations. In 1932 the Emergency Relief and Construction Act empowered the Reconstruction Finance Corporation (RFC) to make such loans. Only New York's Knickerbocker Village, which received a loan of $8.1 million, actually benefited from this program before it was transferred by the National Industrial Recovery Act (NIRA) to the Public Works Administration (PWA).

When NIRA was passed in 1933, funds were included for slum clearance and low-rent housing to be built by public agencies or by private limited-dividend groups. The public agencies failed because NIRA's emphasis was on economic stability rather than on housing and because the states had not passed enabling legislation authorizing the formation of public bodies capable of accepting responsibility for a public housing program. Efforts in the private sector were also unsuccessful because many limited-dividend groups seized the opportunity to sell unprofitable developments to the federal government. As a result, PWA, which supervised the program, assumed greater responsibility for conducting local housing programs.

The PWA continued to solicit applications from limited-dividend housing corporations. It asked that these corporations build outside congested areas and erect homes that would cover only a portion of the site, reserving the remainder for light, air, and recreation. Some applicants totally misunderstood the purposes of the program and applied for loans to finance hotels, tourist camps, and other commercial developments; while others sought merely to dispose of unprofitable properties at inflated prices. But the PWA Housing Division carefully scrutinized applications to insure that building costs would not drive the rentals higher than the rent-paying ability of low-paid workers. Out of 533 applications,

Neighborhood Gardens in St. Louis, Missouri, was one of the public housing projects that received support from the PWA Housing Division's limited-dividend program.

only seven limited-dividend proposals met the Housing Division's criteria.

Neighborhood Gardens in St. Louis received assistance from the PWA Housing Division's limited-dividend program. The project included nine, three-story fireproof brick buildings that covered 35 percent of a cleared slum area within walking distance of the central business district. The 252 apartments in the project were provided with heat, ice boxes, cooking fuel, and laundry facilities; the tenants were required to purchase their own electricity and ice. Neighborhood Gardens also contained a variety of community facilities—a social hall, library, domestic science kitchen, playground, wading pool, and club rooms.

In October 1933, the PWA Housing Division undertook direct federal construction of housing projects. It sought first to identify large tracts of land as sites for proposed projects and then to rebuild whole neighborhoods into better planned communities that would cost local governments less for street mainte-

nance, fire and police protection, and similar services. Large-scale construction would also allow economies in the purchase of building materials, installation of utilities, and construction of needed facilities. The Housing Division desired to build homes for families whose annual income of between $600 and $1,600 rendered them unable to pay rents in standard dwellings constructed on a self-liquidating basis. It wanted to demonstrate the economic feasibility of low-interest rates and long-term amortization for large, carefully planned communities.

But land assembly in the slums and blighted areas of cities often proved difficult, especially when sites were divided into small parcels that had many owners. One absentee owner of a Louisville, Kentucky property refused all reasonable offers and forced the Housing Division to resort to condemnation. Still resisting, the owner challenged the division's right to condemn and won. On January 4, 1935, United States District Court Judge Charles I. Dawson for the Western District of

Kentucky ruled that the federal government had the power of eminent domain only for federal purposes and that building homes for families was not a federal responsibility. Judge Dawson, who held a strict construction of the public purpose requirement, said that "Surely it is not a governmental function to construct buildings in a state for the purpose of selling or leasing them to private citizens for occupancy as homes." He added that the national government has no police power within any state to condemn or destroy properties that are a menace to public health or safety.

The PWA Housing Division appealed Judge Dawson's decision, but on July 15, 1935, the Sixth Circuit Court of Appeals affirmed it. Three months later, the District Court for the Eastern District of Michigan followed Louisville's example and denied the Housing Division's request to condemn certain properties in Detroit. The division appealed to the United States Supreme Court. Influenced by the Louisville and Detroit decisions, landowners across the country began holding out for prices higher than the Housing Division could pay. But on March 5, 1936, the solicitor general of the United States withdrew the government's appeal of the Louisville decision because by that time the Housing Division had allocated all of its funds and abandoned the projects at issue. It had acquired forty-one of fifty-one sites by negotiation and had successfully used condemnation to clear disputed titles on the others.

While the federal government was losing its battle for the right to condemn properties for public housing, the New York City Housing Authority won its case of eminent domain powers in the New York Court of Appeals. On March 17, 1936, New York's highest court ruled that the menace of slum housing was so severe that it endangered the entire community. Its removal and replacement by safe and sanitary housing was, therefore, a public purpose justifying condemnation. Thus, the New York and Louisville decisions helped set the legal framework for American public housing. The federal government's role became primarily one of financial assistance. Local authorities would acquire sites and then carry out the actual building and management of public housing.

In addition to its problem with site acquisition, the PWA Housing Division faced difficulty in obtaining adequate funds from the federal work-relief budget. The planners of economic recovery discovered that other projects generated employment faster than housing construction. Between 1933 and 1934, the funds for twenty-nine authorized projects were severely curtailed; nearly all work was brought to a standstill. Then, on September 25, 1935, President Franklin D. Roosevelt rescinded $120.6 million of the housing appropriation to finance other projects. In spite of the cut in funds, the Housing Division generally refused to economize on quality. During 1936 increases in labor and material costs forced many bids over estimates. Yet the division rejected bids on nineteen projects in an attempt to keep building costs within prescribed limits so that low-income dwellers could pay reasonable rents over the amortization period. In meeting this difficult situation, the division cut back on only one of its requirements—it permitted semi-fireproof construction in place of complete fireproof construction.

The PWA Housing Division discovered that few communities had personnel with an expertise in planning and building low-income housing. The division, therefore, established a program of consultation and education to improve poorly designed projects according to the Housing Division's suitability standards for low-rent housing. It adopted a basic building plan and allowed local communities to determine the exterior work while insisting on hot and cold running water, private toilets, cross-ventilation, and adequate sunlight in every unit. It also required that apartments be built free of long halls and that bedrooms be placed so that occupants could enter them without passing through other rooms. Finally, to prevent overcrowding, the Housing Division insisted that structures cover no more than 30 percent of the building site.

In relocating persons whose homes were demolished to clear sites for new housing, the Housing Division sought the assistance of local agencies. The Detroit Housing Commission was able to avoid relocation problems by building its first projects on vacant sites. When it began slum clearance, the commission simply relocated displaced families in the new projects.

In struggling with problems of land acquisition, budgets, building codes, and relocation, the PWA Housing Divison was often criticized by local officials who complained that it was arbitrary and dictatorial. The Detroit Housing Commission, for instance, objected when the PWA Housing Division overruled contracts which the Detroit agency had made with the lowest bidders on the grounds that the bids were too high. Detroit officials contended that the contractors had bid high not only because of the rising labor and material costs but also because the PWA Housing Division conducted rigid inspections and sometimes issued arbitrary rulings which delayed projects. The New York City Housing Authority argued for decentralization of decision making in public housing. It regarded Harold L. Ickes, PWA administrator and secretary of the interior, as the source of excessive federal regimentation. Few doubted that Ickes was a sincere advocate of public housing, but New York officials felt that his minute supervision and frequent changes in policy almost wrecked their program.

As local governments began to construct new housing, they found themselves confronted with still another problem: who would manage the completed projects. Reflecting their feelings that the PWA Housing Division had unduly restricted them during construction, local housing officials meeting in Chicago on June 16, 1936 resolved that local agencies should manage public housing projects. Two weeks later on June 29, Congress passed the George-Healey Act. This law affirmed state and local jurisdiction over housing projects, allowed the federal government to make payments in lieu of property taxes on the projects, provided that rents should cover maintenance expenses, and permitted only those having incomes less than five times the established rent to be accepted, or to remain, as tenants.

These provisions went into operation on August 15, 1936 when the first families

National Archives and Records Service

Harlem River Houses in New York City were built for black families in the 1930s with funds provided by PWA's Housing Division.

moved into Techwood Homes in Atlanta, Georgia—the PWA Housing Division's first completed project. Rentals ranged from $16.40 to $31.30 per month and served families with annual incomes between $700 and $1,800. Techwood gave preference to self-supporting, low-income families with children. It reached 96 percent occupancy by February 1, 1937. The tenants were largely low-income, white-collar workers or skilled laborers of whom 88 percent earned less than $25.00 per week or $1,300 a year. Their incomes, therefore, clustered at the middle or in the lower half of the $700 to $1,800 range of eligibility.

Tenant and site selection particularly concerned blacks. In many instances, they bore a double burden—low incomes and exclusion from housing developments that they could afford. An advisor on Negro affairs for the Department of Interior observed that the PWA Housing Division often constructed projects for blacks in physically and socially undesirable areas. As examples he cited the Charleston, South Carolina housing project which was built on a former city dump and surrounded by marshland and the Memphis, Tennessee and Jacksonville, Florida projects which were "virtually isolated from Negro colleges, high schools, civic and welfare organizations, churches, businesses and the better residential sections in these cities."

Studies of housing conditions made during the 1930s revealed considerable deficiencies in both the quantity and quality of American dwellings. The Department of Commerce discovered that 18 percent of the houses in sixty-four cities needed structural repairs. The Works Progress Administration (WPA) found that 16 percent of the housing units in 203 standard metropolitan areas, excluding New York City, were unfit for use or required major repairs. These studies, representing the first serious national inventory of housing, stimulated the demand once again for a permanent public housing program.

To create enough political pressure to convince Congress to enact such a program, social workers and urban reform groups sought support from the American Federation of Labor (AFL). They argued that workers in general would benefit from a large supply of low-cost homes and that unemployed construction workers in particular would find employment in federally aided housing projects. In the spring of 1934, labor leaders in New Jersey and Pennsylvania established the Labor Housing Conference. This group first assuaged the anxieties of labor leaders, who feared that public housing might lead to a government monopoly of construction, and then obtained the endorsement of the Building Trades Department at the AFL convention in October 1934. The following year, the convention added resolutions demanding labor and consumer representation on housing authorities and payment of union wages to workers on public housing construction projects.

In 1935 Senator Wagner and Representative Henry Ellenbogen, from Pittsburgh, Pennsylvania, sponsored bills to create a permanent public housing program. Although the House of Representatives took no action on Ellenbogen's bill, the Senate passed Wagner's bill on June 16, 1936. Forty-two members voted for the bill and twenty-four opposed it. Senator Walter George of Georgia summarized the opponents' objections when he said that the proposal cost too much, benefited urban areas at the expense of rural ones, and extended federal authority into a sphere where it had no rightful power.

The Senate's approval failed to convince Chairman Henry Steagall of the House Banking and Currency Committee to schedule hearings on the Wagner bill. The Alabama representative said that he was waiting for Roosevelt's personal request before calling any hearings. But Roosevelt preferred programs that aided individual homeowners in suburban or rural areas rather than those designed for renters in the cities. His preferences were not, however, practical for low-income families. They could not afford to carry a mortgage; private builders were unable to construct homes meeting minimum standards for $2,000 to $4,000; and few workers could move away from their jobs into the country. Furthermore, Roosevelt was running for reelection, and he knew that proponents of housing would vote for him regardless of the fate of the Wagner bill, while real estate and financial interests would desert him if the bill passed. Consequently, no hearings were held in the House in 1936.

After Roosevelt's reelection, Wagner devoted most of his attention to public housing. Since Congress continually refused to appropriate the vast lump sum necessary to build new housing, Wagner devised an installment plan whereby the federal government would pay the interest on the bonds and the amortization of the principal while current rents would supply the operating costs. In the Senate, criticism centered on the expense of such a public housing program as well as on alleged exclusive benefit to large cities. Senator Harry F. Byrd of Virginia, one of the leading proponents of government economy, proposed an amendment to limit construction costs to $1,000 per room and $4,000 per unit. Byrd's amendment allowed cities over 500,000 in population to incur costs up to $1,250 per room and $5,000 per unit. Senator Davis Walsh, a housing advocate from Massachusetts, added the requirement that local housing authorities eliminate one slum dwelling for every unit of public housing they build. This equivalent elimination requirement pleased many urban reformers who believed that the eradication of ugly slums was more desirable than the actual improvement of housing opportunities for the poor.

The 1937 Housing Act

On August 3, 1937, the Senate adopted the cost limitation and equivalent elimination amendments. Three days later, it passed Wagner's bill by a vote of 64 to 16. The House gave its approval—275 to 86—on August 18. Opposition in both instances came from southerners who disliked spending federal funds on public housing. On September 1, 1937, Roosevelt signed the United States Housing Act, the only social reform passed by Congress that year, and subsequently appointed Nathan Straus the chief administrator of the new United States Housing Authority (USHA).

Partial economic recovery in the mid 1930s actually made housing needs more urgent. In 1934 about 30 percent of the slum apartments on New York's Lower East Side were vacant, but by 1937 these vacancies had disappeared. The Detroit Housing Commission observed that "doubling up" and moves to rural areas had increased vacancies and lowered rents during the most severe period of the Depression. The return of some prosperity, however, brought a decrease in vacancies and an increase in rents.

The PWA Housing Division had demonstrated the feasibility of government construction of low-rent housing. It had built 51 projects containing 21,700 family units in 36 widely distributed communities. More than half of these projects stood on cleared slum sites and more than half of the new dwellings were for blacks. The monthly shelter rents averaged $5.10 per room making them comparable to the rents that low-income people paid for slum accommodations. The average construction costs were $4,473 per unit and $1,270 per room.

The USHA inherited the PWA Housing Division's work. By May 1, 1938, USHA had approved projects for eight cities (9,644 units). While New York City gained 5,194 units, Augusta, Georgia; Austin, Texas; Charleston, South Carolina; Jacksonville, Florida; Louisville, Kentucky; New Orleans, Louisiana; Syracuse, New York; and Youngstown, Ohio also received allotments. The estimated cost per unit ranged from $2,549 in Austin to $4,626 in New York City, and the rent per room ranged from $2.75 in Austin to $5.15 in New York City. To relieve the economic downturn in 1937 and 1938, USHA recommended that cities build on vacant sites first to avoid the delays required in acquiring and clearing slum sites. Furthermore, the cost of cleared slum land was four times as great as the cost of vacant land.

To obtain federal financial aid for public housing, the United States Housing Act required local governments to assume 10 percent of a project's construction costs and 20 percent of its operating costs. Few cities made large cash payments toward the construction of public housing, but many municipalities provided land or built streets, sewers, and other utilities to pay their share of the construction costs. Most cities exempted public housing from local real estate taxes as a further contribution to a project's operating expenses. Local housing authorities found a ready market for their bonds with private investors because, unlike most local bonds, these bonds were secured by the credit of the federal government. They were also tax exempt.

Although authorizing direct relations between USHA and local housing authorities, federal law required a state's consent before creating such agencies. By March 1940, all states except Iowa, Kansas, Maine, Minnesota, Nevada, New Hampshire, Oklahoma, South Dakota, Utah, and Wyoming had enacted laws authorizing the establishment of local housing authorities. Several states permitted only large cities and towns to form housing authorities. Missouri, for example, gave this right only to St. Louis. State laws were often restrictive because state officials believed that substandard housing was a "big city" problem. But as the evidence of poor housing conditions grew, small communities succeeded in persuading their state legislatures to repeal these restrictions.

For the most part during this period, state courts sustained the power of local housing authorities to acquire both vacant and slum sites through eminent domain. The courts also permitted local authorities to borrow in excess of municipal debt limits, and they granted real estate tax exemptions on the basis that public housing was either a property of government or a charitable institution. By 1941 the highest courts of twenty-seven states and the District of Columbia had ruled in favor of public housing on one or more of these contested issues.

New York City had particular difficulty with land prices. In some Brooklyn slum areas, the prices for land reached between $3 and $4 a square foot; in Manhattan, prices were often as high as $10 a square foot. Only the land for the Red Hook Project in Brooklyn, which cost $1.41 a square foot, came within the federal limit of $1.50. The net construction cost of $3,155 per unit at Red Hook reflected the higher costs of building in New York City—even with favorable rates on materials and the elimination of certain amenities such as closet doors and elevator stops on the odd-numbered floors. Cities in other sections of the country built public housing at much lower costs. Fort Wayne, Indiana, constructed dwelling units for $1,830 while Phoenix, Arizona, cut costs to a record minimum of $1,648 per dwelling unit. The Phoenix Housing Authority experimented with assembly line methods in its construction and attributed lower costs to these practices.

Critics argued that USHA could have achieved even greater cost reductions if it had refused to abide by union work rules. They insisted that unions contributed to increased costs by forcing the use of obsolete handwork processes rather than mechanization and mass production. Administrator Straus strongly defended the public housing program, contending that good labor relations saved money that would otherwise be lost in strikes. He complained that these critics exhibited a typical American tendency which was to allow experimentation in private business but to demand perfection in public projects from the beginning.

Low-cost housing required low-cost utilities. Local housing authorities sought, therefore, to obtain wholesale utility rates for their projects. Because they looked upon public housing as either government properties or charitable institutions, many cities granted these rates. In addition, local housing authorities claimed that public projects were large-volume users which would receive electricity or gas directly from a utility and distribute it to consumers through their own facilities. This process eliminated the necessity of supplying the connections needed by private homes. Finally, utilities reduced their costs because they did not have to meter and bill individual tenants. By 1941 public utility commissions in Arizona, Arkansas, Illinois, Montana, North Carolina, Pennsylvania, and Washington permitted lower utility rates for public housing projects.

During the late 1930s, many people expressed concern that government programs would become the tools of corrupt politicians rather than the vehicles of social improvement. By separating local housing authorities from municipal governments and by appointing managers whose allegiance rested with public service, political manipulation in public housing was never great. The USHA conducted training courses in both the business management and the social aims of public housing. To insure that only competent people became managers, the Committee on Personnel Standards of the National Association of Housing (and Redevelopment) Officials urged that managers have backgrounds in public administration with specialized study in housing. The committee also proposed that city governments give managers full civil service protection.

In assessing the work of public housing authorities before World War II, housing officials contended that USHA made its most significant contribution by demonstrating that public effort could rebuild depreciated urban areas and rehouse the inhabitants of those areas. By 1940 public housing was building over 10 percent of all new dwellings in the United States. Administrator Straus continued to insist that public housing did not compete with private enterprise because it served low-income groups exclusively. He also cited figures showing that private homebuilding had increased since the 1937 United States Housing Act.

By June 30, 1941, USHA had constructed 230 developments containing 73,132 units open for occupancy; 94.1 percent of those units were occupied. Vacancy losses amounted to only 3.2 percent annually, and

The Jane Addams Houses in Chicago, Illinois, were built in the 1930s on a 24-acre site formerly occupied by slum dwell-ings.

rent delinquency losses were almost nil. To many housing officials, these percentages proved that the rents were low enough that people could pay them; that people wanted to stay in public housing; and that the projects' management was efficient and businesslike.

In its early years, the public housing program came under the jurisdiction of several federal agencies. The 1937 United States Housing Act placed it in the Department of Interior. In 1939 President Roosevelt transferred USHA to the newly created Federal Works Agency, and then in 1942 he grouped all federal housing programs under the jurisdiction of the National Housing Agency and changed the name of the United States Housing Authority to the Federal Public Housing Authority.

Postwar Housing Legislation

World War II halted low-rent housing construction and diverted the energies of the Federal Public Housing Authority (FPHA) to building and operating housing projects for defense workers. Yet the federal government did not repeat the mistakes it made during World War I; it did not neglect planning for peacetime. In 1943 Roosevelt directed federal agencies, including FPHA, to prepare post-war construction plans that could be initiated as soon as funds and materials became available. Anticipating large postwar appropriations from Congress, FPHA encouraged local housing authorities to apply for funds. It also reassured the authorities that it would give priority to projects deferred or suspended by the war.

Americans living in urban areas generally seemed to approve of more public housing. In a poll conducted by the Bureau of Urban Research at Princeton University, city dwellers were asked to name the most important municipal problem. A large majority cited the lack of good low-priced housing as the most serious problem, and over half acknowledged a willingness to pay higher taxes to replace poor housing with better housing.

Some state legislators did not heed this message, however. Instead they drafted bills either to dissolve local housing authorities or to levy full taxes on public housing projects.

In 1943 legislators in Georgia, Idaho, Indiana, Montana, Nebraska, and Washington introduced measures to terminate federally aided public housing. None of the bills passed, but their introduction represented growing opposition to public housing in certain areas of the nation. At the same time, a number of housing reformers began to question the social benefit of large public housing projects that stood isolated from surrounding neighborhoods. Critics contended that in too many instances public housing failed to meet the needs of its tenants who were totally separated by income from the rest of the community. Suggestions were made that public housing be scattered throughout the city with no more than one building in each block.

In 1941 Congress stipulated that government houses built for defense workers during World War II should not become a permanent addition to the nation's housing supply. Housing of this type was, therefore, built quickly and cheaply; few concessions were made to quality or durability. As a result, public housing officials as well as private homebuilders wanted this wartime housing destroyed as soon after hostilities ended as possible. A FPHA commissioner endorsed the removal of these substandard structures but promised to replace them with new standard public housing. In planning for postwar construction, former Administrator Strauss urged local authorities to reduce population densities in urban areas. He reported that FPHA had found a high degree of tenant satisfaction in low- to medium-density, row-house projects. He also stated that more than twenty families to an acre was undesirable and that more than fifty families per acre should be prohibited by law.

By 1945 an acute housing shortage had developed. Ten years of difficult times in the 1930s and five years of war in the 1940s had curtailed nearly all residential building. People were living in basements, attics, and boxcars, and returning veterans were protesting the lack of housing. It became apparent to many that the federal government would have to take action.

On August 2, 1945, Senator Wagner, the principal sponsor of the 1937 United States Housing Act, introduced an omnibus housing bill in which public housing was included with other types of housing. Senator Allen J. Ellender of Louisiana and Senator Robert A. Taft of Ohio joined Wagner as sponsors. Although a leading conservative, Taft deviated from his principles of free enterprise and limited government to back public housing legislation. He concluded from his observations of projects in Cincinnati and Cleveland that local governments lacked the financial resources to provide good housing for low-income people and believed that the family would be preserved if given a decent environment in which to live.

Public housing advocates hoped for the passage of the Wagner-Ellender-Taft bill, but it was blocked in the House Banking and Currency Committee during the Seventy-ninth Congress. Opponents of the bill supported the position of the private homebuilding, real estate, and mortgage lending groups who wanted the federal government to use its money to underwrite private housing construction. In the Eightieth Congress, the omnibus housing bill became the Taft-Ellender-Wagner bill, to reflect the change in majority parties, and was passed by the Senate on April 22, 1948.

President Harry S. Truman demonstrated his support of the housing bill by making it a part of his appeal for reelection. By a one-vote margin, this measure was approved by the Housing Banking and Currency Committee; but the House Rules Committee blocked the Taft-Ellender-Wagner bill and sent to the House a bill that contained no public housing provision. The House, faced with approving it or passing no housing legislation in an election year, accepted the bill as submitted. In the Senate, attempts to add public housing amendments were defeated. As a result, the bill that passed the Senate contained no provisions for public housing.

Truman brought in large Democratic majorities to both houses of Congress when reelected in 1948. Thus, with the President's endorsement, the Taft-Ellender-Wagner bill passed the Senate with ease and won rapid approval from the House Banking and Currency Committee. On June 24, 1949, the House finally passed the bill by a vote of 227 to 186. The 1949 Housing Act authorized the construction of 810,000 new units over the next six years.

Since 1949 was a year of economic uncertainty, cities with high rates of unemployment were particularly urged to apply for public housing funds. On August 8, 1949, the Public Housing Administration (PHA), which had succeeded FPHA in 1947, distributed application forms; and one week later, Galveston, Texas, and Norfolk, Virginia, received the first allocations. Within two weeks, fifteen other cities including Baltimore, Chicago, Detroit, Los Angeles, and New York had reserved 80,750 units. By mid November, 108 cities had received approval for their preliminary loans. These loans, which paid for site surveys, income studies, architectural and engineering plans, and cost estimates that the local housing authorities had to complete before receiving federal approval of their proposals, covered 134,500 units. Only 500 units of the first year's program remained unallocated.

The rapid submission of applications reflected the enthusiasm of local housing authorities. But before they could proceed with their plans, they had to win the approval of their governing bodies. In 1949 public housing opponents—realtors, homebuilders, and mortgage lenders—began shifting pressure from Congress to their local communities. Although a large number of labor, veteran, civic, and church groups supported public housing, they lacked the organization and power of such groups as the National Association of Real Estate Boards, the United States Savings and Loan League, the National Association of Home Builders, and the United States Chamber of Commerce.

In Seattle, Washington, for example, the anti-public housing forces won a referendum on a proposed public housing program by using campaign materials containing the slogan: "Can you afford to pay somebody else's rent?" This slogan became the central theme of several anti-public housing campaigns in different areas of the country. And in each instance, public housing was identified with socialism, corrupt political machines, or racial integration.

The merits of using vacant sites as opposed to cleared slum sites for housing projects became a grim political issue in postwar America. Public housing opponents argued that projects built on vacant sites brought economically and socially undesirable people into good neighborhoods. They also said that large-scale rental housing depressed the value of owner-occupied properties and cheapened the appearance of a community. But public housing proponents maintained that local authorities needed to build on vacant sites so that people whose homes were demolished in slum clearance projects would have a place to live while housing was constructed on cleared sites.

The most significant controversy over site selection occurred in Chicago in 1949. A local housing authority which favored the construction of large and unsegregated public housing projects conflicted with city aldermen who wanted to maintain the political and racial composition of their wards. They especially feared the introduction of Negroes into their neighborhoods. In 1946 and 1947, whites on Chicago's South Side had violently resisted the movement of blacks into previously all white housing projects. Mayor Edward J. Kelly had extended police protection to the blacks, but his successor, Martin H. Kennelly, refused to continue the practice. Conditions on the South Side did not change between 1947 and 1949.

Chicago was one of the first cities to reserve public housing under the 1949 Housing Act. In October the Chicago Housing Authority completed a site proposal that was equally balanced between slum and vacant areas. But on March 2, 1950, the city council rejected the proposed vacant sites and suggested alternatives either in the wards of public housing advocates on the council or in obviously unsuitable locations such as paths of proposed superhighways or areas covered with valuable commercial and industrial properties. The council's final proposal called for 10,500 units on cleared slum land and 2,000 units on vacant land. The plan displaced 12,465 families (almost all of them black) and provided housing on vacant sites for only 2,112 families. Rather than see public housing

The six-story buildings of the Marcy Houses in Brooklyn, New York, won the approval of public housing advocates.

defeated in Chicago—which would have been disastrous when public housing was fighting for its life in Congress and in many local referenda—PHA accepted the Chicago plan with only minor modifications.

New York City implemented its public housing program without encountering any of the difficulties experienced by Chicago. Yet public housing advocates found little to praise in New York's program. Except in Staten Island, Queens, and the outlying areas of the Bronx and Brooklyn, the New York City Housing Authority maintained populations as dense in the projects as had existed in the demolished slums. Although former Administrator Straus strongly disapproved of densities greater than fifty families per acre, the Elliott Project in the Chelsea section of Manhattan placed 120 families per acre; four other projects in Manhattan and one project in the South Bronx contained 100 families per

In Manhattan, New York, the Jacob Riis Houses, which covered less than 25 percent of the site, allowed air and light to enter the apartments.

acre. However, most buildings covered only between 15 and 22 percent of the project sites which allowed more light and air to enter the apartments than often entered those on Park Avenue. The six-story buildings in the Marcy Houses in Brooklyn and the Jacob Riis Houses in Manhattan approached the highest standards of livability. The architects grouped four apartments around a single staircase and elevator permitting full cross-ventilation and short well-lighted public halls.

In 1949 and 1950, New York City contained some 58,000 acres of vacant or unused land, but the housing authority chose to build on expensive land in the center of the city. This enabled slum property to be cleared and dwellings to be constructed in close proximity to places of employment. It was necessary, therefore, to construct high-rise apartments. But such apartments required greater expenditures for structural support; elevators and stairways; and heating, lighting, and plumbing facilities. In addition, the physical differences between the projects and homes in the surrounding neighborhoods, together with the absence of churches, shops, and other private businesses, made the housing projects segregated communities for low-income persons. Former Administrator Straus, disappointed with the New York Housing Authority, suggested that it return to the standards of the Harlem River Houses and Williamsburg Houses which PWA built in the 1930s.

Cutbacks and Problems Slow Progress

The outbreak of the Korean War in June 1950 stopped the momentum of the construction program initiated by the 1949 Housing Act. To conserve building materials for national defense needs and to prevent inflationary pressures in the building industry, on July 18 Truman ordered PHA to limit its construction to 30,000 starts in the remaining months of 1950. The PHA considered many construction bids too high, even though it recognized that costs for decent housing had increased so much since March 1949 that the cost limits in the 1949 Housing Act were obsolete. By November 1, 1950, costs had risen 25 percent over those of March 1949. Nevertheless, in 1950 PHA rejected bids for 6,722 units because they exceeded the cost limits.

On October 13, 1950, PHA announced stringent economy regulations. They reversed the trend toward improving space and livability standards and made former space standards the new maximum limits. In addition, PHA increased project densities, discouraged heavy construction, and prohibited the building of large units. It also demanded that local housing authorities obtain zoning and building code variances if adherence to local codes increased building costs; purchase wholesale utility services whenever possible; and solicit bids from a larger number of contractors. The agency contended that its authority to cut costs extended beyond merely assuring compliance with legal maximums. If it could produce "modest but adequate standards of decency and livability" for less than the legal maximum, it had the duty to do so.

Realtors, homebuilders, and mortgage lenders used the Korean War emergency to defeat public housing in many states and municipalities. The Texas Association of Home Builders persuaded the small Texas cities of Breckenridge and Edinburgh to rescind their public housing programs and donate the money saved to the federal government for national defense. The United States Chamber of Commerce encouraged other cities to follow suit and urged states either to repeal their public housing laws or to require referenda on them. Only Nebraska enacted a mandatory referendum law; Minnesota and Texas passed laws that permitted referenda under certain conditions.

After escaping major damage in state legislative sessions, the public housing program was seriously cut by Congress. Truman requested an appropriation for the construction of 75,000 units in fiscal year 1952; but Congress authorized only 50,000 units. The cutback proved embarrassing for PHA, which had scheduled 83,395 units for bids before February 1, 1952. It decided, therefore, to give priority to projects necessary to maintain racial equality, to those in defense areas, and to those in localities where only one project was scheduled.

In 1951 public housing lost in twenty-five

of thirty-eight municipal referenda. Its foes in Congress used these defeats as arguments in favor of reducing appropriations for public housing. In addition to limiting construction for fiscal year 1953 to 35,000 units, both houses agreed to curtail future public housing construction to 35,000 units a year unless Congress should change that number by legislation. Congressman Ralph Gwinn of New York attached a rider prohibiting annual federal contributions to any local housing authority whose projects housed members of subversive organizations. Even before it became law, the Gwinn Amendment caused the cancellation of bond sales by seventy-three housing authorities; investors refused to buy bonds if federal contributions became subject to such conditions.

At the end of 1952, the last full year of Truman's Administration, local housing authorities had reserved 358,908 units under the 1949 Housing Act. They had, however, placed only 156,060 units under construction and completed 68,472 of the 405,000 units authorized for the entire three-year period. The November 1952 elections brought an increase in approvals for public housing by local referenda. Toledo and Cincinnati, Ohio; River Rouge, Michigan; and Elizabeth, New Jersey voted for public housing projects while Ossining, New York, and Mansfield, Ohio turned them down. But the election of a Republican President and Congress placed the future of public housing in doubt.

The National Association of Real Estate Boards resolved that Congress should abolish the public housing program and sell its project to private interests. The realtors maintained that standard housing could be achieved through code enforcement. But, early in the twentieth century, housing reformers had demonstrated that code enforcement removed bad housing but did nothing to increase the supply of standard housing for low-income people.

President Dwight D. Eisenhower appointed former Representative Albert M. Cole of Kansas, who had consistently opposed public housing during his congressional career, as administrator of the Housing and Home Finance Agency (HHFA). Public housing advocates were not pleased with this appointment, but Cole promised at his confirmation hearing to administer the law as written despite his continuing personal objection to public housing. For PHA commissioner, Eisenhower selected Charles E. Slusser, former mayor of Akron, Ohio. Although he had favored a modest public housing program in Akron, he had done little to prevent its defeat in a 1952 referendum. Finally, after a third contest between the House and Senate over the public housing appropriation, Congress settled on 20,000 units of public housing for fiscal year 1954.

As of July 31, 1953, PHA had 61,500 units under annual contribution contracts. Since it could proceed on only 20,000 units in fiscal year 1954, Slusser notified local housing authorities that the Administration would accept no new applications and take no further action on applications already on file. He ordered more intense reviews of each phase of construction to insure maximum economy and told local housing authorities to discontinue planning and development but to preserve the work that they had already done. Comptroller General Lindsay C. Warren, however, overruled Slusser's order to stop planning and site acquisition. Warren said that such activities might proceed on any project under an annual contribution contract.

On December 15, the President's Committee on Housing Policies and Programs recommended continuation of the public housing program but only as needed for the relocation of families displaced by public clearance activities. The committee also advocated a requirement that localities applying for public housing submit a "workable program" to demonstrate that they were taking positive steps to improve the physical, social, and economic development of their communities. To implement these recommendations, the President asked for the construction of the 35,000 units already under contract in fiscal year 1955. He then proposed that Congress enact another program to build 35,000 units during each of the next three fiscal years. But Congress approved 35,000 units for one year only. And the 1954 Housing Act restricted public housing under the year's allotment to cities with workable programs designed to eliminate urban decay. Since few local housing authorities could comply with these requirements, only 16,200 units were placed under construction in 1954.

In 1955 Commissioner Slusser requested an extension of the cutoff dates for applications and of all authorizations from one year to two years. At the request of the President, he did not ask for repeal of the workable program requirement. Eisenhower and other supporters of the program believed that local housing authorities could satisfy it, if Congress gave them more time to complete applications. Before the June 30, 1955 deadline, thirty-four communities signed contracts for 29,509 units—only 5,500 units short of the maximum authorized. In July 1955, Congress approved the construction of 45,000 units and deleted the workable program requirement as it applied to the building of public housing. Despite rumors that Eisenhower would veto the housing bill, he approved what became the 1955 Housing Act.

On November 7, 1955, and again on February 27, 1956, the United States Supreme Court declined to review lower court decisions holding the Gwinn Amendment invalid. The Department of Justice also refused to appeal a District of Columbia decision invalidating the amendment. Yet in the course of its four-year history, some two dozen courts ruled against the Gwinn Amendment. Still, PHA continued to require loyalty oaths until June 30, 1956, when it announced rescission of the requirement.

During the 1950s, public housing projects became heavily populated by blacks because they were more frequently displaced by urban renewal and public improvement programs. Managers noticed growing feelings of frustration, despair, and revolt among tenants as they came to realize that their incomes lagged far behind those of most Americans in a time of prosperity. The instances of broken families, crime, juvenile delinquency, drug addiction, and vandalism multiplied. Managers began to feel that their postwar rejection of social workers and community development programs might have been hasty. They discovered that they needed the assis-

tance of social service agencies in handling problems within their projects. Contemporary social analysts, however, cautioned housing advocates and officials against expecting that public housing would transform low-income persons into middle-class Americans. Public housing tenants of the 1930s had been middle-class people suffering from a temporary loss of income. But in the 1950s—a period of national prosperity—public housing was occupied chiefly by the problem poor whose very low incomes resulted from physical disabilities, lack of education, or impaired family structures.

In an attempt to improve social conditions within public housing projects, the National Federation of Settlements and Neighborhood Centers recommended that public housing abandon its maximum income limits. The federation argued that these limits branded public housing tenants as failures and excluded persons who were improving their economic status. It suggested, therefore, that the law allow individuals who increase their income to remain in public housing projects and pay higher rents. This practice would not only enlarge a project's revenue, but it would retain tenants who were perhaps community leaders or at least models of self improvement. The federation also recommended abandoning large projects and scattering public housing throughout communities. The National Federation of Settlement and Neighborhood Centers argued that the dispersal of public housing would mitigate both the racial and the economic segregation that was inevitable in large projects.

In 1956 Congress authorized construction of 35,000 public housing units for each of the following two years and reinstated the workable program requirement. In an important new departure, the law permitted single persons over sixty-five years of age to become public housing tenants (originally public housing served only families with children and elderly couples) and allowed local housing authorities to spend up to $500 more per room in building housing for the aged. As this legislation was subsequently enlarged, housing for the elderly developed into a major segment of the public housing program and in

Villas for the elderly in Miami Florida. After 1956 housing for the elderly developed into a major segment of the public housing program.

some communities became its primary use.

When Slusser announced that PHA had no new legislative program for 1957, the National Association of Real Estate Boards moved quickly to encourage Congress to terminate the existing program when the construction authorizations expired on June 30, 1958. The National Association of Home Builders contended that the rise in consumer incomes eliminated the need for additional public housing and that tax-exempt housing bonds drew investors whose money would otherwise support private mortgage loans. In 1957 private investors held more than 96 percent of the local housing authority bonds, giving the private sector a large share in a public program.

Twenty years after the 1937 United States Housing Act, public housing had still not won acceptance as a part of the American system.

Construction under the 1949 Housing Act lagged far behind expectations and never approached the goal of 135,000 units of annual construction. In the opinion of many housing advocates, the long struggle to save public housing from defeat in Congress and in the cities had deepened the defensiveness of public housing officials and deterred them from trying new ideas. They refused to undertake any experimentation in design and tended to perpetuate both the bad and the good in public housing.

Commenting on the condition of public housing, Harrison Salisbury of the *New York Times* contended that the "big low cost projects have no organization, no political interests. Their community structure has been turned into social mush by stupidity and bureaucracy." For in building projects, local housing authorities frequently demolished the local churches and scattered their congregations. Consequently, negligible religious influences existed for tenants. Also, project managers discouraged tenant participation in political organizations because they feared Communist infiltration.

In 1957 Canton and Elyria, Ohio, as well as Shreveport, Louisiana, defeated proposed public housing projects in local referenda. The only major victory came in Jersey City where voters overturned the city commission's decision to stop construction on a housing project after having spent $1.4 million on acquiring and clearing the site. Early in 1958, Cedartown, Georgia, completed the first decentralized, low-rent project with single-family and duplex buildings. Because it was dispersed throughout the community, the project could use existing utilities, street access, and neighborhood facilities; walk-up buildings ensured that the tenant, rather than the housing authority, had the greater maintenance responsibility.

Congress failed to enact any public housing legislation whatsoever in 1958. At hearings, the National Association of Housing and Redevelopment Officials urged relaxation of income limits, variations in design, more autonomy for local housing authorities, and federal payment of the full legal subsidy. Slusser, however, stressed contrary objectives—immediate cost-cutting on construction and curtailment of tenant income exemptions.

Between 1955 and 1959, Senator John Sparkman and Representative Albert Rains, both from Alabama, managed the housing bills and negotiated the shares that Congress allocated to the various federal housing programs. Often these bills authorized more expenditures than the President thought prudent or desirable. Thus, in 1959 Eisenhower vetoed two housing bills before Congress passed what the President considered a sufficiently modest authorization. The 1959 Housing Act authorized construction of 37,000 units and vested in housing agencies "the maximum amount of responsibility in the administration of the low-rent housing program." This addition brought to local authorities some welcome flexibility in gearing their programs to the individual needs of their communities. The PHA retained the right to review decisions of the local authorities to ensure that they considered the rent-paying ability of their tenants and the solvency of their projects.

As civil rights for minorities became a more publicized political issue, whites in many northern cities identified public housing with blacks. In Chicago Negroes occupied 81 percent of the public housing units, but they accounted for only 45 percent of the families earning incomes less than $3,000 and 47 percent of the families earning between $3,000 and $3,999 (the income groups most heavily represented in public housing). According to national statistics, the proportion of blacks in public housing was 44 percent, reflecting their percentage of the nation's low-income population.

Housing built in neighborhoods with a predominantly black population or in adjacent areas attracted few white applicants. In 1956 the Philadelphia Housing Authority proposed a plan to build twenty-one small projects—most of them containing fewer than 100 units—on sites scattered throughout the city. But the opposition of white neighborhoods forced the housing authority to reduce the amount of sites. New York City attempted to increase the number of white tenants in its public housing projects by establishing higher income limits for new projects and encouraging eligible whites to apply. Few whites, however, accepted apartments reserved for them in largely non-white projects. By the same token, most blacks refused to move into apartments set aside for them in projects on the outskirts of the city.

In 1959 the New York State Division of Housing commissioned the Pratt Institute to devise ways of cutting building costs. The institute suggested using less expensive materials and processes, and it recommended limiting elevator stops to every third floor. The eleven-story Pruitt-Igoe Project in St. Louis, which later had to be torn down, was built with a single elevator stopping at the fourth, seventh, and tenth floors. The Pratt Institute study also advised that local housing authorities designate the living room as a sleeping room in 25 percent of their apart-

National Association of Housing and Redevelopment Officials

In St. Louis, Missouri, the Pruitt-Igoe Project, which was built with elevators stopping only at every third floor, was subsequently torn down.

ments. Its proponents contended that this was not the most desirable living arrangement, but "since many middle-income families have to live this way, it does not seem unreasonable that tenants of publicly supported housing should too."

Several cities began to complete small projects built to resemble typical housing patterns in their neighborhoods. Philadelphia opened a group of individual dwellings for families with three and four children and one containing efficiency and single-bedroom apartments for the elderly. In Inkster, Michigan, a project of two-story, one-to-five-bedroom dwellings with tenant-kept gardens and generous yard space won new friends for the public housing program in that community.

By the end of 1960—the last year of the Eisenhower Administration—local housing authorities had reserved 402,325 units, placed 304,512 units under construction, and completed 268,382 units of the 1949 program

authorization (810,000 units in six years). Public housing thus increased under the second half of this program by 43,417 reservations, 148,452 starts, and 199,910 completions. Four states (Iowa, Oklahoma, Utah, and Wyoming) had still not passed enabling legislation for local housing authorities and, therefore, remained outside the public housing program.

The Kennedy-Johnson Era

In 1961 President John F. Kennedy appointed Robert C. Weaver, a black housing official in the federal housing program of the Roosevelt and Truman administrations and later in the New York State housing program, as administrator of HHFA. For commissioner of PHA, Kennedy selected Marie C. McGuire, former executive director of the San Antonio Texas Housing Authority. She was the first federal housing director with previous experience as a housing administrator. Besides being convinced that social services were a necessary component of public housing, McGuire was especially interested in purchasing rehabilitated dwellings from private owners and using them as public housing and in improving project unit design. She, therefore, brought more architectural talent into the agency with the hope of diminishing the institutional atmosphere of public housing. Under McGuire's leadership, PHA expanded its program to Indian reservations through agreements with the Bureau of Indian Affairs and the various Indian tribes.

Congress responded to this new activity by enacting a more generous public housing bill. The 1961 Housing Act authorized spending the full $336 million allowed by the 1949 Housing Act for annual federal contributions. But twelve years of rising construction costs limited the purchasing power of these funds to only 100,000 units.

In the late 1960s, public housing officials became concerned because the revenue from low-rent housing projects failed to increase as rapidly as operating expenses. The difference between rental income and operating expenses dropped from $6.58 per unit in 1951 to $3.17 per unit in 1961. Although local housing authorities were nonprofit institutions, they desired to keep the residual receipts as a reserve fund against emergencies. The federal government, however, preferred that local authorities spend the receipts for their expenses and ask less in annual contributions from the federal government. In 1961 the federal government contributed 87 percent of what the law permitted.

The PHA contended that its management procedures were economical and efficient— that it was the aging of public housing structures together with rapidly increasing labor and material costs that caused the rise in maintenance expenditures. Because the tenants' incomes rose so slowly, public housing authorities could not raise the rents to cover increases in expenditures. Maintaining project solvency under these conditions destroyed the charitable aspect of the housing program. It could not serve those extremely poor persons whose rent-paying ability could not meet the operating expenses of their dwellings.

Local management bore the brunt of these

National Archives and Records Service

These high-rise buildings, constructed in 1963 in New York City, are examples of the kinds of public housing that were common in large cities in the 1960s.

financial problems. While continuing to demand high-rise construction—which most tenants disliked—and to deny popular conveniences such as separate living and dining rooms, federal officials pressed for more revenue. As a result, local management frequently evaded anti-discrimination policies in order to keep their projects solvent. In officially integrated projects, credit ratings or character references eliminated many black applicants, while Pennsylvania found that a marriage license requirement was a successful exclusionary device. Management also manipulated the income and income-exemption regulations to protect over-income tenants from eviction, thereby keeping stable and high rent-paying families in projects.

In spite of the financial stringency of the early 1960s, PHA developed some new programs. In 1959 the public housing law had been amended to authorize special provisions for housing low-income persons who were disabled or handicapped, regardless of age. In 1963 PHA contracted with the Toledo Metropolitan Housing Authority to build the first public housing designed specifically for the disabled. This $2 million facility tested the utility of known structural aids for the disabled and developed new techniques as well. The apartment house was located next to a branch of Goodwill Industries which provided experiments in physical therapy and employment for tenants.

On November 20, 1962, Kennedy issued Executive Order 11063 to end racial discrimination in federally assisted housing programs. He exempted existing public projects from the mandatory provisions for non-discriminatory tenant selection imposed on projects initiated after the order. But PHA did not vigorously combat discrimination, and it failed to use litigation to secure open occupancy. Applying the anti-discrimination pledge only to tenant selection, PHA allowed local housing authorities to continue to build in all black areas where whites refused to live. As of March 31, 1963, PHA had 1,179 all white projects, 1,174 all black projects, and 675 integrated projects. By January 6, 1965, the number of all white projects increased to 1,213; the number of all black projects fell to 942; and the number of integrated projects increased to 852.

President Lyndon B. Johnson continued Kennedy's efforts to raise HHFA to cabinet status as the Department of Housing and Urban Development (HUD), and the department was created in 1965. The HUD incorporated HHFA's former constituent agencies: PHA, which traced its lineage back to the United States Housing Authority established by the 1937 Housing Act; the Urban Renewal Administration; and the Community Facilities Administration. Also brought under the HUD umbrella, but retaining its separate identity, was the Federal Housing Administration. Weaver became the first secretary of this new department.

The 1965 Housing and Urban Development Act provided for the construction of 35,000 units of new public housing each year for the next four years. This act and subsequent laws passed in the late 1960s and early 1970s authorized several innovations: *leased housing*, under which houses and apartments were leased by private owners to low-income families, who received a subsidized rent from the housing authority; the *turnkey* program, which enabled housing authorities to acquire from private developers low-rent housing built to their specifications; *acquisition and rehabilitation* of existing housing; and several programs of *homeownership* for low-income families. Federal housing assistance was extended to *moderate-income housing* sponsored by limited profit developers and non-profit groups such as foundations, labor unions, and churches. A program of *rent supplements* was introduced to enable low-income families to live in privately owned, moderate-income housing.

Conventional (competitive-bid) housing presupposes ownership of a site by the housing authority. Bids for construction are submitted by general contractors in the manner typical of all public construction. In the competitive-bid method, the following steps are necessary: site approval by HUD and the locality; site acquisition by negotiated purchase or condemnation; architect selection and preparation of plans; relocation of families and businesses to be displaced by the contemplated housing; governmental approvals, culminating in the execution of an annual contributions contract; bidding on the job and award of the contract to the lowest qualified bidder; construction; and occupancy. This process sometimes requires as much as three years from commencement of the design to award of the contract. During that time, costs can rise considerably beyond the local authority's estimate. As a result, bids often exceed the money available to build the project. The project may, therefore, have to be abandoned or its design cut back to reduce cost. Such changes can lead to severe management problems after the project is completed.

The turnkey method of building public housing was developed in an attempt to overcome the limitations of the competitive-bid method. A private developer builds housing according to authority specifications on land he owns; when the housing is completed, he sells it to the authority (hence the name "turnkey") at a previously agreed-upon price. Turnkey housing has certain advantages. The developer, who hires the architect and arranges his own construction financing, can maintain tighter control over costs and predict them with greater accuracy. Since there is no public bidding in the turnkey method, the developer and the local authority can work more closely at every stage of development and devise alternative materials and construction techniques when necessary. These practices have resulted in savings in time and money since the turnkey program was initiated in 1966.

The District of Columbia became the first jurisdiction to experiment with turnkey as well as leasing. In February 1967, the National Capital Housing Authority purchased Claridge Towers, a 343-unit apartment for the elderly. It also sought nonprofit developers, such as the Roman Catholic Church's *Sursum Corda,* to build mixed projects of high-rise and townhouse dwellings which the authority later leased. Roseville, Michigan; Bossier City, Louisiana; Miami, Florida; and King County, Washington also developed successful turnkey projects.

By 1967 local housing authorities had reserved all 240,000 units authorized for purchase, leasing, or construction. But, as in 1949, they were slow in undertaking actual housing construction. In many instances, the local authorities were unable to decide whether to scatter housing for low-income minorities and possibly incur the wrath of the city's residents or to continue to concentrate low-income minorities in the ghettos and perpetuate the dreary deadlock of public housing. Cumbersome administrative procedures, high interest rates, and periodic credit crunches also increased the cost of the projects and delayed construction.

Physical unkeep began to absorb almost all of the rental income of large projects built in the 1940s and 1950s. In 1954 the Pruitt-Igoe Project cost $36.8 million to build; twelve years later it required a $7 million renovation. These large public housing projects also created a sense of social irresponsibility among their tenants that manifested itself in vandalism and violence. Pruitt-Igoe demonstrated all too well the consequences of concentrating too

National Archives and Records Service

This development in San Francisco is an example of some of the better postwar public housing projects.

many poor, unstable, and problem-ridden families in one project without adequate social services. As late as 1963, there was a specific injunction against the use of federal funds in public housing developments for social services. Localities that provided such programs did so with state, local, or private funds. Federal legislation authorizing tenant services was enacted in 1968, but efforts to implement the provision with adequate appropriations were unsuccessful.

Although the period from 1956 to 1966 ended in a time of unprecedented prosperity, public housing tenants enjoyed no substantial increases in their purchasing power. Many tenants could not, therefore, pay rents sufficient to cover the cost of maintenance, services, and the 10 percent paid in lieu of taxes to local governments. In cities over 250,000, the income limits for admission to public housing for a single person ranged from $2,400 in Fort Worth, Louisville, Memphis, Minneapolis, and Omaha to $4,200 in Detroit and Honolulu. For a family of twelve or more persons, the limits ranged from $3,000 in Fort Worth to $7,896 in New York. But the question of income limits for very large families was, for the most part, academic; few authorities had built accommodations for such families.

In 1967 public housing had a national vacancy rate of 2.2 percent as compared to the 5 percent normal vacancy rate for private apartments. Turnovers in public housing amounted to only 16.5 percent compared with the 20 percent turnover rate for both owners and renters of private houses. In the fifty largest cities, 6,864 vacancies existed in public housing while 193,072 applicants were on waiting lists for these vacancies. The Housing Assistance Administration reported 705,985 as the total number of public housing units as of December 31, 1968; but this total was still short of the goal set in 1949 to build 810,000 units by 1955.

In the late 1960s, the deficits that resulted from increased operating costs brought on a fiscal crisis for many housing authorities. The St. Louis Housing Authority was one of the first to exhaust its reserves. Yet nearly 27 percent of the St. Louis tenants were already paying at least half of their income in rent, while 86 percent paid more than 25 percent of their income in rent. In December 1968, the tenants staged a rent strike that continued until October 29, 1969. In settling the strike, the housing authority gave tenants more voice in the management of the projects and set their rents at 25 percent of their income. In addition, it promised more housing for the elderly, improved security systems, and an increase in "community, educational, commercial, transportation, and recreational facilities."

Rent strikes led to the passage of the Brooke amendments which limited rents to 25 percent of the occupant's income. The amendments severely reduced revenues to the housing authorities. Congress, responding to this fiscal crisis, enacted legislation in 1969 and 1970 which authorized payment of subsidies designed to stabilize rents, to provide adequate funds for operating and maintenance services, and to restore reserves to reasonable levels. This legislation ensured tenants that they would not have to pay more than 25 percent of their income in rent. It also allowed housing authorities to devote more attention to maintenance and repairs. However, this legislation failed to improve substantially the economic position of the nation's public housing program. Instead, there was continuous controversy over its interpretation and implementation.

A Reassessment Period

In the early 1970s, states became more involved in producing or financing housing programs. In July 1971, there were thirteen state housing finance agencies (HFAs). By January 1972, the number had risen to fifteen; one year later, there were twenty-three. The state legislatures that created these HFAs intended that they deliver sound housing at below market rents by acting as mortgage bankers—by making and servicing low-interest, long-term direct mortgage loans. But a more recent and growing trend has been to go beyond pure financing functions and establish development authorities, such as government agencies or nonprofit organizations, with the power to assemble land and to work with local developers in creating hous-

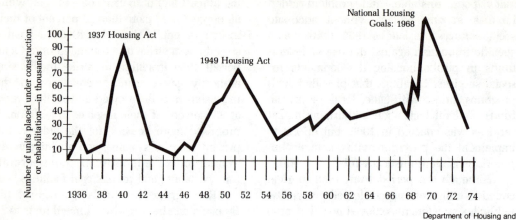

Department of Housing and
Urban Development

Figure 16-2.
Public Housing Production, 1935-1974.

ing for families of varying incomes through state and federal assistance programs. Many state legislators apparently believe that an agency playing all of these roles is their best hope for attacking the housing problems they face.

By the end of 1973, there were 1.1 million federally supported low-rent public housing units under management in the United States. Figure 16-2 shows the annual production of public housing from 1935 to 1974 and indicates the impact of various housing acts. The methods employed to obtain these housing units were conventional (contracted for construction by public housing authorities), turnkey (purchased from private developers), leased (by private owners at subsidized rates to low-income families), and acquisition (purchased by negotiation from private owners). The extent to which each method was used is as follows:

Conventional	818,848
Turnkey	157,640
Leased	101,810
Acquisition	29,610
Total	1,107,908

Over 90 percent of these units were newly constructed, while the others were rehabilitated units. The elderly occupied 258,916 units. Of the total units under management in 8,899 projects at the beginning of 1974, approximately 47 percent of the projects and 74 percent of the units were located in metropolitan areas; and 31 percent of the proj-

ects and 61 percent of the units were located in central cities.

By 1974 a total of 4,373 local housing authority programs had been established in the United States. Only 17 percent of these were functioning in cities of over 25,000 population; however, over 70 percent of the low-rent public housing units built were located in such cities. These units were under the management of 2,633 local housing authorities whose jurisdiction frequently extended to several communities, as in the case of those established by counties. The states with the largest number of authorities were Texas, Georgia, Alabama, Arkansas, Kentucky, Minnesota, Oklahoma, and Nebraska.

The year 1974 marked the beginning of a new era in public housing. For the purpose of aiding low- and moderate-income families in obtaining a decent place to live and of promoting economically mixed housing, the 1974 Housing and Community Development Act provided that assistance payments may be made to individuals rather than the public body for existing, newly constructed, and substantially rehabilitated housing. Besides broadening the definition of rural housing to include mobile homes and mobile home sites, the 1974 act increased appropriations for rural housing programs by $60 million. It also authorized the secretary of agriculture to make loans to persons and families of low or moderate income to assist them in purchasing dwelling units in condominiums in rural areas.

Through the rental assistance program, the 1974 Housing and Community Development Act encouraged HUD to help low-income families find living quarters in locations of their choice as well as to support the construction of low-income housing. Funds from the rental assistance program were used by communities for new housing construction designed to preserve urban neighborhoods. In fact, by the end of fiscal year 1975, such funds had been committed for more than 91,000 housing units. At the same time, $1.6 billion had been appropriated for rental assistance to 400,000 low-income families in fiscal year 1976. Thus, in the mid 1970s, it is evident that greater emphasis is being placed on rent supplements than on the construction of public housing units.

During the past decade, significant national housing and community development legislation has been enacted. Concurrently, there has been a flood of new HUD regulations implementing that legislation. There has also been a burst of activity at the state level as new plans and programs were adopted to supplement federal programs. Existing ones have been radically transformed; their scope has expanded from the single concern of adequately housing the economically disadvantaged, the elderly, and the physically handicapped to concern for the total environment in which they live.

Urban Renewal and Community Development

Since adequate housing is but one element of a total living environment, housing projects were often initiated in conjunction with urban renewal and community development programs. Financial assistance for urban renewal projects was first provided for under Title I of the 1949 Housing Act as amended. Over 2,000 projects, involving the expenditure of approximately $10 billion in federal grants, have been initiated under this program since 1950. These include the demolition of slums, the installation of public improvements of various types, and the reconstruction of homes and businesses by private developers. (see Table 16:1 Urban Renewal—A Statistical Profile).

Some $2 billion has also been invested in over 400 projects initiated under the Neighborhood Development Program (NDP) which was adopted by Congress in 1968. The primary purpose of NDP was to speed up urban renewal projects. Instead of formulating detailed plans for acquiring and disposing of each parcel of property over the entire life of a project, NDP funded incremental activities within designated neighborhoods on an annual basis. To qualify for this and other types of assistance, cities and counties were required by the 1954 Housing Act to adopt a "workable program" for community development—an official plan for using private and public resources to remove urban slums and blight.

By the end of 1974, nearly 4,000 communities had adopted workable programs. However, 70 percent of these plans were classified as "inactive"; the limited funding of federal aid programs did not provide sufficient incentives to keep these plans up-to-date. Thus, many of the so-called categorized grant programs enacted in the 1960s were abandoned in favor of the more flexible block grant approach with the passage of the 1974 Housing and Community Development Act.

This 1974 act authorized the allocation of $8.4 billion to local governments over a three-year period (fiscal years 1975, 1976, and 1977) for comprehensive planning and consolidated community development programs in addition to urban and rural housing. The primary objective of the community development programs was to create viable urban communities, not only by providing decent housing and suitable living environments but also by expanding economic opportunities for persons of low and moderate income. Thus, federal assistance was made available to eliminate conditions detrimental to a neighborhood's health, safety, and public welfare; expand the quantity and quality of community services; conserve and improve the nation's housing stock; develop a more rational utilization of land and other natural resources; and restore and preserve properties of special value for historic, architectural, or aesthetic reasons. Since grants could be made for as much as 100 percent of the ac-

TABLE 16-1
Urban Renewal:
A Statistical Profile

What are urban renewal sites being used for?

Number of projects, June 30, 1969	1601

Planned reuse on land acquired

Housing	19,300 acres, one-third
Commercial, industrial, institutional, other public (part for residential areas).	29,300 acres, one-half
Streets, right-of-way (part for residential areas).	8,700 acres, one-sixth
Total land acquired.	57,300 acres
Private redevelopment	34,600 acres
Public redevelopment.	22,700 acres

Non-residential reuse, building space (in square feet)

Private

Retail.	31.6 million
Office buildings	40.6 million
Other commercial	60.2 million
Industrial	24.1 million
Wholesale	8.5 million
Total Private	165.0 million

Institutional and public

Government and public buildings	29.2 million
Schools	27.3 million
Hospitals	9.4 million
Other	10.9 million
Total institutional and public. . . .	76.8 million

Taxes

Renewal puts more land in public use and leaves less on the tax rolls, yet the values added by redevelopment of renewal sites have resulted in a 240 percent increase in assessed value of taxable land and a corresponding increase in tax revenues. Following are the results in 524 projects with land committed for redevelopment at the end of 1968:

Percent of taxable land before renewal	Three-fourths
Assessed value before renewal. . . .	375 million dollars
Percent of taxable land after renewal	One-half
Assessed value after renewal	1,280 million dollars

Investment

Each dollar of federal renewal grants generates $5.30 in redevelopment investment, a HUD analysis shows. Redevelopment investment on 28,700 acres of renewal land (about half the total acquired) is estimated at 11.6 billion dollars. About two-thirds of this is private investment. Land value at time of disposition was a little more than 1 billion dollars.

Relocation

Reports to HUD show the following results of relocation of people and businesses for urban renewal from its inception through June 30, 1969:

Families

Relocated to standard housing	212,084
Self-relocated to substandard housing	13,996
Whereabout unknown (about half left the city).	33,190
Total displaced.	259,270

Relocation Payments

Families and individuals (moving expenses and rent assistance)	34,8 million dollars

Businesses

Moving expenses, loss of property . .	137.1 million dollars
Small business displacement (with net annual income under $10,000). . . .	44.6 million dollars

Low- and moderate-income housing

Low- and moderate-income housing construction on renewal sites has sharply increased since enactment of new low-income housing assistance programs in recent years.

During the three fiscal years ending June 30, 1969, the number of new low- and moderate-income units started on renewal sites was virtually equal to the total of all such units during the preceding 16 years.

During this three-year period, two-thirds of all new units started on renewal land were for low- and moderate-income use compared to only 40 percent of total renewal housing starts during the preceding years. The figures are shown in the following table.

New Housing Units Started on Renewal Land for Periods Ending in Fiscal Years 1966 and 1969

	Total New Starts	Low-Moderate Income Starts	
		No. of Units	Percent of Total
Cumulative through June 30, 1969	183,213	91,233	50
Cumulative through June 30, 1966	114,829	45,861	40
Three years ending June 30, 1969	68,384	45,372	66

Data from Department of Housing and Urban Development

Of the total units started through fiscal year 1969, 144,317 had been completed, including 63,021 for low- and moderate-income use. This increase in low- and moderate-income housing occurred even before the new interest-subsidy programs, Section 235 and 236, enacted in 1968, had any significant effect. With these programs now a prime support for private financing of moderate-income housing, it can be expected that they will further stimulate the construction of such housing in renewal areas.

Journal of Housing, 27 (October, 1970), 469.

tivity costs, there were no requirements for state or local contributions.

Prior to 1974, community development funds were available for only seven categorical programs. But under Title I of the new Housing and Community Development Act, localities could apply for a single lump sum or block grant, the amount of which was determined by a community's needs. Therefore, on their applications, communities were directed first to identify their development needs and objectives and then to describe how they would meet them. They were also required to include a housing assistance plan assessing housing needs, especially for low-income persons; establishing local housing goals; and indicating the cost and general location of the proposed housing. Finally, communities were requested to submit a three-year plan

designed to eliminate or to prevent slums, blight, and deterioration and to improve community facilities and services.

The HUD's role was limited to ensuring that communities' needs were fairly represented and to seeing that communities allocated the block grant funds as planned. The major task of monitoring the execution of community development programs was, therefore, placed on local governments and their citizens. By June 1975, block grants had been approved for 1,272 cities and 73 urban counties. Thus, these local governments will give the first indication of the 1974 Housing and Community Development Act's effectiveness in providing decent housing, suitable living environments, and expanding economic opportunities for all Americans.

SUGGESTED READINGS

Abrams, Charles. *Forbidden Neighbors.* New York, 1955.

Beyer, Glenn. *Housing and Society.* New York, 1965.

Brown, Robert K. *The Development of the Public Housing Program in the United States.* Atlanta, 1960.

Burghardt, Stephen, ed. *Tenants and the Urban Housing Crisis.* Dexter, Michigan, 1972.

Callendar, John Hancock, and others. *Methods of Reducing the Cost of Public Housing.* Brooklyn, 1960.

Conkin, Paul. *Tomorrow a New World: The New Deal Community Program.* Ithaca, New York, 1959.

Davies, Richard O. *Housing Reform During the Truman Administration.* Columbia, Missouri, 1966.

Downs, Anthony. *Federal Housing Subsidies: How are they Working?* Lexington, Massachusetts, 1973.

Fisher, Robert M. *Twenty Years of Public Housing: Economic Aspects of the Federal Program.* New York, 1959.

Fitzgerald, John L. *Public Housing and the Public Utility Rate Structure.* Washington, D.C., 1940.

Friedman, Lawrence M. *Government and Slum Housing: A Century of Frustration.* Chicago, 1968.

Lubove, Roy. *The Progressives and the Slums: Tenement House Reform in New York City, 1890-1917.* Pittsburgh, 1962.

——————— . *The Urban Community: Housing and Planning in the Progressive Era.* Englewood Cliffs, New Jersey, 1967.

National Association of Housing and Redevelopment Officials. *Journal of Housing.* 1944-

National Commission on Urban Problems. *Building the American City: Report of the National Commission on Urban Problems to the Congress and to the President of the United States.* Washington, D.C., 1968.

Sachs, Daniel Y. *Handbook for Housing and Urban Renewal Commissioners.* Washington, D.C., 1972.

Smith, Wallace F. *Housing: The Social and Economic Elements.* Berkeley, 1971.

Starr, Roger. *Housing and the Money Market.* New York, 1975.

Straus, Nathan. *The Seven Myths of Housing.* New York, 1944.

——————— . *Two Thirds of a Nation: A Housing Program.* New York, 1952.

U.S. Department of Housing and Urban Development. *1973 HUD Statistical Yearbook.* Washington, D.C., 1973.

Wood, Edith Elmer. *The Housing of the Unskilled Wage Earner.* New York, 1919.

CHAPTER 17

PARKS AND RECREATION

One of the continuing challenges of 1976 is to improve the quality of life for all Americans. With the economic progress that has been made, the average person has more time for leisure than ever before. Increased population and rapid growth of cities have created congestion and environmental problems that are most troublesome; yet at the same time, the opportunities for recreation in public as well as private parks and recreational facilities are greater than ever before and are growing. However, there is a need to understand and appreciate the legacy, to enjoy the parks without abuse, and to achieve a balance between preservation and use to best meet human needs and values.

The evolution of America's parks and recreation facilities is a rich history of dynamic and sometimes volatile struggles and triumphs that have created a cornucopia of leisure opportunities. This chapter briefly relates the developments that have been achieved by local, state, and federal governments in providing public parks and recreation facilities to improve the quality of life and the general welfare of America.

In 1976 more than 2,700 municipalities provide public programs involving 805,000

acres of parks and recreation areas within city boundaries. Counties have also developed extensive park and recreation areas and programs, especially in the suburban regions of the East. State park and recreation organizations administer 3,550 parks, totaling 8.9 million acres in scenic areas, recreational forests, and sites of special historical interest. State involvement varies from New York's 169 areas totaling 2.9 million acres to Delaware's nine areas totaling 7,200 acres. Visits to these state parks, forests, and recreation areas exceed 500 million per year.

The magnitude and importance of outdoor activity is further demonstrated by federal park and recreation programs. Fifty agencies in regular departments and forty independent agencies, boards, commissions, or councils administer over 300 separate programs related to parks and recreation. However, the major efforts are included in about ten agencies. For instance, the National Park Service, the steward of natural scenery, wilderness, and historical areas of national significance, administers thirty-eight national parks and 270 other scenic, historic, and recreation areas, totaling 30.5 million acres. The Bureau of Land Management provides special recreational sites on some of the 475 million acres of public lands it administers. Water resource development agencies furnish water-oriented recreational facilities at over 800 major artificial lakes created by federal water control

This chapter is based in part on a special report prepared by the National Recreation and Park Association and on information from the Bureau of Outdoor Recreation of the United States Department of Interior.

projects. The use of the various outdoor recreational areas has been growing at about 10 percent per year for the past several decades.

Over one third of the United States' land area is under federal management and control, mostly in the West. All of these lands have some outdoor recreational value. Lands administered by all governmental levels primarily for this purpose total 319.2 million acres, about 15 percent of America's land area, as represented in Table 17-1.

TABLE 17-1
Government Lands Administered Primarily for Outdoor Recreation — 1972

Government Level	Lands Administered (in millions of acres)
Federal	266.7*
States	41.8
Counties	8.1
Local, other than counties	2.6
Total	319.2

*Total federal land is 755.7 million acres, all of which have some outdoor recreation value.

Expenditures for public parks and

recreation has been steadily growing. In 1973 they totaled about $3.7 billion, of which at least $1.2 billion was for public works construction and improvements, and $681 million was for land procurement. Table 17-2 gives the estimated government expenditures for outdoor recreation, as compiled by the Bureau of Outdoor Recreation in preparing the first nationwide recreation plan.

A 1965 survey indicated that 85,000 commercial enterprises provided outdoor recreational opportunities on a full- or part-time basis on 23 million acres, receiving more than a billion visits per year. An additional 46,000 commercial enterprises furnished outdoor recreation facilities and services related to amusement and spectator sports activities. These enterprises occupied about 18 million acres and received 400 million visits annually. Another million nonprofit enterprises, provided by 47,000 private and quasi-private nonprofit organizations on 7 million acres of recreation lands, had total visits of about one-half billion per year. Indications are that most of these activities have been steadily growing since 1965. Although data is fragmentary, the studies of the Bureau of Outdoor Recreation

U.S. Bureau of Outdoor Recreation

Camping at public grounds in national forests and areas adjacent to lakes or reservoirs is a fast growing recreational activity of the 1970s.

TABLE 17-2
Estimated Government Expenditures for Outdoor Recreation — 1973

Government Level	Expenditures (in millions of dollars)				
	Total	Capital Additions		Operation and Maintenance	
		Land	Development	Salaries	Other
Federal	$573	$117	$172	$179	$105
States	661	134	218	212	97
Local (including counties, cities, districts, regional councils)	2,455	430	786	870	369
Total	$3,689	$681	$1,176	$1,261	$571

indicate government outdoor recreation facilities may receive over 5 billion visits per year. These facts give basis to the claim that recreation is one of America's largest and fastest growing industries.

Early City Parks

Since ancient times, civilized man has sought rejuvenation and beauty in parks. Wealthy Sumerians about 2340 B.C. created parks on private land holdings; and in the tenth century B.C., the Hanging Gardens of Babylonia served as a hunting ground and a setting for feasts and assemblies of great leaders. Gymnasiums and pleasant, natural surroundings were associated in Plato's ancient Greece. Affluent Romans maintained garden-type villas in and on the outskirts of towns. Generally, these early parks were only for the use of the privileged elite. In 1300 A.D., public grounds were provided in Florence, Italy, for the "leisure of people." This practice appeared in England several centuries later when areas were set aside for sports and hunting. In other European countries, natural areas were carefully landscaped; and parks were built that encompassed aviaries, fishponds, summer houses, and replicas of ancient ruins and outdoor theaters.

By the nineteenth century, true "people's parks" emerged, as English gardens or parks became more informal and provided open space for public meetings and gatherings. Famous parks created during the century include Versailles and the Champs Elysees in Paris and Hyde Park and Kensington Gardens

in London. The beauty and pleasure afforded by these areas were gradually shared by the general citizenry as well as the affluent.

Early park developments in the United States are attributable to the impact of the new environment upon the colonists and to the influence of their cultural background and heritage. Initially, colonists were utilitarian and used open lands for cattle grazing. In 1634 the Boston Commons was created as a public pasture ground rather than for leisure activities. The recreational utility of the commons was not officially recognized until 1728. Public park lands emerged gradually. The plan drafted for Philadelphia in 1682 by William Penn included five open squares. James E. Oglethorpe's 1733 plan for Savannah, Georgia, featured twenty-four small squares and open spaces in addition to the public garden and common. Pierre C. L'Enfant's plan in 1791 for the Federal City (Washington, D.C.) envisioned stately parks and pleasure gardens.

Thus, by the early nineteenth century, there were many plazas, commons, squares, and village greens in America's larger cities. These relatively small areas were for the most part intended to improve city environments. However, good park design was generally lacking, and few such spaces were provided in the crowded tenement areas. Utilizing cemeteries as a place to visit on Sundays and holidays became quite common, not only out of respect for the dead, but also to enjoy picnicking in an area of greenery, flowers, shrubs, and trees. Cemeteries were the first to utilize landscaping to provide a harmonious park setting.

In 1851 urban aesthetics began to come to the forefront, when President Millard Fillmore appointed Andrew Jackson Downing, a well-known horticulturist, to prepare landscape designs for several parks in Washington, D.C. However, at the time of Downing's death the following year, the plans were incomplete, except for the Mall, the Ellipse in back of the White House, and the White House grounds.

In the meantime, support was building for the acquisition of America's first large park, to be located in the heart of New York City. The venture received strong backing from Downing, who publicly stated his views on the need for the park from his perspective as an architect and horticulturist. William Cullen Bryant, one of the nation's great journalists and considered the father of American poetry, provided strong support through his *New York Evening Post* and other publications. However, several attempts to acquire acreage failed because of disagreements over location and concern that the extent of the park might foster crime. Finally, in 1856 the city council authorized the purchase of 700 acres of land for $5,000 and designated the site Central Park. Three years later, the area was enlarged to the present 840 acres.

The site was rocky lowland, and development was expected to be costly. Egbert Viele, a civil engineer, was employed as the park's chief engineer. And in 1857 Frederick Law Olmsted was appointed superintendent of Central Park by the nonpartisan park commission. Architects were invited to submit designs and compete for cash awards. Competitors were given detailed specifications upon which to formulate their plans and were told that they were to work within a $1.5 million budget. Only four of the thirty-three plans submitted were considered worthy.

In early 1858, the team of Calvert Vaux, who had assumed Downing's architectural business at the time of his death, and Olmsted was awarded the $2,000 first prize for their design called "Greensward." These men believed that the huge land area would someday be surrounded by buildings and would

give city residents green, open space. They envisioned the park as an "immunity from urban conditions" and wanted to provide a country atmosphere for those unable to leave the city. Vaux and Olmsted varied the landscape and, with great concern for the visitor's experience, separated traffic patterns so that persons could walk, ride horseback, or go in carriages without coming together or crossing at the same elevation.

Although Olmsted was neither a trained horticulturist nor architect, his landscaping concepts had a great effect upon park designers. He was the first to use the designation "landscape architect." Olmsted favored open meadows and lawns in large central areas, use of native trees and shrubs, roads and paths laid out in widespread curves, major roadways circumscribing the parks, preservation of the natural scenery, and informal design. Both Vaux and Olmsted frowned upon large buildings in a park environment. The success of Central Park attested to the architectural skills of both men. Olmsted later designed parks and park systems in many cities, including San Francisco, Boston, Philadelphia, Baltimore, Washington, D.C., Atlanta, and Louisville.

Ice skating, boating, and band concerts were popular recreation activities in the early days of Central Park. The designers and commissioners found it difficult to reconcile the provision of active sports, which might endanger physical features, with their concept of a park as a natural area for relaxation and contemplation. However, controlled sports and games were eventually allowed. This controversy prevailed among park professionals and conservationists for many decades until the consolidation of park and recreation services gained acceptance. Central Park had considerable influence on the park movement in the United States. It was the first major purposely designed and developed public park, and its success was quickly and widely acclaimed. The park's popularity, as evidenced by the attendance records, influenced other cities to establish them.

The next important episode in the nation's public park movement was the active participation of the federal government in the recreation field. It came with the establishment of Yellowstone National Park in 1872, the first of its kind not only in the United States but also in the world. However, major emphasis on park acquisition and planning remained centered in urban areas where there were strong desires to create attractive green spaces in or near the heart of cities.

In 1892 enabling legislation authorized acquisition of property near Boston, which was by then surrounded by suburban communities. This action established a pattern that was followed extensively in the twentieth century and led to the formation of a Boston Metropolitan Park Commission, the first body in the United States authorized to operate a multicity park system. The formation of the park commission, initially a temporary body, occurred after several unsuccessful attempts dating back to 1849 to establish a city park system. The Boston Metropolitan Park District found its leader in Charles Eliot, son of the president of Harvard. He had gained his experience as a landscape architect while an apprentice and later an associate of Olmsted. Eliot helped to stimulate positive action on the proposed bill to establish the park commission. He stressed that the finest scenery of

each district should be included in the public reserves. After the appointment of the permanent commission several years later, Olmsted assumed responsibility for designing the parks within the district.

In an 1893 design for the city of Cambridge, Massachusetts, Eliot included a building, which he called a "field house," that affected future park developments. He proposed this structure as the keystone of the area's design and included in it a meeting room, checkrooms, refreshment concessions, restrooms, and an area for visitors with babies.

Controversy arose in Boston, as it had in New York, about traffic patterns into and within parks. Eliot proposed legislation dealing with boulevards and parkways, passed in 1894, as a means of offsetting unemployment created by an industrial depression in Massachusetts. Recognizing the advantages of the parkway concept, he attempted to correlate recreation and transportation merits of traffic patterns as they related to park design. He envisioned elongated, landscaped parkways that could serve as park and recreation areas. In his design, he provided for a total strip measuring 125 feet in width; in the

National Recreation and Park Association

The croquet field provided active recreation in Prospect Park in Brooklyn, New York, in the early 1900s.

center, he placed a 35-foot-wide electric rail-way area with 30-foot roadways on each side; on the outside of each roadway was a planting strip 7 feet wide. Parkways took on a new meaning, however, shortly after the start of the twentieth century.

Eliot also believed that "small reservations" should provide for the active outdoor recreational pursuits of adults and children. These areas included sand plots, playgrounds, field houses with gymnasiums, and an outdoor concert ground. However, he opposed including large sports fields, which he felt might result in the park being "monopolized by the sports minded." This philosophy represented one view in the controversy over active versus passive use of parks. As a result of Olmsted's principles, most parks in the early 1900s lacked facilities for active recreation—ball grounds, tennis courts, and related constructions; but as the demand for active recreational opportunities increased, playgrounds and outdoor gymnasiums usurped more land within the parks.

A split developed between the advocates of active play and those of passive recreation. It led to the establishment of separate recreation commissions in cities across the country, especially where park authorities resisted accepting playgrounds. During the first quarter of the twentieth century, many of the well-designed park areas were despoiled because of improperly designed facilities and areas for active play. Lack of understanding and intolerance by both recreation leaders and park designers led to this unfortunate occurrence.

L. H. Weir brought this major conflict into greater focus with the publication of his *Manual of Municipal and County Parks* in 1928. He noted the marked confusion in terminology. He understood the importance of Olmsted's concept of parks as places for "peaceful enjoyment of an idealized rural landscape," but noted that parks had also become areas for active recreation for city dwellers. While recognizing the need to retain Olmsted's vision, he felt that "the life needs of people which can be expressed in their leisure are far wider than those comprehended in the early conception, and a wide range of active forms of recreation have come to be included."

The Play Movement

The beginning of the play movement, which directly and indirectly advanced the development of parks, can be traced to Massachusetts, where outdoor physical education classes were first held at the Salem Latin School in 1821. In 1825 outdoor gymnasiums opened at several New England colleges, largely as a result of the efforts of German political refugees. They were instrumental in forming the Turnvereins, an association of gymnasts and athletes, which supported extending gymnastics to the public schools.

In 1866 the first vacation school was created in Boston's First Church. Initiated primarily by women's clubs, these vacation schools stimulated the play movement and gave a new dimension and purpose to education. They featured carpentry, nature study, plant care, drawing, and singing. This educational concept provided an impetus for using school facilities during non-class hours. When the First Church moved to another part of the city in 1868, the vacation school set a precedent by using a public school building and opening its yard as a playground. In 1872 the small community of Brookline, Massachusetts, became the first town to approve funds through a public referendum to acquire land specifically for play purposes; however, no action was taken at the time. In 1876 Chicago made Washington Park a designated play area by constructing play facilities for children.

In the 1880s, attention focused upon providing small play areas for young children. The small park or playground movement took hold in 1882 when Joseph Lee—father of the playground movement and the most influential of the early recreation pioneers—assisted the Family Welfare Society of Boston in making a study of play opportunities in the more highly congested neighborhoods of the city's South End. In 1885 Marie Zakrzewska, a Boston resident recently returned from Germany, proposed to the chairman of the Massachusetts Emergency and Hygiene Association that heaps of sand be provided to the city's children to permit them to "dig as if on a miniature seashore." She had observed such areas in German public gardens.

This led to the creation of the first three of Boston's famous Sand Gardens in 1886. By the following year, ten had been established; and within a few years, the sand garden concept had spread to Philadelphia, New York, Chicago, and other cities. Gymnastic apparatus was the only equipment installed at the Boston sand gardens. They were later called playgrounds when they were moved to school properties and supervised by matrons employed with public funds. Children also had opportunities for group games, arts and crafts, and musical activities. Only $9 were expended for the gardens in 1885; in 1887, $532 were used for toys, construction of the lots, and matrons' salaries.

National Recreation and Park Association

Play areas for children were provided in Boston's South End in the 1880s.

A second major influence upon the municipal park movement occurred in 1889 with the conversion of a 10-acre tract on the Charles River in a congested section of Boston to the first open air gymnasium in the world. Known as the Charlesbank Outdoor Gymnasium, it established a playground pattern that had tremendous influence upon the evolution of both the park and playground movements. It included a men's gymnasium (the women's facility was added in 1891), an apparatus area, and areas for sports, bathing, wading, and rowing.

Joseph Lee helped to create the first "model" playground in a slum area of Boston in 1898. The tract included a small space for younger children, an area for sports, and over 200 individual gardens. Abandoned stables were remodeled for indoor activities. This action was part of a plan of Boston's mayor to establish a series of playgrounds in the city's high-density residential areas. As a result, in 1898 the legislature passed a bill providing that a sum not greater than half a million dollars could be spent by the park commissioners at the rate of not over $200,000 a year to create a "system of playgrounds for the city." About this time, New York City was coming to grips with its highly populated areas and the problems arising in tenements on the Lower East Side. Children were permitted to play on the "little traveled but much used asphalt streets." Boston followed New York's example. The asphalt streets proved far superior as play places than the normal cobblestone streets. By the turn of the century, the sand gardens and playgrounds were so widely publicized that representatives from other cities visited Boston to study the playground committee's work.

National Recreation and Park Association

Supervised street play was introduced in New York City in the early 1900s.

In 1903 Lee reported that the popularity of skating at Charlesbank attracted 5,000 participants each day. However, he found the use of Olmsted's grassy mounds, trees, and shrubs in the center of the recreation park of much greater interest. Thus, Boston's Charlesbank and Franklin Park, seventy acres originally acquired as a community meeting place and training site for the militia, served as areas in which to "play many of the match games for which the local playgrounds were crowded or too small." In Lee's words, these parks were "the keystone of the arch, forming a sort of university for which local playgrounds are the preparatory schools."

Another pioneer, George A. Parker, was superintendent of parks in Hartford, Connecticut, from 1895 to 1915. He was a founder of the New England Association of Park Superintendents in 1898, the first such organization. Parker was the earliest municipal park administrator to recognize that local parks could adhere to the aesthetic park concept and at the same time be designed for active patron use. Hartford was one of the first cities to develop a municipal golf course and sports areas for use by all age groups. In 1903 Parker asserted that city parks had previously been designed "more for the brain worker than for the hand worker" and suggested that the naturalistic park was infrequently used by the working class. He recommended that a municipal park system include a large country park, but it should begin with small parks located near the homes of the workers. He envisioned these areas including playgrounds, shaded areas, grass, seats and tables, flowers but few shrubs, a stadium for contests, and an indoor and outdoor gymnasium. He recommended shelter for rainy days and winter. He believed the areas should be open year-round and all day for the benefit of working families.

Prompted by civic leader Jacob A. Riis, New York developed a series of small parks in the downtown district. This effort involved destruction of the Mulberry Bend slum and creation of an open grassy area; clearing land for Seward Park in 1899; and development of outdoor gymnasiums and playgrounds on the banks of the Hudson River by the New York Outdoor Recreation League. New York City, unlike other communities at the time, provided instructors and a variety of equipment at these sites.

One of the significant events in park and recreation development occurred in Chicago in 1903 when the citizens of South Chicago approved a $5 million bond issue to develop

small neighborhood parks ranging from seven to 300 acres. South Park District Superintendent J. Frank Foster believed the residents would be better served by a number of small neighborhood parks located in high-density areas. The interest of Jane Addams, of Hull House fame, in dealing with neighborhood needs gave him support. Foster envisioned neighborhood parks with field houses, refreshment stands, gymnasiums, assembly halls, clubrooms, and sports areas. Many prominent civic leaders opposed the bond issue, but it was approved by 83 percent of the voters in a public referendum. Ten centers were in operation by 1905.

Chicago had developed large parks over a quarter of a century before it established Lincoln Park, its first major park. It had been acquired for a cemetery but was subsequently redesigned for recreational uses as well. Several large parks had been obtained and developed prior to 1899 when the mayor appointed a special park commission of citizens and city government officials to study the open space demands in Chicago's congested areas. The study pointed out the need for small parks and playgrounds for youngsters in the city's crowded neighborhoods. Steps were taken to finance fifteen small areas between 1900 and 1904. In 1903, 750,000 people visited the parks, attesting to their success.

South Park, one of Chicago's three park districts, contracted with Olmsted to prepare a master plan for the improvement of the district's large Jackson Park, site of the 1893 World's Fair. Although Olmsted's plan did

National Recreation and Park Association

In the early 1900s, the athletic fields at Longfellow School in Pasadena, California, were utilized by the community.

not materialize (because of the site's location in a congested area and because of a fear that it would not attract children), features of the plan were later incorporated into small neighborhood parks. The concept of the recreation center emerged and became an important element of the play movement. The impetus for this development was provided by the construction of field houses included in Olmsted's plans. Year-round indoor activities for all ages were emphasized for the first time. There were men's and women's outdoor gymnasiums patterned after the Charlesbank development in Boston. There were ball fields, athletic houses, tracks, and exercise equipment.

The small neighborhood parks and recreation centers brought play areas to thousands of Chicago residents who had been unable to enjoy the benefits of outdoor recreation. The needs of the working class were met by the addition of recreation centers in the parks. The welfare of the expanding employment core was the main issue of the day, as Chicago grew into a transportation, commercial, and manufacturing center. The South Park commissioners believed that the establishment of parks was essential and that the neighborhood center embodied the highest practical type of public service.

The small neighborhood parks developed by the Chicago South Park District added new dimensions to the recreation movement. The attractiveness of playgrounds and the variety of play facilities were enhanced in park settings. The neighborhood park became a social center that transformed the play movement into a recreation movement encompassing a broad and complex program of year-round activities for adults and youth under professional leadership. The concepts upon which the South Park District's neighborhood parks were established reflected acceptance of public responsibility for administering recreation programs and services in addition to providing and maintaining parks as settings for recreation.

In 1904 Los Angeles appointed the nation's first separate board of playground commissioners to assume independent authority for the administration and operation of activities relating to park and school systems. A superintendent of recreation was employed by the board. Thus, parks (called playgrounds) were in the hands of a non-park authority.

Also during this period, a few cities started actions to make effective use of school plants for civic and social functions in the evenings and summers. The parks and schools generally operated independently and without coordination. In 1902 the American Park and Outdoor Art Association was commended for its efforts in helping school boards lay out grounds, plant trees, improve the aesthetics of playgrounds, and make new school houses physically attractive. Using the school plant for civic and social functions decreased the need to build additional recreation centers. Prior to 1900, several states passed laws permitting the use of school buildings and grounds for this purpose.

In Chicago, after several pioneer efforts to develop "independent" playgrounds through private and volunteer contributions, the first school playground was opened in 1897 by the West End District of Associated Charities. Between 1898 and 1911, New York and Wisconsin created recreation programs in conjunction with school systems. Initially, little attention was given to the design of school plants for purposes other than the academic program. This gradually improved, however, and in September 1908 The Playground, the monthly journal of the Playground Association of America (PAA), described three types of playgrounds: the private yard, the public school yard, and the municipal ground. Design characteristics were presented.

The establishment of PAA in April 1906 greatly influenced the play-recreation movement. Concerned with the needs of children in large cities, the purpose was to guide, support, and stimulate interest in the development and operation of play areas throughout the country. Luther Gulick served as president; Joseph Lee and Jane Addams were vice-presidents; and President Theodore Roosevelt, a staunch supporter of PAA, was elected as the first honorary president. He urged attendance at the initial annual PAA meeting in Chicago in 1907 to see the magnificent system that Chicago had erected in its South Park section, which he termed "one of the notable civic achievements in any American city."

The organization expanded in 1910 and became the Playground and Recreation Association of America (PRAA) to incorporate the broadened concept and serve the rapidly growing national interest in public recreation. Focus was initially placed upon urban and rural recreation, but the commercial and industrial elements were beginning to come to the forefront of the movement. A 1915 recreation census identified 3,294 playgrounds in operation, 573 of which were on a year-round basis.

Through the efforts of PRAA and others, more communities adopted the park-school concept. By 1940 emphasis was being placed upon school site planning standards that included a playground area and development of the entire school plant for community recreation use. In 1946 the National Council on School House Construction specified student-acreage ratios for the construction of elementary school sites and proposed the neighborhood park-school of approximately ten acres as the basic unit in the city's recreation system. The desirability and cost-effectiveness of providing one playground at or near the school site to meet the needs of the school and the neighborhood was emphasized.

A 1950 study by the National Recreation Association revealed extensive use of school plants for community recreation and effective cooperative relationships between school and recreation authorities in conducting programs within these buildings. It also noted the widespread acceptance by school authorities of making their buildings available for such purposes. In later years, public opinion and legislation continued to expand the cooperative approach to education and recreation. Economy and better community programs have resulted from the park-school concept.

World War I and the Recreation Movement

World War I brought an entirely new challenge to recreation. The fusion of voluntary effort and public support and the impact of the mobilization of military and industrial forces required a shift in direction. At the request of the War Department, PRAA initiated the War Camp Community Service (WCCS) to provide soldiers with recreation programs and services through coordination of recreation resources in communities near military camps. Relying upon the American tradition of volunteerism, WCCS created local committees to expand recreational opportunities, with a special concern for service personnel. The program operated in 700 cities for one and a half years during the national emergency.

As a result of these widespread community programs, there was a general public awakening to the value of parks and recreation in postwar America. As soldiers returned home, they sought organized active recreational opportunities similar to those they had had during wartime. However, the momentum of PRAA was greatly diminished as donations and contributions fell drastically after the war. The American Red Cross and other voluntary organizations experienced the same problem. A gradual transfer of services occurred from WCCS to public recreation agencies. Program scopes broadened to include music, dramatics, and community-wide events. There was widespread construction of "community houses" as part of a nationwide campaign to erect war memorials.

The changing concept of parks created new problems. With the greater demand for organized active recreation, a distinct conflict arose. Playground leaders generally had no training in landscape architecture or park design, and Olmsted's followers frequently lacked the breadth of understanding to incorporate recreation into park designs. Barren playgrounds and marred parks often resulted.

During the early 1920s, almost half of the states passed legislation to allow cities to establish public recreation programs and collect and spend tax dollars for that purpose. This period was marked by a growing recognition of the importance of local governments providing leisure and recreational opportunities. The establishment of the National Park Service in the Department of Interior in 1916 had focused attention on national outdoor recreational needs; and after interruption by the war, the interest expanded. Several national organizations were established.

In 1924 the National Conference on Outdoor Recreation was convened by President Calvin Coolidge. It attracted over 300 delegates representing 128 organizations. Called to assist in the development of a national policy and to coordinate the independent activities of scores of public and private agencies providing outdoor recreational opportunities, the conference laid the foundation for a comprehensive survey of municipal and county parks. It helped rectify the division that had been developing between park and recreation forces as park concepts changed and the need emerged for specialized recreation facilities, requiring the redesign of parks and revisions in park policies. The survey formed the basis for the two-volume *Parks: Manual of Municipal and County Parks* by L. H. Weir. Although park-oriented, Weir understood recreation's role in American life and incorporated his views in the publications.

A 1929 recreation census identified 945 communities providing recreation facilities and programs; 22,920 recreation workers, mostly seasonal, were reported, compared to the 7,507 recorded in 1915. Recreation expenditures totaled $33.5 million, an increase of 822 percent over 1915.

Depression, Public Works, and Recreation

The stock market collapse followed by the closing of many businesses, industrial firms, and banks, and the resulting unemployment during the early 1930s had a positive effect on the park and recreation movement. Many families were unable to afford commercial recreation, and they were unable to use automobiles to visit national or state parks. Faced with limited mobility and funds, they sought out local facilities and programs. To meet the challenge posed by the Depression, the federal government allocated billions of dollars for public works projects, many of which provided recreational benefits.

Among the agencies that helped meet the recreation needs of the country were the Civil Works Administration (CWA), the Federal Emergency Relief Administration (FERA), the Works Progress Administration (WPA), and the National Youth Administration (NYA). These agencies assisted state and local governments in providing recreation leadership as well as a far-reaching construction program of parks development and specialized recreation facilities. Unemployed teachers, artists, administrators, musicians, technicians, and laborers were hired for a variety of positions in recreation programs in 467 cities. The impact was tremendous. While only 2,500 persons were working in full-time recreation positions nationwide in 1930; by 1937, 44 states employed 46,000 people in WPA's recreation program.

The emergency work projects facilitated the creation of new crafts programs, summer play schools, and recreational opportunities for municipalities, labor unions, settlement houses, schools, and hospitals. The national impetus also enabled local public and private recreation agencies to continue their social, physical, and cultural activities. Federal funds made facilities and equipment available to communities that could not secure them otherwise. Greater emphasis was placed on adult recreation. Volunteers became more prevalent in community efforts, as citizens became involved in program planning and development through neighborhood and community recreation councils. The work relief programs also built specialized recreation facilities and developed park areas in small towns.

This national thrust to relieve the economic and social problems brought organized recreation into wide acceptance as a governmental service. Thousands of Americans found productive employment and satisfying opportunities in an era of hardship and great insecurity. The federal contribution to recreation benefited American communities for years to come.

One of the greatest contributions to the park and recreation field was that of WPA, which conducted a program in cooperation with state and local governments to provide work for the unemployed. Approximately 10 percent of the WPA projects were devoted to parks and playgrounds, including construction of swimming pools and other outdoor

Public swimming pools were constructed by WPA in many cities during the Depression.

recreation facilities. An additional 2 percent went to the creative and performing arts. In the three-year period ending June 30, 1938, more than 15,000 parks, playgrounds, and athletic fields were built or improved; 11,600 swimming and wading pools, golf courses, tennis courts, skating rinks, ski jumps and trails, outdoor theaters, and band shells were created.

During this period, WPA recreation leaders operated more than 14,700 community centers and assisted with over 7,800 others. They were also directly involved in various recreation activity programs, totaling more than 16 million participant hours in an average week. The Federal Art Project sponsored art classes in many communities, with an average monthly attendance of 60,000 and the operation of sixty-six community art centers. In addition, the Federal Music Project and the Federal Theater Program, which operated only in 1938, averaged a monthly attendance of 3 million and 476,000. The WPA program's success is reflected in a resolution approved by the United States Conference of Mayors in 1938:

The integrity and permanent usefulness of the city projects which have been approved by the federal government need no apology from anyone. They are the cities' own projects. Honest and impartial analysis . . . will reveal that practically every project represents a useful, and in most cases, a permanent public improvement. Finally, it is apparent that the city officials of America will never consent to abandonment of the work principle in giving relief assistance. The dole, based upon idleness and groceries, has no place in our American scheme of society.

In addition to WPA, two sections of the Federal Security Agency (FSA) also provided work for the young unemployed and out-of-school during the Depression. On April 5, 1933, soon after President Franklin D. Roosevelt sent a message to Congress asking for power to launch an experimental project, the Civilian Conservation Corps (CCC) was created. This program—to provide work but not interfere with normal employment—was confined to forestry, soil erosion control, flood control, and similar projects; and it was seen as a significant contribution to the conservation of the country's natural resources. National and state forests and parks were greatly improved through the work of CCC. It planted trees and built camp and picnic sites, trails, roads, dams, and shelters. Under supervision of the War Department, CCC constructed resident camps for the enrollees and for administration; the Department of Labor was charged with selecting the youth. The departments of Interior and Agriculture had the responsibility of planning and supervising the various work projects. The first camp was located in the George Washington National Forest in Virginia. Within six months of the CCC's opening, over 300,000 enrollees were working in more than 1,500 camps, most of which were involved in some type of activity improving outdoor recreational opportunities and facilities.

The National Youth Administration (NYA), another section within FSA, provided part-time employment for needy high school and college students to enable them to continue their education. Many of the students were assigned to local recreation agencies as aides. All agencies conducted ongoing training programs in conjunction with the recreation activity programs and often utilized the specialized training resources of the National Recreation Association. In 1939 there were 375,000 students employed in NYA programs.

The housing programs of the federal government also benefited. Both indoor and outdoor recreation facilities were provided for in public housing projects in accordance with an established per-family housing unit formula. They were developed in cooperation with local recreation agencies and community organizations. These programs recognized the relationship of health and sanitation to recreation. Recreation facilities and services were stressed in the care and rehabilitation of the ill and aged; standards were established for nursing homes and hospitals. Also, sanitary engineers from the Public Health Service worked closely with the National Park Service in the planning, development, and operation of national parks during the 1930s. This effort and technical assistance on sanitation problems as they pertain to park-recreation developments have been continued by both federal and state agencies.

The Impact of World War II

As the United States began to recover from the Great Depression, war broke out in Europe and a new set of problems emerged. With the termination of the government's work relief programs, recreation services were severely curtailed in many areas, although some communities were able to sustain programs. However, another era in the history of organized recreation in America began with the nation's entry into World War II.

The effects of the war upon recreation were both positive and negative. Once again, mobility was limited by gas rationing; industrial expansion received high priority; critical materials were scarce; and recreation development was limited to military installations, neighboring communities, and industrial plants. Prior to America's formal declaration of war, the army established the Morale Division (later Social Services) within the Adjutant General's Office to assume responsibility for on-post recreation programs in the event of mobilization. As military personnel left for war and became less able to participate in leadership roles in community life and recreation programs, the demand for professionally trained personnel increased. In recognition of this need, the National Recreation Association (NRA) assigned its field staff to assist key cities. Community in-service training programs were expanded; local groups served as sponsors.

In 1940 Roosevelt appointed Paul V. McNutt, administrator of FSA, national coordinator of health, welfare, and related defense activities. Several months after his appointment, he established a recreation division, which grew rapidly and employed a trained staff of seventy-five to aid impacted communities by offering technical assistance. This unit duplicated some of the work initiated by NRA and its field staff, which had already organized community defense recreation communities in fifty cities. The FSA's recreation division secured NRA staff assistance for its programming in many of the impacted areas.

In the meantime, the United Service Organization (USO) was formed as a private agency to raise funds and function in a manner similar to the War Camp Community Service of World War I. The USO established servicemen's clubs in large cities and smaller impacted military communities. Federal funds were used to construct and renovate several hundred buildings. The American Red Cross was also involved and established clubs and programs overseas and in hospitals. The Veterans Administration developed a comprehensive recreation program in its hospitals and institutions. The war's social impact led to an expansion of recreation services. Youth centers were established in hundreds of communities to cope with delinquency problems as parents were forced to spend less time at home because of work and war activities.

During this period, states began to develop recreation agencies. The FSA and the NRA provided specialized services to states, but differences developed in the philosophies of these two groups. They remained at odds on several issues, especially the way services should be offered. Top leaders in the FSA recreation division were also influential in the American Recreation Society, and they worked for a congressional bill to establish a new federal bureau of recreation to carry on nationwide consultation work. Despite their efforts, no action was taken by Congress.

U.S. Air Force

Servicemen craft programs during World War II were continued as public recreation programs after the war.

The effects of World War II upon local recreation were even more striking than those of World War I. Large numbers of service personnel for the first time had experienced an opportunity to enjoy extensive recreation facilities and diversified programs. Furthermore, every American community benefited from the effects of home-front recreation during the war. The concept of living war memorials, initiated after World War I, ex-

panded. Construction of recreation centers, playgrounds, parks, athletic fields, swimming pools, band shells, and similar facilities and areas paid tribute to the American war effort. Recreation became established as a valid and necessary American institution, as its value to the lives of Americans became widely recognized.

The Federal Inter-Agency Committee on Recreation (FICR) was established in 1946 to increase the effectiveness of federal public recreation services through joint planning and coordination at the bureau level. Member agencies of the committee included units within the departments of Agriculture; Army; Health, Education, and Welfare; and Interior. The Housing and Home Finance Agency (later the Department of Housing and Urban Development) was also involved. The committee's objectives were to (1) serve as a clearinghouse for information on policies, plans, methods, experiences, and procedures among agencies; (2) consider problems and recommend basic principles; and (3) facilitate distribution of information about federal recreation programs. It also sought to clarify the proper responsibilities of the federal government in the recreation field, fill in gaps in federal programs and services, and stimulate state agencies to develop facilities and services. The NRA (now the National Recreation and Park Association) provided free services of an executive secretary for the seventeen years of the committee's existence.

New Trends and New Concerns

By 1950 recreation expenditures represented 5.1 percent of total consumer expenditures, as compared to 3.0 percent in 1909. Providing recreational opportunities had become a major function of government, and efforts were renewed to acquire and develop park lands and build specialized facilities. There was also a need to renovate existing properties. However, the country once again experienced a shortage of critical materials as the Korean conflict further postponed many projected capital projects.

As the Korean hostilities ceased, capital programs and further advancement of community recreation services resumed. There was a rapid expansion of the hospital recreation programs as a result of casualties suffered in the conflict. Over 2,000 municipalities had established year-round recreation operations utilizing over 58,000 workers, of which 7,000 were employed full-time. Although this was a 300 percent increase over 1930, the community services fell short of recognized standards established by NRA.

A significant step was taken during the 1950s, as park and recreation systems were combined in most cities into a single agency. As a result, college and university curricula were modified to provide courses in both parks and recreation management. Graduates of these programs quickly assumed administrative positions because of the demand for professionally trained personnel that was accentuated by the retirement of those who had entered the field in the 1920s.

During the 1950s, several trends in parks and recreation emerged:

1. Greater expansion of adult recreational opportunities, especially for women;

2. Growing concern for those having physical or mental handicaps, and increasing employment possibilities for this group in hospitals, institutions, and nursing homes;

3. Greater focus on outdoor recreation and management of natural resources, with a tremendous surge in group and family camping and water activity;

4. Expansion of national competitive sports for boys by the public and private sector;

5. Increase in cultural opportunities, with emphasis on the performing arts;

6. Increased concern for land acquisition and planning and action to prevent encroachment upon park and recreation areas;

7. Implementation of the United States Supreme Court decision on racial integration and the need to deal with the effects of new policies on public recreation;

8. Establishment of county level recreation and park systems to meet the rapid growth in the suburbs and unincorporated areas, sometimes resulting in consolidation of city and county services;

9. Development of park-school programs, which involved acquisition and utilization of land adjacent to school buildings for instructional activities.

U.S. Bureau of Outdoor Recreation

Bicycle trails such as this one near Washington, D.C., are proven attractions for family use.

Of major significance in the 1950s were the dramatic increases in the number of hours of leisure time (about 2,200 hours per year) available to the average employed person; the rise in the real income of the average family; and a population growth that exceeded expectations. In 1952 presidential candidates, Dwight D. Eisenhower and Adlai E. Stevenson, both spoke of these developments and urged their supporters to think in terms of the new and abundant America. Eisenhower noted:

Science and technology, labor-saving methods, management, labor organizations, education, medicine, politics, and government have brought within our grasp a world in which back-breaking toil and longer hours will not be necessary. Leisure, together with education and recreation opportunities, will be abundant, so that all can develop the life of the spirit, of reflection, of religion, of the arts, of the full realization of the good things of the world.

During the 1950s, the Federation of National Professional Organizations for Recreation was formed as a vehicle for information exchange among the growing number of national recreation organizations. Greater coordination efforts were made between the major municipal professional groups—the American Recreation Society and the National Recreation Association. These groups jointly sponsored a National Recreation Congress. They also worked closely with state agencies and started state recreation societies.

At the beginning of the 1960s, Americans were enjoying unprecedented prosperity. Advances were occurring in industry, the arts, science, social programs, and parks and recreation. Americans were working less, traveling more, eating more, saving more, spending more, and living longer. The Outdoor Recreation Resources Review Commission (ORRRC), established in June 1958 to study the nation's outdoor recreational resources and needs, completed the extensive report in 1962 and stated:

Leisure is the blessing and could be the curse of a progressive and successful civilization. The amount of leisure already at hand is enough to have made many Americans uneasy. Ours is a culture that has always been inclined to look upon idle time with some misgivings for reasons that trace to the Puritan tradition of industry, but which spring also from the historic and very practical need for hard work in the building of a nation. Certainly a substantial adjustment in perspective will be required as we move into a period in which the leisure available to all citizens will be greatly increased.

In any event most Americans face the prospect of more leisure in the future, and thus, the challenge of using it for their own enrichment and development. This is precisely the contribution that recreation can make. For at its best recreation activity is a "renewing" experience—a refreshing change from the workday world.

With the publication of this study, the federal government recognized as never before the importance of recreation in the life of all Americans. During this period, expanded superhighway networks allowed increased mobility without stress; public recreation programs proliferated; and outdoor recreation boomed. Park and recreation personnel were hired in increasing numbers in the public and private sectors. As attention was directed to functional and aesthetic planning and design of park and recreation areas and facilities, legislative action created new funding programs to enable states and their political subdivisions to acquire park acreage for outdoor and community recreation. Development of coordinated master plans by local, state, and national agencies was mandated.

In accordance with ORRRC's recommendation, the Bureau of Outdoor Recreation was established in the Department of Interior in April 1962. The new bureau was to study the nation's outdoor recreational resources and needs and prepare a nationwide plan. It was later also given the assignment of administering the funds established by the 1965 Land and Water Conservation Fund Act. Some revenues came from the sale of surplus federal real property and the motorboat fuel tax, but the mineral leasing receipts from the Outer Continental Shelf furnished most of the revenue. The purpose of the fund was to finance lands for federally administered recreation areas and to provide matching funds to state and local governments for recreation planning, acquisition, and development. By 1975 about $2 billion had been expended under this fund: 60 percent by the states and their subdivisions and 40 percent by the federal government. The appropriations were at a $300 million per year rate.

Innovative programs responsive to new philosophies of play, recreation, and leisure emerged during the 1960s. Focus shifted from playgrounds and athletics to cultural opportunities, performing arts, and the needs of special groups. These changes resulted in the 1965 consolidation of some of the major organizations in the recreation and park field; and the National Recreation and Park Association was founded after seven years of effort to achieve a united voice.

The 1960s brought new opportunities for urban residents with the creation of vest pocket or mini parks. These small open spaces scattered throughout urban areas became highly valued by city dwellers. When properly developed and maintained, these land parcels provided a refreshing alternative to the cold concrete of the city environment.

The forerunner of the contemporary mini park was the one-half-acre plot leased by authorities in New York City to three residents in 1733 for conversion to a bowling green. Known appropriately as Bowling Green, the area remains a landmark in the center of the city's financial district. This concept was revived in the 1960s when Philadelphia and New York acquired and developed a series of small, centrally located open areas in congested neighborhoods.

U.S. Bureau of Outdoor Recreation

Small areas with playground equipment became attractive neighborhood parks.

In 1961 the City of Philadelphia established a land bank operation to acquire parcels of land through its Department of Licenses and Inspections. The program's unique feature was a provision permitting organizations or groups to lease, at no cost, city-owned parcels for public purposes. An organization called the Neighborhood Park Program was formed to develop the vest pocket park sites as a cooperative venture between citizens and city government to prevent neighborhood blight and to provide for leisure activities for residents.

At the same time, New York City began an extensive vest pocket park program which included Riis Plaza, a three-acre site surrounded by low-income, high-rise apartments in lower Manhattan; Bedford-Stuyvesant Park, a one-block tract located in a deteriorating, depressed area; and Paley Park, perhaps the most publicized mini park of the century, which opened in 1967 on a mere one tenth of an acre in the heart of New York's shopping district. Both Bowling Green and Paley Park were created as a result of intense citizen interest and support rather than as a result of park authority initiative or funding. Considerable controversy surrounded the creation of Paley Park, including the realistic concern that mini park areas could prove to be neighborhood nuisances because of the difficulty of administering and maintaining them. However, with proper planning and maintenance of such areas, the quality of life in many American cities has been improved by the existence of these small, green open spaces.

Another innovation in the use of small land parcels also occurred during the 1960s. Known as X-way parks, these recreation sites and landscaped parks were created within expressway rights-of-way. In 1968 Miami, Florida, pioneered this type of multiuse development by creating parks and erecting playground equipment apparatus at several locations under I-95 in the heart of the city. Some cities followed Miami's lead in later years.

Other potential areas for outdoor open spaces and recreation are America's cemeteries. Many neglected public cemeteries can be and are being turned into community assets. In changing land use areas, cemeteries present a "posture of stability, continuity, open space, and beauty." They also serve as an ecological buffer to urban sprawl. This is not a new concept. Recreational use of cemeteries was common before parks and recreation areas were established in and on the outskirts of cities. The famed Forest Lawn Memorial Park in Los Angeles, for instance, has been a tourist attraction for over fifty years. The fountains, mosaics, statues, and

National Park Service

The Grand Canyon of the Yellowstone River is located in Yellowstone National Park.

lush landscape make it a favorite beauty spot of the nation. With sensitive, careful, innovative design and administration, these areas can provide additional park and recreation facilities close to population centers where the needs are greatest.

The National Park System

Millions of Americans enjoy the natural splendors and outdoor recreation attractions of the National Park System. This part of the development of the nation's parks began on March 1, 1872, when Congress established Yellowstone National Park "as a public park or pleasuring ground for the benefit and enjoyment of the people." The founding of this 2.2-million-acre site in the Wyoming, Idaho, and Montana territories inaugurated a new policy of perpetually reserving public lands for purposes "other than material gain." This action set aside federally owned land for a public park to protect and preserve the natural environment. While it was the first action establishing a federal reservation for park purposes, President Abraham Lincoln had signed an 1864 act in which Congress granted Yosemite Valley and the Mariposa

Sequoia Grove to the State of California for use as a public park. Since the state had great difficulty in administering the grant, the valley was returned to the federal government in 1906 to become part of Yosemite National Park, which was created in 1890.

The national parks serve to preserve wilderness much as it would have been when the colonists landed in the New World. Their purpose is to ensure the uninterrupted flow of nature's processes and maintain intact prehistoric and historic evidences of what has occurred throughout the centuries. Harvesting of timber, hunting, mining, grazing, and commercial enterprises are prohibited. Despite attacks by special interest groups, the national park concept was staunchly defended by members of Congress and solidly confirmed between 1872 and 1916, as parks were established from public lands throughout the West.

The 1891 Forest Reserve Act separated national parks from national forests and created distinct systems. A parallel movement was begun during this time to preserve the cliff dwellings, pueblo ruins, and early missions on the vast public lands of the South-

Public Works Histroical Society

Rainbow Bridge in southeastern Utah was designated a
National Monument in 1910.

west. This preservation movement had its
roots among scientists and civic leaders in
Boston and spread to Washington, D.C., New
York, Denver, Santa Fe, and other centers
during the 1880s and 1890s. The 1906 Antiq-
uities Act established the national momument
concept. It authorized the President to designate as national monuments historic landmarks situated on lands owned or controlled
by the United States. National parks, on the
other hand, could only be established through
congressional action. With this legislation
came recognition of the national and historic
significance of the Indian lands and cliff
dwellings. Between 1906 and 1916, twenty
national monuments, including the Petrified
Forest in Arizona, were designated by three
Presidents.

With the creation of the National Park
Service (NPS) in 1916 within the Department
of Interior, the federal government increased
its involvement in the park and recreation
movement. This agency was established by
Congress to "promote and regulate the usual
federal areas known as national parks, monuments and reservations and to conserve the

scenery and the natural and historic objects
and wildlife unimpaired for the enjoyment of
future generations."

As the first director of the National Park
Service, Stephen T. Mather outlined an administrative policy based upon three major
principles: (1) that the national parks be maintained unimpaired; (2) that the parks be set
apart for the use and pleasure of the people;
and (3) that the national interest must dictate
all decisions affecting public or private enterprise in the parks. The secretary of interior
urged that the parks be used for educational
as well as recreational purposes and that both
low-cost, concessioner-operated camps and
free camps be provided. At its inception, the
Park Service was responsible for fourteen national parks, twenty-one national monuments,
and several reservations.

The railroads provided the first access to
many of the national parks and built hotels
and lodges, such as those at Yellowstone,
Grand Canyon, and Zion national parks,
which still survive. Concessions were granted
from the beginning, usually to one conces-
sioner who controlled most or all the business
in the park. This policy has caused controversy between the "purists" and the "recrea-
tionists" through the years. However, the
course followed by the Park Service has
steered a middle ground which appears to
best meet the overall public interest.

Before 1916 coordinated operation of
parks and monuments was lacking, for the
responsibility was divided among several
federal agencies. The establishment of the National Park Service created the concept of a
National Park System. In 1933 President
Roosevelt signed Executive Order 6166 which
substantially enlarged the National Park
System. Mather and his successor, Horace M.
Albright, with the support of the successive
secretaries of interior, Presidents, and members of Congress, laid the foundations for the
National Park Service as it now exists:
uniformed ranger service; information and interpretive programs; and the professional
wildlife, forestry, historical, architectural, and
landscape services.

President Roosevelt's executive order in
1933 placed all national parks, monuments,

military parks, cemeteries, memorials, and the National Capital Parks (over 300 parks in the Washington, D.C. area) under the direction of the National Park Service. This consolidation created a single agency responsible for all federally owned parks, memorials, and historic monuments; and it increased the system's holdings by adding a dozen areas in nine western states and Alaska and fifty-seven historical areas in the eastern part of the country. This action brought the National Park Service into urban areas, thereby modifying the traditional orientation toward remote areas. Entrance into urban America eventually led to the creation of innovative recreation programs in large cities in the late 1960s.

The emergency work programs of the Depression years had a tremendous impact on the National Park Service and on the national, state, and municipal parks all across the nation. All work done on park lands, whether federal, state, or municipal, was under the supervision of the National Park Service. Over 120 CCC camps, each with 200 enrollees, were employed in nearly all the national park areas in constructing and improving campgrounds, buildings, trails, bridges, utilities, and roads. Historic buildings and battlefields were restored and visitor facilities provided. A total of 482 CCC camps carried out similar work on state park areas under the supervision of the Park Service. Unused land near cities was converted into fifty recreation demonstration areas which were later given to the states. From 1933 to 1940, $130 million was appropriated for the 650 CCC camps operating under the supervision of the Park Service. The technical staff to handle the program required 7,000 landscape architects, engineers, foresters, biologists, historians, architects, and archaeologists, about equal to the total permanent Park Service employment in 1976.

The effect of these programs on the national parks was profound. They served to awaken Americans to their outdoor heritage; they provided public works facilities to visitors at the sites; and they built up a highly professional multidisciplinary staff to operate and manage the nation's outdoor parks. Unfortunately, the tragedy of World War II

cancelled many such programs and reduced activities to a minimum holding action. In 1943 the regular appropriations for managing the National Park System were cut from $21 million to $5 million; the number of full-time employees was reduced from 3,510 to 1,970; and visits to the parks fell from 21 million in 1941 to only 6 million in 1942. After peace came in 1945, the lull before the Korean crisis was short, not enough to provide needed support to the National Park System before military needs again became dominant in funding priorities.

However, after World War II, visits to the national parks increased. From a low of 6 million in 1942, the visits in 1950 grew to 33 million; by 1954 they totaled 54 million; and by 1960 they increased to 72 million. These increases in the face of limited funding and manpower created great problems for the National Park Service. The park facilities were inadequate, run down, and out of date. Trails were washed out, and the narrow roads into park areas were inadequate for automobile traffic and were in dangerous conditions. Employee morale was at a low level because of the difficulties of coping with three times as many visitors as the areas were equipped to handle.

Director Conrad L. Wirth instigated a year's planning effort to develop a coordinated approach to maintaining and expanding the park system to meet the ever-increasing demands. Out of this effort, the far-reaching "Mission 66" program was born which rejuvenated the National Park System. Approved by congressional action in 1956 at a cost of over $1 billion, this ten-year development and acquisition plan provided for the construction of visitor accommodations and other public works facilities—including over 4,000 miles of new roadways to increase accessibility to and through the park areas. More than 130 new visitor centers were constructed, with the museums and information centers serving as the focal points for visitor information and interpretation. For the first time, funds were appropriated to purchase lands to create national parks and historic areas. This program also established two training camps for in-service training for park rangers and other personnel at Harpers Ferry, West Virginia, and Grand Canyon National Park.

Over the years, the National Park System has expanded to include recreation areas, seashores, demonstration sites, lakes, wild and scenic rivers, linear trails, and parkways. The 1936 Park, Parkway and Recreation Area Study had enabled the Park Service to plan facilities on a cooperative basis with state and local agencies. Later the authority led to the creation of four new types of federal park areas: reservoir-related recreation areas, recreation demonstration sites, seashores, and parkways.

In 1964 new directions were chartered as a result of *Parks for America: A Survey of Park and Related Resources in the Fifty States and a Preliminary Plan* prepared by the Park Service. Legislative actions of Congress had established three categories of areas within the National Park System: natural, historical, and recreational. In the postwar years, the great population increases and diminishing open spaces placed urgent emphasis on national recreation areas. This required greater effectiveness by the Park Service as a "people serving" organization. Legislation in the 1960s, including the 1964 Wilderness Act, the 1965 Land and Water Conservation Fund Act, the 1966 Historic Preservation Act, and the 1968 Wild and Scenic River Act, added responsibilities and complexities to the National Park Service and its management problems.

One of the most complex difficulties in the national parks is how best to provide roads into and through the parks. This problem has been under continuing scrutiny, especially since the great increase in automobile travel in the last three decades. With policy established by the National Park Service, the design and construction of the roads are performed under the supervision of the Bureau of Public Roads (now the Federal Highway Administration). The enduring objective has been to find a proper balance between building roadways to move automobiles efficiently and preserving the natural beauty which gives the park visitor a meaningful experience. The problem continues to require multidiscipline cooperation between engineers and park professionals. Positive action to deal with the extreme traffic congestion in Yosemite was taken in 1974 by limiting the number of visitors and by establishing, on a demonstration basis, mass transportation for park visitors in shuttle buses.

The 1970 Public Land Law Review Commission report urged the Park Service to ration the use of certain parks and wilderness areas so as not to compromise the visitors' experience. This policy is under continuing evaluation. In the 1970s, rangers were receiving training for coping with civil protests, drugs, and other stressful situations. Special recruitment procedures were also established to assist in hiring those most suited for the new working conditions.

A performing arts component was added to the National Park System in 1971 when Catherine Filene Shouse donated her 117-acre Virginia estate, Wolf Trap Farm, to the federal government as a center for the performing arts. The outdoor Filene Center, financed by a contribution from Shouse, seats 3,500, with

National Park Service.

The 630-foot-high St. Louis Arch was constructed as a memorial to settlement of the West. The arch and the 90-acre park site was financed one fourth by the City of St. Louis and three fourths by the federal government.

room for 3,000 more on the adjacent lawn. Largely supported by a private foundation, the cultural center also offers a credit course in the performing arts to high school and college students in cooperation with a local university. Other similar facilities will undoubtedly be included in future programs.

In 1975 the total lands administered within the National Park System exceeded 30.5 million acres, including 308 areas. In 1974 there were over 217 million visitor-days at the parks, compared to 33 million in 1950 and 170 million in 1970. The system provides 29,000 developed campsites in 440 campgrounds. The fiscal year 1975 appropriation totaled $209 million for administration and operations and $195 million for constructing and improving the public works facilities of the system.

Future expansion targets for the Park Service will probably be in the urban park area. One of the great social goals of America in the years ahead will be to provide recreational opportunities to the growing numbers of city dwellers. The strength of the National Park System over its almost 100 years of existence has been its ability to respond to the changing needs of American society.

National Forests

Congress authorized the creation of national forests from the public domain in 1891 and established the Yellowstone Timberland Reserve. Gradually over the years, additional large land tracts were set aside as forest reserves. Franklin B. Houg became the first government forestry employee in the Department of Agriculture in 1876 and paved the way for the establishment of a Division of Forestry within the Department of Agriculture. It became the United States Forest Service in 1905. The 1891 act set aside forest resources and prohibited the tracts from being used for other purposes. However, an amendment in 1897 permitted multiple use, provided the other uses did not conflict with supplying and harvesting timber.

Gifford Pinchot, former governor of Pennsylvania, was appointed chief forester in 1898 and became head of the division of forestry. In 1899 Congress passed a law authorizing recreational use of forest reserves, the first legislation recognizing the recreational value of forests. Later legislation permitted leasing forest lands for hotels, resorts, summer dwellings, and sanitariums.

Among the important functions of national forests are providing outdoor recreation and fish and wildlife habitat, along with range, timber, and watersheds—the five primary resources given equal emphasis under the 1960 Multiple Use Act. These outdoor recreational opportunities, along with those in national parks, are among the natural heritage available to the American public. Visitor-days at forest areas nearly equal those at national parks, over 200 million per year by 1976. These visits are made possible by access to the forests from the system of federal aid, state, and county highways and roads. Public works within the national forests include 221,000 miles of roads, 100,000 miles of trails, 85,000 developed family camp sites, and 458 interpretive areas. In addition, there are permits for individuals and concessioners for 19,000 recreation residences, 216 winter sports areas, 558 organization camps, and 370 lodges and resorts. The total capacity can provide facilities for 1.4 million people at one time, although the biggest problems of the increasing number of visitors are furnishing an

U.S. Forest Service

During the 1930s, the Forest Service supervised 1,800 CCC camps in America's forests.

unpolluted water supply and handling liquid and solid wastes.

The recreation support facilities of the national forests received a boost during the Depression years from the various emergency employment programs. For instance, the Forest Service had approximately 1,800 CCC camps under its supervision during the nine years of the program, over half working in national forests and the remainder in state and private forest lands. A large percentage of the camps were involved in providing public works related to outdoor recreation activities. Accomplishments included over 50,000 acres of campsites, 10,000 acres of picnic areas, 120,000 miles of forest roads, and various support facilities such as latrines and toilets, fences, trails, water supply, and wastewater treatment and disposal facilities.

As in other outdoor recreation areas, the surge declined during and after World War II. However, the postwar increase in automobile travel brought more people into forest areas. The growth of suburban communities usurped thousands of acres of open land for population growth, and there was an expanding awareness and appreciation of the role federal forests could play in alleviating the pressures facing urban residents and meeting their needs for leisure opportunities. In the late 1950s, the Forest Service launched the National Forest Recreation Survey to inventory its resources as a first step in achieving maximum multipurpose use of forest tracts. The program stressed the need for coordinated management so that all resources could be put to best use, yet still afford opportunities for recreation. The passage of the 1960 Multiple Use Act marked a turning point in the management of forest lands. It stressed managing renewable resources in a way that would best meet overall needs of people; and it gave additional emphasis to using land for purposes other than timber production.

In recent years, federal aid highways and better county and state roads have made forest lands more accessible; their scenic beauty added another dimension and increased their value. For instance, forests near large urban areas—such as the George Washington National Forest, a few miles from

U.S. Forest Service

A Forest Service guide explains woodland life to a group of city youths in George Washington National Forest in Virginia.

the District of Columbia, and the Los Angeles National Forest—attract thousands of visitors seeking open lands and relief from the stress and congestion of metropolitan areas.

In 1966, 151 million visitor-days were recorded for national forests. Although 34 percent of the United States population lived west of the Mississippi River, over 91 percent of the national forests were located in the West. This concentration was an important factor, for it related to the location of all federal outdoor recreational resources noted by the Outdoor Recreation Resources Review Commission in its 1962 report. The Forest Service developed plans to put recreation facilities where the people were and established goals for expanding recreation in national forests. Subsequently, "Outdoor Patterns for People," a pilot program, was begun in the George Washington National Forest in Virginia to provide experiences and learning opportunities for groups of inner-city youth who normally would not have visited such areas. Schools from metropolitan regions were invited to use national forests as outdoor classrooms.

In 1976 the Forest Service manages 187 million acres, 8.2 percent of the total land area of the United States. Whereas 151 million visitor-days were recorded in 1966, over 193 million were reported in 1974. Nearly 12 million acres of national forests are designated Wilderness Areas, about 95 percent of the nation's wilderness system. A major portion of the National Wild and Scenic Rivers system is in national forests, as is the case with the National Scenic Trails and the National Recreational Trails systems. The 83,000 miles of fishing streams and the 2.2 million acres of natural and created lakes within the national forests provide an environment for many species of fish as well as millions of outdoor recreation hours. A program of managing the landscape to furnish visual effects for man's psychological welfare, is carried out by the multidisciplinary professionals in the Forest Service.

Recreation in national forests differs from recreation in national parks by tradition and definition. Camping is comparatively primitive, and facilities are limited. In national forests, semi-precious stones may be sought and collected; pine cones and common plants may be taken home; game animals, birds, and fish may be hunted or caught in accordance with state laws; and dead timber, forage, and other materials used for camping may be collected. These activities are not permitted in the national parks. The role of the national forests helps fulfill Gifford Pinchot's dream at the turn of the twentieth century that "the rightful use and purpose of our natural resources is to make all the people strong and well, able and wise, well taught, well fed, well clothed, and well housed, full of knowledge and initiative, and with equal opportunity for all and special privilege for none."

State Parks

The 1864 congressional grant of Yosemite Valley and Mariposa Sequoia Grove to California for use as a public park was the only state involvement in park activities for many years. Then the New York State legislature set aside land at Niagara Falls as a public reservation in 1885 and established a forest reserve in the Adirondack Mountains, which several decades later became a state park.

National Recreation and Park Association

New York State set aside land at Niagara Falls as a public reservation in 1885.

Also during that year, the federal government ceded Fort Mackinac to Michigan to start that state's park system. However, the development of state lands for recreational purposes did not take hold until the 1920s, as the national parks concept attracted public attention and interest. As people experienced the wilderness of Yellowstone and Yosemite, they encouraged state political leaders to consider the establishment of large, natural areas as state properties.

At the invitation of Iowa's governor in 1921, several hundred conservationists met in Des Moines. National Park Service Director Stephen T. Mather spoke of the problems confronting his agency in responding to the requests to establish national parks in eastern, southern, and midwestern states. An outgrowth of this meeting was the creation of the National Conference of State Parks (NCSP), an incorporated body of state representatives, whose prime purpose was to stimulate local, county, state, and national governments to acquire land and water areas suitable for recreation, the study of natural history, and the preservation of wildlife. The goal was to provide accessibility to recreation areas for all the people.

In a California State Park Survey, Frederick Law Olmsted in the 1860s set forth principles that had a great impact on state park planning: state parks should be of interest and importance to all visitors; they should contain scenic and recreational resources not likely to be preserved and made available under private ownership; and they should be geographically distributed so as to be accessible to people in each part of the state. There were some differences of opinion with regard to the philosophy of state parks. One faction viewed a park only as a haven for urban residents, a place to relax, play, and picnic; the other faction saw a park as a rich storehouse of scenic views, memories, and reveries that required a special location. In 1953 NCSP adopted a statement for use by state park administrators, "Suggested Criteria for Evaluating Areas Proposed for Inclusion in State Park Systems," which classified sites as parks, monuments, recreation areas, beaches, parkways, and waysides.

State areas and facilities draw more visitors than nationally operated sites because they are more accessible to high-density population centers and provide a variety of facilities as well as natural beauty and undisturbed lands. Jones Beach State Park, begun in 1926, annually attracted more than 15,000,000 persons in the early 1970s. It was built under the leadership of Robert Moses and contains 6 miles of ocean beach and a half mile of bay frontage.

Florida Department of Natural Resources
The lighthouse at Cape Florida State Park is located just south of Key Biscayne.

Prior to World War II, the concern of state governments for recreation centered on park systems. In the 1950s, states began to provide consultation and other forms of recreation assistance to political subdivisions and actively coordinate and cooperate with federal and local agencies charged with park and recreation responsibilities. State involvement enabled smaller communities to meet the needs of residents and thereby avoid gross inequalities of service from community to community.

With the passage of the 1965 Land and Water Conservation Fund Act, states stepped up statewide master planning for parks and recreation. By 1976 some states had developed fifth-generation master plans, and federal funds totaling $1.2 billion had been made available on a 50 percent matching basis and were being provided at a $180 million annual rate. The program has been well administered and has produced impressive results. The open space program of the Department of Housing and Urban Development has been effective in assisting states in acquiring and developing outdoor recreation properties in connection with housing developments.

State personnel are employed to deal with recreation in correctional institutions, institutions for the handicapped, and senior citizen centers. Legislation has been passed in the states to permit greater use of resources for recreation. While state and federal funds are used to assist communities, personnel are employed at Cooperative Extension Service units at state land-grant colleges to assist with recreation development in rural areas. Expanded environmental awareness programs have been developed by state park and recreation administrators in response to the return-to-the-land, back-to-nature, bike-for-health slogans of 1972 and 1973. Nature interpretive programs have also been established and expanded. The recognition of park and recreation needs by states in the past speaks well for the years ahead.

County Parks

Until 1895 when Essex County, New Jersey, pioneered the idea of a county park

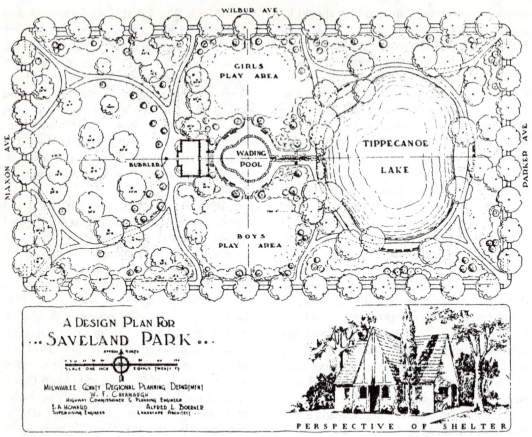

Saveland Park, designed in the 1920s, is a part of the Milwaukee County, Wisconsin park system.

system, the only county-owned properties serving a park function were the county courthouse square and the county fairgrounds. By the 1920s, however, a survey by the Playground Association of America identified 322 county properties totaling 105,943 acres, with 97 of 3,200 counties reporting a park commission or park lands. At the beginning of the 1920s, a few counties were considering turning over the fairgrounds to towns and cities or to other county authorities to further their development and use.

County properties of that era can be classified as (1) parks of 25 to 100 acres found primarily in metropolitan areas; (2) parks of 150 to 500 acres generally located outside the central city boundary; (3) reservations of 500 to 5,000 acres acquired to preserve woodlands and areas of natural beauty; (4) parkways created to preserve and protect natural features

on access ways from the city to the surrounding countryside and occasionally to connect units of the county system; and (5) parks in rural, sparsely populated areas developed to serve as outdoor recreation centers for residents of small communities unable to provide recreation resources.

In general, easily accessible county properties supplemented city areas, offering pleasant settings for outdoor recreation and family gatherings and calling attention to notable historic or physical features. During the Depression years of the 1930s, few counties could afford comprehensive park systems; consequently, many sites were acquired and developed for camping and recreational purposes by private or semi-private organizations, such as the Young Mens-Young Women's Christian associations and 4-H clubs.

Although formal zoos had not been

established in county parks, many parks served as game preserves; some sheltered birds; and Cook and Alleghany counties in Pennsylvania protected buffalo. Hunting was generally prohibited, but fishing was a popular activity.

Opportunities for active recreational participation in county systems gradually increased. But few indoor facilities existed in the 1920s, primarily because of limited funds. There were some pavilions built for dancing, and some structures erected for golf courses or pools. The 5,000-seat County Center Auditorium in Westchester County, New York, was equipped for a variety of functions. Food service facilities were sometimes provided in county parks.

As a result of the post-World War II demand for recreational opportunities and the pressure brought by urban residents for close-to-home outdoor recreation, county parks increased dramatically—from 933 in 1950 to 2,610 in 1960. In 1930 county park acreage totaled 46,565, and by 1960 it had risen to 430,700 acres. A detailed survey by the Bureau of Outdoor Recreation in 1972 showed counties were administering 1.3 million acres of parks and recreation areas; 5.5 million acres of forests and fish and game areas; and 1.3 million acres of wilderness and natural areas, for a total of 8.1 million acres.

In 1962 the National Association of Counties (NACO) formed a special committee to clarify and develop a meaningful policy for county parks and recreation. Its 1964 publication, *National Policy for County Parks and Recreation,* committed NACO and its members to consider parks and recreation as an essential function of county government. The policy statement also paved the way for tax levies, creation of park systems, and liaisons with other levels of government and private agencies.

In 1976 millions of Americans find a variety of leisure pursuits within county parks. For many, close-to-home opportunities are more desirable than ever before, especially in light of financial and fuel constraints. Greater use of flood plains for recreational purposes is also expected to result from the better management of these areas. Thus,

future acquisition, planning, and development strategies will maintain and expand the valuable county park and recreation systems. Energy problems with probable decreased mobility will create greater pressures for expansion of county parks. An excellent base has been established for this expansion.

Water Related Recreation

According to an estimate of the federal Water Resources Council, about one fourth of all recreational activity in the 1960s and 1970s was dependent upon water bodies, and approximately two thirds of all designated publicly administered recreation areas have a body of water within their boundaries or were adjacent to water. Water resource public works developments have created great outdoor recreational opportunities. Not only do they provide for the popular activities of boating, water skiing, swimming, and fishing, but the areas surrounding them support camping, hiking, bicycling, picnicking, horseback riding, hunting, pleasure driving, and outdoor games and sports.

The nation's seashore line totals about 37,000 miles, exclusive of Alaska. Of this amount, 11 percent is federal property and 12 percent is owned by state and local governments. In 1975 there were 3,400 miles of public beaches, which were some of the earliest water-related recreation facilities provided by government. The engineering works built to control rampaging floods, store precious water, harness water power, and support navigation created spacious playgrounds. Recreation was, however, initially incidental to these developments. For instance, legislation for Bureau of Reclamation projects made no provision for recreation facilities until the 1950s, and then usually on the basis of matching fund arrangements with other government agencies operating the recreation features of the project. In the 1944 Flood Control Act, Congress gave the Army Corps of Engineers authority to "construct, maintain, and operate public park and recreational facilities in reservoir areas under the control of the secretary of the army, and to permit the construction, maintenance, and operation of such facilities." By 1976 the corps was operating and managing the largest water resource recreation program in the nation, with 2,700 recreation areas developed and another 3,500 areas with few or no facilities at 400 major lakes with 40,000 miles of shoreline. The public spent over 400 million visitor-days at these areas in 1975. Many of these facilities, as well as the Bureau of Reclamation and Tennessee Valley reservoirs, are near population centers and easily accessible. Pressures on the national parks and wilderness areas are thereby eased, and outdoor water-oriented recreational opportunities are made available to those who otherwise would be unable to afford them.

U.S. Bureau of Reclamation

Reservoirs created by flood control and resource development projects provide boating and related activities to millions.

The 230 reservoirs with 12,200 miles of shoreline administered by the Bureau of Reclamation accounted for 64 million visitor-days of water-related recreation during 1974. The Tennessee Valley Authority reservoirs provided about 61 million. The recreation visits to the small watershed program facilities of the Department of Agriculture and to the recreation facilities built as a part of the Federal Power Commission license requirements of non-federal hydroelectric projects were equally impressive. By the 1970s, the staffs of water resource development agencies included landscape architects, biologists, foresters, recreation planners, and various other disciplines as well as economists and engineers for planning and constructing the projects.

Boating is a particularly popular activity on rivers and lakes. The small pleasure craft industry has mushroomed since World War II. Boat ownership rose from 2.5 million in 1947 to 9 million by 1973. In 1974 an estimated 50 million persons in the United States went boating more than twice. The sport has become big business, with yearly expenditures amounting to over $3 billion for boats, equipment, supplies, and services. Public expenditures for water resource development, including navigation improvements, have laid the basis for the growth of this recreational pastime.

To accommodate pleasure boating, Congress authorized the Army Corps of Engineers to construct small craft harbors. These sheltered areas provide a safe location for local interests to build and operate marinas to serve the needs of the boating public. States, counties, municipalities, private companies, and individuals have constructed launching, docking, and service facilities along America's seacoasts and throughout the inland lakes and waterways system. By 1973 there were over 3,000 marinas in the United States.

Facilities vary widely at marinas, but most offer the boat owner a berth, fuel, dockside electricity, fresh water, laundry facilities, marine stores, waste disposal system, and hauling, repair, and storage facilities. On-shore services may also include a restaurant, lounge, swimming pool, and other sources of entertainment. Most marinas are privately owned, but since the early 1960s many state and local jurisdictions have built marinas and operated them on a direct or leased basis. For instance, Marina del Rey, California, one of the world's largest, is a multimillion-dollar facility operated by the County of Los Angeles. It provides berths for about 6,000 craft.

In seacoast areas and on large lakes, marinas are situated in protected harbors that provide a safe haven for small craft. Protective works such as jetties and breakwaters are constructed at the harbor entrance. These structures furnish a safe, convenient navigation entrance, dissipate waves, and prevent littoral drift from encroaching on the harbor's entrance or mooring areas. The Army Corps

Army Corps of Engineers

This marina at Berkeley, California, is typical of many public works built for recreational boating.

of Engineers will create a harbor by building the outer protection and access channels, if public or private developers supply lands, easements, rights-of-way, public docks, and other facilities. Generally, the federal government assumes the total costs of jetties, breakwaters, and channels for harbors intended for commercial uses such as fishing. If a harbor is used for recreation, local interests furnish 50 percent of the costs. Publicly owned marinas are usually financed by several public agencies. Small craft facilities can be financed by several means including general obligation bonds, revenue bonds, or direct tax levies. Under some circumstances, federal loans are available to assist communities in undertaking harbor improvements.

Boating services are also available on federal property. Several federal agencies, including the Army Corps of Engineers, Forest Service, National Park Service, Bureau of Sport Fisheries and Wildlife, and Bureau of Reclamation, lease waterfront sites to private individuals and companies for the construction and operation of marinas and other recreation facilities. These concession sites are situated on lakes and reservoirs created to provide flood control, hydroelectric power, navigation, and irrigation. Services, including piers, fishing docks, fueling depots, snack

bars, launching ramps, and marine supply and repair facilities are privately built and are periodically expanded to meet the rapid growth of water recreation. Use of water-oriented recreational resources has increased over 10 percent per year in the last two decades. This growth is expected to continue, especially in the more accessible areas.

Trends of The Future

The mobility and increased leisure time of 1976 America, along with the availability of park and recreation areas, have resulted in recognition of recreation as a basic need for and an essential part of a quality life. The domestic and international strife, urban congestion and sprawl, crime and civil disturbances, pollution and environmental abuses of the 1970s have made a return to the land and a more simple life more attractive. Thus, the years ahead are likely to witness a much greater participation in outdoor recreational activities and more visits to areas of natural beauty.

Possible decreased mobility due to the energy problems, increased leisure time, and a slowing or a leveling off of affluence will put greater emphasis on local and more easily accessible areas. However, growing population will insure continuing pressures on all park

U.S. Bureau of Outdoor Recreation

Public tennis courts provide outdoor recreational opportunities to all ages.

and outdoor recreation facilities. Providing public works that will make enjoyment possible, prevent deterioration, make natural areas available, while at the same time perserving them, will be the big challenge. Facilities that will supply access, water, food, and shelter; manage and control wastes; and prevent destructive activities from ever-increasing numbers of people can be built in recreation areas.

For instance, park and recreation programs are receiving greater and more intelligent attention at all levels of government and are becoming more responsive to the changing needs of the American public. New types of programs are being offered in urban areas; new technology makes possible better and more effective facilities and types of equipment; design and construction approaches create new leisure environments more suited to greater numbers of people. Leisure education is being introduced into the public school curriculum. Professional training focuses upon preparing personnel to work with new user groups—ethnic and racial minorities, disabled persons, and senior citizens. Strategies are being developed to offer close-to-home activities as mobility is curtailed by fuel shortages and inflation restrictions.

Some of the developments that can be expected to increase in the future are hiking trails, nature areas, flood plains for recreation activities, outdoor sports such as tennis, better picnicking and camping areas, and more winter activities. The 2,000-mile Appalachian Trail through the East and the Canada to Mexico Pacific Crest Trail in the West will be used more extensively, and the thousands of miles of other scenic trails under study will result in the construction of many more trails and facilities. In 1976 greater value is being placed on parks, forests, wilderness areas, beaches, lakes, and waterways. For they "strengthen bodies, refresh minds, uplift the spirits, and enrich leisure."

Thousands of miles of hiking trails, such as this one in Zion National Park, offer exhilarating outdoor recreation.

SUGGESTED READINGS

American Heritage. *Book of Natural Wonders*. New York, 1963.

Breckman, C. Frank. *Recreation Use of Wild Lands*. New York, 1959.

Douglass, Robert W. *Forest Recreation*. New York, 1969.

Everhart, William C. *The National Park Service*. New York, 1972.

Federal Interagency Committee on Recreation. *Role of the Federal Government in the Field of Public Recreation*. Washington, D.C., 1961.

Fitch, Edwin M., and Shanklin, John E. *The Bureau of Outdoor Recreation*. New York, 1970.

Frome, Michael. *The Forest Service*. New York, 1971.

Hibbard, Benjamin H. *A History of the Public Land Policies*. Madison, Wisconsin, 1965.

LaGasse, Alfred, and Cook, Walter. *History of Parks and Recreation*. Arlington, Virginia, 1965.

Lee, Ronald F. *Family Tree of the National Park System*. Philadelphia, 1972.

National Geographic Society. *America's Wonderlands: The Scenic Natural Parks and Monuments of the United States*. Washington, D.C., 1959.

——————— . *Vacationland U.S.A.* Washington, D.C., 1970.

——————— . *Wilderness U.S.A.* Washington, D.C., 1973.

National Recreation and Park Association. *Play for America: Recreation and Parks*. Arlington, Virginia, 1972.

Olmsted, Frederick Law, Jr., and Kimball, Theodore. *Frederick Law Olmsted: Landscape Architect*. New York, 1922.

Public Land Law Review Commission. *One Third of the Nation's Land*. Washington, D.C., 1970.

Tilden, Freeman. *The National Parks*. Rev. ed. New York, 1968.

——————— . *The State Parks: Their Meaning in American Life*. New York, 1962.

U.S. Department of Agriculture. *Outdoors U.S.A. (1967 Yearbook)*. Washington, D.C., 1967.

U.S. Department of Interior. Bureau of Outdoor Recreation. *Outdoor Recreation: A Legacy for America*. Washington, D.C., 1973.

Van Doren, C.S., and Hodges, Louis. *America's Park and Recreation Heritage*. Prepared for the Bureau of Outdoor Recreation, Department of the Interior. Washington, D.C., 1975.

Weir, L. H. *Parks: A Manual of Municipal and County Parks*. 2 vols. New York, 1928.

CHAPTER 18

MILITARY INSTALLATIONS

Public works are a vital part of the United States military establishment. During the past two centuries, these structures and facilities housed personnel and provided logistical and maintenance support for ground forces, ships, and aircraft. The following discussions of army, navy, air force, and coast guard public works survey the evolution of the facilities that helped the United States to win and preserve its independence and become a world power.

ARMY

The history of the United States Army's public works is a story of growth from stark simplicity to a sophisticated network of global bases. It began with crude breastworks at Bunker Hill and advanced through the fortifications of harbors against powerful foreign enemies. It then spread to the erection of small western forts to guard the vast unsettled frontier. Military installations have armed, sheltered, and provided training facilities for generations of American troops from the eighteenth century to the recent Vietnam conflict. These forts, cantonments, and hospitals com-

This chapter is based on materials provided by the Army Corps of Engineers, Naval Facilities Engineering Command, United States Air Force, and the United States Department of Transportation.

prise a rich heritage of public works achievements.

Building a New Nation

During the Revolutionary War, the American army had little opportunity to construct its own military installations. However, some British-built forts were occupied and played significant roles in the fight for independence. The Americans occupied the strategic position at West Point and constructed Fort Putnam to block the British Hudson River invasion route. In 1775 Colonel Ethan Allen captured Fort Ticonderoga, which sat astride the route from New York to Canada. Once an English stronghold between Lake Champlain and Lake George, it was used by Allen as a jumping off point to attack Montreal. In the South, the heroic defenders of Fort Moultrie at Charleston, South Carolina, inflicted heavy casualties and drove off a British invasion fleet. At the engagement on Bunker Hill (actually fought on the adjoining Breed's Hill), a field fortification was erected by the army's first chief engineer, Colonel Richard Gridley, who fortified the positions by building breastworks.

During the conflict, the movement of the opposing sides precluded construction of training camps or cantonments with the possible exceptions of the American winter quarters at Valley Forge, Pennsylvania

(1777-1778), and Morristown, New Jersey (1778-1779), which were comprised of log huts thrown up by the ragged Continental Army. Some coastal forts were built along the Atlantic seaboard by piling up earth and timbers or whatever materials were at hand. A notable exception to these primitive installations was Whetstone Point near Baltimore, Maryland, which later became famous during the War of 1812 as the site of Fort McHenry. The fort was built by Maryland and consisted of a battery, magazine, military hospital, and barracks. Although it never came under enemy fire, the fort deterred British naval operations in Chesapeake Bay and protected the strategic port behind it from attack.

Army Corps of Engineers

In June 1776, the defenders of Fort Moultrie thwarted a British invasion.

After the close of the American Revolution, the United States Army was demobilized and reduced to only eighty men. The former colonies were bound to one another by the weak Articles of Confederation which made no provision for a national armed force in peacetime. Efforts were made to maintain seacoast fortifications through contracts with civilian engineers. In 1789 the new republic created its present Constitution, a much stronger document which empowered Congress to establish a standing national army. Six years later, Congress revised the contractual system of maintaining fortifications and created a Corps of Artillerists and Engineers to assume active direction of most fortification work.

Concern for national defense was prompted by fears of renewed hostilities with Great Britain and led, in 1794, to congressional authorization of what became known as the First American System of Seacoast Fortifications. Under this system, the secretary of war ordered the repair of three existing positions and the fortification of an additional sixteen harbors on the Atlantic Ocean. This action was not intended to constitute a permanent defense system but was rather a response to the pending emergency. Consequently, the forts were principally open works with earth parapets. However, some permanent installations such as Fort McHenry were built. The strength of these structures varied. The number of guns at each site ranged from eight to several dozen, depending on the nature and importance of the harbor to be protected. The First American System was not exclusively a federal effort. Individual states provided much of the armament and retained ownership of the fortification sites. The armament and design of the resulting fortifications, therefore, were far from uniform.

The new republic also found itself exposed to French and Indian attack in the West. In the 1790s, Indian tribes in the Ohio Territory began to resist the growing encroachment of eastern settlers. The young republic sent Generals Josiah Harmar, Arthur St. Clair, and Anthony Wayne against them. The ensuing campaigns moved the military frontier still farther west, and many of the older forts were abandoned as a new chain of frontier defenses along the Ohio River and its tributaries replaced them. To anchor this defense network, Governor Arthur St. Clair built Fort Washington at the site of present-day Cincinnati.

In 1794 the United States occupied and restored an old French post, Fort Massac, on the north bank of the Ohio River, a few miles above its confluence with the Mississippi.

Fort Pickering was erected in 1797 at the mouth of the Tennessee River; and a year later, a fort was established on the Mississippi at present-day Vicksburg. The southern frontier of the United States was defended against the Spanish and Indians by four hastily constructed posts in Georgia.

On the diplomatic front, the United States acquired additional holdings which had to be governed and defended by military installations. In 1794 the British and Americans signed the Jay Treaty which ended British occupation of American installations. Fort Niagara, New York, located at the union of the Niagara River and Lake Ontario, was taken over by United States troops on August 11, 1796. Fort Mackinac, Michigan, strategically situated on the straits between Lakes Michigan and Huron, was occupied in October 1796. The military center at Detroit was given over to the Americans that same year. In 1795 Thomas Pinckney concluded a treaty with Spain that provided for free navigation of the Mississippi River to citizens of both countries and gave to the United States Fort St. Stephens near Mobile, Alabama.

By the turn of the century, the influence of the United States had spread far to the west and south of the initial coastal strip occupied by the original thirteen states. During the 1790s, military installations were erected or occupied throughout the trans-Appalachian region. With the decline of Spanish strength, the southern frontier was menaced only by Indian tribes. Along the Atlantic seaboard, coastal fortifications protected the republic's harbors.

It had become clear that the regiment of Artillerists and Engineers could not combine effectively the two duties assigned to them. Congress, therefore, passed a law separating them into two corps, declaring that the Corps of Engineers should be stationed at West Point, New York, and "shall constitute a Military Academy." This act of March 16, 1802 set the strength of the new installation at five officers and ten cadets. It also provided that the "principal engineer shall have the superintendence of the Military Academy, under the direction of the President of the United States." Major (later Colonel) Jonathan Williams, a nephew of Benjamin Franklin, was the first chief engineer of the United States under the 1802 act and has been called the father of both the Military Academy and the Army Corps of Engineers. The duties of the engineer officers precluded their remaining full time at West Point. Most of them were soon called out to construct fortifications along the seaboard. Furthermore, the academy not only trained engineers and artillerists but also supplied officers to all branches of the service.

It was a propitious time for America to begin developing its engineering skills. In 1803 the country doubled in size, and engineers were needed as explorers, surveyors, planners, and builders. The Spanish retroceded the Territory of Louisiana to the French in 1800, and the concessions of the Pinckney Treaty appeared lost to the United States. Especially troublesome was the withdrawal from American traders of the right of deposit at New Orleans. This action closed off the main commercial artery for the West, and President Thomas Jefferson feared that the United States soon would have no alternative but to "marry ourselves to the British fleet and nation." In an effort to avoid armed conflict, Ambassador James Monroe went to Paris to try to buy the city and part of Florida from the French.

Before he arrived, however, the French foreign minister called in resident American Minister Robert R. Livingston and asked how much the United States would offer for all of the Louisiana Territory. Within a week, a treaty was signed, tendering to the young republic an area larger than the entire United States in exchange for $15 million.

In its enthusiam of expansion, the United States found that it had assumed the obligation of occupying what had been essentially a huge foreign territory. Initial investment in the area, therefore, had to be military in nature. United States troops first entered New Orleans on December 20, 1803; and they located the first American garrison in the territory at Fort St. Philip in that city. Early in 1804, the army took over five other former French posts and in 1805 built Fort Belle Fontaine on the south bank of the Missouri River,

This 1827 view of West Point shows typical cadet barracks and academic buildings.

a post that became military headquarters for the Middle West.

Building military installations influenced the opening of the Louisiana Territory in three ways. First, the forts reduced the danger of British, French, and Spanish intrigue which had been rampant throughout the area. Second, they opened up for possible settlement the valleys of the Mississippi, Arkansas, and Missouri rivers. And third, they helped to maintain order among the Indians then living in the area.

As the United States expanded, its military installations also grew in number. There was, however, no real plan and certainly no permanence about the structures that dotted the geography of the new nation. Already the fortifications which had been built or rebuilt on the Atlantic seaboard after 1794 were beginning to lapse into disrepair, as Congress neglected to vote appropriations for improvement or upkeep.

But the antagonism between America and Great Britain which led to the War of 1812 evoked a renewed concern for coastal defenses. Between 1807 and 1812, more than $3 million was appropriated for harbor protection. Under the program known as the Second American System of Seacoast Fortifications, Congress authorized construction at practically every port and harbor. For the first time, engineers of American birth supervised the work; most of them were graduates of the Military Academy at West Point.

Unfortunately, the planning for the Second System was still limited and uncoordinated, and there were extreme variations in the armament and structure of the fortifications. Many of the Second System forts were masonry-faced earthen structures. Open batteries in linear, polygonal, and curved shapes continued to be built. These were of low durability and were usually small works constructed at relatively unimportant sites or as supplements to larger forts.

During Jefferson's Administration, the army solidified its control of the Northwest Territory. In 1803 troops erected Fort Dearborn at the present site of Chicago. Five years later, Fort Madison was established in Iowa on the bank of the Mississippi near the mouth of the Des Moines River. These forts thwarted efforts of English traders and agents to incite the Indians against American authority. In 1811 Fort Harrison was built on the Wabash River to further guard against possible Indian attacks.

British intrigue among the Indians continued and contributed to the outbreak of war in 1812. During the conflict, several western and northern forts became the scene of hostilities. In 1812 pro-British Indians descended on Fort Dearborn and massacred American troops and civilians as they evacuated the post after surrendering. In Iowa, the garrison at Fort Madison successfully resisted a threatening band of Indians; but in Michigan, Fort Mackinac fell to a British force, followed by Fort Niagara, New York. The most important American fort to fall was Fort Detroit, which surrendered to the British without a fight in August 1812.

As war flared, American engineers stepped up the construction of harbor defenses, interior forts, arsenals, and winter cantonments. Their most famous endeavor was strengthening the defenses at Fort McHenry near Baltimore. In 1813 a local committee advanced $40,000 to the federal government for restoration of the strategic fort. Engineers repaired the earthen ramparts of the outer batteries and replaced defective wooden gun platforms and carriages. The front and rear of the fort were protected; and in August and early September 1814, when a British attack appeared inevitable, a long line of strong entrenchments was dug to guard the eastern approaches to Baltimore. On September 13, sixteen British warships began the intensive bombardment that inspired the national anthem. Over 400 shells landed within the defenses, but of the thousand defenders, only four were killed and twenty-four injured. Fort McHenry held strong. Indeed, none of the forts built by army engineers fell to the British in battle.

The 1815 Treaty of Ghent which ended the conflict restored the lost forts in the West to the United States, but their capitulation during the war had shaken confidence. In response, the number of western forts was expanded. Most notably, Fort Howard at Green Bay, Wisconsin, for a quarter century would play a key role in western frontier defense between the Great Lakes and Mississippi River.

The state of seacoast installations was of even greater concern. Although by 1815 almost every large harbor was sheltered by military works, they varied widely in size and quality. The First and Second systems had produced few permanent structures since each program had been a response to an emergency. In truth, the two spasms of building hardly merited the name "systems," for they failed to provide a uniform and mutually supportive body of defenses.

In 1816 Congress decided to remedy this by appointing a commission to establish a long-term program for permanent military construction. Accordingly, the Board of Engineers for Fortifications was charged to designate positions requiring fortification, establish general fort designs, and review plans of engineers in charge of specific projects. The board traveled for nearly five years, consulting with engineers and examining sites. Their 1821 report formed the basis for the Third American System of Seacoast Defense. Giving primary attention to the navy, the board indicated locations for major naval bases, repair yards, and anchorages. They also recommended specific fortifications to guard naval facilities, commercial seaports, and river mouths. The commission continued to function until 1850, submitting periodic reports on the nation's defense needs.

The new works developed during the Third System included a group of thirty massive, vertical-walled forts known as "principal forts" and simple, inexpensive detached batteries erected in locations of secondary importance. Of the initial group, Fort Sumter, South Carolina, where the first shots of the Civil War were fired, was a prime example of antebellum military engineering. The magnitude of the task is indicated by the quantities of materials involved, most of which came from the North. Ten-thousand tons of granite and 60,000 tons of other rock were brought in from as far away as Maine. Brick and sand could be obtained locally; but brickyard capacities were small, and millions of bricks were required. Similarly, hundreds of thousands of bushels of seashells were needed to manufacture concrete. By 1860 Fort Sumter was a five-sided masonry fort designed for three tiers of guns. Its 5-foot-thick outer walls, which towered nearly 50 feet above the water, enclosed an acre parade ground, quarters for officers and enlisted men, gunrooms, and storage facilities.

Following the War of 1812, increasing pressure from whites for Indian lands led to consideration of a plan to give Indians property in the West in exchange for their eastern tribal holdings. The first such exchange came in 1817, when a group of Choctaw Indians from Alabama and Mississippi consented to take land in Arkansas. President Monroe backed the program and in 1825 promised the Indians that the federal government would move and protect them in their new homes. The federal authorities entered into treaties with the western (Plains) Indians to secure land for the relocation.

By the 1830 Removal Bill, Congress assigned to the War Department the task of negotiating with tribes of the American South. Between 1820 and 1845, the Indians gradually were forced to move to less habitable lands beyond what was known as the "Permanent Indian Frontier," a line west of Arkansas and Missouri. Army posts were garrisoned in the area to prevent conflict between the newcomers and the Plains Indians, to watch over the immigrants who suffered starvation and degradation during the westward march, and to forestall encroachment of white settlers. To define this Permanent Indian Frontier, the army established a chain of posts, running from Forth Snelling, Minnesota, on the north to Fort Jesup, Louisiana, on the south.

The wholesale removal of Indian tribes was reflective of America's pre-Civil War expanionist fervor which sometimes flouted international law. After the War of 1812, many people regarded Spanish Florida as rightfully belonging to America. Denuded of military forces by the declining imperial power, Florida was a haven for fugitives and belligerent Indians who frequently raided southern Georgia and Alabama. In 1817 Andrew Jackson, commissioned by the President to pacify the border, exceeded his authority by invading the Spanish possession and deposing its governor. In the process, he summarily hanged two Indian chiefs and two British subjects who reportedly abetted them. Bowing to the American occupation, Spain signed the 1819 Adams-Onis Treaty, ceding all of Florida and firmly establishing the western boundaries of the Louisiana Territory. By conquering Florida, the United States took possession of several forts, including Castillo de San Marco at St. Augustine, a relic dating from 1672.

By the 1840s, expansionists believed it was the United States' "manifest destiny" to expand the republic's limits from sea to sea. In 1844 James K. Polk was elected President

Army Corps of Engineers.

A fort on the Potomac River was one of the installations that protected the nation's capital from attack during the Civil War.

on a platform which called for annexing Texas and acquiring Oregon and California. After Texas entered the Union in March 1845, disputes between Mexico and the United States regarding the location of the new state's western boundaries touched off the Mexican War. During this conflict, little attention was given to troop shelter. Most forts were stripped of their personnel, who were transferred to the Mexican front and bivoacked in tents for most of the conflict. The overwhelming American victory over the Mexicans added territory which required establishment of still more military installations. Under the 1848 Treaty of Guadalupe Hidalgo, the United States received half of Mexico's land mass, from which the states of California, Utah, Nevada, and parts of Wyoming, New Mexico, and Arizona were eventually carved.

The extreme northwest corner of the United States was still in dispute. The British claimed the area, but American trappers, missionaries, and farmers settled the region and disdained English authority. Tensions ran high, but a third war with England was averted by a compromise in 1846 which set the boundary between the United States and Canada at the forty-ninth parallel. The nation's grand design was nearly complete, and army posts were soon established to protect the vast region for the swarms of immigrants who trod the western trails.

Discovery of gold in California and southern Oregon upset all previous planning for western military installations. The fever for gold unleashed a tide of migration, and the lines of forts designed to watch over transplanted eastern Indians began to be diverted to protect wagon trains making their way westward. In the decade preceding the Civil War, the army was essentially a western frontier force scattered in small posts over 3 million square miles, guarding the great routes between the Mississippi and the Pacific Ocean. Over such routes as the Oregon Trail, from Independence, Missouri, to the Columbia River, and the Santa Fe Trail, stretching from Fort Leavenworth to Santa Fe, passed gold seekers, settlers, traders, overland stages, and the Pony Express—all protected by the far-ranging system of small forts.

Preserving the Union

The Civil War brought revolutionary changes in military ordnance which made coastal fortifications such as Fort Sumter practically obsolete. The introduction of armorplated ships equipped with rifle-barreled guns rendered existing defenses nearly useless. Both sides discovered very early in the conflict that masonry forts were easily shattered, whereas a defense of earth or sand could suffer the impact of a projectile and be quickly repaired. Fortifications completed during the Civil War, therefore, were mostly earthworks, erected in large numbers on inland rivers, around cities, and in several coastal locations.

The most sophisticated military installations were those guarding the nation's capital. At the outset of the war, Washington, D.C., found itself geographically vulnerable, directly on the line dividing North and South and within shelling range of Virginia. General Winfield Scott of the Union forces organized volunteer and regular troops to defend the city. Engineers began constructing a defensive system. Their plan was to occupy commanding points, locate forts within cannon range of one another, and connect them by infantry parapets.

These positions were occupied by the first Union offensive in May 1861. The Union forces hastily began building lunettes, redoubts, batteries, and forts. They developed a defensive line which cut an arc through the Virginia countryside. This ring of defenses was soon to become a haven for retreating Union forces following their defeat at the first battle of Bull Run. After this sobering lesson, Major John C. Barnard was appointed as chief engineer; and under his direction, the defenses of Washington expanded into a unified protective system. By 1862 a thirty-seven fort defense network had been created. This was expanded to sixty-eight forts by 1865. Lines were extended in a 37-mile perimeter around the capital. Gradually, new blockhouses were built, entrenched positions between forts connected, and military roads constructed.

The Civil War was the first American conflict to involve large masses of troops; and for the first time, troop shelter was a serious problem. Older permanent military installations had barracks, but these were generally either at seacoast fortifications or at frontier posts in the West. The permanent inland installations that did exist could only serve as reception depots where troops seldom remained more than a few days. The regiments pouring into Washington for its defense were temporarily sheltered in public buildings. In other places, state authorities resorted to using empty stores, halls, and courthouses.

Most volunteers were quartered at small camps. The first troops to arrive at new camps built the barracks they occupied. The quartermaster furnished tools, lumber, and other materials, and the men did the work. Under these circumstances, the design had to be simple: generally long, one-story buildings with an entrance at one end, a broad aisle running through the center, and a double row of bunks—one above the other on either side. By the spring of 1864, standardized plans for barracks were provided to the Union quartermasters. They were 24- by 128-foot, two-story structures with provision for ventilation in summer and heat in winter. The first floor provided officer quarters, kitchens, and storerooms. The second floor had a dormitory for troops, and the bunks were arranged in three tiers down the length of the two side walls.

When troops left the training camps for active service in the field, they were quartered in tents. This kind of shelter ranged from large pyramidal and wall tents for command posts to two-man shelter or "pup" tents. In winter the soldiers built huts as they had since the American Revolution. The troops usually settled in a well-timbered area, and within a few days a city of log cabins was erected. In contrast to the earlier army encampments, in the Civil War the huts were ordinarily covered with tents.

Quartermasters distributed supplies to troops in the field through a depot system. The depots were sometimes built by the troops but more often by mechanics and laborers attached to the repair shops that accompanied the armies in the field. These civilian employees also constructed sheds and platforms to protect supplies, stables for animals, guardhouses, quarters for officers, and any other facilities required.

Union armies also constructed permanent arsenals during the war. However, it was not possible to equip the Union Army from stores on hand nor by running the government arsenals at capacity. Therefore, the Ordnance Department had to rely on private firms, even though dependence upon inexperienced manufacturers often resulted in poor quality control.

For the care of sick and wounded in the field, the Medical Department developed a policy of evacuation and hospitalization. Casualties received emergency treatment at a series of medical stations established in the forward areas of combat zones. Nearly every regiment had a medical detachment to provide such treatment and transportation for patients.

As fighting increased, provision for hospital facilities became a matter of deep concern. At the outbreak of hostilities, most hospitals, like other military installations, were situated in the West. There were no general hospitals at first, so hotels, schools, and other buildings in eastern cities were commandeered until more suitable accommodations could be constructed. A national Sanitary Commission raised such a clamor over conditions in these makeshift facilities that in 1862 the Quartermaster Department ordered construction of the first pavilion hospital in Parkersburg, West Virginia. This was followed later in the year by a modest hospital building program. In the South and Midwest, general hospitals were constructed at Memphis, Chattanooga, Louisville, and other locations on the Ohio River. The largest was the Jefferson General Hospital at Jeffersonville, Indiana. This was a 2,600-bed facility with twenty-four pavilions radiating from a circular corridor a half mile in circumference.

Throughout the Civil War and into the 1870s, the western frontier was ablaze with Indian uprisings; and new army posts were constructed to deal with specific outbreaks. When the Civil War ended, large numbers of troops were shifted to the West to quell the hostilities. In 1869 President Ulysses S. Grant instituted a "peace policy" for dealing with the Indians. This new program arose because of a growing concern among eastern humanitarians that after the original Americans were subdued they should be cared for and converted to the white man's way of life. This involved setting aside more reservations to be held inviolate against white intrusion. However, the proposed beneficiaries of this treatment regarded the reservations as enslavement, a compulsory confinement that robbed them of their lands and freedom. Hositlities continued until the Indians were subdued in the 1880s. Subsequently, many of the western forts were either phased out or manned by a smaller complement of personnel.

Elsewhere in the country, little heavy military construction was undertaken except for a brief spurt of building in the 1870s which resulted from Anglo-American tension over British aid to the former Confederacy. This issue was resolved by arbitration, and, subsequently, defense spending for construction lapsed for ten years. In 1885 President Grover Cleveland asked his secretary of war, William C. Endicott, to form and head a special board to review coastal defenses and to recommend an updating program that would take into account advances in weaponry. The board was composed of representatives from the army, navy, and civilian sectors. Early in 1886, it presented a proposed program for a large number of defensive installations to be armed with weapons of unprecedented firepower. Fortifications were to be built at twenty-six coastal locations and three points on the Great Lakes.

Becoming a World Power

Improvements were made in quartering some military personnel in the late nineteenth century. Brick structures with plumbing and heating were made available for officers and their families. Quarters for both officers and enlisted men began to have indoor latrines, baths, and central heating systems. Candlelight gave way to oil lamps and gaslight in the barracks.

Nevertheless, during the Spanish-American War, as in the Civil War, few of the fighting men were stationed at permanent posts. When the war began, the federal government owned 49,000 tents which provided shelter for foot soldiers during the conflict. These were attempts to make a comfortable and safe environment at the camps. This regimental report provides a glimpse of the public works that were undertaken at Camp Wikoff on Long Island:

> The work of the Second Regiment . . . comprised the laying out, pitching, and striking of camps for other troops, the erection, and subsequently the operation, of the camp water supply, including wells, pipe lines, pumps, and filter, much work in connection with the general hospital, road repairs, the erection and starting of the Signal Corps electric lighting plant.
> The main water supply . . . included the supervision of driven wells by contract, the laying of several miles of pipe (in part by civilian labor) from 6 inches to 1 inch, reaching all camps; the erection of tanks, the installation and operation of pumps, and a filter, all for a supply of 500,000 gallons a day.

The defeat of Spain and the acquisition of a colonial empire led the United States to change from its former policy of opposing large peacetime standing armies. At American posts, shelter had to be provided for a much larger force than the 25,000 men on the military rolls prior to the Spanish-American War. Expansion of posts involved more than the mere construction of barracks. It also required building hospitals, storehouses, and other specialized structures. Installations built between 1900 and 1905 were a far cry from the primitive frontier posts of earlier years. Funds were appropriated for constructing, equipping, and maintaining post exchanges, schools, libraries, lunchrooms, amusement rooms, and gymnasiums. During this period, the quartermaster general reported: "It is safe to say that a vastly greater amount of construction work was planned, undertaken, and contracted for during the fiscal year 1902-03 than during any previous year in the history of the Army."

In 1905 President Theodore Roosevelt called together a group to review once more the coastal defenses of the nation. He appointed his secretary of war, future President

William Howard Taft, to head this board. The members studied the program launched by the earlier Endicott board and determined that the harbors of the United States were fairly well protected by a vast body of fortifications. They did, however, recommend an addition of accessory harbor defense equipment—fire-control systems for aiming major caliber guns and mortars, searchlights, and general electrification of all aspects of harbor defense. The Taft board also gave attention to building coastal defenses in Hawaii and the Philippines.

This modernization work progressed until the United States became embroiled in a global conflict. With the outbreak of World War I, the United States was fighting a new kind of war—one that required vast numbers of troops. For the first time in the country's military history, providing adequate shelter for mass armies was recognized as one of the most demanding aspects of the military effort.

From the time of the American Revolution, Congress had charged the Corps of Engineers with combat construction as well as building fortifications, roads, and bridges. Sheltering troops, however, was a responsibility of the Quartermaster Corps. By 1917 the quartermasters had constructed installations for 124,000 men, but these facilities were inadequate to accommodate wartime mobilization. To house the estimated 1 million troops needed, construction of large reception centers and training camps was required.

Responsibility for building cantonments rested with the Construction and Repair Division in the Office of the Quartermaster General and a civilian Committee on Emergency Construction, later replaced by a Cantonment Division. On May 7, 1917, they were ordered by the general staff to build thirty-two cantonments to shelter the conscriptees who were to enter the service in September. They were expected to have suitable quarters for training a million men ready in sixteen weeks. Construction went forward rapidly. On June 11, the first contracts were let. By June 13, work was begun on the first cantonment, Camp Devens, Massachusetts. The following day, construction began at Camp Travis, Texas, and at Camp Dix, New Jersey. By September 4, some 287,000 recruits were housed; and at the year's end, a million men were in training.

The camps were essentially self-contained cities. The largest, Camp Lee, Virginia,

Barracks and lavatories were rapidly constructed at Camp Dix, New Jersey, after the United States' entry into World War I.

accommodated 45,500 men. Each cantonment had a full road system, power lines, and water supply. Unlike most previous American military installations, these centers possessed their own hospitals, bakeries, laundries, theaters, gymnasiums, and other amenities. Army troops lived in barracks. National guardsmen were quartered in wooden-floored tents, equipped with stoves.

Hospitals to accommodate 3 percent of each camp's population were also constructed. These originally provided 1,000 beds at each army camp and 500 to 800 at each National Guard camp. Later, two-story ward barracks were built, thereby increasing the capacity of hospitals by as much as 30 percent. In addition, embarkation hospitals were provided at ports such as Hoboken, New Jersey, and Newport News, Virginia. Meanwhile, general hospitals for returned overseas casualties were set up in widely separated districts, apart from troop concentrations. Among these were facilities for the blind, for tuberculosis patients, and for troops suffering from nervous disorders. To make an additional 5,000 beds a month available, the government also leased hotels, schools, and other public and private buildings.

At the start of the war, the Ordnance Department had nine permanent arsenals. These were expanded during the war to increase facilities for manufacturing small arms, ammunition, rifles, shells, artillery carriages, explosives, and light field artillery. In addition, other Ordnance Department installations added proving grounds, ordnance depots, and housing and cantonment projects. Aberdeen Proving Gound, located on Chesapeake Bay near Baltimore, covered 35,000 acres and was the largest and most extensive proving ground. The huge demand for weapons and ammunition also required the building of 3 million square feet of industrial storage space, 3.3 million square feet of magazine storage, and 13,000 linear feet of docks, together with necessary housing and operating utilities. These were constructed away from thickly populated centers because of danger to the civilian population and near deep water to avoid frequent handling of the high explosives.

By the war's end, the United States could take pride in its military construction record. Shelter for approximately 1.7 million men was provided at thirty-two camps and cantonments, four ports of embarkation, twenty special training centers, and numerous other posts and stations. Work was also completed on airfields, schools, hospitals, supply bases, and depots. Overall, the program included 581 projects, costing approximately $1 billion.

A desire to return to "normalcy" characterized the 1920s and led to a reduction of the army to a traditional skeleton force. Consequently, military installations began to fall apart—so much so that their decay became a national disgrace. In 1924 Secretary of War John W. Weeks proposed a long-range building program to remedy this situation. To support a peacetime army of 150,000 men, Congress enacted legislation to replace the temporary war structures still in use with proper permanent buildings. The army housing program was projected to cover a ten-year period and cost $148 million. As the program developed, careful attention was paid to layout plans for posts, applying modern methods of city planning in order to produce a functional arrangement. Handsome masonry installations replaced the unsightly "tempos" of World War I. Telephones, oil burners, storm doors, screens, and lighted streets enhanced the amenities of life on military reservations. Paradoxically, the Depression years served to expedite this construction of army housing, since the building program complemented efforts to relieve unemployment. By the late 1930s, approximately $150 million had been allotted for military construction.

Military medical facilities received attention during the ten-year construction program, and hospitals improved greatly. The Medical Department of the army was operating seven general hospitals and 119 station hospitals by 1939. Hospitals were designed to serve general and special needs. They received patients who suffered from severe or obscure diseases as well as those who needed complicated surgery. Five of the general hospitals were located in the United States: Walter Reed at Washington, D.C.; Army and Navy at

Hot Springs, Arkansas; Fitzsimons at Denver; Letterman at San Francisco; and William Beaumont at El Paso, Texas. The other two were in overseas possessions: Tripler in Hawaii and Sternberg in the Philippines. Of the station hospitals, 104 were on army posts in the United States and Alaska, and the remainder were divided among the Philippines, Hawaii, and the Panama Canal Zone. Station hospitals served local and ordinary needs, usually treating patients for minor ills and injuries.

The outbreak of war in Europe necessitated the first large-scale emergency construction effort since 1918. Between January 1939 and March 1940, $175 million was provided for strengthening seacoast defenses, modernizing arsenals, enlarging dozens of stations, and establishing ten new installations. This so-called "Expansion Program" was designed to prepare the army for possible global war.

In the spring of 1940, the Quartermaster Corps began to take the first steps toward war mobilization. This involved readying plans for building more than 300 structures of various types and sizes. Included were barracks, mess halls, hospitals, bakeries, laundries, storehouses, shops, administration buildings, recreation halls, post exchanges, theaters, and other structures. It was estimated that housing for 2 million men could be completed within nine months if funds were made available. The air corps also called for quick establishment of fields and training centers for 7,000 pilots a year, plus a much larger ground staff. Sites also had to be found for twenty-nine munitions projects. On May 31, 1940, the President urgently asked Congress for over a billion dollars to be used in "equipping and training in the light of our defense needs."

The Army General Staff, with Chief of Staff George C. Marshall setting most of the criteria, determined the locations for mobilization camps. Marshall decided to establish divisional camps and cantonments and to build a network of reception and training centers in nine corps areas. Old posts were expanded. If additional installations were needed, they were built, whenever possible, on federal- and state-owned lands.

The military success of the Axis powers in 1940 created pressure on all war-related programs of the United States. Many Americans believed it was imperative to begin training a large force of fighting men. A Selective Service Act was passed in September 1940, but it provided that no men could be drafted until "shelter, sanitary facilities, water supplies, heating and lighting arrangements, medical care, and hospital accommodations" had been provided for them. Thus, the problem of construction was critical for the whole mobilization program.

Across the country, as sites were selected to receive new draftees, private architect-engineering firms began designing camp layouts. Incomplete and tentative at first, they served as good working guides. Every unit, large and small, remained intact. Companies were grouped into battalions and battalions into regiments. Regimental areas adjoined a central parade ground, and hospitals were erected in isolated spots away from noise and dirt. Storage depots and motor parks were placed near railway sidings or along main roads. To prevent the spread of fire, buildings were at least 40 feet apart; and firebreaks, no less than 250 feet wide, were spaced at 1,000-foot intervals throughout the length of the camp. By December 1940, more than a half-million men were housed.

In addition to this work performed by the Quartermaster Corps, the Army Corps of Engineers was assigned a quasi-military airfield construction program for the Civil Aeronautics Administration. In September 1940, legislation was passed to share part of the total construction program with the Corps of Engineers. The first of these tasks was outside the continental limits of the United States. As a result of the Destroyer for Bases Agreement with Great Britain, the United States acquired the right to build military bases in the Caribbean and Canada, and the general staff assigned construction to the Corps of Engineers. The corps also assumed responsibility for all construction in Alaska; and in November 1940, the building of all facilities for the air corps was assigned to the Corps of Engineers. By the following March, the engineers were in charge of eighty-one such

A montage of facilities at Perrin Field, Sherman, Texas, illustrates World War II military construction.

projects at an estimated cost of $200 million.

The quarters awaiting the troops in 1941 resembled forty-six modern cities. They contained 1,537 miles of roads, 1,500 miles of sewers, 2,000 miles of water conduits, and 3,500 miles of electric cables. Their supporting storage tanks and reservoirs contained 118 million gallons of water. Structures for the 2-million-man army were well made. According to the quartermaster general, the new posts offered a healthy and comfortable living environment:

> Scientific planning has made barracks warmer than those of World War days. Where a thin strip of wood and tar paper made protection for 1917 soldiers, the 1940 trainee will live in barracks lined inside and out with composition insulating board covered with heavy planks. Many World War cantonments were heated by several small pot-bellied or cannon stoves. The new barracks each have a hot-air heating plant and fans to blow the heat into all corners of the buildings. Showers, wash basins, and toilets are located inside the barracks.

For a modern army of 2 million men,

shelter was not the only consideration. In 1940 legislation was passed for the "30 June Munitions Program" which called for construction of "government-owned, contractor-operated" (GOCO) plants. Unless such munitions plants could be brought quickly into production, however, the rest of the mobilization would be ineffectual. As the army expanded, the primary objects of concern became arsenals, munitions plants, depots, and factories where tanks and other military vehicles could be produced.

The supply of these items to other countries was an added problem. In January 1941, President Franklin D. Roosevelt announced his policy of making the United States the "arsenal of democracy." By March the Lend-Lease program stood ready to divide with Canada and Britain all the materiel the projected munitions program could produce. To expedite work and to save money, temporary plants were designed to last only five years. In all, seventy-three new GOCO plants were built with an investment of approximately $3 billion. The total acreage covered by these facilities was larger than the combined areas of New York City, Chicago, Philadelphia, and Detroit.

Construction of ordnance storage facilities kept pace with production. Five new ammunition depots developed into huge complexes, occupying a total of 110,812 acres. At Ogden, Utah, forty warehouses stored casings for the shell and bomb-loading plant. None of the munitions plants lacked adequate warehousing at any time. Even before the United States entered the war, the new government-owned munitions industry was ready to aid the Allied cause.

To provide medical care for the enlarged army, a coeval expansion of hospital facilities was required. Regular army posts which already possessed hospitals expanded them by converting hospital porches, barracks, and other available buildings into wards. However, new construction was soon required for the new draftees. In September 1940, the War Department changed its policy and instructed that cantonment-type hospitals be built at all new posts and many older ones. Planning for station hospitals was on a short-range basis because changing troop distributions affected their size, number, and location. Planning for general hospitals, on the other hand, was more comprehensive, since they usually served more than one post and were less affected by troop distribution. During 1941 nine general hospitals were added to the five in existence. By the time of the Pearl Harbor attack, the army had approximately 74,250 hospital beds available in the United States.

Meanwhile at air bases and at seacoast harbor fortifications, the Army Corps of Engineers was developing a great construction capability. As larger programs loomed ahead, the supply responsibilities of the Quartermaster Corps were also expanding. In September 1941, at the request of the secretary of war, a bill was introduced in Congress assigning all construction, maintenance, and repair of structures for the army to the Corps of Engineers. On December 1, 1941, six days before the Japanese attacked Pearl Harbor, President Roosevelt signed the measure into law.

Entry into global war meant mobilizing not only for defense of American shores but also for victory over Axis powers in far-flung theaters of operations. To carry out these goals, the United States armed 15 million men. The Army Corps of Engineers placed nearly $12 billion worth of construction inside the United States. The corps was responsible for 3,000 command installation projects undertaken in this program, including 230 cantonments; 140 ports of embarkation and staging areas; 210 general depots representing either new installations or expansion work at existing bases. The Corps of Engineers assumed maintenance responsibility for a vast military area, which included over a billion square feet of buildings, 62,640 miles of roads, 22,600 miles of electric lines, 12,550 miles of sewer lines, 4,260 miles of railroads, 12,860 miles of water mains, 2,860 miles of gas lines, and 1,590 miles of steam lines. In addition, the corps supervised construction of nearly 300 major industrial projects.

Medical facilities were again one of the major construction efforts. In the eighteen months following Pearl Harbor, enough additional hospitals were built to house more than three times the number provided during the peacetime mobilization. Ten general hospitals, including those already begun before the war, were built on a two-story, semi-permanent plan. For buildings at station hospitals, however, temporary construction similar to that used in the theater of operation overseas was common at first. Buildings of this type were of the lightest possible frame construction, with exteriors usually of heavy treated paper or fiberboard. Plumbing was omitted from barracks and placed in separate lavatory buildings. Heat was generally furnished by stoves rather than by a central heating plant. During 1942, as the shortage of materials increased throughout the United States, an even lower quality construction was proposed for some hospitals. For units in field tent camps for advanced stages of training, hospitalization for a time was provided in screened and floored tents. The corps also converted existing civilian buildings into army hospitals. The army acquired enough civilian structures to house twenty-three hospitals and to expand five others by the end of 1943.

Hospitals were also built near ports for troops awaiting shipment overseas and for patients being returned to the United States. During 1942 and 1943, several special port and staging-area hospitals were constructed. By 1944 there was a growing belief that convalescent patients recuperated more rapidly if kept occupied physically and mentally. The surgeon general, therefore, approved construction of libraries, swimming pools, athletic fields, and similar facilities at general and convalescent hospitals.

Outside the area of the forty-eight contiguous states, the Army Corps of Engineers extended the military construction program to the far reaches of Canada and Alaska in such projects as the building of the Alcan Highway and the Canol project. The first of these required creating a permanent gravel highway, approximately 1,500 miles in length through difficult terrain, in order to provide a land transport connection between Dawson Creek in British Columbia and Alaska. On this road,

Army Corps of Engineers

During World War II, the Alcan Highway was pushed through the Canadian and Alaskan wilderness.

in addition to corps personnel, 1,850 federal public roads engineers and over 14,000 civilian employees of contractors were utilized. After a season of surveys and completing a pioneer road, the major part of the project was finished in one four-month season. The Canol project involved the building of a pipeline to supply Canadian oil to the United States. In addition to these construction efforts, the corps also built numerous airfields for the extended protection of the Western Hemisphere.

The American homeland was still unscathed by war when the Axis collapsed. The giant industrial machine which had provided arms for the Western cause had been built to a capacity unparalleled in history, and American military forces were the most potent striking force ever mobilized. Yet, within months of V-J Day, this capability was reduced in traditional American postwar style. The American consumer demanded

reconversion of industrial capacity to the manufacture of civilian goods. Popular demands to "bring the boys back home" were followed by immediate demobilization of the fighting forces, leaving hardly more than the few needed for occupational duties in Germany and Japan.

However, the Cold War tensions which followed led to second thoughts regarding demobilization. The United States first attempted to help threatened nations such as Greece through international aid, both in military arms and in economic assistance. Then, the United States took the lead in organizing groups of states for their common defense. It developed a system of regional security and collective self-defense arrangements in the Western Hemisphere, Europe, and Asia. Finally, the American government recreated its own defense capability. In 1947 the military organizations were brought together within the Department of Defense, with a single cabinet member at its head. Under him came the three secretaries of the army, navy, and air force.

Defense of the continental United States shifted from protection of harbors and ports to defense of the northern skies. Advances in aviation during World War II indicated that enemy attacks would likely come by air over the North Pole. Protecting Alaska and the entire northern hemisphere had first priority in defense efforts. Almost a billion dollars were spent on building a defense base in Alaska. To meet this urgent need, the Corps of Engineers established a new Alaska District, with headquarters in Anchorage. Large permanent military installations were constructed, and the North American Air Defense (NORAD) came into being.

A radar network was created to give quick warning of any enemy attack across the polar reaches. A longer range radar system, called the Distant Early Warning (DEW) Line, was strung across Canada. Later, as the Soviet Union added ballistic missiles to its arsenal, the Ballistic Missile Early Warning System (BMEWS) was built to scan space from three radar posts in Alaska, Greenland, and England. Further deactivation of military installations for ground forces was slowed, and the selling off of military surpluses halted.

The outbreak of the Korean War in 1950 had relatively little permanent effect on military installations in the United States. A few bases underwent expansion and several closed posts were reactivated, but the conflict did not engender extensive military construction. Because of the mobility of the opposing sides, few permanent installations were built in Korea. However, the Corps of Engineers was active in erecting and repairing bridges and lines of communication and in building the port at Inchon under emergency conditions.

During the years between the Korean and Vietnam wars, the United States embarked on an orderly plan of permanent construction at military installations, patterned in five- and ten-year objectives. In this way, the Corps of Engineers was able to maintain a stable design capability. America's anti-aircraft defenses were brought up to date. The latest

in facilities for radar, missiles, planes, and other weapons were phased into the air defense system. As a defense against nuclear bombs from enemy aircraft the Army Air Defense Command, part of NORAD, constructed 262 surface-to-air missile sites.

Few large construction projects were undertaken at American army installations until the Vietnamese conflict. Techniques of fighting in Vietnam were different from previous conflicts, and special training facilities were needed. At Fort Benning, Georgia, for example, replica Vietnamese villages were built. Construction efforts were accelerated to maintain the new mobilization. At Fort Bragg, North Carolina, approximately 600 barracks were rehabilitated on a crash basis to house the sudden influx of recruits and draftees.

Because of the protracted nature of the Vietnam conflict, extensive facilities were erected in the quasi-republic. In 1965 a long-range logistical support plan was drawn up which specified the following priorities: first, improve airfields and related facilities; second, upgrade main supply routes; third, improve railroads; fourth, rehabilitate and expand port installations; and fifth, expand logistic base and support facilities.

The task was gigantic. When American military advisors first came to Vietnam, Saigon was the only port capable of receiving oceangoing ships. In consequence, three new deep-water harbors and their attendant shore installations were built at Da Nang, Qui Nhon, and Cam Ranh Bay. Logistical requirements dictated developing major air bases in each principal port area. Since railroad and road traffic was frequently disrupted by the Viet Cong and North Vietnamese, many supplies were delivered to combat areas by air. The close presence of airfields permitted rapid shuttling of material from the dockside to awaiting aircraft.

As the number of troops in Vietnam rose, cantonments were built throughout the country. Barracks ranged from austere huts and tents, to one- and two-story wooden barracks and pre-engineered metal buildings. For household items in these facilities, service exchanges marketed air conditioners, electric fans, small refrigerators, and radio and televi-

WAC barracks at Fort Monmouth, New Jersey, offer Army personnel an attractive living environment.

sion sets. Several radio and television stations in the country broadcast programs taped in the states to the soldiers.

Direct American participation in the Vietnamese conflict ended in 1973. The conversion from a draft-dominated armed force to a volunteer army produced the most significant changes of the 1970s. Throughout the war years, a clamor persisted to end selective service, which provided most of the manpower for the unpopular conflict. Congress voted to end the draft as of July 1, 1973, and the army began to make the transition to an all volunteer force. As the draft came into its final months, half of the army was still housed in barracks constructed during World War II—originally built for only five years of occupancy. To recruit members for a volunteer military force, the army began to take steps to improve these conditions.

On March 2, 1973, the army announced that building would begin on modern barracks for enlisted men and women at Fort Carson, Colorado; Fort Sill, Oklahoma; and Fort Hood, Texas. In marked contrast to traditional concepts of military shelter, the new barracks program was designed to increase personal privacy and comfort. Occupants would have their own desk, chair, bed, and storage locker, with natural light from a window over each desk. Barracks would include

laundry rooms with washers and driers, individual mail boxes, public telephones, and a lobby for visitors. The complex would include such facilities as chapels, dining areas, post exchange, dispensary, gymnasium, athletic fields, and an administrative and storage building.

These new steps are an example of the army's ability to respond to changing national requirements. Over the past centuries, the evolution of American military installations has paralleled and abetted the nation's growth from a disjointed union of rebellious colonies to the most powerful nation on earth.

NAVY

The facilities of the United States Navy are far more extensive than ships and planes. They include numerous bases to support the navy weapons systems and Marine combat forces. The past two centuries have witnessed rapid advancements in American ships of war and the shore establishment that supports them. The single wooden wharf and storehouse of the navy's early years has evolved into a multifaceted complex of hospitals, training centers, ammunition depots, aviation facilities, radio stations, submarine bases, supply depots, and research centers.

From Sails to Steam

The United States Navy dates it birth from the founding of the Continental Navy in 1775. This first navy, however, was but one of several American fleets fighting the British during the Revolutionary War. In addition to the Continental Navy, individual state fleets patrolled the coasts of eleven of the thirteen original colonies, and a force of American privateers preyed on British supply ships.

There was a great deal of opposition against the Continental government's plans for naval protection. Critics felt that any attempt at naval warfare would be suicidal because Britain had one of the most powerful armadas in the world. But after the burning of Falmouth, Massachusetts, and an urging letter from General George Washington asking for naval assistance, the Continental Congress appropriated $100,000 for naval armament and appointed a naval committee to procure the ships. This first naval committee bought and fitted out two twenty-four-gun frigates and two brigs and furnished them with powder and muskets borrowed from the Pennsylvania Committee of Safety. In December 1775, the Congress organized the first American fleet and granted commissions.

Privately owned colonial shipyards produced the naval craft for the American navy. The ships were laid down in huge sheds called mould lofts. The lines of the vessel were drawn out fully on the floor of the loft and scaled up from the designer's plan or a wooden half-model. Then, the timbers were chosen and hewn to shape. All work was performed manually. Very few of these building yards possessed water-powered sawmills, so the planks had to be cut over a saw pit and then shaped with a broadax and adz.

Ships were usually built in the open, since the effects of weathering were considered beneficial to the timber. Planking was fastened to the ship's frame by means of wooden pegs, called treenails, or by iron nails and bolts. A blacksmith was needed to forge these metal fasteners, and his shop was a standard facility at each building yard. Another facility common to many colonial shipyards was the masthouse, where lumber was worked into the required dimensions for masting. Each shipyard also required a ropewalk and a sail loft. The ropewalk was a long, roofed building where hemp could be combed out through a series of steel prongs. These combed fibers eventually became rope for the rigging of sailing vessels. In the sail loft, bolts of linen were made into sails.

The 1783 Treaty of Paris ended the war and brought an abrupt halt to fledgling American naval operations. Within two years, the United States did not own a single armed vessel. With an empty treasury and a huge debt, the new nation felt it could ill afford a standing navy. Moreover, a navy smacked of monarchy and that might prove a threat to the hard-won liberties of the new republic.

However, America's peaceful isolation was short lived. The seizure of American merchantmen by Algerian pirates forced Congress to pass an act in March 1794 authorizing the formation of a naval armada to protect American commerce. The act provided for six frigates and authorized the President to commission a force of 2,060 naval personnel. Work was immediately begun under Secretary of War Henry Knox, who handled all marine matters. The United States owned no shipyards. The necessary building facilities were leased, and ship construction began under the joint supervision of newly commissioned captains and government-employed naval constructors. While the ships were being built, however, diplomatic efforts finally resulted in a 1795 treaty with Algiers which ended the hostilities. The infant fleet was reduced to three vessels—*United States, Constellation*, and *Constitution*—which were launched during 1797.

Meanwhile, trouble with France developed, resulting in the capture of over 300 American merchantmen. By early 1798, French privateers were defiantly making seizures in American harbors. Consequently, Congress authorized completion of the three unfinished vessels from the Algerian conflict and called for the building, purchase, or hire of up to twelve additional ships to be armed, fitted, and manned.

In April 1798, Congress removed jurisdiction of the navy from the overburdened secretary of war and established a separate Navy Department. President John Adams chose Benjamin Stoddert of Maryland to be the first secretary of the navy. Secretary Stoddert's principal concern was providing construction and support facilities and investigating suitable sites for government-owned yards. His office was immediately besieged by congressmen and delegates urging sites in their own localities. Stoddert selected the present location of the Washington Navy Yard because it was convenient to the new capital in the District of Columbia. It also had an adequate spring to supply water, was close to an abundant source of ship timber, and accessible to all but the heaviest war ships. The deep-water community of Portsmouth, New Hampshire, was chosen for its plentiful supply of lumber and its skilled craftsmen. A parcel of choice land ceded by the Massachusetts legislature was picked for the Boston Yard in 1800. The site chosen for the yard in Brooklyn, New York, was an old Revolutionary War anchorage; and the yard at Norfolk, Virginia, was selected by Stoddert over rival Virginia proposals from Yorktown and Tangiers Island. Acreage at the foot of Broad Street,

Philadelphia, was selected as the site for the Pennsylvania installation.

These navy yards were purchased by Secretary Stoddert with funds from a $1 million appropriation which Congress had authorized for the building of six ships of war. He drew his authorization from the portion of the appropriation which addressed additional expenses incurred in the course of building the vessels. Stoddert felt that the need for government-owned building yards merited his liberal interpretation of the law. Congress disapproved of this action, but Stoddert had President Adams' backing in pointing out the disadvantages of renting private shipyards. Their strong argument was that to build government frigates, the public treasury had to finance permanent ships, wharves, and sheds at private yards which became the property of the owner when the lease ran out. Stoddert and Adams were apparently persuasive, because on March 1, 1801, Congress appropriated $500,000 for the building of six frigates and for completing yards, docks, and wharves.

When Jefferson became President in 1801, the navy was reduced considerably.

Naval Facilities Engineering Command.

Washington Navy Yard in 1837. The facility was rebuilt after its destruction by fire during the War of 1812.

Much of the funding appropriated for naval public works was returned to the treasury. Under the Jeffersonian "peace establishment," all naval personnel were discharged with the exception of 9 captains, 36 lieutenants, 150 midshipmen, and 1,200 seamen. The navy was permitted to maintain thirteen frigates, but only six remained in active service. At the same time, the President called for improvements on the Washington Navy Yard to make it the navy's repair shop and chief supply depot. In 1804 Jefferson appointed Benjamin Latrobe as Engineer of the Navy Department and asked him to submit a master plan for the yard. The yard was then little more than a collection of sheds and slipways. By 1809 a well-equipped, functional naval facility was in operation that included a blacksmith shop, rolling mill, and building for gun-carriage and rigging manufacture. No coordinated plans for the other navy yards were made prior to 1828, though some sporadic building occurred when funds were available.

The War of 1812 taxed American shore facilities to their limits. When the conflict erupted, the navy had eighteen seaworthy vessels, seven of which were frigates. Of the six navy yards, only the yard at Washington was capable of extensive fleet repair and maintenance. In 1813 congressional approval of ten frigates touched off activity at all six naval installations. New ships were rapidly constructed and launched while older vessels were repaired and fitted out. Many ships had to be completely overhauled, requiring an investment of manpower as great as for constructing a new vessel.

As the war spread to the Great Lakes, the need for additional building yards became acute. America carved yards and depots from the wilderness along the shores of Lake Ontario, Erie, and Champlain in order to create a fleet to protect its northern frontier. Although these installations remained in operation throughout the war, the naval shore establishment did suffer one major setback. When Washington came under British attack in August 1814, the Washington Navy Yard was burned to keep it out of the enemy's hands. The yard was restored after the war, but it

never regained its standing as the country's most important naval facility.

The War of 1812 was a powerful lesson in the importance of maintaining a well-equipped navy. When the war ended, generous appropriations were made to allow the United States to build, for the first time, a peacetime fleet comparable to the foremost navies of the world. Additional government-owned and operated shore facilities were necessary to support the growing fleet. Hospitals, barracks, clothing, food, ammunition depots, and magazines were slowly established in the navy yards and their immediate vicinities.

The job of managing this expanding shore establishment became too large for the secretary of the navy. Thus, in February 1815, the authority for building and maintaining ships was delegated to a Board of Navy Commissioners. Under the commission's direction, the next ten years saw a marked increase in public works construction at all naval installations; and new yards were founded at New Orleans and Pensacola Bay.

During this spurt of growth, temporary improvements were often made without regard for long-range planning. Great sums of money were wasted because shoddy, temporary facilities were constructed which required much maintenance and frequent replacement. In the 1825 annual report of the navy secretary, he suggested that a commission be established to study the shore facilities and to prescribe "the buildings which will be required, and the location, and the character of each building, together with such improvements in the grounds and form of the yards as will be most beneficial." In response, the Congress enacted a law which authorized the President to have master plans drawn for each of the existing yards. No deviations were to be made from approved plans except by special presidential order. The board took two years to complete its study, but its report governed yard expansion at many bases for the balance of the nineteenth century. Exceptions were taken only when technological advancements and new equipment made changes necessary.

Perhaps the most important naval engineering feat during the early nineteenth century was the construction of drydocks. As early as 1798, Secretary Stoddert recognized the need for such facilities and recommended the building of a drydock in some northern port, possibly Boston, Portsmouth, or New York, and another near the entrance of Chesapeake Bay. He felt that the need for these docks was acute, as the drydocks would eliminate the "heaving down" of vessels, an expensive and dangerous repair process. In response to the secretary's request, Congress appropriated $50,000 in 1799 to build two drydocks, but the money was inadequate and the docks were never built.

Although the most enlightened naval officers and President Jefferson recommended building the docks, Congress remained unresponsive. In 1815 and again in 1821, the navy commissioners strongly advocated the construction of drydocks. Finally, Secretary Benjamin Southward reviewed the entire subject in 1825, and he recommended the erection of two docks, one at Norfolk and a second at Boston. Congress made the appropriation two years later, and the structures began servicing vessels in 1833. The two nearly identical drydocks were a tribute to the engineering and mechanical skills of nineteenth-century artisans. The Norfolk facility, for example, was a masonry structure 350 feet long and 185 feet wide, which cost in excess of $1 million to build.

The dry dock at the Norfolk, Virginia Navy Yard was an outstanding engineering feat of the early nineteenth century.

Steam power, the ship house, and the marine railway were some of the other innovations which changed the character of the navy's shipyards during the first half of the nineteenth century. The use of steam as power for naval vessels revolutionized the navy. Many years elapsed between the time steam was proved feasible for ships and the widespread use of steam to propel naval vessels. This was due to the reluctance on the part of the navy to engage in the "dirty" business of coal-fired steam engines and to the erratic performance of primitive technology. Once steam power was adopted, however, a new navy emerged, and the transformation from white-sailed schooners to coal-burning craft caused many changes within the naval shore establishment.

But the navy found steam to be a valuable tool in the operation of labor-saving machinery at navy yards. The introduction of steam as a mode of propulsion also caused the navy to reassess its shore defenses. Naval sailing vessels had been confined, for the most part, to the oceans, since the necessary winds were not available on inland waterways. With the introduction of steam power, however, an enemy could steam up almost any river and bombard a town. Inland cities situated near large waterways were henceforth vulnerable to enemy attack. The naval shore establishment could no longer confine its facilities to coastal regions.

A steam-powered fleet led to the establishment of a new kind of naval station—the coaling station. These facilities, which stored quantities of the combustible fuel for use by American vessels, had to be established not only on the American continent but also on foreign soil. American naval vessels could not steam round the world without means of refueling. In 1857 Congress appropriated funds to establish a coaling depot at Key West, Florida, and again in 1886 for a depot at Port Royal, South Carolina. American coaling stations did not become prevalent on foreign soil, however, until the turn of the century.

The ship house was first introduced to the navy's shore establishment by Commodore William Bainbridge in 1813. He was charged with the task of building ships during the cold New England winters in Portsmouth and Boston. He proposed the erection of houses over the ship's ways to protect the workmen and enable them to build quickly, neatly, and efficiently throughout the winter. In addition to protecting the workmen, Bainbridge believed that the houses would protect the vessels themselves.

Bainbridge's arguments were convincing. In August 1813, the secretary of the navy authorized the "erection of a cover of suitable material and dimensions over the building at Charlestown." At Boston Harbor, long hangar-like structures were soon erected throughout the naval shore establishment. By 1850 Boston had four ship houses and every other yard possessed at least two.

The third innovation of the nineteenth century was the marine railway, a mechanism which was capable of hauling a ship of any magnitude out of the water for repairs. The device was constructed in conjunction with a ship house. The railway had two parallel stone walls which were laid at the high water mark and braced sufficiently to withstand a great deal of lateral pressure. Two thick platforms or railways were built on these walls. These constituted the ways. The ways were plated with iron or some other metal, made perfectly smooth, and grooved to admit friction rollers. A large wooden ship cradle with flanged wheels fit onto these rails and could be drawn up the inclined plane by the strength of men or animals. The first of these marine railways was constructed at the Washington Navy Yard in 1822.

Ropewalks constituted another area of major public works for the naval shore establishment. Miles of cordage were neccessary to rig the sailing vessels of the nineteenth-century navy. The ropewalk proper was a long building in which rope was manufactured. The name was derived from the constant walking back and forth of the workmen involved in the hand-spinning of cord fibers. The ropewalk complex included several structures. One building received and cut bailed fibers. Another was used for spinning the fibers into yarn and roping. Facilities for oiling and tarring were required to complete the ropemaking process. There were also storage facilities for the hemp.

During the 1830s, the secretary of the navy requested funds to build ropewalk complexes because the navy was having problems with bad cordage purchased from private manufacturers. The defective cordage could pass unnoticed into a ship's rigging and expose both the ship and her crew to great danger. A navy-owned and operated ropewalk could eliminate the problems of uncertain workmanship. After its completion in 1836, the Boston ropewalk produced about 10 percent of the hemp and manila rope used by the navy.

As progressive technology improved the navy's shore establishment, measures were also taken to update its rather antiquated organization. In the late 1830s, the Board of Naval Commissioners faced a great deal of criticism. It was accused of everything from extravagance, dilatoriness, and vacillation to poor accounting habits. The press clamored for reform. Finally, in 1842 Congress replaced the Board of Naval Commissioners with a bureau system that divided the work functionally among specialists. Five bureaus were created, among which was the Bureau of Yards and Docks.

On August 31, 1842, President John Tyler appointed Commodore Lewis Warrington, president of the Board of Naval Commissioners, to be chief of the Bureau of Yards and Docks. This bureau was granted authority over most of the public works activity of the navy, having responsibility for the navy yards proper, the yards' docks and wharves, and the yards' buildings, including magazines and hospitals.

This bureau had a large mission, and the twenty-year period between the establishment of the bureau and the outbreak of the Civil War was a time of intense growth for the naval shore establishment. During that period, the strategic value of the yard at Pensacola, Florida was recognized, and liberal appropriations for improvements were made available to the yard for the first time. Pensacola became a center for shipbuilding. By 1859 the Pensacola Navy Yard comprised sixty buildings and had become an important component of the naval shore establishment. Many improvements were instituted at other navy yards during those two decades as well. For example, in 1848 the capacity of the New York Navy Yard was greatly enhanced by a purchase of eighty additional acres of land. At the Philadelphia Navy Yard, extensive improvements were made to the waterfront area when, during the 1840s, the channel to the yard was deepened and the wharves were extended.

This antebellum period also witnessed the founding of new shore installations. Introduction of steam-powered vessels made the river systems more vulnerable to hostile intrusion. Because of its strategic location, Memphis was selected as a site for a depot and dockyard to service ships on the Mississippi River, and construction contracts were awarded in 1845. Also in the 1840s, acquisition of California from Mexico, the settlement of the Oregon boundary dispute with Great Britain, and the subsequent discovery of gold in the area enhanced the importance of a Pacific fleet and established the need of founding a naval station to support it. In 1850 the naval secretary was authorized by Congress to select a Pacific coastal harbor and construct a drydock and marine railway. Mare Island, a peninsula located 30 miles north of San Francisco, was selected to serve as the principal shipbuilding and repair station in the West.

At the outbreak of the Civil War, two of the Union's most important naval stations were lost to the Confederacy. In January 1861, the well-equipped complex at Pensacola surrendered without a fight in spite of sufficient men and guns to challenge the opposition. The Norfolk Navy Yard fell to rebel Virginia forces in April. Possession of the Norfolk yard and its supplies was a great boon to the Confederacy. The station's armaments were used to fortify secessionist bulwarks on the Atlantic and Gulf coasts as well as along southern rivers. The yard remained in Confederate hands until May 1862 when it was demolished because of approaching Union forces.

The Pensacola Navy Yard was recaptured the same month, but it too had been destroyed before surrender. Rebuilding began immediately because the facility was urgently needed as a repair and supply depot. By August 1863, the yard was functioning as the repair center for the Gulf Blockading

Naval Facilities Engineering Command

The Norfolk Navy Yard was destroyed by Confederate forces in 1862.

Squadron. This force was a portion of the Union fleet that attempted to choke off Confederate supply lines along the entire southern coast. The Union navy policed 3,500 miles of coastline, 189 rivers, and thousands of inlets. The naval shore establishment worked feverishly to maintain and repair the blockading flotilla.

The five northern navy yards served as depots, manufactories, and naval repair centers during the war. Facilities were improved at all the yards and the workforce increased fourfold. The New York Navy Yard quickly became the Union's most important naval facility. Its metropolitan access to artisans, laborers, and supplies, as well as its comparative nearness to the South, contributed to the yard's prominence. A total of sixteen ships were built, over 400 merchant ships were fitted out as armed cruisers, and several hundred fighting ships were repaired at the New York Navy Yard during the war.

Farther north, the Portsmouth Navy Yard was also active. Ships crowded its piers. The need for expanded facilities was so acute that Secretary Gideon Welles was able to persuade Congress to approve the purchase of the adjacent Seavery's Island for ten times the price of the original yard. The additional ten acres were quickly studded with facilities.

During the course of the war, the Union forces established a series of naval depots and stations in the southern states for the maintenance and repair of northern blockading and patrolling squadrons. These stations were equipped with facilities for repairing vessels, ordnance of all kinds, provisions, coal, and naval stores. In 1861 Union forces drove Confederate forces from Port Royal, South Carolina, and the navy established a repair and supply depot for the South Atlantic Blockading Squadron at that strategic port. Beaufort, South Carolina, one of the few Southern port cities on the Atlantic coast with rail connections to the major cities of the Confederacy, was heavily fortified; but the secessionists were driven from the site on November 7, 1861. For the remainder of the war, Beaufort was used as a coaling and repair facility for the Union Blockading Squadrons. Elsewhere, in the spring of 1862, the navy established a depot at Cairo, Illinois, for equipping and repairing vessels on western rivers.

The Modern Navy

The naval blockade was a major factor in bringing an end to the war. Traditional methods of shipbuilding underwent a radical change during the conflict. The dramatic battle between the *Monitor* and *Merrimac* spawned a different breed of ships and required changes in the shore facilities that serviced them.

During the war, the navy yards were capable of building only wooden hulls for steamers; the engines to propel them had to be constructed by private firms. In December 1863, President Abraham Lincoln asked Congress to authorize funds for a new shipyard on League Island near Philadelphia for building and repairing ironclad warships. For some time, the Philadelphia Navy Yard had been declining in importance because of its confined acreage and the difficulty of its interior position for access by sailing vessels. The merits of the Philadelphia area increased substantially, however, in terms of the requirements for manufacturing iron ships and steam engines. Philadelphia possessed all the natural advantages for a center of iron shipbuilding. The city was situated in the center of one of the country's principal iron and coal mining regions. The location gave access to the Delaware River which never froze, and Philadelphia offered the largest pool of skilled labor in the country. Congress authorized acceptance of the League Island site in 1867, but construction funds were held up for six years. A few permanent buildings were begun in the early 1870s, but the bulk of building did not occur until after 1889.

In the postwar period, American commerce in the Pacific grew substantially. This increased trade and the acquisition of Alaska in 1867 underscored the need for a drydock and navy yard in the Northwest. A great many Pacific ports were over 1,000 miles north of the navy yard at Mare Island, California, and the Pacific Squadron badly needed more northerly repair facilities. In 1891 the Puget Sound Navy Station was founded near Seattle,

Washington, to strengthen support of the Pacific fleet. An increased naval presence in the Pacific also required the building of coaling stations on the small islands which dotted the ocean. After negotiating with King Kalakana of Hawaii, the United States gained the exclusive right to establish the famous station at Pearl Harbor in 1887.

Even with the conversion to steam vessels by the time of the Spanish-American War, the shore establishment was ill-prepared to support a wartime fleet. During the 1880s, activities at the navy's yards and stations were slowed and in some instances halted. For example, Secretary of the Navy William Chandler believed that entirely too much money was being spent to maintain and staff the navy's nine yards. In 1883 he closed the Pensacola, League Island, and New London yards; discontinued the construction and repair of ships at Boston, retaining only the ropewalk and sailmaking operations; and reduced the installation at Portsmouth. The curtailment policy was in effect until the eve of the Spanish-American War. Luckily the conflict was short lived; victory came swiftly, and the shore support establishment was not severely tested. As a result of the 1898 Paris Treaty, the United States became an imperial

power. Cuba was temporarily occupied; and the Philippines, Guam, the Marianas, Hawaii, and American Samoa were annexed. Consequently, the navy was able to establish a valuable chain of overseas coaling stations in its new possessions.

The need for more efficient continental coaling facilities also became apparent during the Spanish-American War period. For many years after steam engines had been installed in naval vessels, captains continued to do most of their cruising under sail. Steam power was used as little as possible. A few coal sheds without mechanical equipment had been provided for storing the small amounts of coal that the navy used. These coaling facilities had not been updated; and at the onset of the Spanish-American War, the navy found its coaling facilities sadly inadequate. In June 1898, Secretary of the Navy John D. Long appointed a board under Rear Admiral George E. Belknap to study the navy's requirements for coaling facilities. The board recommended the establishment of modern coaling stations equipped with mechanized equipment along the Atlantic Coast.

Another naval construction effort which grew out of the events of the Spanish-American War was the Panama Canal project.

Naval Facilities Engineering Command.

The coal shed at the U.S. Naval Station at New London, Connecticut, in 1915. This facility serviced steam-powered vessels.

At the onset of war, the battleship *Oregon* was docked in San Francisco. In order to add her strength to the American fleet at Key West, the *Oregon* had to journey 16,000 miles around the entire continent of South America. The trip took sixty-nine days to complete. This protracted voyage convinced the American public that national security demanded a shortcut between the Pacific and Atlantic coasts. The solution was a canal across the Isthmus of Panama, linking the Pacific with the Atlantic Ocean via the Caribbean Sea.

The canal, which spanned 40 miles from Colon on Limon Bay to Balboa on the Bay of Panama, was completed in 1914. (The construction is described in Chapter 2.) It was of immense strategic military value to the United States, permitting swift transference of naval forces from one seacoast to the other. The Panama Canal was also of vast commercial value, cutting 10,000 miles and a great many dollars in shipping costs from mercantile voyages.

In accordance with the Panamanian treaty ratified by Congress in 1904, the navy established several stations within the Canal Zone. The powerful Darien Naval Radio Station was constructed in 1914. In addition to its steel radio towers, the Darien facility was equipped with a powerhouse, an operator's building, quarters, and a concrete storehouse. Two other naval stations, Coco Solo on the Caribbean terminal of the canal and Balboa on the Pacific Coast, were built a few years later. Both stations maintained secondary radio equipment, coal, fuel oil, and lighterage facilities. Balboa became a repair center, and a large drydock was erected at the facility by 1916. Coco Solo, where more than 2 million cubic yards of coral was dredged from Manzillo Bay to raise the elevation of the station, became a submarine base during the World War I.

The efforts to provide modern shops, improved waterfront areas, more drydocks, and better coaling facilities at navy yards resulted in a large increase in the number of power plants to service these facilities. It soon became apparent that many of these power generating sources were duplicated within a single navy yard because each autonomous unit maintained its own power source. This wasteful duplication was remedied by the 1904 Naval Act, which provided for central power plants and distributing systems at navy yards and stations under the cognizance of the Bureau of Yards and Docks.

The savings garnered from this power centralization led Congress to look for further economies. Another possible area of consolidation was the construction of navy public works. By placing this building function in the hands of experts, the navy could expect better facilities and Congress could expect to avoid duplicate costs of materials, tools, and labor.

On January 28, 1911, the House Committee on Naval Affairs submitted the following report: "In order to facilitate a better coordination of work in the matter of public works, the Committee has consolidated under this Bureau (Yards and Docks) all the public works of the entire Naval Establishment. This Bureau is controlled by the Corps of Civil Engineers in the Navy, which is a corps of officers especially trained in construction work at navy yards and stations." On March 4, 1911, Congress enacted the law, and all future navy public works were constructed by the Bureau of Yards and Docks.

A good deal of that future construction was concerned with the erection of naval radio stations. The navy had been experimenting with "wireless telegraphy" since before the turn of the century in an effort to provide an effective means of communication between the ships and distant stations. The first high-powered radio station was built for the navy at Arlington, Virginia. The station, which was capable of transmitting up to 2,000 miles, had steel towers. The two side towers, each 450 feet high, together with the center tower, measuring 600 feet, formed an isosceles triangle. Brick support facilities, consisting of transmitting, receiving, and administration buildings and a small well house, completed the Arlington radio complex.

The Arlington Naval Radio Station was first put into operation on February 13, 1913. Because of its long-range capacity, the Arlington station was able to reach many navy yards and stations equipped with "wireless telegraphy" equipment. Either by direct transmission or by means of relay through the various transmitting stations, Arlington was able to reach all naval vessels within the continental limits of the coasts.

The number and transmitting capacities at naval radio stations increased during World War I. Contracts were given to construct towers, buildings, and other related facilities. Radio towers 600 feet high were erected at Cavite, Pearl Harbor, and San Diego. Similar naval facilities were built at Cayey, Puerto Rico, in 1917 and on Greenbury Point across the Severn River from Annapolis in 1918.

During this period, the navy entered a new technological area. In 1898 Theodore Roosevelt, who served as assistant secretary of the navy under John D. Long, became enthusiastic about the potential of aircraft. At Roosevelt's coaxing, the navy kept a sharp eye on the developments of heavier-than-air craft. After the successful flights of aviation pioneers, foresighted officers urged the navy to invest in aircraft.

The possibilities of teaming planes and ships were dramatically demonstrated by a civilian pilot, Eugene Ely, in November 1910, when he flew a Curtiss biplane off a specially constructed deck aboard the cruiser *Birmingham*. Two months later, Ely took off from Tanforan near San Francisco, flew 10 miles in as many minutes and made a perfect landing on an improvised platform on the *USS Pennsylvania,* anchored in San Francisco Bay. These demonstrations convinced many skeptics that the airplane did indeed have a place in the navy.

A navy aviation group was organized and, under the supervision of aviation pioneer Captain Washington Irving Chambers, a very primitive airfield was constructed at Greenbury Point in 1911. Trees were felled, a swamp filled in, and tent hangars were erected. Captain Chambers moved the aviation group to the base; but it soon became apparent that the cleared space was perilously small for landplanes, the water near shore was too shallow for hydroplanes, and the whole site was uncomfortably close to the Naval Academy's rifle range. In 1913 a navy board investigated the primitive air program and recommended that the department

establish a formal Naval Air Department, train additional pilots, acquire more planes, and found a new aeronautic station.

The new aeronautic facility was established on the grounds of the abandoned naval station at Pensacola, Florida, which had been in a state of deterioration since 1883. This original aviation unit, which arrived in January 1914 and confronted the stormswept beaches and dilapidated buildings, consisted of nine officers, less than two dozen enlisted men, and eleven airplanes. The rudimentary air facility, which was used primarily as a flying school and an experimental center for the development of aviation equipment, offered little more at first than a row of tent hangars along a sandy beach and wooden ramps to serve as runways. However, within a few years, the Naval Air Station at Pensacola was equipped with facilities for testing airplanes, three steel seaplane hangars, a brick hangar, an airship shed mounted on a barge, and a few service buildings.

The establishment of air facilities greatly multiplied during World War I. The Bureau of Yards and Docks constructed them from Nova Scotia to Panama in order to guard the coast from German submarines. Forty-four American naval air installations dotted Europe, and another network of thirteen stretched from the Atlantic to the Pacific Ocean.

The development of the navy's air arm gave rise to the construction of many specialized aviation facilities over the years. In order to obtain the necessary planes, the navy constructed its own aircraft factory at the Philadelphia Navy Yard. The original contract for $1 million was let on August 17, 1917. The steel and glass facility was completed eighty-seven days later and soon expanded into a large complex of aircraft factory and support buildings.

World War I brought about a monumental expansion of the naval shore establishment. The value of overall navy public works more than doubled during the conflict. One of the most immediate problems confronting the navy at the outbreak of the war was the inadequacy of training facilities. To augment officer training, Congress made a series of appropriations that added four permanent and two temporary buildings to the United States Naval Academy, enabling Annapolis to train a thousand additional midshipmen each year.

Expanding training facilities for naval enlisted personnel posed a greater problem. When the United States entered World War I, the navy had four training stations having a combined capacity for 6,000 men. This was sufficient for a peacetime navy, but hundreds of thousands of well-trained men were required for the global war. The Bureau of Yards and Docks supervised the huge construction program which provided adequate naval training centers. The key to success was a standard station design, adapted at each location to meet specific geographic and climatic conditions. Buildings were added to serve as barracks, schools, mess halls, heating and power plants, hospitals, and support facilities.

The actual construction of these training centers was accomplished by a variety of methods. At some stations, the work was done by navy enlisted personnel; in other locations, navy yard civilian personnel performed the job under the supervision of the public works officer; and the remainder of the building was done by commercial contractors. At the height of the activity, some 50,000 men were employed on the training camp project. By the end of the war, forty training centers were turning out about 400,000 men per year.

Increased medical facilities were also needed for the wartime effort. Just prior to World War I, plans were drawn for constructing two large naval hospital facilities, but these plans were abandoned when hostilities broke out. Instead, many strategically placed smaller units which could be quickly constructed and easily expanded were required. A standard self-sustaining wooden hospital complex was designed to handle 100, 150, or 200 patients. By the end of the war, twenty-seven of these hospital complexes were operating within the United States and Hawaii.

In order to expedite the construction of its war fleet, the navy was faced with a unique construction job. Since the late 1800s, the Navy Department had followed a policy of contracting its shipbuilding to private companies. The navy's shipyards, therefore, were not prepared for the huge shipbuilding requirements of World War I. Private shipyards were quickly taxed beyond their resources. To increase their capability, the department had to fund expansion of private shipyards. In all, some forty-five additions to private shipbuilding and support industrial facilities were constructed by the navy at a cost of $71 million. This massive program was the first such activity undertaken by the government since the eighteenth century, and it helped to create an effective American fleet during World War I.

No consideration had been given prior to the war to the construction of navy bases specifically designed for submarines. However, the emphasis placed on submarine activity during the conflict prompted the navy to design and construct bases for the new vessels. The typical design, developed for the berthing of ten submarines, included two concrete piers approximately 250 feet apart, a storehouse, the crew's barracks, officers' quarters, radio towers, a small magazine, and a combination shop. The first of these self-sufficient submarine bases was developed at New London, Connecticut, in 1917. Other navy submarine stations were established at Pearl Harbor, Hawaii; Coco Solo, Panama; and Hampton Roads, Virginia.

The war also marked the transition from coal to oil fuel for naval combat vessels and gave rise to the construction of navy fuel oil facilities. These depots generally consisted of a rectangular grouping of reinforced concrete storage tanks set underground and equipped with heating coils and a fire protection system. The first navy oil storage facility, built at Guantanamo Bay, Cuba, had a capacity for 6 million gallons of oil. Subsequent stations, such as the Naval Fuel Depot at Yorktown, Virginia, held 30 million gallons.

An Army-Navy Airship Board was convened during the war to study the military potential of lighter-than-air craft. The board recommended that the navy should be given exclusive jurisdiction over the development of rigid dirigibles. The army transferred Camp Kendrick at Lakehurst, New Jersey, to the

Naval Facilities Engineering Command.

The Rigid Air Ship Hanger at the Lakehurst, New Jersey Naval Air Station housed giant dirigibles.

navy for dirigible experimentation and training and to provide a berthing for the lighter-than-air craft that patrolled American shores. The facility passed into the navy's hands in 1921 and was designated the Naval Air Station, Lakehurst, New Jersey. The navy soon added to the facility several dirigible hangars, a powerhouse, a gas cell shop and storage buildings, and an experimental mobile dirigible mooring mast. It was at the Naval Air Station at Lakehurst, that the famous *Hindenburg* disaster occurred in 1937. On May 6, after crossing the Atlantic Ocean for the twenty-first time, the giant zeppelin burst into flames as it prepared to moor at the navy's dirigible station. It fell from the sky in a heap of twisted and smoking wreckage.

During the years following the World War I, activity at the navy's yards and stations diminished. Drastic economy measures and military curtailment were effected under the Administration of President Warren G. Harding. In 1922 a navy board examined its shore establishment and recommended measures to make the navy more efficient and economical. It was suggested that certain shore installations be improved, others maintained on a standby basis, and still others disestablished. In line with this policy, a large personnel layoff was carried out during the early 1920s, and the work week at navy yards was reduced from six to five days.

Despite the austerity, the navy shore establishment was enhanced by several new facilities between World War I and World War II. In 1920 a Naval Experimental and Research Laboratory was established near Washington, D.C., to provide a central facility to develop navy-related technology. The laboratory became the site of research into such fields as gun erosion, torpedo motive power, and the improvement of submarine engines.

Construction of the large naval complex at San Diego was another major naval effort during the postwar period. The extensive naval base included a large fuel oil depot with a 4.2-million-gallon capacity, repair and supply facilities for the fleet, a model training station to accommodate 4,500 officers and enlisted men, and an immense fleet supply storehouse.

A great many drydocks and marine airways were also added to the navy shore establishment during these years. New docking facilities were constructed at navy installations at Boston, Philadelphia, Norfolk, Charleston, Pearl Harbor, Hunter's Point near San Francisco, and Puget Sound near Seattle. New sources of power were installed at most naval facilities, including the first automatic motor electrical generating station, built at the Puget Sound Navy Yard in 1928. During the 1930s, the navy modernized its lighting systems and equipped many of its yards and stations with telephone systems and elevators.

Navy hospital facilities, especially veterans' hospitals, were extended in the years following World War I. The onslaught of returning wounded and disabled servicemen severely overburdened the available accommodations. In 1922 the Veterans Bureau requested the Bureau of Yards and Docks to prepare plans for a series of new hospitals to house the World War I veterans. These facilities were subsequently built at Tupper Lake, New York; Gulfport, Mississippi; and St. Cloud, Minnesota. During the 1930s, a new hospital was constructed at Philadelphia to replace two old naval facilities, and a Naval Medical Center was established in Washington, D.C.

A concerted effort was also made to renovate and revitalize the navy's ordnance facilities. One of the more important construction projects involved the building of the Naval Ordnance Plant in South Charleston, West Virginia. This specialized facility manufactures some of the highest quality armor in the world. By 1925 a large naval ammunition depot was completed at Pearl Harbor and, within a decade, another large munitions plant was built at Oahu.

The powerful German submarine fleet of World War I convinced the United States Navy that the time was ripe to expand its submersible capability. A contract was let in late 1919 for a submarine base at Key West, Florida. A similar facility was established at Astoria, Oregon, four years later. With the addition of a complete submarine facility at Pearl Harbor and extensive additions to existing bases at New London, Hampton Roads, and Coco Solo, the navy was able to maintain and berth a considerable number of submarines by the eve of World War II.

Air power had proven indispensable to the navy during World War I, and the chain of naval air installations continued to expand during the postwar years. An air installation was established at Ford Island near Pearl Harbor in the early 1920s, and another developed at Coco Solo, Canal Zone. New air stations were built at Sand Point, Washington, and in California at Alameda and San Diego. Just prior to America's entry into World War II, an increase of building to support naval aviation was authorized and air facilities were established and improved throughout continental America as well as in island possessions.

Two months after Hitler overran Austria, a major expansion of naval air installations was authorized by the 1938 Vinson Bill. Warlike activity in Europe posed a grave threat to American security, and decisive measures had to be taken to prepare America for any eventuality. In June 1938, the navy appointed a board to make an exhaustive survey of the available strategic naval facilities and to evaluate defense potential should hostilities arise. The board's findings set into motion one of the most massive naval construction efforts ever undertaken.

According to this ambitious program, the navy was to develop three major installations to protect each coast. Extensive base facilities were also scheduled for the Canal Zone, Hawaii, and island possessions. The Naval Air Training Center at Pensacola was to be enlarged, and an additional air training station was to be built at Corpus Christi. New submarine and air bases were to be established in Alaska and in the mid Pacific, and existing facilities were updated.

When war was declared in December 1941, private contractors had already carried out many of the proposals. Although efficient and expeditious completion of these construction projects were vital to America's defense, civilian contractors were unable to complete the job. The work site in the Pacific became a war zone and civilian engineers and construction workers were noncombatants. Moreover, if civilians were discovered in a combat area, they were liable to summary execution.

The navy had a problem and Rear Admiral Ben Moreell, chief of the Bureau of Yards and Docks, offered a solution—builders who could fight. Five weeks before Japan attacked Pearl Harbor, Moreell began to organize a few units of Civil Engineer Corps officers to assume overseas construction jobs if war were declared. After the Pearl Harbor attack, Moreell suggested the navy recruit experienced civilian builders and engineers, give them military training, and send them out to build the desperately needed bases. On January 5, 1942, Moreell was authorized to form naval construction battalions, and the Seabees were born.

The concept of a navy construction battalion had originally been considered during World War I. At that time, the urgent need for training facilities prompted the navy to combine all their recruits with construction skills into a single regiment. The resultant unit, the Twelfth Regiment (Public Works) based at Great Lakes, numbered nearly 1,000 men. The war was over before the regiment could be sent overseas, but their trial performance encouraged the navy to accept Moreell's proposal twenty-five years later.

The World War II Seabees were different from ordinary recruits. They were skilled craftsmen. Although a large percentage of Seabees were engaged in the construction trades, personnel for the navy's construction battalions came from all walks of life. They were plumbers, carpenters, masons, steam shovel operators, stevedores, teachers, dentists, and bakers. The Seabees were, on the whole, at least ten years older than the average World War II fighting man, inspiring the United States Marines to quip: "Never strike a Seabee, he may be the grandfather of a Marine."

These bulldozer commandos had a big job to do. They came ashore immediately after the assault waves, assisted in unloading and rehabilitating equipment and supplies, and, in an incredibly short time, built the wartime naval public works. The Seabees' primary function was to construct advance bases. A mission of this kind involved taking a beachhead, cutting roads through to a protected area, moving supplies inland, clearing the site, finding a source of water, constructing hospital and messing facilities, setting up gun emplacements, installing radio facilities, roughing out access roads, and building an airstrip. After the Seabees had accomplished these initial tasks, they set about building piers, fuel tanks, power plants, warehouses, shops, and quarters until the base was operational.

From the Aleutians in the north to Guadalcanal in the south, Seabee construction projects mounted into the hundreds. Warehouses, hospitals, airfields, harbors, and fleet facilities stood in the wake of the navy's construction battalions. In all, the Seabees built and maintained more than 400 bases of all types and sizes and engaged in every combat theater of the war. Moreell's utilization of American construction workers proved highly successful.

Between 1939 and 1945, a total of $590 million was expended for construction at navy yards. Since Congress had authorized a two-ocean navy in 1940, West Coast facilities received a large portion of this appropriation and Mare Island and Puget Sound were among the earliest yards to benefit. The yards were extensively improved, and facilities were built to accommodate the new World War II vessels. Other super-docks, designed for berthing battleships, were begun at Norfolk and Philadelphia in June 1940. These gargantuan structures measured 1,092 feet long and 150 feet wide. Similar facilities were erected at the navy yard in New York one year later.

In order to extend the overburdened ship repair facilities on the West Coast, a new repair base was established at Terminal Island, near San Pedro, California, in 1940. Later that year, the navy formally acquired and quickly expanded the privately owned ship repair yard near the base at Hunter's Point on San Francisco Bay. A comparable facility was established on the East Coast at Bayonne, New Jersey. The New York Navy Yard was considerably enhanced through the addition of several parcels of land and the construction of shops, storehouses, and piers. These improvements converted the congested and obsolete yard into a modern, well-equipped, and exceptionally efficient plant. Both the Portsmouth and Charleston yards were similarly upgraded to support the war effort.

During the war, the air station took its rightful place alongside the navy yard as a major facility. In 1939 the navy maintained eleven air stations and eight reserve bases. By the end of World War II, the number had grown to eighty air stations and a great many satellite fields. Some of the more comprehensive air facility projects accomplished during

Naval Facilities Engineering Command.

During World War II, the Navy's floating drydocks repaired damaged ships in hostile waters.

the war were the expansion of the Pensacola Naval Air Station and the development of major bases at Corpus Christi, Texas; Astoria, Oregon; Quonset Point, Rhode Island; and Jacksonville, Florida.

A significant factor in the American victory in World War II was the squadron of floating drydocks built by the navy. The navy's fleet, operating in distant and hostile waters, often suffered serious damage far from any accessible repair facility. Each vessel lost for want of repairs sapped the navy's strength. In order to provide repair facilities, even in the most remote seas, the navy developed a series of specialized floating drydocks. The mobile drydocks were able to keep many damaged vessels in action and helped insure ultimate victory.

In 1939 the navy had 110,000 enlisted personnel on record. Five years later, the manpower count had reached 3 million. The navy's four major training stations, which dated from World War I and before, were unable to handle the large influx of recruits. Facilities were expanded at Great Lakes, Newport, San Diego, and Norfolk; and by 1943 new training facilities were founded at Port Deposit, Maryland; Lake Seneca, New York; and Lake Pend Oreille, Idaho. Typical of the new training facilities was the Farragut Naval Training Station in Northern Idaho. The facility, which provided accommodations for a population of 45,000, had a total of 650 frame

buildings used for training unit facilities, schools, outgoing unit facilities, and administrative and operational purposes. In total, the navy added over $173 million worth of improvements to its training capability during World War II.

Construction was also required to meet increased supply demands of the Atlantic and Pacific wars. In 1941 the navy maintained a single continental supply depot on each coast. Four years later, the department had completed another ten continental supply depots and had added over fifty fuel, landing craft equipment, and aviation depots to its shore establishment. In order to meet the prodigious demands for ammunition, four large shipping facilities and five coastal depots were developed to provide the necessary ammunition service to operating bases. As in previous conflicts, medical facilities were inadequate for the large number of sick and wounded navy personnel. Between June 1940 and June 1945, the navy built a total of forty-two new hospitals and extended a great many existing units to meet this increased need.

World War II was still a vivid memory when on June 25, 1950 the Republic of Korea was invaded by over 60,000 North Korean Communist troops. The United Nations Security Council demanded that the Communists cease hostilities and withdraw; and to back the demand, President Harry S. Truman ordered American forces to Korea. Entrance into the Korean conflict again required rapid mobilization. Much of the navy's shore support for the fleet and the air arm had been in mothballs since the end of World War II. As the Seventh Fleet steamed toward Korea, the navy rapidly renovated and modernized its reserve shore facilities and geared up its engineering-construction corps for the emergency. High on the list of priorities was rehabilitation and modernization of naval air facilities. Training fields, longer runways for the heavier and faster planes, and test facilities for aviation research were soon under construction. The outbreak of hostilities also called for renovation and expansion of training centers, increased storage facilities, construction of new ordnance plants, additional hospital facilities, and the overhaul of the World War II floating drydocks.

The invasion of South Korea once again brought the navy's construction battalions into operation. By means of their pontoon causeways, the Seabees were instrumental in putting United Nations forces ashore. Throughout the war zone, Seabees were assigned to constructing, repairing, and servicing airfields. One of the most incredible Seabee construction feats was the building of an airstrip on Yo Do Island on the Bay of Wonsan. This was the location of a key enemy supply and transportation center and was under constant attack by American planes. The attacking aircraft were frequently hit by Communist ground fire, leaving the pilots to choose between ditching at sea or landing in enemy territory. The need for an emergency airstrip was critical. Under the code name "Operation Crippled Chick," the Seabees put ashore at Yo Do Island and, working under constant artillery bombardment, managed to complete a 2,400-foot airstrip in sixteen days. At a prearranged signal, "Steak is Ready," the American pilots were informed the job was complete, and nine damaged aircraft landed on the new field.

The Korean conflict triggered a swift rearrangement of American strategy in the Pacific. The navy determined that an airfield should be built at Cubi Point in the Philippines to support American operations should the Korean War spread to Indochina. Early in 1951, a Seabee detachment landed in the Philippine jungle and proceeded to truncate mountains, fill swamps, and clear jungles to build the air base on strategic Luzon Island. Ultimately, the Seabees moved 17 million cubic yards of dirt, dredged another 7 million of mud from the bay, and filled 200 acres of land. One million cubic yards of rock were quarried with a million pounds of dynamite, and a million sacks of cement were used to complete the airstrip on the eastern shore of Subic Bay. The Seabees battled the rugged terrain, created their own access roads and water supply, moved an entire village intact, and, after five years of labor, completed the Cubi Point Naval Air Station in 1956.

Rapid technological development in such areas as weapons systems, communications, space exploration, and aeronautics had a strong impact on the navy's public works of late 1950s and early 1960s. The Fleet Ballistic Missile Weapons System—which encompassed the Polaris missile, nuclear-powered missile launching submarines, and sea and shore support structures—introduced a new concept in underwater weaponry. This concept placed demands on the navy shore establishment for specialized test and support facilities. The navy complex at the Air Force Eastern Test Range at Cape Canaveral, Florida, was fitted out with launch pads, block houses, missile assembly buildings, missile check buildings, and associated supply, administrative, and maintenance facilities to accommodate testing of the Polaris missile. Two Fleet Ballistic Missile centers, one at the Naval Ammunition Depot at Charleston and another at the Bangor Depot in Washington, were built as assembling and loading points for the Polaris submarines. And the naval shipyards at Charleston and Bremerton were fitted out to receive the nuclear-powered vessels. Other Polaris-related construction included the development of a Polaris Team Training Facility at the Naval Base at New London and construction of an underwater test launcher off San Clemente Island in California.

In support of Project Mercury, in 1961 the navy built a Tracking and Ground Instrumentation Center for the National Aeronautics and Space Administration. This Seabee-built installation, located on Canton Island in the South Pacific, included a telemetry and control building which housed equipment to track and communicate with space vehicles. This sophisticated tracking complex was used to receive and forward scientific information transmitted from the first American in space as he orbited the globe.

To improve naval communications to ships, submarines, and aircraft, the navy built a chain of powerful and unique radio stations operating on Very Low Frequency transmission. A part of this chain, the Naval Radio Station at Cutler, Maine, encompassing a reinforced concrete transmitting building and twenty-six towers spread over 2,850 acres, was dedicated in 1961. One remarkable feature of the navy radio chain was the 1,272-foot-high Tower Zero, the tallest man-made structure in the Southern Hemisphere, built at North West Cape in Australia. This great needle served as the hub of a network of towers and guy wires at the navy's Very Low Frequency Communications Center there, which provided reliable fleet communication in the Far East.

In contrast to their past work in cutting away mountains, filling swamps, and clearing tropical jungles, under Project Deepfreeze the navy builders faced the frozen wasteland of Antarctica. The Seabees were asked to provide logistic support for the construction and maintenance of South Pole scientific stations. By the early 1960s, the Seabees had built snow-compacted roads and airstrips, a series of stations, and a nuclear power generator on the frozen continent. This plant provided McMurdo Station, Antarctica, with a safe and efficient source of electrical and steam power.

The growing sophistication of naval aviation called for a new type of aeronautic support facility, geared to the specialized needs of jet aircraft. These requirements were met through the creation of a series of master jet complexes, designed with a new type of elongated runway tough enough to withstand rigorous use by jet aircraft. The components of these master jet complexes included facilities to support one or more carrier air groups, a seaport industrial air station with adequate berthing for aircraft carriers and facilities for the overhaul and repair of aircraft, and a group of auxiliary landing strips and target areas. In the years following the Korean War, the navy developed master jet complexes at Virginia Beach, Virginia; Cecil Field, Florida; and San Diego, Mountain View, and Lemoore, California.

During the period following the Korean conflict, the navy accomplished a good deal of construction in the Philippines, Japan, and Thailand. However, the navy's most comprehensive Asiatic construction program was concentrated in the tiny and explosive Republic of Vietnam. The artificial division of Vietnam into North and South in 1954 produced an undercurrent of unrest that slowly

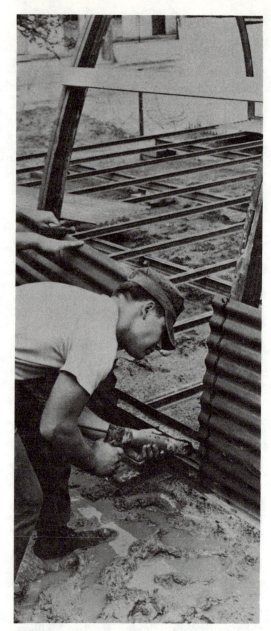

Naval Facilities Engineering Command

Navy personnel constructed facilities in Vietnam during the Asian conflict.

evolved into open war. Guerilla fighting sporadically erupted between the forces of the Communist Vietcong, supported by the North Vietnamese, and the republic in the South. In order to maintain a balance of power in Southeast Asia, the United States materially aided the South Vietnamese, and in 1962 the Department of Defense assigned the Naval Facilities Engineering Command to begin a

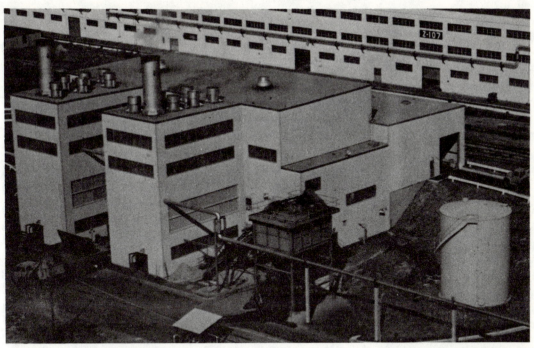

The Navy's Salvage Fuel Boiler Plant at the Norfolk Naval Shipyard converts solid waste into steam power.

program of military construction in the Vietnamese republic. This early building program, intended to bolster South Vietnamese defenses, consisted of improvements at three airfields—Tat Son Nhut, Bien Hoa, and Pleiku—and the construction of a radar site at Da Nang.

The situation changed drastically in 1965 when President Lyndon Johnson ordered active American combat troop participation in Vietnam. A full construction program in support of American forces was quickly developed, and the navy was faced with a huge assignment. Saigon was the only deep-water port in South Vietnam, and the meager air facilities were incapable of sustaining the massive airlift delivery system of men and materials. No cantonments existed to house and feed American troops, electric power was unavailable in sufficient quantities, and even the water was unsuitable for drinking.

Within a decade in South Vietnam, the navy built 15 jet airfields; over 100 small airfields; 7 deep-draft ports; thousands of feet of wharfing; cantonment facilities for over 350,000 troops, hospital accommodations for 8,000 patients; 56 million square feet of covered and open storage areas; 2.5 million cubic feet of cold storage; over 620 miles of streets, roads, and highways; 27,000 lineal feet of bridges; and over 50 miles of railroad.

The requirements of contemporary American society have placed new demands on the navy. Energy conservation and pollution control must now be considered in the design of all navy construction. Specialized facilities to help protect the environment are also emerging. In recent years, the navy built a Waterwall Salvage Fuel Boiler Plant at the Norfolk Naval Shipyard capable of converting solid waste into 100,000 pounds of steam per hour to supply the station's steam distribution system. Modern naval fuel depots have been equipped to reduce oil contamination of harbor waters and to maximize oil recovery for energy-saving purposes. Sandblast and metal preparation facilities have been constructed over the past few years at many of the navy's industrial yards to protect the environment from hazardous emissions. To alleviate the excessive noise given off by jet engines at air installations, the navy is developing fixed enclosures to keep noise at tolerable levels. The prototype noise retardant "hush house" is being constructed at the Naval Air Station at Miramar, California.

In the area of medical facilities, the navy is serving as construction agent for the Department of Defense's Uniformed Services University of the Health Sciences. This unique medical complex, which will be built on the grounds of the Navy National Medical Center in Bethesda, Maryland, will provide training for military physicians. The navy construction effort involves the replacement of aging and obsolete military hospitals throughout the nation. This $500 million medical facilities modernization program, which is scheduled for completion in 1980, has already produced new health care facilities at Charleston and Corpus Christi. Work has begun on a hospital at New Orleans, and plans are being drawn for additional medical facilities at Bremerton, San Diego, and Bethesda.

Another significant part of the contemporary navy construction program involves the Trident submarine support facilities in Bangor, Washington. The Trident project, the largest single navy construction effort in the continental United States, will provide support for the ultra-modern Trident weapons system. Unlike the Polaris system, Trident will operate from a single support site equipped with a refit pier/drydock configuration; explosive handling piers; a large training facility; a group of missile assembly and weapons support buildings; industrial ship, supply, and repair shops; administrative buildings; bachelor officer and enlisted quarters; and a complete personnel support area. The Trident site is scheduled for completion within a five- to eight-year period.

The OMEGA navigational system, a low-frequency radio aid to navigation having a fix accuracy of up to 2 nautical miles, is another technological refinement of the 1970s which is generating a navy construction program. The full OMEGA system calls for the erection of eight transmitting stations in strategic locations around the globe. This multinational effort is well underway. The navy has directly completed an OMEGA station in North Dakota and additional stations are currently under construction in Hawaii, Japan, Liberia,

Argentina, Norway, and La Reunion Island. The OMEGA system, which is scheduled for completion by the end of the decade, should prove an invaluable navigation aid for the ships and planes of all nations.

The naval shore establishment has, in recent years, undergone reorganization to produce the most effective network of shore support for the navy's fleet. Its shore facilities, which originally spread out along the country's coasts, are currently being consolidated within the southern portion of the United States. A shore establishment consolidation program began in 1973 as a result of winding down the Southeast Asian involvement and the consequent reduction of armed forces. The 1973 realignment included closing hospitals, air stations, training centers, and, most notably, the historic Boston Naval Shipyard—one of the original navy yards established by Secretary Stoddert almost two hundred years ago.

Project OMEGA, Trident, the hospital modernization program, and shore establishment reductions are among the factors that will shape future naval public works. Additional requirements will emerge as technological advances and new needs are cited by the American people. These needs have been the motivating force in creating the highly complex and sophisticated navy shore establishment of 1976 from the scattering of wooden wharves and sheds which provided fleet support almost two centuries ago.

AIR FORCE

During the twentieth century, warfare has broadened its theater of operations from the land and sea to the envelope of air which surrounds the earth. In seventy-six years, military air technology has advanced from the observation balloon to the jet bomber and guided missile. From its earlier support role for ground and sea forces, the air force has evolved into a worldwide defense network that comprises the principal strategic deterrent of the United States. This process has required construction of stronger and longer runways; housing for air force personnel and their families; and the training, maintenance, and support facilities that keep today's sophisticated air combat weapons systems flying.

Pioneering Years

Establishment of a balloon park at Fort Logan, Kansas, in 1897 began the history of American air installations. A balloon built and flown there was used in the Spanish-American War to observe the Spanish fleet in the harbor at Santiago and to direct artillery fire at the Battle of San Juan Hill in 1898. Brigadier General Adolphus W. Greely, chief signal officer of the United States Army, had established the Signal Corps balloon section in 1892. Citing European aeronautical achievements and advances in his annual reports between 1892 and 1898, Greely urged appropriations that would enable the War Department to become active in aeronautics. His efforts were finally rewarded when the 1900 Deficiency Act authorized $18,500 for a balloon house and administrative and instruction buildings at Fort Myer, Virginia, near the nation's capital. This apparently was the first federal appropriation used for air installation construction. Although balloon operations were moved to Fort Omaha, Nebraska, in 1908, Fort Myer became the focus of heavier-than-air machines.

The first army airplane, built by the Wright brothers, was delivered to Fort Myer on August 20, 1908 and made its maiden flight on September 3. Airfield size and local weather conditions were among the earliest problems to confront the air pioneers. The Wrights' instruction of the first two army pilots in 1909 had to be conducted on a field at College Park, Maryland, because the parade ground at Fort Myer was considered too small to be safe. A small hangar was built at College Park in the autumn of 1909 as a temporary shelter, but winter weather there proved too severe for flying in open planes without appropriate clothing. Pilot training was conducted in Fort Sam Houston, Texas, and then at Augusta, Georgia, for winter flying. Summer flying continued at College Park, and by 1912 there were eight hangars there, which along with twelve airplanes and fifty-one men comprised "virtually the Government's entire aeronautical capital." Nevertheless, when the lease for the property expired in mid 1913, College Park was abandoned.

As air operations were reduced at Fort Myer and College Park, the pace quickened at

The first army aviators trained at Fort Sam Houston, Texas, during 1910.

a new location near San Diego, California. In November 1912, the army began paying the Curtiss Company $25 per month for the use of their hangars on North Island. The Signal Corps occupied a barn, a shed, and a canvas hangar. In the fall, rent for North Island was discontinued and temporary construction on the installation began, with the proviso that the government could remove the buildings and vacate the premises at any time. Enlisted aviators, assisted by the marines, did most of the construction work during 1913 and 1914. The installation of two hangars, a 10-kilowatt, gasoline-electric generator, and some lathes in February 1915 further improved the site. The following months saw the completion of two permanent hangars, portable field tent hangars, and seaplane hangars. This installation, later a major Signal Corps aviation school, continued as a temporary facility until 1917, when a campaign began to purchase the island for permanent military occupancy. Meanwhile, balloon activities had fallen off as the army focused its attention on the airplanes. In October 1913, all balloon schools were consolidated at Fort Leavenworth, Kansas; but as World War I approached, the Fort Omaha balloon school was reestablished.

The army also conducted air activities overseas in the early years. The first overseas installation was the Philippine Air School which opened in March 1912 at Fort William McKinley near Manila. It consisted of one airplane and a two-plane hangar which the quartermaster built on the edge of the army polo field. In October 1913, a Burgess coast defense seaplane was assigned to service at Fort Mills on Corregidor Island, and a hangar was built on San Jose beach. A series of flights followed which represented some of the earliest attempts at reconnaissance and to direct ground fire from military airplanes. In the winter of 1913-1914, facilities at Fort Mills were improved. A concrete floor was added to the hangar and a 225-foot marine railway was built into the water for the seaplane. From this seaplane, early aviators in 1914 demonstrated two-way radio telegraphy between air and ground.

In April 1914, the secretary of war approved a plan to locate a new air training center at San Antonio. Although funds were appropriated for new construction, no action was taken until March 1915. Captain Benjamin Foulois, commander of the First Aero Squadron, was sent from San Diego to Fort Sam Houston to prepare plans and estimates for buildings and roads on the old target range, about 4 miles north of Fort Sam Houston. The sum of $48,200 included in the appropriation for fiscal year 1915 funded the construction of living quarters for the commanding officer, two six-set bachelor officers' quarters, one barracks building, one garage, a stable, and a machine shop. While assigned to this field in 1916, Foulois and his First Aero Squadron deployed to New Mexico and flew missions in support of General John J. Pershing's punitive expedition against Pancho Villa. The squadron thus became the first and only tested tactical air unit in service prior to World War I.

Air base establishment continued in 1916. In the summer, the army inaugurated an additional flying school at the Signal Corps Aviation Station, Mineola, New York (later named Hazelhurst Field), on land leased from the Wright-Martin Aircraft Company. The men lived in tents and worked in an office building and outmoded hangars which remained from earlier aviation days. Near Chicago, on land obtained from the Aero Club of Illinois, the Signal Corps began yet another flying school in November. Named Ashburn Field, it was used for several months before limited space and adverse weather caused operations to move in August 1917 to a site 90 miles away at Rantoul, Illinois. The men at these early fields lived in a primitive environment while mastering the elements of flight. But the outbreak of World War I transformed American air fields from small, low-cost sites into major public works installations.

Requests from the French government in 1918 for 4,500 American pilots and planes generated the first massive expansion of air installations in United States history. The army had fewer than 200 airplanes and only a few major flying fields. Therefore, plans were drawn up for twenty-four new flying fields to train 1,000 men each month. Rigid requirements were developed for landing areas and weather conditions favorable to winter flying. Fields were to be flat, unobstructed, and well-drained. A three-year lease with an option to buy was the contractual basis for site acquisition, and annual rents ranged from one dollar at Eberts Field, Lonoke, Arkansas, to $20,000 at Wilbur Wright Field, Dayton, Ohio.

Organized within the Signal Corps in May 1917, the Construction Division began work on the new bases. Contractors were usually local people, and they often started work merely on the strength of a letter indicating that a contract was being prepared. Fields such as Wilbur Wright in Ohio and Chanute in Illinois were selected and constructed so rapidly that the installations were able to receive the first aviation training classes in July 1917. Fifteen such fields were in use by December of that year. In July 1917, while these fields were under construction, Congress passed the Aviation Act appropriating $600 million for the expansion program, including aircraft, supplies, and personnel.

During the first year of the program, forty-seven main construction projects were begun and thirty-five were completed at a cost of nearly $50 million. Most training facilities were located in the southern states where year-round flying conditions prevailed. There were twenty-seven major flying fields in the United States by the end of the war, complemented by a long list of schools and other support facilities. A total of 40,900 flying and non-flying personnel were trained at these facilities during the war.

To determine the kinds of combat aircraft the United States would build, a fundamental understanding of air tactics was needed; but these concepts were evolving and engineers were still developing design specifications. Consequently, the War Department ordered its first combat airplanes from the more advanced French factories, and American industry focused its effort on manufacturing training planes. The American aircraft industry was, in effect, created by the government to meet World War I production needs. It involved equipping factories and procuring the raw materials needed in airplane manufacture. Of the ten companies already in existence when the war started, four had built no more than ten airplanes. When the fighting ended, American industry had produced nearly 12,000 airplanes.

The balloon program was also active during this period, though it operated separately from other air activities. Fort Omaha was greatly enlarged in size to accommodate the sixty-one officers and 2,100 enlisted men in the balloon program. Because of adverse

U.S. Air Force

Winter balloon training was conducted at Camp John Wise, Texas, during World War I.

weather conditions at Fort Omaha, in December Camp John Wise was opened near San Antonio as a winter training camp. The average life of a balloon operating on the European front was only fifteen days. To supply the Allies with balloons, the rubber and textile industries cooperated to produce an average of ten balloons per day. The government also established gas plants and expanded private facilities to produce millions of cubic feet of hydrogen and helium.

Massive construction efforts in the United States were paralleled overseas. Original plans called for advanced flight training at schools in Europe, since there were inadequate facilities, aircraft inventories, and resources in the United States. When the Allies were unable to provide facilities, the army had to assume the training burden by establishing its own schools. Initial pilot training was still conducted in the United States, and the European schools were used mainly for briefing and refresher courses. Eventually, sixteen fields were activated in France, Great Britain, and Italy.

The signing of the armistice in November 1918 ushered in an interbellum period of relative austerity for the air forces which lasted until 1939. By 1920 rapid demobilization had taken its toll. Congress reduced funding; aircraft and engine orders were cancelled; the World War I aircraft industry was 90 percent liquidated; uniformed manpower fell far below authorized strength levels; and the air service sold large numbers of surplus planes and equipment to civilian buyers. Even though the war had pointed up the need for military aviation training schools, most of the existing schools were ordered to discontinue flight instruction when hostilities ceased.

Continuing reduction of appropriations during the postwar period also depleted the military airplane inventory to a mere 754 operating aircraft by 1924. Many planes were obsolete, but there was no money for new ones. This consequently reduced the demand for permanent flying fields. As an alternative, the air service actively encouraged the development of civilian facilities which would meet the needs of military aviation. This, along with the development of special aerial maps by air service meteorologists, greatly enhanced infant commercial and civil aviation. By 1925 the Government Printing Office was publishing a bulletin listing data on 3,460 landing fields across the United States.

Despite the postwar austerity from 1919 to 1926, the air service, operating with old airplanes and from worn-out fields, produced an impressive series of aviation spectaculars. These included flights across the continent; aerial photography and radio communications improvements; border and fire patrols; air mail operations; and a long succession of new records for speed, altitude, distance, and endurance.

Conditions changed somewhat after July 2, 1926, when Congress passed the Air Corps Act. In addition to changing the name of the air service to the air corps, the statute provided for significantly enlarging the force to 1,800 airplanes. This statute also authorized a five-year expansion program. Lack of immediate funding, however, set back the expansion plan to the period from July 1927 to June 1932. Increases occurred in more or less equal yearly increments. Congress, however, never provided adequate funds to enable growth at rates originally intended. Expansion took place mainly during the first three years; by 1930 the effects of the Great Depression were felt in the military construction program as elsewhere. Given the problems of implementing the 1926 Air Corps Act, facilities construction and station improvement seemed to fare comparatively better than corresponding manpower and airplane buildups.

For example, in June 1927, General Frank Lahm suggested building a single, large field several miles from San Antonio to house all flight training. Shortly thereafter, $4 million was appropriated for construction of the "West Point of the Air." The field was laid out using a British design which placed the hangars on a knoll in the center of the area bounded by aprons and runways. The site was named Randolph Field in June 1930 while still only partially completed. The Air Corps Training Center was moved from Duncan Field to Randolph in October 1931, and primary and basic training activities were

transferred from other stations. All basic flying training in the air corps was conducted at
Randolph until July 1939.

Military public works were given high
priority during the Depression. In October
1933, the army and navy were granted $15
million by the Public Works Administration
(PWA). While far below the amount
originally requested, these funds were used
both to purchase aircraft and construct
facilities and to provide unemployment relief.

Unfortunately, the ensuing procurement
program encountered severe criticism. Ac-
cusations of irregularities and profiteering
were leveled at its managers. The military
establishment was accused of taking unfair
advantage of emergency public works and
relief programs to fund unnecessary projects.
A congressional investigation in 1934 looked
at the War Department's relations with business and industry, including the department's
alleged "awarding of contracts without competitive bidding." Although these issues involved monies authorized in the PWA grant,
the controversy concerned mainly the air
corps' procurement of aircraft rather than
base construction and improvement. Neither

the air corps, the Budget Bureau, the Congress, nor the White House escaped the blame
leveled by various investigations and critics.
By 1935 the prevailing opinion was that the air
corps expansion program had failed.

Japan's increasing belligerence in the mid
1930s evoked fears in Congress and the War
Department that America's air defenses were
becoming inadequate. Florida Congressman
James M. Wilcox introduced a hotly debated
1935 bill to fund construction of new air bases
in coastal areas and outlying United States
possessions. In order to retain some flexibility
in site selection, air corps officers successfully
obtained modification of the original draft
which had called for bases in specifically
identified locations. Signed by the President
in August 1935, the Wilcox Act authorized the
secretary of war to effect "the selection, construction, and installation of frontier defense
bases for the Army Air Corps" in each of ten
broad geographical areas of the United States.
Only a limited number of construction projects were undertaken, but the influence of the
Wilcox Act was felt later. Because it was already in effect, the pre-World War II expansion program was generally free from logroll-

U.S. Air Force

Randolph Field, Texas, became the "West Point of the Air" in the 1930s.

ing and political pressures. The act also gave the authority for much of the rapid build-up through the early years of World War II.

Prewar expansion of the air corps continued at a slow pace. In 1936 Congress approved and authorized an increase from 1,800 to 2,300 aircraft, but by the crucial autumn of 1938 long production times had kept the aircraft inventory at only 1,600. The air corps was further crippled by the interbellum concept of a totally defensive air force. Augmented by a persistent theory that the navy was responsible for the air above the high seas, defense planners played down any extensive long-range strike capability or oversea operation by the air corps.

Shaken out of lethargy in late 1938 by the crisis over Czechoslovakia, many national leaders recognized the ominous factor of Hitler's Luftwaffe in complex international politics. President Roosevelt and his advisers were alert to the possibility that America's air arm might again be called to action. Roosevelt, at a November 1938 conference, expressed a strong belief that the air corps was the weakest of all American forces and recommended a rapid build-up to 10,000 planes. He did not request a similar increase in bases and men, which led to speculation that many of these planes were destined for the Allies. However, largely due to forceful arguments by General "Hap" Arnold and others that a well-balanced combat force required bases as well as planes, installation expansion was included in the planning. In April 1939, Roosevelt designated $300 million for air expansion, 40 percent of which was for air base and other non-plane items. The army received an additional $3 million in supplemental funds for air corps construction from the Works Progress Administration (WPA).

The build-up during the next several years represented the most intense and concentrated expansion in air history. The existing 17 army air bases and 4 depots grew to 114 major Army Air Force aviation facilities by December 1941. When expansion peaked in 1944, there were 461 major bases, a part of a complex of over 2,200 air installations throughout the nation. In addition, the air corps and WPA worked closely together to de-

velop and improve municipal airports for military use, thereby augmenting civil aviation.

While a philosophy of continental defense governed military expansion in 1939, the existing base structure had not been fashioned with this concept in mind. Geographic locations, physical characteristics, and structural design were often ill-suited to emerging demands of hemispheric defense and the developing weapon systems. Only since 1936 had planners given consideration to confounding attacking enemy aircraft by judicious placement of bases. Subsequently, strategic planners made the location of new bases compatible with the operating range of aircraft in order to maximize air defenses.

Initially, both Congress and the War Department exercised close and detailed control over site selection. By 1940 preliminary site selection was the joint responsibility of the air corps, the Army Corps of Engineers, and the quartermaster general's Construction Division. As the press for rapid rearmament continued, more authority devolved to lower echelon commanders in the various defense sectors. Domestic site selection was based on many new factors. In addition to considerations of weather conditions and strategic location, the topography, soil composition, natural drainage characteristics, accessibility, and obstructions were evaluated. The faster and heavier aircraft imposed requirements not previously confronted. For example, the B-17 bombers needed taxiways and runways of a strength and length not incorporated into the design of earlier fields.

One of the first concerns in mid 1938 was the training of flyers in the large numbers required. Civilian schools handled primary flight training, but in Texas the air corps still was unable to provide adequate basic and advanced instruction at Randolph, Kelly, and Brooks fields. Antiquated construction—much of it pre-World War I and intended to be only temporary—was put to heavy use at these bases. New training bases sprang up of necessity, especially in the South and Southwest where weather was most favorable. By December 1941, there were twenty-eight new training fields in operation or under construction.

Bombing and gunnery ranges, essential to combat training, were too few and small. Air corps headquarters recognized this deficiency as early as 1937 and considered it the limiting factor in combat preparation. One of the best ranges existing in 1939 was the 1,460-acre tract near Valparaiso, Florida. Donated the year before, Eglin Field made use of both the overwater ranges in the Gulf of Mexico and range areas in the Choctawhatchee National Forest. Radio ranges were also needed to serve rapidly increasing communication and navigation requirements. New ranges were installed; and by the end of 1940, the Army Airways Communications System comprised thirty-six operating stations.

Aircraft industry factories, although not properly considered military installations, also experienced phenomenal growth as they responded to the sudden increase in orders for military planes. To expedite production, the government often found it necessary to build facilities at its own expense and lease them to manufacturers. Among factors considered in plant site selection were the proximity to transportation and power sources, availability of raw materials, and vulnerability to enemy attack. The dominant factor, however, was the availability of manpower. The post-Depression years of 1939-1940 produced pockets of both high and low employment, and much attention was given to locating new facilities to bring work to the idle.

The build-up of hemispheric air defenses was not confined to the continental United States. Military appropriations for 1940 provided for new bases in the Alaska-Hawaii-Panama Canal defense triangle. Strategists increasingly viewed Alaska as a logical Japanese invasion route to the Western Hemisphere. Work began in late 1939 on Elmendorf Field near Anchorage, one of the first experiences in air base construction in the far north.

There was no Atlantic counterpart to the Pacific defense triangle, but an urgent need for such a system was apparent by mid 1939. The British Isles, French West Africa, the Canaries, the Azores, and the Cape Verde islands constituted the first line of defense of the Western Hemisphere. Bases existed in the Caribbean area which would satisfy much of the immediate need. Diplomatic negotiations which followed culminated in the celebrated "Destroyers for Bases Deal" in which President Roosevelt and British Prime Minister Winston Churchill agreed to exchange fifty American destroyers for a ninety-nine-year lease for bases in Britian's possessions. Included were stations in the Bahamas, Jamaica, Trinidad, Newfoundland, and Bermuda. The announcement of this transaction in August 1940 was a clear signal to the world that America was aligning itself against Nazi aggression occurring on the European continent. By the end of 1940, defense agreements had been concluded with every country of South America except Argentina, further securing the hemisphere from invasion.

Heretofore responsible for air corps construction, the Quartermaster Corps was overtaxed by the demands of so rapid an expansion. On November 19, 1940, all air corps construction was transferred to the Army Corps of Engineers. This historic transfer took place without appreciable delay in scheduled projects.

Burgeoning Axis naval presence and the growing threat of enemy air attack capability from bases such as those in South America spurred an expansion of the United States Army Air Corps to eighty-four combat groups in March 1941. The new build-up, more than tripling the original twenty-five group structure, required an extensive redistribution of existing facilities and the construction of yet more new bases. The increasingly long list of flying schools, technical schools, tactical bases, reception centers, depots, and ranges was still geared to a hemispheric defense posture. The receipt of funds from War Department, WPA, and Civil Aeronautics Administration (CAA) appropriations; lump construction monies allocated by the President; and the wide use of quickly erected temporary structures enabled expansion to proceed.

Expansion was underway when Pearl Harbor was attacked. A succession of further build-ups quickly followed, increasing the number of combat groups from eighty-four to 273. This acceleration, and the need for base building programs to precede actual force increases, demanded unprecedented support from the nation's construction resources. The multitude of problems faced by installation planners was set against a backdrop of a modified defense philosophy, which included the idea of offensive air power for direct use in World War II.

Plans called for maintaining one third of the air units in the United States, with one major installation and four sub-bases to support each combat group. Training was geared upward to produce 70,000 new pilots per year. Through emergency legislation in the early weeks of 1942, the recently established United States Army Air Forces (AAF) received $700 million for its construction program, and CAA was given $59 million for additional airport development. Decentralization of construction procedures beginning at the site selection stage came into effect. The AAF construction directives were expedited, and initial surveys and acquisitions for a new set of bases began early in 1942.

Flight schools proliferated with amazing speed. An observer wrote: "It was not unusual to find a training field with dozens of planes flying above it, bulldozers on the ground finishing the earthwork, cement mixers turning out concrete for runways yet to be built, and men in the open still clearing the brush off what had been grazing land." New technical training installations also rushed into operation. Initially, construction was unable to keep up with demand, especially in the housing of students. Hangars, tents, leased hotels, and schools were used. By September 1945, the eight stations originally built for Technical Training Command, with combined housing capacity for 131,000, had cost $120 million.

Persistent fear that United States shores were vulnerable to sudden Pearl Harbor-like air attacks persuaded commanders to incorporate passive defense measures into base expansion. Coastal areas were avoided in site selection. Dispersal and concealment of installations received the highest attention. The AAF directed dispersed layouts for all new bases built within 300 miles of the Gulf of Mexico. On the West Coast, AAF, in close coordination with the commissioner of public roads and the state highway departments, constructed flight strips for dispersal of tactical aircraft parallel to major highways in areas from 25 to 75 miles from established bases.

War operations approached their height in early 1943, and by June there were sufficient base facilities to support military air requirements. Housing capacity reached its maximum of 2.4 million persons. The peak count for separate installations, in December 1943, numbered 345 main bases, 116 sub-bases, and 322 auxiliary fields. The AAF promulgated a strict policy of full utilization of existing facilities to replace the massive construction effort of previous years.

Reduction actions were foreseen by December 1943. As the war approached conclusion, preliminary planning and policy formulation began. Excess fields were first put on a "standby" status, pending the clarification redeployment policies at the end of the war. Congress in 1944 began to reassert control of air force real property acquisitions which had devolved to lower command levels during the emergency build-up. Expressing dissatisfaction at some of the purchases and disposals, Congress advocated reestablishing secretarial review of questionable cases and ruled that the value of a base as a permanent military installation should be the guiding principle in deciding its fate. Following V-J Day, surplus facilities were speedily relinquished; and by the end of 1945, AAF domestic installations were reduced to a total of 429, of which 174 were either inactive or on standby status.

Construction had not stopped completely, however. New weapons systems were being introduced into the air force inventory, and existing facilities were not always fully able to accommodate them. Almost all construction during 1943 and 1944 related to the needs of very heavy bombardment aircraft and to the training of their crews. The B-36 bomber, for example, which was then under construction imposed requirements much in excess of anything previously known. The landing surface would have to withstand a load much greater than the upper limits of existing runways built on the basis of highway construction technology. Consequently, during 1943 and 1944, some bases underwent improvements at the very time that nearby bases were being disposed of.

Essentially new facilities were also being established to respond to technological advances. In February 1945, the secretary of war approved plans to establish White Sands Proving Ground in New Mexico as a rocket-firing installation. That same year a WAC Corporal rocket attained a height of 43.5 miles. Shortly thereafter, the army launched from White Sands the first V-2 rocket fired in the United States. White Sands thus presaged the construction requirements of the impending missile age.

Base building activity also continued during 1944 and 1945 to support directly prosecution of the war in combat areas overseas. For example, in Europe tactical air forces accompanied General George S. Patton and the Allied armies' drive across France. The exceptional efforts of the aviation engineers and supply sections in such units as General Hoyt Vandenberg's Ninth Air Force made possible the immediate repair and improvement of forward airfields. This allowed flyers to operate from strips located near the advancing front lines. Construction units were also active in the Pacific. A system of five bomber and six fighter fields was built in China between

January and May 1944 under the direction of General Claire Chenault. This Chengtu Project, in which 400,000 Chinese workers labored with primitive tools and ancient methods of construction, was one of the most outstanding World War II achievements.

The cost of base construction during World War II is difficult to determine. Excluding the cost of land, the estimated capital value of installations used by the air corps in the continental United States as of June 1940 was $104 million. By September 1945, the figure had risen to $3 billion. During the period of the war emergency, 29 percent of the total War Department expenditures for facilities went to the construction of AAF installations.

Supreme in Air and Space

Postwar reduction of forces and bases offered the opportunity to redraw the system of installations in order to better serve a changing military environment. The rapid facilities reduction program attempted to dispose of relatively useless or poorly located sites and concentrate strength in a smaller number of modified and improved bases. Many temporary wartime structures were fast deteriorating to the point at which maintenance expenses were prohibitive. The demands of a changing air defense mission also

U.S. Air Force

French workers repaired bomb craters at this former Luftwaffe airfield that served B-26 Marauders.

influenced decisions regarding base dispositions, for strategic and continental air
defenses demanded larger, more complex
bases dispersed throughout the world.
Furthermore, the many training bases exceeded requirements.

Congress once again began to assert
policy guidance. Although it urged rapid
demobilization, Congress was sensitive to the
pitfalls encountered during post-World War I
reductions. Required levels of military pre-
paredness would be maintained, scarce commodities were to be made available to the
general public, and the national economy was
to be disrupted as little as possible by
demobilization. Congress delegated broad
authority to administrative agencies to dispose
of unwanted holdings. Insofar as new acquisitions were concerned, however, Congress
tightened its control, rescinding surplus war
appropriations, setting dollar limits on the
building of new, permanent facilities, and
restricting transfer of funds into military
public works coffers.

The United States Air Force (USAF)
became a separate and independent branch of
service in 1947. With independence came the
responsibility to manage the expansion and
modification of its own air bases and
ultimately to state requirements for future
facilities in annually prepared budget requests. Coordination of construction projects
was a complicated and time-consuming process in peacetime involving the USAF,
Department of Defense, Bureau of the Budget,
and Congress. A director of air force installations estimated that bureaucratic processing
would necessitate at least a three-year planning lead time. Fund shortages often exacerbated the situation. In most cases, the Army
Corps of Engineers continued to effect actual
real estate purchases and construction contracting for air force projects.

Air planners saw clearly the need to
begin building defenses against a growing
Soviet air capability. The USAF in late 1947
proposed an aircraft control and warning network of 411 radar stations, 347 of which were
to be located in the United States. Costs were
estimated at $400 million. However, neces-
sary funding did not accompany congressional

approval. When the Communists seized
Czechoslovakia in February 1948, the United
States had but one active radar station; four
more were operating in Alaska but only for
part of the day.

A war scare generated by the crisis in
Europe caused an increase in planned air
defenses, especially for the northeast and
northwest sectors of the United States and
Alaska. Several old wartime radar sites were
reoccupied. The Joint Chiefs of Staff assigned
primary responsibility for continental air
defense to the air force. Since funds were not
yet appropriated for the proposed radar complex, the air force submitted a modified plan
to build a permanent system of seventy-five
early warning radar stations and ten control
centers on government-owned land in the
United States and Alaska. Congress put funds
toward its estimated cost of $86 million in
1949, but several years of development and
construction time were anticipated before the
system could be fully operative. Supplemental
funds enabled some expansion of the planned
network.

Russia's first explosion of an atomic
device in August 1949 convinced the government to step up the pace of air defense by accelerating the radar build-up. The air force
expedited completion of a net of forty-four stations in California and instituted dispersal of
defense aircraft to alternate bases.

Housing for men and their families posed
one of the air force's most critical problems
after 1945. Because some bases were located
far from urban centers, there were military
housing shortages which could not be relieved
by civilian residential communities. Although
the air force did what it could with the limited
funds available, the situation continued to
worsen, lowering morale and affecting the retention of airmen in service. In 1948 the
secretary of the air force stated that family
quarters were available to only a fourth of
those legally entitled to them. Half of these
structures were makeshift conversions of antiquated barracks and other buildings.

Congress, in August 1949, authorized
$500 million to underwrite Federal Housing
Authority mortgage insurance for privately financed housing on or near military installa-

tions. Known as the Wherry-Spence Act, it provided some relief. The air force also planned to construct 26,595 units at forty-nine stateside bases. Even if the complete program had been finished, it would have provided less than half the required houses; but by mid June 1950, work had begun on only 4,292 units.

U.S. Air Force

The Wherry-Spence Act enabled construction of this housing at Patrick Air Force Base, Florida, in the mid 1950s.

More than half of the 207,000 bachelor airmen still lived in temporary wartime barracks at the beginning of 1950, and the remainder lived in obsolete permanent-type barracks. Over half of the USAF bases in 1950 were temporaries and had been deteriorating for five years. The deterioration required recurrent maintenance, further complicated by the chronic shortage of funds. In 1950 the air force estimated that a five-year program of major repairs would cost $90 million. Emergency repairs and base modifications depleted most of the funds appropriated for repair and maintenance from 1945 to 1950. Often funds had to be diverted from one base to pay for badly needed repairs at another. Because of the temporary construction at many bases, air force fire losses were serious, running to about $150,000 a month in the United States and even more overseas. Nevertheless, before the airbase, radar, and

housing problems of the postwar period could be resolved, the invasion of South Korea launched USAF into yet another expansion effort.

Changing world conditions demanded further expansion of air facilities during the 1950-1953 period. The Korea conflict provided the catalyst for a speed-up in acquiring foreign bases. The need for airfields in direct support of combat on the Korean peninsula drew much attention. Simultaneously, the global deterrence mission of the Strategic Air Command (SAC), the heightened air defense measures for the United States homeland, and the progress of the Tactical Air Command (TAC) toward a global strike force created additional requirements. President Truman's policy was to modernize existing bases and utilize surplus resources if at all possible; if not, build new bases. As a result, few new facilities were built in the United States, but overseas areas saw extensive installation construction.

No single factor so seriously handicapped air force operations in the war in Korea as the persistent lack of adequate air facilities. Obstacles to base construction were many, but the principal problem was a shortage of properly qualified aviation engineers. Nevertheless, key strategic bases were built at Taegu, Kunsan, and elsewhere in the face of adversity.

Existing World War II airfields in other overseas areas did not provide alternate strategic bases which the air force considered vital to its operations. Therefore, construction began on new bases in Germany, Greenland, Morocco, and Spain. In France, Germany, Libya, Japan, and elsewhere existing fields were improved and expanded. The history of these endeavors is one of human and technological successes over innumerable obstacles of geography, topography, weather, international tensions, military logistics, and high costs. From the ordeal came not only a responsive and modern global airbase system, but the development of innovative and pioneering concepts in airfield design and construction.

Inadequate bases in the continental United States prompted a domestic rebuilding program during the years of the Korean conflict. The decision to expand from forty-eight wings to 143 exacerbated an already critical problem of shortages especially in the area of flying training facilities. Flight line modifications, required by the advent of new aircraft, demanded the acquisition of more space, extension of runways, building of longer overruns, and the widening of aircraft approach corridors. As new bases were established, USAF sought to locate them at least 15 miles from the nearest major community to avoid conducting flying operations close to crowded urban areas. Engineers responded to problems in safety, maintenance, and firefighting by developing new construction materials with improved fire-protective qualities. During this expansion period, many existing structural safety hazards were eliminated, and safer building materials were used.

The specter of atomic warfare following the Korean War led to a resumption of the World War II policy of dispersing aircraft to as many fields as possible. Construction, begun in many areas during the Korean conflict, continued to completion. Airfields became operational in places such as Thule, Greenland, and Zaragoza, Spain, linking a system of air force installations which extended three quarters of the way around the world. The SAC's offensive bomber force added five new bases within the United States in 1955 and 1956. The fear of a devastating air attack on the United States also exposed a need for more strategically located air defense bases. In 1955 Congress approved construction of six interceptor bases just below the Canadian border.

Typical of problems encountered in upgrading existing bases to the standards of Cold War defenses was runway pavement failure. During the period of rapid expansion after 1950, most runways and taxiways were built of flexible pavements with insufficient base support, particularly on bases not considered permanent. On the refueling aprons and warm-up pads, asphalt presented difficulties because spilled jet fuel caused it to disintegrate. As planes became heavier and the number of takeoffs and landings increased, pavement failures became more fre-

quent. Finally, in early 1956, the air force command determined that all primary airfield pavement for combat or combat support aircraft would be of portland cement concrete with adequate base materials and thicknesses to support the greater weights.

Challenges of defense against the threat of atomic weapons and their supersonic delivery systems added to the lexicon of military installations such terms as the DEW Line, Texas Towers, and SAGE buildings. The transformation of these concepts into physical entities is a story of rapid and radical expansion of air facilities construction.

Limited use of search radars by the United States military began during World War II. Secretary of Defense James V. Forrestal announced publicly in November 1947 that planning for a nationwide early warning system was underway. By the end of 1952, the United States was under the protective vigilance of a seventy-five-station radar network. These were to be augmented by another 108 "mobile" stations and several Canadian sites. The construction of them, under the direction of the Army Corps of Engineers, was often plagued by indecision on the part of the air force as to location and on the obstacles of building the facilities on isolated mountaintop outposts. By 1955, however, the number of search radars in the United States had grown to ninety.

It was the Distant Early Warning (DEW) Line that presented the most formidable challenge to the military defense construction program. Across 3,000 miles of the Arctic circle, a series of sites, whose radar coverage overlapped, was erected to provide a continuous electronic warning shield against penetration by hostile aircraft. Conceived and built between 1952 and 1958, the DEW Line included three types of sites. The main stations provided a rotating radar and an accompanying complex of full service and support facilities; secondary or auxiliary stations contained everything but complete service stations; and "gap fillers" primarily housed a non-rotating radar device.

Variable temperatures from −65 degrees to +65 degrees Fahrenheit and gale winds exceeding 100 miles per hour characterized the climate over most of the DEW Line. The surface was a "muskeg," a sludgy marsh 2 to 6 feet in depth, frozen in winter, and thawed in summer, with a permafrost below it. Experience in building the $400 million DEW Line produced not only a formidable defense complex but also basic research on the arctic polar cap, arctic survival methods, and the ability of an individual to subsist on lichens, lemmings, and sea cucumbers.

In the autumn of 1953, the United States Air Force authorized the construction of five stationary offshore observation platforms. They were called "Texas Towers" after similarly designed oil-drilling platforms in the Gulf of Mexico. The initial cost of $4 million per copy was funded from 1954 and 1955 appropriations. Located about 100 miles into the Atlantic Ocean, the towers were equipped with radar detection devices to search out and identify approaching aircraft. In addition, the navy was authorized to use facilities on the towers to house recording equipment for collecting oceanographic data.

Because of the increasing speed and complexity of hostile aircraft, radar and communications technology was called upon to supplement other defense systems, such as the DEW Line and the Texas Towers, with a high-speed digital computer network to

Army Corps of Engineers

This DEW Line station in Alaska guarded against enemy attack.

receive, process, and transmit air surveillance identification and weapons guidance information. Called the Semi-Automatic Ground Environment system, or SAGE, it was made up of a series of direction and combat centers housing advanced electronic equipment, display consoles, and communication gear. Testing began in late 1953. Computer refinement problems and a 1957 Defense Department in-depth review of all military construction programs caused some delays in building the complex, but the system became fully operational under the North American Air Defense Command in December 1961.

Obtaining family housing for its officers and airmen at rentals they could afford continued to present difficulties for the air force in the post-Korean era. In 1954 it needed at its semipermanent installations 185,000 housing units—160,000 in the United States, its territories, and possessions. It had only 64,000 units of all kinds available, including trailers and temporary housing. Within the United States, the air force depended on Title VIII of the National Housing Act (Wherry housing). Although never enough, Wherry housing helped relieve the shortage. But overseas and at isolated locations such as aircraft control and warning stations, building was difficult and shortages remained acute.

Congress passed the Capehart Amendment to Title VIII of the National Housing Act in August 1955. The amendment permitted expansion of Wherry housing by authorizing the use of quarters allowances of occupants to pay off mortgages. The air force contracted for housing to be built on government land in the United States or its territories. The average cost of quarters was not to exceed $13,500 per unit. By June 1956, the air force had drawn up plans to build more than 46,500 of these at eighty-eight bases.

The combat debut of the German V-2 rocket in September 1944 marked the beginning of long-range guided missile development. During the following decade, progress in research and development in the United States was substantial, though plagued by conservative, budget-balancing constraints common to new scientific endeavors. When the Soviet Sputnik was launched in 1957,

USAF was already proceeding with a fully approved and funded ballistic missile program. The Sputnik "spectacular" added a sense of urgency to the missile program. Dollars earmarked for guided missiles and their components, which comprised 9 percent of the air force budget for procurement of aircraft and related items in 1954, rose to 37.5 percent by 1962. During this period, construction and site activation proceeded simultaneously with missile development and the organizing of support systems.

Training facilities for missile men were first established by the air force at Cooke Air Force Base, California (redesignated Vandenberg Air Force Base in 1958) to provide training in the new field of missile launching and operations. The air force took over a 64,000-acre former army camp, and in 1957 the Army Corps of Engineers began a $100 million construction program at the facility. The barracks area, worn from service in World War II and the Korean conflict, was thoroughly rehabilitated; and an $11 million, 800-unit Capehart housing project was undertaken. This installation has been in the forefront of missile defenses since a strategic missile squadron was first activated there in January 1958.

The paramount consideration in selecting and preparing sites to house operational missile units was survival. Dispersal, reminiscent of earlier days, was the axiom of the missile age. The protection afforded by physically separating missile sites was augmented by the hardening of missile silos to withstand the shock of high megaton blasts from attacking enemy missiles or bombs. The construction of these complex facilities dominated the period from 1957 to 1964.

Sites were located in areas ranging from Malstrom Air Force Base, Montana, with temperatures as low as − 42 degrees to Davis-monthan Air Force Base, Arizona, with + 110 degrees, and from the 11-inch annual rainfall of Davis-Monthan to 47 inches at Little Rock, Arkansas. Some were located near existing construction industries; others were isolated. By any measure, the size of the task achieved in constructing the missile system was formidable. The combined area of the sites was approximately that of the state of Colorado.

These various kinds of facilities illustrate the extent to which the air force was involved in missile operations by the early 1960s. They required the construction and maintenance of launch pads, fuel storage areas, telemetry stations, computer and laboratory buildings, and auxiliary airfields as well as office space and living quarters. Much of the construction during the period preceding the Vietnam conflict was in support of the air force role in the missile age.

U.S. Air Force

This Tital missile launch facility was built at Vandenberg Air Force Base, California, in 1961.

Involvement of USAF in open aerial warfare in Southeast Asia dominated air installations in the mid 1960s. The build-up of the war created an immediate need for a number of new jet airfields in Vietnam. Typical of these was the field at Cam Ranh Bay. Starting from nothing in mid August 1965, engineers had to have interim facilities ready to receive operational aircraft by November and permanent facilities in place by the following summer. Cam Ranh Bay was on a remote sand peninsula in a primitive area. It was in a zone of open hostilities, sniping, and sabotage. There was no laterite or other subgrade material for constructing the airstrip. Lumber was in critical supply, and often exotic Philippine mahogany plywood was used as form lumber in placing concrete. Deep sand and intense heat added to the problems of the construction workers. Labor was provided by American contractors, with frequent assistance from military personnel.

There was heavy reliance on "instant construction"—new concepts of using prefabricated materials and structures for both interim and permanent facilities. The air force developed a pre-packaged, 1,100-man "tent city" deployment kit called the "Grey Eagle Kit." This complex housed advance party personnel and supported initial aircraft operations. Although readily available and quick to erect, the kit was not designed for continued use. The two kits initially erected at Cam Ranh Bay were later replaced with Quonset huts and newly developed inflatable shelters.

The urgent need in Vietnam for runways capable of handling jet combat and cargo aircraft could not await the time needed to place concrete pavement. An aluminum plank, called AM-2, was developed as a temporary expedient for the Southeast Asia environment. Measuring 2 feet by 12 feet or 6 feet by 12 feet, it had interlocking and keyed joints. Fitting them loosely together facilitated placement of the mats and allowed for the thermal expansion caused by 100 degree temperature changes. The mats could be laid on undisturbed earth after necessary grading and leveling. The mats were used for entire runways, including the 10,000-foot ones at Cam Ranh Bay and Phan Rang air bases.

Several new air bases in the Southeast Asia theater of operations were constructed under these organization and contracting arrangements as the increase of forces progressed into the 1966-1967 period. The creation of Tuy Hoa Air Base, 70 miles north of Cam Ranh Bay, was especially interesting. It involved a new and untried management concept of installation construction. Under a project called "Turn Key," the air force administered a contract which gave to a single contractor the responsibility for constructing the entire installation. The Air Force Logistics Command competitively selected the contractor who then signed a letter of agreement in May 1966. Construction began in August. Except for real estate acquisition and security measures, the contractor furnished everything needed to build the base—designs, engineering, transportation, materials, equipment, the labor force, and the actual construction. Prohibited from using existing facilities, he had to construct his own port area to bring incoming supplies and equipment ashore. Construction moved rapidly. The first combat airmen arrived three months later. With only minor deviations and exceptions to contract provisions, the builder completed the project in mid 1967, proving the viability of the approach.

U.S. Air Force

Facilities at Tug Hoa Air Base in Vietnam included fire vehicles, revetments, aircraft shelters, and runways.

Demands of the Vietnam War generated some interesting new ways of using the civil engineering resources of the air force. In 1965 Rapid Engineering Deployment and Heavy Operational Repair Squadrons, Engineering (RED HORSE) were formed. Their primary mission was to make emergency repairs to airfields damaged by enemy action or natural disasters. The Vietnam War also brought about another innovation in civil engineering support—the operation of mobile teams capable of responding on short notice to tactical and special warfare requirements. The Base Engineering Emergency Force, known by the combination nickname and acronym Prime BEEF, was conceived in 1963. Operating commands organized teams of specialists to erect aircraft revetments and cantonments complete with electricity and running water.

Military construction programs in the Vietnam era involved far more than support of combat operations in Southeast Asia. Funds were spent on construction and expansion of facilities in other parts of the world to maintain an effective response to ever-changing global defense requirements. Space systems, missile sites, satellite programs, and radar warning complexes were established and improved. Research and development activity involved exotic new aircraft, vast computer hardware, intricate electronics systems, and nuclear test facilities. Physical plants at training institutions like the Air Force Academy and Officer Training School were continually modernized. Operational requirements ranged from dispersal of fighter aircraft to foreign military assistance and perfecting a worldwide communication network. All of these efforts required a wide variety of skills and talents and substantial expenditures of construction funds.

In the competition for federal funds for military construction, Congress generally required detailed justification of proposed projects on a case-by-case basis. Occasional broad policy changes were sometimes superimposed on annual budget formulations. In 1964 and 1970, the Defense Department ordered far-reaching base closure actions, which involved not only real property disposals but relocation of military units and modification of existing active installations. In October 1967, the Department of Defense imposed a freeze on military construction programs. The stoppage affected $140 million of construction funds in 1967 and 1968. Again in September 1969, President Richard M. Nixon made a blanket 75 percent reduction in federal construction, resulting in a deferral of $146 million in air force construction monies. Foreign exchange expenditure limitations (gold flow) imposed additional constraints on the use of available dollars for overseas procurements.

Real property acquisitions and dispositions since the mid 1960s have shown a trend toward a reduction in air force holdings. Changing requirements made it necessary for the air force to continue to purchase real property at various times for such purposes as runway extension, family housing sites, Minuteman missile complexes, and facilities' expansions. At the same time, installations that were no longer needed were deactivated. The Department of Defense in 1964 directed the closure of a long list of bases and stations, including many radar sites, missile sites, and associated family housing areas.

Surplus real property holdings in the United States were put to a variety of uses. Excess family housing complexes were made available to municipalities for use as low-income housing projects and to universities for student housing. In January 1966, a pilot program was begun with 735 housing units at Schilling Air Force Base, Kansas, which had been closed in 1964. The air force reassumed accountability for the housing complex, although they were later transferred to the army's jurisdiction. These Capehart housing units are still being used by army, navy, and air force families while their husbands and fathers are stationed overseas. Other inactive bases were put to similar use. Obsolete missile launch complexes were converted to civil defense facilities, college laboratories, and other useful facilities. Municipalities voiced a growing desire in the early 1970s to annex military bases lying adjacent to their city limits. Although not all annexation requests were approved, there have been some successes. Dover Air Force Base (excluding the housing area) was annexed to the City of Dover, Delaware, and Nellis Air Force Base, Nevada, was made a part of the City of North Las Vegas.

Pressures from escalating Southeast Asia expenditures were evident in family housing construction programs during the 1960s and 1970s, as they were either stretched or postponed. Since 1966 yearly programs for new family housing, improvements, and minor construction projects have experienced deferrals, "holds," and close financial and budgetary controls. Although the early 1970s saw a slight increase in authorized units, the problem continued to be a serious one for air force planners and servicemen alike.

These events in overseas and stateside operations, facilities construction, and real property activities illustrate the nature of air installations and related construction during the years of the Vietnam conflict and the first months of the post-Vietnam era. The recent past is prologue to the decades to come, and the air force has shown itself to be dynamic, sensitive to changing requirements, and open to innovative concepts and methods in order to create the bases and buildings necessary to keep the air arm of the United States second to none.

COAST GUARD

Although one of the nation's armed forces, the United States Coast Guard has a dual role—serving as a bridge between the military and civil branches of government. Because of the variety of tasks assigned to it, the coast guard has developed an integral system of men, ships, aircraft, and related public works facilities capable of responding to a wide range of assignments. In fact, the coast guard can be described as a maritime police force, rescue squad, inspection agency, and traffic department all in one. Its varied responsibilities include search and rescue, pollution prevention and control, maritime safety, navigation aids, icebreaking, boating safety, and enforcement of all federal laws in American waters and on the high seas. Its 38,000 men and women make up the smallest American military service, but it has compiled a rich heritage of war and peacetime achievements.

A Colorful and Varied Service

The coast guard's special character dates back to the nation's earliest days. One of the first acts of the newly created Congress was to place a tariff on imported goods designed to provide much needed revenue as well as to protect infant American\ industries from destructive competition. The stumbling block to this noble plan was American smugglers who had become highly skilled evaders of British laws and regarded the new nation's tariff act in the same light.

Secretary of the Treasury Alexander Hamilton espoused the necessity of a seagoing police force for the custom laws. Accordingly, on August 5, 1790, Congress authorized con-struction of "ten boats" to patrol the Atlantic Coast in order to prevent contraband cargoes from landing, thereby creating the coast guard's ancestor. Its formation preceded the United States Navy by eight years. Despite numerous attempts to transfer control of the service to the navy during the next 177 years, it remained in the Treasury Department until 1967, when it became part of the newly created Department of Transportation.

For over a century, the service was known variously as the revenue service, revenue marine, and revenue cutter service. The present name—the coast guard—was adopted in 1915 upon its merger with the lifesaving service. It is from the latter agency that the coast guard acquired its principal humanitarian mission. As early as 1848, Congress appropriated $5,000 for federal lifeboat stations. Congressional interest grew, and by 1854 there were 137 lifeboat stations along the coasts. These were, however, manned by volunteers who were often unavailable when need arose. Beginning in 1871, full-time crews were employed, and in 1878 the lifesaving service was created. The new agency worked closely with the revenue cutter service until the 1915 merger.

Marine safety is a major peacetime responsibility of the coast guard. In fact, it is the hub around which most day-to-day activities of the agency revolve. A substantial number of its personnel are involved in the service's comprehensive program for making the American merchant marine the world's safest. Supplementing its traditional roles in marine safety, the coast guard absorbed most of the functions of the Bureau of Marine Inspection and Navigation on March 1, 1942. Since then, the coast guard has been the sole federal agency charged with responsibility for safety at sea. In performing this role, the service administers an intensive merchant vessel inspection program, extending from approval of plans on the drafting board, through the ship's operating life, to its final trip to the scrap yard. Besides regular inspection of American merchant ships to insure their compliance with safety regulations, the coast guard is also concerned with the qualifications of their officers and crews. It licenses the officers and certifies the seamen, investigates any casualties or personnel problems, supervises the proper shipment and discharge of crews, and institutes disciplinary action when needed. The coast guard also investigates all violations of American navigation laws as well as develops and promulgates new or revised standards and rules for marine safety for the entire country.

The aids to navigation mission of the coast guard dates from 1716, when the first lighthouse in America was built on Brewster Island in Boston Harbor. During colonial times, governments shouldered the responsibility of creating aids to navigation to reduce marine accidents. On August 7, 1789, the new Congress passed the first federal public works law which provided for federal control of navigation aids. The Cape Henry Lighthouse, an octagonal sandstone tower which was lighted in 1792 at the Virginia entrance to Chesapeake Bay, was the first public work built by the United States. During the period 1789-1842, the supply, construction, and inspection of the lighthouses of the United States were performed mainly by contract. Under this system, the contractors virtually administered the lighthouse organization and exercised wide discretion in performing their duties. Subletting of contracts was also a common practice under this arrangement. In many cases, those actually engaged in the lighthouse work were not directly responsible to the government.

U.S. Departments of Transportation

The Montauk Point Light Station has protected ships from the east end of Long Island since 1797.

In 1852 Congress created a nine-member Lighthouse Board to be composed of naval officers, army engineers, and civilians. This new board divided the country into twelve lighthouse districts. For each district, it appointed an inspector and charged him "with building the lighthouses, with keeping them in repair, and with the purchase, the setting up, and the repairs of the illuminating apparatus." Within a few years, the Lighthouse Board found that the duties of the district inspectors had expanded so greatly that they felt it necessary to appoint an engineer in each district—an army officer, who supervised lighthouse construction and repair. It also set up at Staten Island a central depot for dispersing supplies to light stations. Eventually, each district had its own depot, to which the Staten Island depot shipped the necessary supplies and materials.

Under the Lighthouse Board, aids to navigation in the United States were improved dramatically. As soon as possible, the dark sections of the American coasts were lighted and marked by new lighthouses, lightships, and buoys. The members of the board brought their experience and knowledge to all facets of lighthouse establishment, seeking out and training employees as well as giving them adequate and explicit instructions in writing. One historian later wrote that the "board raised the reputation of the United States' lighthouses from the bottom of the heap to the top . . . in providing the mariner with the latest and fullest aids to make his occupation safer."

As successful as the Lighthouse Board was, its nine-member composition made it too cumbersome to manage effectively and efficiently the country's aids to navigation. Congress finally abolished it in 1910 and created the Bureau of Lighthouses which was later named the Lighthouse Service. President Roosevelt, by means of his 1939 Reorganization Act, abolished the Lighthouse Service and incorporated its activities in the United States Coast Guard on July 7 "in the interest of economy and efficiency."

Today, the aids-to-navigation elements of the coast guard guide ships past dangerous rocks and shoals until they are safe in port. The service does this by means of lighthouses, lightships, buoys, fog signals, and radio beacons. Currently, there are over 40,000 such aids, of which about 170 are manned lighthouses.

The lights no longer depend upon smoky oil lamps that have to be cleaned, filled, and have their wicks trimmed by the keeper. Now, electricity makes the task more efficient, and some lights and fog signals are even turned on and off by remote control. Other electronic improvements are RACON (radar beacons), which indicate the distance (up to 120 miles) and bearing of ships and aircraft from the beacon; and LORAN (Long Range Aid to Navigation), which provides navigational information to ships and aircraft. Coast guard LORAN stations are located in many countries in Europe and Asia as well as other parts of the world. Although a few lightships still remain, most have been replaced either by offshore towers or giant sea buoys.

Long after its creation in 1790, the rescue service had no need for shore support facilities. The construction of its revenue cutters and the lifesaving boats used at the lifeboat stations was done in private shipyards. Necessary repairs and overhauls were likewise done under contract. Over the years, however, as the service's activities grew to meet the needs, the picture changed. The mounting cost of cutter construction and upkeep became a matter of concern. Too often, the quality of work and the prices charged by private shipyards were unsatisfactory.

The service started a small yard manned by workers drawn from among its personnel. In April 1899, Lieutenant John C. Moore, commander of the cutter *Colfax,* established the experimental yard at Curtis Bay, Maryland. Moore, the founder of the present Coast Guard Yard, started by erecting four small buildings—a mill for sawing, shaping and dressing lumber; a boat shop proper for actual assembly and construction; a storage structure to house a sail loft where sails, hatch covers, tarpaulins and other canvas work could be produced; and an administration building. The entire work force consisted of twenty men, all officers and enlisted men from the

Colfax. The cutter itself served as the construction crew's living quarters.

Yard facilities were enlarged and improved between 1910 and World War I to better support the coast guard's small fleet. After war was declared, the service became an integral part of the navy and was in the midst of military action convoying cargo ships and troop transports. Besides handling the vastly increased demands upon its facilities by coast guard vessels, the yard expedited repairs and conversion work on many navy ships.

The yard facilities became antiquated during the 1920s and the Depression years; but in spite of aging equipment and limited working space, the mixed force of military and civilian personnel gained a reputation for fine craftsmanship. The small crafts were famed throughout the world, wherever lifesaving stations were located or cutters patrolled the seas. When the lighthouse service was transferred to the coast guard in 1939, buoy construction became another major yard function. And, during World War II, Curtis Bay became active in supporting cutters engaged in the global struggle. From its modest beginnings as a small boatyard in 1899, consisting of 36 acres of land, 4 small buildings, and 20 employees, the present-day Coast Guard Yard at Curtis Bay, Maryland, has developed into a modern ship building, repair, supply, and manufacturing facility of 112 acres, 69 large shops and buildings, with over 1,000 civilian employees and 100 military personnel.

The yard is the service's largest industrial plant. It is primarily devoted to the construction and repair of ships and boats and the manufacturing of buoys and industrial equipment and components. It does design work for new ships as well as modernization of older ones. In addition, it makes many special shipboard installations such as search radars, torpedo launchers, and oceanographic laboratories; and it frequently manufactures special items for the army, navy, and air force. Moreover, the yard provides supply support for coast guard units in its immediate area and serves as a storage facility for decommissioned vessels.

When the coast guard was formed in 1915, it acquired the system of coastal lifeboat stations maintained for the rescue of those involved in shipwrecks along the American

The Lifesaving Station at Salisbury Beach, Massachusetts, helped save shipwrecked mariners in the late nineteenth and early twentieth centuries.

coasts. The former lifesaving service employed a small staff of workmen and civil engineers who constructed and maintained the lifeboat stations. These stations consisted essentially of housing and handling equipment for the surfboats and living quarters for surfmen. Few men were required for this work and, at the time of the consolidation, they were retained in a civil status to perform the same functions. Some twenty years later, a civil engineer was employed at the Coast Guard Yard at Curtis Bay to be responsible to the military commander of the yard. Another civil engineer, responsible to the officer directing coast guard aviation, was assigned the mission of constructing air stations.

On July 1, 1939, when the lighthouse service became part of the coast guard, the coast guard acquired not only an extensive system of shore establishments but also a corps of engineers. The lighthouse service was essentially an engineering service, requiring construction engineers for its many types of structures; electrical and mechanical engineers for its intricate operating and signal equipment and sound propagation and transmission; as well as marine engineers and naval architects. The only shore establishment then maintained by the revenue cutter service was the Curtis Bay boat yard and a former navy station acquired in 1910 at New London, Connecticut, which was destined to become the service's academy in 1914.

To properly care for the greatly augmented shore establishment, a Civil Engineering Division was begun in 1939. Headed by a chief of civil engineering, the division undertook all needs pertaining to shore establishments. This work included investigations and surveys preliminary to acquisition of property and to the design, construction, and maintenance of structures, appurtenances, utilities, and equipment essential to the operation of shore facilities. This division was given increased responsibilities following Pearl Harbor. The first major undertaking was to provide shore facilities for receiving and training recruits for both the coast guard and the merchant marine. Next came housing for the SPARS (the women's military reserve of the coast guard), buildings at the academy, and

bases and moorings for coastal picket patrols and fireboat stations.

As World War II progressed, regional supply depots were established; garages were provided for motor pools; and telephone section stations, weather reporting stations, and rifle ranges were erected. Many lookout stations and towers were also constructed to supplement the coastal network of lighthouses and lifeboat stations. After the organizing of the Beach Patrol, it was necessary to provide housing and living facilities for the men, kennels for their dogs, and barns for their horses over the entire periphery of the continental coastline. Of equal importance was the performance of the construction detachments working outside the United States, which built networks of LORAN stations. In all, the Civil Engineering Division planned and carried out a wide variety of projects during the war, covering all shores and waterways of the continental United States and extending to advance bases in the North Atlantic, the Caribbean Sea, and to all combat areas of the Pacific.

The end of the fighting brought an immediate demand for demobilization. Accordingly, the wartime complement of 175,000 personnel was reduced to 18,687 by 1947. This drastic reduction brought problems, for in the immediate post-World War II years, the service was performing missions and duties that properly required between 25,000 and 30,000 people.

When the Korean conflict broke out in June 1950, the coast guard was not transferred to the navy as in previous emergencies. Nevertheless, the air force and navy aircraft operating over Korea needed facilities for accurate navigation and search and rescue. The coast guard responded by building new LORAN chains, covering the areas around Korea, Japan, Formosa, and the Philippines. Following the Korean Armistice in July 1953, it either discontinued or turned over to the navy all of the search and rescue units that had been established to support American armed forces in the Pacific. Other activities were cut back accordingly, but LORAN stations remained manned and were upgraded to permanent installations.

U.S. Department of Transportation

Completed in 1967, the Ambrose Offshore Light Structure guards the entrance to New York Harbor.

The physical plant of the coast guard had deteriorated badly through the years. Not only did most of its vessels date back to prohibition days, but they showed the wear of their strenuous wartime duty and were becoming more and more expensive to maintain. The shore establishment was in even worse condition. Nearly all lifeboat and light stations were old and had received only minimum maintenance.

A gradual modernization program was begun. In at least one instance, replacement was not the best answer. By 1960 the coast guard found itself with thirty lightships, the majority of which were quite antiquated. Faced with the problem of mass replacement, the service decided to use fixed structures in their place. The Texas Tower type of offshore structure was finally adopted and modified to meet this need. The Texas Tower principle consisted of performing all basic construction ashore and then towing the structure to its offshore position. Supporting columns were then hydraulically lowered to the ocean floor, supporting the platform at the desired height above the water. The first of the new offshore light structures replaced the Buzzards Bay Lightship on November 1, 1961. With helicopter platforms and built-in facilities for oceanographic and meteorological equipment, these fixed structures are much more efficient than a lightship.

During the Vietnam conflict, the coast guard assisted the navy by halting the infiltration of Communist forces and supplies into South Vietnam by sea. In April 1965, the service began sending to the waters around Vietnam highly maneuverable, heavily armed 82-foot-long boats. Besides boarding all suspicious looking craft, searching for weapons, ammunition, and other contraband, the personnel of these cutters took part in hundreds of naval gunfire support missions, assisting ground forces with mortar fire on selected enemy targets. Two years later, again at the navy's request, the coast guard began sending its larger cutters to strengthen coastal defenses. Eventually, nearly all of the major cutters from the 255-foot to the 378-foot classes were deployed to Vietnam.

Other coast guard servicemen performed little noticed but extremely important missions during the Vietnam conflict. These activities included unloading highly explosive munitions, port security, marine safety, and maintaining aids to navigation in addition to flying "Jolly Green Giant" helicopters in the recovery of downed American airmen. The service also built and manned LORAN transmitting stations in Vietnam and neighboring Thailand to aid air and sea navigation in the area.

Involvement in the tragic Asian conflict illustrates that in time of national emergencies combat roles are merely added to the coast guard's normal activities of search and rescue, marine safety, and maintaining navigational aids. Construction of shore facilities continues to meet changing technology, additional responsibility, and replacement needs. Public works support of the service's missions is reflected in the physical shore installations and equipment in the coast guard inventory. At Curtis Bay, Maryland, the shipyard keeps twenty-six cutters and 2,000 small boats in operating condition. Its Aircraft Repair and Supply Center at the Coast Guard Air Station in Elizabeth City, North Carolina, maintains 150 fixed-wing aircraft and helicopters. In addition, it operates 700 shore stations and manages 40,000 aids to navigation, including 170 manned lighthouses. These facilities enable the coast guard to function as an efficient humanitarian-military force, ready to carry out its widespread and varied duties.

SUGGESTED READINGS

Abbot, Henry L. *Course of Lectures upon the Defence of the Sea-Coast of the United States.* New York, 1888.

Adamson, Hans C. *Keepers of the Lights.* New York, 1955.

Bloomfield, Howard V. L. *The Compact History of the United States Coast Guard.* New York, 1966.

Bowman, Walter G., and others. *Bulldozers Came First.* New York, 1944.

Capron, Walter C. *The U.S. Coast Guard.* New York, 1965.

Carrison, Daniel J. *The Navy from Wood to Steel.* New York, 1964.

Castillo, Edmund L. *The Seabees of World War II.* New York, 1963.

Coggins, Jack. *Ships and Seamen of the American Revolution.* Harrisburg, Pennsylvania, 1969.

Conn, Stetson; Engelman, Rose C.; and Fairchild, Byron. *Guarding the United States and its Outposts*. Washington, D.C., 1964.

Craven, Wesley F., and Cate, James, eds. *The Army Air Force in World War II*. 5 vols. Chicago, 1957-1962.

Cunliffe, Marcus. *Soldiers and Civilians: The Martial Spirit in America, 1775-1885*. Boston, 1968.

Dunn, Carroll H. *Vietnam Studies: Base Development in South Vietnam, 1965-1970*. Washington, D.C., 1972.

Fine, Lenore, and Remington, Jesse A. *The Corps of Engineers: Construction in the United States*. U.S. Army in World War II: The Technical Services. Washington, D.C., 1972.

Goldberg, Alfred, and others. *A History of the United States Air Force, 1907-1957*. Princeton, New Jersey, 1957.

Hammond, P. Y. *Organization for Defense: The American Military Establishment in the Twentieth Century*. New York, 1961.

Huzar, Elias. *The Purse and the Sword: Control of the Army by Congress through Military Appropriations, 1933-1950*. Ithaca, New York, 1950.

King, Ernest J. *U.S. Navy at War*. Washington, D.C., 1946.

Kreidberg, Marvin, and Henry, Merton G. *History of Mobilization in the United States Army, 1775-1945*. Washington, D.C., 1955.

Morenus, Richard. *DEW Line*. New York, 1957.

Paullin, Charles O. *History of the Naval Administration, 1776-1911*. Annapolis, Maryland, 1968.

Risch, Erna. *Quartermaster Support of the Army: History of the Corps, 1775-1939*. Washington, D.C., 1962.

U.S. Coast Guard. *Historically Famous Lighthouses*. Washington, D.C., 1972.

U.S. Department of War. *Citadels of Democracy: Camps and Plants for Men and Munitions*. Washington, D.C., 1941.

Williams, T. Harry. *Americans at War: The Development of the American Military System*. New York, 1960.

CHAPTER 19

AEROSPACE

Conquering the mysteries of flight and traveling in outer space have been two of the twentieth century's most outstanding technological achievements. Seventy years ago, aeronautics was a primitive, arcane science. Mankind has since mastered the air and set foot on the moon, the fulfillment of centuries-old ambitions. Attaining these goals has involved large expenditures of public funds and the joint cooperation of government, industry, and universities to produce a sophisticated public works system of research centers, ground support installations, and exotic vehicles. Rapid progress in this field has been a tribute to the United States' ability to set a goal, marshal the resources to attain it, and thereby better understand the earth's environment and the mysteries of the universe.

Flight Research

In 1913 as war clouds gathered across Europe, a few Americans were alarmed at the state of aeronautics in the United States. Most of the leading nations of Europe had already established aeronautical research facilities and were subsidizing a developing aviation industry, but the United States lagged far behind. Among the small group of concerned men was Charles D. Wolcott, secretary of the

Smithsonian Institution. Convinced that the situation called for federal sponsorship of aviation development, he worked hard to convince Congress to support aeronautical research, and eventually he succeeded. On March 3, 1915, President Woodrow Wilson signed a navy appropriations bill that contained a rider establishing an independent National Advisory Committee for Aeronautics (NACA). The sum of $5,000 was appropriated for the committee's first year of operations. Its organizational structure was unique. Twelve presidentially appointed members, serving without pay and drawn from government and the scientific community, were charged "to supervise and direct the scientific study of the problems of flight, with a view to their practical solution" and to "direct and conduct research and experiments in aeronautics."

The committee's first task was to survey the status of aeronautics in the United States. At that time, aviation was generally regarded as a daredevil sport practiced by a handful of wealthy young men. Research was virtually non-existent; facilities were few in number; and the aviation "industry" consisted of a scattered collection of small shops. The military services had fewer than 200 airplanes, and they were obsolete by European standards. None of the government work in aeronautics previously undertaken by the Weather Bureau, Bureau of Standards, and the military services was coordinated. A

This chapter is based on a special report prepared by the National Aeronautics and Space Administration

NASA

In the 1920s, the Langley Memorial Aeronautical Laboratory's wind tunnel was used for pioneer aviation research.

federal laboratory was urgently needed. Subsequently, the army, navy, and NACA agreed to establish a joint research center near Hampton, Virginia. The three-building complex was formally dedicated in June 1920 as the Langley Memorial Aeronautical Laboratory in honor of Samuel P. Langley, aeronautical pioneeer.

By the end of the 1920s, the research facility had achieved impressive results. In 1929 a distinguished British engineer declared: "The only people so far who have been able to get at something like accurate results from wind tunnel experiments are the workers at the experimental station at Langley Field." Among the most important achievements of Langley's aerodynamic research were the NACA cowling (whose streamlined shape increased aircraft speed); systematic studies of aerodynamic drag; and determining the inefficiency of using fixed, exposed landing gear instead of retracting wheels.

Ironically, the Great Depression of the 1930s was a boon to NACA. Additional research facilities were constructed with money appropriated for the Public Works Administration and other federal agencies. Government salaries and the modern research facilities were attractive to young engineers. For example, in 1931 a 30- by 60-foot wind tunnel, then the largest in the world, was completed at Langley at a cost of $900,000. The NACA's staff grew from 181 in 1930 to 523 by 1939. The researchers designed a series of wing shapes that affected the design of military and civil aircraft throughout the world. As aircraft speeds increased, other aerodynamic problems were solved. Stalls and spins, which caused one fourth of all aircraft accidents, were investigated and largely countered.

By 1936 NACA officials were concerned with two interrelated problems: (1) European nations were rapidly building new research facilities; (2) Langley lacked growth space. In 1938 a special committee on expanded facilities was formed and recommended the creation of a second research center in

California. Congress authorized the new laboratory in 1939. Ground was broken at Moffett Field, a navy airfield 40 miles south of San Francisco, in September 1939 to create the Ames Aeronautical Laboratory. The facility's most impressive structure was a 60-by 80-foot wind tunnel that dwarfed the tunnel at Langley. Construction also commenced on an array of high-speed research facilities.

Another research center was built just after war broke out in Europe in September 1939. In October a special committee, headed by Charles A. Lindbergh, recommended building a third laboratory to conduct research on aircraft power plants. Funds were authorized in 1940 to acquire a site at Cleveland, Ohio's municipal airport to create the Lewis Research Center. Construction commenced on facilities to develop and test aircraft engines, study fuels and combustion, and perform research in the physics, chemistry, and metallurgy of power plants.

War and Cold War

During World War II, NACA turned its attention to solving problems of military aircraft in production or on the drawing boards. The increase in performance and the demands of combat flying spawned new aerodynamic and structural problems. From 1941 through 1945, the NACA laboratories worked on 115 different airplane types and achieved impressive results. Fighter aircraft speeds and altitudes were increased; buffeting and stalls were cured; and the tail design of the B-29 was saved from a dangerous weakness.

The war drastically altered the world's balance of power. The United States and Soviet Russia became superpowers, and each nation sought to exploit the expansion of technology. The atomic bomb was the war's most important legacy. Both nations began building long-range aircraft and sought to develop weapons systems that could deliver the bomb across intercontinental distances. The intercontinental rocket was theoretically promising but did not seem feasible for the immediate future. Atomic bombs were bulky and heavy, and a rocket to lift such a payload would be enormous and expensive. The Soviet Union planned to build such rockets. However, the

American military temporarily focused on jet aircraft and on tactical rocket research. The army imported Wernher von Braun and the other German scientists who created the wartime V-1 and V-2 rockets, and it set them to refurbishing and launching V-2's at White Sands, New Mexico. The air force developed groups of missiles, including the jet Bomarc and Matador air battlefield missiles and the rocket-propelled Navaho, an intercontinental weapon.

By 1951 progress on a hydrogen bomb accelerated interest in long-range ballistic missiles. Two months before President Harry S. Truman announced that the United States would develop the thermonuclear bomb, the air force began development of the Atlas intercontinental ballistic missile. During the next four years, four intermediate range missiles, the army's Jupiter, the navy's Polaris, and the air force's Thor and Titan, were added to the list of American rocket projects. In the 1953 fiscal year, the Department of Defense for the first time spent more than $1 million on missile research, development, and procurement. By 1957 the amount went over $1 billion.

Postwar technological progress had a dramatic effect on NACA. The rise of aircraft speeds and altitudes outran the technological data base that NACA had developed. The jet engine increased aircraft speed and required overcoming the problems of exceeding the sound barrier. The wind tunnel, NACA's principal tool for aerodynamic research, yielded accurate data for subsonic and supersonic speeds; but at transonic speeds (Mach 0.9 to 1.1), it suffered a "choking" effect that garbled data. Until this problem was remedied, other research methods were used. In 1943 NACA began dropping test models from high altitudes and gathering flight data during their fall. This was only partially successful, since radar and telemetry were too primitive to provide sophisticated data. The next step was to use rockets to launch models to transonic and supersonic speeds. For this purpose, NACA acquired a surplus naval station on Wallops Island, Virginia, which became the Wallops Flight Center.

The long-term flight research plan was to

The X-l was the first aircraft to break the sound barrier.

build and operate, in concert with the air corps and the navy, a series of special research aircraft. The Flight Research Center was established at Edwards, California, on Muroc Dry Lake to undertake advanced aeronautical research. On October 14, 1947, air force Captain Charles E. Yeager flew the X-1 aircraft faster than the speed of sound. On November 20, 1953, NACA's Scott Crossfield reached Mach 2 in the D-588-2. During the next two decades, the X-1, X-2, X-15, and other research aircraft provided design data that was used to develop generations of post-World War II military aircraft.

By the mid 1950s, NACA had a staff of 7,200 and modern research facilities that cost $300 million to construct; and it was enlarging its missile research program. Major NACA contributions to the military missile program occurred in the mid 1950s. A research team at Langley developed a means of controlling the intense heat generated by warheads and other bodies re-entering the earth's atmosphere. Other teams demonstrated the blunt body shape as the most effective design for re-entry devices, and work was done on the mechanics of ballistic re-entry.

Space Age Beginnings

By the mid 1950s, America's infant space program was burgeoning with promise. As part of its participation in the International Geophysical Year, the United States proposed to launch a small satellite into orbit around the earth. In 1954, after a spirited design competition between the National Academy of Sciences-navy proposal (Vanguard) and the army-Jet Propulsion Laboratory competitor (Explorer), the navy design was chosen. By 1957 the first test vehicles were being built, but the USSR won the space race by orbiting *Sputnik I* on October 4, 1957.

The American public's response to Sputnik was both alarm and chagrin. The country's certainty that it was technologically superior to Russia was rudely challenged. The Sputnik weighed an impressive 184 pounds compared to the first Vanguard's intended three pounds. In the Cold War environment, the contrast had obvious military implications. Less than one month after *Sputnik I*, the Russians launched *Sputnik II*, which weighed 1,120 pounds and carried a dog. President Dwight D. Eisenhower tried to lessen concern by assuring the public of America's progress in space research and by denying there was any implied military threat in Russian space achievements. As the White House announced the impending launch of the first Vanguard test vehicle in December 1957, the Department of Defense authorized von Braun's army research team in Huntsville, Alabama, to launch a Jupiter-Explorer combination. But pressures for dramatic action mounted. The press ballyhooed the White House announcement on Vanguard into great expectations of America's success. On December 6, 1957, the Vanguard test vehicle rose 4 feet from the launch platform, shuddered, and collapsed in flames. Its tiny three-

NASA

The Explorer I satellite, a duplicate of which is shown here in ceremonies following launching, was the United States' first successful space shot.

pound payload broke away and lay at the edge of the inferno, beeping impotently. On January 31, 1958, an American satellite finally went into orbit. The thirty-pound army *Explorer I* was joined in orbit by *Vanguard I* on March 17.

America was at last in space, but future endeavors remained uncertain because of rivalries within the federal government. The military services, Atomic Energy Commission, and NACA all fought for control of America's expanding space commitment. The NACA had devoted more of its facilities, budget, and expertise to missile research in the mid and late 1950s and developed a long-term, scientifically based proposal for aeronautic and space research. The agency was experienced at working closely with the military services on research problems, while at the same time translating these findings into civil applications. But NACA's greatest asset was its peaceful, research-oriented image. President Eisenhower and congressional leaders wanted to avoid projecting Cold War tensions into the new arena of outer space.

By March 1958, the official opinion in Washington had solidified to create a national space program with a military branch under the Defense Department and a civil branch lodged in a new agency. The latter would assume control of existing space projects and forge a program of space exploration in close concert with the military. On July 29, 1958, Eisenhower signed the National Aeronautics and Space Act. The law established a broad charter for civilian aeronautical and space research. The NACA was absorbed into the new National Aeronautics and Space Administration (NASA) as its nucleus, and space projects from other government agencies were acquired by the new agency. Plans were immediately formulated for building another center for space science research, satellite development, flight operations, and tracking. A 550-acre tract of the Department of Agriculture's research center in Beltsville, Maryland, was chosen, and in March 1961 the Robert H. Goddard Space Flight Center (named for America's rocket pioneer) was dedicated.

A two-year period of organization, build-up, and planning followed. Only one week after NASA was formed, the go-ahead was given to Project Mercury, America's first manned space flight program. Long-range planning was accelerated, and a NASA ten-year plan was presented to Congress in February

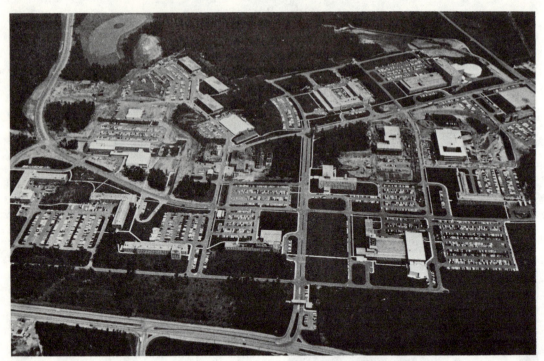

NASA

The Goddard Space Flight Center in Beltsville, Maryland, was dedicated in March 1961.

1960. It called for an expanding program on a broad front: manned flight; scientific satellites to measure radiation and other features of the near-space environment and to photograph the moon; planetary probes to measure and photograph Mars and Venus; weather satellites to improve understanding of earth's weather patterns; continued aeronautical research; and development of larger launch vehicles for lifting heavier payloads. The cost of the program was estimated to vary between $1 billion and $1.5 billion a year over the ten-year period.

The NASA became markedly different from NACA in two important ways. First, it was operational as well as research and development oriented. That is, it would not only design and build launch vehicles and satellites but would launch, operate, track, and acquire and interpret data. Second, it would do the greatest part of its work by contract with universities and private companies rather than by relying on federal employees.

Launch vehicles occupied the agency's attention in these first few years. A series of existing and future launch vehicles had to be built for diverse missions and spacecraft. In addition, work continued with the Atomic Energy Commission on the Nerva, a promising nuclear-propelled upper stage, and on a family of long-life electric power systems. The NASA also sought to improve the reliability of the existing boosters. By December 1959, the United States had attempted thirty-seven satellite launches, but less than one third attained orbit. Virtually every booster component had to be redesigned to withstand the stresses of launch. New production standards were instilled in workmen and managers, and repeated testing was undertaken to confirm the reliability of each component before vehicle assembly. Since the existing vehicles were Defense Department products, NASA persuaded the Pentagon to impose these stringent standards on its contractors. By 1960 initial reorganization and planning were completed, and a viable organization was functioning.

Meeting the Challenges

Although not a direct issue in the 1960 presidential campaign, the space program, as an expensive item in the federal budget, faced an uncertain future. After John F. Kennedy was elected, he appointed his science advisor to chair a committee that prepared a report critical of the space program's progress and skeptical of its future. However, once again the Russians captured the world's attention. On April 12, 1961, Major Yuri Gagarin piloted *Vostok I* into a 187- by 108-mile orbit of the earth. After one orbit, he re-entered the atmosphere and landed safely. There was some consolation for Americans on May 5, 1961, when astronaut Alan B. Shepard, Jr., piloted the *Freedom 7* Mercury spacecraft for a fifteen-minute suborbital flight and was picked up 297 miles downrange. In spite of Shepard's flight, the United States was clearly still behind, especially in rocket power. A dejected President Kennedy stated: "We are behind . . . . the news will be worse before it is better, and it will be some time before we catch up."

The public reaction was less emphatic than after *Sputnik I*, but congressional concern was strong. The NASA officials were hard put to restrain Congress from forcing more money on them than could be effectively used. President Kennedy was also troubled. His inaugural address promised bold new initiatives that would "get this country moving again." The succeeding three months were marked by the Bay of Pigs invasion and the Gagarin flight. As one of several new initiatives, the President asked Vice President Lyndon B. Johnson to head a study of what would be required to surpass the Soviets in space. Johnson found strong support in NASA, and the agency accelerated and expanded the central elements of its ten-year plan.

A manned lunar landing became the focal point of the space program. On May 25, 1961, the President stood before a joint session of Congress and proposed a historic national goal: "before this decade is out, of landing a man on the moon and returning him safely to the earth." The President correctly assessed the national mood. The decision to land a man on the moon was endorsed virtually without dissent. Editorial support was widespread and congressional debate perfunctory.

The earlier assumption was to build a large booster, fly directly to the moon, land a large vehicle on the lunar surface, and return it to the earth. But there was disagreement as to whether the lunar surface could support such a load. The other initial alternative was to place components of a lunar vehicle into earth orbit, assemble and refuel them, and take off for a direct landing on the moon. This approach was fraught with hazards, including whether payloads could rendezvous in space, whether men could assemble complex equipment in this environment, and whether operations such as refueling could be safely performed in space.

Regardless of these questions, some points were clear. This massive effort was different from anything previously attempted. It would require new organizational modes and a much stronger headquarters team to oversee the project and coordinate mobilization of support from American industry and universities. In addition, there were problems requiring long lead times such as developing a big, reliable rocket engine. Work on the million-pound-thrust F-1 engine, already in progress for three years, was accelerated. The navigation system was another major concern. Accurately vectoring a spacecraft from the earth to a precise point on the moon was a formidable problem in celestial mechanics. Therefore, a large Apollo contract was let to the Massachusetts Institute of Technology to develop the requisite navigational system.

A new system of earth-based logistics was also needed. Every step from factory to launch exceeded normal sizes and transportation modes. New factories, mammoth test stands, and launch complexes had to be built. Railroads and highways could not accommodate the larger components, so water transportation had to be planned. A massive facility design and site location program was underway even before the final configuration of the vehicle was determined. Limited in its facilities construction capability, NASA called on the Army Corps of Engineers to plan and supervise construction of its facilities.

As planning went forward in 1961 and 1962, a concept for how to get to the moon gradually emerged—lunar-orbit rendezvous. Project Apollo involved a set of spacecraft going into orbit around the moon. The mother craft would dispatch a smaller one to land on the lunar surface, reconnoiter, and rejoin the mother ship in orbit for the return to the earth. Once made, this decision enabled rapid development of the Apollo spacecraft combination. The objective was to put a payload of nearly 150 tons in earth orbit and 50 tons around the moon. To do this required a three-stage vehicle: the first stage employed a cluster of engines to provide 7.5 million pounds of thrust at launch; the second stage combined five of a 200,000-pound-thrust, liquid hydrogen and liquid oxygen engine, the J-2; the third stage, powered by a single J-2 engine, would boost the Apollo three-man spacecraft out of earth orbit and impart enough speed to enable it to escape the earth's gravitational field. At that point the three-spacecraft combination would take over: a command module housing the astronauts, a service module providing propulsion for maneuvers, and a two-part lunar module for the moon landing. The engine on the service module would ignite to slow the spacecraft enough to be captured into lunar orbit. The lunar module would then leave the mother craft and descend to land its two passengers on the moon.

The grand design was complete, but important technological questions remained. At three critical points, the plan depended on the successful rendezvous and docking of spacecraft. Although theoretically feasible, it had never been done and was not within the scope of Project Mercury. How could practical experience be gained with rendezvous and docking short of an experimental and possibly disastrous series of tests with Apollo hardware? Could men and their equipment function in space outside the artificial environment of their spacecraft?

While these questions remained unanswered, the Mercury program moved forward. In September 1961, an unmanned Mercury capsule was orbited and landed east of Bermuda. Two months later the final test flight took chimpanzee Enos on a successful two-orbit ride. The system was qualified for manned orbital flight; and on February 20, 1962, Astronaut John H. Glenn, Jr., who piloted *Friendship 7*, became the first American to orbit the earth.

That same year the young American space program experienced other important successes. Two more Mercury flights were made, and the powerful Saturn booster made its first two test flights. The first communications satellite, *Telstar I*, was launched; and Britain's *Ariel I* was launched by NASA to take scientific measurements of the ionosphere. *Mariner II* became the first satellite to fly by another planet. On December 14, it passed within 21,400 miles of Venus and scanned the surface of the cloud-shrouded body, measuring its temperature. It continued into orbit around the sun and eventually set a new communications distance record of 54.7 million miles. Tiros meterological satellites were placed in earth orbit and reported on the world's weather. Tiros was so successful that the Weather Bureau regularly integrated Tiros data into its forecasting and

NASA

Astronaut John H. Glenn, Jr. rose off the launch pad at Cape Canaveral on February 20, 1962 to become the first American to orbit the earth.

began planning a full-scale weather satellite system.

The Ranger, designed to photograph the moon while falling to the lunar surface, encountered serious problems. A complex program, Ranger closed 1962 with five straight failures, and NASA and its contractors came under heavy pressure from Congress. After studies were made, the program was reorganized, and the last three Ranger flights in 1963 were spectacularly successful. They provided close-up lunar photography that exceeded by 2,000 times the best telescopic detail of the moon and dispelled many theories about the lunar surface's composition.

All lunar reconnaissance programs were designed to support the Apollo project. The surveyor program was developed to provide photography of the lunar surface and televised digging for a better understanding of soil composition. To acquire detailed mapping photography of the moon, a third program was initiated—Lunar Orbiter—a photographic mapping satellite that went into orbit around the moon and took photographs to determine the areas that offered potential Apollo landing sites.

Despite these achievements, however, the vexing problems of rendezvous and extravehicular activity remained. Therefore, on January 3, 1962, NASA announced the creation of Gemini, a new manned space flight project. Using the basic design of the Mercury capsule, but increasing its size to hold a two-man crew, Gemini was a transition program between Mercury and Apollo that aided design work on Apollo. Its launch vehicle was the Titan II missile developed by the air force. Innovations were incorporated into the program and contracts and subcontracts let for design and fabrication. Soon the monthly bills for Gemini were running far ahead of the budget. Cost overruns became severe by late 1962; and by March 1963, the original program cost of $350 million had risen to over $1 billion. But by early 1964, most of the engineering problems were being solved.

To the Moon

Even before Gemini was proposed, it was clear that NASA needed additional facilities. On September 19, 1961, the agency announced that a new Manned Spacecraft Center would be built on the outskirts of Houston, Texas. It was designed as NASA's primary facility for (1) design, development, and manufacture of manned spacecraft; (2) selection and training of astronaut crews; and (3) the control of space flight missions. The enormous complex of buildings, located on a 1,620-acre tract 20 miles southeast of Houston, cost over $800 million to construct and became NASA's nerve center for manned space exploration.

Water access played a role in site selection for all Apollo facilities. The big Michoud Ordnance Plant, where the 33-foot diameter Saturn first stage would be fabricated, was located near New Orleans, Louisiana. The facility included a main assembly plant covering 43 acres under one roof. The Mississippi Test Facility, with its huge test stands for booster stages, was built on 138,870 acres 55 miles northeast of New Orleans. The center's primary responsibility was testing the Saturn launch vehicles for the Apollo program. The complex cost $333 million to build. The site afforded deep-water transportation for the large booster via the East Pearl River and the Intracoastal Waterway.

All this effort would come together at the launch site at Cape Canaveral, Florida, where NASA used the air force's launch facilities and tracking range. But Apollo required facilities much too large for the crowded cape. In the interest of safety, large buffer zones of land were required around the launch pads; if all stages of the launch vehicle exploded, the force would approximate a small atomic bomb. Therefore, NASA received congressional approval to purchase 88,000 acres of Merritt Island, just northwest of the air force facilities, to build a new launch complex. Named the John F. Kennedy Space Center, the facility is about 34 miles long and occupies 87,760 acres of land. By 1972, $1.3 billion had been spent to construct facilities at this location. It serves as the primary center for test, checkout, and launch of space vehicles. The site, with its adjoining bodies of water, provides enough space to insure the safety of the

NASA

Saturn launch vehicles were erected in the cavernous Vehicle Assembly Building and transported by a crawler to the launch complex 3 miles away.

surrounding civilian community. The NASA reached agreements with the Interior Department for using portions of the facility as a wildlife refuge and parts of the shoreline for recreation.

To acquire data from manned and unmanned spacecraft, NASA established the Spaceflight Tracking and Data Network, a worldwide system of twenty-two tracking and communications stations. In addition to fixed bases, the network includes mobile land-based stations, communications ships, and specially equipped aircraft. Information received from manned spacecraft is relayed to the Mission Control Center at Houston, Texas, the operational headquarters for manned space flights. Data from satellites is gathered at the Goddard Flight Center in Greenbelt, Maryland, where a computer complex was built to monitor and analyze the constant flow of telemetric information.

The NASA struggled with a wide range of concepts for the best launch system for Apollo. The agency was hampered by a limited knowledge of how the vehicle would be configured, what the missions involved, and how frequently launches would occur. On July 21, 1962, NASA announced its choice. The Advanced Saturn (later Saturn V) launch vehicle would be transported to the new Launch Operations Center on Merritt Island stage by stage; the stages would be erected and checked out in one of four bays of the world's largest building, the enormous 525-foot-high Vehicle Assembly Building which covered an area of nearly 1.8 million square feet; and the assembled missile would be transported to one of the four launch pads several miles away by a 2,500-ton crawler tractor. This system was a major departure from previous practices of erecting vehicles on the launch pad. Under the new concept, the vehicle was on the pad a much shorter time, allowing better protection from lightning, hurricanes, and salt water corrosion. As in the case of the other new Apollo facilities, the Army Corps of Engineers supervised the vast construction project.

Building facilities and hardware took a great deal of money and a large force of skilled technicians. The NASA budget, $966.7 million in fiscal year 1961, rose to $1.8 billion in 1962. It hit $3.74 billion the next year and reached $5.1 billion in 1964. It remained in that range for the next three years. During this period, NASA personnel increased from 17,471 to 35,860. However, this total was small compared to the contractor and university force where 90 percent of NASA's money was spent. When the Apollo program peaked in 1967, more than 400,000 people were working on some aspect of the project.

The NASA made great progress in 1963. The master plan for Apollo was drawn and key men were in place. Mercury ended with L. Gordon Cooper's twenty-two orbit flight, far beyond the original design limits of the spacecraft. Of thirteen NASA launches during the year, eleven were successful. In addition to improved performance from the established launch vehicles, Saturn I had another successful test flight. The *Syncom II* communications satellite transmitted voice and teletype communications between North America, South America, and Africa; and the *Explorer XVIII* scientific satellite sailed out in a long elliptical orbit to measure radiation levels most of the distance to the moon.

By early 1964, the Gemini program had overcome earlier difficulties and was preparing for a rapid series of launches. Trial launches in April 1964 and January 1965 confirmed the reliability of the hardware. One of the program objectives was to orbit men in space for at least the week it would take the Apollo flight to go to the moon, land, and return. Seven manned flights were made during 1965, culminating with *Gemini 7* which lasted fourteen days. Of more importance than the durability of the equipment was evidence that no long-term harmful effects to man resulted from weightlessness. Subsequent launches proved that rendezvous and

docking maneuvers planned for every lunar flight were feasible. Astronauts also learned to "walk" in space and perform mechanical tasks on the outside of spacecraft as they orbited the earth. But perhaps the most valuable benefit from Gemini was developing coordination between the space vehicle and the ground team.

While the Apollo spacecraft was being developed throughout the Gemini operational period, Saturn I finished its ten-flight program in 1964 and 1965 with six launches featuring a second liquid-hydrogen stage. Meanwhile, the larger booster, the Saturn IB, was aborning. It was the first launch vehicle to be affected by the new concept of "all-up" testing. Besieged by budgetary constraints, NASA abandoned its stage-by-stage testing program. With intensive ground testing of components, NASA could examine the entire stock of vehicles at great budget and schedule savings. This procedure was successful; and on February 26, 1966, the Saturn IB flew with the Apollo command and service module spacecraft in suborbital flight.

The lunar module encountered difficulties because it was a unique spacecraft. There were two craft within the lunar module: one that would descend to the lunar surface from lunar orbit; another that would discard the descent stage and blast off the surface into orbit and rendezvous with the command module. The engine for each stage had to work perfectly for the one time it fired. Weight was a constant problem with the lunar module. Each small change in a system, each substitution of one material for another had to be considered in terms of pounds added or pounds saved.

By the end of 1966, the Saturn IB and the first Apollo command and service module were considered operational. On January 27, 1967, astronauts Virgil I. Grissom, Edward H. White II, and Roger B. Chaffee were suited up in the command module, moving through a simulated launch count-down, when tragedy struck. Ground crew members saw a flash fire break through the spacecraft and envelop the astronauts in smoke. Rescue attempts failed, and the three men died of asphyxiation. Shock swept the nation. The day following the fire, an eight-member board was appointed to investigate the accident. For months the board probed the evidence, heard witnesses, and studied documentation. The fire had apparently been started by an electrical short circuit that ignited the oxygen-rich atmosphere and fed on combustible materials in the spacecraft. There had been errors in design and faults in testing procedures, but the basic spacecraft design was sound. A thorough review of the spacecraft's design, wiring, combustible materials, and test procedures was undertaken. The hatch was redesigned for quick opening, and hundreds of miles of wiring were fireproofed and protected against damage. An intensive materials research program developed substitutes for combustibles. This effort caused eighteen months delay in the manned flight schedule and cost at least $50 million.

Before the Apollo spacecraft flew, NASA began developing long-range plans. With the long lead times and heavy costs inherent in manned space programs, advance planning was essential. President Johnson asked NASA to outline its future program in 1964, and the agency responded during congressional hearings on the 1965 budget. Funds were requested for study contracts to investigate using Apollo hardware for other programs. Proposals included lunar surface exploration operating out of an unmanned Apollo lunar module, lunar orbital missions to survey and map the moon, and earth orbital operations leading to creation of space stations. Through 1965 and 1966, these and other projects were studied. The 1965 Woods Hole Conference brought together a broad spectrum of the American science community and identified some 150 scientific experiments that were candidates for such missions.

By 1966 there was a sense of urgency in NASA planning; the Apollo program was peaking and would begin to decline in less than two years. Unless firm requirements for additional boosters and other systems could be funded, the Apollo production lines would shut down. In the 1967 congressional hearings, NASA presented further details and fixed the next fiscal year as the latest that contractural commitments could be deferred if

Apollo hardware were to be used for future programs. The NASA began the 1968 budget cycle with a fairly ambitious Apollo applications proposal. It asked for a 1968 appropriation of $626 million to start constructing six Saturn IB's, six Saturn V's, and eight Apollo spacecraft per year. The Bureau of the Budget approved a budget request of $454 million. This cut the program by one third. However, Congress appropriated only $253 million; so that by mid 1968, many future missions were curtailed.

Manned space flight, with its overwhelming priority, had both a direct and indirect impact on the NASA space science program. From 1958 to 1963, scientific satellites had made impressive discoveries such as the Van Allen radiation belts, the earth's magnetosphere, and the existence of the solar wind. Much of the space science effort was directed toward gathering additional detailed data on these phenomena. The radiation belts were found to be plural with definite shifting altitudes. The magnetosphere's elongated tail which reached out beyond the moon was discovered. The solar wind was shown to vary greatly in intensity with solar activity.

These momentous discoveries about the space environment led NASA to plan more sophisticated, versatile satellites that would reveal other aspects of how the universe works. Therefore, a second generation of spacecraft was planned and developed; they were called the observatory class and were designed to support up to twenty experimental instruments that could be varied from one flight to the next. These complex spacecraft were developed and launched in the mid 1960s; but because of electrical failures, the first results were disappointing. By the late 1960s, the budgetary demands of manned spaceflight reduced or eliminated space science programs. However, smaller satellites, such as the Pioneer series, survived and made observations on the solar wind, solar plasma, and the interplanetary magnetic field.

Lunar scientific programs fared better. The moon missions were in support of Apollo and were allowed to run their course. Surveyor soft-landed six out of its seven

Lunar orbiter satellites mapped the rocky lunar surface to locate potential Apollo landing sites.

spacecraft on the moon from 1966 to 1968 and sent back television pictures of the lunar landscape. Its instruments revealed that the soil had the consistency of wet sand, strong enough to support landings by the lunar module. In addition, five lunar orbiters were put into orbit around the moon to photograph more than 90 percent of the surface and to survey potential Apollo landing sites.

Planetary programs encountered heavy reductions. The Mariner series was cut back, but its two flights provided exciting new glimpses of Mars. *Mariner IV* flew past Mars on July 14, 1965 and gave man his first close-up view of this planet, which showed that it was battered by meteor impacts. *Mariner V* passed Venus on October 19, 1967. This second mission to the mysterious planet discovered that the atmosphere was dense and very hot; temperatures of 500 degrees Fahrenheit were recorded, and the satellite revealed that 80 percent of the atmosphere was carbon dioxide gas. Despite these flights, the future of more sophisticated planetary ex-

ploration seemed bleak by the late 1960s.

The applications satellites were NASA's crowning achievement in the early 1960s. In 1962 the Kennedy Administration proposed formation of a Communications Satellite Corporation, a unique concept in government-industry-international cooperation. The fifteen-member board of directors was composed of representatives of the communications industry, public stockholders, and presidential appointees. The corporation was empowered to invite other nations to share the system's ownership and services. This precedent-setting proposal stirred strong political emotions, especially in the Senate. A twenty-day debate ensued before Congress approved the Administration proposal. On August 31, 1962, President Kennedy signed the bill that established the Communications Satellite Corporation (ComSatCorp). In April 1965, its first satellite, *Early Bird I*, was launched into orbit by NASA. By the end of 1968, there was a network of five communications satellites in synchronous orbits, twenty of an expected forty ground stations in operation, and forty-eight nations participating in the International Telecommunications Satellite Consortium. The Soviets introduced a competitive system, Molniya, in 1965. They also sought international partnership, but outside of the Iron Curtain countries, only France signed up. By 1968 they had launched ten Molniya satellites.

Weather satellites continued to be put in orbit. The highly successful Tiros was developed by the Weather Bureau as the model for its operational satellite series. There was also a new satellite—the earth resources satellite. Impressed by the Tiros and Gemini photographs, the Department of Interior proposed development of an earth resources satellite program in 1966, which got underway in the early 1970s.

The research activities of NASA had application outside the space programs. Its basic and applied research projects were designed to develop new ideas and equipment. The most visible portion was flight research. The X-15 climaxed the series of air force-NASA research aircraft with a series of speed and altitude records and a solid base of aerodynamic data. The prototype B-70 bomber was turned over to NASA for research on supersonic aircraft. The quiet-engine program for commercial aircraft grew out of public protest against noise levels near the approaches to city airports. Research into all aspects of the jet engine (air inlets, turbine blades, exhaust characteristics) led to findings that would lower the level of aircraft engine noise during takeoff and landing.

While modifications of the Apollo capsule progressed, launch vehicle testing continued. On November 9, 1967, *Apollo 4* was launched by the awesome Saturn V. A 363-foot-high, three-stage launch vehicle and spacecraft, weighing a total of 6 million pounds, slowly lifted off Launch Complex 39, propelled by a first-stage thrust of 7 million pounds. A record 278,699 pounds went into earth orbit. An unmanned flight test of the lunar module immediately followed. On January 22, 1968, a Saturn IB launched a 31,700-pound lunar module into earth orbit; and its ascent and descent engines were successfully fired. The stage was set for the first manned

space flight in Apollo since the tragic fire. *Apollo 7* was another milestone. Launched on October 11, 1968, it used a Saturn IB to put three astronauts into earth orbit. They remained in space for eleven days, testing the spacecraft's complex systems. On December 21, a Saturn V lifted the manned *Apollo 8* off Launch Complex 39 at the Cape. The first phases were duplicated, but then the Saturn third stage fired and *Apollo 8* headed for the moon. On Christmas eve, *Apollo 8* disappeared behind the moon and fired the service module engine to reduce its speed enough to be captured into lunar orbit.

Television provided breathtaking views of the lunar landscape to hundreds of millions on earth. On Christmas eve, the crew read the creation story from Genesis and wished their viewers a Merry Christmas. On Christmas day, they fired their service module engine once again, acquired the 3,500-feet per second speed needed to escape lunar gravity, and headed back to earth. This mission verified lunar landing sites and demonstrated the reliability of the spacecraft and lunar communications.

The lunar module remained a major concern to NASA and two more test flights were made to confirm its readiness for lunar landings. The *Apollo 9* flight (March 3-13, 1969), the first manned test of the lunar orbiter in

NASA

Apollo 11 astronaut Edwin E. Aldrin deployed seismic experiments at Tranquility Base.

earth orbit, was successful. On May 18, 1969, *Apollo 10* took off for the moon. Once in lunar orbit, the lunar orbiter separated from the command module, descended to within 9 miles of the surface, fired its ascent engine, and docked with the command module. All elements of the Apollo system had been tested.

Apollo 11 took off for the moon on July 16, 1969 amid much fanfare. On July 20, the lunar module separated and descended to the surface. At 4:18 p.m., astronaut Neil A. Armstrong announced "Houston—Tranquility Base here—the *Eagle* has landed." A few hours later, Armstrong set foot on the lunar surface. The eight-year national commitment had been fulfilled. Armstrong set up the television camera, and Edwin E. Aldrin, Jr., joined him on the surface, as Astronaut Michael Collins circled the moon in the *Columbia* command module. More than one fifth of the earth's population watched television pictures of two space-suited men plodding around gingerly in a surreal moonscape of boulders and craters. The astronauts implanted the United States flag, deployed scientific experiments, collected rock samples, and climbed back into the lunar module. The next day they blasted off and rendezvoused with the command module. The astronauts returned to an ecstatic worldwide reception.

Beyond Apollo

The worldwide euphoria over mankind's greatest voyage of exploration did not rescue the NASA budget. At its moment of greatest triumph, the space program was drastically cut back from the $5 billion budgets that had characterized the mid 1960s. Part of the reduction resulted from the end of Apollo hardware production; but most of the cut stemmed from changes in the political climate, including the unpopular Vietnam War and domestic problems. The 1970 fiscal year budget was $3.7 billion. The basic Apollo mission continued, but the last two flights were eliminated. Space science projections were also cut back. The $2 billion Voyager program for planetary exploration was eliminated and later resurfaced as the much more modest Viking program. A $60 million Electronics

Research Center at Cambridge, Massachusetts, under construction since 1964, was transferred to the Department of Transportation.

In spite of NASA budget cuts, however, projects continued to move forward. An Orbiting Astronomical Observatory was launched December 7, 1968. It was the heaviest and most complex automated spacecraft in the space science program and took the first ultraviolet photographs of the stars. *Mariner VI* and *VII,* launched in early 1969, journeyed to Mars, flew past as close as 2,000 miles, took photos of the planet, and analyzed its atmosphere and surface. In 1971 *Mariner IX* became the first spacecraft to orbit another planet. Its initial months in orbit were discouraging; an impenetrable dust storm covered most of the Martian surface for two months. But the dust storm gradually cleared and photographs in 1972 showed startling detail. Mapping 85 percent of the Martian surface, *Mariner IX* photographs revealed higher mountains and deeper valleys than exist on earth. The Martian moons, Deibus and Phobus, were also photographed. *Oso VII,* launched September 29, 1971, was the first satellite to film the beginning of a solar flare and the streamers of hot gases that extend 6.5

NASA

The Deep Space Network's 210-foot diameter antenna at Goldstone, California, picks up and amplifies signals from spacecraft at lunar and planetary distances.

million miles out from the sun. It also discovered "polar ice caps" on the sun, dark areas several million degrees cooler than the normal surface temperatures.

Planetary exploration was continued by *Pioneer X*, which began a voyage to the huge, misty planet Jupiter in March 1972. *Pioneer X* traveled through space for a year and a half until it flew past Jupiter on December 3, 1973. It survived the fierce magnetic field of the huge planet, photographed the planet and

several of its moons, and measured its searing temperatures and magnetic field. *Pioneer XI* took off on April 6, 1973 and sent back data on Jupiter in December 1974.

Meanwhile, NASA continued the Apollo launches in the face of declining public interest. *Apollo 12* featured a pinpoint landing 600 feet from the *Surveyor III* spacecraft. *Apollo 13* was forced to abort its lunar mission because of a ruptured oxygen tank, but it safely returned to earth using the lunar

NASA

The *Skylab I* orbital satellite collected data on earth resources.

module for life support and propulsion. Succeeding missions attained their pre-flight goals of collecting geological samples and deploying sophisticated scientific experiments. Beginning with *Apollo 15,* astronauts explored lunar terrain in the Lunar Rover, an electric-powered, four-wheel-drive vehicle developed at a cost of $60 million. *Apollo 17,* launched December 7, 1972, completed the Apollo program, perhaps the most ambitious technological project ever undertaken. The program lasted over eleven years, cost $23.5 billion, and produced an enormous amount of knowledge and data.

Scientific discoveries from Apollo will continue for several decades. A Lunar Receiving Laboratory has been constructed in Houston to house the 1,000 pounds of geological samples that were returned from the moon by six lunar-landing crews. Scientists in the United States and fifty-four foreign countries continue to analyze the samples. Investigators have established that the moon is a separate entity and not a fragment of the earth, though formed at the same time as earth some 4.5 billion years ago. With no protective atmosphere, it was bombarded for eons by meteors which plowed up the surface and triggered lava flows from the lunar interior. Refinement of this data will continue for many years.

Apollo also proved the ability of government, industry, and universities to mobilize behind a common national goal and produce an immense and diverse technological system directed to a common purpose. It not only proved that man could live and work in space, but it indicated that many major problems such as pollution, food supply, and natural disasters could be ameliorated by space technology.

Skylab was the next manned space program. Trimmed back to one orbital workshop and three astronaut flights, it had a hectic financial and planning career. The plan called for a Saturn V to be outfitted as a two-story orbiting laboratory with one floor for living quarters, the other for a work room. The major objective of Skylab was to determine whether men could withstand extended stays in space. Medical evidence from the Gemini

and Apollo flights had not completely answered this question. Since there would be far more room in the 85-foot-long orbital workshop than in any previous spacecraft, NASA developed an extensive experiment schedule. The most ambitious in terms of hardware was the Apollo telescope mount; five major experiments would cover the entire range of solar physics and make it the most powerful astronomical observatory ever orbited. The other major areas of experimentation involved earth-resources observations and medical experiments involving the three-man crew.

Launched in 1973, the three-manned Skylab missions gathered astronomical and earth-resources data that will take years to analyze. The missions proved that there was no physiological barrier to how long man could survive and function in space. The crew's biological functions stabilized after several weeks in zero gravity, and they maintained their muscle tone by regular exercise. Industrial experiments offered evidence that the melting and solidification processes were much different in a weightless environment. Crystal growth experiments produced crystals five times larger than on earth, suggesting that some high-cost industrial processes were apparently more efficient in space.

Skylab's earth sensors gathered information about the planet and tested instruments that will be used on future satellites and manned space stations. Seven fixed cameras and the astronauts' hand-held cameras photographed surface features. Other instruments automatically measured the reflectivity of plants, soils, and water and determined the altitude of land and water surfaces. The Skylab missions gathered data on croplands and forests, soils, urban development, pollution, clouds, and ice and snow cover. Other teams simultaneously gathered data from aircraft and ground stations. Comparing their "ground truth" to Skylab's findings will enable scientists to recognize special radiation "signatures" of earth objects that will improve the design of future automated spacecraft.

The Skylab program was closely allied with another NASA earth resources project. The Earth Resources Technology Satellite,

ERTS I, was launched on July 23, 1972 into polar orbit so that as the earth rotated beneath it, the satellite could survey the surface of the earth every eighteen days. *ERTS II* was launched on January 22, 1975. The two satellites have been subsequently renamed *LANDSAT I* and *LANDSAT II.* Their multispectral sensors provide data on geology, crop inventory and health, water storage, air and water pollution, forest fires and diseases, and shifts in urban population that affect urban planning, zoning, and needs for sewers and highways.

One practical application of LANDSAT data involved a project to compile a land use map of the 191 counties in the United States that border the Great Lakes. The job was completed in nine months at an average cost to the Environmental Protection Agency of $785 per county. The information was used to prepare an International Joint Commission study of boundary water pollution in the Great Lakes Basin. The results of the effort were so successful that Canada began considering making a similar study on its side of the border.

WASHINGTON, D. C.

NASA

LANDSAT observations, such as this photograph of the Potomac River and Chesapeake Bay, can assist government agencies in planning public works systems.

Preliminary findings indicate that LANDSAT data is valuable for water resources monitoring. The principal areas of application are snow cover mapping, surface water mapping, watershed surveys, and river monitoring. The Army Corps of Engineers estimates that millions of dollars can be saved by using the LANDSAT data collection techniques. In August 1972, the National Dam Safety Program was authorized by the Dam Safety Act. The program requires an inventory of all dams that are more than 25 feet high or have impoundment capacities of more than 50 acre-feet. The NASA and the Army Corps of Engineers developed computer techniques in conjunction with the LANDSAT satellites that gather water resource data at a cost of $50 to $70 per thousand square miles. This program provides a low-cost means of locating a significant portion of the water impoundments for the national dam inventory.

LANDSAT is essentially a technology development program. The data it gathers is used by hundreds of scientists in universities, state and local governments, and federal agencies who conduct experiments to determine the usefulness of the information in solving problems on earth. The foregoing examples suggest that this satellite system will be upgraded in the future to deliver data rapidly to a broad spectrum of users throughout the world.

While Skylab was underway, cooperation developed between the United States and Russian manned space programs. The first proposal called for a linkup with the Skylab Orbital Workshop, but the USSR was unreceptive. Further discussions evoked interest in a project to develop compatible docking and rescue systems for manned space flights. The plan called for a mutual docking and crew exchange mission that could develop equipment for international rescue and establish criteria for both nations' future manned systems. A Soyuz spacecraft would lift off and establish itself in orbit. An Apollo spacecraft would rendezvous and join with the Soviet craft using a specially designed docking unit between the two. The crews would adjust pressure differences of the spacecraft and spend a day joined together ex-

The Space Shuttle will accommodate up to 65,000 pounds of space cargo and passengers.

changing crews and conducting experiments. This plan became a significant part of President Richard M. Nixon's policy of detente with the Soviet Union. At the Nixon-Brezhnev summit conference in 1973, the prospective launch date was set. On July 17, 1975, the Soyuz and Apollo spacecraft united in orbit over the Atlantic Ocean.

With Apollo completed, NASA began developing future manned space programs. Nixon established a President's Space Task Group to recommend broad outlines for the next ten years of space exploration. This committee recommended development of the Space Shuttle. It would be a rocket-boosted, airplane-like structure that would take off from a regular airport runway, fly to orbital speed and altitude, and deploy satellites into orbit. Development of the Space Shuttle was approved on January 5, 1972. It offered a new approach to spaceflight: multiple payloads that could be placed into and picked out of orbit and new satellite designs free from the expensive precautions for the vibrations and shocks of rocket launch. Costs of putting a pound of payload into orbit should drop from $200 to $100. The $5.5 billion program called for the production of two prototypes by 1979.

As the United States celebrates its two-hundredth birthday, the aerospace program's future is somewhat clouded. The thaw in Cold War tensions, domestic economic problems, and the resulting reordering of national priorities have brought about a de-emphasis of many aerospace projects. Though it is doubtful that this public works program will again capture the nation's attention as it did in the 1960s, it will continue to enhance understanding of earth's environment and the universe.

SUGGESTED READINGS

Akens, David S. *Historical Origins of the George C. Marshall Space Flight Center*. Huntsville, Alabama, 1960.

Corliss, William R. *History of the Goddard Networks*. Greenbelt, Maryland, 1969.

Crowell, Benedict. *America's Munitions, 1917-1918*. Washington, D.C., 1919.

Emme, Eugene M. *Aeronautics and Astronautics: An American Chronology of Science and Technology in the Exploration of Space, 1915-1960*. Washington, D.C. 1961.

Gray, George W. *Frontiers of Flight: The Story of NACA Research*. New York, 1948.

Green, Constance M., and Lomask, Milton. *Vanguard: A History*. Washington, D.C., 1971.

Hartman, Edwin P. *Adventures in Research: A History of the Ames Research Center, 1940-1965*. Washington, D.C., 1970.

Logsden, John M. *The Decision to Go to the Moon: Project Apollo and the National Interest*. Cambridge, Massachusetts, 1970.

Rosenthal, Alfred. *Venture into Space: Early Years of the Goddard Space Flight Center*. Washington, D.C., 1968.

Rosholt, Robert L. *An Administrative History of NASA, 1958-1963*. Washington, D.C., 1966.

U.S. National Advisory Committee for Aeronautics. *Annual Report of the NACA*. Washington, D.C., 1916-1959.

U.S. National Aeronautics and Space Administration. *Preliminary History of the National Aeronautics and Space Administration During the Administration of President Lyndon B. Johnson, November 1963-January 1969*. 2 vols. Washington, D.C., 1969.

CHAPTER 20

THE PROFESSION IN PERSPECTIVE

Public works provide the physical infrastructure essential to the social and economic development of American civilization. They make human settlements possible and are indispensable to commerce and industry. Effective public works facilities and services are of utmost importance in every community and, in the United States, account for federal, state, and local expenditures of more than $60 billion annually. Together with defense, welfare, and education, this constitutes one of the largest public outlays. Additional billions are also invested in similar privately developed and operated facilities such as schools, utilities, and sports arenas.

Yet it is not money that ultimately determines the effectiveness of these systems—it is people. The planning, design, construction, operation, and maintenance of public works facilities demand a high level of training and proficiency in a variety of disciplines. Although an engineering capability is indispensable, it alone is insufficient. It must be complemented by the work of other professions and by public affairs and administrative competences. The skyrocketing cost of government, the rapid advances in science and technology, and the pressing need for public works to serve an increasingly urbanized populace make it imperative that public works professionals be able to respond to the gamut of social, economic, environmental, and political factors inherent in program planning, policy resolution, and project management.

Engineer-administrators concerned with public works programs, whether employed by government or private enterprise, must be qualified to give reliable answers to the questions of *whether, when,* and *how* public works facilities should be provided. Besides understanding social, economic, environmental, and political factors, they must be technically proficient and above all possess a deep concern for human needs. If they do not, the more than $60 billion of public funds spent yearly for public works plus the large sum expended in the private sector for similar purposes will not be properly related to the quality of life and to the balanced growth of American communities.

In the past, some federal, state, and local public works projects have failed to reach their potential because of inadequate planning and administration. Insufficient time frames, a lack of continuity in policies, and an unawareness of local realities have at times characterized federal grant programs. At the state and local level, management has often left much to be desired, and the advice of public works officials in executive and

This chapter was prepared by Suellen M. Hoy, Associate Editor.

legislative councils has sometimes been deficient. Although a combination of forces—scientific and technological developments, social change, sluggish government, an expanding population—are responsible for many of these problems, they have frequently been solved in whole or in part through measures that have upgraded and retrained public works personnel at all levels. Thus, formal and informal education has been and continues to be a critical agent in the evolution of the public works profession.

Engineering Education in the Early Years

The primary concerns of the earliest American colonists centered on providing the food and shelter necessary to sustain life and in developing the small commercial enterprises encouraged by the mother country. But as the colonists became more independent and began to rebel against British policies, they realized the need for political and social unity. They also recognized that there were benefits to be gained by conducting business not only within a particular colony or with the mother country but between two or more colonies. The colonists, therefore, began to single out those members of their communities who possessed commercial and engineering capabilities.

America's military leaders too began a careful search for individuals with engineering potential as war broke out with Great Britain. Given the military operations that were being planned and executed, persons with technical and mechanical abilities were in high demand for the first time in the nation's history. Unable to find a sufficient number of men with engineering talent, the Continental Congress and others—especially General George Washington—turned to France. Not only was France an ally, but during the reign of Louis XIV the French had become aware of the value of a trained engineering corps and in response had created their own cadre of engineers.

During the American Revolution, engineering capabilities were most needed for mapping as well as for the construction of fortifications and inland transportation routes. Therefore, in June 1775, the Continental Con-gress provided for a chief engineer of the Grand Army, a position to which Washington appointed Colonel Richard Gridley. Although sixty-five years old, he was one of the few colonists who possessed engineering experience. He had laid out the fortifications on Breed's Hill near Boston.

Even with Gridley's appointment, Washington continued to be distressed by the colonies' lack of qualified engineers. After reviewing the military operations around Boston and New York in 1775 and 1776, he shared his sentiments with Congress. Congress responded by passing a resolution in December 1776 which, among other things, authorized Washington to establish a Corps of Engineers. Lacking local talent, Washington appealed directly to France. Thaddeus Kosciuszko, a Pole who had been educated in France, and Louis Du Portail were two of those who answered the general's plea. In July 1777, Washington appointed Du Portail to replace Gridley as chief engineer, but no engineering troops were placed under Du Portail's command until May 1778.

With the peace of 1783, the young nation's engineering needs began to shift. Military fortifications were soon to rank second to internal improvements. But, although the construction of canals and roadways gradually became the United States' primary concern, Washington could not forget the war experience. He remembered how he had been forced to look to a foreign country for engineering talent. He wanted to remedy this situation by developing among the American people an engineering capability that could respond adequately to the nation's defense needs.

Washington argued for the establishment of a school devoted to the teaching and the practical application of military science. He was supported in his arguments by such men as Henry Knox, Alexander Hamilton, John Adams, Thomas Jefferson, James Monroe, James McHenry, and Du Portail. Hamilton proved the most interested. He presented Washington with specific proposals that would have created a military academy with four schools—a fundamental school, a school for engineers and artillerists, a school

U.S. Military Academy

Under a portrait of George Washington, cadets worked diligently in the drafting laboratory at West Point.

for cavalry and infantry, and a school for the navy. In the academy, students were to learn mathematics, geography, natural philosophy, chemistry, mineralogy, architecture, drawing, riding, and fencing.

These arguments and proposals bore fruit in 1794. Congress gave President Washington the authority to construct fortifications for the protection of the country's coastal harbors and to raise a Corps of Artillerists and Engineers who would be educated and stationed at West Point, New York. The curriculum of this new school was not, however, as complete as that outlined by Hamilton. It included only subjects of a military nature. In 1796 the school was destroyed by fire, and it was not reopened until 1801. But by December of that year, the curriculum had been expanded to include mathematics, natural philosophy, fortifications, artillery, and surveying.

The academy responded well to the nation's need for military engineers, but it soon became apparent that there was an even more urgent need for civil engineers. In 1800, for

example, Secretary of War McHenry contended that "We must not conclude that service of the engineer is limited to constructing fortifications. This is but a single branch of the profession; their utility extends to almost every department of war; besides embracing whatever respects public buildings, roads, bridges, canals, and all such works of a civil nature." Statements such as this had their effect. On March 16, 1802, Congress constituted the United States Military Academy at West Point. One provision of the act passed by Congress stipulated that engineers and cadets enrolled in the academy were at all times subject to duty in places and on projects as directed by the President of the United States. Although officers from the Army Corps of Engineers were not employed as civil engineers under this law until 1824, it is noteworthy that in 1802 Congress recognized that there might be occasions when West Point's engineering talent would be needed for internal improvements.

The United States Military Academy was

the first school in America to teach the principles of engineering and their application. Yet in its early years, the academy was small, had only meager resources, and possessed only an informal system of instruction and examination. In fact, if it were not for the successes of the academy's graduates in the War of 1812, the school might well have closed. But in 1817, with the appointment of Major Sylvanus Thayer as superintendent, West Point began operating under a new organizational structure.

Sylvanus Thayer's philosophy is embodied in this early nineteenth-century lithograph. Classrooms were sparse and small so that maximum attention could be given to each cadet.

Thayer brought greater discipline and definite pedagogical procedures to West Point. During his sixteen years as superintendent, he repeatedly emphasized the importance of developing and maintaining high standards of achievement. He grouped students according to their academic abilities because he believed that this practice would insure better instruction and more learning. He demonstrated his interest in the academy's curriculum by introducing new courses and expanding old ones. Under Thayer's supervision, courses in mechanics, hydraulics, pneumatics, optics, chemistry, magnetism, and astronomy became an integral part of the curriculum. And these courses were improved in the 1820s and 1830s with the introduction of analytical textbooks and laboratory experiments.

Courses in the engineering department also evolved gradually. They initially emphasized the practical aspects of military engineering and fortifications, but in 1817

Professor Claude Crozet introduced descriptive geometry into his classes. In 1823 a course entitled "civil engineering" was offered in which students were taught how to construct bridges, roads, and canals. Never before had the academy made such a distinction between civil engineering and that in support of military operations. By 1832 the usual military engineering courses of field fortifications, permanent fortifications, mines, and attack and defense of fortifications were complemented with classes in civil engineering, architecture, masonry, mechanics, and technical drawing.

The value of West Point engineers was demonstrated early in the nineteenth century by their work on a fortification built to protect New York Harbor. Castle Williams—probably the most significant fortress of the period—was designed and constructed between 1807 and 1812 under the direction of Colonel Jonathan Williams, superintendent of the military academy at the time. The first all masonry fort, Castle Williams had high vertical walls in which several floor of guns were mounted (rather than stationed on the top of the exterior walls). It proved to be the most formidable seacoast defense built in the United States to that date, and it became the prototype for all major forts designed and constructed during the following half century.

Castle Williams on Governor's Island in New York Harbor served for many years not only as a deterrent to attack but also as a military prison.

Rensselaer Polytechnic Institute, founded in 1824 in Troy, New York, was another of the earliest and most influential schools which trained the nation's engineers. Although its beginnings were tenuous, the school was completely reorganized in 1850 by Director B. Franklin Greene and became a model for other polytechnic institutions. Patterning Rensselaer's curriculum on those of the French École Polytechnique (a preparatory school for governmental technical institutions) and École Centrale des Arts et Manufactures (a professional school for civil engineers and professors of applied science), Greene incorporated elements of both schools into one three-year engineering program. After 1852, when a preparatory course was added as an introduction to the first year of the program, the basic outline of the modern engineering curriculum was established.

According to Greene's plan, instruction at Rensselaer was divided into three parts. The preparatory course introduced the students to chemistry, physics, algebra, and geometry, and offered them work in English, history, geography, and mechanical drawing. The general course included classes in advanced mathematics as well as lectures and laboratories in chemistry, physics, and mechanics. During this phase, the students were also taught some modern languages, ethics, logic, and jurisprudence. The technical course, which was the final level of instruction, emphasized engineering problems in building, mining, manufacturing, and transportation.

Rensselaer's graduates were the first in the nation to receive a civil engineering degree. Although an 1827 catalogue had referred to "land surveying" and "general engineering," Professor Amos Eaton did not offer his lectures in "civil engineering" until the following year. (The first civil engineering course outside of West Point was given in 1821 at the American Literary, Scientific and Military Academy, renamed Norwich University in 1834.) In 1835 the trustees established a department "for the purpose of giving instruction in Engineering and Technology," and Rensselaer graduated its first class in civil engineering.

Until the middle of the nineteenth century, when the Lawrence Scientific School was created at Harvard and the Sheffield Scientific School at Yale, West Point,

Rensselaer, and Norwich supplied the country with its formally trained civil engineers. Some of them prepared maps and surveyed new lands for Americans as they moved westward; many others planned, constructed, and operated the nation's first roads, canals, and railroads. Engineers who had not attended West Point, Rensselaer, or Norwich acquired their training—often beginning as rodmen or axmen in surveying parties—on these large public works projects.

From 1802 to 1860, West Point graduated some 2,000 men—200 of whom became civil engineers. But, by the 1860s, the academy ceased to be a major source of civil engineers. Although some West Point instructors and graduates played prominent roles either as founders or professors in civil engineering schools, the academy no longer trained a high percentage of men who would eventually become civil engineers. The diminishing number of public works projects supervised by military engineers paralleled West Point's declining influence in the civil engineering field. From 1840 to 1865, the federal government appropriated only $6 million for projects directed by the Corps of Engineers. It is true that these appropriations were substantially increased in the decade after the Civil War. Still the total expenditure of $51 million in the thirty-five years prior to 1875 was insignificant in comparison with the multimillion-dollar public works projects supervised by nonmilitary engineers during this period.

In the third quarter of the nineteenth century, American engineering education developed rapidly. Many new institutions combining formal science with functional application were organized with funds provided by the 1862 Morrill Act. Under this act, large tracts of federal lands were released to the states for the establishment of schools of agriculture and the engineering arts. With a need for technically trained men to develop the country's abundant resources, with the objectives and techniques of higher technical education already outlined by Greene, and with financial backing from the federal government, numerous land grant colleges, scientific schools, and departments of applied science were founded.

The Engineering Profession, 1850-1880

Civil engineers were for the most part civilian in training and personnel. Thus, the term *civil engineer* came to signify those persons who designed, constructed, operated, and maintained public works as well as those who were employed by private corporations engaged in manufacturing and transportation. And it was this group of engineers that was most influential in the rapid professionalization of engineering that took place after 1850. Engineers in the military were too preoccupied with the more traditional and Civil War-related public works projects. However, civil engineers, who had become specialized, began to carry out a wide variety of projects undertaken by state and local governments and private corporations.

Raymond H. Merritt's *Engineering in American Society, 1850-1875* chronicles the growth and professionalization of engineering during this period. Merritt indicates from a tabulation of statistics published in the *United States Census Reports* from 1850 to 1880 that, "while the number of physicians and clergymen more than doubled and architects increased sixfold, the number of civil engineers multiplied sixteen times." In 1840 there were six schools where engineering was taught; in 1880 there were eighty-five. Engineering graduates increased from less than 900 in the 1860s to more than 3,800 in the 1880s.

In response to this rapid growth, there developed a need for a national engineering organization. The first attempt to establish such a body occurred in 1839, when a group of forty engineers met in Baltimore and resolved to form a Society of Civil Engineers in the United States. Benjamin Wright was chosen to chair the next meeting in Philadelphia, a committee of five was appointed "to draft an address to the Civil Engineers of the United States," and a committee of seventeen was elected to prepare a constitution.

In its statement to the nation's civil engineers, the committee of five first observed that "public works are now so extended in our country, and the mass of experimental knowledge to be gained from those in use so great . . . that it is even more valuable to the

American Engineer than what he can learn in Europe . . . ." But because these works were so widespread, the committee noted that "few, if any, members are able to give even the most important of them a personal examination." Therefore, the committee concluded that this is "the strongest argument in favour of a society that shall, by a concert of action, bring the experience of the whole country within the reach of each member."

The committee of seventeen was unable to agree on a constitution that would govern this national engineering organization. Instead, the committee recommended the formation of four independent regional societies. In February 1840, the *American Railroad Journal* carried an explanation of the committee's failure to organize nationally by its secretary, Edward Miller. He contended that the committee was too large to fulfill its task, that many members were unknown to each other, and that some were either hostile or indifferent to any form of institution.

In 1848 engineers in both New York and Boston established local societies. Within two years, the New York group had ceased activity because of lack of support. The Boston Society of Civil Engineers, which was composed of older and more established engineers due to its rigid membership qualifications, remained vital and became the first permanent engineering organization in the United States. James Laurie, one of the original directors of the Boston society, later became a founder and the first president of the American Society of Civil Engineers (ASCE).

This new society was founded in 1852 in the office of Alfred W. Craven, chief engineer of the New York Croton Aqueduct Department. During the following three years, Craven and a few New York City engineers prevented the organization from dying. But, suffering from the lack of a publication for its professional papers and a permanent meeting place for its extremely mobile members, the society languished from 1855 to 1867.

The ASCE was, however, successfully reorganized after the Civil War. Its officers immediately acquired permanent headquarters for the organization in New York City. And through the publication of its transactions, the society began an exchange of technical information among its members. It also started scheduling annual meetings at specific times to enable more engineers to participate. Committed to "the advancement of science and practice in Engineering, the acquisition and dissemination of experimental knowledge, the comparison of professional experience, and the encouragement of social intercourse among its members," the society's membership grew from 179 in 1870 to 408 in 1875 to 2,221 in 1900.

Since many of its prominent members were either immigrants or had international careers, ASCE had a certain cosmopolitan character. James Laurie, a native of Scotland, Albert Fink of Germany, James B. Francis of England, and Octave Chanute of France all served as presidents. Although not an immigrant, William M. Roberts, who became the society's president in 1878, had spent eight years with the Don Pedro Segunda Railroad in Brazil. In 1866 he returned to the United States to work on Mississippi and Ohio River navigation projects and later became associate chief engineer on the Eads Bridge in St. Louis. Following his year as president of ASCE, Roberts returned to Brazil to become chief engineer of all its public works.

In *Engineering in American Society,* Merritt discusses at length the cosmopolitan quality of these early professionals. Besides their enormous mobility, he noted "the amazing extent of the correspondence" among engineers during the second half of the nineteenth century. For instance, in the personal papers of Samuel Nott, a Boston railroad engineer; William Hutton, a Washington, D.C. aqueduct engineer; and Chanute, a Kansas City bridge engineer, there is correspondence "with E. S. Chesbrough, the city engineer of Chicago, about sewer and water problems, and with William McAlpine, the state engineer of New York, about canal, foundation work, and railroad development."

At the end of the nineteenth century, George S. Morison, an internationally known American civil engineer, acknowledged that interdependence had become one of the marks of his profession. In *The New Epoch as Developed by the Manufacture of Power,* he maintained individuals could no longer afford to work independently of one another; the technological revolution had made that impossible. And he perceived that the most serious problems facing the United States at the time originated from the demands of its highly industrialized and urbanized population. Threatened by "bad air, bad water, bad construction and corrupt administration," Americans needed a profession that could minimize air pollution, build water systems, supervise construction projects, and counsel public officials.

Engineering in Urban America

By the end of the nineteenth century, Americans had not only settled their continent, but they had dramatically altered their way of living. From 1820 to 1870, the rate of urbanization climbed sharply. Nearly 25 percent of the total population lived in cities in 1870; only 7 percent did so in 1820. A national network of cities gathered scattered farms and villages into a system of regional and manufacturing and commercial centers. By the 1880s, according to Robert H. Wiebe in *The Search for Order, 1877-1920,* "publicists were savoring the word 'nation' " in the sense of "a continent conquered and tamed."

Yet many individuals living in the second half of the nineteenth century found these fundamental changes bewildering. City dwellers especially felt victimized by the forces of industrialization and urbanization. Their densely populated cities had open sewers, polluted water, unpaved and garbage-filled streets, inadequate drainage, and insufficient housing. They desperately needed basic facilities and services, but neither the rugged individualism nor the spontaneous voluntarism of an earlier age were able to produce them. Under these circumstances, it is not surprising that one of the most significant developments in the engineering profession during this period was the emergence of the city engineer.

After the Civil War, the planning, design, construction, operation, and maintenance of public works facilities became an important responsibility of municipal governments. And public-spirited engineers were willing to put their professional training at the disposal of rising urban centers. The growth of cities created immense problems of administration, which engineers often found similar to those they had encountered and mastered in the building of large public works projects. Thus, engineers with design and construction competences directed their energies to the improvement of urban centers. They supervised the development of water and sewer systems, refuse collection and disposal programs, parks and gardens, paved sidewalks and streets, markets, docks, and bridges.

Chesbrough, the city engineer of Chicago, has been described as "the man who raised Chicago from the mud." In 1855 he planned and directed the work which elevated the city's streets several feet, designed a new sewer system, and committed himself to eliminating Chicago's swampiness. After studying the drainage and water supply problems of major European cities, he returned to Chicago and in 1868 completed the building of a 2-mile water intake tunnel under Lake Michigan to secure fresher water for Chicago residents. He also played a key role in dredging the Chicago River to provide adequate drainage of the city. Chesbrough encouraged the construction of the Chicago Sanitary and Ship Canal, which opened in 1900 and which helped reverse the flow of the Chicago River in an attempt to free the city from the "menace of a contaminated water supply."

George E. Waring, Jr., also became nationally known for his activities in the field of municipal engineering and sanitation. Among his greatest accomplishments was the development of a sewer system for the City of Memphis, Tennessee. Waring strongly believed that disease was the direct result of filth. Thus, when a yellow fever epidemic killed nearly 5,000 people in Memphis in 1878, he blamed it on the city's filthy condition. Two years later, he was hired to design a sewer system. From 1895 to 1898, as New York City's commissioner of street cleaning, Waring again attracted attention for his successful efforts in removing garbage and manure from the streets and sidewalks.

Many city engineers participated in the programs and activities of national engineering organizations such as ASCE and the American Society of Mechanical Engineers. Others, however, became members of local engineering societies. For the most part, they were more social in nature and included members from all branches of engineering. And these societies seemed especially attractive to engineers who were involved in the municipal or regional affairs of a particular locale and who shared a common interest in civic improvements.

American Public Works Association

The Chicago Sanitary and Ship Canal, completed in 1900, winds past a powerhouse and dam at Lockport, Illinois.

Urbanization placed new burdens on local governmental officials. Growing populations necessitated an ever increasing extension and refinement of public services and facilities. In *The Growth of City Government*, Lent D. Upson stated that between 1860 and 1910 Detroit's municipal government became responsible for 147 new activities; and during the next decade, 1910-1920, another eighty functions were added. These included electric street lighting; motorized fire, police, and refuse collection and disposal services; public health nursing; community centers; and airports. This extension of local public services and facilities gave rise to numerous specialized organizations which attempted to provide the expertise needed in a nation of cities. The 1893 World's Columbian Exposition in Chicago also sparked widespread interest in civic improvements. The exposition, in fact, defined the aesthetic principles that governed the design of city halls, public libraries, museums, and union stations for two decades.

Shortly thereafter, in 1894, George H. Frost, publisher of *Engineering News* (now *Engineering News-Record)*, suggested in his editorial column the possibility of organizing municipal engineers and city officials into a national association. Its purpose, according to Frost, would be to promote "special engineering knowledge and efficient practice in the field of civic improvements." Michael J. Murphy, street commissioner of St. Louis, acted on Frost's suggestion by sending letters of inquiry regarding the formation of such an organization to engineers and public officials in cities throughout the United States. The responses Murphy received were positive, and Buffalo's municipal authorities invited him to schedule the association's first meeting in their city.

On September 18, 1894, fifty-seven officials from seventeen cities gathered in Buffalo for the first meeting of the American Society of Municipal Improvements (ASMI). Due to illness, Murphy was unable to attend, but R. E. McMath, president of the St. Louis Board of Public Improvements, represented him and presided over the meeting. Although no one present bore the title "director of public works," those in attendance were either city engineers, elected officials, or employees of boards of "public works" or "public improvements" or "public services." Before concluding their meeting, they resolved to form a national organization "to diffuse and advance the best and most economic methods of managing municipal departments and constructing public works" by means of "annual conventions and the presentation of papers upon municipal improvements," and they elected Murphy president.

When ASMI met in Cincinnati the following year, three times as many cities were represented and twice as many persons attended as in 1894. Ten technical papers were presented and later published in the society's proceedings. The executive committee reported a revised constitution, which was unanimously adopted, and appointed standing committees on such subjects as street paving, street traffic, electric street lighting, water works and water supply, sewerage and sanitation, disposition of garbage and street cleaning, municipal franchises, and taxation and assessments.

Membership in ASMI continued to grow until 1897. One week before its scheduled meeting in Nashville, the executive committee received an invitation to attend the organizational meeting of a new association to be known as the League of American Municipalities. The ASMI executive committee declined the invitation but suggested a joint meeting in Nashville instead. The league, however, failed to respond. During the ensuing year, nearly all the mayors and councilmen who had been members of ASMI withdrew and joined the league. Although the league was defunct by 1916, its short-lived existence not only caused ASMI's membership to decline but altered its whole character as well. Composed almost entirely of city engineers, ASMI began to focus more of its attention on technical problems relating to the design and construction of public works than on those relating generally to city government.

U.S. Department of Transportation

One of the early functions of the American Society of Municipal Improvements was to adopt standards for asphalt paving of city streets.

One of the results of ASMI's meeting in Nashville was representative of this new direction. For the first time, it adopted model provisions for asphalt pavement contracts as recommended by the chairman of the committee on street paving. The document described the expected condition of asphalt pavement at the end of a five-year guaranty period. Although later modified in part, the model provisions approved at this meeting subsequently appeared in the paving contract documents of many cities.

The ASMI had adopted paving specifications for use by its members during the early 1900s, but it had made no effort to standardize them. Municipal engineers who believed that there was a need for such standardization formed a new organization for that particular purpose in 1910. It was called the Association for Standardizing Paving Specifications and was composed largely of city engineers who were also ASMI members. Shortly thereafter, the executive committee of ASMI suggested that the two groups merge and that steps be taken to adopt and standardize comprehensive paving specifications.

In February 1913, a committee appointed by the president of the Association for Standardizing Paving Specifications reported that "it is advisable for the amalgamation to take place." The ASMI gained only fifty-three members who had never before been enrolled in the society and added a modest .$738.68 to its treasury. But in 1914 at its Boston meeting, ASMI members adopted specifications for stone block paving, brick paving, cement and concrete paving, broken stone and gravel roads, sheet asphalt, and sewer construction. They also resolved to make them available "for use in every little town or hamlet in this broad land."

The ASMI, which changed its name to the American Society of Municipal Engineers (AME) in 1930, continued to place major emphasis on technical problems of design and construction. It hired a part-time secretary who also served the Engineers' Club of St. Louis in a similar capacity. Most of AME's members were design and supervising engineers. Thus, its standard specifications, special reports, annual proceedings, and committee findings served as reference material for nearly 800 members by 1935.

In 1919 another organization, the International Association of Street and Sanitation Officials whose name was changed in 1925 to the International Association of Public Works

Public Works Historical Society

In 1936 the Joint Administrative Board of AME and IAPWO planned the consolidation of the organizations to form APWA. Left to right are Norman Hebden, Mark B. Owen, George B. Gascoigne, Thomas Buckley, W. J. Galligan, Alfred E. Roche, J. Eugene Root, Harold D. Bradley, Harrison P. Eddy, and Guy Brown, members of the board.

Officials (IAPWO), was established to advance both the knowledge and practices related to the operation, maintenance, and management of public works facilities. The IAPWO stepped up its activities in 1931 when it created a committee to cooperate with the International City Managers Association (ICMA) to design a national cost accounting and reporting system to facilitate the planning, programming, and budgeting of public works operations. Demonstration installations in Brunswick, Georgia; Kenosha, Wisconsin; Troy, New York; Flint, Michigan; and Cincinnati, Ohio resulted in the development of a comprehensive management system. The demonstration manuals and a textbook entitled *Municipal Public Works Management,* outgrowths of this collaborative effort, were not only widely used but sparked other initiatives and programs which played an important role in improving public works administration in the United States.

By the mid 1930s, it became increasingly evident to public works engineers and administrators that the design, construction, operation, maintenance, and management of public works were inseparable. And the contacts of AME and IAPWO with other nonprofit, public service organizations increased the desire of both associations to have a full-time executive director and a broad program of services. Therefore, in 1935 AME and IAPWO agreed to establish a joint secretariat and requested Donald C. Stone, who had supervised IAPWO's demonstration projects and was then serving as executive director of the Public Administration Service (PAS), to also act as its executive director. Since AME and IAPWO were lacking in funds during these Depression years, Stone consented to contribute his services on condition that the two organizations merge. In 1937 AME and IAPWO joined to form the American Public Works Association (APWA).

Engineers in Municipal Government

To cushion the impact of industrialism, citizens sought assistance from their local governments. But instead of the help they were seeking, they often found waste, extravagance, lack of vision, low standards, and even corruption, particularly in the large cities where problems were most severe. Confounded by these conditions, many persons from business and the professions began meeting in citizen groups to exchange what knowledge they possessed concerning the exigencies of city government. Early in 1894, a group of Philadelphians invited representatives from other cities to attend the first annual Conference for Good City Government. From this gathering emerged the National Municipal League in the following year.

The league proposed to end boss rule, to elect honest men to city hall, and to make local government more efficient and responsive to the people's will. To attain these goals, it recognized that it had to change the basic structure of city government. In 1898 the league adopted a model charter, incorporating what its experts considered the best proposals for local government. The charter called for a strong mayor, an independent comptroller, limitations on the granting of franchises, extensive civil service, and considerable home rule.

The cities were the true leaders of municipal reform. Individual cities across the country experimented with every provision eventually adopted by the league in its model charter. Most importantly, it was the cities that initiated the most decisive of structural changes—the commission and council-manager plans. But the National Municipal League's appearance did mark an important point in the development of American attitudes toward city government. It signalled the nationalization of previously isolated reform movements.

In 1900 a hurricane devastated Galveston, Texas. Since the regular city government was unable to handle the situation, the state legislature appointed a commission of five prominent local businessmen to govern Galveston during the emergency period. They managed the city like a large business corporation. Each of the four commissioners took charge of a distinct area of community responsibility; the fifth served as a coordinator and acted in some respects like a mayor. The system proved so successful that the state legislature provided for its continuance under a new city charter. The citizens of Galveston elected all five commissioners who collectively assumed responsibility for making legislative policy and individually for supervising city departments.

By 1911 over 160 cities had adopted the commission plan. But its popularity soon declined. In some cities, people became disenchanted when they discovered that the plan did not automatically increase efficiency nor did it always eliminate "politics" from city government. In other municipalities, citizens were attracted to the council-manager form of government first tried in Staunton, Virginia, in 1908.

Chicago Association of Commerce & Industry

The problems of providing public works facilities for large cities require engineers in municipal government.

The council-manager plan was a good compromise between two essential elements in early twentieth-century reform thought. It provided efficient administrative systems and permitted democracy to function in a more satisfactory manner. Many reformers had become committed to a better planned, more rationally managed society that could resolve

the cities' pressing problems. By centralizing administrative authority in the office of a trained individual, this commitment could be met. Others had urged greater participation in government by the people. By electing councilmen at large, the desire for decentralized grass-roots participation in public policy making was also satisfied.

Municipal reform represented in large measure the application of business ideology and practices to city government. The commission and manager plans were frequently compared to the organization of business corporations. And the success of both plans was due to the widespread belief that city government ought to be conducted on business principles. Another important assumption underlying the municipal reform movement was that expert administrators were essential. In 1914 Henry M. Waite, Dayton, Ohio's first city manager, observed that "a city is a great business enterprise whose stockholders are the people . . . . Our municipal affairs would be placed upon a strict business basis and directed, not by partisans . . . but by men who are skilled in business management . . . ."

When the city council of Staunton, Virginia, decided to appoint its first "general manager" in 1908, it chose Charles E. Ashburner. An engineer who had received his degree from the University of Heidelberg, Ashburner had held positions with the Army Corps of Engineers, highway bureaus of the United States and Virginia, and the Chesapeake and Ohio Railroad before becoming Staunton's general manager. It was while he was employed by the railroad that Ashburner earned the respect of Staunton's city council. The council had been informed by a local contractor that it would cost $4,000 to repair a nearby dam that had given way. However, Ashburner estimated that the necessary work could be done for $737 if his recommendations were followed. His counsel proved correct.

In 1906 Staunton was required by state law to reorganize its government from a unicameral to a bicameral legislative body because the city's population had increased beyond 10,000. The council was expanded from twelve to twenty-two, and the city's government came under the direction of thirty legislative committees. Since Staunton had no full-time municipal employees in 1906, the enlarged government brought almost all work to a halt. By the end of 1907, an enormous backlog of administrative tasks and public works projects threatened the city's future. The council knew that it had to act. But the commission plan, which many members found appealing, was precluded by Virginia law. Thus, in January 1908, the city council established the office of general manager and hired Ashburner. He was given "entire charge and control of all executive work of the city in its various departments."

Many other cities chose the manager plan over the commission plan and selected municipal engineers to administer their affairs. According to Leonard D. White's *The City Manager,* there were 373 managers in office at the end of 1926. During the eighteen years in which the plan had been in existence, there had been 863 individuals serving as city managers. Of the 709 whose prior occupations were known, engineers comprised 56 percent; businessmen, 14 percent; and former public officials, 10 percent.

Three of Dayton, Ohio's first four city managers were municipal engineers. Waite, who became Dayton's manager in 1914, had studied at the Massachusetts Institute of Technology and had been city engineer in Cincinnati. He was succeeded four years later by James E. Barlow, an engineer whom Waite had brought from Cincinnati in 1914 to serve as Dayton's director of public service. Barlow's successor was a businessman whose term ended after only six months, when he failed to display effective leadership during a local strike. In 1921 Dayton's city council chose Fred O. Eichelberger, an engineering official with twenty-one years of service, as its fourth manager.

Pasadena, California, also hired a municipal engineer as its city manager in 1921. Before becoming superintendent of Pasadena's municipal electric light plant, C. Wellington Koiner had been city engineer in Laurel, Maryland; and general manager and chief engineer of the Oneida (New York) Gas Light Company and the National Light and Improvement Company of St. Louis, Missouri. When Koiner was selected as Pasadena's manager, he was widely known as a utility engineer and as an active participant in numerous engineering organizations—ASMI, the American Association of Engineers, the American Gas Institute, and the American Institute of Electrical Engineering. Another of California's most successful city managers was John N. Edy of Berkeley. In 1909 he received the B.S. degree in civil engineering from the University of Missouri and in 1927 (while city manager) the M.A. degree in political science from the University of California. Except for ten years' experience in railroad construction, his early career had been in the public works field; he was assistant street engineer in St. Louis, county engineer in Missouri and Montana, and chief engineer and managing executive of the Montana State Highway Department. He later served as Dallas' city manager and as assistant director of the United States Bureau of the Budget.

The major problems of community life during the early decades of the twentieth century involved engineering technology. City dwellers were in need of such physical structures as water and sewer systems, improved roads, lighted streets, and refuse disposal facilities. Thus, most city managers with engineering backgrounds were eminently capable of finding the best solutions. White described them in his book as "men who do things" and talk very little. Primarily concerned with "specific, definite, immediate matters" within their specialty of municipal government, they were above all interested in engineering and physical construction. As a result, they often neglected the more theoretical and less technical aspects of city government. Yet they were intensely loyal to the municipality as a whole. They generally refused to cater to groups with influence, to play politics, or to advise the council in a manner inconsistent with the city's long-range goals.

In small communities of less than 100,000 population, city managers assumed direct responsibility for most public works. Financial resources did not allow them to hire an expert engineer, a sanitation superintendent, a superintendent of streets, and a building inspector. Since funds were limited and problems were essentially practical and technical, city councils commonly retained engineers as managers who, because of the nature of their office, also supervised other municipal services.

The responsibilities of managers in cities over 100,000 population were different from those of their colleagues in small communities. Managers of large cities with sizeable work forces performed more executive functions. They concerned themselves especially with the formulation of policy; they were vitally involved in planning, financing, personnel administration, and organizational procedures. Since they had specialists at the head of each major department, the diversified functions of municipal government were conducted without their personal supervision. As the years passed, fewer engineers became managers of large cities, since city councils increasingly sought persons trained in public administration for such positions.

Engineers in the public sector who displayed executive ability but who did not become city managers often became public works administrators. They directed those departments engaged in public works activities whose titles varied depending upon the scope of functions for which they were responsible. In a 1929 study of the organization of *The Public Works Department in American Cities,* Clarence E. Ridley reported that for the most part these activities included street design, improvement, and maintenance;

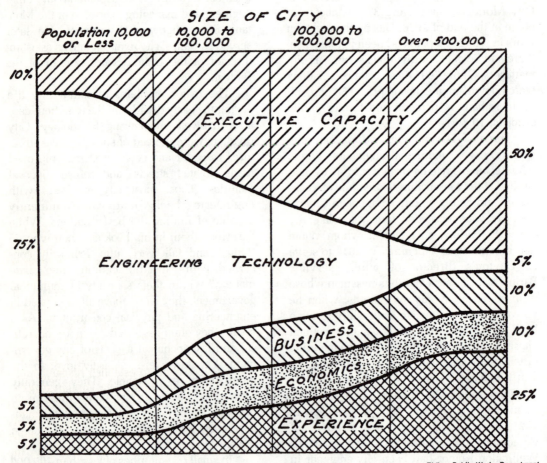

Ridley, *Public Works Department*

Figure 20-1.
The essential technical qualifications for the administrative head of a public works department vary with the size of the city.

street cleaning; sidewalks; street lighting; excavation permits; street name signs; house numbering; bridge design, construction, and maintenance; sewage disposal; water works; refuse collection and disposal; maintenance of all city-owned equipment; inspection of the construction of public improvements; operation and supervision of utilities; and care of public buildings and grounds. In a highly urbanized society, most of these activities were indispensable to community life.

The Transition Years

In many respects, the responsibilities of public works administrators in the early twentieth century were not unlike those of present-day administrators. To insure that their departments performed effectively and economically, these officials were required to develop improved engineering techniques, new administrative methods, and sounder principles of organization. Current operations necessitated the proper use of personnel, equipment, and materials as well as proven standards of practice and technical methods. Future operations demanded the formulation of master plans and zoning regulations for community development, scheduling the construction of specific improvements, budgeting expenses on an annual and long-range basis, and research into technical and management problems.

Although the fundamental nature of these responsibilities remains the same, the society in which early public works administrators functioned has changed. During the first decades of the twentieth century, population was less concentrated in urban areas, and technology was less sophisticated. Not only were citizens less active in community decisionmaking, but they were also less demanding of public works operations. Thus, public works officials generally learned "on the job" by trial and error. Their decisions were based on the primary elements of utility, economy, and convenience. And they customarily valued technical competence over managerial ability.

Proficiency by engineers in a technical capacity was not, however, always a good indicator of their suitability for administrative duties. Ridley graphically demonstrated in his 1929 study of public works departments that, although engineering knowledge was vitally necessary for public works administrators in small departments, it was only a part of the qualifications required of public works directors in large departments (see Figure 20-1). But prior to World War II, opportunities for obtaining formal training in public works administration were limited.

Some officials acquired a better understanding of "management" through institutions such as the New York Bureau of Municipal Research. In "Early Development of Education in Public Administration," Alice B. and Donald C. Stone explain the origins of the bureau and describe the ways in which it contributed to the many improvements in budgeting, accounting, and purchasing in the fields of public works and public health. Incorporated in 1906, the bureau's first research project was a study of the conditions of Manhattan's streets. A research staff collected and analyzed information on appropriations for street construction and maintenance and then demonstrated how the streets would appear if the money had been spent effectively. When the bureau's findings were made known, New York City's committee of accounts immediately filed a report denying them; and Manhattan's borough president sued the bureau's chairman for $100,000 libel. The mayor of New York City ordered an investigation of the entire matter. When it verified the facts in the bureau's report, Manhattan's borough president was removed from office for incompetence.

Public administrators, impressed by the Manhattan street survey and subsequent studies, requested assistance from the New York Bureau of Municipal Research. In response, the bureau encouraged state and local governments to establish research units of their own and to sponsor similar kinds of studies. A number of officials, such as Robert Moses who subsequently served in many public works positions, began their careers with the bureau; while others who saw the value of its programs organized similar institutions in other cities. The New York bureau soon had counterparts in Cleveland,

Detroit, Dayton, Philadelphia, Cincinnati, and Chicago. And in 1916 the Institute of Government Research (predecessor of the Brookings Institution) was established in Washington, D.C., by Robert Brookings as a means of applying to federal problems the analytical approach that the New York bureau had used so effectively in cities and states. By 1925 some 230 surveys of public service problems had been made.

In case after case, these surveys proved helpful to public works administrators. Not only did the survey use hard facts to describe how government agencies should function, but they outlined the advantages and disadvantages of specific administrative policies, arrangements, and procedures. The principles and requisites of responsible and effective government were thereby delineated. As a consequence, the New York Bureau of Municipal Research became the advocate of such measures as the executive budget, the consolidation of overlapping agencies, and the elimination of administrative boards.

Many of the measures supported by the New York bureau incorporated the principles of scientific management developed in the late nineteenth and early twentieth centuries by Frederick W. Taylor. Besides stressing the need to use factual and standardized methods, Taylor encouraged careful selection, training, and assignment of personnel as well as cooperation between management and

American Public Works Association

In 1937 numerous professional and public interest associations moved into the "1313" center for public administration, located on the campus of the University of Chicago. Many of these same organizations remain there today.

employees in executing the work of their organizations. Taylor's methods were not applied extensively in government agencies before World War I. They were, however, adopted by many public agencies during the 1930s.

An equally important development for early public works administrators was the increased activity of professional and public interest associations. In the early 1920s, a plan was devised by John Stutz, executive secretary of the League of Kansas Municipalities, to bring the principal organizations together in one building and to enlist the aid of Charles Merriam of the University of Chicago in seeking foundation funds. The center that emerged with Merriam's assistance was the Public Administration Clearing House (PACH). It was located in temporary quarters in Chicago, Illinois, for the first few years of its existence; but in 1937 PACH moved into a new building, financed by a grant from the Spelman Fund, at 1313 East 60th Street. It subsequently became known as the "1313" center for public administration; and its director was Louis Brownlow, a former journalist, commissioner of the District of Columbia, and city manager. The International City Management Association arrived in Chicago first in 1929. It was soon followed by the Civil Service Assembly (now the International Personnel Management Association), the Municipal Finance Officers Association, the American Municipal Association (now the National League of Cities), the American Legislators Association (now the Council of State Governments), the American Public Welfare Association, and APWA. In 1933 the Public Administration Service—a joint consulting, research, and publications agency—was established at the center. From the beginning, these "1313" associations emphasized the need for in-service training for public officials and better pre-service education by universities. They also circulated information on new administrative procedures in their newsletters, reports, and conference proceedings.

Membership in these associations grew during the 1930s as their activities increased and as more individuals entered public service. For many of the entrants, government was not their first choice but business offered few opportunities for employment. According to the 1962 report of the Municipal Manpower Commission, "security" and "only position available" were important motives for choosing a career in government during the Depression. It also became evident that great sums of money would be wasted unless cities, counties, and states had effective planning agencies and public works departments to implement the large public works programs spearheaded by the federal government. Thus, many engineers competed for positions at all levels of government during this critical period in the nation's history.

Public works policy broke with previous tradition in the 1930s. This reversal was not heralded in any one pronouncement; rather it was stated quite matter-of-factly by President Franklin D. Roosevelt on various occasions. According to the President, public works policy had a twofold objective: "to relieve the unemployment [and] to develop great regions of our country . . . for the benefit of future Americans." But the results of this policy seemed revolutionary to many public officials. In 1936, during an address before a joint conference of AME and IAPWO, Cincinnati's city manager, C. A. Dykstra, expressed a common belief: "in the last four years . . . we have revolutionized our ideas about public works . . . . Today federal aid in all local projects has become a matter of course."

Public works during the New Deal years was essentially a federal story. In "Public Works in the 1930s: A Preliminary Reconnaissance," Roger Daniels summarized the magnitude and impact of federal public works spending. He noted that, although the total dollar volume of public works did not increase greatly, there was a spectacular increase in federal spending on public works construction. From 1925 to 1932, such federal spending averaged slightly over a quarter of a billion dollars annually. During the first six years of the New Deal, federal spending on construction averaged $1.6 billion. Yet, even with this massive increase, the total dollar volume of new construction during the New Deal years was less than two thirds of that

spent during the previous eight years: $48.1 billion for 1933-1940 as opposed to $76.6 billion for 1925-1932. These figures reflected the decrease in state and local expenditures as well as the atrophy of the private sector.

The 1930s public works programs fulfilled their twofold objective. They created several billion hours of employment and accomplished a significant amount of worthwhile public improvements. However, it was the massive spending during World War II that finally brought prosperity to the nation. But the New Deal with its large public works programs held the country together during its most severe economic crisis.

Equally as important as the magnitude of New Deal spending was the impact that the experience had on postwar attitudes. Never again would public works policy be as limited as it had been. This was illustrated in a 1948 report prepared for the Hoover Commission by Robert Moses, a prominent public works administrator. In a section entitled "Advance Plans for Depressions and Public Works," Moses wrote: "There is not a State, city or municipal subdivision in the country which can, on its own, finance a depression-construction program sufficient to make a real dent in the employment problem." Moses did not mention income production or liquidation, nor was he concerned with the size of the federal deficit. He accepted as axiomatic the basic New Deal premise of massive counter-cyclical spending. As Daniels concluded in his article, "this acceptance is perhaps the ultimate tribute to the New Deal public works experience: it had transformed once radical doctrine into conventional wisdom."

Public Works Engineers in State and Federal Government

During the first half of the twentieth century, public works activities at the state and federal levels grew to provide facilities and services beyond the capabilities of local governmental entities. However, state involvement in the public works field varied widely. Since each state is governed by its own constitution, each reserves certain responsibilities for itself and delegates a variety of others to the cities and counties within its boundaries. For example, nine states construct and maintain all rural roads within their jurisdiction; while the remaining ones care for only those highways on the state system.

The states became actively involved in the public works field during the nineteenth century when they either directly or indirectly built canals, toll roads, railroads, and public buildings. Although the engineering work was usually executed by private engineers who were retained for a specific project, their instructions customarily originated with state boards of public improvements or public works. In the early twentieth century, especially with the advent of the automobile, states became increasingly concerned about the conditions of public roads. In 1904 only nine had highway departments; in 1916 there were thirty-two. And by the end of 1917, all states except Indiana had complied with a 1916 federal highway act requiring the establishment of state highway departments as a condition for aid. Indiana organized a highway department in 1919.

During the 1930s, when employment opportunities in the private sector were limited, engineers who did not enter public service at the municipal level often did so at the state level. Many engineers became employees of state highway departments, and some remained there through the 1940s. Thus, with the impetus given highway development in the 1950s, the majority of public works engineers and administrators in state government today are found in highway or transportation departments.

The number of engineers working in the field of water resources at the state level varies according to the needs of each state. In the late nineteenth century, many western states created state engineering offices to administer water rights. These offices have since either expanded or become separate organizations (for example, state water and power boards) and presently supervise all water development programs. Few eastern, southern, or midwestern states have such extensive agencies for water resources.

According to a 1967 survey by the Department of Labor, state governments employed 34,190 engineers. Ninety percent of this number were civil engineers, and nearly all were engaged in some facet of public works. The same survey recorded that state governments also employed 61,920 technicians—90 percent of whom were involved in public works activities. Six years later, when ASCE polled its membership, it learned that 10.2 percent of the 40,000 responding members were employees of state governments and that 15.5 percent were employees of the federal government (see Table 20-1). And according to the ASCE survey, of the 36.5 percent in government, 32.1 percent in consulting engineering firms (engineers in private practice), and 9.4 percent in construction, most reported that their responsibilities were directly related to public works.

TABLE 20-1
Employment of Civil Engineers

Industry	Percent of Total Civil Engineering Employment
Federal Government	15.5
State Highway Department	7.2
State Government (non-highway)	3.0
County or Municipal Government	8.1
Other Governmental Agency	2.7
Consulting Engineer	32.1
Construction	9.4
Railroad or Utility	2.9
Education	6.0
Industry	7.2
Other	5.9
Total	100.0

ASCE 1973 Survey

In many instances, direct federal public works operations are not unlike those at the state level except that federal operations are carried out on federal property such as national parks or military reservations. These operations include activities related to flood control; the disposal of hazardous wastes; the building of offices for governmental employees and installations and housing for military personnel; and the use of water for irrigation, hydroelectric power, and community consumption. Indirect federal public works operations take the form of federal aid. Although all states are eligible to receive support, their participation (and that of their subdivisions) in federal aid public works programs requires adherence to established laws, rules, and regulations.

Cape Henry Lighthouse, built in Virginia in 1791, was the first federal public works project in the United States. Its construction was directed by Secretary of the Treasury Alexander Hamilton, who administered the $15,200 contract that had required the personal approval of President Washington. During the first half of the nineteenth century, the federal government became more involved in public works activities as it helped in the planning and supervision of the nation's internal improvements. The Army Corps of Engineers was employed extensively to undertake mapping, surveying, and exploratory assignments and to oversee the construction of various types of projects.

The corps remains one of the principal public works agencies in the federal government. It has been joined by the Naval Facilities Engineering Command, the Department of the Interior's Bureau of Reclamation, the Department of Agriculture's Soil Conservation Service, the Department of Transportation's Federal Highway Administration, and the General Services Administration. Initially, these agencies were made up mostly of engineers and were responsible for providing the physical construction needed to meet rela-

California Department of Transportation

Government engineers plan, design, and supervise many public works projects. Construction is usually by private contractors.

tively easily defined objectives. But as public works facilities and services became more complex and their impact more widespread, these agencies became increasingly multidisciplinary in composition. Yet their professional staffs continued to consist largely of engineers, many of whom assumed important administrative positions.

The corps is the largest engineering organization in the country. It is presently composed of 4,850 military engineering officers and nearly 45,000 civilians, of whom 8,000 are professional engineers. Over 2,000 of the 8,500 persons employed by the Bureau of Reclamation are engineers and play key roles in the management of the nation's water resources. The Federal Highway Administration, which is responsible for administering funds for the federal aid highway programs in the states, has 5,300 employees, of which about 1,700 are engineers.

Several attempts have been made to streamline federal public works operations by placing non-military engineering functions in a Department of Public Works. Presidents Warren G. Harding and Calvin Coolidge recommended such action in the 1920s as did President Roosevelt in 1937. It was their hope that a federal public works department would eliminate duplication in those instances where different agencies were involved in the same area of concern. But Congress consistently rejected these presidential recommendations.

Although relatively large numbers of engineers are employed by federal and state governmental agencies in what has been called "the age of technology," few engineers have been elected to Congress or state legislatures. In 1974 there were 535 members in the House and Senate, but only seven members had some training as engineers or scientists. There were, however, 288 lawyers, 162 businessmen or bankers, and 72 educators. Six members had medical backgrounds, and five had been educated in the ministry. State legislatures did not fare much better. According to a 1974 survey of 3,926 members in the legislatures of thirty-two states, Brian J. Lewis, a professional engineer and former legislator in Oregon, reported that 26.3 percent were in business or banking, 20.0 percent were in law, 13.0 percent were in agriculture, 9.5 percent were in government, 8.1 percent were in real estate or insurance, 11.7 percent were in miscellaneous occupations, and only 1.1 percent were in engineering. Since many programs enacted by Congress and state legislatures involve the planning and design of extensive networks of public works facilities, the views of professional engineers need to be heard and given serious consideration in debates on public works policies. Engineers should, therefore, be encouraged to seek elective offices and become more active participants in the legislative process.

Consultants and Contractors

Although government agencies customarily own, operate, and maintain public works, private enterprise plays a large and important role in their creation. Planning and design work is frequently performed by private engineering firms and consultants, while most construction work is done by private contractors. Private companies also furnish the equipment, materials, and many of the services required in the building of the nation's public works.

In the public works field, there are two broad categories of clients served by private engineering firms. One consists of public agencies that do not generally maintain an extensive design and construction management staff. These include, among others, the various toll bridge and turnpike authorities, water supply and sewage districts, port authorities, public power agencies, and rapid transit authorities. Planning, design, and management services provided to these types of public agencies are comprehensive and similar to those rendered to clients in the private sector.

The second category of public works clients consists of agencies of federal, state, county, and local governments. At the federal level, these agencies include the Department of Transportation, Department of Defense, Department of Interior, Department of Housing and Urban Development, General Services Administration, and Environmental Protection Agency. At state, county, and local

levels, there are public works and transportation departments, water resources agencies, urban redevelopment administrations, building and housing agencies, parks and recreation departments, and others. These clients have varying degrees of design and construction management capabilities, depending upon the size of their professional staffs, and sufficient expertise to plan, design, and manage projects within their normal sphere of activities.

This second category of public works agencies uses private consulting engineering firms either on projects which require specialized skills or on projects where in-house competence exists but time is not available. There often is not the expertise on agency staffs to handle such projects as vehicular tunnels, rapid transit facilities, long-span and movable bridges, water treatment and sewage disposal plants, water supply structures, and airport master planning and design. For these kinds of projects, consulting firms provide services similar to those extended to special purpose public authorities. However, public agencies normally direct the administrative work involved in the non-engineering aspects of these assignments. On projects that are not unusual but assist public agencies in meeting peak demands, consultants customarily plan, design, and manage services which are extensions of the agencies' capabilities. Thus, the consultants' services may be comprehensive or they may be limited.

The oldest consulting firms in the United States were founded in the second half of the nineteenth century. Lockwood, Greene Engineers, Inc., one of the earliest, was organized in New York in 1858. It was later followed in the 1880s by Fromherz Engineers, New Orleans; Parsons, Brinckerhoff, Quade & Douglas, New York; and Lockwood, Kessler & Bartlett, Inc., New York. Among those firms established in the 1890s were Albright & Friel, Inc., Philadelphia; Alexander Potter Associates, New York; Sargent & Lundy, Chicago; Charles T. Main, Boston; Modjeski and Masters, Harrisburg; Weiskopf & Pickworth, New York; and Burns & McDonnell, Kansas City.

There were only 907 private engineering

firms practicing in the United States in 1940. But by 1950 the number of new firms had increased to 1,287 and to 4,943 in 1960. Although 3,113 engineering firms came into being between 1961 and 1971, the total number in practice only rose from 6,250 in 1961 to 8,056 in 1971—a net gain of 1,806 firms. The reason for this development, beyond normal attrition, was that many firms merged to meet the growing demand for more types of design services from a single qualified source.

Power Authority of the State of New York

The St. Lawrence Power Project was designed and construction contracts supervised by private engineering firms. The project was built by construction contractors selected by competitive bidding.

During the early 1970s, consulting firms of all sizes greatly expanded the types of projects they designed and the scope of services they provided. For example, in 1970 firms of less than twenty-five employees averaged 2.7 types of projects. In 1973 the average was 3.2 types. Firms with over 100 employees averaged 3.2 types of projects in 1970. Three years later, they handled an average of 3.8 types. The averages indicate that large firms differed from small ones mainly in the number and size of projects they designed, not in the types they handled. During 1973 there was also a sharp increase in services (planning, econometrics, life-cycle costing, rate studies, environmental quality, for examples) to local government. This occurred, in many instances, in direct response to the pressure placed on local public agencies to modernize their water treatment and wastewater processing facilities.

Of the many consulting firms practicing in 1972, only about 1,500 confined their services to the states where they were located. Over 6,500 firms worked in the territorial United States, while approximately 150 operated internationally. More than half of the domestic firms had one or more branch offices, and practically all of the firms engaged in international work had branches. Since many of these were established near job sites to supervise and expedite construction projects, they were often temporary. But a growing number of large firms maintained full design capabilities at permanent branch offices, which functioned in the same manner as smaller consulting firms.

The major end product of engineering design is construction. A construction team of owner, architect or engineer, and contractor can transform the design engineer's calculations and drawings into such public works facilities as public buildings, highways, dams, or airports. And few industries equal construction in importance, either in terms of size or of influence on general economic activity. It ranks among the nation's largest industries as an employer and as a consumer of materials, and it is regarded by many economists as a major determinant of the size of the gross national product.

Construction contractors range in size from the small company that builds a few one-family homes to the giant firm that annually does more than $1 billion worth of work. Within a given company, there may be only two employees or there may be hundreds of permanent workers representing the various building trades as well as managers, engineers, clerks, accountants, architects, attorneys, and planners. Like private engineering firms during the 1960s and 1970s, construction firms tended to grow in size and to expand their services. In April 1974, *Engineering News-Record* reported that the 400 largest construction contractors did $55 billion of work, a 38 percent increase over the $40 billion reported in 1972.

Contractors are classified according to the kinds of work they do. There are highway, heavy construction, general building (including home builders as a subdivision), and special trade contractors. Although some large construction firms accept jobs in all of the first three categories, most roads, streets, bridges, and airports are built by highway contractors, who work primarily under contract for some department of federal, state, county, or municipal government. Heavy construction contractors are responsible for the large earthmoving projects that are necessary in building foundations, dams, and tunnels; while virtually every kind of public building and commercial and industrial shelter is constructed by general building contractors. Skyscrapers are by far the most spectacular of their accomplishments, but fire stations, city halls, and homes and apartments are the most common. Special trade contractors confine themselves to a specialty such as heating, plumbing, electrical work, air conditioning, tile setting, roofing, plastering, or pipe fitting.

Most construction work is performed under contract. A construction contract sets forth the rights and obligation of the owner and the contractor with regard to a particular project. Once a contract is agreed upon, the contractor becomes responsible for completing the project and the owner (which is the public agency in the case of government work) for paying the contractor in accordance with the terms of the agreement. Although construction contracts may be awarded either by direct selection and negotiation or by competitive bidding, the competitive contract is used for public works projects unless they are of an emergency nature.

Emergence of the Engineer-Administrator

Early twentieth-century public works organization and administration were rudimentary in comparison to the intricate system of rules, regulations, statutes, and highly mechanized operations that developed in postwar America. Intergovernmental relations were far less complex; public pressure was neither as direct nor as demanding; and the social and economic factors engendered by freeway routings, urban renewal, airport construction, and countless other activities were not matters of special concern to public works officials. Although the pace accelerated in most parts of the United States in the immedi-

ate postwar years, by the 1950s the problems of the following two decades were still only portents on the horizon. Many local communities and states had accumulated surpluses during the war years which were used at the war's end to construct long-delayed public works projects; resistance to bond issues to finance needed improvements was slight; and since the exodus to the suburbs had just begun, the impact of this trend on public works facilities and services was not yet realized.

Public works departments in the first half of the twentieth century tended to use a *line* type of organization. Since fewer considerations were given to external influences of a social, economic, or environmental nature and since the majority of the employees were blue collar, these departments found themselves best served by a hierarchical structure where the lines of authority were clearly defined and the decision making was centralized. But in the postwar years, as society became more urbanized, technology more sophisticated, and citizens more involved in the processes of government, public agencies changed. By the 1970s, they had become larger, more complex, and less rigid. And the new breed of public works executives who emerged to administer them were better trained in management and more knowledgeable in the social sciences. Drawing on the expertise of staff specialists and colleagues in related government departments, they made the integration of public works systems their primary concern.

Most public works administrators serving in the 1950s and 1960s began their careers in the 1930s when the private sector offered few employment opportunities to engineering graduates. Although the number and caliber of persons that entered government at the time proved to be an unexpected dividend, in most cases their engineering education had not prepared them for their new roles as public works administrators. They were forced to meet organizational goals under trying conditions and without the benefit of today's modern machines and management tools. But as they did so, they grew into their positions and often contributed to the expanding technology of their profession and the administrative art

Public Works Historical Society

Representatives from different disciplines meet in interagency meetings to coordinate public works plans and programs.

that became an integral component of their work.

During the 1950s and especially during the 1960s, when suburban populations expanded and the federal government became involved in a growing array of local activities, the number and variety of services performed by local public works organizations increased (see Table 20-2). Not all of these functions were assigned to a single department. In large communities, some of these activities were grouped together and performed by two or more departments or agencies. However, in small communities, it became quite common for nearly all the public works activities to be centralized in one department.

The complex organizational structures of public works agencies and the diversity of their functions involved public works administrators in the difficult tasks of planning, design, construction, institutional development, resource mobilization, personnel motivation, application of changing technologies, and public relations. In the 1950s and 1960s, public works directors were among the best educated and most experienced officials in local government. Ac-

TABLE 20-2
THE "TOP 25" FUNCTIONS TYPICALLY ALLOCATED TO MUNICIPAL PUBLIC WORKS DEPARTMENTS

Public Works departmental function	No. and % of cities (who report the function) that put it in the Public Works Dept.	
Snow removal	528	98.0
Street maintenance	735	97.2
Street cleaning	724	96.4
Drainage maintenance	673	93.7
Storm sewer maintenance	680	92.0
Vehicle maintenance	575	83.8
Street sign maintenance	607	82.2
Street sign installation	607	82.0
Construction inspection	587	80.4
Street construction	570	78.7
Subdivision review	471	78.4
Sewerage system maintenance	568	78.3
Surveying	558	77.9
Street & highway design	563	77.0
Traffic sign maintenance	548	77.0
Right-of-way	512	76.3
Traffic sign installation	547	76.0
Weed control	464	73.8
Street striping (marking)	529	73.1
Storm sewer construction	502	71.1
Building maintenance	407	66.1
Sewerage system design	459	65.0
Street sign manufacturing	418	64.9
Refuse collection	429	64.8
Refuse disposal (landfill)	374	61.8

APWA, *Local Public Works Organizations.*

cording to data gathered by the Municipal Manpower Commission in 1962, 61 percent of the public works directors in cities over 250,000 had college degrees; 48 percent of the directors in cities under 250,000 were college graduates. Approximately 85 percent of them had specialized in civil engineering.

In 1969 APWA surveyed 957 local public works organizations and reported that the level of education had increased. Two thirds of the directors had bachelors or masters degrees and an additional 14 percent had some college work. In cities of over 250,000, 76 percent had graduated from college; while 57 percent had in cities of less than 250,000. Nine out of ten public works directors in cities of over 100,000 who were college graduates had specialized in civil engineering and were registered engineers. And two thirds of the directors in cities with populations of 250,000 to 500,000 had more than twenty years experience in government. Yet many lacked the formal public affairs and managerial training that would have enhanced their effectiveness as public works administrators.

To complement their engineering education, those who aspired to top management positions in the public works field were encouraged to pursue graduate studies in public administration or to enroll in specialized programs such as the one offered at the University of Pittsburgh. The Graduate Center of Public Works Engineering and Administration at the University of Pittsburgh was established in 1965 with assistance from APWA to develop professional skills in management, planning, and systems analysis in public works engineers. This center was sponsored jointly by the School of Engineering, the Graduate School of Public Health, and the Graduate School of Public and International Affairs. Therefore, besides taking courses in public works planning and management, students received instruction in public health, environmental science, urban planning, and public administration according to their specific interests and needs.

In many respects, the University of Pittsburgh's Graduate Center for Public Works Engineering and Administration has served as a model for other institutions of higher learn-

University of Pittsburgh

The first graduates with masters degrees in public works met with the University of Pittsburgh's chancellor in 1967.

ing. Over the last ten years, at least a dozen universities have announced new programs for educating public works administrators. Some of these programs are very similar to that at the University of Pittsburgh and have considerable depth; others are more specialized and feature training, for example, in transportation engineering. But even more significant is the increasing number of engineering schools that have strengthened their civil engineering programs by offering courses in public works administration, engineering management, public affairs, or environmental engineering.

One Among Many

Many professional groups serve the public works field, but APWA holds a unique position among them. Not only does it offer programs that promote clearer understanding and improved practices in the broad field of public works engineering and administration, but it provides a common ground for developing harmonious working relations among the individuals who make up the memberships of the more specialized organizations. From its beginning in 1894, APWA has been especially concerned with public works problems, particularly at the local level of government. Its membership, until recent years, was composed almost entirely of directors of public works; city engineers; superintendents of streets, water, sewers, sanitation, and building inspection; plus some mayors; consulting engineers to cities and towns; and a few other persons who had a special interest in municipal government. But following World War II, as the problems of urban society grew more complex and intricate, many county, state, and federal officials joined APWA and the character of the association changed.

Widely recognized in 1976 as the one organization in the United States that exists for all persons involved in providing public works facilities and services, APWA stresses the importance of integrating and coordinating the efforts of all segments of the public works profession. It understands that the problems of water and air pollution, solid wastes disposal, water supply, location of highways and mass transit systems, for examples, are rarely solved through the expertise of those in any one specialized organization or within the boundaries of a single political jurisdiction. Thus, APWA, directly and through a network of state and local chapters, strongly encourages "cooperation among all public, quasi-public and private persons, firms, corporations, bodies, utilities and agencies which have interests in the field of public works."

Because of this commitment, APWA has established a liaison relationship with a variety of allied associations. It has created joint cooperative committees with such organizations as the Associated Equipment Distributors, Associated General Contractors, American Road Builders Association, ASCE, and the National Safety Council. Membership on these committees is customarily divided equally between APWA and the association

The APWA annually sponsors an International Public Works Congress and Equipment Show which provides an opportunity for the association's members to learn about the latest developments and see the newest products in this field.

identified on the joint committee. Besides maintaining good relationships with the interest groups involved, these committees have prepared statistical data, manuals, and special reports in an attempt to keep pace with the broad spectrum of public works activities and problems.

The APWA has also created seven institutes for professional development. Composed of especially knowledgeable and interested association members, these institutes encompass the fields of solid wastes, municipal engineering, equipment services, transportation, water resources, buildings and grounds, and administrative management. Each institute maintains close working relationships with allied organizations serving their respective fields of specialization. They develop a wide variety of publications and are the focal point for the accumulation of professional knowledge about their functional fields of activity.

The APWA Education and Research foundations assist the institutes in developing and disseminating knowledge about public works problems to their members. Each foundation is governed by a separate board of trustees which oversees its operations. Scores of projects, costing in excess of $3 million, have been completed by the Research Foundation since it was founded in 1959. Many of these projects were financed by different agencies of the federal government; however, some were jointly funded by state and local units of government. The Education Foundation was established in 1965 to assist in disseminating research findings, aid in the development of graduate level programs in public works administration, and provide members and their subordinates with greater opportunities to keep abreast of developments in all branches of public works. Approximately 2,000 persons participated in workshops and seminars sponsored by the foundation in 1975.

Responding to a request of the National Transportation Safety Board, APWA in 1974 established a Utility Location and Coordination Council which brings together officially designated representatives of governmentally and privately owned public utilities of all kinds (including contractors and regulatory officials) which place their utility facilities in public rights-of-way. The purpose of this council is to develop programs to reduce accidents which cause the loss of life, damage to property, and inconvenience to the public resulting from the construction and maintenance of utility operations in street rights-of-way. The newest of APWA's constituent groups is its Council on International Collaboration which was formed in 1975 to facilitate member contacts with public works officials and organizations around the world. As its literature states, APWA is dedicated to "the protection and enhancement of the human environment." It and other professional associations have helped to improve the quality of public works facilities and services in the past and can be expected to make noteworthy contributions in the future.

SUGGESTED READINGS

American Public Works Association. *Dynamic Technology Transfer & Utilization: The Key to Progressive Public Works Management.* Chicago, 1974.

——————— . *Local Public Works Organizations: A Survey-Report on Management Personnel, Association of Functions, and Related Information.* Chicago, 1970.

——————— . *Public Works Engineers Yearbook.* Chicago, 1936-1944.

——————— . *Public Works for the Future: A Report on Research Needs and the Transfer of Knowledge.* Chicago, 1963.

——————— and National Association of Schools of Public Affairs and Administration. *Professional Education in Public Works Environmental Engineering and Administration: A Handbook for Establishing University Centers and Programs.* Chicago, 1974.

American Society of Municipal Improvements. *Proceedings.* Chicago, 1894-1930.

Brown, Esther Lucille. *The Professional Engineer.* New York, 1936.

Calhoun, Daniel Hovey. *The American Civil Engineer: Origins and Conflict.* Cambridge, Massachusetts, 1960.

Daniels, Roger. "Public Works in the 1930s: A Preliminary Reconnaissance." *The Relevancy of Public Works History: The 1930s —A Case Study.* Chicago, 1976.

Healy, Patrick III. *The Nation's Cities: Change and Challenge.* New York, 1974.

International City Managers' Association. *Municipal Public Works Administration.* 5th ed. Chicago, 1967.

Layton, Edwin T., Jr. *The Revolt of the Engineers: Social Responsibility and the American Engineering Profession.* Cleveland, 1971.

McKelvey, Blake. *The Urbanization of America, 1860-1915.* New Brunswick, New Jersey, 1963.

Merritt, Raymond H. *Engineering in American Society, 1850-1875.* Lexington, Kentucky, 1969.

Ricketts, Palmer C. *Rensselaer Polytechnic Institute: A Short History.* Troy, New York, 1930.

Ridley, Clarence E. *The Public Works Department in American Cities.* Chicago, 1929.

Stillman, Richard J. II. *The Rise of the City Manager: A Public Professional in Local Government.* Albuquerque, 1974.

Stone, Alice B., and Stone, Donald C. "Early Development of Education in Public Administration." Edited by Frederick C. Mosher, *American Public Administration: Past, Present, Future.* Tuscaloosa, Alabama, 1975.

Stone, Donald C. *The Management of Municipal Public Works.* Chicago, 1939.

Whinery, S. *Municipal Public Works: Their Inception, Construction, and Management.* London, 1903.

White, Leonard. *The City Manager.* Chicago, 1927.

Wiebe, Robert H. *The Search for Order, 1877-1920.* New York, 1967.

Wisely, William A. *The American Civil Engineer, 1852-1974: The History, Traditions and Development of the American Society of Civil Engineers.* New York, 1974.

INDEX